PRODUCTION AND OPERATIONS MANAGEMENT

Strategic and Tactical Decisions

PRENTICE HALL SERIES IN
DECISION SCIENCES

Barry Render, Consulting Editor
Roy E. Crummer Graduate School of Business, Rollins College

Applied Statistics

Basic Business Statistics, 6th Edition
Berenson, Levine

Statistics for Business and Economics, 2nd Edition
Berenson, Levine

Intermediate Statistical Methods and Applications
Berenson, Levine, Goldstein

Elementary Business Statistics, 6th Edition
Freund, Williams, Perles

Business Statistics for Quality and Productivity
Levine, Ramsey, Berenson

Statistics for Management, 6th Edition
Levine, Rubin

Short Course in Business Statistics
Levine, Rubin

Cases in Business Statistics
Klimberg, Arnold, Berger

Applied Statistics, 4th Edition
Neter, Wasserman, Whitmore

Statistics for Business and Economics, 4th Edition
Newbold

Business Cases in Statistical Decision Making
Peters, Gray

Brief Business Statistics
Watson, Billingsley, Croft, Huntsberger

Statistics for Management and Economics, 5th Edition
Watson, Billingsley, Croft, Huntsberger

Production and Operations Management

Readings in Production and Operations
Ahmadian, Afifi, Chandler

Business Logistics Management, 3rd Edition
Ballou

Operations Strategy
Garvin

Business Forecasting, 5th Edition
Hanke, Reitsch

Games and Exercises for Operations Management
Heineke, Meile

Production and Operations Management, 4th Edition
Heizer, Render

Cases and Readings in Production and Operations Management
Latona, Nathan

Managing Services, 2nd Edition
Lovelock

Cases in Manufacturing and Service System Management
Mabert

Operations Management, 3rd Edition
McClain, Thomas, Mazzola

Service Operations Management
Murdick, Render, Russell

Production Planning and Inventory Control, 2nd Edition
Narasimhan, McLeavy, Billington

Principles of Operations Management
Render, Heizer

Production and Operations Management
Russell, Taylor

Plant and Service Tours in Operations Management, 4th Edition
Schmenner

Production/Operations Management, 5th Edition
Schmenner

Service Operations Management
Schmenner

Topics in Just-In-Time Management
Schneiderjans

Production and Management Systems for Business (book/disk)
Sherrard, Smolin, Rodenrys

Production and Operation Management: Self-Correcting Approach, 3rd Edition
Stair, Render

Operations Strategy
Stonebraker, Leong

PRODUCTION AND OPERATIONS MANAGEMENT

Strategic and Tactical Decisions

FOURTH EDITION

JAY HEIZER

Jesse H. Jones Professor of Business Administration
Texas Lutheran College

BARRY RENDER

Charles Harwood Professor of Operations Management
Crummer Graduate School of Business
Rollins College

PRENTICE HALL, UPPER SADDLE RIVER, NEW JERSEY 07458

Library of Congress Cataloging-in-Publication Data

Heizer, Jay H.
    Production and operations management : strategic and tactical
decisions / Jay Heizer, Barry Render. — 4th ed.
      p.   cm.
    Includes bibliographical references and index.
    ISBN 0-13-199423-9
    1. Production management.   I. Render, Barry.   II. Title.
TS155.H373   1995
658.5—dc20   95-7787
                                           CIP

Production Service: *Marbern House*
Copy Editor: *Peter Zurita*
Senior Project Manager: *Kathleen Kelly*
Cover Designer: *Suzanne Behnke*
Graphic Artist: *Suzanne Behnke*
Design Director: *Patricia Wosczyk*
Manufacturing Buyer: *Marie McNamara*
Proofreader: *Maine Proofreading Services*
Developmental Editors: *Steve Deitmer and David Cohen*
Permissions Editor: *The Permissions Group*
Acquisitions Editor: *Tom Tucker*
Assistant Editor: *Diane Peirano*

© 1996 by Prentice-Hall, Inc.
A Simon & Schuster Company
Upper Saddle River, New Jersey 07458

All rights reserved. No part of this book may be
reproduced, in any form or by any means,
without permission in writing from the publisher.

Printed in the United States of America
10 9 8 7 6 5 4 3 2 1

ISBN: 0-13-199423-9 (student edition)
0-13-438342-7 (instructor's edition)

Prentice-Hall International (UK) Limited, *London*
Prentice-Hall of Australia Pty. Limited, *Sydney*
Prentice-Hall Canada Inc., *Toronto*
Prentice-Hall Hispanoamericana, S.A., *Mexico*
Prentice-Hall of India Private Limited, *New Delhi*
Prentice-Hall of Japan, Inc., *Tokyo*
Simon & Schuster Asia Pte. Ltd., *Singapore*
Editora Prentice-Hall do Brasil, Ltda., *Rio de Janeiro*

PRODUCTIVITY INCREASES MAKE A DIFFERENCE AT WHIRLPOOL

Productivity makes a big difference at Whirlpool's washing-machine factory in Benton Harbor, Michigan. It makes a difference to employees, to customers, and to stockholders.

For employees, enhanced productivity means that, in recent years, each employee has received more than $2,000 in extra pay.

For customers, Whirlpool continues to defy inflation by holding the line on consumer prices. Even in the face of a consumer price index that is up about 20% in the last 4 years, some Whirlpool washers have dropped in price.

Productivity increases have benefitted stockholders, too. Whirlpool has gained market share while outpacing its rivals on profitability. Consequently, Whirlpool's stock price is also up.

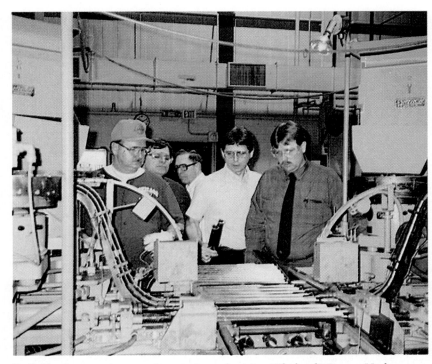

By linking increases in pay to increase in productivity, Whirlpool's Benton Harbor employees are encouraged to take greater control of their jobs and become more involved in the facility's daily operation. Here they participate in a discussion of techniques for continuous improvement.

Visual inspection takes place as parts are packed for shipment. A focus on total quality and reduction in scrap has been a major ingredient in Benton Harbor's productivity improvement.

None of this happens without increases in productivity. How did Whirlpool do it? First, there was a change in attitude by management and employees who now "live" quality as well as talk about it. Second, training stressed that employees use their heads as well as their hands. Third, flexible work rules allowed employees to work where needed. Fourth, a gain-sharing agreement keeps everyone focused on productivity improvements. Specific results include increases in parts manufactured per labor-hour (from 92.8 to 110.6) and reductions in rejected parts per million (from 837 to a world-class 47).

Although the United States still has the highest level of productivity in the world, its rate of increase, as Chapter 1 discusses, trails a number of other countries. But in the manufacturing sector, a comeback is being led by the men and women of facilities such as Whirlpool.

1

PRODUCTION/OPERATIONS MANAGEMENT

LEARNING OBJECTIVES

When you complete this chapter you should be able to:

Identify or define:

   Production and Productivity

   Production/Operations Management (P/OM)

   What Production/Operations Managers Do

   The Three Major Functions of a Business

Describe or Explain

   A brief history of operations management

   Career opportunities in production/operations management

   The future of the discipline

PRODUCTION AND OPERATIONS MANAGEMENT

Strategic and Tactical Decisions

12 Supplement: Learning Curves 554

13 Inventory Management and Just-in-Time Tactics 571

13 Supplement: Simulation 617

14 Material Requirements Planning (MRP) 647

PART FOUR
TACTICAL DECISIONS FOR
MEETING CUSTOMER'S
NEEDS

12 Purchasing Management and
Just-in-Time Strategies 527

8 State-of-the-Art Technology in P/OM 321

9 Location Strategies 343

9 Supplement: Transportation Modeling 373

10 Operations Layout Strategy 401

CONTENTS

BRIEF CONTENTS

FOREWORD

FOREWORD TO THE FOURTH EDITION OF PRODUCTION AND OPERATIONS MANAGEMENT

When I first entered a production operation in 1952 the world of business was divided into two parts, like the Red Sea had been. One part made big things out of little things; the other part purchased the little things, found the customers, took care of the money, sold stuff, and complained about the activities of the first part. The two portions of the company had nothing in common and little interest in each other.

Over the years it was discovered that there are no separate parts of an organization. It is a body that requires all components to function together as a unit if a successful life is to be obtained.

However everyone knew that the world was made up of separate parts. Markets were described as domestic and international. The latter was not part of the organization and often had a great deal of difficulty obtaining information about plans, products, and people. Now we have learned that the world of business has no boundaries and there are only domestic markets. We have also learned that we have suppliers and customers who do not speak our language or observe our holidays.

Functional operations used to be responsible for whatever noun was in their title. Manufacturing manufactured, purchasing purchased, personnel personneled, and quality was done by the quality department. When I was a quality manager top management held me personally responsible if a customer received something that was not proper. Everyone else were "bad guys" trying to get stuff by quality, and we were the "good guys." When enough things went wrong the practice was to find a tougher, smarter cop. There was no thought of getting things done right.

When I began preaching the prevention of problems, called quality management, it took a while for people to catch on. The breakthrough came with the determination of the "price of nonconformance." How much did it cost to do things wrong, and then fix them. Most companies came to the realization that it took 25% and more of their revenues to live that way. That was the beginning of the quality revolution.

When I talk to Professor Render's classes each year I am always impressed that the students are learning to look at the world from a platform that did not exist in my early career. The broad scope of this book assures that this will happen. It provides a place to begin the future by reviewing the past. The students always want to know about the "reality" of quality management, which is the general subject of my chat. I tell them that basic concepts are the important part of business management, that there are no "systems" to do the executive's work. Concepts come from understanding, understanding begins with learning, and learning comes from examining credible resources with an open mind.

I know you will enjoy yourself in this course.

PHILIP CROSBY
Winter Park, Fl.

Leonard Presby
William Patterson State College of
   New Jersey

M. J. Riley
Kansas State University

Narendra K. Rustagi
Howard University

Teresita S. Salinas
Washburn University

Robert J. Schlesinger
San Diego State University

Avanti P. Sethi
Wichita State University

Girish Shambu
Canisius College

Susan Sherer
Lehigh University

Viki L. Smith-Daniels
University of Minnesota–Twin
   Cities

Stan Stockton
Indiana University

John Swearingen
Bryant College

Kambiz Tabibzadeh
Eastern Kentucky University

Rao J. Tatikonda
University of Wisconsin–Oshkosh

Bruce M. Woodworth
University of Texas–El Paso

In addition, we appreciate the fine people at Prentice Hall who provided both help and encouragement during a multiyear revision: Rich Wohl, our editor-in-chief; Tom Tucker, our editor; David Cohen and Steven Deitmer, our developmental editors; Kathleen Kelly, our production editor; Terri Stratford, our photo researcher; and the Permissions Group, our permissions editor. Reva Shader developed the three superb indices for the text. Kay Heizer and Jessie Render provided invaluable proofreading.

We also appreciate the efforts of colleagues who have helped to shape the entire learning package that accompanies this text: Professor Howard Weiss (Temple University) developed AB:POM microcomputer software; Ted Ashford (Rollins College) prepared the transparency masters and presentation graphics. Finally, the following professors provided the excellent case studies found in this edition:

Michael Ballot
University of the Pacific

James Evans
University of Cincinnati

Roger Gagnon
Wake Forest University

Marilyn Helms
University of Tennessee–Chattanooga

Jerry Kinard
Western Carolina University

William M. Lindsay
Northern Kentucky University

Curtis P. McLaughlin
University of North Carolina–Chapel Hill

Zbignew H. Przasnyski
Loyola Marymount University

Roger W. Schmenner
Indiana University

Kala Chand Seal
Loyola Marymount University

Bruce Simmons
University of Akron

Victor E. Sower
Sam Houston State University

Ralph M. Stair, Jr.
Florida State University

Richard J. Tersine
University of Oklahoma

Timothy L. Urban
University of Tulsa

We have been fortunate to have been able to work with all of these people.

We wish you a pleasant and productive introduction to *Production and Operations Management*.

We have, for the sake of completeness, included a great deal of material in this text. However, to cover all of the topics in a one-semester course would be unusual. Consequently, we developed the organization shown in the figure that allows substantial flexibility for the instructor. Instructors may skip over many of the technical chapter supplements (such as linear programming, learning curves, work measurement, simulation, transportation models, and queuing). On the other hand, those instructors preferring a quantitative treatment will especially appreciate many of the supplements, and the numerous quantitative examples, solved problems, AB:POM software, and the spreadsheet formulations. Those preferring a more qualitative treatment of P/OM may stress the numerous case studies and our unique "Critical Thinking Exercises." We think the result is a text that allows instructors to teach the course in their own way and at their own pace.

ACKNOWLEDGMENTS

We thank the many individuals who were kind enough to assist us in this huge endeavor, from writing the first edition in 1986 all the way to this fourth edition 10 years later. Without the help of these fellow professors, we would never have received the feedback needed to put together a teachable text. The reviewers are listed in alphabetical order:

Sema Alptekin
University of Missouri–Rolla

Jean-Pierre Amor
University of San Diego

Moshen Attaran
California State University–Bakersfield

John H. Blackstone
University of Georgia

Theodore Boreki
Hofstra University

Mark Coffin
East Carolina University

Henry Crouch
Pittsburgh State University

Barbara Flynn
Iowa State University

Damodar Golhar
Western Michigan University

Jim Goodwin
University of Richmond

James R. Gross
University of Wisconsin–Oshkosh

Marilyn K. Hart
University of Wisconsin–Oshkosh

James S. Hawkes
University of Charleston

George Heinrich
Wichita State University

Ziaul Huq
University of Nebraska–Omaha

Paul Jordan
University of Alaska

Arthur C. Meiners, Jr.
Marymount University

Larry LaForge
Clemson University

Hugh Leach
Washburn University

Laurie E. MacDonald
Bryant College

Mike Maggard
Northeastern University

Joao Neves
Trenton State College

Niranjan Pati
University of Wisconsin–La Crosse

David W. Pentico
Duquesne University

authors who are noted in the book. The company index illustrates the large number of real-world organizations that are described in the book.

ALSO AVAILABLE TO INSTRUCTORS.   A comprehensive *Annotated Instructor's Edition*, as well as a *Test Bank, Transparency Masters*, a *DataDisk* that contains problem data, a complete *Solutions Manual*, and a wide variety of videos are all available with this edition.

ORGANIZATION OF THE BOOK

We have identified ten decisions that are critical to effective production/operations management. These ten decisions are divided into strategic and tactical decisions, and are presented in a realistic, global, and dynamic environment. We hope this approach presents P/OM decisions in a way that will assist current and future managers in understanding how to manage operations effectively.

Part One provides an introduction to P/OM, productivity, P/OM strategy, and international issues that drive operations decisions.

Part Two focuses on identifying the customer's needs. Its three chapters deal with quality and forecasting. Quality provides an overview because setting a quality plan is both strategic (Chapter 3) and tactical (Chapter 4) in nature.

Part Three focuses on six strategic management decisions beyond quality for meeting customers needs. These are product design, process-technology selection, facility location, facility layout, human resources, and purchasing/JIT.

Part Four introduces three tactical decisions of operations management for meeting customer needs. These are scheduling (short-term in Chapter 16, intermediate-term in Chapter 15, and project-oriented in Chapter 17), inventory control, and maintenance. This philosophy of four parts in the book is summarized in the figure.

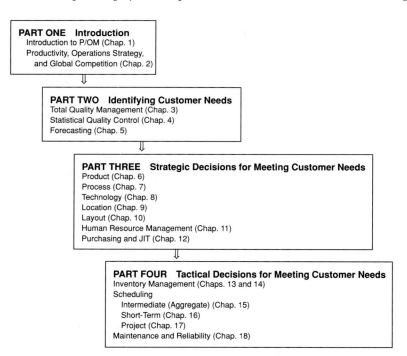

PART ONE   Introduction
Introduction to P/OM (Chap. 1)
Productivity, Operations Strategy,
  and Global Competition (Chap. 2)

PART TWO   Identifying Customer Needs
Total Quality Management (Chap. 3)
Statistical Quality Control (Chap. 4)
Forecasting (Chap. 5)

PART THREE   Strategic Decisions for Meeting Customer Needs
Product (Chap. 6)
Process (Chap. 7)
Technology (Chap. 8)
Location (Chap. 9)
Layout (Chap. 10)
Human Resource Management (Chap. 11)
Purchasing and JIT (Chap. 12)

PART FOUR   Tactical Decisions for Meeting Customer Needs
Inventory Management (Chaps. 13 and 14)
Scheduling
  Intermediate (Aggregate) (Chap. 15)
  Short-Term (Chap. 16)
  Project (Chap. 17)
Maintenance and Reliability (Chap. 18)

today. We call this feature in each chapter and supplement a "Critical Thinking Exercise." Students working in small groups or teams may be an appropriate way to tackle the subject presented. Many critical thinking exercises deal with ethical issues and decisions or with issues for which no clear answer exists. We hope they lead to lively classroom debate.

WORLD-CLASS PROFILES.   In this edition, we have dramatically expanded our exciting feature of full-color tours of world-class organizations. Each of the 18 chapters now begins with a photo essay of a firm chosen for its leadership in the area of POM covered in that chapter. Most of the photo tours in this edition are new.

PHOTOS.   In addition, to the world-class tours, over 150 full-color photos appear in this edition, along with very detailed captions tying them to the contents of their chapters and to specific components. These photos and captions increase student interest and add a depth not found in other textbooks.

AB:POM SOFTWARE.   A microcomputer software package, AB:POM (developed by Howard Weiss, Temple University), is again available with the text. This package, the most popular Decision Support Software in college P/OM use, continues to improve in both breadth of functions and user friendliness. The software includes more than a dozen P/OM application programs that range from forecasting to queuing to line balancing to project scheduling to MRP. We think most students appreciate the experience of using a computer to solve problems. Instructors, however, can structure the course with or without the use of the software. At the end of each problem-oriented chapter, the student will also find an explanation of how to use the software for that particular application. In addition, detailed instructions for using the software are located in Appendix E. For most effective learning, the software has been structured to closely match the approach, notation, and terms found in this text. STORM and QSOM software are also available at reduced prices, through Prentice Hall, with this book.

SYMBOLIC SPREADSHEET PRINTOUTS.   A "symbolic" spreadsheet is one that illustrates the actual formulas used to make calculations. In addition to the "black box" approach of AB:POM, instructors and students can also develop their own formulas via spreadsheet to solve problems in forecasting, simulation, time studies, PERT, and most other application areas. As a new feature, this edition is one of the first P/OM texts to show this alternative approach. Spreadsheet software is illustrated along with AB:POM printouts at the end of eleven of the chapters and supplements.

CD-ROM AND PRESENTATION GRAPHICS.   An exciting new feature in this edition is lecture/classroom material for the course on two colorful media—CD-ROMs and Presentation Graphics disks. Key features from each chapter are highlighted in both. The CD-ROM also includes photographs and video highlights.

STUDY GUIDE.   Another supplement available with the text is a student *Study Guide*. The *Study Guide* comes complete with alternate narrative, solved problems, and answered review questions on a chapter-by-chapter basis.

NAME INDEX, COMPANY INDEX, AND GENERAL INDEX.   We have expanded to three indices in this fourth edition. A new index provides a listing of

This helps us develop an approach for every other P/OM decision. With expanded coverage of European (ISO 9000) and Japanese quality standards, the Baldrige Awards, house of quality, benchmarking, poka-yoke, Kaizen, and fishbone diagrams, we introduce the latest concepts in the quality discipline.

A BALANCE OF SERVICE AND MANUFACTURING APPLICATIONS.   P/OM has a service as well as a traditional manufacturing aspect. This fourth edition takes special note of services. Many chapters include service aspects of operations, and others have special sections that note the distinction between service and manufacturing in P/OM. For instance, in the work measurement sections, we have used service jobs as examples. Similarly, office layouts receive added emphasis, as do service location issues, quality management, and project management applied to services.

Pedagogy

SOLVED PROBLEMS.   Once again, solved problems are included in this edition. They are provided as models for students as they work unsolved problems on their own.

DATA BASE APPLICATIONS.   A feature called "Data Base Applications" appears in chapters on quality control, linear programming, forecasting, location strategy, transportation models, layout, aggregate planning, material requirements planning, short-term scheduling, and project management. These very large problems are intended for analysis by computer. They permit students to spend more time interpreting outputs of realistic problems to supplement problem-solving skills developed with the regular programs.

CASES.   We have introduced 17 new cases into the fourth edition. Most of these have been developed by leading P/OM academics throughout the United States. The cases are generally one to two text pages in length, making them short enough to cover in weekly assignments. But they also deal with situations in a realistic, detailed manner that adds depth to each chapter. Almost all cases are based on real-world companies.

THREE LEVELS OF PROBLEMS.   The number of end-of-chapter problems has been increased by 25%, and each is identified as one of three levels: introductory (one dot), moderate (two dots), and challenging (three dots). In addition, these problems focus on problem formulation and interpretation as well as calculation. Over 100 new discussion questions have been added as well.

POM IN ACTION BOXES.   Recent examples of P/OM practice, from a variety of sources such as the *Wall Street Journal*, *Fortune*, *Harvard Business Review*, and *Forbes*, are included in all chapters and supplements. These boxes bring P/OM to life and help drive home the points made in the chapters. These real P/OM issues can spark the students' interest and enliven class discussion. Sixty-five new *POM in Action* boxes appear in this fourth edition.

CRITICAL THINKING EXERCISES.   Our fourth edition is the first P/OM text to provide a new feature that challenges the student to face critical issues of business

PREFACE

Production and operations management (P/OM) can be one of the most exciting and challenging topics in the business curriculum. This fourth edition of *Production and Operations Management: Strategic and Tactical Decisions* is intended to provide you with a current, complete, and practical introduction to the field. The text is designed for introductory classes at either the undergraduate or MBA level.

We stress the decisions that managers make and the manager's role in increasing productivity in a world economy. We hope that students, after completing the course, will appreciate the role of operations managers in enriching the lives of everyone. The authors are aware that the majority of our readers are not P/OM majors. However, we think that management, marketing, finance, economics, accounting, quantitative methods, and information systems students will find the material both interesting and useful. Over 100,000 readers of the first three editions seem to have endorsed this premise.

FOCUS OF THE FOURTH EDITION

Contents

STRATEGIC AND TACTICAL DECISIONS FOR MEETING CUSTOMER NEEDS. As in the previous editions, we balance the coverage of managerial and strategic issues with a series of decisions for meeting the needs of customers. To provide maximum flexibility, we have included eight chapter supplements that deal with decision-making techniques such as linear programming, queuing, simulation, and learning curves. This allows instructors to spend as much or as little time as needed on each component of the course.

INTERNATIONAL EXAMPLES. As productivity and the world economy are so closely linked with our own, we have made a special effort to include international illustrations in our narrative, problems, cases, and *POM in Action* boxes. This emphasis is also tied to our focus in each chapter on how to achieve world-class standards in performance. We discuss scores of international firms; Volvo, British Airways, Nissan, Toyota, Komatsu, Michelin, and Siemens are just some of the examples discussed. Our coverage of P/OM strategy in Chapter 2 has been expanded to discuss issues of international competitiveness.

STATE-OF-THE-ART DEVELOPMENTS. In order to keep up to date, we have added to or expanded our coverage of total quality management (TQM) tools, house of quality, benchmarking, finite scheduling, time-based competition, work cells, animated simulation, keiretsu, virtual organizations, and Japanese layout.

QUALITY MANAGEMENT. Due to its increasingly important role throughout the operations process, we have significantly revised and expanded the chapters that deal with the important issue of quality. We have moved this material to Chapters 3 and 4.

BARRY RENDER is the Charles Harwood Distinguished Professor of Operations Management at the Crummer Graduate School of Business at Rollins College, in Winter Park, Florida. He received his M.S. in Operations Research and his Ph.D. in Quantitative Analysis at the University of Cincinnati (1975). He previously taught at George Washington University, University of New Orleans, Boston University, and George Mason University, where he held the GM Foundation Professorship in Decision Sciences and was Chair of the Decision Science Department. Dr. Render has also worked in the aerospace industry for General Electric, McDonnell Douglas, and NASA.

Professor Render has co-authored nine textbooks with Prentice-Hall, including *Quantitative Analysis for Management*, *Service Operations Management*, *Principles of Operations Management*, *Introduction to Management Science*, and *Cases and Readings in Management Science*. His more than one hundred articles on a variety of management topics have appeared in *Decision Sciences*, *Interfaces*, *Information and Management*, *Journal of Management Information Systems*, *Socio-Economic Planning Sciences*, and *Operations Management Review*, among others.

Dr. Render has also been honored as an AACSB Fellow and named as a Senior Fulbright Scholar in 1982 and again in 1993. He was twice vice president of the Decision Science Institute Southeast Region and served as Software Review Editor for *Decision Line* for six years. He is Prentice-Hall's consulting editor for Decision Sciences textbooks. Finally, Professor Render has been actively involved in consulting for government agencies and for many corporations, including NASA, FBI, U.S. Navy, Fairfax County, Virginia, and C&P Telephone. He teaches production and operations management courses in Rollins College's MBA and Executive MBA programs. In 1995 he was named as that school's Outstanding Professor of the Year.

JAY HEIZER holds the Jesse H. Jones Chair of Business Administration at Texas Lutheran College in Seguin, Texas. He received his B.B.A. and M.B.A. from the University of North Texas and his Ph.D. in Management and Statistics from Arizona State University (1969). He was previously a member of the faculty at Memphis State University, the University of Oklahoma, Virginia Commonwealth University, and the University of Richmond. He has also held visiting positions at Boston University and George Mason University.

Dr. Heizer's industrial experience is extensive. He learned the practical side of production/operations management as a machinist apprentice at Foringer and Company, production planner for Westinghouse Airbrake, and at General Dynamics, where he worked in engineering administration. Additionally, he has been actively involved in consulting in the P/OM and MIS areas for a variety of organizations including Philip Morris, Firestone, Dixie Container Corporation, Columbia Industries, and Tenneco. He holds the CPIM certification from the American Production and Inventory Control Society.

Professor Heizer has co-authored four books and has published three dozen articles on a variety of management topics. His papers have appeared in the *Academy of Management Journal, Journal of Purchasing, Personnel Psychology, Production & Inventory Control Management, APICS-The Performance Advantage,* and *Engineering Management,* among others. He has taught production and operations management courses in undergraduate, graduate, and executive programs.

Keith Davis,
teacher, scholar, mentor, friend
and
Albert J. Simone,
for always setting the standards
for high-quality academics

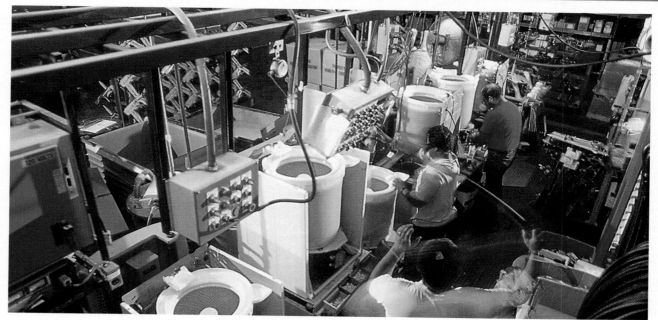

This is a scene from Whirlpool's Clyde, Ohio, plant, where washing machines are assembled with perfect parts received on time from Benton Harbor.

Benton Harbor makes about 5% of the parts that go into a Whirlpool washing machine. Here steel rods for those parts are loaded for processing.

I t was August 1913 in Detroit and Ford Motor managers Clarence Avery and C. W. Klann struggled to build cars. Men had been building cars for decades, but Avery and Klann wanted to do it faster and cheaper. Their plan was to put the car together while it moved and the men assembling it stood still—a revolutionary change. For centuries, men had moved and the work stood still. Moving work while men stand still is difficult. But they succeeded. In 9 months, they reduced the time spent on assembly from over 12 hours to just 93 minutes. They revolutionized production and before they were through, they put America on wheels with 15 million Model T Fords. ◆

Production
Production management and operations management

In this text, we discuss how managers continue to revolutionize production and how you, too, can manage resources to improve production and our quality of life. **Production** is the creation of goods and services. **Production management and operations management (P/OM)** are activities that transform resources into goods and services. Activities creating goods and services take place in all organizations.

In companies that manufacture goods, the production activities that create those goods are usually quite obvious. For instance, we can watch the creation of a tangible product such as a Sony television set or a Chevy truck. When referring to such activity, we tend to use the term *production management*.

In other organizations that do not create physical products, the production function may be less obvious. The "production" that takes place when your check is processed at your bank, or when you make an airline reservation, or when a patient is taken care of in a hospital, is called *operations*. The product that is produced may take some unusual forms, such as placing machine-readable marks on paper, filling an empty seat on an airplane, or prescribing medication. We call the companies that do this type of work *service organizations*. The production activity that goes on in these service organizations is usually referred to as *operations* or *operations management*. The *POM in Action* box "Moving Money at 111 Wall Street" provides a brief glimpse of the role of an operations manager at First National City Bank in New York City.

As we progress through the text, we examine exciting examples of production and operations functions, ranging from General Motors to McDonald's. We see how production managers in these firms create the goods and services that enrich our lives. Production/operations managers make the decisions that transform resources into goods and services. In this text we use the words *production and operations*, as well as the combination *production/operations management* (or P/OM), when we discuss this transformation process.

Frederick W. Taylor's *Principles of Scientific Management* revolutionized manufacturing. A scientific approach to the analysis of daily work and the tools of industry frequently increased productivity 400%. For instance, by 1913, Model T Fords were being assembled with less than two hours of labor.

HERITAGE OF OPERATIONS MANAGEMENT

The field of P/OM is relatively young, but its history is rich and interesting. Our lives and the P/OM discipline have been enhanced by the innovations and contributions of numerous individuals. We introduce you to a few of these individuals in this section.

Eli Whitney (1800) is credited with the early popularization of interchangeable parts, which he achieved by standardizing parts and through effective quality control. In a contract he signed with the U.S. government for 10,000 muskets, he was able to command a premium price because the muskets had interchangeable parts.

Moving Money at 111 Wall Street

There's a factory on Wall Street in a tall building of concrete and smoky glass that looks identical to the neighboring 24-story structures. However, when workers from the other downtown office buildings complete their day's labors and leave for home, activity at 111 Wall Street continues.

Huge, noisy sorting machines and scurrying robot forklift trucks create an atmosphere of factory-like activity, and trucks carrying raw materials descend on the loading docks. In other large rooms, workers at electric machines produce deafening noise equal to a hundred machine guns.

During one year, $2.5 trillion will be processed in the Operating Group of First National City Bank, where 6,500 laborers perform the physical acts of the otherwise ephemeral business of banking. Accounts are debited and credited. Checks drawn on other banks are put through the clearing houses and sent back to the original writers. First National City Bank's own customers are mailed their canceled checks and bank statements on a monthly basis.

Every 24 hours, approximately 1.5 million checks are delivered by 38 trucks to the loading docks of 111 Wall Street. Hopefully, the last check is put through the mill by 6 A.M. The goal is to send out as many checks as come in.

In the encoding room, dozens of people working feverishly at their keyboards complete an average of 1,200 checks an hour. When they leave the encoding area, the checks are placed into trays and "handed off" to the climate-controlled computer room where 40-foot "Trace" machines sort them for delivery to a multitude of institutions from Chase Manhattan Bank to the Bank of China.

Sources: World of Banking, 9, no. 2 (March/April 1990): 12–18, 30–31; *Wall Street Journal* (June 6, 1975).

Frederick W. Taylor (1881) contributed to personnel selection, planning and scheduling, and motion study.[1] One of his major contributions was his belief that management should be much more resourceful and aggressive in the improvement of work methods. Taylor and his colleagues, Henry L. Gantt and Frank and Lillian Gilbreth, were among the first to seek scientifically the best way to produce. Because

Frank and Lillian Gilbreth were interested in finding the one best way to accomplish work tasks. In pursuit of this effort, they invented a wide variety of techniques and devices. One technique was to use cameras to record movement by attaching lights to an individual's arms and legs. In that way they could track the movement of individuals while performing various jobs.

[1]Frederick W. Taylor, *Principles of Scientific Management* (New York: Harper & Brothers, 1911).

of his work, Taylor is known as the father of scientific management. Taylor made a distinction between management (for example, those who plan, organize, staff, direct, and control) and labor (those who do the physical work). He believed that management should assume more responsibility for

1. matching employees to the job
2. providing the proper training
3. providing proper work methods and tools
4. establishing legitimate incentives for work accomplished

As suggested earlier, by 1913, Henry Ford had provided the leadership that combined standardized parts with the quasi-assembly lines of the meat-packing and mail-order industries and had added the concept of the modern moving assembly line. Based on his experience at Ford, Charles Sorensen designed the Willow Run assembly line during World War II, which eventually produced one B-24 "Liberator" bomber each hour.

Quality control is another historically significant contribution to the field of P/OM. Walter Shewhart (1924), who understood statistics and the need for evaluating quality, provided the foundations for statistical sampling and quality control. W. Edwards Deming (1950), another leader in quality control, believed, as did Frederick Taylor, that management must do more to improve the work environment and processes so that quality can be improved.

Industrial engineering

Management science

Physical sciences

Production/operations management will continue to progress based on contributions from other disciplines, including **industrial engineering** and **management science.** These disciplines, along with statistics, management, and economics, have contributed substantially to greater productivity.

Innovations from the **physical sciences** (biology, anatomy, chemistry, and physics) have also contributed to advances in P/OM. These advances include new adhesives, chemical processes for printed-circuit boards, gamma rays to sanitize food products, and molten tin tables on which to float a higher-quality molten glass as it cools. The design of products and processes often depend on the biological and physical sciences.

Information sciences

An especially important contribution to P/OM has come from **information sciences.** In a modern organization, information management implies the use of computers that turn raw data into information—and the rapid flow of accurate information is critical to effective management. Information science is a discipline that has grown due to the contributions of a variety of people, including Charles Babbage and John Vincent Atanasoff. Babbage, in 1832, was the first person to design a prototype computer. Ada, the Countess of Lovelace and daughter of the poet Byron, was the first person to design a way to program it. A century later John Atanasoff, while on the faculty of Iowa State, described and built the first digital computer (the ABC computer) in the winter of 1937–1938. These and subsequent contributions to computing and information sciences have provided operations management with an ability to handle problems that previously could not have been addressed and to provide society with a great diversity of goods and services.

Understanding the history of P/OM provides a basis for both studying the discipline today and planning a future in it. In this chapter, we look at the diverse ways you can prepare for a career in production/operations management. Let us first look, though, at how we organize firms to create goods and services.

FIGURE 1.1 ■ Three Functions Required of All Organizations

ORGANI-ZATION	MARKETING	OPERATIONS	FINANCE/ACCOUNTING
Fast food restaurant	Advertise on TV Give away promotional materials Sponsor kids' leagues	Make hamburgers/fries Maintain equipment Design new facilities	Pay suppliers Collect cash Pay employees Pay bank loans
University	Mail catalogs Call on high schools	Research for truth Disseminate truth	Pay faculty/staff Collect tuition
Automobile manufacturer	Advertise on TV, in newspapers, etc. Support auto racing Offer rebates	Design automobiles Manufacture parts Assemble automobiles Develop suppliers	Pay suppliers, employees Prepare budgets Pay dividends Sell stock
Church/synagogue	Call on newcomers	Conduct weddings Conduct funerals Conduct services	Count contributions Keep track of pledges Pay the mortgage, other bills

ORGANIZING FOR THE CREATION OF GOODS AND SERVICES

To create goods and services, all organizations perform three functions (see Figure 1.1). These functions are the necessary ingredients not only for production, but also for an organization's survival. The functions are

1. *Marketing*, which generates the demand or, at least, takes the order for a product or service.
2. *Production/operations*, which creates the product.
3. *Finance/accounting*, which tracks how well the organization is doing, pays the bills, and collects the money.

Universities, churches and synagogues, and businesses all perform these functions. Any institution, even a volunteer group such as the Boy Scouts of America, is organized to perform these three basic functions. Figure 1.2 shows how an airline, a bank, and a manufacturing firm organize themselves to perform these functions. The shaded areas of Figure 1.2 show the production and operations in these organizations.

WHY STUDY P/OM?

We study P/OM for four reasons. First, P/OM is one of the three major functions of any organization and is essential to understanding what organizations do. Only by studying P/OM do we understand how people organize themselves for productive enterprise.

FIGURE 1.2 ■ Organization Charts for (a) an Airline, (b) a Bank, and (c) a Manufacturing Organization. The blue areas are P/OM tasks.

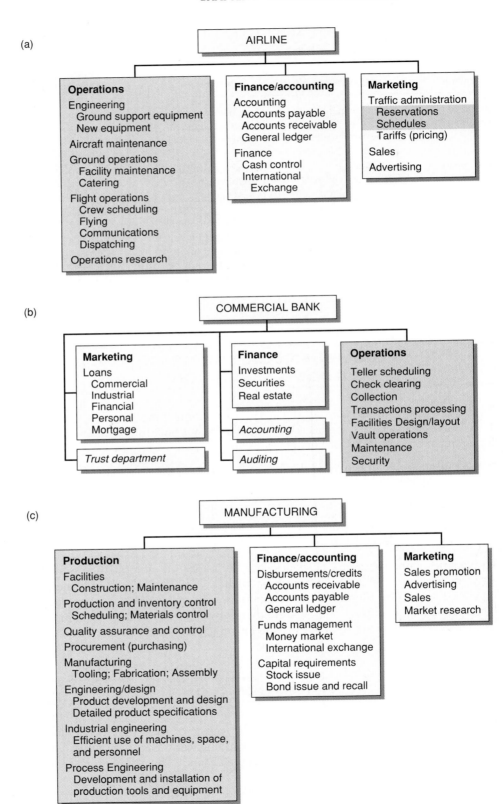

(a)

AIRLINE

Operations
Engineering
  Ground support equipment
  New equipment
Aircraft maintenance
Ground operations
  Facility maintenance
  Catering
Flight operations
  Crew scheduling
  Flying
  Communications
  Dispatching
Operations research

Finance/accounting
Accounting
  Accounts payable
  Accounts receivable
  General ledger
Finance
  Cash control
  International
    Exchange

Marketing
Traffic administration
  Reservations
  Schedules
  Tariffs (pricing)
Sales
Advertising

(b)

COMMERCIAL BANK

Marketing
Loans
  Commercial
  Industrial
  Financial
  Personal
  Mortgage

Trust department

Finance
Investments
Securities
Real estate

Accounting

Auditing

Operations
Teller scheduling
Check clearing
Collection
Transactions processing
Facilities Design/layout
Vault operations
Maintenance
Security

(c)

MANUFACTURING

Production
Facilities
  Construction; Maintenance
Production and inventory control
  Scheduling; Materials control
Quality assurance and control
Procurement (purchasing)
Manufacturing
  Tooling; Fabrication; Assembly
Engineering/design
  Product development and design
  Detailed product specifications
Industrial engineering
  Efficient use of machines, space,
  and personnel
Process Engineering
  Development and installation of
  production tools and equipment

Finance/accounting
Disbursements/credits
  Accounts receivable
  Accounts payable
  General ledger
Funds management
  Money market
  International exchange
Capital requirements
  Stock issue
  Bond issue and recall

Marketing
Sales promotion
Advertising
Sales
Market research

Second, we study P/OM because we want to know how goods and services are produced. The production function is the segment of our society that creates the products we use. Third, we study P/OM because it is one of the most costly parts of any organization. Table 1.1 shows the large percentage of revenue spent in the P/OM functions of selected businesses. This cost makes it a legitimate focus as societies strive to increase productivity. Indeed, P/OM may provide the best opportunity for an organization to improve its profitability as it provides goods or services. Example 1 shows us how a firm might increase its profitability via the production function.

EXAMPLE 1

Landrum Technologies is a small firm that must double its dollar contribution to overhead in order to be profitable enough to purchase the next generation of production equipment. The management has determined that if the firm fails to increase contribution, its bank will not make the loan and the equipment cannot be purchased. If the firm cannot purchase the equipment, the limitations of the old equipment will preclude Landrum Technologies from remaining in business, and the firm will be unable to provide jobs for its employees or goods and services for its customers. The data below show a simple income statement and three strategic options for the firm. The first strategic option is a *marketing option*, where good marketing management may increase sales by 50%. By increasing sales by 50%, contribution will in turn increase 71%. But increasing sales by 50% may be more than difficult; it may even be impossible.

Second is a *finance/accounting* option, where finance costs are cut in half through good financial management. But elimination of all finance costs is still inadequate for generating the necessary increase in contribution. Contribution is increased by only 21%.

Third is a *P/OM option*, where management reduces production costs by 20% and increases contribution by 114%!

Given the conditions of our brief example, we now have a bank willing to lend additional funds to Landrum Technologies.

OPTIONS FOR INCREASING CONTRIBUTION

	CURRENT	MARKETING OPTION* INCREASE SALES REVENUE 50%	FINANCE OPTION† REDUCE FINANCE COSTS 50%	PRODUCTION OPTION‡ REDUCE PRODUCTION COSTS 20%
Sales	$100,000	$150,000	$100,000	$100,000
Costs of goods	− 80,000	−120,000	− 80,000	− 64,000
Gross margin	20,000	30,000	20,000	36,000
Finance costs	− 6,000	− 6,000	− 3,000	− 6,000
Contribution§	14,000	24,000	17,000	30,000

*Increasing sales 50% increases contribution by $10,000, or 71.4% (10,000/14,000).
†Reducing finance costs 50% increases contribution by $3,000, or 21.4%.
‡Reducing production costs 20% increases contribution by $16,000, or 114.2% (16,000/14,000).
§Contribution to fixed cost (excluding finance costs) and profit.

The Hawthorne studies began to determine the impact of lighting on productivity. They concluded by recognizing the importance of a social system at the workplace. Shown here is part of the relay assembly room at the Hawthorne plant of Western Electric.

TABLE 1.1 ■ PERCENTAGE OF SALES SPENT ON THE P/OM FUNCTION FOR SELECTED ORGANIZATIONS

	MEAT-PACKING INDUSTRY	FURNITURE MANUFAC-TURING	RESTAURANT	HEAVY EQUIPMENT MANUFACTURING
Production/Operations				
Material	79%	40%	38%	42%
Direct labor	8%	15%	20%	12%
Fringes, supervision, supplies	3%	22%	16%	23%
	90%	77%	74%	77%
Selling, Finance, General, and Administrative	9%	15%	22%	20%
Interest, Extraordinary Items, Taxes, and Profits	1%	8%	4%	3%

Note: All figures are approximate because standardized categories are grouped and rounded.

The production option taken in Example 1 is the successful strategy recently used by Cummins Engine. As you see from the *POM in Action* box "The Yankee Samurai," this strategy was the only one that made sense. The Cummins case is not unusual. An efficient production function has a high payoff for the company and the managers concerned.

The fourth reason for studying P/OM is to understand what production/operations managers do. By understanding what these managers do, you can build the decision-making skills necessary to be such a manager. Such an understanding is integral to exploring the numerous and lucrative career opportunities in P/OM.

WHAT PRODUCTION/OPERATIONS MANAGERS DO

Management process

All good managers perform the basic functions of the management process.[2] The **management process** consists of the following:

1. *Planning.* Managers determine objectives and goals for organizations and develop programs, policies, and procedures that will help organizations attain them. Managers also determine subordinate plans for every department, group, and individual.

2. *Organizing.* Managers develop a structure of individuals, groups, departments, and divisions to achieve objectives.

3. *Staffing.* Managers determine personnel requirements, including the best way to recruit, train, retain, and terminate employees for achieving objectives.

4. *Leading.* Managers lead, supervise, and motivate personnel to achieve objectives.

[2]See Henri Fayol, *General and Industrial Administration* (London: Pitman, 1969); Harold Koontz, *Toward a Unified Theory of Management* (New York: McGraw-Hill, 1964); and J. G. March and H. Simon, *Organizations* (New York: John Wiley, 1958).

The Yankee Samurai

It all began when the first truck engines marked "Komatsu" and "Nissan" appeared on a California dock. Soon after, calls were received from good customers such as Navistar and Freightliner, telling Cummins that they were trying out these Japanese medium-truck engines.

Cummins, a company that held almost 60% of the U.S. heavy-duty diesel-truck engine market, had a lot to lose. After all, if the Japanese were gaining momentum in the medium-engine market, the heavy-engine market could be their next target. To protect themselves, Cummins decided to become more competitive. They cut their prices 10 to 40%. That was the easy part.

Next came cost cutting and simultaneously dealing with inflation. Costs needed to be cut by a minimum of 33%, and this was no easy task.

But Cummins decided to learn from the Japanese and studied their production methods. They found that U.S. accounting systems tended to hide certain costs. Cummins also discovered that by using more flexible machinery, they could reduce their inventory from 60 days' supply down to 3 or 4 days' supply.

Now it was time to tackle their big item, cutting material costs, which represented 50% of the production budget. Cummins turned to their suppliers for suggestions. Could they help? Yes. It turned out that no one had ever asked before. In 3 years, Cummins was able to lower material costs an impressive 18%. Relationships with suppliers have gone from adversarial to cooperative. In the Cummins's chairman's own words, "We're trying to do everything with our suppliers that we want to do with our customers."

Sources: Forbes (July 14, 1986). *Accountancy*, 103 (May 1991): 39–43; *Business Week* (October 2, 1993): 222–224.

5. *Controlling.* Managers develop the standards and communication networks necessary to ensure that the enterprise is pursuing appropriate plans and achieving objectives.

Production/operations managers apply this management process to the decisions they make in the P/OM function. In a complex organization, managers contribute to production and operations through the activities shown in Table 1.2. Each of these activities requires planning, organizing, staffing, directing, and controlling.

The activities shown in Table 1.2 require that operations managers make decisions. These decisions allocate resources that affect the efficiency and strategy of the firm. In this text, we provide an introduction to the proper way to make these decisions.

WHERE ARE THE P/OM JOBS?

Figure 1.3 shows jobs in the United States by sector. Manufacturing, which has a high portion of P/OM jobs, now constitutes about 18% of all jobs; construction and mining industries, about 6%; and services, the remaining 76%. The service sector includes government, education, food and lodging, trade, utilities, transportation, finance, insurance, real estate, legal, medical, and repair and maintenance. Table 1.3 is a list of firms in these various categories.

TABLE 1.2 ■ ACTIVITIES OF TYPICAL PRODUCTION AND OPERATIONS DEPARTMENTS

DEPARTMENT	ACTIVITY
Research and development (R & D)	Conducts product research, product development.
Product design	Fine-tunes product design to enhance production efficiency.
Process design	Selects or designs and develops production tools, equipment, and processes.
Facilities planning, construction	Plans, constructs, and repairs facilities.
Purchasing	Determines the best source for given specification, delivery, and price.
Industrial engineering (IE)	Determines most efficient use of machines, space, and personnel; work measurement.
Methods and procedures	Directs efforts toward improvement in procedures at the workplace.
Production planning and inventory control (PIC)	Schedules the manufacturing processes; manages inventory.
Management science	Applies the methodology, models, and procedures of mathematics or management information systems to manufacturing operations.
Quality management/quality control	Reviews designs, products, and processes to ensure quality objectives are met.
Maintenance	Focuses on designing systems and procedures that will create and maintain a reliable system.

If two-thirds of all jobs in manufacturing and the extractive industries are production/operations jobs and one-third of all jobs in the service sector are production/operations jobs, then about 40% of *all* jobs are in production and operations. In the United States, which has about 128 million people employed, there would be 51 million jobs in the production/operations function; most of these jobs are professional

FIGURE 1.3 ■ Jobs in the United States

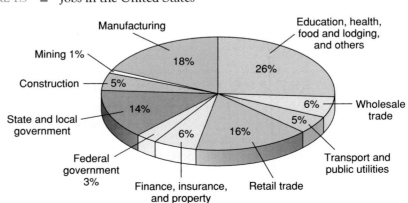

(*Source:* U.S. Department of Labor, *Monthly Labor Review.*)

TABLE 1.3 ■ EXAMPLES OF ORGANIZATIONS IN EACH SECTOR

COMPANY/ORGANIZATION	EXAMPLE
Manufacturing sector	General Electric, Ford, U.S. Steel
Construction sector	Bechtel, McDermott
Mining sector	Homestake Mining
Service sector	
Government	Federal, state, local
Education	Public and private schools
Food	McDonald's, Luby's Cafeteria
Lodging	Motel 6, Hilton Hotels
Entertainment	Walt Disney, Paramount Pictures
Trade (retail, wholesale)	Walgreen's, Wal-Mart, Kmart
Utilities	Pacific Gas & Electric
Transportation	
Airlines	American Airlines, Southwest Airlines
Railroad	CSX, Santa Fe
Trucking	Overnight, J. B. Hunt
Finance	Citicorp, American Express
Insurance	Prudential, Aetna
Real estate	
Development	Trammell Crow
Sales	Coldwell Bankers
Legal	Hunton & Williams, Local Law Offices
Medical	Mayo Clinic, Humana Hospitals
Repair and maintenance	IBM Computer Maintenance, Xerox Maintenance, Pitney-Bowes

and managerial. These positions require education, training, and professional qualifications, and also a knowledge of P/OM concepts. Now let us examine some of these P/OM jobs.

PREPARING FOR A CAREER IN P/OM?

How does one get started on a career in production/operations? Let us review the qualifications for individuals seeking entry-level positions in P/OM. The activities identified in Table 1.2 require decisions by individuals trained in P/OM. The more background the competent business student has in P/OM, accounting, statistics, information systems, and mathematics, the more job opportunities will be available.

In the *production and inventory control* area, entry-level jobs often go to P/OM graduates. A P/OM graduate can enhance his or her qualifications by becoming a certified practitioner in inventory management (CPIM). The *American Production and Inventory Control Society (APICS)* offers this certification.[3] Membership in a student or local chapter of APICS is also an excellent way to enhance qualifications for positions in this field. Jobs are available in virtually all sectors from hospitals and banks to aircraft maintenance to manufacturing.

[3]American Production and Inventory Control Society, Certification Department, 500 W. Annandale, Falls Church, VA 22046–4274.

Management science is a term used to describe a wide variety of quantitative and computer-related tasks. Consequently, the term encompasses a wide variety of opportunities. Most entry-level positions in this area go to majors in mathematics, quantitative management, information systems, management, or P/OM, depending on the exact nature of the assignment. The *Society of Manufacturing Engineers (SME)* is one source of information about P/OM careers in manufacturing,[4] and the *Institute for Operations Research and the Management Sciences (INFORMS)*[5] and *Decision Sciences Institute*[6] can provide career information in other sectors, such as government and transportation.

The jobs in *cost analysis, industrial engineering, labor standards, work methods,* and management aspects of *maintenance* often go to business and P/OM graduates, particularly if the student has completed some special course work in these areas. The *Institute of Industrial Engineers (IIE)* has nationwide chapters, usually with monthly meetings at which students are welcome.[7]

Entry-level *purchasing* jobs are often as expediters or assistant buyers. Business and P/OM graduates have the inside track for such positions which exist in all sectors from retail to medicine, to manufacturing. Students can enhance their qualifications by taking a series of exams to become certified purchasing managers (CPMs). If purchasing interests you, you might contact the *National Association for Purchasing Management* (NAPM) for information about membership and the exam.[8]

Quality management positions, of course, are ideal for students with a solid background in statistics, either as statistics majors or business majors. The *American Society for Quality Control* (ASQC)[9] can provide information about careers in quality control and their certification examinations. Quality management has been critical in such fields as food and hospitality management, hospitals, and airlines.

Students with an *information science* background often possess the necessary skills to get P/OM jobs. These students can carve their niche by assisting in developing computerized accounting, ordering, inventory control, forecasting, or personnel systems or in creating mathematical models that help the firm make better decisions. You can turn to your local chapter of the *Data Processing Management Association* (DPMA)[10] or the *Association for Systems Management* (ASM)[11] for contacts and more information.

Many opportunities exist for individuals with other backgrounds as well. Students in the *physical sciences*, for example, can find opportunities in a wide variety of jobs related to production and operations. These jobs range from protecting the environment to developing new adhesives or production processes.

Whatever the job and career, the task is to transform effectively resources into products and services. This transformation must take place efficiently because the production/operations manager is responsible, more than anyone else in our society, for improving productivity.

---

[4]Society of Manufacturing Engineers, One SME Drive, P.O. Box 930, Dearborn, MI 48121.

[5]The Institute for Operations Research and the Management Sciences, 290 Westminster Street, Providence, RI 02903.

[6]Decision Sciences Institute, University Plaza, Atlanta, GA 30303.

[7]Institute of Industrial Engineers, 25 Technology Park, Norcross, GA 30092.

[8]National Association for Purchasing Management, P.O. Box 418, Oradell, NJ 07649.

[9]American Society for Quality Control, 230 W. Wells Street, Milwaukee, WI 53203.

[10]Data Processing Management Association (DPMA), 505 Busse Highway, Park Ridge, IL 60068.

[11]Association for Systems Management, 1433 W. Bogley Road, P.O. Box 38370, Cleveland, OH 44130–0370.

THE PRODUCTIVITY CHALLENGE

Production, as defined earlier, is the creation of goods and services. **Productivity** is the enhancement of the production process. Enhancement of production means a favorable comparison of the quantity of resources employed (inputs) to the quantity of goods and services produced (outputs) (see Figure 1.4). Productivity can be improved by either reducing *inputs* while keeping *output* constant or increasing *output* while keeping *inputs* constant. Inputs, as defined by economists, are land, labor, capital, and management. Managers combine these inputs in a production system that converts inputs to outputs. Outputs are goods and services, including such diverse items as guns, butter, education, improved judicial systems, and ski resorts.

Productivity

Productivity allows both firms and countries to maintain their competitiveness. Measurement of productivity is an excellent way to evaluate performance of a firm or a country. Productivity management is also an excellent way to evaluate a firm's or a country's ability to provide an improving standard of living for its people. Figure 1.5 shows that productivity improvement at Whirlpool Corporation allowed the company to reduce prices to customers and at the same time to increase wages. Similarly, while the recent resurgence of productivity in the United States is welcome, the modest gains of the last two decades (see Figure 1.6(a)) have allowed other industrialized countries to approach U.S. productivity (see Figure 1.6(b)). *Only through increases in productivity can the standard of living improve.* Moreover, only through increases in productivity can labor, capital, and management receive additional payments. If payments to labor, capital, or management are increased without increased productivity, then prices rise. On the other hand, prices tend to drop as productivity increases, because the same inputs are producing more outputs.

Since 1889, the United States has been able to increase productivity at an average rate of nearly 2.5% per year. Such growth doubles wealth every 30 years. However, in recent decades, the United States has been unable to sustain that annual rate

FIGURE 1.4 ■ The Economic System Transforms Inputs to Outputs. An effective feedback loop evaluates process performance against a plan. It also evaluates customer satisfaction and sends signals to the institutions controlling the inputs and process.

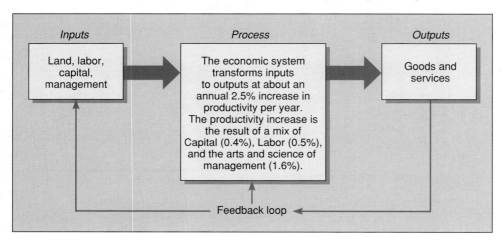

FIGURE 1.5 ■ What Happens When Productivity Improves? When productivity increases, costs can drop and wages increase. These gains occurred at Whirlpool's Benton Harbor, Michigan, plant.

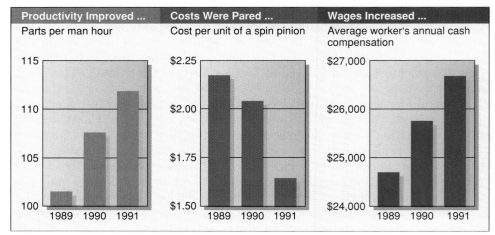

(*Source:* Whirlpool Corp.; American Productivity and Quality Centers, as reported in the *Wall Street Journal* [May 4, 1992]: A1–A4.)

of productivity increase. But as the *POM in Action* box "The United States Maintains World Leadership in Productivity" shows, recent productivity gains in the United States are encouraging. When productivity lags, so does improvement in the quality of life. Companies, like countries, must first determine the reasons for low levels of productivity improvement and then address them. In this text, we examine how to improve productivity by studying the strategic and tactical decisions made by operations managers.

FIGURE 1.6 ■ A Comparison of Productivity in the United States, Japan, and Germany

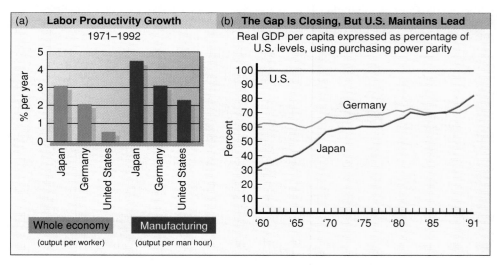

(*Sources:* [a] Adapted from *The Economist* [February 13, 1993]: 67; [b] Bureau of Labor Statistics, based on OECD price calculation, as reported in *Forbes* [September 14, 1992]: 43.)

The United States Maintains World Leadership in Productivity

Just a few years ago, the descent of the United States into second-rate status was a widely accepted *fait accompli*. No more. Europe and Japan have stumbled while the U.S. economy is growing, its inflation rate is low, and productivity and employment are rising. After more than a decade of painful change and dislocation, many U.S. industries are leaner and nimbler, and many have seized the leadership in sophisticated technologies that are ushering in the information age.

Start with the most basic yardstick of economic health, the growth of productivity or output per worker. Productivity determines how fast living standards can rise. The American worker remains the most productive in the world, producing on average $49,600 in goods and services—$5,000 to $10,000 more per worker than their Japanese and German counterparts.

The reasons. First, there is much less corporate restructuring under way in Japanese and German companies than in the United States. Second, at current exchange rates, German manufacturing workers are paid about $26 an hour, $10 more than U.S. and Japanese factory workers. Third, compared with Japan, the United States has three times as many personal computers per worker. "More American firms have learned to use technology to improve productivity," says Merrill Lynch's Bruce Steinberg. U.S. firms such as Intel, Hewlett-Packard, and Microsoft are also in the lead in virtually all important areas of the computer revolution: software, workstations, laser printers, networks, and microprocessors.

The U.S. lead is actually widest in services. Retailing is twice as productive in the United States as in Japan, where laws protect shopkeepers from discount chains. The U.S. telephone industry is at least twice as productive as Germany's government monopoly. And the U.S. banking system is 33% more efficient than Germany's banking oligopolies.

Sources: New York Times (February 27, 1994): 3–1, *Forbes*, Sept. 14, 1992, p. 43; and *Forbes*, March 29, 1993, p. 517.

Productivity Measurement

Measuring productivity is, in some cases, quite direct. Such is the case when productivity can be measured as labor-hours required per ton of steel or as the energy (BTUs) necessary to generate a kilowatt of electricity.[12] An example is

$$\text{Productivity} = \frac{\text{units produced}}{\text{input used}}$$

$$= \frac{\text{units produced}}{\text{labor-hours used}} = \frac{1000}{250} = 4$$

In many instances, however, substantial measurement problems do exist.[13] Some of these measurement problems are as follows:

1. *Quality* of inputs and outputs may change while the quantity remains constant.

---

[12]The quality of units produced and the time period are assumed to remain constant.

[13]See John W. Henrici, "How Deadly Is the Productivity Disease?" *Harvard Business Review*, 59 (November/December 1981): 123–129, for discussion of measurement problems at the national level; and David J. Sumanth, *Productivity Engineering and Management* (New York: McGraw-Hill, 1984), for an excellent discussion at the company level.

2. *External elements* may cause an increase or decrease in productivity for which the system under study may not be directly responsible.[14] For instance, a more reliable electric power service may greatly improve production, thereby improving the firm's productivity because of this support system rather than because of managerial decisions made within the firm.

3. *Precise units of measure* may be lacking. Not all automobiles require the same inputs—some cars are subcompacts, and others are Porsches.

Service sector

The measurement problems noted here are particularly acute in the service sector. We earlier identified the **service sector** as repair and maintenance, government, food and lodging, transportation, insurance, trade, financial, real estate, education, legal, medical, and other professional occupations. Note, for instance, the measurement problems in a law office where each case is different. Every legal case will vary, altering the accuracy of the measure "cases per labor-hour" or "cases per employee." Despite these measurement problems, the operations manager must strive for productivity improvement and the information that documents that progress. Indeed, productivity increases in service firms are just as critical as in manufacturing.

Productivity Variables

Productivity variables

Productivity increases exist because of the management of three variables.[15] These **productivity variables** are

1. *labor*, which contributes 0.5% to the increase;
2. *capital*, which contributes 0.4% to the increase;
3. *management*, which contributes 1.6%.

These three factors (Figure 1.7) are critical to productivity improvement. They represent the broad areas in which managers can take action to obtain better productivity.

LABOR.   Historically, the quality of labor contributes about one-half of one percent to productivity improvement each year. Three traditional variables for improved labor productivity have been

1. basic education appropriate for an effective labor force;
2. diet of the labor force;
3. social overhead that makes labor available, such as transportation and sanitation.

Under some conditions, such as a major construction job in an underdeveloped country, the manager may find these three variables important. However, in developed nations, basic education, diet of the labor force, and social overhead do not now appear to be the critical variables to increase productivity. In developed and postindustrialized nations, however, the real challenge to management is *maintaining and enhancing the skills of labor*. This issue is particularly acute in the midst of rapidly expanding technology and knowledge. Indeed, the variations between countries can be substan-

---

[14]These are exogenous variables, that is, variables outside of the system under study that influence it.

[15]See the work of Solomon Fabricant, *A Primer on Productivity* (New York: Random House, 1969); Dale W. Jorgensen, *Productivity and U.S. Economic Growth* (Cambridge, MA: Harvard University Press, 1987); and Angus Maddison, "Growth and Slowdown in Advanced Capitalist Economics: Technique of Quantitative Assessment," *Journal of Economic Literature*, 25, no. 2 (June 1987): 649–698.

FIGURE 1.7 ■ The Contribution of Capital, Labor, and Management to the Annual Increase in Productivity in the United States

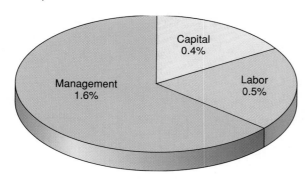

tial. While Germany has outstanding apprenticeship programs, many nations do not. Recent data suggest that the average American 17-year-old knows only half the mathematics known by the average Japanese of the same age (see Figure 1.8). More generally, elementary and secondary students in the United States fall near the bottom of any comparative international test.[16]

Education will remain an important high-cost item in postindustrial societies. Most Western societies are postindustrial, or knowledge, societies. A **knowledge society** is one in which much of the labor force has migrated from manual work to work based on knowledge. Consequently, improving the quality of labor in both developing and developed nations remains a challenge. Perhaps improvements can be found not only through increasing the competence of labor, but also via a fifth item, *better utilized labor with a stronger commitment*. Improvements in labor productivity are possible. However, they can be expected to be increasingly difficult and expensive. What one company does to find workers skilled for today's needs is described in the *POM in Action* box about Carrier, a manufacturer of air conditioners.

Knowledge society

CAPITAL. Human beings are tool-using animals. Capital investment provides those tools. These tools can range from desk computers to complex machinery and new airports. Capital investment has increased in the United States every year except for a few very severe recession periods. Capital investment adds about .4% to productivity each year. Annual capital investment in the United States has increased (until recent years) at the rate of 1.5% of the base investment. This means that the amount of capital invested after allowances for depreciation has grown by 1.5% per year.

However, as inadequate depreciation and taxes drive up the cost of capital, capital investment becomes increasingly expensive.[17] When the capital invested per employee drops, as it has in recent years, we can expect a drop in productivity. Production can often be accomplished with some trade-off between labor and capital. That is, if we want to build a road, we can do so with crews of thousands using shovels

[16]Michael L. Dertouzos, Richard K. Lester, and Robert M. Solow, *Made in America: Regaining the Productive Edge* (Cambridge, MA: MIT Commission on Industrial Productivity, MIT Press, 1989); also see "U.S. Science Students Near Root of Class," *Science*, 239 (March 1988): 1237; also see Richard M. Wolf, "The NAEP and International Comparisons," *Phi Delta Kappan* (April 1988): 580–581.

[17]For instance, the U.S. minimum alternative tax in many instances fails to allow companies to recover their investment. *Economic Effects of the Corporate Alternative Minimum Tax* (Washington, DC: American Council for Capital Formation, Center for Policy Research, 1991).

FIGURE 1.8   ■   About Half (48.9%) of the 17-Year-Olds in the United States Cannot Correctly Answer Questions of This Type.

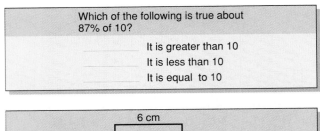

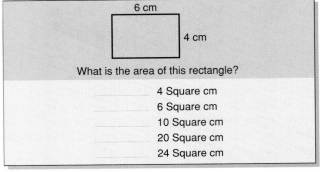

If $7x + 4 = 5x + 8$ then $x =$

| | 1 | | 4 |
| | 2 | | 6 |

(*Source:* Education Testing Service.)

or we can invest in earth-moving equipment. Using labor rather than capital may reduce unemployment in the short run, but it also makes economies less productive and therefore lowers wages in the long run. The trade-off between capital and labor is continually in flux. The more expensive capital is, the more projects requiring capital are squeezed out. Managers adjust their investment plans to changes in capital cost.

In this text, we examine numerous opportunities for P/OM to enhance productivity through improved utilization of capital.

Improving the reading, writing, and arithmetic abilities of workers so that they are capable of handling more difficult jobs is a major concern if productivity is to improve. When the New York Telephone Company recently arranged to have 57,000 applicants take its entry-level examination (a simple test measuring basic skills in reading, math, and reasoning), the severity of the problem was clear—less than 4 percent (only 2,100 applicants) passed.

A Job at Carrier Is Like Applying for College

On a pothole-filled road across from a chicken processor in the remote town of Arkadelphia, Arkansas, sits a Carrier Corp. plant that could be a blueprint for the future of U.S. manufacturing.

The sleek, spotless plant looks more like an insurance office than a factory. Full of automation, with a lean work force of only 150, quiet enough to hear a whisper, it is "probably cleaner than most of our houses," says Fred Cobb, a Carrier worker.

This plant, however, is distinguished by its workers, who are a breed apart from most factory workers. Instead of knuckling under to foreign competition, Carrier, a world-class supplier of air conditioners, is opening small plants that require small, educated work forces. Job applicants at Carrier must complete a grueling course. The selection process results in a job for only 1 of every 16 applicants, and yields a top-quality work force.

The application process starts with a standard state test for applicants who already hold high school diplomas. Only those scoring in the top third advance to having their references checked. Then applicants are interviewed by managers *and* assembly-line workers to see how well they would fit in. Those who survive the interviews enter a six-week course. For five nights a week plus Saturdays, applicants learn blueprint reading, math, computer skills, and quality control. They still receive no assurance of a job at Carrier—and they do not get paid!

But if hired, they have a say in how the plant is run and have unusual authority. They can shut down production if they spot a problem and can order their own supplies. Carrier and the workers at this plant have found a way to build and maintain teamwork while improving productivity.

Sources: Wall Street Journal (March 13, 1993): A-1; and *Quality Digest*, May 1994, p. 40.

MANAGEMENT. Management is a factor of production and an economic resource.[18] It is responsible for ensuring that labor and capital are effectively used to increase productivity. Management accounts for almost two-thirds of the annual 2.5% increase in productivity. The arts and sciences of management include improvements made by using technology and knowledge. Such improvements require training and education as well as dynamic organizations. However, although the United States is a high-technology society, the country invests less in civilian research and development than do any of its major industrial competitors.[19] The research, utilization, and dissemination of knowledge specific to technique and technology may be a current shortcoming of the United States. Moreover, Japan seems to be disseminating information faster and more ably than is the United States.[20]

As we move through the text, we note legal and cultural values that distinguish the U.S. economy from the economies of other nations. We now live in a world economy, and the production/operations manager must adjust to both the opportunities and the realities of the global economy.

PRODUCTIVITY ACTIONS OF THE PRODUCTION/OPERATIONS MANAGER.
Because society and commerce are changing, education and training requirements continue to increase. For instance, not only did the introduction of computers re-

---

[18]For an excellent discussion of management as an economic resource, see Frederick Harbison and Charles A. Myers, *Management in the Industrial World: International Analysis* (New York: McGraw-Hill, 1959).

[19]"A Time to Dismantle the World Economy," *The Economist* (November 9, 1985): 22.

[20]Robert S. Cuttler, "A Survey of High-Technology Transfer Practices in Japan and in the United States," *Interfaces*, 19, no. 6 (November/December 1989): 62–77.

quire added training, but each generation of new computers also requires more training. Each additional management science technique requires education, and new organizational designs require more organizational development. These requirements for more training and education are the inevitable results of the knowledge explosion and the development of a high-technology society. The effective operations manager will *ensure that available knowledge and technology are disseminated and utilized.*

The *more effective utilization* of capital, as opposed to additional capital, is also important. The manager, as a productivity catalyst, is charged with the task of making improvements in the use of capital.

Recent increases in effectiveness in oil exploration, airline scheduling, inventory management, and feedlot operations, for example, show the strides that can be made through the *utilization of management and management science.* Productivity gains in knowledge societies require managers who are comfortable with technology, management science, and management. In this text, we have organized the P/OM aspects of management into ten strategic and tactical decisions. We begin discussion of these ten decisions in Chapter 2.

The productivity challenge is difficult. A country cannot be a world-class competitor with second-class inputs. Poorly educated labor inputs, inadequate capital inputs, and dated technologies are second-class inputs. Low-quality, second-class inputs must be changed to high-quality, first-class inputs. High productivity and high-quality outputs require high-quality inputs.

Productivity and the Service Sector

The service sector provides a challenge to the accurate measurement of productivity and productivity improvement. Productivity of the service sector has proven difficult to improve. This is happening because in the service sector work is

1. typically labor-intensive
2. frequently individually processed
3. often an intellectual task performed by professionals
4. often difficult to mechanize and automate

The more intellectual and personal the task, the more difficult it has been to achieve increases in productivity. The low productivity of the service sector is reflected in the fact that, although more than two-thirds of the U.S. labor force is engaged in service, the service sector contributes only about half of the gross national product (GNP). Productivity improvement in the service sector is a continuing challenge to P/OM.

SUMMARY

Production/operations, marketing, and finance/accounting are the three functions basic to all organizations. The production/operations function creates goods and services. Much of the progress of operations management has been made in the twentieth century, but since the beginning of time, humankind has been attempting to improve its material well-being. P/OM is the primary vehicle for making that improvement.

The effective use of labor, capital, and management by production/operations managers increases productivity. Most productivity improvements are available to assertive, innovative, entrepreneurial managers. Production/operations managers function as productivity catalysts. Moreover, improvements in productivity are the responsibility of the professional manager, and professional managers are among the few people in our society who *can* make this improvement. Modern technological society consists of complex organizations that cry out for effective management. The challenge is great but exciting, and the rewards to the manager and to society are substantial.

KEY TERMS

Production (p. 4)
Production management and operations
   management (P/OM) (p. 4)
Industrial engineering (p. 6)
Management science (p. 6)
Physical sciences (p. 6)

Information sciences (p. 6)
Management process (p. 10)
Productivity (p. 15)
Service sector (p. 18)
Productivity variables (p. 18)
Knowledge society (p. 19)

SOLVED PROBLEM

Solved Problem 1.1

Productivity can be measured in a variety of ways, such as labor, capital, energy, material usage, and so on. In this example, Boe Warren, a noted producer of apple pies sold to supermarkets, has been able, with his current equipment, to produce 24 pies per bushel of apples. He currently purchases 100 bushels per day, and each bushel requires 3 labor-hours to process. He believes that he can hire a professional food broker, who can buy a better-quality apple at the same cost. If this is the case, he can increase his production to 26 pies per bushel. His labor-hours will increase by 8 hours per day.

What will be the impact on productivity (pies per labor-hour) if the food broker is hired?

$$\text{Current labor productivity} = \frac{24 \text{ pies} \times 100 \text{ bushels}}{100 \text{ bushels} \times 3 \text{ hours}} = \frac{2400}{300}$$

$$= 8.0 \text{ pies per labor-hour}$$

$$\text{Labor productivity with food broker} = \frac{26 \text{ pies} \times 100 \text{ bushels}}{(100 \text{ bushels} \times 3 \text{ hours}) + 8 \text{ hours}}$$

$$= \frac{2600}{308} = 8.44$$

Using last year (i.e., 8.0) as a base, the increase is 5.5%: 8.44/8.0 = 1.055, or a 5.5% increase over last year.

DISCUSSION QUESTIONS

1. Define production/operations management in your own words. Will your definition accommodate both manufacturing and service operations?

2. Consider the potential contribution of information sciences to P/OM. Why is the management of information of such great importance in the management of "production"?

3. Figure 1.2 outlines the marketing, operations, and finance/accounting function of three organizations. Prepare a chart similar to Figure 1.2 outlining the same functions for
   (a) a large metropolitan newspaper
   (b) a local drugstore
   (c) a college library
   (d) a local service organization (Boy Scouts, Girl Scouts, Rotary International, Lions, Grange, etc.)
   (e) a doctor's or dentist's office
   (f) a jewelry factory

4. Do the preceding assignment for some other enterprise of your choosing, perhaps an organization where you have worked.

5. What is the difference between production and operations?

6. Identify some disciplines that will contribute in a major way to the future development of P/OM.

7. Can you identify the operation function(s) of a past or current employer? Draw an organization chart for the operations function of that firm.

8. What are the three classic functions of a firm?

9. What departments might you find in the P/OM function of a home appliance manufacturer?

10. Productivity increases as the result of change in what three variables?

11. Which of the three variables noted in Question 10 provide the best opportunity for increase in productivity?

12. How did U.S. productivity compare with productivity changes in Germany and Japan between 1971 and 1992?

13. What are the problems in the measurement of productivity?

14. Identify the contributions to P/OM of Eli Whitney, Henry Ford, and W. Edwards Deming.

CRITICAL THINKING EXERCISE

As Figure 1.8 and the discussion in this chapter suggest, the U.S. educational system is far from being a world leader. Other nations, such as Japan and Israel, excel in academic education, and Germany is the leader in technical training through apprenticeship programs. What are the strengths and weaknesses of the U.S. educational system? What features would we want to emulate from Japan, Germany, or other nations? What is the role of business and the production/operations manager when the education system fails to provide world-class inputs, but consumers expect world-class outputs?

PROBLEMS

• 1.1 Boe and Ann Warren bake apple pies for resale to local supermarkets. They and their three employees invest 50 hours per day making 150 pies.
   (a) What is their productivity?
   (b) They have discussed reassigning work so the flow through the bakery is smoother. If they are correct and they can do the necessary training, they think they can increase apple pie production to 155 per day. What is their new productivity?
   (c) What is their increase in productivity?

• 1.2 Joan Blasco-Paul produces Christmas tree ornaments for resale at local craft fairs and Christmas bazaars. She is currently working a total of 15 hours per day to produce 300 ornaments.
   (a) What is Joan's productivity?

(b) Joan thinks that by redesigning the ornaments and switching from use of a contact cement to a hot-glue gun she can increase her total production to 400 ornaments per day. What is her new productivity?

(c) What is the increase in productivity?

: 1.3 Brewerton's Tennessee Sip'n Whiskey is an extraordinary organization established by John Brewerton shortly after the Treasury Department began using infrared photography to find distillers that showed little interest in purchasing revenue stamps. Because Frank's expenses have gone up, he has a new-found interest in efficiency. Frank is interested in determining the productivity of his organization. He has last year's records and good current data. He would like to know if his organization is maintaining the national average of 2.5% annual increase in productivity. He has the following data:

	LAST YEAR	NOW
Production	1,000	1,000
Labor (hours)	300	275
Corn mash (bushels)	50	45
Capital invested ($)	10,000	11,000
Energy (BTUs)	3,000	2,850

Show the productivity increase for each category and then determine the annual improvement for labor-hours, the typical standard for comparison.

· 1.4 Lackey's, a local bakery, is worried about increased costs—particularly energy. Last year's records can provide a fairly good estimate of the parameters for this year. Charles Lackey, the owner, does not believe things have changed much, but he did invest an additional $3,000 for modifications to the bakery's ovens to make them more energy efficient. The modifications were supposed to make the ovens at least 15% more efficient, but extra labor-hours were required to become familiar with the process changes. Charles has asked you to check the energy savings of the new ovens and also to look over other measures of the bakery's productivity to see if the modifications were beneficial. You have the following data to work with:

	LAST YEAR	NOW
Production (dozen)	1,500	1,500
Labor	350	325
Capital	15,000	18,000
Energy	3,000	2,750

· 1.5 The approximate figures for service jobs in certain countries are shown. Overall productivity increases are highest in Japan, Germany, and the United States (in that order). What conclusions might you draw about productivity and the percentage of services in the economy?

PERCENTAGE OF JOBS THAT ARE SERVICE JOBS	
United States	78
Japan	57
Germany	62

- **1.6** As a library assignment, find the U.S. productivity rate for the (a) latest quarter and (b) latest year.

- **1.7** As a library assignment, find the U.S. productivity rate (increase) last year for the (a) national economy, (b) manufacturing sector, and (c) service sector.

CASE STUDY

National Air Express

National Air is a competitive air express firm with offices around the country. Frank Smith, the Chattanooga, Tennessee, station manager, is preparing his quarterly budget report, which will be presented at the Southeast regional meeting next week. He is very concerned about adding capital expense to the operation when business has not increased appreciably. This has been the worst first quarter he can remember: snowstorms, earthquakes, and bitter cold. He has asked Martha Lewis, field services supervisor, to help him review the available data and offer possible solutions.

SERVICE METHODS

National Air offers door-to-door overnight air express delivery within the United States. Smith and Lewis manage a fleet of 24 trucks to handle freight in the Chattanooga area. Routes are assigned by area, usually delineated by zip code boundaries, major streets, or key geographical features, such as the Tennessee River. Pickups are generally handled between 3:00 P.M. and 6:00 P.M., Monday through Friday. Driver routes are a combination of regularly scheduled daily stops and pickups that the customer calls in as needed. These call-in pickups are dispatched by radio to the driver. Commitments are made in advance with regular pickup stops concerning the time the package will be ready, but most call-in customers want as late a pickup as possible, but before they close (usually at 5:00 P.M.).

When the driver arrives at each pickup location, he or she provides supplies as necessary (an envelope or box if requested) and must receive a completed air waybill for each package. Because the industry is extremely competitive, a professional, courteous driver is essential to retaining customers. Therefore, Smith has always been concerned about drivers not rushing a customer to complete his or her package and paperwork.

BUDGET CONSIDERATIONS

Smith and Lewis have found that they have been unable to meet their customers' requests for a scheduled pickup on many occasions in the past quarter. While on average, drivers are not handling any more business, some days they are unable to arrive at each location on time. Smith does not think he can justify increasing costs by $1,200 per week for additional trucks and drivers while productivity (measured in shipments per truck/day) has remained flat. The company has established itself as the low-cost operator in the industry but at the same time has committed itself to offering quality service and value for its customers.

DISCUSSION QUESTIONS

1. Is the productivity measure of shipments per day per truck still useful? Are there alternatives that might be effective?

2. What, if anything, can be done to reduce the daily variability in pickup call-ins? Can the driver be expected to be at several locations at once at 5:00 P.M.?

3. How should we measure package pickup performance? Are standards useful in an environment that is affected by the weather, traffic, and other random variables? Are other companies having similar problems?

Source: Adapted from a case by Phil Pugliese under the supervision of Professor Marilyn M. Helms, University of Tennessee at Chattanooga.

BIBLIOGRAPHY

Babbage, C. *On the Economy of Machinery and Manufacturers*, 4th ed. London: Charles Knight, 1835.

Drucker, P. F. *The Concept of the Corporation*. New York: Mentor, 1946.

Drucker, P. F. "The New Productivity Challenge." *Harvard Business Review*, 69, no. 6 (November/December 1991): 69.

Fabricant, S. *A Primer on Productivity*. New York: Random House, 1969.

Ferdows, K., and A. De Meyer. "Lasting Improvements in Manufacturing Performance: In Search of a New Theory." *Journal of Operations Management*, 9, no. 2 (April 1990): 168.

Garvin, D. A. *Operations Strategy: Text and Cases*. Englewood Cliffs, NJ: Prentice Hall, 1992.

Harbison, F., and C. A. Myers. *Management in the Industrial World*. New York: McGraw-Hill, 1959.

Hounshell, D. A. *From the American System to Mass Production 1800–1932: The Development of Manufacturing*. Baltimore: Johns Hopkins University Press, 1985.

Malhotra, M. K., D. C. Steele, and V. Grover. "Important Strategic and Tactical Manufacturing Issues in the 1990s." *Decision Sciences*, 25, no. 2 (March/April 1994): 189–214.

Smith, A. *An Inquiry into the Nature and Causes of the Wealth of Nations*. London: Strahan and Cadell, 1776.

Taylor, F. W. *The Principles of Scientific Management*. New York: Harper & Brothers, 1911.

———. *Shop Management*. New York: Harper & Brothers, 1919.

Vora, J. A. "Productivity and Performance Measures: Who Uses Them?" *Production and Inventory Management Journal*, 33, no. 1 (First Quarter 1992): 46–49.

Wrege, C. D. *Frederick W. Taylor, the Father of Scientific Management: Myth and Reality*. Homewood, IL: Business One Irwin, 1991.

Wren, D. A. *The Evolution of Management Thought*. New York: Ronald Press, 1994.

2

P/OM STRATEGY AND INTERNATIONAL COMPETITION

LEARNING OBJECTIVES

When you complete this chapter you should be able to:

Identify or define:

  Strategy

  Mission

  Competitive Advantage

  World-Class

Describe or explain:

  How to establish a mission and strategies

  The contribution of the P/OM function to strategy

  Strategies and tactical decisions of P/OM

Komatsu Dresser Modifies Its Strategy to Obtain Competitive Advantage

Komatsu, a long-time Japanese manufacturer of construction and mining equipment, competes worldwide in some very competitive markets. Like other organizations, Komatsu must constantly review how to organize its resources for maximum benefit. This review and change of resource allocation means modifications in Komatsu's strategy. Over the years, these modifications have taken many forms.

In the 1960s, Komatsu augmented its product line and reduced development costs by licensing designs and technology from others, such as Cummins Engine and International Harvester. This period also saw a strategic move toward improved quality.

In the 1970s, Komatsu's strategy was to become an international enterprise and build export markets, while reducing costs because of the increasing value of the yen. It expanded into Eastern bloc countries and established subsidiaries in Europe and America, as well as service departments in newly industrializing countries.

In the 1980s, Komatsu responded to an even stronger yen through joint ventures with Dresser Industries (to form the Komatsu Dresser Company) and manufacturing outside of Japan. By the 1990s, the strategy includes the latest in manufacturing technology to improve quality and drive down costs, as well as added focus on electronic engine controls for environmentally friendly engines.

The battle for construction equipment is fierce. World-class competitors such as Caterpillar, John Deere, Champion, and Ingersoll-Rand fight for these markets. But Komatsu's constant strategic adjustments to its environment have allowed Komatsu to be number one or two in a variety of markets throughout the world.

Komatsu Dresser sells products (crawler tractors, loaders, hydraulic excavators, and wheel loaders) to construction and mining markets in North America in direct competition with Caterpillar.

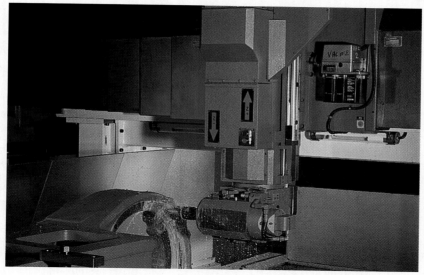

Advanced manufacturing equipment like this welding robot helps Komatsu Dresser turn out some of the highest quality products on the market.

The strategic changes mean more emphasis on environmental issues. Here research is being conducted on exhaust gas emission control for diesel engines to make Komatsu equipment more environmentally friendly.

Komatsu, in its continuing fierce worldwide battle with Caterpillar for the global heavy equipment customer, is building equipment throughout the world as cost and logistics dictate. This worldwide strategy allows Komatsu to move production as markets and exchange rates change.

G eneral Electric is number two in the world, behind Philips, in the light bulb business. Light bulbs are big business, generating over $2 billion in sales for GE in the United States alone. But GE cannot become number one in the world without a strong presence in Europe, where it holds a paltry 2% of the market. GE's European strategy obviously needed help, and GE wanted a foot in the door to Eastern European markets. Therefore, in January, 1990, GE bought a controlling interest in Tungsram Company, the declining state-owned Hungarian light bulb maker. Tungsram has become GE's strategic vehicle to European competition.[1] ♦

The job of GE's production function is to use its resources to produce goods and services effectively and efficiently, and that may mean opening a plant in Hungary. Operations managers are *effective* when they operate a system that supports the firm's strategy and goals. They are *efficient* when that system supports the firm with economical use of resources.

THE P/OM MISSION AND STRATEGY

In this section, we describe how to develop missions (i.e., a firm's purpose) and strategies (i.e., a specific plan for achieving the mission). The operations manager determines missions and strategies for very complex systems; so let us first say a few words about systems.

Systems

System

The word *system* implies order and arrangement. A **system** is a set of interacting variables. The operations manager takes these interacting variables and designs a system to achieve a particular objective or mission. One kind of system designed to achieve a particular objective is a *transformation system* that converts inputs into goods and services. The economy is such a system; the firm is such a system; and the production function is such a system. These systems provide the goods and services of our society. Such systems have inputs, transformations, and outputs. To function properly, such systems also have an information flow, called a feedback loop. Figure 2.1 shows the production system and its particular inputs, transformation, outputs, and feedback loops. This feedback lets the inputs and the transformation process know what the customer thinks of its performance.

    Production/operations managers manage a variety of systems *within the P/OM function*. There are many P/OM systems, including inventory and scheduling systems, purchasing systems, and maintenance systems. Production/operations managers also respond to a variety of systems *outside the P/OM function, but within the firm*. Among these systems are marketing and finance systems. Still other systems are *outside the firm*, such as economic systems, a system of world trade, and political systems. Managers who understand both the internal and external systems will be better managers.

[1]John S. McClenahen, "Light in the East," *Industry Week*, Vol. 241, No. 5 (March 2, 1992): 14–19; and Richard Bruner, "Tungsram's Leading Light," *International Management*, 47, no. 11 (December 1992): 42–46.

FIGURE 2.1 ■ The Production System Transforms Inputs to Outputs

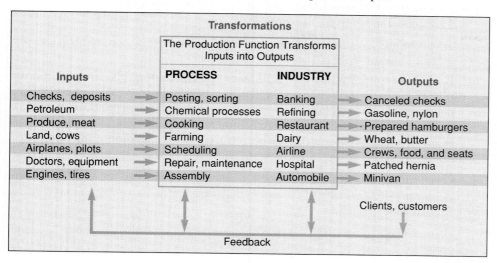

They will be able to coordinate the linkages of people, material, money, and information that are essential for effective and efficient performance.

Viewing the enterprise as a system within other systems allows managers to see the organization in its environment. This insight provides managers a perspective that allows them to design a P/OM system that supports the company's mission and objectives.

SUBSYSTEMS. Complex systems also contain smaller systems. These subsystems sometimes have their own relatively narrow objectives. Therefore, the manager must keep subsystems focused on the goals of the overall system. For example, a finance department may perceive its goal as holding inventory levels close to zero. The sales department, however, may want to keep large stocks of inventory in the hopes that this will help achieve sales goals. When conflicting objectives such as these occur, the larger system (the firm) may not be operating at its best or optimum level. When a system is not operating at its best level, it is said to be **suboptimized**. By understanding the goals of the subsystem and the linkages between systems, the operations manager has an opportunity to avoid suboptimization. Understanding systems, both internal and external, allows the operations manager to make good decisions that improve the productivity of the operations function.

Suboptimize

Mission

To satisfy opportunities in the economic system, managers identify what goods or services the firm will contribute to society. *This contribution is the organization's (or system's) reason for being, that is, its **mission**.* Establishing a mission ensures a focus on a common purpose, a concept around which the firm can rally. The mission states the rationale for the organization's existence. Developing a good plan is difficult, but is easier if the mission has been well defined. The mission can also be thought of as the intent of the plan—what is to be achieved. Once an organization decides upon its mission, each "functional area" within the firm, namely, marketing, finance/

Mission

accounting, and production/operations, develops its supporting mission. Figure 2.2 provides a hierarchy of sample missions for a manufacturing firm.

Examples of missions for two firms are:

Telephone and Data Systems, Inc.: "to be the finest in total communications services for our subscribers."[2]

Ford Motor Company: "to be a worldwide leader in automotive and automotive related products and services as well as in newer industries such as aerospace, communications, and financial services . . . and to improve continually our products and services to meet our customers' needs, allowing us to prosper as a business and to provide a reasonable return to our stockholders, the owners of our business."[3]

These brief mission statements provide a rationale and purpose for each firm's existence. Once missions are identified, a plan must be identified to achieve that mission. We call such plans strategies.

Strategy

Strategy

A **strategy** is a plan designed to achieve a mission. Each functional area has a strategy for achieving its mission and for helping the organization reach the overall mission. A strategy should be established in light of the threats and opportunities in the environment and the strengths and weaknesses of the organization.

Only when these external threats/opportunities and internal strengths/ weaknesses are understood can the firm begin to build an effective strategy. A brief look at strategic implications of developments in the world economy is presented in Example 1.

EXAMPLE 1

Global Strategy. Postindustrial societies such as those in the European Community (EC) and North America have global as well as local opportunities and threats to consider. Let us take a look at global changes taking place in the economic environment.

First, as we will discuss in Chapter 9, exchange rates, labor rates, productivity, and local attitude and values make a major difference in the location decision. But even with those constraints, we should notice that most of the products made in America (or anywhere else) are also made elsewhere in the world. Virtually no product is still available from only one national source. Those other places in the world where American products are likely to be produced are places where high-volume, standardized products can be built by productive low-cost labor with few fringe benefits and a burning desire to sell to affluent Western markets. This desire to sell to the Western world is often augmented by national policies such as low taxes, export credits, and subsidies that support such sales.

Second, although the EC is not a low-labor-cost competitor, it is maturing into one huge market. Volume in this market, and therefore the optimum size of facilities in this market, is increasing. This allows surviving firms in the EC to

[2]Annual Report.
[3]*Quality Progress* (October 1989): 49.

FIGURE 2.2 ■ Sample Mission for a Company, the Production/Operations Function, and the Major Departments in a Production/Operations Function

---

SAMPLE COMPANY MISSION

To pursue a diversified, growing, and profitable worldwide manufacturing business in electronic components, apparatus, and systems; and to service these products for industry, commerce, agriculture, government, and home.

SAMPLE PRODUCTION/OPERATIONS MANAGEMENT MISSION

To produce products consistent with the company's mission as the worldwide low-cost manufacturer.

SAMPLE P/OM DEPARTMENTAL MISSION

Quality Management	To attain the exceptional quality that is consistent with our company mission and marketing objectives, by close attention to design, procurement, production, and field service opportunities for enhancing design.
Product Design	To lead in research and engineering competencies in all areas of our primary business, designing and producing products and services with outstanding quality and inherent customer value.
Process Design	To determine and design or produce the production process and equipment that will be compatible with low-cost product, high quality, and a good quality-of-work life for our employees at economical cost.
Layout	To achieve, through skill, imagination, and resourcefulness in plant layout and work methods, production effectiveness and efficiency while supporting a high quality-of-work life for our employees.
Location	To locate, design, and build efficient and economical facilities that will yield high value to the company, its employees, and the community.
Human Resources	To provide a good quality-of-work life, with well-designed, safe, rewarding jobs, stable employment, and equitable pay, in exchange for outstanding individual contribution from employees at all levels.
Purchasing	To cooperate with suppliers and subcontractors to develop stable, effective, and efficient sources of supply for those components that are to be procured from outside sources.
Scheduling	To achieve high utilization of manufacturing facilities through effective scheduling.
Inventory	To achieve low investment in inventory consistent with high customer service levels and high facility utilization.
Maintenance	To achieve high utilization of facilities and equipment by effective preventive maintenance and prompt repair of facilities and equipment.

---

spread their fixed expenses over more units. Therefore, these firms could very well be low-cost producers even with high labor costs. And depending upon the trade arrangements that develop with Eastern Europe, low labor cost could be available for the next decade.

Third, communication, travel, and shipments between continents are relatively easy, inexpensive, and rapid. This means that both markets and sources are truly global.

Fourth, the affluent world itself is demanding quality, immediate delivery, and options. Affluence allows this market to purchase the latest technology and readily discard the old.

The U.S. home appliance market is growing annually at 2% or less, about half of that projected for Europe. Therefore, Whirlpool chairman David Whitwam's strategy is to take Whirlpool global. Whirlpool recently acquired major interest in Ingils Limited of Canada, Vitromatic of Mexico, and a 53% stake in N. V. Philips in the Netherlands. Whirlpool has also moved toward global procurement of 35 strategic materials and components. Appliance giants Maytag, Electrolux, and GE have similarly developed and implemented global strategies to enable them to compete internationally and to be a part of the new European Community. They are also positioned for the next round of tariff reductions, which should result from the recently concluded GATT negotiations.

What are the strengths and weaknesses for Western firms in such an environment? What are the potential competitive advantages for Western firms in this changing world? Perhaps sophisticated, flexible production systems that produce high-quality, innovative, option-filled products for wealthy consumers are a reasonable strategy. The products produced would utilize the strengths found in higher skills, technology, and education that are unique to the postindustrialized society. And they would bypass a potential weakness, low labor costs.

Western manufacturing firms that remain in competition with the high-volume, relatively low-technology facilities of the world will be in lean, focused plants (see Chapter 10, Operations Layout Strategy), utilizing both a high degree of automation (see Chapter 7, Process Strategies) and worker commitment (see Chapter 11, Human Resource Strategy).

As Example 1 suggests, firms evaluate their internal strengths and weaknesses and their external opportunities and threats. Mission and strategy development requires that an organization find an opportunity in the environment for which it is uniquely qualified. That is, the company identifies its own unique competencies—its own special capabilities—that fit an opportunity. A firm does not want to attack the market with exactly the same mission and strategy as a competitor. Instead, the firm wants to find those voids or opportunities in the environment that provide a chance for it to mobilize uniquely its resources for a competitive advantage. Many Japanese companies are matching their strengths with opportunities in Southeast Asia, as shown in the *POM In Action* box "Japan Flocks to Southeast Asia to Build Its Products."

The significant role that P/OM can play to support a competitive strategy is evident from a study done by Prof. David Aaker. Of 32 broad categories that contribute to competitive advantage, 28% fall into the production category that includes product, process, location, and scheduling.[4] From this and similar studies, the major role P/OM can play in strategy development is clear.[5] A list of typical strategies to be supported by P/OM is shown in Figure 2.3.

The production manager's task is to mobilize the resources of P/OM to contribute to a successful strategy. We have identified ten P/OM decisions as critical to this effort.

Strategic and Tactical Decisions of P/OM

The 10 strategic and tactical P/OM decisions that support missions and implement strategies are as follows:[6]

1. **Quality Strategy.** The customer's quality expectations must be determined and policies and procedures established to identify and achieve that quality.

[4]See David A. Aaker, "Creating a Sustainable Competitive Advantage," *California Management Review* (Winter 1989): 91–106.

[5]Shawnee K. Vickery, Cornelia Droge, and Robert E. Markland, "Production Competence and Business Strategy: Do They Affect Business Performance?" *Decision Sciences*, 24, no. 2 (March/April 1993): 435–455; Robert H. Hayes and Steven C. Wheelwright, *Restoring Our Competitive Edge* (New York: John Wiley, 1984).

[6]For another perspective see Manoj K. Malhotra, Daniel C. Steel, and Varun Grover, "Important Strategic and Tactical Manufacturing Issues in the 1990s," *Decision Sciences*, 25, no. 2 (March/April 1994): 189–214.

FIGURE 2.3 ■ Typical Strategies to Be Supported by P/OM

COMPETITIVE ADVANTAGE	DEFINED AS THE CAPABILITY TO:
Flexibility	
Design	Make rapid design changes and/or introduce new products quickly
Volume	Respond to swings in volume
Quality	
Conformance	Offer consistent quality
Performance	Provide high-performance products
Delivery	
Speed	Deliver products quickly
Dependability	Deliver on time (as promised)
Low price	Compete on price
After-sale service	Provide after-sale service
Broad line	Produce a broad product line

Source: Adapted from Jeffrey G. Miller and Aleda Roth, "A Taxonomy of Manufacturing Strategies," *Management Science,* 40, no. 3 (March 1994): 285–304.

2. **Product Strategy.** Product strategy defines much of the transformation process. Production costs, quality and human resource decisions interact strongly with the design of products. Product designs often set the lower limits of cost and the upper limits of quality.

3. **Process Strategy.** Process options are available for a product. Process decisions commit management to basic approaches to technology, quality, human resource utilization, and maintenance. These expense and capital commitments will determine much of the firm's basic cost structure.

4. **Location Strategy.** Facility location decisions for both manufacturing and service organizations may determine the ultimate success of the operation. Errors made at this juncture may overwhelm other efficiencies.

5. **Layout Strategy.** Capacity needs, personnel levels, purchasing decisions, and inventory requirements influence layout. Additionally, the processes and material must be sensibly located in relation to each other.

6. **Human Resource Strategy.** Human resources are an integral and expensive part of the total system design. Therefore, the quality-of-work life provided, the talent and skills required, and their costs must be determined.

7. **Purchasing and Just-in-Time Strategy.** These decisions determine what is to be made and what is to be purchased. Consideration is also given to quality, delivery, and innovation, at a satisfactory price. An atmosphere of mutual respect between buyer and supplier is necessary for effective purchasing.

8. **Inventory Tactics.** Inventory decisions can be optimized only when considered in light of customer satisfaction, suppliers, production schedules, and human resource planning.

9. **Scheduling Tactics.** Feasible and efficient schedules of production must be developed; the demands on human resources and facilities must be determined and controlled.

Cummins Engine Company manufactures diesel engines for buses, trucks, and heavy-duty equipment for sale worldwide. Cummins is an American organization operating internationally. Since the introduction of its fuel-efficient L10 engine in the United Kingdom, its share of the UK bus market increased steadily. Cummins prospers by keeping in touch with its suppliers and customers, stressing quality, service, and innovation.

Japan Flocks to Southeast Asia to Build Its Products

Joseph Romm's recent book, *The Once and Future Superpower*, provides a scholarly look at an important new trend in Japanese industry. Romm claims that Japan's strategy, called the New Asian Industrial Development plan, is to gather Asian economies into an economic flock with Japan at the head. It is doing so by targeting Indonesia, Malaysia, the Philippines, Thailand, Vietnam, India, and Bangladesh not only as primary suppliers of basic materials like rubber, oil, and timber, but also as manufacturers of low-value-added products.

Malaysia, for example, has been selected by Japanese investors to become the world's largest manufacturer of window unit air conditioners for the global market. Sony uses Malaysia to build its compact disc players. Overall, Japanese investment in

Malaysia has ballooned ($1.5 billion in 1990) with some 550 Japanese manufacturing and service businesses already in place.

Thailand, with a population of 55 million, is even more dramatically affected, with $3.6 billion in Japanese investment in 1989 alone (compared to only $565 million from the United States). The Japanese have been opening factories in Thailand at the incredible rate of one every three days. This boosts exports of Japanese VCRs and color TVs to the United States, while giving the appearance of increased U.S. trade with Thailand.

Elsewhere in Southeast Asia, Sumitomo Electric is moving labor-intensive assembly of auto-wiring systems to Indonesia; Suzuki has opened an auto plant in India; and JVC has contracted with Hanoi Electronics in Vietnam to produce its TVs.

These decisions, reflecting a systematic strategy by world-class Japanese firms, pose new low-labor-cost threats to competitors.

Sources: Joseph Romm, *The Once and Future Superpower* (New York: Morrow, 1992) and *Forbes* (November 23, 1992): pp. 108–112.

10. **Maintenance and Reliability Tactics.**   Decisions must be made regarding desired levels of reliability and maintenance. Plans for implementation and control of reliability and maintenance are necessary.

Each of the foregoing decisions discussed is presented in one or more chapters in the text. These 10 areas do not, of course, represent all that operations managers do or all that they should know. For instance, our discussion of organization theory, accounting, staffing, or human behavior and communication skills is limited, but all are important for the effective operations manager. Moreover, as we shall see in subsequent chapters, these 10 P/OM decision areas interact strongly with each other. When the 10 decisions are not made in such a way as to contribute to the company's strategy, the operations manager has failed. Notice in the *POM in Action* box "Michelin Tire Rolls On" how Michelin has used P/OM decisions related to product design, quality, and location to support its goals.

DEVELOPING A P/OM STRATEGY

The operations manager is an active participant in determining the firm's mission and strategy because so many resources are a P/OM responsibility. Only when operations managers understand the organization's overall strategy can optimal decisions be made. The best utilization of resources requires more than effective marketing and finance. Jazzy ads and new financial leverage schemes do not create better products delivered on time to the customer. Only the production function does that. The production function is a vital element in building a competitive advantage. By

Michelin Tire Rolls On

After World War II, France's Michelin family forged into the development of its controversial new product, the radial tire. Although it experienced great success with that tire, Michelin still ranked only seventh in the worldwide tire industry by the late 1960s. At that point, the company decided that international growth would be its future.

Michelin ran up heavy debts and losses as it proceeded to build new factories at the rate of two a year in the late 1970s. A few years later, the oil shock deflated the tire market, but the company bounced back. Michelin's secret is that it is continuously willing to sacrifice short-term concerns for its two long-term objectives: quality and market share.

Hoping to avoid unions, Michelin prefers to build plants in the Southern United States. Eighty percent of production is in numerous countries outside France, and the French represent only a small minority of employees.

Michelin consistently spends 5% of sales on research, which is the same percentage as Japan's Bridgestone. Goodyear attributes its heavy research spending of less than 4% as the reason why it alone of the U.S. majors has avoided a takeover.

Although Michelin concentrates on tires and tire components, it does make maps and restaurant guides for motorists. Goodyear and Bridgestone produce more than 25% of revenue from nontire products, but tires represent more than 90% of Michelin's sales. Almost all materials, including the steel belting and synthetic rubber used in its tires, are produced by Michelin.

Michelin is mainly concerned about its long-term position as exemplified by its purchase of Uniroyal Goodrich. This transaction clearly will push up debt and hold down profits. But for Michelin the acquisition is strategic; its cost is secondary.

Sources: Adapted from the *Wall Street Journal* (January 5, 1990): 1–8; *Business Marketing* (May 1994): 11; and *Economist* (June 8, 1991): 65–66.

---

competitive advantage, we mean an advantage that competitors do not have. Johnson Electric, as indicated in the *POM in Action* box on page 42 "Strategy at Hong Kong's Johnson Electric Is Global," found competitive advantage in speed of manufacture, staying informed of customer needs, and efficient manufacturing.

The production function can contribute to a competitive advantage in a variety of ways. However, P/OM is only one-third of the strategic triad, which also includes marketing and finance/accounting. Figure 2.4 provides a synopsis of strategic options for marketing, finance, and P/OM. These functions, as well as other functions of the firm, make contributions to strategy. In this text, we note a variety of specific examples of how firms do so.

Competitive advantage

P/OM Strategy Considerations

A successful P/OM strategy is not only consistent with the organization's strategy, but also recognizes product life cycles. Every product has a life cycle. A few products and their approximate life cycle are shown in Figure 2.5. That figure also shows some specific strategic issues to be addressed at various stages in each phase of a product's life cycle.

Strategy Implementation

Because every organization has limitations, the operations manager identifies what the P/OM function can and cannot accomplish. The idea is not only to have a supportive P/OM strategy, but also to implement that strategy successfully.

FIGURE 2.4 ■ Developing Operations Strategy

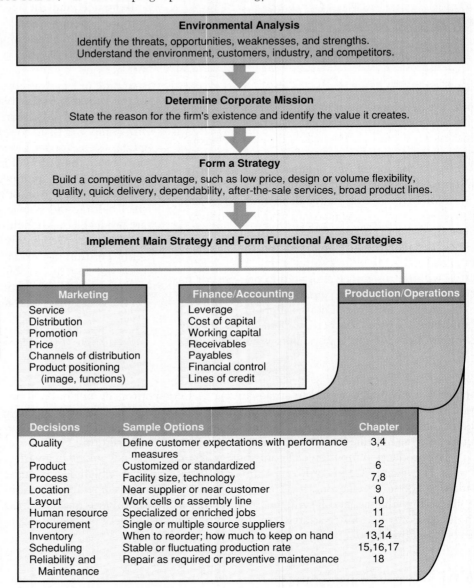

KEY TASKS. Successful strategy implementation requires identifying those tasks that are key to success. The operations manager asks, "What tasks must be done particularly well for a given operations strategy to succeed? Which elements contain the highest likelihood of failure, and which will require additional commitment of managerial, monetary, technological, and human resources? Which activities will help the P/OM function provide a competitive advantage?" For example, in a manufacturing firm, the most important ingredient in the P/OM mission may be on-time shipment to customers (scheduling tactics) or product design (heart valves). In an emergency care center, however, the focus may be on having the proper personnel present (human resource strategy) and pharmaceuticals (inventory tactics) available.

FIGURE 2.5 ■ Strategy and Issues During a Product's Life Cycle.

	Introduction	Growth	Maturity	Decline
Company Strategy / Issues	Best period to increase market share R&D engineering are critical Sales CD-ROM	Practical to change price or quality image Marketing critical Strengthen niche Fax machines Cellular phones Color copiers	Poor time to increase market share or change image, price, or quality Color monitors Competitive costs become critical Defend position via fresh promotion and distribution approaches	Cost control critical 3 1/2" Floppy disks 5 1/4" Floppy disks
P/OM Strategy / Issues	Product design and development critical Frequent product and process design changes Overcapacity Short production runs High-skilled labor High production costs Limited number of models Utmost attention to quality Quick elimination of defects in design	Forecasting critical Product and process reliability Competitive product improvements and options Increase capacity Shift toward product oriented Enhance distribution	Standardization Less rapid product changes—more minor annual model changes Optimum capacity Increasing stability of manufacturing process Lower labor skills Long production runs Attention to product improvement and cost cutting Reexamination of necessity of design compromises	Little product differentiation Cost minimization Overcapacity in the industry Prune line to eliminate items not returning good margin Reduce capacity

(*Source:* Various; see, for instance, Michael E. Porter, *Techniques for Analyzing Industries and Competitors* (New York, Free Press, 1980).)

Each firm must determine its own way of finding competitive advantage. The *POM in Action* box "Strategy at Compaq and Microsoft" discusses approaches to strategy implementation.

ORGANIZATION. Each firm will make its own choices about how to organize so the key tasks can be accomplished. The organization charts shown in Chapter 1 (Figure 1.2) indicate the way that some firms have organized to make these decisions. The organization of the operations function and its relationship to other parts of the organization vary with the P/OM mission. For example, volatile customer travel patterns dominate short-term scheduling in the airline industry. Day-of-the-week preference, holidays, seasonality, and college schedules all play a role in changing flight

Strategy at Hong Kong's Johnson Electric Is Global

Patrick Wang, managing director of Johnson Electric Holdings, Ltd., walks through his Hong Kong headquarters with a micromotor in his hand. This tiny motor, about twice the size of his thumb, powers a Dodge Viper power door lock. Although most people have never heard of Johnson Electric, we all have several of their micromotors nearby. This is because Johnson is the world's leading producer of micromotors for cordless tools, household appliances (such as coffee grinders and food processors), personal care items (such as hair dryers and electric shavers), and cars. A luxury Mercedes, with its headlight wipers, power windows, power seat adjustments, and power side mirrors, may use 50 Johnson micromotors per vehicle.

Like all truly global businesses, Johnson spends liberally on communications to tie together its global network of factories, R&D and design centers. For example, Johnson Electric is installing a $20 million videoconferencing system that allows engineers in Cleveland, Ohio, and Stuttgart, Germany, to monitor trial production of their micromotors in China.

Johnson's first strength is speed—13 million motors a month, mostly assembled in China. Its second strength is the ability to stay close to its customers. Johnson has design and technical centers scattered across the United States, Europe, and Japan. "The physical limitations of the past are gone" when it comes to deciding where to locate a new center, says Patrick Wang. "Customers talk to us where they feel most comfortable, but products are made where they are most competitive."

Sources: Forbes (November 8, 1993): 292–293; and *Asian Business* (February 1993): 12.

---

schedules. Consequently, airline scheduling, although a P/OM activity, can be a part of a marketing organization. (Refer to Figure 1.2 a on page 8.) Effective scheduling in the trucking industry is reflected in the amount of time trucks travel loaded. However, scheduling trucks is usually part of the P/OM function, although information from delivery and pickup points, drivers, and other parts of the organization is required. When the organization of the P/OM function results in effective scheduling in the air passenger and commercial trucking industries, a competitive advantage can exist.

The production/operations manager develops strategy, identifies key tasks, groups activities into an organized structure, and staffs with personnel who will get the job done. The manager works with subordinate managers to build plans, budgets, and programs that will successfully implement strategies that achieve missions. When the operations manager has done the foregoing, the basics for an efficient system that transforms inputs into outputs exist. Then the operations manager should be able to implement a P/OM strategy that will increase productivity and provide competitive advantage.

Strategy Dynamics

Strategies change. They change for two reasons. First, *strategy is dynamic because of changes within the organization.* All areas of the firm are subject to change. Changes may be in a variety of areas including purchasing, finance, technology, and product life. All may make a difference in an organization's strengths and weaknesses and therefore its strategy. Figure 2.5 shows possible change in both overall strategy and

Strategy at Compaq and Microsoft

Two world-class companies, Compaq and Microsoft, lead in bringing new products to market with quality and marketability. They share these five traits in doing so:

They focus on one business. For example, Compaq makes only one product, personal computers, and more specifically, business PCs. "We don't spend a lot of time worrying about the home marketing or the educational market . . . [but] focus on developing new products to meet the needs of the business PC user," says Michael Swavely, division president.

They are global. Both Microsoft and Compaq are so strong that they are able to compete globally. And they pursue international markets that have stiff competition, which forces them to remain world-class. Compaq is the second leading supplier

of business PCs in the U.S., Canadian, and European markets, and has 45% of its sales abroad.

Their senior management is actively involved in defining and improving the product development process. Microsoft's Bill Gates, for example, keeps in contact with his engineers by electronic mail memos, sometimes 30 in a day.

They recruit and retain the top people in their fields. Microsoft is always known for hiring the best and brightest possible. Thousands have become millionaires by staying on and helping the company grow.

They understand that speed to market reinforces product quality. Microsoft's Windows NT, with a staggering 4.3 million lines of code, almost killed the 200 programmers on the project in rushing it to market in 1993. But it redefined the concept of network software and windows software by marrying them. It also reflects Gates' aggressive goals of continuous improvement.

Sources: Wall Street Journal (August 6, 1990): A12 (May 26, 1993): A1, A12.

P/OM strategy during the product's life cycle. Second, *strategy is dynamic because of changes in the environment.* Komatsu, the international manufacturer of large earthmoving equipment shown in this chapter's World-Class Profile, provides an example of how strategy must change as the environment changes. Komatsu, in its worldwide competition with Caterpillar, has had to adopt strategies of quality enhancement, product-line growth, and cost reduction.[7] P/OM strategies are increasingly global.

INTERNATIONAL ISSUES IN P/OM

The world has increasingly turned into one interconnected economy, a *global village*, where the economy of one country is affected by the economies of many others. For example, as other countries have targeted the United States as an export destination, American companies have had to turn more to foreign markets for sales and profits. And, as we saw in the opening quote of this chapter, GE has turned to Hungary for a strategic alliance to produce and market light bulbs.

GE is not alone in its global P/OM strategy. Note that every firm in Table 2.1 generates the majority of its sales outside its home country. An enormous 98% of Nestlé's sales come from beyond its home in Switzerland. It is no wonder that writers such as Alvin Toffler think that international firms will become *stateless*.[8] They are

[7]Gary Hamel and C. K. Prahalad, "Strategic Intent," *Harvard Business Review*, 67, no. 3 (May/June 1989): 63–76.

[8]Lois F. Lunin, "Recipe for Intelligence," *Information Today* (March 1994): 61–63.

TABLE 2.1 ■ WORLD-CLASS FIRMS HAVE INTERNATIONAL STRATEGIES			
COMPANY	HOME COUNTRY	% SALES OUTSIDE HOME COUNTRY	% ASSETS OUTSIDE HOME COUNTRY
Avon Products	United States	61	48
Bayer	Germany	65	NA
Citicorp	United States	66	51
Colgate-Palmolive	United States	65	47
Daimler-Benz	Germany	61	NA
Dow Chemical	United States	54	45
Gillette	United States	68	66
Hoechst	Germany	77	NA
Honda	Japan	63	36
IBM	United States	59	55
ICI	Britain	78	50
Nestlé	Switzerland	98	95
Philips	Netherlands	94	85
Procter & Gamble	United States	52	41
Siemens	Germany	51	NA
Sony	Japan	66	NA
Unilever	Britain/Netherlands	75	70

NA: Not available.

Sources: Business Week (May 4, 1990): 103; and *Forbes* (July 18, 1994): 277.

no longer German or Swiss or Canadian. National identities do not matter in many decisions. Decisions are made on economic, not national, merits.

As firms increasingly position their production function in a dynamic global environment, they will also have substantial investments outside their "home" country. Variations in labor skills and cost, capital availability and cost, local infrastructures and markets, and political risk are the challenges firms face.[9]

As a test of *your* knowledge about international companies, try to answer the questions in our quiz in Table 2.2. You will probably be surprised regarding ownership of the eleven famous product lines listed in the first column.

ACHIEVING A WORLD-CLASS P/OM STRATEGY

World-class firms
World-class P/OM function

Firms that compete successfully in the international arena are known as **world-class firms.** A **world-class P/OM function** is one that obtains excellence in meeting customer requirements through continuous improvement. Most world-class firms, whether manufacturing or service, will have P/OM functions that are also world-class. These firms have been successful in putting together an operations strategy that

[9]See the discussion in M. E. McGrath and R. W. Hoole, "Manufacturing's New Economies of Scale," *Harvard Business Review* (May/June 1992): 94–99.

| TABLE 2.2 ■ INTERNATIONAL QUIZ: CAN YOU MATCH THE PRODUCT WITH THE PROPER PARENT COMPANY AND COUNTRY? |||
PRODUCT	PARENT COMPANY	COUNTRY OF PARENT
Arrow Shirts		
Braun Household Appliances		
Burger King		
Firestone Tires		
Godiva Chocolate		
Haagen-Dazs Ice Cream		
Jaguar Autos		
MGM Movies		
Lamborghini Autos		
Goodrich Tires		
Alpo Petfoods		

Choose from these parent companies:
a Automobili Lamborghini
b Bidermann International
c Bridgestone
d Campbell Soup
e Credit Lyonnais
f Ford Motor Company
g Gillette
h Grand Metropolitan
i Michelin
j Nestlé

Choose from these countries:
1 France
2 Great Britain
3 Indonesia
4 Japan
5 United States
6 Switzerland

Answers: Arrow: b, 1; Braun: g, 5; Burger King: h, 2; Firestone: c, 4; Godiva: d, 5; Haagen-Dazs: h, 2; Jaguar: f, 5; MGM: e, 1; Lamborghini: a, 3; Goodrich: i, 1; Alpo: j, 6.

Like its main competitor, Komatsu, Caterpillar has a global strategy. It sells, manufactures, and services products in more than 100 countries. Plant capability, labor and schedule availability, and costs are evaluated prior to decisions being made about manufacturing and shipping of Caterpillar products. Here Caterpillar equipment is loaded for export to Europe.

supports the overall company objectives by creating a competitive advantage. Each of the 10 decisions of P/OM in its own way can contribute to this competitive advantage. For each of these 10 decisions, Table 2.3 suggests some characteristics of world-class firms. These characteristics are addressed in their respective chapters. A world-class P/OM function contributes to competitive advantage, making the organization successful today and providing products, services, and jobs for tomorrow.

SUMMARY

P/OM is a major function that can contribute in a significant way to an organization's competitiveness. Organizations must understand their environment and realistically identify their own abilities. Then they implement a strategy that utilizes those abilities within the environment to achieve the mission. Only when all of the above are done well can the organization have a competitive advantage and be a world-class performer. In our global economy, in which companies easily operate and compete across international borders, world-class performance is increasingly required.

TABLE 2.3 ■ WHAT ARE THE CHARACTERISTICS OF WORLD-CLASS FIRMS IN THE STATEGIC AND TACTICAL AREAS OF P/OM? HERE ARE EXAMPLES OF HOW WORLD-CLASS FIRMS DEAL WITH IMPORTANT P/OM ISSUES.

QUALITY STRATEGY

Improves systems via empowered employees.

Reduces costs and wins orders via quality.

PRODUCT STRATEGY

Produces one or only a few products.

Introduces new products continually.

Links product strategy to market share and product life cycles.

HUMAN RESOURCES STRATEGY

Trains employees to perform a variety of jobs.

Fosters mutual trust and respect, resulting in a high level of morale.

Builds an outstanding staff via effective recruiting, selection, training, and retention.

PROCESS STRATEGY

Develops uniquely efficient equipment or process.

Generates a dollar of sales with low capital requirements relative to the competition.

SCHEDULING TACTICS

Schedules effectively for high utilization.

Wins orders with conformance to delivery promises.

Enhances use of facilities by effective scheduling.

Develops stable production schedules.

LOCATION STRATEGY

Finds locations that yield an advantage in cost, revenue, customer service, and market penetration.

Pursues opportunities internationally.

INVENTORY TACTICS

Minimizes investment in inventory.

Uses JIT techniques to control inventory and to ensure consistent quality.

LAYOUT STRATEGY

Uses work cells and flexible facilities.

Streamlines movement of material for efficiency and value.

PROCUREMENT STRATEGY

Evaluates and develops suppliers into world-class performers.

Integrates suppliers into the production system.

MAINTENANCE TACTICS

Performs effective preventive maintenance, reducing product variability.

Trains employees to do equipment inspection and minor preventive maintenance.

KEY TERMS

SOLVED PROBLEM

Solved Problem 2.1

How does a company in the very mature and established meatpacking industry win a competitive advantage?[10] Iowa Beef Packers (IBP) was able to win a strong competitive advantage by restructuring traditional beef-processing operations. In beef packing, traditional operations involved raising cattle on scattered farms and ranches, shipping them live to labor-intensive, unionized slaughtering plants, and then transporting whole sides of beef to grocery retailers whose butcher departments cut them into smaller pieces and packaged them for sale to grocery shoppers.

Solution

Iowa Beef Packers revamped traditional operations with a radically different strategy. Large automated plants employing nonunion labor were built near economically transportable supplies of cattle. Then the meat was partially butchered at the processing plant into smaller, high-yield cuts (sometimes sealed in plastic ready for purchase), boxed, and shipped to retailers. IBP's inbound cattle transportation expenses, traditionally a major cost item, were cut significantly by avoiding major losses that occurred when live animals were shipped long distances. Additionally, major outbound shipping-cost savings were achieved by not having to ship whole sides of beef with their high waste factor. IBP's strategy was so successful that it was, by 1985, the largest U.S. meatpacker, surpassing the former industry leaders, Swift, Wilson, and Armour.

[10]Adapted from information in Michael E. Porter, *Competitive Advantage* (New York: Free Press, 1985), p. 109; Arthur A. Thompson, Jr., and A. J. Strickland III, *Strategy Formulation and Implementation* (Homewood, IL: BPI/Irwin, 1989).

DISCUSSION QUESTIONS

1. Describe the registration system at your university. What are its inputs, transformations, and outputs?

2. Would the complex system in which productions/operations managers operate be different with faster feedback loops?

3. What are the similarities and differences in the transformation process between a fast-food restaurant and a computer manufacturer?

4. Identify the 10 strategic and tactical decisions of operations management.

5. Identify the transformation that takes place in your automobile repair garage. What are the manifestations of

the 10 production and operation management (P/OM) decisions at the garage? That is, how is each of the ten decisions accomplished? (Figure 2.4 may be helpful.)

6. Answer Question 5 for some other enterprise of your choosing.

7. Based on what you know of the automobile industry, how has the P/OM strategy of General Motors or Ford changed in the last 10 years?

8. As a library assignment, identify the mission of a firm and the strategy that supports that mission.

9. What is an example of suboptimization?

10. In this chapter, we have identified 10 strategic and tactical decisions of P/OM. What are some strategic and tactical decisions of finance and marketing?

11. What are the implications to the United States of Japan's strategy for dominance in Southeast Asia, as described in the *P/OM in Action* box?

CRITICAL THINKING EXERCISE

IBM at one time had a 70% market share in the computer business. Most of that business was in large computers, known as mainframe computers. Throughout the 1980s and 90s technology and markets favored computer networks, then PCs, and now computer networks *and* PCs. IBM has had a difficult time adjusting. IBM's sales, employment, and percent of installed computers have dropped. From a P/OM perspective, how might IBM have matched its strengths and weaknesses with the opportunities and threats of the environment?

PROBLEMS

- **2.1** Find an article in the business literature (*Business Week, Wall Street Journal, Forbes, Fortune,* and so on) that (1) documents an organization's current P/OM strategy and (2) documents a *change* in an organization's P/OM strategy.

- **2.2** Identify how changes in the external environment affect the P/OM strategy for a company. For instance, discuss what impact the following external factors might have on P/OM strategy:

  a) major increases in oil prices

  b) water- and air-quality legislation

  c) fewer young prospective employees entering the labor market in 1985 through 1995

  d) inflation vs. stable prices

  e) legislation moving health insurance from a benefit to taxable income

- **2.3** Identify how changes in the internal environment affect the P/OM strategy for a company. For instance, discuss what impact the following internal factors might have on P/OM strategy:

  a) maturing of a product

  b) technology innovation in the manufacturing process

  c) changes in product design that move Compaq's disk drives from 3½-in. floppy drives to CD-ROM drives.

CASE STUDY

Minit-Lube, Inc.

In recent years, a substantial market has developed for automobile tune-up and lubrication shops. This demand came about because of the change in consumer buying patterns as self-service gas stations proliferated. Consumers started pumping their own gas, which made a second stop necessary for oil and lubrication. Consequently, Minit-Lube and Jiffy-Lube developed a strategy to accommodate this opportunity.

Minit-Lube stations perform oil changes, lubrication, and interior cleaning in a spotless environment. The buildings are clean, painted white, and surrounded by neatly trimmed landscaping. To facilitate fast service, cars can be driven through three abreast. At Minit-Lube, the customer is greeted by service representatives who are graduates of the Minit-Lube school in Salt Lake City. The Minit-Lube school is not unlike McDonald's

(Continued)

Hamburger University near Chicago or Holiday Inn's training school in Memphis. The greeter takes the order, which typically includes fluid checks (oil, water, brake fluid, transmission fluid, differential grease) and the necessary lubrication, as well as filter changes for air and oil. Service personnel in neat uniforms then move into action. The standard three-person team has one person checking fluid levels under the hood, another is assigned interior vacuuming and window cleaning, and the third is in the garage pit, removing the oil filter, draining the oil, checking the differential and transmission, and lubricating as necessary. Precise task assignments and good training are designed to put the car in and out of the bay in 10 minutes. The idea is to charge no

more, and hopefully less, than gas stations, automotive repair chains, and auto dealers, while providing better service.

DISCUSSION QUESTIONS

1. What constitutes the mission of Minit-Lube?
2. How does the Minit-Lube operations strategy provide competitive advantage? (*Hint:* Evaluate how Minit-Lube's traditional competitors perform the 10 decisions of operations management vs. how Minit-Lube performs them.)
3. Is it likely that Minit-Lube or Jiffy-Lube have increased productivity over their more traditional competitors? Why? How would we measure productivity in this industry?

CASE STUDY

Johannsen Steel Company

Johannsen Steel Company (JSC) was established by three Johannsen brothers in 1928 in Pittsfield, Rhode Island. The brothers began JSC by concentrating on high-quality, high-carbon, high-margin steel wire. Products included "music wire" for instruments such as pianos and violins; copper, tin, and other coated wires; and high tensile wire for the newly emerging aircraft industry. JSC even pioneered new types of wire.

Throughout the 1930s and 40s JSC prospered while maintaining its reputation for high-quality products and in-house design/construction of its own equipment. In 1946, the last remaining Johannsen brother sold the company to West Virginia Steel for $4 million. For its investment, West Virginia Steel (WVS) obtained three Johannsen steel mills located in Pittsfield, Rhode Island (500 employees), Akron, Ohio (100 employees), and Los Angeles (16 employees), and two steel wire warehouses—one in Chicago (8 employees) and one in Los Angeles (4 employees). WVS kept Johannsen completely intact as a wholly owned subsidiary.

The 1940s and 50s witnessed increasing JSC sales to the U.S. military and to U.S. automakers and tire makers. JSC also sold wire for use

in staples, nails, cables, cookie cutters, steel brushes/wire wheels, and electrical products, leading to a continued healthy upward climb in sales and profits.

1960 was a climactic year for the U.S. steel industry. A prolonged steel strike of 14 weeks caught steel customers off guard. With stocks nearly exhausted, steel customers throughout the United States looked for alternative sources. Up to this point, competition from Japanese steel plants had been minimal. However, with few options, steel customers turned to the Japanese. They found the quality, price, and even delivery of steel to be very acceptable. No longer was competition from offshore steel makers to be insignificant.

The combination of offshore steel competition and a productivity-minded economy drove steel prices down to very competitive levels throughout the 1960s and 70s. Attention in the industry and in JSC turned toward cost cutting and sales expansion as means to maintain profit levels.

The selection of Joe Thomas, formerly the sales manager of JSC, as its president in 1978 resulted in a further emphasis on sales expansion. And indeed sales grew by nearly 2 million pounds per year through the 1970s and 80s. The growth in sales revenue paralleled the tonnage sold. However, after-tax profits on sales throughout the late 1980s were never above 2%.

(Continued)

Because profits had been meager since the mid-1970s for both JSC and WVS, the "mother corporation" was spending little on capital investment unless a 40% return on investment (ROI) before taxes could be demonstrated. WVS had other restrictions on its JSC subsidiary. Sixty percent of JSC's total purchase of steel rod (the raw material for steel wire) had to be purchased from WVS, even though it was well acknowledged throughout the industry that WVS's steel rod was the lowest in quality. Also the smaller size of WVS rod coils (300 lb), compared to the newest industry sizes from Bethlehem Steel (1500 and 3000 lb), increased the number of machine setups and production cost.

To use up their quota of WVS steel rods and spread overhead costs over more tonnage (thus reducing allocated overhead per ton), Joe Thomas ordered his sales people to increase sales at least 10% per year. And they did. Orders and revenue for the more common grades of steel wire products such as staple wire, stitching wire, tire bead wire, and brush wire continued to increase. The prices of these steel wire products slowly continued to fall as the Japanese, in particular, manufactured these products with greater efficiency.

Johannsen Steel nonetheless maintained its reputation for high quality throughout the 1970s and 80s. It won prestigious NASA and computer industry contracts and still produced "music wire" and other high-carbon grades. The percentage of these high-quality/high-margin sales to total sales continued to decrease, however.

Wire-drawing machinery now was so sophisticated that JSC no longer designed or produced its own machines. In fact, by the 1980s JSC often purchased used equipment.

Although several new JSC product innovations had appeared every few years, these were highly irregular and not significant. To control costs, the R&D lab staff had not increased in size or funding for many years. JSC had much of its original equipment (some over 50 years old), which was in good working order. However, equipment and building maintenance costs continued to rise.

The sales salaries were low, with 6% commissions paid on all sales generated. To cut costs, sales staff travel was considerably reduced.

In conversation with John Green, JSC's operations manager, Joe Thomas was overheard to say, "I can't understand why our profits are now at zero. Sales are up again. Scrap rates are reasonable (5%), even our raw material costs per ton shipped are lower. John, if we can just lower our labor cost and maintenance costs per shipped ton and spread our fixed overhead costs over more tonnage, I am sure we can pull ourselves out of this."

DISCUSSION QUESTIONS

1. What would be a good mission statement for (a) Johannsen Steel and (b) for the production function of Johannsen Steel?

2. What does an analysis of external threats, opportunities, and internal strengths and weaknesses suggest?

3. Review the ten P/OM decisions discussed in this chapter and determine the reasons (both strategic and tactical) behind JSC's problems. What are JSC's options and what strategic or tactical decisions should it make?

4. What tools/techniques would help you in your analysis of JSC and/or in explaining your recommendations to top management?

Source: Professor Roger J. Gagnon. Names of the firm and principals have been changed, but the situation and issues described are actual.

Barro, R. J. "Economic Growth in a Cross Section of Countries." *Quarterly Journal of Economics,* 106 (May 1991): 407–443.

Chase, R. B., and R. H. Hayes. "Beefing Up Operations in Service Firms." *Sloan Management Review,* 33, no. 1 (Fall 1991): 15–26.

Committee on Analysis of Research. *The Competitive Edge: Research Priorities for U.S. Manufacturing.* Washington, DC: National Academy Press, 1991.

De Long, J. B., and L. H. Summers. "Equipment Investment and Economic Growth." *Quarterly Journal of Economics,* 106 (May 1991): 445–502.

Drucker, P. F. "The Emerging Theory of Manufacturing." *Harvard Business Review* (May/June 1990): 94.

Egelhoff, W. G. "Great Strategy or Great Strategy Implementation—Two Ways of Competing in Global Markets." *Sloan Management Review,* 34, no. 2 (Winter 1993): 37.

Forrester, J. *Industrial Dynamics.* Cambridge: MIT Press, 1964.

Gerwin, D. "Manufacturing Flexibility: A Strategic Perspective." *Management Science,* 39, no. 4 (April 1993): 395–410.

Hamel, G., and C. K. Prahalad. "Strategy as Stretch and Leverage." *Harvard Business Review,* 71, no. 2 (March/April 1993): 75–84.

Hayes, R. H., and G. P. Pisano. "Beyond World-Class: The New Manufacturing Strategy." *Harvard Business Review,* 72, no. 1 (January/February 1992): 77–86.

Hayes, R. H., S. Wheelwright, and K. B. Clark: *Dynamic Manufacturing.* New York: Free Press, 1988.

Heim, J. A., and W. D. Compton, eds. *Manufacturing Systems: Foundations of World-Class Practice.* Washington, DC: National Academy Press, 1992.

Kiernan, M. J. "The New Strategic Architecture: Learning to Compete in the Twenty-First Century." *The Executive,* 7, no. 1 (February 1993): 7–21.

Kim, Y., and J. Lee. "Manufacturing Strategy and Production Systems: An integrated framework." *Journal of Operations Management,* 11, no. 1 (March 1993): 3–15.

Kogut, B., and N. Kulatilaka. "Operating Flexibility, Global Manufacturing, and the Option Value of a Multina-tional Network." *Management Science,* 40, no. 1 (January 1994): 123–139.

Little, J. D. C. "Tautologies, Models, and Theories: Can We Find 'Laws' of Manufacturing?" *Industrial Research & Development,* 24, no. 3 (July 1992): 7.

National Center for Manufacturing Sciences. *Competing in World-Class Manufacturing: America's 21st Century Challenge.* Homewood, IL: Business One Irwin, 1990.

Ohmae, K. "The Borderless World." *Sloan Management Review,* 32 (Winter 1991): 117.

Peteraf, M. A. "Commitment: The Dynamic of Strategy." *Academy of Management Executive,* 6, no. 3 (August 1992): 97.

Pine, B. J. II, B. Victor, and A. C. Boynton. "Making Mass Customization Work." *Harvard Business Review,* 71, no. 5 (September/October 1993): 108–119.

Porter, M. E. *The Competitive Advantages of Nations.* New York: Free Press, 1990.

Rich, P. "The Organizational Taxonomy: Definition and Design." *The Academy of Management Review,* 17, no. 4 (October 1992): 758.

Rockart, J. F., and J. D. Hofman. "Systems Delivery: Evolving New Strategies." *Sloan Management Review,* 33, no. 4 (Summer 1992): 21.

Schmenner, R. W. "International Factory Productivity Gains." *Journal of Operations Management,* 10, no. 2 (April 1991): 229–254.

Shaw, M. J., J. J. Solberg, and T. C. Woo. "System Integration in Intelligent Manufacturing: An Introduction." *Industrial Engineering Research & Development,* 24, no. 3 (July 1992): 2.

Skinner, W. *Manufacturing: The Formidable Competitive Weapon.* New York: John Wiley, 1985.

Sloan, A. P. *My Years with General Motors.* New York: Doubleday, 1972.

Stephanou, S. *The Manufacturing Challenge from Concept to Production.* New York: Van Nostrand Reinhold, 1991.

Stonebraker, P. W., and G. K. Leong. *Operations Strategy: Focusing Competitive Excellence.* Boston: Allyn & Bacon, 1994.

2 SUPPLEMENT

DECISION-MAKING TOOLS

The wildcatter's decision was a tough one. Which of his new Kentucky lease areas—Blair East or Blair West—should he drill for oil? A wrong decision in this type of wildcat oil drilling could mean the difference between success and bankruptcy for the company. Talk about decision making under uncertainty and pressure! But using a decision tree, Tomco Oil's President Thomas E. Blair identified 74 different options, each with its own net profit. What had begun as an overwhelming number of geological, engineering, economic, and political factors now became much clearer. Says Blair, "Decision tree analysis provided us with a systematic way of planning these decisions and clearer insight into the numerous and varied financial outcomes that are possible." ◆

Source: Adapted from J. Hosseini, "Decision Analysis and Its Application in the Choice Between Two Wildcat Oil Ventures," *Interfaces* (March/April 1986): 75–85.

Operations managers are decision makers. To achieve the goals of their organizations, managers must understand how decisions are made and know what decision-making tools to use. To a great extent, the success or failure of people and companies depends on the quality of their decisions. The manager who insisted on launching the space shuttle *Challenger* (which exploded in 1986), despite being told that it should not be launched, did not rise to power within NASA. William Gates, who developed DOS and Windows, operating systems for personal computers, became president of the most powerful software firm in the world (Microsoft) and the youngest billionaire in the United States.

In this supplement and throughout the text, we use the term *model* over and over. Models lie at the heart of P/OM decision making. A **model** is a representation of reality. It can be a physical model, such as a scale model of a factory or a model of an airplane for use in a wind tunnel. Or it can be a mathematical model, which is even more common. One simple mathematical model you learned in geometry is the formula Area = length × width. Other models can be much more complex and can even represent the operation of a business. Such a model would have variables to account for production costs, transportation costs, inventory costs, and data-handling costs, as well as a wide variety of other possible inputs and outputs.

Model

Models and the techniques of scientific management can help managers:

1. understand how their own companies work
2. understand how other companies work
3. see a way of reducing, or at least understanding, uncertainty that surrounds business plans and actions.

Throughout this book, we introduce you to a broad range of models and tools that help operations managers make better decisions. This supplement first examines the analytic decision-making process, then categorizes the models you will be dealing with, and finally introduces decision theory, which is one of the most popular decision-making tools in use.

THE ANALYTIC DECISION PROCESS

What makes the difference between a good decision and a bad decision? A "good" decision, using analytic decision making, is based on logic and considers all available data and possible alternatives. It also follows these six steps:

1. **Define the problem and the factors that influence it.** The problem to be decided must be stated clearly and concisely, which in many cases is the most important and difficult step.
2. **Establish decision criteria and goals.** Managers must develop specific and measurable objectives. Most firms have more than just a goal of maximizing profit.
3. **Formulate a model or relationship between goals and variables.** In other words, we want to develop a representation of the situation—a model. Most models presented in this book contain one or more variables. A variable, as the name implies, is a measurable quantity that may vary or is subject to change.
4. **Identify and evaluate alternatives.** Managers need to generate as many solutions to the problem as possible (and usually quickly). Most managers like to have a *range* or set of options so they can evaluate each option for its merits and drawbacks.

Back in 1969, Robert Freitag was head of the NASA team responsible for landing the *Apollo II* safely on the moon. Here are Freitag's comments about that task:

"What you do is break it down into pieces: the launch site, the launch vehicles, the spacecraft, the lunar module, and worldwide tracking networks. Then, once these pieces are broken down, you assign them to one organization or another. They, in turn, take those small pieces, like the rocket, and break it down into engines or structures or guidance equipment. And this breakdown, or 'tree,' is the really tough part about managing. You need to be sure that the pieces come together at the right time, and that they work when put together. Mathematical models help with that. The total number of people who worked on the Apollo was about 400,000 to 500,000, all working toward a single objective."

5. **Select the best alternative.** This is the alternative that best satisfies and is most consistent with the stated goals.

6. **Implement the decision.** Putting into action the steps of the chosen alternative can be the most difficult phase of decision making. Implementation involves making task assignments and a timetable for their completion.

We should point out that these steps do not always follow one another without some looping back to an earlier step. Modifying one or more steps before the final results are implemented is not unusual. Still, making "good" decisions in operations problems means performing all six steps.

MODELS FOR DECISION MAKING

When applied to operations management decisions, the decision process is closely tied to the use of mathematical models and "quantitative" analysis.

There are advantages and disadvantages of modeling. We use models to try to represent the reality of a real system by duplicating its important features, appearance, and characteristics. Models are not a panacea: Indeed, most models are simplifications of the real world. The emphasis in this book is not on model building per se, but on the use of models to help operations managers make decisions. We think you should know:

1. when a model is appropriate and what its assumptions and limitations are

2. what purpose a model might serve in a particular problem

3. how to use the model and produce results

4. how to interpret, in management terms, the results of the model

Advantages and Disadvantages of Using Models

The mathematical models presented in this book are tools that have become widely accepted by managers for several reasons.

1. They are less expensive and disruptive than experimenting with the real-world system.

2. They allow operations managers to ask "what if" types of questions (that is, questions such as "what if" my inventory cost increases 3% next year—how will profits change?).

3. They are built for management problems and encourage management input.

4. They force a consistent and systematic approach to the analysis of problems.

5. They require managers to be specific about constraints and goals relating to a problem.

6. They can help reduce the time needed in decision making.

The main limitations of models are as follows:

1. They may be expensive and time-consuming to develop and test.

2. They are often misused and misunderstood (and feared) because of their mathematical complexity.

3. They tend to downplay the role and value of nonquantifiable information.

4. They often have assumptions that oversimplify the variables of the real world.

DECISION THEORY

Decision theory, an analytic approach to choosing the best alternative or course of action, is one of the most widely used and useful of all decision-making tools. Decision theory can be separated into three decision models. These are based on the degree of certainty of the possible outcomes or consequences facing the decision maker. The three types of decision models are as follows:

1. *Decision making under certainty*—the *decision maker knows with certainty* the consequence or outcome of any alternative or decision choice. For example, a decision maker knows with complete certainty that a $100 deposit in a checking account will result in an increase of $100 in the balance of that account.

2. *Decision making under uncertainty*—the *decision maker does not know the probability* of occurrence of the outcomes for each choice. For example, the probability that the U.S. Postal Service will be replaced by home-to-home computer networks is unknown.

3. *Decision making under risk*—the *decision maker knows the probability* of occurrence of the outcomes or consequences for each choice. For instance, Chrysler may not know how many of its successful minivans it will sell next year, but the probability of selling more than 450,000 is 0.30.

A temporary island in the Beaufort Sea off the northern coast of Alaska has been created by sea water projected into the sky. The water freezes immediately into cascading ice crystals and forms a solid mass. For the drilling of a test well, Amoco executives considered several decision alternatives: (1) an offshore platform, (2) a drill ship, (3) a gravel island, (4) a concrete island, or (5) the temporary island of ice. Using decision theory, they opted for the ice island, because the cost would be less than half that of the gravel island. In the summer, the ice would melt back into its natural state.

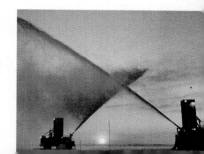

Fundamentals of Decision Theory

Regardless of the complexity of a decision, all decision makers are faced with alternatives and states of nature. An *alternative* is a course of action or a strategy that a decision maker might choose. For example, Amoco Oil managers had as an alternative the building of a temporary island of ice to drill for oil in Alaska (see the photo on page 55). A *state of nature* is an occurrence or a situation over which the decision maker has no control. For example, if the Alaskan weather was unseasonably warm, a temporary ice island for Amoco's drilling would melt and thus prove to be a very costly decision.

Decision Tables

Decision table

Decision tables are, quite simply, charts that help define alternatives. For any alternative and a particular state of nature, there is a consequence or outcome, which, in business, is usually expressed as a monetary value. This is called a conditional value. Note that all of the alternatives in Example S1 are listed down the left side of the table, that states of nature are listed across the top, and that conditional values are in the body of the decision table.

EXAMPLE S1

The Getz Products Company is investigating the possibility of producing and marketing backyard storage sheds. Undertaking this project would require the construction of either a large or a small manufacturing plant. The market for the product produced—storage sheds—could be either favorable or unfavorable. Getz, of course, has the option of not developing the new product line at all. With a favorable market, a large facility would give Getz Products a net profit of $200,000. If the market is unfavorable, a $180,000 net loss would occur. A small plant would result in a net profit of $100,000 in a favorable market, but a net loss of $20,000 would be encountered if the market was unfavorable. The following table shows the decision table based on this information.

DECISION TABLE WITH CONDITIONAL VALUES FOR GETZ PRODUCTS

	STATES OF NATURE	
ALTERNATIVES	**FAVORABLE MARKET**	**UNFAVORABLE MARKET**
Construct large plant	$200,000	−$180,000
Construct small plant	$100,000	−$ 20,000
Do nothing	$0	$0

In Examples S2 and S3, we see how to use decision tables.

DECISION MAKING UNDER CERTAINTY.   This is the easiest situation a manager can face. If, for example, Getz Products, the company in Example S1, knows that the market for storage sheds will be favorable, the firm will build a large plant. If the firm is certain the market will be unfavorable, it will do nothing.

DECISION MAKING UNDER UNCERTAINTY. When there is complete *uncertainty* as to which state of nature in a decision table may occur (that is, when we cannot even assess probabilities for each possible outcome), we rely on three decision methods:

1. **Maximax**—this method finds an alternative that *maximizes* the *maximum* outcome for every alternative. First, we find the maximum outcome within every alternative, and then we pick the alternative with the maximum number. Because this decision criterion locates the alternative with the *highest* possible *gain*, it has been called an "optimistic" decision criterion.   **Maximax**

2. **Maximin**—this method finds the alternative that *maximizes* the *minimum* outcome for every alternative. First, we find the minimum outcome within every alternative, and then we pick the alternative with the maximum number. Because this decision criterion locates the alternative that has the *least* possible *loss*, it has been called a "pessimistic" decision criterion.   **Maximin**

3. **Equally likely**—this method finds the alternative with the highest average outcome. First, we calculate the average outcome for every alternative, which is the sum of all outcomes divided by the number of outcomes. We then pick the alternative with the maximum number. The equally likely approach assumes that each state of nature is equally likely to occur.   **Equally likely**

Example S2 applies each of these approaches to the Getz Products Company.

EXAMPLE S2

Given Getz's decision table of Example S1, determine the maximax, maximin, and equally like decision criteria.

1. The maximax choice is to construct a large plant. This is the *maximum* of the *maximum* number within each row, or alternative.

2. The maximin choice is to do nothing. This is the *maximum* of the *minimum* number within each row, or alternative.

3. The equally likely choice is to construct a small plant. This is the maximum of the average outcome of each alternative. This approach assumes that all outcomes for any alternative are *equally likely.*

| | STATES OF NATURE | | | | |
| | FAVORABLE | UNFAVORABLE | MAXIMUM | MINIMUM | ROW |
ALTERNATIVES	MARKET	MARKET	IN ROW	IN ROW	AVERAGE
Construct large plant	$200,000	−$180,000	$200,000 ←	−$180,000	$10,000
Construct small plant	$100,000	−$20,000	$100,000	−$20,000	$40,000 ←
Do nothing	$0	$0	$0	$0 ←	$0
			Maximax ⌐	Maximin ⌐	Equally likely ⌐

Expected monetary value (EMV)

DECISION MAKING UNDER RISK.   Decision making under risk, a more common occurrence, relies on probabilities. Several possible states of nature may occur, each with an assumed probability. Given a decision table with conditional values and probability assessments for all states of nature, we can determine the **expected monetary value (EMV)** for each alternative. This figure represents the expected value or *average* return for each alternative if we could repeat the decision a large number of times. Picking the alternative that has the maximum EMV is one of the most popular decision criteria.

The EMV for an alternative is the sum of possible payoffs of the alternative, each weighted by the probability of that payoff occurring.

$$EMV\ (\text{Alternative } i) = (\text{payoff of 1st state of nature}) \times (\text{probability of 1st state of nature})$$

$$+ (\text{payoff of 2nd state of nature}) \times (\text{probability of 2nd state of nature})$$

$$+ \ldots + (\text{payoff of last state of nature}) \times (\text{probability of last state of nature})$$

Example S3 shows how a sample EMV is calculated.

EXAMPLE S3

Getz Products' P/OM manager believes that the probability of a favorable market is exactly the same as that of an unfavorable market. This is, each state of nature has a 0.50 chance. We can now determine the EMV for each alternative (see the following table).

	STATES OF NATURE	
ALTERNATIVES	**FAVORABLE MARKET**	**UNFAVORABLE MARKET**
Construct large plant	$200,000	−$180,000
Construct small plant	$100,000	−$20,000
Do nothing	$0	$0
Probabilities	0.50	0.50

1. EMV (large plant) = (0.5)($200,000) + (0.5)(−$180,000) = $10,000
2. EMV (small plant) = (0.5)($100,000) + (0.5)(−$20,000) = $40,000
3. EMV (do nothing) = (0.5)($0) + (0.5)($0) = $0

The maximum EMV is seen in the second alternative, constructing a small plant. Thus, according to the EMV decision criterion, we would build the small facility.

EXPECTED VALUE OF PERFECT INFORMATION (EVPI).   If a manager were able to determine which state of nature would occur, then he or she would know which decision to make. Once a manager knows which decision to make, the payoff increases because the payoff is now a certainty, not a probability. Because the payoff will increase if we know which state of nature will occur, this knowledge, or "perfect information," has value. Therefore, we now look at how to determine the value of this information. We call this difference between the payoff under certainty and the payoff under risk the **expected value of perfect information (EVPI)**.

Expected value of perfect information (EVPI)

$$\text{EVPI} = \text{expected value under certainty} - \text{maximum EMV}$$

To find the EVPI, we must first compute the **expected value under certainty**, which is the average return based on perfect information. In order to calculate this value, we choose the best alternative for each state of nature and multiply its payoff by the probability for that state of nature.

Expected value under certainty

Expected value under certainty = (best outcome or consequence for 1st state of nature) × (probability of 1st state of nature) + (best outcome for 2nd state of nature) × (probability of 2nd state of nature) + . . . + (best outcome for last state of nature) × (probability of last state of nature)

In Example S4, we use the data and decision table from Example S3 to examine the expected value of perfect information.

EXAMPLE S4

Suppose Getz Products' P/OM manager has been approached by a marketing research firm that proposed to help him make the decision about whether or not to build the plant to produce storage sheds. The marketing researchers claim that their technical analysis will tell Getz with certainty whether or not the market is favorable for the proposed product. In other words, it will change Getz's environment from one of decision making under risk to one of decision making under certainty. This information could prevent Getz Products from making a very expensive mistake. The marketing research firm would charge Getz $65,000 for the information. What would you recommend to Getz? Should the P/OM manager hire the firm to make the marketing study? Even if the information from the study is perfectly accurate, is it worth $65,000? What would it be worth? Determining the value of such *perfect information* can be very useful. It places an upper bound on what Getz would be willing to spend on information.

By referring to the table in Example S3, Getz's manager can calculate the maximum that he would pay for information, that is, the EVPI. First, he computes the expected value under certainty. Then, using this information, he calculates the EVPI. The procedure is outlined as follows.

1. The best outcome for the state of nature "favorable market" is "build a large facility" with a payoff of $200,000. The best outcome for the state of nature "unfavorable market" is "do nothing" with a payoff of $0.

   Expected value under certainty = ($200,000)(0.50) + ($0)(0.50) = $100,000.

   Thus, if we had perfect information, we would expect (on the average) $100,000 if the decision could be repeated many times.

2. The maximum EMV is $40,000, which is the expected outcome without perfect information.

$$\text{EVPI} = \text{expected value under certainty} - \text{maximum EMV}$$

$$= \$100,000 - \$40,000 = \$60,000$$

Thus, the *most* Getz Products should be willing to pay for perfect information is $60,000. This, of course, is again based on the assumption that the probability of each state of nature is 0.50.

Decision Trees

Decision tree

Any decision that can be placed in a decision table can also be placed in a decision tree. A **decision tree** is a graphic display of the decision process that indicates decision alternatives, states of nature and their respective probabilities, and payoffs for each combination of alternative and state of nature. Decision trees are most useful for problems that include *sequential* decisions and states of nature. When later decisions depend on the outcomes of prior ones, decision tables are too difficult to structure. Decision trees are *much* easier to visualize.

Two symbols are used in decision trees:

1. □—a decision node from which one of several alternatives may be selected.

2. ○—a state of nature node out of which one state of nature will occur.

In constructing a decision tree, we must be sure that all alternatives and states of nature are in their correct and logical places and that we include *all* possible alternatives and states of nature. Example S5 presents a sample decision tree.

EXAMPLE S5

Figure S2.1 presents a decision tree for Getz Products, using the symbols just introduced.

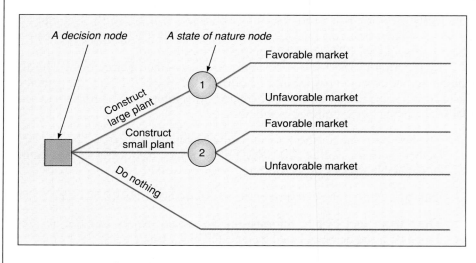

FIGURE S2.1   ■   Getz's Decision Tree

Although all previously discussed decision criteria apply to decision trees, expected monetary value (EMV) is the most commonly used and usually the most appropriate criterion for decision-tree analysis. Early steps in the analysis are to graph the decision tree and to specify the monetary consequences of all possible outcomes on the tree for a particular siuation.

Analyzing problems with *decision trees* involves five steps:

1. Define the problem.
2. Structure or draw the decision tree.
3. Assign probabilities to the states of nature.
4. Estimate payoffs for each possible combination of alternatives and states of nature.
5. Solve the problem by computing monetary values (EMV) for each state of nature node. This is done by working *backward*, that is, by starting at the right of the tree and working back to decision nodes on the left.

EXAMPLE S6

We present a completed and solved decision tree for Getz Products in Figure S2.2. Note that the payoffs are placed at the right-hand side of each of the tree's branches. The probabilities (first used by Getz in Example S3) are placed in parentheses next to each state of nature. The expected monetary values for each state of nature node are then calculated and placed by their respective nodes. The EMV of the first node is $10,000. This represents the branch from the decision node to construct a large plant. The EMV for node 2, to construct a small plant, is $40,000. Building no plant or doing nothing has, of course, a payoff of $0. The branch leaving the decision node leading to the state of nature node with the highest EMV will be chosen. In Getz's case, a small plant should be built.

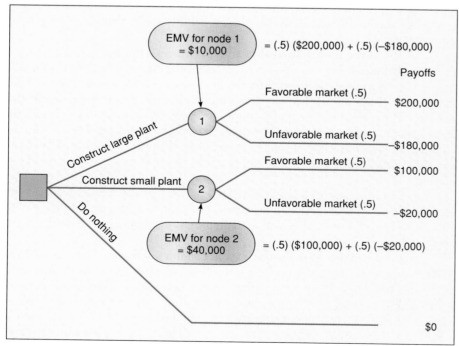

FIGURE S2.2 ■ Completed and Solved Decision Tree for Getz Products

A MORE COMPLEX DECISION TREE.   As we mentioned before, when a *sequence* of decisions must be made, decision trees are much more powerful tools than are decision tables. Let us say that Getz Products has two decisions to make, with the second decision dependent on the outcome of the first. Before deciding about building a new plant, Getz has the option of conducting its own marketing research survey, at a cost of $10,000. The information from this survey could help the company decide whether to build a large plant or a small plant, or not to build at all. Getz Products recognizes that such a market survey will not provide it with *perfect* information, but may *help* quite a bit nevertheless.

Getz's new decision tree is represented in Figure S2.3 of Example S7. Take a careful look at this more complex tree. Note that *all possible outcomes and alternatives* are included in their logical sequence. This is one strength of using decision trees in making decisions. The manager is forced to examine all possible outcomes, including unfavorable ones. He or she is also forced to make decisions in a logical, sequential manner.

EXAMPLE S7

Examining the tree in Figure S2.3, we see that Getz's first decision point is whether to conduct the $10,000 market survey. If it chooses *not* to do the study (the lower part of the tree), it must decide to build a large plant, a small plant, or no plant. This is Getz's second decision point. The market will either be favorable (0.50 probability) or unfavorable (also 0.50 probability) if it builds. The payoffs for each of the possible consequences are listed along the right-hand side. In fact, this lower portion of Getz's tree is *identical* to the simpler decision tree shown in Figure S2.2.

The upper part of Figure S2.3 reflects the decision to conduct the market survey. State of nature node number 1 has two branches coming out of it. Let us say there is a 45% chance that the survey results will indicate a favorable market for the storage sheds. We also note that the probability is .55 that the survey results will be negative.

The rest of the probabilities shown in parentheses in Figure S2.3 are all *conditional* probabilities. For example, 0.78 is the probability of a favorable market for the sheds *given* a favorable result from the market survey. Of course, you would expect to find a high probability of a favorable market given that the research indicated that the market was good. Do not forget, though, that there is a chance that Getz's $10,000 market survey did not result in perfect or even reliable information. Any market research study is subject to error. In this case, there's a 22% chance that the market for sheds will be unfavorable given that the survey results are positive.

Likewise, we note that there is a 27% chance that the market for sheds will be favorable given that Getz's survey results are negative. The probability is much higher (0.73) that the market will actually be unfavorable given that the survey was negative.

Finally, when we look to the payoff column in Figure S2.3, we see that $10,000—the cost of the marketing study—had to be subtracted from each of the top 10 tree branches. Thus, a large plant with a favorable market would normally net a $200,000 profit. But because the market study was conducted, this figure is reduced by $10,000. In the unfavorable case, the loss of $180,000 would increase to $190,000. Similarly, conducting the survey and building *no plant* now result in a −$10,000 payoff.

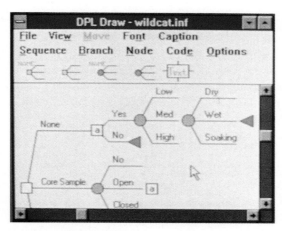

Decision tree software is a relatively new advance that permits users to solve decision analysis problems with flexibility, power, and ease. Programs such as DPL and Supertree allow decision problems to be analyzed with less effort and in greater depth than ever before. Full-color presentations of options open to managers always have impact. In this photo wildcat drilling options are explored with DPL, a product of Applied Decision Analysis in Menlo Park, CA.

With all probabilities and payoffs specified, we can start calculating the expected monetary value of each of the branches. We begin at the end or right-hand side of the decision tree and work back toward the origin. When we finish, the best decision will be known.

1. Given favorable survey results,

$$\text{EMV(node 2)} = (.78)(\$190{,}000) + (.22)(-\$190{,}000) = \$106{,}400$$

$$\text{EMV(node 3)} = (.78)(\$90{,}000) + (.22)(-\$30{,}000) = \$63{,}600$$

The EMV of no plant in this case is −$10,000. Thus, if the survey results are favorable, a large plant should be built.

2. Given negative survey results,

$$\text{EMV(node 4)} = (.27)(\$190{,}000) + (.73)(-\$190{,}000) = -\$87{,}400$$

$$\text{EMV(node 5)} = (.27)(\$90{,}000) + (.73)(-\$30{,}000) = \$2{,}400$$

The EMV of no plant is again −$10,000 for this branch. Thus, given a negative survey result, Getz should build a small plant with an expected value of $2,400.

3. Continuing on the upper part of the tree and moving backward, we compute the expected value of conducting the market survey.

$$\text{EMV(node 1)} = (.45)(\$106{,}400) + (.55)(\$2{,}400) = \$49{,}200$$

4. If the market survey is *not* conducted,

$$\text{EMV(node 6)} = (.50)(\$200{,}000) + (.50)(-\$180{,}000) = \$10{,}000$$

$$\text{EMV(node 7)} = (.50)(\$100{,}000) + (.50)(-\$20{,}000) = \$40{,}000$$

The EMV of no plant is $0. Thus, building a small plant is the best choice, given the marketing research is not performed.

5. Because the expected monetary value of conducting the survey is $49,200— versus an EMV of $40,000 for not conducting the study—the best choice is to *seek marketing information*. If the survey results are favorable, Getz should build the large plant. But if the research is negative, it should build the small plant.

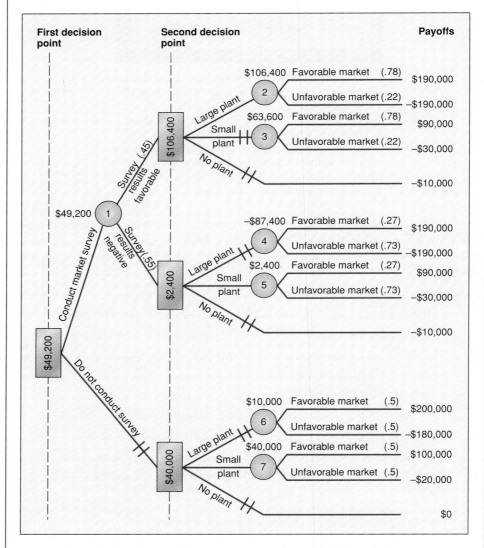

FIGURE S2.3 ■ Getz's Decision Tree with Probabilities and EMVs Shown. The short parallel lines mean "prune" that branch; it is less favorable than another available option and thus can be dropped.

SUMMARY

Operations managers make many important decisions. They must decide on investment levels for product development, for plants and equipment, and for new buildings. They decide what inventory levels are appropriate, when to schedule workers, and when to perform maintenance. Successful decision makers use all the tools available to them, including mathematical models. They also follow a process that involves six steps:

1. defining the problem
2. setting goals
3. formulating a model
4. identifying alternative solutions
5. selecting the best alternative
6. implementing the decision

Decision theory provides a useful framework for decision making. Problems are categorized as decision making under (1) certainty, (2) risk, or (3) uncertainty. Decision trees and tables are especially useful for making decisions under risk and uncertainty.

KEY TERMS

Model (p. 53)
Decision table (p. 56)
Maximax (p. 57)
Maximin (p. 57)
Equally likely (p. 57)

Expected monetary value (EMV) (p. 58)
Expected value of perfect information
 (EVPI) (p. 59)
Expected value under certainty (p. 59)
Decision tree (p. 60)

USING AB:POM AND SPREADSHEETS TO SOLVE DECISION-THEORY PROBLEMS

Solving Examples S1–S4 with AB:POM

AB:POM is a powerful yet user-friendly microcomputer program that is available with this text. It can be used in many chapters to solve homework problems (which are marked with computer logos) and textbook examples. This section shows how AB:POM can be used to calculate all of the information found in decision tables. We provide more details on the program in Appendix E. Programs S2.1 and S2.2 illustrate how Getz Products can use AB:POM to provide decision-theory calculations.

PROGRAM S2.1 ■ AB:POM's Decision Table Program with Screens Shown for a Three-Alternative, Two States-of-Nature Problem. Once we respond with three alternatives, Two states-of-nature, and maximize profit, the table below appears. In Program S2.2, inputs and outputs are all shown.

	3 Decision Tables		2
Number of alternatives (2–10)	Number of nature states (2–8)		
Profits -maximize profits			
		Sample Screen	
Probability→	0.000	0.000	
	state 1	state 2	
alternatv 1	0	0	
alternatv 2	0	0	
alternatv 3	0	0	

PROGRAM S2.2 ■ AB:POM Output for Example S1–S4 (Getz Products). We entered all the shaded data, including the labels "LG. FACILITY", "FAV MKT", and so on. Probabilities must sum to 1.

GETZ PRODUCTS EXAMPLES S2–S5

	FAV MKT	BAD MKT	EMV	Row Min	Row Max
Probability →	0.500	0.500			
LG. FACILITY	200000	-180000	10000	-180000	200000
SM. FACILITY	100000	-20000	40000	-20000	100000
DO NOTHING	0	0	0	0	0
column maximum →			40000	0	200000

The maximum expected monetary value is 40000 given by SM. FACILITY
The maximin is   0   given by DO NOTHING
The maximax is   200000   given by LG. FACILITY

PERFECT   200000   0   100000←EV under certainty
The expected value of perfect information is 60000

Using a Spreadsheet to Solve Examples S1–S4

An entirely different approach to working with decision-theory calculations is to build your own model, unique to each problem, with a spreadsheet program such as Lotus, Excel, Quattro, Visicalc, or others.

Program S2.3 shows the spreadsheet formulas needed to compute the expected monetary values and EVPI for Getz Products. For example, the formula +$B$12*B8 + $C$12*C8 is used to multiply the probability values times the monetary outcomes to get an EMV of $10,000 for the large facility in cell D8. Note the use of $, which creates an absolute cell. An absolute cell makes copying the general formula in Cell D8 to cells D9 and D10 easier.

Cells D9 and D10 contain EMV values for the other alternatives. Cell D14 computes the maximum EMV with the formula @MAX(D8 . . D10) to be $40,000. Cell D15 computes a value for EVPI using the same type of approach discussed in the chapter.

PROGRAM S2.3 ■ Using a Spreadsheet to Compute EMV Values for Getz Products (Examples S1–S4). This "symbolic" spreadsheet shows Getz's data and the formulas used in calculations.

	A	B	C	D
1	Expected Monetary Value			
2				
3	States	Favorable	Unfavorable	EMV
4	• of Nature	Market	Market	Computed
5				
6	Alternatives			
7				
8	Large Facility	200000	-180000	+$B$12*B8+$C$12*C8
9	Small Facility	100000	-20000	+$B$12*B9+$C$12*C9
10	Do Nothing	0	0	+$B$12*B10+$C$12*C10
11				
12	Probabilities	0.5	0.5	
13				
14	Maximum EMV =			@MAX(D8 . . D10)
15	EVPI =			@MAX(B8 . . B10)*B12+ @MAX(C8 . . C10)*C12−D14

SOLVED PROBLEM

Solved Problem S2.1

Daily demand for cases of Tidy Bowl cleaner at Ravinder Nath's Supermarket has always been 5, 6, or 7 cases. Develop a decision tree that illustrates her decision alternatives as to whether to stock 5, 6, or 7 cases.

Solution

The decision tree is shown in Figure S2.4.

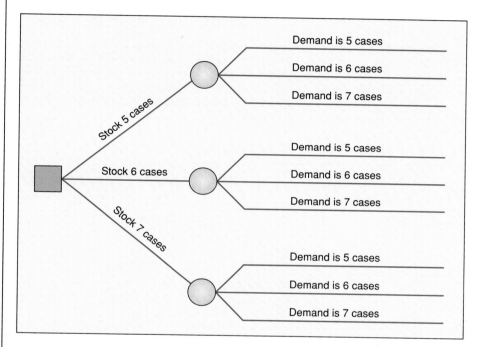

FIGURE S2.4   ■   Demand at Ravinder Nath's Supermarket

DISCUSSION QUESTIONS

1. Describe each step in the decision process.
2. Why do operations managers build models? What kind of models are most useful?
3. Give an example of a good decision you made that resulted in a bad outcome. Also give an example of a bad decision you made that had a good outcome. Why was each decision good or bad?
4. What is an alternative? What is a state of nature?
5. Discuss the differences between decision making under certainty, under risk, and under uncertainty.
6. Jenine Duffey is trying to decide whether to invest in real estate, stocks, or certificates of deposit. How well she does depends on whether the economy enters a period of recession or inflation. Develop a decision table (excluding the conditional values) to describe this situation.
7. Describe the meaning of EMV and EVPI. Provide an example in which EVPI can help a manager.
8. What techniques are used to solve decision-making problems under uncertainty? Which technique results

in an optimistic decision? Which technique results in a pessimistic decision?

9. What is the most conservative method of making a decision under uncertainty? Why?

10. What are the five steps used in analyzing a problem with a decision tree?

11. When is a decision tree preferred over a decision table?

CRITICAL THINKING EXERCISE

A robust 60-year-old male college professor has just been diagnosed as having a defective heart valve. Although he is otherwise healthy, his condition could prove fatal if left untreated. Based on current research, chances of survival *without* surgery would be as follows: a 50% chance of living 1 year, a 20% chance of surviving for 2 years, a 20% rate for 5 years, and a 10% chance of living to age 68. The probability of survival beyond age 68 without an operation is extremely low.

The operation, however, is a serious surgical procedure. Five percent of the patients succumb during the operation or its recovery stage, with an additional 45% dying during the first year after surgery. Twenty percent survive for 5 years, 13% survive for 10 years, and 8%, 5%, and 4% survive for 15, 20, and 25 years, respectively.

How would you evaluate this critical situation if the person described was a close relative? Discuss all the factors to be considered.

PROBLEMS

· **S2.1** Given the following conditional value table, determine the appropriate decision under uncertainty using:

a) maximax

b) maximin

c) equally likely

d) minimax

	STATES OF NATURE		
ALTERNATIVES	**VERY FAVORABLE MARKET**	**AVERAGE MARKET**	**UNFAVORABLE MARKET**
Large plant	$275,000	$100,000	–$150,000
Small plant	$200,000	$60,000	–$10,000
Overtime	$100,000	$40,000	–$1,000
Do nothing	$0	$0	$0

· **S2.2** G. W. Willis's company is considering expansion of its current facility to meet increasing demand. If demand is high in the future, the major expansion would result in an additional net profit of $800,000, but if demand is low, there would be a loss of $300,000. If demand is high, the minor expansion will result in an increase in net profits of $200,000, but if demand is low, there is a loss of $100,000. The company has the option of not expanding. If there is a 50% chance the demand will be high, what should the company do to maximize the long-run average profits?

: **S2.3** Foto Color is a small supplier of chemicals and equipment used by some photographic stores to process 35-mm film. One product that Foto Color supplies is BC–6. Doug Niles, president of Foto Color, normally stocks 11, 12, or 13 cases of BC–6 each week. For each case that Doug sells, he receives a profit of $35. BC–6, like many photographic chemicals, has a very short shelf life. If a case is not sold by the end of the week Doug must discard it. Since each case costs Doug $56, he loses $56 for every case that is not sold by the end of the week. There is a probability of 0.45 of selling 11 cases, a probability of 0.35 of selling 12 cases, and a probability of 0.2 of selling 13 cases.

a) What is your recommended course of action?

b) If Doug is able to develop BC–6 with an ingredient that stabilizes BC–6 so that it no longer has to be discarded, how would this change your recommended course of action?

: S2.4 Young Cheese Company is a small manufacturer of several different cheese products. One product is a cheese spread that is sold to retail outlets. Peg Young must decide how many cases of cheese spread to manufacture each month. The probability that the demand will be 6 cases is 0.1, for 7 cases it is 0.3, for 8 cases it is 0.5, and for 9 cases it is 0.1. The cost of every case is $45, and the price Peg gets for each case is $95. Unfortunately, any cases not sold by the end of the month are of no value as a result of spoilage. How many cases of cheese should Peg manufacture each month?

: S2.5 Kamlesh Mehta, chief engineer at San Antonio Chemical, Inc., has to decide whether or not to build a new processing facility, using the latest technology. If the new processing facility works, the company could realize a profit of $200,000. If the processing facility fails, the company could lose $150,000. At this time, Mehta estimates there is a 60% chance that the new process will fail.

The other option is to build a pilot plant and then decide whether or not to build a complete facility. The pilot plant would cost $10,000 to build. Mehta estimates there is a 50/50 chance the pilot plant will work. If the pilot plant works, there is a 90% probability that the complete plant, if it is built, will work. If the pilot plant project does not work, there is only a 20% chance that the complete project (if it is constructed) will work. Mehta faces a dilemma. Should he build the plant? Should he build the pilot project and then make a decision? Help Mehta by analyzing this decision-theory problem.

: S2.6 Stanley Shader, president of SS Industries, is considering whether or not to build a manufacturing plant in the Ozarks. His decision is summarized in the following table:

ALTERNATIVES	FAVORABLE MARKET	UNFAVORABLE MARKET
Build large plant	$400,000	–$300,000
Build small plant	$80,000	–$10,000
Don't build	$0	$0
Market probabilities	0.4	0.6

a) Construct a decision tree.

b) Determine the best strategy, using expected monetary value (EMV).

c) What is the expected value of perfect information (EVPI)?

: S2.7 Varzandeh Mfg. Corp. buys on–off switches from two suppliers. The quality of the switches from the suppliers is indicated below:

PERCENT DEFECTIVE	PROBABILITY FOR SUPPLIER A	PROBABILITY FOR SUPPLIER B
1	0.70	0.30
3	0.20	0.40
5	0.10	0.30

For example, the probability of getting a batch of switches that are 1% defective from supplier A is 0.70. Because Varzandeh orders 10,000 switches per order, this would mean that there is a 0.7 probability of getting 100 defective switches out of the 10,000 switches if supplier A is used to fill the order. A defective switch can be repaired for $0.50. Although the quality of supplier B is lower, it will sell an order of 10,000 switches for $37 less than supplier A.

a) Develop a decision tree.

b) Which supplier should Varzandeh use?

▪ : **S2.8** Mary Fischer, a concessionaire for the local ballpark, has developed a table of conditional values for the various alternatives (stocking decision) and states of nature (size of crowd).

	STATES OF NATURE (SIZE OF CROWD)		
ALTERNATIVES	**LARGE**	**AVERAGE**	**SMALL**
Large inventory	$20,000	$10,000	−$2,000
Average inventory	$15,000	$12,000	$6,000
Small inventory	$9,000	$6,000	$5,000

If the probabilities associated with the states of nature are 0.30 for a large crowd, 0.50 for an average crowd, and 0.20 for a small crowd, determine:

a) the alternative that provides the greatest expected monetary value (EMV)

b) the expected value of perfect information (EVPI)

▪ : **S2.9** Even though independent gasoline stations have been having a difficult time, Susan Helms has been thinking about starting her own independent gasoline station. Susan's problem is to decide how large her station should be. The annual returns will depend on both the size of her station and a number of marketing factors related to the oil industry and demand for gasoline. After a careful analysis, Susan developed the following table.

SIZE OF FIRST STATION	GOOD MARKET ($)	FAIR MARKET ($)	POOR MARKET ($)
Small	50,000	20,000	−10,000
Medium	80,000	30,000	−20,000
Large	100,000	30,000	−40,000
Very large	300,000	25,000	−160,000

For example, if Susan constructs a small station and the market is good, she will realize a profit of $50,000.

a) Develop a decision table for this decsion.

b) What is the maximax decision?

c) What is the maximin decision?

d) What is the equally likely decision?

:S2.10 Using the data in Problem S2.9, develop a decision tree and determine the best decision based on the highest expected monetary value criteria. Assume each outcome is equally likely.

:S2.11 Lynn Heinrichs is hospital administrator for Lowell Hospital. She is trying to determine whether to build a large wing on the existing hospital, a small wing, or no wing at all. If the population of Lowell continues to grow, a large wing could return $150,000 to the hospital each year. If the small wing were built, it would return $60,000 to the hospital each year if the population continues to grow. If the population of Lowell remains the same, the hospital would encounter a loss of $85,000 if the large wing were built. Furthermore, a loss of $45,000 would be realized if the small wing were constructed and the population remains the same. Unfortunately, Lynn does not have any information about the future population of Lowell.

a) Construct a decision tree.

b) Construct a decision table.

c) Using the equally likely criterion, determine the best alternative.

d) If the likelihood of growth is 0.6 and that of remaining the same is 0.4, and the decision criterion is expected monetary value, what decision should Lynn make?

·S2.12 Jim Higgins is considering opening a bicycle shop in Oshkosh. Jim enjoys biking, but this is to be a business endeavor from which he expects to make a living. Jim can open a small shop, a large shop, or no shop at all. Because there will be a 5-year lease on the building that Jim is thinking about using, he wants to make sure he makes the correct decision. Jim is also thinking about hiring his old marketing professor to conduct a marketing research study to see if there is a market for his services. From the studies conducted, the results could be either favorable or unfavorable. Develop a decision tree for Jim.

:S2.13 Jim Higgins (of Problem S2.12) has done some analysis of his bicycle shop decision. If Jim builds a large shop he will earn $60,000 if the market is favorable, but he will lose $40,000 if the market is unfavorable. The small shop will return a $30,000 profit with a favorable market and a $10,000 loss if the market is unfavorable. At the present time, he believes there is a 50/50 chance that there will be a favorable market. His old marketing professor will charge him $5,000 for the market research. He has estimated that there is a 0.6 probability that the market will be favorable. Furthermore there is a 0.9 probability that the market will be favorable given a favorable outcome of the study. However, the marketing professor has warned Jim that there is a probability of only 0.12 of a favorable market if the marketing research results are not favorable. Expand the decision tree of Problem S2.12 to help Jim decide what to do.

·S2.14 Dick Szecsy is not sure what he should do. He can build either a large video rental section or a small one in his drugstore. He can also gather additional information, or simply do nothing. If he gathers additional information, the results could suggest either a favorable or an unfavorable market, but it would cost him $3,000 to gather the information. Dick believes that there is a 50/50 chance that the information will be favorable. If the rental market is favorable, Dick will earn $15,000 with the large section or $5,000 with the small. With an unfavorable video rental market, however, Dick could lose $20,000 with the large section or $10,000 with the small section. Without gathering additional information, Dick estimates that the probability of a favorable rental market is 0.7. A favorable report from the study would increase the probability of a favorable rental market to 0.9. Furthermore, an unfavorable report from the additional information would decrease the probability of a favorable rental market to 0.4. Of course, Dick could forget all of these numbers and do nothing. What is your advice to Dick?

:S2.15 Bakery Products is considering the introduction of a new line of products. In order to produce the new line, the bakery is considering either a major or a minor renovation of the current plant. The following conditional values table has been developed by the bakery.

ALTERNATIVES	FAVORABLE MARKET	UNFAVORABLE MARKET
Major renovation	$100,000	–$90,000
Minor renovation	$40,000	–$20,000
Do nothing	$0	$0

Under the assumption that the probability of a favorable market is equal to the probability of an unfavorable market, determine:

a) the appropriate decision tree showing payoffs and probabilities

b) the best alternative using expected monetary value (EMV)

: S2.16 Assume that the research and development department at BRK Labs, Inc., a small pharmaceutical company, has tentatively found an ointment that grows hair. This discovery adds substantial value to BRK Labs. As president of BRK, you must make a recommendation to the investors. You face three choices: first, to sell the discovery to a larger drug company—it is worth $10 million; second, to begin experimental laboratory testing and *then* make a decision; or third, to arrange financing for an all-out, aggressive marketing program, with the hope that testing and development will go well along the way. The real goal of this third option is to move so fast that the competition is left with little chance of catching up.

The experimental laboratory testing program will cost $5 million, and there is a 50/50 chance that favorable results will be found and survive FDA review prior to a larger company's preempting BRK Labs. Occasionally, even with unfavorable test results, alternative uses for a drug are found; but this occurs only about once in 10 cases, and the value of the formula still drops to only $1 million. On the other hand, if a favorable formulation is found, you estimate the discovery and results are worth $20 million. But because BRK Labs is a small company with limited resources and marketing ability, even with favorable laboratory test results, the chance of BRK Labs successfully getting the product approved and on the market is only about 40%. Even with favorable laboratory test results and a decision to market, costs will include not only $5 million in test costs but also an additional $3 million for marketing.

The third choice for BRK Labs is to proceed aggressively on its own and aim for the marketing coup of the decade. As president, you figure there is only about one chance in five of BRK's doing this. However, the payoff from BRK's doing this successfully is $100 million. (This figure is five times greater than the results mentioned earlier because the $20 million reflects the potential for a competitor to enter the market while BRK is in experimental testing.) Under this third choice, marketing costs are $3 million and testing will cost $5 million. Both of these expenses apply for this option whether the product is ultimately successful or not.

a) Draw the decision tree.

b) Determine the expected monetary value (EMV).

c) What do you recommend to the investors? How might this recommendation differ based on the firm's financial status?

d) How sensitive is this solution to changes in probabilities? Does this change your conclusion?

CASE STUDY

Toledo Leather Company

The Toledo Leather Company has been producing leather goods for more than 30 years. It purchases prepared hides from tanners and produces leather clothing accessories such as wallets, belts, and handbags. The firm has just developed a new leather product and has prepared a 1-year production and sales plan for it. The new product is best described as a combination billfold, key case, and credit card carrier. As company president Peggy Lane has noted, "It is a super carryall for small this-and-thats." Lane has placed her administrative assistant, Harold Hamilton, in charge of the project.

Hamilton has established that material and variable overhead for the carryall should be about $1.50 per case over the next year, given a 5-day week and no overtime. Unit labor and machining costs, however, depend on the choice of machine that will be used for production. Hamilton has narrowed the choice down to two specialized pieces of equipment. Machine 1 is a semiautomated machine that will cut the material to the size needed for one unit and also will sew it, install the rings and snaps, and emboss it with two types of designs. This machine costs $250,000 and will add $2.50 to the average variable cost for labor and other machine-related costs. This piece of equipment has a production capacity of 640 units per day. However, estimated downtime for maintenance and repairs is 12.5% (1/8 the time).

Machine 2 is fully automated. It cuts, sews, installs rings and snaps, and is capable of embossing the case with three types of designs. This machine costs $350,000 and will add $1.75 to the average variable cost for labor and other machine-related costs. Machine 2 has a higher production capacity (estimated at 800 units per day) than the semiautomated machine. However, estimated downtime is 25% (1/4 the time), consistent with its greater complexity.

Marketing estimates for the next year have been more difficult to project than production costs and capacity estimates. However, $6.00 seems the likeliest selling price for the carryall. This price brings it in line with comparable products on the market, but because it offers more than these products it has the potential to outsell them. Sales volume estimates seem to center on 140,000 units for the year. Analysis of the potential market has been difficult because this new product is different from similar ones now being sold. Hamilton's best estimates of sales at $6.00 per unit and the probabilities attached to these volumes are in Table 1.

TABLE 1 ■ THE TOLEDO LEATHER COMPANY FIRST-YEAR SALES VOLUME ESTIMATE	
SALES VOLUME	PROBABILITY
120,000 units	0.15
130,000 units	0.25
140,000 units	0.40
150,000 units	0.15
160,000 units	0.05

Given these marketing estimates and the machine capacities, the company will have to decide either to modify the machines in order to increase capacity or work overtime if demand is at the higher levels. Overtime premiums would raise the costs by $1.20 per case on the semiautomated machine and by $0.90 on the fully automated machine. Modification of Machine 1, the semiautomatic one, would cost $15,000 to meet the highest levels of sales. Modifications of Machine 2 would cost $20,000.

Lane has directed Hamilton to make a decision based on first-year sales, since demand for a product such as this is uncertain after its initial popularity passes. Toledo operates on a fifty-week year because the company usually closes down for the holidays.

DISCUSSION QUESTIONS

1. Using a decision tree (show *all* work) based on maximizing expected profit, decide which machine Toledo Leather should select. Should overtime be scheduled or should the machine be modified, and under what circumstances?

(Continued)

2. Set up a payoff matrix for the sales volumes given (assume the machines cannot be modified and overtime is used) and assume that the probability of occurrence of the five levels of sales are not known. Then, decide which machine should be purchased using:

(a) the maximax criterion
(b) the maximin criterion
(c) the equally likely criterion.

Source: Professor Michael Ballot, University of the Pacific.

BIBLIOGRAPHY

Brown, R. "Do Managers Find Decision Theory Useful?" *Harvard Business Review* (May/June 1970): 78–89.

Brown, R. V. "The State of the Art of Decision Analysis: A Personal Perspective." *Interfaces*, 22, no. 6 (November/December 1992): 5–14.

Dantzig, G. B. "The Diet Problem." *Interfaces*, 20, no. 4 (July/August 1990): 43–47.

Gass, S. I. "Model World: Models at the OK Corral." *Interfaces*, 21, no. 6 (November/December 1991): 80.

Green, A. E. S. "Finding the Japanese Fleet." *Interfaces*, 23, no. 5 (September/October 1993): 62.

Hess, S. W. "Swinging on the Branch of a Tree: Project Selection Applications." *Interfaces*, 23, no. 6 (November/December 1993): 5–12.

Kirkwood, C. W. "An Overview of Methods for Applied Decision Analysis." *Interfaces*, 22, no. 6 (November/December 1992): 28–39.

Lane, M. S., A. H Mansour, and J. L. Harpell. "Operations Research Techniques: A Longitudinal Update 1973–1988." *Interfaces*, 23, no. 2 (March/April 1993): 63–68.

Lev, B. "Airline Operations Research." *Interfaces*, 20, no. 3 (May/June 1990): 99.

Moore, E. W., Jr., J. M. Warke, and L. R. Gorban. "The Indispensable Role of Management Science in Centralizing Freight Operations at Reynolds Metals Company." *Interfaces*, 21, no. 1 (January/February 1991): 107–129.

Pratt, J. W., H. Raiffa, and R. Schlaifer. *Introduction to Statistical Decision Theory*. New York: McGraw-Hill, 1965.

Raiffa, H. *Decision Analysis: Introductory Lectures on Choices Under Certainty*. Reading, MA: Addison-Wesley, 1968.

Render, B., and R. M. Stair, Jr. *Introduction to Management Science*. Boston: Allyn and Bacon, 1992.

————. *Quantitative Analysis for Management*, 5th ed. Boston: Allyn and Bacon, 1994.

Schlaifer, R. *Analysis of Decisions Under Certainty*. New York: McGraw-Hill, 1969.

3

TOTAL QUALITY MANAGEMENT

LEARNING OBJECTIVES

When you complete this chapter you should be able to:

Identify or define:

Quality

Malcolm Baldrige Awards

Deming, Juran, and Crosby

Taguchi Technique

Explain:

Why Quality is Important

Total Quality Management (TQM)

House of Quality

Pareto Charts

Process Charts

Quality Robust Products

Inspection

TOTAL QUALITY MANAGEMENT PROVIDES A COMPETITIVE ADVANTAGE AT MOTOROLA

Motorola decided some years ago to be a world leader in quality. Indeed, Motorola is so good that it became the first winner of the Malcolm Baldrige National Quality Award. Motorola believes in total quality management and practices it from the top, specifically from Honorary Chairman Robert Galvin. It achieves outstanding quality through demonstrated top management commitment that permeates the entire organization.

To make the quality focus work, Motorola did a number of things:

- Aggressively began a worldwide education program to be sure that employees understood quality and statistical process control.

- Established goals, namely, its Six Sigma program. Motorola's Six Sigma program means that it can expect to have a defect rate of no more than a few parts per million.

- Established extensive employee participation and a competitive system where employees vie for awards based on performance of their particular work group. This is a worldwide competition.

Motorola's divisions can expect a quality service review every two years. Five member teams are selected from various parts of the company to perform the review. After the review, the general manager and staff have a session with the teams and go over the review. The strengths and weaknesses are discussed and recommendations are given to the local management about improvements that must be made. The system is working; it gives Motorola uniformity and consistency. Corporate goals receive commitment throughout the organization and that is a powerful quality tool.

Total quality management (TQM) provides a competitive advantage for Motorola.

The development of robust products requires good experimental design and extensive testing. Here Motorola's portable phones, in an Accelerated Life Testing (ALT) facility.

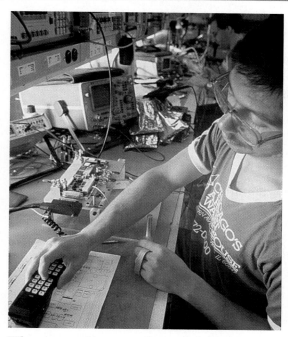

When automated inspection devices work, they are used. However, when manual intervention in the testing process is appropriate, as is shown here, it is used.

Motorola's Accelerated Life Testing (ALT) facility also tests extreme conditions of temperature shock, dust, water, and vibrations. Here cellular phones are undergoing a water test.

With Motorola's strong emphasis on total quality management, Motorola employees are responsible for evaluating their own work, including locating and recording defects. Here employees are evaluating printed circular boxes.

W orld-class textile producer Milliken and Company in Spartanburg, South Carolina, is obsessed with quality. But even at Milliken, 25% of the company's cost was attributed to quality problems. Roger Milliken wanted the quality problems solved. He wanted quality to be management's first commitment. So at a meeting of 400 managers, he jumped up on a chair, raised his right arm, and asked others to raise theirs and to repeat after him:

> I will listen; I will not shoot the messenger; I will recognize that management is the problem.

Milliken believes that was the breakthrough moment. "That day we started to commit . . . and to embark upon an entirely new approach to quality: one of leadership through listening and coaching . . . without realizing the magic of what we were about to do, we were indeed beginning to enable and empower each and every one of our associates to do what they know and can do best."[1] ◆

There is no topic in organizations today more important than quality. The future of Milliken, Motorola, and every other firm hinges on its ability to provide quality goods and services for both domestic and international consumption. Determining quality expectations is critical to identifying and meeting customer needs. Quality affects the *entire organization*, from supplier to customer and from product design to maintenance. In this chapter, we deal with two quality issues. We first define *quality* and discuss why it is important. We then present the concept of Total Quality Management (TQM) and its tools. In Chapter 4, we explore the subject of statistical quality control.

DEFINING QUALITY

The American Society for Quality Control defines *quality* as: "The totality of features and characteristics of a product or service that bear on its ability to satisfy stated or implied needs."[2] Although this definition is widely accepted, others believe that definitions of *quality* fall into several categories.[3] Some definitions are *user-based*. They propose that quality "lies in the eyes of the beholder." Marketing people like this approach, and so do customers. To them, higher quality means better performance, nicer features, and other (sometimes costly) improvements. To production managers, quality is *manufacturing-based*. They believe that quality means conforming to specifications and "making it right the first time." Yet a third approach is the *product-based* definition, which views quality as a precise and measurable variable. This approach views a high-quality ice cream as having high-butterfat content.

[1] Adopted from Jeremy Maine, *Quality Wars* (New York: Free Press, 1994), pp. 45–46.

[2] Ross Johnson and William O. Winchell, *Production and Quality* (Milwaukee: American Society for Quality Control, 1989), p. 2; also see Carol A. Reeves and David A. Bednar, "Defining Quality: Alternatives and Implications," *Academy of Management Review*, 19, no. 3 (1994): 419–445.

[3] David A. Garvin, "What Does 'Product Quality' Really Mean?" *Sloan Management Review*, 26, no. 1 (Fall 1984): 25–43.

In this text, we address all three categories of quality. Quality characteristics are first identified through market research, which identifies what the customer wants (a user-based approach to quality). These characteristics are then translated into specific product attributes (a product-based approach to quality). Then the manufacturing process ensures that the products are made precisely to specifications (a manufacturing-based approach to quality). A process that ignores any one of these steps will not result in a product that meets or exceeds the customer's expectations.[4]

"Well, as a last ditch measure, we could improve the corporate image by improving the product."

Source: Wall Street Journal, with permission of Cartoon Features Syndicate.

WHY QUALITY IS IMPORTANT

Quality goods and services are strategically important to firms and to countries. The quality of a firm's products, the prices it charges, and the supply it makes available are all factors that determine demand. In particular, quality affects a firm in four ways:

1. *Costs and market share*. Figure 3.1 shows that improved quality can lead to both increased market share and cost savings. Both can also affect profitability. Likewise, adhering to quality standards means fewer defects and lower service costs. One analysis of air conditioner manufacturers even showed that quality and productivity were positively related. In that study, companies with the highest quality were five times as productive (as measured by units produced per labor-hour) as companies with the poorest quality.[5] Indeed, when the implications of an organization's long-term costs and the potential for increased market share are considered, total costs may well be at a minimum when 100% of the goods or services are perfect and defect-free.

FIGURE 3.1　■　Two Ways Quality Can Improve Profitability

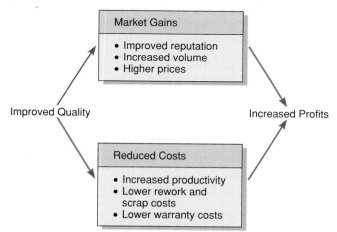

---

[4]See Garvin (Fall 1984): 29.
[5]Garvin (Fall 1984): 36.

An emphasis on quality has helped many businesses improve profitability. Mobil Oil's lubricant-blending plant in Bogota, Colombia, attained ISO certification in 1993 and, through a number of quality initiatives, reached record production. Here Luis Pineda monitors a filling machine.

ISO 9000

2. *Company's reputation.* An organization can expect its reputation for quality—be it good or bad—to follow it. Quality will show up in perceptions about the firm's new products, employment practices, and supplier relations. Self-promotion is not a substitute for quality products.

3. *Product liability.* The courts increasingly hold organizations that design, produce, or distribute faulty products or services liable for damages or injuries resulting from their use. The Consumer Product Safety Act of 1972 sets and enforces product standards by banning products that do not reach those standards. Drugs that accidentally cause birth defects, insulation that leads to cancer, or auto fuel tanks that explode upon impact can all lead to huge legal expenses, large settlements or losses, and terrible publicity.

4. *International implications.* In this technological age, quality is an international, as well as P/OM, concern. For both a company and a country to compete effectively in the global economy, products must meet global quality and price expectations. Inferior products harm a firm's profitability and a nation's balance of payments.

INTERNATIONAL QUALITY STANDARDS

Quality is so important internationally that a number of quality standards have been developed. Japan, the European Community, and the United States have each developed their own quality standards.

JAPAN'S INDUSTRIAL STANDARD. The Japanese specification for quality management is published as Industrial Standard Z8101–1981. The standard states:

> Implementing quality control effectively necessitates the cooperation of all people in the company, involving top management, managers, supervisors, and workers in all areas of corporate activities such as market research, research and development, product planning design, preparations for production, purchasing, vendor management, manufacturing, inspection, sales, and afterservices, as well as financial control, personnel administration, and training and education.

EUROPE'S ISO 9000 STANDARD. The European Community (EC) has developed the **ISO 9000** series of quality standards. The focus of the EC standards is to force the establishment of quality management procedures on firms doing business in the EC.

Several factors make the ISO 9000 series the subject of interest: (1) the standards may achieve worldwide acceptance, (2) the standards are now being applied to some products made or imported by the EC, and (3) adherence to the standards may be necessary for product certification. The *POM in Action* box "Rice Aircraft's New Strategy" suggests that ISO 9000 is becoming increasingly important.

AMERICAN STANDARDS. The United States has long had military specifications for defense contracts, and in recent years, the American Quality Control Society has developed specifications equivalent to those of the EC. They are Q90, Q91, Q92, Q93, and Q94. Q90 provides an overview and introduction to the other standards, definitions, and concepts related to quality.

Q91 is the general standard for design, development, manufacturing, installation, and servicing of products or services.

Rice Aircraft's New Strategy: International Quality Standards

Faced with shrinking sales, Rice Aircraft discovered an unusual survival strategy: compliance with new international quality control standards. The so-called ISO 9000 series of rules, drawn up by a standards-setting body in Geneva, have been endorsed in about 60 countries. The rules spell out how companies should set up quality assurance systems, especially focusing on procedures, controls, and documentation. Increasingly, both large and small U.S. firms recognize that they must meet these voluntary standards to compete for business abroad and win domestic contracts from U.S.-based multinational companies.

Rice's efforts set this family-owned Hauppage, New York, aircraft parts distributor apart from many of its competitors. Under rigorous rules, Rice made sure it kept inventory lists current, procedures for every job documented, office manuals up to date, and shipments logged into a computer as soon as they hit the loading dock.

Executive VP Paula Rice says the company's new strategy, tied to ISO 9000, has improved profits and helped win significant new business. For instance, Rice recently won a $3 million contract with American Airlines, which confirms that American was impressed that a company as small as Rice was meeting international quality standards.

Sources: Wall Street Journal (November 19, 1992): and *Incentive* (October 1991): 60–68.

Q92 provides more detail than Q91 for organizations involved in production, installation, and servicing of products or services.

Q93 provides more detail than Q91 for organizations specifically involved in inspection and tests and for distributors and value-added contractors.

Q94 provides guidelines for managing and auditing a quality control system.

The international implications of quality are so important that, in 1988, the United States established the *Malcolm Baldrige National Quality Award* for quality achievement. The award is named for former Secretary of Commerce Malcolm Baldrige. Winners include Motorola (1988); Milliken and Xerox (1989); IBM, Federal Express, and Cadillac (1990); Solectron, Zytec, and Marlow (1991); Ritz-Carlton Hotels, AT&T, and Texas Instruments (1992); Eastman Chemical, Ames Rubber (1993), and GTE, and Wainwright Industries (1994). Figure 3.2 presents the criteria framework for the awards.

TOTAL QUALITY MANAGEMENT

Total quality management (TQM) refers to a quality emphasis that encompasses the entire organization, from supplier to customer. TQM stresses a commitment by management to have a continuing companywide drive toward excellence in all aspects of products and services that are important to the customer.[6]

TQM is important because quality decisions influence each of the 10 strategic and tactical decisions made by production/operations managers. Every chapter that

Total quality management

[6]The term *companywide quality control* (CWQC) is sometimes used to describe an organization's commitment to quality; see L. P. Sullivan, "The Seven Stages in Company-Wide Quality Control," *Quality Progress* (May 1986): 78.

FIGURE 3.2   ■   Baldrige Award Criteria Framework

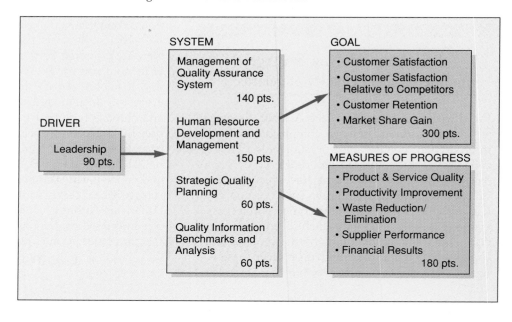

follows deals with some aspect of identifying and meeting customer expectations. Meeting those expectations requires an emphasis on TQM if a firm is to compete as a leader in world markets.

Quality expert W. Edwards Deming used 14 points (see Table 3.1) to indicate how he implemented TQM.[7] We develop these into five concepts for an effective TQM program: (1) continuous improvement, (2) employee involvement, (3) benchmarking, (4) just-in-time (JIT), and (5) knowledge of tools.

Continuous Improvement

Total quality management (TQM) requires a never-ending process of continuous improvement. The end goal is perfection, which is never achieved but always sought.

The Japanese use the word **Kaizen** to describe this ongoing process of unending improvement—the setting and achieving ever-higher goals. In the United States, TQM, *zero defects,* and *six sigma* are used to describe such efforts. Whatever word or phrase is used, P/OM managers are key players in building a work culture that endorses continuous improvement.

Employee Empowerment

Kaizen

Employee empowerment

TQM requires **employee empowerment**, or involving employees in every step of the production process. Consistently, business literature suggests that some 85% of quality problems have to do with materials and processes, not with employee performance. Therefore, the task is to design equipment and processes that produce the desired quality. This is best done with a high degree of involvement by those who un-

[7]John C. Anderson, Manus Rungtusanatham, and Roger G. Schroeder, "A Theory of Quality Management Underlying the Deming Management Method," *Academy of Management Review,* 19, no. 3 (1994): 472–509.

TABLE 3.1 ■ DEMING'S 14 POINTS FOR IMPLEMENTING QUALITY IMPROVEMENT

1. Create consistency of purpose.
2. Lead to promote change.
3. Build quality into the product; stop depending on inspections to catch problems.
4. Build long-term relationships based on performance instead of awarding business on the basis of price.
5. Continuously improve product, quality, and service.
6. Start training.
7. Emphasize leadership.
8. Drive out fear.
9. Break down barriers between departments.
10. Stop haranguing workers.
11. Support, help, and improve.
12. Remove barriers to pride in work.
13. Institute a vigorous program of education and self-improvement.
14. Put everybody in the company to work on the transformation.

Source: Deming revised his 14 points a number of times over the years. See W. E. Deming, "Transformation of Western Style of Management," *Interfaces,* 15, no. 3 (May/June 1985): 6–11; W. Edwards Deming, "Improvement of Quality and Productivity Action Through Action by Management," *National Productivity Review* (Winter 1981–1982): 12–22; W. Edwards Deming, "Philosophy Continues to Flourish," *APICS—The Performance Advantage,* 1, no. 4 (October 1991): 20.

derstand the shortcomings of the system. Those dealing with the system on a daily basis understand it better than anyone else. When nonconformance occurs, the worker is seldom wrong. Either the product was designed wrong, the system that makes the product was designed wrong, or the employee was improperly trained.[8] Although the employee may be able to help solve the problem, the employee rarely causes it.

Techniques for building employee empowerment include (1) building communication networks that include employees; (2) open, supportive supervisors; (3) moving responsibility from both managerial and staff responsibilities to production employees; (4) building high-morale organizations; (5) and formal techniques such as team building and quality circles.

Teams can be built to address a variety of issues. One popular approach to team building is a focus on quality via quality circles. A **quality circle** is a group of between 6 and 12 employees who volunteer to meet regularly to solve work-related problems. The members, all from the same work area, receive training in group planning, problem solving, and statistical quality control. They generally meet about 4 hours per month (usually after work, but sometimes on company time). Although the circle members are not rewarded financially, they do receive recognition from the firm. A specially trained team member, called the facilitator, usually helps train the circle members and keeps the meetings running smoothly. Quality circles have proven to be a cost-effective way to increase productivity as well as quality.

Quality circle

[8]See a related discussion in Asher Israeli and Bradley Fisher, "The Worker Is Never Wrong," *Quality Progress* (October 1989): 95.

Leaders in the Fight for Quality
W. Edwards Deming. (left) The awarding of the Deming Prize for quality control on Japanese TV is a national event. After World War II, Dr. Deming went to Japan to teach quality. And the Japanese learned. In his quality crusade, Deming insisted that management accept responsibility for building good systems. The employee, he believed, cannot produce products that on the average exceed the quality of what the process is capable of producing. Dr. Deming died in 1993.
J. M. Juran. (middle) A pioneer in teaching the Japanese how to improve quality, Juran believes strongly in top management commitment, support, and involvement in the quality effort. He is also a believer in teams that continually seek to raise quality standards. Juran varies from Deming somewhat in focusing on the customer and defining quality as fitness for use, not necessarily the written specifications.
Philip B. Crosby. (right) *Quality Is Free* was Crosby's attention-getting book published in 1979. Crosby's traditional view has been "with management and employee commitment great strides can be made in improving quality." He also believes that in the traditional trade-off between the cost of improving quality and the cost of poor quality, the cost of poor quality is understated. The cost of poor quality should include all of the things that are involved in *not* doing the job right the first time.

Benchmarking

Benchmarking

Benchmarking is another ingredient in an organization's TQM program. **Benchmarking** involves selecting a demonstrated standard of performance that represents the very best performance for processes or activities very similar to yours. The idea is to develop a target at which to shoot and then to develop a standard or benchmark against which to compare your performance. The steps for developing benchmarks are:[9]

- Determine what to benchmark
- Form a benchmark team
- Identify benchmarking partners
- Collect and analyze benchmarking information
- Take action to match or exceed the benchmark

In the ideal situation, you find one or more similar organizations that have proved to be leaders in the particular areas that you want to study. Then you compare

[9]Adapted from Michael J. Spendolini, *The Benchmarking Book* (New York: AMACOM, 1992).

In an effort to bring the total quality management message to Northrop employees working on the Stealth Bomber program, Northrop had each employee sign a giant scroll. The scroll, which reads "Total Quality Control on the B-2 Begins with Me," hangs above the B-2 assembly line, symbolizing employee commitment to quality.

yourself (benchmark yourself) against them. The company need not be in your industry. Indeed, to establish world-class standards, it may be best to look outside of your industry. If one industry has learned how to compete via rapid product development, but your industry has not, it does no good to study your industry. As discussed in the *POM in Action* box "L. L. Bean's Reputation Makes It a Benchmark Favorite," this is exactly what Xerox and Chrysler did when they went to L. L. Bean for order-filling benchmarks. However, competitive data need not be elaborate or sophisticated. Even casually developed data can suggest areas for further investigation. This is the case in Table 3.2, which indicates that in 1991, General Motors only generated sales of $162,700 per employee, while Ford and Chrysler were at $265,400 and $238,800, respectively. This information suggests that a true benchmark study may be warranted.

Benchmarks can and should be established in a variety of areas. Total quality management requires measurable benchmarks.

TABLE 3.2 ■ SALES PER EMPLOYEE			
1991	SALES $ (BILLIONS)	EMPLOYEES (1000S)	SALES $ PER EMPLOYEE (1000S)
Ford 88.3	333	265.4	
Chrysler	29.4	123	238.8
General Motors	123.1	756	162.7

L. L. Bean's Reputation Makes It a Benchmark Favorite

Managers in the United States smiled knowingly in the 1950s when Japanese engineers made the rounds at trade shows, endlessly snapping photos. The smiles faded in the 1970s and 80s as those photos led to world-class products. Now, the United States is embracing an effective response: benchmarking. "Too many companies suffer because they refuse to believe others can do things better," says Robert Camp, Xerox's manager of benchmarking.

The spread of benchmarking has created many role models at home. When Xerox set out to improve its order filling, for example, it went to L. L. Bean. What did copier parts have in common with Bean's outdoor paraphernalia? Nothing. But Xerox managers felt that their order-filling processes were similar: they both involve handling products so varied in size and shape that the work must be done by hand. Bean, it turns out, was able to "pick" orders three times as fast as Xerox. Lesson learned, Xerox pared its warehouse costs by 10%.

Then Chrysler came to study Bean's warehousing methods. Bean employees use flowcharts to spot wasted motions. This practice resulted in an employee suggestion to stock high-volume items close to packing stations. So impressed was Chrysler that it decided to follow suit and rely more on problem solving at the worker level.

L. L. Bean now receives up to five requests a week for benchmark visits—too many to handle. They schedule only those with a "genuine interest in quality, not the merely curious," says Robert Olive, Bean's plant manager.

Sources: Business Week (November 30, 1992): 74–75; and R. C. Camp, *Making Total Quality Happen* (New York: Conference Board, 1990), p. 42.

Just-in-Time (JIT)

The philosophy behind Just-in-Time (JIT) is one of continuing improvement and enforced problem solving. When implemented, JIT reduces the amount of inventory a firm has on hand by establishing quality and purchasing controls that bring inventory to the firm just-in-time for use. JIT is related to quality in three ways.

First, JIT cuts the cost of quality. This occurs because scrap, rework, inventory investment, and damage costs are directly related to inventory on hand. Because there is less inventory on hand with JIT, costs are lower. Additionally, inventory *hides* bad quality, while JIT immediately *exposes* bad quality.

Second, JIT improves quality. As JIT shrinks lead time, it keeps evidence of errors fresh and limits the number of potential sources of error. JIT creates, in effect, an early warning system for quality problems, both within the firm and with vendors.

Finally, better quality means less inventory and a better, easier-to-employ JIT system. Often the purpose of keeping inventory is to protect against poor production performance resulting from unreliable quality. If consistent quality exists, JIT allows us to reduce all the costs associated with inventory.

Knowledge of TQM Tools

To empower employees and implement TQM as a continuing effort, managers must train everyone in the organization in the techniques of TQM. In the following section, we focus on some of the diverse and expanding tools that are used in the TQM crusade.

TOOLS FOR TQM

Six tools/techniques that aid the TQM effort are (1) quality function deployment (house of quality), (2) Taguchi techniques, (3) Pareto charts, (4) process charts, (5) cause-and-effect diagrams (fish-bone charts), and (6) statistical process control. We will now introduce these tools.

Quality Function Deployment (QFD)

An effective TQM program translates customer desires into specific, designable features. **Quality function deployment (QFD)** refers to both (1) determining what will satisfy the customer and (2) translating those customer desires into the target design.[10] We use QFD early in the production process to help us determine where to deploy quality efforts.

Quality function deployment (QFD)

One of the tools of QFD is the house of quality. The **house of quality** is a graphic technique for defining the relationship between customer desires and product (or service). Only by defining this relationship in a rigorous way can operations managers build products and processes with features desired by customers. Defining this relationship is the first step in building a world-class production system. To build the house of quality, we perform six basic steps:

House of quality

1. Identify customer *wants*.
2. Identify product/service attributes. (Think of attributes as *how* the product/service will meet the *wants*.)
3. Relate the customer *wants* to the product/service *hows*.
4. Conduct an evaluation of competing products.
5. Develop performance specifications for product or service *hows*.
6. Assign (deploy) *hows* to the appropriate place in the transformation process.

Example 1 shows how to construct a house of quality.

EXAMPLE 1

Through extensive market research, Great Cameras, Inc., determined customer *wants*. Those *wants* are shown on the left of the house of quality on page 88 and are lightweight, easy to hold steady, no double exposures, easy to use, and reliable. Then the product development team determined *how* the organization is going to translate those customer *wants* into product design and process attribute targets. These *hows* are entered across the top portion of the house of quality. These attributes are low electricity requirements, aluminum components, auto focus, auto exposure, auto film advance, and ergonomic design.

The product team then evaluated each of the customer *wants* against the *hows*. In the matrix of the house, the team evaluated how well its design will meet customer needs. Similarly, in the "roof" of the house, the product development

[10]See Yoji Akao (ed.), *Quality Function Deployment* (Cambridge, MA: Productivity Press, 1990).

team developed the relationship between the attributes. Finally, the team developed importance ratings for its design attributes and a ranking of how to proceed with product and process design.

A variety of modifications can be made to the house of quality. For instance, it can be used to evaluate how a competitor meets customer demands.

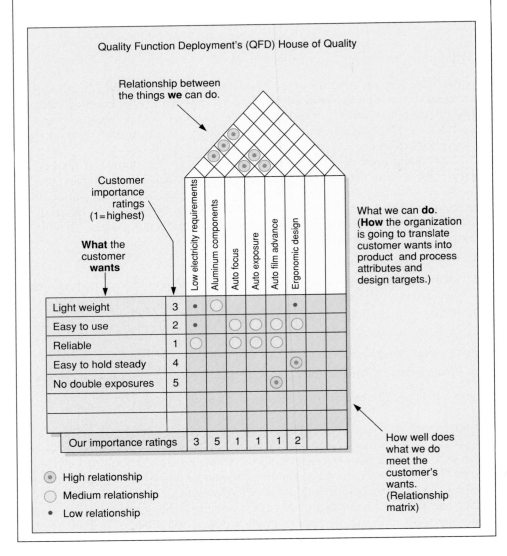

Taguchi Technique

Taguchi technique

Most quality problems are the result of product and process design. Therefore, tools are needed to address these areas. One of those tools is the **Taguchi technique**, named after Japanese engineer, Genichi Taguchi.[11]

[11]R. N. Kackar, "Taguchi's Quality Control, Parameter Design, and the Taguchi Method," *Journal of Quality Technology* (October 1985): 176–188; Lance Ealey, "Taguchi Basics," *Quality* (November 1988): 30–32; and Glen Stuart Peace, *Taguchi Methods* (Reading, MA: Addison-Wesley, 1993).

TAGUCHI CONCEPTS.   Three concepts are important to understanding Taguchi's approach and method. These concepts are *quality robustness, quality loss factor,* and *target-oriented quality.*

The Taguchi method calls for making products and processes that are *quality robust.* **Quality robust** products are products that can be produced uniformly and consistently in adverse manufacturing and environmental conditions. Taguchi's idea is to remove the *effects* of adverse conditions instead of removing the causes. Taguchi suggests that removing the effects is often cheaper than removing the causes and more effective in producing a robust product. In this way, small variations in materials and process do not destroy product quality.

Quality robust

Taguchi has also defined what he calls a quality loss function. A **quality loss function (QLF)** identifies all costs connected with poor quality and shows how these costs increase as the product moves away from being exactly what the customer wants. These costs include not just customer dissatisfaction, but also warranty and service costs; internal inspection, repair, and scrap costs; and costs that can best be described as costs to society. Notice that Figure 3.3 (a) shows the quality loss function as a curve that increases at an increasing rate. It takes the general form of a simple quadratic formula:

Quality loss function (QLF)

$$L = D^2C$$

where L = loss
D^2 = square of the deviation from the target value
C = cost of avoiding the deviation

FIGURE 3.3   ■   (a) Quality Loss Function; (b) Distribution of Product Produced. Taguchi aims for the target, because products produced near the upper and lower acceptable specifications result in higher quality loss function.

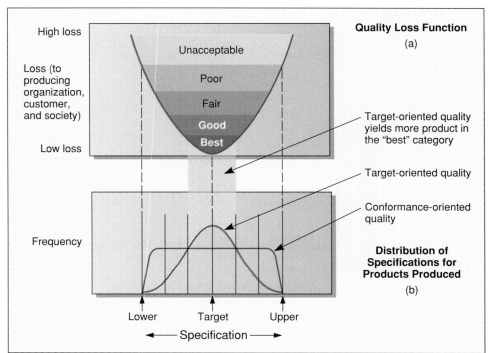

All the losses to society due to poor performance are included in the loss function. The smaller the loss, the more desirable the product. The farther the product is from the target value, the more severe the loss.

Taguchi observed that the traditional way of looking at specifications (that is, the product is good until it fails to fall within the tolerance limits) is too simplistic. As shown in Figure 3.3(b), conformance-oriented quality produces more units farther from the target. Therefore, the loss (cost) is higher in terms of customer satisfaction and benefits to society.

Target-oriented quality

Target-oriented quality is a philosophy of continuous improvement to bring the product exactly on target.

Pareto Charts

Pareto charts

Pareto charts organize errors, problems, or defects to help production personnel focus on problem-solving efforts. They are based on the work of Vilfredo Pareto, a nineteenth-century economist. Joseph M. Juran popularized Pareto's work when he suggested that 80% of a firm's problems are a result of only 20% of the causes. As the *POM in Action* box "Pacific Bell Takes Care of Screaming Customers" suggests, Pareto charts, although simple, can identify problems and focus effort. Pareto analysis, as shown in Example 2, indicates which problems may yield the greatest payoff.

EXAMPLE 2

Custom Wine Glasses of Leadville, Colorado, has just collected the data from 75 defects from the day's production. The boss decides to prepare a Pareto analysis of the defects. The data provided are scratches 61; porosity 5; nicks 4; contamination 3; and miscellaneous 2.

The Pareto chart shown indicates that about 80% of the defects were the result of one cause, scratches.

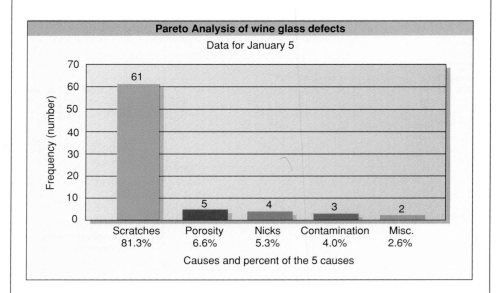

The majority of defects will be eliminated when this one cause is corrected.

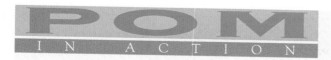

Pacific Bell Takes Care of Screaming Customers

For a telephone company, quality of service comes down to a simple test: You pick up the phone . . . either there is a dial tone or there is not. When there is not, "It's a killer," says a Pacific Bell technician. "You work around the clock for days to restore services. And you've got people driving by and yelling at you because their phones don't work."

Screaming customers—and lost revenue—were powerful incentives to change. Pacific Bell formed a 15-member quality improvement team to find a way to reduce damage to buried cable, the number 1 cause of phone outages. Team members included a lawyer, managers, and cable technicians—all volunteers, but many skeptical at first that TQM was just "another fad we were going through."

Team member Dale Bouguennec worked nights and weekends for 3 months to log 2,441 incidents that cost Pac Bell $18 million in repairs and revenue losses. Pareto analysis showed that 41% of cable damage was caused by construction work, and further analysis identified the main factors that increased the likelihood of damage.

Armed with this information, the team was able to make changes that improved responsiveness on the part of both the construction industry and Pac Bell. Cable cuts were reduced by 24% in 1 year. These changes saved Pac Bell $6 million and won it a 1994 *USA Today* Quality Cup in the service category.

Sources: USA Today (April 8, 1994): 2B; and the *Wall Street Journal* (February 24, 1994): A–1.

Example 2 indicates that of the five types of defects identified, the vast majority were of one type, scratches; so 20% (1 of 5) of the causes result in 81.3% (61 of 75) of the defects.

Process Charts

Process charts are designed to help us understand a sequence of events (that is, the process) through which a product or service travels. The process flow chart graphs the steps of the process and their relationship. This type of analysis can:

Process charts

1. help identify the best data collection points;
2. isolate and track the origin of problems;
3. identify the best place for process audits; and
4. identify opportunities for travel distance reduction.

As shown in Example 3, a process chart organizes information about a process in a graphical matter, using five standard symbols and distance. The standard American Society of Mechanical Engineers (ASME) process symbols are O = operation; ⇓ = transportation; □ = inspection; D = delay; ▽ = storage.

EXAMPLE 3

The WJC Chicken Processing Plant in Little Rock, Arkansas, would like to understand more about its packing and shipping process. After observation of the packing and shipping line and discussion with the operators, you prepare the following process chart:

Present Method	X	PROCESS CHART		
Proposed Method	X			

SUBJECT CHARTED _Packing and Shipping Process_   DATE _1 / 1 / 96_

CHART BY _HRC_

CHART NO. _1_

DEPARTMENT _Packing and Shipping_   SHEET NO. _1_ OF _1_

DIST. IN FEET	TIME IN MINS.	CHART SYMBOLS	PROCESS DESCRIPTION
10'		○ ⇨ □ D ▽	To Packing Station
—		○ ⇨ □ D ▽	Pack
2'		○ ⇨ □ D ▽	To Weigh Station
—		○ ⇨ □ D ▽	Weigh
2'		○ ⇨ □ D ▽	To Airtight Sealing, Weighing and Labeling
—		○ ⇨ □ D ▽	Airtight Sealing, Weighing and Labeling
50'		○ ⇨ □ D ▽	To Quick Freeze Storage
—		○ ⇨ □ D ▽	Quick Freeze Storage
25'		○ ⇨ □ D ▽	To Bulk Packing
—		○ ⇨ □ D ▽	Bulk Packing
40'		○ ⇨ □ D ▽	To Shipping Dock
		○ ⇨ □ D ▽	Load on Shipping Truck
		○ ⇨ □ D ▽	
		○ ⇨ □ D ▽	
		○ ⇨ □ D ▽	
		○ ⇨ □ D ▽	
		TOTAL	

This type of analysis should help you determine (1) where inspection and data collection could take place (perhaps after automatic weighing and labeling and after automatic sealing and after quick freeze), (2) the opportunities for reducing the distance traveled (perhaps to quick freeze storage, bulk packing, and the shipping dock), and (3) where to look should certain types of problems arise.

As you will see in our discussion of people and work systems in Chapter 11, process charts can be useful analytical tools in a wide variety of other applications.

Cause-and-Effect Diagram

Cause-and-effect diagram
Ishikawa diagram
Fish-bone chart

Another tool for identifying possible locations of quality problems and inspection points is the **cause-and-effect diagram**, also known as an **Ishikawa diagram** or a **fish-bone chart**. Figure 3.4 illustrates a chart (note the shape resembling the bones of a fish) for an everyday quality control problem—a dissatisfied airline customer. Each "bone" represents a possible source of error.

FIGURE 3.4 ■ Fish-Bone Chart (or Cause-and-Effect Diagram) for Problems in Airline Customer Service

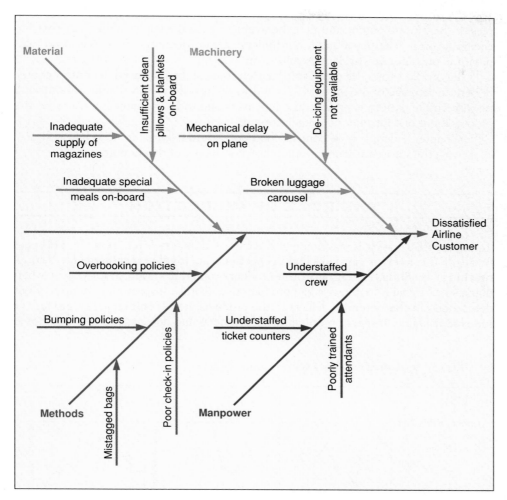

The way to get started on any cause-and-effect diagram is to have four categories: material, machinery/equipment, manpower, and methods. These four "M's" are the "causes." They provide a good checklist for initial analysis. When such a chart is systematically developed, possible quality problems and inspection points are highlighted.

Statistical Process Control (SPC)

Statistical process control monitors standards, makes measurements, and takes corrective action as a product or service is being produced. Samples of process outputs are examined; if they are within acceptable limits, the process is permitted to continue. If they fall outside certain specific ranges, the process is stopped and, typically, the assignable cause is located and removed.

Statistical process control

Control charts

Control charts are graphic presentations of data over time that show upper and lower limits for the process we want to control. Control charts are constructed in such a way that new data can be quickly compared to past performance data. We take samples of the process output and plot the average of these samples on a chart that has the limits on it. The upper and lower limits in a control chart can be in units of temperature, pressure, weight, length, and so on.

Figure 3.5 shows the useful information that can be portrayed in control charts. When the average of the samples falls within the upper and lower control limits and no discernible pattern is present, the process is said to be in control. Otherwise, the process is out of control or out of adjustment.

Chapter 4 details how control charts of different types are developed. It also deals with the statistical foundation underlying the use of this important tool.

THE ROLE OF INSPECTION

Inspection

To make sure a system is producing at the expected quality level, inspection of some or all of the items is needed. This **inspection** can involve measurement, tasting, touching, weighing, or testing of the product (sometimes even destroying it when doing so). Its goal is to detect a bad product immediately. Inspection does not correct deficiencies in the system or defects in the products; nor does it change a product or increase its value. Inspection only finds deficiencies and defects; and it is expensive.

FIGURE 3.5   ■   Patterns to Look for on Control Charts

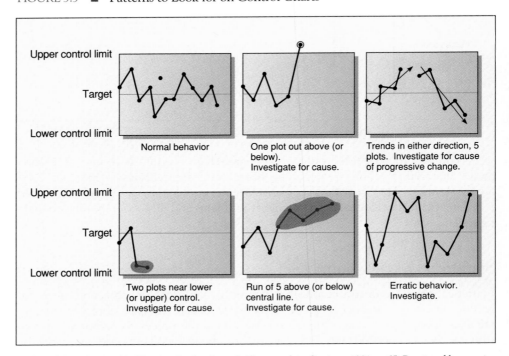

(Adapted from Bertrand L. Hansen, *Quality Control: Theory and Applications*, 1991, p. 65. Reprinted by permission of Prentice-Hall, Englewood Cliffs, New Jersey.)

Inspection should be thought of as an audit. Audits do not add value to the product. But production/operations managers, like financial managers, need audits and they need to know when and where to audit. So there are two basic issues relating to inspection. They are (1) *when to inspect* and (2) *where to inspect*.

When and Where to Inspect

Deciding when and where to inspect depends on the type of process and the value added at each stage. Inspection in manufacturing firms can take place at any of the following six points.

1. Inspect at your supplier's plant while the supplier is producing.
2. Inspect at your plant upon receipt of goods from your supplier.
3. Inspect before costly or irreversible processes.
4. Inspect during the step-by-step production process.
5. Inspect when production is complete.
6. Inspect before shipment from your plant.

Pareto charts, process charts, and cause-and-effect diagrams, as discussed in the previous section, are TQM tools to aid in this "when and where" to inspect decision. However, inspection is not a substitute for a robust product produced by a good process. In one well-known experiment conducted by an independent research firm, 100 defective pieces were added to a "perfect" lot of items and then subjected to 100% inspection.[12] The inspectors found only 68 of the defective pieces in their first inspection. It took another three passes by the inspectors to find the next 30 defects. The two last defects were never found. So the bottom line is that there is variability in the inspection process. Additionally, inspectors are only human: They become bored, they become tired, and the inspection equipment itself has variability. Even with 100% inspection, inspectors cannot guarantee perfection.

Source Inspection

The best inspection is inspection at the source. This is called **source inspection** and is consistent with the concept of employee empowerment where individual employees self-check their own work. The idea is that each process and each employee *treat the next step in the process as the customer,* ensuring perfect product to the next "customer." This inspection may be assisted by the use of checklists and controls such as a fail-safe device called a poka-yoke, a name borrowed from the Japanese.

A **poka-yoke** is a foolproof device or technique that ensures production of good units every time.[13] These special devices avoid errors and provide quick feedback of problems. A simple example of a poka-yoke device is the diesel or leaded gas pump nozzle that will not fit into the "unleaded" gas tank opening on your car. This same poka-yoke technique is used by airplane fuel service companies at airports. The idea of source inspection and poka-yokes is to ensure that 100% good product or service is provided.

At TRW's new plant in Dijon, France, technician Patrick Debonne inspects power-steering system pinions. TRW's internal quality audit program includes such aspects as measuring quality costs, procedures to make sure new products are designed and delivered with quality, inspection at all points in the process, quality circles, close relations with suppliers, and a business plan stressing quality.

Source inspection

Poka-yoke

[12]*Statistical Quality Control* (Springfield, MA: Monsanto Chemical Company, n.d.), p. 19.
[13]For further discussion, see Alan Robinson, *Modern Approaches to Management Improvement: The Shingo System* (Cambridge, MA: Productivity Press, 1990).

TABLE 3.3 ■ INSPECTION POINTS IN THREE SERVICE ORGANIZATIONS

TYPE OF ORGANIZATION	SOME POINTS OF INSPECTION	ISSUES TO CONSIDER
Bank	Teller stations	Shortages, courtesy, speed, accuracy
	Loan processing	Collateral, proper credit checks, rates, terms of loans, default rates, loan ratios
	Check clearing	Accuracy, speed of entry, percent of checks cleared each day
Department store	Stockrooms	Clean, uncluttered, organized, level of stockouts, ample supply, rotation of goods
	Display areas	Attractive, well-organized and stocked, visible goods, good lighting
	Sales counters	Neat, courteous, knowledgeable personnel; waiting time; accuracy in credit checking and sales entry
Restaurant	Kitchen	Clean, proper storage, unadulterated food, health regulations observed, well-organized
	Cashier station	Speed, accuracy, appearance
	Dining areas	Clean, comfortable, regular monitoring by personnel

Service Industry Inspection

Both service and manufacturing organizations have similar inspection needs. And in both, the when-and-where-to-inspect decision presents many options. However, Pareto charts and process charts prove very useful tools to successfully address these issues. Some specific examples of locations where inspection may prove particularly useful in service organization are illustrated in Table 3.3. The service manager, like the production manager, must maximize source inspection through employee empowerment and poka-yoke-like techniques such as checklists.

Inspection of Attributes vs. Variables

Attribute inspection

Variable inspection

When inspections take place, quality characteristics may be measured as either *attributes* or *variables*. **Attribute inspection** classifies items as being either good or defective. It does not address the degree of failure. For example, the lightbulb burns or it does not. **Variable inspection** measures such dimensions as weight, speed, height, or strength to see if the item falls within an acceptable range. If a piece of electrical wire is supposed to be 0.01 inch in diameter, a micrometer can be used to see if the product is close enough to pass inspection.

Knowing whether attributes or variables are being inspected helps us decide which statistical quality control approach to take.

TOTAL QUALITY MANAGEMENT IN SERVICES

Quality of services is more difficult to measure than quality of manufactured goods.[14] Generally though, a user of a service has a few features in mind as a basis for compari-

---

[14]This section is adapted from Robert Murdick, Barry Render, and Roberta Russell, *Service Operations Management* (Boston: Allyn and Bacon, 1990), pp. 421–422.

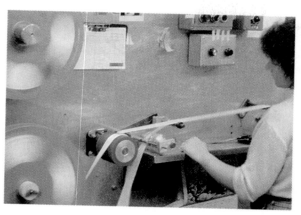

At Velcro Industries N.V., as in many organizations, quality was viewed by machine operators as the job of "those QC people." Inspections were based on random sampling, and if a part showed up bad, it was thrown out. The company decided to pay more attention to operators, to machine repair and design, to measurement methods, communications, and responsibilities, and to invest more money in training. Over time, Velcro was able to pull half its quality control people out of the process, as defects continued to decline.

son among alternatives. Lack of one feature may eliminate a service firm from consideration. Quality also may be perceived as a bundle of attributes in which many lesser characteristics are superior to those of competitors.

Extensive, in-depth interviews with consumer focus groups identified 10 general attributes or determinants of service quality[15] (see Table 3.4). The same study also drew the following conclusions:

1. *Consumers' perceptions of service quality result from a comparison of their expectations before they receive their actual experience with the service.* In other words, service quality is judged on the basis of whether it meets expectations.

2. *Quality perceptions are derived from the service process as well as from the service outcome.* The way the service is performed can be as important as the actual service from the consumer's point of view.

3. *Service quality is of two types, normal and exceptional.* First, there is the quality level at which the regular service is delivered, such as the bank teller's handling of a transaction. Second, there is the quality level at which "exceptions" or "problems" are handled. This implies that a quality control system must recognize and have prepared a set of alternate plans for less-than-optimal operating conditions. In addition, when a problem occurs, the low-contact firm may suddenly become a high-contact firm. Thus, good customer relations are important in maintaining quality, regardless of the type of service.

Follow-up interviews with service managers suggest that service quality can be measured by how effectively a service can close the gaps between expectations and the service provided. The *POM in Action* box "TQM Principles at Work in the Service Sector" provides another glimpse of how P/OM managers improve quality in services.

[15]L. Berry, V. Zeithaml, and A. Parasuraman, "Quality Counts in Services, Too," *Business Horizons* (May/June 1985): 45–46.

TABLE 3.4 ■ DETERMINANTS OF SERVICE QUALITY

Reliability involves consistency of performance and dependability. It means that the firm performs the service right the first time and also means that the firm honors its promises.

Responsiveness concerns the willingness or readiness of employees to provide service. It involves timeliness of service.

Competence means possession of the required skills and knowledge to perform the service.

Access involves approachability and ease of contact.

Courtesy involves politeness, respect, consideration, and friendliness of contact personnel (including receptionists, telephone operators, etc.).

Communication means keeping customers informed in language they can understand and listening to them. It may mean that the company has to adjust its language for different consumers—increasing the level of sophistication with a well-educated customer and speaking simply and plainly with a novice.

Credibility involves trustworthiness, believability, and honesty. It involves having the customer's best interests at heart.

Security is the freedom from danger, risk, or doubt.

Understanding/knowing the customer involves making the effort to understand the customer's needs.

Tangibles include the physical evidence of the service.

Source: Excerpted from A. Parasuraman, Valerie A. Zeithaml, and Leonard L. Berry, "A Conceptual Model of Service Quality and Its Implications for Future Research," *Journal of Marketing* (Fall 1985): 44.

ACHIEVING WORLD-CLASS STANDARDS

Designing a high-quality process that fills these pharmaceutical bottles in sterile conditions is much more fruitful than having an inspector evaluate the bacteria count on bottles filled in a poor system. Good-quality systems focus on quality processes, not via after-the-fact inspections.

Quality is a tremendous competitive weapon. World-class firms such as Milliken, L.L. Bean, and Motorola achieve outstanding quality performance in a variety of ways. They understand that:

- Top management provides total quality management (TQM) leadership, with an emphasis on doing it correctly the first time.

- Customer requirements are understood and achieved.

- Quality is approached via total quality management (TQM), not quality inspection systems.

- Systems and procedures are designed to deliver quality products and services.

- Continuous improvement programs are in place to ensure that quality in all phases of the organization is always improving.

- Employees know the cost of quality and are trained in TQM tools.

- Performance measurers for quality are included in manager evaluation.

- Benchmarking procedures are in place and are used.

- Quality is a competitive weapon because quality forces so many other things, such as design, processes, inventory, schedules, maintenance, and training to be right.

TQM Principles at Work in the Service Sector

The service industry in the 1990s distinctly resembles manufacturing in the United States in the 1970s. Quality is inconsistent, costs are high, profit margins are narrow, and competition increases each year.

Savin Corp., a copier manufacturer in Stamford, Connecticut, decided to try out a Deming-style quality management approach to improve its service programs. As Robert Williams, Savin's VP, stated, "A company's fortunes ride on the quality of its service."

Here are just two ways Savin cut service expenses in the past 12 months, while improving service quality:

- Using statistical analysis, Savin found that significant time was being wasted on service calls when engineers had to go back to their trucks for spare parts. The firm assembled a "call kit," to carry onto customer premises, that contained parts with highest probability for use. Now service calls are faster and cost less, and more can be made per day.

- The Pareto principle, that 20% of your staff cause 80% of your errors, was used to tackle the "call-back" problem. Call-backs meant the job was not done right the first time and a second visit, at Savin's expense, was needed. Retraining only the 11% of customer engineers with the most call-backs resulted in a 19% drop in return visits.

"Total quality management," according to Williams, "is an approach to doing business that should permeate every job in the service industry."

Sources: Wall Street Journal (November 4, 1991): A18; *Office* (October 1993): 26, 69.

SUMMARY

Quality is a term that means different things to different people. But it is defined in this chapter as the totality of features and characteristics of a product or service that bear on its ability to satisfy stated or implied needs. Defining quality expectations is critical to effective and efficient operations.

Quality requires building a Total Quality Management (TQM) environment because quality cannot be inspected into a product. The chapter also addresses five TQM concepts. They are continuous improvement, employee empowerment, benchmarking, Just-in-Time, and knowledge of TQM tools. The six TQM tools introduced in this chapter are house of quality, Taguchi method, Pareto charts, process charts, cause-and-effect diagrams, and statistical process control (SPC).

ISO 9000 (p. 80)
Total Quality Management (TQM) (p. 81)
Kaizen (p. 82)
Employee empowerment (p. 82)
Quality circle (p. 83)
Benchmarking (p. 84)
Quality function deployment (QFD) (p. 87)

House of quality (p. 87)
Taguchi technique (p. 88)
Quality robust (p. 89)
Quality loss function (p. 89)
Target-oriented quality (p. 90)
Pareto charts (p. 90)
Process charts (p. 91)

KEY TERMS

Cause-and-effect diagram (p. 92)
Ishikawa diagram (p. 92)
Fish-bone chart (p. 92)
Statistical Process Control (p. 93)
Control charts (p. 94)

Inspection (p. 94)
Source inspection (p. 95)
Poka-yoke (p. 95)
Attribute inspection (p. 96)
Variable inspection (p. 96)

DISCUSSION QUESTIONS

1. Provide your own definition of product quality.
2. Name several products that do not require high quality.
3. Do you think the establishment of the *Malcolm Baldrige National Quality Award* had much effect on the quality of products actually produced in the United States?
4. How can a university control the quality of its output (that is, its graduates)?
5. What are the major concepts of TQM?
6. Find a recent article on quality circles and summarize its major points. Do you think quality circles will be commonplace in all U.S. firms? Why?
7. How can a firm build a climate of continuous improvement?

8. What are the three basic concepts of the Taguchi method?
9. What are six tools of TQM?
10. What is the "house of quality"?
11. Why is the target-oriented performance better than conformance-oriented performance?
12. What are 10 determinants of service quality?
13. What is the quality loss function (QLF)?
14. What does the formula $L = D^2C$ mean?
15. How would you change the Baldrige Award criteria?
16. What are the four "M's" of a cause-and-effect diagram?

CRITICAL THINKING EXERCISE

The Oklahoma City plant of Tursine Electronics assembles printed circuit boards with a quality rating that is both deplorable and dropping. Indeed, it is worse than any of the company's other plants. To complicate matters, labor relations are difficult and morale low, resulting in high turnover and absenteeism. The new plant manager, who had been sent in to straighten things out, believes that the facility will be closed unless dramatic productivity and quality improvements are made. Quality has become too important a factor in the industry.

How can the manager turn this plant around, build a quality product, and instill quality into the work force?

PROBLEMS

: 3.1 Use the quality function deployment's house of quality technique to construct a relationship matrix between customer *wants* and *how* you as a production manager would address them. Consider the *wants* and *hows* of the following:

a) ice cream

b) a soft drink

· 3.2 Conduct an interview with a prospective purchaser of a new bicycle and translate the customer's *wants* into the specific *hows* of the firm.

· 3.3 Use Pareto analysis to investigate the following data collected on a printed-circuit-board assembly line.

a) Prepare a graph of the data.

b) What conclusions do you reach?

DEFECT	NUMBER OF DEFECT OCCURRENCES
Wrong component	217
Components not adhering	146
Excess adhesive	64
Misplaced transistors	600
Defective board dimension	143
Mounting holes improperly positioned	14
Circuitry problems on final test	92

3.4 Develop a process chart for one of the following:

a) changing an automobile tire

b) paying a bill in a restaurant

c) making a deposit at your bank

3.5 Prepare a process chart for one of the following:

a) a fast-food drive-thru window (single window)

b) a two-station drive-thru window (pay at one, pick up at second)

c) the registration process at your college

3.6 Draw a fish-bone chart detailing reasons why a bolt might not be correctly matched to a nut on an assembly line.

3.7 Draw a fish-bone chart showing why a typist you paid to prepare a term paper produced a document with numerous errors.

CASE STUDY

Westover Electrical, Inc.

Westover Electrical, Inc., is a medium-sized Houston manufacturer of wire windings used in making electric motors. Joe Wilson, Operations Manager, has experienced an increasing problem with rejected product found during the manufacturing operation. "I'm not sure where to begin," said Joe at the weekly staff meeting with his boss. "Rejects in the Winding Department have been killing us the past 2 months. Nobody in operations has any idea why. I have just brought in a consultant, Roger Gagnon, to take a look at the situation and make recommendations about how we can find out what is going on. I don't expect Roger to make technical recommendations—just see if he can point us in the right direction."

Gagnon's first stop later that day was the production floor. His discussions with the production supervisors in the Winding Department indicated they had no real grasp of what the problem was or what to do to correct it. A tour of the winding operation indicated that there were three machines that wound wire onto plastic cores to produce the primary and secondary electric motor windings. After inspection by quality control (QC), these windings then went to the Packaging Department. Packaging personnel, Gagnon found, inspect their own work and make corrections on the spot. The problem is that too many windings are found to be defective and require reworking before they can be packaged.

Gagnon's next stop was the Quality Control Department where he obtained the records for the past month's Winding Department rejects (Table 1).

DISCUSSION QUESTIONS

1. Prepare an outline for Roger Gagnon's report.

2. What charts, graphs, computer printouts, and so forth might be included in the report?

(Continued)

3. Prepare Gagnon's recommendation, with justification, on one page.

4. Prepare the detail necessary to supplement Gagnon's recommendation and justification so Joe Wilson will understand how he arrived at your recommendations.

Source: Professor Victor E. Sower, Ph.D., C.Q.E., Sam Houston State University.

TABLE 1 ■ JANUARY TRANSFORMER REJECT LOG: WINDING PROCESS

			No. of Reject Units by Cause						
DATE	NO. INSPECTED	WINDER	BAD WIND	TWISTED WIRE	BROKEN LEADS	ABRADED WIRE	WRONG CORE	WRONG WIRE	FAILED ELECTRICAL TEST
1	100	1	1	0	4	1	0	0	1
	100	2	2	1	0	0	1	5	0
	100	3	0	0	0	5	0	0	3
2	100	1	0	1	3	0	0	0	0
	100	2	3	1	0	0	2	3	0
	100	3	0	0	1	6	0	0	0
3	100	1	1	0	0	2	0	0	0
	100	2	0	0	0	0	0	3	3
	100	3	0	0	1	4	0	0	0
4	100	1	0	0	3	0	0	2	0
	100	2	0	0	0	0	1	0	3
	100	3	0	0	0	3	0	0	0
5	100	1	0	1	5	0	0	0	1
	100	2	0	0	0	0	0	2	2
	100	3	0	0	0	3	0	0	0
8	100	1	0	0	2	0	0	0	0
	100	2	0	0	0	0	0	1	3
	100	3	0	0	0	3	0	0	0
9	100	1	0	1	2	0	0	0	0
	100	2	0	0	0	0	0	1	4
	100	3	0	0	0	3	0	0	0
10	100	1	0	0	5	0	1	0	0
	100	2	1	0	0	0	0	0	4
	100	3	0	0	0	5	0	0	0
11	100	1	0	0	4	0	0	0	0
	100	2	0	0	0	0	0	0	0
	100	3	0	0	0	4	0	0	4
12	100	1	0	0	3	0	1	0	0
	100	2	1	0	1	0	0	0	0
	100	3	0	0	0	5	0	0	4
15	100	1	0	0	2	0	0	1	0
	100	2	0	0	0	0	0	1	0
	100	3	0	0	0	3	0	0	3
16	100	1	0	0	6	0	0	0	0
	100	2	0	0	0	0	0	0	3
	100	3	0	0	0	3	0	0	0
17	100	1	0	1	1	0	0	0	1
	100	2	0	0	0	0	0	0	3
	100	3	0	0	0	3	0	0	

(Continued)

TABLE 1 ■ JANUARY TRANSFORMER REJECT LOG: WINDING PROCESS (CONTINUED)

| | | | NO. OF REJECT UNITS BY CAUSE | | | | | | |
DATE	NO. INSPECTED	WINDER	BAD WIND	TWISTED WIRE	BROKEN LEADS	ABRADED WIRE	WRONG CORE	WRONG WIRE	FAILED ELECTRICAL TEST
18	100	1	1	0	2	0	0	0	0
	100	2	0	0	0	0	0	1	0
	100	3	0	0	0	4	0	0	1
19	100	1	0	0	2	0	0	0	0
	100	2	0	0	0	0	0	0	0
	100	3	0	0	0	3	0	0	1
22	100	1	0	1	4	0	0	0	0
	100	2	0	0	0	0	0	0	0
	100	3	0	0	0	3	0	1	2
23	100	1	0	0	4	0	0	0	0
	100	2	0	0	0	0	0	0	1
	100	3	0	0	0	4	0	0	3
24	100	1	0	0	2	0	0	1	0
	100	2	0	1	0	0	0	0	0
	100	3	0	0	0	4	0	0	3
25	100	1	0	0	3	0	0	0	0
	100	2	0	0	0	1	0	0	0
	100	3	0	0	0	2	0	0	4
26	100	1	0	0	1	0	0	0	0
	100	2	0	1	0	1	0	0	0
	100	3	0	0	0	2	0	0	3
29	100	1	0	0	2	0	0	0	0
	100	2	0	0	1	0	0	0	0
	100	3	0	0	0	2	0	0	3
30	100	1	0	0	2	0	0	0	0
	100	2	0	0	0	0	1	0	0
	100	3	0	0	0	2	0	0	3

Note: Assume that each defective unit was rejected because of one, single defect.

CASE STUDY

Quality Cleaners

The owner of Quality Cleaners has decided that a quality improvement program must be implemented in its dry cleaning service. Customers bring clothes to one of five stores or pickup stations. Orders are then delivered to the cleaning plant twice (morning and afternoon) each day, with deliveries of orders being made to the stores at the same time, allowing for same-day service by customer request.

The stores are opened at 7:00 A.M. by a full-time employee. This person is relieved at 3:00 P.M. by a part-time employee, who closes the store at 6:00 P.M.

When the clothes are received from the customer, a five-ply ticket showing the customer name, phone number, due date, and special requests is prepared. One ply is given to the customer as a claim

(Continued)

check and the store keeps one ply (to show what they have in process). The clothes and the remaining plies of the ticket are put in a nylon laundry bag for delivery to the plant.

At the cleaning plant the departments are:

Mark-in.   Each order is removed from the bag; items are tagged for identification later and sorted into large buggies according to due date, type of garment, and cleaning requirements. The buggies are moved to the cleaning department as they become full. Also at mark-in, garments are checked for spots, stains, tears, or other special handling. The problem is written on a strip-tag (a ½-in. wide paper tape) and attached to the garment with the identification tag.

Cleaning.   The buggies are emptied into the cleaning machine one item at a time to allow for inspection. The primary items checked for are spots and stains requiring special attention and foreign objects. For example, an ink pen left in a pocket could ruin the whole load. As items are removed from the cleaning machine, they are placed on hangers and moved by conveyor to the pressing department.

Pressing.   There are four presses: one for silks, one for pants, and two general-purpose. On an ordinary day, three of the presses will be operating, but which three of the four are operating will depend upon the total demand and product mix that particular day. As items are pressed, they are placed on a conveyor that delivers them to the assembly department.

Assembly.   Cleaned items are grouped into customer orders, bagged, and put in the appropriate queue for delivery to the respective store. At this time, two plies (of the remaining three) of the ticket are attached to the order, and one ply stays at the plant to show this order was completed. When the customer picks up the order, one ply will stay on the order.

The store will retain the last ply and pull the corresponding ply from its work-in-process file to show that this order is complete.

Note: Although Quality Cleaners is a larger-than-average cleaning operation, total annual revenues are approximately $500,000. Therefore, any suggestions must be relatively inexpensive.

At present, a majority of the employees are cross-trained to allow for flexibility. Table 2 indicates the production employees and the positions for which they are trained. P indicates this is the primary duty, or the one they perform most often. A check indicates they are also trained in that function.

		PRESSES		
EMPLOYEE	**CLEANING**	**GENERAL PURPOSE**	**SILKS**	**PANTS**
David	P	✓		✓
Tasha	✓	✓		P
Len	✓	P	✓	
Mary		✓	P	✓
Betty (part-time)	✓	✓		✓
Mike (part-time)	✓	✓		✓

TABLE 2

For example, one day David may only clean; the next day he cleans a while and then presses pants. This presents a problem in determining who put a double crease in Mrs. Jones's slacks, but the owner believes this flexibility in scheduling is valuable and must be maintained.

DISCUSSION QUESTIONS

1. Design the quality program. Consider the following issues:
   a) Where should inspection(s) occur?
   b) How will accountability be achieved?
   c) What factors (variables, attributes, other considerations) should be checked?
   d) Is statistical process control (SPC) appropriate?
      i. Variable or attribute?
      ii. At what point?

(Continued)

2. What are the cost items for implementing your plan? Give a budget, including equipment, supplies, and labor-hours (divided into types of labor).

3. What records should be kept to measure the success of the program in terms of cost, quality performance, and service to the customer?

Source: Professor Marilyn S. Jones, Winthrop University.

BIBLIOGRAPHY

Akao, Y., ed. *Quality Function Deployment: Integrating Customer Requirements into Product Design.* Cambridge, MA: Productivity Press, 1990.

Berry, L. L., A. Parasuraman, and V. A. Zeithaml. "Improving Service Quality in America: Lessons Learned." *The Academy of Management Executive,* 8, no. 2 (May 1994): 32–52.

Besterfield, D. H. *Quality Control,* 4th ed. Englewood Cliffs, NJ: Prentice Hall, 1994.

Blackburn, R., and B. Rosen. "Total Quality and Human Resources Management: Lessons Learned from Baldrige Award-Winning Companies." *The Academy of Management Executive,* 7, no. 3 (August 1993): 49–66.

Caporaletti, L., E. Gillenwater, and J. Jaggers. "The Application of Taguchi Methods to a Coil Spring Manufacturing Process." *Production and Inventory Management Journal,* 34, no. 4 (Fourth Quarter 1993): 22–27.

Carr, L. P. "Applying Cost of Quality to a Service Business." *Sloan Management Review,* 33, no. 4 (Summer 1992): 72.

Costin, H. *Readings in Total Quality Management.* New York: Dryden Press, 1994.

Crosby, P. B. *Let's Talk Quality.* New York: McGraw-Hill, 1989.

———. *Quality Is Free.* New York: McGraw-Hill, 1979.

———. "Working Like a Chef." *Quality* (January 1989): 24–25.

Deming, W. E. *Out of the Crisis.* Cambridge, MA: Center for Advanced Engineering Study, 1986.

Denton, D. K. "Lessons on Competitiveness: Motorola's Approach." *Production and Inventory Management Journal,* 32, no. 3 (Third Quarter 1991): 22.

DeVor, R. E., T. Chang, and J. W. Sutherland. *Statistical Quality Design and Control: Contemporary Concepts and Methods.* New York: Macmillan, 1992.

Dobyns, L., and C. Crawford-Mason. *Quality or Else: The Revolution in World Business.* New York: Houghton Mifflin, 1991.

Elsayed, E. A., and D. Dietrich. "Quality Control and Its Applications in Production Systems." *Industrial Engineering Research & Development,* 24, no. 5 (November 1992): 2–3.

Evans, J. R., and W. M. Lindsay. *The Management and Control of Quality,* 2d ed. New York: West, 1993.

Feigenbaum, A. V. *Total Quality Control,* 3d ed. New York: McGraw-Hill, 1991.

Forker, L. B. "Quality: American, Japanese, and Soviet Perspectives." *The Academy of Management Executive,* 5, no. 4 (November 1991): 63–73.

Foster, S. T., Jr. "Designing and Initiating a Taguchi Experiment in a Services Setting." *OM Review,* 9, no. 3: 37–50.

Gehani, R. R. "Quality Value-Chain: A Meta-Synthesis of Frontiers of Quality Movement." *The Academy of Management Executive,* 7, no. 2 (May 1993): 29–42.

Hart, M. K. "Quality Tools for Decreasing Variation and Defining Process Capability." *Production and Inventory Management Journal,* 33, no. 2 (Second Quarter 1992): 6.

———. "Quality Control Training for Manufacturing." *Production and Inventory Management Journal,* 32, no. 3 (Third Quarter 1991): 35.

Hauser, J. R. "How Puritan-Bennett Used the House of Quality." *Sloan Management Review,* 34, no. 3 (Spring 1993): 61–70.

Hauser, J. R., and D. Clausing. "The House of Quality." *Harvard Business Review,* 3 (May/June 1988): 63–70.

Hill, R. C. "When the Going Gets Rough: A Baldrige Award Winner on the Line." *The Academy of Management Executive,* 7, no. 3 (August 1993): 75–79.

Juran, J. M. "Made in the U.S.A.: A Renaissance in Quality." *Harvard Business Review,* 14, no. 4 (July/August 1993): 35–38.

Krishnan, R., A. B. Shani, R. M. Grant, and R. Baer. "In Search of Quality Improvement: Problems of Design and Implementation." *The Academy of Management Executive,* 7, no. 4 (November 1993): 7.

Miller, J. G. *Benchmarking*. Homewood, IL: Business One Irwin, 1992.

Nandakumar, P., S. M. Datar, and R. Akella. "Models for Measuring and Accounting for Cost of Conformance Quality." *Management Science*, 39, no. 1 (January 1993): 1–16.

Peace, G. S. *Taguchi Methods: A Hands-On Approach*. Reading, MA: Addison-Wesley, 1993.

Porteus, E. L. "Note: The Impact of Inspection Delay on Process and Inspection Lot Sizing." *Management Science*, 36, no. 8 (August 1990): 999–1007.

Price, F. *Right Every Time: Using the Deming Approach*. New York: Marcel Dekker, 1990.

Ryan, T. P. *Statistical Methods for Quality Improvement*. New York: John Wiley, 1989.

Schonberger, R. J. "Is Strategy Strategic? Impact of Total Quality Management on Strategy." *The Executive*, 6, no. 3 (August 1992): 80.

Tsui, K. "An Overview of Taguchi Method and Newly Developed Statistical Methods for Robust Design." *Industrial Engineering Research & Development*, 24, no. 5 (November 1992): 44–57.

Vaziri, H. K. "Using Competitive Benchmarking to Set Goals." *Quality Progress*, 25, no. 10 (October 1992): 81.

4

STATISTICAL QUALITY CONTROL

LEARNING OBJECTIVES

*When you complete this
chapter you should be able to:*

Identify or define:

Assignable causes of variations

Natural causes of variations

Central limit theorem

Attribute inspection

Variable inspection

Process control

$\bar{x}$-charts

R-charts

LCL and UCL

Acceptance sampling

OC curve

AQL and LTPD

Producer's risk

Consumer's risk

AOQ

Explain:

The role of statistical quality
control

STATISTICAL PROCESS CONTROL ASSURES QUALITY PRODUCTS AT AVX-KYOCERA

In Raleigh, North Carolina, in the former Dow-Corning plant, war has been declared. To satisfy customers, employees of AVX, a maker of electronic chip components, have declared war on defects. The Japanese-owned company's objective is zero defects at very low tolerance for variable data and nearly zero defects for parts per million (ppm) for attribute data.

AVX-Kyocera's first step was to evaluate samples at each machine to ensure that the processes were indeed capable of achieving the desired results. Simultaneously, all quality control inspectors were transferred to manufacturing duties, and all engineering and plant personnel were trained in statistical methodology. "Ownership" of processes and product quality was given to empowered operators. Work teams were then established to take charge of clusters of machines in the production process. The result is six teams that are now an integral part of the plant's operation.

Empowered employees and statistical process control (SPC) are now the norm. Employees take plot after plot to generate SPC charts that track trends, comparing them with process limits and final customer specifications.

The process at AVX is typical of many firms that are now world-class. Prior to the 1980s, these firms focused on inspectors evaluating finished products. In the 1980s, they focused on improving the process and educating and empowering employees. Now, world-class firms like AVX-Kyocera focus on identifying customer expectations and achieving total customer satisfaction in both products and services.

Sources: Basile A. Denisson, "War with Defects and Peace with Quality," *Quality Progress* (September 1993): 97–101; *Profiles in Quality: Blueprints for Action from 50 Leading Companies* (Boston: Allyn & Bacon with Bureau of Business Practice, 1991), pp. 131–134.

Operator Responsibility. This casting operator measures the thickness of a periodic sample he took from his process and is going to plot the results on his statistical process control chart to verify that his process is still within required control limits.

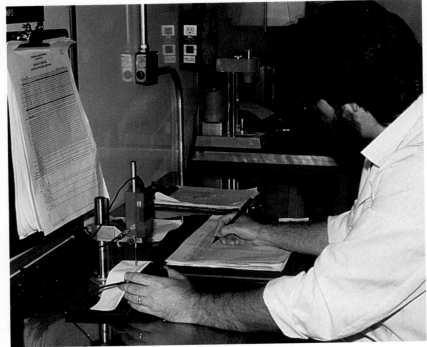

Reviewing Trends. This operator reviews the trends of her process. The quality trend board includes not only statistical process control charts, but also procedures, process document change approvals, and the names of all certified operators.

Communication. As this view of a production process at AVX shows, quality data is posted where all can see it. A quality trend board is shown on the back wall.

AVX CORPORATION

RE
4-2
PR

RALEIGH PLANT

CASE SIZE 02, 03

CHIP SILVER PROCESS CONTROL CHART

DATE: 9-1-89   SHIFT: 1ST   OPERATORS: Vonda / Sandy   MACH. NO. 1

Time	7³⁰	8:00	8³⁰	9:00	9:³⁰	10:⁰⁰	10:³⁰	11:⁰⁰	11:³⁰	12:⁰⁰	12:³⁰	1:⁰⁰			
Lot No.	DS9162				DS9161										
Style	024B				024B										
Value	1003				1003										

WRAPAROUND: 10 Pcs. ACC. 1/REJ. 2

# Rej.	o	o	o	o	o	o	o	o	o	o	o	o			
Acc/Rej.	Acc	Acc	Acc	Acc	Acc	Acc	Acc	Acc	Acc	Acc	Acc				

PINHOLES: ACC. 1/REJ. 2 (4 pin. max. per end of chip)

Pinhole	o	o	o	o	o	o	o	o	o	o	o				

VISUAL INSPECTION 10 PCS. ACC. 1/Rej. 2

Coverage	o	o	o	o	o	o	o	o	o	o	o	o			
Smeared	o	o	o	o	o	o	o	o	o	o	o	o			
Smashed	o	o	o	o	o	o	o	o	o	o	o	o			
TOTAL # REJ.	o	o	o	o	o	o	o	o	o	o	o	o			
ACC/REJ.	Acc	Acc	Acc	Acc	Acc	Acc	Acc	Acc	Acc	Acc	Acc				

SILVER LOT NO. OPKS
CORRECT SILVER ✓

X̄ CHART THICKNESS (MILS)
7.5
7.0
6.5
6.0
5.5
5.0
4.5

Process Capability Indexes. Process capability indexes take into consideration both process variation vs. specification limits and process mean location vs. targets.

In the mid-1980s, Motorola was in trouble. Japanese companies such as NEC, Toshiba, and Hitachi were gobbling up the company's markets in pagers, cellular phones, and semiconductor chips. Something had to be done. Motorola's management responded with a bold plan that included rapid product development, sharply upgraded quality, and a determination to reduce manufacturing costs. A key element in this plan was a statistical way of measuring quality called *six sigma*. In an era when many organizations viewed *three sigma* as acceptable, *six sigma* was radical. For example, *three sigma* is equivalent to 15,000 out of every million newborn babies being dropped by doctors and nurses each year, while *six sigma* means not having more than 3.4 errors per million. Motorola is now well on its way to performing at this exceptional world-class level. ♦

In this chapter, we address statistical process control—the same techniques used at Motorola to achieve six sigma. We also introduce acceptance sampling. *Statistical process control* is the application of statistical techniques to the control of processes. *Acceptance sampling* is used to determine acceptance or rejection of a lot of material evaluated by inspection or test of a sample.

STATISTICAL PROCESS CONTROL (SPC)

Statistical process control (SPC) is a statistical technique that is widely used to ensure that processes are meeting standards. All processes are subject to a certain degree of variability. Walter Shewhart of Bell Laboratories, while studying process data in the 1920s, made the distinction between the common and special causes of variation. Many people now refer to these variations as *natural* and *assignable* causes. He developed a simple but powerful tool to separate the two—the **control chart**. A use of control charts at DuPont is discussed in the *POM in Action* box "Statistical Process Control Helps DuPont and the Environment."

Control chart

    We use statistical process control to measure performance of a process. A process is said to be operating in statistical control when the only source of variation is common (natural) causes. The process must first be brought into statistical control by detecting and eliminating special (assignable) causes of variation.[1] Then its performance is predictable, and its ability to meet customer expectations can be assessed. The *objective* of a process control system is *to provide a statistical signal when assignable causes of variation are present.* Such a signal can quicken appropriate action to eliminate assignable causes.

    NATURAL VARIATIONS. Natural variations affect almost every production process and are to be expected. **Natural variations** are the many sources of variation

Natural variations

---

[1] Removing assignable causes is work. As W. Edwards Deming observed, "a state of statistical control is not a natural state for a manufacturing process. It is instead an achievement, arrived at by elimination, one by one, by determined effort, of special causes of excessive variation." See W. Edwards Deming, "On Some Statistical Aids Toward Economic Production," *Interfaces*, 5, no. 4 (1975): 5.

Statistical Process Control Helps DuPont and the Environment

DuPont has found that statistical process control (SPC) is an excellent approach to solving environmental problems. With a goal of slashing manufacturing waste and hazardous waste disposals by 35%, DuPont brought together information from its quality control systems and its material management data bases.

Cause-and-effect diagrams and Pareto charts revealed where major problems occurred. Then the company began reducing waste materials through improved SPC standards for production. Tying together shop-floor information-based monitoring systems with air-quality standards, DuPont identified ways to reduce emissions. And using a vendor evaluation system linked to JIT purchasing requirements, the company initiated controls over incoming hazardous materials.

DuPont now saves more than 15 million pounds of plastics annually by recycling them into products rather than dumping them into landfills. Through electronic purchasing, the firm has reduced wastepaper to a trickle, and by using new packaging designs, has cut in-process material wastes by nearly 40%.

By integrating SPC with environmental compliance activities, DuPont has made major quality improvements that far exceed regulatory guidelines and at the same time the company has realized huge cost savings.

Sources: Business Week/Quality (October 25, 1991): 44–46, 49; and E. E. Dwinells and J. P. Sheffer, *APICS—The Performance Advantage* (March 1992): 30–31.

within a process that is in statistical control. They behave like a constant system of chance causes. Although individual values are all different, as a group, they form a pattern that can be described as a distribution. When these distributions are *normal*, they are characterized by two parameters. These parameters are

- mean, μ (the measure of central tendency, in this case, the average value)
- standard deviation, σ (variation, the amount by which the smaller values differ from the larger ones)

As long as the distribution (output precision) remains within specified limits, the process is said to be "in control," and the modest variations are tolerated.

ASSIGNABLE VARIATIONS.   Assignable variation in a process can be traced to a specific reason. Factors such as machine wear, misadjusted equipment, fatigued or untrained workers, or new batches of raw material are all potential sources of **assignable variations**.

Natural and assignable variations distinguish two tasks for the P/OM manager. The first is to ensure that the process will have only natural variation that is capable of operating under control. The second is, of course, to identify and eliminate assignable variations so that the processes will remain under control.

SAMPLES.   Because of natural and assignable variation, statistical process control uses averages of small samples (often of five items or parts) as opposed to data on individual parts. Individual pieces tend to be too erratic to make trends quickly visible.

Assignable variations

FIGURE 4.1   ■   Natural and Assignable Variation

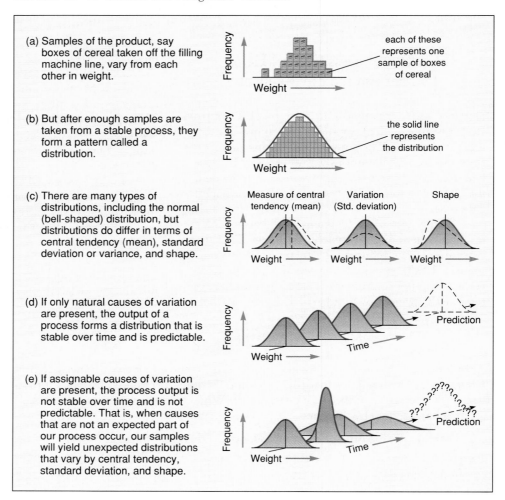

Figure 4.1 provides a detailed look at the important steps in determining process variation. The horizontal scale can be weight (as in the number of ounces in boxes of cereal), or length (as in fence posts), or any physical measure. The vertical scale is frequency.

CONTROL CHARTS.   The process of building control charts is based on the concepts presented in Figure 4.2. This figure shows three distributions that are the result of outputs from three types of processes. We plot small samples and then examine characteristics of the resulting data to see if the process is within "control limits." The purpose of control charts is to help distinguish between natural variations and variations due to assignable causes. As seen in Figure 4.2, a process is (a) in control *and the process is capable of producing within established control limits,* (b) in control, *but the process is not capable of producing within established limits,* or (c) out of control. We now look at how to build control charts that help the P/OM manager keep a process under control.

FIGURE 4.2 ■ Process Control: Three Types of Process Outputs

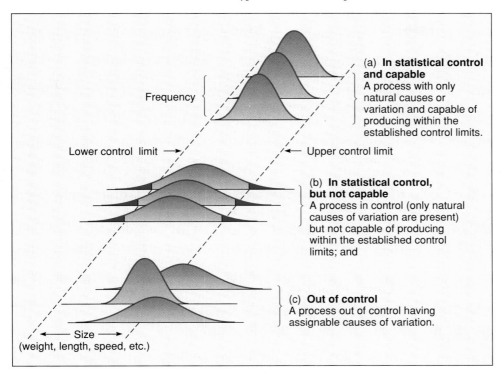

Control Charts for Variables

Variables are characteristics that have continuous dimensions. They have an infinite number of possibilities. Examples are weight, speed, length, or strength. Control charts for the mean, $\bar{x}$, and the range, R, are used to monitor processes that have continuous dimensions. The $\bar{x}$- (x-bar) **chart** tells us whether changes have occurred in the central tendency of a process. This might be due to such factors as tool wear, a gradual increase in temperature, a different method used on the second shift, or new and stronger materials. The **R-chart** values indicate that a gain or loss in uniformity has occurred. Such a change might be due to worn bearings, a loose tool part, an erratic flow of lubricants to a machine, or to sloppiness on the part of a machine operator. The two types of charts go hand in hand when monitoring variables.

$\bar{x}$-chart

R-chart

The Central Limit Theorem

The theoretical foundation for $\bar{x}$-charts is the **central limit theorem**. In general terms, this theorem states that regardless of the distribution of the population of all parts or services, the distribution of $\bar{x}$'s (each of which is a mean of a sample drawn from the population) will tend to follow a normal curve as the sample size grows larger. And, fortunately, even if the sample (n) is fairly small (say, 4 or 5), the distributions of the averages will still roughly follow a normal curve. The theorem also states that (1) the mean of the distribution of the $\bar{x}$'s (called $\bar{\bar{x}}$) will equal the mean of the overall population (called μ); and (2) the standard deviation of the sampling distribution, $\sigma_{\bar{x}}$, will

Central limit theorem

"All quality control does is find our mistakes. I want to start avoiding them."

be the population standard deviation, σ_x, divided by the square root of the sample size, n. In other words,

$$\bar{\bar{x}} = \mu \qquad \text{and} \qquad \sigma_{\bar{x}} = \frac{\sigma_x}{\sqrt{n}}$$

Figure 4.3 shows three possible population distributions, each with its own mean, μ, and standard deviation σ_x. If a series of random samples ($\bar{x}_1, \bar{x}_2, \bar{x}_3, \bar{x}_4$, and so on) each of size n is drawn from any one of these, the resulting distribution of $\bar{x}_i$'s will appear as in the bottom graph of that figure. Because this is a normal distribution, we can state that

1. 99.7% of the time, the sample averages will fall within $\pm 3\sigma_{\bar{x}}$ if the process has only random variations; and
2. 95.5% of the time, the sample averages will fall within $\pm 2\sigma_{\bar{x}}$ if the process has only random variations.

If a point on the control chart falls outside of the $\pm 3\sigma_{\bar{x}}$ control limits, then we are 99.7% sure the process has changed. This is the theory behind control charts.

Setting Mean Chart Limits ($\bar{x}$ Charts)

If we know, through past data, the standard deviation of the process population, σ_x, we can set upper and lower control limits by these formulas:

$$\text{Upper control limit (UCL)} = \bar{\bar{x}} + z\sigma_{\bar{x}} \qquad (4.1)$$

$$\text{Lower control limit (LCL)} = \bar{\bar{x}} - z\sigma_{\bar{x}} \qquad (4.2)$$

where $\bar{\bar{x}}$ = mean of the sample means
        z = number of normal standard deviations (2 for 95.5% confidence, 3 for 99.7%)

FIGURE 4.3 ■ The Relationship Between Population and Sampling Distributions. Regardless of the population distribution (e.g., beta, normal, uniform), each with its own mean (μ) and standard deviation (σ_x), the distribution of sample means is always normal.

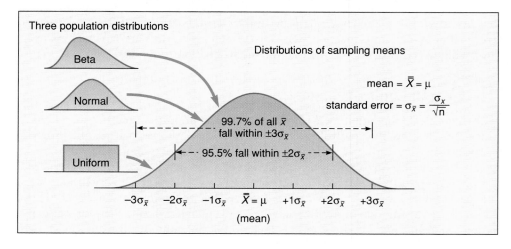

$\sigma_{\bar{x}}$ = standard deviation of the sample means = $\sigma_x / \sqrt{n}$
n = sample size

Example 1 shows how to set control limits for sample means using standard deviations.

EXAMPLE 1

The weights of boxes of Oat Flakes within a large production lot are sampled each hour. To set control limits that include 99.7% of the sample means, samples of nine boxes are randomly selected and weighed. Here are the results for the past 12 hours:

HOUR	AVG. OF 9 BOXES	HOUR	AVG. OF 9 BOXES	HOUR	AVG. OF 9 BOXES
1	17.1	5	16.5	9	16.3
2	16.8	6	16.4	10	16.5
3	14.5	7	15.2	11	14.2
4	14.8	8	16.4	12	17.3

The average mean of all 12 of the samples is easily calculated to be exactly 16 ounces and the population standard deviation is calculated to be 1 ounce. We therefore have $\bar{\bar{x}}$ = 16 ounces, σ_x = 1 ounce, n = 9, and z = 3. The control limits are:

$$UCL_{\bar{x}} = \bar{\bar{x}} + z\sigma_{\bar{x}} = 16 + 3\left(\frac{1}{\sqrt{9}}\right) = 16 + 3\left(\frac{1}{3}\right) = 17 \text{ ounces}$$

$$LCL_{\bar{x}} = \bar{\bar{x}} - z\sigma_{\bar{x}} = 16 - 3\left(\frac{1}{\sqrt{9}}\right) = 16 - 3\left(\frac{1}{3}\right) = 15 \text{ ounces}$$

Because process standard deviations are either not available or difficult to compute, we usually calculate control limits based on the average *range* values rather than on standard deviations. Table 4.1 provides the necessary conversion for us to do so. The range is defined as the difference between the largest and smallest items in one sample. For example, if the heaviest box of Oat Flakes in hour 1 of Example 1 was 19 ounces and the lightest was 14 ounces, the range for that hour would be 5 ounces. We use Table 4.1 and the equations

$$UCL_{\bar{x}} = \bar{\bar{x}} + A_2 \bar{R} \tag{4.3}$$

and

$$LCL_{\bar{x}} = \bar{\bar{x}} - A_2 \bar{R} \tag{4.4}$$

where $\bar{R}$ = average range of the samples
A_2 = value found in Table 4.1
$\bar{\bar{x}}$ = mean of the sample means

Example 2 shows how to set control limits for sample means using Table 4.1 and the average range.

TABLE 4.1 ■ FACTORS FOR COMPUTING CONTROL CHART LIMITS

SAMPLE SIZE, N	MEAN FACTOR, A_2	UPPER RANGE, D_4	LOWER RANGE, D_3
2	1.880	3.268	0
3	1.023	2.574	0
4	.729	2.282	0
5	.577	2.114	0
6	.483	2.004	0
7	.419	1.924	0.076
8	.373	1.864	0.136
9	.337	1.816	0.184
10	.308	1.777	0.223
12	.266	1.716	0.284
14	.235	1.671	0.329
16	.212	1.636	0.364
18	.194	1.608	0.392
20	.180	1.586	0.414
25	.153	1.541	0.459

Source: Reprinted by permission of American Society for Testing Materials. Copyright 1951. Taken from Special Technical Publication 15-C, "Quality Control of Materials," pp. 63 and 72.

EXAMPLE 2

Super Cola bottles soft drinks labeled "net weight 16 ounces." An overall process average of 16.01 ounces has been found by taking several batches of samples, in which each sample contained five bottles. The average range of the process is .25 ounce. Determine the upper and lower control limits for averages in this process.

Looking in Table 4.1 for a sample size of 5 in the mean factor A_2 column, we find the number .577. Thus, the upper and lower control chart limits are

$$\text{UCL}_{\bar{x}} = \bar{\bar{x}} + A_2\bar{R}$$
$$= 16.01 + (.577)(.25)$$
$$= 16.01 + .144$$
$$= 16.154 \text{ ounces}$$

$$\text{LCL}_{\bar{x}} = \bar{\bar{x}} - A_2\bar{R}$$
$$= 16.01 - .144$$
$$= 15.866 \text{ ounces}$$

Setting Range Chart Limits (R Charts)

In Examples 1 and 2, we determined the upper and lower control limits for the process *average*. In addition to being concerned with the process average, operations managers are interested in the process *dispersion,* or *variability*. Even though the process average is under control, the variability of the process may not be. For example, something may have worked itself loose in a piece of equipment. As a result, the average of the samples may remain the same, but the variation within the samples could be entirely too large. For this reason, P/OM managers use control charts for ranges in order to monitor the process variability, as well as control charts for the process average, which monitor the process average. The theory behind the control charts for ranges is the same as that for the process average control charts. Limits are established that contain ±3 standard deviations of the distribution for the average range $\overline{R}$. We can use the following equation to set the upper and lower control limits for ranges:

$$UCL_R = D_4\overline{R} \tag{4.5}$$

$$LCL_R = D_3\overline{R} \tag{4.6}$$

where $\quad UCL_R$ = upper control chart limit for the range
$\quad\quad\quad LCL_R$ = lower control chart limit for the range
$\quad\quad D_4$ and D_3 = values from Table 4.1

Example 3 shows how to set control limits for sample ranges using Table 4.1 and the average range.

Acceptable tolerance levels on auto body parts at this New United Motor Manufacturing (NUMMI) plant in Fremont, California, are so small that the company uses computers to see whether the process is in or out of control. Workers at NUMMI (which makes the Toyota Corolla and GM Prizm) are empowered to stop the entire production line by pulling the overhead cord if any quality problems are spotted.

EXAMPLE 3

The average *range* of a process loading is 5.3 pounds. If the sample size is 5, determine the upper and lower control chart limits.

Looking in Table 4.1 for a sample size of 5, we find that $D_4 = 2.114$ and $D_3 = 0$. The range control limits are

$$
\begin{aligned}
UCL_R &= D_4\overline{R} \\
&= (2.114)(5.3 \text{ pounds}) \\
&= 11.2 \text{ pounds}
\end{aligned}
$$

$$
\begin{aligned}
LCL_R &= D_3\overline{R} \\
&= (0)(5.3 \text{ pounds}) \\
&= 0
\end{aligned}
$$

STEPS TO FOLLOW IN USING CONTROL CHARTS. There are five steps that are generally followed in using $\overline{x}$- and R-charts:

1. Collect 20 to 25 samples of $n = 4$ or $n = 5$ each from a stable process and compute the mean and range of each.

2. Compute the overall means ($\overline{\overline{x}}$ and $\overline{R}$), set appropriate control limits, usually at the 99.7% level, and calculate the preliminary upper and lower control limits. If the process is not currently stable, use the desired mean, μ, instead of $\overline{\overline{x}}$ to calculate limits.

3. Graph the sample means and ranges on their respective control charts and determine whether they fall outside the acceptable limits.

4. Investigate points or patterns that indicate the process is out of control. Try to assign causes for the variation and then resume the process.

5. Collect additional samples and, if necessary, revalidate the control limits using the new data.

An application of control charts with the Madison, Wisconsin, police department is discussed in the following *POM in Action* box.

Madison's Police Department Learns Some Hard Quality Lessons

The Police Department in Madison, Wisconsin, has been implementing the concepts of TQM since 1986, using new and creative ways to improve employee and citizen satisfaction. Surveys are sent to people involved in every 35th case number (including to those arrested) to track progress, and control charts are used to monitor variations in department performance.

But David Couper, chief of police, has found that improving quality in a government agency is difficult. Here are some of his observations about TQM and politics:

- Politics is like war. Most newly elected politicians attempt to negate their predecessor's programs.

- If TQM is viewed as one particular politician's program, it will only last for the tenure of that politician.

- Government likes to maintain traditional work systems and the status quo.

- When bosses fear a major failure, they will try anything, even quality improvement.

- Unions cannot be expected to carry the torch for quality improvement.

- Politicians have fragile egos and have trouble with the teamwork approach needed in TQM.

Despite these observations, more and more leaders like Chief Couper are using TQM with control charts to satisfy the external customer—taxpayers.

Sources: Quality Progress (October 1990): 37–40; and National Productivity Review (Autumn 1992): 453–461.

Control Charts for Attributes

Control charts for $\bar{x}$ and R do not apply when we are sampling *attributes*, which are typically classified as defective or nondefective. Measuring defectives involves counting them (for example, number of bad light bulbs in a given lot or number of letters or data entry records typed with errors), whereas *variables* are usually measured for length or weight. There are two kinds of attribute control charts: (1) those that measure the percent defective in a sample—called *p*-charts, and (2) those that count the number of defects—called *c*-charts.

p-charts

P-CHARTS.   Using *p*-charts is the chief way to control attributes. Although attributes that are either good or bad follow the binomial distribution, the normal distribution can be used to calculate *p*-chart limits when sample sizes are large. The procedure resembles the $\bar{x}$-chart approach, which was also based on the central limit theorem.

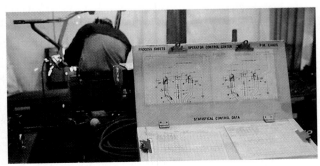

Harley-Davidson, like other world-class firms, makes extensive use of statistical process control (SPC). At the work cell shown here, an employee measures the dimensions of a part and posts the data on the control chart.

The formulas for p-chart upper and lower control limits follow:

$$UCL_p = \bar{p} + z\sigma_{\hat{p}} \tag{4.7}$$

$$LCL_p = \bar{p} - z\sigma_{\hat{p}} \tag{4.8}$$

where $\bar{p}$ = mean fraction defective in the sample
   z = number of standard deviations ($z = 2$ for 95.5% limits; $z = 3$ for 99.7% limits)
   $\sigma_{\hat{p}}$ = standard deviation of the sampling distribution

$\sigma_{\hat{p}}$ is estimated by the formula:

$$\sigma_{\hat{p}} = \sqrt{\frac{\bar{p}(1 - \bar{p})}{n}} \tag{4.9}$$

where n = size of each sample.

Example 4 shows how to set control limits for p-charts for these standard deviations.

EXAMPLE 4

Data entry clerks at ARCO key in thousands of insurance records each day. Samples of the work of 20 clerks are shown in the table. One hundred records entered by each clerk were carefully examined to make sure they contained no errors. The fraction defective in each sample was then computed.

Set the control limits to include 99.7% of the random variation in the entry process when it is in control.

SAMPLE NUMBER	NUMBER OF ERRORS	FRACTION DEFECTIVE	SAMPLE NUMBER	NUMBER OF ERRORS	FRACTION DEFECTIVE
1	6	.06	11	6	.06
2	5	.05	12	1	.01
3	0	.00	13	8	.08
4	1	.01	14	7	.07
5	4	.04	15	5	.05
6	2	.02	16	4	.04
7	5	.05	17	11	.11
8	3	.03	18	3	.03
9	3	.03	19	0	.00
10	2	.02	20	$\underline{4}$	.04
				80	

$$\bar{p} = \frac{\text{total number of errors}}{\text{total number of records examined}} = \frac{80}{(100)(20)} = .04$$

$$\sigma_{\hat{p}} = \sqrt{\frac{(.04)(1 - .04)}{100}} = .02$$

(*Note*: 100 is the size of each sample = n)

$$UCL_p = \bar{p} + z\sigma_{\hat{p}} = .04 + 3(.02) = .10$$

$$LCL_p = \bar{p} - z\sigma_{\hat{p}} = .04 - 3(.02) = 0$$

(because we cannot have a negative percent defective)

When we plot the control limits and the sample fraction defectives, we find that only one data entry clerk (number 17) is out of control. The firm may wish to examine that individual's work a bit more closely to see if a serious problem exists (see Figure 4.4.)

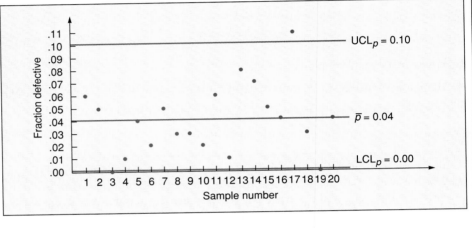

FIGURE 4.4　■　*p*-Chart for Data Entry for Example 4

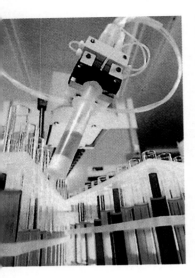

Space-age robotics and computerized analytical equipment are used by Waste Management to protect groundwater. Waste management processing and disposal centers analyze up to 60,000 samples annually in its attempt to assure the highest standards of environmental quality.

c-charts

C-CHARTS.　In Example 4, we counted the number of defective records entered. A defective record was one that was not exactly correct. A bad record may contain more than one defect, however. We use **c-charts** to control the *number* of defects per unit of output (or per insurance record in the preceding case).

Control charts for defects are helpful for monitoring processes in which a large number of potential errors can occur but the actual number that do occur is relatively small. Defects may be errors in newspaper words, bad circuits in a microchip, blemishes on a table, or missing pickles on a fast-food hamburger.

The Poisson probability distribution, which has a variance equal to its mean, is the basis for c-charts. Because c is the mean number of defects per unit, the standard deviation is equal to $\sqrt{c}$. To compute 99.7% control limits for $\bar{c}$, we use the formula

$$\bar{c} \pm 3\sqrt{\bar{c}} \qquad\qquad (4.10)$$

Example 5 shows how to set control limits for a $\bar{c}$ chart.

EXAMPLE 5

Red Top Cab Company receives several complaints per day about the behavior of its drivers. Over a 9-day period (where days are the units of measure), the owner received the following numbers of calls from irate passengers: 3, 0, 8, 9, 6, 7, 4, 9, 8, for a total of 54 complaints.

To compute 99.7% control limits, we take

$$\bar{c} = \frac{54}{9} = 6 \text{ complaints per day}$$

Thus,

$$UCL_c = \bar{c} + 3\sqrt{\bar{c}} = 6 + 3\sqrt{6} = 6 + 3(2.45) = 13.35$$

$$LCL_c = \bar{c} - 3\sqrt{\bar{c}} = 6 - 3\sqrt{6} = 6 - 3(2.45) = 0$$

After the owner plotted a control chart summarizing these data and posted it prominently in the drivers' locker room, the number of calls received dropped to an average of three per day. Can you explain why this occurred?

Note that although we have discussed process charts and control limits, a focus on the target value, not the limits, is best. An example of the advantage of such a focus is provided in the *POM in Action* box "Robust Quality at Mazda."

ACCEPTANCE SAMPLING

Acceptance sampling is a form of testing that involves taking random samples of "lots" or batches of finished products and measuring them against predetermined standards. Sampling, as mentioned earlier in this chapter, is more economical than 100% inspection. The quality of the sample is used to judge the quality of all items in the lot. Although either attributes or variables can be inspected by acceptance sampling, attribute inspection is more commonly used in business and is illustrated in this section.

Acceptance sampling

Acceptance sampling can be applied when raw materials arrive at a plant during a production process, or in final inspection, but it is usually used to control incoming lots of purchased products. A lot of items rejected, based on an unacceptable level of defects found in the sample, can (1) be returned to the supplier or (2) be 100% inspected to cull out all defects, with the cost of this screening usually billed to the supplier. However, acceptance sampling is not a substitute for adequate process controls. In fact, the current approach is to build statistical quality controls at the supplier level so that acceptance sampling can be eliminated.

Sampling Plans

A lot of items can be inspected in several ways, including the use of single, double, or sequential sampling.

SINGLE SAMPLING. Two numbers specify a **single sampling** plan: They are the number of items to be sampled (n) and a prespecified acceptable number of defects (c). If there are fewer or equal defects in the lot than the acceptance number, c, then the whole batch will be accepted. If there are more than c defects, the whole lot will be rejected or subjected to 100% screening.

Single sampling

Robust Quality at Mazda

Ford Motor Company, which owns 25% of the Japanese-based Mazda Company, asked Mazda to build transmissions for one of Ford's models sold in the United States. Although the transmissions built by Mazda were identical in specification to those built by Ford, the Ford transmissions produced higher rates of malfunction and customer complaints. Consequently, Ford incurred increased levels of warranty costs.

Wanting to correct the situation, Ford investigated by comparing samples of transmissions from both companies. Ford found that whereas their own transmissions fell within a preset range of acceptability on a zero defect standard, the Mazda samples were more exact with virtually little, if any, variation from the engineering specs. In some Ford transmissions, many components fell near the *outer limits* of tolerance from the target. When randomly assembled together, a series of deviations tended to "stack up." Otherwise, trivial variations in one part exacerbated a variation in another. Because of deviations, parts interacted with greater friction than they could withstand individually or with greater vibration than customers were prepared to endure.

Further investigation also indicated that creative management played a part in Mazda's more reliable transmissions. Instead of focusing on a range of acceptability, Mazda management aimed at manufacturing products that consistently met target values.

Sources: Harvard Business Review (January/February 1990): 65–75; and *Business Week* (July 22, 1991): 82–83.

DOUBLE SAMPLING.   Often a lot of items is so good or so bad that we can reach a conclusion about its quality by taking a smaller sample than would have been used in a single sampling plan. If the number of defects in this smaller sample (of size n_1) is less than or equal to some lower limit (c_1), the lot can be accepted. If the number of defects exceeds an upper limit (c_2), the whole lot can be rejected. But if the number of defects in the n_1 sample is between c_1 and c_2, a second sample (of size n_2) is drawn. The cumulative results determine whether to accept or reject the lot. The concept is called **double sampling**.

Double sampling

SEQUENTIAL SAMPLING.   Multiple sampling is an extension of double sampling, with smaller samples used sequentially until a clear decision can be made. When units are randomly selected from a lot and tested one by one, with the cumulative number of inspected pieces and defects recorded, the process is called **sequential sampling**.

Sequential sampling

If the cumulative number of defects exceeds an upper limit specified for that sample, the whole lot will be rejected. Or if the cumulative number of rejects is less than or equal to the lower limit, the lot will be accepted. But if the number of defects falls within these two boundaries, we continue to sample units from the lot. It is possible in some sequential plans for the whole lot to be tested, unit by unit, before a conclusion is reached.

Selection of the best sampling approach—single, double, or sequential—depends on the types of products being inspected and their expected quality level. A very low-quality batch of goods, for example, can be identified quickly and more cheaply with sequential sampling. This means that the inspection, which may be costly and/or destructive, can end sooner. On the other hand, there are many cases where a single sampling plan is easier and simpler for workers to conduct even though the number sampled may be greater than under other plans.

Operating Characteristic (OC) Curves

The **operating characteristic (OC) curve** describes how well an acceptance plan discriminates between good and bad lots. A curve pertains to a specific plan, that is, a combination of n (sample size) and c (acceptance level). It is intended to show the probability that the plan will accept lots of various quality levels.

Naturally, we would prefer a highly discriminating sampling plan and OC curve. If the entire shipment of parts has an unacceptably high level of defects, we hope the sample will reflect that fact with a very high probability (preferably 100%) of rejecting the shipment.

Figure 4.5(a) shows a perfect discrimination plan for a company that wants to reject all lots with more than 2½% defectives and accept all lots with less than 2½% defectives. Unfortunately, the only way to assure 100% acceptance of good lots and 0% acceptance of bad lots is to conduct a full inspection, which is often very costly.

Figure 4.5(b) reveals that no OC curve will be as steplike as the one in Figure 4.5(a); nor will it be discriminating enough to yield 100% error-free inspection. Figure 4.5(b) does indicate, though, that for the same sample size ($n = 100$ in this case), a smaller value of c (of acceptable defects) yields a steeper curve than does a larger value of c. So one way to increase the probability of accepting only good lots and rejecting only bad lots with random sampling is to set very tight acceptance levels.

A second way to develop a steeper, and thereby sounder, OC curve is to increase the sample size. Figure 4.5(c) illustrates that even when the acceptance number is the same proportion of the sample size, a larger value of n will increase the likelihood of accurately measuring the lot's quality. In this figure, both curves use a maximum defect rate of 4% (equal to $4/100 = 1/25$). Yet if you take a straightedge or ruler and carefully examine Figure 4.5(c), you will be able to see that the OC curve for $n = 25$, $c = 1$ rejects more good lots and accepts more bad lots than the second plan. Here are a few measurements to illustrate that point.

FIGURE 4.5 ■ (a) Perfect Discrimination for Inspection Plan. (b) OC Curves for Two Different Acceptable Levels of Defects ($c = 1$, $c = 4$) for the Same Sample Size ($n = 100$). (c) OC Curves for Two Different Sample Sizes ($n = 25$, $n = 100$) but Same Acceptance Percentages (4%). Larger sample size shows better discrimination.

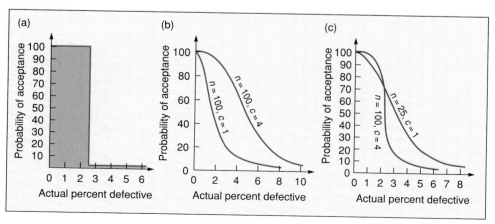

WHEN THE ACTUAL PERCENT OF DEFECTS IN THE LOT IS:	THEN THE PROBABILITY (APPROXIMATE) OF ACCEPTING THE WHOLE LOT IS:	
	FOR N = 100, C = 4	FOR N = 25, C = 1
1%	97%	90%
3%	15%	47%
5%	3%	18%
7%	1%	6%

In other words, the probability of accepting a more than satisfactory lot (one with only 1% defects) is 97% for $n = 100$, but only 90% for $n = 25$. Likewise, the chance of accepting a "bad" lot (one with 5% defects) is only 3% for $n = 100$, whereas it is 18% using the smaller sample size.[2] Of course, were it not for the cost of extra inspection, every firm would opt for larger sample sizes.

Producer's and Consumer's Risk

In acceptance sampling, two parties are usually involved: the producer of the product and the consumer of the product. In specifying a sampling plan, each party wants to avoid costly mistakes in accepting or rejecting a lot. The producer wants to avoid the mistake of having a good lot rejected (*producer's risk*) because he or she usually must replace the rejected lot. Conversely, the customer or consumer wants to avoid the mistake of accepting a bad lot because defects found in a lot that has already been accepted are usually the responsibility of the customer (*consumer's risk*). The OC curve shows the features of a particular sampling plan, including the risks of making a wrong decision.

Figure 4.6 illustrates four sampling concepts:

Acceptable quality level (AQL)

1. The **acceptable quality level (AQL)** is the poorest level of quality we are willing to accept. We wish to accept lots that have this level of quality. If an acceptable quality level is 20 defects in a lot of 1,000 items or parts, then AQL is $20/1,000 = 2\%$ defectives.

Lot tolerance percent defective (LTPD)

2. The **lot tolerance percent defective (LTPD)** is the quality level of a lot we consider bad. We wish to reject lots that have this level of quality. If it is agreed that an unacceptable quality level is 70 defects in a lot of 1,000, then the LTPD is $70/1,000 = 7\%$ defective.

   To derive a sampling plan, the producer and the consumer must define not only "good lots" and "bad lots" through the AQL and LTPD, but they must also specify risk levels.

Producer's risk

3. **Producer's risk (α)** is the probability that a "good" lot will be rejected. This is the risk of taking a random sample that results in a much higher proportion of

[2]It bears repeating, even at the risk of sounding repetitive, that sampling always runs the danger of leading to an erroneous conclusion. Let us say in this example, that the total population under scrutiny is a load of 1,000 computer chips, of which in reality only 30 (or 3%) are defective. This means that we would want to accept the shipment of chips, because 4% is the allowable defect rate. But if a random sample of $n = 50$ chips were drawn, we could conceivably end up with zero defects and accept that shipment (that is, it is OK) or we could find all 30 defects in the sample. If the latter happened, we could wrongly conclude that the whole population was 60% defective and reject them all.

FIGURE 4.6 ■ An Operating Characteristic (OC) Curve Showing Producer's and Consumer's Risk. *Note:* A good lot for this particular acceptance plan has less than or equal to 2% defectives. A bad lot has 7% or more defectives.

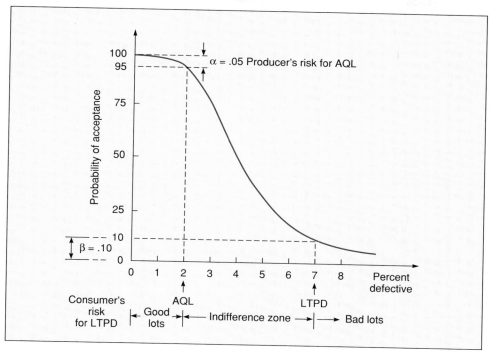

defects than the population of all items. A lot with an acceptable quality level of AQL still has an α chance of being rejected. Sampling plans are often designed to have the producer's risk set at $\alpha = .05$, or 5%.

4. **Consumer's risk** (β) is the probability that a "bad" lot will be accepted. This is the risk of taking a random sample that results in a lower proportion of defects than the overall population of items. A common value for consumer's risk in sampling plans is $\beta = .10$, or 10%.

Consumer's risk

In statistics, the probability of rejecting a good lot is called a **Type I error**. The probability of a bad lot being accepted is referred to as a **Type II error**.

Type I error
Type II error

Sampling plans and OC curves can be developed by computer (as seen in the computer programs supplied with this text), by published tables such as the U.S. Military Standard MIL-STD-105 or the Dodge–Romig table, or by calculation, using the binomial or Poisson distributions.[3] To help you understand the theory underlying the use of sampling plans, we will illustrate how an OC curve is constructed statistically.

In attribute sampling, where products are determined to be either good or bad, a binomial distribution is usually employed to build the OC curve. The binomial equation is

$$P(x) = \frac{n!}{x!(n-x)!}\, p^x (1-p)^{n-x} \tag{4.11}$$

[3]The two most frequently used tables for acceptance plans are *Military Standard Sampling Procedures and Tables for Inspection by Attributes* (MIL-STD–105D) (Washington, DC: U.S. Government Printing Office, 1963); and H. F. Dodge and H. G. Romig, *Sampling Inspection Tables—Single and Double Sampling,* 2nd ed. (New York: John Wiley, 1959).

where n = number of items sampled (called trials)
         p = probability that an x (defect) will occur on any one trial
      $P(x)$ = probability of exactly x results in n trials

When the sample size (n) is large and the percent defective (p) is small, however, the Poisson distribution can be used as an approximation of the binomial formula. This is convenient because binomial calculations can become quite complex, and because cumulative Poisson tables are readily available. Our Poisson table appears in Appendix B.

In a Poisson approximation of the binomial distribution, the mean of the binomial, which is np, is used as the mean of the Poisson, which is λ; that is,

$$\lambda = np \tag{4.12}$$

EXAMPLE 6

A shipment of 2,000 portable battery units for microcomputers is about to be inspected by a Malaysian importer. The Korean manufacturer and the importer have set up a sampling plan in which the α risk is limited to 5% at an AQL of 2% defective, and the β risk is set to 10% at LTPD = 7% defective. We want to construct the OC curve for the plan of $n = 120$ sample size and an acceptance level of $c \leq 3$ defectives. Both firms want to know if this plan will satisfy their quality and risk requirements.

To solve the problem, we turn to the cumulative Poisson table in Appendix B, whose columns are set up in terms of the acceptance level, c. We are interested only in the $c = 3$ column for this example. The rows in the table are λ (= np), which represents the number of defects we would expect to find in each sample.

By varying the percent defectives (p) from .01 (1%) to .08 (8%) and holding the sample size at $n = 120$, we can compute the probability of acceptance of the lot at each chosen level. The values for P (acceptance) calculated in what follows are then plotted to produce the OC curve shown in Figure 4.7

FIGURE 4.7   ■   OC Curve Constructed for Example 6

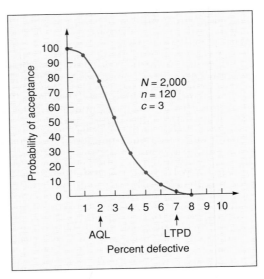

Although we increasingly rely upon automated inspection techniques, much inspection is still done manually. Here, an employee of Bausch & Lomb in Indonesia inspects contact lenses.

SELECTED VALUES OF % DEFECTIVE	MEAN OF POISSON, $\lambda = np$	P (ACCEPTANCE) FROM APPENDIX B
.01	1.20	.966
.02	2.40	.779 $\leftarrow 1 - \alpha$ at AQL
.03	3.60	.515
.04	4.80	.294
.05	6.00	.151
.06	7.20	.072
.07	8.40	.032* $\leftarrow \beta$ level at LTPD
.08	9.60	.014*

*Interpolated from value.

Now back to the issue of whether this OC curve satisfies the quality and risk needs of the consumer and producer of the batteries. For the AQL of $p = .02 = 2\%$ defects, the P (acceptance) of the lot = .779. This yields an α risk of $1 - .779 = .221$, or 22.1%, which exceeds the 5% level desired by the producer. The β risk of .032, or 3.2%, is well under the 10% sought by the consumer. It appears that new calculations are necessary with a larger sample size if the α level is to be lowered.[4]

[4]Indeed, as AB:POM's quality control module will verify, the sample size should be 165.

In Example 6, we set n and c values for a sampling plan and then computed the α and β risks to see if they were within desired levels. Often, organizations instead develop an OC curve for preset values and an AQL and then substitute values of n and c until the plan also satisfies the β and LTPD demands.

Average Outgoing Quality

In most sampling plans, when a lot is rejected, the entire lot is inspected and all of the defective items are replaced. Use of this replacement technique improves the average outgoing quality in terms of percent defective. In fact, given (1) any sampling plan that replaces all defective items encountered and (2) the true incoming percent defective for the lot, it is possible to determine the **average outgoing quality (AOQ)** in percent defective. The equation for AOQ is

Average outgoing quality (AOQ)

$$AOQ = \frac{(P_d)(P_a)(N - n)}{N} \qquad (4.13)$$

where
P_d = true percent defective of the lot
P_a = probability of accepting the lot
N = number of items in the lot
n = number of items in the sample

EXAMPLE 7

The percent defective from an incoming lot in Example 6 is 3%. An OC curve showed the probability of acceptance to be .515. Given a lot size of 2,000 and a sample of 120, what is the average outgoing quality in percent defective?

$$\text{AOQ} = \frac{(P_d)(P_a)(N - n)}{N}$$

$$= \frac{(.03)(.515)(2,000 - 120)}{2,000} = .015$$

Thus, an acceptance sampling plan changes the quality of the lots in percent defective from 3% to 1.5% on the average. Acceptance sampling significantly increases the quality of the inspected lots.

In most cases, we do not know the value of P_a; we must determine it from the particular sampling plan. The fact that we seldom know the true incoming percent defective presents another problem. In most cases, several different incoming percent defective values are assumed. Then we can determine the average outgoing quality for each value.

EXAMPLE 8

To illustrate the AOQ relationship, let us use the data we developed for the OC curve in Example 6. The lot size in that case was $N = 2,000$ and the sample size was $n = 120$. We assume that any defective batteries found during inspection are replaced by good ones. Then using the formula for AOQ given before and the probabilities of acceptance from Example 6, we can develop the following numbers:

P_D	×	P_A	×	$(N - n)/N$	=	AOQ
.01		.966		.94		.009
.02		.779		.94		.015
.03		.515		.94		.015
.04		.294		.94		.011
.05		.151		.94		.007
.06		.072		.94		.004
.07		.032		.94		.002
.08		.014		.94		.001

These numbers are graphed in Figure 4.8 as the average outgoing quality as a function of incoming quality.

FIGURE 4.8 ■ A Typical AOQ Curve Using Data from Example 8

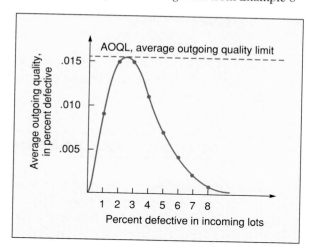

Did you notice how AOQ changed for different percent defectives? When the percent defective of the incoming lots is either very high or very low, the percent defective of the outgoing lots is low. AOQ at 1% was .009, and AOQ at 8% was .001. For moderate levels of the incoming percent defective, AOQ is higher: AOQ at 2–3% was .015. Thus, AOQ is low for small values of the incoming percent defective. As the incoming percent defective increases, the AOQ increases up to a point. Then, for increasing incoming percent defective, AOQ decreases.

A few years ago, IBM Canada Ltd. ordered some parts from a new supplier in Japan. IBM stated in its order that acceptable quality allowed for 1.5% defects—a demanding standard in North America at that time. The Japanese sent the order, with a few parts packaged separately in plastic. Their letter said: "We don't know why you want 1.5% defective parts, but for your convenience we have packaged them separately."

The maximum value on the AOQ curve corresponds to the highest average percent defective or the lowest average quality for the sampling plan. It is called the *average outgoing quality limit (AOQL)*. In Figure 4.8, the AOQL is just over 1.5%, meaning the batteries are about 98.4% good when the incoming quality is between 2 and 3%.

Acceptance sampling is useful for screening incoming lots. When the defective parts are replaced with good parts, acceptance sampling helps to increase the quality of the lots by reducing the outgoing percent defective.

ACHIEVING WORLD-CLASS STANDARDS

World-class organizations establish an environment of total quality management (TQM) where employees know and use the tools of TQM. This is accomplished via an aggressive education program. The education to build and maintain a work force comfortable with TQM cannot be overemphasized. World-class Motorola requires that 1.5% of revenue be spent on education. Other world-class organizations require up to 200 hours of training per person per year. Another approach to ensure a major commitment to TQM and its tools is taken at Xerox where each manager is evaluated on quality performance in his or her organization.

Statistical process control (SPC) is one step on the way to quality. SPC requires understanding process capability, control charting, and timely corrections. Processes are designed and maintained so they are capable of producing products that meet customer expectations. Consequently, in world-class organizations, employees are provided facilities, education, and training for TQM and SPC. SPC permeates world-class organizations.

SUMMARY

Statistical process control and acceptance sampling are major statistical tools of quality control. Control charts for SPC help the operations manager distinguish between natural and assignable variations. The $\bar{x}$-chart and the R-chart are used for variable sampling and the p-chart and the c-chart for attribute sampling. Sampling plans and operating characteristic (OC) curves facilitate acceptance sampling and provide the manager with tools to evaluate the quality of a production run or shipment.

KEY TERMS

Control chart (p. 110)
Natural variations (p. 110)
Assignable variations (p. 111)
$\bar{x}$-chart (p. 111)
R-chart (p. 112)
Central limit theorem (p. 112)
p-charts (p. 118)
c-charts (p. 120)
Acceptance sampling (p. 121)
Single sampling (p. 121)
Double sampling (p. 122)

Sequential sampling (p. 122)
Operating characteristic (OC) curve (p. 123)
Acceptable quality level (AQL) (p. 124)
Lot tolerance percent defective (LTPD) (p. 124)
Producer's risk (p. 124)
Consumer's risk (p. 125)
Type I error (p. 125
Type II error (p. 125)
Average outgoing quality (AOQ) (p. 127)

Solving Example 4 with AB:POM's Quality Control Module

AB:POM's quality control module addresses a number of quality issues through an initial screen that provides these options: (1) $\bar{x}$- and R-charts, (2) p-charts, (3) c-charts, (4) attribute sampling, (5) variable sampling, and (6) OC curves. We illustrate the p-chart option in Program 4.1 using the data from Example 4.

PROGRAM 4.1 ■ AB:POM's p-Chart Option. AB:POM computes the average percentage of defects (the center line of the p-bar chart), which is displayed as .04 for Example 4 data. Using these data, the program presents the limits for four different control charts at the bottom of the screen. There is one chart with 95% confidence, one with 98%, one with 99%, and one with 3 standard deviations (99.7%) confidence.

		Quality Control				Solution

Number of samples (1–99) `20`   Sample size (n) (2–9999) `100`

ARCO Insurance Records

Sample Number	Number of Defects	Percent Defects	Sample Number	Number of Defects	Percent Defects
1	6	0.0600	13	8	0.0800
2	5	0.0500	14	7	0.0700
3	0	0.0000	15	5	0.0500
4	1	0.0100	16	4	0.0400
5	4	0.0400	17	11	0.1100
6	2	0.0200	18	3	0.0300
7	5	0.0500	19	0	0.0000
8	3	0.0300	20	4	0.0400
9	3	0.0300			
10	2	0.0200			
11	6	0.0600			
12	1	0.0100			

	95%	98%	99%	99.7%
Upper Control Limit	0.0784	0.0857	0.0906	0.0988
Center Line (p-bar)	0.0400	0.0400	0.0400	0.0400
Lower Control Limit	0.00159	0.0000	0.0000	0.0000

F1=Help   F3=Graph   F9=Print   Esc

A Spreadsheet Approach to Example 1's $\bar{x}$-Chart

Program 4.2 illustrates how easy it is to compute upper and lower control limits for an $\bar{x}$-chart with spreadsheets. The @STD and @AVG formulas compute the standard deviations (σ_x) and average ($\bar{\bar{x}}$) of the 12 observed sample averages. These are used to compute $\sigma_{\bar{x}}$ (in cell D7) and control limits (in cells D9 and D10).

PROGRAM 4.2 ■ A "Symbolic" Spreadsheet for Computing Upper and Lower Control Chart Limits

	A	B	C	D	E
1	Spreadsheet used to solve Example 1				
2					
3	Sample	Sample			
4	Number	Weight		Sample Size =	9
5	1	17.1		X bar bar =	(B19)
6	2	16.8		Z value =	3
7	3	14.5		Sigma X bar =	(B18) / @SQRT(E4)
8	4	14.8			
9	5	16.5		UCL xbar =	(B19+(E6∗E7))
10	6	16.4		LCL xbar =	(B19−(E6∗E7))
11	7	15.2			
12	8	16.4			
13	9	16.3			
14	10	16.5			
15	11	14.2			
16	12	17.3			
17		- - - - - - - - - -			
18		@STD(B5. .B16)		Standard deviation (sigma)	
19		@AVG(B5. .B16)		Average mean (x bar bar)	

SOLVED PROBLEMS

Solved Problem 4.1

The manufacturer of precision parts for drill presses produces round shafts for use in the construction of drill presses. The average diameter of a shaft is .56 inch. The inspection samples contain six shafts each. The average range of these samples is .006 inch. Determine the upper and lower control chart limits.

Solution
The mean factor A_2 from Table 4.1, where the sample size is 6, is seen to be .483. With this factor, you can obtain the upper and lower control limits:

$$UCL = .56 + (.483)(.006)$$
$$= .56 + .0029$$
$$= .5629$$

$$LCL = .56 - .0029$$
$$= .5571$$

Solved Problem 4.2

Nocaf Drinks, Inc., a producer of decaffeinated coffee, bottles Nocaf. Each bottle should have a net weight of 4 ounces. The machine that fills the bottles with coffee is new, and the operations manager wants to make sure that it is properly adjusted. The operations manager takes a sample of $n = 8$ bottles and records the average and range in ounces for each sample. The data for several samples are in the following table. Note that every sample consists of 8 bottles.

SAMPLE	SAMPLE RANGE	SAMPLE AVERAGE	SAMPLE	SAMPLE RANGE	SAMPLE AVERAGE
A	.41	4.00	E	.56	4.17
B	.55	4.16	F	.62	3.93
C	.44	3.99	G	.54	3.98
D	.48	4.00	H	.44	4.01

Is the machine properly adjusted and in control?

Solution

We first find that $\bar{\bar{x}} = 4.03$ and $\bar{R} = .51$. Then, using Table 4.1, we find

$$\text{UCL}_{\bar{x}} = \bar{\bar{x}} + A_2\bar{R} = 4.03 + (.373)(.51) = 4.22$$

$$\text{LCL}_{\bar{x}} = \bar{\bar{x}} - A_2\bar{R} = 4.03 - (.373)(.51) = 3.84$$

$$\text{UCL}_R = D_4\bar{R} = (1.864)(.51) = .95$$

$$\text{LCL}_R = D_3\bar{R} = (.136)(.51) = .07$$

It appears that the process average and range are both in control.

Solved Problem 4.3

Altman Electronics, Inc., makes resistors, and among the last 100 resistors inspected, the percent defective has been 5%. Determine the upper and lower limits for this process for 99.7% confidence.

Solution

$$\text{UCL}_p = \bar{p} + 3\sqrt{\frac{\bar{p}(1-\bar{p})}{n}} = .05 + 3\sqrt{\frac{(.05)(1-.05)}{100}}$$

$$= .05 + 3(0.0218) = .1154$$

$$\text{LCL}_p = \bar{p} - 3\sqrt{\frac{\bar{p}(1-\bar{p})}{n}} = .05 - 3(.0218)$$

$$= .05 - .0654 = 0 \text{ (because percent defective cannot be negative)}$$

Solved Problem 4.4

In an acceptance sampling plan developed for lots containing 1,000 units, the sample size n is 85 and c is 3. The percent defective of the incoming lots is 2%, and the probability of acceptance, which was obtained from an OC curve, is 0.64.

What is the average outgoing quality?

Solution

$$AOQ = \frac{(P_d)(P_a)(N-n)}{N} = \frac{(.02)(.64)(1,000-85)}{1,000} = .012 \text{ or } AOQ = 1.2\%$$

DISCUSSION QUESTIONS

1. Why is the central limit theorem so important in statistical quality control?

2. Why are $\bar{x}$- and R-charts usually used hand in hand?

3. Explain the difference between an $\bar{x}$- and an R-chart.

4. What might cause a process to be out of control?

5. Explain why a process can be out of control even though all samples fall within the upper and lower control limits.

6. What is the difference between variable and attribute sampling?

7. What charts are used for variable sampling?

8. What charts are used for attribute sampling?

9. What do the terms *producer's risk* and *consumer's risk* mean?

10. Define Type I and Type II errors.

11. Explain the difference between single, double, and sequential sampling.

12. Define AQL and LTPD.

13. What is "average outgoing quality"?

14. What is the AOQL?

CRITICAL THINKING EXERCISE

When Nashua Corp., a large paper company, had quality problems, they called noted quality guru W. Edwards Deming. Deming discovered that the Nashua technicians did not understand natural variations. They frequently stopped the paper-coating machinery to make adjustments to the coating head. But by assuming any variation had to be corrected, they were inadvertently *increasing* the variation. What they did was the equivalent of trying to adjust a scale while someone was jumping up and down on it. When they stopped meddling with the machine, it turned out to be in fairly good statistical control. The special (assignable) cause of variation was eliminated. Nashua then went back to work at reducing the common (natural) causes of variation in the machine.[5]

Prepare a brief explanation for foremen at Nashua Corp. of special (assignable) vs. common (natural) variations.

PROBLEMS

💻 · **4.1** The overall average on a process you are attempting to monitor is 75 units. The average range is 6 units. What are the upper and lower control limits if you choose to use a sample size of 10?

💻 · **4.2** The overall average on a process you are attempting to monitor is 50 units. The average range is 4 units. What are the upper and lower control limits if you choose to use a sample size of 5?

· **4.3** Your supervisor, Mike Perman, has asked that you check and report on the output of a machine on the factory floor. This machine is supposed to be producing widgets that have a mean weight of 50 grams, and a range of 3.5 grams. The table contains the data taken during the past 3 hours:

[5]Adopted from Jeremy Maine, *Quality Wars* (New York: Free Press, 1994), p. 110.

	SAMPLE NUMBER									
	1	2	3	4	5	6	7	8	9	10
Sample Average	55	47	49	50	52	57	55	48	51	56
Sample Range	3	1	5	3	2	6	3	2	2	3

What are the control limits and what conclusions do you draw?

- **4.4** Food Storage Technologies produces refrigeration units for food producers and retail food establishments. The overall average temperature that these units maintain is 46°F. The average range is 2°F. Samples of 6 are taken to monitor the process. Determine the upper and lower control-chart limits for averages and ranges for these refrigeration units.

- **4.5** Autopitch devices are made for both major- and minor-league teams to help them improve their batting averages. When set at the standard position, Autopitch can throw hard balls toward a batter at an average speed of 60 mph. Company executives take samples of 10 Autopitch devices at a time to monitor these devices and to maintain the highest quality. The average range is 3 mph. Using control-chart techniques, determine control-chart limits for averages and ranges for Autopitch.

- **4.6** Major Products, Inc., produces granola cereal, granola bars, and other natural food products. Its natural granola cereal is sampled to ensure proper weight. Each sample contains eight boxes of cereal. The overall average for the samples is 17 ounces. The range is only 0.5 ounce. Determine the upper and lower control-chart limits for averages for the boxes of cereal.

- **4.7** Small boxes of NutraFlakes cereal are labeled "net weight 10 ounces." Each hour, random samples of size $n = 4$ boxes are weighed to check process control. Five hours of observation yielded the following:

	WEIGHTS			
TIME	BOX 1	BOX 2	BOX 3	BOX 4
9 A.M.	9.8	10.4	9.9	10.3
10 A.M.	10.1	10.2	9.9	9.8
11 A.M.	9.9	10.5	10.3	10.1
Noon	9.7	9.8	10.3	10.2
1 P.M.	9.7	10.1	9.9	9.9

Using these data, construct limits for $\bar{x}$- and R-charts. Is the process in control? What other steps should the QC department follow at this point?

- **4.8** Sampling four pieces of precision-cut wire (to be used in computer assembly) every hour for the past 24 hours has produced the following results:

	HOUR											
	1	2	3	4	5	6	7	8	9	10	11	12
$\bar{x}$ (in.)	3.25	3.10	3.22	3.39	3.07	2.86	3.05	2.65	3.02	2.85	2.83	2.97
R (in.)	.71	1.18	1.43	1.26	1.17	.32	.53	1.13	.71	1.33	1.17	.40

	HOUR										
	13	14	15	16	17	18	19	20	21	22	23	24
$\bar{x}$ (in.)	3.11	2.83	3.12	2.84	2.86	2.74	3.41	2.89	2.65	3.28	2.94	2.64
R (in.)	.85	1.31	1.06	.50	1.43	1.29	1.61	1.09	1.08	.46	1.58	.97

Develop appropriate control charts and determine whether there is any cause for concern in the cutting process.

4.9 In the past, the defect rate for your product has been 1.5%. What are the upper and lower control-chart limits if you wish to use a sample size of 500 and $z = 3$?

4.10 In the past, the defect rate for your product has been 3.5%. What are the upper and lower control-chart limits if you wish to use a sample size of 500 and $z = 3$?

4.11 You are attempting to develop a quality monitoring system for some parts purchased from Warton & Kotha Manufacturing Co. These parts are either good or defective. You have decided to take a sample of 100 units. Develop a table of the appropriate upper and lower control-chart limits for various values of the fraction defective in the sample taken. The values for p in this table should range from .02 to .1 in increments of .02. Develop the upper and lower control limits for a 99.7% confidence level.

4.12 Due to the poor quality of various semiconductor products used in their manufacturing process, Microlaboratories has decided to develop a quality control program. Because the semiconductor parts it receives from suppliers are either good or defective, George Haverty has decided to develop control charts for attributes. The total number of semiconductors in every sample is 200. Furthermore, George would like to determine the upper control-chart limit and the lower control-chart limit for various values of the fraction defective (p) in the sample taken. To allow more flexibility, he has decided to develop a table that lists values for p, UCL, and LCL. The values for p should range from .01 to .1, incrementing by .01 each time. What are the UCLs and the LCLs for 99.7% confidence?

4.13 For the last 2 months, Robin Russo has been concerned about the number 5 machine at the West Factory. In order to make sure that the machine is operating correctly, samples are taken, and the average and range for each sample are computed. Each sample consists of 12 items produced from the machine. Recently, 12 samples were taken, and for each, the sample range and average were computed. The sample range and sample average were 1.1 and 46 for the first sample, 1.31 and 45 for the second sample, .91 and 46 for the third sample, and 1.1 and 47 for the fourth sample. After the fourth sample, the sample averages increased. For the fifth sample, the range was 1.21 and the average was 48; for sample number 6 it was .82 and 47; for sample number 7, it was .86 and 50; and for the eighth sample, it was 1.11 and 49. After the eighth sample, the sample average continued to increase, never going below 50. For sample number 9, the range and average were 1.12 and 51; for sample number 10, they were .99 and 52; for sample number 11, they were .86 and 50; and for sample number 12, they were 1.2 and 52.

Although Robin's boss was not overly concerned about the process, Robin was. During installation, the supplier set an average of 47 for the process with an average range of 1.0. It was Robin's feeling that something was definitely wrong with machine number 5. Do you agree?

4.14 Pet Products, Inc., caters to the growing market for cat supplies, with a full line of products ranging from litter to toys to flea powder. One of its newer products, a tube of paste that prevents hair balls in long-haired cats, is produced by an automated machine that is set to fill each tube with 63.5 grams of paste.

To keep this filling process under control, four tubes are pulled randomly from the assembly line every 4 hours. After several days, the data shown in the table resulted. Set control limits for this process and graph the sample data for both the $\bar{x}$- and R-charts.

	SAMPLE NUMBER												
	1	2	3	4	5	6	7	8	9	10	11	12	13
$\bar{x}$	63.5	63.6	63.7	63.4	63.0	63.2	63.3	63.7	63.7	63.5	63.3	63.2	63.6
R	2.0	1.0	1.7	0.9	1.2	1.6	1.8	1.3	1.6	1.3	1.8	1.0	1.8

	SAMPLE NUMBER											
	14	15	16	17	18	19	20	21	22	23	24	25
$\bar{x}$	63.3	63.4	63.4	63.5	63.6	63.8	63.5	63.9	63.2	63.3	64.0	63.4
R	1.5	1.7	1.4	1.1	1.8	1.3	1.6	1.0	1.8	1.7	2.0	1.5

· **4.15** The smallest defect in a computer chip will render the entire chip worthless. Therefore, tight quality control measures must be established to monitor these chips. In the past, the percentage defective for these chips for a California-based company has been 1.1%. The sample size is 1,000. Determine upper and lower control-chart limits for these computer chips. Use $z = 3$.

∶ **4.16** Chicago Supply Company (CSC) manufactures paper clips and other office products. Although inexpensive, paper clips have provided the firm with a high margin of profitability. The percentage defective for paper clips produced by CSC has been averaging 2.5%. Samples of 200 paper clips are taken. Establish upper and lower control-chart limits for this process at 99.7% confidence.

∶ **4.17** Daily samples of 100 power drills are removed from Drill Master's assembly line and inspected for defects. Over the past 21 days, the following information has been gathered. Develop a 3 standard deviation (99.7% confidence) p-chart and graph the samples. Is the process in control?

DAY	1	2	3	4	5	6	7	8	9	10	11
Number of Defective Drills	6	5	6	4	3	4	5	3	6	3	7

DAY	12	13	14	15	16	17	18	19	20	21
Number of Defective Drills	5	4	3	4	5	6	5	4	3	7

∶ **4.18** A random sample of 100 Modern Art dining room tables that came off the firm's assembly line is examined. Careful inspection reveals a total of 2,000 blemishes. What are the 99.7% upper and lower control limits for the number of blemishes? If one table had 42 blemishes, should any special action be taken?

▣ ⋮ **4.19** Eighty items are randomly drawn from a lot of 6,000 talking toy animals, and the total lot is accepted if there are $c \leq 2$ defects. Develop an OC curve for this sample plan.

▣ ⋮ **4.20** A load of 200 desk lamps has just arrived at the warehouse of Lighting, Inc. Random samples of $n = 5$ lamps are checked. If more than one lamp is defective, the whole lot is rejected. Set up the OC curve for this plan.

▣ ⋮ **4.21** Develop the AOQ curve for Problem 4.20.

▣ ⋮ **4.22** Each week, Melissa Bryant Ltd. receives a batch of 1,000 popular Swiss watches for its chain of East Coast boutiques. Bryant and the Swiss manufacturer have agreed on the following sampling plan: $\alpha = 5\%$, $\beta = 10\%$, AQL = 1%, LTPD = 5%. Develop the OC curve for a sampling plan of $n = 100$ and $c \leq 2$. Does this plan meet the producer's and consumer's requirements?

▣ ⋮ **4.23** Kristi Conlin's firm in Waco, Texas, has designed an OC curve that shows a ⅔ chance of accepting lots with a true percentage defective of 2%. Lots of 1,000 units are produced at a time, with 100 of each lot sampled randomly. What is the average outgoing quality level?

DATA BASE APPLICATION

▣ ⋮ **4.24** West Battery Corp. has recently been receiving complaints from retailers that its 9-volt batteries are not lasting as long as other name brands. James West, head of the TQM program at the Austin plant, believes there is no problem, because his batteries have had an average life of 50 hours, about 10% longer than competitors' models. To raise the lifetime above this would require a new level of technology not available to West. Nevertheless, he is concerned enough to set up hourly assembly line checks. He decides to take 5 samples of 9-volt batteries for each of the next 25 hours to create the standards for control-chart limits (see the table):

WEST BATTERY DATA—BATTERY LIFETIMES (IN HOURS)

	SAMPLE						
HOUR	1	2	3	4	5	X̄	R
1	51	50	49	50	50	50.0	2
2	45	47	70	46	36	48.8	34
3	50	35	48	39	47	43.8	15
4	55	70	50	30	51	51.2	40
5	49	38	64	36	47	46.8	28
6	59	62	40	54	64	55.8	24
7	36	33	49	48	56	44.4	23
8	50	67	53	43	40	50.6	27
9	44	52	46	47	44	46.6	8
10	70	45	50	47	41	50.6	29
11	57	54	62	45	36	50.8	26
12	56	54	47	42	62	52.2	20
13	40	70	58	45	44	51.4	30
14	52	58	40	52	46	49.6	18
15	57	42	52	58	59	53.6	17
16	62	49	42	33	55	48.2	29
17	40	39	49	59	48	47.0	20

WEST BATTERY DATA—BATTERY LIFETIMES (IN HOURS)—CONTINUED

	SAMPLE						
HOUR	1	2	3	4	5	$\overline{X}$	R
18	64	50	42	57	50	52.6	22
19	58	53	52	48	50	52.2	10
20	60	50	41	41	50	48.4	19
21	52	47	48	58	40	49.0	18
22	55	40	56	49	45	49.0	16
23	47	48	50	50	48	48.6	3
24	50	50	49	51	51	50.2	2
25	51	50	51	51	62	53.0	12

With this limits in place, West now takes five more hours of data, shown in the following sample:

	SAMPLE				
HOUR	1	2	3	4	5
26	48	52	39	57	61
27	45	53	48	46	66
28	63	49	50	45	53
29	57	70	45	52	61
30	45	38	46	54	52

a) Is the manufacturing process in control?

b) Comment on the lifetimes observed.

CASE STUDY

Bayfield Mud Company

In November 1994, John Wells, a customer service representative of Bayfield Mud Company, was summoned to the Houston warehouse of Wet-Land Drilling, Inc., to inspect three boxcars of mud-treating agents that Bayfield Mud Company had shipped to the Houston firm. (Bayfield's corporate offices and its largest plant are located in Orange, Texas, which is just west of the Louisiana–Texas border.) Wet-Land Drilling had filed a complaint that the 50-pound bags of treating agents that it had just received from Bayfield were short-weight by approximately 5%.

The light-weight bags were initially detected by one of Wet-Land's receiving clerks, who noticed that the railroad scale tickets indicated that the net weights were significantly less on all three of the boxcars than those of identical shipments received on October 25, 1994. Bayfield's traffic department was called to determine if lighter-weight dunnage or pallets were used on the shipments. (This might explain the lighter net weights.) Bayfield indicated, however, that no changes had been made in the loading or palletizing procedures. Hence, Wet-Land randomly checked 50 of the bags and discovered

(Continued)

that the average net weight was 47.51 pounds. They noted from past shipments that the bag net weights averaged exactly 50.0 pounds, with an acceptable standard deviation of 1.2 pounds. Consequently, they concluded that the sample indicated a significant short-weight. (The reader may wish to verify this conclusion.) Bayfield was then contacted, and Wells was sent to investigate the complaint. Upon arrival, Wells verified the complaint and issued a 5% credit to Wet-Land.

Wet-Land's management, however, was not completely satisfied with only the issuance of credit for the short shipment. The charts followed by their mud engineers on the drilling platforms were based on 50-pound bags of treating agents. Lighter-weight bags might result in poor chemical control during the drilling operation and might adversely affect drilling efficiency. (Mud-treating agents are used to control the pH and other chemical properties of the cone during drilling operation.) This could cause severe economic consequences because of the extremely high cost of oil and natural gas well-drilling operations. Consequently, special use instructions had to accompany the delivery of these shipments to the drilling platforms. Moreover, the light-weight shipments had to be isolated in Wet-Land's warehouse, causing extra handling and poor space utilization. Hence, Wells was informed that Wet-Land Drilling might seek a new supplier of mud-treating agents if, in the future, it received bags that deviated significantly from 50 pounds.

The quality control department at Bayfield suspected that the light-weight bags may have resulted from "growing pains" at the Orange plant. Because

of the earlier energy crisis, oil and natural gas exploration activity had greatly increased. This increased activity, in turn, created increased demand for products produced by related industries, including drilling muds. Consequently, Bayfield had to expand from a one-shift (6:00 A.M. to 2:00 P.M.) to a two-shift (2:00 P.M. to 10:00 P.M.) operation in mid-1992, and finally to a three-shift operation (24 hours per day) in the fall of 1994.

The additional night-shift bagging crew was staffed entirely by new employees. The most experienced foremen were temporarily assigned to supervise the night-shift employees. Most emphasis was placed on increasing the output of bags to meet the ever-increasing demand. It was suspected that only occasional reminders were made to double-check the bag weight-feeder. (A double-check is performed by systematically weighing a bag on a scale to determine if the proper weight is being loaded by the weight-feeder. If there is significant deviation from 50 pounds, corrective adjustments are made to the weight-release mechanism.)

To verify this expectation, the quality control staff randomly sampled the bag output and prepared the following chart. Six bags were sampled and weighed each hour.

DISCUSSION QUESTIONS

1. What is your analysis of the bag weight problem?
2. What procedures would you recommend to maintain proper quality control?

Source: Professor Jerry Kinard, Western Carolina University.

Time	Average Weight (Pounds)	Range		Time	Average Weight (Pounds)	Range	
		Smallest	Largest			Smallest	Largest
6:00 A.M.	49.6	48.7	50.7	1:00 P.M.	49.0	46.4	50.0
7:00	50.2	49.1	51.2	2:00	49.0	46.0	50.6
8:00	50.6	49.6	51.4	3:00	49.8	48.2	50.8
9:00	50.8	50.2	51.8	4:00	50.3	49.2	52.7
10:00	49.9	49.2	52.3	5:00	51.4	50.0	55.3
11:00	50.3	48.6	51.7	6:00	51.6	49.2	54.7
12 Noon	48.6	46.2	50.4	7:00	51.8	50.0	55.6

(Continued)

Time	Average Weight (Pounds)	Range		Time	Average Weight (Pounds)	Range	
		Smallest	Largest			Smallest	Largest
8:00	51.0	48.6	53.2	1:00 A.M.	49.6	48.4	51.7
9:00	50.5	49.4	52.4	2:00	50.0	49.0	52.2
10:00	49.2	46.1	50.7	3:00	50.0	49.2	50.0
11:00	49.0	46.3	50.8	4:00	47.2	46.3	50.5
12 Midnight	48.4	45.4	50.2	5:00	47.0	44.1	49.7
1:00 A.M.	47.6	44.3	49.7	6:00	48.4	45.0	49.0
2:00	47.4	44.1	49.6	7:00	48.8	44.8	49.7
3:00	48.2	45.2	49.0	8:00	49.6	48.0	51.8
4:00	48.0	45.5	49.1	9:00	50.0	48.1	52.7
5:00	48.4	47.1	49.6	10:00	51.0	48.1	55.2
6:00	48.6	47.4	52.0	11:00	50.4	49.5	54.1
7:00	50.0	49.2	52.2	12 Noon	50.0	48.7	50.9
8:00	49.8	49.0	52.4	1:00 P.M.	48.9	47.6	51.2
9:00	50.3	49.4	51.7	2:00	49.8	48.4	51.0
10:00	50.2	49.6	51.8	3:00	49.8	48.8	50.8
11:00	50.0	49.0	52.3	4:00	50.0	49.1	50.6
12 Noon	50.0	48.8	52.4	5:00	47.8	45.2	51.2
1:00 P.M.	50.1	49.4	53.6	6:00	46.4	44.0	49.7
2:00	49.7	48.6	51.0	7:00	46.4	44.4	50.0
3:00	48.4	47.2	51.7	8:00	47.2	46.6	48.9
4:00	47.2	45.3	50.9	9:00	48.4	47.2	49.5
5:00	46.8	44.1	49.0	10:00	49.2	48.1	50.7
6:00	46.8	41.0	51.2	11:00	48.4	47.0	50.8
7:00	50.0	46.2	51.7	12 Midnight	47.2	46.4	49.2
8:00	47.4	44.0	48.7	1:00 A.M.	47.4	46.8	49.0
9:00	47.0	44.2	48.9	2:00	48.8	47.2	51.4
10:00	47.2	46.6	50.2	3:00	49.6	49.0	50.6
11:00	48.6	47.0	50.0	4:00	51.0	50.5	51.5
12 Midnight	49.8	48.2	50.4	5:00	50.5	50.0	51.9

CASE STUDY

SPC at the *Gazette*

Of critical importance to a newspaper is accurate typesetting. To assure typesetting quality, a quality improvement team was established in the printing department at the *Gazette* in Geronimo, Texas. The team developed a procedure for monitoring the performance of typesetters over a period of time. Such a procedure involves sampling output, establishing control limits, comparing the *Gazette*'s accuracy with that of the industry, and occasionally updating the information.

(Continued)

The team randomly selected 30 of the *Gazette's* newspapers published during the preceding 12 months. From each paper, 100 paragraphs were randomly chosen and were read for accuracy. The number of paragraphs with errors in each paper was recorded, and the fraction of paragraphs with errors in each sample was determined. The table shows the results of the sampling.

SAMPLE	PARAGRAPHS WITH ERRORS IN THE SAMPLE	FRACTION OF PARAGRAPHS WITH ERRORS (PER 100)	SAMPLE	PARAGRAPHS WITH ERRORS IN THE SAMPLE	FRACTION OF PARAGRAPHS WITH ERRORS (PER 100)
1	2	.02	16	2	.02
2	4	.04	17	3	.03
3	10	.10	18	7	.07
4	4	.04	19	3	.03
5	1	.01	20	2	.02
6	1	.01	21	3	.03
7	13	.13	22	7	.07
8	9	.09	23	4	.04
9	11	.11	24	3	.03
10	0	.00	25	2	.02
11	3	.03	26	2	.02
12	4	.04	27	0	.00
13	2	.02	28	1	.01
14	2	.02	29	3	.03
15	8	.08	30	4	.04

DISCUSSION QUESTIONS

1. Plot the overall fraction of errors (p) and the upper and lower control limits on a control chart using a 95.45% confidence level.

2. Assume the industry upper and lower control limits are .1000 and .0400, respectively. Plot them on the control chart.

3. Plot the fraction of errors in each sample. Do all fall within the firm's control limits? When one falls outside the control limits, what should be done?

Source: Professor Jerry Kinard, Western Carolina University.

BIBLIOGRAPHY

Besterfield, D. H. *Quality Control,* 2nd ed. Englewood Cliffs, NJ: Prentice Hall, 1986.

Das, T. K., and M. A. Wortman. "Asymmetric Patrolling Repairman Systems with General Repair Time and Walk Time Distributions: Cost Analysis of Service Schedule." *IIE Transactions,* 25, no. 6 (November 1993): 19.

Hwarng, H. B., and N. F. Hubele. "X Control Chart Pattern Identification Through Efficient Off-Line Neural Network Training." *IIE Transactions,* 25, no. 3 (May 1993): 27–40.

Kumar, S., and Y. P. Gupta. "Statistical Process Control at Motorola's Austin Assembly Plant." *Interfaces,* 23, no. 2 (March/April 1993): 84–92.

Runger, G. C., and D. C. Montgomery. "Adaptive Sampling Enhancements for Shewhart Control Charts." *IIE Transactions,* 25, no. 3 (May 1993): 41–51.

See additional references at the end of Chapter 3.

4 SUPPLEMENT

STATISTICAL TOOLS FOR MANAGERS

When the ship *S.S. Central America* sank roughly 200 miles off the coast of South Carolina in the great hurricane of 1857, some 425 people lost their lives. Also lost to the ocean floor, some 8,000 feet below, were gold bars and coins worth $400 million. In 1985, the Columbus-America Discovery Group hired Lawrence Stone to develop a series of probability distributions for the location of the gold cargo. Stone's probability maps of several hundred square miles of ocean provided estimates of the success of finding the wreck at each grid point. By 1989, the project was successful, recovering 1 ton of gold. Thirty-nine insurance companies filed their claims to the recovered gold, but the Discovery Group won the rights to the gold in every case. Part of the gold recovered from the *S.S. Central America* is shown below.

(Source: Adapted from L. Stone, "Search for the *SS Central America*," *Interfaces* [January/February 1992]: 32–54.)

Statistics and probabilities are important not only in the search for gold. Statistics applications permeate the subject of operations management because so much of decision making depends on probabilities that are based on limited or uncertain information. This supplement provides you with a review of several important statistical tools that you will find useful in many chapters of the text. An understanding of the concepts of probability distributions, expected values, and variances is needed in the study of decision trees (Chapters 2 Supplement, 6, and 7), quality control (Chapters 3 and 4), forecasting (Chapter 5), queuing models (Chapter 10 Supplement), work measurement (Chapter 11 Supplement), learning curves (Chapter 12 Supplement), inventory (Chapter 13), simulation (Chapter 13 Supplement), project management (Chapter 17), and maintenance (Chapter 18).

DISCRETE PROBABILITY DISTRIBUTIONS

Discrete probability distribution

In this section, we explore the properties of **discrete probability distributions**, that is, distributions in which outcomes are not continuous. When we deal with discrete variables, there is a probability value assigned to each event. These values must be between 0 and 1, and they must sum to 1. Example S1 relates to a sampling of student grades.

EXAMPLE S1

The Dean at East Florida University, Nancy Beals, is concerned about the undergraduate statistics training of new MBA students. In a sampling of 100 applicants for next year's MBA class, she asked each student to supply his or her final grade in the course in statistics taken as a sophomore or junior. To translate from letter grades to a numeric score, the Dean used the following system:

5. A   **4.** B   **3.** C   **2.** D   **1.** F

The responses to this query of the 100 potential students are summarized in the table below. Also shown is the probability for each possible grade outcome. This discrete probability distribution is computed using the relative frequency approach. Probability values are also often shown in graph form as in Figure S4.1.

PROBABILITY DISTRIBUTION FOR GRADES

GRADE LETTER OUTCOME	SCORE VARIABLE (X)	NUMBER OF STUDENTS RESPONDING	PROBABILITY, P(X)
A	5	10	0.1 = 10/100
B	4	20	0.2 = 20/100
C	3	30	0.3 = 30/100
D	2	30	0.3 = 30/100
F	1	10	0.1 = 10/100
		Total = 100	1.0 = 100/100

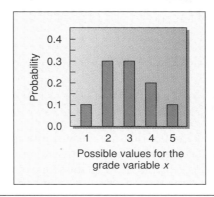

FIGURE S4.1 ■ Probability Function for Grades

This distribution follows the three rules required of all probability distributions:

1. the events are mutually exclusive and collectively exhaustive
2. the individual probability values are between 0 and 1 inclusive
3. the total of the probability values sum to 1

The graph of the probability distribution in Example S1 gives us a picture of its shape. It helps us identify the central tendency of the distribution (called the expected value) and the amount of variability or spread of the distribution (called the variance). Expected value and variance are discussed next.

Expected Value of a Discrete Probability Distribution

Once we have established a probability distribution, the first characteristic we are usually interested in is the "central tendency" or average of the distribution.[1] We compute the **expected value**, a measure of central tendency, as a weighted average of the values of the variable:

Expected value

$$E(x) = \sum_{i=1}^{n} x_i P(x_i) = x_1 P(x_1) + x_2 P(x_2) + \cdots + x_n P(x_n) \qquad (S4.1)$$

where x_i = variable's possible values
$P(x_i)$ = probability of each of the variable's possible values

The expected value of any discrete probability distribution can be computed by: (1) multiplying each possible value of the variable x_i by the probability $P(x_i)$ that outcome will occur, and (2) summing the results, indicated by the summation sign, Σ. Example S2 shows such a calculation.

---

[1]If the data we are dealing with have not been grouped into a probability distribution, the measure of central tendency is called the arithmetic mean, or simply, the average. Here is the mean of the following seven numbers: 10, 12, 18, 6, 4, 5, 15.

$$\text{Arithmetic mean, } \overline{X} = \frac{\Sigma X}{n} = \frac{10 + 12 + 18 + 6 + 4 + 5 + 15}{7} = 10$$

EXAMPLE S2

Here is how the expected grade value can be computed for the question in Example S1.

$$E(x) = \sum_{i=1}^{5} x_i P(x_i) = x_1 P(x_1) + x_2 P(x_2) + x_3 P(x_3) + x_4 P(x_4) + x_5 P(x_5)$$

$$= (5)(.1) + (4)(.2) + (3)(.3) + (2)(.3) + (1)(.1)$$

$$= 2.9$$

The expected grade of 2.9 implies that the mean statistics grade is between D (2) and C (3), and that the average response is closer to a C, which is 3. Looking at Figure S4.1, we see that this is consistent with the shape of the probability function.

Variance of a Discrete Probability Distribution

Variance

In addition to the central tendency of a probability distribution, most decision makers are interested in the variability or the spread of the distribution. The **variance** of a probability distribution is a number that reveals the overall spread or dispersion of the distribution.[2] For a discrete probability distribution, it can be computed using the following equation:

$$\text{Variance} = \sum_{i=1}^{n} (x_i - E(x))^2 P(x_i) \qquad (S4.2)$$

where x_i = variable's possible values
                $E(x)$ = expected value of the variable
                $P(x_i)$ = probability of each possible value of the variable

To compute the preceding variance, the expected value is subtracted from each value of the variable squared, and multiplied by the probability of occurrence of that value. The results are then summed to obtain the variance.

Standard deviation

A related measure of dispersion or spread is the **standard deviation**. This quantity is also used in many computations involved with probability distributions. The standard deviation, σ, is just the square root of the variance:

$$\sigma = \sqrt{\text{variance}} \qquad (S4.3)$$

Example S3 shows a variance and standard deviation calculation.

---

[2]Just as the variance of a probability distribution shows the dispersion of the data, so does the variance of ungrouped data, that is, data not formed into a probability distribution. The formula is: Variance = $\Sigma(X - \overline{X})^2 / n$. Using the numbers 10, 12, 18, 6, 4, 5, and 15, we find that $\overline{X} = 10$. Here are the variance computations:

$$\text{Variance} = \frac{(10-10)^2 + (12-10)^2 + (18-10)^2 + (6-10)^2 + (4-10)^2 + (5-10)^2 + (15-10)^2}{7}$$

$$= \frac{0 + 4 + 64 + 16 + 36 + 25 + 25}{7}$$

$$= \frac{170}{7} = 24.28$$

We should also note that when the data we are looking at represent a *sample* of a whole set of data, we use the term $n - 1$ in the denominator, instead of n, in the variance formula.

EXAMPLE S3

Here is how this procedure is done for the statistics grade survey question:

$$\text{Variance} = \sum_{i=1}^{5} (x_i - E(x))^2 P(x_i)$$

$$= (5 - 2.9)^2(.1) + (4 - 2.9)^2(.2) + (3 - 2.9)^2(.3) + (2 - 2.9)^2(.3) + (1 - 2.9)^2(.1)$$

$$= (2.1)^2(.1) + (1.1)^2(.2) + (.1)^2(.3) + (-.9)^2(.3) + (-1.9)^2(.1)$$

$$= .441 + .242 + .003 + .243 + .361$$

$$= 1.29$$

The standard deviation for the grade question is

$$\sigma = \sqrt{\text{variance}}$$

$$= \sqrt{1.29} = 1.14$$

CONTINUOUS PROBABILITY DISTRIBUTIONS

There are many examples of continuous variables. The time it takes to finish a project, the number of ounces in a barrel of butter, the high temperature during a given day, the exact length of a given type of lumber, and the weight of a railroad car of coal are all examples of continuous variables. Variables can take on an infinite number of values, so the fundamental probability rules must be modified for continuous variables.

As with discrete probability distributions, the sum of the probability values must equal 1. Because there are an infinite number of values of the variables, however, the probability of *each value* of the variable *must be 0*. If the probability values for the variable values were greater than 0, then the sum would be infinitely large.

The Normal Distribution

One of the most popular and useful continuous probability distributions is the **normal distribution**, which is characterized by a bell-shaped curve. The normal distribution is completely specified when values for the mean, μ, and the standard deviation, σ, are known.

Normal distribution

THE AREA UNDER THE NORMAL CURVE. Because the normal distribution is symmetrical, its midpoint (and highest point) is at the mean. Values of the *x*-axis are then measured in terms of how many standard deviations they are from the mean.

The area under the curve (in a continuous distribution) describes the probability that a variable has a value in the specified interval. The normal distribution requires complex mathematical calculations, but tables that provide areas or probabilities are readily available. For example, Figure S4.2 illustrates three commonly

FIGURE S4.2 ■ Three Common Areas Under Normal Curves

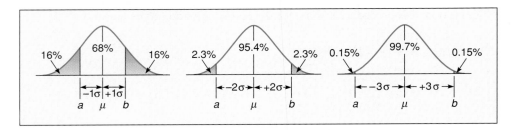

used relationships that have been derived from standard normal tables (a procedure we discuss in a moment). The area from point a to point b in the first drawing represents the probability, 68%, that the variable will be within 1 standard deviation of the mean. In the middle graph, we see that about 95.4% of the area lies within plus or minus 2 standard deviations of the mean. The third figure shows that 99.7% lies between $\pm 3\sigma$.

Translated into an application, Figure S4.2 implies that if the expected lifetime of an experimental computer chip is $\mu = 100$ days, and if the standard deviation is $\sigma = 15$ days, then we can make the following statements:

1. 68% of the population of computer chips studied have lives between 85 and 115 days (namely, $\pm 1\sigma$).

2. 95.4% of the chips have lives between 70 and 130 days ($\pm 2\sigma$).

3. 99.7% of the computer chips have lives in the range from 55 to 145 days ($\pm 3\sigma$).

4. Only 16% of the chips have lives greater than 115 days (from first graph, the area to the right of $+1\sigma$).

USING THE STANDARD NORMAL TABLE.   To use a table to find normal probability values, we follow two steps.

Step 1. Convert the normal distribution to what we call a *standard normal distribution*. A standard normal distribution is one that has a mean of 0 and a standard deviation of 1. All normal tables are designed to handle variables with $\mu = 0$ and $\sigma = 1$. Without a standard normal distribution, a different table would be needed for each pair of μ and σ values. We call the new standard variable z. The value of z for any normal distribution is computed from the equation:

$$z = \frac{x - \mu}{\sigma} \tag{S4.4}$$

where x = value of the variable we want to measure
           μ = mean of the distribution
           σ = standard deviation of the distribution
           z = number of standard deviations from x to the mean, μ

For example, if $\mu = 100$, $\sigma = 15$, and we are interested in finding the probability that the variable x is less than 130, then we want $P(x < 130)$.

$$z = \frac{x - \mu}{\sigma} = \frac{130 - 100}{15} = \frac{30}{15} = 2 \text{ standard deviations}$$

FIGURE S4.3 ■ Normal Distribution Showing the Relationship Between z Values and x Values

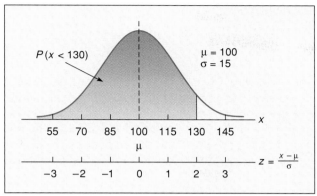

This means that the point x is 2.0 standard deviations to the right of the mean. This is shown in Figure S4.3

Step 2. Look up the probability from a table of normal curve areas. Appendix A is such a table of areas for the standard normal distribution. It is set up to provide the area under the curve to the left of any specified value of z.

Let us see how Appendix A can be used. The column on the left lists values of z, with the second decimal place of z appearing in the top row. For example, for a value of $z = 2.00$ as just computed, find 2.0 in the left-hand column and .00 in the top row. In the body of the table, we find that the area sought is .97725, or 97.7%. Thus.

$$P(x < 130) = P(z < 2.00) = 97.7\%$$

This suggests that if the mean lifetime of a computer chip is 100 days with a standard deviation of 15 days, the probability that the life of a randomly selected chip is less than 130 is 97.7%. By referring to Figure S4.2, we see that this probability could also have been derived from the middle graph. (Note that $1.0 - .977 = .023 = 2.3\%$, which is the area in the right-hand tail of the curve.)

Example S4 illustrates the use of the normal distribution further.

EXAMPLE S4

Holden Construction Co. builds primarily three- and four-unit apartment buildings (called triplexes and quadraplexes) for investors, and it is believed that the total construction time in days follows a normal distribution. The mean time to construct a triplex is 100 days, and the standard deviation is 20 days. If the firm finishes this triplex in 75 days or less, it will be awarded a bonus payment of $5,000. What is the probability that Holden will receive the bonus?

FIGURE S4.4 ■ Probability Holden Will Receive the Bonus by Finishing in 75 Days

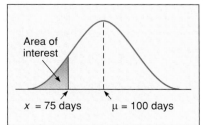

Figure S4.4 illustrates the probability we are looking for in the shaded area. The first step is to compute the z value:

$$z = \frac{x - \mu}{\sigma} = \frac{75 - 100}{20} = \frac{-25}{20} = -1.25$$

This z value indicates that 75 days is -1.25 standard deviations to the left of the mean. But the standard normal table is structured to handle only positive z values. To solve this problem, we observe that the curve is symmetric. The probability Holden will finish in *less than 75 days is equivalent* to the probability it will finish in *more than 125 days*. We first find the probability Holden will finish in less than 125 days. That value was .89435. So the probability it will take more than 125 days is

$$P(x > 125) = 1.0 - P(x < 125) = 1.0 - .89435 = .10565$$

Thus, the probability of completing the triplex in 75 days is .10565, or about 10%.

A second example: What is the probability the triplex will take between 110 and 125 days? We see in Figure S4.5 that

$$P(110 < x < 125) = P(x < 125) - P(x < 110)$$

FIGURE S4.5   ■   Probability of Holden Completion Between 110 and 125 Days

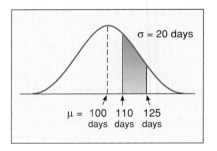

That is, the shaded area in the graph can be computed by finding the probability of completing the building in 125 days or less *minus* the probability of completing it in 110 days or less.

Recall that $P(x < 125 \text{ days})$ is equal to .89435. To find $P(x < 110 \text{ days})$, we follow the two steps developed earlier.

1. $z = \dfrac{x - \mu}{\sigma} = \dfrac{110 - 100}{20} = \dfrac{10}{20} = .50$ standard deviation

2. From Appendix A, we see that the area for $z = .50$ is .69146. So the probability the triplex can be completed in less than 110 days is .69146. Finally,

$$P(110 < x < 125) = .89435 - .69146 = .20289$$

The probability that it will take between 110 and 125 days is about 20%.

SUMMARY

The purpose of this supplement is to assist readers in tackling decision-making issues that involve probabilistic (uncertain) information. A background in statistical tools is quite useful in studying operations management. We examined two types of probability distributions, discrete and continuous. Discrete distributions assign a probability to each specific event. Continuous distributions, such as the normal, describe variables that can take on an infinite number of values. The normal, or bell-shaped, distribution is very widely used in business decision analysis and is referred to throughout this book.

KEY TERMS

Discrete probability distribution (p. 144)
Expected value (p. 145)
Variance (p. 146)
Standard deviation (p. 146)
Normal distribution (p. 147)

USING SPREADSHEETS TO COMPUTE EXPECTED VALUES AND VARIANCES

Program S4.1 shows the formulas used to compute the expected value for Example S1 and the variances for Example S2. If data are not grouped into a probability distribution, the computations are much simpler, because the @avg and @var formulas can be applied directly.

PROGRAM S4.1 ■ A Spreadsheet Approach to Expected Value and Variance Calculations. Examples S1 and S2 are illustrated with formulas.

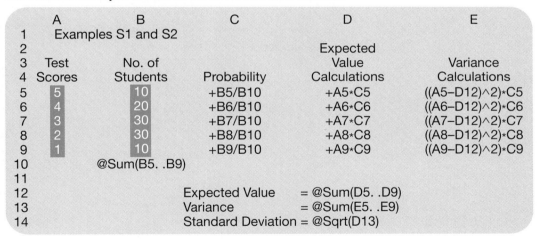

	A	B	C	D	E
1	Examples S1 and S2				
2				Expected	
3	Test	No. of		Value	Variance
4	Scores	Students	Probability	Calculations	Calculations
5	5	10	+B5/B10	+A5*C5	((A5–D12)^2)*C5
6	4	20	+B6/B10	+A6*C6	((A6–D12)^2)*C6
7	3	30	+B7/B10	+A7*C7	((A7–D12)^2)*C7
8	2	30	+B8/B10	+A8*C8	((A8–D12)^2)*C8
9	1	10	+B9/B10	+A9*C9	((A9–D12)^2)*C9
10		@Sum(B5. .B9)			
11					
12			Expected Value	= @Sum(D5. .D9)	
13			Variance	= @Sum(E5. .E9)	
14			Standard Deviation	= @Sqrt(D13)	

DISCUSSION QUESTIONS

1. What is the difference between a discrete probability distribution and a continuous probability distribution? Give your own example of each.

2. What is the expected value and what does it measure? How is it computed for a discrete probability distribution?

3. What is the variance and what does it measure? How is it computed for a discrete probability distribution?

4. Name three business processes that can be described by the normal distribution.

CRITICAL THINKING EXERCISE

The normal probability distribution is clearly the most widely used and understood continuous distribution in business. Its parameters, as we discuss in this supplement, are μ and σ. Yet there are many other continuous distributions that are not bell-shaped. Find information to describe three of them. What are their parameters and shapes? Describe business applications of each and when they would be more appropriate than the normal distribution.

PROBLEMS

• **S4.1**   Sami Abbasi Health Food stocks five loaves of Vita-Bread. The probability distribution for the sales of Vita-Bread is listed in the following table. How many loaves will Sami sell on the average?

NUMBER OF LOAVES SOLD	PROBABILITY
0	.05
1	.15
2	.20
3	.25
4	.20
5	.15

⋮ **S4.2**   What are the expected value and variance of the following probability distribution?

VARIABLE, X	PROBABILITY
1	.05
2	.05
3	.10
4	.10
5	.15
6	.15
7	.25
8	.15

• **S4.3**   Sales for Hobi-cat, a 17-foot catamaran sailboat, have averaged 250 boats per month over the last 5 years with a standard deviation of 25 boats. Assuming that the demand is about the same as past years and follows a normal curve, what is the probability that sales will be less than 280 boats next month?

⋮ **S4.4**   Refer to Problem S4.3. What is the probability that sales will be more than 265 boats during the next month? What is the probability that sales will be under 250 boats next month?

⋮ **S4.5**   Precision Parts is a job shop that specializes in producing electric motor shafts. The average shaft size for the E300 electric motor is .55 inch, with a standard deviation of .10 inch. It is normally distributed. What is the probability that a shaft selected at random will be between .55 and .65 inch?

S4.6 Refer to Problem S4.5. What is the probability that a shaft size will be greater than .65 inch? What is the probability that a shaft size will be between .53 and .59 inch? What is the probability that a shaft size will be under .45 inch?

S4.7 An industrial oven used to cure sand cores for a factory manufacturing engine blocks for small cars is able to maintain fairly constant temperatures. The temperature range of the oven follows a normal distribution, with a mean of 450°F and a standard deviation of 25°F. Kamvar Farahbod, president of the factory, is concerned about the large number of defective cores that have been produced in the last several months. If the oven gets hotter than 475°F, the core is defective. What is the probability that the oven will cause a core to be defective? What is the probability that the temperature of the oven will range from 460° to 470°F?

S4.8 Bill Hardgrave, production foreman for the Virginia Fruit Company, estimates that the average sales of oranges is 4,700 and the standard deviation is 500 oranges. Sales follow a normal distribution.

a) What is the probability that sales will be greater than 5,500 oranges?

b) What is the probability that sales will be greater than 4,500 oranges?

c) What is the probability that sales will be less than 4,900 oranges?

d) What is the probability that sales will be less than 4,300 oranges?

S4.9 Lori Becher has been the production manager of Medical Suppliers, Inc. (MSI), for the last 17 years. MSI is a producer of bandages and arm slings. During the last 5 years, the demand for the No-Stick bandage has been fairly constant. On the average, sales have been about 87,000 packages of No-Stick. Lori has reason to believe that the distribution of No-Stick follows a normal curve, with a standard deviation of 4,000 packages. What is the probability sales will be less than 81,000 packages?

BIBLIOGRAPHY

Campbell, S. *Flaws and Fallacies in Statistical Thinking.* Englewood Cliffs, NJ: Prentice Hall, 1974.

Canavos, G. C., and D. M. Miller. *An Introduction to Modern Business Statistics.* Belmont, CA: Duxbury Press, 1993.

Huff, D. *How to Lie with Statistics.* New York: Norton, 1954.

Levin, R. I., D. S. Rubin, J. P. Stinson, and E. S. Gardner. *Quantitative Approaches to Management,* 8th ed. New York: McGraw-Hill, 1992.

Render, B., and R. M. Stair. *Quantitative Analysis for Management,* 5th ed. Boston: Allyn and Bacon, 1994.

Tsokos, C. *Probability Distributions: An Introduction to Probability Theory with Applications.* North Scituate, MA: Duxbury Press, 1972.

5

FORECASTING

LEARNING OBJECTIVES

When you complete this chapter you should be able to:

Identify or Define:
Forecasting
Types of forecasts
Time horizons
Approaches to forecasts

Explain:
Moving averages
Exponential smoothing
Trend projections
Regression and correlation analysis
Measures of forecast accuracy

FORECASTING IS CRITICAL
TO TUPPERWARE'S COMPETITIVE ADVANTAGE

Stainless steel alloy molds, each requiring over 1,000 hours of skilled hand-crafting, are the heart of the manufacturing process. Each mold creates the exact shape of a new product: the mold's costs average $100,000 and their weight can be up to 5 tons. When a specific product is scheduled for a production run, its mold is carefully placed, as we see in the photo, into an injection molding machine.

map the sales of each product, the test market results of each *new* product (since 20% of the firm's sales come from products less than 2 years old), and where each product is in its own life cycle.

Three factors are key in the sales forecast: (1) the number of "consultants" or sales representatives that are registered, (2) the percentage of these dealers that are currently "active" (this number changes each week and month), and (3) the sales per active dealer, on a weekly basis. Forecasts incorporate historical data, recent events, and promotional events.

Tupperware maintains its edge over strong competitors such as

The plastic pellets which are melted at 500 degrees into Tupperware products are dropped through pipes from second floor bins into the machine holding a mold. After being injected into the water-cooled molds at a pressure up to 20,000 pounds per square inch, the product cools and is removed and inspected.

When many people think of Tupperware, they envision plastic food storage containers sold through home parties. That image is correct, but Tupperware also happens to be a successful global manufacturer with over 80% of its $1.3 billion in sales outside the United States. A household name in nearly 100 countries, the firm has 14 plants: one in Hemingway, S.C., four in Latin America, one in Africa, five in Europe, and three in Asia. Throughout the world, Tupperware stands for quality, providing a lifetime warranty that each of its 400 plastic products will not chip, crack, break, or peel.

Forecasting demand at Tupper-

ware is a critical, never-ending process, with each of its fifty profit centers around the world responsible for computerized monthly, quarterly, and 12-month sales projections. These are aggregated by region and then globally at Tupperware's World Headquarters in Orlando, Florida. The forecasts drive production at each plant.

The variety of statistical forecasting models used at Tupperware includes every technique discussed in this chapter, including moving averages, exponential smoothing, and regression analysis. At world headquarters, huge databases are maintained that

Rubbermaid by using a group process to refine its statistical forecasts. Inputs come from sales, marketing, finance, and production, but final forecasts are the consensus of all participating managers. This final step is Tupperware's version of the "jury of executive opinion" described in this chapter.

This packing line assembles and packs thousands of products daily. Tupperware's semi-automated order, distribution, and storage system uses a robotic line to automatically "pick" individual orders and place them in plastic cartons. From enormous warehouses, orders are shipped throughout North America.

Tupperware's Manufacturing Process

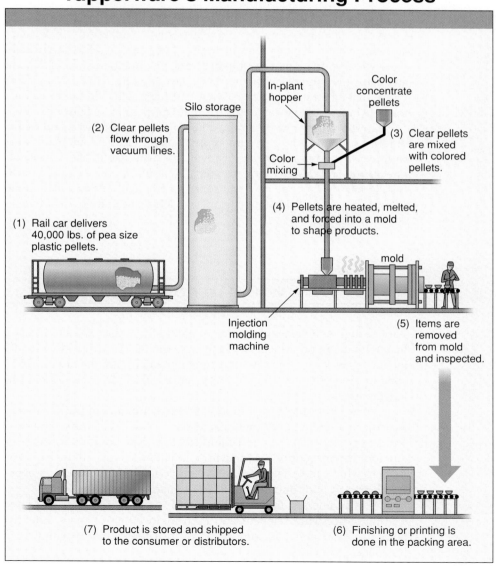

Silo storage

(2) Clear pellets flow through vacuum lines.

In-plant hopper

Color concentrate pellets

Color mixing

(3) Clear pellets are mixed with colored pellets.

(4) Pellets are heated, melted, and forced into a mold to shape products.

(1) Rail car delivers 40,000 lbs. of pea size plastic pellets.

mold

Injection molding machine

(5) Items are removed from mold and inspected.

(7) Product is stored and shipped to the consumer or distributors.

(6) Finishing or printing is done in the packing area.

I n 1970, Boeing, McDonnell Douglas, and Lockheed, all U.S. firms, dominated the global market for commercial aircraft. To counterbalance these American powerhouses, a group of European countries began to subsidize the European-based Airbus Industries so that it could improve the quality and productivity of its jet production. In 1990, about 85% of the world's airline jets were still made in the United States, but Airbus was capturing one-third of new worldwide contracts. Using forecasting techniques that you will study in this chapter, Airbus predicts that the huge, multibillion dollar investments made in it will see a payoff. Between 1990 and 2008, forecasts are that 11,500 planes, worth $600 billion will be sold. Airbus, now second in sales to Boeing, predicts a significant increase in that market share. ◆

Every day managers like those at Airbus and Tupperware make decisions without knowing what will happen in the future. They order inventory without knowing what sales will be, purchase new equipment despite uncertainty about demand for products, and make investments without knowing what profits will be. Managers are always trying to make better estimates of what will happen in the future in the face of uncertainty. Making good estimates is the main purpose of forecasting.

In this chapter, we examine different types of forecasts, and we present a variety of forecasting models. Our purpose is to show that there are many ways for managers to forecast the future. We also provide an overview of the subject of business sales forecasting and describe how to prepare, monitor, and judge the accuracy of a forecast. Good forecasts are an *essential* part of efficient service and manufacturing operations. They are also an important modeling tool in both strategic and tactical decision making.

WHAT IS FORECASTING?

Forecasting

Forecasting is the art and science of predicting future events. It may involve taking historical data and projecting them into the future with some sort of mathematical model. It may be a subjective or intuitive prediction of the future. Or it may involve a combination of these, that is, a mathematical model adjusted by a manager's good judgment.

As we introduce different forecasting techniques in this chapter, you will realize that there is seldom one single superior method. What works best in one firm under one set of conditions may be a complete disaster in another organization, or even in a different department of the same firm. In addition, you will realize that there are limits as to what can be expected from forecasts. They are seldom, if ever, perfect. They are also costly and time-consuming to prepare and monitor.

Few businesses, however, can afford to avoid the process of forecasting by just waiting to see what happens and then taking their chances. Effective planning in both the short and long run depends on a forecast of demand for the company's products.

Forecasting Time Horizons

Forecasts are usually classified by the future time horizon that they cover.[1] The three categories are as follows:

1. *Short-range forecast.* This forecast has a time span of up to 1 year but is generally less than 3 months. It is used for planning purchasing, job scheduling, work-force levels, job assignments, and production levels.

2. *Medium-range forecast.* A medium-range, or intermediate, forecast generally spans from 3 months up to 3 years. It is useful in sales planning, production planning and budgeting, cash budgeting, and analyzing various operating plans.

3. *Long-range forecast.* Generally 3 years or more in time span, long-range forecasts are used in planning for new products, capital expenditures, facility location or expansion, and research and development.

Intermediate and long-run forecasts have three features that differentiate them from short-range forecasts. First, intermediate and long-run forecasts deal with more comprehensive issues and support management decisions regarding planning and products, plants, and processes. Implementing some facility decisions, such as GM's opening a new Saturn auto manufacturing plant, can take 5 to 8 years from inception to completion. Second, short-term forecasting usually employs different methodologies than do longer-term ones. Mathematical techniques such as moving averages, exponential smoothing, and trend extrapolation (all of which we shall examine shortly) are common to short-run projections. Broader, *less* quantitative methods are useful in predicting such issues as whether a new product, like the optical disk recorder, should be introduced in a company's product line. And third, as you would expect, short-range forecasts tend to be more accurate than longer-range forecasts. Factors that influence demand change every day. Thus, as the time horizon lengthens, it is likely that one's forecast accuracy will diminish. It almost goes without saying, then, that sales forecasts need to be updated regularly in order to maintain their value and integrity. After each sales period, the forecast should be reviewed and revised.

The Influence of Product Life Cycle

Another factor to consider when developing sales forecasts, especially longer ones, is the product's life cycle. Products, and even services, do not sell at a constant level throughout their lives. Most successful products pass through four stages: (1) introduction, (2) growth, (3) maturity, and (4) decline.

Products in the first two stages of their life cycle need longer forecasts than those in the maturity and decline stages. Forecasts are useful in projecting different staffing levels, inventory levels, and factory capacity as the product passes from the first to the last stage. The subject of introducing new products, and their life cycles, is treated in more detail in Chapter 6.

---

[1]For details, see Peter W. Stonebraker and G. Keong Leong, *Operations Strategy* (Boston: Allyn and Bacon, 1994).

TYPES OF FORECASTS

Organizations use three major types of forecasts in planning the future of their operations.

Economic forecasts

1. **Economic forecasts** address the business cycle by predicting inflation rates, money supplies, housing starts, and other planning indicators.

Technological forecasts

2. **Technological forecasts** are concerned with rates of technological progress, which can result in the birth of exciting new products, requiring new plants and equipment.

Demand forecasts

3. **Demand forecasts** are projections of demand for a company's products or services. These forecasts, also called sales forecasts, drive a company's production, capacity, and scheduling systems and serve as inputs to financial, marketing, and personnel planning.

Economic and technological forecasting are specialized techniques that may be outside the role of the operations manager. The emphasis in this book therefore will be on demand forecasting.

FORECASTING APPROACHES

There are two general approaches to forecasting, just as there are two ways to tackle all decision modeling. One is quantitative analysis; the other is a qualitative approach. **Quantitative forecasts** employ a variety of mathematical models that use historical data and/or causal variables to forecast demand. Subjective or **qualitative forecasts** incorporate important factors such as the decision maker's intuition, emotions, personal experiences, and value system in reaching a forecast. Some firms use one approach and some use the other. In practice, a combination or blending of the two styles is usually most effective.

Quantitative forecasts

Qualitative forecasts

Overview of Qualitative Methods

In this section, we consider four different *qualitative* forecasting techniques.

Jury of executive opinion

1. **Jury of Executive Opinion.** Under this method, the opinions of a group of high-level managers, often in combination with statistical models, are pooled to arrive at a group estimate of demand.

Sales force composite

2. **Sales Force Composite.** In this approach, each salesperson estimates what sales will be in his or her region. These forecasts are then reviewed to ensure they are realistic and then combined at the district and national levels to reach an overall forecast.

Delphi method

3. **Delphi Method.** There are three different types of participants in the Delphi method: decision makers, staff personnel, and respondents. The decision makers usually consist of a group of 5 to 10 experts who will be making the actual forecast. The staff personnel assist the decision makers by preparing, distributing, collecting, and summarizing a series of questionnaires and survey results.

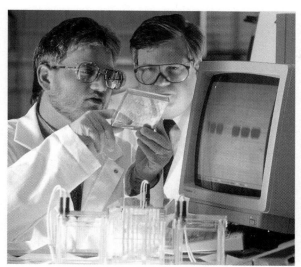

To get a grasp on future trends in the world of medical research, Bristol-Myers Squibb Company questioned 220 well-known research scientists. These leaders made a *jury of executive opinion* suggesting that the future treatment of disease will concentrate on the disease's cause. In other words, rather than treat diseases like cancer through symptom elimination, medical treatment will focus on attacking individual cells of the disease itself. As a result of this qualitative forecasting, Bristol-Myers created the fluorescence-activated cell sorter, which targets antibodies of tumor cells through the use of lasers and computers.

The respondents are a group of people, often located in different places, whose judgments are valued and are being sought. This group provides inputs to the decision makers before the forecast is made. An application of this technique is noted in the photo on page 162 describing how the State of Alaska used the Delphi method to develop its long-range forecast.

4. **Consumer Market Survey.** This method solicits input from customers or potential customers regarding their future purchasing plans. It can help not only in preparing a forecast, but also in improving product design and planning for new products.

Consumer market survey

Overview of Quantitative Methods

Five quantitative forecasting methods are addressed in this chapter. They are as follows:

1. Naive approach
2. Moving averages
3. Exponential smoothing ⎫
4. Trend projection ⎬ time-series models
5. Linear-regression causal model ⎬ causal model

TIME-SERIES MODELS. **Time-series** models predict on the assumption that the future is a function of the past. In other words, they look at what has happened over a period of time and use a series of past data to make a forecast. If we are predicting weekly sales of lawn mowers, we use the past weekly sales for lawn mowers in making the forecast.

Time series

Alaska's economy is dominated by oil. An amazing 90% of the state's budget is derived from 1.5 million barrels of oil pumped daily through this pipeline at Prudhoe Bay. To develop a long-range economic forecast, the State of Alaska turned to the Delphi method. The large Delphi panel of experts had to represent all groups and opinions in the state and all geographic areas. But Delphi was the perfect forecasting tool because panelist travel could be avoided. It also meant leading Alaskans could participate because their schedules were not impacted by meetings and distances.

CAUSAL MODELS.   Causal models, such as linear regression, incorporate the variables or factors that might influence the quantity being forecast. For example, a causal model for lawn-mower sales might include factors such as new housing starts, advertising budget, and competitors' prices.

Eight Steps to a Forecasting System

Forecasting always follows the same eight steps, regardless of the method used:

1. Determine the use of the forecast—what objectives are we trying to obtain?
2. Select the items that are to be forecasted.
3. Determine the time horizon of the forecast—is it short-, medium-, or long-term?
4. Select the forecasting model(s).
5. Gather the data needed to make the forecast.
6. Validate the forecasting model.
7. Make the forecast.
8. Implement the results.

These steps present a systematic way of initiating, designing, and implementing a forecasting system. When the system is to be used to generate forecasts regularly over time, data must be routinely collected. Then the actual computations used to make the forecast are usually done by computer. This is the process that virtually every retailer, from Wal-Mart to Sears to Bloomingdales, follows daily, using point-of-sale computer terminals as the data collection device. The *POM in Action* box "Expert Systems Change the Way Xerox Does Forecasting" describes how that firm developed its current forecasting system.

TIME-SERIES FORECASTING

A time series is based on a sequence of evenly spaced (weekly, monthly, quarterly, and so on) data points. Examples include weekly sales of Nike Air Jordans, quarterly earnings reports of Microsoft stock, daily shipments of Coors beer, and annual consumer price indices. Forecasting time-series data implies that future values are predicted *only* from past values and that other variables, no matter how potentially valuable, are ignored.

Decomposition of a Time Series

Analyzing time series means breaking down past data into components and then projecting them forward. A time series typically has four components: trend, seasonality, cycles, and random variation.

1. *Trend* is the gradual upward or downward movement of the data over time.
2. *Seasonality* is a data pattern that repeats itself after a period of days, weeks, months, or quarters (the latter being from where the term *seasonality* arose, that is, the seasons, fall, winter, spring, and summer). There are six common seasonality patterns:

PERIOD OF PATTERN	SEASON LENGTH	NUMBER OF SEASONS IN PATTERN
Week	Day	7
Month	Week	4–4½
Month	Day	28–31
Year	Quarter	4
Year	Month	12
Year	Week	52

3. *Cycles* are patterns in the data that occur every several years. They are usually tied into the business cycle and are of major importance in short-term business analysis and planning.
4. *Random variations* are "blips" in the data caused by chance and unusual situations. They follow no discernible pattern.

Figure 5.1 shows a time series and its components.

There are two general forms of time-series models in statistics. The most widely used is a multiplicative model, which assumes that demand is the product of the four components:

$$\text{Demand} = \text{trend} \times \text{seasonality} \times \text{cycle} \times \text{random variation}$$

Expert Systems Change the Way Xerox Does Forecasting

"Expert systems" and "artificial intelligence" are not the most commonly used terms in the corporate boardroom. Becoming increasingly popular, they describe computer systems that use knowledge about a specific complex application area to act as an expert consultant to users. Using this new software, which in effect permits a computer to mimic human reasoning, has made planning at Xerox Corp. much more flexible than ever.

Until 1990, the copier giant's seven-member sales forecasting team used a hodgepodge of forecasting models and methods to do its job. At one extreme, analysts graphed historical data and extrap-

olated it into the future for each line of copier. These graphs were then distributed within the company. At the other extreme, some analysts used spreadsheet models such as Lotus 1-2-3. This patchwork approach was so laborious and took so long to develop that next year's forecast was started in July of the preceding year. Further, the team could only manage to forecast out the next 12 months.

Now, after 2 years of development, a new forecasting model using expert systems is up and running. Not only can Xerox wait until October to start developing the next forecast, but the firm can now make forecasts for 3 years out. And the new system constantly analyzes actual results versus the forecast, updating its parameters to refine its accuracy. Further, the time saved allows the Xerox team to consider how factors outside the firm, such as inflation or rivals' activities, might affect future sales.

Sources: Business Week (November 2, 1992): 133–136; *CIO* (August 1993): 38–46; and *MIS Quarterly* (September 1990): 323–329.

An additive model provides an estimate by adding the components together. It is stated as

$$\text{Demand} = \text{trend} + \text{seasonality} + \text{cycle} + \text{random variation}$$

In most real-world models, forecasters assume that the random variations are averaged out over time. They then concentrate on only the seasonal component and a component that is a combination of trend and cyclical factors.

FIGURE 5.1   ■   Product Demand Charted over 4 Years with Trend and Seasonality Indicated

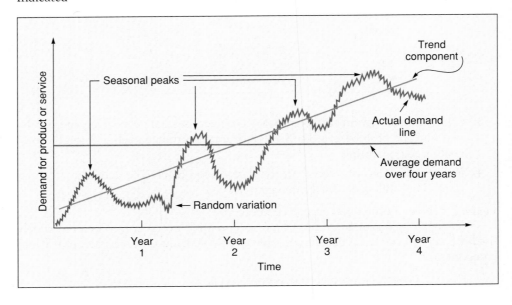

Naive Approach

The simplest way to forecast is to assume that demand in the next period is just equal to demand in the most recent period. In other words, if sales of a product, say, Motorola cellular phones, were 68 units in January, we can forecast that February's sales will also be 68 phones. Does this make any sense? It turns out that for some product lines, selecting this **naive approach** is the most cost-effective and efficient objective forecasting model. It at least provides a starting point against which the more sophisticated models that follow can be compared.

Naive approach

Moving Averages

A **moving-average** forecast uses a number of recent actual data values to generate a forecast. Moving averages are useful if we can assume that market demands will stay fairly steady over time. A 4-month moving average is found by simply summing the demand during the past 4 months and dividing by 4. With each passing month, the most recent month's data are added to the sum of the previous 3 months' data, and the earliest month is dropped. This tends to smooth out short-term irregularities in the data series.

Moving averages

Mathematically, the simple moving average (which serves as an estimate of the next period's demand) is expressed as

$$\text{Moving average} = \frac{\Sigma \text{ demand in previous } n \text{ periods}}{n} \qquad (5.1)$$

where n is the number of periods in the moving average—for example, 4, 5, or 6 months, respectively, for a 4-, 5-, or 6-period moving average.

Example 1 shows how moving averages are calculated.

EXAMPLE 1

Storage shed sales at Donna's Garden Supply are shown in the middle column of the table. A 3-month moving average appears on the right.

MONTH	ACTUAL SHED SALES	3-MONTH MOVING AVERAGE
January	10	
February	12	
March	13	
April	16	$(10 + 12 + 13)/3 = 11\frac{2}{3}$
May	19	$(12 + 13 + 16)/3 = 13\frac{2}{3}$
June	23	$(13 + 16 + 19)/3 = 16$
July	26	$(16 + 19 + 23)/3 = 19\frac{1}{3}$
August	30	$(19 + 23 + 26)/3 = 22\frac{2}{3}$
September	28	$(23 + 26 + 30)/3 = 26\frac{1}{3}$
October	18	$(26 + 30 + 28)/3 = 28$
November	16	$(30 + 28 + 18)/3 = 25\frac{1}{3}$
December	14	$(28 + 18 + 16)/3 = 20\frac{2}{3}$

When there is a detectable trend or pattern, weights can be used to place more emphasis on recent values. This makes the techniques more responsive to changes because more recent periods may be more heavily weighted. Choice of weights is somewhat arbitrary because there is no set formula to determine them. Therefore, deciding which weights to use requires some experience and a bit of luck. If the latest month or period is weighted too heavily, the forecast might reflect a large unusual change in the demand or sales pattern too quickly.

A weighted moving average may be expressed mathematically as

$$\frac{\text{Weighted}}{\text{moving average}} = \frac{\Sigma \,(\text{weight for period } n)\,(\text{demand in period } n)}{\Sigma \,\text{weights}} \qquad (5.2)$$

Example 2 shows how to calculate a weighted moving average.

EXAMPLE 2

Donna's Garden Supply (see Example 1) decides to forecast storage shed sales by weighting the past 3 months as follows:

WEIGHTS APPLIED	PERIOD
③	Last month
②	Two months ago
①	Three months ago
6	Sum of weights

Forecast for this month =

$$\frac{③ \times \text{sales last mo.} + ② \times \text{sales 2 mos. ago} + ① \times \text{sales 3 mos. ago}}{6 \longleftarrow \text{sum of the weights}}$$

The results of this weighted average forecast are as follows:

MONTH	ACTUAL SHED SALES	THREE-MONTH WEIGHTED MOVING AVERAGE
January	10	
February	12	
March	13	
April	16	$[(3 \times 13) + (2 \times 12) + (10)]/6 = 12\frac{1}{6}$
May	19	$[(3 \times 16) + (2 \times 13) + (12)]/6 = 14\frac{1}{3}$
June	23	$[(3 \times 19) + (2 \times 16) + (13)]/6 = 17$
July	26	$[(3 \times 23) + (2 \times 19) + (16)]/6 = 20\frac{1}{2}$
August	30	$[(3 \times 26) + (2 \times 23) + (19)]/6 = 23\frac{5}{6}$
September	28	$[(3 \times 30) + (2 \times 26) + (23)]/6 = 27\frac{1}{2}$
October	18	$[(3 \times 28) + (2 \times 30) + (26)]/6 = 28\frac{1}{3}$
November	16	$[(3 \times 18) + (2 \times 28) + (30)]/6 = 23\frac{1}{3}$
December	14	$[(3 \times 16) + (2 \times 18) + (28)]/6 = 18\frac{2}{3}$

In this particular forecasting situation, you can see that weighting the latest month more heavily provides a much more accurate projection.

Both simple and weighted moving averages are effective in smoothing out sudden fluctuations in the demand pattern in order to provide stable estimates. Moving averages do, however, have three problems. First, increasing the size of n (the number of periods averaged) does smooth out fluctuations better, but it makes the method less sensitive to *real* changes in the data. Second, moving averages cannot pick up trends very well. Because they are averages, they will always stay within past levels and will not predict a change to either a higher or lower level. Finally, moving averages require extensive records of past data.

Figure 5.2, a plot of the data in Examples 1 and 2, illustrates the lag effect of the moving-average models.

Exponential Smoothing

Exponential smoothing is a sophisticated weighted moving-average forecasting method that is still fairly easy to use. It involves very *little* record keeping of past data. The basic exponential smoothing formula can be shown as follows:

Exponential smoothing

New forecast = last period's forecast +
$\quad\quad\quad$ α(last period's actual demand − last period's forecast) $\quad\quad$ (5.3)

where α is a weight, or **smoothing constant,** chosen by the forecaster, that has a value from 0 and 1. Equation (5.3) can also be written mathematically as

Smoothing constant

$$F_t = F_{t-1} + \alpha(A_{t-1} - F_{t-1}) \tag{5.4}$$

FIGURE 5.2 ■ Actual Demand vs. Moving-Average and Weighted Moving-Average Methods for Donna's Garden Supply

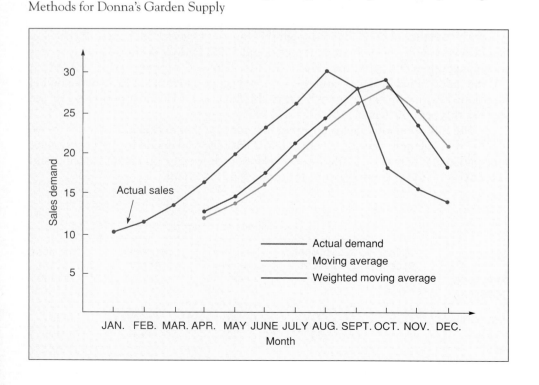

where F_t = new forecast
F_{t-1} = previous forecast
α = smoothing constant $(0 \leq \alpha \leq 1)$
A_{t-1} = previous period's actual demand

The concept is not complex. The latest estimate of demand is equal to our old estimate adjusted by a fraction of the difference between the last period's actual demand and the old estimate. Example 3 shows how to use exponential smoothing to derive a forecast.

EXAMPLE 3

In January, a car dealer predicted a February demand for 142 Ford Mustangs. Actual February demand was 153 autos. Using a smoothing constant chosen by management, of $\alpha = .20$, we can forecast the March demand using the exponential smoothing model. Substituting into the formula, we obtain

$$\text{New forecast (for March demand)} = 142 + .2(153 - 142)$$
$$= 144.2$$

Thus, the demand forecast for Ford Mustangs in March is rounded to 144.

The *smoothing constant*, α, is generally in the range from .05 to .50 for business applications. It can be changed to give more weight to recent data (when α is high) or more weight to past data (when α is low). To demonstrate this weighting concept, Equation 5.4 can be rewritten algebraically in the form

$$F_t = \alpha A_{t-1} + \alpha(1 - \alpha)A_{t-2} + \alpha(1 - \alpha)^2 A_{t-3} +$$
$$\alpha(1 - \alpha)^3 A_{t-4} + \cdots + \alpha(1 - \alpha)^n A_{t-n} \quad (5.5)$$

where the weights add to 1. Even though this time series goes back n periods (where n can be a very long time), the importance of older past periods declines quickly as α is increased. When α reaches the extreme of 1.0, then in Equation (5.5), $F_t = 1.0A_{t-1}$. All the older values drop out, and the forecast becomes identical to the naive model mentioned earlier in this chapter. That is, the forecast for the next period is just the same as this period's demand.

The following table helps illustrate this concept. For example, when $\alpha = .5$, we can see that the new forecast is based almost entirely on demand in the last three or four periods. When $\alpha = .1$, the forecast places little weight on recent demand and takes *many* periods (about 19) of historic values into account.

	WEIGHT ASSIGNED TO				
SMOOTHING CONSTANT	MOST RECENT PERIOD (α)	2ND MOST RECENT PERIOD $\alpha(1 - \alpha)$	3RD MOST RECENT PERIOD $\alpha(1 - \alpha)^2$	4TH MOST RECENT PERIOD $\alpha(1 - \alpha)^3$	5TH MOST RECENT PERIOD $\alpha(1 - \alpha)^4$
$\alpha = .1$	.1	.09	.081	.073	.066
$\alpha = .5$	.5	.25	.125	.063	.031

SELECTING THE SMOOTHING CONSTANT. The exponential smoothing approach is easy to use, and it has been successfully applied in virtually every type of business. The appropriate value of the smoothing constant, α, however, can make the difference between an accurate forecast and an inaccurate forecast. In picking a value for the smoothing constant, the objective is to obtain the most accurate forecast. The overall accuracy of a forecasting model can be determined by comparing the forecasted values for past known periods with the actual or observed demand for those periods.

The forecast error is defined as

$$\text{Forecast error} = \text{demand} - \text{forecast}$$

MEAN ABSOLUTE DEVIATION. One measure of the overall forecast error for a model is the **mean absolute deviation (MAD)**. This value is computed by taking the sum of the absolute values of the individual forecast errors and dividing by the number of periods of data (n):

Mean absolute deviation (MAD)

$$\text{MAD} = \frac{\Sigma \, |\text{forecast errors}|}{n} \tag{5.6}$$

Example 4 applies this concept with a trial-and-error testing of two values of α.

EXAMPLE 4

The Port of Baltimore has unloaded large quantities of grain from ships during the past eight quarters. The port's operations manager wants to test the use of exponential smoothing to see how well the technique works in predicting tonnage unloaded. He guesses that the forecast of grain unloaded in the first quarter was 175 tons. Two values of α are examined: $\alpha = .10$ and $\alpha = .50$. The following table shows the *detailed* calculations for $\alpha = .10$ only:

QUARTER	ACTUAL TONNAGE UNLOADED	ROUNDED FORECAST USING $\alpha = .10$*	ROUNDED FORECAST USING $\alpha = .50$*
1	180	175	175
2	168	$176 = 175.00 + .10(180 - 175)$	178
3	159	$175 = 175.50 + .10(168 - 175.50)$	173
4	175	$173 = 174.75 + .10(159 - 174.75)$	166
5	190	$173 = 173.18 + .10(175 - 173.18)$	170
6	205	$175 = 173.36 + .10(190 - 173.36)$	180
7	180	$178 = 175.02 + .10(205 - 175.02)$	193
8	182	$178 = 178.02 + .10(180 - 178.02)$	186
9	?	$179 = 178.22 + .10(182 - 178.22)$	184

*Forecasts rounded to the nearest ton.

To evaluate the accuracy of each smoothing constant, we can compute the absolute deviations and MADs.

Quarter	Actual Tonnage Unloaded	Rounded Forecast with $\alpha = .10$	Absolute Deviation for $\alpha = .10$	Rounded Forecast with $\alpha = .50$	Absolute Deviation for $\alpha = .50$
1	180	175	5	175	5
2	168	176	8	178	10
3	159	175	16	173	14
4	175	173	2	166	9
5	190	173	17	170	20
6	205	175	30	180	25
7	180	178	2	193	13
8	182	178	4	186	4
		Sum of absolute deviations	84		100
	$\text{MAD} = \dfrac{\Sigma \,\lvert\text{deviations}\rvert}{n}$		10.50		12.50

On the basis of this analysis, a smoothing constant of $\alpha = .10$ is preferred to $\alpha = .50$ because its MAD is smaller.

Most computerized forecasting software includes a feature that automatically finds the smoothing constant with the lowest forecast error. Some software modifies the alpha value if errors become larger than acceptable.

Mean squared error (MSE)

MEAN SQUARED ERROR.   The **mean squared error (MSE)** is another way of measuring overall forecast error. MSE is the average of the squared differences between the forecasted and observed values. Its formula is

$$\text{MSE} = \frac{\Sigma \,\text{forecast errors}^2}{n} \tag{5.7}$$

Example 5 finds the MSE for the Port of Baltimore noted in Example 4.

EXAMPLE 5

Quarter	Actual Tonnage Unloaded	Forecast for $\alpha = .10$	$(\text{Error})^2$
1	180	175	$5^2 = 25$
2	168	176	$8^2 = 64$
3	159	175	$(16)^2 = 256$
4	175	173	$2^2 = 4$
5	190	173	$(17)^2 = 289$
6	205	175	$(30)^2 = 900$
7	180	178	$2^2 = 4$
8	182	178	$4^2 = 16$
			Sum of errors squared $= 1,558$

$$\text{MSE} = \frac{\Sigma \,\text{forecast errors}^2}{n} = 1{,}558/8 = 194.75$$

Is this MSE good or bad? The answer is, it all depends on the MSEs for other values of α. As a practice exercise, find the MSE for $\alpha = .50$. (You should get MSE = 201.5.) This indicates that $\alpha = .10$ is a better choice because we want to minimize MSE. Coincidentally, this confirms the conclusion we reached in Example 4 using MAD.

Exponential Smoothing with Trend Adjustment

As with any moving-average technique, simple exponential smoothing fails to respond to trends. To illustrate a more complex exponential smoothing model, let us consider one that adjusts for trend. The idea is to compute a simple exponential smoothing forecast as before and then adjust for positive or negative lag in trend. The formula is

Forecast including trend (FIT_t) = new forecast (F_t) + trend correction (T_t)

To smooth out the trend, the equation for the trend correction uses a smoothing constant, β, in the same way the simple exponential model uses α. T_t is computed by

$$T_t = (1 - \beta)T_{t-1} + \beta(F_t - F_{t-1}) \qquad (5.8)$$

where T_t = smoothed trend for period t

T_{t-1} = smoothed trend for previous period

β = trend-smoothing constant that we select

F_t = simple exponential smoothed forecast for period t

F_{t-1} = forecast for previous period

There are three steps to compute a trend-adjusted forecast.

Step 1. Compute a simple exponential forecast for time period t (F_t).

Step 2. Compute the trend by using the equation

$$T_t = (1 - \beta)T_{t-1} + \beta(F_t - F_{t-1})$$

To start step 2 for the first time, an initial trend value must be inserted (either by a good guess or by observed past data). After that, trend is computed.

Step 3. Calculate the trend-adjusted exponential smoothing forecast (FIT_t) by the formula

$$FIT_t = F_t + T_t$$

Example 6 shows how to use trend-adjusted exponential smoothing.

EXAMPLE 6

A large Portland manufacturer uses exponential smoothing to forecast demand for a pollution-control equipment product. It appears that an increasing trend is present.

MONTH	DEMAND	MONTH	DEMAND
1	12	6	26
2	17	7	31
3	20	8	32
4	19	9	36
5	24		

Smoothing constants are assigned the values of $\alpha = .2$ and $\beta = .4$. Assume the initial forecast for month 1 was 11 units.

Step 1. Forecast for month 2 (F_2) = forecast for month 1 (F_1) + α (month 1 demand − forecast for month 1):

$$F_2 = 11 + .2(12 − 11)$$
$$= 11.0 + .2 = 11.2 \text{ units}$$

Step 2. Compute the trend present. Assume an initial trend adjustment of zero, that is, $T_1 = 0$.

$$T_2 = (1 − \beta)T_1 + \beta(F_2 − F_1)$$
$$= 0 + 4(11.2 − 11.0)$$
$$= .08$$

Step 3. Compute the forecast including trend (FIT_t):

$$FIT_2 = F_2 + T_2$$
$$= 11.2 + .08$$
$$= 11.28 \text{ units}$$

We will do the same calculations for the third month also.

Step 1. $F_3 = F_2 + \alpha(\text{demand in month } 2 − F_2)$
$$= 11.2 + .2(17 − 11.2) = 12.36$$

Step 2. $T_3 = (1 − \beta)T_2 + \beta(F_3 − F_2)$
$$= (1 − .4)(.08) + .4(12.36 − 11.2) = .51$$

Step 3. $FIT_3 = F_3 + T_3$
$$= 12.36 + .51 = 12.87$$

So the simple exponential forecast (without trend) for month 2 was 11.2 units, and the trend-adjusted forecast was 11.28 units. In month 3, the simple forecast (without trend) was 12.36 units, and the trend-adjusted forecast was 12.87 units. Naturally, different values of T_1 and β can produce even better estimates.

The following table completes the forecasts for the 9-month period. Figure 5.3 compares actual demand, forecast without trend (F_t), and forecast with trend (FIT_t). Note that although FIT_t is better than F_t in this case, it is still not perfect in predicting actual demand. Perhaps a higher value of β would help.

Month	Actual Demand	Forecast, F_T (Without Trend)	Trend	Adjusted FIT_T
1	12	11.00	0	—
2	17	11.20	.08	11.28
3	20	12.36	.51	12.87
4	19	13.89	.92	14.81
5	24	14.91	.96	15.87
6	26	16.73	1.30	18.03
7	31	18.58	1.52	20.10
8	32	21.07	1.91	22.98
9	36	23.25	2.02	25.27

FIGURE 5.3 ■ Actual Compared to Forecasts

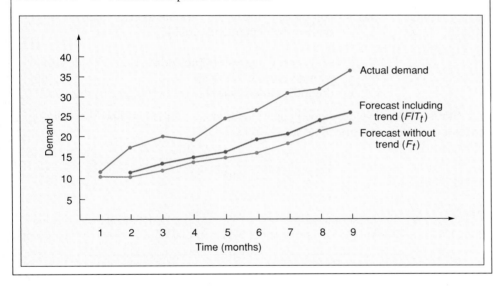

The value of the trend-smoothing constant, β, resembles the α constant because a high β is more responsive to recent changes in trend. A low β gives less weight to the most recent trends and tends to smooth out the present trend. Values of β can be found by the trial-and-error approach, or by using sophisticated commercial forecasting software, with the MAD used as a measure of comparison.

Simple exponential smoothing is often referred to as first-order smoothing, and trend-adjusted smoothing is called second-order, or double, smoothing. Other advanced exponential smoothing models are also in use, including seasonal-adjusted and triple smoothing, but these are beyond the scope of this book.[2]

---

[2]For more details, see E. S. Gardner, "Exponential Smoothing: The State of the Art." *Journal of Forecasting*, 4, no. 1 (March 1985) or R. Brown, *Smoothing, Forecasting and Prediction* (Englewood Cliffs, NJ: Prentice Hall, 1973).

₴nd Projections

₴ last time-series forecasting method we will discuss is **trend projection**. This tech-
₴ue fits a trend line to a series of historical data points and then projects the line
₴ the future for medium-to-long-range forecasts. Several mathematical trend equa-
₴s can be developed (for example, exponential and quadratic), but in this section,
₴will look at *linear* (straight-line) trends only.

If we decide to develop a linear trend line by a precise statistical method, we
₴ apply the *least squares method*. This approach results in a straight line that minimizes the sum of the squares of the vertical differences from the line to each of the actual observations. Figure 5.4 illustrates the least squares approach.

A least squares line is described in terms of its *y*-intercept (the height at which
it intercepts the *y*-axis) and its slope (the angle of the line). If we can compute the
y-intercept and slope, we can express the line with the following equation:

$$\hat{y} = a + bx \tag{5.9}$$

where $\hat{y}$ (called "y hat") = computed value of the variable to be predicted
               (called the dependent variable)

a = y-axis intercept

b = slope of the regression line (or the rate of change in
               y for given changes in x)

x = the independent variable (which is *time* in this case)

Statisticians have developed equations that we can use to find the values of a
and b for any regression line. The slope b is found by

$$b = \frac{\Sigma xy - n\overline{x}\,\overline{y}}{\Sigma x^2 - n\overline{x}^2} \tag{5.10}$$

FIGURE 5.4   ■   The Least Squares Method for Finding the Best-Fitting Straight Line,
Where the Asterisks Are the Locations of the Seven Actual Observations or Data Points

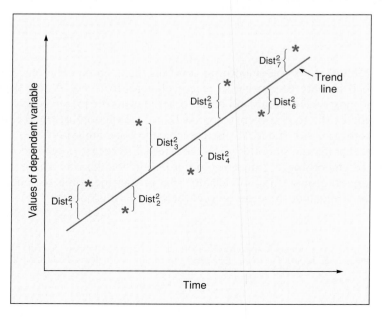

where b = slope of the regression line
        Σ = summation sign
        x = values of the independent variable
        y = values of the dependent variable
        $\bar{x}$ = average of the value of the x's
        $\bar{y}$ = average of the value of the y's
        n = number of data points or observations

We can compute the y-intercept a as follows:

$$a = \bar{y} - b\bar{x} \qquad (5.11)$$

Example 7 shows how to apply these concepts.

EXAMPLE 7

The demand for electrical power at N.Y. Edison over the period 1989–95 is shown below, in megawatts. Let us fit a straight-line trend to these data and forecast 1996 demand.

YEAR	ELECTRICAL POWER DEMAND	YEAR	ELECTRICAL POWER DEMAND
1989	74	1993	105
1990	79	1994	142
1991	80	1995	122
1992	90		

With a series of data over time, we can minimize the computations by transforming the values of x (time) to simpler numbers. Thus, in this case, we can designate 1989 as year 1, 1990 as year 2, and so on.

YEAR	TIME PERIOD	ELECTRIC POWER DEMAND	x^2	XY
1989	1	74	1	74
1990	2	79	4	158
1991	3	80	9	240
1992	4	90	16	360
1993	5	105	25	525
1994	6	142	36	852
1995	7	122	49	854
	$\Sigma x = 28$	$\Sigma y = 692$	$\Sigma x^2 = 140$	$\Sigma xy = 3,063$

$$\bar{x} = \frac{\Sigma x}{n} = \frac{28}{7} = 4 \qquad \bar{y} = \frac{\Sigma y}{n} = \frac{692}{7} = 98.86$$

$$b = \frac{\Sigma xy - n\bar{x}\bar{y}}{\Sigma x^2 - n\bar{x}^2} = \frac{3,063 - (7)(4)(98.86)}{140 - (7)(4^2)} = \frac{295}{28} = 10.54$$

$$a = \bar{y} - b\bar{x} = 98.86 - 10.54(4) = 56.70$$

Hence, the least squares trend equation is $\hat{y} = 56.70 + 10.54x$. To project demand in 1996, we first denote the year 1996 in our new coding system as $x = 8$:

$$\text{Demand in 1996} = 56.70 + 10.54(8)$$
$$= 141.02, \text{ or } 141 \text{ megawatts}$$

We can estimate demand for 1997 by inserting $x = 9$ in the same equation:

$$\text{Demand in 1997} = 56.70 + 10.54(9)$$
$$= 151.56, \text{ or } 152 \text{ megawatts}$$

To check the validity of the model, we plot historical demand and the trend line in Figure 5.5. In this case, we may wish to be cautious and try to understand the 1994–1995 swings in demand.

FIGURE 5.5 ■ Electrical Power and the Computed Trend Line

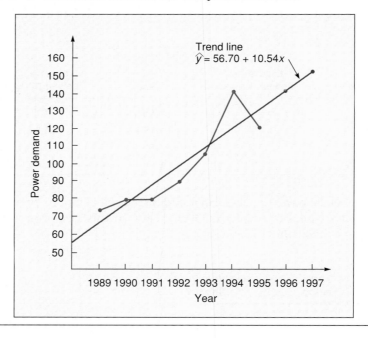

SEASONAL VARIATIONS IN DATA

Time-series forecasting such as that in Example 7 involves looking at the *trend* of data over a series of time observations. As we stated before, however, seasonality sometimes makes adjustment in the trend-line forecast necessary. Demand for coal and fuel oil, for example, usually peaks during cold winter months. Demand for golf clubs or suntan lotion may be highest in summer. Analyzing data in monthly or quarterly terms usually makes it easy for a statistician to spot seasonal patterns. Seasonal indices can then be developed by several common methods. Example 8 illustrates one way to compute seasonal factors from historical data.

EXAMPLE 8

Monthly sales of Compaq Company laptop computers at Reva Computerland are shown below for 1993–1994.

Month	Sales Demand 1993	Sales Demand 1994	Average 1993–1994 Demand	Average Monthly Demand*	Seasonal Index[†]
Jan.	80	100	90	94	.957
Feb.	75	85	80	94	.851
Mar.	80	90	85	94	.904
Apr.	90	110	100	94	1.064
May	115	131	123	94	1.309
June	110	120	115	94	1.223
July	100	110	105	94	1.117
Aug.	90	110	100	94	1.064
Sept.	85	95	90	94	.957
Oct.	75	85	80	94	.851
Nov.	75	85	80	94	.851
Dec.	80	80	80	94	.851
			Total average demand = 1,128		

*Average monthly demand $= \dfrac{1,128}{12 \text{ months}} = 94$

[†]Seasonal index $= \dfrac{\text{average 1993–94 demand}}{\text{average monthly demand}}$

Using these seasonal indices, if we expected the 1995 annual demand for computers to be 1,200 units, we would forecast the monthly demand as follows:

Month	Demand	Month	Demand
Jan.	$\dfrac{1,200}{12} \times .957 = 96$	July	$\dfrac{1,200}{12} \times 1.117 = 112$
Feb.	$\dfrac{1,200}{12} \times .851 = 85$	Aug.	$\dfrac{1,200}{12} \times 1.064 = 106$
Mar.	$\dfrac{1,200}{12} \times .904 = 90$	Sept.	$\dfrac{1,200}{12} \times .957 = 96$
Apr.	$\dfrac{1,200}{12} \times 1.064 = 106$	Oct.	$\dfrac{1,200}{12} \times .851 = 85$
May	$\dfrac{1,200}{12} \times 1.309 = 131$	Nov.	$\dfrac{1,200}{12} \times .851 = 85$
June	$\dfrac{1,200}{12} \times 1.223 = 122$	Dec.	$\dfrac{1,200}{12} \times .851 = 85$

For simplicity, trend calculations were ignored and only two periods were used for each monthly index in the above example. Example 9 illustrates how indices that have already been prepared can be applied to adjust trend line forecasts.

EXAMPLE 9

Management of Davis's Department Store has used time-series regression to forecast retail sales for the next four quarters. The sales estimates are $100,000, $120,000, $140,000, and $160,000 for the respective quarters. Seasonal indices for the four quarters have been found to be 1.30, .90, .70, and 1.15, respectively.

To compute a seasonalized or adjusted sales forecast, we just multiply each seasonal index by the appropriate trend forecast:

$$\hat{y}_{seasonal} = \text{Index} \times \hat{y}_{trend\ forecast}$$

Hence for

Quarter I:	$\hat{y}_I = (1.30)(\$100,000) = \$130,000$
Quarter II:	$\hat{y}_{II} = (.90)(\$120,000) = \$108,000$
Quarter III:	$\hat{y}_{III} = (.70)(\$140,000) = \$98,000$
Quarter IV:	$\hat{y}_{IV} = (1.15)(\$160,000) = \$184,000$

CAUSAL FORECASTING METHODS: REGRESSION AND CORRELATION ANALYSIS

Unlike time-series forecasting, *causal forecasting* models usually consider *several* variables that are related to the quantity being predicted. Once these related variables have been found, a statistical model is built and used to forecast the item of interest. This approach is more powerful than the time-series methods that use only the historic values for the forecasted variable.

Many factors can be considered in a causal analysis. For example, the sales of IBM PCs might be related to IBM's advertising budget, the price charged, competitors' prices and promotional strategies, or even the economy and unemployment rates. In this case, PC sales would be called the *dependent variable* and the other variables would be called *independent variables*. The manager's job is to develop the best statistical relationship between PC sales and the independent variables. The most **Linear-regression analysis** common quantitative causal forecasting model is **linear-regression analysis**.

Using Regression Analysis to Forecast

We can use the same mathematical model we employed in the least squares method of trend projection to perform a linear-regression analysis. The dependent variables that we want to forecast will still be $\hat{y}$. But now the independent variable, x, need no longer be time.

$$\hat{y} = a + bx$$

where $\hat{y}$ = value of the dependent variable, sales here

a = y-axis intercept
b = slope of the regression line
x = independent variable

Example 10 shows how to use linear regression.

EXAMPLE 10

Tongren Construction Company renovates old homes in Orono, Maine. Over time, the company has found that its dollar volume of renovation work is dependent on the Orono area payroll. The following table lists Tongren's revenues and the amount of money earned by wage earners in Orono during the years 1990–1995.

TONGREN'S SALES ($000,000), Y	LOCAL PAYROLL ($000,000,000), X	TONGREN'S SALES ($000,000), Y	LOCAL PAYROLL ($000,000,000), X
2.0	1	2.0	2
3.0	3	2.0	1
2.5	4	3.5	7

Tongren's management wants to establish a mathematical relationship that will help it predict sales. First, it needs to determine whether there is a straight-line (linear) relationship between area payroll and sales, so it plots the known data on a scatter diagram.

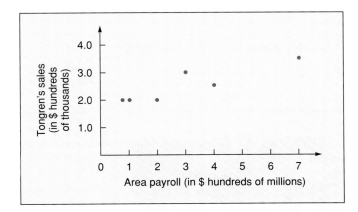

It appears from the six data points that there is a slight positive relationship between the independent variable, payroll, and the dependent variable, sales. As payroll increases, Tongren's sales tend to be higher.

We can find a mathematical equation by using the least-squares regression approach.

SALES, Y	PAYROLL, X	x^2	XY
2.0	1	1	2.0
3.0	3	9	9.0
2.5	4	16	10.0
2.0	2	4	4.0
2.0	1	1	2.0
3.5	7	49	24.5
$\Sigma y = 15.0$	$\Sigma x = 18$	$\Sigma x^2 = 80$	$\Sigma xy = 51.5$

$$\bar{x} = \frac{\Sigma x}{6} = \frac{18}{6} = 3$$

$$\bar{y} = \frac{\Sigma y}{6} = \frac{15}{6} = 2.5$$

$$b = \frac{\Sigma xy - n\bar{x}\bar{y}}{\Sigma x^2 - n\bar{x}^2} = \frac{51.5 - (6)(3)(2.5)}{80 - (6)(3^2)} = .25$$

$$a = \bar{y} - b\bar{x} = 2.5 - (.25)(3) = 1.75$$

The estimated regression equation, therefore, is

$$\hat{y} = 1.75 + .25x$$

or

$$\text{Sales} = 1.75 + .25 \text{ (payroll)}$$

If the local chamber of commerce predicts that the Orono area payroll will be $6 hundred million next year, we can estimate sales for Tongren with the regression equation:

$$\text{Sales (in hundred thousands)} = 1.75 + .25(6)$$
$$= 1.75 + 1.50 = 3.25$$

or

$$\text{Sales} = \$325,000$$

Glidden Paints assembly lines fill thousands of cans per hour. To predict demand for its products, the firm uses causal forecasting methods such as linear regression, with independent variables such as disposable personal income and GNP. Although housing starts would be a natural variable, Glidden found it correlated poorly with past sales. It turns out that most Glidden paint is sold through retailers to customers who already own homes or businesses.

FIGURE 5.6 ■ Distribution about the Point Estimate of $600 Million Payroll

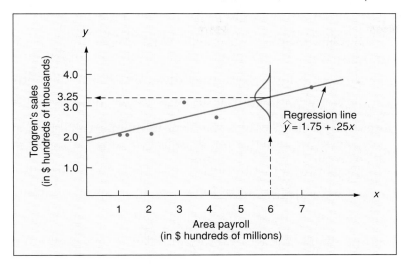

The final part of Example 10 shows a central weakness of causal forecasting methods like regression. Even when we have computed a regression equation, it is necessary to provide a forecast of the independent variable x—in this case, payroll—before estimating the dependent variable y for the next time period. Although this is not a problem for all forecasts, you can imagine the difficulty of determining future values of *some* common independent variables (such as unemployment rates, gross national product, price indices, and so on).

Standard Error of the Estimate

The forecast of $325,000 for Tongren's sales in Example 10 is called a *point estimate* of y. The point estimate is really the mean, or expected value, of a distribution of possible values of sales. Figure 5.6 illustrates this concept.

To measure the accuracy of the regression estimates, we need to compute the **standard error of the estimate**, $S_{y,x}$. This is called the *standard deviation of the regression*. Equation (5.12) is a similar expression to that found in most statistics books for computing the standard deviation of an arithmetic mean:

Standard error of the estimate

$$S_{y,x} = \sqrt{\frac{\Sigma(y - y_c)^2}{n - 2}} \tag{5.12}$$

where y = y-value of each data point
  y_c = computed value of the dependent variable, from the regression equation
  n = number of data points

Equation (5.13) may look more complex, but it is actually an easier-to-use version of Equation (5.12). Either formula provides the same answer and can be used in setting up prediction intervals around the point estimate.[3]

[3]When the sample size is large ($n > 30$), the prediction interval value of y can be computed using normal tables. When the number of observations is small, the t-distribution is appropriate. See J. Neter, W. Wasserman, and S. Whitmore, *Applied Statistics*, 3rd ed. (Newton, MA: Allyn & Bacon, 1991).

$$S_{y,x} = \sqrt{\frac{\Sigma y^2 - a\Sigma y - b\Sigma xy}{n-2}} \qquad (5.13)$$

Example 11 shows how we would calculate the standard error of the estimate in Example 10.

EXAMPLE 11

Let us compute the standard error of the estimate for Tongren's data in Example 10. The only number we need that is not available to solve for $S_{y,x}$ is Σy^2. Some quick addition reveals $\Sigma y^2 = 39.5$. Therefore,

$$S_{y,x} = \sqrt{\frac{\Sigma y^2 - a\Sigma y - b\Sigma xy}{n-2}}$$

$$= \sqrt{\frac{39.5 - 1.75(15.0) - .25(51.5)}{6-2}}$$

$$= \sqrt{.09375} = .306 \text{ (in \$ hundred thousands)}$$

The standard error of the estimate is then $30,600 in sales.

Correlation Coefficients for Regression Lines

The regression equation is one way of expressing the nature of the relationship between two variables. Regression lines are not "cause-and-effect" relationships. They merely describe the relationship between variables. The regression equation shows how one variable relates to the value and changes in another variable.

Coefficient of correlation

   Another way to evaluate the relationship between two variables is to compute the **coefficient of correlation**. This measure expresses the degree or strength of the linear relationship. Usually identified as r, the coefficient of correlation can be any number between $+1$ and -1. Figure 5.7 illustrates what different values of r might look like.

FIGURE 5.7 ■ Four Values of the Correlation Coefficient

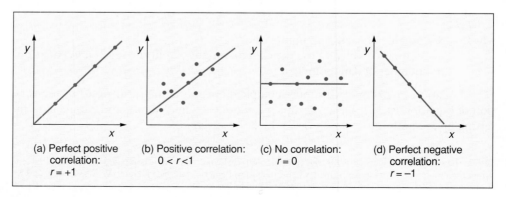

(a) Perfect positive correlation: $r = +1$

(b) Positive correlation: $0 < r < 1$

(c) No correlation: $r = 0$

(d) Perfect negative correlation: $r = -1$

To compute r, we use much of the same data needed earlier to calculate a and b for the regression line. The rather lengthy equation for r is

$$r = \frac{n\Sigma xy - \Sigma x \Sigma y}{\sqrt{[n\Sigma x^2 - (\Sigma x)^2][n\Sigma y^2 - (\Sigma y)^2]}} \tag{5.14}$$

Example 12 shows how to calculate the coefficient of correlation for the data in Examples 10 and 11.

EXAMPLE 12

In Example 10, we looked at the relationship between Tongren Construction Company's renovation sales and payroll in Orono. To compute the coefficient of correlation for the data shown, we need only add one more column of calculations (for y^2) and then apply the equation for r.

Y	X	x^2	XY	Y^2	
2.0	1	1	2.0	4.0	
3.0	3	9	9.0	9.0	
2.5	4	16	10.0	6.25	New
2.0	2	4	4.0	4.0	column
2.0	1	1	2.0	4.0	
3.5	7	49	24.5	12.25	
$\Sigma y = 15.0$	$\Sigma x = 18$	$\Sigma x^2 = 80$	$\Sigma xy = 51.5$	$\Sigma y^2 = 39.5$	

$$r = \frac{(6)(51.5) - (18)(15.0)}{\sqrt{[(6)(80) - (18)^2][(6)(39.5) - (15.0)^2]}}$$

$$= \frac{309 - 270}{\sqrt{(156)(12)}} = \frac{39}{\sqrt{1,872}}$$

$$= \frac{39}{43.3} = .901$$

This r of .901 appears to be a significant correlation and helps to confirm the closeness of the relationship between the two variables.

Although the coefficient of correlation is the measure most commonly used to describe the relationship between two variables, another measure does exist. It is called the *coefficient of determination* and is simply the square of the coefficient of correlation, namely, r^2. The value of r^2 will always be a positive number in the range of $0 \leq r^2 \leq 1$. The coefficient of determination is the percent of variation in the dependent variable (y) that is explained by the regression equation. In Tongren's case, the value of r^2 is .81, indicating that 81% of the total variation is explained by the regression equation.

Multiple-Regression Analysis

Multiple regression

Multiple regression is a practical extension of the simple regression model we just explored. It allows us to build a model with several independent variables instead of just one variable. For example, if Tongren Construction wanted to include average annual interest rates in its model to forecast renovation sales, the proper equation would be

$$\hat{y} = a + b_1 x_1 + b_2 x_2 \tag{5.15}$$

where
$\hat{y}$ = dependent variable, sales
a = y-intercept
x_1 and x_2 = values of the two independent variables,
area payroll and interest rates, respectively
b_1 and b_2 = slopes for the two independent variables

The mathematics of multiple regression becomes quite complex (and is usually tackled by computer), so we leave the formulas for a, b_1, and b_2 to statistics textbooks. However, Example 13 shows how to interpret Equation (5.15) in forecasting Tongren's sales.

EXAMPLE 13

The new multiple-regression line for Tongren Construction, calculated by computer software, is

$$\hat{y} = 1.80 + .30x_1 - 5.0x_2$$

We also find that the new coefficient of correlation is .96, implying the inclusion of the variable x_2, interest rates, adds even more strength to the linear relationship.

We can now estimate Tongren's sales if we substitute values for next year's payroll and interest rate. If Orono's payroll will be $600 million and the interest rate will be .12 (12%), sales will be forecast as

$$\text{Sales (\$ hundred thousands)} = 1.80 + .30(6) - 5.0(.12)$$
$$= 1.8 + 1.8 - .6$$
$$= 3.00$$

or

$$\text{Sales} = \$300,000$$

MONITORING AND CONTROLLING FORECASTS

Once a forecast has been completed, it should not be forgotten. No manager wants to be reminded when his or her forecast is horribly inaccurate, but a firm needs to determine why the actual demand (or whatever variable is being examined) differed significantly from that projected. If the forecaster *is* accurate, that individual usually makes sure that everyone is aware of his or her talents. Very seldom does one read articles in *Fortune*, *Forbes*, or the *Wall Street Journal*, however, about money managers who are consistently off by 25% in their stock market forecasts.

Some of the best brains in the United States are concentrated in the field of short-term economic forecasting. However, even these forecasters sometimes make large errors. For example, in the summer of 1981, the median 1-year-ahead forecast of five prominent forecasters had predicted 2.1% growth in U.S. GNP for 1982. Instead, the economy plunged into a deep recession, with a GNP *decline* of 1.8%. As one journalist commented, "This is like forecasting partly cloudy and getting a 10-inch snowstorm instead."

One way to monitor forecasts to ensure they are performing well is to employ a tracking signal. A **tracking signal** is a measurement of how well the forecast is predicting actual values. As forecasts are updated every week, month, or quarter, the newly available demand data are compared to the forecast values.

Tracking signal

The tracking signal is computed as the *running sum of the forecast errors (RSFE)* divided by the *mean absolute deviation (MAD)*:

$$\binom{\text{Tracking}}{\text{signal}} = \frac{\text{RSFE}}{\text{MAD}}$$

$$= \frac{\Sigma(\text{actual demand in period } i - \text{forecast demand in period } i)}{\text{MAD}} \qquad (5.16)$$

where

$$\text{MAD} = \frac{\Sigma|\text{forecast errors}|}{n}$$

as seen earlier in Equation (5.6).

Positive tracking signals indicate that demand is greater than forecast. Negative signals mean that demand is less than forecast. A good tracking signal, that is, one with a low RSFE, has about as much positive error as it has negative error. In other words, small deviations are okay, but the positive and negative ones should balance one another so the tracking signal centers closely around zero.

Once tracking signals are calculated, they are compared to predetermined control limits. When a tracking signal exceeds an upper or lower limit, there is a problem with the forecasting method, and management may want to reevaluate the way it forecasts demand. Figure 5.8 shows the graph of a tracking signal that is exceeding the range of acceptable variation. If the model being used is exponential smoothing, perhaps the smoothing constant needs to be readjusted.

How do firms decide what the upper and lower tracking limits should be? There is no single answer, but they try to find reasonable values—in other words, limits not so low as to be triggered with every small forecast error, and not so high as to allow bad forecasts to be regularly overlooked. George Plossl and Oliver Wight, two inventory control experts, suggested using maximums of ±4 MADs for high-volume stock items and ±8 MADs for lower-volume items.[4] Other forecasters suggest slightly lower ranges. One MAD is equivalent to approximately .8 standard deviations, so that ±2 MADs = ±1.6 standard deviations, ±3 MADs = ±2.4 standard deviation, and ±4 MADs = ±3.2 standard deviations. This suggests that for a forecast to be "in control," 89% of the errors are expected to fall within ±2 MADs, 98% within ±3 MADs, or 99.9% within ±4 MADs.[5]

Example 14 shows how the tracking signal and RSFE can be computed.

EXAMPLE 14

Tom Tucker Bakery's quarterly sales of croissants (in thousands), as well as forecast demand and error computations, are shown below. The objective is to compute the tracking signal and determine whether forecasts are performing adequately.

QUARTER	FORECAST DEMAND	ACTUAL DEMAND	ERROR	RSFE	|FORECAST ERROR|	CUMULATIVE ERROR	MAD	TRACKING SIGNAL
1	100	90	−10	−10	10	10	10.0	−1
2	100	95	−5	−15	5	15	7.5	−2
3	100	115	+15	0	15	30	10.0	0
4	110	100	−10	−10	10	40	10.0	−1
5	110	125	+15	+5	15	55	11.0	+.5
6	110	140	+30	+35	30	85	14.2	+2.5

$$\text{MAD} = \frac{\Sigma |\text{forecast errors}|}{n} = \frac{85}{6} = 14.2$$

$$\text{Tracking signal} = \frac{\text{RSFE}}{\text{MAD}} = \frac{35}{14.2} = 2.5 \text{ MADs}$$

This tracking signal is within acceptable limits. We see that it drifted from −2.0 MADs to +2.5 MADs.

Adaptive Smoothing

A lot of research has been published on the subject of adaptive forecasting. Adaptive forecasting refers to computer monitoring of tracking signals and self-adjustment if a signal passes its preset limit. For example, when applied to exponential smoothing, the α and β coefficients are first selected on the basis of values that minimize error forecasts, and then adjusted accordingly whenever the computer notes an errant tracking signal. This is called **adaptive smoothing**.

Adaptive smoothing

---

[4]See G. W. Plossl and O. W. Wight, *Production and Inventory Control* (Englewood Cliffs, NJ: Prentice Hall, 1967).

[5]To prove these three percentages to yourself, just set up a normal curve for ±1.6 standard deviations (z values). Using the normal table in Appendix A, you find that the area under the curve is .89. This represents ±2 MADs. Likewise, ±3 MADs = ±2.4 standard deviations encompass 98% of the area, and so on for ±4 MADs.

FIGURE 5.8 ■ A Plot of Tracking Signals

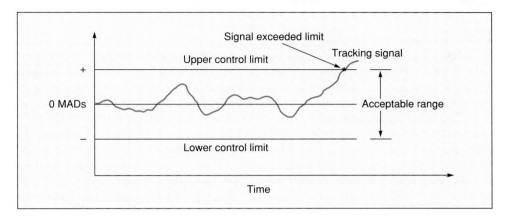

Focus Forecasting

Rather than adapt by choosing a smoothing constant, computers allow us to try a variety of forecasting models. Such an approach is called focus forecasting. **Focus forecasting** is based on two principles. The first is that very sophisticated forecasting models are not always better than simple ones. The second is that there is no single technique that should be used for all products or services.

Bernard Smith, inventory manager for American Hardware Supply, is the man who coined the term focus forecasting. Smith's job was to forecast quantities for 100,000 hardware products purchased by American's 21 buyers.[6] He found that buyers neither trusted nor understood the exponential smoothing model then in use. They instead used very simple approaches of their own. So Smith developed his new computerized system for selecting forecasting methods.

Smith chose seven forecasting methods to test. They ranged from the simple ones buyers used (such as the naive approach) to some of the more statistical models. Every month, Smith applied the forecasts of all seven models to each item in stock. In these simulated trials, the forecast values were subtracted from the most recent actual demands, giving a simulated forecast error. The forecast method yielding the least error is selected by the computer, which then uses it to make next month's forecast. Buyers still have an override capability, but American Hardware finds that focus forecasting provides excellent results.

Focus forecasting

The Computer's Role in Forecasting

As we can see from American Hardware Supply, forecast calculations are seldom performed by hand in this day of computers. Many academic and commercial packaged programs are readily available to handle time-series and causal projections.

Popular commercial packages include General Electric's *Time Series Forecasting* and IBM's IMPACT (Inventory Management Program and Control Technique). Popular university packages available for PCs are SAS, SPSS, STORM, QSB, AB:POM, and Minitab.

[6]Bernard T. Smith, *Focus Forecasting: Computer Techniques for Inventory Control* (Boston: CBI Publishing, 1978).

ACHIEVING WORLD-CLASS STANDARDS

World-class firms view forecasting as an integral part of business planning. For example, when Compaq Computer makes new product and manufacturing capacity decisions, it forecasts the size, direction, and price trends in the microcomputer market. With competitors like IBM, Dell, NEC, and dozens of others, Compaq attributes much of its phenomenal success to its correct forecasts.

To gain a competitive advantage, world-class firms develop excellent short-term forecasts of production capacity, materials to be purchased, inventory levels, workforce size, and cash. Compaq and other world-class forecasters also maintain high-quality long-range business planning systems, driven by formal forecasting models. Because long-range planning is an important job that affects all employees, forecasting input comes from many sources and departments. In fact, world-class firms even hire outside analysts who specialize in using the most sophisticated technology, models, and data bases available to their industry. Sources of useful data outside the firm may include global and industry data gathered by universities, trade associations, consulting firms, and government agencies.

World-class organizations continuously track the accuracy of their forecasts. They want their business plans and management decisions to be based on the latest and most valid data available.

SUMMARY

Forecasts are a critical part of the operations manager's function. Demand forecasts drive the production, capacity, and scheduling systems in a firm and affect the financial, marketing, and personnel planning functions.

There are a variety of qualitative and quantitative forecasting techniques. Qualitative approaches employ judgment, experience, intuition, and a host of other factors that are difficult to quantify. Quantitative forecasting uses historical data and causal relations to project future demands. No forecasting method is perfect under all conditions. And even once management has found a satisfactory approach, it must still monitor and control its forecasts to make sure errors do not get out of hand. Forecasting can often be a very challenging, but rewarding, part of managing.

KEY TERMS

Forecasting (p. 158)
Economic forecasts (p. 160)
Technological forecasts (p.160)
Demand forecasts (p. 160)
Quantitative forecasts (p. 160)
Qualitative forecasts (p. 160)
Jury of executive opinion (p. 160)
Sales force composite (p. 160)
Delphi method (p. 160)
Consumer market survey (p. 161)
Time series (p. 161)
Naive approach (p. 165)
Moving averages (p. 165)

Exponential smoothing (p. 167)
Smoothing constant (p. 167)
Mean absolute deviation (MAD) (p. 169)
Mean squared error (MSE) (p. 170)
Trend projection (p. 174)
Linear-regression analysis (p. 178)
Standard error of the estimate (p. 181)
Coefficient of correlation (p. 182)
Multiple regression (p. 184)
Tracking signal (p. 185)
Adaptive smoothing (p. 186)
Focus forecasting (p. 187)

Examples of AB:POM in Exponential Smoothing and Regression

AB:POM's forecasting program provides an initial menu screen asking whether you wish to do a time-series forecast or a least squares causal forecast. If time series is selected, you may use (1) moving averages, (2) weighted moving averages, (3) exponential smoothing, (4) exponential smoothing with trend, (5) least squares trend analysis, (6) deseasonalize data, or (7) deseasonalize data then regress. If you select the causal model, you may do simple or multiple regression. We provide two sample printouts in Programs 5.1 and 5.2 to illustrate one of the time-series approaches and linear regression. These programs solve Examples 4 and 10.

PROGRAM 5.1 ■ AB:POM's Exponential Smoothing Program Using Example 4 Data. This program demonstrates the input/output for exponential smoothing, using Example 4's data. We entered (1) the number of data periods, (2) the model desired, (3) alpha, (4) the eight demands, (5) the initial forecast of 175, and (6) the titles for each period (i.e., QTR1, QTR2, and so on).

If you look back to Examples 4 and 5, note that the MAD and MSE are slightly different. This is because AB:POM does not calculate an error for this initial forecast (Period 1). So the error terms are based on seven periods, not the eight we used earlier. Conclusions reached tend to be the same with either approach. Bias, a third type of forecast error, is also provided by AB:POM. Bias is a measure of the *direction* of forecast error. It tells us whether our forecasts tend, on average, to be too high or too low.

Forecasting   Solution

Number of past data periods (2–99) 8

PORT OF BALTIMORE, EXAMPLE 4

Method –> Exponential Smoothing

alpha (α) 0.100

	Period (x)	Demand (y)	Forecast	Error	|Error|	Error^2
QTR 1	1	180.00	175.00			
QTR 2	2	168.00	175.50	–7.50	7.50	56.25
QTR 3	3	159.00	174.75	–15.75	15.75	248.063
QTR 4	4	175.00	173.175	1.82500	1.82500	3.33061
QTR 5	5	190.00	173.357	16.6425	16.6425	276.97
QTR 6	6	205.00	175.022	29.9783	29.9783	898.70
QTR 7	7	180.00	178.020	1.98042	1.98042	3.92208
QTR 8	8	182.00	178.218	3.78	3.78	14.31
TOTALS	36.00	1439.00		30.9586	77.4586	1501.54
AVERAGE	4.50	0.5625		4.42265	11.0655	214.506
				(Bias)	(MAD)	(MSE)

Next period's forecast   178.60   Standard error = 17.3294

F1 = Help   F2 = Summary   F3 = Graph   F9 = Print   Esc

PROGRAM 5.2 ■ AB:POM's Linear Regression Program Using Example 10 Data. There is only one independent variable, so this is also called simple regression. Outputs include the regression line, correlation coefficient, and standard error.

In this and other cases, the data points can also be graphed by pressing the F3 function key. This program is accessed off the Forecasting Menu by requesting the "Least Squares" option.

Number of past data periods (2–99) 6				Number of independ. variables (1–6) 1	

TONGREN

Method -> Least Squares–Simple and Multiple Regression

	B 0	B 1				
Coef ->	1.75	0.25				

	SALES	PAYROLL	Forecast	Error	|Error|	Error^2
1990	2.00	1.00	2.00	0.00	0.00	0.00
1991	3.00	3.00	2.50	0.50	0.50	0.25
1992	2.50	4.00	2.75	−0.25	0.25	0.0625
1993	2.00	2.00	2.25	−0.25	0.25	0.0625
1994	2.00	1.00	2.00	0.00	0.00	0.00
1995	3.50	7.00	3.50	0.00	0.00	0.00
TOTALS				0.00	1.00	0.375
AVERAGE				0.00	.166667	0.0625
				(Bias)	(MAD)	(MSE)

Regression line = SALES = 1.75   +0.25*PAYROLL
Correlation coefficient = 0.9013878   Standard error = .3061862

F1 = Help	F2 = Summary	F3 = Graph	F9 = Print	Esc

Examples of Spreadsheet Software for Exponential Smoothing and Regression

Program 5.3 uses Example 4's data to illustrate exponential smoothing via spreadsheets. This "symbolic spreadsheet" shows all the formulas used in forecasting in cells D6 through D13. $B$3 is called an "absolute reference" to the value of alpha in B3. Cells E6 through E13 hold the formulas for computing the absolute differences of forecast tonnage in column C and actual in column B. They are also rounded off. The @SUM and @AVG commands in cells E14 and E15, respectively, total the absolute values and then provide their mean (the MAD).

Program 5.4 shows the use of spreadsheets in regression analysis using the /Data Regression (/DR) command. When we press /DR, the following submenu appears:

X-Range   Y-Range   Output-Range   Intercept   Reset   Go   Quit

We first use the x-Range option to select the independent variable(s). We specify B5..B10 (payroll) as our only independent variable in Example 10. We then use the Y-Range option to specify the dependent variable of sales. We enter range A5..A10.

The Output-Range option specifies where to display the regression results. This needs to be an unused area of the spreadsheet and must be at least nine rows long and two columns wider than the number of independent variables. We need only specify the upper left corner of the output range. Because we want the results to appear in the range A12..D20, we specify A12 at the prompt.

PROGRAM 5.3 ■ Using Spreadsheets to Compute the Port of Baltimore's Exponential Smoothing Forecast. The symbolic spreadsheet, showing formulas in cells, is provided.

	A	B	C	D	E
1	Port of Baltimore Exponential Smoothing Forecast from Example 4				
2					
3	Alpha =	0.1			
4					
5	Quarter	Act.Tons	Frcst	$F_{t-1} + \alpha(A_{t-1} - F_{t-1})$	Abs. Error
6	1	180	175	+C6+$B$3*(B6–C6)	@ROUND(@ABS(B6–C6),0)
7	2	168	+D6	+C7+$B$3*(B7–C7)	@ROUND(@ABS(B7–C7),0)
8	3	159	+D7	+C8+$B$3*(B8–C8)	@ROUND(@ABS(B8–C8),0)
9	4	175	+D8	+C9+$B$3*(B9–C9)	@ROUND(@ABS(B9–C9),0)
10	5	190	+D9	+C10+$B$3*(B10–C10)	@ROUND(@ABS(B10–C10),0)
11	6	205	+D10	+C11+$B$3*(B11–C11)	@ROUND(@ABS(B11–C11),0)
12	7	180	+D11	+C12+$B$3*(B12–C12)	@ROUND(@ABS(B12–C12),0)
13	8	182	+D12	+C13+$B$3*(B13–C13)	@ROUND(@ABS(B13–C13),0)
14	Total				@SUM(E6. .E13)
15	Average				@AVG(E6. .E13)

PROGRAM 5.4 ■ Regression Analysis with Spreadsheet Software and the /Data Regression Command. Tongren's data from Example 11 are shown. The constant value output is the Y-intercept. The X-coefficient is the slope of the independent variable, i.e., payroll.

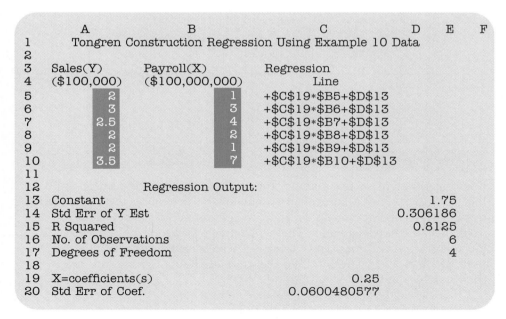

	A	B	C	D	E	F
1	Tongren Construction Regression Using Example 10 Data					
2						
3	Sales(Y)	Payroll(X)	Regression			
4	($100,000)	($100,000,000)	Line			
5	2	1	+$C$19*$B5+$D$13			
6	3	3	+$C$19*$B6+$D$13			
7	2.5	4	+$C$19*$B7+$D$13			
8	2	2	+$C$19*$B8+$D$13			
9	2	1	+$C$19*$B9+$D$13			
10	3.5	7	+$C$19*$B10+$D$13			
11						
12		Regression Output:				
13	Constant			1.75		
14	Std Err of Y Est			0.306186		
15	R Squared			0.8125		
16	No. of Observations			6		
17	Degrees of Freedom			4		
18						
19	X=coefficients(s)		0.25			
20	Std Err of Coef.		0.0600480577			

SOLVED PROBLEMS

Solved Problem 5.1

Sales of Green Line Jet Skis have grown steadily during the past 5 years (see table). The sales manager had predicted in 1990 that 1991 sales would be 410 air conditioners. Using exponential smoothing with a weight of $\alpha = .30$, develop forecasts for 1992 through 1996.

YEAR	SALES	FORECAST
1991	450	410
1992	495	
1993	518	
1994	563	
1995	584	
1996	?	

Solution

YEAR	FORECAST
1991	410.0
1992	$422.0 = 410 + .3 (450 - 410)$
1993	$443.9 = 422 + .3 (495 - 422)$
1994	$466.1 = 443.9 + .3 (518 - 443.9)$
1995	$495.2 = 466.1 + .3 (563 - 466.1)$
1996	$521.8 = 495.2 + .3 (584 - 495.2)$

Solved Problem 5.2

Room registrations in the Toronto Towers Plaza Hotel have been recorded for the past nine years. Management would like to determine the mathematical trend of guest registration in order to project future occupancy. This estimate would help the hotel determine whether a future expansion will be needed. Given the following time series data, develop a regression equation relating registrations to time. Then forecast 1996 registrations. Room registrations are in the thousands:

1987: 17	1988: 16	1989: 16	1990: 21	1991: 20
1992: 20	1993: 23	1994: 25	1995: 24	

Solution

YEAR	TRANSFORMED YEAR, X	REGISTRANTS, Y (IN THOUSANDS)	x^2	XY
1987	1	17	1	17
1988	2	16	4	32
1989	3	16	9	48
1990	4	21	16	84
1991	5	20	25	100
1992	6	20	36	120
1993	7	23	49	161
1994	8	25	64	200
1995	9	24	81	216
	$\Sigma x = 45$	$\Sigma y = 182$	$\Sigma x^2 = 285$	$\Sigma xy = 978$

$$\bar{x} = \frac{45}{9} = 5, \qquad \bar{y} = \frac{182}{9} = 20.22$$

$$b = \frac{\Sigma xy - n\bar{x}\bar{y}}{\Sigma x^2 - n\bar{x}^2} = \frac{978 - (9)(5)(20.22)}{285 - (9)(25)} = \frac{978 - 909.9}{285 - 225} = \frac{68.1}{60} = 1.135$$

$$a = \bar{y} - b\bar{x} = 20.22 - (1.135)(5) = 20.22 - 5.675 = 14.545$$

$$\hat{y} \text{ (registrations)} = 14.545 + 1.135x$$

The projection of registrations in 1997 (which is $x = 11$ in the coding system used) is

$$\hat{y} = 14.545 + (1.135)(11) = 27.03$$

$$\text{or } 27,030 \text{ guests in 1997.}$$

Solved Problem 5.3

Quarterly demand for Jaguar XJ6's at a New York auto dealer is forecast with the equation

$$\hat{y} = 10 + 3x$$

where x = quarters, and

Quarter I of 1994 = 0
Quarter II of 1994 = 1
Quarter III of 1994 = 2
Quarter IV of 1994 = 3
Quarter I of 1995 = 4
and so on

and

$\hat{y}$ = quarterly demand

The demand for sports sedans is seasonal, and the indices for Quarters I, II, III, and IV are 0.80, 1.00, 1.30, and 0.90, respectively. Forecast demand for each quarter of 1996. Then seasonalize each forecast to adjust for quarterly variations.

> **Solution**
> Quarter II of 1995 is coded $x = 5$; Quarter III of 1995, $x = 6$; and Quarter IV of 1995, $x = 7$. Hence, Quarter I of 1996 is coded $x = 8$; Quarter II, $x = 9$; and so on.
>
> $\hat{y}(1996 \text{ Quarter I}) = 10 + 3(8) = 34$ Adjusted forecast = $(.80)(34) = 27.2$
> $\hat{y}(1996 \text{ Quarter II}) = 10 + 3(9) = 37$ Adjusted forecast = $(1.00)(37) = 37$
> $\hat{y}(1996 \text{ Quarter III}) = 10 + 3(10) = 40$ Adjusted forecast = $(1.30)(40) = 52$
> $\hat{y}(1996 \text{ Quarter IV}) = 10 + 3(11) = 43$ Adjusted forecast = $(.90)(43) = 38.7$

DISCUSSION QUESTIONS

1. Briefly describe the steps that are used to develop a forecasting system.
2. What is a time-series forecasting model?
3. What is the difference between a causal model and a time-series model?
4. What is a qualitative forecasting model, and when is it appropriate?
5. What is the meaning of least squares in a regression model?
6. What are some of the drawbacks of the moving-average forecasting model?
7. What effect does the value of the smoothing constant have on the weight given to the past forecast and the past observed value?
8. Briefly describe the Delphi technique.
9. What is MAD, and why is it important in the selection and use of forecasting models?
10. Describe the three forecasting time horizons and their use.
11. Name and discuss three *qualitative* forecasting methods.
12. Which of the forecasting techniques can place the most emphasis on recent values? How does it do this?
13. What does it mean to decompose a time series?
14. What is the basic difference between a weighted moving average and exponential smoothing?
15. Describe two popular measures of forecast accuracy.
16. What is the difference between a dependent and an independent variable?
17. Define the meaning of the coefficient of determination in your own words. Provide an example.
18. What is the purpose of a tracking signal?

CRITICAL THINKING EXERCISE

In 1994, the Board of Regents, responsible for all public higher education funding in a large midwestern state, hired a consultant to develop a series of enrollment forecasting models, one for each college. These models used historical data and exponential smoothing to forecast next year's enrollments. Based on the model, which included a smoothing constant (α) for each school, each college's budget was set by the Board. The head of the Board personally selected each smoothing constant, based on what she called her "gut reactions and political acumen."

What do you think the advantages and disadvantages of this system are? Answer from the perspective of (a) the Board of Regents and (b) the President of each college. How can this model be abused and what could be done to remove any biases? How can a *regression model* be used to produce results that favor one forecast over another?

PROBLEMS

• **5.1** Daily high temperatures in the city of Houston for the last week have been as follows: 93, 94, 93, 95, 96, 88, 90 (yesterday).
   a) Forecast the high temperature today, using a 3-day moving average.
   b) Forecast the high temperature today, using a 2-day moving average.
   c) Calculate the mean absolute deviation based on a 2-day moving average.

• **5.2** For the data below, develop a 3-month moving-average forecast.

MONTH	AUTOMOBILE BATTERY SALES	MONTH	AUTOMOBILE BATTERY SALES
January	20	July	17
February	21	August	18
March	15	September	20
April	14	October	20
May	13	November	21
June	16	December	23

· **5.3** Given the following data, develop a 3-year moving-average forecast of demand.

YEAR	1	2	3	4	5	6	7	8	9	10	11
DEMAND	7	9	5	9	13	8	12	13	9	11	7

· **5.4** Eli Cohen has developed the following forecasting model:

$$\hat{y} = 36 + 4.3x$$

where $\hat{y}$ = demand for Aztec air conditioners and
        x = the outside temperature (°F).

a) Forecast demand for the Aztec when the temperature is 70°F.

b) What is demand for a temperature of 80°F?

c) What is demand for a temperature of 90°F?

· **5.5** Data collected on the yearly demand for 50-lb bags of grass seed at Bob's Hardware Store are shown in the following table. Develop a 3-year moving average to forecast sales. Then estimate demand again with a weighted moving average in which sales in the most recent years are given a weight of 2 and sales in the other two years are each given a weight of 1. Which method do you think is best?

YEAR	1	2	3	4	5	6	7	8	9	10	11
DEMAND FOR GRASS SEED (THOUSANDS OF BAGS)	4	6	4	5	10	8	7	9	12	14	15

· **5.6** Develop a 2- and a 4-year moving average for the demand for bags of grass seed in Problem 5.5.

· **5.7** In Problems 5.5 and 5.6, four different forecasts were developed for the demand for grass seed. These four forecasts are a 2-year moving average, a 3-year moving average, a weighted moving average, and a 4-year moving average. Which one would you use? Explain your answer.

· **5.8** Use exponential smoothing with a smoothing constant of .3 to forecast the demand for grass seed given in Problem 5.5. Assume that last period's forecast for year 1 is 5,000 bags to begin the procedure. Would you prefer to use the exponential smoothing model or the weighted-average model developed in Problem 5.5? Explain your answer.

- **5.9** Using smoothing constants of .6 and .9, develop a forecast for the sales of Green Line Jet Skis. See Solved Problem 5.1.

- **5.10** What effect did the smoothing constant have on the forecast for Green Line Jet Skis? See Solved Problem 5.1 and Problem 5.9. Which smoothing constant gives the most accurate forecast?

- **5.11** Use a 3-year moving-average forecasting model to forecast the sales of Green Line Jet Skis. See Solved Problem 5.1.

- **5.12** Using the trend-projection method, develop a forecasting model for the sales of Green Line Jet Skis. See Solved Problem 5.1.

- **5.13** Would you use exponential smoothing with a smoothing constant of .3, a 3-year moving average, or trend to predict the sales of Green Line Jet Skis? Refer to Solved Problem 5.1 and Problems 5.11 and 5.12.

- **5.14** Demand for heart transplant surgery at Washington General Hospital has increased steadily in the past few years, as seen in the following table.

Year	1	2	3	4	5	6
Heart Transplant Surgeries Performed	45	50	52	56	58	?

The director of medical services predicted 6 years ago that demand in year 1 would be for 41 surgeries.

a) Use exponential smoothing, first with a smoothing constant of .6 and then with one of .9, to develop forecasts for years 2 through 6.

b) Use a 3-year moving average to forecast demand in years 4, 5, and 6.

c) Use the trend-projection method to forecast demand in years 1 through 6.

d) With MAD as the criterion, which of the above four forecasts is best?

- **5.15** A careful analysis of the cost of operating an automobile was conducted by a firm. The following model was developed:

$$Y = 4,000 + 0.20X$$

where Y is the annual cost and X is the miles driven.

a) If a car is driven 15,000 miles this year, what is the forecasted cost of operating this automobile?

b) If a car is driven 25,000 miles this year, what is the forecasted cost of operating this automobile?

c) Suppose that one car was driven 15,000 miles and the actual cost of operating this was $6,000, and a second car was driven 25,000 miles and the actual operating cost was $10,000. Calculate the mean absolute deviation for this.

- **5.16** Given the following data, use exponential smoothing ($\alpha = 0.2$) to develop a demand forecast. Assume the forecast for the initial period is 5.

Period	1	2	3	4	5	6
Demand	7	9	5	9	13	8

: **5.17** Consulting income at Dr. Thomas W. Jones Associates for the period February–July has been as follows:

MONTH	February	March	April	May	June	July
INCOME (IN THOUSANDS)	70.0	68.5	64.8	71.7	71.3	72.8

Use trend-adjusted exponential smoothing to forecast August's income. Assume that the initial forecast for February is $65,000 and the initial trend adjustment is 0. The smoothing constants selected are $\alpha = .1$ and $\beta = .2$.

: **5.18** Resolve Problem 5.17 with $\alpha = .1$ and $\beta = .8$. Using MAD, which smoothing constants provide a better forecast?

: **5.19** Calculate (a) MAD and (b) MSE for the following forecast versus actual sales figures.

FORECAST	100	110	120	130
ACTUAL	95	108	123	130

: **5.20** Given the following data, use the least squares regression to derive a forecasting equation. What is your estimate of the demand in period 7?

PERIOD	1	2	3	4	5	6
DEMAND	7	9	5	11	10	13

: **5.21** Given the following data, use least squares regression to develop a relation between the number of rainy summer days and the number of games lost by the Boca Raton Cardinal baseball team.

YEAR	1986	1987	1988	1989	1990	1991	1992	1993	1994	1995
RAINY DAYS	15	25	10	10	30	20	20	15	10	25
GAMES LOST	25	20	10	15	20	15	20	10	5	20

: **5.22** Sales of industrial vacuum cleaners at Gary Williams Supply Co. over the past 13 months are shown below.

MONTH	Jan.	Feb.	March	April	May	June	July
SALES (IN THOUSANDS)	11	14	16	10	15	17	11
MONTH	Aug.	Sept.	Oct.	Nov.	Dec.	Jan.	
SALES (IN THOUSANDS)	14	17	12	14	16	11	

a) Using a moving average with three periods, determine the demand for vacuum cleaners for next February.

b) Using a weighted moving average with three periods, determine the demand for vacuum cleaners for February. Use 3, 2, and 1 for the weights of the most recent, second most recent, and third most recent periods, respectively. For example, if you were forecasting the demand for February, November would have a weight of 1, December would have a weight of 2, and January would have a weight of 3.

c) Evaluate the accuracy of each of these methods.

d) What other factors might Williams consider in forecasting sales?

: 5.23 The operations manager of a musical instrument distributor feels that demand for bass drums may be related to the number of television appearances by the popular rock group Green Shades during the previous month. The manager has collected the data shown in the following table.

DEMAND FOR BASS DRUMS	3	6	7	5	10	8
GREEN SHADES TV APPEARANCES	3	4	7	6	8	5

a) Graph these data to see whether a linear equation might describe the relationship between the group's television shows and bass drum sales.

b) Use the least squares regression method to derive a forecasting equation.

c) What is your estimate for bass drum sales if the Green Shades performed on TV nine times last month?

· 5.24 A study to determine the correlation between bank deposits and consumer price indices in Birmingham, Alabama, revealed the following (which was based on $n = 5$ years of data):

$$\Sigma x = 15$$
$$\Sigma x^2 = 55$$
$$\Sigma xy = 70$$
$$\Sigma y = 20$$
$$\Sigma y^2 = 130$$

a) Find the coefficient of correlation. What does it imply to you?

b) What is the standard error of the estimate?

: 5.25 The accountant at Barbara Herdman Coal Distributors, Inc., notes that the demand for coal seems to be tied to an index of weather severity developed by the U.S. Weather Bureau. That is, when weather was extremely cold in the United States over the past 5 years (and hence the index was high), coal sales were high. The accountant proposes that one good forecast of next year's coal demand could be made by developing a regression equation and then consulting the *Farmer's Almanac* to see how severe next year's winter will be. For the data in the following table, derive a least squares regression and compute the coefficient of correlation of the data. Also compute the standard error of the estimate.

COAL SALES, Y (IN MILLIONS OF TONS)	4	1	4	6	5
WEATHER INDEX, X	2	1	4	5	3

: **5.26** Thirteen students entered the P/OM program at Rollins College 2 years ago. The following table indicates what their grade point averages (GPAs) were after being in the program for 2 years and what each student scored on the SAT exam when he or she was in high school. Is there a meaningful relationship between grades and SAT scores? If a student scores a 350 on the SAT, what do you think his or her GPA will be? What about a student who scores 800?

STUDENT	A	B	C	D	E	F	G	H	I	J	K	L	M
SAT SCORE	421	377	585	690	608	390	415	481	729	501	613	709	366
GPA	2.90	2.93	3.00	3.45	3.66	2.88	2.15	2.53	3.22	1.99	2.75	3.90	1.60

· **5.27** Dr. Jerilyn Ross, a New York City psychologist, specializes in treating patients who are agoraphobic (afraid to leave their homes). The following table indicates how many patients Dr. Ross has seen each year for the past 10 years. It also indicates what the robbery rate was in New York City during the same year.

YEAR	1	2	3	4	5	6	7	8	9	10
NUMBER OF PATIENTS	36	33	40	41	40	55	60	54	58	61
CRIME RATE (ROBBERIES) PER 1,000 POPULATION	58.3	61.1	73.4	75.7	81.1	89.0	101.1	94.8	103.3	116.2

Using trend analysis, how many patients do you think Dr. Ross will see in years 11, 12, and 13? How well does the model fit the data?

: **5.28** Using the data in Problem 5.27, apply linear regression to study the relationship between the crime rate and Dr. Ross's patient load. If the robbery rate increases to 131.2 in year 11, how many phobic patients will Dr. Ross treat? If the crime rate drops to 90.6, what is the patient projection?

· **5.29** Accountants at the firm Doke and Reed believed that several traveling executives submit unusually high travel vouchers when they return from business trips. The accountants took a sample of 200 vouchers submitted from the past year; they then developed the following multiple-regression equation relating expected travel cost ($\hat{y}$) to number of days on the road (x_1) and distance traveled (x_2) in miles:

$$\hat{y} = \$90.00 + \$48.50x_1 + \$.40x_2$$

The coefficient of correlation computed was .68.

a) If Bill Tomlinson returns from a 300-mile trip that took him out of town for 5 days, what is the expected amount he should claim as expenses?

b) Tomlinson submitted a reimbursement request for $685. What should the accountant do?

c) Should any other variables be included? Which ones? Why?

· **5.30** In the past, Kelly Gibson's tire dealership sold an average of 1,000 radials each year. In the past 2 years 200 and 250, respectively, were sold in fall, 350 and 300 in winter, 150 and 165 in spring, and 300 and 285 in summer. With a major expansion planned, Ms. Gibson projects sales next year to increase to 1,200 radials. What will the demand be each season?

· **5.31** Suppose the number of auto accidents in a certain region is related to the regional number of registered automobiles in thousands (b_1), alcoholic beverage sales in $10,000s (b_2), and rainfall in inches (b_3). Furthermore, imagine that the regression formula has been calculated as

$$Y = a + b_1X_1 + b_2X_2 + b_3X_3$$

where Y = number of automobile accidents,
$a = 7.5$, $b_1 = 3.5$, $b_2 = 4.5$, and $b_3 = 2.5$

Calculate the expected number of automobile accidents under the following conditions:

	X_1	X_2	X_3
a)	2	3	0
b)	3	5	1
c)	4	7	2

· **5.32** The following multiple-regression model was developed to predict job performance as measured by a company job performance evaluation index based on a preemployment test score and college grade point average (GPA).

$$Y = 35 + 20X_1 + 50X_2$$

where Y = job performance evaluation index
X_1 = preemployment test score
X_2 = college GPA

a) Forecast the job performance index for an applicant who had a 3.0 GPA and scored 80 on the preemployment score.

b) Forecast the job performance index for an applicant who had a 2.5 GPA and scored 70 on the preemployment score.

⊞ ⋮ **5.33** City government has collected the following data on annual sales tax collections and new car registrations:

ANNUAL SALES TAX COLLECTIONS (IN MILLIONS)	1	1.4	1.9	2	1.8	2.1	2.3
NEW CAR REGISTRATIONS (IN THOUSANDS)	10	12	15	16	14	17	20

Determine the following:

a) The least squares regression equation.

b) Using the results of part (a), find the estimated sales tax collections if new car registrations total 22.

c) The coefficients of correlation and determination.

⊞ ⋮ **5.34** Passenger miles flown on Northeast Airlines, a commuter firm serving the Boston hub, are shown for the past 12 weeks.

WEEK	1	2	3	4	5	6
ACTUAL PASSENGER MILES (IN THOUSANDS)	17	21	19	23	18	16

WEEK	7	8	9	10	11	12
ACTUAL PASSENGER MILES (IN THOUSANDS)	20	18	22	20	15	22

a) Assuming an initial forecast for week 1 of 17,000 miles, use exponential smoothing to compute miles for weeks 2 through 12. Use $\alpha = .2$.

b) What is the MAD for this model?

c) Compute the RSFE and tracking signals. Are they within acceptable limits?

: **5.35** Bus and subway ridership in Washington, DC, during the summer months is believed to be heavily tied to the number of tourists visiting that city. During the past 12 years, the following data have been obtained:

YEAR	NUMBER OF TOURISTS (IN MILLIONS)	RIDERSHIP (IN MILLIONS)	YEAR	NUMBER OF TOURISTS (IN MILLIONS)	RIDERSHIP (IN MILLIONS)
1	7	1.5	7	16	2.4
2	2	1.0	8	12	2.0
3	6	1.3	9	14	2.7
4	4	1.5	10	20	4.4
5	14	2.5	11	15	3.4
6	15	2.7	12	7	1.7

a) Plot these data and decide if a linear model is reasonable.

b) Develop a regression relationship.

c) What is expected ridership if 10 million tourists visit the city in a year?

d) Explain the predicted ridership if there are no tourists at all.

e) What is the standard error of the estimate?

f) What is the model's correlation coefficient and coefficient of determination?

: **5.36** Emergency calls to the 911 system of Gainesville, Florida, for the past 24 weeks are shown:

WEEK	1	2	3	4	5	6	7	8	9	10	11	12
CALLS	50	35	25	40	45	35	20	30	35	20	15	40

WEEK	13	14	15	16	17	18	19	20	21	22	23	24
CALLS	55	35	25	55	55	40	35	60	75	50	40	65

a) Compute the exponentially smoothed forecast of calls for each week. Assume an initial forecast of 50 calls in the first week, and use $\alpha = .1$. What is the forecast for week 25?

b) Reforecast each period using $\alpha = .6$

c) Actual calls during week 25 were 85. Which smoothing constant provides a superior forecast? Explain and justify the measure of error used.

: 5.37 Using the 911 call data in Problem 5.36, forecast calls for weeks 2 through 25 with a trend-adjusted exponential smoothing model. Assume an initial forecast for 50 calls for week 1 and an initial trend of zero. Use smoothing constants of $\alpha = .3$ and $\beta = .1$. Is this model better than that of Problem 5.36? What adjustment might be useful for further improvement? (Again, assume actual calls in week 25 were 85.)

: 5.38 Des Moines Power and Light has been collecting data on demand for electric power in its west subregion for only the past 2 years. Those data are shown:

MONTH	DEMAND IN MEGAWATTS LAST YEAR	THIS YEAR	MONTH	DEMAND IN MEGAWATTS LAST YEAR	THIS YEAR
Jan.	5	17	July	23	44
Feb.	6	14	Aug.	26	41
Mar.	10	20	Sept.	21	33
Apr.	13	23	Oct.	15	23
May	18	30	Nov.	12	26
June	15	38	Dec.	14	17

The utility needs to be able to forecast demand for each month next year in order to plan for expansion and to arrange to borrow power from neighboring utilities during peak periods. Yet the standard forecasting models discussed in this chapter will not fit the data observed for the 2 years.

a) What are the weaknesses of the standard forecasting techniques as applied to this set of data?

b) Because known models are not really appropriate here, propose your own approach to forecasting. Although there is no perfect solution to tackling data such as these (In other words, there are no 100% right or wrong answers.), justify your model.

c) Forecast demand for each month next year using the model you propose.

: 5.39 Attendance at Orlando's newest Disneylike attraction, Vacation World, has been as follows:

QUARTER	GUESTS (IN THOUSANDS)	QUARTER	GUESTS (IN THOUSANDS)
Winter '92	73	Summer '93	124
Spring '92	104	Fall '93	52
Summer '92	168	Winter '94	89
Fall '92	74	Spring '94	146
Winter '93	65	Summer '94	205
Spring '93	82	Fall '94	98

Compute seasonal indices using all of the data.

· **5.40** Claude Simpson, manager of Simpson's Department Store, has used time-series extrapolation to forecast retail sales for the next four quarters. The sales estimates are $120,000, $140,000, $160,000, and $180,000 for the respective quarters. Seasonal indices for the four quarters have been found to be 1.25, .90, .75, and 1.15, respectively. Compute a seasonalized or adjusted sales forecast.

: **5.41** Thornton Savings and Loan is proud of its long tradition in Tampa, Florida. Begun by Angela Thornton 4 years after World War II, the S&L has bucked the trend of financial and liquidity problems that has plagued the industry since 1985. Deposits have increased slowly but surely over the years, despite recessions in 1960, 1983, 1988, and 1991. Ms. Thornton believes it necessary to have a long-range strategic plan for her firm, including a 1-year forecast and preferably even a 5-year forecast of deposits. She examines the past deposit data and also peruses Florida's Gross State Product (GSP) over the same 44 years. (GSP is analogous to Gross National Product, GNP, but on the state level.)

DATA BASE APPLICATION

a) Using exponential smoothing, with $\alpha = .6$, then trend analysis, and finally linear regression, discuss which forecasting model fits best for Thornton's strategic plan. Justify why one model should be selected over another.

b) Carefully examine the data. Can you make a case for excluding a portion of the information? Why? Would that change your choice of model?

YEAR	DEPOSITS*	GSP†	YEAR	DEPOSITS*	GSP†	YEAR	DEPOSITS*	GSP†
1951	.25	.4	1967	2.3	1.6	1982	24.1	3.9
1952	.24	.4	1968	2.8	1.5	1983	25.6	3.8
1953	.24	.5	1969	2.8	1.6	1984	30.3	3.8
1954	.26	.7	1970	2.7	1.7	1985	36.0	3.7
1956	.25	.9	1971	3.9	1.9	1986	31.1	4.1
1957	.30	1.0	1972	4.9	1.9	1987	31.7	4.1
1958	.31	1.4	1973	5.3	2.3	1988	38.5	4.0
1959	.32	1.7	1974	6.2	2.5	1989	47.9	4.5
1960	.24	1.3	1975	4.1	2.8	1990	49.1	4.6
1961	.26	1.2	1976	4.5	2.9	1991	55.8	4.5
1962	.25	1.1	1977	6.1	3.4	1992	70.1	4.6
1963	.33	.9	1978	7.7	3.8	1993	70.9	4.6
1964	.50	1.2	1979	10.1	4.1	1994	79.1	4.7
1965	.95	1.2	1980	15.2	4.0	1995	94.0	5.0
1966	1.7	1.2	1981	18.1	4.0			

*In $ millions.
†In $ billions.

CASE STUDY

The North-South Airline

In 1994, Northern Airlines* merged with Southeast Airlines to create the fourth largest U.S. carrier. The new North-South Airline inherited both an aging fleet of Boeing 727-200 aircraft and Stephen Ruth. Ruth was a tough former Secretary of the Navy who stepped in as new President and Chairman of the Board.

Ruth's first concern in creating a financially solid company was maintenance costs. It was commonly surmised in the airline industry that maintenance costs rose with the age of the aircraft. He quickly noticed that historically there has been a significant difference in the reported B727-200 maintenance costs (from ATA Form 41s) both in the airframe and engine areas between Northern Airlines and Southeast Airlines, with Southeast having the newer fleet.

On November 12, 1994, Peg Young, Vice President for Operations and Maintenance, was called into Ruth's office and asked to study the issue. Specifically, Ruth wanted to know (1) whether the average fleet age was correlated to direct airframe maintenance costs and (2) whether there was a relationship between average fleet age and direct engine

maintenance costs. Young was to report back with the answer, along with quantitative and graphical descriptions of the relationship, by November 26.

Young's first step was to have her staff construct the average age of Northern and Southeast B727-200 fleets, by quarter, since the introduction of that aircraft to service by each airline in late 1985 and early 1986. The average age of each fleet was calculated by first multiplying the total number of calendar days each aircraft had been in service at the pertinent point in time by the average daily utilization of the respective fleet to total fleet hours flown. The total fleet hours flown was then divided by the number of aircraft in service at that time, giving the age of the "average" aircraft in the fleet.

The average utilization was found by taking the actual total fleet hours flown at September 30, 1993, from Northern and Southeast data, and dividing by total days in service for all aircraft at that time. The average utilization for Southeast was 8.3 hours per day, and the average utilization for Northern was 8.7 hours per day. Because the available cost data were calculated for each yearly period ending at the end of the first quarter, average fleet age was calculated at the same points in time.

The Fleet data are shown in Table 1. Airframe cost data and engine cost data are both shown paired with fleet average age in that table.

DISCUSSION QUESTION

1. Prepare Peg Young's response to Stephen Ruth.

*Dates and names of airlines and individuals have been changed in this case to maintain confidentiality. The data and issues described here are actual.

TABLE 1 ■ **NORTH-SOUTH AIRLINE DATA FOR BOEING 727-200 JETS**

YEAR	NORTHERN AIRLINE DATA			SOUTHEAST AIRLINE DATA		
	AIRFRAME COST PER AIRCRAFT	ENGINE COST PER AIRCRAFT	AVERAGE AGE (HOURS)	AIRFRAME COST PER PER AIRCRAFT	ENGINE COST PER AIRCRAFT	AVERAGE AGE (HOURS)
1987	$51.80	$43.49	6,512	$13.29	$18.86	5,107
1988	54.92	38.58	8,404	25.15	31.55	8,145
1989	69.70	51.48	11,077	32.18	40.43	7,360
1990	68.90	58.72	11,717	31.78	22.10	5,773
1991	63.72	45.47	13,275	25.34	19.69	7,150
1992	84.73	50.26	15,215	32.78	32.58	9,364
1993	78.74	79.60	18,390	35.56	38.07	8,259

CASE STUDY

The Akron Zoological Park

During the late 1970s, global changes in consumer preferences for radial tires, inflation, and changes in governmental priorities almost resulted in the permanent closing of the Akron Children's Zoo. Lagging attendance and a low level of memberships did not help matters. Faced with uncertain prospects of continuing, the City of Akron opted out of the zoo business. In response, the Akron Zoological Park was organized as a corporation to contract with the city to operate the zoo.

The Akron Zoological Park is an independent organization that manages the Akron Children's Zoo for the city. To be successful, the zoo must maintain its image as a quality place for its visitors to spend their time. Its animal exhibits are clean and neat. The animals, birds, and reptiles look well cared for. As resources become available for construction and continuing operations, the zoo keeps adding new exhibits and activities. Efforts seem to be working, because attendance increased from 53,353 in 1986 to an all-time record of 133,762 in 1991.

Due to its northern climate, the zoo conducts its open season from mid-April until mid-October. It reopens for 1 week at Halloween and for the month of December. Zoo attendance depends largely on the weather. For example, attendance was down during the month of December 1992, which established many local records for the coldest temperature and the most snow. Variations in weather also affect crop yields and prices of fresh animal foods, thereby influencing the costs of animal maintenance.

In normal circumstances, the zoo may be able to achieve its target goal and attract an annual attendance equal to 40% of its community. Akron has not grown appreciably during the past decade. But the zoo became known as an innovative community resource, and as indicated in Table 2, annual paid attendance has doubled. Approximately 35% of all visitors are adults. Children accounted for one-half of the paid attendance. Group admissions remain a constant 15% of zoo attendance.

The zoo does not have an advertising budget. To gain exposure in its market, then, the zoo depends on public service announcements, the zoo's public television series, and local press coverage of its activities and social happenings. Many of these activities are but a few years old. They are a strong reason that annual zoo attendance has increased.

Although the zoo is a nonprofit organization, it must ensure that its sources of income equal or exceed its operating and physical plant costs. Its continued existence remains totally dependent on its ability to generate revenues and to reduce its expenses.

TABLE 2 ■ **ANNUAL ATTENDANCE**

YEAR	TOTAL PERSONS	ADMISSION FEE ($)		
		ADULT	CHILD	GROUP
1995	117,874	4.00	2.50	1.50
1994	125,363	3.00	2.00	1.00
1993	126,853	3.00	2.00	1.50
1992	108,363	2.50	1.50	1.00
1991	133,762	2.50	1.50	1.00
1990	95,504	2.00	1.00	.50
1989	63,034	1.50	.75	.50
1988	63,853	1.50	.75	.50
1987	61,417	1.50	.75	.50
1986	53,353	1.50	.75	.50

DISCUSSION QUESTIONS

1. The President of the Akron Zoo asked you to calculate the expected gate admittance figures and revenues for both 1996 and 1997. Would simple linear-regression analysis be the appropriate forecasting technique?

2. Besides admission price, what other factors that influence annual attendance should be considered in the forecast?

Source: Professor F. Bruce Simmons, III, The University of Akron.

BIBLIOGRAPHY

Box, G. E. P., and G. Jenkins. *Time Series Analysis: Forecasting and Control.* San Francisco: Holden Day, 1970.

Brown, R. G. *Statistical Forecasting for Inventory Control.* New York: McGraw-Hill, 1959.

Chambers, J. C., C. Satinder, S. K. Mullick, and D. D. Smith. "How to Choose the Right Forecasting Techniques." *Harvard Business Review*, 49 (July/August 1971): 45–74.

Collopy, F., and J. S. Armstrong. "Rule-Based Forecasting: Development and Validation of an Expert Systems Approach to Combining Time Series Extrapolations." *Management Science*, 38, no. 10 (October 1992): 1094.

Gardner, E. S. "Exponential Smoothing: The State of the Art." *Journal of Forecasting*, 4 (March 1985)

Georgoff, D. M., and R. G. Murdick. "Managers Guide to Forecasting." *Harvard Business Review*, 64 (January/February 1986): 110–120.

Gips, J., and B. Sullivan. "Sales Forecasting—Replacing Magic with Logic." *Production and Inventory Management Review*, 2 (February 1982)

Murdick, R., B. Render, and R. Russell. *Service Operations Management.* Boston: Allyn and Bacon, 1990.

Murdick, R., and D. M. Georgoff. "Forecasting: A Systems Approach." *Technological Forecasting and Social Change*, 44 (1993): 1–16.

Render, B., and R. M. Stair. *Cases and Readings in Management Science*, 2nd ed. Boston: Allyn and Bacon, 1988.

———. *Quantitative Analysis for Management*, 5th ed. Boston: Allyn and Bacon, 1994.

6

PRODUCT STRATEGY

LEARNING OBJECTIVES

When you complete this chapter you should be able to:

Identify or Define:
  Product Life Cycle
  Product Development Team
  Value Engineering
  Value Analysis
  Group Technology
  Configuration Management
  Time-Based Competition
Explain:
  Product-by-value analysis
  Product documentation

PRODUCT STRATEGY PROVIDES
COMPETITIVE ADVANTAGE AT REGAL MARINE

Twenty-five years after its founding by potato farmer Paul Kuck, Regal Marine has become a powerful force on the waters of the world. Product design is critical in the highly competitive pleasure boat business, where Regal is one of the largest manufacturers in the United States. "We keep in touch with our customers and we respond to the marketplace," says Kuck. "We're introducing six new models this year alone. I'd say we're definitely on the aggressive end of the spectrum." With changing consumer tastes, compounded by material changes, and ever-improving marine engineering, the design function is under constant pressure. Added to these pressures is the constant issue of cost competitiveness combined with providing good value for customers.

Consequently, Regal Marine is a frequent user of computer-aided design (CAD). New designs come to life via Regal's three-dimensional CAD system, borrowed from automotive technology. Regal's naval architects' goal is to continue to reduce the time from concept to prototype to production. Their latest product, the *Rush*, is a radical 14-foot design that seats four people, operates in shallow water, and can pull a water skier or kneeboarder. The sophisticated CAD system not only has reduced product development time, but also has reduced problems with tooling and production, while resulting in a superior product.

All of Regal's products, from the $9,000 Rush to the $225,000 40-foot Commodore yacht, follow a similar production process. Hulls and bows are separately hand-produced by spraying preformed molds with three to five layers of a fiberglass laminate. This product hardens and is removed to become the upper and lower structure of the boat. As this "superstructure" moves to an assembly line and is joined, components are added at each workstation.

Wooden decks, precut in house by computer-driven routers, are

Once a hull has been pulled from the mold, it travels down a monorail assembly path. JIT inventory delivers engines, wiring, seats, flooring, and interiors when needed.

CAD/CAM is used to design the hull of a new product. This process results in faster and more efficient design and production.

delivered on a just-in-time basis for installation at one station. Engines, one of the few purchased components, are installed at another. Racks of electrical wiring harnesses, engineered and rigged in-house, are then installed. An in-house upholstery department delivers the customized seats, beds, dashboards, or other cushioned components. Finally, chrome fixtures are put in place, and the boat is sent to Regal's test tank for watertight, gauge, and system inspection.

At the final stage, boats are placed in this test tank where a rain machine ensures water-tight fits.

The Rush, designed and produced in record time, entered the hot new market for small, fast, and powerful pleasure boats.

A computer numerically controlled device (a CNC router) cuts out wood parts (flooring, cabinets, supports) used in a boat. The computer stores each part in memory and allows Regal to maximize cuts for top efficiency.

Experience suggests that when Toyota and General Motors (GM) each design an auto for 1998, Toyota will take 2 years and GM 5. Speed of design will provide Toyota with a number of advantages. First, Toyota will be able to design next year's technology into the car and the production process, but GM will be using 3-year-old technology. Additionally, Toyota will only need to forecast customer needs 2 years into the future, but GM will require a 5-year time horizon. Consequently, GM is more likely to be wrong. And, of course, Toyota's design organization is gaining development experience more than twice as fast as General Motors'.[1] ◆

As Toyota and GM know, the basis for any organization's existence is the product or service it provides society. Companies that meet customer needs with exciting, useful high-quality products or services find customers. Those that do not will not last. So one of the critical decisions for managers in world-class firms is the selection, definition, and design of products. Products and services are diverse: They range from a GE toaster, to an appendectomy, to a KFC chicken nugget dish, or a Citicorp 401K account. The objective of a **product strategy** is to meet the demands of the marketplace with a competitive advantage.

Product strategy

The production function itself should have available the necessary managerial ability, technological skills, and financial and human resources. When these abilities, skills, and resources do not support a product with a competitive advantage, the product should probably not be produced or offered.

Product selection and design decisions should involve the entire organization, because they affect the entire organization. Additionally, changing a strategic product commitment can be a lengthy and expensive process. In this chapter, we look at efficiently performing product selection, development, and documentation. Moving a product from idea to market is critical to organizational success.

PRODUCT SELECTION

Product Options

Management has many options in the selection, definition, and design of products. Product selection is choosing the product or service to provide customers or clients. For instance, hospitals specialize in various types of patients and various types of medical procedures. A hospital's management may decide to operate a general-purpose hospital, a maternity hospital, or, as in the case of Shouldice, a hospital specializing in hernias, as shown in the photo. Hospitals select their product when they decide what kind of hospital to be. Numerous other options exist for hospitals, just as they exist for McDonald's or General Motors.

Product decisions are fundamental and have major implications throughout the operations function. The strategy implications are substantial and pervasive. The

---

[1]See related discussion in James P. Womack, Daniel T. Jones, and Daniel Roos, *The Machine That Changed The World* (New York: Macmillan, 1990), p. 111.

Product selection occurs in services as well as manufacturing. Shown here is Shouldice Hospital, renowned for its world-class specialization in hernia repair—no emergency room, no maternity ward, no open heart surgery, just hernias. Shouldice became world-class by selecting and then focusing on a product (service) at which it could excell. Discharging its patients 3 days earlier than other hospitals, Shouldice's cost is about one-third of general purpose hospitals. Local anesthetics are used; patients enter and leave the operating room on their own; rooms are spartan, discouraging patients from remaining in bed; and all meals are served in a common dining room. As Shouldice has demonstrated, product selection impacts the entire production system.

example that follows indicates the strategic implications of a rather minor design change.

> An appliance maker found that it could extend the life of a product and save $1.75 per unit in warranty costs by substituting a newly designed part. Against expectation, it turned out that the new part would add more than $2 to the cost of each unit—hardly an attractive proposition, operationally speaking. But on strategic grounds the move still made excellent sense. By sparing the end user cost and inconvenience over the product's lifetime, it would strengthen the company's sales message and increase the product's value in the customer's eye. Management's decision to go ahead has since been rewarded by a hefty gain in market share.[2]

Identifying New Product Opportunities

An organization cannot survive without introducing new products. Older products are maturing and others in periods of decline must be replaced. This requires a constant successful introduction of new products and active participation by the operations manager. Successful firms have learned how to turn opportunities into successful products.

Product selection, definition, and design take place on a continuing basis because so many new product opportunities exist.[3] Factors influencing market opportunities include *economic change, sociological and demographic change, technological change,* and *political change.* In addition, other changes and opportunities may be brought

---

[2]Reprinted by permission of the *Harvard Business Review.* Excerpt from "Breakthrough Manufacturing," by Elizabeth A. Hass (March/April 1987). Copyright © 1987 by the President and Fellows of Harvard College; all rights reserved.

[3]See, for instance, an interesting article by Tom Peters, "All Markets Are Now Immature," *Industry Week* (July 3, 1989): 14–16.

about through *market practice, professional standards, suppliers,* and *distributors.* Operations managers must be aware of these factors and be able to anticipate changes in products, product volume, and product mix.

Product Life Cycles

Products are born. They live and they die. They are cast aside by a changing society. It may be helpful to think of a product's life as divided into four phases. Those phases, introduction, growth, maturity, and decline, are illustrated for several products in Figure 6.1. That figure also reveals the relative positions of a number of products.

Product life cycles may be a matter of a few hours (a newspaper), months (seasonal fashions and personal computers), years (Betamax video recorders), or decades Volkswagen Beetle). Regardless of the length of the cycle, the task for the operations manager is the same: to design a system that helps introduce new products successfully. If the operations function cannot perform effectively at this stage, the firm may be saddled with losers—products that cannot be produced efficiently and perhaps not at all. The *POM in Action* box "Cannibalism at Tandem Computer" indicates just how vicious the product life cycle can be.

Figure 6.2 shows the four life cycles and the relationship of product sales, costs, and profit over the life cycle of a product. Note that typically a firm has a negative cash flow while it develops a product. When the product is successful, those losses may be recovered. Eventually, the successful product may yield a profit prior to its decline. However, the profit is fleeting. As Figure 6.3 shows, leading companies generate a substantial portion of their sales from products less than 5 years old.

FIGURE 6.1   ■   Examples of Products in Various Life Cycle Stages

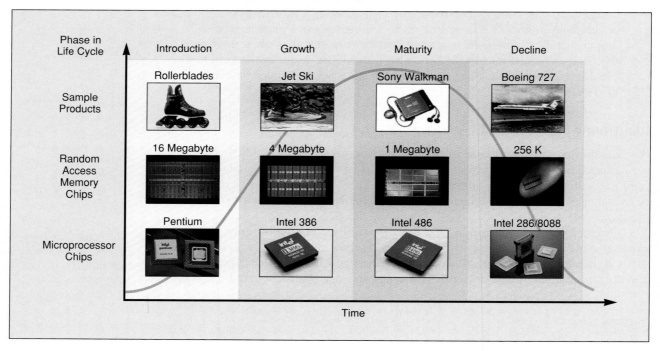

Cannibalism at Tandem Computer

For two decades, Tandem Computer Inc. provided the world with powerful "fault-tolerant" computers at a premium price. The company was uncommonly successful. But when revenue skidded and customers were screaming for an "open" operating system and lower prices, a change in product strategy was required.

The strategy used is cannibalism: gutting an existing product line, even when it is selling well, by introducing better versions at competitive prices—then slashing prices on the old line. "When you are at the top, you have to have the courage to say, 'I have to stop investing in this great product, and I'm going to use the money to generate a new product that will kill it,'" says Willem Roelandts, head of Hewlett-Packard's successful computer business. "If you're not going to do that, let me tell you, there's going to be some competitor that's going to do it for you."

Increased competition and shorter product cycles have made cannibalizing a means of survival, especially in the hypercompetitive world of computers and consumer electronics. To keep up, high-tech companies must constantly find ways to cut costs and prices while marketing new products that eventually destroy their own previous creations. To demonstrate their competence, Tandem expects to come out with low-priced, more powerful computers every 15 months.

Sources: Electronic News (July 26, 1993): 15; and *Wall Street Journal* (August 24, 1994): A1.

Despite efforts to introduce new products, many new products do not succeed. Consequently, product selection, definition, and design occur frequently. In fact, it is estimated that only 1 out of 25 products introduced actually succeeds! However, many more products go through product development, final production design, and preliminary stages of production but are judged too marginal for further investment. Therefore, they are not introduced.

This means that the number of products that must be reviewed for production and, in some cases, actually produced can be substantial, perhaps as many as 500 for each financially successful product. The relative number of products surviving a given development state is shown in Figure 6.4. Production managers and their

FIGURE 6.2 ■ Product Life Cycle, Sales, Cost, and Profit

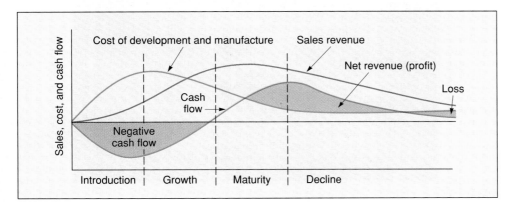

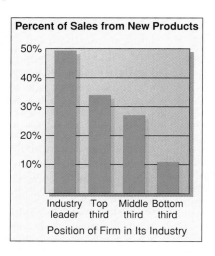

Percent of Sales from New Products

FIGURE 6.3 ■ Percent of Sales from Products Introduced in the Last 5 Years. The higher the percent of sales from products introduced in the last 5 years, the more likely the firm is to be a leader.

organizations must be able to accommodate this volume of new product ideas while maintaining activities to which they are already committed.[4]

Life Cycle and Strategy

Just as operations managers must be prepared to develop new products, they must also be prepared to develop strategies for new and existing products. Periodic examination of products is appropriate to determine their position in the life cycle because

The high rate of product failures can claim casualties on what sometimes looks like sure things. Such a case is the high-definition television (HDTV) which just a few years ago looked like a sure bet for the next generation of television sets. HDTV incorporated more computer power and memory combined with new tube; high definition television was going to result in huge sales for those companies who mastered the technology. It now seems that the whole concept is dead and will be replaced by other technologies.

[4]See a discussion of this issue in Rosabeth Moss Kanter, "Swimming in New Streams: Mastering Innovation Dilemmas," *California Management Review*, 31, no. 4 (Summer 1989): 45–69.

strategies change as products move through their life cycle. Successful product strategies require determining the best strategy for each product based on its position in its life cycle. A firm, therefore, identifies products or families of products and their position in the life cycle. Let us review some strategy options as products move through their life cycle.

INTRODUCTORY PHASE. Because products in the introductory phase are still being "fine-tuned" for the market, as are their production techniques, they may warrant unusual expenditures for (1) research, (2) product development, (3) process modification and enhancement, and (4) supplier development. For example, when video cassette recorders (VCRs) were first introduced, the features desired by the public were still being determined. At the same time, production managers were still groping for the best manufacturing techniques.

GROWTH PHASE. In the growth phase, product design has begun to stabilize, and effective forecasting of capacity requirements is necessary. Adding capacity or enhancing existing capacity to accommodate the increase in product demand may be necessary.

MATURITY PHASE. With product maturity come competitors, so high-volume, innovative production may be appropriate. Improved cost control, reduction in options, and a paring down of the product line may be effective or necessary for profitability and market share.

PRODUCT DECLINE. Management may need to be ruthless with those products whose life cycle is at an end. Dying products are typically poor products in which to invest resources and managerial talent. Unless dying products make some unique contribution to the firm's reputation or its product line or can be sold with an unusually high contribution, their production should be terminated.[5]

FIGURE 6.4 ■ Product Development Yields Few Successes

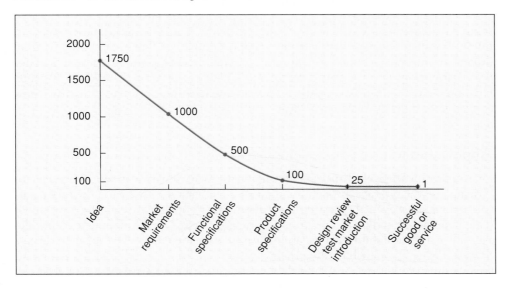

[5]Contribution is defined as the difference between direct cost and selling price. Direct costs are labor and material that go into the product.

TABLE 6.1 ■ HOW PRODUCT DEVELOPMENT IS MANAGED MAKES A DIFFERENCE: PRODUCT DEVELOPMENT PERFORMANCE OF REGIONAL AUTO INDUSTRIES			
	JAPANESE PRODUCERS	EUROPEAN VOLUME PRODUCERS	AMERICAN PRODUCERS
Average engineering hours per new car (millions)	1.7	2.9	3.1
Average development time per new car (in months)	46.2	57.3	60.4
Number of employees in project team	485.0	904.0	903.0
Number of body types per new car	2.3	2.7	1.7
Average ratio of shared parts	18%	28%	38%
Ratio of delayed products	1 in 6	1 in 3	1 in 2

Source: Adapted from James P. Womack, Daniel T. Jones, and Daniel Roos, *The Machine That Changed the World*, New York: Macmillan, 1990, p. 118. Data are representative of performance in the mid-1980s. The world auto industry has become more competitive in the ensuing decade.

NCR corporation has demonstrated the success of the team approach with their new 2760 electronic cash register. The cash register goes together with no screws or bolts. The entire terminal consists of just fifteen vendor produced components. Assembly is so easy that this engineer can put the terminal together blindfolded. NCR has reduced the number of parts by 85%, the number of suppliers by 65, and the time to assemble by 25%.

PRODUCT DEVELOPMENT

Management of the product development process may well determine not only product success, but also the firm's future. Table 6.1 provides a view of six important factors in product development in the automobile industry. In this section, we examine how to be successful at product development.

The Product Development System

Figure 6.5 shows a product development system. In this system, product options go through eight stages, starting with ideas that may be from either internal or external sources, and ending with the evaluation of a new product. The initial stage of successful new product development may put emphasis on factors that are external (market driven) or internal (technology and innovation driven) or a combination. Outstanding organizations find the best combination for idea generation. The *POM in Action* box "Stryker's Product Development Ideas Come from Its Customers" discusses how Stryker maintains its flow of new ideas.

Approaches to Product Development

One approach to overall product development is to assign a product manager to "champion" the product through the product development system and the related organizations. However, the best product development approach seems to be a formal team approach. Such teams are known variously as product development teams, design for manufacturability teams, and value engineering teams. The Japanese bypass the team issue by not subdividing their organization into research and development, engineering, production, and so forth. Consistent with the Japanese style of group effort and teamwork, these activities are all in one organization. The Japanese culture

Stryker's Product Development Ideas Come from Its Customers

Homer Stryker's hospital products firm has made Forbes' list of the Best Small Companies in America for 10 years straight. From its humble start 50 years ago by its clever orthopedist founder, Stryker Corporation now offers an array of niche products including bone drills and saws, hospital beds, hip implants, and video cameras for internal surgery.

Churning out new products has been Stryker's strength. By operating with autonomous divisions, each with its own highly trained, specialized sales staff, Stryker knows how to listen to its customers. Stryker's salespeople act as a de facto research-and-development team. Most of the company's new product ideas come from salespeople standing in the operating room next to the physician. There they can observe the doctor in action, write down his or her comments, and come up with ways to improve a saw, a hip implant, or a bed.

As a case in point, eye surgeons kept complaining about a bed's lack of flexibility at the head level. It was hard, they said, to position a patient's head. Stryker people took note and the firm rolled out a profitable bed with a moveable headrest.

Another hot new product is a tiny $18,000 video camera used inside a long tube through the abdomen for gall bladder surgery. Aided by the camera, the surgeon can swiftly remove the gall bladder with only a minute incision. Instead of a 1-week hospital stay, the patient is out the next day. This product holds down health care costs while producing a brisk seller for Stryker.

Sources: Forbes (November 11, 1991): 243–244; and *Marketing News* (February 1, 1993): 14.

FIGURE 6.5 ■ Product Development Stages

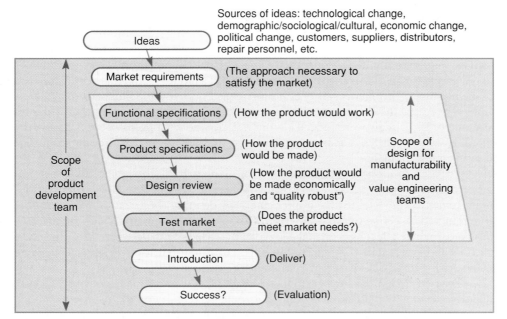

Product concepts are developed from a variety of sources, both external and internal to the firm. Concepts that survive the product idea stage progress through various stages with nearly constant review in a highly participative environment to minimize failure.

Product development teams

and management style are more collegial and the organization less structured than in most Western countries. Therefore, they find it unnecessary to have "teams" provide the necessary communication and coordination. However, the typical Western style and the conventional wisdom is to use teams. **Product development teams** are charged with the responsibility of moving from market requirements for a product to achieving a product success (Figure 6.5). Such teams often include marketing, manufacturing, purchasing, quality assurance, and field service personnel. Many teams also include representatives from vendors. Regardless of the formal nature of the product development effort, research suggests that success is more likely to occur in an open, highly participative environment where those with potential contributions are allowed to make them. The objective of a product development team is to make the product or service a success. This includes marketability, manufacturability, and serviceability.

Design for manufacturability and value engineering teams

Design for manufacturability and value engineering teams, on the other hand, have a somewhat narrower charge. They are charged with improvement of designs and specifications at the research, development, design, and production stages of product development. In addition to immediate, obvious cost reduction, design for manufacturability and value engineering may produce other benefits. These include

1. reduced complexity of the product;
2. additional standardization of components;
3. improvement of functional aspects of the products;
4. improved job design and job safety;
5. improved maintainability (serviceability) of the product;
6. quality robust design.

Quality robust design

Quality robust design means that the product is designed so that small variations in production or assembly do not adversely affect the product. For instance, AT&T developed an integrated circuit that could be used in many products to amplify voice signals. As originally designed, the circuit had to be manufactured very precisely to avoid variations in the strength of the signal. Such a circuit would have been costly to make because of stringent quality controls needed during the manufacturing process. But AT&T's engineers, after testing and analyzing the design, realized that if the resistance of the circuit were reduced—a minor change with no associated costs—the circuit would be far less sensitive to manufacturing variations. The result was a 40% improvement in quality.[6]

Product development teams, design for manufacturability teams, and value engineering teams may be the best cost-avoidance technique available to operations management. They yield value improvement by defining the essential function(s) of the item and by achieving that function without lowering quality. Value engineering programs, when effectively managed, typically reduce cost between 15% and 70% without reducing quality. Some studies have indicated that for every dollar spent on value engineering, $10 to $25 in savings can be realized!

Product design has impact on virtually all aspects of operating expense. Consequently, development teams, regardless of their makeup, need to ensure a thorough evaluation of the product's design prior to a commitment to produce. The cost reduction achieved for a specific bracket via value engineering is shown in Figure 6.6.

---

[6]John Mayo, "Process Design as Important as Product Design," *Wall Street Journal* (October 29, 1984): 32.

FIGURE 6.6 ■ Cost Reduction of a Bracket via Value Engineering. Each time the bracket is redesigned and simplified, we are able to produce it for less.

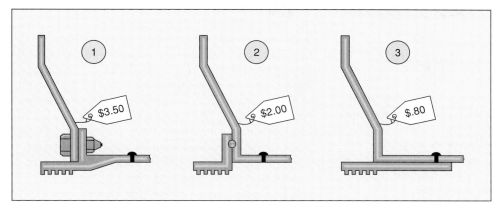

(*Source:* Adapted from Robert Goodell Brown, *Management Decisions for Production Operations*, Hinsdale, IL: Dryden Press, Inc., 1971, p. 353.)

Value Analysis

Whereas value engineering focuses on preproduction design improvement, value analysis, a related technique, takes place during the production process when it is clear that a new product is a success. **Value analysis** teams are charged with improvements that lead to either a better product or a product made more economically. The techniques and advantages for value analysis are the same as for value engineering, although minor changes in implementation may be necessary because analysis is taking place while the product is being produced.

Time-Based Competition

A firm may make a substantial investment to place a new product to market. With many products, the first company into production may have its product adopted for use in a variety of applications that will generate sales for years. It may become the "standard." Consequently, there is often more concern with getting the product to market than with optimum product design or process efficiency. Rapid introduction to the market may be good management because until competition begins to introduce copies or improved versions, the product can sometimes be priced high enough to earn a profit even using somewhat inefficient production design and methods. For example, when Kodak first introduced its Ektar film, the film sold for 10% to 15% more than conventional film. Motorola's pocket-sized cellular telephone was 50% smaller than any Japanese competitor's and sold for twice the price.[7]

The technology and affluence of modern society is also shortening product life. This increases the importance of product development because faster developers of new products continually gain a competitive advantage over slower developers.[8]

Value analysis

The new washer transmission designed by Maytag can switch from slow reciprocal motion of the agitator shaft during the wash cycle to fast rotary motion of the wash tub during the wring cycle. The new design using only 40 pieces is more reliable. The reduction in parts means a substantial reduction in cost with fewer designs and purchases, as well as less inventory and manufacturing expense.

[7]J. Dean and J. Evans, *Total Quality*, (St. Paul, West Publishing, 1994), p. 251.

[8]See related discussion in George Stalk, Jr., "Time—The Next Source of Competitive Advantage," *Harvard Business Review* (July/August 1988): 41–51; Joseph Blackburn, *Time-Based Competition: The Next Battleground in American Manufacturing* (Homewood, IL: Business One/Irwin, 1990); "Manufacturing: About Time," *Economist* (April 11, 1990): 72.

Developing a Successful New Printer at Hewlett-Packard

Hewlett-Packard (H-P) needed a blockbuster product. Research had shown that personal computer users wanted a new printer on the market. It could be *relatively* slow, but it had to print as clearly as a laser model and sell for less than half the price for a laser. A team of researchers, engineers, and marketing experts met to study the possibilities.

In its first step, the team defined exactly what customers needed and examined the shortcomings of existing low-cost printers such as Japan's Epson, which dominated the market. Still in the conceptualizing phase, product engineers were brought in to confirm that H-P could produce the printer and print head. The team then, as a second step, submitted a plan of action. Management quickly stamped its approval.

Now the team had to design a prototype that could be tested: It had to meet performance, reliability, cost, and manufacturability goals. H-P started with an assembly of components, handwired to printed-circuit boards, to represent the technical core of the printer. As soon as the prototype proved feasible and on target for market needs, the project team was enlarged. Specialists in mechanical design, control software, and parts sourcing were added to help produce several working prototypes. These models were assembled complete with cabinets, software, panel, and paper handlers, and handed to consumers to try out. Based on this trial, print quality still had to be improved, but the DeskJet was ready for production.

Just 26 months after H-P first explored the idea, the DeskJet printer was launched. It was an immediate success, as was H-P's color jet printer. The company's share of the U.S. printer market jumped from 2% in 1984 to 35% by 1993.

Sources: Harvard Business Review (May/June 1990): 156; and *Wall Street Journal* (September 8, 1994): A1, A9.

Time-based competition

Those who develop products faster are learning faster. Faster product introduction has a cumulative and positive effect not only in the marketplace, but also on innovative design, quality improvements, and cost reduction. **Time-based competition** is the concept that faster product development has a competitive advantage. As an example, see the *POM in Action* box describing Hewlett-Packard's new printer introduction. Products must be developed fast, but they must also be developed well, and economically. Doing so is difficult.

Product by Value

Product-by-value analysis

The effective operations manager directs efforts toward those items that show the greatest promise. This is the Pareto principle applied to product mix. Resources are invested in the critical few and not the trivial many. **Product-by-value analysis** lists products in descending order of their *individual dollar contribution* to the firm. It also lists the *total annual dollar contribution* of the product. Low contribution on a per unit basis by a particular product may look substantially different if it represents a large portion of the company's sales.

A product-by-value report allows management to evaluate possible strategies for each product. These might include increasing cash flow (for example, increasing contribution by raising selling price or lowering cost), increasing market penetration (for example, improving quality and/or reducing cost or price), or reducing costs (for example, improving the production process). The report may also tell management

Product design can also mean a change of materials. Automobile manufacturers are currently evaluating a number of non-steel materials like plastic and fiberglass, as well as aluminum, to reduce the weight of cars and thereby improve mileage. Aluminum components, for instance, can weigh half as much as steel. However, aluminum has its own drawbacks, notably its cost—four times as much as that of steel—and usually more expensive manufacturing processes. Here two technicians lift the aluminum shell of a Mercury Sable.

which product offerings should be eliminated and which fail to justify further investment in research and development or capital equipment. The report focuses management's attention on the strategic direction for each product.

DEFINING AND DOCUMENTING THE PRODUCT

Once new products or services are selected for introduction, they must be defined. First, a product or service is defined in terms of its functions, that is, what it is to do. The product is then designed, that is, it is determined how the functions are to be achieved. Management typically has a variety of options as to how a product is to achieve its functional purpose. For instance, when an alarm clock is produced, aspects of design such as the color, size, or location of buttons may make substantial differences in ease of manufacture, quality and market acceptance.

Rigorous specifications of a product are necessary to assure efficient production. Equipment, layout, and human resources cannot be decided upon until the product is defined, designed, and documented. Therefore, every organization needs documents to define its products. This is true of everything from meat patties, to cheese, to computers, to a medical procedure. In the case of cheese, a written specification is typical. Indeed, written specifications or standard grades exist and provide the definition for many products. For instance, Monterey Jack cheese has a written description that specifies the characteristics necessary for each Department of Agriculture grade. A portion of the Department of Agriculture grade for Monterey Jack Grade AA is shown in Figure 6.7. Similarly, McDonald's Corp. has 60 specifications for potatoes that are to be made into McDonald's french fries (see the photo on page 223).

Most manufactured items as well as their components are typically defined by a drawing, usually referred to as an engineering drawing. An **engineering drawing** shows the dimensions, tolerances, materials, and finishes of a component. The engineering drawing will be an item on a bill of material. An engineering drawing is shown in Figure 6.8. The **bill of material** lists the components, their description, and the quantity of each required to make one unit of a product. A bill of material for a manufactured item is shown in Figure 6.9(a). A bill of material is often referred to as a BOM. An engineering drawing shows how to make one item on the bill of material.

Engineering drawing

Bill of material (BOM)

FIGURE 6.7 ■ Monterey Jack. A portion of the general requirements for the U.S. grades of Monterey cheese is shown here.

---

§ 58.2469   Specifications for U.S. grades of Monterey (Monterey Jack) cheese

(a) *U.S. grade AA.* Monterey cheese shall conform to the following requirements:

(1) *Flavor.* Is fine and highly pleasing, free from undesirable flavors and odors. May possess a very slight acid or feed flavor.

(2) *Body and texture.* A plug drawn from the cheese shall be reasonably firm. It shall have numerous small mechanical openings evenly distributed throughout the plug. It shall not possess sweet holes, yeast holes, or other gas holes.

(3) *Color.* Shall have a natural, uniform, bright attractive appearance.

(4) *Finish and appearance—bandaged and paraffin-dipped.* The rind shall be sound, firm, and smooth providing a good protection to the cheese.

Code of Federal Regulation, Parts 53 to 109, Revised as of Jan. 1, 1985, General Service Administration.

GE Motors has completely redesigned its washing machine motors, reducing individual parts from 87 to 23, manufacturing processes from 61 to 20 and the production cycle from 5 days to 12 hours. Here, Sheri Nemeth, who is leader of the site team responsible for getting manufacturing systems on line and employees trained, inspects one of the new Form W motors.

In the food-service industry, bills of material manifest themselves in portion-control standards. The portion-control standard for a "Juicy Burger" is shown in Figure 6.9(b). In a more complex product, a bill of material is referenced on other bills of material of which they are a part. In this manner, subunits (subassemblies) are part of the next higher unit (their parent bill of material), which ultimately make a final product. Products, in addition to being defined by a written specification, a portion-control document, or bill of material, can be defined in other ways. For example, products such as chemicals, paints, and petroleums may be defined by formulas or proportions that describe how they are to be made.

Make or Buy

For many components of products, firms have the option of producing the component themselves or purchasing it from an outside source. Choosing between these options

FIGURE 6.8 ■ Engineering Drawings Such as This One Show Dimensions, Tolerances, Materials, and Finishes

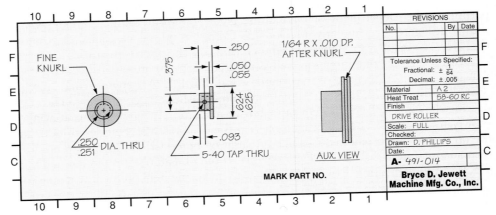

FIGURE 6.9 ■ Bills of Material Take Different Forms in a Manufacturing Plant (a) and a Fast-Food Restaurant (b), but in Both Cases, the Product Must Be Defined

Bill of Material for a Panel Weldment

NUMBER	DESCRIPTION	QTY
A 60-71	PANEL WELDM'T	1
A 60-7	LOWER ROLLER ASSM.	1
R 60-17	ROLLER	1
R 60-428	PIN	1
P 60-2	LOCKNUT	1
A 60-72	GUIDE ASSM. REAR	1
R 60-57-1	SUPPORT ANGLE	1
A 60-4	ROLLER ASSEM.	1
02-50-1150	BOLT	1
A 60-73	GUIDE ASSM. FRONT	1
A 60-74	SUPPORT WELDM'T	1
R 60-99	WEAR PLATE	1
02-50-1150	BOLT	1

(a)

Portion Control Standard for a Hamburger

PRODUCT: Juicy Burger

DESCRIPTION	QTY
Buns	1
Cheese	1 slice
Meat patties	2
Pickle slice	2
Dehydrated onions	1/250 pkg.
Sauce	1/137.5
Lettuce	1/26 head

(b)

is known as the make or buy decision. The **make-or-buy decision** distinguishes between what the firm is willing to produce and what it is willing to purchase. Because of variations in quality, cost, and delivery schedules, the make-or-buy decision is critical to product definition. Many items can be purchased as a "standard item"

Make-or-buy decision

The J. R. Simplot potato processing facility in Caldwell, Idaho, is responsible for making many of the billions of french fries McDonald's uses each year. Sixty specifications define how these strips of potatoes become french fries at McDonald's. These specifications define this product by first specifying a russet Burbank potato. The russet Burbank potato has a distinctive taste and high ratio of solids to water. It specifies special blend of frying oil and the unique steaming process. The fries are then prefried and dried; the exact time and heat being covered by a patent. Mac fries are sprayed, in lieu of dipping in sugar as are other fries, to brown them evenly. The product is further defined by requiring that 40% of all fries be between two and three inches long and another 40% must be over three inches long. A few stubby ones constitute the final 20%.

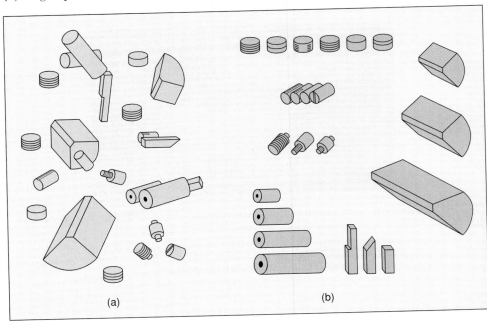

produced by someone else. Such a standard item does not require its own bill of material or engineering drawing because its specification as a standard item is adequate. Examples are the standard bolts listed on the bill of material shown in Figure 6.9(a), for which there will be SAE (Society of Automotive Engineers) specifications. Therefore, there typically is no need for the firm to duplicate this specification in another document. We discuss what is known as the make-or-buy decision in more detail in Chapter 12.

Group Technology

Group technology

Engineering drawings may also include codes to facilitate group technology. **Group technology** requires that components be identified by a coding scheme that specifies the type of processing (such as drilling) and the parameters of the processing (such as size). Machines can then process families of parts as a group, minimizing setups, routings, and material handling. An example of how families of parts may be grouped is shown in Figure 6.10. Group technology provides a systematic way to review a family of components to see if an existing component might suffice on a new project. Using an existing component eliminates all the costs connected with the design and development of the new part, which is a major cost reduction. For these reasons, successful implementation of group technology leads to

1. improved design because more design time can be devoted to fewer products,
2. reduced raw material and purchases,
3. simplified production planning and control,

FIGURE 6.10 ■ A Variety of Coding Schemes Move Manufactured Components from (a) Ungrouped to (b) Grouped

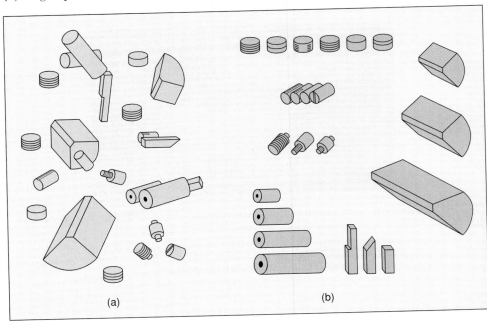

(a)   (b)

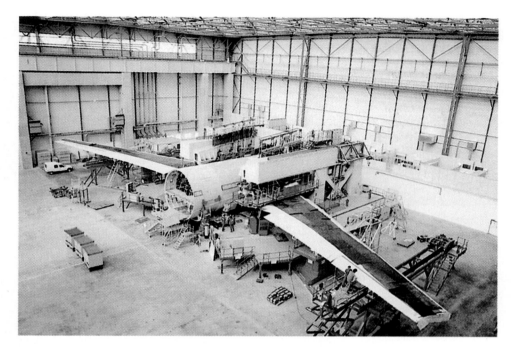

Group technology also opens the door to consideration of the exact same part in other applications. For instance, on the Airbus A340 assembly shown near Toulouse, France, much of the wing is the same as that used on the Airbus A330. The differences are limited to engine installation. This commonality of components can save an enormous amount in design and tooling, reducing both costs and development time.

4. improved routing and machine loading,
5. reduced tooling setup time, and work-in-process and production time.

The application of group technology helps the entire organization, as many costs are reduced.

Computer-Aided Design

Product design is greatly enhanced through the use of **computer-aided design (CAD)**. Increasingly, manufactured products are designed and documented on CAD.

Where CAD is used, a design engineer starts by developing a rough sketch or, conceivably, just an idea. The designer then utilizes a graphic display as a drafting board to construct the geometry of a design. As a geometric definition is completed, a sophisticated CAD system will allow the designer to determine various kinds of engineering data, such as strength or heat transfer. CAD will also allow the designer to ensure that parts fit together so there will be no interferences when parts are subsequently assembled. Thus, if the designer is sketching the fender for an automobile, the brackets and related panels are changed as the fender is changed. Analysis of existing, as well as new, designs can be done expediently and economically. These advances in CAD systems are discussed further in the *POM in Action* box "Paperless Design at Boeing" and in Chapter 8.

Computer-aided design (CAD)

Paperless Design at Boeing

When designers of Boeing's new 777 wide-body plane want to make design changes, there is no going back to the drawing board: There are no drawing boards. Nor are there any drawings. All the design and engineering for the 777 have been done on computer screens, making it the first fully "paperless" airliner.

The paperless approach saves money by greatly reducing the number of last-minute changes that are needed to make the two million pieces in an airplane fit together. It also makes it unnecessary to build a full-scale mockup of the plane.

"Every engineer since Leonardo da Vinci has had to think in three dimensions but draw in two dimensions on paper," says Boeing VP Philip Condit. New computing tools allow design in 3D. By completely eliminating paper and putting 2 to 3 *trillion* bytes of information into computers, Boeing is trying to retain its dominance as the world's leading jet maker. Since World War II, 54% of all airliners ordered in the world have been Boeing.

The design effort for the 777 involves 5,600 people scattered over 18 locations in the Puget Sound area. Computers provide the essential link, with a lot riding on the change. The 777, with its first test flight in 1994, represents a $7 billion gamble by Boeing.

Sources: New York Times (November 10, 1991): 3–1; and *Business Week* (October 28, 1991): 120–121.

Once the designer is satisfied with the design, it becomes part of a drawing data base on electronic media. The CAD system, through a library of symbols and details, also helps to ensure adherence to the drafting standards. Additionally, because CAD data are available for subsequent use by others, tool design personnel and programmers of numerically controlled machines are aided. They can now proceed to design tooling and programs with confidence that they have the latest accurate engineering data and engineering drawings.

Computer aided design: B. F. Goodrich engineers and managers use software from Structural Dynamics Research Corporation (SDRC) to model wheel and brake assemblies. By analysis of stress and heat, they can often avoid costly design and production mistakes. Errors that are found at the design stage on a CRT screen can often be fixed for a nominal cost, but the cost is substantial once production has begun.

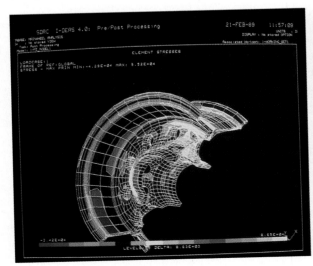

Once again, we see how decisions made when a product is designed have ramifications in many other P/OM decisions.

PREPARING FOR PRODUCTION

Once a product is selected and designed, a number of issues remain. Among these are (a) documentation to aid the production process, (b) configuration management, and (c) determining the exact time to stop design and move the product to production.

Documentation

An **assembly drawing** simply shows an exploded view of the product. An assembly drawing is usually a three-dimensional drawing, known as an isometric drawing. The relative locations of the components are shown in relation to each other to show how to assemble the unit (see Figure 6.11(a)).

Assembly drawing

The **assembly chart** shows in schematic form how a product is assembled. Manufactured components, purchased components, or a combination of both may be shown on an assembly chart. The assembly chart identifies the point of production where components flow into subassemblies and ultimately into a final product. An example of an assembly chart is shown in Figure 6.11(b).

Assembly chart

The **route sheet** lists the operations (including assembly and inspection) necessary to produce the component with the material specified in the bill of material. The

Route sheet

FIGURE 6.11 ■ Assembly Drawing and Assembly Chart

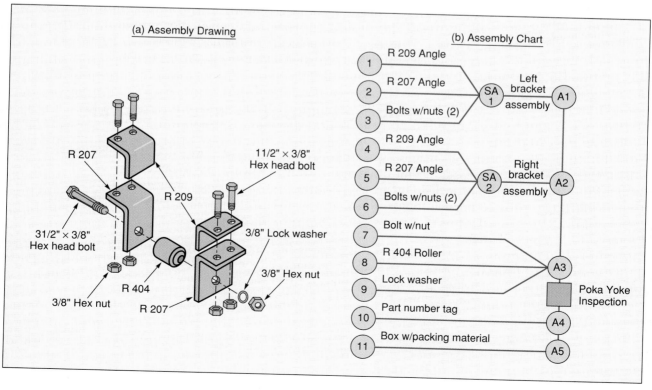

route sheet for an item will have one entry for each operation to be performed on the item. When route sheets include specific methods of operation and labor standards, they are often known as *process sheets*.

Job instructions

Organizations also often find it necessary to develop **job instructions**, which provide detailed instructions about how to perform the task. Where there are a large variety of jobs, job instructions change often. Instruction manuals are used where the jobs seldom change. Various **standards manuals** provide standard times for setup and information about speed, capacity, and tolerances, and perhaps other pertinent data for each operation in a process. Standards manuals are found not only in manufacturing environments, but also in most operating areas, such as a well-organized institutional kitchen or a computer center.

Standards manuals

Work order

The **work order** is an instruction to make a given quantity of a particular item, usually to a given schedule. The ticket that a waiter writes in your favorite restaurant is a work order. In a hospital or factory, the work order is a more formal order that provides authorization to draw various pharmaceuticals or items from inventory, to perform various functions, and to assign personnel to perform those functions. Increasingly, job instructions, standards manuals, and work orders are maintained on computer.

Configuration Management

Engineering change notice (ECN)

Engineering change notices (ECNs) change some aspect of the product's definition or documentation, such as an engineering drawing or a bill of material. For a complex product that has a long manufacturing cycle, such as a Boeing 747 jumbo jet, the changes may be so numerous that no two 747s are built exactly alike—which is indeed the case. Such dynamic design change has fostered the development of a discipline known as configuration management, which is concerned with product identification, control, and documentation. **Configuration management** is the system by which a product's planned and changing configurations are accurately identified and for which control and accountability of change are maintained.

Configuration management

SERVICE PRODUCTS ARE DIFFERENT

Much of our discussion so far has focused on what we can call tangible products, that is, goods. On the other side of the product coin are, of course, services. Service industries include intangibles such as banking, finance, insurance, transportation, and communications.[9] They also include those medical procedures that leave only the tiniest scar after an appendectomy, as well as the shampoo and cut at a hair salon.

Thus, the first thing that is different about service is that it is *usually intangible* (your purchase of a ride in an empty airline seat between two cities) as opposed to a tangible product. Note, however, that the service may still be precisely defined. The airline seat may be defined by row, flight number, date, and class.

---

[9]The *Statistical Abstract of the United States* considers services as wholesale and retail trade, finance, insurance, real estate, and government. Most definitions also include education, health care, and the legal and lodging industries.

The second thing is that services are often *produced and consumed simultaneously*; there is no stored inventory. For instance, the beauty salon produces a haircut that is consumed simultaneously, or the doctor produces an operation that is consumed as it is produced.

The third item that makes services different is that although many goods are standardized or have standardized components, *many services are unique*. Your mix of financial coverage, which manifests itself in investments and insurance policies, may not be the same as anyone else's.

The fourth thing that makes the service product unique is *high customer interaction*. It is often difficult to standardize, automate, and be as efficient as we would like because customer interaction demands a uniqueness. This uniqueness in many cases is what the customer is paying for; therefore, the operations manager must ensure that the product is designed so that it can be delivered in the required unique manner.

The fifth item that makes service unique is *inconsistent product definition*. Product definition may be rigorous, as in the case of an insurance policy, or casual, as in the case of a haircut. Moreover, the haircut definition not only varies with each customer, but often with each haircut, even for the same customer.

In spite of these differences between products and services, there is still an operations function to be performed. This occurs when the insurance company defines the product (say, an insurance policy), processes the purchase transaction, issues premium statements, and processes those premiums. The same would be the case for a stock transaction where the "back room," which is the operations center, handles the transaction. In the case of an airline, the operations function schedules the planes, crews, and meals, and usually manages the maintenance function. So, although service products are often unique, the operations function continues to perform a transformation function, as was shown in the organization charts of Chapter 1.

APPLICATION OF DECISION TREES TO PRODUCT DESIGN

Decision trees, introduced in the supplement to Chapter 2 can be used for new product decisions as well as for a wide variety of other management problems. They are particularly helpful when there are a series of decisions and various outcomes that lead to *subsequent* decisions, followed by other outcomes. You may recall from our earlier discussions that to form a decision tree, we use the following procedure:

1. Be sure that all possible alternatives and states of nature are included in the tree. This includes an alternative of "doing nothing."

2. Payoffs are entered at the end of the appropriate branch. This is the place to develop the payoff of achieving this branch.

3. The objective is to determine the expected value of each course of action. We accomplish this by starting at the end of the tree (the right-hand side) and working toward the beginning of the tree (the left), calculating values at each step and "pruning" alternatives that are not as good as others from the same node.

Example 1 shows the use of a decision tree applied to product design.

EXAMPLE 1

Silicon, Inc., a semiconductor manufacturer, is investigating the possibility of producing and marketing a microprocessor. Undertaking this project will require either purchasing a sophisticated CAD system or hiring and training several additional engineers. The market for the product could be either favorable or unfavorable. Silicon, Inc., of course, has the option of not developing the new product at all.

With favorable acceptance by the market, sales would be 25,000 processors selling for $100 each, and with unfavorable acceptance, sales would be only 8,000 processors selling for $100 each. The cost of the CAD equipment is $500,000, but that of hiring and training three new engineers is only $375,000. However, manufacturing cost should drop from $50 each when manufacturing without CAD to $40 each when manufacturing with CAD.

The probability of favorable acceptance of the new microprocessor is .40; the probability of unfavorable acceptance is .60. See Figure 6.12.

FIGURE 6.12   ■   Decision Tree for Development of a New Product

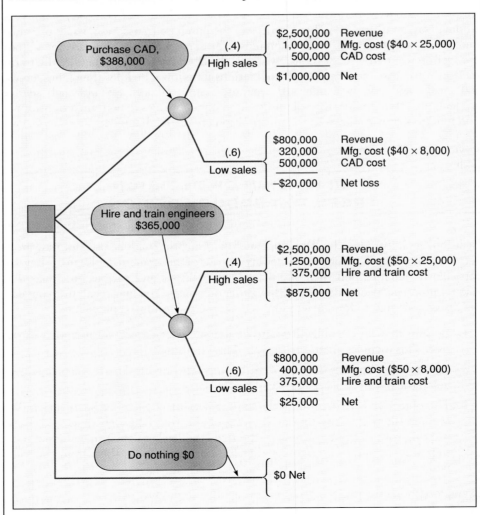

The expected monetary values (EMVs) have been circled at each step of the decision tree. For the top branch:

$$\text{EMV (purchase CAD system)} = (.4)(\$1,000,000) + (.6)(-\$20,000)$$
$$= \$388,000$$

This represents the results that will occur if Silicon, Inc., purchases CAD.

The expected value of hiring and training engineers is the second series of branches:

$$\text{EMV (hire/train engineers)} = (.4)(\$875,000) + (.6)(\$25,000)$$
$$= \$365,000$$

The EMV of doing nothing is $0.

Because the top branch has the highest expected monetary value (an EMV of $388,000 vs. $365,000 vs. $0), it represents the best decision. Management should purchase the CAD system.

TRANSITION TO PRODUCTION

Eventually, our product has been selected, designed, and defined. The product has progressed from an idea, to a functional definition, and then perhaps to a design. Now, management must make a decision as to further development, production, or termination of the product idea. One of the arts of modern manage is knowing when to move a product from development to production; this movement is known as *transition to production*. The product development staff is always interested in making improvements in the product. Because this staff tends to see product development as evolutionary, they may never have a completed product, but as noted in our earlier discussion, the cost of late product introduction is high. Although these conflicting pressures exist, management must make a decision—more development or production.

Once this decision is made, there is usually a period of trial production to ensure that the design is indeed producible. This is the manufacturability test. This also gives the production staff the opportunity to develop proper tooling, quality control procedures, and training of personnel to ensure that production can be initiated successfully. Finally, when the product is deemed both marketable and producible, line management will assume responsibility.

Some companies appoint a project manager and others use the product development teams we discussed earlier to ensure that the transition from the development phase to production is successful. Both approaches allow a wide range of resources and talents to be brought to bear to ensure satisfactory production of a product that is still in flux. A third approach is integration of the product development and manufacturing organizations. This allows for easy shifting of resources between the two organizations as needs change. The production manager's job is to make the transition from R&D to production smooth and without gaps.

ACHIEVING WORLD-CLASS STANDARDS

World-class firms recognize that anything less than an excellent product strategy can be devastating. Consequently, these firms focus on only a few businesses or technologies. For instance Honda's focus is engines. Virtually all of Honda's sales (for example, autos, motorcycles, generators, lawn mowers, etc.) are based on its outstanding engine technology. The same is true of Intel (microcomputer components) and Microsoft (PC software products). World-class firms design these products to be "quality robust" while continually improving them. Managers of world-class firms insist upon strong communication between customer, product, processes, and suppliers that results in a high success rate for their new products. Benchmarks, of course, vary by industry, but Rubbermaid introduces a new product each day!

World-class firms often allow customization around existing products or services. This approach allows the customer to choose product variations while reinforcing the organization's strength. This is the way Dell Computers has built a huge market. Dell delivers computers with the exact hardware and software desired by the end user. And they do it fast—which brings us to the next attribute of world-class companies. They understand that speed to market is important. They provide quick response. Motorola built its pager business based on quick response. The firm reduced the time from order to delivery from over a month to less than 3 hours, providing a benchmark for others. Finally, a world-class product strategy links product strategy to investment, market share, product life cycles, and breadth of the product line. Product development and design are key to a successful business strategy.

SUMMARY

Selecting, designing, and defining a product has implications for all subsequent operations decisions. The operations manager must be imaginative and resourceful in the product development process. Products are defined by written specification, bills of material, and engineering drawings. Group technology, computer-aided design, and value engineering are helpful product design techniques. Assembly drawings, assembly charts, route sheets, job instruction, work orders, and standards manuals assist the manager in defining a product for production.

Once a product is in production, value analysis is appropriate for quality and production review. Configuration management allows the manager to track and document the product that has been produced.

How products move through their life cycle of introduction, growth, maturity, and decline influences the strategy the operations manager should pursue. And decision trees are particularly useful techniques in many product strategy decisions.

KEY TERMS

Product strategy (p. 210)
Product development teams (p. 218)
Design for manufacturability and value engineering teams (p. 218)
Quality robust design (p. 218)
Value analysis (p. 219)
Time-based competition (p. 220)
Product-by-value analysis (p. 220)
Engineering drawing (p. 220)
Bill of material (BOM) (p. 221)
Make or buy decision (p. 223)

Group technology (p. 224)
Computer-aided design (CAD) (p. 225)
Assembly drawing (p. 227)
Assembly chart (p. 227)
Route sheet (p. 227)
Job instructions (p. 228)
Standards manuals (p. 228)
Work order (p. 228)
Engineering change notice (ECN) (p. 228)
Configuration management (p. 228)

SOLVED PROBLEM

Solved Problem 6.1

Kris King, president of King Electronics, Inc., has two design options for her new line of high-resolution cathode-ray tubes (CRTs) for computer-aided design workstations. The life cycle sales forecast for the CRT is 100,000 units.

Design option A has a .90 probability of yielding 59 good CRTs per 100 and a .10 probability of yielding 64 good CRTs per 100. This design will cost $1,000,000.

Design option B has a .80 probability of yielding 64 good units per 100 and a .20 probability of yielding 59 good units per 100. This design will cost $1,350,000.

Good or bad, each CRT will cost $75. Each good CRT will sell for $150. Bad CRTs are destroyed and have no salvage value. There is little disposal cost as they break up when thrown in the trash. Therefore, we ignore any disposal costs in this problem.

Solution

We draw the decision tree to reflect the two decisions and the probabilities associated with each decision. We then determine the payoff associated with each branch. This is shown in Figure 6.13.

FIGURE 6.13 ■ Decision Tree for Solved Problem 6.1

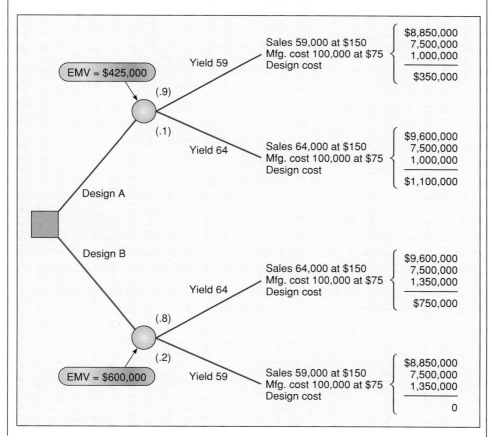

For design A,

$$\text{EMV (design A)} = (.9)(\$350,000) + (.1)(\$1,100,000)$$
$$= \$425,000$$

For design B,

$$\text{EMV (design B)} = (.8)(\$750,000) + (.2)(\$0)$$
$$= \$600,000$$

The highest payoff is design option B at $600,000.

DISCUSSION QUESTIONS

1. What management techniques may prove helpful in making the transition from design to production?

2. Why is it necessary to document a product explicitly?

3. What techniques do we use to document a product?

4. Configuration management has proved particularly useful in what industries? Why?

5. How does computer-aided design help other departments?

6. What is group technology and why is it proving helpful in our quest for productivity improvement?

7. What savings can be expected by computer-aided design?

8. How does computer-aided design help computer-aided manufacture?

9. What are the four phases of the product life cycle?

10. How does product selection (and design) affect quality?

11. Once a product is defined, what documents are used to assist production personnel in the manufacture of that product?

12. How does configuration management manifest itself when you ask for service on your automobile?

13. What are the similarities and dissimilarities between a manufactured product and a new type of life insurance policy referred to by the salesmen as their new "product."

CRITICAL THINKING EXERCISE

Rubbermaid's record of new product innovation is remarkable. With almost five thousand products, the firm continues to crank out a new one almost every day . . . and with great success. Rubbermaid has divided its product line into four dozen categories. Then it creates entrepreneurial teams of five to seven members in each category. Each team includes a product manager, research and manufacturing engineers, and financial sales and marketing executives. The teams conceive their own products, shepherding them from design stage to the marketplace.

Compare Rubbermaid's product approach to the American and Japanese approaches discussed in this chapter.

PROBLEMS

- 6.1 Prepare a bill of material for a ballpoint pen.
- 6.2 Draw an assembly chart for a ballpoint pen.
- 6.3 Prepare a bill of material for a simple table lamp. Identify the items that you, as manufacturer of the body and related components, are likely to make and that you are likely to purchase. Justify your decision for each.

• **6.4** Prepare an assembly chart for the table lamp in Problem 6.3.

• **6.5** As a library project, find a series of group technology codes.

⁞ **6.6** Given the contribution made on each of the three products in the table and their position in the life cycle, identify a reasonable operations strategy for each.

TABLE FOR PROBLEM 6.6

PRODUCT	PRODUCT CONTRIBUTION (PERCENT OF SELLING PRICE)	COMPANY CONTRIBUTION (PERCENT OF TOTAL ANNUAL CONTRIBUTION DIVIDED BY TOTAL ANNUAL SALES)	POSITION IN LIFE CYCLE
Portable computer	30	40	Growth
Laptop computer	30	50	Introduction
Hand calculator	50	10	Decline

⁞ **6.7** The product planning group of Hawkes Electric Supplies, Inc., has determined that it needs to design a new series of switches. They must decide upon one of three design strategies. The market forecast is for 200,000 units. The better and more sophisticated the design strategy and the more time spent on value engineering, the less will be the variable cost. The chief of engineering design, Dr. Gerry Johnson has decided that the following costs are a good estimate of the initial and variable costs connected with each approach. These are

  a) Low-tech: a low-technology, low-cost process consisting of hiring several new junior engineers. This has a cost of $45,000 and variable cost probabilities of .2 for $.55 each, .5 for $.50, and .3 for $.45.

  b) Subcontract: a medium-cost approach utilizing a good outside design staff. This approach would have an initial cost of $65,000 and variable cost probabilities of .7 of $.45, .2 of $.40 and .1 of $.35.

  c) High-tech: a high-technology approach utilizing the very best of the inside staff and the latest computer-aided design technology. This approach has a fixed cost of $75,000 and variable cost probabilities of .9 of $.40 and .1 of $.35.

What is the best decision based on an expected monetary value (EMV) criterion? (*Note:* We want the lowest EMV as we are dealing with costs in this problem.)

⁞ **6.8** Faber Manufacturing, Inc., of St. Paul, Minnesota, has the option of (a) proceeding immediately with production of a new top-of-the-line stereo TV, which has just completed prototype testing or (b) having the value analysis team complete a study. If Karita France, VP for Operations, proceeds with the existing prototype (option A), the firm can expect sales to be 100,000 units at $550 each with a probability of .6, and a .4 probability of 75,000 at $550. If, however, she uses the value analysis team (option B), the firm expects sales of 75,000 units at $750 with a probability of .7, and a .3 probability of 70,000 units at $750. Cost of the value analysis is $100,000. Which option has the highest expected monetary value (EMV)?

⁞ **6.9** Ritz Products' materials manager, Houston Griffin, must make a determination to make or buy a new semiconductor for the wrist TV it is about to produce. One million units are expected to be produced over the life cycle. If the product is made, the start-up and production cost of the make decision is $1,000,000, with a probability of .4 that the product will be satisfactory and .6 probability that it will not. If the product is not satisfactory, the firm will have to reevaluate the decision. If the decision is reevaluated, the choice will be to spend another $1,000,000 to redesign the semiconductor or to purchase. Likelihood of success the second time the make decision is made is .9. If the second make decision also fails, the firm must purchase. Regardless of when the purchase takes place, the best judgment Houston Griffin has of cost is that Ritz Products will pay $.50 for each purchased semiconductor plus $1,000,000 in vendor development cost.

   a) Assuming that Ritz Products must have the semiconductor (stopping or doing without is not a viable option), what is their best decision?

   b) What criteria did you use to make this decision?

   c) What is the worst that can happen to Ritz Products on this particular decision? What is the best that can happen?

: **6.10** Use the data in Solved Problem 6.1 to examine what happens to the decision if Ms. King can increase the yield when the yield is 59 out of each 100. If the yield is 59 per 100, a special expensive phosphorous for the screen can be used at an added cost of $50.00 per CRT. This procedure will be good for only 5 units per 100 (that is, this procedure can bring the yield up to only 64 per 100). Prepare the modified decision tree. What are the payoffs and which branch has the greatest EMV?

CASE STUDY

GE's Rotary Compressor

In 1981, market share and profits in General Electric's appliance division were falling. The company's technology was antiquated compared to foreign competitors. For example, making refrigerator compressors required 65 minutes of labor in comparison to 25 minutes for competitors in Japan and Italy. Moreover, GE's labor costs were higher. The alternatives were obvious: Either purchase compressors from Japan or Italy or design and build a better model.

By 1983, the decision to build a new rotary compressor in house was made, along with a commitment for a new $120 million factory. GE was not a novice in rotary compressor technology; it had invented the technology and had been using it in air conditioners for many years. A rotary compressor weighed less, had one-third fewer parts, and was more energy-efficient than the current reciprocating compressors. The rotary compressor took up less space, thus providing more room inside the refrigerator and better meeting customer requirements.

Some engineers argued to the contrary, citing the fact that rotary compressors run hotter. This is not a problem in most air conditioners, because the coolant cools the compressor. In a refrigerator, however, the coolant flows only one-tenth as fast, and

the unit runs about four times longer in 1 year than an air conditioner. GE had problems with the early rotary compressors in air conditioners. Although the bugs had been eliminated in smaller units, GE quit using rotaries in larger units due to frequent breakdowns in hot climates.

GE managers and design engineers were concerned about other issues. Rotary compressors make a high-pitched whine, and managers were afraid that this would adversely affect consumer acceptance. Many hours were spent on this issue by managers and consumer test panels. The new design also required key parts to work together with a tolerance of only 50 millionths of an inch. Nothing had been mass produced with such precision before, but manufacturing engineers felt sure they could do it.

The compressor they finally designed was nearly identical to that used in air conditioners, with one change. Two small parts inside the compressor were made out of powdered metal, rather than the hardened steel and cast iron used in air conditioners. This material was chosen because it could be machined to much closer tolerances, and reduced machining costs. Powdered metal had been tried a decade earlier on air conditioners but did not work. The design engineers who were new to designing compressors did not consider the earlier failure important.

A consultant suggested that GE consider a joint venture with a Japanese company that had a

(Continued)

rotary refrigerator compressor already on the market. The idea was rejected by management. The original designer of the air conditioner rotary compressor, who had left GE, offered his services as a consultant. GE declined his offer, writing him that they had sufficient technical expertise.

About 600 compressors were tested in 1983 without a single failure. They were run continuously for 2 months under elevated temperatures and pressures that were supposed to simulate 5 years' operation. GE normally conducts extensive field testing of new products; its original plan to test models in the field for 2 years was reduced to 9 months due to time pressure to complete the project.

The technician who disassembled and inspected the parts thought they did not look right. Parts of the motor were discolored, a sign of excessive heat. Bearings were worn, and it appeared that high heat was breaking down the lubricating oil. The technician's supervisors discounted these findings and did not relay them to upper levels of management. Another consultant who evaluated the test results believed that something was wrong because only one failure was found in 2 years and recommended that test conditions be intensified. This suggestion was also rejected by management.

By 1986, only 2.5 years after board approval, the new factory was producing compressors at a rate of 10 per minute. By the end of the year, more than 1 million had been produced. Market share rose and the new refrigerator appeared to be a success. But in July 1987, the first compressor failed. Soon after, reports of other failures in Puerto Rico arrived. By September, the appliance division knew it had a major problem. In December, the plant stopped making the compressor. Not until 1988 was the problem diagnosed as excessive wear in the two powdered-metal parts that burned up the oil. The cost in 1989 alone was $450 million. By mid-1990, GE had voluntarily replaced nearly 1.1 million compressors with ones purchased from six suppliers, five of them foreign.

DISCUSSION QUESTIONS

1. What factors in the product development process caused this disaster? What individuals were responsible?

2. How might this disaster have been prevented? What lessons do you think GE learned for the future?

3. On what basis was GE attempting to achieve a competitive advantage? How did they fail?

Source: James Dean and James Evans, *Total Quality* (St. Paul West Publishing, 1994) pp. 256–257.

BIBLIOGRAPHY

Akao, Y., ed. *Quality Function Deployment: Integrating Customer Requirements into Product Design.* Cambridge, MA: Productivity Press, 1990.

Ali, A., M. U. Kalwani, and D. Kovenock. "Selecting Product Development Projects: Pioneering versus Incremental Innovation Strategies." *Management Science,* 39, no. 3 (March 1993): 255–274.

Berliner, C., and J. A. Brimson. *Cost Management for Today's Advanced Manufacturing.* Boston: Harvard Business School Press, 1988.

Bower, J. L., and T. M. Hout. "Fast Cycle Capacity for Competitive Power." *Harvard Business Review* (November/December 1988): 110–118.

Burbidge, J. L. "Production Flow Analysis for Planning Group Technololgy." *Journal of Operations Management,* 10, no. 1 (January 1991): 5–27.

Capon, N., J. U. Farley, D. R. Lehmann, and J. M. Hulbert. "Profiles of Product Innovators Among Large U. S. Manufacturers." *Management Science,* 38, no. 2 (February 1992): 157.

Choi, M. and W. E. Riggs. "GT Coding and Classification Systems for Manufacturing Cell Design." *Production and Inventory Management Journal,* 32 (First Quarter 1991): 28.

Clark, K., and S. Wheelwright. "Organizing and Leading 'Heavyweight' Development Teams." *The California Management Review,* (Spring 1992)

Eppen, G. D., W. A. Hanson, and R. K. Martin. "Bundling-New Products, New Markets, Low Risk." *Sloan Management Review*, 32 (Summer 1991): 7.

Fitzsimmons, J. A., P. Kouvelis, and D. N. Mallick. "Design Strategy and Its Interface with Manufacturing and Marketing: A Conceptual Framework." *Journal of Operations Management*, 10, no. 3 (August 1991): 398.

Garza, O., and T. L. Smunt. "Countering the Negative Impact of Intercell Flow in Cellular Manufacturing." *Journal of Operations Management*, 10, no. 1 (January 1991): 92–118.

Hastings, N. A., and C. Yeh. "Bill of Manufacture." *Production and Inventory Management Journal*, 33, no. 4 (Fourth Quarter 1992): 27–31.

Iansiti, M. "Real-World R&D: Jumping the Product Generation Gap." *Harvard Business Review*, 71, no. 3 (May/June 1993): 131–147.

Miltenburg, J., and W. Zhang. "A Comparative Evaluation of Nine Well-Known Algorithms for Solving the Cell Formation Problem in Group Technology." *Journal of Operations Management*, 10, no. 1 (January 1991): 44–72.

Otis, I., "Designing for Manufacture and Assembly to Improve Efficiency and Quality." *Industrial Engineering*, 24, no. 8 (August 1992): 60.

Samoras, T. T., and F. L. Czerwinski. *Fundamentals of Configuration Management*. New York: John Wiley, 1971.

Smith, P. G., and D. G. Reinertsen. *Developing Products in Half the Time*. New York: Van Nostrand Reinhold, 1991.

Stalk, G., Jr., and T. M. Hout. *Competing Against Time*. New York: Free Press 1990.

Suri, R., and S. de Treville. "Full Speed Ahead: A Timely Look at Rapid Modeling and Operations Management." *OR/MS Today* (June 1991): 34–42.

Ulrich, K., D. Sartorius, S. Pearson, and M. Jakiela. "Including the Value of Time in Design-for-Manufacturing Decision Making." *Management Science*, 39, no. 4 (April 1993): 429–447.

6 SUPPLEMENT

LINEAR PROGRAMMING

The storm front closed in quickly on Chicago's O'Hare Airport, shutting it without warning. The heavy thunderstorms, lightning, and poor visibility sent American Airlines passengers and ground crew scurrying. Because American Airlines uses linear programming (LP) to schedule flights, hotels, crews, and refueling, LP has a direct impact on profitability. As Thomas Cook, president of AA's Decision Technology Group, says, "Finding fast solutions to LP problems is essential. If we get a major weather disruption at one of the hubs, such as Dallas or Chicago, then a lot of flights may get canceled, which means we have a lot of crews and airplanes in the wrong places. What we need is a way to put that whole operation back together again." LP is the tool that helps airlines such as American unsnarl and cope with this weather mess.[1] ◆

[1]Adapted from *Introduction to Contemporary Mathematics*, 2nd ed. (New York: W. H. Freeman, 1990), p. 82–83.

Linear programming (LP)

Many operations management decisions involve trying to make the most effective use of an organization's resources. Resources typically include machinery (such as planes), labor (such as pilots), money, time, and raw materials (such as jet fuel). These resources may be used to produce products (such as machines, furniture, food, or clothing) or services (such as airline schedules, advertising policies, or investment decisions). **Linear programming (LP)** is a widely used mathematical technique designed to help production and operations managers plan and make the decisions necessary to allocate resources.

A few examples of problems in which LP has been successfully applied in operations management are

1. selecting the product mix in a factory to make best use of machine- and labor-hours available while *maximizing* the firm's profit;

2. picking blends of raw materials in feed mills to produce finished feed combinations at *minimum* cost;

3. determining the distribution system that will *minimize* total shipping cost from several warehouses to various market locations;

4. developing a production schedule that will satisfy future demands for a firm's product and at the same time *minimize* total production and inventory costs.

As the *POM in Action* box "Using LP to Select Tenants in a Shopping Mall" suggests, LP can be used in a very broad range of applications.

REQUIREMENTS OF A LINEAR PROGRAMMING PROBLEM

All LP problems have four properties in common.

Objective function

1. LP problems seek to *maximize* or *minimize* some quantity (usually profit or cost). We refer to this property as the **objective function** of an LP problem. The major objective of a typical firm is to maximize dollar profits in the long run. In the case of a trucking or airline distribution system, the objective might be to minimize shipping costs.

Constraints

2. The presence of restrictions, or **constraints**, limits the degree to which we can pursue our objective. For example, deciding how many units of each product in a firm's product line to manufacture is restricted by available labor and machinery. We want, therefore, to maximize or minimize a quantity (the objective function) subject to limited resources (the constraints).

3. There must be *alternative courses of action* to choose from. For example, if a company produces three different products, management may use LP to decide how to allocate among them its limited production resources (of labor, machinery, and so on). If there were no alternatives to select from, we would not need LP.

4. The objective and constraints in linear programming problems must be expressed in terms of *linear equations* or inequalities.

Using LP to Select Tenants in a Shopping Mall

Homart Development Company is one of the largest shopping-center developers in the United States. When developing a new center, Homart produces a tentative floor plan, or footprint, for the mall. This plan outlines sizes, shapes, and spaces for large department stores. Leasing agreements are reached with the two or three major department stores that will become anchor stores in the mall. The anchor stores are able to negotiate highly favorable occupancy agreements. Typically, they either pay low rent or receive other concessions. Homart's profits come primarily from the rent paid by the nonanchor tenants—the smaller stores that lease space along the aisles of the mall. The decisions allocating space to potential tenants and establishing the tenant mix are therefore crucial to the success of the investment.

The tenant mix describes the desired stores in the mall by their size, general location, and type of merchandise or service provided. For example, the tenant mix might specify two small jewelry stores in a central section of the mall and a medium-sized shoe store and a large restaurant in one of the side aisles. In the past, Homart developed a plan for tenant mix using "rules of thumb" developed over years of experience in mall development.

Now, to improve its bottom line in an increasingly competitive marketplace, Homart treats the tenant-mix problem as a *linear programming* model. First, the model assumes that tenants can be classified into categories according to the type of merchandise or service they provide. Second, the model assumes that for each store type, store sizes can be made into distinct categories. For example, a small jewelry store is said to contain about 700 square feet and a large one about 2,200 square feet. The tenant-mix model is a powerful tool for enhancing Homart's mall planning and leasing activities.

(*Source:* Adapted from James Bean et al., "Selecting Tenants in a Shopping Mall," *Interfaces* (March/April 1988): 1–9.)

FORMULATING LINEAR PROGRAMMING PROBLEMS

One of the most common linear programming applications is the *product mix problem*. Two or more products are usually produced using limited resources. The company would like to determine how many units of each product it should produce in order to maximize overall profit given its limited resources. Let us look at an example.

Shader Electronics Example

The Shader Electronics Company produces two products: (1) the Shader Walkman, a portable AM/FM cassette player, and (2) the Shader Watch-TV, a wristwatch-sized black-and-white television. The production process for each product is similar in that both require a certain number of hours of electronic work and a certain number of labor hours in the assembly department. Each Walkman takes 4 hours of electronic work and 2 hours in the assembly shop. Each Watch-TV requires 3 hours in electronics and 1 hour in assembly. During the current production period, 240 hours of electronic time are available and 100 hours of assembly department time are available. Each Walkman sold yields a profit of $7; each Watch-TV produced may be sold for a $5 profit.

New England Apple Products, the manufacturing of the *Very Fine* beverage line, has 16 different juice beverages, ranging from apple-cherry to cranapple to grapefruit. A large number of combinations of fruit juices are possible, but New England Apple has only limited supplies of each juice as ingredients. The firm has used linear programming to decide which combinations to market and how much of each to make. The bottom-line question is: "What product mix will yield the best profit?" Although there are many listed ingredients on the side of each bottle of fruit juice blend, LP is one *hidden ingredient.*

Shader's problem is to determine the best possible combination of Walkmans and Watch-TVs to manufacture in order to reach the maximum profit. This production-mix situation can be formulated as a linear programming problem.

We begin by summarizing the information needed to formulate and solve this problem (see Table S6.1). Further, let us introduce some simple notation for use in the objective function and constraints. Let

$$X_1 = \text{number of Walkmans to be produced}$$
$$X_2 = \text{number of Watch-TVs to be produced}$$

Now we can create the LP *objective function* in terms of X_1 and X_2:

$$\text{Maximize profit} = \$7X_1 + \$5X_2$$

Our next step is to develop mathematical relationships to describe the two constraints in this problem. One general relationship is that the amount of a resource *used* is to be less than or equal to ($\leq$) the amount of resource *available*.

First Constraint: Electronic time used is $\leq$ electronic time available.

$$4X_1 + 3X_2 \leq 240 \text{ (hours of electronic time)}$$

Second Constraint: Assembly time used is $\leq$ assembly time available.

$$2X_1 + 1X_2 \leq 100 \text{ (hours of assembly time)}$$

Both of these constraints represent production capacity restrictions and, of course, affect the total profit. For example, Shader Electronics cannot produce 70 Walkmans during the production period because if $X_1 = 70$, both constraints will be violated. It also cannot make $X_1 = 50$ Walkmans and $X_2 = 10$ Watch-TVs. This constraint brings out another important aspect of linear programming. That is, certain interactions will exist between variables. The more units of one product that a firm produces, the fewer it can make of other products.

GRAPHICAL SOLUTION TO A LINEAR PROGRAMMING PROBLEM

The easiest way to solve a small LP problem such as that of the Shader Electronics Company is the graphical solution approach. The graphical procedure can be used

TABLE S6.1 ■ SHADER ELECTRONICS COMPANY PROBLEM DATA

	HOURS REQUIRED TO PRODUCE 1 UNIT		
DEPARTMENT	**(X_1) WALKMANS**	**(X_2) WATCH-TVS**	**AVAILABLE HOURS THIS WEEK**
Electronic	4	3	240
Assembly	2	1	100
Profit/unit	$7	$5	

only when there are two decision variables (such as number of Walkmans to produce, X_1, and number of Watch-TVs to produce, X_2). When there are more than two variables, it is *not* possible to plot the solution on a two-dimensional graph; we then must turn to more complex approaches described later in this supplement.

Graphical Representation of Constraints

In order to find the optimal solution to a linear programming problem, we must first identify a set, or region, of feasible solutions. The first step in doing so is to plot the problem's constraints on a graph.

The variable X_1 (Walkmans, in our example) is usually plotted as the horizontal axis of the graph, and the variable X_2 (Watch-TVs) is plotted as the vertical axis. The complete problem may be restated as:

$$\text{Maximize profit} = \$7X_1 + \$5X_2$$

Subject to the constraints:

$$4X_1 + 3X_2 \leq 240 \quad \text{(electronics constraint)}$$
$$2X_1 + 1X_2 \leq 100 \quad \text{(assembly constraint)}$$
$$X_1 \geq 0 \quad \text{(Number of Walkmans produced is greater than or equal to 0.)}$$
$$X_2 \geq 0 \quad \text{(Number of Watch-TVs produced is greater than or equal to 0.)}$$

The first step in graphing the constraints of the problem is to convert the constraint *inequalities* into *equalities* (or equations).

$$\text{Constraint A:} \quad 4X_1 + 3X_2 = 240$$
$$\text{Constraint B:} \quad 2X_1 + 1X_2 = 100$$

The equation for constraint A is plotted in Figure S6.1 and for constraint B in Figure S6.2.

FIGURE S6.1 ■ Constraint A

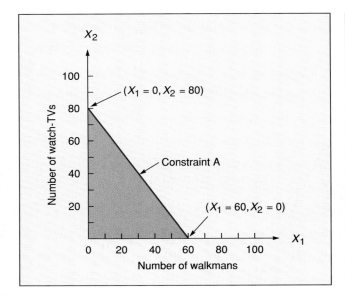

FIGURE S6.2 ■ Constraint B

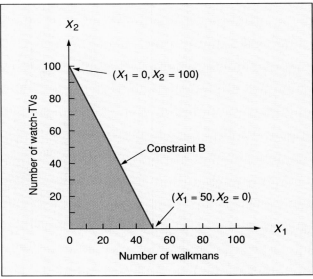

To plot the line in Figure S6.1, all we need to do is to find the points at which the line $4X_1 + 3X_2 = 240$ intersects the X_1 and X_2 axes. When $X_1 = 0$ (the location where the line touches the X_2 axis), it implies that $3X_2 = 240$ or that $X_2 = 80$. Likewise, when $X_2 = 0$, we see that $4X_1 = 240$ and that $X_1 = 60$. Thus, constraint A is bounded by the line running from $(X_1 = 0, X_2 = 80)$ to $(X_1 = 60, X_2 = 0)$. The shaded area represents all points that satisfy the original *inequality*.

Constraint B is illustrated similarly in Figure S6.2. When $X_1 = 0$, then $X_2 = 100$; and when $X_2 = 0$, then $X_1 = 50$. Constraint B then is bounded by the line between $(X_1 = 0, X_2 = 100)$ and $(X_1 = 50, X_2 = 0)$. The shaded area represents the original inequality.

Figure S6.3 shows both constraints together. The shaded region is the part that satisfies both restrictions. The shaded region in Figure S6.3 is called the *area of feasible solutions*, or simply the *feasible region*. This region must satisfy *all* conditions specified by the program's constraints and thus is the region where all constraints overlap. Any point in the region would be a *feasible solution* to the Shader Electronics Company problem. Any point outside the shaded area would represent an *infeasible solution*. Hence, it would be feasible to manufacture 30 Walkmans and 20 Watch-TVs ($X_1 = 30, X_2 = 20$), but it would violate the constraints to produce 70 Walkmans and 40 Watch-TVs. This can be seen by plotting these points on the graph of Figure S6.3.

Iso-Profit Line Solution Method

Now that the feasible region has been graphed, we can proceed to find the optimal solution to the problem. The optimal solution is the point lying in the feasible region that produces the highest profit.

FIGURE S6.3   ■   Feasible Solution Region for the Shader Electronics Company Problem

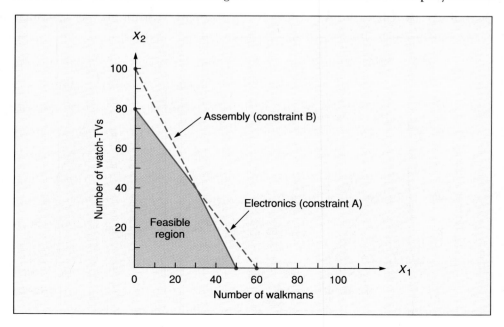

Once the feasible region has been established, several approaches can be taken in solving for the optimal solution. The speediest one to apply is called the **iso-profit line method.**[2]

Iso-profit line method

We start by letting profits equal some arbitrary but small dollar amount. For the Shader Electronics problem, we may choose a profit of $210. This is a profit level that can easily be obtained without violating either of the two constraints. The objective function can be written as $\$210 = 7X_1 + 5X_2$.

This expression is just the equation of a line; we call it an *iso-profit line*. It represents all combinations (of X_1, X_2) that would yield a total profit of $210. To plot the profit line, we proceed exactly as we did to plot a constraint line. First, let $X_1 = 0$ and solve for the point at which the line crosses the X_2 axis.

$$\$210 = \$7(0) + \$5X_2$$
$$X_2 = 42 \text{ Watch-TVs}$$

Then let $X_2 = 0$ and solve for X_1.

$$\$210 = \$7X_1 + \$5(0)$$
$$X_1 = 30 \text{ Walkmans}$$

We can now connect these two points with a straight line. This profit line is illustrated in Figure S6.4. All points on the line represent feasible solutions that produce a profit of $210.

We see that the iso-profit line for $210 does not produce the highest possible profit to the firm. In Figure S6.5, we try graphing two more lines, each yielding a higher profit. The middle equation, $\$280 = \$7X_1 + \$5X_2$, was plotted in the same fashion as the lower line. When $X_1 = 0$,

$$\$280 = \$7(0) + \$5X_2$$
$$X_2 = 56$$

FIGURE S6.4 ■ A Profit Line of $210 Plotted for the Shader Electronics Company

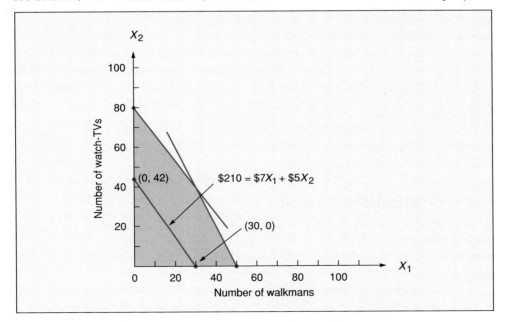

FIGURE S6.5   ■   Four Iso-Profit Lines Plotted for the Shader Electronics Company

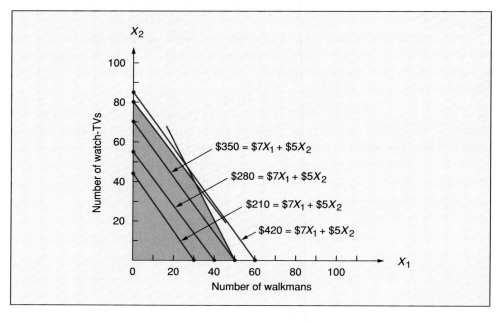

When $X_2 = 0$,

$$\$280 = \$7X_1 + \$5(0)$$
$$X_1 = 40$$

Again, any combination of Walkmans (X_1) and Watch-TVs (X_2) on this iso-profit line will produce a total profit of $280.

Note that the third line generates a profit of $350, even more of an improvement. The farther we move from the 0 origin, the higher our profit will be. Another important point to note is that these iso-profit lines are parallel. We now have two clues as to how to find the optimal solution to the original problem. We can draw a series of parallel profit lines (by carefully moving our ruler in a plane parallel to the first profit line). The highest profit line that still touches some point of the feasible region will pinpoint the optimal solution. Notice that the fourth line ($420) is too high to count because it does not touch the feasible region.

The highest possible iso-profit line is illustrated in Figure S6.6. It touches the tip of the feasible region at the corner point ($X_1 = 30$, $X_2 = 40$) and yields a profit of $410.

Corner Point Solution Method

Corner point method

A second approach to solving linear programming problems employs the **corner point method**. This technique is simpler in concept than is the iso-profit line approach, but it involves looking at the profit at every corner point of the feasible region.

The mathematical theory behind linear programming states that an optimal solution to any problem (that is, the values of X_1, X_2 that yield the maximum profit) will lie at a *corner point*, or *extreme point*, of the feasible region. Hence, it is necessary

FIGURE S6.6 ■ Optimal Solution for the Shader Electronics Problem

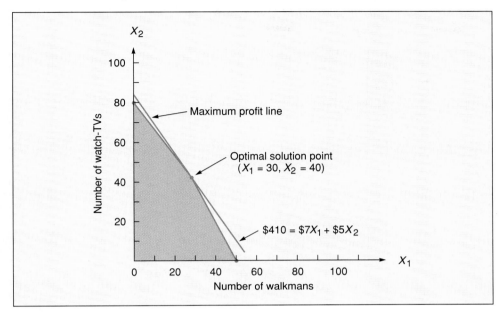

to find only the values of the variables at each corner; the maximum profit or optimal solution will lie at one (or more) of them.

Once again we can see (in Figure S6.7) that the feasible region for the Shader Electronics Company problem is a four-sided polygon with four corner, or extreme, points. These points are labeled①, ②, ③, and ④ on the graph. To find the (X_1, X_2) values producing the maximum profit, we find out what the coordinates of each corner point are and test their profit levels.

Point ①: $(X_1 = 0, X_2 = 0)$ Profit $7(0) + 5(0) = 0$
Point ②: $(X_1 = 0, X_2 = 80)$ Profit $7(0) + 5(80) = 400$
Point ④: $(X_1 = 50, X_2 = 0)$ Profit $7(50) + 5(0) = 350$

We skipped corner point ③ momentarily because in order to find *accurately* its coordinates, we will have to solve for the intersection of the two constraint lines. As you may recall from algebra, we can apply the method of *simultaneous equations* to the two constraint equations.

$$4X_1 + 3X_2 = 240 \quad (electronics\ line)$$
$$2X_1 + 1X_2 = 100 \quad (assembly\ line)$$

To solve these equations simultaneously, we multiply the second equation by –2:

$$-2(2X_1 + 1X_2 = 100) = -4X_1 - 2X_2 = -200$$

and then add it to the first equation:

$$\begin{array}{r} +4X_1 + 3X_2 = 240 \\ -4X_1 - 2X_2 = -200 \\ \hline + 1X_2 = 40 \end{array}$$

FIGURE S6.7   ■   The Four Corner Points of the Feasible Region

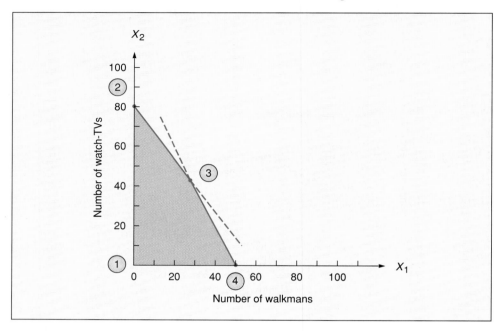

One of the early applications of LP is called the *diet problem*, which was originally used by hospitals to determine the most nutritious but economical diet for patients. Known in agricultural circles as the *feed mix problem*, the diet problem involves specifying a feed ingredient combination that will keep cows healthy. Dairy farmers find that they can use LP to minimize total feed cost, yet still provide a high protein diet that increases the efficiency of milk production in their cows.

or

$$X_2 = 40$$

Doing this has enabled us to eliminate one variable, X_1, and to solve for X_2. We can now substitute 40 for X_2 in either of the original equations and solve for X_1. Let us use the first equation. When $X_2 = 40$, then

$$4X_1 + 3(40) = 240$$
$$4X_1 + 120 = 240$$

or

$$4X_1 = 120$$
$$X_1 = 30$$

Thus, point ③ has the coordinates ($X_1 = 30$, $X_2 = 40$). We can compute its profit level to complete the analysis.

Point ③: ($X_1 = 30, X_2 = 40$)   Profit $= \$7(30) + \$5(40) = \$410$

Because point ③ produces the highest profit of any corner point, the product mix of $X_1 = 30$ Walkmans and $X_2 = 40$ Watch-TVs is the optimal solution to Shader Electronics' problem. This solution will yield a profit of \$410 per production period; it is the same solution we obtained using the iso-profit line method.

Solving Minimization Problems

Many linear programming problems involve *minimizing* an objective such as cost, instead of maximizing a profit function. A restaurant, for example, may wish to develop a work schedule to meet staffing needs while minimizing the total number of employees. Also, a manufacturer may seek to distribute its products from several factories to its many regional warehouses in such a way as to minimize total shipping costs.

Minimization problems can be solved graphically by first setting up the feasible solution region and then using either the corner point method or an **iso-cost** line approach (which is analogous to the iso-profit approach in maximization problems) to find the values of X_1 and X_2 that yield the minimum cost.

Example S1 shows how to solve a minimization problem.

EXAMPLE S1

Mark Cohen Chemicals, Inc., produces two types of photo-developing fluids. The first, a black-and-white picture chemical, costs Cohen $2,500 per ton to produce. The second, a color photo chemical, costs $3,000 per ton.

Based on an analysis of current inventory levels and outstanding orders, Cohen's production manager has specified that at least 30 tons of the black-and-white chemical and at least 20 tons of the color chemical must be produced during the next month. In addition, the manager notes that an existing inventory of a highly perishable raw material needed in both chemicals must be used within 30 days. In order to avoid wasting the expensive raw material, Cohen must produce a total of at least 60 tons of the photo chemicals in the next month.

We may formulate this information as a minimization LP problem. Let

X_1 = number of tons of black-and-white picture chemical produced
X_2 = number of tons of color picture chemical produced

Subject to:

$$X_1 \geq 30 \text{ tons of black-and-white chemical}$$
$$X_2 \geq 20 \text{ tons of color chemical}$$
$$X_1 + X_2 \geq 60 \text{ tons total}$$
$$X_1, X_2 \geq 0 \text{ nonnegativity requirements}$$

To solve the Cohen Chemicals' problem graphically, we construct the problem's feasible region, shown in Figure S6.8.

FIGURE S6.8 ■ Cohen Chemical's Feasible Region

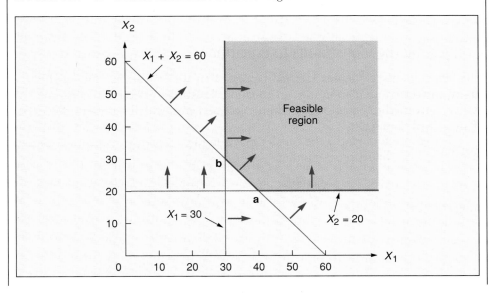

Iso-cost

Minimization problems are often unbounded outward (that is, on the right side and on the top), but this characteristic causes no problem in solving them. As long as they are bounded inward (on the left side and the bottom), we can establish corner points. The optimal solution will lie at one of the corners.

In this case, there are only two corner points, **a** and **b** in Figure S6.8. It is easy to determine that at point **a**, $X_1 = 40$ and $X_2 = 20$ and that at point **b**, $X_1 = 30$ and $X_2 = 30$. The optimal solution is found at the point yielding the lowest total cost. Thus

$$\text{Total cost at } \mathbf{a} = 2{,}500X_1 + 3{,}000X_2$$
$$= 2{,}500(40) + 3{,}000(20)$$
$$= \$160{,}000$$
$$\text{Total cost at } \mathbf{b} = 2{,}500X_1 + 3{,}000X_2$$
$$= 2{,}500(30) + 3{,}000(30)$$
$$= \$165{,}000$$

The lowest cost to Mark Cohen Chemicals is at point **a**. Hence the production manager should produce 40 tons of the black-and-white chemical and 20 tons of the color chemical.

THE SIMPLEX METHOD OF LP

Simplex method

Most real-world linear programming problems have more than two variables and thus are too complex for graphical solution. A procedure called the **simplex method** may be used to find the optimal solution to multivariable problems. The simplex method is actually an algorithm (or a set of instructions) with which we examine corner points in a methodical fashion until we arrive at the best solution—highest profit or lowest cost. Computer programs and spreadsheets (both described at the end of this supplement) are available to handle the simplex calculations for you. But you need to know what is involved behind the scenes in order to best understand their valuable outputs.

Converting the Constraints to Equations

The first step of the simplex method requires that we convert each inequality constraint in an LP formulation into an equation. Less-than-or-equal-to constraints ($\leq$) can be converted to equations by adding *slack variables*, which represent the amount of an unused resource.

Earlier, we formulated the Shader Electronics Company's product mix problem as follows, using linear programming:

$$\text{Maximize profit} = \$7X_1 + \$5X_2$$

Subject to LP constraints:

$$2X_1 + 1X_2 \leq 100$$
$$4X_1 + 3X_2 \leq 240$$

where X_1 equals the number of Walkmans produced and X_2 equals the number of Watch-TVs produced.

To convert these inequality constraints to equalities, we add slack variables S_1 and S_2 to the left side of the inequality. The first constraint becomes

$$2X_1 + 1X_2 + S_1 = 100$$

and the second becomes

$$4X_1 + 3X_2 + S_2 = 240$$

To include all variables in each equation (a requirement of the next simplex step), we add slack variables not appearing in each equation with a coefficient of zero. The equations then appear as

$$2X_1 + 1X_2 + 1S_1 + 0S_2 = 100$$
$$4X_1 + 3X_2 + 0S_1 + 1S_2 = 240$$

Because slack variables represent unused resources (such as time on a machine or labor-hours available), they yield no profit, but we must add them to the objective function with zero profit coefficients. Thus, the objective function becomes

$$\text{Maximize profit} = \$7X_1 + \$5X_2 + \$0S_1 + \$0S_2$$

Setting Up the First Simplex Tableau

To simplify handling the equations and objective function in an LP problem, we place all of the coefficients into a tabular form. We can express the preceding two constraint equations as:

SOLUTION MIX	X_1	X_2	S_1	S_2	QUANTITY (RHS)
S_1	2	1	1	0	100
S_2	4	3	0	1	240

The numbers (2, 1, 1, 0) and (4, 3, 0, 1) represent the coefficients of the first equation and second equation, respectively.

As in the earlier graphical approach, we begin the solution at the origin, where $X_1 = 0$, $X_2 = 0$, and profit $= 0$. The values of the two other variables, S_1 and S_2, then, must be nonzero. Because $2X_1 + 1X_2 + 1S_1 = 100$, we see that $S_1 = 100$. Likewise, $S_2 = 240$. These two slack variables comprise the initial solution mix—as a matter of fact, their values are found in the quantity column across from each variable. Because X_1 and X_2 are not in the solution mix, their initial values are automatically equal to zero.

Some production-operations management books call this initial solution a *basic feasible solution* and describe it in vector, or column, form as

$$\begin{bmatrix} X_1 \\ X_2 \\ S_1 \\ S_2 \end{bmatrix} = \begin{bmatrix} 0 \\ 0 \\ 100 \\ 240 \end{bmatrix}$$

Variables in the solution mix, which is often called the *basis* in LP terminology, are referred to as *basic variables*. In this example, the basic variables are S_1 and S_2. Variables not in the solution mix—or basis—(X_1 and X_2, in this case) are called *nonbasic variables*.

Table S6.2 shows the complete initial simplex tableau for Shader Electronics. The terms and rows that you have not seen before are as follows:

C_j: Profit contribution per unit of each variable. C_j applies to both the top row and first column. In the row, it indicates the unit profit for all variables in the LP objective function. In the column, C_j indicates the unit profit for each variable *currently* in the solution mix.

Z_j: In the quantity column, Z_j provides the total contribution (gross profit in this case) of the given solution. In the other columns (under the variables) it represents the gross profit *given up* by adding one unit of this variable into the current solution. The Z_j value for each column is found by multiplying the C_j of the row by the number in that row and jth column and summing.

The calculations for the values of Z_j in Table S6.2 are as follows:

$$Z_j \text{ (for column } X_1) = 0(2) + 0(4) = 0$$
$$Z_j \text{ (for column } X_2) = 0(1) + 0(3) = 0$$
$$Z_j \text{ (for column } S_1) = 0(1) + 0(0) = 0$$
$$Z_j \text{ (for column } S_2) = 0(0) + 0(1) = 0$$
$$Z_j \text{ (for total profit)} = 0(100) + 0(240) = 0$$

$C_j - Z_j$: This number represents the net profit (that is, the profit gained minus the profit given up), which will result from introducing one unit of each product (variable) into the solution. It is not calculated for the quantity column. To compute these numbers, we simply subtract the Z_j total from the C_j value at the very top of each variable's column.

The calculations for the net profit per unit ($C_j - Z_j$) row in this example are as follows:

		COLUMN		
	X_1	X_2	S_1	S_2
C_j for column	$7	$5	$0	$0
Z_j for column	0	0	0	0
$C_j - Z_j$ for column	$7	$5	$0	$0

It was obvious to us when we computed a profit of $0, that this initial solution was not optimal. Examining numbers in the $C_j - Z_j$ row of Table S6.2, we see that total profit can be increased by $7 for each unit of X_1 (Walkmans) and by $5 for each unit of X_2 (Watch-TVs) added to the solution mix. A negative number in the $C_j - Z_j$ row would tell us that profits would *decrease* if the corresponding variable were added to the solution mix. An optimal solution is reached in the simplex method when the $C_j - Z_j$ row contains no positive numbers. Such is not the case in our initial tableau.

TABLE S6.2 ■ COMPLETED INITIAL SIMPLEX TABLEAU

$C_j \rightarrow$		$7	$5	$0	$0	
	SOLUTION MIX	X_1	X_2	S_1	S_2	QUANTITY (RHS)
$0	S_1	2	1	1	0	100
$0	S_2	4	3	0	1	240
	Z_j	$0	$0	$0	$0	$0
	$C_j - Z_j$	$7	$5	$0	$0	(total profit)

Simplex Solution Procedures

Once we have completed an initial tableau, we proceed through a series of five steps to compute all of the numbers we need for the next tableau. The calculations are not difficult, but they are sufficiently complex that the smallest arithmetic error can produce a very wrong answer.

We first list the five steps and then apply them in determining the second and third tableau for the data in the Shader Electronics example.

1. Determine which variable to enter into the solution mix next. Identify the column—hence the variable—with the largest positive number in the $C_j - Z_j$ row of the previous tableau. This step means that we will now be producing some of the product contributing the greatest additional profit per unit.

2. Determine which variable to replace. Because we have just chosen a new variable to enter into the solution mix, we must decide which variable currently in the solution to remove to make room for it. To do so, we divide each amount in the quantity column by the corresponding number in the column selected in step 1. The row with the *smallest nonnegative number* calculated in this fashion will be replaced in the next tableau (this smallest number, by the way, gives the maximum number of units of the variable that we may place in the solution). This row is often referred to as the **pivot row**, and the column identified in step 1 is called the **pivot column**. The number at the intersection of the pivot row and pivot column is the **pivot number**.

Pivot row
Pivot column
Pivot number

3. Compute new values for the pivot row. To find them, we simply divide every number in the row by the *pivot number*.

4. Compute new values for each remaining row. (In our sample problems there have been only two rows in the LP tableau, but most larger problems have many more rows.) All remaining row(s) are calculated as follows:

$$\begin{pmatrix} \text{New row} \\ \text{numbers} \end{pmatrix} = \begin{pmatrix} \text{numbers} \\ \text{in old row} \end{pmatrix} - \left[\begin{pmatrix} \text{number in old row} \\ \text{above or below} \\ \text{pivot number} \end{pmatrix} \times \begin{pmatrix} \text{corresponding number in} \\ \text{the new row, i.e., the row} \\ \text{replaced in step 3} \end{pmatrix} \right]$$

5. Compute the Z_j and $C_j - Z_j$ rows, as demonstrated in the initial tableau. If all numbers in the $C_j - Z_j$ row are zero or negative, we have found an optimal solution. If this is not the case, we must return to step 1.

All of these computations are best illustrated by using an example. The initial simplex tableau computed in Table S6.2 is repeated below. We can follow the five steps just described to reach an optimal solution to the LP problem.

<table>
<tr><td></td><td>$C_j \rightarrow$
$\downarrow$</td><td></td><td>$7</td><td>$5</td><td>$0</td><td>$0</td><td></td></tr>
<tr><td></td><td></td><td>SOLUTION
MIX</td><td>X_1</td><td>X_2</td><td>S_1</td><td>S_2</td><td>QUANTITY</td></tr>
<tr><td rowspan="2">1st tableau</td><td>$0
$0</td><td>$S_1$
S_2</td><td>②
4</td><td>1
3</td><td>1
0</td><td>0
1</td><td>100   ← pivot
240   row</td></tr>
<tr><td></td><td></td><td colspan="4" style="text-align:center">pivot number</td><td></td></tr>
<tr><td></td><td>Z_j</td><td>$0</td><td>$0</td><td>$0</td><td>$0</td><td>$0</td></tr>
<tr><td></td><td>$C_j - Z_j$</td><td>$7</td><td>$5</td><td>$0</td><td>$0</td><td>$0</td></tr>
</table>

↑
pivot column
(maximum $C_j - Z_j$ values)

Step 1. Variable X_1 enters the solution next because it has the highest contribution to profit value, $C_j - Z_j$. Its column becomes the pivot column.

Step 2. Divide each number in the quantity column by the corresponding number in the X_1 column: $100/2 = 50$ for the first row and $240/4 = 60$ for the second row. The smaller of these numbers—50—identifies the pivot row, the pivot number, and the variable to be replaced. The pivot row is identified above by an arrow, and the pivot number is circled. Variable X_1 replaces variable S_1 in the solution mix column, as shown in the second tableau.

Step 3. Replace the pivot row by dividing every number in it by the pivot number ($2/2 = 1, 1/2 = 1/2, 1/2 = 1/2, 0/2 = 0, 100/2 = 50$). This new version of the entire pivot row appears below.

C_j	SOLUTION MIX	X_1	X_2	S_1	S_2	QUANTITY
$7	X_1	1	1/2	1/2	0	50

Step 4. Calculate the new values for the S_2 row.

$$\begin{pmatrix}\text{Number in}\\\text{new } S_2 \text{ row}\end{pmatrix} = \begin{pmatrix}\text{number in}\\\text{old } S_2 \text{ row}\end{pmatrix} - \left[\begin{pmatrix}\text{number below}\\\text{pivot number}\\\text{in old row}\end{pmatrix} \times \begin{pmatrix}\text{corresponding}\\\text{number in the}\\\text{new } X_1 \text{ row}\end{pmatrix}\right]$$

0	=	4	−	[(4)	×	(1)]
1	=	3	−	[(4)	×	(1/2)]
−2	=	0	−	[(4)	×	(1/2)]
1	=	1	−	[(4)	×	(0)]
40	=	240	−	[(4)	×	(50)]

C_j	SOLUTION MIX	X_1	X_2	S_1	S_2	QUANTITY
$7	X_1	1	1/2	1/2	0	50
0	S_2	0	1	−2	1	40

Step 5. Calculate the Z_j and $C_j - Z_j$ rows.

Z_j (for X_1 column) = $7(1) + 0(0) = \$7$ $C_j - Z_j = \$7 - \$7 = 0$
Z_j (for X_2 column) = $7(1/2) + 0(1) = \$7/2$ $C_j - Z_j = \$5 - \$7/2 = \$3/2$
Z_j (for S_1 column) = $7(1/2) + 0(-2) = \$7/2$ $C_j - Z_j = 0 - \$7/2 = -\$7/2$
Z_j (for S_2 column) = $7(0) + 0(1) = 0$ $C_j - Z_j = 0 - 0 = 0$
Z_j (for total profit) = $7(50) + 0(40) = \$350$

	$C_j \rightarrow$ $\downarrow$	$7	$5	$0	$0	
	SOLUTION MIX	X_1	X_2	S_1	S_2	QUANTITY
$7	X_1	1	1/2	1/2	0	50
$0	S_2	0	①	−2	1	40 ←pivot row
			pivot number			
	Z_j	$7	$7/2	$7/2	$0	$350
						(total profit)
	$C_j - Z_j$	$0	$3/2	−$7/2	$0	

2nd tableau

↑
pivot
column

Because not all numbers in the $C_j - Z_j$ row of this latest tableau are zero or negative, the solution (that is, $X_1 = 50$, $S_2 = 40$, $X_2 = 0$, $S_1 = 0$; profit = $350) is not optimal; we then proceed to a third tableau and repeat the five steps.

Step 1. Variable X_2 enters the solution next because its $C_j - Z_j = 3/2$ is the largest (and only) positive number in the row. Thus, for every unit of X_2 that we start to produce, the objective function will increase in value by $3/2, or $1.50.

Step 2. The pivot row becomes the S_2 row because the ratio $40/1 = 40$ is smaller than the ratio $50/(\frac{1}{2}) = 100$.

Step 3. Replace the pivot row by dividing every number in it by the (circled) pivot number. Because every number is divided by one, there is no change.

Step 4. Compute the new values for the X_1 row.

$$\begin{pmatrix} \text{Number in} \\ \text{new } X_1 \text{ row} \end{pmatrix} = \begin{pmatrix} \text{number in} \\ \text{old } X_1 \text{ row} \end{pmatrix} - \left[\begin{pmatrix} \text{number above} \\ \text{pivot number} \end{pmatrix} \times \begin{pmatrix} \text{corresponding} \\ \text{number in the} \\ \text{new } X_2 \text{ row} \end{pmatrix} \right]$$

1	=	1	−	[(1/2)	×	(0)]
0	=	1/2	−	[(1/2)	×	(1)]
3/2	=	1/2	−	[(1/2)	×	(−2)]
−1/2	=	0	−	[(1/2)	×	(1)]
30	=	50	−	[(1/2)	×	(40)]

Step 5.   Calculate the Z_j and $C_j - Z_j$ rows.

Z_j (for X_1 column) = $\$7(1) + \$5(0) = \$7$ $C_j - Z_j = \$7 - 7 = \$0$
Z_j (for X_2 column) = $\$7(0) + \$5(1) = \$5$ $C_j - Z_j = \$5 - 5 = \$0$
Z_j (for S_1 column) = $\$7(3/2) + \$5(-2) = \$1/2$ $C_j - Z_j = \$0 - 1/2 = -\$1/2$
Z_j (for S_2 column) = $\$7(-1/2) + \$5(1) = \$3/2$ $C_j - Z_j = \$0 - 3/2 = -\$3/2$
Z_j (for total profit) = $\$7(30) + \$5(40) = \$410$

The results for the third and final tableau are seen in Table S6.3.

Because every number in the third tableau's $C_j - Z_j$ row is zero or negative, we have reached an optimal solution. That solution is: $X_1 = 30$ (Walkmans), and $X_2 = 40$ (Watch-TVs), $S_1 = 0$ (slack in first resource), $S_2 = 0$ (slack in second resource), and profit = $\$410$.

Summary of Simplex Steps for Maximization Problems

The steps involved in using the simplex method to help solve an LP problem in which the objective function is to be maximized can be summarized as follows:

1. Choose the variable with the greatest positive $C_j - Z_j$ to enter the solution.
2. Determine the row to be replaced by selecting the one with the smallest (nonnegative) ratio of quantity to pivot column.
3. Calculate the new values for the pivot row.
4. Calculate the new values for the other row(s).
5. Calculate the C_j and $C_j - Z_j$ values for this tableau. If there are any $C_j - Z_j$ numbers greater than zero, return to step 1.

Shadow Prices

Shadow price

A **shadow price** is the value of one additional unit of a resource in the form of one more hour of machine time, labor time, or other scarce resource. Exactly how much should a firm be willing to pay to make additional resources available? Is it worthwhile to pay workers an overtime rate to stay one extra hour each night in order to increase production output? Fortunately, such valuable management information is available to us in the final simplex tableau of an LP problem. An important property of the $C_j - Z_j$ row is that the *negatives of the numbers in its slack variable* (S_i) *columns* provide *shadow prices*.

TABLE S6.3   ■   THIRD AND FINAL TABLEAU

$C_j \rightarrow$		$\$7$	$\$5$	$\$0$	$\$0$	
$\downarrow$	SOLUTION MIX	X_1	X_2	S_1	S_2	QUANTITY
$\$7$	X_1	1	0	3/2	−1/2	30
$\$5$	X_2	0	1	−2	1	40
	Z_j	$\$7$	$\$5$	$\$1/2$	$\$3/2$	$\$410$
	$C_j - Z_j$	$\$0$	$\$0$	$-\$1/2$	$-\$3/2$	

Table S6.3 indicates that the optimal solution to Shader's problem is $X_1 = 30$ Walkmans, $X_2 = 40$ Watch-TVs, $S_1 = 0$, $S_2 = 0$, and profit = $410, where S_1 represents slack hours in the electronics department and S_2 represents slack or unused assembly department time.

Suppose Shader is considering adding an extra assembler at a salary of $5.00 per hour. Should the firm do so? The answer is *no*—the shadow price of the assembly department resource is only 50¢. Thus, the firm will lose $4.50 for every hour the new assembler works.

Sensitivity Analysis

Sensitivity analysis

Shadow pricing is actually one form of **sensitivity analysis**, that is, the study of how sensitive the optimal solution would be to errors or changes in inputs to the LP problem. For example, if the manager at Shader Electronics had been off by 100% in setting the net profit per Walkman at $7, would that error drastically alter the decision to produce 30 Walkmans and 40 Watch-TVs? What would be the impact of 265 electronic hours being available instead of 240?

Program S6.1 is part of the AB:POM computer-generated output available to help a decision maker know whether or not a solution is relatively insensitive to reasonable changes in one or more of the parameters of the problem. (The complete computer run for these data, including input and full output, is illustrated in Program S6.2 later in this supplement.)

First, let us consider changes to the right-hand side of a constraint. In Program S6.1, we assume changes are made in only one constraint at a time, while the other one remains fixed at its original values. *Right-hand side ranging* tells us over what range of right-hand side values the shadow prices for that constraint will remain valid. In the Shader example, the $1.50 shadow price for the electronic constraint will apply even if the current allowance of 240 hours drops as low as 200 or increases as high as 300.

This concept that the right-hand side range limits the shadow price is important in sensitivity analysis. Suppose Shader Electronics could obtain additional electronic hours at a cost less than the shadow price. The question of how much to obtain is answered by the upper limit in Program S6.1, that is, secure 60 hours more than the current 240 hours.

PROGRAM S6.1 ■ Sensitivity Analysis for Shader Electronics Using AB:POM

SHADER ELECTRONICS EXAMPLE

Solution value = 410

Constraint	Shadow Prices		Original RHS	Lower Limit	Upper Limit
ASSEMBLY	0.50		100.00	80.00	120.00
ELECTRONIC	1.50		240.00	200.00	300.00

Variable	Optimal Value	Reduced Cost	Original Coef	Lower Limit	Upper Limit
WALKMANS	30.00	0.00	7.00	6.666667	10.00
WATCH-TVS	40.00	0.00	5.00	3.50	5.25

Now let us look at changes in one of the objective function coefficients. Sensitivity analysis provides, for each decision variable in the solution, the range of profit values over which the answer will be the same. For example, the net profit of $7 per Walkman ($X_1$) in the objective function could range from $6.67 to $10.00 without the final solution of $X_1 = 30$, $X_2 = 40$ changing. Of course, if a profit coefficient changed at all, the total profit of $410 would change, even if the optimal quantities of X_1 and X_2 did not.

Artificial and Surplus Variables

Constraints in linear programming problems are seldom all of the "less-than-or-equal-to" ($\leq$) variety seen in the examples thus far in this supplement. Just as common are "greater-than-or-equal-to" ($\geq$) constraints and equalities. To use the simplex method, each of these also must be converted to a special form. If they are not, the simplex technique is unable to set an initial feasible solution in the first tableau. Example S2 shows how to convert such constraints.

EXAMPLE S2

The following constraints were formulated for an LP problem for the Claire Burns Publishing Company. We shall convert each constraint for use in the simplex algorithm.

Constraint 1. $25X_1 + 30X_2 = 900$. To convert an *equality*, we simply add an "artificial" variable (A_1) to the equation:

$$25X_1 + 30X_2 + A_1 = 900$$

An *artificial variable* is a variable that has no physical meaning in terms of a real-world LP problem. It simply allows us to create a basic feasible solution to start the simplex algorithm. An artificial variable is not allowed to appear in the final solution to the problem.

Constraint 2. $5X_1 + 13X_2 + 8X_3 \geq 2{,}100$. To handle $\geq$ constraints, a "surplus" variable (S_1) is first subtracted and then an artificial variable (A_2) is added to form a new equation:

$$5X_1 + 13X_2 + 8X_3 - S_1 + A_2 = 2{,}100$$

Surplus variable

A **surplus variable** *does* have a physical meaning—it is the amount over and above a required minimum level set on the right-hand side of a greater-than-or-equal-to constraint.

Whenever an artificial or surplus variable is added to one of the constraints, it must also be included in the other equations and in the problem's objective function, just as was done for slack variables. Each artificial variable is assigned an extremely high cost to ensure that it does not appear in the final solution. Rather than set an actual dollar figure of $10,000 or $1 million, however, we simply use the symbol $M to represent a very large number. Surplus variables, like slack variables, carry a zero cost. Example S3 shows how to figure in such variables.

EXAMPLE S3

The Memphis Chemical Corp. must produce 1,000 lb of a special mixture of phosphate and potassium for a customer. Phosphate costs \$5/lb and potassium costs \$6/lb. No more than 300 lb of phosphate can be used, and at least 150 lb of potassium must be used.

We wish to formulate this as a linear programming problem and to convert the constraints and objective function into the form needed for the simplex algorithm. Let

$$X_1 = \text{number of pounds of phosphate in the mixture}$$
$$X_2 = \text{number of pounds of potassium in the mixture}$$

Objective function: minimize cost $= \$5X_1 + \$6X_2$.
Objective function in simplex form:

$$\text{Minimize costs} = \$5X_1 + \$6X_2 + \$0S_1 + \$0S_2 + \$MA_1 + \$MA_2$$

REGULAR FORM	SIMPLEX FORM			
1st constraint: $1X_1 + 1X_2 = 1,000$	$1X_1 + 1X_2$		$+1A_1$	$= 1,000$
2nd constraint: $1X_1 \leq 300$	$1X_1$	$+ 1S_1$		$= 300$
3rd constraint: $1X_2 \geq 150$	$1X_2$	$-1S_2$	$+ 1A_2 =$	150

Solving Minimization Problems

Now that you have worked a few examples of LP problems with the three different types of constraints, you are ready to solve a minimization problem using the simplex algorithm. Minimization problems are quite similar to the maximization problems tackled earlier in this supplement. The one significant difference involves the $C_j - Z_j$ row. Because our objective is now to minimize costs, the new variable to enter the solution in each tableau (the pivot column) will be the one with the *largest negative* number in the $C_j - Z_j$ row. Thus, we will be choosing the variable that decreases costs the most. In minimization problems, an optimal solution is reached when all numbers in the $C_j - Z_j$ row are *zero* or *positive*—just the opposite from the maximization case. All other simplex steps, as shown, remain the same.

1. Choose the variable with the largest negative $C_j - Z_j$ to enter the solution.
2. Determine the row to be replaced by selecting the one with the smallest (non-negative) quantity-to-pivot-column ratio.
3. Calculate new values for the pivot row.
4. Calculate new values for the other rows.
5. Calculate the $C_j - Z_j$ values for this tableau. If there are any $C_j - Z_j$ numbers less than zero, return to step 1.

SOLVING LP PROBLEMS BY COMPUTER

Large-scale LP problems, which you may be called on to formulate some day, could, with some long and careful computations, be solved by hand by following the steps of

Delta Air Lines became the first commercial airline to use the Karmarkar program, called KORBX, developed and sold by AT&T. Delta found that this program streamlined the monthly scheduling of 7,000 pilots who fly more than 400 airlines to 166 cities worldwide. With increased efficiency in allocating limited resources, Delta thinks it will save millions of dollars in crew time and related costs. Another user is the U.S. Military Airlift Command (MAC). Prior to the arrival of KORBX, MAC's LP problem was too big to run on one computer. Even a scaled-down problem that had 36,000 variables and 10,000 constraints took four hours with simplex-based LP software on a mainframe computer. Today, however, models that include the entire, previously unsolvable Pacific Ocean system run in just 20 minutes on KORBX.

the simplex algorithm. It is, indeed, important to understand how that algorithm works. The only good way to master the algorithm is to solve several problems by hand. Once you comprehend the mechanics of the simplex technique, however, it should not be necessary to struggle with the manual method again.

Every university and most business and government organizations have access to programs that are capable of solving fairly large linear programming problems. Popular microcomputer software capable of handling such LP problems include such products as LINDO, STORM, QSB, and AB:POM.

KARMARKAR'S ALGORITHM

The biggest change in the field of linear programming solution techniques in four decades was the arrival in 1984 of an alternative to the simplex algorithm. Developed by Narendra Karmarkar, the new method, called Karmarkar's algorithm, often takes significantly less computer time to solve very large-scale LP problems.[3]

[3]For details, see Narendra Karmarkar, "A New Polynomial Time Algorithm for Linear Programming," *Combinatorica*, 4, no. 4 (1984): 373–395; or J. N. Hooker, "Karmarkar's Linear Programming Algorithm," *Interfaces*, 16, no. 4 (July/August 1986): 75–90.

As we saw, the simplex algorithm finds a solution by moving from one adjacent corner point to the next, following the outside edges of the feasible region. The major difference is that Karmarkar's method follows a path of points on the *inside* of the feasible region. Its uniqueness is its ability to handle an *extremely* large number of constraints and variables, giving LP users the capability to solve previously unsolvable problems. Although the simplex method will likely continue to be used for many LP problems, a new generation of LP software built around Karmarkar's algorithm is already being used.

SUMMARY

This chapter introduces a special kind of model, linear programming. LP has proven to be especially useful when trying to make the most effective use of an organization's resources.

The first step in dealing with LP models is problem formulation, which involves identifying and creating an objective function and constraints. The second step is to solve the problem. If there are only two decision variables, the problem can be solved graphically, using the corner point method or the iso-profit/iso-cost line method. With either approach, we first identify the feasible region, then find the corner point yielding the greatest profit or least cost.

All LP problems can also be solved with the simplex method, either by computer or by hand. This method is more complex mathematically than graphical LP, but it also produces such valuable economic information as shadow prices. LP is used in a wide variety of business applications, as the examples and homework problems in this chapter reveal.

KEY TERMS

Linear programming (LP) (p. 240)
Objective function (p. 240)
Constraints (p. 240)
Iso-profit line method (p. 245)
Corner point method (p. 246)
Iso-cost (p. 249)
Simplex method (p. 250)

Pivot row (p. 253)
Pivot column (p. 253)
Pivot number (p. 253)
Shadow price (p. 256)
Sensitivity analysis (p. 257)
Surplus variable (p. 258)

USING AB:POM AND SPREADSHEETS TO SOLVE LP PROBLEMS

Using AB:POM's LP Module

AB:POM can handle linear programming problems with up to 99 constraints and 99 variables. Data entry and output for the Shader Electronics example used earlier in this chapter are provided in Program S6.2. A nice feature of the program is that it allows us to give names to the variables (instead of just calling them X_1 and X_2) and to give names to the constraints.

As output, AB:POM provides optimal values for the variables, optimal cost/profit, shadow prices (duals), and sensitivity analysis. A further option on the LP module is the ability to "step through" the simplex tableau one at a time. This procedure allows us to observe changes in the solution from one iteration to the next. In addition, AB:POM provides graphical output for problems with only two variables, as shown in Program S6.3.

PROGRAM S6.2   ■   AB:POM's Computer Analysis of Shader Electronics Data Including Optional Output of
Tableaux

Data file: SHADER   Linear Programming   Solution

Number of constraints (2–99) 2   Number of variables (2–99) 2
maximize

SHADER ELECTRONICS EXAMPLE

Options ->   Step   Cmputr   PrtOFF

	WALKMANS	WATCH-TV		RHS	
Objective	7	5			Shadow
Electronics	4	3	≤	240.00	1.50
Assembly	2	1	≤	100.00	0.50
Values ->	30.00	40.00		$410.00	

                                        Phase 2   Iteration 3   0.38 seconds

F1 = Display solution table   F3 = Graph   F9 = Print   Esc

Press <Esc> key to continue or highlight key or function key for options

Iteration 1

	WALKMAN	WATCH-TV	slk 1	slk 2	RHS
maximize	– 7.00	– 5.00	0.00	0.00	0.00
slk 1	2.00	1.00	1.00	0.00	100.00
slk 2	4.00	3.00	0.00	1.00	240.00

Iteration 2

	WALKMAN	WATCH-TV	slk 1	slk 2	RHS
maximize	0.00	– 1.50	3.50	0.00	350.00
WALKMAN	1.00	0.50	0.50	0.00	50.00
slk 2	0.00	1.00	– 2.00	1.00	40.00

Iteration 3

	WALKMAN	WATCH-TV	slk 1	slk 2	RHS
maximize	0.00	0.00	0.50	1.50	410.00
WALKMAN	1.00	0.00	1.50	– 0.50	30.00
WATCH-TV	0.00	1.00	– 2.00	1.00	40.00

PROGRAM S6.3 ■ Shader Electronics Optional Graphic Output

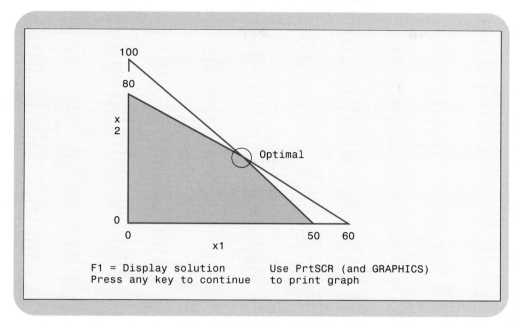

Using Spreadsheet Software

Program S6.4 shows a "symbolic spreadsheet" with each of the formulas needed to solve the Shader Electronics LP problem. Known user-supplied numbers and labels are shown in appropriate cells. We see the profit contributions per Walkman ($7) and Watch-TV ($5) in cells B5 and C5, respectively.

The empty boxes in cells B4 and C4 are highlighted to draw your attention to them. In a what-if analysis (which is a major strength of the spreadsheet approach to LP) the user supplies values to these cells. The user can then see what effect different numbers of Walkmans and Watch-TVs have on total profit (cell D6), total resource use (cells D9 and D12), and slack or unused resources (cells F9 and F12). Alternately, with a spreadsheet optimizing program such as *What's Best!*, the software finds the optimal values and places the answers in cells B4 and C4. Even if you do not have *What's Best!* available, you can still perform the what-if analysis in the spreadsheet by simply entering a series of values, using a trial-and-error approach, into cells B4 and C4.

PROGRAM S6.4 ■ Symbolic Spreadsheet (with Formulas) for Shader Electronics Walkmans and Watch-TVs

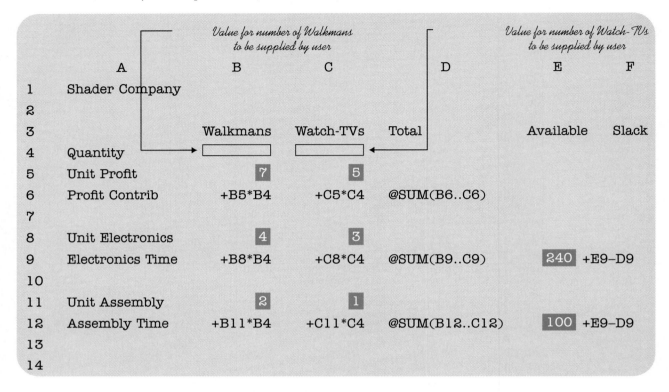

SOLVED PROBLEMS

Solved Problem S6.1

Smitty's, a clothing manufacturer that produces men's shirts and pajamas, has two primary resources available: sewing-machine time (in the sewing department) and cutting-machine time (in the cutting department). Over the next month, Smitty can schedule up to 280 hours of work on sewing machines and up to 450 hours of work on cutting machines. Each shirt produced requires 1 hour of sewing time and 1.5 hours of cutting time. Outputting each pair of pajamas requires .75 hour of sewing time and 2 hours of cutting time.

To express the LP constraints for this problem mathematically, we let

$$X_1 = \text{number of shirts produced}$$
$$X_2 = \text{number of pajamas produced}$$

Solution

First Constraint: $1X_1 + .75X_2 \le 280$ hours of sewing-machine time available—our first scarce resource

Second Constraint: $1.5X_1 + ②X_2 \le 450$ hours of cutting-machine time available—our second scarce resource

Note: This means that each pair of pajamas takes 2 hours of the cutting resource.

Smitty's accounting department analyzes cost and sales figures and states that each shirt produced will yield a $4 contribution to profit and that each pair of pajamas will yield a $3 contribution to profit.

This information can be used to create the LP *objective function* for this problem:

Objective function: maximize total contribution to profit = $4X_1 + $3X_2$

Solved Problem S6.2

We want to solve the following LP problem for Failsafe Computers using the corner point method.

$$\text{Maximize profit} = \$9X_1 + \$7X_2$$
$$2X_1 + 1X_2 \leq 40$$
$$X_1 + 3X_2 \leq 30$$

Solution

Figure S6.9 illustrates these constraints.

Corner point **a**:	$(X_1 = 0, X_2 = 0)$	Profit = 0
Corner point **b**:	$(X_1 = 0, X_2 = 10)$	Profit = $9(0) + 7(10) = \$70$
Corner point **d**:	$(X_1 = 20, X_2 = 0)$	Profit = $9(20) + 7(0) = \$180$

FIGURE S6.9 ■ Failsafe Computer Corp.'s Feasible Region

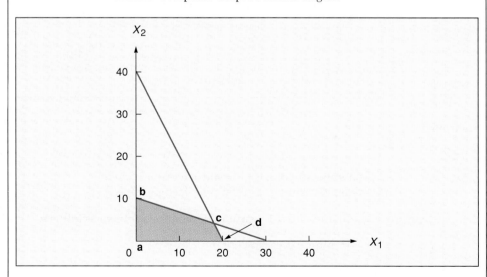

Corner point **c** is obtained by solving equations $2X_1 + 1X_2 = 40$ and $X_1 + 3X_2 = 30$ simultaneously. Multiply the second equation by –2 and add it to the first.

$$2X_1 + 1X_2 = 40$$
$$\underline{-2X_1 - 6X_2 = -60}$$
$$-5X_2 = -20$$

Thus $X_2 = 4$.

$$X_1 + 3(X_2 = 4) = 30 \quad \text{or} \quad X_1 + 12 = 30 \quad \text{or} \quad X_1 = 18$$

Corner point **c**: $(X_1 = 18, X_2 = 4)$ Profit $= 9(18) + 7(4) = \$190$

Hence the optimal solution is

$$(X_1 = 18, X_2 = 4) \quad \text{Profit} = \$190$$

Solved Problem S6.3

The Holiday Meal Turkey Ranch is considering buying two different types of turkey feed. Each feed contains, in varying proportions, some or all of the three nutritional ingredients essential for fattening turkeys. Brand Y feed costs the ranch $.02 per pound. Brand Z costs $.03 per pound. The rancher would like to determine the lowest-cost diet that meets the minimum monthly intake requirement for each nutritional ingredient.

The following table contains relevant information about the composition of Brand Y and Brand Z feeds, as well as the minimum monthly requirement for each nutritional ingredient per turkey.

INGREDIENT	COMPOSITION OF EACH POUND OF FEED		MINIMUM MONTHLY REQUIREMENT
	BRAND Y FEED	BRAND Z FEED	
A	5 oz	10 oz	90 oz
B	4 oz	3 oz	48 oz
C	.5 oz	0	1.5 oz
Cost/lb	$.02	$.03	

Solution

If we let

$X_1 =$ number of pounds of Brand Y feed purchased
$X_2 =$ number of pounds of Brand Z feed purchased

then we may proceed to formulate this linear programming problem as follows:

$$\text{Minimize cost (in cents)} = 2X_1 + 3X_2$$

subject to these constraints:

$$5X_1 + 10X_2 \geq 90 \text{ ounces} \qquad \textit{(ingredient A constraint)}$$
$$4X_1 + \ \ 3X_2 \geq 48 \text{ ounces} \qquad \textit{(ingredient B constraint)}$$
$$\tfrac{1}{2}X_1 \geq \qquad \ \ 1\tfrac{1}{2} \text{ ounces} \qquad \textit{(ingredient C constraint)}$$

Figure S6.10 illustrates these constraints.

FIGURE S6.10 ■ Feasible Region for the Holiday Meal Turkey Ranch Problem

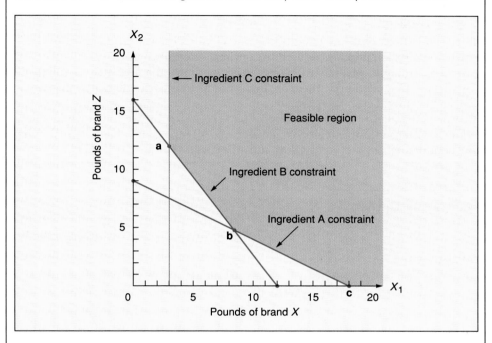

FIGURE S6.11 ■ Graphical Solution to the Holiday Meal Turkey Ranch Problem Using the Iso-Cost Line. Note that the last line parallel to the 54¢ iso-cost line that touches the feasible region indicates the optimal corner point.

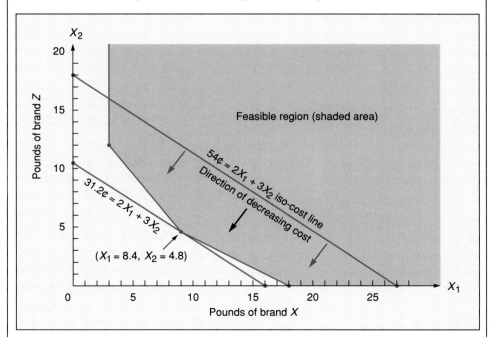

The iso-cost line approach may be used to solve LP minimization problems such as that of the Holiday Meal Turkey Ranch. As with iso-profit lines, we need not compute the cost at each corner point, but instead draw a series of parallel cost lines. The lowest cost line (that is, the one closest in toward the origin) to touch the feasible region provides us with the optimal solution corner.

For example, we start in Figure S6.11 by drawing a 54¢ cost line, namely, $54 = 2X_1 + 3X_2$. Obviously, there are many points in the feasible region that would yield a lower total cost. We proceed to move our iso-cost line toward the lower left, in a plane parallel to the 54¢ solution line. The last point we touch while still in contact with the feasible region is the same as corner point **b** of Figure S6.10. It has the coordinates ($X_1 = 8.4$, $X_2 = 4.8$) and an associated cost of 31.2 cents.

Solved Problem S6.4

Convert the following constraints and objective function into the proper form for use in the simplex method.

$$\text{Objective function:} \qquad \text{Minimize cost} = 4X_1 + 1X_2$$
$$\text{Subject to the constraints:} \qquad
\begin{aligned}
3X_1 + X_2 &= 3 \\
4X_1 + 3X_2 &\geq 6 \\
X_1 + 2X_2 &\leq 3
\end{aligned}$$

Solution

$$\text{Minimize cost} = 4X_1 + 1X_2 + 0S_1 + 0S_2 + MA_1 + MA_2$$
$$\text{Subject to:} \qquad
\begin{aligned}
3X_1 + 1X_2 \qquad\qquad\quad + 1A_1 \qquad\quad &= 3 \\
4X_1 + 3X_2 - 1S_1 \qquad\qquad\; + 1A_2 &= 6 \\
1X_1 + 2X_2 \qquad\; + 1S_2 \qquad\qquad\quad &= 3
\end{aligned}$$

DISCUSSION QUESTIONS

1. Discuss the similarities and differences between minimization and maximization problems, using the graphical solution approach of linear programming.

2. It has been said that each linear programming problem that has a feasible region has an infinite number of solutions. Explain.

3. The production manager of a large Cincinnati manufacturing firm once made this statement: "I should like to use linear programming, but it's a technique that operates under conditions of certainty. My plant doesn't have that certainty; it's a world of uncertainty. So LP can't be used here." Do you think this statement has any merit? Explain why the manager may have said it.

4. Should people who will be using the results of a new quantitative model such as linear programming become involved in the technical aspects of the problem-solving procedure?

5. C. W. Churchman once said "mathematics . . . tends to lull the unsuspecting into believing that he who thinks elaborately thinks well." Do you think that the best models are the ones that are the most elaborate and complex mathematically? Why?

6. Explain the purpose and procedures of the simplex method.

7. How do the graphic and simplex methods of solving linear programming problems differ? In what ways are they the same? Under what circumstances would you prefer to use the graphic approach?

8. What are the simplex rules for selecting the pivot column? The pivot row? The pivot number?

9. A particular linear programming problem has the following objective function:

$$\text{Maximize profit} = \$8X_1 + \$6X_2 + \$12X_3 - \$2X_4$$

Which variable should enter at the second simplex tableau? If the objective function was

$$\text{Minimize cost} = \$2.5X_1 + \$2.9X_2 + \$4.0X_3 + \$7.9X_4$$

which variable would be the best candidate to enter the second tableau?

10. To solve a problem by the simplex method, when are slack variables added?

11. What is a shadow price?

12. Explain how to use the iso-profit line in a graphical maximization problem.

13. Explain how to use the iso-cost line in a graphical minimization problem.

14. Compare how the corner point and iso-profit line methods work for solving graphical problems.

15. Define the feasible region of a graphical LP problem. What is a feasible solution?

16. What are the properties of all LP problems?

17. List the steps in a simplex maximization problem.

18. What is a surplus variable? What is an artificial variable?

One of the many areas of LP application is called the diet problem. Because many people who eat at McDonald's are concerned about how nutritionally complete their diet is, your assignment is to construct a daily diet that (1) meets the nutritional standards shown in the next paragraph, (2) is comprised entirely of foods from McDonald's, and (3) is provided at the least cost. To complete this project, you will also need a copy of "McDonald's Food: the Facts," available at your local store or by calling the restaurant's Nutritional Information Center at 708–575–FOOD.

Your diet should provide at least 100% of the U.S. RDA of vitamins A, C, B_1, B_2, niacin, calcium, and iron; supply at least 55 grams of protein; contain at most 3 grams of sodium; and obtain at most 30% of its calories from fat (each gram of fat contains 9 calories). Choose at least 10 foods from the McDonald's menu in formulating your LP problem.

CRITICAL THINKING EXERCISE

PROBLEMS

· **S6.1** Ray Christiansen is trying to determine how many units of two cordless telephones to produce each day. One of these is the standard model; the other is the deluxe model. The profit per unit on the standard model is $40; the profit per unit on the deluxe model is $60. Each unit requires 30 minutes of assembly time. The standard requires 10 minutes of inspection time; the deluxe model requires 15 minutes of inspection time. The company must fill an order for six standard phones. There are 450 minutes of assembly time and 180 minutes of inspection time available each day. How many units of each product should be manufactured to maximize profits?

· **S6.2** Solve the following linear programming problem, using the corner point method.

$$\begin{aligned}
\text{Maximize} \quad & X + 10Y \\
\text{subject to:} \quad & 4X + 3Y \le 36 \\
& 2X + 4Y \le 40 \\
& Y \ge 3 \\
& X, Y \ge 0
\end{aligned}$$

· **S6.3** Solve the following linear programming problem, using the corner point method.

$$\begin{aligned}
\text{Maximize} \quad & 3X + 5Y \\
\text{subject to:} \quad & 4X + 4Y \le 48 \\
& 1X + 2Y \le 20 \\
& Y \ge 2 \\
& X, Y \ge 0
\end{aligned}$$

: S6.4 Consider the following linear programming problem:

$$\begin{aligned}
\text{Maximize} \quad & Z = 30X_1 + 10X_2 \\
\text{subject to:} \quad & 3X_1 + X_2 \leq 300 \\
& X_1 + X_2 \leq 200 \\
& X_1 \leq 100 \\
& X_2 \geq 50 \\
& X_1 - X_2 \leq 0 \\
& X_1, X_2 \geq 0
\end{aligned}$$

a) Solve the problem graphically.

b) Is there more than one optimal solution? Explain.

· S6.5 Suppose a linear programming (maximization) problem has been solved and the optimal value of the objective function is $300. Suppose an additional constraint is added to this problem. Explain how this might affect each of the following:

a) the feasible region

b) the optimal value of the objective function

: S6.6 John Bragg's Dog Food Company wishes to introduce a new brand of dog biscuits composed of chicken- and liver-flavored biscuits that meet certain nutritional requirements. The liver-flavored biscuits contain 1 unit of nutrient A and 2 units of nutrient B; the chicken-flavored ones contain 1 unit of nutrient A and 4 units of nutrient B. According to federal requirements there must be at least 40 units of nutrient A and 60 units of nutrient B in a package of the new mix. In addition, the company has decided that there can be no more than 15 liver-flavored biscuits in a package. If it costs 1 cent to make a liver-flavored biscuit and 2 cents to make a chicken-flavored one, what is the optimal product mix for a package of the biscuits in order to minimize the firm's cost?

a) Formulate this as a linear programming problem.

b) Solve this problem graphically, giving the optimal values of all variables.

c) What is the total cost of a package of dog biscuits using the optimal mix?

· S6.7 The Electrocomp Corporation manufactures two electrical products: air conditioners and large fans. The assembly process for each is similar in that both require a certain amount of wiring and drilling. Each air conditioner takes 3 hours of wiring and 2 hours of drilling. Each fan must go through 2 hours of wiring and 1 hour of drilling. During the next production period, 240 hours of wiring time are available and up to 140 hours of drilling time may be used. Each air conditioner sold yields a profit of $25. Each fan assembled may be sold for a $15 profit.

Formulate and solve this LP production-mix situation and find the best combination of air conditioners and fans that yields the highest profit. Use the corner point graphical approach.

· S6.8 The Greg Duncan Tub Company manufactures two lines of bathtubs, called Model A and Model B. Every tub requires blending a certain amount of steel and zinc; the company has available a total of 25,000 pounds of steel and 6,000 pounds of zinc. Each Model A bathtub requires a mixture of 125 pounds of steel and 20 pounds of zinc, and each yields a profit to the firm of $90. Each Model B tub produced can be sold for a profit of $70; it in turn requires 100 pounds of steel and 30 pounds of zinc.

Find by graphical linear programming the best production mix of bathtubs.

· S6.9 The Outdoor Furniture Corporation manufactures two products, benches and picnic tables, for use in yards and parks. The firm has two main resources: its carpenters (labor force) and a supply of redwood for use in the furniture. During the next production cycle, 1,200 hours of labor are available under a union agreement. The firm also has a stock of 3,500 board feet of quality redwood. Each bench that Outdoor Furniture produces requires 4 labor-hours and 10 board feet of redwood; each picnic table takes

6 labor-hours and 35 board feet of redwood. Completed benches will yield a profit of $9 each, and tables will result in a profit of $20 each. How many benches and tables should Outdoor Furniture produce in order to obtain the largest possible profit? Use the graphical linear programming approach.

· **S6.10** MSA Computer Corporation manufactures two models of minicomputers, the Alpha 4 and the Beta 5. The firm employs five technicians, working 160 hours each per month, on its assembly line. Management insists that full employment (that is, *all* 160 hours of time) be maintained for each worker during next month's operations. It requires 20 labor-hours to assemble each Alpha 4 computer and 25 labor-hours to assemble each Beta 5 model. MSA wants to see at least 10 Alpha 4's and at least 15 Beta 5's produced during the production period. Alpha 4's generate a $1,200 profit per unit, and Beta's yield $1,800 each.

Determine the most profitable number of each model of minicomputer to produce during the coming month.

· **S6.11** Solve the following linear programming problem, using the corner point graphic method:

$$\text{Maximize profit} = 4X_1 + 4X_2$$
$$\text{Subject to: } 3X_1 + 5X_2 \leq 150$$
$$X_1 - 2X_2 \leq 10$$
$$5X_1 + 3X_2 \leq 150$$
$$X_1, X_2 \geq 0$$

· **S6.12** Consider this linear programming formulation:

$$\text{Minimize cost} = \$1X_1 + \$2X_2$$
$$\text{Subject to: } X_1 + 3X_2 \geq 90$$
$$8X_1 + 2X_2 \geq 160$$
$$3X_1 + 2X_2 \geq 120$$
$$X_2 \leq 70$$

a) Graphically illustrate the feasible region and apply the iso-cost line procedure to indicate which corner point produces the optimal solution.

b) What is the cost of this solution?

· **S6.13** Develop your own individual set of constraint equations and inequalities and use them to illustrate graphically each of the following conditions:

a) An "unbounded" problem. That is, a problem that has no constraints forcing profit limitation.

b) An "infeasible" problem. That is, a problem that has no solution, but satisfies all of the constraints.

c) A problem containing redundant constraints. That is, a problem that has one or more constraints that do not affect the solution.

· **S6.14** The mathematical relationships that follow were formulated by an operations research analyst at the Jennifer Black Chemical Company. Which ones are invalid for use in a linear programming problem, and why?

$$\text{Maximize profit} = 4X_1 + 3X_1X_2 + 5X_3$$
$$\text{Subject to: } 2X_1X_2 + 2X_3 \leq 50$$
$$8X_1 - 4X_2 \geq 6$$
$$1.5X_1 + 6X_2 + 3X_3 \geq 21$$
$$19X_2 - \tfrac{1}{3}X_3 = 17$$
$$5X_1 + 4X_2 + 3\sqrt{X_3} \leq 80$$
$$-X_1 - X_2 + X_3 = 5$$

:S6.15 Paul Feyen Corp. makes three products, and it has three machines available as resources as given in the following LP problem.

$$\text{Maximize profit} = 4X_1 + 4X_2 + 7X_3$$

Subject to:
$$1X_1 + 7X_2 + 4X_3 \leq 100 \text{ (hours on machine 1)}$$
$$2X_1 + 1X_2 + 7X_3 \leq 110 \text{ (hours on machine 2)}$$
$$8X_1 + 4X_2 + 1X_3 \leq 100 \text{ (hours on machine 3)}$$

a) Determine the optimal solution.

b) Is there unused time available on any of the machines with the optimal solution?

:S6.16 Using the data from Paul Feyen Corp. in Problem S6.15, determine:

a) What would it be worth to the firm to make an additional hour of time available on the third machine?

b) How much would the firm's profit increase if an extra ten hours of time were made available on the second machine at no extra cost?

:S6.17 The Denise Davis Mfg. Corp. has $250,000 available to invest for 12 months prior to its plant expansion. The money can be placed in treasury notes yielding an 8% return or in municipal bonds at an average rate of 9%. Management requires that at least 50% of the investment be placed in treasury notes. Because of defaults in municipal bonds, it is decided that no more than 40% of the investment be placed in bonds.

How much should be invested in each security to maximize return on investment?

:S6.18 Malek Furniture manufactures two different types of china cabinets, a French provincial model and a Danish modern model. Each cabinet produced must go through three departments: carpentry, painting, and finishing. The accompanying table contains all relevant information concerning production times per cabinet produced and production capacities for each operation per day, along with net revenue per unit produced. The firm has a contract with an Indiana distributor to produce a minimum of 300 of each cabinet per week (or 60 cabinets per day). Owner Tom Malek would like to determine a product mix to maximize his daily revenue.

CABINET STYLE	CARPENTRY (HR/CABINET)	PAINTING (HR/CABINET)	FINISHING (HR/CABINET)	NET REVENUE/ CABINET
French provincial	3	1½	¾	$28
Danish modern	2	1	¾	$25
Department capacity (hours)	360	200	125	

Formulate this as a linear programming problem and solve.

:S6.19 The famous Sylvia Bonadio Restaurant is open 24 hours a day. Servers report for duty at 3 A.M., 7 A.M., 11 A.M., 3 P.M., 7 P.M., or 11 P.M., and each works an 8-hour shift. The following table shows the minimum number of workers needed during the six periods into which the day is divided.

PERIOD	TIME	NUMBER OF SERVERS REQUIRED
1	3 A.M.– 7 A.M.	3
2	7 A.M.–11 A.M.	12
3	11 A.M.– 3 P.M.	16
4	3 P.M.– 7 P.M.	9
5	7 P.M.–11 P.M.	11
6	11 P.M.– 3 A.M.	4

Bonadio's scheduling problem is to determine how many servers should report for work at the start of each time period in order to minimize the total staff required for 1 day's operation: (*Hint:* Let X_i equal the number of servers beginning work in time period i, where $i = 1, 2, 3, 4, 5, 6$.)

:S6.20 This is the slack time of year at JES, Inc. JES, Inc., would actually like to shut down the plant, but if the company laid off its core employees, they would probably go to work for a competitor. JES, Inc., could keep its core (full-time, year-round) employees busy by making 10,000 round tables per month, or by making 20,000 square tables per month (or some ratio thereof). JES, Inc., does, however, have a contract with a supplier to buy precut table tops for a minimum of 5,000 square tables per month. Handling and storage costs per round table will be $10; these costs would be $8 per square table.

Draw a graph, algebraically describe the constraint inequalities and the objective function, identify the points bounding the feasible solution area, and find the cost at each point and the optimum solution. Let X_1 equal the thousands of round tables per month and X_2 equal the thousands of square tables per month.

:S6.21 Each coffee table produced by John Alessi Designers nets the firm a profit of $9. Each bookcase yields a $12 profit. Alessi's firm is small and its resources limited. During any given production period (of one week), 10 gallons of varnish and 12 lengths of high-quality redwood are available. Each coffee table requires approximately 1 gallon of varnish and 1 length of redwood. Each bookcase takes 1 gallon of varnish and 2 lengths of wood.

Formulate Alessi's production mix decision as a linear programming problem, and solve, using the simplex method. How many tables and bookcases should be produced each week? What will the maximum profit be?

:S6.22 a) Set up an initial simplex tableau, given the following two constraints and objective function:

$$1X_1 + 4X_2 \leq 24$$
$$1X_1 + 2X_2 \leq 16$$
$$\text{Maximize profit} = \$3X_1 + \$9X_2$$

You will have to add slack variables.

b) Briefly list the iterative steps necessary to solve the problem in part (a).

c) Determine the next tableau from the one you developed in part (a). Determine whether or not it is an optimum solution.

d) If necessary, develop another tableau and determine whether or not it is an optimum solution. Interpret this tableau.

e) Start with the same initial tableau from part (a) but use X_1 as the first pivot column. Continue to iterate it (a total of twice) until you reach an optimum solution.

:S6.23 Solve the following linear programming problem graphically. Then set up a simplex tableau and solve the problem, using the simplex method. Indicate the corner points generated at each iteration by the simplex on your graph.

$$\text{Maximize profit} = \$3X_1 + \$5X_2$$
$$\text{Subject to:} \quad X_2 \leq 6$$
$$3X_1 + 2X_2 \leq 18$$
$$X_1, X_2 \geq 0$$

:S6.24 Solve the following linear programming problem, first graphically and then by the simplex algorithm.

$$\text{Minimize cost} = 4X_1 + 5X_2$$
$$\text{Subject to:} \quad X_1 + 2X_2 \geq 80$$
$$3X_1 + X_2 \geq 75$$
$$X_1, X_2 \geq 0$$

What are the values of the basic variables at each iteration? Which are the non-basic variables at each iteration?

:S6.25 Barrow Distributors packages and distributes industrial supplies. A standard shipment can be packaged in a Class A container, a Class K container, or a Class T container. A single Class A container yields a profit of $8; a Class K container, a profit of $6; and a Class T container, a profit of $14. Each shipment prepared requires a certain amount of packing material and a certain amount of time.

CLASS OF CONTAINER	RESOURCES NEEDED PER STANDARD SHIPMENT	
	PACKING MATERIAL (POUNDS)	PACKING TIME (HOURS)
A	2	2
K	1	6
T	3	4
Total amount of resource available each week	120 pounds	240 hours

Joe Barrow, head of the firm, must decide the optimal number of each class of container to pack each week. He is bound by the previously mentioned resource restrictions but also decides that he must keep his six full-time packers employed all 240 hours (6 workers × 40 hours) each week.

Formulate and solve this problem, using the simplex method.

:S6.26 Set up a complete initial tableau for the data (repeated below) that were first presented in Solved Problem S6.4.

$$\text{Minimize cost} = 4X_1 + 1X_2 + 0S_1 + 0S_1 + MA_1 + MA_2$$
$$\text{Subject to:} \quad 3X_1 + 1X_2 \qquad\qquad + 1A_1 \qquad\quad = 3$$
$$4X_1 + 3X_2 - 1S_2 \qquad\qquad\quad + 1A_2 = 6$$
$$1X_1 + 2X_2 \qquad + 1S_2 \qquad\qquad\qquad = 3$$

a) Which variable will enter the solution next?

b) Which variable will leave the solution?

:S6.27 Solve Problem S6.26 for the optimal solution, using the simplex method.

:S6.28 Using the data from Problem S6.7 and LP software:

a) Determine the range within which the unit profit contribution of an air conditioner must fall for the current solution to remain optimal.

b) Determine the shadow price for the wiring constraint and range within which that value holds.

:S6.29 Using the data from Problem S6.8 and LP software:

a) Determine the range within which the unit profit contribution of a Model A tub must fall for the current solution to remain optimal.

b) Determine by how much the unit profit contribution of a Model B tub must increase before it would be desirable to produce any of them.

c) Determine the shadow price for the steel constraint and the range within which that value holds.

d) Determine the shadow price for the zinc constraint and the range within which that value holds.

: S6.30 Using the data from Problem S6.20 and LP software:

    a) Determine the range within which the unit cost of a square table must fall for the current solution to remain optimal.

    b) Determine the shadow price for the labor constraint and the range within which that value holds.

    c) Determine the shadow price for the contract constraint and the range within which that value holds.

: S6.31 John DeBruzzi, the advertising director for Diversey Paint and Supply, a chain of four retail stores on Chicago's North Side, is considering two media possibilities. One plan is for a series of half-page ads in the Sunday *Chicago Tribune* newspaper, and the other is for advertising time on Chicago TV. The stores are expanding their lines of do-it-yourself tools, and the advertising director is interested in an exposure level of at least 40% within the city's neighborhoods and 60% in northwest suburban areas.

    The TV viewing time under consideration has an exposure rating per spot of 5% in city homes and 3% in the northwest suburbs. The Sunday newspaper has corresponding exposure rates of 4% and 3% per ad. The cost of a half-page *Tribune* advertisement is $925; a television spot costs $2000.

    Diversey Paint would like to select the least costly advertising strategy that would meet desired exposure levels. Formulate and solve this LP problem.

: S6.32 Bill Bilderback Manufacturing has three factories (1, 2, and 3) and three warehouses (A, B, and C). The diagram below shows the shipping costs between each factory and warehouse, the factory manufacturing capabilities (in 1000's) and the warehouse capacities (in 1000's). Write the objective function and the constraint inequations. Let X1A = 1000's of units shipped from factory 1 to warehouse A, et cetera.

TO FROM	A	B	C	PRODUCTION CAPABILITY
Factory 1	$ 6	$ 5	$ 3	6
Factory 2	$ 8	$10	$ 8	8
Factory 3	$11	$14	$18	10
Capacity	7	12	5	

: S6.33 Andy's Bicycle Company (ABC) has the hottest new product on the upscale toy market—boys' and girls' bikes in bright fashion colors, with oversized hubs and axles, shell design safety tires, a strong padded frame, chrome-plated chains, brackets, and valves, and a nonslip handlebar. Due to the seller's market for high-quality toys for the newest baby boomers, ABC can sell all the bicycles it manufactures at the following prices: boys' bikes—$220, girls' bikes—$175. This is the price payable to ABC at its Orlando plant.

    The firm's accountant has determined that direct labor costs will be 45% of the price ABC receives for the boys' model and 40% of the price received for the girls' model. Production costs other than labor, but excluding painting and packaging, are $44 per boys' bicycle and $30 per girls' bicycle. Painting and packaging are $20 per bike, regardless of model.

    The Orlando plant's overall production capacity is 390 bicycles per day. Each boys' bike requires 2.5 labor-hours, each girls' model takes 2.4 hours to complete. ABC currently employs 120 workers, who each puts in an 8-hour day. The firm has no desire to hire or fire to affect labor availability for it believes its stable work force is one of its biggest assets.

Using a graphic approach, determine the best product mix for ABC.

: **S6.34** New Orleans's Mt. Sinai Hospital is a large, private, 600-bed facility complete with laboratories, operating rooms, and X-ray equipment. In seeking to increase revenues, Mt. Sinai's administration has decided to make a 90-bed addition on a portion of adjacent land currently used for staff parking. The administrators feel that the labs, operating rooms, and X-ray department are not being fully utilized at present and do not need to be expanded to handle additional patients. The addition of 90 beds, however, involves deciding how many beds should be allocated to the medical staff (for medical patients) and how many to the surgical staff (for surgical patients).

The hospital's accounting and medical records departments have provided the following pertinent information. The average hospital stay for a medical patient is 8 days, and the average medical patient generates $2,280 in revenues. The average surgical patient is in the hospital 5 days and receives a $1,515 bill. The laboratory is capable of handling 15,000 tests per year more than it *was* handling. The average medical patient requires 3.1 lab tests, and the average surgical patient takes 2.6 lab tests. Furthermore, the average medical patient uses one X-ray; the average surgical patient requires two X-rays. If the hospital were expanded by 90 beds, the X-ray department could handle up to 7,000 X-rays without significant additional cost. Finally, the administration estimates that up to 2,800 additional operations could be performed in existing operating room facilities. Medical patients, of course, require no surgery, while each surgical patient generally has one surgery performed.

Formulate this problem so as to determine how many medical beds and how many surgical beds should be added in order to maximize revenues. Assume that the hospital is open 365 days per year.

DATA BASE APPLICATION

: **S6.35** Mann Enterprises is a Houston manufacturer of tables and accessories for personal computers. The company is caught in a vicious cross fire between rapidly dropping market prices from competitors worldwide for its products and stable domestic costs for its materials. The 15 different products noted below must be scheduled to maximize profits or there will be no jobs and no firm in another three months. Your job as the new P/OM graduate is to address the issues raised this morning by Laura Mann, the president, in an emergency meeting in her office. Without being told so explicitly, you concluded that if you didn't get the schedule done accurately and in a timely manner you would be history. To your relief the industrial engineers and accountants have provided the data shown below. The issues, as recorded in your notes, are shown in **a** through **f** below.

Product	Steel Alloy Required (Lb.)	Plastic Required (Sq. Ft)	Wood Required (Bd. Ft)	Aluminum Required (Lb.)	Formica Required (Bd. Ft)	Labor Required (Hr)	Minimum Monthly Demand (Units)	Contribution to Profit
A158	—	.4	.7	5.8	10.9	3.1	—	$18.79
B179	4	.5	1.8	10.3	2.0	1.0	20	6.31
C023	6	—	1.5	1.1	2.3	1.2	10	8.19
D045	10	.4	2.0	—	—	4.8	10	45.88

(Continued on next page)

Product	Steel Alloy Required (Lb.)	Plastic Required (Sq. Ft)	Wood Required (Bd. Ft)	Aluminum Required (Lb.)	Formica Required (Bd. Ft)	Labor Required (Hr)	Minimum Monthly Demand (Units)	Contribution to Profit
E388	12	1.2	1.2	8.1	4.9	5.5	—	63.00
F422	—	1.4	1.5	7.1	10.0	.8	20	4.10
G366	10	1.4	7.0	6.2	11.1	9.1	10	81.15
H600	5	1.0	5.0	7.3	12.4	4.8	20	50.06
I701	1	.4	—	10.0	5.2	1.9	50	12.79
J802	1	.3	—	11.0	6.1	1.4	20	15.88
K900	—	.2	—	12.5	7.7	1.0	20	17.91
L901	2	1.8	1.5	13.1	5.0	5.1	10	49.99
M050	—	2.7	5.0	—	2.1	3.1	20	24.00
N150	10	1.1	5.8	—	—	7.7	10	88.88
P259	10	—	6.2	15.0	1.0	6.6	10	77.01
Availability per month	980	400	600	2,500	1,800	1,000		

a) How many of each of the 15 products should be produced each month?

b) Clearly explain the meaning of each shadow price.

c) A number of workers interested in saving money for the holidays have offered to work overtime next month at a rate of $12.50 per hour. What should the response of management be?

d) Two tons of steel alloy are available from an overstocked supplier at a total cost of $8,000. Should the steel be purchased? All or part of the supply?

e) The accountants have just discovered that an error was made in the contribution to profit for product N150. The correct value is actually $8.88. What are the implications of this error?

f) Management is considering the abandonment of five product lines (those beginning with letters A through E). If no minimum monthly demand is established, what are the implications? Note that there already is no minimum for two of these products. Use the corrected value for N150.

CASE STUDY

Golding Landscaping and Plants, Inc.

Kenneth and Patricia Golding spent a career as a husband-and-wife real estate investment partnership in Washington, DC. When they finally retired to a 25-acre farm in northern Virginia's Fairfax County, they became ardent amateur gardeners. Kenneth Golding planted shrubs and fruit trees, and Patricia spent her hours potting all sizes of plants. When the volume of shrubs and plants reached the point where

the Goldings began to think of their hobby in a serious vein, they built a greenhouse adjacent to their home and installed heating and watering systems in it.

By 1984, the Goldings realized their retirement from real estate had really only led to a second career—in the plant and shrub business—and they filed for a Virginia business license. Within a matter of months, they asked their attorney to file incorporation documents and formed the firm Golding Landscaping and Plants, Inc.

Early in the new business's existence, Kenneth Golding recognized the need for a high-quality

(Continued)

commercial fertilizer that he could blend himself, both for sale and for his own nursery. His goal was to keep his costs to a minimum while producing a top-notch product that was especially suited to the northern Virginia climate.

Working with chemists at Virginia Tech and George Mason Universities, Golding blended "Golding-Grow." It consists of four chemical compounds, C-30, C-92, D-21, and E-11. The cost per pound for each compound is indicated in Table 1.

TABLE 1

CHEMICAL COMPOUND	COST PER POUND
C-30	$.12
C-92	.09
D-21	.11
E-11	.04

The specifications for Golding-Grow are established as:

a) Chemical E-11 must comprise at least 15% of the blend.

b) C-92 and C-30 must together constitute at least 45% of the blend.

c) D-21 and C-92 can together constitute no more than 30% of the blend.

d) Golding-Grow is packaged and sold in 50-pound bags.

DISCUSSION QUESTIONS

1. Formulate an LP problem to determine what blend of the four chemicals will allow Golding to minimize the cost of a 50-pound bag of the fertilizer.

2. Solve to find the best solution.

Source: Barry Render and Ralph Stair, *Introduction to Management Science* (Boston: Allyn and Bacon, 1992) p. 84.

CASE STUDY

Mexicana Wire Works

Ron Garcia felt good about his first week as management trainee at Mexicana Wire Winding, Inc. He had not yet developed any technical knowledge about the manufacturing process, but he had toured the entire facility, located in the suburbs of Mexico City, and had met many people in various areas of the operation.

Mexicana, a subsidiary of Westover Wire Works, a Texas firm, is a medium-sized producer of wire windings used in making electrical transformers. Carlos Alverez, the production control manager, described the windings to Garcia as being of standardized design. Garcia's tour of the plant, laid out by process type (see Figure S6.12), followed the manufacturing sequence for the windings: drawing, extrusion, winding, inspection, and packaging. After inspection, good product is packaged and sent to finished product storage; defective product is stored separately until it can be reworked.

On March 8, Vivian Espania, Mexicana's general manager, stopped by Garcia's office and asked him to attend a staff meeting at 1:00 P.M.

"Let's get started with the business at hand," Vivian said, opening the meeting. "You all have met Ron Garcia, our new management trainee. Ron studied operations management in his MBA program in Southern California, so I think he is competent to help us with a problem we have been discussing for a long time without resolution. I'm sure that each of you on my staff will give Ron your full cooperation."

Vivian turned to José Arroyo, production control manager. "José, why don't you describe the problem we are facing?"

"Well," José said, "business is very good right now. We are booking more orders than we can fill. We will have some new equipment on line within the next several months, which will take care of our capacity problems, but that won't help us in April. I have located some retired employees who used to work in the drawing department, and I am planning

(Continued)

FIGURE S6.12 ■ Mexicana Wire Winding, Inc.

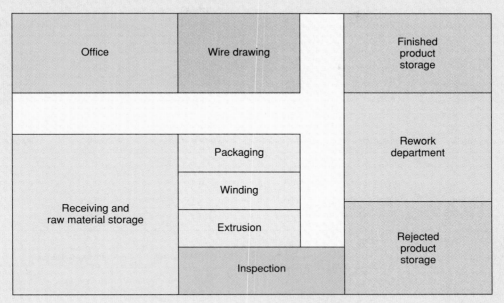

to bring them in as temporary employees in April to increase capacity there. Because we are planning to refinance some of our long-term debt, Vivian wants our profits to look as good as possible in April. I'm having a hard time figuring out which orders to run and which to back-order so that I can make the bottom line look as good as possible. Can you help me with this?"

Garcia was surprised and apprehensive to receive such a high profile, important assignment so early in his career. Recovering quickly, he said, "Give me your data [Table 2] and let me work with it for a day or two."

DISCUSSION QUESTIONS

1. What recommendations should Ron Garcia make, with what justification? Provide a detailed analysis with charts, graphs, and computer printouts included.
2. Discuss the need for temporary workers in the drawing department.
3. Discuss the plant layout.

Source: Professor Victor E. Sower, Sam Houston State University. This case material is based on an actual situation, with names and data altered for confidentiality.

TABLE 2

APRIL ORDERS

Product No. W0075C	1,400 units
Product No. W0033C	250 units
Product No. W0005X	1,510 units
Product No. W0007X	1,116 units

Note: Vivian Espania has given her word to a key customer that we will manufacture 600 units of Product No. W0007X and 150 units of Product No. W0075C for him during April.

(Continued)

TABLE 2

STANDARD COST	PRODUCT	MATERIAL	LABOR	O/H	SELLING PRICE
	W0075C	$33.00	$9.90	$23.10	$100.00
	W0033C	$25.00	$7.50	$17.50	$80.00
	W0005X	$35.00	$10.50	$24.50	$130.00
	W0007X	$75.00	$11.25	$63.75	$175.00

BILL OF LABOR (HOURS/UNIT)	PRODUCT	DRAWING	EXTRUSION	WINDING	PACKAGING
	W0075C	1.0	1.0	1.0	1.0
	W0033C	2.0	1.0	3.0	0.0
	W0005X	0.0	4.0	0.0	3.0
	W0007X	1.0	1.0	0.0	2.0

PLANT CAPACITY: (HOURS)	DRAWING	EXTRUSION	WINDING	PACKAGING
	4,000	4,200	2,000	2,300

Note: Inspection capacity is not a problem—we can work overtime as necessary to accommodate any schedule.

Selected Operating Data

Average output per month = 2,400 units

Average machine utilization = 63%

Average percentage of production sent to rework dept. = 5% (mostly from Winding Dept.)

Average no. of rejected units awaiting rework = 850 (mostly from Winding Dept.)

BIBLIOGRAPHY

Bodington, C. E., and T. E. Baker. "A History of Mathematical Programming in the Petroleum Industry." *Interfaces*, 20, no. 4 (July/August 1990): 117–132.

Farley, A. A. "Planning the Cutting of Photographic Color Paper Rolls for Kodak (Australasia) Pty. Ltd." *Interfaces*, 21, no. 1 (January/February 1991): 92–106.

Ferris, M. C., and A. B. Philpott. "On the Performance of Karmarkar's Algorithm." *Journal of the Operational Research Society*, 39 (March 1988): 257–270.

Gass, S. I. *An Illustrated Guide to Linear Programming*. New York: Dover, 1990.

Greenberg, H. J. "How to Analyze the Results of Linear Programs—Part 1: Preliminaries." *Interfaces*, 23, no. 4 (July/August 1993): 56–68.

———. "How to Analyze the Results of Linear Programs—Part 3: Infeasibility Diagnosis." *Interfaces*, 23, no. 6 (November/December 1993): 120–139.

Hirshfeld, D. S. "Some Thoughts on Math Programming Practice in the '90s." *Interfaces*, 20, no. 4 (July/August 1990): 158–165.

Oliff, M., and E. Burch. "Multiproduct Production Scheduling at Owens-Corning Fiberglass." *Interfaces*, 15 (September/October 1985): 25–34.

Orden, A. "LP from the '40s to the '90s." *Interfaces*, 23, no. 5 (September/October 1993): 2.

Quinn, P., B. Andrews, and H. Parsons. "Allocating Telecommunications Resources at L.L. Bean, Inc." *Interfaces*, 21, no. 1 (January/February 1991): 75–91.

Render, B., and R. M. Stair. *Introduction to Management Science*. Boston: Allyn and Bacon, 1992.

———. *Quantitative Analysis for Management*, 5th ed. Boston: Allyn & Bacon, 1994.

Rubin, D. S., and H. M. Wagner. "Shadow Prices: Tips and Traps for Managers and Instructors." *Interfaces*, 20, no. 4 (July/August 1990): 150–157.

Saltzman, M. J. "Survey: Mixed Integer Programming." *OR/MS Today*, 21, no. 2 (April 1994): 42–51.

Schindler, S., and T. Semmel. "Station Staffing at Pan American World Airways." *Interfaces*, 23, no. 3 (May/June 1993): 91.

Sexton, T. R., S. Sleeper, and R. E. Taggart, Jr. "Improving Pupil Transportation in North Carolina." *Interfaces*, 24, no. 1 (January/February 1994): 87–104.

Zangwill, W. I. *Lightning Strategies for Innovation: How the World's Best Firms Create New Products*. New York: Lexington Books, 1993.

Zappe, C., W. Webster, and I. Horowitz. "Using Linear Programming to Determine Post-Facto Consistency in Performance Evaluations of Major League Baseball Players." *Interfaces*, 23, no. 6 (November/December 1993): 107–119.

7

PROCESS STRATEGY AND CAPACITY PLANNING

LEARNING OBJECTIVES

When you complete this chapter you should be able to:

Identify or define:
  Process Focus
  Product Focus
  Repetitive Focus
Explain:
  Lean production
  The capacity issue
  Break-even analysis
  Financial considerations
  Strategy-driven investments

PROCESS SELECTION YIELDS A COMPETITIVE ADVANTAGE AT NUCOR

In Crawfordsville, Indiana, Nucor produces sheet steel in a nearly *continuous process* with small variety. But with modest changes in the steel mix, alloys, and in size and finish of the steel, a wide variety of market requirements are met.

Nucor builds and operates a type of steel mill known as the "minimill." Minimills are smaller, cheaper, and less complex, and have proven more efficient than integrated mills. Minimills typically make steel from scrap rather than from ore. About half of the steel consumed in the United States is produced this way.

Steel is produced in two phases. First, scrap is loaded into two 125-ton electric-arc furnaces. A massive electric charge with a thunderous roar melts the scrap. Then an analysis is made of the alloy and a variety of additional ingredients are added, depending upon the nature of the scrap and the product desired. The melted steel, at about 3,000°F, is called a *heat*. It is poured into a ladle and carried by an overhead crane to a casting machine. There steel solidifies as a red-hot 2-inch-thick ribbon of steel and is cut into lengths as it cools. The lengths are called *slabs* and weigh about 25 tons.

In the second phase, the characteristics of the steel can be modified modestly; the second stage primarily determines shape and finish. The Crawfordsville facility typically makes sheet steel. This is accomplished in a rolling mill

This AC electric-arc furnace holds 125 tons. Electrodes lowered into cold scrap steel in the furnace produce arc heat to melt the scrap.

This ladle, equipped with magnetic stirring and vacuum degassing features, pours steel via a ceramic nozzle into a metering vessel called a tundish, *and then to a special mold that can adjust the slab's dimensions.*

and related operations. The rolling mill, with steel flying by at 30 miles per hour, progressively presses the red-hot slabs into the desired shapes.

Subsequent finishing operations can modify the characteristics of the sheet steel depending on customer desires and market.

Here the coiling of rolled sheet steel results in rolls of about 25 tons.

At Nucor, process selection provides a competitive advantage in several ways.

First, Nucor casts steel close to the final shape of the product, eliminating unnecessary capital equipment and personnel.

Second, the continuous process eliminates a substantial amount of reheating prior to rolling. This yields major savings in energy cost.

Third, an efficient process, combined with an effective incentive system, yields the highest productivity found in any steel mill in the world. Nucor's labor hours per ton of steel may be half that of competitors.

Fourth, the process technology used at Crawfordsville results in high productivity *and* high quality. The process results in excellent control of steel characteristics, and reduced labor, energy, and work-in-process, as well as a net savings in capital investment.

How does Nucor maintain a competitive advantage? Through excellent operations management, including the right process strategy.

Here the shaped steel exits the caster mold as a 2-inch-thick by 52-inch-wide slab, and enters the hot tunnel furnace, where its temperature is uniformly raised to the level needed for rolling. A higher-quality sheet can be produced if slab temperature is uniform.

B uilding compressors for air conditioners, Carrier Corporation faced severe worldwide competition. To fight back, Carrier recently decided to
change its strategy to building compressors only to customer order.
This means that the firm's big plants, built in the 1970s and 1980s, with their
high fixed cost and inflexible production lines, are no good. It also means that
Carrier has to build manufacturing processes that are flexible enough to respond
to customer orders—and have no finished goods inventory. To be a world-class
organization, Carrier has no choice but to change its process strategy.[1] ♦

In Chapter 6, we examined the need for the selection, definition, and design of products. We now turn to selection of the processes to be used in making these products
and examine the advantages and disadvantages of process changes, such as the ones
made by Carrier and Nucor. A major decision for the operations manager is finding
the best way to produce a product. This chapter looks at ways to help managers develop what is called a process strategy.

Process strategy   A **process** (or transformation) **strategy** is the approach that an organization
takes to transform resources into goods and services. The *objective of a process strategy*
is to find a way to produce goods that meet customer requirements and product speci-
fications within cost and other managerial constraints.

The process selected will have a long-term effect on an organization's performance, efficiency, and production, as well as the flexibility, cost, and quality of the
goods produced. Therefore, much of a firm's strategy is determined at the time of the
process decision. The payoff from effective process selection prior to initial production is much more fruitful than the same effort expended later trying to improve the
wrong process.

THREE PROCESS STRATEGIES

Virtually everything in the world is made by using some variation of one of three
process strategies: process, repetitive, and product.

Process Focus

Perhaps as much as 75% of U.S. production is devoted to making *low-volume, high-*
variety products—in places called "job shops." The facilities are organized to perform
a *process*. In a factory, these processes might be welding or painting departments, and
Process focus   in an office environment, they might be accounts payable, sales, and payroll departments. Such facilities have a **process focus** in terms of equipment, layout, and supervision. They provide a high degree of product flexibility because they are designed to
Intermittent processes   process a wide variety of requirements and handle frequent changes. Consequently,
they are also known as **intermittent processes**.

---

[1]Erle Norton, "Future Factories," *Wall Street Journal* (January 13, 1993): A1.

In 1947, like most restaurants, McDonald's paid out between 35% and 40% of gross income as wages. In 1948, Richard and Mac McDonald switched their process to a limited and rigidly standardized menu. The brothers developed specific portions to be served with each menu item. This included such things as dispensers that put an exact amount of catsup or mustard on each bun and paper goods to replace glassware and china. By 1952, it took 20 seconds for McDonald's to serve a customer a hamburger, a drink, french fries, and ice cream; labor costs had dropped to 17% of gross income and McDonald's was on its way to becoming the world-class fast-food restaurant.

Product Focus

High-volume, low-variety production is **product-focused**. The equipment, layout, and supervision are organized to make a *product*. Because product-focused facilities have very long continuous production runs, they are also called **continuous processes**. A continuous process is used to make products such as glass, paper, tin sheets, light bulbs, and nuts and bolts. Some products, such as light bulbs, are discrete, that is, distinct, separate units. Others, such as rolls of paper, are not discrete. An organization producing the same light bulb or hot dog bun day after day can invest in, and organize around, a product. Such an organization with a continuous process has an inherent ability to set standards and maintain a given quality, as opposed to an organization that is producing unique products every day. Note in the *POM in Action* box "Uniform Pigs Contribute to Efficiency" that the hog industry's effort to standardize products is an attempt to be more efficient by moving toward a continuous process.

Product focus

Continuous processes

Repetitive Process

Production need not be either process- or product-focused, as other possibilities exist. A third approach is a repetitive process. **Repetitive processes** use modules. **Modules** are parts or components previously prepared, often in a continuous process. An example of the repetitive process is the classic assembly line. The repetitive process is widely used, including the assembly of virtually all automobile and household appliances. The repetitive strategy has less flexibility than a process-focused facility, but more flexibility than a product-focused facility.

Repetitive processes

Modules

Fast-food firms provide another example of a repetitive process using modules. This type of production allows more customizing than a continuous process; so modules (for example, meat, cheese, sauce, tomato, onion) are assembled to get a quasi-custom product, a cheeseburger. In this manner, the firm obtains both the low-unit-cost advantages of the continuous model (where many of the modules are prepared) and the custom advantage of the low-volume, high-variety model.

Table 7.1 compares the major characteristics of process-focus, repetitive, and product-focused strategies.

TABLE 7.1 ■ COMPARISON OF THE CHARACTERISTICS OF THREE TYPES OF PROCESSES

LOW-VOLUME, HIGH-VARIETY PROCESS (PROCESS FOCUS) (E.G., HOSPITALS)	MODULAR PROCESS (REPETITIVE FOCUS) (E.G., BURGER KING)	HIGH-VOLUME, LOW-VARIETY PROCESS (PRODUCT FOCUS) (E.G., NUCOR STEEL)
1. Small quantity and large variety of products are produced.	1. Long runs, usually a standardized product with options, are produced from modules.	1. Large quantity and small variety of products are produced.
2. Equipment used is general-purpose.	2. Special equipment aids in use of an assembly line.	2. Equipment used is special-purpose.
3. Operators are broadly skilled.	3. Employees are modestly trained.	3. Operators are less broadly skilled.
4. There are many job instructions because each job changes.	4. Repetitive operations reduce training and changes in job instructions.	4. Work orders and job instructions are few, because they are standardized.
5. Raw material inventories are high relative to the value of the product.	5. Just-in-time procurement techniques are used.	5. Raw materials inventories are low relative to the value of the product.
6. Work-in-process is high compared to output.	6. Just-in-time inventory techniques are used.	6. Inventory of work-in-process is low compared to output.
7. Units move slowly through the plant.	7. Movement is measured in hours and days.	7. Swift movement of units through the facility is typical.
8. Materials are moved via small flexible equipment.	8. Materials move by conveyor, transfer machines, AGVs, etc.	8. Materials move by connected pipes, material guides, etc.
9. Wide aisles and ample storage are typical.	9. Medium or narrow aisles, little storage space.	9. The facility is built around equipment, machinery, and product flows.
10. Finished goods are usually made to order and not stored.	10. Finished goods are made to frequent forecasts.	10. Finished goods are usually made to a forecast and stored.
11. Scheduling to orders is complex and concerned with the trade-off between inventory availability, capacity, and customer service.	11. Scheduling is based on building various models from a variety of modules to forecasts.	11. Scheduling is relatively simple and concerned with establishing a rate of output sufficient to meet sales forecasts.
12. Fixed costs tend to be low and variable costs high.	12. Fixed costs are dependent on flexibility of the facility.	12. Fixed costs tend to be high and variable costs low.
13. Costing, often done by the job, is estimated prior to doing the job, but known only after the job.	13. Costs are usually known, because of extensive prior experience.	13. Because fixed costs are high, costs are highly dependent on utilization of capacity.

Uniform Pigs Contribute to Efficiency

Taking shape in the secluded hills of Princeton, Missouri, is a multibillion dollar food revolution: technopork.

Inside Barn No. 5 of Premium Standard Farms Inc.'s sprawling complex, 1,100 hogs are being bred to a lean uniformity, with lower body fat than the average American adult. Pellets rattle down plastic tubes when feed gets low. A computer closes curtains as the night grows chilly, and heaters whir into action. (Because bigger pigs like it cooler, a computer lowers the temperature a half degree per day as they age.) Just when the odor seems a bit ripe, a whoosh of water flushes away manure.

A door cracks open and suddenly the pigs grunt and turn in unison to face two men in spotless blue jumpsuits—the hog farmer outfit of the twenty-first century. VP Dan Skadburg gently pokes the ribs of a 235-pounder. Five days to slaughter, he figures.

Factorylike operations such as this, which bring together technology and finance, are changing the face of the pork industry. Long a messy sideline for family farmers, megafarms can produce a healthy, lean hog for 10% less than their smaller counterpart.

And because Premium Standard's hogs are so uniform, its $50 million slaughterhouse will be mechanized as never before. Loins will be pulled off by robots. Disassembling heads, a job requiring a dozen knife-wielding workers, will be automated. It all adds up to higher-quality, lower-priced pork at the market. It is a lesson learned long ago in manufacturing: standardized products are necessary for efficient processes.

Sources: Wall Street Journal (March 28, 1994): A–1; December 1, 1994: A–1, 8; and May 4, 1995: A1-6.

Moving Toward World-Class Performance with Lean Production

Lean producers is the term used to describe repetitive producers who are world-class.[2] The lean producer's mission is to achieve perfection. Lean production also means reducing staff positions so that those responsible are doing the entire job, from housekeeping chores, to execution, to planning. Lean production calls for continuous learning, creativity, and teamwork. It requires the full commitment and application of everyone's capabilities.

Lean producers

Lean producers understand what the customer wants and they rapidly design quality products to meet those requirements. The advantages held by lean producers are spectacular (see Table 7.2). The documented attributes of lean producers include the following:

- They remove waste by focusing on *inventory reduction*. They eliminate virtually all inventory. The removal of inventory removes the safety nets that allow a poor product to make its way through the product process.

- They use *just-in-time* techniques to reduce inventory and the waste caused by inventory. They drive down the time and cost of switching production from one product to another.

- They *build systems that help employees* produce a perfect part every time.

- They *reduce space requirements*. The technique is to minimize the distance a part travels.

[2]*Synchronous manufacturing* is another term currently in vogue to describe efficient repetitive processes. General Motors has gone so far as to add the title synchronous manufacturing manager to its lexicon.

TABLE 7.2 ■ SUMMARY OF AUTOMOTIVE ASSEMBLY PLANT PERFORMANCE

	LEAN PRODUCERS	OTHERS		
	JAPANESE IN JAPAN	JAPANESE IN NORTH AMERICA	AMERICAN IN NORTH AMERICA	ALL EUROPE
Inventories (days for 8 sample parts)	.2	1.6	2.9	2.0
Quality (assembly defects/100 vehicles)	60.0	65.0	82.3	97.0
Space (square feet/vehicle/year)	5.7	9.1	7.8	7.8
Supplier share of engineering	51%	14%	37%	32%
Work force:				
Productivity (hours/vehicle)	16.8	21.2	25.1	36.2
% of work force in teams	69.3	71.3	17.3	.6
Number of job classes	11.9	8.7	67.1	14.8
Training of new production workers (hours)	380.3	370.0	46.4	173.3
Suggestions/employee	61.6	1.4	.4	.4
Absenteeism	5.0	4.8	11.7	12.1

Source: Adapted from James P. Womack, Daniel T. Jones, and Daniel Roos, *The Machine That Changed the World* (New York: Macmillan, 1990), pp. 92, 118.

- They *develop close relationships with suppliers;* suppliers understand their needs and their customers' needs.
- They *educate suppliers* to accept responsibility for helping meet customer needs.
- They strive for continually declining costs by *eliminating all but value-added activities.* They eliminate material handling, inspection, inventory, and rework jobs because they do not add value to the product. They retain only those activities that add value. Waste is eliminated.
- They *develop the work force.* They constantly improve job design, training, employee participation and commitment, and work teams.
- They *make jobs more challenging,* pushing responsibility to the lowest level possible. They reduce the number of job classes.

Viewed in this context, we see that traditional production techniques have set *limited* goals. For instance, traditionally, managers have accepted the production of a limited number of defective parts and have accepted safety stock as a limit on inventory reduction. Lean producers, on the other hand, set their sights on perfection; no bad parts and no inventory. The results are continually declining costs that are obtained via quality workmanship, zero inventory, a focus on teamwork and communications, and continuous self-improvement as employees broaden their skills. Lean producers are constantly building a better production system. A better system allows evermore challenging work for the employee and more rapid response to the market.

Lean production requires a commitment to remove continuously those activities that do not add value to the product. Thus, we can think of lean production as a waste-reduction philosophy. Lean producers enter a never ending battle to reduce idle time, changeover time, inventory, poor quality, poor suppliers, poor product design, and poor performance. Only when this is done is the organization lean and world-class.

We note successful lean production at Westinghouse in the *POM in Action* box.

Comparison of Process Strategies

Figure 7.1 further compares the three process strategies we have described. Advantages exist across the continuum. Unit costs will be less in the continuous process case if high volume exists because of specialized equipment and facilities. However, low-volume, unique service or product is more economical when produced under process focus. The bottom row of Figure 7.1 indicates that equipment utilization in a process-focused facility is often in the range of 5% to 25%. Utilization above 15% suggests moving to the right on the process strategy continuum. McDonald's started a whole new industry by moving from the left toward the right of the continuum.

Pharmaceutical and petrochemicals are examples of "process industries." Process industries typically deal with liquids and bulk raw materials. Here, chemical operator John Walsh monitors a continuous reaction step in the chemical process for the active ingredient of Fosaxmax, Merck's new medicine for postmenopausal osteoporosis. This plant in Baloydine, Ireland, will be the worldwide source for the active ingredient.

FIGURE 7.1 ■ Process Continuum

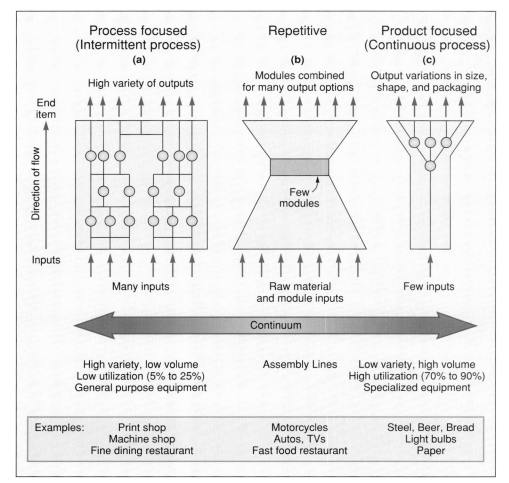

However, changing a production system from the process-focused model to the product-focused model is usually expensive. In some cases, this switch may necessitate starting over. Consequently, choosing where to operate on the process strategy continuum may determine the transformation strategy for an extended period.

Movement to the right of the continuum is desirable if the

1. *cash flows* to pay the fixed cost are adequate, and
2. risk of *lower demand* is insignificant, and
3. necessary *product variety* can be maintained.

The idea is to move to the right as far as possible to increase utilization without fixed costs becoming intolerable or the necessary product variety being destroyed.

Selection of Machinery and Equipment

Ultimately, the decisions about a particular process require decisions about machinery and equipment. Those decisions can be complex because alternative methods of production are present in virtually all operations functions, be they hospitals, restaurants, or manufacturing facilities. Picking the best equipment means understanding the specific industry, established processes, and technology (see photos of Plastic Recycling Corp.). That choice of equipment, be it an X-ray machine for a hospital, a computer-controlled lathe for a factory, or a new computer for an office, requires considering cost, quality, capacity, and flexibility. To make this decision, operations per-

Technology can result in new processes. Shown here is a process developed by Floyd Hammer (right) that converts plastic into weather-resistant park benches, parking lot curbs, and landscaping timbers. Hammer's company, Plastic Recycling Corp., based in Iowa Falls, expects to grow from only 2 plants to more than 16 as this new process provides an environmentally friendly product.

Lean Production Methods Are a Success at Westinghouse

To Westinghouse, the problems were clear: Worldwide competition was increasing; the company was pressed to lower prices, yet cost of materials, employees, and overhead kept increasing; and higher customer expectations demanded shorter cycle times, superior quality, and customer satisfaction.

Lean production (known as reengineering at Westinghouse) was the answer. The phrase embraces such techniques as work teams—training employees in multiple skills so that they can do more than one job—and "empowerment," which means pushing decision-making authority as far down in the organization as possible. It also entails reorganizing assembly lines and offices to simplify and speed the flow of work.

The company's solution focused on 12 years of experience to develop WESTIP (Westinghouse Technology to Improve Process), a method to radically reengineer or improve business processes. Cross-functional employee teams used WESTIP to perform process analysis, redesign, and implementation quickly and simply.

The result was a Baldrige National Quality Award and these benefits: $22 million in savings in 1 year, two-thirds reduction in material costs, reduced drawing time from 90 down to 10 days, 30% lower manufacturing costs through improved cellular layout, a drop in the time it takes to handle purchase orders from 14 days to 6 hours, and reduced order cost from $86 to $12. Finally, a factory that used to take 100,000 square feet to build Westinghouse components now only needs 40,000 square feet.

Sources: Westinghouse Productivity and Quality Center Workshop, Pittsburgh, December 1–3, 1993; and *Wall Street Journal* (March 16, 1993): A-1.

---

sonnel develop documentation that indicates the capacity, size, and tolerances of each option, and its maintenance requirements. Any one of these attributes may be the deciding factor regarding the use of a process.

As discussed in the *POM in Action* box "Automating Pizza Crust Production" the selection of machinery and equipment for a particular type of process can also provide competitive advantage. Many firms, for instance, develop a unique machine or technique within the established processes that provides an advantage. This advantage may result in added flexibility in meeting customer requirements, lower cost, or higher quality. Innovations and modification of equipment might also allow for a

Moving from a welding process to an investment-casting process made a major difference at Precision Castparts Corp. In the past, some of the firm's parts, like the fan for a GE jet engine, were made of hundreds of small stainless steel parts welded together. Precision Castparts Corp. replaced the traditional welding process with a single, large titanium casting. With this casting process, engine manufacturers have a lighter-weight frame at a cost savings approaching 50%.

Automating Pizza Crust Production

Even in the pizza business, craftsmen are being replaced by machine. The classic pizza parlor's star is the guy in the white apron who kneads the dough just to the right consistency, spins it dramatically in the air for shape, adds the toppings, and pops it into an oven. All this handiwork is intended to produce a pizza with the ideal combination of a crunchy, chewy crust.

Now, Chicago's AM Manufacturing has developed a system that can produce a similar crust, untouched by human hands. Its crusts are to be sold in grocery stores for ordinary people to make their own pizzas at home.

Here is how it works: The first step involves mixing the flour, water, and such. Then the dough is placed on a conveyor leading to a machine that measures out portions by weight, depending on the desired crust size. The dough is then rolled into balls to allow for motion to add firmness. The balls are dropped onto another belt, which carries them to a press that converts each ball to a disk. Thus flattened, the dough heads into another press where heated dies raise the edges of the crust.

Baking time on AM's assembly line takes only about 3 minutes, leaving more moisture in the chewy crust. Older methods, which yield less tasty crusts, simply stamp crusts out of sheets of cold dough and bake them for longer periods.

Sources: Restaurant Business (Sept. 1, 1992): 148-150; and *The New York Times* (June 27, 1993): F10.

more stable production process that takes less adjustment, maintenance, and training of operators. In any case, specialized unique equipment often provides a way to win orders.

The study of specific industries and their technology is outside the scope of this book. However, the technological advances that influence P/OM process strategy, and the selection of machinery and equipment are substantial and are discussed in Chapter 8.

SERVICE PROCESS STRATEGY

Figure 7.1 can be applied to services as well as manufacturing. For instance, much of the service industry produces in very small lots. This is true for legal services, medical services, dental services, and many restaurants. They are often producing in lot sizes as small as one. Such organizations would be on the left of Figure 7.1.

Service Sector Considerations

As Figure 7.1 indicates, equipment utilization is extremely low in process-focused facilities—perhaps as low as 5%. This is true not only for manufacturing, but also for services. An X-ray machine in a dentist's office and much of the equipment in a fine dining restaurant have low utilization. Hospitals, too, can be expected to be in that range, which would suggest why their costs are considered high. Why such low utilization? In part because excess capacity for peak loads is desirable. Hospital administrators, as well as managers of other service facilities and their patients and customers, expect equipment to be available as needed. Another reason utilization is low is poor scheduling (although substantial efforts have been made to forecast demand in the service industry) and the resulting imbalance in the use of facilities.

The service industry moves to the right of Figure 7.1 by establishing fast-food restaurants, legal clinics, auto lubrication shops, auto tune-up shops, and so forth. Notice how the hog industry and pizza business moved to the right on our process continuum, as indicated in the *POM in Action* boxes earlier in this chapter. As the variety of services is reduced, we would expect per unit cost to drop also. This is typically what happens.

Customer Contact and Process Strategy

Customer contact is an important variable in a transformation system. In a process that directly interfaces with the customer, one expects the customer to affect process performance adversely. In a restaurant, a medical facility, a law office, or a retail store, interaction between the customer and the process keeps the process from operating as smoothly as it otherwise might. Individual attention and customizing of the product or service for the customer can play havoc with a process. The more the process can be insulated from the customer's unique requirements, the lower will be the cost. Improving productivity can be accomplished in a variety of ways, as shown in Table 7.3.

Restaurants, such as General Mills' Red Lobster, are part of the service industry, but they are also the end of a long production line. At the beginning of the line, raw material goes in—at Red Lobster that means 60 million pounds of seafood a year. The seafood is purchased from all over the world. The shrimp arrives in frozen boxes from Ecuador and Thailand at a General Mills processing plant in St. Petersburg, Florida. There the shrimp is loaded onto a conveyor belt to be peeled, deveined, cooked, quick frozen (above), sorted (below), and repacked for ultimate delivery to individual restaurants.

CAPACITY

After considering the process options, a number of issues remain. In the rest of this chapter, we deal with three issues that are important for good process decisions. These issues are capacity, break-even analysis, and the investment itself.

TABLE 7.3 ■ CUSTOMER CONTACT AND PROCESS STRATEGY. THESE TECHNIQUES ARE USED TO IMPROVE PRODUCTIVITY.	
TECHNIQUE	**EXAMPLE**
Restrict the offerings	Limited-menu restaurant
Structure service so customers must go where the service is offered	Banks where customers go to a service representative to open a new account, to loan officers for loans, or to tellers for deposits and withdrawals
Provide self-service so customers examine, compare, and evaluate at their own pace	Supermarkets and department stores
Separate services that may lend themselves to some type of automation	Automatic teller machines
Customize at delivery	Customize vans at delivery rather than at production

 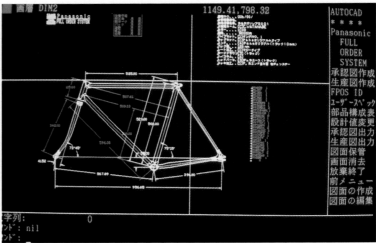

Flexible manufacturing can improve customer service and provide a competitive advantage. National Bicycle's customized Panasonic bicycle production process begins by defining individual customer needs. The customer mounts the special frame in a Panasonic bicycle store from which measurements are taken. These custom measurements are sent to the factory where CAD software produces a blueprint in about 3 minutes. At the same time, a bar-code label is prepared that will identify bicycle components as they move through production. Time—from beginning to end—is only 3 hours.

Capacity

Capacity is defined as the maximum output of a system in a given period under ideal conditions. In a process-focused facility, capacity is often determined by some measure of size such as the number of beds in a hospital or seating capacity in a restaurant. In a repetitive process the number of units assembled each shift, such as number of refrigerators, may be the criterion for capacity. And in a product-focused facility, such as Nucor, tons of steel processed per shift may be the measure of capacity. Whatever the measure, the capacity decision is critical to an organization because everything from cost to customer service depends upon the capacity of the process.

Many organizations operate their facilities at a rate less than capacity. They do so because they have found that they can operate more efficiently when their resources are not stretched to the limit. Instead, they operate at perhaps 92% of capacity. This concept is called effective capacity, or utilization. **Effective capacity**, or **Effective capacity utilization**, is simply the percent capacity *expected*. It can be computed from the following formula:

$$\text{Effective capacity, or utilization} = \frac{\text{expected capacity}}{\text{capacity}}$$

Effective capacity, or utilization, is the capacity a firm can *expect* to achieve given its product mix, methods of scheduling, maintenance, and standards of quality.

Another capacity consideration is efficiency. Depending on how facilities are used and managed, it may be difficult or impossible to reach 100% efficiency. Typically, **efficiency** is expressed as a percentage of the effective capacity. Efficiency is a measure of actual output over effective capacity:

Efficiency

$$\text{Efficiency} = \frac{\text{actual output}}{\text{effective capacity}}$$

The **rated capacity** is a measure of the maximum usable capacity of a particular **Rated capacity** facility. Rated capacity will always be less than or equal to the capacity. The equation used to compute rated capacity is

$$\text{Rated capacity} = (\text{capacity})(\text{utilization})(\text{efficiency})$$

We determine rated capacity in the following example.

EXAMPLE 1

The Sara James Bakery has a plant for processing breakfast rolls. The facility has an efficiency of 90%, and the utilization is 80%. Three process lines are used to produce the rolls. The lines operate 7 days a week and three 8-hour shifts per day. Each line was designed to process 120 standard (that is, plain) rolls per hour. What is the rated capacity?

In order to compute the rated capacity, we multiply the capacity (which is equal to the number of lines times the number of hours times the number of rolls per hour) times the utilization times the efficiency. Each facility is used 7 days a week, three shifts a day. Therefore, each process line is utilized for 168 hours per week (168 = 7 days × 3 shifts per day × 8 hours per shift). With this information, the rated capacity can be determined as follows:

$$\text{Rated capacity} = (\text{capacity})(\text{utilization})(\text{efficiency})$$
$$= [(120)(3)(168)](.8)(.9) = 43{,}546 \text{ rolls/week}$$

Forecasting Capacity Requirements

Determining future capacity requirements can be a complicated procedure, one based in large part on future demand. When demand for goods and services can be forecasted with a reasonable degree of precision, determining capacity requirements can be straightforward. It normally requires two phases. During the first phase, future demand is forecasted with traditional methods such as regression analysis. During the second phase, this forecast is used to determine capacity requirements.

Once the rated capacity has been forecasted, managers must decide the size of each addition to capacity. The assumption here is that management knows the technology and the *type* of facilities to be employed to satisfy these future demands.

Figure 7.2 shows two ways new capacity can be planned for growth of future demand. In Figure 7.2(a), new capacity is acquired at the beginning of year 1. This capacity will be sufficient to handle increased demand until the beginning of year 2. At the beginning of year 2, new capacity is again acquired, which will allow the organization to meet demand until the beginning of year 3. This process can be continued indefinitely into the future.

An alternative is presented in Figure 7.2(b). In the figure, a large increase in capacity is acquired at the beginning of year 1, which will satisfy future demand until the beginning of year 3.

Figures 7.2(a) and 7.2(b) reveal only two of many possible alternatives. In some cases, determining capacity requirements and deciding between alternatives can be relatively easy. Managers determine the total cost of each alternative and select the alternative with the least total cost. In most cases, however, determining the capacity of future facilities can be much more complicated. Many factors are difficult to quan-

The capital expenditures for a capacity change can be tremendous. Many companies address this by making incremental changes when possible. Others adjust by modifying old equipment or using older equipment even though it may not be as efficient. For instance, managers at family-owned Chelsea Milling Company, makers of Jiffy brand mixes, decided that their company and P/OM strategy did not support additional capital investment in new equipment. Consequently, when making repairs, modifying equipment, or adjusting for peak loads, they draw on spare, often old, equipment.

tify and measure. A major factor is market acceptance for the goods and services being produced. However, other factors include changing technology, actions by competitors, building restrictions, future cost of capital, availability of human resource, and laws and regulations.

When the future is subject to significant unknowns, the direct approach suggested in Figure 7.2 may not be adequate. In these cases, "probabilistic" models may be more appropriate. One technique for making successful capacity planning decisions with an uncertain demand is decision theory, including the use of decision trees.

Decision Trees Applied to Capacity Decisions

Decision trees, as we saw in Chapter 2's supplement, require specifying alternatives and various states of nature. For capacity planning situations, the state of nature usually is future demand or market favorability. By assigning probability values to the

FIGURE 7.2   ■   Adding Capacity

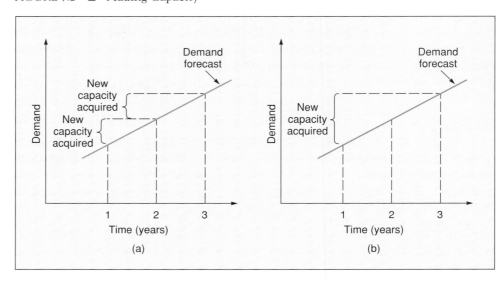

various states of nature, it is possible to make decisions that maximize the expected value of the alternatives. Example 2 shows how to apply decision trees to a capacity decision.

EXAMPLE 2

Southern Hospital Supplies, a company that makes hospital gowns, is considering capacity expansion. Its major alternatives are to do nothing, build a small plant, build a medium plant, or build a large plant. The new facility would produce a new type of gown, and currently the potential or marketability for this product is unknown. If a large plant is built and a favorable market exists, a profit of $100,000 could be realized. An unfavorable market would yield a $90,000 loss. However, a medium plant would earn a $60,000 profit with a favorable market. A $10,000 loss would result from an unfavorable market. A small plant, on the other hand, would return $40,000 with favorable market conditions and lose only $5,000 in an unfavorable market. Of course, there is always the option of doing nothing.

Recent market research indicates that there is a .4 probability of a favorable market, which means that there is also a .6 probability of an unfavorable market. With this information, the alternative that will result in the highest expected monetary value (EMV) can be selected:

$$\text{EMV (large plant)} = (.4)(\$100{,}000) + (.6)(-\$90{,}000) = -\$14{,}000$$
$$\text{EMV (medium plant)} = (.4)(\$60{,}000) + (.6)(-\$10{,}000) = +\$18{,}000$$
$$\text{EMV (small plant)} = (.4)(\$40{,}000) + (.6)(-\$5{,}000) = +\$13{,}000$$
$$\text{EMV (do nothing)} = \$0$$

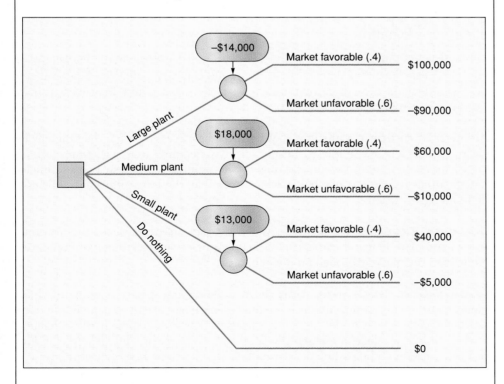

Based on EMV criteria, Southern should build a medium plant.

Forecasting capacity can be difficult even in the relatively stable electric utility industry. OPEC price fixing, restrictions on sulfur emissions from coal and oil, and changes in nuclear plant approvals all make long-range capacity planning difficult. Southern Edison's forecasting techniques looked ahead 10 years and envisioned 12 alternative futures. The results were forecasts that varied 30% on the upside and 30% on the downside. With these forecasts, management's job became building flexibility into their system, not just building more power stations. They now have plans to meet demand through sale or purchase of electricity, depending upon the scenario that occurs. Other options include demand management through programs urging consumers to reduce or expand their electricity consumption.

Rather than strategically manage capacity, P/OM managers may tactically manage demand. We now discuss some techniques for managing demand.

Managing Demand

Even with good forecasting and facilities built to that forecast, there may be a poor match between the actual demand that occurs and capacity available. A poor match may mean demand exceeds capacity or capacity exceeds demand. However, in both cases firms have options.

DEMAND EXCEEDS CAPACITY.   When *demand exceeds capacity*, the firm may be able to curtail demand simply by raising prices, scheduling long lead times (which may be inevitable), and discouraging marginally profitable business. Because inadequate facilities reduce revenue below what is possible, the long-term solution is usually to increase capacity.

CAPACITY EXCEEDS DEMAND.   When *capacity exceeds demand*, the firm may want to stimulate demand through price reductions or aggressive marketing, or accommodate the market through product changes.

ADJUSTING TO SEASONAL DEMANDS.   Another capacity issue with which management may be confronted is a seasonal or cyclical pattern of demand. In such cases, management may find it helpful to offer products with complementing demand patterns, that is, products for which the demand is the opposite. For example, in Figure 7.3 the firm is adding a line of snowmobile engines to its line of lawn mower engines to smooth demand. With appropriate complementing products, perhaps the utilization of facility, equipment, and personnel can be smoothed.

FIGURE 7.3 ■ By Combining Products That Have Complementary Seasonal Patterns, Capacity Can Be Better Utilized. A smoother demand for sales also contributes to improved scheduling and better human resource strategies.

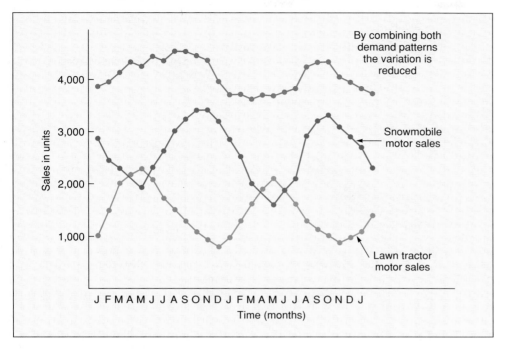

TACTICS FOR MATCHING CAPACITY TO DEMAND. Various tactics for matching capacity to demand exist. Internal changes include adjusting the process to a given volume through:

1. staffing changes;
2. adjusting equipment and processes, which might include purchasing additional machinery or selling or leasing existing equipment;
3. improving methods to increase throughput; and/or
4. redesigning the product to facilitate more throughput.

The foregoing tactics can be used to adjust demand to existing facilities. The strategic issue is, of course, how to have a facility of the correct size. Break-even analysis may help with that decision.

BREAK-EVEN ANALYSIS

The objective of **break-even analysis** is to find the point, in dollars and units, at which costs equal revenues. This point is the break-even point. Break-even analysis requires an estimation of fixed costs, variable cost, and revenue.

Break-even analysis

FIGURE 7.4 ■ Basic Break-Even Point

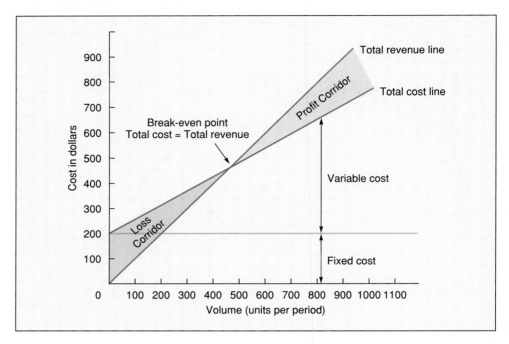

Fixed costs

Variable costs

Revenue function

     Fixed costs are costs that continue even if no units are produced. Examples include depreciation, taxes, debt, and mortgage payments. **Variable costs** are those that vary with the volume of units produced. The major components of variable costs are labor and materials. However, other costs, such as the portion of the utilities that varies with volume, are also variable costs.

     Another element in break-even analysis is the **revenue function**. It begins at the origin and proceeds upward to the right, increasing by the selling price of each unit. This revenue line is shown in Figure 7.4. Where the revenue function crosses the total cost line is the break-even point, with a profit corridor to the right and a loss corridor to the left.

     Break-even analysis assumes that costs and revenue increase in direct proportion to the volume of units being produced. However, neither fixed costs nor variable costs (nor, for that matter, the revenue function) need be a straight line. For example, fixed costs change as more capital equipment or warehouse space is used; labor costs change with overtime or as marginally skilled workers are employed; and the revenue function may change with such factors as volume discounts.

     The first step in break-even analysis is to define those costs that are fixed and sum them. The variable costs are then estimated by an analysis of labor, materials, and other costs connected with the production of each unit. The fixed costs are drawn as a horizontal line beginning at that dollar amount on the vertical axis, as we see in Figure 7.4. The variable costs are then shown as an incrementally increasing cost, originating at the intersection of the fixed cost on the vertical axis and increasing with each change in volume as we move to the right on the volume (or horizontal) axis. Both fixed and variable cost information is usually available from a firm's cost accounting department, although an industrial engineering department may also maintain cost information.

The respective formulas for the break-even point in units and dollars are developed as follows:

$$BEP(x) = \text{break-even point in units}$$
$$BEP(\$) = \text{break-even point in dollars}$$
$$P = \text{price per unit (dollars received per unit after all discounts)}$$
$$x = \text{number of units produced}$$
$$TR = \text{total revenue} = Px$$
$$F = \text{fixed costs}$$
$$V = \text{variable costs per unit}$$
$$TC = \text{total costs} = F + Vx$$

Setting total revenue equal to total costs, we get

$$TR = TC$$

or

$$Px = F + Vx$$

Solving for x, we get

$$BEP(x) = \frac{F}{P - V}$$

and

$$BEP(\$) = BEP(x)P$$

$$= \frac{F}{P - V}P = \frac{F}{(P - V)/P}$$

$$= \frac{F}{1 - V/P}$$

$$\text{Profit} = TR - TC$$

$$= Px - (F + Vx)$$

$$= Px - F - Vx$$

$$= (P - V)x - F$$

Using these equations, we can solve directly for break-even point and general profitability. The two formulas that are of particular interest are

$$BEP(x) = \text{Break-even in units} = \frac{\text{total fixed cost}}{\text{price} - \text{variable cost}} \qquad (7.1)$$

$$BEP(\$) = \text{Break-even in dollars} = \frac{\text{total fixed cost}}{1 - \dfrac{\text{variable cost}}{\text{selling price}}} \qquad (7.2)$$

CROSSOVER CHARTS. Break-even analysis aids process selection by identifying the processes with the lowest total cost for the volume expected. Such a point will, of course, also indicate the largest profit corridor. We are, therefore, able to address two issues: the low-cost process and the absolute amount of profit. Only by directly ad-

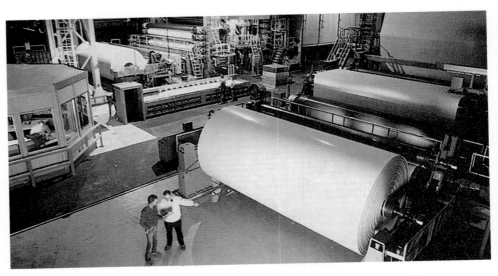

These paper machines, recently upgraded at a cost of $500 million by International Paper in Texarkana, Texas, produce bleached board, which is used in cigarette cartons, signs, pharmaceutical boxes, and so on. This huge capital expenditure will result in a high fixed cost, but will allow production of these products at a very low variable cost. The production manager's job is to maintain utilization above the break-even point to achieve profitability.

Crossover chart

dressing both issues can the process decision be successful. Figure 7.5 shows three alternative processes compared on a single chart. Such a chart is sometimes called a **crossover chart**. Process A has the lowest total cost for volumes below V_1. Process B has the lowest cost between V_1 and V_2. Process C has the lowest cost at volumes above V_2.

Single-Product Case

In Example 3 we determine the break-even point in dollars and units for one product.

EXAMPLE 3

Jimmy Stephens, Inc., has fixed costs of $10,000 this period. Direct labor is $1.50 per unit, and material is $.75 per unit. The selling price is $4.00 per unit.

The break-even point in dollars is computed as follows:

$$BEP(\$) = \frac{F}{(1 - V/P)} = \frac{\$10,000}{1 - [(1.50 + .75)/(4.00)]} = \frac{\$10,000}{.4375} = \$22,857.14$$

and the break-even point in units is

$$BEP(x) = \frac{F}{P - V} = \frac{\$10,000}{4.00 - (1.50 + .75)} = 5714$$

Note that in this example, we must use the *total* variable costs (that is, both labor and material).

FIGURE 7.5 ■ Crossover Charts. Three different processes can be expected to have three different costs. However, at any given volume, only one will have the lowest cost.

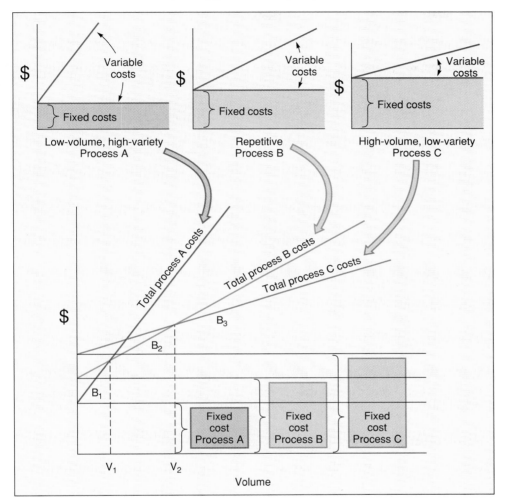

Multiproduct Case

Most firms, from manufacturers to restaurants (even fast-food restaurants), have a variety of offerings. Each offering may have a different selling price and variable cost. Utilizing break-even analysis, we modify Equation (7.2) to reflect the proportion of sales for each product. We do this by "weighting" each product's contribution by its proportion of sales. The formula is then

$$BEP(\$) = \frac{F}{\sum\left[\left(1 - \frac{V_i}{P_i}\right) \times \left(W_i\right)\right]} \tag{7.3}$$

where V = variable cost per unit
   P = price per unit
   F = fixed cost
   W = percent each product is of total dollar sales
   i = each product

  Example 4 shows how to determine the break-even point for the multiproduct case.

EXAMPLE 4

The costs from Le Bistro, a French-style deli, follow. Fixed costs are $3,500 per month.

ITEM	PRICE	COST	FORECASTED UNIT SALES
Sandwich	$2.95	$1.25	7,000
Soft drink	.80	.30	7,000
Baked potato	1.55	.47	5,000
Tea	.75	.25	5,000
Salad bar	2.85	1.00	3,000

With a variety of offerings, we proceed with break-even analysis just as in a single-product case, except that we weight each of the products by its proportion of total sales here.

MULTIPRODUCT BREAK-EVEN—DETERMINING CONTRIBUTION

1	2	3	4	5	6	7	8
ITEM (i)	SELLING PRICE (P)	VARIABLE COST (V)	(V/P)	1 − (V/P)	FORECASTED SALES	% OF SALES	WEIGHTED CONTRIBUTION (= COL. 5 × COL. 7)
Sandwich	$2.95	$1.25	.42	.58	$20,650	.446	.259
Soft drink	.80	.30	.38	.62	5,600	.121	.075
Baked potato	1.55	.47	.30	.70	7,750	.167	.117
Tea	.75	.25	.33	.67	3,750	.081	.054
Salad bar	2.85	1.00	.35	.65	8,550	.185	.120
					$46,300	1.000	.625

For instance, revenue for sandwiches is $20,650, which is 44.6% of the total revenue of $46,300. Therefore, the contribution for sandwiches is "weighted" by .446. The weighted contribution is .446 × .58 = .259. In this manner, its relative contribution would be properly reflected.

  Using this approach for each product, we find that the total weighted contribution is .625 for each dollar sales, and the break-even point in dollars is $67,200:

$$BEP(\$) = \frac{F}{\Sigma\left[\left(1 - \frac{V_i}{P_i}\right) \times \left(W_i\right)\right]}$$

$$= \frac{\$3,500 \times 12}{.625} = \frac{\$42,000}{.625}$$

$$= \$67,200$$

The information given in this example implies total daily sales (52 weeks at 6 days each) of

$$\frac{\$67,200}{312 \text{ days}} = \$215.38$$

Break-even figures by product provide the manager with added insight as to the realism of his or her sales forecast. They indicate exactly what must be sold each day, as we have done in Example 5.

EXAMPLE 5

Using the data in Example 4, we take the forecast sandwich sales of 44.6% times the daily break-even of $215.38 divided by the selling price of each sandwich ($2.75). Then the sandwich sales must be

$$\frac{.446 \times \$215.38}{\$2.75} = \text{number of sandwiches} = 34.9 \approx 35 \text{ sandwiches each day}$$

Once break-even analysis of this type has been prepared, analyzed, and judged to be reasonable, decisions can be made about the types of equipment needed. Indeed, a better judgment of the likelihood of success of the enterprise can now be made.

STRATEGY-DRIVEN INVESTMENTS

Let us now address the integration of strategy and investment with our process decision. Increasingly, managers realize that sustained profits come from building competitive advantage, not from a good financial return on a specific process.[3] We recommend that the traditional approach to investment analysis (just looking at financial returns) be enhanced by strategic considerations. Specifically, the strategic considerations we suggest are

1. that investments be made as *part of a coordinated strategic plan*. Where are these investments taking the organization? Investments should not be made as isolated expenditures, but as part of a coordinated strategic plan that will place the firm in an advantageous position. The question to be asked is, "Will these investments eventually win customers?"

[3]For an excellent discussion on investments that support competitive advantage, see Terry Hill, *Manufacturing Strategy: Text and Cases* (Homewood, IL: Irwin, 1989). Also see "Selling Rockwell on Automation," *Business Week* (June 6, 1988): 104.

2. that investments *yield a competitive advantage* (process flexibility, speed of delivery, quality, and so on);

3. that investments *consider product life cycles;*

4. that a *variety of operating factors be included in the financial return analysis* (for instance, reductions in scrap, rework, floor space, and inventory increase returns);

5. that investments be *tested in light of several revenue projections* to ensure that upside potential and down-side risk are considered.

Once the strategy implications of potential investments have been considered, traditional investment analysis is appropriate. We introduce the investment aspects of process selection next.

Investment, Variable Cost, and Cash Flow

Because process alternatives exist, so do options with regard to capital investment and variable cost. Managers must choose from among different financial options as well as process alternatives. The number of initial alternatives may be large, but analysis of six major factors (cost, volume, human resource constraints, technology, quality, and reliability) typically reduces the number of alternatives to a few. Analysis should show the capital investment, variable cost, and cash flows as well as net present value for each alternative.

Net Present Value

Net present value

Determining the discount value of a series of future cash receipts is known as the **net present value** technique. By way of introduction, let us consider the time value of money. Say you invest $100.00 in a bank at 5% for 1 year. Your investment will be worth $100.00 + ($100.00)(.05) = $105.00. If you invest the $105.00 for a second year, it will be worth $105.00 + ($105.00)(.05) = $110.25 at the end of the second year. Of course, we could calculate the future value of $100.00 at 5% for as many years as we wanted by simply extending this analysis. But there is an easier way to express this relationship mathematically. For the first year:

$$\$105 = \$100(1 + .05)$$

For the second year:

$$\$110.25 = \$105(1 + .05) = \$100(1 + .05)^2$$

In general,

$$F = P(1 + i)^N \tag{7.4}$$

where F = future value (such as $110.25 or $105)
  P = present value (such as $100.00)
  i = interest rate (such as .05)
  N = number of years (such as 1 year or 2 years)

In most investment decisions, however, we are interested in calculating the present value of a series of future cash receipts. Solving for P, we get

$$P = \frac{F}{(1 + i)^N} \tag{7.5}$$

When the number of years is not too large, the preceding equation is effective. When the number of years, N, is large, the formula is cumbersome. For 20 years, you would have to compute $(1 + i)^{20}$. Without a sophisticated calculator, this computation would be difficult indeed. Interest-rate tables, such as Table 7.4, alleviate this situation. First, let us rearrange the present value equation:

$$P = \frac{F}{(1 + i)^N} = FX$$

where

$$X = \text{a factor defined as}$$

$$= 1/(1 + i)^N \qquad (7.7)$$

and

$$F = \text{future value}$$

Thus, all we have to do is find the factor X and multiply it by F to calculate the present value P. The factors, of course, are a function of the interest rate, i, and the number of years, N. Table 7.4 lists some of these factors.

Equations (7.4), (7.5), and (7.6) are used to determine the present value of one future cash amount, but there are situations in which an investment generates a series of uniform and equal cash amounts. This type of investment is called an *annuity*. For example, an investment might yield $300 per year for 3 years. Of course, you could use Equation 7.4 three times, for 1, 2, and 3 years, but there is a shorter method. Although there is a formula that can be used to solve for the present value of an annual series of uniform and equal cash flows (an annuity), an easy-to-use table has been developed for this purpose. Like the customary present value computations, this calculation involves a factor. The factors for annuities are in Table 7.5. The basic relationship is

$$S = RX$$

TABLE 7.4 ■ PRESENT VALUE OF $1								
YEAR	5%	6%	7%	8%	9%	10%	12%	14%
1	.952	.943	.935	.926	.917	.909	.893	.877
2	.907	.890	.873	.857	.842	.826	.797	.769
3	.864	.840	.816	.794	.772	.751	.712	.675
4	.823	.792	.763	.735	.708	.683	.636	.592
5	.784	.747	.713	.681	.650	.621	.567	.519
6	.746	.705	.666	.630	.596	.564	.507	.456
7	.711	.665	.623	.583	.547	.513	.452	.400
8	.677	.627	.582	.540	.502	.467	.404	.351
9	.645	.592	.544	.500	.460	.424	.361	.308
10	.614	.558	.508	.463	.422	.386	.322	.270
15	.481	.417	.362	.315	.275	.239	.183	.140
20	.377	.312	.258	.215	.178	.149	.104	.073

TABLE 7.5 ■ PRESENT VALUE OF AN ANNUITY OF $1

YEAR	5%	6%	7%	8%	9%	10%	12%	14%
1	.952	.943	.935	.926	.917	.90	.893	.877
2	1.859	1.833	1.808	1.783	1.759	1.73	1.690	1.647
3	2.723	2.673	2.624	2.577	2.531	2.48	2.402	2.322
4	3.546	3.465	3.387	3.312	3.240	3.17	3.037	2.914
5	4.329	4.212	4.100	3.993	3.890	3.79	3.605	3.433
6	5.076	4.917	4.766	4.623	4.486	4.35	4.111	3.889
7	5.786	5.582	5.389	5.206	5.033	4.86	4.564	4.288
8	6.463	6.210	5.971	5.747	5.535	5.33	4.968	4.639
9	7.108	6.802	6.515	6.247	5.985	5.75	5.328	4.946
10	7.722	7.360	7.024	6.710	6.418	6.14	5.650	5.216
15	10.380	9.712	9.108	8.559	8.060	7.60	6.811	6.142
20	12.462	11.470	10.594	9.818	9.128	8.51	7.469	6.623

where X = factor from Table 7.5

S = present value of a series of uniform annual receipts

R = receipts that are received every year for the life of the investment (the annuity)

The present value of a uniform annual series of amounts is an extension of the present value of a single amount, and thus Table 7.5 can be directly developed from Table 7.4. The factors for any given interest rate in Table 7.5 are nothing more than the cumulative sum of the values in Table 7.4. In Table 7.4, for example, .952, .907, and .864 are the factors for years 1, 2, and 3 when the interest rate is 5%. The cumulative sum of these factors is 2.723 = .952 + .907 + .864. Now look in Table 7.5 to where the interest rate is 5% and the number of years is 3. The factor for the present value of an annuity is 2.723, as you would expect. Table 7.5 can be very helpful in reducing the computations necessary to make financial decisions.

Example 6 shows how to determine the present value of an annuity.

EXAMPLE 6

River Road Medical Clinic is thinking of investing in a sophisticated new piece of medical equipment. It will generate $7,000 per year in receipts for 5 years. What is the present value of this cash flow? Assume an interest rate of 6%.

$$S = RX = \$7,000(4.212) = \$29,484$$

The factor from Table 7.5 (4.212) was obtained by finding that value when the interest rate is 6% and the number of years is 5. There is another way of looking at this example. If you went to a bank and took a loan for $29,484 today, your payments would be $7,000 per year for 5 years if the bank used an interest rate of 6% compounded yearly. Thus, $29,484 is the *true* present value of the investment.

The net-present-value method is considered to be one of the best methods of ranking investment alternatives. The procedure is straightforward; you simply compute the present value of all cash flows for each investment alternative. When deciding among investment alternatives, you pick the investment that has the highest net present value. Similarly, when making several investments, those with higher net present values are preferable to investments with lower net present values.

Example 7 shows how to use the net present value to choose between investment alternatives.

EXAMPLE 7

Quality Plastics, Inc., is considering two different investment alternatives. Investment A has an initial cost of $25,000, and investment B has an initial cost of $26,000. Both investments have a useful life of 4 years. The cash flows for these investments follow. The cost of capital or the interest rate (i) is 8%.

INVESTMENT A'S CASH FLOW	INVESTMENT B'S CASH FLOW	YEAR	PRESENT VALUE FACTOR AT 8%
$10,000	$9,000	1	.926
9,000	9,000	2	.857
8,000	9,000	3	.794
7,000	9,000	4	.735

To find the present value of the cash flows for each investment, we multiply the present value factor by the cash flow for each investment for each year. The sum of these present-value calculations minus the initial investment is the net present value of each investment. The computations appear in the following table.

YEAR	INVESTMENT A'S PRESENT VALUES	INVESTMENT B'S PRESENT VALUES
1	$ 9,260 = (.926)($10,000)	$ 8,334 = (.926)($9,000)
2	7,713 = (.857)($9,000)	7,713 = (.857)($9,000)
3	6,352 = (.794)($8,000)	7,146 = (.794)($9,000)
4	5,145 = (.735)($7,000)	6,615 = (.735)($9,000)
Totals:	$28,470	$29,808
Minus initial investment	− 25,000	− 26,000
Net present value	$3,470	$3,808

The net present value criterion shows investment B to be more attractive than investment A because it has a higher present value.

In Example 7, it was not necessary to make all of those present-value computations for investment B. Because the cash flows are uniform, Table 7.5, the annuity table, gives the present value factor. Of course, we would expect to get the same answer. As you recall, Table 7.5 gives factors for the present value of an annuity. In this example, for payments of $9,000, cost of capital is 8% and the number of years is 4. Looking at Table 7.5 under 8% and 4 years, we find a factor of 3.312. Thus, the present value of this annuity is (3.312)($9,000) = $29,808, the same value as in Example 7.

Although net present value is one of the best approaches to evaluating investment alternatives, it does have its faults. Limitations of the net present value approach include the following:

1. Investments with the same present value may have significantly different project lives and different salvage values.

2. Investments with the same net present value may have different cash flows. Different cash flows may make substantial differences in the company's ability to pay its bills.

3. The assumption is that we know future interest rates, which we do not.

4. Payments are always made at the end of the period (week, month, or year).

ACHIEVING WORLD-CLASS STANDARDS

World-class producers use their process strategy as a competitive weapon. Operations managers select a production process with the necessary quality, flexibility, and cost structure to meet product and volume requirements. Increasingly, world-class competitors find ways to combine the low unit cost of high-volume, low-variety manufacturing with the customization available through low-volume, high-variety facilities. We began this chapter with a discussion of how Carrier Corporation is making such a change. Additionally, managers find ways to use the techniques of lean production and employee participation to build quality products as demanded by the customer.

World-class firms encourage the development of uniquely efficient proprietary equipment and processes. They design their equipment and processes to have capabilities beyond the tolerance required by their customers, while ensuring the flexibility needed for adjustments in technology and volumes.

Additionally, world-class firms make process investments that are efficient by ensuring that the investments support a long-term strategy. The criteria for investment decisions are contribution to the overall strategic plan and winning profitable orders, not just return on investment. World-class firms select the correct process and the correct capacity that contributes to their long-term strategy.

SUMMARY

The processes that operations managers use to perform transformations can be as important as the products themselves. Transformation processes determine much of the fixed and variable cost, as well as quantity and quality of the product. The process decision can result in selection of a transformation technology that is process-focused or product-focused or someplace in between. However, it must be of a capacity and technology that will provide a competitive advantage.

Good forecasting, break-even analysis, crossover charts, decision trees, cash flow, and net present value (NPV) techniques are particularly useful to operations managers when making the process decision.

SOLVED PROBLEMS

Solved Problem 7.1

Sara James Bakery, described earlier in Example 1, has decided to increase its facilities by adding one additional process line. The firm will have four process lines, each working 7 days a week, three shifts per day, 8 hours per shift. Utilization is 90%. This addition, however, will reduce its overall system efficiency to 85%. Compute the new rated capacity with this change in facilities.

Solution

$$\text{Rated capacity} = \text{capacity} \times \text{utilization} \times \text{efficiency}$$
$$= [(120)(4 \times 7 \times 3 \times 8)] \times (.9) \times (.85)$$
$$= (80,640) \times (.9) \times (.85)$$
$$= 61,689.6 \text{ per week}$$
$$\text{or}$$
$$= 120 \times 4 \times .9 \times .85$$
$$= 367.2 \text{ per hour}$$

Solved Problem 7.2

Marty McDonald works part-time making canoe paddles in Wisconsin. His annual fixed cost is $10,000, direct labor is $3.50 per paddle, and material is $4.50 per paddle. The selling price will be $12.50 per paddle. What is break-even in dollars? What is break-even in units?

Solution

$$BEP(\$) = \frac{F}{1 - V/P} = \frac{\$10,000}{1 - (\$8.00/\$12.50)} = \frac{\$10,000}{.36} = \$27,777$$

$$BEP(x) = \frac{F}{P - V} = \frac{\$10,000}{\$12.50 - \$8.00} = \frac{\$10,000}{\$4.50} = 2,222 \text{ units}$$

DISCUSSION QUESTIONS

1. What are the advantages of standardization? How do we obtain variety while maintaining standardization?

2. What type of process is used for each of the following?
    (a) beer
    (b) business cards
    (c) automobiles
    (d) telephone
    (e) "Big Macs"
    (f) custom homes

3. In an affluent society, how do we produce a wide number of options for products at low cost?

4. What products would you expect to have made by a repetitive process?

5. Where does the manager obtain data for break-even analysis?

6. What keeps plotted variable and fixed-cost data from falling on a straight line?

7. What keeps plotted revenue data from falling on a straight line?

8. What are the assumptions of break-even analysis?

9. How might we isolate the production/operations process from the customer?

10. What are assumptions of the net-present-value technique?

11. Identify two services located at the process-focused side of the process strategy continuum (Figure 7.1).

12. Identify two services located at the product-focused side of the process strategy continuum (Figure 7.1).

13. Identify two services that are organized as repetitive.

14. Distinguish between designed capacity, effective capacity, and efficiency.

15. Refer to the discussion of Carrier's manufacturing process that opened this chapter. How is its process strategy changing?

CRITICAL THINKING EXERCISE

Premium Standard Farms, the firm described in the *POM in Action* box "Uniform Pigs Contribute to Efficiency," has turned pig production into a commodity—like toasters. Impregnated female sows wait for 40 days in metal stalls so small that they cannot turn around. After an ultrasound test, they wait 67 days in a similar stall till they give birth. Two weeks after delivering 10 or 11 piglets, the sows are moved back to breeding rooms for another cycle. After 3 years, the sow is slaughtered. Animal-welfare advocates say such confinement drives pigs crazy. Premium Standard replies that its hogs must be comfortable, because only 1% die before Premium Standard wants them to. Discuss the business/ethical implications of this industry and these two divergent opinions.

PROBLEMS

7.1 River Road Medical Clinic, which runs an optometrist lab, has been blessed with substantial growth over the last decade. Additionally, it was able to buy additional increments of lens-grinding equipment in relatively small units. Prior analysis of its data (since its growth has been steady and constant) suggests that regression analysis (as described in Chapter 5) is adequate to determine its capacity demands. Data for the past decade follow:

	YEAR									
	1984	1985	1986	1987	1988	1989	1990	1991	1992	1993
Units Produced (in thousands)	15.0	15.5	16.25	16.75	16.9	17.24	17.5	17.3	17.75	18.1

· a) Determine its capacity needs in units for 1994, 1996, and 2000.

  b) If each machine is capable of producing 2,500 lenses, how many machines should it expect to have in 1996?

· **7.2** Assume River Road Medical Clinic (Problem 7.1) in 1994 has eight machines, each capable of producing 2,500 lenses per year. However, the new and best machine then on the market has the capability of producing 5,000 per year.

  a) What is the status of capacity at the firm in the year 2000 if it buys the new and best machine in 1994?

  b) What is the status of capacity at the firm in the year 2000 if it buys the standard machine with a capacity of 2,500?

· **7.3** A work center operates two shifts per day 5 days per week (8 hours per shift) and has four machines of equal capability. If the machines are utilized 80% of the time at a system efficiency of 95%, what is the rated output in standard hours per week?

· **7.4** The minutes available for the next quarter of 1996 at MMU Mfg. in Waco, Texas, for each of three departments is shown. Recent data on utilization and efficiency are also shown.

DEPARTMENT	MINUTES AVAILABLE	EFFECTIVE UTILIZATION	RECENT EFFICIENCY
Design	93,600	.92	.95
Fabrication	156,000	.95	1.03
Finishing	62,400	.96	1.05

Compute the expected capacity for next quarter for each department.

· **7.5** Butch Porter Manufacturing intends to increase capacity by overcoming a bottleneck operation through addition of new equipment. Two vendors have presented proposals. The fixed costs for Proposal A are $50,000 and for Proposal B, $70,000. The variable cost for A is $12.00 and for B, $10.00. The revenue generated by each of these units is $20.00.

  a) What is the break-even point in units for Proposal A?

  b) What is the break-even point in units for Proposal B?

· **7.6** You are given the data in Problem 7.5:

  a) What is the break-even point in dollars for Proposal A?

  b) What is the break-even point in dollars for Proposal B?

· **7.7** Given the data in Problem 7.5, at what volume (units) of output would the two alternatives yield the same profit?

· **7.8** Use the same data in Problem 7.5:

  a) If the expected volume is 8,500 units, which alternative should be chosen?

  b) If the expected volume is 15,000 units, which alternative should be chosen?

∶ **7.9** What is the net present value of an investment that costs $123,545, and has a salvage value of $44,560? The annual profit from the investment is $14,667 each year for 5 years. The cost of capital at this risk level is 12%.

· **7.10** The initial cost of an investment is $65,000 and the cost of capital is 10%. The return is $16,000 per year for 8 years. What is the net present value?

· **7.11** An investment will produce $1,000 2 years from now. What is the amount worth today? That is, what is the present value if the interest rate is 9%?

· **7.12** What is the present value of $5,600 when the interest rate is 8% and the return of $5,600 will not be received for 15 years?

: **7.13** Mr. Kulonda, VP Operations at McClain Manufacturing, has to make a decision between two investment alternatives. Investment A has an initial cost of $61,000, and investment B has an initial cost of $74,000. The useful life of investment A is 6 years; the useful life of investment B is 7 years. Given a cost of capital of 9% and the following cash flows for each alternative, determine the most desirable investment alternative according to the net present value criterion.

INVESTMENT A'S CASH FLOW	INVESTMENT B'S CASH FLOW	YEAR
$19,000	$19,000	1
19,000	20,000	2
19,000	21,000	3
19,000	22,000	4
19,000	21,000	5
19,000	20,000	6
19,000	11,000	7

: **7.14** An electronics firm is currently manufacturing an item that has a variable cost of $.50 per unit and a selling price of $1.00 per unit. Fixed costs are $14,000. Current volume is 30,000 units. The firm can substantially improve the product quality by adding a new piece of equipment at an additional fixed cost of $6,000. Variable cost would increase to $.60, but volume should jump to 50,000 units due to a higher-quality product. Should the company buy the new equipment?

: **7.15** The electronics firm in Problem 7.14 is now considering the new equipment with a price increase to $1.10 per unit. With the higher-quality product, the new volume is expected to be 45,000 units. Under these circumstances, should the company purchase the new equipment and increase the selling price?

· **7.16** Given the following data, calculate $BEP(x)$, $BEP(\$)$, and the profit at 100,000 units:

$$P = \$8/\text{unit} \qquad V = \$4/\text{unit} \qquad F = \$50,000$$

: **7.17** Kathleen Bentley has been asked to evaluate two machines. After some investigation, she determines that they have the following costs. She is told to assume that

a) the life of each machine is 3 years

b) the company thinks it knows how to make 12% on investments no more risky than this one.

	MACHINE A	MACHINE B
Original cost	$10,000	$20,000
Labor per year	2,000	4,000
Maintenance per year	4,000	1,000
Salvage value	2,000	7,000

Determine, via the present value method, which machine Kathleen should recommend.

⦂ **7.18** Your boss has told you to evaluate two ovens for Tink-the-Tinkers, a gourmet sandwich shop. After some questioning of vendors and receipt of specifications, you are assured the ovens have the following attributes and costs. The following two assumptions are appropriate:

  1. the life of each machine is 5 years

  2. the company thinks it knows how to make 14% on investments no more risky than this one.

	THREE SMALL OVENS AT $1,250 EACH	TWO LARGE HIGH-QUALITY OVENS AT $2,500 EACH
Original cost	$3,750	$5,000
Labor per year in excess of larger models	$750 (total)	
Cleaning/maintenance	$750 ($250 each)	$400 ($200 each)
Salvage value	$750 ($250 each)	$1,000 ($500 each)

  a) Determine via the present value method which machine to tell your boss to purchase.

  b) What assumption are you making about the ovens?

  c) What assumptions are you making in your methodology?

⦂ **7.19** Tom Miller and Jeff Vollman have opened a copy service on Commonwealth Avenue. They estimate their fixed cost at $12,000 and their variable cost of each copy sold at $.01. They expect their selling price to average $.05.

  a) What is their break-even point in dollars?

  b) What is their break-even point in units?

⦂ **7.20** Dr. Aleda Roth, a prolific author, is considering starting her own publishing company. She will call it DSI Publishing, Inc. DSI's estimated costs are

  Fixed $250,000.00

  Variable cost per book $20.00

  Selling price per book $30.00

  How many books must DSI sell to break even?

⦂ **7.21** In addition to the costs in Problem 7.20, Dr. Roth wants to pay herself a salary of $50,000 per year.

  a) Now what is her break-even point in units?

  b) What is her break-even point in dollars?

⦂ **7.22** As a prospective owner of a club known as the Red Rose, you are interested in determining the volume of sales dollars necessary for the coming year to reach the break-even point. You have decided to break down the sales for the club into four categories, the first category being liquor and beer. Your estimate of the beer sales is that 30,000 drinks will be served. The selling price for each unit will average $1.50; the cost is $.75. The second major category is meals, which you expect to be 10,000 units with an average price of $10.00 and a cost of $5.00. The third major category is desserts and wine, of which you also expect to sell 10,000 units, but with an average price of $2.50 per unit sold and a cost of $1.00 per unit. The final category is lunches and inexpensive sandwiches, which you expect to total 20,000 units at an average price of $6.25 with a food cost of $3.25. Your fixed cost (that is, rent, utilities, and so on) is $1,800 per month plus $2,000 per month for entertainment.

a) What is your break-even point in dollars?

b) What is the expected number of meals each day if you are open 360 days a year?

: **7.23** Using the data in Problem 7.22, make the problem more realistic by adding labor cost at one-third of meals and sandwiches cost. Also add variable expenses (kitchen supplies, tablecloths, napkins, and so on) at 10% of cost for all categories.

a) What is your break-even point?

b) If you expect to make a profit of $35,000 (before taxes) for your 12-hour days, what must your total sales be?

: **7.24** As operations manager of Baby Furniture, Inc., you must make a decision about expanding your line of nursery furniture (that is, cribs, toy chests, dressers, and so on). In discussing the possibilities with your sales manager, Betsy Waugh-McCollum, you decide that there definitely will be a market and that your firm should enter that market. However, because nursery furniture is often painted rather than stained, you decide you need another process line. There is no doubt in your mind about the decision, and you are sure that you should have a second process. But you do question how large to make it. A large process line is going to cost $300,000; a small process line will cost $200,000. The question, therefore, is the demand for nursery furniture. After extensive discussion with Mrs. Waugh-McCollum and Mr. Utecht of Utecht Market Research, Inc., you determine that the best estimate you can make is that there is a two-out-of-three chance of profit from sales as large as $600,000 and a one-out-of-three chance as low as $300,000.

With a large process line, you could handle the high figure of $600,000. However, with a small process line you could not and would be forced to expand (at a cost of $150,000), after which time your profit from sales would be $500,000 rather than the $600,000 because of the lost time in expanding the process. If you do not expand the small process, your profit from sales would be held to $400,000. If you build a small process and the demand is low, you can handle all of the demand.

Should you open a large or small process line?

: **7.25** You are the new manager of the university basketball concession booths. You have been told in no uncertain terms that concession sales will support themselves. The following table provides the information you have been able to put together thus far.

ITEM	SELLING PRICE	VARIABLE COST	% OF REVENUE
Soft drink			
Large	$1.10	$ .65	10
Medium	.75	.45	10
Small	.60	.40	20
Hot dog	.75	.45	10
Coffee	.50	.25	20
Miscellaneous snacks	.40	.30	30

Last year's manager, La Tonya Thompson, has advised you to be sure to add 10% of variable cost as a waste allowance for all categories.

You estimate labor cost to be (five booths with three people each) $250.00. Even if nothing is sold, your cost will be $250.00, so you decide to consider this a fixed cost. Booth rental, which is a contractual cost at $50 *each* per game, is also a fixed cost.

a) What is break-even volume for all booths per game?

b) How many hot dogs would you expect to sell at the break-even point?

: **7.26** Rank the following investments according to net present value. Each alternative requires an initial investment of $20,000. Assume a 10% cost of capital.

YEAR	CASH FLOWS FROM INVESTMENT 1	CASH FLOWS FROM INVESTMENT 2	CASH FLOWS FROM INVESTMENT 3
1	$ 1,000	$ 7,000	$10,000
2	1,000	6,000	5,000
3	3,000	5,000	3,000
4	15,000	4,000	2,000
5	3,000	4,000	1,000
6	1,000	4,000	1,000
7	—	4,000	1,000
8	1,000	2,000	—
9	—	—	1,000

CASE STUDY

Matthew Yachts, Inc.

Matthew Yachts, located in Montauk, Long Island, manufactured sailing yachts of all descriptions. The company had begun by building custom-designed yachts for a largely New York-based clientele. Custom-designed yachts still accounted for three-fifths of Matthew's unit sales and four-fifths of its dollar sales and earnings. Over the years, as Matthew Yachts' reputation for quality design and workmanship spread, sales broadened to cover all of the eastern seaboard.

In an effort to capitalize on this increased recognition and to secure a piece of the fastest growing market in sailing, Matthew Yachts began manufacturing a new standard, fixed-design craft. Matthew attacked only the high end of this market, as the boat measured 37 feet long. Nevertheless, even this end of the market was more price-sensitive and less conscious of performance than Matthew Yachts' custom-design customers were.

All of the company's yachts were manufactured at the Montauk plant and shared the same equipment and skilled labor force. Custom designs were given priority in scheduling, and the new boat was rotated into the schedule only when demand slackened. As sales of the fixed-design boat increased, however, scheduling the new boat on a regular basis became necessary.

Matthew Yachts were built basically from the bottom up. Fabricating hulls was the first step. Increasingly, fiberglass hulls were demanded for their speed and easy maintenance. Afterward came the below-decks woodworking, followed by the fiberglass and woodworking on the deck itself. The masts were turned and drilled separately. Masts and hull were then joined and the finish work completed.

Over the past year, as the fixed-design craft continued its steady increase in sales, costs and deliveries began to slide precipitously, especially on the fixed-design yachts. During this period, when push came to shove, construction of the fixed-design craft always yielded time and resources to the higher-profit-margin custom designs. As a result, many fixed-design yachts were strewn around the yard in various stages of construction. Moreover, space in the existing shipyard was becoming scarce, and a plant expansion of one sort or another appeared inevitable.

DISCUSSION QUESTIONS

1. Should Matthew Yachts, Inc., stay in the business of building standard, fixed-design yachts?
2. If Matthew does so, how should it continue?

Source: Roger W. Schmenner, *Production/Operations Management,* 5th ed., New York: Macmillan, 1993, p. 517.

BIBLIOGRAPHY

Berry, W. L., C. C. Bozarth, T. J. Hill, and J. E. Klompmaker. "Factory Focus: Segmenting Markets from an Operations Perspective." *Journal of Operations Management,* 10, no. 3 (August 1991): 363.

Burbidge, J. L. "Production Flow Analysis for Planning Group Technology." *Journal of Operations Management,* 10, no. 1 (January 1991): 5–27.

Ettlie, J. E. "What Makes a Manufacturing Firm Innovative." *The Executive* (November 1990): 10.

Ettlie, J. E., and E. M. Reza. "Organizational Integration and Process Innovation." *The Academy of Management Journal* (October 1992): 795.

Ferguson, J. T., and J. H. Heizer. *Real Estate Investment Analysis.* Boston: Allyn and Bacon, 1990.

Grant, R. M., R. Krishnan, A. B. Shani, and R. Baer. "Appropriate Manufacturing Technology: A Strategic Approach." *Sloan Management Review,* 33, no. 1 (Fall 1991): 43–54.

Heizer, J. H. "Manufacturing Productivity: Japanese Techniques Not Enough." *Industrial Management* (September/October 1986): 21–23.

Hounshell, D. A. *From the American System to Mass Production, 1800–1932.* Baltimore: Johns Hopkins University Press, 1984.

Kim, D., V. A. Mabert, and P. A. Pinto. "Integrative Cycle Scheduling Approach for a Capacitated Flexible Assembly System." *Decision Sciences,* 24, no. 1 (January/February 1993): 126–147.

Kwan, C. C. Y., and Y. Yuan. "The Present Value Issue in a Sequential Selection Problem." *Decision Sciences,* 24, no. 5 (September/October 1993): 1057.

Leachman, R. C., and T. F. Carmon. "On Capacity Modeling for Production Planning with Alternative Machine Types." *Industrial Engineering Research & Development,* 24, no. 4 (September 1992): 62.

Mansfield, E. "The Diffusion of Flexible Manufacturing Systems in Japan, Europe, and the United States." *Management Science,* 39, no. 2 (February 1993): 149–159.

McCutcheon, D. M., A. S. Raturi, and J. R. Meredith. "The Customization-Responsiveness Squeeze." *Sloan Management Review,* 35, no. 2 (Winter 1994): 89–100.

Morris, J. S., and R. J. Tersine. "A Simulation Analysis of Factors Influencing the Attractiveness of Group Technology Cellular Layout." *Management Science,* 36 (December 1990): 1567–1578.

Parsaei, H. R., and A. Mital. *Economic Aspects of Advanced Production and Manufacturing Systems.* New York: Van Nostrand Reinhold, 1991.

Pine, B. J., II. *Mass Customization: The New Frontier in Business Competition.* Boston: Harvard Business School Press, 1993.

Quinn, J. B., and J. A. Mueller. "Transferring Research Results to Operations." *Harvard Business Review* (January/February 1991): 39–40.

Sekine, K. *One-Piece Flow.* Cambridge, MA: Productivity Press, 1992.

Womack, J. P., and D. T. Jones. "From Lean Production to the Lean Enterprise." *Harvard Business Review,* 72, no. 2 (March/April 1992): 93–103.

Young, S. M. "A Framework for Successful Adoption and Performance of Japanese Manufacturing Practices in the United States." *The Academy of Management Review,* 17, no. 4 (October 1992): 677.

8

STATE-OF-THE-ART TECHNOLOGY IN P/OM

LEARNING OBJECTIVES

When you complete this chapter you should be able to:

Identify and define:

Computer-Aided Design (CAD)

Computer-Aided Manufacturing (CAM)

Numerical Control

Process Control

Fuzzy Logic

Neural Networks

Explain:

Flexible manufacturing systems (FMS)

Computer-integrated manufacturing (CIM)

Expert systems

Manufacturing uses of MIS

TECHNOLOGY PROVIDES THE COMPETITIVE ADVANTAGE AT AT&T

AT&T Microelectronics, a winner of the Shingo quality prize for manufacturing, is truly a global producer of computer chips. With fabrication plants in Allentown and Reading, Pennsylvania, Orlando, Florida, and Madrid, Spain, and with manufacturing facilities in Malmsburg, England, Matamoros, Mexico, Bangkok, Thailand, and Singapore, AT&T is one of the world's largest producer of chips that go into disk drives, cellular phones, and network switches.

Touring a fabrication plant is like entering a vacuum-sealed bag. It is not a place made for people, who by nature are "dirty," with flaking skin that creates showers of dust. Today's chips can be contaminated by a single particle of dust, ¹⁄₁₀₀ the width of a human hair. The chips themselves are less than one-millionth of a meter (called a micron) in size.

What goes on in a fabrication or "fab" plant? Blank silicon wafers, valued at perhaps $200, are the starting product. The output is a wafer with complicated patterns transferred on it, now valued at $20,000 or more.

The real center of a fab is the photolithography bays. Here a photo-sensitive gel is sprayed onto the wafers; they then go into a machine that projects the circuit elements onto the wafer. The projector is called a "stepper" because it projects the same image about 100 times onto each wafer, moving the wafer in steps to receive each successive image.

A designer of integrated circuits adjusts the tiny electro-optic crystal probe to try to tell what's going on within the circuits without taking them apart. Pointing the optic tip and micron-sized spot of laser light provides an electrical "window" into the world of the integrated circuit. The photo shows the microscope, crystal, laser, circuit board and computer used to measure the electrical currents.

Workers in "bunny suits" complete one step in the photolithographic process of developing a wafer full of chips. The process of producing thousands of chips onto a silicon wafer is like printing a silk-screen reproduction with 20 different colors of ink. At each step a fresh layer of silicon dioxide is baked on, parts of the new layer are etched away, and chemical elements are added to the exposed areas.

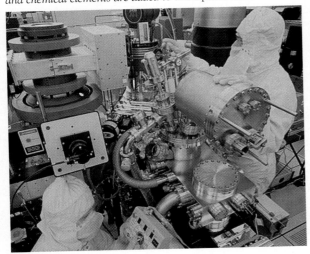

The photolithography equipment needed to print the circuit patterns is cutting-edge technology and can cost over $2 million per machine. It is not unusual for one production "clean room" to cost over half a billion dollars to build.

The fab room's cleanliness is specified in terms of the number of particles larger than one-half of one micron found in a cubic foot of air. A typical college classroom might have a few hundred thousand particles per cubic foot. A surgical operating room brings the level down to about 20,000. In AT&T's wafer-handling areas of the fab, the level is brought down to one!

To maximize the use of the capital equipment, AT&T's fab plant operates 24 hours a day, seven days a week. Workers pull 12-hour shifts, working 3 shifts one week and four the next.

A magnified view of AT&T's new technique to make internal measurements of integrated circuits.

These three researchers are examining a wafer in a "cleanroom." Their cleanroom "suits" consist of coats, gloves, and hoods, which are donned after the workers themselves are brushed and vacuumed. In some cleanroom environments, only non-smokers are permitted, as even a particulate of smoke residual in a man's mustache may contaminate the chip process.

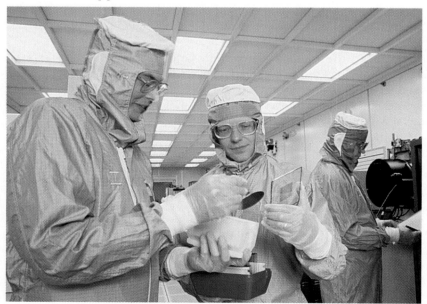

The process of completing a wafer's worth of chips takes as long as 12 weeks. It's not so much a linear assembly line as it is a loop. Over and over, the wafers are heat-treated, printed, etched, and doped with chemicals.

When the fab finishes a wafer, the wafer is sent to an overseas plant where it is sawed into chips. The chips are then put onto the familiar-looking plastic cases with wires coming out and are shipped to customers throughout the world.

In an industry where the life of a new product is measured in months, not years, AT&T must use its technology to maintain a global competitive edge.

Gillette is in the business of making razors and blades—and lots of other things that sell for very little. It has honed the art of using technology to cut fractions of a cent off production costs year after year. In just over 2 years, Gillette cut unit costs of its *Sensor* razor by 30%. How? By using advanced technology such as computers for tracking parts inventory and custom-designed laser welders for making the twin-blade *Sensor* cartridges. The company also uses specialized "vision" cameras to monitor and ensure product quality. Thanks to its use of technology, Gillette has become both a low-cost *and* high-quality manufacturer. The company is a world-class leader, not just with its *Sensor* razor, but with its other brands as well.[1] ◆

In this chapter, we introduce the use of technology in P/OM. As Gillette and AT&T can testify, technology can be a powerful tool in developing a competitive advantage.[2] Firms that achieve competitive advantage through technology

- plan for a more distant time horizon;
- have a narrow product line and know their product and customer exceedingly well;
- have strong internal technical capabilities that are tied to their strategic analysis;
- have consistent and stable strategic management;
- have effective ways to implement the changes necessary for the constructive use of technology.

Opportunities for innovative uses of technology exist throughout P/OM—from product development to maintenance.[3] Because information technology is so pervasive, most of this chapter focuses on its application to P/OM.

TECHNOLOGY IN MANUFACTURING

Information sciences are the driving technology for both manufacturing and services. Among the tools provided by the information sciences are computer-aided design (CAD), computer-aided manufacturing (CAM), flexible manufacturing systems (FMSs), computer-integrated manufacturing (CIM), vision systems, automated storage and retrieval systems (ASRs), and automated guided vehicles (AGVs).

The electronic flow of data that ultimately becomes information is the communication that ties ever improving equipment together. This electronic flow of

One of the great advantages of robots is that they can be reprogrammed for different movements by merely changing the electronic signals that control them. However, one of the limitations of robots has been their inability to "sense" their strength or position or the pressure that is being exerted when they "grab" or "bump" something. Consequently, substantial effort has been made in recent years in this area. This picture indicates the tremendous strides being made in this area as robotic "fingers" pick up and hold a semiconductor chip.

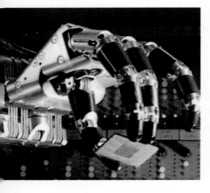

[1] *Wall Street Journal* (April 6, 1992): A1; and *AME News*, 7, no. 4 (July/August 1994): 3.

[2] See, for example, S. C. Fleming, "Using Technology for Competitive Advantage," *Research Technology Management*, 11, no. 5 (September/October 1994): 34–41; P. H. Biranbaum-Moore, A. R. Weiss, and R. W. Wright, "How do Rivals Compete: Strategy, Technology, and Tactics," *Research Policy*, 23, no. 3 (May 1994): 249–265; Andrew Bartmess and Keith Cerny, "Building Competitive Advantage Through a Global Network of Capabilities," *California Management Review*, 35, no. 2 (Winter 1993): 78–103; and M. E. Porter, "The Technological Dimension of Competitive Strategy," in R. S. Rosenbloom, ed., *Research on Technology Innovation, Management and Policy* (Greenwich, CT: JAI Press), p. 3.

[3] For instance, see an excellent discussion on the strategic uses of technology in product innovation by Joseph Morone, "Strategic Use of Technology," *California Management Review* (Summer 1989): 81–110.

Design for Manufacture and Assembly (DFMA): Success Stories at Ford, IBM, and Brown & Sharpe

A new software program is reducing design-to-product launch times by as much as 50%. Called design for manufacture and assembly (DFMA), the software helps increase product quality while producing the product faster and for less. It allows engineers and designers to examine product design alternatives before the product is manufactured. Here are three success stories.

IBM used DFMA to design its successful Proprinter. The printer, previously made for IBM in Japan, had 152 parts and took ½ hour to assemble.

The new Proprinter, now completely manufactured and assembled in the United States, has just 61 parts and takes 3 minutes to assemble.

Brown & Sharpe Manufacturing, a large tool company, used DFMA to help design its Micro Measuring Machine. Before using the software, the original plan called for 57 parts: The DFMA based design reduced this to four parts, allowing the company to sell its product competitively at half the cost of the competition and market it successfully overseas.

Finally, more than 1,000 engineers at Ford used DFMA on the Taurus model and reduced its manufacturing costs by 30%-more than $1 billion. "You can use DFMA on everything from footware to automotive supplies to aerospace components" says John Ingalls, a Boston management consultant.

Sources: Industrial Engineering (August 1992): 60–62; and *Manufacturing Issues* (Winter 1995): 1–5.

---

information allows the replacement of manual operations with automatic operations. The impact of information runs across the entire manufacturing spectrum, from design to manufacturing and from purchasing to shipping.

Computer-Aided Design (CAD) and Computer-Aided Manufacturing (CAM)

Computer-aided design (CAD) is the use of computers to interactively prepare engineering drawings. Although the variety of CAD software is extensive, most of it is used for drafting and three-dimensional drawings. Specialized CAD software exists for applications from electronic circuits to printed-circuit-board design. Still other CAD software is suited for mechanical applications including analysis of heat or stress. Additionally, some software focuses on how design affects processes as discussed in the *POM in Action* box "Design for Manufacture and Assembly (DFMA)."

As we saw in Chapter 6, most of the manufacturing costs are determined at the design stage.[4] CAD software allows designers to save time and money by shortening development cycles for virtually all products. The speed and ease with which sophisticated designs can be manipulated, analyzed, and modified with CAD makes review of numerous options possible before final commitments are made. Faster development, better products, accurate flow of information to other departments, all contribute to a tremendous payoff for CAD.

The electronic transfer of product design information has proven so important that a standard for its exchange has been developed. That standard is known as the

Computer-aided design

---

[4]See Mohan V. Tatikunda, "Design for Assembly: A Critical Methodology for Product Reengineering and New Product Development," *Production and Inventory Management Journal* (First Quarter 1994): 31–38.

Electronic Design Speeds Development of Ford's Next "World Car"

The key to its future, as Ford sees it, is a "world car" approach—the global manufacturing of a family of cars that share identical components produced in plants throughout the world. Its new series of common-component cars—the Ford Contour, the Mercury Mystique, and the Mondeo (their European version)—cost a whopping $6 billion to develop.

To dramatically cut costs of the 1999 rollout of its next new sedan, Ford is turning to an interactive process of design intended to cut lead time to 24 months. This compares positively to the 35 months it took to design the 1994 Mustang and the 54 months to design the average U.S. auto.

Here is how it works: A Ford engineer in England transmits a massive computer file of 3-D detailed drawings of the car to designers in Dearborn, Michigan, which takes only 15 minutes. The information is scrambled for satellite transmission. With revisions on hand, the Dearborn designers call England and coordinate final changes with their European counterpart. Each sees the latest images as they are made. The revised drawings are transmitted to Ford's design studio in Turin, Italy, where a computerized milling machine can turn out a clay or plastic-foam model in a matter of hours.

This interactive computer-aided design structure lets engineers, manufacturers, and suppliers worldwide get involved early in the automotive design stage. Not only does this technology reduce costs and speed development, but designers hope it will also mean that prototypes will not require substantial alteration once they hit the road.

Sources: New York Times (August 29, 1993): and *Forbes* (March 15, 1993): 54.

Standard for the Exchange of Product Data (STEP)

Standard for the Exchange of Product Data (STEP). This standard allows manufacturers to express three-dimensional product information in a standard format so it can be exchanged internationally. STEP allows geographically dispersed manufacturers to integrate design, manufacture, and support processes. It also results in a reduction in design lead time and development costs. The *POM in Action* box "Electronic Design Speeds Development of Ford's Next 'World Car'" suggests the efficiencies that can be obtained with this technology.

Computer-aided manufacturing (CAM)

Computer-aided manufacturing (CAM) refers to the use of specialized computer programs to direct and control manufacturing equipment. When computer-aided design (CAD) information is translated into instructions for computer-aided manufacturing (CAM), the result of these two technologies is CAD/CAM.

The benefits of CAD and CAM include

1. *Product quality.* CAD provides an opportunity for the designer to investigate more alternatives, potential problems, and dangers.

2. *Shorter design time.* Because time is money, the shorter the design phase, the lower the cost.

3. *Production cost reductions.* Reduced inventory, more efficient use of personnel through improved scheduling, and faster implementation of design changes lower costs.

4. *Database availability.* Consolidating accurate product data so everyone is operating from the same information results in dramatic cost reductions.

5. *New range of capabilities.* For instance, the ability to rotate and depict objects in three-dimensional form, to check clearances, to relate parts and attachments, to improve use of numerically controlled machine tools—all provide new

capability for manufacturing. CAD/CAM removes substantial detail work, allowing designers to concentrate on the conceptual and imaginative aspects of their task.

Numerical Control

CAD/CAM works because much of the machinery in the world can now be controlled electronically. Machinery can be designed for electronic control rather than manual and mechanical control. Electronic control increases both speed and flexibility. Machinery that can be controlled electronically, usually with magnetic tape, is called **numerical control (NC)** machines. When machines have their own microcomputer *and* memory to store computer programs, they are called **computer numerical control (CNC)** machinery. Electronic control is accomplished by writing computer programs that are stored on the magnetic tape in the case of NC machines and in computer memory in the case of CNC machines. The computer program is written much as one might write a BASIC or COBOL program to produce a paycheck. The languages used include APT (Automatically Programmed Tool) and Compact II.

Numerical control (NC)
Computer numerical control (CNC)

The third phase of numerical control is **direct numerical control (DNC)**. DNC machines are wired to a central computer that can send (download) the necessary code to the memory in DNC machines.

Direct numerical control (DNC)

Process Control

Process control is the use of information technology to monitor and control a physical process. These processes usually meet our definition of a *continuous process*. For instance, process control is used to measure the moisture content and thickness of paper as it travels over a paper machine at thousands of feet per minute. Process control is also used to determine and control temperatures, pressures, and quantities in petroleum refineries, petrochemical processes, cement plants, steel mills, nuclear reactors, and other continuous processes.

Process control

Process control systems operate in a number of ways, but the following is typical:

- They have sensors—often analog devices collecting data.
- The analog devices read data on some periodic basis, perhaps once a minute, or once every second.
- The measurements are translated into digital signals, which are transmitted to a digital computer.
- Computer programs read the file (the digital data) and analyze the data.
- The resulting output may take numerous forms. These include a message on a computer console or printer, a signal to a motor to change a valve setting, a warning light or horn, or a statistical process control chart.

Vision Systems

Vision systems combine video cameras and computer technology. These systems are primarily used in inspection roles. Visual inspection is an important task in most

Vision systems

food-processing and manufacturing organizations. Moreover, in many applications, visual inspection performed by humans is tedious, mind numbing, and error-prone. This is why vision systems are widely used when the items being inspected are very similar. For instance, vision systems are used to inspect french fries so that imperfections can be identified as the fries proceed down the production line. Vision systems are used to ensure that sealant is present and in the proper amount on Whirlpool's washing-machine transmissions. Such systems are also used to inspect switch assemblies at the Foster Plant in Des Plaines, Illinois. Vision systems are consistently accurate, do not become bored, and are of modest cost. Consequently, these systems are vastly superior to individuals trying to perform these tasks.

Robots

A large automated guided vehicle (AGV) shuttles paper at the Wisconsin Rapids plant of Consolidated Papers, Inc.

Robot

When a machine is flexible and has the ability to hold, move, and perhaps "grab" items, we tend to use the word **robot**. However, in spite of movies, cartoons, and stories about robots, they are not mechanical people. They are mechanical devices that may have a few electronic impulses stored on semiconductor chips that will activate motors or switches. When robots are part of a production process, they usually provide the movement of material between machines. They may also be used effectively to perform tasks that are especially monotonous, or dangerous, or when the task can be improved by the substitution of mechanical for human effort. This would be the case where consistency, accuracy, speed, or the necessary strength or power can be enhanced by the substitution of machines for people.

Robots and programmable machines are now cost competitive for a wide range of applications from small-batch jobs through long, continuous jobs. Less flexible and, consequently, less expensive robots may substitute for specialized equipment even in continuous processes. Robot control and instructions are similar to those used for numerically controlled machine tools. These instructions provide complete task control providing position, orientation, velocity, and acceleration. Communication between the operator and the robot is typically provided by a computer terminal, although robots can also be instructed via a "lead-through" method. Once instructions are entered, they are stored in computer memory and modified or edited as changes are made in the product or processing. Robots are not a panacea for every company and every task, as we see in the *POM in Action* box "The Robot's Role Is Not in Every Factory."

Automated Storage and Retrieval Systems (ASRSs)

Automated storage and retrieval systems (ASRSs)

Because of the tremendous labor involved in error-prone warehousing, computer-controlled warehouses have been developed. These systems, known as **automated storage and retrieval systems (ASRSs)**, provide for the automatic placement and withdrawal of parts into and from designated places in a warehouse. The systems are commonly used in distribution facilities of retailers such as Wal-Mart, Tupperware, and Benetton. (See the *POM in Action* box "Benetton, The World's Fastest Clothing Manufacturer on page 332.") These systems are also found in inventory and test areas of manufacturing firms.

The Robot's Role Is Not in Every Factory

Steve Antenen runs the nation's largest employment agency for laid-off robots. His 70 industrial robots all look impeccable, most having worked no more than a few thousand hours before their former owners, some of the nation's leading companies, showed them the door.

It was not supposed to be this way. To labor unions, robots presented the threat of driving real people out of their jobs. To industry, they were to be an uncomplaining solution to round-the-clock production needs and to tasks too unpleasant for human workers. However, companies have found that people still work better than robots in many jobs, and the U.S. robot population is not the hundreds of thousands once predicted, but closer to 45,000.

As it turns out, robots on occasion show behavioral lapses. There have been instances at General Motors of robots painting each other rather than cars, and rumors of one wayward robot spinning around and smashing windshields that another had just installed. In other words, the care and feeding of a robot may sometimes be more costly than the care and feeding of a human.

"Robots are just machines," says MIT's Walter Seering. "They have a place like all machines." They are particularly good for working in rooms where paint spray or fiberglass particulates cloud the air. "Robots don't have to breathe," notes Seering.

Sources: New York Times (July 1, 1990): 16; and *Fortune* (September 21, 1992): 62–74.

Automated Guided Vehicles (AGVs)

Automated material handling can take the form of monorails, conveyors, robots, or automated guided vehicles (AGVs). **Automated guided vehicles (AGVs)** are electronically guided and controlled carts used in manufacturing to move parts and equipment. They are also used in offices to move mail and in hospitals and in jails to deliver meals.

Automated guided vehicles (AGVs)

Flexible Manufacturing Systems (FMSs)

In the sophisticated case, material handling equipment is used to complement direct numerical control (DNC) machines. The material handling equipment can be robots, transfer machines, or automated guided vehicles; it moves materials from one workstation to another. The material handling equipment and the workstation may be connected to a common centralized computer facility, which provides the instructions for routing jobs to the appropriate workstation and the instructions for each workstation. Such an arrangement is an automated work cell or, as it is more commonly known, a **flexible manufacturing system (FMS)**. (See Figure 8.1.)

While technological challenging, computer-aided scheduling and the improved utilization possible with FMS are making these systems ever more popular.

Flexible manufacturing system (FMS)

Computer-Integrated Manufacturing (CIM)

A flexible manufacturing system can be extended backward electronically into the engineering (computer-aided design), production, and inventory control departments. In this way, computer-aided drafting can ultimately generate the necessary electronic code (instructions) to control a direct numerically controlled (DNC)

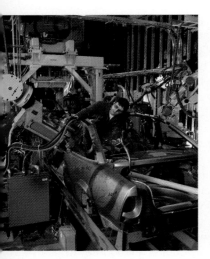

Robots can do a variety of dangerous and monotonous tasks for which they are much better suited than people. However, even robots have to be taught to perform those tasks. Here a General Electric engineer, after analysis using motion studies, is using a "teaching" box to train an industrial robot to perform those tasks.

FIGURE 8.1 ■ Flexible Manufacturing Systems (FMS) place machines and various computer-controlled material handling devices under computer control. Machines and material handling devices can be of different types. Setups and tool changing for each job are handled automatically.

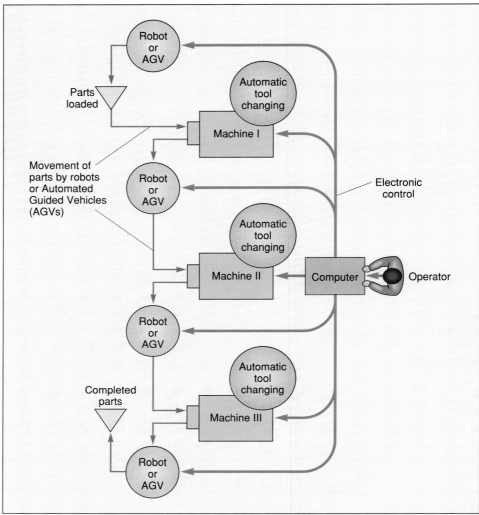

Computer-integrated manufacturing (CIM)

machine. If this machine is connected to others and to material handling equipment as a part of a flexible manufacturing system, then the entire system would be **computer-integrated manufacturing (CIM)** (Figure 8.2).

In a computer-integrated manufacturing environment, a design change initiated at a computer-aided design (CAD) terminal can result in that change being made in the part produced in a matter of minutes.

Expansion of FMS and CIM

Flexible manufacturing systems (FMS) and computer-integrated manufacturing (CIM) are reducing the distinction between low-volume, high-variety and high-

FIGURE 8.2 ■ **Computer-Integrated Manufacturing (CIM)**. Computer-aided design (CAD), computer-aided manufacturing (CAM), flexible manufacturing systems (FMSs), brought together with automated storage and retrieval systems (ASRSs) and automated guided vehicles (AGVs).

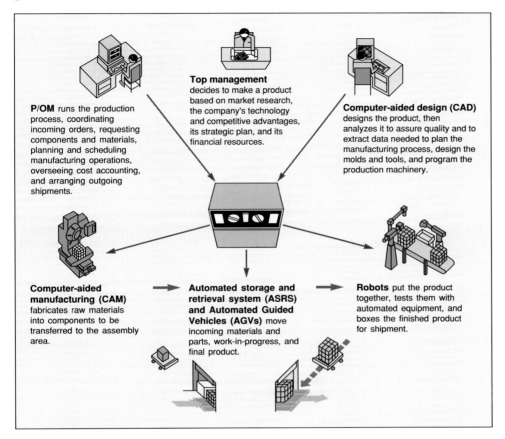

Top management decides to make a product based on market research, the company's technology and competitive advantages, its strategic plan, and its financial resources.

P/OM runs the production process, coordinating incoming orders, requesting components and materials, planning and scheduling manufacturing operations, overseeing cost accounting, and arranging outgoing shipments.

Computer-aided design (CAD) designs the product, then analyzes it to assure quality and to extract data needed to plan the manufacturing process, design the molds and tools, and program the production machinery.

Computer-aided manufacturing (CAM) fabricates raw materials into components to be transferred to the assembly area.

Automated storage and retrieval system (ASRS) and Automated Guided Vehicles (AGVs) move incoming materials and parts, work-in-progress, and final product.

Robots put the product together, tests them with automated equipment, and boxes the finished product for shipment.

Robots are used not only for labor savings, but more importantly, for those jobs that are dangerous, or monotonous, or require consistency, as in the even spraying of paint on an automobile.

Benetton: The World's Fastest Clothing Manufacturer

Benetton, the Italian sportswear company, can probably claim to have the world's fastest factory *and* the most efficient distributor in the garment industry. Located in Ponzano, Italy, Benetton makes and ships 50 million pieces of clothing—mostly slacks, dresses, and sweaters worldwide each year. Its one and only warehouse serves Benetton's 5,000 stores in 60 countries around the world. It cost $60 million, but this distribution center, run by only eight people, ships 230,000 pieces of clothing each day.

Here is how efficient Benetton is in meeting market demands: Let us say a salesperson in a Boston shop finds she is running out of a best-selling blue sweater. She calls a Benetton sales agent, who enters the order in a PC, which electronically forwards the order to the mainframe computer in Italy. Because the blue sweater was originally created by computer-aided design (CAD), the mainframe retains all the proper measurements, which it passes on to a knitting machine. The machine makes the sweaters, which are boxed with a bar code addressed to the Boston store, and the box goes to the Italian warehouse.

Once the blue sweaters are snugly sitting in one of the 300,000 slots in the warehouse, a robot flies by, reading bar codes. It picks out the right box and any other boxes ready for the Boston store and loads them for shipment.

Including manufacturing time, Benetton gets the order to Boston in 4 weeks if none is in stock, 1 week if a supply is already in the warehouse. In the notoriously slow garment industry, Benetton responded to the customer by using electronic communication, a CAD/CAM, robots, and bar codes and became a world-class leader.

Sources: Fortune (February 13, 1989): 54–59; and *Distribution* (October 1993): 62–66.

Firms often link several types of automated equipment together into a single, integrated system. Here an AGV feeds an ASRS.

volume, low-variety production. Information technology is allowing FMS and CIM to be extremely flexible and expand to include a growing range of volumes, as shown in Figure 8.3. Table 8.1 provides a synopsis of some of the major advances in manufacturing technology.

TECHNOLOGY IN SERVICES

The use of technology extends beyond manufacturing. Technology also has a wide range of applications in the services industry. These include everything from diagnostic equipment at an auto repair shop, to blood and urine testing equipment at a hospital, to improved materials for a knee replacement. The lodging industry provides a good example of the many ways technology can be used in the service industry (see the *POM in Action* box "Working Smart" on page 334). As you may have experienced, you can now authorize payment of your bill from your hotel room via a channel on the room's television set. The labor savings at the registration desk and enhanced service for the customer are currently providing a competitive advantage to Sheraton Hotels.

Table 8.2 provides a glimpse of the impact of technology on services. Operations managers in services, as in manufacturing, must be able to evaluate the impact of technology on their firm. This requires particular skill when evaluating reliability, investment analysis, human resource requirements, and maintenance/service.

FIGURE 8.3 ■ Different Production Processes Provide Different Combinations of Volume and Variety. As FMS and CIM expand, more overlap among options will occur.

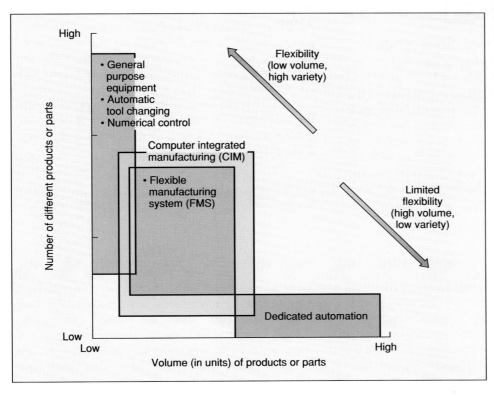

In an effort to manage the time and paper-work associated with insurance claims, State Farm Mutual Automobile Insurance is testing "notepad" computers. A "notepad" computer uses an electric pen that claims adjusters use to fill out insurance forms and mark damage on a schematic of a car. The computer then uses stored parts and price lists to calculate damage. The information, along with digitized versions of signatures is then transferred to the central computer at the end of the day. The hope is that the system will improve accuracy and reduce time and costs associated with automobile insurance claims.

INFORMATION SCIENCES IN OPERATIONS

The information sciences are making a major impact in additional areas that have applications in operations. These areas are transaction processing, management information systems, and decision support systems. Figure 8.4 shows these information systems.

TABLE 8.1 ■ MAJOR INNOVATIONS IN MANUFACTURING TECHNOLOGY

MACHINERY	TECHNOLOGICAL INNOVATION
Numerical control (NC)	Electronic instructions read from a tape.
Computer numerical control (CNC)	Computer memory resident at machine.
Direct numerical control (DNC)	Computer memory resident at machine and machine wired to a central computer.
Flexible machining center (FMC)	Electronic control of several DNC machines and the equipment (such as robots and AGVs) necessary to move material between those machines.
Computer-integrated manufacturing (CIM)	An FMS expanded to include design (CAD), inventory control, warehousing, and shipping.

Working Smart: Service Firms Struggle to Raise Productivity

Information technology is making a difference in the hotel industry. Hotel owners can now precisely track a maid's time through the use of a security system. When a maid enters a room, a card is inserted that notifies the front desk computer as to the maid's location. "We can show her a printout of how long she takes to do the room," says a major investor in a Salisbury franchise.

The security system also enables guests to use their own credit cards as keys to unlock their door. And there are other uses for the system. The computer can bar a guest's access to the room after checkout time and automatically controls the air conditioning or heat, turning it on at check-in and off at check-out.

A 92-room hotel with the system opened with the equivalent of only 11 full-time employees—a general manager, 4.5 desk clerks, five housekeepers, and a part-time maintenance person.

Sources: Lodging Hospitality (June 1992): 38–40; and *Hotel and Motel Management* (September 7, 1992): 31–33, and (May 26, 1992): 21.

Transaction Processing

Transaction processing system

A **transaction processing system** is a system that addresses the many transactions that occur within and between firms. These transactions have traditionally been paper transactions and include payroll, order entry, invoicing, receipt of checks, inventory, personnel, and so on. When these transactions are moved from paper to computerized processing and storage, we have a computer-based transaction system. The paperwork transactions at General Motors were so horrendous that GM bought Electronic Data Systems, Inc. (EDS) so that these transactions could be computerized

TABLE 8.2 ■ EXAMPLES OF TECHNOLOGY'S IMPACT ON SERVICES

SERVICE INDUSTRY	EXAMPLE
Financial services	Debit cards, electronic funds transfer, automatic teller machines.
Education	Multimedia presentations, electronic bulletin boards, library cataloging systems.
Utilities and government	Automated one-man garbage trucks, optical mail scanners, airborne warning and control systems.
Restaurant and foods	Optical check-out scanners, coupons based on specific purchases issued at check-out counters, wireless orders from waiters to the kitchen, robot butchering.
Communications	Electronic publishing, interactive TV, voicemail, "notepad" computers, cellular phones.
Hotels	Electronic check-in and check-out systems, electronic key/lock systems.
Wholesale/retail trade	Point-of-sale electronic terminals, dry cleaner's conveyors, barcoded data, automated security systems.
Transportation	Automatic toll booths, space shuttle, satellite-directed navigation systems.
Health care	MRI scanners, sonograms, patient-monitoring systems, on-line medical information systems.

FIGURE 8.4 ■ DSS, MIS, and Transaction Processing in Production/Operations Management

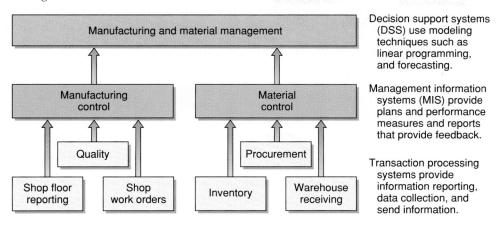

Decision support systems (DSS) use modeling techniques such as linear programming, and forecasting.

Management information systems (MIS) provide plans and performance measures and reports that provide feedback.

Transaction processing systems provide information reporting, data collection, and send information.

and the cost reduced. To the extent that such systems can be automated beyond those of competitors, a competitive advantage in speed, accuracy, or cost reduction may be obtained. If General Motors has one billion paper transactions a year and is able to reduce the cost of each transaction by $5, the savings is tremendous.

Modern transaction processing systems rely on electronic signals, which are a great vehicle for transmitting information, but they have a major limitation—most P/OM data do not start out in bits and bytes. Therefore, we must get the data into an electronic form; **automatic identification systems (AISs)** are the technologies that provide the translation of data into electronic bits and bytes. Bar codes, radio frequencies, and those optical characters on bank checks are automatic identification systems that help us move data to electronic media. Bar codes are used by Litton Industries for checking inventory and by nurses in hospitals to match bar codes on medication to ID bracelets on patients. For another application, see the *POM in Action* box "TRW and Ford Learn the Importance of Tracking in Airbag Production."

Automatic identification systems (AISs)

Management Information System (MIS)

The second form of information system is the **management information system (MIS)**. MIS systems are dedicated to obtaining, formatting, manipulating, and presenting data in the form of information to managers when needed. Much of the control information for a firm is provided by the MIS system. Information systems make their presence known in P/OM in a variety of ways, from scheduling to material requirements planning (MRP).

Management information system (MIS)

Decision Support System (DSS)

Another area where information science is helping operations in service as well as in manufacturing is through the use of a decision support system. A **decision support system (DSS)** is a logical extension of MIS that aids managers in *modeling* and decision making. Rather than simply providing information, a DSS allows a manager to perform "what-if" analysis given certain financial or operating parameters. A DSS

Decision support system (DSS)

TRW and Ford Learn the Importance of Tracking in Airbag Production

Airbags are supposed to allay fears of injury, but the one in Audrey Baker's 1990 Ford had just the opposite effect. Ms. Baker's car was part of a 165,000-car, multimillion dollar recall by Ford, which feared that defective bags could leak burning gases on occupants. The 1991 experience was an expensive lesson to Ford in the value of bar codes.

The airbags, supplied by TRW, Inc., show the hazards of converting an experimental technology into a mass-produced good. An airbag is a complex system made up of sensors that detect an impact and then explode a small canister of gas, which temporarily inflates a parachutelike balloon to cushion the auto occupant's impact. To meet demand, TRW accelerated production by using robots to automate previously manual tasks. But an out-of-tolerance machine damaged a joint in the airbag module, which *might* have allowed a few bags to spill their gases. No injuries occurred because of the defect, and TRW stressed that only 3,133 airbags had the problem.

The only problem was that no one knew *which* airbags had the defect, for neither TRW nor Ford had used bar coding or any other system to identify individual airbags or their production lot. What should Ford do? The legal and moral implications caused the company to play it safe with a total recall. Ford also announced that it expected TRW to share in the expense. At the same time, it canceled its exclusive contract with TRW and began plans to buy from multiple sources by 1996. This major blow to TRW left executives shaking their heads over the hidden expense of not tracking products, which can be done economically with bar codes.

Sources: Wall Street Journal (March 12, 1991): A4; and J.A.F. Stoner and R.E. Freeman, *Management*, 5th ed. (Englewood Cliffs, NJ: 653. Prentice-Hall, 1992)

---

also can incorporate a wide variety of management science models and graphical outputs. A spreadsheet model that is used to examine various alternatives is one form of a DSS.

Artificial Intelligence

MIS and DSS are supported by recent advances in artificial intelligence. Three tools, *expert systems, fuzzy logic,* and *neural networks,* can be thought of as part of a general discipline known as artificial intelligence. We will now introduce each of these tools.

Expert systems (ESs)

Expert systems (ESs) are computer programs that mimic human logic and "solve" problems much as a human expert would. The idea behind the use of an expert system is to capture in a computer program the knowledge and skills of a person who is an expert in a given field. Indeed, five advantages of ESs are that they

1. make decisions faster than the expert;
2. derive the benefits of having an expert at its disposal without having the expert present;
3. equal and surpass, at least in terms of consistency, the human expert;
4. free the human expert for other work;
5. can be disseminated to numerous nonexperts for education and training.

Although the idea is quite simple, the mechanics of making an expert system work are difficult. To make the system function there must be a knowledge base that is supplied by an expert. Every step of the process must be programmed meticulously, including any and all options to decisions made throughout the process. This computerized knowledge base is designed to be updated periodically to include new rules and facts. An electronic representation of the expert's thought process is called the "inference engine"—this fuels the knowledge base.

Table 8.3 provides an indication of the areas in which expert systems have been developed. Their names and a brief explanation are also included. The *POM in Action* box "Credit Authorization at American Express" discusses a specific example of an expert system. A number of expert systems are discussed in more detail in the appropriate chapters of this text.

Although the use of expert systems is widespread and rapidly expanding, limitations do exist. Among these are determining the relevance of data and recognizing the lack of data—these abilities have yet to be incorporated into expert systems. However, these limitations are being addressed by fuzzy logic and neural networks.

Many decisions are not clear-cut enough for the use of expert systems. A yes or no may not be sufficient. Consequently, another tool, *fuzzy logic*, has been developed for the operations manager's tool kit. **Fuzzy logic** can deal with approximate values, influences, and incomplete or ambiguous data to make decisions. For example, when making concrete or steel, the expertise of years of training is often the critical ingredient for a good batch. Knowing when to add material, heat, or a minor ingredient may be critical. Adding fuzzy rules—such as "if too hot, cut back on fuel" or "if mix is not consistent or if mix is too moist, mix longer"—deals with such ambiguities. Fuzzy logic is now written into computer programs to make both concrete and steel.It is also being used to add new features to consumer products, as we see in the *POM in Action* box "Matsushita's 'Fuzzy Logic' Microwaves and Washing Machines on page 339."

Fuzzy logic

Neural networks, modeled on the brain's meshlike network of interconnected cells, recognize patterns and program themselves to solve related problems on their own. The advantage to the operations manager is that they are programmed to learn.

Neural networks

TABLE 8.3 ■ EXPERT SYSTEMS IN P/OM		
NAME	**USE**	**EXPLANATION**
XCON (eXpert CONfigurer), Digital Equipment Corp.	Configuration	Checks sales orders and specifies components needed to configure the system
Authorizer's Assistant, American Express	Credit	Helps determine the appropriate level of credit, based on a variety of criteria
CONSULTANT, IBM	Bids	Helps field representatives prepare bids by analyzing the request for quotation
PROPLAN	Scheduling	Schedules parts based on their features and on machine capability and availability
SPC (Statistical Process Control), Automatix, Inc.	Process control	Data are analyzed to help the manufacturing process anticipate malfunctions
DELTA (Diesel Electric Locomotive Trouble-shooting), General Electric	Maintenance	Assists maintenance staff isolate and repair various faults in locomotives
FADES (Facilities Design Expert System)	Layout	Develops a good facility design mixing quantitative tools and human judgment.

Sources: Adapted from H. Raghav Rao and B. P. Lingaraj, "Expert Systems in Production and Operations Management: Classification and Prospects," *Interfaces*, 18 (November/December 1988): 80–91; and Dorothy Leonard-Barton and John J. Sviokla, "Putting Expert Systems to Work," *Harvard Business Review*, 66 (March/April 1988): 92.

Credit Authorization at American Express

The American Express Company has no set charging limits. To help the company decide whether to approve a specific charge, an expert system is used to sort through as many as 13 data bases. This feature has value for competitive reasons, but more importantly, it has eased the stiff administrative challenge of determining a customer's credit level. A merchant calls AMEX to authorize a charge whenever a customer makes a large purchase. Before the expert system was in place, the AMEX employee had to use his or her own discretion. If a specific purchase was outside a customer's normal buying pattern, the AMEX employee had to search through other data bases to gather more information. Now, the authorizer's assistant ES conducts the search and makes recommendations to the person who authorizes the approval decision. The whole process takes place in seconds, while the merchant is still on the phone.

Sources: ComputerWorld (January 25, 1993): 27; and *Datamation* (December 1, 1992): 95–96.

They can, for instance, recognize unnatural patterns, such as cycles and trends in control charts. Because of this unique ability to learn and recognize patterns, they can provide valuable information for real-time process control.[5]

These three tools, and indeed the discipline of artificial intelligence, have developed to the point where they are now making a major impact on operations management.

ACHIEVING WORLD-CLASS STANDARDS

World-class firms distinguish themselves not just by using the latest technology, but by the way they *strategically* use technology. The objective is not to just grab hold of the latest technological gimmick, but to use technology to achieve the long-term strategic objectives of the firm. For world-class firms, return on investment is only one criterion for technological investment. Such companies also ask, "Does the technology win orders?" Moreover, these firms ensure that they have the financial and human resources to make the technology work. That was obviously not the case for many companies in the earlier *POM in Action* box "The Robot's Role Is Not in Every Factory."

Bar codes have been with us for a long time. Now, however, Symbol Technologies has developed what they call a two-dimensional bar code that is capable of storing about a hundred times more information. This means that we can automate the reading of huge amounts of information and facilitate a wide variety of additional tasks. For instance, besides the typical product code and price, a bar code can now include such items as vendor, serial number, and even instructions for a robot in the next stage of production.

SUMMARY

Technology is a major source of competitive advantage. Advances are being made in a number of areas, but particularly in the information sciences. Information sciences are improving management information systems, transaction processing systems, and decision support systems. Information technology is also enhancing machine controls, from numerical controls to computer-integrated manufacturing. These advances are, with proper management, providing improved flexibility in meeting customer requirements, higher quality, and greater utilization of resources.

[5]H. Brian Hwarng and Norma Faris Habele, "X Control Chart Pattern Identification Through Efficient Off-Line Neural Network Training," *IIE Transactions*, 25, no. 3 (May 1993): 27–40.

Matsushita's "Fuzzy Logic" Microwaves and Washing Machines

Matsushita Electric Industries (MEI), Japan's giant appliance manufacturer, is building machines that mimic human logic. The cornerstone of its technology is neuro-fuzzy logic controllers. Instead of responding to yes–no, on–off digital commands, the fuzzy system can answer with "sort of" and "maybe, but let's see" actions based on if–then logic programming.

MEI's fuzzy logic microwave ovens, for example, simulate a cook's judgment, setting temperatures according to feedback from the cooking process. It monitors air temperature, food texture, and moisture content to trigger electronic controls with minute adjustments in timing and heat levels.

The firm also uses fuzzy logic to control washing machines so that wash cycles, water heat, and spinning speeds are adjusted in predetermined ways to match types of clothing. MEI claims its washers and dryers do a much better job at selecting settings than humans, who guess which is best and then walk away.

MEI's technology is also embedded in 2,000 other experimental home and office mechanisms, including camera processors. These processors improve automatic focusing features, trigger light-sensitive, flash-photo equipment, and operate shutter speed and aperture controls. Fuzzy logic technology is now using "neuro-networks" that can "learn" from preprogrammed expert data and from their own accumulation of process data.

Sources: Business Week (September 26, 1994): 144; and *Wall Street Journal* (October 21, 1991): R18.

KEY TERMS

Computer-Aided Design (CAD) (p. 325)
Standard for the Exchange of Product Data (STEP) (p. 326)
Computer-Aided Manufacturing (CAM) (p. 326)
Numerical control (NC) (p. 327)
Computer numerical control (CNC) (p. 327)
Direct numerical control (DNC) (p. 327)
Process control (p. 327)
Vision systems (p. 327)
Robot (p. 328)
Automated storage and retrieval systems (ASRSs) (p. 328)
Automated guided vehicles (AGVs) (p. 329)
Flexible manufacturing system (FMS) (p. 329)
Computer-integrated manufacturing (CIM) (p. 330)
Transaction processing system (p. 334)
Automated identification system (AIS) (p. 335)
Automatic identification systems (AISs) (p. 335)
Management information system (MIS) (p. 335)
Decision support system (DSS) (p. 335)
Expert systems (ESs) (p. 336)
Fuzzy logic (p. 337)
Neural networks (p. 337)

DISCUSSION QUESTIONS

1. What are possible applications of an expert system?

2. In what kind of situations are expert systems being used?

3. What is the difference between a management information system (MIS) and a decision support system (DSS)?

4. Give some recent examples of information technology successfully applied to new products and new processes in (a) manufacturing and (b) services.

5. Distinguish between flexible manufacturing systems (FMSs) and computer-integrated manufacturing (CIM).

6. What kinds of enhancements are being made to computer-aided design (CAD) systems?

7. Distinguish between expert systems, fuzzy logic, and neural networks.

8. How do "vision systems" work and where might they be used?

9. What are the advantages of a system like the Standard for the Exchange of Product Data (STEP)?

10. Explain the difference between NC, CNC, and DNC machines.

11. What are the different types of computer-aided design systems?

CRITICAL THINKING EXERCISES

1. Do you see any problems with an expert system such as the one discussed in the *POM in Action* box "Credit Authorization at American Express" determining your credit limit? What are the ethical issues of your doctor using an expert system to diagnose your ailment and prescribe a cure?

2. What are the implications for an organization that develops an expert system based on the years of experience of personnel in the scheduling department and then reduces that department's staffing? What happens under such conditions if the expert system is no longer valid because of a change in such things as technology, setup cost, and staffing levels?

PROBLEMS

8.1 Heyl Machine Shop, Inc., has a 1-year contract for the production of 200,000 gear housings for a new off-road vehicle. The owner, Jeff Heyl hopes the contract will be extended and the volume increased next year. Mr. Heyl has developed costs for three alternatives (see Figure 8.3). They are general-purpose equipment (GPE), flexible manufacturing system (FMS), and dedicated automation (DA). The cost data follow:

	GENERAL-PURPOSE EQUIPMENT (GPE)	FLEXIBLE MANUFACTURING SYSTEM (FMS)	DEDICATED AUTOMATION (DA)
Annual contracted units	$200,000	$200,000	$200,000
Annual fixed cost	100,000	200,000	500,000
Per unit variable cost	15.00	14.00	13.00

What process is best for this contract?

8.2 Using the data in Problem 8.1, determine the economical volume for each process.

8.3 Using the data in Problem 8.1, determine the best process for each of the following volumes: (1) 50,000, (2) 250,000, and (3) 350,000.

8.4 Refer to Problem 8.1. If a contract for the second and third years is pending, what are the implications for process selection.

CASE STUDY

Rochester Manufacturing Corporation

Rochester Manufacturing Corporation (RMC) was considering moving some of its production from traditional numerically controlled machines to a flexible machining system (FMS). Its traditional numerical control machines have been operating in a high-variety, low-volume, intermittent manner. Machine utilization, as near as it can determine, is hovering around 10%. The machine tool sales people and a consulting firm want to put the machines together in an FMS. They believe that a $3,000,000 expendi-

(Continued)

ture on machinery and the transfer machines will handle about 30% of RMC's work. The firm has not yet entered all its parts into a comprehensive group technology system, but believes that the 30% is a good estimate. This 30% fits very nicely into a "family." A reduction, because of higher utilization, should take place in the number of pieces of machinery. The firm should be able to go from fifteen to about four machines and personnel should go from fifteen to perhaps as low as three. Similarly, floor space reduction will go from 20,000 feet to about 6,000. Throughput of orders should also improve with this family of parts being processed in 1 to 2 days rather than 7 to 10. Inventory reduction is estimated to yield a one-time $750,000 savings, and annual labor savings should be in the neighborhood of $300,000.

Although the projections all look very positive, an analysis of the project's return on investment showed it to be between 10% and 15% per year. The company has traditionally had an expectation that projects should yield well over 15% and have payback periods of substantially less than 5 years.

DISCUSSION QUESTIONS

1. As a production manager for RMC, what do you recommend? Why?

2. Prepare a case by a conservative plant manager for maintaining the status quo until the returns are more obvious.

3. Prepare the case for an optimistic sales manager that you should move ahead with the FMS now.

BIBLIOGRAPHY

Beatty, C. A. "Implementing Advanced Manufacturing Technologies: Rules of the Road." *Sloan Management Review*, 33, no. 4 (Summer 1992): 49.

Byrd, T. A. "Expert Systems in Production and Operations Management: Results of a Survey." *Interfaces*, 23, no. 2 (March/April 1993): 118–129.

Davenport, T. H. *Process Innovation*, Cambridge, MA: Harvard Business School Press, 1993.

Grant, R. M., R. Krishnan, A. B. Shani, and R. Baer. "Appropriate Manufacturing Technology: A Strategic Approach." *Sloan Management Review*, 33 (Fall 1991): 43.

Roberts, E. B. "The Success of High-Technology Firms: Early Technological and Marketing Influences." *Interfaces*, 22, no. 4 (July/August 1992): 3.

Rodriquiz, A. A., and O. R. Mitchell. "A Vision System for Manufacturing Applications Under Moderately Un-

constrained Conditions." *Industrial Engineering Research & Development*, 25, no. 4 (July 1993): 15–25.

Roth, A. V., C. Gaimon, and L. Krajewski. "Optimal Acquisition of FMS Technology Subject to Technological Progress." *Decision Sciences*, 22 (Spring 1991): 308.

Stefik, M., J. Aikins, R. Balzer, J. Benoit, L. Birnbaum, F. Hayes-Roth, and E. Sacerdoti. "The Organization of Expert Systems: A Tutorial." *Artificial Intelligence*, 13 (March 1986): 135–173.

Turban, E. *Decision Support and Expert Systems: Managerial Perspectives*. New York: Macmillan, 1988.

Van Weelderen, J. A., and H. G. Sol. "MEDESS: A Methodology for Designing Expert Support Systems." *Interfaces*, 23, no. 3 (May/June 1993): 51–61.

Wu, B. *Fundamentals of Manufacturing Systems Design and Analysis*. New York: Van Nostrand Reinhold, 1991.

9

LOCATION STRATEGIES

LEARNING OBJECTIVES

When you complete this chapter you should be able to:

Identify or Define:

Objective of Location Strategy

International Location Issues

Explain:

Three methods of solving the location problem:

- Factor-rating method
- Locational break-even analysis
- Center-of-gravity method

LOCATION PROVIDES COMPETITIVE ADVANTAGE FOR FEDERAL EXPRESS

Fred Smith, founder and president of Federal Express, received a C on a college paper in which he proposed the "hub concept" (that Delta Airlines uses at Atlanta Airport), but for small packages. Since then, he has proven that the hub concept provides a radial distribution system that is unique and effective. He selected Memphis, Tennessee, as the central hub.

Memphis provides Federal Express with an uncongested airport, centrally located in the United States, with very few hours of closure because of weather. Competing carriers fly out of airports with substantially more weather problems. Location may be a contributor to the firm's safety record. In its 25 years of existence, Federal Express has never had an aircraft crash.

Each night, except Sunday, Federal Express brings to Memphis packages from throughout the world that are going to cities for which Federal Express does not have direct flights. The central hub permits service to a far greater number of points with fewer aircraft than the traditional city A to city B system. It also allows Federal Express to match aircraft flights with package loads each night and to reroute flights when load volume requires it, a major cost savings. Moreover, Federal Express also believes that the central hub system helps reduce mishandling and delay in transit because there is total control over the packages from pickup point through delivery.

At the Federal Express hub in Memphis, Tennessee, approximately 100 Federal Express aircraft converge each night around midnight with more than 700,000 documents and packages.

At the preliminary sorting area, packages and documents are sorted and sent to a secondary sorting area. The Memphis facility covers 1,500,000 square feet; it is big enough to hold 33 football fields. Packages are sorted and exchanged until 4 A.M.

At the outbound slide/load area, the packages and documents that have already gone through the primary and secondary sorts are checked by city, state, and zip code. They are then placed in containers that will be loaded onto aircraft for delivery to their final destinations in 170 countries.

Containers carrying documents and packages are loaded onto a Federal Express aircraft. A series of rollers moves the containers into position on the aircraft; a system of locking mechanisms secures the containers in place on the floor.

At a Federal Express station, employees are picking the items for a particular route and are loading them into a Federal Express van for delivery to their final destination.

Shipping company Sea-Land Service was headquartered in New Jersey's heavily settled Eastern corridor. But in 1992, the $3.2 billion company picked up stakes and resettled 25 miles up the road in Liberty Corner, New Jersey, in search of lower rents and greener surroundings. And why not? As a Sea-Land executive says, "All I need is a PC to track any of the 1.2 million containers we have in our company system. I can do that just as well from my house, or a hotel suite in Hong Kong, as I can from a high-rise office building overlooking the docks. Who needs to be near the ships?"[1] ◆

One of the most important long-term decisions companies like Federal Express and Sea-Land make is where to locate their operation. Location greatly affects costs, both fixed and variable. It can even have a large impact on the overall profit of the company. For instance, depending on the product and type of production or service taking place, transportation costs alone can total as much as 25% of the product's selling price. That is, one-fourth of the total revenue of a firm may be needed just to cover freight expenses of the raw materials coming in and the finished product going out. Other costs that may be influenced by location include taxes, wages, raw material costs, and, as we see in the quote above, rents.

Once management has committed an organization to a specific location, many costs are firmly in place and difficult to reduce. For instance, if a new factory location is in a region with high energy costs, even good management with an outstanding energy strategy is starting at a disadvantage. Management is in a similar bind with its human resource strategy if labor in the selected location is expensive, or ill-trained, or has a poor work ethic. Consequently, hard work to determine an optimal facility location is a good investment.

THE OBJECTIVE OF LOCATION STRATEGY

The best location for a given firm depends on its type of business. Industrial location decisions focus on minimizing costs, whereas retail and professional service organizations typically have a focus of maximizing revenue. Warehouse location, however, may be determined by a combination of cost and speed of delivery. In general though, the *objective of location strategy* is to maximize the benefit of location to the firm.

FACTORS THAT AFFECT LOCATION DECISIONS

Selecting a facility location is becoming much more difficult with the globalization of the workplace. Globalization has taken place because of the push to find new markets for products and because of several major changes. These changes include (1) better international communications, (2) more rapid, reliable travel and shipping, (3) ease of capital flow between countries, and (4) high differences in labor costs. Whereas only a decade ago few firms considered opening new offices, factories, retail stores, or

[1]"The Virtual Workplace," *Forbes* (November 23, 1992): 184.

FIGURE 9.1 ■ Some Considerations and Factors That Affect Location Decisions

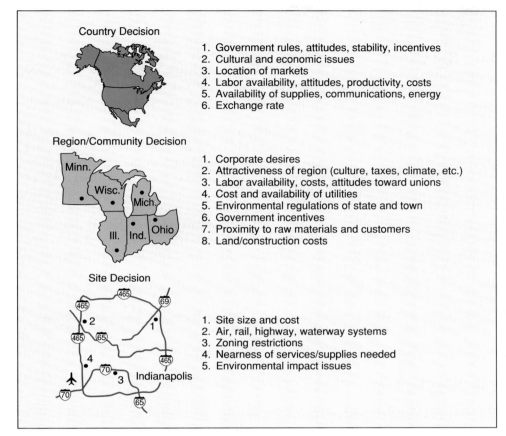

Country Decision

1. Government rules, attitudes, stability, incentives
2. Cultural and economic issues
3. Location of markets
4. Labor availability, attitudes, productivity, costs
5. Availability of supplies, communications, energy
6. Exchange rate

Region/Community Decision

1. Corporate desires
2. Attractiveness of region (culture, taxes, climate, etc.)
3. Labor availability, costs, attitudes toward unions
4. Cost and availability of utilities
5. Environmental regulations of state and town
6. Government incentives
7. Proximity to raw materials and customers
8. Land/construction costs

Site Decision

1. Site size and cost
2. Air, rail, highway, waterway systems
3. Zoning restrictions
4. Nearness of services/supplies needed
5. Environmental impact issues

Masaki Kaneho, Plant Manager of Motorola's integrated semiconductor plant in Aizu, Japan, with author Jay Heizer. As a world-class manufacturer, Motorola has located facilities throughout the world. Where labor costs are a significant part of product cost, S.E. Asia may be appropriate. For other countries, such as Japan, exchange rates or a local presence may be critical. While a S.E. Asian worker can wire 120 integrated circuits to metal frames each hour, an automated machine can do 640. And one worker can monitor eight machines for a total hourly production of 5,120. Clearly, in integrated circuit production direct labor costs have become less critical and other considerations relatively more important.

banks outside their own country, location decisions now transcend national borders. In fact, as Figure 9.1 shows, the sequence of location decisions often begins with choosing a country in which to operate. Before Germany's Mercedes-Benz chose Alabama as the location of its first major overseas plant, it first considered Mexico. In the end, the fear of marketing a $50,000 Mercedes that was "Made in Mexico" drove the firm back to the United States. The *POM in Action* box that deals with Mercedes' decision provides an interesting insight from Alabama's perspective.

Once a firm decides which country is best for its location, it focuses on a region of the chosen country and a community. In the United States, the South has become a popular destination for a variety of reasons, including the hospitality so often found in smaller towns. It is easy to see why Canada's Norbord Industries found a home in Tupelo, Mississippi, when you read the *POM in Action* box telling that firm's story.

The final step in the location decision process is choosing a specific site within a community. The company must pick the one location that is best suited for shipping and receiving, zoning, utilities, size, and cost. Again, Figure 9.1 summarizes this series of decisions and the factors that affect them.

Besides globalization, a number of other factors affect the location decision. Among these are labor productivity, foreign exchange, and changing attitudes toward the industry, unions, employment, zoning, pollution, taxes, and so forth.

Alabama Rolls Out the Red Carpet for Mercedes

When Mercedes-Benz announced its plans to build its first overseas plant in Vance, Alabama, the state hailed the German automaker as an industrial savior. Alabama's euphoria came after a year of competition among 170 sites in 30 states. Losers included finalists North Carolina and South Carolina and semifinalists Tennessee, Georgia, and Nebraska. Alabama Governor Jim Folsom warmly welcomed the $300-million-dollar complex and 1,500 high-paying new jobs as a symbol of prosperity. The city of Birmingham even spent $75,000 to erect a huge Mercedes hood ornament at the Legion Field football stadium as a way of thanking the company.

But as details of the state's economic incentives to Mercedes leaked out, not everyone was as happy as the Governor. Besides a gift of $253 million in capital investments and tax breaks, the fawning over a foreign company raised some ire. In a state where "Buy American" fever runs high, word that Governor Folsom had just ordered a new $82,000 Mercedes as his official car, ending the Alabama custom of purchasing U.S. cars, was not exactly welcome.

Alabama also promised to buy as many as 25,000 new Mercedes for government agencies and colleges. That brought out images of state workers driving luxury vehicles costing more than a lot of houses in Alabama.

The trade-offs, say state officials, will be clearer in 1997, when the plant opens and starts producing 60,000 sports-utility vehicles annually. And by the year 2017, an additional 13,500 jobs are supposed to be generated.

Sources: Economist (January 8, 1994): 32; *Business Week* (October 11, 1993): 138–139; and *Orlando Sentinel* (December 31, 1993): B-1.

Labor Productivity

When deciding on a location, management may be tempted by an area's low wage rates (see Figure 9.2 for a comparison of hourly manufacturing costs in 17 countries). However, wage rates cannot be considered by themselves, as Quality Coils discovered in the *POM in Action* box on page 350. Management must also consider productivity.

As discussed in Chapter 1, differences exist in productivity in various countries. What management is really interested in is the combination of productivity and the wage rate. For example, a firm paying $12.00 per hour with 1.25 units produced per hour will spend less on labor than one paying $10.00 per hour with productivity of 1.0 units per hour.

$$\frac{\text{Labor cost per hour}}{\text{Productivity (that is, units per hour)}} = \text{cost per unit}$$

$$\text{Case 1:} \quad \frac{\$12 \text{ Wages per hour}}{1.25 \text{ Units produced per hour}} = \frac{\$12}{\$1.25} = \$9.60$$

$$\text{Case 2:} \quad \frac{\$10 \text{ Wages per hour}}{1.00 \text{ Units produced per hour}} = \frac{\$10}{\$1.00} = \$10.00$$

Employees with poor training, poor education, or poor work habits may not be a good buy even at low wages. By the same token, employees who cannot or will not always reach their place of work are not much good to the organization even at low wages. Labor cost per unit is sometimes called the *labor content* of the product.

Why Canada's Norbord Industries Headed to Mississippi

Why would Canadian wood-products manufacturer Norbord Industries select Tupelo, Mississippi, as the site for a new $83 million factory? It turns out that Tupelo, although a poor, low-wage town of 30,000, is the envy of economic development recruiters all across the United States. It has a proven track record of drawing the likes of Norbord, Sara Lee, Philip Morris, and Cooper Tire and Rubber—as well as a large number of furniture makers from as far away as Switzerland, Brazil, and Australia. And it does not give away the keys to the city.

What makes Tupelo so seductive is its good old-fashioned Southern hospitality, like answering phone calls. One Canadian CEO stated, "In New York, just to get someone to talk to me, I had to make three phone calls. With Tupelo, six guys met me at the airport. They had five different sites ready for me to look at." For another, Tupelo is smart in investing its small marketing budget.

Knowing that Norbord needed to be near its raw material, pine trees, Tupelo spent $15,000 to buy 300,000 pine seedlings even before Norbord scouts arrived. It then gave the seedlings to farmers, to other landowners, and even to 600 kids to plant in their yards. Because pines grow three times faster in Mississippi than in Canada, Norbord was impressed. The result: Norbord chose Tupelo over competitors.

The payoff to Tupelo: 1,000 new jobs/year on average over the past decade, second highest per capita income in the state, its own symphony orchestra, and the nation's largest rural hospital.

Sources: Wall Street Journal (March 4, 1994): A-1 and *Economic Development Review* Vol 12 (Fall 1994): 78-82.

FIGURE 9.2 ■ Manufacturing Labor Costs of 17 Nations, 1993. These average hourly costs, in U.S.$, include benefits.

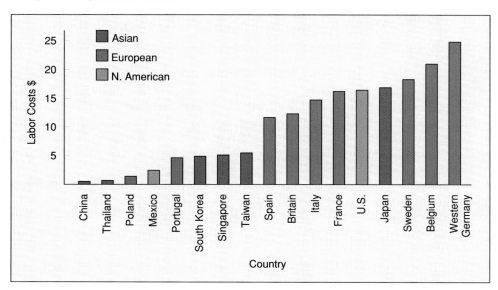

Sources: Wall Street Journal (September 30, 1994): R4; Morgan Stanley Research; and DRI McGraw-Hill.)

Quality Coils Pulls the Plug on Mexico

Keith Gibson, President of Quality Coils Inc., saw the savings of low Mexican wages and headed South. He shut down a factory in Connecticut and opened one in Juarez, where he could pay Mexicans one-third the wage rates he was paying Americans. "All the figures pointed out we should make a killing," says Gibson.

Instead, his company was nearly destroyed. The electromagnetic coil maker regularly lost money during 4 years in Mexico. High absenteeism, low productivity, and problems of long-distance management wore Gibson down until he finally pulled the plug on Juarez.

Moving back to the United States and rehiring some of his original workers, Gibson learned, "I can hire one person in Connecticut for what three were doing in Juarez."

When American unions complain that they cannot compete against the low wages in other countries and when teamster rallies chant "$4 a day/No way!," they overlook several factors. First, productivity in low-wage countries often erases a wage advantage, one that is not nearly as great as people believe. Second, a host of problems, from poor roads to corrupt governments, run up operating costs. And most importantly, the cost of labor for most U.S. manufacturers is less important than such factors as the skill of the work force, the quality of transportation, and access to technology.

Sources: Wall Street Journal (September 15, 1993): A-1 and *CFO* Vol 10 (March 1994): 63–65.

Exchange Rates

Although wage rates and productivity may make different countries seem economical, unfavorable exchange rates might negate any savings. Sometimes, though, companies can take advantage of a particularly favorable exchange rate by relocating or exporting to a foreign country. However, the values of foreign currencies continually rise and fall in most countries. Such changes could well make what was a good location in 1995 a disastrous one in 1999. Many of the *maquiladora* plants, U.S.-owned factories in Juarez, Tijuana, and Matamoros, Mexico, opened shortly after the Mexican peso decreased by 200% in relation to the dollar in the 1980s.

"May I have my allowance in Deutsche Marks, Dad?"

Costs

Tangible costs

We can divide location costs into two categories, tangible and intangible. **Tangible costs** are those costs that are readily identifiable and precisely measured. They include utilities, labor, material, taxes, depreciation, and other costs the accounting department and management can identify. In addition, such costs as transportation of raw materials, transportation of finished goods, and site construction are all factored into the overall cost of a location.

Intangible costs

Intangible costs are less easily quantified. They include quality of education, public transportation facilities, community attitudes toward the industry and the company, and quality and attitude of prospective employees. They also include quality-of-life variables, such as climate and sports teams, that may influence personnel recruiting.

Attitudes

Attitudes of national, state, and local governments toward private property, zoning, pollution, and employment stability may be in flux. Governmental attitudes at the time a location decision is made may not be lasting ones. Moreover, management may find that these attitudes can be influenced by leadership.

METHODS OF EVALUATING LOCATION ALTERNATIVES

There are four major methods for solving location problems: the factor-rating method, locational break-even analysis, the center-of-gravity method, and the transportation model.

The Factor-Rating Method

There are many factors, both qualitative and quantitative, to consider in choosing a location. Some of these factors are more important than others, so managers can use weightings to make the decision process more objective. The **factor-rating method** is popular because a wide variety of factors from education to recreation to labor skills can be included.

To give you an idea what a set of typical location factors and their relative weights are in manufacturing, we present Table 9.1. This table was developed by Grant Thornton, a consulting firm headquartered in Chicago, based on a survey of state manufacturing associations.

Factor-rating method

Assembly plants operating along the Mexican side of the border, from Texas to California, are called *maquiladoras*. Some 1,400 firms such as RCA, General Motors, Zenith, Hitachi, and GE operate these plants, which were designed to help both sides of the impoverished border region. After the 1982 devaluation of the peso, the number of *maquiladoras* nearly tripled, and it is believed that by the year 2000 as many as three million workers will be employed in these cross-border plants. Mexican wages are low, and at current exchange rates, companies don't look to the Far East as they once did.

TABLE 9.1 ■ LOCATIONAL FACTORS AND WEIGHTS

THE FOLLOWING 19 FACTORS HAVE BEEN IDENTIFIED AS IMPORTANT TO MANUFACTURING FIRMS:

FACTOR	WEIGHT (%)	FACTOR	WEIGHT (%)
Labor costs		**Government fiscal policies**	
Wages	8	Personal income growth	9
Unionization	6	Tax effort	4
Changes in wages	5	Changes in taxes	4
Changes in unionization	5	State business incentives	4
	24		21
Resource availability and productivity		**State-regulated employment costs**	
Available work force	7	Workers' compensation insurance	6
Energy costs	5	Unemployment compensation benefits	9
Value added	5	Average insurance cost per case	5
Labor-hours lost	4		20
	21	**Selected quality-of-life issues**	
		Education	5
		Cost of living	3
		Transportation	3
		Health care	3
			14

Sources: A series of annual Grant Thornton Manufacturing Climates studies. The factors were developed in discussion with state manufacturing associations, state economic development directors, and state Chambers of Commerce.

The factor-rating method has six steps:

1. Develop a list of relevant factors (such as those in Table 9.1).
2. Assign a weight to each factor to reflect its relative importance in the company's objectives.
3. Develop a scale for each factor (for example, 1–10 or 1–100 points).
4. Have management score each location for each factor, using the scale in step 3.
5. Multiply the score by the weights for each factor, and total the score for each location.
6. Make a recommendation based on the maximum point score, considering the results of quantitative approaches as well.

Example 1 shows how to use the factor-rating method.

EXAMPLE 1

Mademoiselle Linda Cosmetics of New Hampshire has decided to expand its production of Musk Cologne by opening a new factory location. The expansion is due to limited capacity at its existing plant. The rating sheet in Table 9.2 provides a list of qualitative factors that management has decided are important. Their weightings and their rating for two possible sites—St. Cloud, Minnesota, and Billings, Montana, are shown.

TABLE 9.2 ■ WEIGHTS, SCORES, AND SOLUTION

FACTOR	WEIGHT	SCORES (OUT OF 100) ST. CLOUD	BILLINGS	WEIGHTED SCORES ST. CLOUD	BILLINGS
Labor costs and attitude	.25	70	60	(.25)(70) = 17.5	(.25)(60) = 15.0
Transportation system	.05	50	60	(.05)(50) = 2.5	(.05)(60) = 3.0
Education and health	.10	85	80	(.10)(85) = 8.5	(.10)(80) = 8.0
Tax structure	.39	75	70	(.39)(75) = 29.3	(.39)(70) = 27.3
Resources and productivity	.21	60	70	(.21)(60) = 12.6	(.21)(70) = 14.7
Totals	1.00			70.4	68.0

Table 9.2 also shows the weights used to evaluate alternative site locations. Given the option of 100 points assigned to each factor, the St. Cloud location is preferable. By changing the points or weights slightly for some factors, we can analyze the sensitivity of the decision. For instance, we can see that changing the scores for labor costs and attitudes by 10 points can change the decision.

When a decision is sensitive to minor changes, further analysis of either the weighting or the points assigned may be appropriate. Alternatively, management may conclude that these intangible factors are not the proper criteria on which to base a location decision and may therefore place primary weight on the more quantitative aspects of the decision.

Locational Break-Even Analysis

Locational break-even analysis is the use of cost–volume analysis to make an economic comparison of location alternatives. By identifying fixed and variable costs and graphing them for each location, we can determine which one provides the lowest cost. This graphic approach also provides the range of volume over which each location is preferable.

Locational break-even analysis

The three steps to locational break-even analysis are:

1. Determine the fixed and variable cost for each location.

2. Plot the costs for each location, with costs on the vertical axis of the graph and annual volume on the horizontal axis.

3. Select the location that has the lowest total cost for the expected production volume.

Example 2 shows how to use locational break-even analysis.

EXAMPLE 2

A manufacturer of automobile carburetors is considering three locations—Akron, Bowling Green, and Chicago—for a new plant. Cost studies indicate that fixed costs per year at the sites are $30,000, $60,000, and $110,000, respectively. Variable costs are $75 per unit, $45 per unit, and $25 per unit, respectively. The expected selling price of the carburetors produced is $120. The company wishes to find the most economical location for an expected volume of 2,000 units per year.

For each of the three, we can plot the fixed costs (those at a volume of zero units) and the total cost (fixed costs + variable costs) at the expected volume of output. These lines have been plotted in Figure 9.3.

For Akron,

$$\text{Total cost} = \$30,000 + \$75(2,000) = \$180,000$$

For Bowling Green,

$$\text{Total cost} = \$60,000 + \$45(2,000) = \$150,000$$

For Chicago,

$$\text{Total cost} = \$110,000 + \$25(2,000) = \$160,000$$

With an expected volume of 2,000 units per year, Bowling Green provides the lowest cost location. The expected profit is

$$\text{Total revenue} - \text{total cost} = \$120(2,000) - \$150,000 = \$90,000/\text{year}$$

FIGURE 9.3   ■   Crossover Chart for Locational Break-Even Analysis

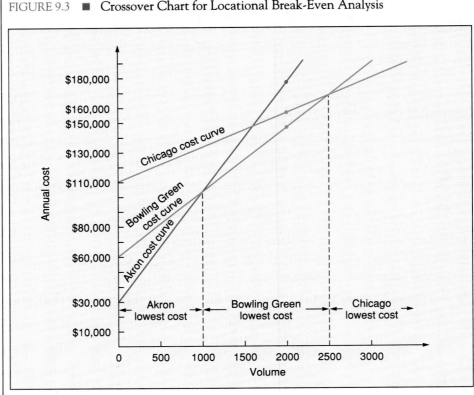

The chart also tells us that for a volume of less than 1,000, Akron would be preferred, and for a volume greater than 2,500, Chicago would yield the greatest profit. The crossover points are 1,000 and 2,500.

The Center-of-Gravity Method

Center-of-gravity method

The **center-of-gravity method** is a mathematical technique used for finding the location of a distribution center that will minimize distribution costs. The method takes into account the location of markets, the volume of goods shipped to those markets, and shipping costs in finding a best location for a distribution center.

The first step in the center-of-gravity method is to place the locations on a coordinate system. The origin of the coordinate system and the scale used are arbitrary, just as long as the relative distances are correctly represented. This can be done easily by placing a grid over an ordinary map. The center of gravity is determined by Equations (9.1) and (9.2):

$$C_x = \frac{\sum_i d_{ix} W_i}{\sum_i W_i} \tag{9.1}$$

The Third Wave of Urban Emigration Leads to a New Geography

Why would Citicorp locate its credit card operations in South Dakota and clothing vendor Patagonia put its customer service staff in Montana? Why did Utah turn into a national center for software development? And why would U.S. West pick tiny Lusk, Wyoming (population 1,504), as a telecommunications center? The answers are the same: explosive advances in fiber-optic cables, digital switches, and computing make sites in the previous hinterlands ever closer. "Geography is irrelevant" in location selection, says real estate consultant Chris Leinberger.

Employers have, of course, been trickling out of big cities for a long time. In the first wave of urban emigration, manufacturers took their factories out of settled areas and put them wherever electric power lines and railroads reached. The interstate highway system was the driving force in the second wave, which chased more assembly lines and textile mills

into rural areas; it also saw the exodus of corporate headquarters from city centers to more congenial suburban sites.

The third wave—call it the fiber-optic wave—is electrifying the United States by crisscrossing it with glass fibers. It has taken scarcely 15 years. The third wave is one reason why Fidelity Investments relocated many of its employees in 1993 from Boston to Covington, Kentucky. Now employees in the low-cost Covington region connect by phone line to their colleagues in the Boston office at a cost of less than a penny per minute. That is less than Fidelity spends on local connections.

Who will be the winners in the fiber-optic location movement? States with smaller tax burdens and owners of property in fringe suburbs and scenic rural areas should come out ahead. And so should E-mail providers (like MCI), telecommuting software makers (like Lotus), videoconferencing firms (like Picture-Tel), makers of office electronic equipment (like Dell and Hewlett-Packard), and delivery firms (like UPS and Federal Express).

Sources: Forbes (November 23, 1992): 184–190 and *Telemarketing Magazine* Vol 12 (Feb. 1994): 42–43.

$$C_y = \frac{\sum_i d_{iy} W_i}{\sum_i W_i} \qquad (9.2)$$

where C_x = x-coordinate of the center of gravity
C_y = y-coordinate of the center of gravity
d_{ix} = x-coordinate of location i
d_{iy} = y-coordinate of location i
W_i = volume of goods moved to or from location i

Note that Equations (9.1) and (9.2) include the term W_i, the volume of supplies transferred to or from location i.

Because the number of containers shipped each month affects cost, volume must be considered in the location decision. The center-of-gravity method assumes that cost is directly proportional to both distance and volume shipped. The ideal location is that which minimizes the weighted distance between the warehouse and its retail outlets, where the distance is weighted by the number of containers shipped.

Example 3 shows how to use the center-of-gravity method to choose a warehouse location.

EXAMPLE 3

Consider the case of Quain's Discount Department Stores, a chain of four large K-Mart-type outlets. The firm's store locations are in Chicago, Pittsburgh, New York, and Atlanta; they are currently being supplied out of an old and inadequate warehouse in Pittsburgh, the site of the chain's first store. Data on demand rates at each outlet are shown in Table 9.3.

TABLE 9.3 ■ DEMAND FOR QUAIN'S DISCOUNT STORES

STORE LOCATION	NUMBER OF CONTAINERS SHIPPED PER MONTH
Chicago	2,000
Pittsburgh	1,000
New York	1,000
Atlanta	2,000

FIGURE 9.4 ■ Coordinate Locations of Four Quain's Department Stores

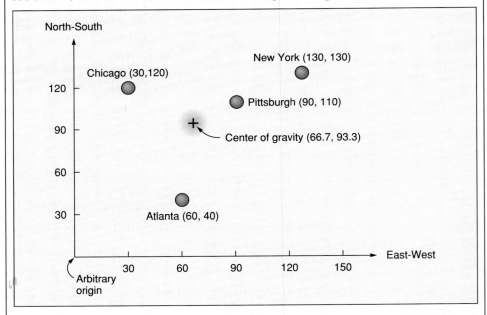

The firm has decided to find some "central" location in which to build a new warehouse. Its current store locations are shown in Figure 9.4. For example, location 1 is Chicago, and from Table 9.3 and Figure 9.4, we have

$$d_{1x} = 30$$
$$d_{1y} = 120$$
$$W_1 = 2,000$$

Using the data in Table 9.3 and Figure 9.4 for each of the other cities, in Equations (9.1) and (9.2), we find

$$C_x = \frac{(30)(2000) + (90)(1000) + (130)(1000) + (60)(2000)}{2000 + 1000 + 1000 + 2000} = \frac{400,000}{6,000}$$

$$= 66.7$$

$$C_y = \frac{(120)(2000) + (110)(1000) + (130)(1000) + (40)(2000)}{2000 + 1000 + 1000 + 2000} = \frac{560,000}{6,000}$$

$$= 93.3$$

This location (66.7, 93.3) is shown by the crosshair in Figure 9.4. By overlaying a U.S. map on this exhibit, we find that this location is near central Ohio. The firm may well wish to consider Columbus, Ohio, or a nearby city as an appropriate location.

The Transportation Model

The objective of the **transportation model** is to determine the best pattern of shipments from several points of supply (sources) to several points of demand (destinations) so as to minimize total production and transportation costs. Every firm with a network of supply and demand points faces such a problem. The complex Volkswagen supply network (shown in Figure 9.5) provides one such illustration.

Transportation model

Although the linear programming (LP) technique introduced in the supplement to Chapter 6 can be used to solve this type of problem, more efficient, special-purpose algorithms have been developed for the transportation application. As in the LP approach, the transportation model finds an initial feasible solution and then makes step-by-step improvement until reaching an optimal solution. Unlike the LP simplex method, the transportation method is fairly simple to compute.

A description of how the transportation model works and examples of its use in location decisions are found in detail in the supplement to this chapter.

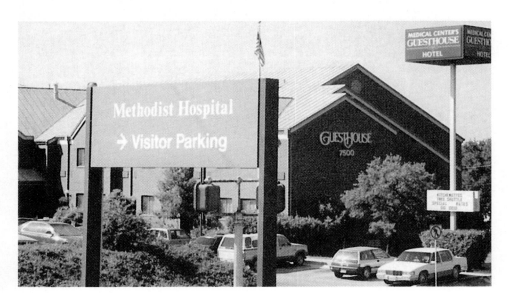

Even with reduced tax benefits and a saturated hotel market, opportunities still exist when hotel/motel locations are right. Good sites include those near hospitals and medical centers. As medical complexes in metropolitan areas continue to increase, so does the need for hotels to house patients' families. Additionally, medical services such as outpatient care, shorter hospital stays, and more diagnostic tests increase the need for hotels near hospitals.

FIGURE 9.5   ■   Worldwide Distribution of Volkswagens and Parts

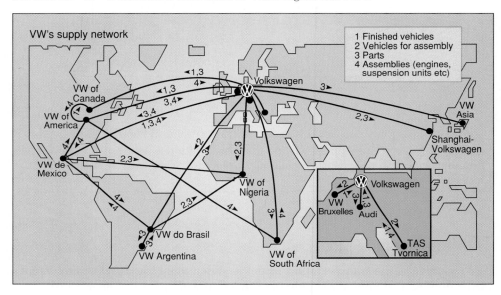

(*Source*: Copyright 1985, *The Economist*, *Ltd*. Distributed by The New York Times/Special Features.)

SERVICE/RETAIL/PROFESSIONAL SECTOR

Whereas the focus in industrial sector location analysis is on minimizing cost, the focus in the service sector is on maximizing revenue. This is because manufacturing costs tend to vary substantially between locations, but in service firms, costs vary little

Volkswagen has found substantial markets in many nations outside of Germany. The market in Mexico or Brazil may not now be big enough to support a major investment, but VW moved in and invested heavily because the market tomorrow is going to be 100 million people. Global location strategy demands bases that can reach the world's markets.

How La Quinta Motor Inns Selects Profitable Hotel Sites

One of the most important decisions a lodging chain makes is location. Hotel chains that pick good sites more accurately and quickly than competitors have a distinct advantage. La Quinta Motor Inns, headquartered in San Antonio, Texas, is a moderately priced chain of 150 inns oriented toward frequent business travelers. To model motel selection behavior and predict success of a site, La Quinta turned to statistical regression analysis.

The hotel started by testing 35 independent variables, trying to find which of them would have the highest correlation with predicted profitability, the dependent variable. "Competitive" independent variables included the number of hotel rooms in the vicinity and average room rates. "Demand generator" variables were such local attractions as office buildings and hospitals that drew potential customers to a 4-mile-radius trade area. "Demographic"

variables, such as local population and unemployment rate, can also affect the success of a hotel. "Market awareness" factors, such as the number of inns in a region were a fourth category. And, finally, "physical characteristics" of the site, such as ease of access or sign visibility, provided the last group of the 35 independent variables.

In the end, the regression model chosen, with an R^2 of 51%, included just four predictive variables. They are the price of the inn, median income levels, the state population per inn, and the location of nearby colleges (which serves as a proxy for other demand generators). La Quinta then used the regression model to predict profitability and developed a cutoff that gave the best results for predicting success or failure of a site. A Lotus spreadsheet is now used to implement the model, which applies the decision rule and suggests "build" or "don't build." Sam Barshop, La Quinta's founder and president, likes the model so much that he no longer feels obliged to personally select new sites.

Source: Sheryl Kimes and James Fitzsimmons, "Selecting Profitable Hotel Sites at La Quinta Motor Inns," *Interfaces* (March/April 1990): 12–20.

within a market area. Therefore, for the service firm, a specific location influences revenue more than it does cost. This means that the location focus for service firms should be on determining the volume of business and revenue. There are eight major components of volume and revenue for the service firm. These are

1. purchasing power of the customer drawing area;
2. service and image compatibility with demographics of the customer drawing area;
3. competition in the area;
4. quality of the competition;
5. uniqueness of the firm's and competitor's locations;
6. physical qualities of facilities and neighboring businesses;
7. operating policies of the firm;
8. quality of management.

Realistic analysis of these factors can provide a reasonable picture of the revenue expected. Table 9.4 provides a summary of location strategies for both service and industrial organizations. La Quinta Motor Inns, described in the POM in Action box, used one of the techniques listed in Table 9.4, regression and correlation analysis, in selecting new locations.

SERVICE/RETAIL/PROFESSIONAL	INDUSTRIAL LOCATION
REVENUE FOCUS	**COST FOCUS**
Volume/revenue	**Tangible costs**
Drawing area; purchasing power	Transportation cost of raw material
Competition; advertising/pricing	Shipment cost of finished goods
	Energy and utility cost; labor; raw material; taxes, etc.
Physical quality	
Parking/access; security/lighting; appearance/image	**Intangible and future costs**
	Attitude toward union
Cost determinants	Quality of life
Management caliber	Education expenditures by state
Operation policies	Quality of state and local government
TECHNIQUES	**TECHNIQUES**
Regression models to determine importance of various factors	Transportation method
Traffic counts	Weighted approach to intangibles
Demographic analysis of drawing area	Break-even analysis
Purchasing power analysis of area	Crossover charts
ASSUMPTIONS	**ASSUMPTIONS**
Location is a major determinant of revenue	Location is a major determinant of cost
High customer contact issues are critical	Most major costs can be identified explicitly for each site
Costs are relatively constant for a given area; therefore, the revenue function is critical	Low customer contact allows focus on the identifiable costs
	Intangible costs can be evaluated

TABLE 9.4 ■ LOCATION STRATEGIES—SERVICE VS. INDUSTRIAL ORGANIZATIONS

ACHIEVING WORLD-CLASS STANDARDS

World-class organizations recognize that facility location decisions are critical long-term commitments. Because these firms want to be located optimally, they search globally for their new sites and are not bound by national borders. Mercedes and BMW have opened plants in the United States, Volkswagen is now in Mexico and Brazil, and, as we saw in the *POM in Action* box, Canada's Norbord Industries has found a home in Tupelo, Mississippi. At the same time, Quality Coils has left Mexico and returned to Connecticut.

The factors considered in these decisions differ, depending on the type of facility and the type of operation. However, all world-class firms take the time to gather the data needed for the analytic techniques we just described. They also watch their competition closely and fight hard for the economic incentives that each country, region, and local government will offer. Clearly, location is one of the most important strategic choices an organization can make.

SUMMARY

Location may determine up to 10% of the total cost of an industrial firm. Location is also a critical element in determining revenue for the service/retail/professional firm. Industrial firms need to consider both tangible and intangible costs. We typically address industrial location problems via the factor-rating method, locational break-even analysis, the center-of-gravity method, and the transportation method of linear programming.

For service/retail/professional organizations, analysis is typically made of a variety of variables including purchasing power of a drawing area, competition, advertising and promotion, physical qualities of the location, and operating policies of the organization.

KEY TERMS

Tangible costs (p. 350)
Intangible costs (p. 350)
Factor-rating method (p. 351)
Locational break-even analysis (p. 353)
Center-of-gravity method (p. 354)
Transportation model (p. 357)

USING AB:POM AND SPREADSHEETS TO SOLVE LOCATION PROBLEMS

Solving Examples 1 and 3 with AB:POM's Facility Location Module

The facility location module in AB:POM includes two different models. The first, the Qualitative Weighting Model (also known as the factor-rating method), is used to solve Example 1. The second, Two-Dimensional Siting, is applied to the center-of-gravity problem described in Example 3.

PROGRAM 9.1 ■ AB:POM's Factor-Rating Model Applied to Example 1. When running this module, we first enter the number of factors (up to 99) and locations (up to 6) to consider. In Example 1, we rated two cities over five factors. The program's particular strength is in demonstrating the sensitivity of one or more weights or scores on the final selection.

——— Plant Location ———				Solution ———
Number of factors (1–99) 5			Number of locations (1–6) 2	
COSMETIC COMPANY, EXAMPLE 1				
FACTORS	Weight	city 1	city 2	
LABOR	0.25	70.00	60.00	
TRANSPORT	0.05	50.00	60.00	
EDUCATION	0.10	85.00	80.00	
TAXES	0.39	75.00	70.00	
POWER	0.21	60.00	70.00	
Weighted score		70.35	68.00	

The location with the best (highest) score is city 1

PROGRAM 9.2 ■ AB:POM's Plant Location Program, Center-of-Gravity Method for Example 3. This screen shows both the input and output for Quain's Department Store.

─────────────────── Plant Location ─────────────── Solution ───

Number of sites (1–99)   [4]

───────────── QUAIN'S DEPARTMENT STORES ─────────────

				WEIGHTED COORDINATES	
SITES	Weight/trips	x coord	y coord	X-coord	Y-coord
CHICAGO	2000.00	30.00	120.00	60000	240000
PITTSBURGH	1000.00	90.00	110.00	90000	110000
NEW YORK	1000.00	130.00	130.00	130000	130000
ATLANTA	2000.00	60.00	40.00	120000	80000
TOTAL	6000.00	310.00	400.00	400000	560000
AVERAGE		77.50	100.00	66.6667	93.3333

The unweighted center of gravity is x = 77.5   y = 100

The weighted center of gravity is   x = 66.66666   y = 93.33334

Solving Example 1 with Spreadsheet Software

Program 9.3 provides a spreadsheet alternative to Program 9.1. Program 9.3 illustrates how straightforward it is to solve a factor-rating problem with spreadsheet formulas.

PROGRAM 9.3 ■ Spreadsheet Solution to Example 1.

	A	B	C	D	E	F
1						
2			SCORES		WEIGHTED SCORES	
3			(OUT OF 100)			
4						
5	FACTOR	WEIGHT	St. Cloud	Billings	St. Cloud	Billings
6						
7	Labor costs	0.25	70	60	+B7*C7	+B7*D7
8	Transportation	0.05	50	60	+B8*C8	+B8*D8
9	Education	0.1	85	80	+B9*C9	+B9*D9
10	Tax structure	0.39	75	70	+B10*C10	+B10*D10
11	Resources	0.21	60	70	+B11*C11	+B11*D11
12						
13	Totals	@sum(B7..B11)			@sum(E7..E11)	@sum(F7..F11)

SOLVED PROBLEMS

Solved Problem 9.1

Just as cities and communities can be compared for location selection by the weighted approach model, as we saw earlier in this chapter, so can actual site decisions within those cities be helped. Table 9.5 illustrates four factors of importance to Washington, DC, health officials charged with opening that city's first public AIDS clinic. Of primary concern (and given a weight of 5) was location of the clinic so it would be as accessible as possible to the largest number of patients. The annual lease cost also was of some concern due to a tight budget. A suite in the new City Hall, at 14th and U Streets, was highly rated because its rent would be free. An old office building near the downtown bus station received a much lower rating because of its cost. Equally important as lease cost was the need for confidentiality of patients and, therefore, for a relatively inconspicuous clinic. Finally, because so many of the staff at the AIDS clinic would be donating their time, the safety, parking, and accessibility of each site were of concern as well.

TABLE 9.5 ■ POTENTIAL AIDS CLINIC SITES IN WASHINGTON, DC

		POTENTIAL LOCATIONS*			WEIGHTED SCORES		
FACTOR	IMPORTANCE WEIGHT	HOMELESS SHELTER (2ND AND D, SE)	CITY HALL (14TH AND U, NW)	BUS TERMINAL AREA (7TH AND H, NW)	HOMELESS SHELTER	CITY HALL	BUS TERMINAL AREA
Accessibility for infectives	5	9	7	7	45	35	35
Annual lease cost	3	6	10	3	18	30	9
Inconspicuous	3	5	2	7	15	6	21
Accessibility for health staff	2	3	6	2	6	12	4
				Total scores:	84	83	69

*All sites are rated on a 1 to 10 basis, with 10 as the highest score and 1 as the lowest.

Solution

From the three rightmost columns in Table 9.5, the weighted scores are summed. It appears that the bus terminal area can be excluded from further consideration, but that the other two sites are virtually identical in total score. The city may now consider other factors, including political ones, in selecting between the two remaining sites.

Source: From R. Murdick, B. Render, and R. Russell, *Service Operations Management.* Copyright © 1990 by Allyn and Bacon. Reprinted by permission.

Solved Problem 9.2

Chuck Bimmerle is considering opening a new foundry in Denton, Texas, Edwardsville, Illinois, or Fayetteville, Arkansas, to produce high-quality rifle sights. He has assembled the following fixed- and variable-cost data:

		PER UNIT COSTS		
LOCATION	FIXED COST PER YEAR	MATERIAL	LABOR	VARIABLE OVERHEAD
Denton	$200,000	$ .20	$ .40	$ .40
Edwardsville	$180,000	$ .25	$ .75	$ .75
Fayetteville	$170,000	$1.00	$1.00	$1.00

(a) Graph the total cost lines.

(b) Over what range of annual volume is each facility going to have a competitive advantage?

(c) What is the point volume at the intersection of Edwardsville and Fayetteville?

Solution

(a) A graph of the total cost lines is shown in Figure 9.6.

(b) Below 8,000 units, the Fayetteville facility will have a competitive advantage (lowest cost); between 8,000 units and 26,666 units, Edwardsville has an

FIGURE 9.6 ■ Graph of Total Cost Lines for Solved Problem 9.2

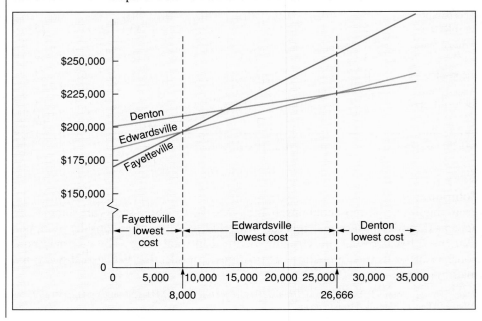

advantage; and above 26,666, Denton has the advantage. (We have made the assumption in this problem that other costs, that is, delivery and intangible factors, are constant regardless of the decision.)

(c) From the chart, we can see that the cost line for Fayetteville and the cost line for Edwardsville cross at about 8,000. We can also determine this point with a little algebra:

$$\$180{,}000 + 1.75Q = \$170{,}000 + 3.00Q$$
$$\$10{,}000 = 1.25Q$$
$$8{,}000 = Q$$

DISCUSSION QUESTIONS

1. In terms of the strategic objective, how do industrial and service location decisions differ?

2. In recent years, the federal government has increased the latitude that railroads have in setting rates and deregulated much of the rate-setting structure of trucks and airlines. What will be the long-range impact of this deregulation on location strategies?

3. Beth Wood, city manager of a large Eastern city, responding to a group of manufacturers who were complaining about the impact of increased taxes, said that taxes levied by a city were not an important consideration to a new business contemplating moving to that city. If you were president of the local Chamber of Commerce, how would you respond? If you are a person who is concerned about the unemployment rate in the inner city, how would you respond?

4. Explain the assumptions behind the center-of-gravity method. How can the model be used in a service facility location?

5. How do service facility location decisions differ from industrial location decisions in terms of the techniques used to analyze them?

6. What is the objective of location strategy?

7. What are the three steps to locational break-even analysis?

8. What are the major factors firms consider when choosing a country in which to locate?

9. What factors affect region/community location decisions?

10. Name several factors that affect site location.

11. How can quantitative and qualitative factors both be considered in a location decision?

12. The Grant Thornton studies generated the factor weights similar to those shown in Table 9.1. Would all companies rate these factor weights of equal importance? If so, why? If not, why not?

CRITICAL THINKING EXERCISE

In this chapter, we have discussed a number of location decisions, including Mercedes' selection of Vance, Alabama, for its first U.S. plant. Similarly, United Airlines recently announced its competition to select a town for a new billion dollar aircraft repair base. The bidding for the prize of 7,000 jobs was fast and furious, with Orlando offering $154 million in incentives, and Denver more than twice that amount. Kentucky's Governor Wilkinson angrily rescinded Louisville's offer of $300 million, likening the bidding to "squeezing every drop of blood out of a turnip." What are the ethical/legal/economic implications of location wars such as these? Who pays for such giveaways? Are local citizens allowed to vote on offers made by their cities, countries, or states? Should there be the limits on these incentives?

PROBLEMS

9.1 Consolidated Refineries, headquartered in Houston, must decide among three sites for the construction of a new oil processing center. The firm has selected the six factors listed as a basis for evaluation and has assigned rating weights from 1 to 5 on each factor.

FACTOR NO.	FACTOR NAME	RATING WEIGHT
1	Proximity to port facilities	5
2	Power source availability and cost	3
3	Work-force attitude and cost	4
4	Distance from Houston	2
5	Community desirability	2
6	Equipment suppliers in area	3

Management has rated each location for each factor on a 1-to-100-point basis.

FACTOR NO.	LOCATION A	LOCATION B	LOCATION C
1	100	80	80
2	80	70	100
3	30	60	70
4	10	80	60
5	90	60	80
6	50	60	90

What site will be recommended?

9.2 The fixed and variable costs for four potential plant sites for a ski equipment manufacturer are shown.

SITE	FIXED COST PER YEAR	VARIABLE COST PER UNIT
Atlanta	$125,000	$ 6
Burlington	75,000	5
Cleveland	100,000	4
Denver	50,000	12

a) Graph the total cost lines for the four potential sites.

b) Over what range of annual volume is each location the preferable one (which location has the lowest expected cost)?

c) If expected volume of the ski equipment is 5,000 units, which location would you recommend?

: **9.3** A Detroit seafood restaurant is considering opening a second facility in the suburb of West Bloomfield. The table shows its ratings of five factors at each of four potential sites. Which site should be selected?

		SITE			
FACTOR	WEIGHT	1	2	3	4
Affluence of local population	10	70	60	85	90
Construction and land cost	10	85	90	80	60
Traffic flow	25	70	60	85	90
Parking availability	20	80	90	90	80
Growth potential	15	90	80	90	75

: **9.4** In placing a new medical clinic, county health offices wish to consider three sites. The pertinent data are given in the table. Which is the best site?

		SCORES		
LOCATION FACTOR	WEIGHT	DOWNTOWN	SUBURB A	SUBURB B
Facility utilization	9	9	7	6
Average time per emergency trip	8	6	6	8
Employee preferences	5	2	5	6
Accessibility to major roadways	5	8	4	5
Land costs	4	2	9	6

: **9.5** The main post office in Tampa, Florida, is due to be replaced with a much larger, more modern facility that can handle the tremendous flow of mail that has followed the city's growth since 1970. Because all mail, incoming or outgoing, travels from the seven regional post offices in Tampa through the main post office, its site selection can mean a big difference in overall delivery and movement efficiency. Using the data in the following table, calculate the center of gravity for the proposed new facility.

REGIONAL POST OFFICE	MAP COORDINATES (X, Y)	TRUCK ROUND-TRIPS PER DAY
Ybor City	(10, 5)	3
Davis Island	(3, 8)	3
Dale-Mabry	(4, 7)	2
Palma Ceia	(15, 10)	6
Bayshore	(13, 3)	5
Temple Terrace	(1, 12)	3
Hyde Park	(5, 5)	10

9.6 Gretchen Harris owns two exclusive women's clothing stores in Miami. In her plan to expand to a third location, she has narrowed her decision down to three sites—one in a downtown office building, one in a shopping mall, and one in an old Victorian house in the suburban area of Coral Gables. She feels that rent is absolutely the most important factor to be considered, while walk-in traffic is 90% as important as rent. Further, the more distant the new store is from her two existing stores, the better, she thinks. She weights this factor to be 80% as important as walk-in traffic. Gretchen developed the following table, in which she graded each site on the same system used in her MBA program. Which site is preferable?

	DOWNTOWN	SHOPPING MALL	CORAL GABLES HOUSE
Rent	D	C	A
Walk-in traffic	B	A	D
Distance from existing stores	B	A	C

9.7 The following table gives the map coordinates and the shipping loads for a set of cities that we wish to connect through a central "hub." Near what map coordinates should the hub be located?

CITY	MAP COORDINATE (X, Y)	SHIPPING LOAD
A	(5, 10)	5
B	(6, 8)	10
C	(4, 9)	15
D	(9, 3)	5
E	(7, 9)	15
F	(3, 2)	10
G	(2, 6)	5

9.8 Nancy Hard Retailers is attempting to decide upon a location for a new retail outlet. At the moment, they have three alternatives—stay where they are, but enlarge the facility; locate along the main street in nearby Newbury; or locate in a new shopping mall in Hyde Park. They have selected the four factors listed in the following table as the basis for evaluation, and have assigned weights from 1 to 5 for each factor.

FACTOR	FACTOR DESCRIPTION	WEIGHT
1	Average community income	.30
2	Community growth potential	.15
3	Availability of public transportation	.20
4	Labor availability, attitude, and cost	.35

Ms. Hard has rated each location for each factor, on a 100-point basis. These ratings follow:

	LOCATION		
FACTOR	PRESENT LOCATION	NEWBURY	HYDE PARK
1	40	60	50
2	20	20	80
3	30	60	50
4	80	50	50

Which site should be recommended?

: **9.9** The fixed and variable costs for three potential manufacturing plant sites for Marty McDonald's firm follow:

SITE	FIXED COST PER YEAR	VARIABLE COST PER UNIT
Site 1	$ 500	$11
Site 2	1000	7
Site 3	1700	4

a) Over what range of production is each location optimal?

b) For a production of 200 units, which site is best?

: **9.10** The unification of Europe has brought about changes in airline regulation that dramatically affect major European carriers such as British International Air, SAS, KLM, Air France, Alitalia, and Sabena. With ambitious expansion plans, British International Air (BIA) has decided it needs a second service hub on the continent, to complement its large Heathrow (London) repair facility. The location selection is critical, and with the potential for 4,000 new skilled blue-collar jobs on the line, virtually every city in Western Europe is actively bidding for BIA's business.

After initial investigations by Harry Zipper, head of the Operations Department, BIA has narrowed the list to 16 cities. Each is then rated on 12 factors, with the following table resulting.

a) Help Zipper rank the top three cities that BIA should consider as its new site for servicing aircraft.

b) After further investigation, Harry Zipper decides that an existing set of hangar facilities for repairs is not nearly as important as earlier thought. In lowering the weight of that factor to 30, does the ranking change?

c) After Zipper makes the change in part (b), Germany announces it has reconsidered its offer of financial incentives, with an additional 200 million deutsche mark package to entice BIA. Accordingly, BIA has raised Germany's rating to 10 on that factor. Is there any change in top rankings in part (b)?

DATA BASE APPLICATION

TABLE FOR DATA BASE APPLICATION 9.10

| | | LOCATION | | | | | | | | | | | | | | | |
| | | ITALY | | | FRANCE | | | GERMANY | | | SPAIN | SWITZERLAND | | HOLLAND | | DENMARK | PORTUGAL |
FACTOR	IMPORTANCE WEIGHT	MILAN	ROME	GENOA	PARIS	LYON	NICE	MUNICH	BONN	BERLIN	MADRID	BERN	ZURICH	AMSTERDAM	THE HAGUE	COPENHAGEN	LISBON
Financial incentives	85	8	8	8	7	7	7	7	7	7	9	8	8	9	9	8	10
Skilled labor pool	80	4	6	5	9	9	7	10	8	9	4	9	10	9	8	7	3
Existing facility	70	5	3	2	9	6	5	9	9	2	5	7	8	8	2	8	6
Wage rates	70	9	8	9	4	6	6	4	5	5	10	3	3	5	9	5	10
Competition for jobs	70	7	3	8	2	8	7	4	8	9	6	5	4	3	7	6	6
Ease of air traffic access	65	5	4	6	2	8	8	4	8	9	5	5	5	3	9	4	6
Real estate cost	40	6	4	7	4	6	6	3	4	5	8	2	1	3	5	4	7
Communication links	25	6	7	6	9	9	9	10	9	8	2	8	8	8	6	9	2
Attractiveness to relocating executives	15	4	8	3	9	6	6	2	3	3	4	9	8	9	6	7	3
Political considerations	10	6	6	6	8	8	8	8	8	8	5	9	9	8	8	8	2
Expansion possibilities	10	10	2	8	1	5	4	4	5	6	5	3	2	3	8	4	6
Union strength	10	1	1	1	5	5	5	6	6	6	9	8	8	7	7	5	9

CASE STUDY

Southern Recreational Vehicle Company

In October 1994, top management of Southern Recreational Vehicle Company of St. Louis, Missouri, announced its plans to relocate its manufacturing and assembly operations by constructing a new plant in Ridgecrest, Mississippi. The firm, a major producer of pickup campers and camper trailers, had experienced five consecutive years of declining profits as a result of spiraling production costs. The costs of labor and raw materials had increased alarmingly; utility costs had gone up sharply; and taxes and transportation expenses had climbed upward steadily. In spite of increased sales, the company suffered its first net loss since operations were begun in 1977.

When management initially considered relocation, they closely scrutinized several geographic areas. Of primary importance to the relocation decision were the availability of adequate transportation facilities, state and municipal tax structures, an adequate labor supply, positive community attitudes, reasonable site costs, and financial inducements. Although several communities offered essentially the same incentives, the management of Southern Recreational Vehicle Company was favorably impressed by the efforts of the Mississippi Power and Light company to attract "clean, labor-intensified" industry and the enthusiasm exhibited by state and local officials who actively sought to bolster the state's economy by enticing manufacturing firms to locate within its boundaries.

Two weeks prior to the announcement, management of Southern Recreational Vehicle Company finalized its relocation plans. An existing building in Ridgecrest's industrial park was selected (the physical facility had previously housed a mobile home manufacturer that had gone bankrupt due to inadequate financing and poor management); initial recruiting was begun through the State Employment Office; and efforts to lease or sell the St. Louis property were initiated. Among the inducements offered Southern Recreational Vehicle Company to locate in Ridgecrest were as follows:

1. Exemption from county and municipal taxes for 5 years,

2. Free water and sewage services,

3. Construction of a second loading dock—free of cost—at the industrial site,

4. An agreement to issue $500,000 in industrial bonds for future expansion,

5. Public-financed training of workers in a local industrial trade school.

In addition to these inducements, other factors weighed heavily in the decision to locate in the small Mississippi town. Labor costs would be significantly less than those incurred in St. Louis; organized labor was not expected to be as powerful (Mississippi is a right-to-work state); and utility costs and taxes would be moderate. All in all, management of Southern Recreational Vehicle Company felt that its decision was sound.

On October 15, the following announcement was attached to each employee's paycheck:

To: Employees of Southern Recreational Vehicle Company

From: Gerald O'Brian, President

The Management of Southern Recreational Vehicle Company regretfully announces its plans to cease all manufacturing operations in St. Louis on December 31. Because of increased operating costs and the unreasonable demands forced upon the company by the union, it has become impossible to operate profitably. I sincerely appreciate the fine service that each of you has rendered to the company during the past few years. If I can be of assistance in helping you find suitable employment with another firm, please let me know. Thank you again for your cooperation and past service.

DISCUSSION QUESTIONS

1. Evaluate the inducements offered Southern Recreational Vehicle Company by community leaders in Ridgecrest, Mississippi.

2. What problems would a company experience in relocating its executives from a heavily populated industrialized area to a small rural town?

3. Evaluate the reasons cited by Mr. O'Brian for relocation. Are they justifiable?

4. What responsibilities do you think a firm has to its employees when a decision to cease operations is made?

Source: Professor Jerry Kinard, Western Carolina University.

BIBLIOGRAPHY

Craig, C. S., et al., "Models of the Retail Location Process." *Journal of Retailing*, 60 (April 1984): 5–36.

DeForest, M. E. "Thinking of a Plant in Mexico?" *The Academy of Management Executive*, 8, no. 1 (February 1994): 33–40.

Domich, P. D., K. L. Hoffman, R. H. F. Jackson, and M. A. McClain. "Locating Tax Facilities: A Graphics-Based Microcomputer Optimization Model." *Management Science*, 37 (August 1991): 960.

Fitzsimmons, J. A. "A Warehouse Location Model Helps Texas Comptroller Select Out-of-State Audit Officers." *Interfaces*, 13 (October 1983): 40–45.

Kimes, S. E., and J. A. Fitzsimmons. "Selecting Profitable Hotel Sites at La Quinta Motor Inns." *Interfaces*, 20 (March/April 1990): 12–20.

Murdick, R., B. Render, and R. Russell. *Service Operations Management*. Boston: Allyn and Bacon, 1990.

Price, W. L., and M. Turcotte. "Locating a Blood Bank." *Interfaces*, 16 (September/October 1986): 17–26.

Render, B., and R. M. Stair. *Introduction to Management Science*. Boston: Allyn and Bacon, 1992.

———. *Quantitative Analysis for Management*, 5th ed. Boston: Allyn and Bacon, 1994.

"The Checklist of Site Selection Factors." In *Site Selection Handbook*. Atlanta, GA: Conway, 1978.

Vargas, G. A., and T. W. Johnson. "An Analysis of Operational Experience in the US/Mexico Production Sharing (Maquiladora) Program." *Journal of Operations Management*, 11, no. 1 (March 1993): 17–34.

9 SUPPLEMENT

TRANSPORTATION MODELING

The problem facing this Avis car rental company last year was cross-country travel. Lots of it. Cars rented in New York ended up in Chicago, cars from LA came to Philadelphia, and cars from Boston came to Miami. The scene was repeated in over 100 cities around the United States. As a result, there were many too many cars in some cities and way too few in others. Avis operations managers had to decide how many of these rentals should be trucked (by costly auto carriers) from each city with excess capacity to each city that needed more rentals. The process required quick action at the most economical routing. What did Avis do? It turned to the transportation method of linear programming for an optimal solution. ♦

The purpose of transportation modeling is to find the least cost means of shipping supplies from several origins to several destinations. Origin points (or sources) can be factories, warehouses, car rental agencies like Avis, or any other points from which goods are shipped. Destinations are any points that receive goods. To use the transportation model, we need to have the following:

1. The origin points and the capacity or supply per period at each.
2. The destination points and the demand per period at each.
3. The cost of shipping one unit from each origin to each destination.

The transportation model is actually a class of the linear programming model discussed in the Supplement to Chapter 6. As it is for linear programming, software is available to solve transportation problems. To fully use such programs, though, you need to understand the assumptions that underlie the model. To illustrate one transportation problem, we will look in this supplement at a company called Arizona Plumbing, which makes, among other products, a full line of bathtubs. Data for Arizona Plumbing's bathtubs are presented in Figure S9.1 and Table S9.1. The firm needs to decide which factories should supply which warehouses.

TABLE S9.1 ■ TRANSPORTATION COSTS PER BATHTUB FOR ARIZONA PLUMBING

From \ To	Albuquerque	Boston	Cleveland
Des Moines	$5	$4	$3
Evansville	$8	$4	$3
Fort Lauderdale	$9	$7	$5

FIGURE S9.1 ■ Transportation Problem

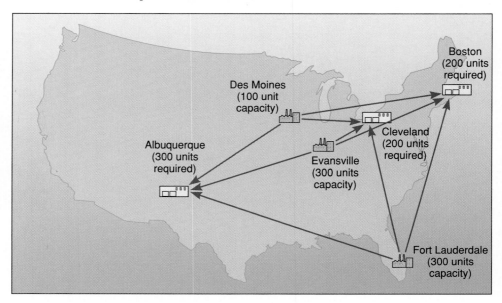

FIGURE S9.2 ■ Transportation Matrix for Arizona Plumbing

The first step in the modeling process is to set up a transportation matrix. Its purpose is to summarize conveniently and concisely all relevant data and to keep track of algorithm computations. Using the information from Arizona Plumbing displayed in Figure S9.1 and Table S9.1, we can construct a transportation matrix as shown in Figure S9.2.

DEVELOPING AN INITIAL SOLUTION—THE NORTHWEST-CORNER RULE

Once the data are arranged in tabular form, we must establish an initial feasible solution to the problem. One systematic procedure, known as the **northwest-corner rule**, requires that we start in the upper left-hand cell (or northwest corner) of the table and allocate units to shipping routes as follows:

Northwest-corner rule

1. Exhaust the supply (factory capacity) of each row before moving down to the next row.
2. Exhaust the (warehouse) requirements of each column before moving to the next column on the right.
3. Check that all supplies and demands are met.

Example S1 applies the northwest corner rule to the Arizona Plumbing problem.

EXAMPLE S1

In Figure S9.3 we use the northwest-corner rule to find an initial feasible solution to the Arizona Plumbing problem. Five steps are required in this example to make the initial shipping assignments:

1. Assign 100 tubs from Des Moines to Albuquerque (exhausting Des Moines' supply).
2. Assign 200 tubs from Evansville to Albuquerque (exhausting Albuquerque's demand).

3. Assign 100 tubs from Evansville to Boston (exhausting Evansville's supply).
4. Assign 100 tubs from Fort Lauderdale to Boston (exhausting Boston's demand).
5. Assign 200 tubs from Fort Lauderdale to Cleveland (exhausting Cleveland's demand and Fort Lauderdale's supply).

FIGURE S9.3 ■ Northwest-Corner Solution to Arizona Plumbing Problem

To From	(A) Albuquerque	(B) Boston	(C) Cleveland	Factory capacity
(D) Des Moines	$5 100	$4	$3	100
(E) Evansville	$8 200	$4 100	$3	300
(F) Fort Lauderdale	$9	$7 100	$5 200	300
Warehouse requirements	300	200	200	700

Means that the firm is shipping 100 bathtubs from Fort Lauderdale to Boston

The total cost of this shipping assignment is $4,200 (see Table S9.2).

TABLE S9.2 ■ COMPUTED SHIPPING COST

ROUTE				
FROM	TO	TUBS SHIPPED	COST PER UNIT	TOTAL COST
D	A	100	$5	$ 500
E	A	200	8	1,600
E	B	100	4	400
F	B	100	7	700
F	C	200	5	1,000
				Total: $4,200

The solution given is feasible because it satisfies all demand and supply constraints. However, we would be very lucky if this solution yielded the minimum transportation cost for the problem. It is more likely we will have to employ an additional procedure to reach an optimal solution because the northwest-corner method is only meant to provide us with a starting point.

THE STEPPING-STONE METHOD

Stepping-stone method

The stepping-stone method helps to move from an initial feasible solution to an optimal solution. It is used to evaluate the cost effectiveness of shipping goods via transportation routes not currently in the solution. We test each unused cell, or square, in the transportation table by asking: "What would happen to total shipping costs if one unit of the product (for example, one bathtub) were tentatively shipped on an unused route?" We conduct the test as follows:

1. Select any unused square to evaluate.

2. Beginning at this square, trace a closed path back to the original square via squares that are currently being used (only horizontal and vertical moves are permissible). You may, however, step over either an empty or an occupied square.

3. Beginning with a plus (+) sign at the unused square, place alternate minus signs and plus signs on each corner square of the closed path just traced.

4. Calculate an improvement index by first adding the unit cost figures found in each square containing a plus sign, and then by subtracting the unit costs in each square containing a minus sign.

5. Repeat steps 1 through 4 until you have calculated an improvement index for all unused squares. If all indices computed are greater than or equal to zero, you have reached an optimal solution. If not, it is possible to improve the current solution and decrease total shipping costs.

Example S2 illustrates how to use the stepping-stone method to move toward an optimal solution.

Moving sand to help expand Australia's Brisbane International Airport became a classic transportation problem. It involved the shipment of almost 2 million cubic meters of sand from 26 source sites to 35 final fill destinations. Using the transportation approach saved over $800,000, or about 27% of total hauling costs.

EXAMPLE S2

We can apply the stepping-stone method to the Arizona Plumbing data in Figure S9.3 to evaluate unused shipping routes. The four currently unassigned routes are Des Moines to Boston, Des Moines to Cleveland, Evansville to Cleveland, and Fort Lauderdale to Albuquerque.

Steps 1 and 2. Beginning with the Des Moines-to-Boston route, first trace a closed path using only currently occupied squares (see Figure S9.4). Place alternate plus signs and minus signs in the corners of this path. Note that we can use only squares currently used for shipping to turn the corners of the route we are tracing. Hence, the path Des Moines–Boston to Des Moines–Albuquerque to Fort Lauderdale–Albuquerque to Fort Lauderdale–Boston to Des Moines–Boston would not be acceptable, because the Fort Lauderdale–Albuquerque square is empty. It turns out that *only one closed route exists for each empty square.* Once this one closed path is identified, we can begin assigning plus and minus signs to these squares in the path.

Step 3. How do we decide which squares get plus signs and which squares get minus signs? The answer is simple. Because we are testing the cost effectiveness of the Des Moines–Boston shipping route, we try shipping one bathtub from Des Moines to Boston. This is one more unit than we *were* sending between the two cities, so place a plus sign in the box. But if we ship one more unit than before from Des Moines to Boston, we end up sending 101 bathtubs out of the Des Moines factory. Because the Des Moines factory's capacity is only 100 units, we must ship one bathtub less from Des Moines to Albuquerque. This change prevents us from violating the limit constraint.

To indicate that we have reduced the Des Moines–Albuquerque shipment, place a minus sign in its box. Continuing along the closed path, notice that we are no longer meeting the warehouse requirement for 300 units. In fact, if we reduce the Des Moines–Albuquerque shipment to 99 units, we must increase the Evansville–Albuquerque load by one unit, to 201 bathtubs. Therefore, place a plus sign in that box to indicate the increase. You may also observe that those squares where we turn (and only those squares) will have plus or minus signs.

Finally, note that if we assign 201 bathtubs to the Evansville–Albuquerque route, then we must reduce the Evansville–Boston route by one unit, to 99 bathtubs, in order to maintain the Evansville factory's capacity constraint of 300 units. Thus, we insert a minus sign in the Evansville–Boston box. As a result, we have balanced supply limitations among all four routes on the closed path.

FIGURE S9.4 ■ Stepping-Stone Evaluation of Alternative Routes for Arizona Plumbing

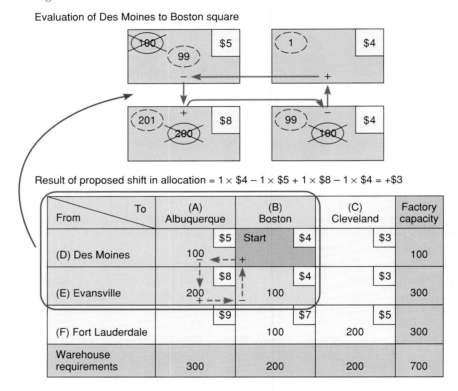

Step 4. Compute an improvement index for the Des Moines–Boston route by adding unit costs in squares with plus signs and subtracting costs in squares with minus signs.

$$\text{Des Moines–Boston index} = \$4 - \$5 + \$8 - \$4 = +\$3$$

This means that for every bathtub shipped via the Des Moines–Boston route, total transportation costs will increase by \$3 over their current level.

Let us now examine the Des Moines–Cleveland unused route, one slightly more difficult to trace with a closed path. Again, notice that we turn each corner along the path only at squares on the existing route. The path can go through the Evansville–Cleveland box but cannot turn a corner, and we cannot place a plus or minus sign there. We may use only an occupied square as a stepping stone (see Figure S9.5):

FIGURE S9.5 ■ Testing Des Moines to Cleveland

From ⟍ To	(A) Albuquerque	(B) Boston	(C) Cleveland	Factory
(D) Des Moines	$5 100	$4	Start $3 +	100
(E) Evansville	$8 200+	$4 – 100	$3	300
(F) Fort Lauderdale	$9 +	$7 100	$5 – 200	300
Warehouse requirements	300	200	200	700

Des Moines–Cleveland index = $3 − $5 + $8 − $4 + $7 − $5 = +$4

Thus, opening this route will also not lower total shipping costs.
The other two routes can be evaluated in a similar fashion:

Evansville–Cleveland index = $3 − $4 + $7 − $5 = +$1
(Closed path = EC − EB + FB − FC)

Fort Lauderdale–Albuquerque index = $9 − $7 + $4 − $8 = −$2
(Closed path = FA − FB + EB − EA)

Because this last index is negative, a cost savings can be attained by making use of the (currently unused) Fort Lauderdale–Albuquerque route.

In Example S2, we saw that a better solution is possible due to the presence of a negative improvement index on one of the unused routes. Each negative index represents the amount by which total transportation costs could be decreased if one unit or product were shipped by the source–destination combination. The next step, then, is to choose that route (unused square) with the largest negative improvement index. We can then ship the maximum allowable number of units on that route and reduce the total cost accordingly.

What is the maximum quantity that can be shipped on the new money-saving route? That quantity is found by referring to the closed path of plus signs and minus signs drawn for the route and selecting the smallest number found in the squares containing minus signs.

To obtain a new solution, we add that number to all squares on the closed path with plus signs and subtract it from all squares on the path assigned minus signs.

One iteration of the stepping-stone method is now complete. Again, we must test to see if the solution is optimal or whether we can make any further improvements. This is done by evaluating each unused square, as previously described. Example S3 continues Arizona Plumbing's move toward a final solution.

EXAMPLE S3

To improve Arizona Plumbing's solution, we can use the improvement indices calculated in Example S2. The largest (and only) negative index is the Fort Lauderdale–Albuquerque route, as shown in Figure S9.6.

The maximum quantity that may be shipped on the newly opened route (FA) is the smallest number found in squares containing minus signs—in this case, 100 units. Why 100 units? Because the total cost decreases by $2 per unit shipped, we know we would like to ship the maximum possible number of units. Previous stepping-stone calculations indicate that each unit shipped over the FA route results in an increase of one unit shipped from E to B and a decrease of one unit in both amounts shipped from F to B (now 100 units) and from E to A (now 200 units). Hence, the maximum we can ship over the FA route is 100 units. This solution results in zero units being shipped from F to B. Now we add 100 units (to the zero now being shipped) on route FA; then proceed to subtract 100 from route FB, leaving zero in that square (but still balancing the row total for F); then add 100 to route EB, yielding 200; and, finally, subtract 100 from route EA, leaving 100 units shipped. Note that the new numbers still produce the correct row and column totals as required. The new solution is shown in Figure S9.7.

FIGURE S9.6   ■   Transportation Table: Route FA

From \ To	(A) Albuquerque	(B) Boston	(C) Cleveland	Factory
(D) Des Moines	$5 100	$4	$3	100
(E) Evansville	$8 200	$4 100	$3	300
(F) Fort Lauderdale	$9	$7 100	$5 200	300
Warehouse	300	200	200	700

FIGURE S9.7   ■   Solution at Next Iteration (Still Not Optimal)

From \ To	(A) Albuquerque	(B) Boston	(C) Cleveland	Factory
(D) Des Moines	$5 100	$4	$3	100
(E) Evansville	$8 100	$4 200	$3	300
(F) Fort Lauderdale	$9 100	$7	$5 200	300
Warehouse	300	200	200	700

Total shipping cost has been reduced by (100 units) × ($2 saved per unit) = $200 and is now $4,000. This cost figure, of course, can also be derived by multiplying each unit shipping cost by the number of units transported on its route, namely:

$$100(\$5) + 100(\$8) + 200(\$4) + 100(\$9) + 200(\$5) = \$4,000$$

Looking carefully at Figure S9.7, you can see that it, too, is not yet optimal. Route EC (Evansville–Cleveland) has a negative cost improvement index. See if you can find the final solution on your own. Programs S9.1 and S9.2, at the end of this supplement, provide the AB:POM solution.

DEMAND NOT EQUAL TO SUPPLY

A common situation in real-world problems is the case in which total demand is not equal to total supply. We can handle these "unbalanced" problems easily with the solution procedures discussed before if we first introduce **dummy sources** or **dummy destinations**. In the event that total supply is greater than total demand, we create a dummy destination, so the demand exactly equals the surplus. If total demand is greater than total supply, we introduce a dummy source (factory) with a supply equal to the excess of demand over supply. In each case, we assign cost coefficients of zero to each square on the dummy location because in fact these units will not be shipped. Hence, the cost is zero.

Dummy sources
Dummy destinations

Example S4 demonstrates the use of a dummy destination.

EXAMPLE S4

Arizona Plumbing increases the rate of production of bathtubs in its Des Moines factory to 250. To reformulate this unbalanced problem, we refer back to the data presented in Example S1 and present the new matrix in Figure S9.8. We use the northwest-corner rule to find the initial feasible solution. Once the problem is balanced, solution can proceed in the normal way.

FIGURE S9.8 ■ Northwest-Corner Rule with Dummy

From \ To	(A) Albuquerque	(B) Boston	(C) Cleveland	Dummy	Factory capacity
(D) Des Moines	$5 / 250	$4	$3	0	250
(E) Evansville	$8 / 50	$4 / 200	$3 / 50	0	300
(F) Fort Lauderdale	$9	$7	$5 / 150	0 / 150	300
Warehouse requirements	300	200	200	150	850

New Des Moines capacity

Total cost = 250($5) + 50($8) + 200($4) + 50($3) + 150($5) + 150(0) = $3,350

DEGENERACY

To apply the stepping-stone method to a transportation problem, we must observe a rule about the number of shipping routes being used: *The number of occupied squares in*

When the navy in Thailand drafts a young man, he first reports to the drafting center closest to his home. From the country's 36 drafting centers, he is transported by truck to one of the four Thai naval bases. Deciding how many men should be assigned and transported from each center to each base is solved using the transportation model. This way each base gets the number of recruits it needs and costly extra trips are avoided.

Degeneracy

any solution (initial or later) must be equal to the number of rows in the table plus the number of columns minus 1. Solutions that do not meet this rule are called degenerate.

Degeneracy occurs when there are too few squares or shipping routes being used. As a result, it becomes impossible to trace a closed path for one or more unused squares. No problem discussed in this chapter so far has been degenerate. The original Arizona Plumbing problem, for example, had five assigned routes (three rows or factories + 3 columns or warehouses − 1). Example S4, employing a dummy warehouse, had six assigned routes (3 rows + 4 columns − 1) and was not degenerate either.

To handle degenerate problems, we artificially create an occupied cell. That is, we place a zero or *very* small amount (representing a fake shipment) in one of the unused squares and *then treat that square as if it were occupied*. The square chosen, it should be noted, must be in such a position as to allow all stepping-stone paths to be closed or traced. We illustrate this in Example S5.

EXAMPLE S5

Martin Shipping Company has three warehouses from which it supplies its three major retail customers in San Jose. Martin's shipping costs, warehouse supplies, and customer demands are presented in the transportation table below. To make the initial shipping assignments in the table, we apply the northwest-corner rule (see Figure S9.9).

FIGURE S9.9   ■   Martin's Northwest-Corner Rule

From \ To	Customer 1	Customer 2	Customer 3	Warehouse supply
Warehouse 1	$8 100	$2	$6	100
Warehouse 2	$10 0	$9 100	$9 20	120
Warehouse 3	$7	$10	$7 80	80
Customer demand	100	100	100	300

The initial solution is degenerate because it violates the rule that the number of used squares must equal the number of rows plus the number of columns minus one. To correct the problem, we may place a zero in the unused square that permits evaluation of all empty cells. Some experimenting may be needed because not every cell will allow tracing a closed path for the remaining cells. Also, we want to avoid placing the 0 in a cell that has the negative sign in a closed path. No reallocation will be possible if we do this.

For this example, we try the empty square that represents the shipping route from warehouse 2 to customer 1. Now we can close all stepping-stone paths and compute improvement indices.

THE MODI METHOD

The **MODI (modified distribution) method** allows us to compute improvement indices for each unused square without drawing all of the closed paths. Thus, it can often save considerable time over the stepping-stone method for solving transportation problems.

Modified distribution (MODI) method

In applying the MODI method, we begin with an initial solution obtained by using the northwest-corner rule. We must compute a value for each row (call the values R_1, R_2, R_3, if there are three rows) and for each column (K_1, K_2, K_3, if there are three columns) in the transportation table. In general, we let

R_i = value assigned to row i
K_j = value assigned to column j
C_{ij} = cost in square ij (cost of shipping from source i to destination j)

The MODI method consists of five steps:

1. To compute the values for each row and column, set $R_i + K_j = C_{ij}$ but only for those squares that are currently used or occupied. For example, if the square at the intersection of row 2 and column 1 is occupied, we set $R_2 + K_1 = C_{21}$.
2. After you have written all equations, set $R_1 = 0$.
3. Solve the system of equations for all R and K values.
4. Compute the improvement index for each unused square by the formula

$$\text{Index} = C_{ij} - R_i - K_j$$

5. Select the largest negative index and proceed to solve the problem as you did using the stepping-stone method.

Example S6 uses the MODI method for the Arizona Plumbing problem.

EXAMPLE S6

Given the initial solution to the Arizona Plumbing problem (Example S1), we can use the MODI method to calculate an improvement index for each unused square. The initial transportation table is repeated in Figure S9.10.

First, set up an equation for each occupied square:

1. $R_1 + K_1 = 5$
2. $R_2 + K_1 = 8$
3. $R_2 + K_2 = 4$
4. $R_3 + K_2 = 7$
5. $R_3 + K_3 = 5$

Letting $R_1 = 0$, we can easily solve, step by step, for K_1, R_2, K_2, R_3, and K_3.

1. $0 + K_1 = 5 \Rightarrow K_1 = 5$
2. $R_2 + 5 = 8 \Rightarrow R_2 = 3$
3. $3 + K_2 = 4 \Rightarrow K_2 = 1$
4. $R_3 + 1 = 7 \Rightarrow R_3 = 6$
5. $6 + K_3 = 5 \Rightarrow K_3 = -1$

FIGURE S9.10 ■ Transportation Table

K_j		K_1	K_2	K_3	
R_i	To / From	Albuquerque	Boston	Cleveland	Factory capacity
R_1	Des Moines	$5 100	$4	$3	100
R_2	Evansville	$8 200	$4 100	$3	300
R_3	Fort Lauderdale	$9	$7 100	$5 200	300
	Warehouse requirements	300	200	200	700

The improvement index for each unused cell is $C_{ij} - R_i - K_j$:

$$\text{Des Moines–Boston} = C_{12} - R_1 - K_2 = 4 - 0 - 1 = \$3$$
$$\text{Des Moines–Cleveland} = C_{13} - R_1 - K_3 = 3 - 0 - (-1) = \$4$$
$$\text{Evansville–Cleveland} = C_{23} - R_2 - K_3 = 3 - 3 - (-1) = \$1$$
$$\text{Fort Lauderdale–Albuquerque} = C_{31} - R_3 - K_1 = 9 - 6 - 5 = -\$2$$

Note that these indices are exactly the same as the ones calculated in Example S2. Now only one closed path, from Fort Lauderdale–Albuquerque, is necessary in order to proceed with the stepping-stone solution procedures.

FACILITY LOCATION ANALYSIS

As noted earlier, the location of a new factory or warehouse is an issue of major financial importance to a firm. Ordinarily, several alternative locations must be considered and evaluated. Even though a wide variety of subjective factors must be considered, rational decisions are needed to minimize costs.

The transportation methods just studied prove useful when considering alternative facility locations within the framework of an existing production–distribution system. Each new potential plant or warehouse will produce a different allocation of shipments, depending on its own production and shipping costs and the costs of each existing facility. The choice of a new location depends on which will yield the minimum cost for the entire system. This concept is illustrated in Example S7.

EXAMPLE S7

Williams Auto Top Carriers currently maintains plants in Atlanta and Tulsa to supply major distribution centers in Los Angeles and New York. Because of an expanding demand, Williams has decided to open a third plant and has narrowed the choice to one of two cities—New Orleans and Houston. Table S9.3 gives the pertinent production and distribution costs as well as the plant capacities and distribution demands.

TABLE S9.3 ■ PRODUCTION COSTS, DISTRIBUTION COSTS, PLANT CAPABILITIES, AND MARKET DEMANDS FOR WILLIAMS AUTO TOP CARRIERS

| | FROM PLANTS | TO DISTRIBUTION CENTERS | | NORMAL PRODUCTION | UNIT PRODUCTION COST |
		LOS ANGELES	NEW YORK		
Existing plants	Atlanta	$8	$5	600	$6
	Tulsa	$4	$7	900	$5
Proposed locations	New Orleans	$5	$6	500	$4 (anticipated)
	Houston	$4	$6*	500	$3 (anticipated)
Forecast demand		800	1,200	2,000	

*Indicates distribution cost (shipping, handling, storage) will be $6 per carrier between Houston and New York.

The important question that Williams faces is: "Which of the new locations will yield a lower cost for the firm in combination with the existing plants and distribution centers?" To determine the answer, we need to solve two transportation problems, one for each possible combination. The location that shows a lower total cost of distribution and production to the existing system will be recommended.

We begin by setting up a transportation table that represents the opening of a third plant in New Orleans (see Figure S9.11). Use the northwest-corner method to find an initial solution. The total cost of this first solution is $23,600. Note that the cost of each individual "plant-to-distribution-center" route is found by adding the distribution costs (in the body of Table S9.3) to the respective unit production costs (in the right-hand column of Table S9.3). Thus, the total production-plus-shipping cost of one auto top carrier from Atlanta to Los Angeles is $14 ($8 for shipping plus $6 for production).

FIGURE S9.11 ■ Williams Transportation Table for New Orleans Plant

From \ To	Los Angeles	New York	Production capacity
Atlanta	$14 600	$11	600
Tulsa	$9 200	$12 700	900
New Orleans	$9	$10 500	500
Demand	800	1,200	2,000

Total cost $= (600 \text{ units} \times \$14) + (200 \text{ units} \times \$9)$
$+ (700 \text{ units} \times \$12) + (500 \text{ units} \times \$10)$
$= \$8,400 + \$1,800 + \$8,400 + \$5,000$
$= \$23,600$

Is this initial solution optimal? The stepping-stone method can be employed to test it and to compute improvement indices for unused routes.

$$\text{Improvement index for Atlanta–New York route} = +\$11 \text{ (Atlanta–N.Y.)} - \$14 \text{ (Atlanta–L.A.)} + \$9 \text{ (Tulsa–L.A.)} - \$12 \text{ (Tulsa–N.Y.)}$$

$$= -\$6$$

$$\text{Improvement index for New Orleans–Los Angeles route} = +\$9 \text{ (New Orleans–L.A.)} - \$10 \text{ (New Orleans–N.Y.)} + \$12 \text{ (Tulsa–N.Y.)} - \$9 \text{ (Tulsa–L.A.)}$$

$$= \$2$$

Because the firm can save $6 for every unit it ships from Atlanta to New York, it will want to improve the initial solution and send as many as possible (600, in this case) on this currently unused route (see Figure S9.12).

FIGURE S9.12 ■ Improved Transportation Table for Williams

From \ To	Los Angeles	New York	Production capacity
Atlanta	$14	$11 600	600
Tulsa	$9 800	$12 100	900
New Orleans	$9	$10 500	500
Demand	800	1,200	2,000

You may want to confirm that the total cost is now $20,000, a saving of $3,600 over the initial solution.

Now, we must test the two unused routes to see if their improvement indices are negative numbers.

$$\text{Index for Atlanta–Los Angeles} = \$14 - \$11 + \$12 - \$9 = \$6$$

$$\text{Index for New Orleans–Los Angeles} = \$9 - \$10 + \$12 - \$9 = \$2$$

Because both indices are greater than zero, we have reached an optimal solution using the New Orleans plant. If Williams elects to open the New Orleans plant, the firm's total production and distribution cost will be $20,000.

Example S7, however, provides only half the answer to Williams' problem. The same procedure would be followed to determine the minimum cost with the new plant in Houston. Determining this cost is left as an exercise. You can help provide complete information and recommend a solution by solving Problem S9.4.

SUMMARY

This supplement introduced the transportation model, a form of linear programming used to help find the least cost solutions to systemwide shipping problems. The northwest-corner method, which begins in the upper-left corner of the transportation table, is used for finding an initial feasible solution. The stepping-stone and MODI algorithm methods are then used for finding optimal solutions. We introduced degeneracy (that is, the case in which the number of rows + the number of columns − 1) is not equal to the number of occupied squares. We also illustrated unbalanced problems—problems in which the total demand is not equal to the total supply. Finally, we showed how to use the transportation model to help solve facility location problems. This approach is one of the four location models described earlier in Chapter 9.

KEY TERMS

Northwest-corner rule (p. 375)
Stepping-stone method (p. 376)
Dummy sources (p. 381)
Dummy destinations (p. 381)

Degeneracy (p. 382)
Modified distribution (MODI) method (p. 383)

USING AB:POM TO SOLVE TRANSPORTATION PROBLEMS

In this transportation modeling example, we use the data from Arizona Plumbing. After entering the number of origins and destinations, we are prompted in Program S9.1 to provide demand data, supply data, and unit shipping costs. Program S9.2 displays the output screen computed by AB:POM.

PROGRAM S9.1 ■ Data Entry Screen for Transportation Problem in Examples S1, S2, and S3. AB:POM adds dummy rows and columns automatically, if needed. The program can handle up to 99 rows or columns. We *do* need to instruct AB:POM as to whether we want to *maximize* or *minimize*. Origin and destination names are entered below as an option.

——————— Transportation ——————— Data Screen ———————

Number of sources (1–99) 3   Number of Destinations (1–99) 3

minimize

——————— ARIZONA PLUMBING, EXAMPLES S1–S3 ———————

Options -> NO steps   Comptr   PrntOFF

	ALBUQ	BOSTON	CLEVELAND	Supply
DES MOINE	5	4	3	100
EVANSVILL	8	4	3	300
FT. LAUD	9	7	5	300
Demand	300	200	200	

Esc

PROGRAM S9.2   ■   AB:POM Solution to Transportation Problem in Examples S1, S2, and S3. Part (b) illustrates cell improvement indices.

(a)

ARIZONA PLUMBING, EXAMPLES S1–S3

SHIPMENTS	ALBUQ	BOSTON	CLEVELD	Supply
DES MOINE	100			100
EVANSVILL		200	100	300
FT. LAUD	200		100	300
Demand	300	200	200	

The minimum total cost = $3,900

(b)

ARIZONA PLUMBING, EXAMPLES S1–S3

IMPROV IND	ALBUQ	BOSTON	CLEVELD	Supply
DES MOINE		+2	+2	100
EVANSVILL	+1			300
FT. LAUD		+1		300
Demand	300	200	200	

The minimum total cost = $3,900

SOLVED PROBLEM

Solved Problem S9.1

Marion Sobol, president of Sobol Concrete Company, has plants in three locations and is currently working on three major construction projects, located at different sites. The shipping cost per truckload of concrete, plant capacities, and project requirements are provided below:

(a) Formulate an initial feasible solution to Sobol's transportation problem, using the northwest-corner rule.

(b) Then evaluate each unused shipping route (each empty cell) by applying the stepping-stone method and computing all improvement indices. Remember to

 1. check that supply and demand are equal

 2. load the table via the northwest-corner method

 3. check that there is the proper number of occupied cells for a "normal" solution (number of rows + number of columns − 1 = number of occupied cells)

 4. find a closed path to each empty cell

 5. determine the index for each unused cell

 6. move as many units as possible to the cell that provides the most improvement (if there is one)

 7. repeat steps 3 through 6 until no further improvement can be found

FROM	To			
	PROJECT A	PROJECT B	PROJECT C	PLANT CAPACITY
Plant 1	$10	$ 4	$11	70
Plant 2	$12	$ 5	$ 8	50
Plant 3	$ 9	$ 7	$ 6	30
Project requirements	40	50	60	150

Solution

(a) Northwest-corner solution:

$$\text{Initial cost} = 40(\$10) + 30(\$4) + 20(\$5) + 30(\$8) + 30(\$6) = \$1,040$$

To From	Project A	Project B	Project C	Plant capacities
Plant 1	$10 40	$4 30	$11	70
Plant 2	$12	$5 20	$8 30	50
Plant 3	$9	$7	$6 30	30
Project requirements	40	50	60	150

(b) By using the stepping-stone method, the following improvement indices are computed:

$$\text{Path: plant 1 to project C} = \$11 - \$4 + \$5 - \$8 = +\$4$$
$$\text{(Closed path} = \text{1C to 1B to 2B to 2C)}$$

To From	Project A	Project B	Project C	Plant capacities
Plant 1	10	4 –	11 +	70
Plant 2	12	5 +	8 –	50
Plant 3	9	7	6	30
Project requirements	40	50	60	150

Path: plant 1 to project C

$$\text{Path: plant 2 to project A} = \$12 - \$5 + \$4 - \$10 = +\$1$$
$$\text{(Closed path} = \text{2A to 2B to 1B to 1A)}$$

Path: plant 2 to project A

To From	Project A	Project B	Project C	Plant capacities
Plant 1	10	4	11	70
Plant 2	12	5	8	50
Plant 3	9	7	6	30
Project requirements	40	50	60	150

Path: plant 3 to project A = $9 − $6 + $8 − $5 + $4 − 10 = $0
(Closed path = 3A to 3C to 2C to 2B to 1B to 1A)

Path: plant 3 to project A

To From	Project A	Project B	Project C	Plant capacities
Plant 1	10	4	11	70
Plant 2	12	5	8	50
Plant 3	9	7	6	30
Project requirements	40	50	60	150

Path: plant 3 to project B = $7 − $6 + $8 − $5 = $4
(Closed path = 3B to 3C to 2C to 2B)

Path: plant 3 to project B

To From	Project A	Project B	Project C	Plant capacities
Plant 1	10	4	11	70
Plant 2	12	5	8	50
Plant 3	9	7	6	30
Project requirements	40	50	60	150

Because all indices are greater than or equal to zero (all are positive or zero), this initial solution provides the optimal transportation schedule, namely, 40 units from 1 to A, 30 units from 1 to B, 20 units from 2 to B, 30 units from 2 to C, and 30 units from 3 to C.

Had we found a path that allowed improvement, we would move all units possible to that cell and then check every empty cell again.

1. What is a *balanced* transportation problem? Describe the approach you would use to solve an *unbalanced* problem.

2. How do the MODI and stepping-stone methods differ?

3. Develop a *northeast* corner rule and explain how it would work. Set up an initial solution for the Arizona Plumbing problem in Example S1.

4. Explain what happens when the solution to a transportation problem does not have M + N −1 occupied squares.

5. When, in solving a transportation problem:

a) is a northwest corner solution optimal?

b) is a MODI solution optimal?

6. How can the transportation method address production costs in addition to transportation costs?

7. What is the difference between a feasible solution and an optimal one?

8. What is the purpose of the stepping stone method?

9. What is the solution to the problem of degeneracy?

10. What are the purposes of *dummy sources* or *dummy destinations* in a transportation problem?

11. Identify the three "steps" in the northwest corner rule.

CRITICAL THINKING EXERCISE

Cahill May Roberts (CMR) is Ireland's largest wholesale drug distributor. Its head office and three warehouses are in Dublin, with five more warehouses scattered around Ireland. CMR supplies about 400 retail druggists in Dublin and over 800 customers in 300 outlying villages. Customers are reached by a fleet of delivery vans, with drop-off frequency varying from twice a day to once per week. It is common for customers to receive supplies from more than one warehouse. Make specific recommendations to improve CMR's efficiency and to satisfy druggists' demands.

PROBLEMS

: S9.1 The following table presents data for a transportation problem in Judeth Hall's furniture company. Set up the appropriate transportation table and find the initial solution, using northwest-corner data.

From \ To	1	2	3	Capacity
A	30	10	5	20
B	10	10	10	30
C	20	10	25	75
Supply	40	60	55	

: S9.2 The following table is the result of one or more iterations:

To From	1	2	3	Capacity
A	30 / 40	10	5 / 10	50
B	10	10 / 30	10	30
C	20	10 / 30	25 / 45	75
Demands	40	60	55	155

a) Complete the next iteration using the stepping-stone method.

b) Calculate the "total cost" incurred if your results were to be accepted as the final solution.

: S9.3 Determine whether the new solution table presented in Example S3 contains the optimal transportation allocation for Arizona Plumbing. If not, compute an improved solution and test it for optimality.

: S9.4 In Example S7, Williams Auto Top Carrier proposed opening a new plant in either New Orleans or Houston. The firm's management found that the total system cost (of production plus distribution) would be $20,000 if they chose the New Orleans site.

What would be the total cost if Williams opened a plant in Houston? At which of the two proposed locations (New Orleans or Houston) should Williams open the new facility?

: S9.5 After one iteration of the stepping-stone method, G. W. Willis Paint Company produced the transportation table below.

Complete the analysis, determining an optimal shipping solution.

G. W. Willis Paint Company

To From	Warehouse 1	Warehouse 2	Warehouse 3	Factory capacity
Factory A	$8 / 120	$5	$6	120
Factory B	$15	$10 / 80	$14	80
Factory C	$3 / 30	$9	$10 / 50	80
Warehouse requirements	150	80	50	280

Cost = $2350

⊞ : **S9.6** The initial solution for the Hardrock Concrete Company's shipping problem, derived by using the northwest-corner rule, is presented below. Apply the MODI method in order to determine whether this allocation is optimal.

Hardrock Concrete Company

From \ To	Project A		Project B		Project C		Plant capacity
Plant 1	40	$10	30	$4		$11	70
Plant 2		$12	20	$5	30	$8	50
Plant 3		$9		$7	30	$6	30
Project requirements	40		50		60		150

⊞ : **S9.7** The JC Clothing Group owns factories in three towns (W, Y, and Z), which distribute to three JC retail dress shops in three other cities (in A, B, and C). The table below summarizes factory availabilities, projected store demands, and unit shipping costs.

JC Clothing Group

From \ To	Dress shop A		Dress shop B		Dress shop C		Factory availability
Factory W		$4		$3		$3	35
Factory Y		$6		$7		$6	50
Factory Z		$8		$2		$5	50
Store demand	30		65		40		135

a) Complete the analysis, determining the optimal solution for shipping at the JC Clothing Group.

b) How do you know if it is optimal or not?

⊞ : **S9.8** Sound Track Stereos assembles its high-fidelity stereophonic systems at three plants and distributes systems from three regional warehouses. The production capacities at each plant, demand at each warehouse, and unit shipping costs are presented below.

a) Set up this transportation problem by adding a dummy plant. Then use the north-west-corner rule to find an initial basic feasible solution.

b) What is the optimal solution?

Sound Track Stereos

To From	Warehouse A	Warehouse B	Warehouse C	Plant supply
Plant W	$6	$4	$9	200
Plant Y	$10	$5	$6	175
Plant Z	$12	$7	$8	75
Warehouse demand	250	100	150	500 / 450

: S9.9 Whybark Mill Works (WMW) ships French doors to three building supply houses from its mills in Mountpelier, Nixon, and Oak Ridge. Determine the best shipment schedule for WMW from the data provided by Tad Hixon, the traffic manager at WMW. Use the northwest-corner starting procedure and the stepping-stone method. Refer to the table below.

Whybark Mill Works

To From	Supply house 1	Supply house 2	Supply house 3	Mill capacity (in tons)
Mountpelier	$3	$3	$2	25
Nixon	$4	$2	$3	40
Oak Ridge	$3	$2	$3	30
Supply house demand (in tons)	30	30	35	95

: S9.10 Using the data in Problem S9.8, resolve via the MODI method.

: S9.11 Using the data in Problem S9.9, resolve via the MODI method.

: S9.12 Jim Lloyd, vice president for operations of HHN, Inc., a manufacturer of cabinets for telephone switches, is constrained from meeting the 5-year forecast by limited capacity at the existing three plants. These three plants are Waterloo, Pusan, and Bogota. You, as his able assistant, have been told that because of existing capacity constraints and the expanding world market for HHN cabinets, a new plant is to be added to the existing three plants. The real estate department has advised Mr. Lloyd that two sites seem particularly good because of a stable political situation and tolerable exchange rate. These two acceptable locations are Dublin, Ireland, and Fontainebleau, France. Mr. Lloyd suggests that you should be able to take the data below and determine where the fourth plant should be located on the basis of production costs and transportation costs. *Note*: This problem is degenerate with the data for both locations.

MARKET AREA	PLANT LOCATION				
	WATERLOO	PUSAN	BOGOTA	FONTAINEBLEAU	DUBLIN
Canada: Demand 4,000					
Production cost	50	30	40	50	45
Transportation cost	10	25	20	25	25
South America: Demand 5,000					
Production cost	50	30	40	50	45
Transportation cost	20	25	10	30	30
Pacific Rim: Demand 10,000					
Production cost	50	30	40	50	45
Transportation cost	25	10	25	40	40
Europe: Demand 5,000					
Production cost	50	30	40	50	45
Transportation cost	25	40	30	10	20
Capacity	8,000	2,000	5,000	9,000	9,000

: S9.13 Susan Helms Manufacturing Company has hired you to evaluate its shipping costs. The table that follows shows its present demand, capacity, and freight costs between each factory and each warehouse. Find the shipping pattern with the lowest cost.

Susan Helms Manufacturing Data

From \ To	Warehouse 1	Warehouse 2	Warehouse 3	Warehouse 4	Plant capacity
Factory 1	4	7	10	12	2,000
Factory 2	7	5	8	11	2,500
Factory 3	9	8	6	9	2,200
Warehouse demand	1,000	2,000	2,000	1,200	

: S9.14 Cerveny Corporation is considering adding an additional plant to its three existing facilities in Decatur, Minneapolis, and Carbondale. Both St. Louis and East St. Louis are being considered. Evaluating only the transportation costs per unit as shown in the table, which site is best?

| | FROM EXISTING PLANTS | | | |
To	DECATUR	MINNEAPOLIS	CARBONDALE	DEMAND
Blue Earth	$20	$17	$21	250
Ciro	25	27	20	200
Des Moines	22	25	22	350
Capacity	300	200	150	

| | FROM PROPOSED PLANTS | |
To	EAST ST. LOUIS	ST. LOUIS
Blue Earth	$29	$27
Ciro	30	28
Des Moines	30	31
Capacity	150	150

:S9.15 Using the data from Problem S9.14 and the unit production costs shown below, which locations yield the lowest cost?

LOCATION	PRODUCTION COSTS
Decatur	$50
Minneapolis	60
Carbondale	70
East St. Louis	40
St. Louis	50

:S9.16 Find the result for the next iteration of the following transportation table for David Chou's chain of clothing stores.

David Chou's Store Data

To \ From	1	2	3	Demand
A	1 — 9	6	7	9
B	2	5	3 — 8	8
C	3 — 10	2	4	10
D	6	3 — 24	9 — 7	31
Capacity	19	24	15	

:S9.17 Duffy Pharmaceuticals holds a dominant position in the southeast United States, with over 800 discount retail outlets. These stores are served with twice-weekly deliveries from Duffy's 13 warehouses, which in turn are supplied daily by seven factories that manufacture about 70% of all of the chain's products.

It is clear to Jo Ann Duffy, VP Operations, that an additional warehouse is desperately needed to handle growth and backlogs. Three cities, Mobile, Tampa, and Huntsville, are under final consideration. The following table illustrates the current and proposed factory/warehouse capacities/demands and shipping costs per average box of supplies.

a) Based on shipping costs only, which city should be selected for the new warehouse?

b) Ocala's capacity, a study shows, can increase to 500 boxes per day. Would this affect your decision in part (a)?

c) Because of a new intrastate shipping agreement, rates for shipping from each factory in Florida to each warehouse in Florida drop by $1 per carton. How does this affect your answer to parts (a) and (b)?

TABLE FOR DATA BASE APPLICATION S9.17

WAREHOUSE / FACTORY	ATLANTA, GA	NEW ORLEANS, LA	JACKSON, MS	BIRMINGHAM, AL	MONTGOMERY, AL	RALEIGH, NC	ASHVILLE, NC	COLUMBIA, SC	CAPACITY (CARTONS PER DAY)
Valdosta, GA	$3	$5	$4	$3	$4	$6	$8	$8	500
Ocala, FL	4	6	5	5	6	7	6	7	300
Augusta, GA	1	4	3	2	2	6	7	8	400
Stuart, FL	3	5	2	6	6	5	5	6	200
Biloxi, MS	4	1	4	3	3	8	9	10	600
Starkville, MS	3	3	1	2	2	6	5	6	400
Durham, NC	4	8	8	7	7	2	2	2	500
Requirements (cartons/day)	150	250	50	150	100	200	150	300	

TABLE FOR DATA BASE APPLICATION S9.17 (CONTINUED)

WAREHOUSE / FACTORY	ORLANDO, FL	MIAMI, FL	JACKSONVILLE, FL	WILMINGTON, NC	CHARLOTTE, NC	MOBILE, AL	TAMPA, FL	HUNTSVILLE, AL	CAPACITY (CARTONS PER DAY)
Valdosta, GA	$9	$10	$8	$8	$11	$4	$6	$3	500
Ocala, FL	2	3	2	6	7	5	2	5	300
Augusta, GA	7	9	6	8	9	3	5	2	400
Stuart, FL	2	2	3	5	5	6	3	5	200
Biloxi, MS	7	13	9	8	8	2	6	3	600
Starkville, MS	6	8	7	7	8	3	6	2	400
Durham, NC	6	8	5	1	2	8	7	8	500
Requirements (cartons/day)	250	300	300	100	150	300	300	300	

CASE STUDY

Custom Vans, Inc.

Custom Vans, Inc., specializes in converting standard vans into campers. Depending on the amount of work and customizing to be done, the customizing could cost less than $1,000 to over $5,000. In less than four years, Tony Rizzo was able to expand his small operation in Gary, Indiana, to other major outlets in Chicago, Milwaukee, Minneapolis, and Detroit.

Innovation was the major factor in Tony's success in converting a small van shop into one of the largest and most profitable custom van operations in the Midwest. Tony seemed to have a special ability to design and develop unique features and devices that were always in high demand by van owners. An example was Shower-Rific, which was developed by Tony only six months after Custom Vans, Inc., was started. These small showers were completely self-contained, and they could be placed in almost any type of van and in a number of different locations within a van. Shower-Rific was made of fiberglass, and contained towel racks, built-in soap and shampoo holders, and a unique plastic door. Each Shower-Rific took 2 gallons of fiberglass and 3 hours of labor to manufacture.

Most of the Shower-Rifics were manufactured in Gary in the same warehouse where Custom Vans, Inc., was founded. The manufacturing plant in Gary could produce 300 Shower-Rifics in a month, but this capacity never seemed to be enough. Custom Van shops in all locations were complaining about not getting enough Shower-Rifics, and because Minneapolis was farther away from Gary than the other locations, Tony was always inclined to ship Shower-Rifics to the other locations before Minneapolis. This infuriated the manager of Custom Vans at Minneapolis, and after many heated discussions, Tony decided to start another manufacturing plant for Shower-Rifics at Fort Wayne, Indiana. The manufacturing plant at Fort Wayne could produce 150 Shower-Rifics per month.

The manufacturing plant at Fort Wayne was still not able to meet current demand for Shower-Rifics, and Tony knew that the demand for his unique camper shower would grow rapidly in the

next year. After consulting with his lawyer and banker, Tony concluded that he should open two new manufacturing plants as soon as possible. Each plant would have the same capacity as the Fort Wayne manufacturing plant. An initial investigation into possible manufacturing locations was made, and Tony decided that the two new plants should be located in Detroit, Michigan; Rockford, Illinois; or Madison, Wisconsin. Tony knew that selecting the best location for the two new manufacturing plants would be difficult. Transportation costs and demands for the various locations should be important considerations.

The Chicago shop was managed by Bill Burch. This Custom Van shop was one of the first established by Tony, and it continued to outperform the other locations. The manufacturing plant at Gary was supplying 200 Shower-Rifics each month, although Bill knew that the demand for the showers in Chicago was 300 units. The transportation cost per unit from Gary was $10, and although the transportation cost from Fort Wayne was double that amount, Bill was always pleading with Tony to get an additional 50 units from the Fort Wayne manufacturer. The two additional manufacturing plants would certainly be able to supply Bill with the additional 100 showers he needed. The transportation costs would, of course, vary, depending on which two locations Tony picked. The transportation cost per shower would be $30 from Detroit, $5 from Rockford, and $10 from Madison.

Wilma Jackson, manager of the Custom Van shop in Milwaukee, was the most upset about not getting an adequate supply of showers. She had a demand for 100 units, and at the present time, she was only getting half of this demand from the Fort Wayne manufacturing plant. She could not understand why Tony didn't ship her all 100 units from Gary. The transportation cost per unit from Gary was only $20, while the transportation cost from Fort Wayne was $30. Wilma was hoping that Tony would select Madison for one of the manufacturing locations. She would be able to get all of the showers needed, and the transportation cost per unit would be only $5. If not Madison, a new plant in Rockford would be able to supply her total needs, but the transportation cost per unit would be twice as much as it would be from Madison. Because the trans-

(Continued)

portation cost per unit from Detroit would be $40, Wilma speculated that even if Detroit became one of the new plants, she would not be getting any units from Detroit.

Custom Vans, Inc., of Minneapolis was managed by Tom Poanski. He was getting 100 showers from the Gary plant. Demand was 150 units. Tom faced the highest transportation costs of all locations. The transportation cost from Gary was $40 per unit. It would cost $10 more if showers were sent from the Fort Wayne location. Tom was hoping that Detroit would not be one of the new plants, as the transportation cost would be $60 per unit. Rockford and Madison would have a cost of $30 and $25, respectively, to ship one shower to Minneapolis.

The Detroit shop's position was similar to Milwaukee's—only getting half of the demand each month. The 100 units that Detroit did receive came directly from the Fort Wayne plant. The transportation cost was only $15 per unit from Fort Wayne, while it was $25 from Gary. Dick Lopez, manager of Custom Vans, Inc., of Detroit, placed the probability of having one of the new plants in Detroit fairly high. The factory would be located across town, and the transportation cost would be only $5 per unit. He could get 150 showers from the new plant in Detroit and the other 50 showers from Fort Wayne. Even if Detroit were not selected, the other two locations were not intolerable. Rockford had a transportation cost per unit of $35, and Madison had a transportation cost of $40.

Tony pondered the dilemma of locating the two new plants for several weeks before deciding to call a meeting of all managers of the van shops. The decision was complicated, but the objective was clear—to minimize total costs. The meeting was held in Gary, and everyone was present except Wilma.

Tony: Thank you for coming. As you know, I have decided to open up two new plants at Rockford, Madison, or Detroit. The two locations, of course, will change our shipping practices, and I sincerely hope that they will supply you with the Shower-Rifics that you have been wanting. I know you could

have sold more units, and I want you to know that I am sorry for this situation.

Dick: Tony, I have given this situation a lot of consideration, and I feel strongly that at least one of the new plants should be located in Detroit. As you know, I am now getting only half of the showers that I need. My brother, Leon, is very interested in running the plant, and I know he would do a good job.

Tom: Dick, I am sure that Leon could do a good job, and I know how difficult it has been since the recent layoffs by the auto industry. Nevertheless, we should be considering total costs and not personalities. I believe that the new plants should be located in Madison and Rockford. I am farther away from the other plants than any other shop, and these locations would significantly reduce transportation costs.

Dick: That may be true, but there are other factors. Detroit has one of the largest suppliers of fiberglass, and I have checked prices. A new plant in Detroit would be able to purchase fiberglass for $2 less than any of the other existing or proposed plants.

Tom: At Madison, we have an excellent labor force. This is primarily due to the large number of students attending the University of Madison. These students are hard workers, and they will work for $1 less per hour than the other locations that we are considering.

Bill: Calm down, you two. It is obvious that we will not be able to satisfy everyone in locating the new plants. Therefore, I would like to suggest that we vote on the two best locations.

Tony: I don't think that voting would be a good idea. Wilma was not able to attend, and we should be looking at all of these factors together in some type of logical fashion.

DISCUSSION QUESTION

1. Where would you locate the two new plants and why?

Source: Written by R. M. Stair, Jr., in Barry Render and Ralph M. Stair, *Quantitative Analysis for Management*, 5th ed., Boston: Allyn & Bacon, 1994.

See the references at the end of Chapter 9.

10

OPERATIONS LAYOUT STRATEGY

LEARNING OBJECTIVES

When you complete this chapter you should be able to:

Identify or Define:
   Fixed-position layout
   Process-oriented layout
   Work cells
   Focused work center
   Retail/service layout
   Warehouse layout
   Product-oriented layout
   Assembly line factory

Explain:
   How to achieve a good layout for the process facility
   How to balance production flow in a repetitive or product-oriented facility

LAYOUT PROVIDES A COMPETITIVE ADVANTAGE FOR AIRLINES AT PITTSBURGH AIRPORT

Pittsburgh International's X-shaped terminal reduces taxi time and improves gate access, thereby reducing airline fuel cost substantially. These dual taxiways contribute to reduced taxiing time for aircraft at the Pittsburgh airport as well as higher takeoff speeds.

Just as operations techniques can assist in layouts for factories, stores, and hospitals, they can also aid in airport layout. Important layout criteria include reducing congestion, distance, and delays. These criteria have been successfully applied to the new Pittsburgh airport. The Pittsburgh airport layout also had to accommodate passenger convenience, cost, and expandability as well as the traditional P/OM criterion of operational efficiency.

The terminal layout provides a mall-like environment for travelers.

A variety of people movers—from shuttle trains to escalators to these moving walkways—improve passenger convenience.

To address passenger convenience, designers created a revolutionary X-shaped airport. The airport includes a central shopping mall, a variety of people movers, and a $34 million baggage-handling system. The X shape positively influences the movement of passengers and aircraft. Combinations of escalators, moving sidewalks, and shuttle trains move passengers to any of the 75 gates in about 11 minutes.

The X-shaped terminal also proved to be an excellent vehicle for operational efficiency. Elaborate simulations were done to evaluate flight activity and its impact on runways, taxiways, and gates early in the design stage.

The layout also provides dual apron taxilanes around the jet gates to allow efficient aircraft access in and out of all positions. These are coupled with complementary dual taxiways running in opposite directions to and from existing runways. The combination is contributing to reduced delays and allowing faster take-offs. The resultant efficiencies mean airlines using the Pittsburgh airport can expect to save as much as $15 million per year in operating expenses.

Pittsburgh airport, through the use of P/OM techniques, is setting a new standard for efficiency.

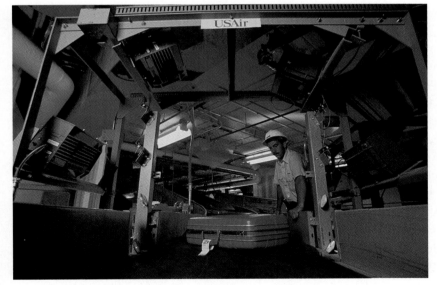

This $34 million dollar automated baggage handling system uses a 10-digit tag to sort bags. The system uses computer-directed laser scanners to route bags along six miles of conveyor belts.

On entering the Wal-Mart in Rogers, Arkansas, customers expecting the usual warehouse-like atmosphere of discount stores are shocked. With wide aisles, open displays, sitting areas for customers, and classy clothing racks, Wal-Mart looks like an upscale department store. Displays organize related products such as shower curtains, towels, and bathroom fixtures into visual vignettes that encourage what the store calls "multiple sales." What makes Wal-Mart a leader in layout? Retail executives say it's the store's attention to layout details that help shape shoppers' attitudes.[‡] ◆

Layout is one of the strategic areas that determines the long-run efficiency of operations. Layout issues apply to Wal-Mart, to Pittsburgh International Airport, and, in fact, to every organization in the world. The *objective of the layout strategy* is to develop an economic layout that will meet the requirements of

1. product design and volume,
2. process equipment and capacity,
3. quality of work life,
4. building and site constraints.

A layout specifies the arrangement of processes (such as welding, milling, and painting), the related equipment, and work areas, including customer service and storage areas. An effective layout also facilitates the flow of materials and people within and between areas. Management's layout decisions must be made with this effectiveness and efficiency in mind. Layout decisions include the best placement of machines (in a production setting), offices and desks (in an office setting), or service centers (in settings such as hospitals or department stores).

TYPES OF LAYOUT

To achieve these layout objectives, a variety of classes have been developed. Among them are six that we discuss in this chapter:

Fixed-position layout

1. **Fixed-position layout**—addresses the layout requirements of large, bulky projects such as ships and buildings.

Process-oriented layout

2. **Process-oriented layout**—deals with low-volume, high-variety production (also called "job shop" or intermittent production).

Office layout

3. **Office layout**—positions workers, their equipment, and spaces/offices to provide for movement of information.

Retail/service layout

4. **Retail/service layout**—allocates shelf space and responds to customer behavior.

Warehouse layout

5. **Warehouse layout**—addresses trade-offs between space and material handling.

Product-oriented layout

6. **Product-oriented layout**—seeks the best personnel and machine utilization in repetitive or continuous production.

Examples for each of these classes of layout problems are noted in Table 10.1.

[‡]*Source: Wall Street Journal* (May 17, 1991).

TABLE 10.1 ■ LAYOUT STRATEGIES

PROJECT (FIXED-POSITION)	JOB SHOP (PROCESS-ORIENTED)	OFFICE	RETAIL (SERVICE/RETAIL)	WAREHOUSE (STORAGE)	REPETITIVE/CONTINUOUS (PRODUCT-ORIENTED)
Example:					
Ingall Ship Building Co.	Shouldice Hospital	Allstate Insurance	Kroger's Supermarket	Federal-Mogul's warehouse	Sony's TV assembly line
Trump Plaza	Olive Garden Restaurants	Microsoft Corp.	Walgreens Drug Co. Bloomingdales		Dodge Caravan Minivans
Problem:					
Move material to the limited storage areas around the site.	Manage varied material flow for each product.	Locate workers requiring frequent contact close to one another.	Expose customer to high-margin items.	Balance low-cost storage with low-cost material handling.	Arrange product flow from one workstation to the next.

Only a few of these six classes can be modeled mathematically, so the layout and design of physical facilities are still something of an art. However, we do know that a good layout requires determining:

1. *Material handling equipment.* Managers must decide about the equipment to be used, including conveyors, cranes, and automatic carts to deliver material or the mail.

2. *Capacity and space requirements.* Only when we know the personnel, machines, and equipment required can we proceed with the layout and provide space for each component. In the case of office work, operations managers must make judgments about the space requirements for each employee. It may be a 6 × 6-foot cubicle plus allowance for hallways, aisles, rest rooms, cafeterias, stairwells,

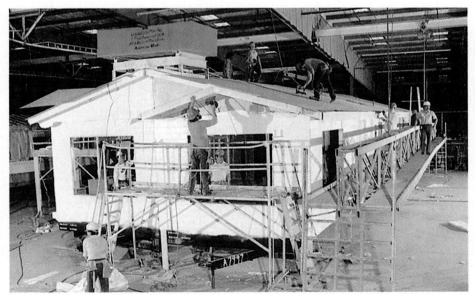

A house built via traditional fixed position layout would be constructed on-site, with equipment, materials, and workers brought to that site. However, imaginative P/OM solutions allow this home to be built at a much lower cost. The house is built in two movable modules (shown joined here) in a factory where equipment and materials handling are expedited. The indoor work environment means no weather delays and no overnight thefts. Prepositioned work scaffolding and hoists mounted on the factory ceiling make the job easier, quicker, and cheaper.

elevators, and so forth, or it may be spacious executive offices and conference rooms. Management must also consider allowances for safety requirements that address noise, dust, fumes, temperature, and space around equipment and machines.

3. *Environment and aesthetics.* Layout concerns often require decisions about windows, planters, and height of partitions to facilitate air flow, to reduce noise, to provide privacy, and so forth.

4. *Flows of information.* Communication is important to any company and must be facilitated by the layout. This may require decisions about proximity as well as open spaces versus half-height dividers versus private offices.

5. *Cost of moving between the various work areas.* There may be unique considerations related to moving materials or the importance of certain areas being next to each other. For example, the movement of molten steel is more difficult than the movement of cold steel.

FIXED-POSITION LAYOUT

In a *fixed-position layout*, the project remains in one place and workers and equipment come to that one work area. Examples of this type of project are a ship, a highway, a bridge, a house, and an oil well.

The techniques for addressing the fixed-position layout are not well developed and are complicated by three factors.

First, there is limited space at virtually all sites. Second, at different stages in the construction process, different materials are needed; therefore, different items become critical as the project develops. And third, the volume of materials needed is dynamic. For example, the rate of use of steel panels for the hull of a ship changes as the project progresses.

Different industries handle these problems in different ways. The construction industry usually has a "meeting of the trades" to assign space for various time periods. As you would suspect, this often yields less than an optimum solution, as the discussion may be more political than analytical. Shipyards, however, have loading areas called "platens" adjacent to the ship, which are loaded by a scheduling department.

Because the fixed-position layout is so difficult to solve well at the site, an alternative strategy is to complete as much of the project as possible off site. This approach is used in the shipbuilding industry when standard units, say, pipe-holding brackets, are assembled in a nearby assembly line process (a product-oriented facility). Ingall Ship Building Corporation has built similar sections of a ship (modules) or the same section of several similar ships in a product-oriented line in an attempt to add efficiency to shipbuilding.[1] Similarly, other shipbuilding firms are experimenting with group technology to produce components.[2] As the photo on the previous page shows, even some home builders are trying to move to an off-site environment.

---

[1]"Ingall's 130 Million Dollar Ship Factory," *Shipbuilding and Shipping Record*, **115**, 22 (London: Transport and Technical Publications Ltd.): 25–26.

[2]Naboru Yamamoto, Kiyohi Terai, and Tatsumi Kurioka, "The Continuous Flow Production System Which Has Applied to Hull Works in Shipbuilding Industry," *Selected Journal of the Society of Naval Architects of Japan*, No. 35, Society of Naval Architects of Japan, Shiba-Kotohiracho, Minato-Ku, Tokyo, Japan, **5**, 70: 153–174.

PROCESS-ORIENTED LAYOUT

The *process-oriented layout* can handle a wide variety of products or services at the same time. In fact, it is most efficient when making products that have different requirements or when handling customers who have different needs. A process-oriented layout is typically the low-volume, high-variety strategy discussed in Chapter 7. In this job shop environment, each product or each small group of products has a different sequence of operations. A product or small order is produced by moving it from one department to another in the sequence required for that product. Machines are arranged according to the type of process being performed.

Figure 10.1 illustrates this process for two products, electric saws and electric drills. Another example of the process-oriented layout is a hospital or clinic. A continuous inflow of patients, each with his or her own processing needs, requires routing through records areas, admissions, laboratories, operating rooms, intensive care units, pharmacies, nursing stations, and so on.

A big advantage of process-oriented layout is its flexibility in equipment and labor assignments. The breakdown of one machine, for example, need not halt an entire process, because work can be transferred to other machines in the department. Process-oriented layout is also especially good for handling the manufacture of parts in small batches, or **job lots**, and for the production of a wide variety of parts in different sizes or forms.

Job lots

The disadvantages of process-oriented layout come from the general-purpose use of the equipment. Orders take more time and money to move through the system because of difficult scheduling, setups, and material handling. In addition, labor skill requirements and work-in-process inventories are higher because of larger imbalances in the production process. High labor skill needs increase the required level of training and experience; high work-in-process increases capital investment.

FIGURE 10.1 ■ A Process Layout Showing the Routing of Two Families of Parts

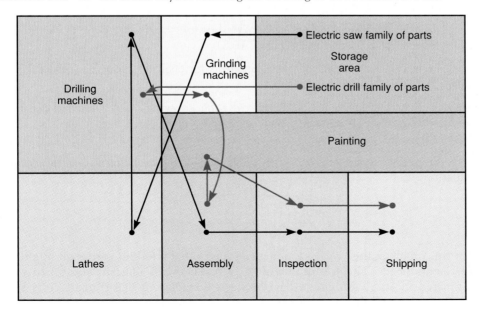

In process-layout planning, the most common tactic is to arrange departments or work centers so as to minimize the costs of material handling. In other words, departments with large flows of parts or people between them should be placed next to one another. Material handling cost in this approach depends on: (1) the number of loads (or people) to be moved during some period of time between two departments (i or j) and (2) the distance-related costs between departments. Cost can be a function of distance between departments. The objective can be expressed as follows:

$$\text{Minimize cost} = \sum_{i=1}^{n} \sum_{j=1}^{n} X_{ij} C_{ij} \tag{10.1}$$

where n = total number of work centers or departments
        i, j = individual departments
        X_{ij} = number of loads moved from department i to department j
        C_{ij} = cost to move a load between department i and department j

Process-oriented facilities (and fixed-position layouts as well) try to minimize the loads or trips times distance-related costs. The term C_{ij} combines distance and other costs into one factor. We thereby assume not only that the difficulty of movement is equal but also that the pickup and setdown costs are constant. Although they are not always constant, for simplicity's sake we summarize these data (that is, cost, difficulty, and pickup and setdown cost) into this one variable. The best way to understand the steps of process layout is to look at an example.

EXAMPLE 1

The Walters Company's management wants to arrange the six departments of its factory in a way that will minimize interdepartmental material handling costs. They make an initial assumption (to simplify the problem) that each department is 20 × 20 feet and that the building is 60 feet long and 40 feet wide. The process layout procedure that they follow involves six steps.

Step 1. *Construct a "from-to matrix"* showing the flow of parts or materials from department to department (Figure 10.2)

Step 2. *Determine the space requirements* for each department. (Figure 10.3 shows the available plant space.)

Step 3. *Develop an initial schematic diagram* showing the sequence of departments through which parts will have to move. Try to place departments with a heavy flow of materials or parts next to one another. (See Figure 10.4.)

Step 4. *Determine the cost* of this layout by using the material-handling cost equation:

$$\text{Cost} = \sum_{i=1}^{n} \sum_{j=1}^{n} X_{ij} C_{ij}$$

For this problem, the Walters Company assumes that a forklift carries all interdepartmental loads. The cost of moving one load between adjacent departments is estimated to be $1. Moving a load between nonadjacent departments costs $2. Hence, the handling cost between departments 1 and 2 is $50 ($1 × 50 loads),

$200 between departments 1 and 3 ($2 × 100 loads), $40 between departments 1 and 6 ($2 × 20 loads), and so on. The total cost for the layout shown in Figure 10.4 then is

$$
\begin{aligned}
\text{Cost} = \quad & \$50 \quad + \quad \$200 \quad + \quad \$40 \quad + \quad \$30 \quad + \quad \$50 \\
& \text{(1 and 2)} \quad \text{(1 and 3)} \quad \text{(1 and 6)} \quad \text{(2 and 3)} \quad \text{(2 and 4)} \\
& + \quad \$10 \quad + \quad \$40 \quad + \quad \$100 \quad + \quad \$50 \\
& \text{(2 and 5)} \quad \text{(3 and 4)} \quad \text{(3 and 6)} \quad \text{(4 and 5)} \\
= \quad & \$570
\end{aligned}
$$

Step 5. By trial and error (or by a more sophisticated computer program approach that we discuss shortly), *try to improve this layout* to establish a reasonably good arrangement of departments.

FIGURE 10.2 ■ Interdepartmental Flow of Parts. The high flows between 1 and 3, and 3 and 6 are immediately apparent. Departments 1, 3, and 6, therefore, should be close together.

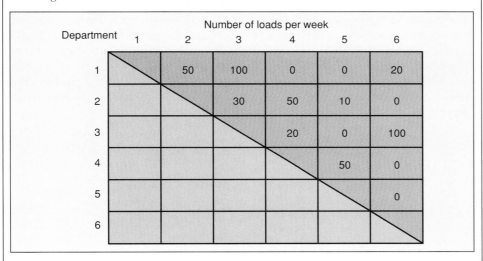

FIGURE 10.3 ■ Building Dimensions and a Possible Department Layout

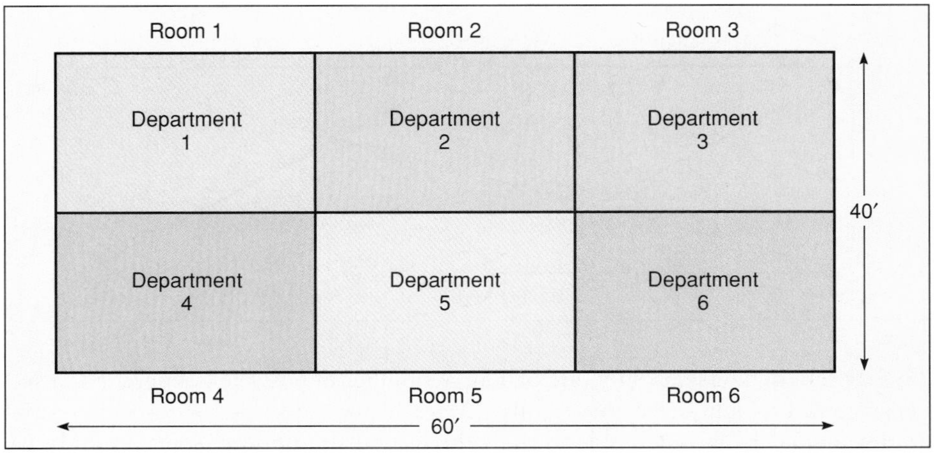

FIGURE 10.4 ■ Interdepartmental Flow Graph Showing Number of Weekly Loads

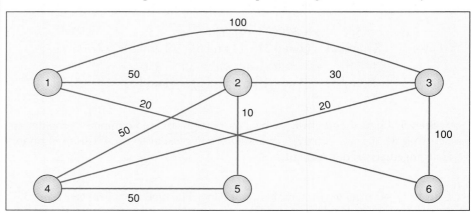

By looking at both the flow graph and the cost calculations, it appears desirable to place departments 1 and 3 closer together. They currently are nonadjacent, and the high volume of flow between them causes a large handling expense. Looking the situation over, we need to check the effect of shifting departments and possibly raising, instead of lowering, overall costs.

One possibility is to switch departments 1 and 2. This exchange produces the second departmental flow graph (Figure 10.5), which shows that it is possible to reduce the cost to $480, a savings in material handling of $90.

$$
\begin{array}{cccccccccc}
\text{Cost} = & \$50 & + & \$100 & + & \$20 & + & \$60 & + & \$50 \\
& (1 \text{ and } 2) & & (1 \text{ and } 3) & & (1 \text{ and } 6) & & (2 \text{ and } 3) & & (2 \text{ and } 4) \\
& + \$10 & + & \$40 & + & \$100 & + & \$50 \\
& (2 \text{ and } 5) & & (3 \text{ and } 4) & & (3 \text{ and } 6) & & (4 \text{ and } 5) \\
= \$480
\end{array}
$$

FIGURE 10.5 ■ Second Interdepartmental Flow Graph

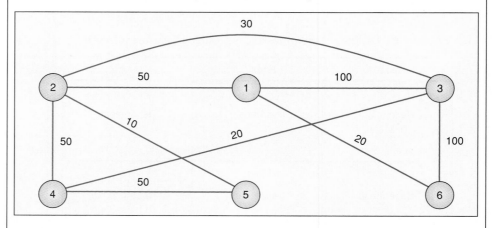

This switch, of course, is only one of a large number of possible changes. For a six-department problem there are actually 720 (or $6! = 6 \times 5 \times 4 \times 3 \times 2 \times 1$) potential arrangements! In layout problems, we seldom find the optimal solution and may have to be satisfied with a "reasonable" one reached after a few trials. Suppose the Walters Company is satisfied with the cost figure of $480 and the flow graph of Figure 10.5. The problem may not be solved yet. Often a sixth step is necessary.

Step 6. *Prepare a detailed plan* arranging the departments to fit the shape of the building and its nonmovable areas (such as the loading dock, washrooms, and stairways). Often this step involves making certain that the final plan can be accommodated by the electrical system, floor loads, aesthetics, and other factors.

In the case of the Walters Company, space requirements are a simple matter (see Figure 10.6).

FIGURE 10.6 ■ A Feasible Layout for the Walters Company

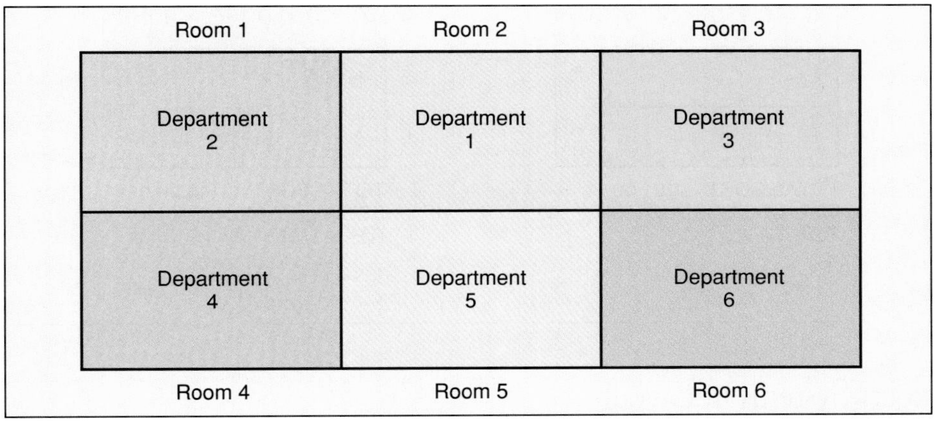

The graphic approach in Example 1 is fine for small problems.[3] However, this method does not suffice for larger problems. When 20 departments are involved in a layout problem, more than 600 *trillion* different department configurations are possible. Fortunately, computer programs have been written to handle layouts of up to 40 departments. The best-known of these is **CRAFT** (Computerized Relative Allocation of Facilities Technique),[4] a program that produces "good" but not always "optimal" solutions. CRAFT is a search technique that systematically examines alternative departmental rearrangements to reduce the total material handling cost (see Figure 10.7). CRAFT has the added advantage of allowing not only load and distance to be examined, but also a third factor, a difficulty rating.

Computerized techniques have been developed for both the two-dimensional and three-dimensional cases—the two-dimensional case is a one-story facility successfully addressed by CRAFT. The three-dimensional case is a multi-story facility and is addressed by **SPACECRAFT**.[5] Manual techniques also exist, but they are more difficult to use than are computer techniques.

CRAFT

SPACECRAFT

[3]See also Richard Muther, *Systematic Layout Planning*, 2nd ed. (Boston: Cahners, 1976), for a similar approach to what the author calls simplified layout planning.

[4]E. S. Buffa, G. S. Armor, and T. E. Vollman, "Allocating Facilities with CRAFT," *Harvard Business Review*, **42**, 2 (March–April 1964): 136–159.

[5]R. V. Johnson, "SPACECRAFT for Multi-Floor Layout Planning," *Management Science*, **28**, 4 (1982): 407–417. A discussion of CRAFT, COFAD, PLANET, CORELAP, and AIDED is available in James M. Moore and James A. Tompkins, *Computer Aided Layout: A User's Guide*, Publication Number 1 in the monograph series, *Facilities Planning and Design Division* (American Institute of Industrial Engineers) p. 77–1. Norcross, GA.

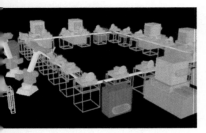

Historically, 3-dimensional physical models were often built to address the layout problem. We now use 3-dimensional computer models to achieve the same purpose, but at greatly reduced cost. Here a transmission assembly line using AutoMod II, a computer simulation program, is shown.

FIGURE 10.7 ■ In This Six-Department Example, CRAFT Has Rearranged the Initial Layout (a) with a Cost of $201.00, to the New Layout with a Lower Cost of $143.90 as Shown in (b).

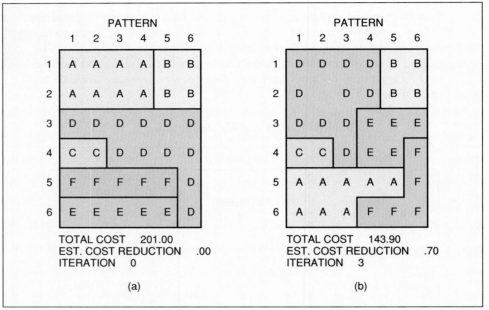

Expert Systems in Layout

CRAFT and SPACECRAFT are just two of the computerized techniques to aid in the design and layout of facilities. But these and the other popular programs, such as CORELAP, ALDEP, and COFAD, do not consider expert knowledge in ranking alternative plans. They do not have built-in rules to consider the creative aspects that a human designer would.

FADES (Facilities Design Expert System) is an *expert system*, that is a program that combines judgmental rules of human experts with the mathematical tools we have introduced earlier in this section.[6] It develops good facility designs for unstructured situations. FADES reflects the new breed of artificial intelligence decision-making aids described in detail in Chapter 8.

Work Cells

A special case of process-oriented layout is the work cell. Although the idea of work cells was first presented by R. E. Flanders in 1925,[7] it is only with the increasing use of group technology (see Chapter 6) that the technique has reasserted itself. Cellular work arrangements are used where volume warrants a special arrangement of machinery and equipment. In a manufacturing environment, group technology identifies products that have similar characteristics and allows not just a particular batch (for example, several units of the same product), but also a family of batches, to be

[6]See E. L. Fisher, "An AI Based Methodology for Factory Design," *AI Magazine*, **3**, 4 (Fall 1986): 72–85, and E. L. Fisher and S. F. Nof, "FADES," *Proceedings of the Annual IIE Meeting* (1984): 74–82.

[7]R. E. Flanders, "Design Manufacture and Production Control of a Standard Machine," *Transactions of ASME*, **46** (1925).

FIGURE 10.8 ■ Improving Layouts by Moving to the Work Cell Concept

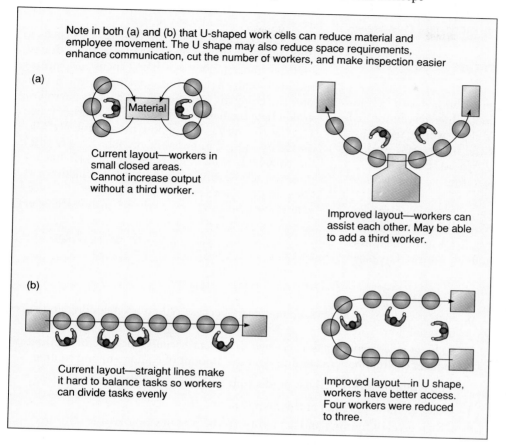

Note in both (a) and (b) that U-shaped work cells can reduce material and employee movement. The U shape may also reduce space requirements, enhance communication, cut the number of workers, and make inspection easier

(a)

Material

Current layout—workers in small closed areas. Cannot increase output without a third worker.

Improved layout—workers can assist each other. May be able to add a third worker.

(b)

Current layout—straight lines make it hard to balance tasks so workers can divide tasks evenly

Improved layout—in U shape, workers have better access. Four workers were reduced to three.

processed in a particular work cell.[8] The **work cell** idea is to take people and machines that would ordinarily be dispersed in various process departments and temporarily arrange them in a small group so that they can focus on making a single product or a group of related products (Figure 10.8). The work cell is built around the product. The advantages of work cells are:[9]

Work cell

1. *Reduced work-in-process inventory* because the work cell is set up to provide a balanced flow from machine to machine.
2. *Less floor space* required because less space is needed between the machines to accommodate the work-in-process inventory.
3. *Reduced raw material and finished goods inventories* because less work-in-process allows more rapid movement of materials through the work cell.
4. *Reduced direct labor cost* because of better flow of material and improved scheduling.
5. *Heightened sense of employee participation* in the organization and the product because employees accept the added responsibility of product quality being directly associated with them and the work cell.

---

[8]Small batches in a process-oriented facility (e.g., a job shop) are called *job lots*.
[9]Burton I. Zisk, "Flexibility Is Key to Automated Material Transport System for Manufacturing Cells," *Industrial Engineering* (November 1983): 58–64 and Williams J. Dumoliem and William P. Santen, "Cellular Manufacturing Becomes Philosophy of Management at Components Facility," *Industrial Engineering* (November 1983): 72–76.

The Factory of the Future at Square D

Square D, the $1.6 billion Illinois-based manufacturer of electrical products, has revolutionized the way its employees think about work. At its Lexington, Kentucky, plant of the future, 800 workers are divided into teams of 20 to 30. Each team operates like a small business run by the workers themselves.

To accomplish this feat, Square D's plant layout has been redesigned into small factories within a factory. Each team is responsible for its product from start to finish. Now, without consulting manage-

ment, a decision to change the order in which parts are assembled is made on the spot.

The transformation of Square D began in 1988, when chairman and CEO Jerre Stead discovered that more money was being spent on painting buildings than on training employees. Just 5 years later the company was spending 4% of its payroll on worker development, versus 1% at most other firms.

With today's shift almost over, employee Gloria Henry says, "I'm proud of my job. I really think I'm somebody now." Her team, Team 440, has finished its fifty-seventh day without a rejected part. Overall, the plant's rejection rate is down 75%. And whereas it used to take 6 weeks to process the average order, Team 440 now does it in 3 days.

Source: Adapted from "American Agenda" ABC News (February 24, 1993).

6. *Increased use of equipment and machinery* because of better scheduling and faster material flow.
7. *Reduced investment in machinery and equipment* because good facility utilization reduces the number of machines and the amount of equipment and tooling.[10]

The requirements of cellular production include:

1. group technology codes or their equivalent
2. a high level of training and flexibility on the part of employees
3. either staff support or flexible, imaginative employees to establish the work cells initially.

Work cells are sometimes organized in a U-shape. U-shaped work cells, as shown in Figure 10.8, have several advantages over the straight ones. They help in five ways: (1) tasks can be grouped so inspection is immediate; (2) fewer workers are needed; (3) workers can reach more linear feet of the line; (4) the line can be more efficiently balanced; and (5) communication is enhanced.

Focused Work Center and the Focused Factory

Focused work center

Focused factory

When a firm has *identified a large family of similar products that have a large and stable demand*, it may organize a focused work center. A **focused work center** moves production from a general-purpose, process-oriented facility to a large work cell. The large work cell may be a part of the present plant, in which case it may be called a focused work center. Or it may be separated and called a **focused factory**. A fast-food

---

[10]In conflict with advantages 6 and 7, two researchers have reported an increase in capital investment and lower machine use when work cells are utilized. Perhaps different firms achieve different utilization depending on their ability to switch cell configuration and move personnel, as well as on the initial cost of their particular machinery and equipment. See Timothy J. Greene and Randall P. Sadowski, "A Review of Cellular Manufacturing Assumptions, Advantages and Design Techniques," *Journal of Operations Management*, **4**, 2 (February 1984): 85–97.

TABLE 10.2 ■ WORK CELLS, FOCUSED WORK CENTERS, AND THE FOCUSED FACTORY		
WORK CELL	**FOCUSED WORK CENTER**	**FOCUSED FACTORY**
A work cell is a temporary product-oriented arrangement of machines and personnel in what is ordinarily a process-oriented facility.	A focused work center is a permanent product-oriented arrangement of machines and personnel in what is ordinarily a process-oriented facility.	A focused factory is a permanent facility to produce a product or component in a product-oriented facility. Many of the focused factories currently being built in the United States were originally part of a process-oriented facility.
Example: A job shop with machinery and personnel rearranged to produce 30 unique control panels.	*Example:* Pipe bracket manufacturing at a shipyard.	*Example:* A plant to produce car radios.

restaurant is a focused factory. Burger King, for example, changes the number of personnel and task assignments rather than moving machines and equipment. In this manner, the company balances the assembly line to meet changing production demands. In effect, the "layout" changes numerous times each day.

The term *focused factories* may also refer to facilities that are focused in ways other than by product line or layout. For instance, facility may be focused in regard to meeting quality, new product introduction, or flexibility requirements.[11]

Focused facilities in manufacturing and in services appear to be better able to stay in tune with their customers, to produce quality products, and to operate at higher margins. This is true whether they are steel mills such as SMI, Nucor, or Chaparral, or restaurants such as McDonald's and Burger King.

Table 10.2 summarizes our discussion of work cells, focused work centers, and focused factories.

OFFICE LAYOUT

The main difference in the layout of offices and factories is the importance placed on information. In a manufacturing environment, work relies on the flow of parts and material, but office work relies on the movement of information.

Figure 10.9 shows a relationship chart. It is an extremely effective way to plan office activities. This chart, prepared for an office of consulting engineers, indicates that Ms. Payne must be (1) near the engineers' area, (2) less near the secretary and central files, and (3) not at all near the photocopy or storage room.

General office area guidelines allot an average of about 100 square feet per person (including corridors). A major executive is allotted about 400 square feet, and a conference room area is based on 25 square feet per person, up to 30 people. In contrast, restaurants provide from 16 to 50 square feet per customer (total kitchen and dining area divided by capacity). By making effective use of the vertical dimension in a workstation, some office designers expand upward instead of outward. This keeps each workstation unit (what designers call the "footprint") as small as possible.

Siemens, Germany's electronics giant, inherited this manufacturing plant in Lake Mary, Florida from Britain's Plessey Co. in 1989. To bring the plant up to world-class standards, it invested millions of dollars in a new layout. Siemens turned the flow of production from north-south to a U-shaped east-west layout that begins with receiving at one dock and shipping at another. Siemens also "cleaned up its act." Its P/OM head states: "In most companies that can lay claims to world-class operations, one of the first things you'll notice when you walk into their operations is that they're absolutely sparkling."

---

[11]See, for example, Wickham Skinner, "The Focused Factory," *Harvard Business Review*, **52**, 3 (May–June 1974): 113–121.

Once the material and information flows of any layout provide a general arrangement, the layout details must be added. This has traditionally been done on a drafting board, cardboard cutouts, or a 3-dimensional model. However, AutoDesk of Sausalito, California, has a new program, Office Layout, that has many of the features of a CAD (Computer-Aided Design) product that allows dimensions, walls, dividers, and furniture, as well as people and even plants to be included and then printed.

FIGURE 10.9   ■   Office Relationship Chart

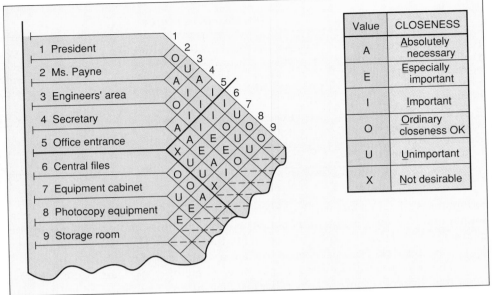

(*Source:* Adapted from Richard Muther, *Systematic Layout Planning,* 2nd ed. Boston: Cahners Publishing Company, 1973. Used by permission of the publisher.)

These American concepts of space are not universal, however. In the Tokyo office of Toyota, for example, about 110 people work in one large room.[12] As is typical of Japanese offices, they work out in the open, with desks crammed together in clusters called islands. The islands are arranged in long rows; managers sit at the ends of the rows, with their subordinates in full view. (When important visitors arrive for meetings, they are ushered into special rooms and do not see these cramped offices.)

There are additional layout considerations that are universal (some of which apply as well as to an office). They have to do with teamwork, authority, and status. Should all or only part of the work area be air conditioned? Should all employees use the same entrance, rest rooms (see the *POM in Action* box on "Potty-Parity"), lockers, and cafeteria? As mentioned earlier, layout decisions are part art and part science. Only the science part, flow of paper in an office, can be analyzed in the same manner as the flow of parts in a process layout.

RETAIL STORE LAYOUT

Retail store layouts are based on the idea that sales vary directly with customer exposure to products. Thus, most retail store operations managers try to expose customers to as many products as possible. Studies do show that the greater the rate of exposure, the greater the sales and the higher return on investment. The operations manager can alter *both* with the overall arrangement of the store and the allocation of space within that arrangement to various products.

Although the *POM in Action* box "Lettuce in Aisle 4, Loans in Aisle 10 at Kroger" suggests that there is no longer any set pattern for store layouts, we can still

[12]"Think Japan Inc. Is Lean and Mean? Step into This Office," *The New York Times* (March 20, 1994).

Potty-Parity Lead to Calls for New Bathroom Layouts

In Texas, an aide to a legislator spent one-third of his evening at a rock festival, keeping his girlfriend company in a forty-five-minute line for the ladies bathroom. In Washington, DC, a congresswoman missed the entire show of her home-state Ohio University marching band as she waited in a queue at the women's room. And a legal secretary in Houston, Denise Wells, was arrested for using the men's room at a concert when she found twenty people waiting to enter the women's room and none the men's. (She was found not guilty after the jury deliberated just twenty-three minutes.)

Events such as these have led to a spate of new legislation that would require theaters, stadiums, and convention halls to provide twice as many toilets for women as for men. Over a dozen states now mandate "potty parity," and more have bills pending. Pro-parity legislators have been able to tap into a well-spring of academic research to support their views. Virginia Tech professors, for example, found that women needed about twice as much time in restrooms as men. In sports arenas, women needed 3 minutes, whereas men a mere 83.6 seconds.

But Denver's new Colorado Convention Center has tackled the problem as one of creative layout. Men's and women's rooms are now separated with a movable wall. When the mostly female Nurses Society hits town, the convention center can produce women's rooms that are three times bigger than men's. For the predominantly male Petroleum Geologists, the center will reverse the ratio. Other proposals by architects call for unisex hand-washing areas or unisex restrooms, which many European centers have had for decades.

Source: Adapted from the *Wall Street Journal* (February 24, 1994): A1.

note five ideas that are helpful for determining the overall arrangement of retail stores such as supermarkets and drug stores.

1. Locate the high-draw items around the periphery of the store. Thus, we tend to find dairy products on one side of a supermarket and bread and bakery products on another. An example of this is shown in Figure 10.10.

2. Use prominent locations for high-impulse and high-margin items such as housewares, beauty aids, and shampoos.

FIGURE 10.10 ■ Store Layout with Dairy and Bread, High-Draw Items, in Different Corners of the Store

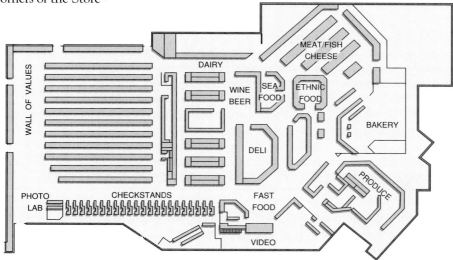

Lettuce in Aisle 4, Loans in Aisle 10 at Kroger

One reason supermarkets look much as they did 40 years ago is that they have all been using the same layout. But demographics and shopping patterns are changing. More and more, food is being purchased in restaurants, from fine dining to fast-food and carry-out. This is partly because both parents work in more families, and also because we have become more of a grazing, or nibbling, society. The bottom line is that the number of home-prepared meals, and the related purchase of groceries, is declining. Consequently, supermarkets are rethinking their layouts.

The modern supermarket may now include a fast-food restaurant, a deli, a photo lab, a video store, and a place to pay your bills. The high-draw items, such as meats, dairy, bakery, and produce items, are still at the far ends of the store, but high-margin items like deli, gourmet foods, pharmacy, beer and wine, and cosmetics are positioned for maximum exposure. And a variety of other services have been added to draw customers.

One of them is banking. NCB, for example, has added fourteen branches in Kroger's Memphis supermarkets. Enthusiastic young NCB bankers stop people in the aisles and use the public address system to push loans and promote the consumer banking services available from the NCB office in the store. The bright, verbal, and attractive (BVAer's, they're called) supermarket bankers do triple duty as tellers, loan officers, and salespeople who even know where to find the Cheez Whiz.

Sources: Adapted from *Forbes* (August 3, 1992): 39–40; *Forbes*, (February 17, 1992): 58–63; and the *Wall Street Journal* (May 20, 1994): B1.

Federal-Mogul, a large manufacturer of auto engine parts, took a radical approach to the layout of its state-of-the-art distribution center in Alabama. With over 50,000 different stock items that must be stored, retrieved, picked, packed, and shipped, a non-automated system simply wouldn't work. The solution was a 70-foot-high, 7-mile automated storage and retrieval system, a 26-aisle, 24-foot-high rail guided picking vehicle system, and a generous dose of computer control.

3. Distribute what are known in the trade as "power items"—items that may dominate a shopping trip—to both sides of an aisle, and disperse them to increase the viewing of other items.

4. Use end aisle locations because they have a very high exposure rate.

5. Convey the image of the store by careful selection in the positioning of the lead-off department. Some stores position the bakery and deli up front to appeal to convenience-oriented customers who want prepared foods.

Once the overall layout of a retail store has been decided, the products need to be arranged for sale. Many considerations go into this arrangement. However, the main *objective of retail layout is to maximize profitability per square foot of shelf space* (some stores may base this profitability on linear foot of shelf space in lieu of square foot of shelf space). Big-ticket, or expensive, items may yield greater dollar sales, but the profit per square foot may be lower. A number of computerized programs exist that can assist managers in evaluating the profitability of various merchandise. One, SLIM (Store Labor and Inventory Management), can help store managers determine when shelf space is adequate to accommodate another full case. Another software package is COSMOS (Computerized Optimization and Simulation Modeling for Operating Supermarkets), which matches shelf space with delivery schedules, allocating sufficient space to minimize out-of-stock between receipts.

WAREHOUSING AND STORAGE LAYOUTS

The objective of *warehouse layout* is to find the optimum trade-off between handling cost and warehouse space. Thus, management must maximize the use of the total "cube" of the warehouse—that is, use its full volume while maintaining low material handling costs. We define material handling costs as all the costs related to the incoming transport, storage, and outgoing transport of the material. These costs include equipment, people, material, supervision, insurance, and depreciation. Effective warehouse layout must, of course, also minimize the damage and spoilage of material within the warehouse. Management minimizes the sum of the resources spent on retrieving material plus the deterioration and damage to the material itself. The variety of items stored and the number of items "picked" have direct bearing on the optimum layout. A warehouse storing a few items lends itself to higher density more than does a warehouse storing a variety of items. Modern warehouse management is, in many instances, an automated procedure utilizing automatic stacking cranes, conveyors, and sophisticated controls that manage the flow of materials. Examples of firms that use the latest technology include Federal-Mogul and The Gap, both illustrated in photos.

PRODUCT-ORIENTED LAYOUT

Product-oriented layouts are organized around a product or a family of similar high-volume, low-variety products. Repetitive production and continuous production, discussed in Chapter 7, use product layouts. The assumptions are:

1. Volume is adequate for high equipment utilization.
2. Product demand is stable enough to justify high investment in specialized equipment.
3. Product is standardized or approaching a phase of its life cycle that justifies investment in specialized equipment.
4. Supplies of raw material and components are adequate and of uniform quality (adequately standardized) to ensure that they will work with the specialized equipment.

Two types of a product-oriented layout are a fabrication line and an assembly line. The **fabrication line** builds components, such as automobile tires or metal parts for a refrigerator, on a series of machines. An **assembly line** puts the fabricated parts together at a series of workstations. Both are repetitive processes, and in both cases, the line must be "balanced." That is, the work performed on one machine must balance with the work performed on the next machine in the fabrication line, just as the work done at one workstation by an employee on an assembly line must match up in time with the work done at the next workstation by the next employee.

Fabrication lines tend to be machine-paced and require mechanical and engineering changes to facilitate balancing. Assembly lines, on the other hand, tend to be paced by work tasks assigned to individuals or to workstations. Assembly lines, therefore, can be balanced by moving tasks from one individual to another. In this manner, the amount of *time* required by each individual or station is equalized. The Boeing photo shows that the final assembly of even some huge products, such as a Boeing 747 airplane, is done in a product layout.

The central problem in product-oriented layout planning is to balance the output at each workstation on the production line so that it is nearly the same, while obtaining the desired amount of output. Management's goal is to create a smooth, continuous flow along the assembly line with a minimum of idle time at each person's workstation. A well-balanced assembly line has the advantage of high personnel and

Fabrication line
Assembly line

Flex Time for Galleys?

Galleys and lavatories are headaches for aircraft builders and airlines alike. Because they define the areas of a plane, separating coach, business, and first class, each airline wants a different layout based on its route and passenger configurations.

For example, an airline that flies long-distance routes carrying a high proportion of business travelers would probably specify an airplane with expanded first- and business-class sections and a shrunken coach cabin. But an airline that caters more to cost-conscious tourists might eliminate the high-priced seats entirely.

"We have to redesign each time we get a new customer," says Boeing designer Ron Ostrowski. "It is a nightmare in the factory and it wastes engineering time."

Airlines have a problem of buying planes with one type of market in mind and then having conditions change. For example, grounding a 747 for as much as 3 weeks to redo the interior results in substantial revenue loss.

To deal with this problem, Boeing has developed an optional layout for its new 777 that allows galleys and lavatories to be repositioned in as little as 1 day, despite the complexity of the wiring and plumbing.

But the penalty for flexibility is added weight, because of extra fittings and plumbing equipment. The more an empty airplane weighs, the fewer revenue-producing passengers and less cargo it can carry. The plane's range also is limited. Layout flexibility in planes, as in factories, is not cheap.

Sources: The New York Times (Nov. 10, 1991): 3–1 and *Aviation Week* (July 19, 1993): 56–7.

Assembly line balancing

facility utilization *and* equity between employees' work loads. Some union contracts include a requirement that work loads must be nearly equal among those on the same assembly line. The term most often used to describe this process is **assembly line balancing**. Indeed, the *objective of the product-oriented layout is to minimize imbalance in the fabrication or assembly line.*

The main advantage of product-oriented layout is the low variable cost per unit usually associated with high-volume, standardized products. The product-oriented layout also keeps material handling costs low, reduces work-in-process inventories, and makes training and supervision easier. These advantages often outweigh the disadvantages of product layout. These disadvantages are as follows:

1. High volume is required because of the large investment needed to set up the process.
2. Work stoppage at any one point ties up the whole operation.
3. There is a lack of flexibility in handling a variety of products or production rates.

Because the problems of fabrication lines and assembly lines are similar, we phrase our discussion in terms of an assembly line. On an assembly line, the product typically moves via automated means, such as a conveyor, through a series of workstations until completed (Figure 10.11). This is the way automobiles are assembled, television sets and ovens are produced, and fast-food hamburgers are made. Product-oriented layout uses more automated and specially designed equipment than is found in a process layout.

Assembly Line Balancing

Line balancing is usually done to minimize imbalance between machines or personnel while meeting a required output from the line. To balance a line, management must

FIGURE 10.11 ■ An Assembly-Line Layout

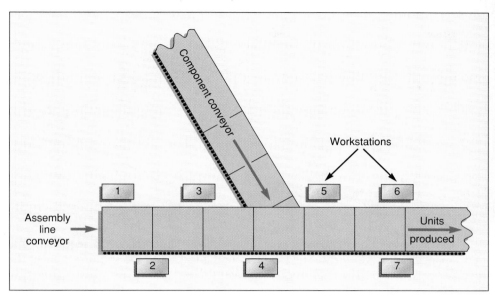

The Gap, Inc., strives for both high quality and low costs. It does this by (1) designing its own clothes, (2) quality control at the vendors, and (3) maintaining downward pressure on distribution costs. A new automatic distribution center near Baltimore, Maryland, is designed to allow The Gap to stock East Coast stores daily, rather than three times a week.

know the tools, equipment, and work methods used. Then the time requirements for each assembly task (such as drilling a hole, tightening a nut, or spray painting a part) must be determined. Management also needs to know the precedence relationship among the activities, that is, the order in which various tasks need to be performed. Example 2 shows how to turn these task data into a precedence diagram.

EXAMPLE 2

We want to develop a precedence diagram for an electrostatic copier that requires a total assembly time of sixty-six minutes. Table 10.3 and Figure 10.12 give the tasks, assembly times, and sequence requirements for the copier.

TABLE 10.3 ■ PRECEDENCE DATA

TASK	PERFORMANCE TIME (MINUTES)	TASK MUST FOLLOW TASK LISTED BELOW	
A	10	—	
B	11	A	This means that
C	5	B	tasks B and E
D	4	B	cannot be done
E	12	A	until task A has
F	3	C, D	been completed.
G	7	F	
H	11	E	
I	3	G, H	
Total time	66		

FIGURE 10.12   ■   Precedence Diagram

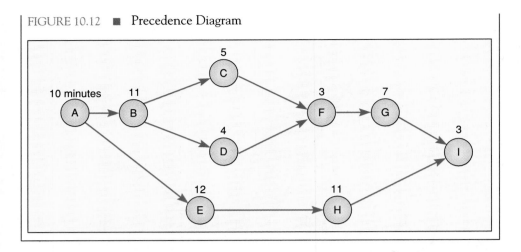

Once we have constructed a precedence chart summarizing the sequences and performance times, we turn to the job of grouping tasks into job stations to meet the specified production rate. This process involves three steps:

Cycle time

1. Take the demand (or production rate) per day and divide it into the productive time available per day (in minutes or seconds). This operation gives us the **cycle time**, namely, the time the product is available at each workstation:

$$\text{Cycle time} = \frac{\text{production time available per day}}{\text{demand per day or production per day}} \qquad (10.2)$$

2. Calculate the theoretical minimum number of workstations. This is the total task-duration time divided by the cycle time. Fractions are rounded to the next higher whole number:

$$\text{Minimum number of workstations} = \frac{\sum_{i=1}^{m} \text{time for task } i}{\text{cycle time}} \qquad (10.3)$$

where m is the number of assembly tasks.

3. Perform the line balance by assigning specific assembly tasks to each workstation. An efficient balance is one that will complete the required assembly, follow the specified sequence, and keep the idle time at each workstation to a minimum. A formal procedure for doing this is:

   (a) Identify a master list of work elements and separate the available work elements from the unavailable work elements.

   (b) Eliminate those work elements that have been assigned.

   (c) Eliminate those work elements whose precedence relationship has not been satisfied.

   (d) Eliminate those elements for which there is inadequate time available at the workstation.

   (e) Identify a unit of work that can be assigned, such as the first unit of work in the list, the last unit of work in the list, the unit of work with the shortest time, the unit of work with the longest time, a randomly selected unit of work, or some other criterion.

(f) Switch the work elements to find the best balance available.

Example 3 illustrates a simple line-balancing procedure.

EXAMPLE 3

On the basis of the precedence diagram and activity times given in Example 2, the firm determines that there are 480 productive minutes of work available per day. Furthermore, the production schedule requires that 40 units be completed as output from the assembly line each day. Hence,

$$\text{Cycle time (in minutes)} = \frac{480 \text{ minutes}}{40 \text{ units}}$$

$$= 12 \text{ minutes/unit}$$

$$\text{Minimum number of workstations} = \frac{\text{total task time}}{\text{cycle time}} = \frac{66}{12}$$

$$= 5.5 \text{ or } 6 \text{ stations}$$

FIGURE 10.13 ■ A Six-Station Solution to the Line-Balancing Problem

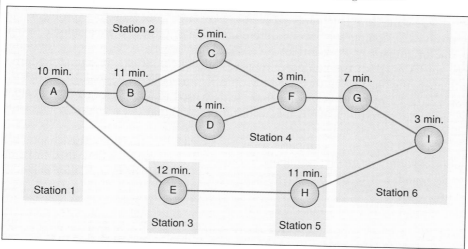

Boeing, Seattle's largest employer and the world's largest manufacturer of commercial jetliners, employs a modular construction to assemble its "parts." These "parts" of tail, aft body section, center body section, wings, front body, and nose are joined above. Workers "inch" the body sections together, measuring and leveling them for a perfect fit. Landing gear is installed and the airplane is ready for its final five assembly line operations.

Figure 10.13 shows one solution that does not violate the sequence requirements and in which the tasks are grouped into six stations. To obtain this solution, appropriate activities were moved into workstations that use as much of the available cycle time of 12 minutes as possible. The first workstation consumes 10 minutes and has an idle time of 2 minutes.

The second workstation uses 11 minutes, and the third consumes the full 12 minutes. The fourth workstation groups three small tasks and balances perfectly at 12 minutes. The fifth has 1 minute of idle time, and the sixth (consisting of tasks G and I) has 2 minutes of idle time per cycle. Total idle time for this solution is 6 minutes per cycle.

We can compute the efficiency of a line balance by dividing the total task time by the product of the number of workstations times the assigned cycle time:

$$\text{Efficiency} = \frac{\sum \text{task times}}{(\text{number of workstations}) \times (\text{assigned cycle time})} \quad (10.4)$$

Management often compares different levels of efficiency for various numbers of workstations. In this way, the firm can determine the sensitivity of the line to changes in the production rate and workstation assignments.

In the case of slaughtering operations, the assembly line is actually a disassembly line. The line balancing procedures described in this chapter are the same as for an assembly line. The chicken processing plant shown here must balance the work of several hundred employees. Division of labor produces efficiency. Because one's skills develop with repetition, there is less time lost in changing tools, and specialized tools are developed. The total labor content in each of the chickens processed is a few minutes. How long would it take you to process a chicken by yourself?

EXAMPLE 4

We can calculate the balance efficiency for Example 3 as follows:

$$\text{Efficiency} = \frac{66 \text{ minutes}}{(6 \text{ stations}) \times (12 \text{ minutes})} = \frac{66}{72} = 91.7\%$$

Opening a seventh workstation, for whatever reason, would decrease the efficiency of the balance to 78.6%:

$$\text{Efficiency} = \frac{66 \text{ minutes}}{(7 \text{ stations}) \times (12 \text{ minutes})} = 78.6\%$$

Large-scale line-balancing problems, like large process-layout problems, are often solved by computers. Several different computer programs are available to handle the assignment of workstations on assembly lines with 100 (or more) individual work activities. Both the computer routine called COMSOAL (Computer Method for Sequencing Operations for Assembly Lines)[13] and ASYBL (General Electric's Assembly Line Configuration program) are widely used in larger problems to evaluate the thousands or millions of possible workstation combinations much more efficiently than could ever be done by hand.

The AB:POM microcomputer software described at the end of this chapter also handles a variety of smaller problems and illustrates the problem described in Examples 2, 3, and 4. It offers five different heuristics (or "rules of thumb") for balancing the line.

ACHIEVING WORLD-CLASS STANDARDS

World-class organizations pay a great deal of attention to facility layouts because layout affects the whole company's performance. As service-oriented firms compete for customers, they focus on strategies that keep the customers' needs in mind. The opening quotation in this chapter describes Wal-Mart's redesign to make shopping more comfortable and organized. World-class retailers increase their sales by optimizing shelf layout with computer programs such as COSMOS and SLIM.

---

[13]A. L. Arcus, "COMSOAL: A Computer Method of Sequencing Operations for Assembly Line," *International Journal of Production Research*, **4**, 4 (1966).

Automobile Disassembly Lines: The Wave of the Ecologically Correct Future

Visionaries like Walter Chrysler and Louis Chevrolet could not have imagined the sprawling graveyards of rusting cars and trucks that bear testimony to the automotive culture they helped invent. These days, the graveyards are shrinking slightly, however. "By the end of the century we think people will be buying cars based on how 'green' they are," says David Millerick, Ford's manager of vehicle recycling. Millerick's counterpart at BMW, Horst Wolf, agrees: "In the long term, all new vehicles will have to be designed in such a way that their materials can be easily reused in the next generation of cars."

BMW, sensitive to the political power of Germany's Green movement, has already built a pilot "auto disassembly" plant. In the United States, the company offers $500 toward the purchase of a new-model BMW to anyone bringing a junked BMW to its salvage centers in New York, Los Angeles, or Orlando.

The disassembly line involves removing most of a car's plastic parts and sorting them for recycling. But this is not easy. Disassembly alone might take five people an hour. BMW also had to invent tools to safely puncture and drain fuel tanks with gas in them. Various plastics are recycled differently, so each must be labeled or color-coded. Some types of plastics can be remelted and turned into new parts, such as intake manifolds. Nissan Motor, with disassembly plants in Germany and Japan, now turns 2,000 bumpers a month into air ducts, foot rests, bumper parts, and shipping pallets.

The scrap metal part of the disassembly line is easier. With shredders and magnets, baseball-sized chunks of metal are sorted after the engines, transmissions, radio, batteries, and exhausts have been removed. Steel makers have helped over the past 20 years by building minimills that use scrap metal.

The ironic twist for an industry pushed to improve the crashworthiness of its vehicles is that automakers now also need to design cars and trucks that will come apart more easily.

Sources: Adapted from *The New York Times* (September 8, 1992): and *Machine Design* (February 12, 1993): 56–57.

World-class manufacturers look for flexibility in layouts, so that changes in product models and in production rates are easy and quick. To obtain flexibility in layout, they cross-train their workers, maintain equipment in top condition, keep their inventories low, place workstations close together, and use small, flexible equipment. By following the Japanese model, layouts are close and compact, with more U-shaped production lines that permit worker interaction and job rotation. World-class companies also use more cellular manufacturing layouts.

In terms of material handling and warehousing, world-class firms keep costs low with automation. "Dark warehouses," run by a handful of employees and their fleet of automated guided vehicles (AGVs), use sophisticated computer-driven systems. At Tupperware International's South Carolina facility, for example, human hands need not touch an order as it is plucked from its shelf and boxed.

SUMMARY

Good layout strategies make a substantial difference in operating efficiency. The six classic layout situations are (1) fixed position, (2) process-oriented, (3) office, (4) retail, (5) warehouse, and (6) product-oriented. A variety of techniques have been developed in attempts to solve these layout problems. Industrial firms focus on reducing material movement and assembly line balancing. Retail firms focus on product exposure. Storage layouts focus on the optimum trade-offs between storage costs and material handling costs.

Often the variables in the layout problem are so wide-ranging and numerous as to preclude finding an optimal solution. For this reason, layout decisions, although having received substantial research effort, remain something of an art.

KEY TERMS

Fixed-position layout (p. 404)
Process-oriented layout (p. 404)
Office layout (p. 404)
Retail/service layout (p. 404)
Warehouse layout (p. 404)
Product-oriented layout (p. 404)
Job lot (p. 407)
CRAFT (p. 411)

SPACECRAFT (p. 411)
Work cell (p. 413)
Focused work center (p. 414)
Focused factory (p. 414)
Fabrication line (p. 419)
Assembly line (p. 419)
Assembly line balancing (p. 420)
Cycle time (p. 422)

USING AB:POM TO SOLVE LAYOUT PROBLEMS

Solving Example 1 Using AB:POM's Operations Layout Module

AB:POM's facility layout module can be used to place up to ten departments in ten rooms in order to minimize the total distance traveled as a function of the distances between the rooms and the flow between departments. The program performs pairwise comparisons, exchanging departments until no exchange will reduce the total amount of movement.

After the number of departments is entered (which is 6 in the case of Example 1), then the data screen will be generated and appear as in Program 10.1. The data essentially consist of two tables of numbers—one for the flows and one for the distances.

PROGRAM 10.1 ■ AB:POM's Operations Layout Program Applied to Example 1's Walter's Company Data. Departments may be named in their columns. Typically, the distance matrix will be symmetric. If not, all entries must be made. The solution appears on the right-hand side of the printout.

Data file: WALTERS			Operations Layout			Solution	
Number of departments (3–10)	6					Symmetric distances	

WALTERS COMPANY, EXAMPLE 1

Flow matrix

	Dept 1	Dept 2	Dept 3	Dept 4	Dept 5	Dept 6	Department in Room	
Dept 1	0	50	100	0	0	20	Dept 1 in	Room 3
Dept 2	0	0	30	50	10	0	Dept 2 in	Room 5
Dept 3	0	0	0	20	0	100	Dept 3 in	Room 2
Dept 4	0	0	0	0	50	0	Dept 4 in	Room 4
Dept 5	0	0	0	0	0	0	Dept 5 in	Room 1
Dept 6	0	0	0	0	0	0	Dept 6 in	Room 6
								(cont'd)

(Program 10.1 cont'd)

Distance Matrix

	Room 1	Room 2	Room 3	Room 4	Room 5	Room 6
Room 1	0	1	2	1	1	2
Room 2	1	0	2	1	1	1
Room 3	2	1	0	2	1	1
Room 4	1	1	2	0	1	2
Room 5	1	1	1	1	0	1
Room 6	2	1	1	2	1	0

The total movement is 430

Solving Examples 2, 3, and 4 Using AB:POM's Assembly Line-Balancing Module

AB:POM's module for line balancing can handle a line with up to 99 tasks, each with up to six immediate predecessors. Programs 10.2 and 10.3 illustrate the input and output computer screens for this module applied to Examples 2, 3, and 4.

PROGRAM 10.2 ■ AB:POM's Assembly Line-Balancing Program Data Entry Screen. Cycle time can be entered in two ways: (1) either directly to the right of "cycle time" if known or (2) demand rate can be entered with time available as shown below. Five "heuristic rules" may be used: (1) longest operation time, (2) most following tasks, (3) ranked positional weight, (4) shortest operation time, and (5) least number of following tasks. No one rule can guarantee an optimal solution. The default rule is the longest operation time.

——————— Balancing, Assembly line ——————— Data Screen ———————

Number of tasks (1–99)   9

——————— ASSEMBLY LINE BALANCING, EXAMPLES 2–4 ———————

Rule   Longest operation time

Demand rate   40 units per   480.00 minutes

Cycle Time   0.00

Task	minutes	Predecessors						
a	10.00	– –	– –	– –	– –	– –	– –	– –
b	11.00	A	– –	– –	– –	– –	– –	– –
c	5.00	B	– –	– –	– –	– –	– –	– –
d	4.00	B	– –	– –	– –	– –	– –	– –
e	12.00	A	– –	– –	– –	– –	– –	– –
f	3.00	C	D	– –	– –	– –	– –	– –
g	7.00	F	– –	– –	– –	– –	– –	– –
h	11.00	E	– –	– –	– –	– –	– –	– –
i	3.00	G	H	– –	– –	– –	– –	– –

PROGRAM 10.3   ■   AB:POM's Assembly Line-Balancing Output for Examples 2–4 and Program 10.2. Note that longest operation time heuristic provides a different solution than the one we found in Figure 10.13.

─────────────────────── ASSEMBLY LINE BALANCING, EXAMPLES 2–4 ───────────────────────

Longest operation time   cycle time = 12 minutes

Station	Task	Time	Time left	ready tasks
				a
1	a	10.00	2.00	b, e
2	e	12.00	0.00	b, h
3	b	11.00	1.00	h, c, d
4	h	11.00	1.00	c, d
5	c	5.00	7.00	d
	d	4.00	3.00	f
	f	3.00	0.00	g
6	g	7.00	5.00	i
	i	3.00	2.00	

Time allocated (cyc*sta) =   72.00; Min (theoretical) # of stations = 6
Time needed (sum task)   =   66.00; EFFICIENCY = 91.67%;
Idle time (alloc-needed) =   6.00 minutes per cycle

─────────────────────────────────────

SOLVED PROBLEMS

Solved Problem 10.1

The Snow-Bird Hospital is a small emergency-oriented facility located in a popular ski resort area in northern Michigan. Its new administrator, Mary Lord, decides to reorganize the hospital, using the process-layout method she studied in business school. The current layout of Snow-Bird's eight emergency departments is shown in Figure 10.14.

FIGURE 10.14   ■   Snow-Bird Hospital Layout

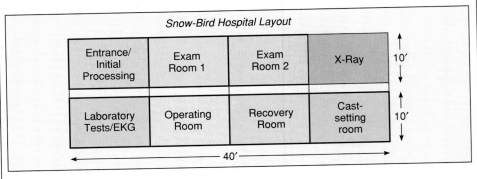

The only physical restriction Lord perceives is the need to keep the entrance and initial processing room in its current location. All other departments or rooms (each 10 feet square) can be moved if the layout analysis indicates this would be beneficial.

Mary's first step is to analyze records in order to determine the number of trips made by patients between departments in an average month. The data are shown in Figure 10.15. The objective, Lord decides, is to lay out the rooms so as to minimize the total distance walked by patients who enter for treatment. She writes her objective as:

$$\text{Minimize patient movement} = \sum_{i=1}^{8} \sum_{j=1}^{8} X_{ij} C_{ij}$$

where X_{ij} = number of patients per month (loads or trips) moving from department i to department j

C_{ij} = distance in feet between departments i and j (which, in this case, is the equivalent of cost per load to move between departments)

Note that this is only a slight modification of the cost-objective equation shown earlier in the chapter.

FIGURE 10.15 ■ Number of Patients Moving between Departments in One Month

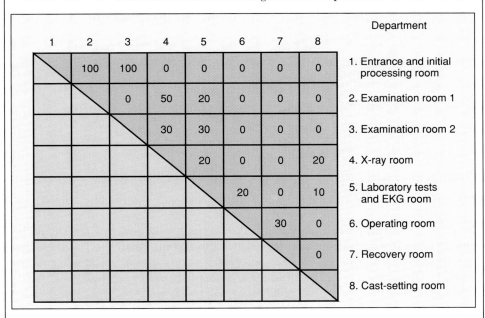

	1	2	3	4	5	6	7	8	Department
		100	100	0	0	0	0	0	1. Entrance and initial processing room
			0	50	20	0	0	0	2. Examination room 1
				30	30	0	0	0	3. Examination room 2
					20	0	0	20	4. X-ray room
						20	0	10	5. Laboratory tests and EKG room
							30	0	6. Operating room
								0	7. Recovery room
									8. Cast-setting room

Departments next to one another, such as the entrance and examination room 1, are assumed to carry a walking distance of 10 feet. Diagonal departments are also considered adjacent and assigned a distance of 10 feet. Nonadjacent departments such as the entrance and examination room 2 or the entrance and recovery room are 20 feet apart, and nonadjacent rooms such as entrance and X-ray are 30 feet apart. (Hence, 10 feet is considered 10 units of cost, 20 feet is 20 units of cost, and 30 feet is 30 units of cost.)

Given the above information, redo the layout of Snow-Bird Hospital to improve its efficiency in terms of patient flow.

Solution

First, establish Snow-Bird's current layout, as shown in Figure 10.16. By using Snow-Bird's current layout, the patient movement may be computed.

$$
\begin{aligned}
\text{Total movement} = &\underset{\text{1 to 2}}{(100 \times 10')} + \underset{\text{1 to 3}}{(100 \times 20')} + \underset{\text{2 to 4}}{(50 \times 20')} + \underset{\text{2 to 5}}{(20 \times 10')} \\
&+ \underset{\text{3 to 4}}{(30 \times 10')} + \underset{\text{3 to 5}}{(30 \times 20')} + \underset{\text{4 to 5}}{(20 \times 30')} + \underset{\text{4 to 8}}{(20 \times 10')} \\
&+ \underset{\text{5 to 6}}{(20 \times 10')} + \underset{\text{5 to 8}}{(10 \times 30')} + \underset{\text{6 to 7}}{(30 \times 10')} \\
= &\ 1{,}000 + 2{,}000 + 1{,}000 + 200 + 300 + 600 + 600 \\
&+ 200 + 200 + 300 + 300 \\
= &\ 6{,}700 \text{ feet}
\end{aligned}
$$

FIGURE 10.16　■　Current Snow-Bird Patient Flow

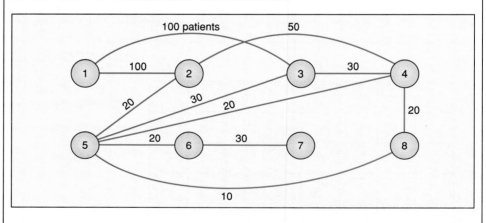

It is not possible to prove a mathematically "optimal" solution, but you should be able to propose a new layout that will reduce the current figure of 6,700 feet. Two useful changes, for example, are to switch rooms 3 and 5 and to interchange rooms 4 and 6. This change would result in the schematic shown in Figure 10.17.

$$
\begin{aligned}
\text{Total movement} = &\underset{\text{1 to 2}}{(100 \times 10')} + \underset{\text{1 to 3}}{(100 \times 10')} + \underset{\text{2 to 4}}{(50 \times 10')} + \underset{\text{2 to 5}}{(20 \times 10')} \\
&+ \underset{\text{3 to 4}}{(30 \times 10')} + \underset{\text{3 to 5}}{(30 \times 20')} + \underset{\text{4 to 5}}{(20 \times 10')} + \underset{\text{4 to 8}}{(20 \times 20')} \\
&+ \underset{\text{5 to 6}}{(20 \times 10')} + \underset{\text{5 to 8}}{(10 \times 10')} + \underset{\text{6 to 7}}{(30 \times 10')} \\
= &\ 1{,}000 + 1{,}000 + 500 + 200 + 300 + 600 + 200 \\
&+ 400 + 200 + 100 + 300 \\
= &\ 4{,}800 \text{ feet}
\end{aligned}
$$

FIGURE 10.17 ■ Improved Layout

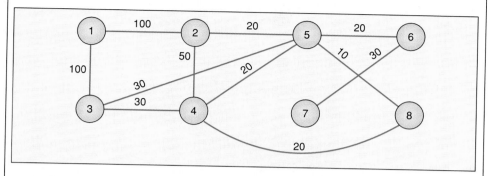

Do you see any room for further improvement? (See Homework Problem 10.2.)

Solved Problem 10.2

An assembly line, whose activities are shown in Figure 10.18, has an 8-minute cycle time. Draw the precedence graph and find the minimum possible number of workstations. Then arrange the work activities into workstations so as to balance the line. What is the efficiency of this line balance?

TASK	PERFORMANCE TIME (MINUTES)	TASK MUST FOLLOW THIS TASK
A	5	—
B	3	A
C	4	B
D	3	B
E	6	C
F	1	C
G	4	D, E, F
H	$\dfrac{2}{28}$	G

Solution

The theoretical minimum number of workstations is

$$\frac{\sum t_i}{\text{Cycle time}} = \frac{28 \text{ minutes}}{8 \text{ minutes}} = 3.5 \text{ or 4 stations}$$

The precedence graph and one good layout are shown in Figure 10.18.

$$\text{Efficiency} = \frac{\text{total task time}}{(\text{number of workstations}) \times (\text{cycle time})} = \frac{28}{(4)(8)} = 87.5\%$$

FIGURE 10.18   ■   A Four-Station Solution to the Line-Balancing Problem

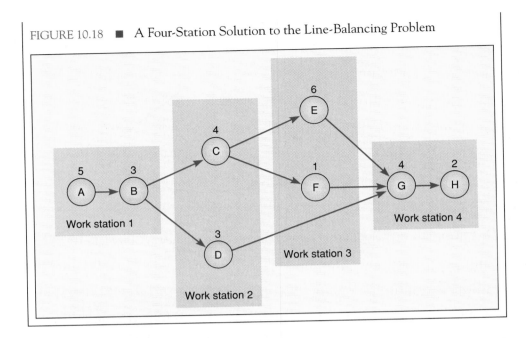

DISCUSSION QUESTIONS

1. What is the layout strategy of your local print shop?

2. How would you go about collecting data to help a small business, like a print shop, improve its layout?

3. What are the six layout strategies presented in this chapter?

4. What are the advantages and disadvantages of product layout?

5. What are the advantages and disadvantages of process layout?

6. What are the advantages and disadvantages of work cells?

7. What layout innovations have you noticed recently in retail establishments?

8. What techniques can be used to overcome the inherent problems of fixed-position layout?

9. What layout variables might you want to consider as particularly important in an office layout where computer programs are written?

10. What is required for a focused work center or focused factory to be appropriate?

11. Which of the layout types described in this chapter assume that demand is stable?

12. What are the variables that a manager can manipulate in a retail store layout?

13. Visit a local supermarket and sketch its layout. What are your major observations regarding departments and their locations?

14. Given that most engineering students in the United States are male, and that most nursing students are female, should colleges build classroom buildings to accommodate the actual ratio of the sexes? (See the "Potty-Parity" P/OM in Action box.)

CRITICAL THINKING EXERCISE

Our discussion of office layout included a note about the difference between U.S. and Japanese firms. Offices are more cramped and less automated in Japan; it also is not uncommon for two workers to share a telephone. No one at Tokyo's Toyota office has his or her own PC; rather, there is an alcove of machines to share.

Discuss your perceptions of the importance of the U.S. and Japanese styles of office layout. Which yields greater productivity?

: **10.1** Given the following flow and distance matrices in Roy Martin's job shop, what is the appropriate layout?

FLOW MATRIX

	DEPT. A	DEPT. B	DEPT. C	DEPT. D	DEPT. E	DEPT. F
Dept. A	0	100	50	0	0	50
Dept. B	25	0	0	50	0	0
Dept. C	25	0	0	0	50	0
Dept. D	0	25	0	0	20	0
Dept. E	50	0	100	0	0	0
Dept. F	10	0	20	0	0	0

DISTANCE MATRIX

	DEPT. A	DEPT. B	DEPT. C	DEPT. D	DEPT. E	DEPT. F
Dept. A	0	1	2	3	4	5
Dept. B	1	0	5	4	3	2
Dept. C	2	5	0	6	7	6
Dept. D	3	4	6	0	4	3
Dept. E	4	3	7	4	0	5
Dept. F	5	2	6	3	5	0

: **10.2** In Solved Problem 10.1 we improved Snow-Bird's layout to 4,800 feet of movement. Is an improved layout possible? What is it?

: **10.3** Registration period at Southeastern University has always been a time of emotion, commotion, and lines. Students must move among four stations to complete the trying semiannual process. Last semester's registration, held in the fieldhouse, is described in Figure 10.19. You can see, for example, that 450 students moved from the paper-work station (A) to advising (B), and 550 went directly from A to picking up their class cards (C). Graduate students, who for the most part had preregistered, proceeded directly from A to the station where the registration was verified and payment collected (D). The layout used last semester is also shown in Figure 10.19. The registrar is preparing to set up this semester's stations and is anticipating similar numbers.

a) What is the "load × distance," or cost, of the layout shown?

b) Provide an improved layout and compute its cost.

FIGURE 10.19 ■ Registration Flow of Students

Interstation Activity Mix

	Pickup paperwork and forms (A)	Advising station (B)	Pickup class cards (C)	Verification of status and payment (D)
Paperwork/forms (A)	---	450	550	50
Advising (B)	250	---	200	0
Class cards (C)	0	0	---	750
Verification/payment (D)	0	0	0	---

Existing Layout

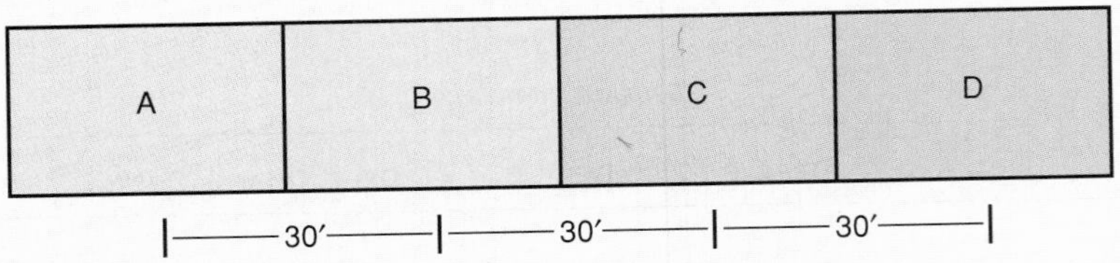

: **10.4** You have just been hired as the Director of Operations for Bellas Chocolates, in Blacksburg, Virginia, a purveyor of exceptionally fine chocolates. Bellas Chocolates has two kitchen layouts under consideration for its recipe-making and testing department. The strategy is to provide the best kitchen layout possible so the food scientists can devote their time and energy toward product improvement, not wasted effort in the kitchen. You have been asked to evaluate these two kitchen layouts and to prepare a recommendation for your boss, Mr. Bellas, so that he can proceed with placing the contract for building the testing kitchens. (See Figure 10.20.)

FIGURE 10.20 ■ Layout Options

Number of trips between work centers:

From: \ To:	Refrigerator 1	Counter 2	Sink 3	Storage 4	Stove 5
Refrig. 1	0	8	13	0	0
Counter 2	5	0	3	3	8
Sink 3	3	12	0	4	0
Storage 4	3	0	0	0	5
Stove 5	0	8	4	10	0

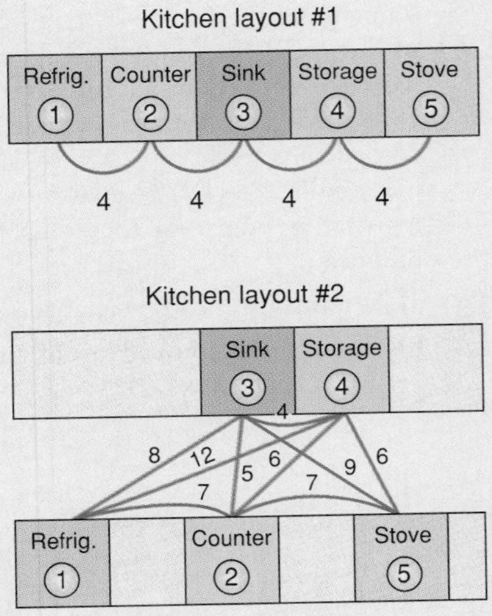

Kitchen layout #1

Kitchen layout #2

: **10.5** Bellas Chocolates (see Problem 10.4) is considering a third layout, as shown below. Evaluate its effectiveness in trip-distance feet.

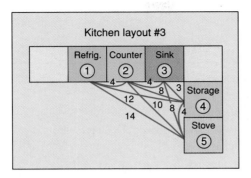

: **10.6** Bellas Chocolates (see Problems 10.4 and 10.5) has yet two more layouts to consider.

   a) Layout #4 is shown below. What is the total trip distance?

   b) Layout #5, also below, has what total trip distance?

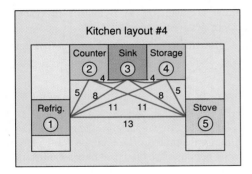

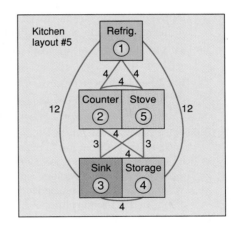

· **10.7** Given the following task, times, and sequence, develop a balanced line capable of operating with a 10-minute cycle time at Paul Reed's company. What is the efficiency of that line?

TASK ELEMENT	TIME (MINUTES)	ELEMENT PREDECESSOR
A	3	—
B	5	A
C	7	B
D	5	—
E	3	C
F	3	B, D
G	5	D
H	6	G

: **10.8** The preinduction physical examination given by the U.S. Army involves the following seven activities:

ACTIVITY	AVERAGE TIME (MINUTES)
Medical history	10
Blood tests	8
Eye examination	5
Measurements (i.e., weight, height, blood pressure)	7
Medical examination	16
Psychological interview	12
Exit medical evaluation	10

These activities can be performed in any order, with two exceptions: The medical history must be taken first and the exit medical evaluation is the final step. At present, there are three paramedics and two physicians on duty during each shift. Only a physician can perform the exit evaluation or conduct the psychological interview. Other activities can be carried out by either physicians or paramedics.

a) Develop a layout and balance the line. How many people can be processed per hour?

b) What activity is the current bottleneck?

c) If one more physician and one more paramedic can be placed on duty, how would you redraw the layout? What is the new throughput?

: **10.9** A final assembly plant for Dictatape, a popular dictation company, produces the DT, a hand-held dictation unit. There are 400 minutes available in the final assembly plant for the DT, and the average demand is 80 units per day. The final assembly requires six separate tasks. Information concerning these tasks is given in the following table. What tasks should be assigned to various workstations, and what is the overall efficiency of the assembly line?

TASK	PERFORMANCE TIME (MINUTES)	TASK MUST FOLLOW TASK LISTED BELOW
1	1	—
2	1	1
3	4	1, 2
4	1	2, 3
5	2	4
6	4	5

: **10.10** SCFI, South Carolina Furniture, Inc., produces all types of office furniture. The Executive Secretary is a chair that has been designed using ergonomics to provide comfort during long work hours. The chair sells for $130. There are 480 minutes available during the day, and the average daily demand has been 50 chairs. There are eight tasks. Given the information below, solve this assembly line-balancing problem.

TASK	PERFORMANCE TIME (MINUTES)	TASK MUST FOLLOW TASK LISTED BELOW
1	4	—
2	7	1
3	6	1, 2
4	5	2, 3
5	6	4
6	7	5
7	8	5
8	6	6, 7

:10.11 Tailwind, Inc., produces high-quality but expensive training shoes for runners. The Tailwind shoe, which sells for $110, contains both gas- and liquid-filled compartments to provide more stability and better protection against knee, foot, and back injuries. Manufacturing the shoes requires 10 separate tasks. How should these tasks be grouped into workstations? There are 400 minutes available for manufacturing the shoes in the plant each day. Daily demand is 60. The information for the tasks is as follows:

TASK	PERFORMANCE TIME (MINUTES)	TASK MUST FOLLOW TASK LISTED BELOW
1	1	—
2	3	1
3	2	2
4	4	2
5	1	3, 4
6	3	1
7	2	6
8	5	7
9	1	5, 8
10	3	9

25

:10.12 Mach 10 is a one-person sailboat designed to be used in the ocean. Manufactured by Creative Leisure, Mach 10 can handle 40-mph winds and over 10-foot seas. The final assembly plant for Creative Leisure is in Cupertino, California. At this time, 200 minutes are available each day to manufacture Mach 10. The daily demand is 60 boats. Given the following information, how many workstations would you recommend?

TASK	PERFORMANCE TIME (MINUTES)	TASK MUST FOLLOW TASK LISTED BELOW
1	1	—
2	1	1
3	2	1
4	1	3
5	3	3
6	1	3
7	1	4, 5, 6
8	2	2
9	1	7, 8

: **10.13** Because of the expected high demand for Mach 10, Creative Leisure has decided to increase the manufacturing time available to produce the Mach 10 (see Problem 10.12). What impact would 300 available minutes per day have on the assembly line? What impact would 400 minutes have?

: **10.14** Nearbeer Products, Inc., manufactures drinks that taste the same as a good draft beer but do not contain any alcohol. With changes in drinking laws and demographics, there has been an increased interest in Nearbeer Lite. Nearbeer Lite has fewer calories than the regular beer, is less filling, and tastes great. The final packing operation for Nearbeer Lite requires 13 tasks. Nearbeer bottles Nearbeer Lite 5 hours a day, 5 days a week. Each week there is a demand for 3,000 bottles of Nearbeer Lite. Given the following information, solve this assembly line-balancing problem.

DATA FOR PROBLEMS 10.14 AND 10.15		
TASK	PERFORMANCE TIME (MINUTES)	TASK MUST FOLLOW TASK LISTED BELOW
1	0.1	—
2	0.1	1
3	0.1	2
4	0.2	2
5	0.1	2
6	0.2	3, 4, 5
7	0.1	1
8	0.1	7
9	0.2	7, 8
10	0.1	9
11	0.2	6
12	0.2	10, 11
13	0.1	12

: **10.15** Nearbeer's president, Reed Doke, believes that weekly demand for Nearbeer Lite could explode (see Problem 10.14). What would happen if demand doubled?

:10.16 Suppose production requirements in Solved Problem 10.2 increase and necessitate a reduction in cycle time from 8 minutes to 7 minutes. Balance the line once again using the new cycle time. Note that it is not possible to combine task times so as to group tasks into the minimum number of workstations. This condition occurs in actual balancing problems fairly often.

:10.17 Marilyn Hart, operations manager at Nesa Electronics, prides herself on excellent assembly line balancing. She has been told that the firm needs 1,400 electronic relays completed per day. There are 420 minutes of productive time in each working day (which is equivalent to 25,200 seconds). Group the assembly line activities below into appropriate workstations and calculate the efficiency of the balance.

TASK	TIME (SECONDS)	MUST FOLLOW TASK	TASK	TIME (SECONDS)	MUST FOLLOW TASK
A	13	—	G	5	E
B	4	A	H	6	F, G
C	10	B	I	7	H
D	10	—	J	5	H
E	6	D	K	4	I, J
F	12	E	L	15	C, K

:10.18 Given the following data describing a line-balancing problem at Mayur Mehta's company, develop a solution allowing a cycle time of 3 minutes. What is the efficiency of that line?

TASK ELEMENT	TIME (MINUTES)	ELEMENT PREDECESSOR
A	1	—
B	1	A
C	2	B
D	1	B
E	3	C, D
F	1	A
G	1	F
H	2	G
I	1	E, H

:10.19 As the Williams Bicycle Co., in Omaha, completes plans for its new assembly line, it identifies 25 different tasks in the production process. R. Don Williams, the VP-Operations, now faces the job of balancing the line. He lists precedences and provides time estimates for each step based on work-sampling techniques. Williams's goal is to produce 1,000 bicycles per standard 40-hour work week.

DATA BASE APPLICATION

TASK	TIME (SECONDS)	PRECEDESSOR TASKS	TASK	TIME (SECONDS)	PRECEDESSOR TASKS
K3	60	—	E3	109	F3
K4	24	K3	D6	53	F4
K9	27	K3	D7	72	F9, E2, E3
J1	66	K3	D8	78	E3, D6
J2	22	K3	D9	37	D6
J3	3	—	C1	78	F7
G4	79	K4, K9	B3	72	D7, D8, D9, C1
G5	29	K9, J1	B5	108	C1
F3	32	J2	B7	18	B3
F4	92	J2	A1	52	B5
F7	21	J3	A2	72	B5
F9	126	G4	A3	114	B7, A1, A2
E2	18	G5, F3			

a) Balance this operation, using various "heuristics." Which is best?

b) What happens if the firm can change to a 41-hour work week?

CASE STUDY

Des Moines National Bank

Des Moines National Bank (DNB) recently finished construction on a new building in the downtown business district. Moving into a new building provides an opportunity to arrange the various departments to optimize the efficiency and effectiveness of the operations.

One primary operation of DNB is its check-processing division. This division acts as a clearing-house for commercial and personal checks. These checks are received from the tellers downstairs as well as from other, smaller financial institutions that DNB has contracted for check processing. Checks are sorted to be sent to the bank from which they are drawn, using the magnetic-ink characters located at the bottom of the check. The reconcilement area ensures that the incoming and outgoing totals balance, and the crediting area makes the entries to complete the transaction. Finally, the sorted checks are bundled and shipped from the distribution area.

The personnel in this division are also responsible for processing government checks and for handling any returned checks coming back through the system. Because these checks require very different processing operations, they are placed in separate departments from the commercial check operations but are located on the same floor.

The service elevator only travels from the basement to the second floor, so it has been decided that the check-processing division will be located on the second floor of the new DNB building. The second floor is divided into eight equal-sized rooms, as shown in Figure 10.21. (We call them rooms even though they are not separated by walls.) Each room is 75 feet square. Fortunately, this will not be a concern to bank management as each of the eight departments to be located on this floor require roughly 5,000 square feet; these rooms will allow for some additional storage space and for future expansion.

The physical flow of materials—such as the checks being processed and computer printouts for the reconcilement and crediting areas—will be on aisles that run between the centers of the rooms, as shown in Figure 10.21. The checks will arrive and be distributed from the service elevator, so it is necessary to put the distribution department in the room with the elevator.

(Continued)

There are no other physical restrictions that require any department to be placed in a given room.

FIGURE 10.21 ■ Floor Plan of the Second Floor of the DNB Building

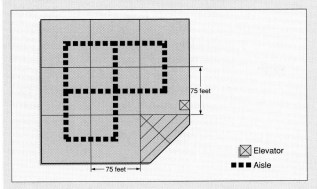

75 feet

75 feet

⊠ Elevator
■ ■ ■ Aisle

For the first step in this analysis, it was necessary to determine the amount of workflow that travels between the departments. Data collected for several weeks determined the average daily traffic—measured in the number of trips between departments. Although there is some fluctuation in the number of checks processed during the different days of the week, these average figures provide a good estimate of the relative workflow between each pair of departments.

A review of the workflow data revealed that several important relationships were not being considered. For example, although no material flows directly between the commercial check-sorting area and the government check area, they use the same type of equipment This equipment is very noisy and requires a "soundproof" wall to control the noise, so it is necessary to keep all of this equipment together to minimize the construction cost. Also, due to this noise, it is desirable to keep this department removed from areas that require concentration, such as the reconcilement area and the offices. To account for these types of concerns, closeness ratings were identified for each pair of departments using the following rating scheme:

A—Absolutely necessary
E—Especially important
I—Important
O—Ordinary closeness OK
U—Unimportant
X—*Not* desirable

Table 10.4 provides the average daily workflow between departments in the upper-right portion and the closeness ratings in the lower-left portion. For example, the workflow between the check sorting and reconcilement departments is 50 units per day, and there is a closeness rating of "X".

DISCUSSION QUESTIONS

1. Develop a layout that minimizes the total workflow.
2. Develop a layout using the relationships defined by the closeness ratings.
3. Develop a layout that considers both the workflow and closeness relationships between departments.
4. Comment on the various layouts developed.
5. Discuss any other factors that should be considered when developing a layout of the check-processing division.

Source: Professor Timothy L. Urban, The University of Tulsa.

TABLE 10.4 ■ WORKFLOW AND CLOSENESS RELATIONSHIPS BETWEEN DEPARTMENTS								
DEPARTMENT	1	2	3	4	5	6	7	8
1. Check sorting	—	50	0	250	0	0	0	0
2. Check reconcilement	X	—	50	0	0	0	0	0
3. Check crediting	X	A	—	0	0	0	0	10
4. Check distribution	U	U	U	—	40	60	0	0
5. Government checks	A	U	U	E	—	0	0	0
6. Returned checks	U	U	U	E	U	—	12	0
7. Credit adjustment	X	A	A	U	U	E	—	10
8. Offices	X	I	I	U	O	O	I	—

CASE STUDY

State Automobile License Renewals

Henry Coupe, the manager of a metropolitan branch office of the state Department of Motor Vehicles, attempted to perform an analysis of the driver's license renewal operations. Several steps were to be performed in the process. After examining the license renewal process, he identified the steps and associated times required to perform each step, as shown in the following table:

STATE AUTOMOBILE LICENSE RENEWALS PROCESS TIMES

Step	Average Time To Perform (seconds)
1. Review renewal application for correctness	15
2. Process and record payment	30
3. Check file for violations and restrictions	60
4. Conduct eye test	40
5. Photograph applicant	20
6. Issue temporary license	30

Coupe found that each step was assigned to a different person. Each application was a separate process in the sequence shown above. Coupe determined that his office should be prepared to accommodate the maximum demand of processing 120 renewal applicants per hour.

He observed that the work was unevenly divided among the clerks, and the clerk who was responsible for checking violations tended to shortcut her task to keep up with the other clerks. Long lines built up during the maximum demand periods.

Coupe also found that steps 1 to 4 were handled by general clerks who were each paid $6.00 per hour. Step 5 was performed by a photographer paid $8 per hour. Step 6, the issuing of a temporary license, was required by state policy to be handled by a uniformed motor vehicle officer. Officers were paid $9.00 per hour, but they could be assigned to any job except photography.

A review of the jobs indicated that step 1, reviewing the application for correctness, had to be performed before any other step could be taken. Similarly, step 6, issuing the temporary license, could not be performed until all the other steps were completed.

The branch offices were charged $5 per hour for each camera to perform photography.

Henry Coupe was under severe pressure to increase productivity and reduce costs, but he was also told by the regional director of the Department of Motor Vehicles that he had better accommodate the demand for renewals. Otherwise, "heads would roll."

DISCUSSION QUESTIONS

1. What is the maximum number of applications per hour that can be handled by the present configuration of the process?

2. How many applications can be processed per hour if a second clerk is added to check for violations?

3. Assuming the addition of one more clerk, what is the maximum number of applications the process can handle?

4. How would you suggest modifying the process in order to accommodate 120 applications per hour?

Source: W. Earl Sasser, Paul R. Olson, and D. Daryl Wyckoff, *Management of Services Operations: Text, Cases, and Readings* (Boston: Allyn and Bacon, 1978).

BIBLIOGRAPHY

Balakrishnan, J. "Notes: The Dynamics of Plant Layout." *Management Science*, **39**, 5 (May 1993): 654–655.

Ding, F., and L. Cheng. "An Effective Mixed-Model Assembly Line Sequencing Heuristic for Just-In-Time Production Systems." *Journal of Operations Management*, **11**, 1 (March 1993): 45–50.

Faaland, B. H., T. D. Klastorin, T. G. Schmitt, and A. Shtub. "Assembly Line Balancing with Resource Dependent Task Times." *Decision Sciences*, **23**, 2 (March–April 1992): 343.

Francis, R. L., L. F. McGinnis, and J. A. White. *Facility Layout and Location*, 2nd ed. Englewood Cliffs, NJ: Prentice Hall, 1992.

Huang, P. Y., and B. L. W. Houck. "Cellular Manufacturing: An Overview and Bibliography." *Production and Inventory Management*, **26** (Fourth Quarter 1985): 83–92.

Joshi, S., and M. Sudit. "Procedures for Solving Single-Pass Strip Layout Problems." *IIE Transactions*, **26**, 1 (January 1994): 27–37.

Leung, J. "A New Graph-Theoretic Heuristic for Facility Layout." *Management Science*, **38**, 4 (April 1992): 594.

Makens, P. K., D. F. Rossin, and M. C. Springer. "A Multivariate Approach for Assessing Facility Layout Complexity." *Journal of Operations Management*, **9**, 2 (April 1990): 185.

Montreuil, B., U. Venkatadri, and H. D. Ratliff. "Generating a Layout from a Design Skeleton." *Industrial Engineering Research & Development*, **25**, 1 (January 1993): 3–15.

Morris, J. S., and R. J. Tersine. "A Comparison of Cell Loading Practices in Group Technology." *Journal of Manufacturing and Operations Management*, **2**, 4 (Winter 1989): 299.

Vakharia, A. J., and B. K. Kaku. "Redesigning a Cellular Manufacturing System to Handle Long-Term Demand Changes: A Methodology and Investigation. *Decision Sciences*, **24**, 5 (September–October 1993): 909.

10 SUPPLEMENT

WAITING-LINE MODELS

The situation at Zayres had taken a turn for the worse. Once the leading discount department store chain in the United States, Zayres was losing market share, and sales were dropping dramatically. K-Mart, Wal-Mart, J. C. Penney, and others had closed the gap, and one reason was clear. A customer could enter a huge Zayres store at almost any time of day or night, pick up 30 items or just one, and then be stuck in a check-out line for what seemed like an eternity. It was time for decisive action and Zayres took it. An extensive and costly national ad campaign touted "If there are 3 or more people in a line, we'll open another cash register." But it was too late. Zayres folded. No one likes a long queue.

The body of knowledge about waiting lines, often called **queuing theory**, is an important part of P/OM and a valuable tool for the operations manager. **Waiting lines** are a common situation—they may, for example, take the form of cars waiting for repair at a Midas Muffler Shop, jobs waiting to be completed at a Kinkos print shop, or unhappy customers waiting to check out at a Zayres type of store. Table S10.1 lists just a few P/OM uses of waiting-line models.

Queuing theory
Waiting line

TABLE S10.1 ■ COMMON QUEUING SITUATIONS		
SITUATION	**ARRIVALS IN QUEUE**	**SERVICE PROCESS**
Supermarket	Grocery shoppers	Check-out clerks at cash register
Highway toll booth	Automobiles	Collection of tolls at booth
Doctor's office	Patients	Treatment by doctors and nurses
Computer system	Programs to be run	Computer processes jobs
Telephone company	Callers	Switching equipment to forward calls
Bank	Customers	Transactions handled by teller
Machine maintenance	Broken machines	Repair people fix machines
Harbor	Ships and barges	Dock workers load and unload

Waiting-line models are useful in both manufacturing and service areas. Analysis of queues in terms of waiting-line length, average waiting time, and other factors helps us to understand service systems (such as bank teller stations), maintenance activities (that might repair broken machinery), and shop-floor control activities. As a matter of fact, patients waiting in a doctor's office and broken drill presses waiting in a repair facility have a lot in common from a P/OM perspective. Both use human resources and equipment resources to restore valuable production assets (people and machines) to good condition.

QUEUING COSTS

Operations managers recognize the trade-off that must take place between the cost of providing good service and the cost of customer or machine waiting time. Managers want queues that are short enough so that customers do not become unhappy and either leave without buying or buy but never return. However, managers are willing to allow some waiting if it is balanced by a significant savings in service costs.

One means of evaluating a service facility is to look at total expected cost (Figure S10.1). Total cost is the sum of expected service costs plus expected waiting costs.

Service costs increase as a firm attempts to raise its level of service. Managers in *some* service centers can vary their capacity by having standby personnel and machines that can be assigned to specific service stations to prevent or shorten excessively long lines. In grocery stores, managers and stock clerks can operate extra check-out counters when needed. In banks and airport check-in points, part-time workers may be called in to help. As service improves (that is, speeds up), however, the cost of time spent waiting in lines decreases. Waiting cost may reflect lost productivity of workers while their tools or machines are awaiting repairs, or may simply be an estimate of the cost of customers lost because of poor service and long queues. In

FIGURE S10.1   ■   The Trade-Off between Waiting Costs and Service Costs

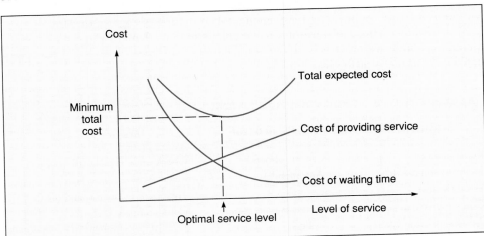

some service systems (for example, an emergency ambulance service), the cost of long waiting lines may be intolerably high.

CHARACTERISTICS OF A WAITING-LINE SYSTEM

In this section, we take a look at the three parts of a waiting-line, or queuing, system:

1. arrivals or inputs to the system;
2. queue discipline, or the waiting line itself;
3. the service facility.

Arrival Characteristics

The input source that generates arrivals or customers for a service system has three major characteristics: the *size* of the arrival population, the *pattern* of arrivals at the queuing system, and the *behavior* of the arrivals.

SIZE OF THE SOURCE POPULATION.   Population sizes are considered to be either unlimited (essentially infinite) or limited (finite). When the number of customers or arrivals on hand at any given moment is just a small portion of potential arrivals, the arrival population is considered **unlimited**, or **infinite**. Examples of unlimited populations include cars arriving at a highway toll booth, shoppers arriving at a supermarket, and students arriving to register for classes at a large university. Most queuing models assume such an infinite arrival population. An example of a **limited**, or **finite**, population is a copying shop with only eight copying machines, which might break down and require service.

PATTERN OF ARRIVALS AT THE SYSTEM.   Customers either arrive at a service facility according to some known schedule (for example, one patient every 15 minutes or one student every half-hour) or else they arrive *randomly*. Arrivals are

Unlimited, or infinite, population

Limited, or finite, population

FIGURE S10.2   ■   Two Examples of the Poisson Distribution for Arrival Times

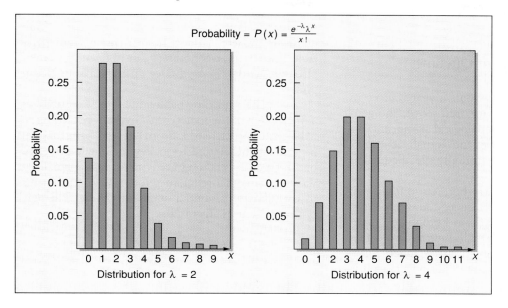

considered random when they are independent of one another and their occurrence cannot be predicted exactly. Frequently in queuing problems, the number of arrivals per unit of time can be estimated by a probability distribution known as the **Poisson distribution**. For any given arrival time (such as two customers per hour, or four trucks per minute), a discrete Poisson distribution can be established by using the formula

$$P(x) = \frac{e^{-\lambda}\lambda^x}{x!} \qquad \text{for } x = 0, 1, 2, 3, 4, \ldots \qquad (S10.1)$$

where $P(x)$ = probability of x arrivals
  x = number of arrivals per unit of time
  λ = average arrival rate
  e = 2.7183 (which is the base of the natural logarithms)

With the help of the table in Appendix C, these values are easy to compute. Figure S10.2 illustrates the Poisson distribution for $\lambda = 2$ and $\lambda = 4$. This means that if the average arrival rate is $\lambda = 2$ customers per hour, the probability of 0 customers arriving in any random hour is about 13%, probability of 1 customer is about 27%, 2 customers about 27%, 3 customers about 18%, 4 customers about 9%, and so on. The chances that 9 or more will arrive are virtually nil. Arrivals, of course, are not always Poisson distributed (they may follow some other distribution) and should be examined to make certain that they are well-approximated by Poisson before that distribution is applied.

BEHAVIOR OF THE ARRIVALS.   Most queuing models assume that an arriving customer is a patient customer. Patient customers are people or machines that wait in the queue until they are served and do not switch between lines. Unfortunately, life is complicated by the fact that people have been known to balk or to renege. Customers who *balk* refuse to join the waiting line because it is too long to suit their needs or interests. *Reneging* customers are those who enter the queue but then become impatient

Poisson distribution

The Culture of Queuing

Americans spend 37 billion hours a year waiting in lines, during which they fidget, fret, scowl, and generally miss the larger anthropological significance of what they are doing. Queues are actually complex social systems, embodying culturally specific principles of fairness and justice.

Sociologists have shown that, left to their own devices, homo sapiens do not queue. And in certain parts of the world, particularly in Europe and Latin America, the practice is virtually unknown—a fact that Disney found out when it first opened Euro-Disney in France and expected ticket buyers to line up in an orderly fashion.

An important factor in queuing is the extent to which a culture values equality. In many Arab countries, where women hold a subordinate position, it is common for men to cut in front of women at ticket windows—a practice unthinkable in North America.

"People's queuing behavior can be explained as a microcosm of the society they live in," according to MIT professor Richard Larson. "In Southern Europe, it's part of the culture to jockey for queue position, but in Britain and the United States, first-come, first-served is almost a religion." Note that the problems in this chapter assume a queue discipline that may not be present in all cultures.

Sources: San Antonio Express-News (February 7, 1993): 3-G; *Orlando Sentinel* (December 18, 1992): E7; and *Cornell Hotel and Restaurant Quarterly* (February 1991): 94–99.

and leave without completing their transaction. Actually, both of these situations just serve to accentuate the need for queuing theory and waiting line analysis (see the *POM in Action* box "The Culture of Queuing").

Waiting-Line Characteristics

The waiting line itself is the second component of a queuing system. The length of a line can be either limited or unlimited. A queue is *limited* when it cannot, by law or physical restrictions, increase to an infinite length. This may be the case in a small barbershop that has only a limited number of waiting chairs. Analytic queuing models are treated in this supplement under an assumption of *unlimited* queue length. A queue is *unlimited* when its size is unrestricted, as in the case of the toll booth serving arriving automobiles.

First-in, first-out (FIFO) rule

A second waiting-line characteristic deals with *queue discipline*. This refers to the rule by which customers in the line are to receive service. Most systems use a queue discipline known as the **first-in, first-out (FIFO) rule**. In a hospital emergency room or an express check-out line at a supermarket, however, various assigned priorities may preempt FIFO. Patients who are critically injured will move ahead in treatment priority over patients with broken fingers or noses. Shoppers with fewer than 10 items may be allowed to enter the express check-out queue (but are *then* treated as first-come, first-served). Computer programming runs are another example of queuing systems that operate under priority scheduling. In most large companies, when computer-produced paychecks are due out on a specific date, the payroll program has highest priority over other runs.[1]

---

[1]The term *FIFS* (first in, first served) is often used in place of FIFO. Another discipline, LIFS (last in, first served) also called last in, first out (LIFO), is common when material is stacked or piled and the items on top are used first.

A P_3 of .0625 means the chance of having more than three customers in an airport check-in line at a certain time of day is one chance in sixteen. If this British Airways office in Barbados can live with four or more passengers in line about 6% of the time, one service agent will suffice. If not, more check-in positions and staff will have to be added.

Service Facility Characteristics

The third part of any queuing system is the service facility. Two basic properties are important: (1) the configuration of the service system and (2) the pattern of service times.

BASIC QUEUING SYSTEM CONFIGURATIONS. Service systems are usually classified in terms of their number of channels (for example, number of servers) and number of phases (for example, number of service stops that must be made). A **single-channel queuing system**, with one server, is typified by the drive-in bank that has only one open teller, or by a drive-through fast-food restaurant. If, on the other hand, the bank had several tellers on duty, and each customer waited in one common line for the first available teller, then we would have a **multiple-channel queuing system** at work. Most banks today are multichannel service systems, as are most large barber shops, airline ticket counters, and post offices.

    A **single-phase system** is one in which the customer receives service from only one station and then exits the system. A fast-food restaurant in which the person who takes your order also brings you the food and takes your money is a single-phase system. So is a driver's license agency in which the person taking your application also grades your test and collects the license fee. But if the restaurant requires you to place your order at one station, pay at a second, and pick up the food at a third service stop, it becomes a **multiphase system**. Likewise, if the driver's license agency is large or busy, you will probably have to wait in a line to complete the application (the first service stop), then queue again to have the test graded (the second service stop), and

Single-channel queuing system

Multiple-channel queuing system

Single-phase system

Multiphase system

FIGURE S10.3   ■   Basic Queuing System Configurations

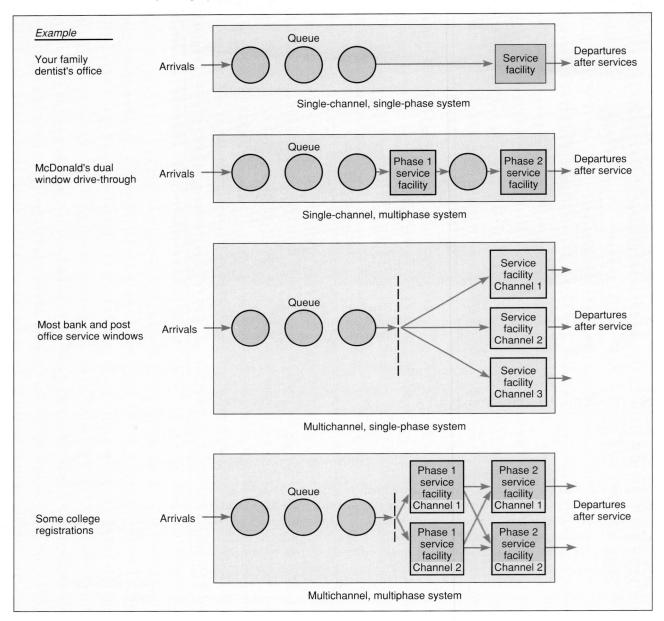

finally go to a third service counter to pay the fee. To help you relate the concepts of channels and phases, Figure S10.3 presents four possible configurations.

SERVICE TIME DISTRIBUTION.   Service patterns are like arrival patterns in that they may be either constant or random. If service time is constant, it takes the same amount of time to take care of each customer. This is the case in a machine-performed service operation such as an automatic car wash. More often, service times are randomly distributed. In many cases, we can assume that random service times are described by the **negative exponential probability distribution**.

Negative exponential probability distribution

FIGURE S10.4 ■ Two Examples of the Negative Exponential Distribution for Service Times

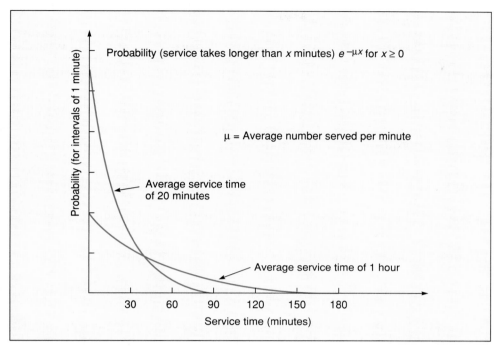

Figure S10.4 illustrates that if *service times* follow a negative exponential distribution, the probability of any very long service time is low. For example, when an average service time is 20 minutes, seldom if ever will a customer require more than 90 minutes in the service facility. If the mean service time is 1 hour, the probability of spending more than 180 minutes in service is virtually zero.

Measuring the Queue's Performance

Queuing models help managers make decisions that balance desirable service costs with waiting-line costs. Some of the many measures of a waiting-line system's performance that are commonly obtained in a queuing analysis are as follows:

1. average time each customer or object spends in the queue;
2. average queue length;
3. average time each customer spends in the system (waiting time plus service time);
4. average number of customers in the system;
5. probability that the service facility will be idle;
6. utilization factor for the system;
7. probability of a specific number of customers in the system.

Years of listening to howling customers have taught the airlines some baggage-retrieval lessons. When American designed its baggage-claim area in the Dallas-Fort Worth Airport, it put it close to the gates, so disembarking passengers would not have to trudge too far. But even though passengers reach the area quickly, they must wait for their luggage. At Los Angeles International Airport, passengers have to walk quite some distance to the claim area, but when they arrive, their suitcases are usually there. Even though the Los Angeles travelers spend more total time picking up their baggage, American has found they do not grouse as much about baggage delays as do the Dallas passengers.

THE VARIETY OF QUEUING MODELS

A wide variety of queuing models may be applied in operations management. We will introduce you to four of the most widely used models. These are outlined in

TABLE S10.2 ■ QUEUING MODELS DESCRIBED IN THIS CHAPTER

MODEL	NAME (TECHNICAL NAME IN PARENTHESES)	EXAMPLE	NUMBER OF CHANNELS	NUMBER OF PHASES	ARRIVAL RATE PATTERN	SERVICE TIME PATTERN	POPULATION SIZE	QUEUE DISCIPLINE
A	Simple system (M/M/1)	Information counter at department store	Single	Single	Poisson	Exponential	Unlimited	FIFO
B	Multichannel (M/M/S)	Airline ticket counter	Multi-channel	Single	Poisson	Exponential	Unlimited	FIFO
C	Constant service (M/D/1)	Automated car wash	Single	Single	Poisson	Constant	Unlimited	FIFO
D	Limited population (finite population)	Shop with only a dozen machines that might break	Single	Single	Poisson	Exponential	Limited	FIFO

Table S10.2, and examples of each follow in the next few sections. More complex models are described in queuing theory textbooks[2] or can be developed through the use of simulation (which is the topic of the supplement to Chapter 13). Note that all four queuing models listed in Table S10.2 have three characteristics in common. They all assume

1. Poisson-distribution arrivals;
2. FIFO discipline;
3. a single-service phase.

In addition, they describe service systems that operate under steady, ongoing conditions. This means that arrival and service rates remain stable during the analysis.

Model A: Single-Channel Queuing Model with Poisson Arrivals and Exponential Service Times

The most common case of queuing problems involves the *single-channel*, or single-server, waiting line. In this situation, arrivals form a single line to be serviced by a single station (Figure S10.3). We assume that the following conditions exist in this type of system:

1. Arrivals are served on a first-in, first-out (FIFO) basis, and every arrival waits to be served, regardless of the length of the line or queue.
2. Arrivals are independent of preceding arrivals, but the average number of arrivals (arrival rate) does not change over time.

[2]See, for example, W. Griffin, *Queuing: Basic Theories and Applications* (Columbus: Grid Publishing, 1978); or R. B. Cooper, *Introduction to Queuing Theory,* 2nd ed. (New York: Elsevier-North Holland, 1980).

TABLE S10.3 ■ QUEUING FORMULAS FOR MODEL A: SIMPLE SYSTEM, ALSO CALLED M/M/1

λ = Mean number of arrivals per time period

μ = Mean number of people or items served per time period

L_s = Average number of units (customers) in the system

$$= \frac{\lambda}{\mu - \lambda}$$

W_s = Average time a unit spends in the system (waiting time plus service time)

$$= \frac{1}{\mu - \lambda}$$

L_q = Average number of units in the queue

$$= \frac{\lambda^2}{\mu(\mu - \lambda)}$$

W_q = Average time a unit spends waiting in the queue

$$= \frac{\lambda}{\mu(\mu - \lambda)}$$

ρ = Utilization factor for the system

$$= \frac{\lambda}{\mu}$$

P_0 = Probability of 0 units in the system (that is, the service unit is idle)

$$= 1 - \frac{\lambda}{\mu}$$

$P_{n>k}$ = Probability of more than k units in the system, where n is the number of units in the system

$$= \left(\frac{\lambda}{\mu}\right)^{k+1}$$

3. Arrivals are described by a Poisson probability distribution and come from an infinite (or very, very large) population.

4. Service times vary from one customer to the next and are independent of one another, but their average rate is known.

5. Service times occur according to the negative-exponential probability distribution.

6. The service rate is faster than the arrival rate.

When these conditions are met, the series of equations shown in Table S10.3 can be developed. Examples S1 and S2 illustrate how Model A (which in technical journals is known as the M/M/1 model) may be used.

EXAMPLE S1

Jones, the mechanic at Golden Muffler Shop, is able to install new mufflers at an average rate of three per hour (or about one every 20 minutes), according to a negative exponential distribution. Customers seeking this service arrive at the shop on the average of two per hour, following a Poisson distribution. The customers are served on a first-in, first-out basis and come from a very large (almost infinite) population of possible buyers.

L.L. Bean Turns to Queuing Theory

L.L. Bean faced severe problems. It was the peak selling season, and the service level to incoming calls was simply unacceptable. Widely known as a high-quality outdoor goods retailer, about 65% of L.L. Bean's sales volume is generated through telephone orders via its toll-free service centers located in Maine.

Here is how bad the situation was: During certain periods, 80% of the calls received a busy signal, and those that did not often had to wait up to 10 minutes before speaking with a sales agent. L.L. Bean estimated it lost $10 million in profit because of the way it allocated telemarketing resources. Keeping customers waiting "in line" (on the phone)

was costing $25,000 per day. On exceptionally busy days, the total orders lost because of queue problems approached $500,000 in gross revenues.

Developing queuing models similar to those presented here, L.L. Bean was able to set the number of phone lines and the number of agents to have on duty for each half-hour of every day of the season. Within a year, use of the model resulted in 24% more calls answered, 17% more orders taken, and 16% more revenues. It also meant 81% fewer abandoned callers, and 84% faster answering time. The percent of calls spending less than 20 seconds in the queue increased from 25% to 77%. Queuing theory changed the way L.L. Bean thinks about telecommunications.

Sources: P. Quinn, B. Andrews, and H. Parsons, *Interfaces* (January/February 1991): 75–91; and B. Render and R. Stair, *Quantitative Analysis for Management*, 5th ed. (Boston: Allyn and Bacon, 1994): 645

From this description, we are able to obtain the operating characteristics of Golden Muffler's queuing system:

$$\lambda = 2 \text{ cars arriving per hour}$$

$$\mu = 3 \text{ cars serviced per hour}$$

$$L_s = \frac{\lambda}{\mu - \lambda} = \frac{2}{3 - 2} = \frac{2}{1}$$

$$= 2 \text{ cars in the system, on average}$$

$$W_s = \frac{1}{\mu - \lambda} = \frac{1}{3 - 2} = 1$$

$$= 1\text{-hour average waiting time in the system}$$

$$L_q = \frac{\lambda^2}{\mu(\mu - \lambda)} = \frac{2^2}{3(3 - 2)} = \frac{4}{3(1)} = \frac{4}{3}$$

$$= 1.33 \text{ cars waiting in line, on average}$$

$$W_q = \frac{\lambda}{\mu(\mu - \lambda)} = \frac{2}{3(3 - 2)} = \frac{2}{3} \text{ hour}$$

$$= 40\text{-minute average waiting time per car}$$

$$\rho = \frac{\lambda}{\mu} = \frac{2}{3}$$

$$= 66.6\% \text{ of time mechanic is busy}$$

$$P_0 = 1 - \frac{\lambda}{\mu} = 1 - \frac{2}{3}$$

$$= .33 \text{ probability there are 0 cars in the system}$$

PROBABILITY OF MORE THAN K CARS IN THE SYSTEM

K	$P_{N>K} = (2/3)^{K+1}$
0	.667 ← Note that this is equal to $1 - P_0 = 1 - .33 = .667$.
1	.444
2	.296
3	.198 ← Implies that there is a 19.8% chance that more than 3 cars are in the system.
4	.132
5	.088
6	.058
7	.039

Once we have computed the operating characteristics of a queuing system, it is often important to do an economic analysis of their impact. The waiting-line model described above is valuable in predicting potential waiting times, queue lengths, idle times, and so on, but it does not identify optimal decisions or consider cost factors. As we saw earlier, the solution to a queuing problem may require management to make a trade-off between the increased cost of providing better service and the decreased waiting costs derived from providing that service.

Example S2 examines the costs involved in Example S1.

EXAMPLE S2

The owner of the Golden Muffler Shop estimates that the cost of customer waiting time, in terms of customer dissatisfaction and lost goodwill, is $10 per hour of time spent *waiting* in the line. Since the average car has a 2/3-hour wait (W_q) and there are approximately sixteen cars serviced per day (two per hour times eight working hours per day), the total number of hours that customers spend waiting for mufflers to be installed each day is

$$\frac{2}{3}(16) = \frac{32}{3} = 10\frac{2}{3} \text{ hour}$$

Hence, in this case,

$$\text{Customer waiting-time cost} = \$10 \left(10\frac{2}{3}\right) = \$107 \text{ per day}$$

The only other major cost that Golden's owner can identify in the queuing situation is the salary of Jones, the mechanic, who earns $7 per hour, or $56 per day. Thus,

$$\text{Total expected costs} = \$107 + \$56$$
$$= \$163 \text{ per day}$$

This approach will be useful in Solved Problem S10.2.

The Epcot Center and Disney World in Orlando, Disneyland in California, EuroDisney near Paris, and Disney Japan near Tokyo all have one feature in common— long lines and seemingly endless waits. But Disney is one of the world's leading companies in the scientific analysis of queuing theory. It analyzes queuing behaviors and can predict which rides will draw what length crowds. To keep visitors happy, Disney does three things: (1) it makes lines appear to be constantly moving forward; (2) it entertains people while they wait; and (3) it posts signs telling visitors how many minutes in line they are away from each ride. That way parents can decide whether a 20-minute wait for Small World is worth more than a 30-minute wait for Mr. Frog's Wild Ride.

Model B: Multiple-Channel Queuing Model

Now let us turn to a multiple-channel queuing system in which two or more servers or channels are available to handle arriving customers. Let us still assume that customers awaiting service form one single line and then proceed to the first available server. An example of such a multichannel, single-phase waiting line is found in many banks today. A common line is formed, and the customer at the head of the line proceeds to the first free teller. (Refer back to Figure S10.3 for a typical multichannel configuration.)

The multiple-channel system presented in Example S3 again assumes that arrivals follow a Poisson probability distribution and that service times are exponentially distributed. Service is first-come, first-served, and all servers are assumed to perform at the same rate. Other assumptions listed earlier for the single-channel model apply as well.

The queuing equations for Model B (which also has the technical name of M/M/S) are shown in Table S10.4. These equations are obviously more complex than the ones used in the single-channel model; yet they are used in exactly the same fashion and provide the same type of information as the simpler model. The AB:POM microcomputer software described later in this chapter proves very useful in solving multiple-channel, as well as other, queuing problems.

TABLE S10.4 ■ QUEUING FORMULAS FOR MODEL B: MULTICHANNEL SYSTEM, ALSO CALLED M/M/S

M = number of channels open

λ = average arrival rate

μ = average service rate at each channel

The probability that there are zero people or units in the system is

$$P_0 = \frac{1}{\left[\displaystyle\sum_{n=0}^{M-1} \frac{1}{n!}\left(\frac{\lambda}{\mu}\right)^n\right] + \frac{1}{M!}\left(\frac{\lambda}{\mu}\right)^M \frac{M\mu}{M\mu - \lambda}} \qquad \text{for } M\mu > \lambda$$

The average number of people or units in the system is

$$L_s = \frac{\lambda\mu(\lambda/\mu)^M}{(M-1)!(M\mu - \lambda)^2} \, P_0 + \frac{\lambda}{\mu}$$

The average time a unit spends in the waiting line or being serviced (namely, in the system) is

$$W_s = \frac{\mu(\lambda/\mu)^M}{(M-1)!(M\mu - \lambda)^2} \, P_0 + \frac{1}{\mu} = \frac{L_s}{\lambda}$$

The average number of people or units in line waiting for service is

$$L_q = L_s - \frac{\lambda}{\mu}$$

The average time a person or unit spends in the queue waiting for service is

$$W_q = W_s - \frac{1}{\mu} = \frac{L_q}{\lambda}$$

EXAMPLE S3

The Golden Muffler Shop has decided to open a second garage bay and to hire a second mechanic to handle muffler installations. Customers, who arrive at the rate of about $\lambda = 2$ per hour, will wait in a single line until one of the two mechanics is free. Each mechanic installs mufflers at the rate of about $\mu = 3$ per hour.

To find out how this system compares to the old single-channel waiting-line system, we will compute several operating characteristics for the $M = 2$ channel system and compare the results with those found in Example S1.

$$P_0 = \cfrac{1}{\left[\displaystyle\sum_{n=0}^{1} \frac{1}{n!} \left(\frac{2}{3}\right)^n\right] + \frac{1}{2!} \left(\frac{2}{3}\right)^2 \frac{2(3)}{2(3) - 2}}$$

$$= \cfrac{1}{1 + \frac{2}{3} + \frac{1}{2} \left(\frac{4}{9}\right)\left(\frac{6}{6 - 2}\right)} = \cfrac{1}{1 + \frac{2}{3} + \frac{1}{3}} = \frac{1}{2}$$

$$= .5 \text{ probability of zero cars in the system}$$

Then,

$$L_s = \frac{(2)(3)(2/3)^2}{1![2(3) - 2]^2} \left(\frac{1}{2}\right) + \frac{2}{3} = \frac{8/3}{16} \left(\frac{1}{2}\right) + \frac{2}{3} = \frac{3}{4}$$

$$= .75 \text{ average number of cars in the system}$$

$$W_s = \frac{L_s}{\lambda} = \frac{3/4}{2} = \frac{3}{8} \text{ hour}$$

$$= 22.5 \text{ minutes average time a car spends in the system}$$

$$L_q = L_s - \frac{\lambda}{\mu} = \frac{3}{4} - \frac{2}{3} = \frac{1}{12}$$

$$= .083 \text{ average number of cars in the queue}$$

$$W_q = \frac{L_q}{\lambda} = \frac{.083}{2} = .0415 \text{ hour}$$

$$= 2.5 \text{ minutes average time a car spends in the queue}$$

We can summarize these characteristics and compare them to those of the single-channel model as follows:

	SINGLE CHANNEL	TWO CHANNELS
P_0	.33	.5
L_s	2 cars	.75 car
W_s	60 minutes	22.5 minutes
L_q	1.33 cars	.083 car
W_q	40 minutes	2.5 minutes

The increased service has a dramatic effect on almost all characteristics. In particular, time spent waiting in line drops from 40 minutes to only 2.5 minutes.

TABLE S10.5 ■	QUEUING FORMULAS FOR MODEL C: CONSTANT SERVICE, ALSO CALLED THE M/D/1 MODEL

Average length of queue: $L_q = \dfrac{\lambda^2}{2\mu(\mu - \lambda)}$

Average waiting time in queue: $W_q = \dfrac{\lambda}{2\mu(\mu - \lambda)}$

Average number of customers in system: $L_s = L_q + \dfrac{\lambda}{\mu}$

Average waiting time in system: $W_s = W_q + \dfrac{1}{\mu}$

Queues exist throughout industry and around the world. Here, the Moscow McDonald's on Puskin Square, four blocks from the Kremlin, boasts 700 indoor and 200 outdoor seats, employs 800 Russian citizens, and generates annual revenues of 80 million dollars. In spite of its size and volume, it still has queues and had to develop a strategy for dealing with them.

Model C: Constant Service Time Model

Some service systems have constant, instead of exponentially distributed service times. When customers or equipment are processed according to a fixed cycle, as in the case of an automatic car wash or an amusement park ride, constant service times are appropriate. Because constant rates are certain, the values for L_q, W_q, L_s, and W_s are always less than they would be in Model A, which has variable service rates. As a matter of fact, both the average queue length and the average waiting time in the queue are halved with Model C. Constant service model formulas are given in Table S10.5. Model C also has the technical name of M/D/1 in the literature of queuing theory. Example S4 gives a constant service time analysis.

EXAMPLE S4

Garcia-Golding Recycling, Inc., collects and compacts aluminum cans and glass bottles in New York City. Its truck drivers, who arrive to unload these materials for recycling, currently wait an average of 15 minutes before emptying their loads. The cost of the driver and truck time while in queue is valued at $60 per hour. A new automated compactor can be purchased that will process truckloads at a constant rate of 12 trucks per hour (that is, 5 minutes per truck). Trucks arrive according to a Poisson distribution at an average rate of 8 per hour. If the new compactor is put in use, its cost will be amortized at a rate of $3 per truck unloaded. The firm hires a summer college intern, who conducts the following analysis to evaluate the costs vs. benefits of the purchase:

Current waiting cost/trip = (1/4 hr. waiting now) ($60/hr. cost) = $15/trip

New system: $\lambda = 8$ trucks/hr. arriving $\mu = 12$ trucks/hr. served

Average waiting time in queue = $W_q = \dfrac{\lambda}{2\mu(\mu - \lambda)} = \dfrac{8}{2(12)(12-8)} = \dfrac{1}{12}$ hr

Waiting cost/trip with new compactor = (1/12 hr. wait) ($60/hr. cost)	= $ 5/trip
Savings with new equipment = $15 (current system) – $5 (new system)	= $10/trip
Cost of new equipment amortized	= $ 3/trip
Net savings	$ 7/trip

Model D: Limited Population Model

When there is a limited population of potential customers for a service facility, we need to consider a different queuing model. This model would be used, for example, if you were considering equipment repairs in a factory that has five machines, if you were in charge of maintenance for a fleet of 10 commuter airplanes, or if you ran a hospital ward that has 20 beds. The limited population model permits any number of repair people (servers) to be considered.

The reason this model differs from the three earlier queuing models is that there is now a *dependent* relationship between the length of the queue and the arrival rate. To illustrate the extreme situation, if your factory had five machines and all were broken and awaiting repair, the arrival rate would drop to zero. In general, as the waiting line becomes longer in the limited population model, the arrival rate of customers or machines drops lower.

Table S10.6 displays the queuing formulas for the limited population model. Note that they employ a different notation than seen in Models A, B, and C. To simplify what can become very time-consuming calculations, finite queuing tables have been developed that determine D and F. D represents the probability a machine needing repair will have to wait in line. F is a waiting-time efficiency factor. D and F are needed to compute most of the other finite model formulas.

A small part of the published finite queuing tables is illustrated in this section. Table S10.7 on page 462 provides for a population of $N = 5$.[3]

To use Table S10.7, we follow four steps:

1. Compute X (the service factor, where $X = T(T + U)$).

2. Find the value of X in the table and then find the line for M (where M is the number of service channels).

3. Note the corresponding values for D and F.

4. Compute L, W, J, H, or whichever are needed to measure the service system's performance.

Example S5 illustrates these steps.

---

[3]Limited, or finite, queuing tables are available to handle arrival populations of up to 250. Although there is no definite number that we can use to divide limited from unlimited populations, the general rule of thumb is this: If the number in the queue is a significant proportion of the arrival population, use a limited population queuing model. For a complete set of N values, see L. G. Peck and R. N. Hazelwood *Finite Queuing Tables* (New York: John Wiley, 1958).

TABLE S10.6 ■ **QUEUING FORMULAS AND NOTATION FOR MODEL D: LIMITED POPULATION**

FORMULAS

Service factor: $X = \dfrac{T}{T+U}$

Average number waiting: $L = N(1-F)$

Average waiting time: $W = \dfrac{L(T+U)}{N-L} = \dfrac{T(1-F)}{XF}$

Average number running: $J = NF(1-X)$

Average number being serviced: $H = FNX$

Number of population: $N = J + L + H$

NOTATION

D = probability that a unit will have to wait in queue

F = efficiency factor

H = average number of units being served

J = average number of units not in queue or in service bay

L = average number of units waiting for service

M = number of service channels

N = number of potential customers

T = average service time

U = average time between unit service requirements

W = average time a unit waits in line

X = service factor

Source: L. G. Peck and R. N. Hazelwood, *Finite Queuing Tables* (New York: John Wiley, 1958).

EXAMPLE S5

In office buildings and hotels, mirrors next to elevators or on elevator doors seem to make people happier to wait. People comb their hair; they check their clothes. One study showed that guests in hotels with mirrors thought elevators were faster in arriving than guests in hotels where there were no mirrors near the elevators. The *reality* was that elevator delays were exactly the same—the only difference was *perception*.

Past records indicate that each of the five laser computer printers at the U.S. Department of Energy, in Washington, D.C. needs repair after about 20 hours of use. Breakdowns have been determined to be Poisson-distributed. The one technician on duty can service a printer in an average of 2 hours, following an exponential distribution. Printer downtime costs $120 per hour. Technicians are paid $25 per hour. Should the DOE hire a second technician?

Assuming the second technician can repair a printer in an average of 2 hours, we can use Table S10.7 (because there are $N = 5$ machines in this limited population) to compare the costs of one vs. two technicians.

1. First, we note that $T = 2$ hours and $U = 20$ hours.

2. Then, $X = \dfrac{T}{T+U} = \dfrac{2}{2+20} = \dfrac{2}{22} = .091$ (close to .090).

3. For $M = 1$ server, $D = .350$ and $F = .960$.

4. For $M = 2$ servers, $D = .044$ and $F = .998$.

5. The average number of printers *working* is $J = NF(1-X)$.
   For $M = 1$, this is $J = (5)(.960)(1 - .091) = 4.36$.
   For $M = 2$, it is $J = (5)(.998)(1 - .091) = 4.54$.

6. The cost analysis follows:

Using Queuing Theory in Finland to Implement Time-Based Competition

The Finnish company Helkama Bica Oy faced two severe economic blows in 1990: a rapid increase in competition due to European integration into one market bloc and the loss of the Soviet Union as a customer. With sales of $50 million, the bicycle and cable manufacturer had been able, until then, to compete based on short delivery times and high quality. In 1988, Helkama was ranked first in Finland in profitability and fifth in growth.

Helkama's response to the pressure has been to increase its focus on time-based competition, yet invest as frugally as possible. Queuing theory is now used throughout the firm to calculate and reduce lead times, aid in capacity planning, and reduce lot sizes. Even more importantly, the queuing models built to describe the factory operation serve as a control against traditional ways of tackling efficiency problems, such as increasing lot sizes.

Using computer software produced by a Massachusetts firm, Helkama's attempts to reduce production lead times have been rapid and successful. Reductions of as much as 40% have reinforced the company's ability to use time-based competition as a strategic weapon. The result has been increased sales and profits.

Sources: OR/MS Today (October 1992): 30–34; and *OR/MS Today* (June 1991): 34–42.

NUMBER OF TECHNICIANS	AVERAGE NUMBER PRINTERS DOWN (N − J)	AVERAGE COST/HR. FOR DOWNTIME (N − J)($120/HR)	COST/HR. FOR TECHNICIANS (AT $25/HR)	TOTAL COST/HR
1	.64	$76.80	$25.00	$101.80
2	.46	$55.20	$50.00	$105.20

This analysis suggests that having only one technician on duty will save a few dollars per hour ($105.20 − $101.80 = $3.40).

OTHER QUEUING APPROACHES

Many practical waiting-line problems that occur in production and operations service systems have characteristics like the four mathematical models described before. Often, however, *variations* of these specific cases are present in an analysis. Service times in an automobile repair shop, for example, tend to follow the normal probability distribution instead of the exponential. A college registration system in which seniors have first choice of courses and hours over all other students is an example of a first-come, first-served model with a preemptive priority queue discipline. A physical examination for military recruits is an example of a multiphase system, one that differs from the single-phase models discussed in this supplement. A recruit first lines up to have blood drawn at one station, then waits to take an eye exam at the next station, talks to a psychiatrist at the third, and is examined by a doctor for medical problems at

TABLE S10.7 ■ FINITE QUEUING TABLES FOR A POPULATION OF N = 5

X	M	D	F	X	M	D	F	X	M	D	F	X	M	D	F	X	M	D	F
.012	1	.048	.999		1	.404	.945		1	.689	.801	.330	4	.012	.999		3	.359	.927
.019	1	.076	.998	.110	2	.065	.996	.210	3	.032	.998		3	.112	.986	.520	2	.779	.728
.025	1	.100	.997		1	.421	.939		2	.211	.973		2	.442	.904		1	.988	.384
.030	1	.120	.996	.115	2	.071	.995		1	.713	.783		1	.902	.583	.540	4	.085	.989
.034	1	.135	.995		1	.439	.933	.220	3	.036	.997	.340	4	.013	.999		3	.392	.917
.036	1	.143	.994	.120	2	.076	.995		2	.229	.969		3	.121	.985		2	.806	.708
.040	1	.159	.993		1	.456	.927		1	.735	.765		2	.462	.896		1	.991	.370
.042	1	.167	.992	.125	2	.082	.994	.230	3	.041	.997		1	.911	.569	.560	4	.098	.986
.044	1	.175	.991		1	.473	.920		2	.247	.965	.360	4	.017	.998		3	.426	.906
.046	1	.183	.990	.130	2	.089	.933		1	.756	.747		3	.141	.981		2	.831	.689
.050	1	.198	.989		1	.489	.914	.240	3	.046	.996		2	.501	.880		1	.993	.357
.052	1	.206	.988	.135	2	.095	.993		2	.265	.960		1	.927	.542	.580	4	.113	.984
.054	1	.214	.987		1	.505	.907		1	.775	.730	.380	4	.021	.998		3	.461	.895
.056	2	.018	.999	.140	2	.102	.992	.250	3	.052	.995		3	.163	.976		2	.854	.670
	1	.222	.985		1	.521	.900		2	.284	.955		2	.540	.863		1	.994	.345
.058	2	.019	.999	.145	3	.011	.999		1	.794	.712		1	.941	.516	.600	4	.130	.981
	1	.229	.984		2	.109	.991	.260	3	.058	.944	.400	4	.026	.977		3	.497	.883
.060	2	.020	.999		1	.537	.892		2	.303	.950		3	.186	.972		2	.875	.652
	1	.237	.983	.150	3	.012	.999		1	.811	.695		2	.579	.845		1	.996	.333
.062	2	.022	.999		2	.115	.990	.270	3	.064	.994		1	.952	.493	.650	4	.179	.972
	1	.245	.982		1	.553	.885		2	.323	.944	.420	4	.031	.997		3	.588	.850
.064	2	.023	.999	.155	3	.013	.999		1	.827	.677		3	.211	.966		2	.918	.608
	1	.253	.981		2	.123	.989	.280	3	.071	.993		2	.616	.826		1	.998	.308
.066	2	.024	.999		1	.568	.877		2	.342	.938		1	.961	.471	.700	4	.240	.960
	1	.260	.979	.160	3	.015	.999		1	.842	.661	.440	4	.037	.996		3	.678	.815
.068	2	.026	.999		2	.130	.988	.290	4	.007	.999		3	.238	.960		2	.950	.568
	1	.268	.978		1	.582	.869		3	.079	.992		2	.652	.807		1	.999	.286
.070	2	.027	.999	.165	3	.016	.999		2	.362	.932		1	.969	.451	.750	4	.316	.944
	1	.275	.977		2	.137	.987		1	.856	.644	.460	4	.045	.995		3	.763	.777
.075	2	.031	.999		1	.597	.861	.300	4	.008	.999		3	.266	.953		2	.972	.532
	1	.294	.973	.170	3	.017	.999		3	.086	.990		2	.686	.787	.800	4	.410	.924
.080	2	.035	.998		2	.145	.985		2	.382	.926		1	.975	.432		3	.841	.739
	1	.313	.969		1	.611	.853		1	.869	.628	.480	4	.053	.994		2	.987	.500
.085	2	.040	.998	.180	3	.021	.999	.310	4	.009	.999		3	.296	.945	.850	4	.522	.900
	1	.332	.965		2	.161	.983		3	.094	.989		2	.719	.767		3	.907	.702
.090	2	.044	.998		1	.638	.836		2	.402	.919		1	.980	.415		2	.995	.470
	1	.350	.960	.190	3	.024	.998		1	.881	.613	.500	4	.063	.992	.900	4	.656	.871
.095	2	.049	.997		2	.117	.980	.320	4	.010	.999		3	.327	.936		3	.957	.666
	1	.368	.955		1	.665	.819		3	.103	.988		2	.750	.748		2	.998	.444
.100	2	.054	.997	.200	3	.028	.998		2	.422	.912		1	.985	.399	.950	4	.815	.838
.100	1	.386	.950	.200	2	.194	.976		1	.892	.597	.520	4	.073	.991		3	.989	.631
.105	2	.059	.997																

Source: From L. G. Peck and R. N. Hazelwood, *Finite Queuing Tables* (New York: John Wiley, 1958, p. 4) © 1985, John Wiley & Sons, Inc.

the fourth. At each phase, the recruit must enter another queue and wait his or her turn. Many models, some very complex, have been developed to deal with situations such as these.

SUMMARY

Queues are an important part of the world of operations management. In this supplement, we describe several common queuing systems and present mathematical models for analyzing them.

The models we illustrate are Model A, the basic single-channel, single-phase system with Poisson arrivals and exponential service times; Model B, the multichannel equivalent of Model A; Model C, a constant service rate model; and Model D, a limited population system. All four of these allow for Poisson arrivals, first-in, first-out service, and a single-service phase. Typical operating characteristics we examine include average time spent waiting in queue and in the system, average number of customers in the queue and system, idle time, and utilization rate.

A variety of queuing models exist for which all of the assumptions of the traditional models need not be met. In these cases, we use more complex mathematical models or turn to a technique called simulation. The application of simulation to problems of queuing systems is addressed in the Supplement to Chapter 13.

KEY TERMS

Queuing theory (p. 445)
Waiting line (p. 445)
Unlimited, or infinite, population (p. 446)
Limited, or finite, population (p. 446)
Poisson distribution (p. 447)
First-in, first-out (FIFO) rule (p. 448)

Single-channel queuing system (p. 449)
Multiple-channel queuing system (p. 449)
Single-phase system (p. 449)
Multiphase system (p. 449)
Negative exponential probability
  distribution (p. 450)

USING AB:POM AND SPREADSHEETS TO SOLVE QUEUING PROBLEMS

Solving Example S3 With AB:POM's Queuing Module

As in this chapter, there are four AB:POM queuing models from which to select, each with or without cost analysis (see Program S10.1): The programs that include cost can compute waiting costs charged against either the time a customer spends in the system or the time spent waiting in the queue.

PROGRAM S10.1 ■ AB:POM's Queuing Options

```
───────────────── Model ─────────────────
          Single Channel
          Multiple Channel
          Constant Service Time
          Limited Population
```

The left-hand side of Program S10.2 shows the input data for Example S3, the Golden Muffler Shop with two mechanics. The right-hand side illustrates the program's outputs.

PROGRAM S10.2 ■ AB:POM's Queuing Program Using Example S3's Data With Optional Conversion of Times into Minutes. AB:POM can also handle the other three queuing models in this supplement, and is capable of conducting economic cost analysis on each model. As a further option, the F3 function key was used to display probabilities of various numbers of people/items in the system.

```
─────────────────── Waiting Line Models ─────────── Solution ───────
Multiple Channel
───────────────────── GOLDEN MUFFLER SHOP, EXAMPLE S3 ───────────────

arrival rate (lambda)  2.00    Average server utilization            .3333333
service rate (mu)      3.00    Average number in the queue (Lq)     0.083333
number of servers        2     Average number in the system (Ls)    0.7500

                               Average time in the queue (Wq)       0.041667
                                   Answer * 60                          2.50
                               Average time in the system (Ws)       0.3750
                                   Answer * 60                         22.50

F1 = Help    F2 = Multiply times by 60    F3 = Display Probabilities  F9 = Print   Esc

                    Number in    Probability   Cumulative    Decum
                    system, k    P (n=k)       P (n<k)       P (n>k)
                        0         .5000        0.5000        0.5000
                        1         .3333        0.8333        0.1667
                        2         .1111        0.9444        0.0556
                        3         .0370        0.9815        0.0185
                        4         .0123        0.9938        0.0062
                        5         .0041        0.9979        0.0021
                        6         .0014        0.9993        0.0007
                        7         .0005        0.9998        0.0002
                        8         .0002        0.9999        0.0001
                        9         .0001        1.0000        0.0000
```

Queuing Analysis with Spreadsheets

The four queuing models developed in this supplement can be analyzed by spreadsheet as well as with software such as AB:POM. Program S10.3 provides an example of a *single* channel analysis using the data from the Golden Muffler Shop in Example S1.

This "symbolic" spreadsheet shows the formulas and the input data for an arrival rate of 2 (in cell B4) and service rate of 3 (in cell B5). Cells D4 through D9 contain the output parameters such as average time and average number of people or items in the system, average number and time in the queue, utilization, and idle percent. Cells D12 through D20 provide the probabilities of more than 0 through 8 customers in the system.

PROGRAM S10.3 ■ Using Spreadsheets to Develop Queuing Parameters. The symbolic spreadsheet, showing formulas in cells, is provided.

	A	B	C	D
1	Golden Muffler Shop Queuing With M/M/1			Single Channel Model
2				
3	Inputs			Outputs
4	Arrival rate (lambda)	2	Av.#system (L)	+B4/(B5–B4)
5	Service rate (mu)	3	Av. time sys (W)	1/(B5–B4)
6			Av.#queue (Lq)	+B4^2/B5*(B5–B4)
7			Av. time queue (Wq)	+B4/B5*(B5–B4)
8			Util. factor (rho)	+B4/B5
9			Percent idle (Po)	1–B4/B5
10				
11			K	P(n>k) cust in system
12			0	($B$4/$B$5) ^ (C12+1)
13			1	($B$4/$B$5) ^ (C13+1)
14			2	($B$4/$B$5) ^ (C14+1)
15			3	($B$4/$B$5) ^ (C15+1)
16			4	($B$4/$B$5) ^ (C16+1)
17			5	($B$4/$B$5) ^ (C17+1)
18			6	($B$4/$B$5) ^ (C18+1)
19			7	($B$4/$B$5) ^ (C19+1)
20			8	($B$4/$B$5) ^ (C20+1)

SOLVED PROBLEMS

Solved Problem S10.1

Sid Das and Sons Brick Distributors currently employ one worker whose job is to load bricks on outgoing company trucks. An average of 24 trucks per day, or three per hour, arrive at the loading gate, according to a Poisson distribution. The worker loads them at a rate of four per hour, following approximately the exponential distribution in his service times.

Das believes that adding a second brick loader will substantially improve the firm's productivity. He estimates that a two-person crew at the loading gate will double the loading rate from four trucks per hour to eight trucks per hour. Analyze the effect on the queue of such a change and compare the results to those found with one worker. What is the probability that there will be more than three trucks either being loaded or waiting?

Solution

	NUMBER OF BRICK LOADERS	
	1	2
Truck arrival rate (λ)	3/hr	3/hr
Loading rate (μ)	4/hr	8/hr
Average number in system (L_s)	3 trucks	.6 truck
Average time in system (W_s)	1 hr	.2 hr
Average number in queue (L_q)	2.25 trucks	.225 truck
Average time in queue (W_q)	.75 hr	.075 hr
Utilization rate (ρ)	.75	.375
Probability system empty (P_0)	.25	.625

PROBABILITY OF MORE THAN K TRUCKS IN SYSTEM		
	PROBABILITY N > K	
K	ONE LOADER	TWO LOADERS
0	.75	.375
1	.56	.141
2	.42	.053
3	.32	.020

These results indicate that when only one loader is employed, the average truck must wait three-quarters of an hour before it is loaded. Furthermore, there are an average of 2.25 trucks waiting in line to be loaded. This situation may be unacceptable to management. Note the decline in queue size after the addition of a second loader.

Solved Problem S10.2

Truck drivers working for Sid Das and Sons (see Solved Problem S10.1) earn $10 per hour on the average. Brick loaders receive about $6 per hour. Truck drivers waiting *in the queue or at the loading gate* are drawing a salary but are productively idle and unable to generate revenue during that time. What would be the *hourly* cost savings to the firm associated with employing two loaders instead of one?

Referring to the data in Solved Problem S10.1, we note that the average number of trucks *in the system* is 3 when there is only one loader and .6 when there are two loaders.

Solution

	NUMBER OF LOADERS	
	1	2
Truck driver idle time costs [(average number of trucks) × (hourly rate)] = (3)($10) = $30		$ 6 = (.6)($10)
Loading costs	6	12 = (2)($6)
Total expected cost per hour	$36	$18

The firm will save $18 per hour by adding the second loader.

Solved Problem S10.3

Sid Das and Sons Brick Distributors are considering building a second platform or gate to speed the process of loading their brick trucks. This system, they think, will be even more efficient than simply hiring another loader to help out on the first platform (as in Solved Problem S10.1).

Assume that workers at each platform will be able to load four trucks per hour each and that trucks will continue to arrive at the rate of three per hour. Then apply the appropriate equations to find the waiting line's new operating conditions. Is this new approach indeed more speedy than the other two considered?

Solution

$$P_0 = \cfrac{1}{\left[\displaystyle\sum_{n=0}^{1} \frac{1}{n!}\left(\frac{3}{4}\right)^n\right] + \frac{1}{2!}\left(\frac{3}{4}\right)^2 \frac{2(4)}{2(4)-3}}$$

$$= \cfrac{1}{1 + \frac{3}{4} + \frac{1}{2}\left(\frac{3}{4}\right)^2\left(\frac{8}{8-3}\right)} = .454$$

$$L_s = \frac{3(4)(3/4)^2}{(1)!(8-3)^2}(.4545) + \frac{3}{4} = .873$$

$$W_s = \frac{.873}{3} = .291 \text{ hr}$$

$$L_q = .873 - 3/4 = .123$$

$$W_q = \frac{.123}{3} = .041 \text{ hr}$$

Looking back at Solved Problem S10.1, we see that although length of the *queue* and average time in the queue are lowest when a second platform is open, the average number of trucks in the *system* and average time spent waiting in the system are smallest when two workers are employed loading at a *single* platform. Hence, we would probably recommend not building a second gate.

Solved Problem S10.4

St. Elsewhere Hospital's Cardiac Care Unit (CCU) has five beds, which are virtually always occupied by patients who have just undergone major heart surgery. Two registered nurses are on duty in the CCU in each of the three 8-hour shifts. About every 2 hours (following a Poisson distribution), one of the patients requires a nurse's attention. The nurse will then spend an average of 30 minutes (exponentially distributed) assisting the patient and updating medical records regarding the problem and care provided.

Because immediate service is critical to the five patients, two important questions are: What is the average number of patients being attended by the nurses? What is the average time a patient spends waiting for one of the nurses to arrive at bedside?

Solution

$$N = 5 \text{ patients}$$
$$M = 2 \text{ nurses}$$
$$T = 30 \text{ minutes}$$

$$U = 120 \text{ minutes}$$

$$X = \frac{T}{T+U} = \frac{30}{30+120} = .20$$

From Table S10.7, with $X = .20$ and $M = 2$, we see that

$$F = .976$$

$$H = \text{average number being attended to} = FNX$$
$$= (.976)(5)(.20) = .98 \approx \text{one patient at any given time}$$

$$W = \text{average waiting time for a nurse} = \frac{T(1-F)}{XF}$$

$$= \frac{30(1-.976)}{(.20)(.976)} = 3.69 \text{ minutes}$$

DISCUSSION QUESTIONS

1. What is the waiting-line problem? What are the components in a waiting-line system?

2. What are the assumptions underlying the queuing models described in this chapter?

3. Describe the important operating characteristics of a queuing system.

4. Why must the service rate be greater than the arrival rate in a single-channel queuing system?

5. Briefly describe three situations in which the first-in, first-out (FIFO) discipline rule is not applicable in queuing analysis.

6. Provide examples of four situations in which there is a limited, or finite, waiting line.

7. What are the components of the following queuing systems? Draw and explain the configuration of each.
   (a) Barber shop
   (b) Car wash
   (c) Laundromat
   (d) Small grocery store

8. Do doctors' offices generally have random arrival rates for patients? Are service times random? Under what circumstances might service times be constant?

9. Do you think the Poisson distribution, which assumes independent arrivals, is a good estimation of arrival rates in the following queuing systems? Defend your position in each case.

   (a) School cafeteria
   (b) Barber shop
   (c) Hardware store
   (d) Dentist's office
   (e) College class
   (f) Movie theater

10. What is the utilization factor for a system?

11. What happens if two single-channel systems have the same mean arrival and service rates, but the service time is constant in one and exponential in the other?

12. What dollar value do you place on yourself per hour that you spend waiting in lines? What value do your classmates assess? Why do they differ?

13. Provide an example of a situation where a manager actually wants to have a queue. Why would the manager do so?

14. Most banks have changed from having a line in front of each teller to a system whereby one line feeds all tellers. Which system is better, and why?

15. Justify the queuing system used in most supermarkets today (i.e., a line for each register, with those customers having 10 items or less going to special registers).

16. What cost trade-offs need to be considered in queuing analysis?

CRITICAL
THINKING
EXERCISE

Queues are a critical component in the operation of service organizations. Yet most managers understand very little about this important subject. Visit two service organizations in your community and observe the use of waiting lines. (Examples might be airline check-ins, fast-food restaurants, muffler or oil-change shops, movie theaters, sports arenas, or banks.) What approaches are taken? Diagram the service areas that involve queuing. Do you have any suggestions for improvement in service?

PROBLEMS

· S10.1 Due to a recent increase in business, a secretary in a certain law firm is now having to word process 20 letters a day on the average (assume a Poisson distribution). It takes him approximately 20 minutes to type each letter (assume an exponential distribution). Assuming the secretary works eight hours a day:

a) What is the secretary's utilization rate?

b) What is the average waiting time before the secretary word processes a letter?

c) What is the average number of letters waiting to be done?

d) What is the probability that the secretary has more than five letters to do?

· S10.2 Sam the Vet is running a rabies vaccination clinic for dogs at the local grade school. Sam can "shoot" a dog every 3 minutes. It is estimated that the dogs will arrive independently and randomly throughout the day at a rate of one dog every 6 minutes according to a Poisson distribution. Also assume that Sam's shooting times are exponentially distributed. Find the following:

a) the probability that Sam is idle

b) the proportion of the time that Sam is busy

c) the average number of dogs being shot and waiting to be shot

d) the average number of dogs waiting to be shot

e) the average time a dog waits before getting shot

f) the average amount (mean) of time a dog spends between waiting in line and being shot

· S10.3 Refer to Problem S10.2. It turns out that dogs arrive at the rate of one dog every 4 minutes (*not* every 6 minutes). Recompute your answers to parts (a) through (f) in Problem S10.2.

· S10.4 Calls arrive at Timothy Cronan's hotel switchboard at a rate of two per minute. The average time to handle each of these is 20 seconds. There is only one switchboard operator at the current time. The Poisson and exponential distributions appear to be relevant in this situation.

a) What is the probability that the operator is busy?

b) What is the average time that a call must wait before reaching the operator?

c) What is the average number of calls waiting to be answered?

· S10.5 At the start of football season, the ticket office gets very busy the day before the first game. Customers arrive at the rate of four every 10 minutes, and the average time to transact business is 2 minutes.

a) What is the average number of people in line?

b) What is the average time that a person would spend in the ticket office?

c) What proportion of time is the server busy?

· S10.6 The Charles Leitle Electronics Corporation retains a service crew to repair machine breakdowns that occur on an average of $\lambda = 3$ per day (approximately Poisson in nature). The crew can service an average of $\mu = 8$ machines per day, with a repair time distribution that resembles the exponential distribution.

a) What is the utilization rate of this service system?

b) What is the average down time for a machine that is broken?

c) How many machines are waiting to be serviced at any given time?

d) What is the probability that more than one machine is in the system? The probability that more than two are broken and waiting to be repaired or being serviced? More than three? More than four?

: S10.7 Dan Bower's Car Wash is open 6 days a week, but its heaviest day of business is always Saturday. From historical data, Dan estimates that dirty cars arrive at the rate of 20 per hour all day Saturday. With a full crew working the hand wash line, he figures that cars can be cleaned at the rate of one every 2 minutes. One car at a time is cleaned in this example of a single-channel waiting line.

Assuming Poisson arrivals and exponential service times, find the following:

a) The average number of cars in line.

b) The average time a car waits before it is washed.

c) The average time a car spends in the service system.

d) The utilization rate of the car wash.

e) The probability no cars are in the system.

f) Dan is thinking of switching to an all-automated car wash that uses no crew. The equipment under study washes one car every minute at a constant rate. How will your answers to parts (a) and (b) change with the new system?

: S10.8 Lisa Kennally manages a large Montgomery, Alabama, movie theater complex called Cinema I, II, III, and IV. Each of the four auditoriums plays a different film; the schedule is set so that starting times are staggered to avoid the large crowds that would occur if all four movies started at the same time. The theater has a single ticket booth and a cashier who can maintain an average service rate of 280 movie patrons per hour. Service times are assumed to follow an exponential distribution. Arrivals on a normally active day are Poisson-distributed and average 210 per hour.

In order to determine the efficiency of the current ticket operation, Lisa wishes to examine several queue operating characteristics.

a) Find the average number of moviegoers waiting in line to purchase a ticket.

b) What percentage of the time is the cashier busy?

c) What is the average time a customer spends in the system?

d) What is the average time spent waiting in line to get to the ticket window?

e) What is the probability that there are more than two people in the system? More than three people? More than four?

: S10.9 A university cafeteria line in the student center is a self-serve facility in which students select the food items they want and then form a single line to pay the cashier. Students arrive at a rate of about four per minute according to a Poisson distribution. The single cashier takes about 12 seconds per customer, following an exponential distribution.

a) What is the probability there are more than two students in the system? More than three students? More than four?

b) What is the probability that the system is empty?

c) How long will the average student have to wait before reaching the cashier?

d) What is the expected number of students in the queue?

e) What is the average number in the system?

f) If a second cashier is added (who works at the same pace), how will the operating characteristics computed in parts (b), (c), (d), and (e) change? Assume customers wait in a single line and go to the first available cashier.

⌨ ፧S10.10 The wheat harvesting season in the American Midwest is short, and farmers deliver their truckloads of wheat to a giant central storage bin within a 2-week span. Because of this, wheat-filled trucks waiting to unload and return to the fields have been known to back up for a block at the receiving bin. The central bin is owned cooperatively, and it is to every farmer's benefit to make the unloading/storage process as efficient as possible. The cost of grain deterioration caused by unloading delays and the cost of truck rental and idle driver time are significant concerns to the cooperative members. Although farmers have difficulty quantifying crop damage, it is easy to assign a waiting and unloading cost for truck and driver of $18 per hour. The storage bin is open and operated 16 hours per day and 7 days per week during the 2-week harvest season and is capable of unloading 35 trucks per hour according to an exponential distribution. Full trucks arrive all day long (during the hours the bin is open) at a rate of about 30 per hour, following a Poisson pattern.

To help the cooperative get a handle on the problem of lost time while trucks are waiting in line or unloading at the bin, find the following:

a) The average number of trucks in the unloading system.

b) The average time per truck in the system.

c) The utilization rate for the bin area.

d) The probability that there are more than three trucks in the system at any given time.

e) The total daily cost to the farmers of having their trucks tied up in the unloading process.

f) The cooperative, as mentioned, uses the storage bin heavily only 2 weeks per year. Farmers estimate that enlarging the bin would cut unloading costs by 50% next year. It will cost $9,000 to do so during the off-season. Would it be worth the cooperative's while to enlarge the storage area?

⌨ ፧S10.11 Michael Hanna's Department Store in Clear Lake, Texas, maintains a successful catalog sales department in which a clerk takes orders by telephone. If the clerk is occupied on one line, incoming phone calls to the catalog department are answered automatically by a recording machine and asked to wait. As soon as the clerk is free, the party that has waited the longest is transferred and answered first. Calls come in at a rate of about 12 per hour. The clerk is capable of taking an order in an average of 4 minutes. Calls tend to follow a Poisson distribution, and service times tend to be exponential.

The clerk is paid $5 per hour, but because of lost goodwill and sales, Hanna's loses about $25 per hour of customer time spent waiting for the clerk to take an order.

a) What is the average time that catalog customers must wait before their calls are transferred to the order clerk?

b) What is the average number of callers waiting to place an order?

c) Hanna's is considering adding a second clerk to take calls. The store would pay that person the same $5 per hour. Should it hire another clerk? Explain.

⌨ •S10.12 Customers arrive at an automated coffee-vending machine at a rate of four per minute, following a Poisson distribution. The coffee machine dispenses a cup of coffee at a constant rate of 10 seconds.

a) What is the average number of people waiting in line?

b) What is the average number in the system?

c) How long does the average person wait in line before receiving service?

💻 :S10.13 Robert Olney's Barber Shop is a popular haircutting and styling salon near the campus of the University of New Haven. Four barbers work full-time and spend an average of 15 minutes on each customer. Customers arrive all day long at an average rate of 12 per hour. Arrivals tend to follow the Poisson distribution, and service times are exponentially distributed. The software described in this supplement may be used to answer these questions.

a) What is the probability that the shop is empty?

b) What is the average number of customers in the barber shop?

c) What is the average time spent in the shop?

d) What is the average time that a customer waits to be called to the barber chair?

e) What is the average number waiting to be served?

f) What is the shop's utilization factor?

g) Robert is thinking of adding a fifth barber. How will this affect the utilization rate?

💻 :S10.14 The administrator at a large hospital emergency room faces a problem of providing treatment for patients who arrive at different rates during the day. There are four doctors available to treat patients when needed. If not needed, they can be assigned to other responsibilities (for example, lab tests, reports, X-ray diagnoses) or else rescheduled to work at other hours.

It is important to provide quick and responsive treatment, and the administrator feels that, on the average, patients should not have to sit in the waiting area for more than 5 minutes before being seen by a doctor. Patients are treated on a first-come, first-served basis and see the first available doctor after waiting in the queue. The arrival pattern for a typical day is as follows:

TIME	ARRIVAL RATE
9 A.M.–3 P.M.	6 patients/hour
3 P.M.–8 P.M.	4 patients/hour
8 P.M.–midnight	12 patients/hour

These arrivals follow a Poisson distribution, and treatment times, 12 minutes on the average, follow the exponential pattern.

How many doctors should be on duty during each period in order to maintain the level of patient care expected?

💻 :S10.15 One mechanic services five drilling machines for a steel plate manufacturer. Machines break down on an average of once every 6 working days, and breakdowns tend to follow a Poisson distribution. The mechanic can handle an average of one repair job per day. Repairs follow an exponential distribution.

a) How many machines are waiting for service, on the average?

b) How many drills are in running order, on the average?

c) How much would the waiting time be reduced if a second mechanic were hired?

💻 :S10.16 Two technicians monitor a group of five computers that run an automated manufacturing facility. It takes an average of 15 minutes (exponentially distributed) to adjust a computer that develops a problem. The computers run for an average of 85 minutes (Poisson-distributed) without requiring adjustments. Determine the following:

a) The average number of computers waiting for adjustment.

b) The average number being adjusted.

c) The average number of computers not in working order.

:S10.17 The Duffy Department Store has approximately 300 customers shopping in its store between 9 A.M. and 5 P.M. on Saturdays. In deciding how many cash registers to keep open each Saturday, Jo Ann Duffy, the owner, considers two factors: customer waiting time (and the associated waiting cost) and the service costs of employing additional check-out clerks. Check-out clerks are paid an average of $4 per hour. When only one is on duty, the waiting time per customer is about 10 minutes (or 1/6 of an hour); when two clerks are on duty, the average check-out time is 6 minutes per person; 4 minutes when three clerks are working; and 3 minutes when four clerks are on duty.

Ms. Duffy has conducted customer satisfaction surveys and has been able to estimate that the store suffers approximately $5 in lost sales and goodwill for every *hour* of customer time spent waiting in check-out lines. Using the information provided, determine the optimal number of clerks to have on duty each Saturday in order to minimize the store's total expected cost.

CASE STUDY

New England Castings

For over 75 years, New England Castings, Inc. (NECI), has manufactured wood stoves for home use. In recent years, with increasing energy prices, George Mathison, president, has seen sales triple. This dramatic increase in sales has made it difficult for George to maintain quality in all of the wood stoves and related products.

Unlike other companies manufacturing wood stoves, NECI is *only* in the business of making stoves and stove-related products. Their major products are the Warmglo I, the Warmglo II, the Warmglo III, and the Warmglo IV. The Warmglo I is the smallest wood stove, with a heat output of 30,000 BTUs, and the Warmglo IV is the largest, with a heat output of 60,000 BTUs.

The Warmglo III outsold all of the other stoves by a wide margin. The heat output and available accessories were ideal for the typical home. The Warmglo III also had a number of outstanding features that made it one of the most attractive and heat-efficient stoves on the market. These features, along with the accessories, resulted in expanding sales and prompted George to build a new factory to manufacture Warmglo III stoves. An overview diagram of the factory is shown in Figure S10.5.

The new foundry used the latest equipment, including a new Disamatic that helped in manufacturing stove parts. Regardless of new equipment or procedures, casting operations have remained

FIGURE S10.5 ■ Overview of Factory

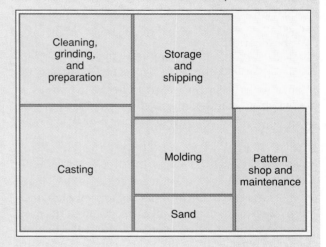

basically unchanged for hundreds of years. To begin with, a wooden pattern is made for every cast-iron piece in the stove. The wooden pattern is an exact duplication of the cast-iron piece that is to be manufactured. NECI has all of its patterns made by Precision Patterns, Inc., and these patterns are stored in the pattern shop and maintenance room. Then, a specially formulated sand is molded around the wooden pattern. There can be two or more sand molds for each pattern. Mixing the sand and making the molds is done in the molding room. When the wooden pattern is removed, the resulting sand molds form a negative image of the desired casting. Next, the molds are transported to the casting room, where molten iron is poured into the molds and allowed to

(Continued)

cool. When the iron has solidified, the molds are moved into the cleaning, grinding, and preparation room. The molds are dumped into large vibrators that shake most of the sand from the casting. The rough castings are then subjected to both sand-blasting to remove the rest of the sand and grinding to finish some of the surfaces of the castings. The castings are then painted with a special heat-resistant paint, assembled into workable stoves, and inspected for manufacturing defects that may have gone undetected thus far. Finally, the finished stoves are moved to storage and shipping, where they are packaged and shipped to the appropriate locations.

At present, the pattern shop and the maintenance department are located in the same room. One large counter is used by maintenance personnel to get tools and parts, and by sand molders who need various patterns for the molding operation. Pete Nawler and Bob Dillman, who work behind the counter, are able to service a total of 10 people per hour (about 5 per hour each). On the average, four people from maintenance and three people from the molding department arrive at the counter per hour. People from the molding department and from maintenance arrive randomly, and to be served, they form a single line.

Pete and Bob have always had a policy of first come, first served. Because of the location of the pattern shop and maintenance department, it takes about 3 minutes for an individual from the maintenance department to walk to the pattern and maintenance room, and it takes about 1 minute for an individual to walk from the molding department to the pattern and maintenance room.

After observing the operation of the pattern shop and maintenance room for several weeks, George decided to make some changes to the layout of the factory. An overview of these changes appears in Figure S10.6.

FIGURE S10.6 ■ Overview of Factory after Changes

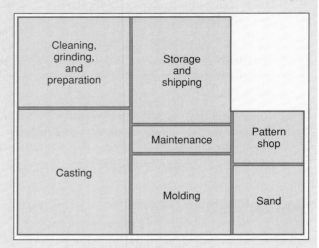

Separating the maintenance shop from the pattern shop had a number of advantages. It would take people from the maintenance department only 1 minute instead of 3 to get to the new maintenance department. Using motion and time studies, George was also able to determine that improving the layout of the maintenance department would allow Bob to serve six people from the maintenance department per hour, and improving the layout of the pattern department would allow Pete to serve seven people from the molding shop per hour.

DISCUSSION QUESTIONS

1. How much time would the new layout save?
2. If maintenance personnel were paid $9.50 per hour and molding personnel were paid $11.75 per hour, how much could be saved per hour with the new factory layout?
3. Should George have made the change in layout?

Source: B. Render and R. M. Stair, Jr., *Quantitative Analysis for Management*, 5th ed. (Boston: Allyn and Bacon, 1994): p. 673–4.

CASE STUDY

The Winter Park Hotel

Donna Shader, manager of the Winter Park Hotel, is considering how to restructure the front desk to reach an optimum level of staff efficiency and guest service. At present, the hotel has five clerks on duty, each with a separate waiting line, during peak check-in time of 3:00 P.M. to 5:00 P.M. Observation of arrivals during this time show that an average of 90 guests arrive each hour (although there is no upward limit on the number that could arrive at any given time). It takes an average of 3 minutes for the front-desk clerk to register each guest.

Ms. Shader is considering three plans for improving guest service by reducing the length of time guests spend waiting in line. The first proposal would designate one employee as a quick-service clerk for guests registering under corporate accounts, a market segment that fills about 30% of all occupied rooms. Because corporate guests are preregistered, their registration takes just 2 minutes. With these guests separated from the rest of the clientele, the average time for registering a typical guest would climb to 3.4 minutes. Under plan one, noncorporate guests would choose any of the remaining four lines.

The second plan is to implement a single-line system. All guests could form a single waiting line to be served by whichever of five clerks became available. This option would require sufficient lobby space for what could be a substantial queue.

The use of an automatic teller machine (ATM) for check-ins is the basis of the third proposal. Given that initial use of this technology might be minimal, Shader estimated that 20% of customers, primarily frequent guests, would be willing to use the machines. (This might be a conservative estimate if the guests perceive direct benefits from using the ATM, as bank customers do. Citibank reports that some 80% of its Manhattan customers use its ATMs.) Ms. Shader would set up a single queue for customers who prefer human check-in clerks. This would be served by the five clerks, although Shader is hopeful that the machine will allow a reduction to four.

DISCUSSION QUESTIONS

1. Determine the average amount of time that a guest spends checking in. How would this change under each of the state options?
2. Which option do you recommend?

Source: B. Render and R. M. Stair, Jr., *Quantitative Analysis for Management,* 5th ed. (Boston: Allyn and Bacon, 1994): p. 672.

BIBLIOGRAPHY

Becker, L. C., and E. G. Landauer. "Reducing Waiting Time at Security Checkpoints." *Interfaces,* 19, no. 5 (September/October 1989): 57–65.

Byrd, J. "The Value of Queuing Theory." *Interfaces,* 8, no. 3 (May 1978): 22–26.

Cooper, R. B. *Introduction to Queuing Theory,* 2nd ed. New York: Elsevier-North Holland, 1980.

Foote, B. L. "Queuing Case Study of Drive-In Banking." *Interfaces,* 6, no. 4 (August 1976): 31.

Grassmann, W. K. "Finding the Right Number of Servers in Real-World Queuing Systems." *Interfaces,* 18, no. 2 (March/April 1988): 94–104.

Ho, C., and H. Lau. "Minimizing Total Cost in Scheduling Outpatient Appointments." *Management Science,* 38, no. 12 (December 1992): 1750.

Katz, K., B. Larson, and R. Larson. "Prescription for the Waiting-in-Line Blues: Entertain, Enlighten, and Engage." *Sloan Management Review* (Winter 1991): 44–53.

Morse, P. M. *Queues, Inventories and Maintenance.* New York: John Wiley, 1958.

Render, B., and R. M. Stair. *Introduction to Management Science.* Boston: Allyn and Bacon, 1992.

———. *Quantitative Analysis for Management.* 5th ed. Boston: Allyn and Bacon, 1994.

Solomon, S. *Simulation of Waiting Lines.* Englewood Cliffs, NJ: Prentice Hall, 1983.

Sze, D. Y. "A Queuing Model for Telephone Operator Staffing." *Operations Research,* 3, no. 2 (March/April 1984): 229–249.

Worthington, D. J. "Queuing Models for Hospital Waiting Lists." *Journal of the Operational Research Society,* 38, no. 5 (May 1987): 413–422.

11

HUMAN RESOURCE STRATEGY

LEARNING OBJECTIVES

*When you complete this
chapter you should be able to:*

Identify or Define:

  Job Specialization

  Job Expansion

  Tools of Methods Analysis

  Ergonomics

  Job Design

  Lean Production

  Labor Standards

Explain:

  Requirements of good job design

ALASKA AIRLINES DEVELOPS A COMPETITIVE ADVANTAGE VIA HUMAN FACTORS

Ergonomics and human factors provide an opportunity to improve human performance. Such opportunities exist in a variety of applications, including commercial aircraft. New cockpit displays are designed to reduce the chance of human error, which is estimated to be a factor in about two-thirds of commercial air accidents. Fractions of a second in the cockpit can literally mean the difference between life and death.

One approach to improved cockpit displays is to simplify the instrument panel. Newer contemporary "glass cockpits" display information in more concise form than the traditional rows of round dials by using cathode-ray tubes (CRTs). CRTs allow pilots to determine more

Traditional round analog dials and gauges can present a lot of difficult-to-interpret information.

A glass cockpit with less clutter because of fewer dials and gauges can net a faster pilot-response time.

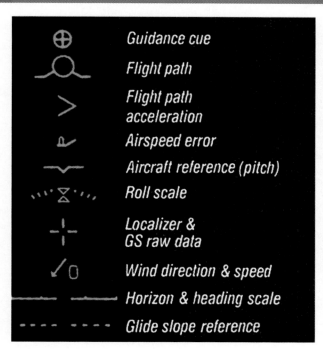

⊕	Guidance cue
	Flight path
>	Flight path acceleration
	Airspeed error
	Aircraft reference (pitch)
	Roll scale
	Localizer & GS raw data
	Wind direction & speed
	Horizon & heading scale
	Glide slope reference

The symbols in the "heads-up" display (shown in the photo to the right) are interpreted above.

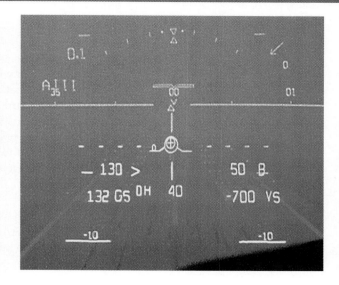

Alaska Airlines has begun using heads-up displays. Displays such as the ones shown above allow images and critical flight information to be projected on a fold-down screen, as shown in the bottom photo, so the pilot can fly "heads-up."

rapidly a variety of control variables including air speed, altitude, and rate of climb.

Demands on the human system have led to a second innovation, which uses our knowledge of human factors to present 19 critical controls directly on a "heads-up" display. A "heads-up" display allows the pilot to look through the data that appear on the visor of a helmet, a fold-down screen, or a windshield. This technology is being introduced in commercial aircraft. And Alaska Airlines is leading the way.

With fleet operations in Seattle, Washington, an area often hit with fog and low-visibility conditions, Alaska Airlines believes installation of the new heads-up displays improves operating capabilities. This improvement in human factors should reduce pilot error *and* improve pilot response. Such a focus on human resources, the subject of this chapter, yields safer flights and ultimately a competitive advantage at Alaska Airlines.

A t 9 A.M. the assembly line has been moving for only 1 hour, but already the day is dragging. In position five on line four, Annette Fullbright catches the next circuit board crawling down the line. At the current pace, one board passes her workstation every minute and a half. Forty down, 280 left to go today. Over in quality control, Ismael Hernandez puts his soldering gun back in its holster, fidgets with his left shirt sleeve and steals a quick glance at his watch. Thirty more minutes before coffee break. Two and a half hours to lunch. Seven and a half more until quitting time.[1] ◆

Assembly line scenes such as these are repeated a thousand times over every day all over the world. Why are Annette's and Ismael's jobs like this? Is it a good human resource strategy for firms to have such jobs? In this chapter, we will examine these and related questions.

HUMAN RESOURCE STRATEGY

Human performance is crucial to an organization's performance. An organization does not function without people. It does not function well without competent people. It does not excel without competent, motivated people. Consequently, how the operations manager formulates a human resource strategy determines the talents available to operations. Moreover, people are expensive; in many organizations, a third of total cost is in wages and salaries. Therefore, this chapter considers human resource strategy options.

Objective of the Human Resource Strategy

The *objective of a human resource strategy* is to manage labor and design jobs so people are *efficiently utilized*. This must be done within the constraints of other P/OM decisions, while maintaining a *reasonable quality of work life* in an atmosphere of *mutual commitment and trust*.

Quality of work life

Mutual commitment
Mutual trust

By reasonable **quality of work life**, we mean a job that not only is reasonably safe and for which the pay is equitable, but also that achieves an appropriate level of both physical and psychological requirements. By **mutual commitment**, we mean both management and employee strive to meet common objectives. By **mutual trust**, we mean reasonable, documented employment policies that are honestly and equitably implemented to the satisfaction of both management and employee.[2] When management has a genuine respect for its employees and their contribution to the firm, establishing a reasonable quality of work life and mutual trust is not particularly difficult.

Constraints on Human Resource Strategy

Human resource strategies are constrained by other strategic decisions. First, the product mix may determine seasonality and stability of employment. Second,

---

[1]Roger Thurow, "Life On The Job," *Wall Street Journal* (June 1, 1981): 1.
[2]With increasing frequency, we find companies calling their employees *associates, individual contributors,* or members of a particular *team.*

FIGURE 11.1 ■ Constraints on Human Resource Strategy. The effective operations manager understands how decisions blend together to constrain the human resource strategy.

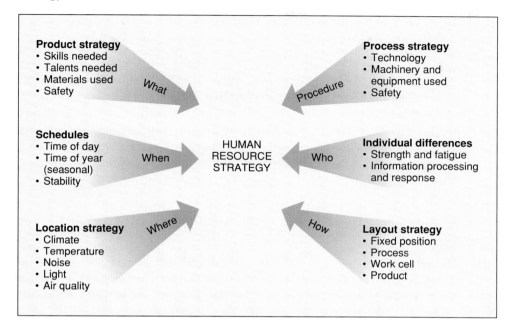

technology, equipment, and processes may affect safety and job content. Third, location may have an impact on the ambient environment in which the employees work. Finally, decisions regarding layout influence job content.

The technology decision imposes substantial constraints. For instance, some of the jobs in steel mills are dirty, noisy, and dangerous; slaughterhouse jobs may be stressful and include a stomach-crunching stench; and assembly line jobs are often boring and mind-numbing.

We are not going to change these jobs without making changes in our other strategic decisions. So, the trade-offs necessary to reach a tolerable quality of work life are difficult.

Much of our human resource strategy is a result of other operation design decisions (Figure 11.1). It behooves a prudent manager to ensure that such decisions are considered simultaneously. The manager blends ingredients so that the result is an effective, efficient system where individuals have optimum job design.

Acknowledging the constraints imposed on human resource strategy, we now look at three distinct decision areas of human resource strategy. These three areas are labor planning, job design, and labor standards. The supplement to this chapter expands on the discussion of labor standards and introduces work measurement.

LABOR PLANNING

Labor planning is determining staffing policies that deal with (1) employment stability and (2) work schedules.

Labor planning

Employment Stability Policies

Employment stability deals with the number of employees that are maintained by an organization at any given time. There are two very basic policies for dealing with stability.

1. *Follow Demand Exactly.* Following demand exactly keeps direct labor costs tied to production, but incurs other costs. These other costs include (a) hiring and termination costs, (b) unemployment insurance, and (c) premium wages to entice personnel to accept unstable employment. This policy tends to treat labor as a variable cost.

2. *Hold Employment Constant.* Holding employment levels constant maintains a trained work force and keeps hiring, termination, and unemployment costs to a minimum. However, with employment held constant, employees may not be utilized fully when demand is low, and the firm may not have the human resources it needs when demand is high. This policy tends to treat labor as a fixed cost.

Maintaining a stable work force may allow a firm to pay lower wages than a firm that follows demand. This savings may provide a competitive advantage. However, firms with highly seasonal work and little control over demand may be best served by a fluctuating work force. For example, a salmon canner on the Columbia River can only process salmon when the salmon are running. However, the firm may find complementary labor demands in other products or operations, such as making the cans and labels or repairing and maintaining facilities.

Firms must determine policies about employment stability. The above policies are only two of many that can be efficient *and* provide a reasonable quality of work life.

Work Schedules

Standard work schedule

Flextime

Although the **standard work schedule** in the United States is five 8-hour days, variations do exist. A currently popular variation is a work schedule called flextime. **Flextime** allows employees, within limits, to determine their own schedules. A flextime policy might allow an employee (with proper notification) to be at work at 8 A.M. plus or minus 2 hours. This allows more autonomy and independence on the part of the employee. Some firms have found flextime a low-cost fringe benefit that enhances job satisfaction. The problem from the P/OM perspective is that much production work requires full staffing for efficient operations. A machine that requires three people cannot run at all if only two show up. Having a waiter show up to serve lunch at 1:30 P.M. rather than 11:30 A.M. is not much help either.

Some industries find that their process strategy has severely constrained their human resource scheduling option. For instance, paper manufacturing, petroleum refining, and power stations must be staffed around the clock except for maintenance and repair shutdown. Firms in these industries are severely constrained when implementing variable-time policies.

Flexible work week

Another work schedule is a **flexible work week**. This often manifests itself in fewer but longer days, such as four 10-hour days. These schedules are viable for many operations functions, provided suppliers and customers can be accommodated. Firms that have high process startup times (say, to get a boiler up to operating temperature) find longer workday options particularly appealing. A 1994 Gallup survey showed that two-thirds of working adults would prefer toiling four 10-hour days to the standard 5-day schedule. Duke Power Co., Los Angeles county, AT&T, and General Motors are just a few organizations to offer the 4-day week.

Another option is to have shorter days rather than longer days. This often moves employees to **part-time status**. Such an option is particularly attractive in service industries, where staffing for peak loads is necessary. Banks and restaurants often hire part-time workers. Also, many firms reduce labor costs by reducing fringe benefits for part-time employees. **Part-time status**

Job Classifications and Work Rules

Many organizations have strict job classifications and work rules that specify who can do what, when they can do it, and under what conditions they can do it. These job classifications and work rules restrict employee flexibility on the job, which in turn reduces the flexibility of the production/operations function. But, part of an operations manager's task is to manage the unexpected. Therefore, the more flexibility a firm has when staffing and establishing work schedules, the more efficient it can be. Building morale and meeting staffing requirements that result in an efficient production function are easier if managers have fewer job classifications and work-rule constraints.

JOB DESIGN

Job design is specifying the tasks that constitute a job for an individual or a group. We examine six components of job design: (1) job specialization, (2) job expansion, (3) psychological components, (4) self-directed teams, (5) motivation and incentive systems, and (6) ergonomics and work methods. **Job design**

Job Specialization

Job design's importance as a management variable is credited to Adam Smith.[3] Smith suggested that a division of labor, also known as **labor specialization** and job specialization, would assist in reducing labor costs in several ways. **Labor specialization**

1. *development of dexterity* and faster learning by the employee because of repetition,
2. *less loss of time* because the employee would not be changing jobs or tools,
3. *development of specialized tools* and the reduction of investment because each employee has only a few tools needed for a particular task.

Charles Babbage determined that a fourth consideration was also important for labor efficiency.[4] Because pay tends to follow skill with a rather high correlation, Babbage suggested *paying exactly the wage needed for the particular skill required*. If the entire job consists of only one skill, then we would pay for only that skill. Otherwise, we

[3] Adam Smith, *On the Creation of the Wealth of Nations* (London, 1876).
[4] Charles Babbage, *On the Economy of Machinery and Manufacturers* (London, 1832), Chapter 18.

would tend to pay for the highest skill contributed by the employee. These four advantages of labor specialization are still valid today.

A classic example of labor specialization is the assembly line, as described in the opening paragraph of this chapter. Such systems are often very efficient, although they may require employees to do repetitive, mind-numbing jobs. The wage rate for many of these jobs, however, is very good. Given the relatively high wage rate for the modest skills required in many of these jobs, there is often a large pool of employees from which to choose. This is not an incidental consideration for the manager with responsibility for staffing the operations function. It is estimated that 2% to 3% of the work force in industrialized nations perform highly specialized, repetitive, assembly-line jobs. The traditional way of developing and maintaining worker commitment under labor specialization has been good selection (matching people to the job), good wages, and incentive systems.

Job Expansion

Job enlargement
Job rotation

Job enrichment

In recent years, there has been an effort to improve the quality of work life by moving from the labor specialization toward a more varied job design. The theory is that variety makes the job "better" and the employee therefore finds a higher quality of work life. This in turn benefits the employee and the organization. We modify jobs in a variety of ways. The first approach is **job enlargement**, which occurs when we add tasks of similar skill to the existing job. **Job rotation** is a version of job enlargement that occurs when the job per se is not enlarged, but rather the employee is allowed to move from one specialized job to another. Variety has been added to the employee's perspective of the job. Another approach is **job enrichment**, which adds planning and control to the job. Job enrichment can be thought of as *vertical expansion*, as opposed to job enlargement, which is *horizontal*. These ideas and others are shown in Figure 11.2.

Employee empowerment

The GE process for empowering employees is generating ideas in offices and on factory floors. Here at Appliance Park in Louisville, Kentucky, for example, employees like utility operator Leo Porter (left) and shop steward Ron Rowe of IUE Local 761 are constantly coming up with ideas—and putting them into action.

Employee empowerment is the practice of enriching jobs so employees accept responsibility for a variety of decisions normally associated with staff specialists.[5] Employee empowerment is a popular extension of job enrichment. Empowering employees helps them take ownership of their jobs so they have a personal interest in improving performance. (See the *POM in Action* box "Empowerment at the Ritz-Carlton.")

Psychological Components of Job Design

An effective human resources strategy also requires consideration of the psychological components of job design. Psychological components of job design focus on how to design jobs that meet some minimum psychological requirements.

HAWTHORNE STUDIES. The Hawthorne studies introduced psychology to the workplace. They were conducted in the late 1920s at GE's Hawthorne Plant near Chicago. Publication of the findings in 1939[6] showed conclusively that there is a dynamic social system at the workplace. Ironically, these studies were initiated to determine the impact of lighting on productivity. Instead they found the social system

---

[5] See W. C. Byham, *Zapp! The Lightning of Empowerment* (New York: Ballantine, 1992).
[6] F. J. Roethlisberger and William J. Dickinson, *Management and the Workers* (New York: John Wiley, 1964, copyright 1939, by the President & Fellows of Harvard College).

Empowerment at the Ritz-Carlton

When the president of the Ritz-Carlton hotel chain introduces himself to employees, he begins with these lines: "My name is Horst Schulze. I'm president of this company; I'm very important. [Pause] But so are you. Absolutely. Equally important." This attitude may be the cause of a turnover rate that is less than half the industry average, and may be why the Ritz recently received a Malcolm Baldrige National Quality Award.

Schulze describes customer service in his organization as "Ladies and gentlemen serving ladies and gentlemen." He stresses that *both* groups be treated with dignity and respect.

To empower employees, Ritz front-desk clerks and sales managers can spend up to $2,000 and $5,000 of company money, respectively—to ensure that guests leave satisfied. For example, when the New York Ritz was overbooked once, 20 guests were sent in three limousines packed with champagne and caviar. The cost: $5,000. "The idea was to please guests," says the Ritz manager.

Empowerment also includes taking suggestions of all employees seriously. When a room service waiter proposed the company spend $50,000 to implement a recycling plan, Schulze took a deep breath and then agreed. The idea paid off: Weekly garbage pickups have been reduced and the hotel now sells its paper products rather than paying others to haul it off. The changes have saved $80,000 a year and typify the hotel's reliance on employee suggestions for quality improvement.

Sources: Wall Street Journal (April 22, 1994): B-1; J. Dean and J. Evans, *Total Quality* (West, 1994): 207–208; and *Hotel and Motel Management* (September 6, 1993): 20–21.

and distinct roles played by employees to be more important than the intensity of the lighting. They also found that individual differences may be dominant in what an employee expects from the job and what the employee thinks her or his contribution to the job should be.

CORE JOB CHARACTERISTICS. In the six decades since the Hawthorne studies, substantial research regarding the psychological components of job design has

FIGURE 11.2 ■ Job Design Continuum

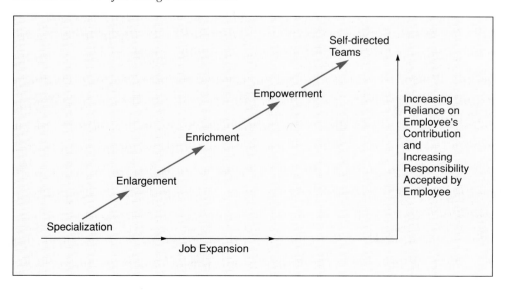

taken place.[7] Hackman and Oldham have incorporated much of that work into five desirable characteristics of job design.[8] Their summary suggests that jobs should include:

1. *Skill Variety.* The job should require the worker to use a variety of skills and talents.
2. *Job Identity.* The job should allow the worker to perceive the job as a whole and recognize a start and a finish.
3. *Job Significance.* The job should provide a sense that the job has impact on the organization and society.
4. *Autonomy.* The job should permit freedom, independence, and discretion.
5. *Feedback.* The job should provide clear, timely information about performance.

Including these five ingredients in job design is consistent with job enlargement, job enrichment, and employee empowerment. We now want to look at teams to expand jobs and achieve these five job characteristics.

Self-Directed Teams

Self-directed team

Many world-class organizations have adopted teams to foster mutual trust and commitment, and provide the core job characteristics. This is illustrated in the *POM in Action* box dealing with Mazda's worker selection. One team concept of particular note is the self-directed team. A **self-directed team** is a group of empowered individuals working together to reach a common goal. These teams may be organized for long-term or short-term objectives. The major reasons teams are effective are because they can easily provide employee empowerment, core job characteristics, and many of the psychological needs of team members.[9]

Of course, many good job designs *can* provide these psychological needs. Therefore, to maximize team effectiveness, managers do more than just form "teams." For instance, they (1) ensure that those who have a legitimate contribution are on the team, (2) provide management support, (3) ensure the necessary training, and (4) endorse a clear objective for the team. Successful teams should also receive rewards and recognition. Finally, managers must recognize that teams have a life cycle and that achieving an objective may suggest disbanding the team. However, teams may be renewed with a change in members or new assignments. Empowered employees working in teams can make a powerful contribution to world-class performance.

Teams and other approaches to job expansion should not only improve the quality of work life and job satisfaction, but also motivate employees to achieve organizational objectives. Both managers *and* employees need to be committed to achieving organizational objectives. However, employee contribution is fostered in a variety of ways, including organizational climate, supervisory action, *and* job design.

---

[7]See, for instance, the work of Abraham H. Maslow, "A Theory of Human Motivation," *Psychological Review*, 50 (1943): 370–396; and Frederick Herzberg, B. Mausner, and B. B. Snyderman, *The Motivation to Work* (New York: John Wiley, 1965).

[8]See "Motivation Through the Design of Work," in Jay Richard Hackman and Greg R. Oldham, *Work Redesign* (Reading, MA: Addison-Wesley, 1980).

[9]Per H. Engelstad, "Sociotechnical Approach to Problems of Process Control," in Louis E. Davis and James C. Taylor, eds., *Design of Jobs* (Santa Monica: Goodyear Publishing, 1979), pp. 184–205.

How Does Mazda Pick Workers for Its U.S. Plants? Very Carefully.

It was not long ago that the auto industry did not want educated people in its factories. As former United Auto Worker's President Douglas Fraser said, "You don't need to be a rocket scientist to assemble a car." But a new breed of auto worker is emerging. Over a quarter of the workers just hired for a new shift at a Chrysler plant in Ontario, Canada, have college degrees.

Mazda Motors' assembly plant in Flat Rock, Michigan, is even pickier, hiring only 1,300 of nearly 10,000 applicants who passed its five-step screening process. It spent about $40 million—roughly $13,000 per employee—to staff the plant. The Japanese firm believes the key to success is picking the best employees and training them well.

A clear goal emerges. Interpersonal skills and team participation are mandatory. The basic philosophy: Reward flows not so much from your personal performance as from your impact on team and company.

In Mazda training rooms, employees learn to chart quality by building paper airplanes and checking their flight performance. "If a part doesn't meet specifications," they are told, "you reject it. That's your job." Mazda devotes 3 training days just to the philosophy of *Kaizen,* or continual improvement. After 3 weeks of this "basic training," each new hire spends 5 to 7 weeks on specific technical training and then 3 to 4 weeks being supervised on the assembly line.

Overkill? Maybe, but Mazda is not taking any chances. The company believes that teams are the key to its success and wants to build its plant around that concept from scratch.

Sources: Wall Street Journal (March 11, 1994): A-1; and *Business Week* (October 3, 1988): 84–85.

Expanded job designs allow the employee to accept more responsibility. For employees who accept this responsibility, we may well expect some enhancement in productivity and product quality. Among the other positive aspects of job expansion are reduced turnover, tardiness, and absenteeism. Managers who expand jobs and build communication systems that elicit suggestions from employees have an added potential for efficiency. But as the *POM in Action* box "World-Class Standards Are Tough" suggests, there is no guarantee that productivity or quality will improve with the use of job expansion. These job designs have a number of limitations.

LIMITATIONS OF JOB EXPANSION. If job designs that enlarge, enrich, empower, and use teams are so good, why are they not universally used? Let us identify some limitations of these expanded job designs:

1. *Higher Capital Cost.* Job expansion requires facilities that cost more than a conventional layout. This extra expenditure must be generated through savings (greater efficiency) or through higher prices.

2. *Many Individuals Prefer Simple Jobs.* Some studies indicate that many employees opt for the less complex jobs.[10] In a discussion about improving the quality of work life, we cannot forget the importance of individual differences. Differences in individuals provide latitude for the resourceful operations manager when designing jobs.

[10]Michell Fein, "Job Enrichment Does Not Work," *Atlanta Economic Review* (November/December 1975): 50–54.

World-Class Standards Are Tough

In 1988, Volvo opened its car-assembly factory in Uddevalla, Sweden, and claimed leadership in a bold experiment in job design. Volvo's chairman wanted to prove that the craftsman approach of having a small team of highly skilled workers build an entire car, when linked with advanced materials handling, could compete after all.

The Uddevalla approach of cutting out layers of management and removing all foremen aimed to give workers more control over their jobs, reduce the tedium of the assembly line, and encourage workers to broaden their skills. In doing so, Volvo hoped also to tackle the special Swedish problems of absenteeism and turnover, which are among the highest in the developed world.

But as the chart shows, it took 50 hours of labor to assemble a car at Uddevalla, compared with 37 hours at Volvo's 17-year-old plant at Kalmar, and 25 hours at its conventional assembly line in Ghent, Belgium. Finally, Volvo conceded that the Uddevalla plant could not achieve world-class productivity levels, and it closed the plant. The Kalmar plant may be the next victim of world-class standards.

COMPANY	LOCATION	HOURS	REGIONAL AVERAGES	
Volvo	Ghent, Belgium	25	Japan— domestic	17
Volvo	Kalmar, Sweden	17	Japan— United States	22
Volvo	Uddevalla, Sweden	50	United States— domestic	25
			Europe	36

Sources: Sloan Management Review (Winter 1994): 32–39, and (Spring 1993): 85–94; and *Personnel Management* (June 1993): 34–38.

3. *Higher Wage Rates Are Required.* People often receive wages for their highest skills, not their lowest.[11] So, expanded jobs may well require a higher average wage than jobs that are not.

4. *Smaller Labor Pool Exists.* Because expanded jobs require more skill and acceptance of more responsibility, the job requirements have increased. Depending upon the availability of labor, this may be a constraint.

5. *Increased Accident Rates May Occur.* Expanded jobs may contribute to a higher accident rate.[12] This indirectly increases wages, insurance costs, and workmen's compensation.

6. *Current Technology May Not Lend Itself to Job Expansion.* The disassembly jobs at a slaughterhouse and computer assembly jobs are that way because alternative technologies (if any) are thought to be unacceptable.

These six points provide the constraints on job expansion. These practices increase costs. Therefore, for the firm to have a competitive advantage, its savings must be greater than its cost. It is not always obvious that such is the case. The strategic decision is not an easy one.

Motivation and Incentive Systems

Our discussion of psychology provides insight into the factors that may contribute to job satisfaction and motivation. In addition to these psychological factors, there are

[11]Charles Babbage, *On the Economy of Machinery and Manufacturers* (London, 1832), Chapter 18.
[12]J. Tsaari and J. Lahtella, "Job Enrichment: Cause of Increased Accidents?" *Industrial Engineering* (October 1978): 41–45.

monetary factors. Money often serves as a psychological, as well as a financial motivator. Monetary rewards take the form of bonuses, profit and gain sharing, and incentive systems.

Bonuses, typically in cash or stock options, are often used at executive levels to reward management. **Profit-sharing** systems provide some part of the profit for distribution to employees. A variation of profit sharing is gain sharing. **Gain-sharing** techniques reward employees for improvements made in an organization's performance. The most popular of these is the Scanlon plan, where any reduction in the cost of labor is shared between management and labor.[13] **Incentive systems** based on individual or group productivity are used in close to half of the manufacturing firms in America. These systems are often based on the employee or crew achieving production above a predetermined standard. The standard can be based on a standard time per task or number of pieces made. Standard time systems are sometimes called **measured daywork**, where employees are paid based on the amount of standard time accomplished. A **piece-rate** system assigns a standard time for each piece, and the employee is paid based on the number of pieces made. Both measured daywork and piece-rate systems typically guarantee the employee at least a base rate for the shift.

Bonus
Profit sharing
Gain sharing

Incentive system

Measured daywork
Piece rate

Lean Production

When mutual trust and commitment are combined with good job designs, lean production may be possible. Under **lean production**, highly trained employees are committed to removing waste and doing only those activities where value is added. Empowered employees analyze every detail of serving the customer and are increasingly successful in squeezing out waste. The concept of lean production varies substantially from a more traditional effort to make jobs ever more simple and require ever less training. Indeed, when effectively implemented, lean production utilizes the employee's *mental* as well as physical attributes to continually improve the production system. Because of a reasonable quality of work life and mutual trust, the employee buys into mutual commitment. In this way, the production process is constantly improving and ever higher levels of efficiency are achieved. Under lean production, the employee is not a robot; he or she is an empowered member of the organization who uses both mental and physical abilities to help serve the customer through ever higher levels of productivity.

Lean production

Ergonomics and Work Methods

As mentioned in Chapter 1, Frederick W. Taylor began the era of scientific management in the late 1800s.[14] He and his contemporaries began to examine personnel selection, work methods, labor standards, and motivation.

With the foundation provided by Taylor, we have developed a body of knowledge about people's capabilities and limitations. This knowledge is necessary because humans are a hand/eye animal possessing exceptional capabilities and some limitations. Because managers must design jobs that can be done, we now introduce a few of the issues related to people's capabilities and limitations.

Ergonomics has a place in sports as well as in the workplace. Here, a stationary swimmer in a 50,000 gallon tank swims against a pump-generated current while her oxygen intake is measured and evaluated.

[13]Fred G. Lesieur, and Elbridge S. Puckett, "The Scanlon Plan Has Proved Itself," *Harvard Business Review*, 47, no. 5 (September/October 1969): 109–118.
[14]Frederick W. Taylor, *Scientific Management* (New York: Harper & Row, 1911), p. 204.

Ergonomics issues occur in the office as well as in the factory. Here an ergonomics consultant is measuring the angle of a terminal operator's neck. Posture, which is related to desk height, chair height and position, keyboard placement, and CRT screen, is an important factor in reducing back and neck pain that can be caused by extended hours at a CRT.

Ergonomics

ERGONOMICS.   The operations manager is interested in building a good interface between human and machine. Studies of this interface are known as **ergonomics**. Ergonomics means "the study of work." (*Ergo* is from the Greek word for *work*.) In the United States, the term *human factors* is often substituted for the word *ergonomics*.

Male and female adults come in limited configurations.[15] Therefore, design of tools and the workplace depends on the study of people to determine what they can and cannot do. Substantial data have been collected that provide basic strength and measurement data needed to design tools and the workplace. The design of the workplace can make the job easier or impossible. Additionally, we now have the ability, through the use of computer modeling, to analyze human motions and efforts.

Let us look briefly at one instance of human measurements, to determine the proper height for a writing desk. The desk has an optimum height depending on the size of the individual and the task to be performed. The common height for a writing desk is 29 inches. For typing or data entry at a CRT, the surface should be lower. The preferred chair and desk height should result in a very slight angle between the body and arm when the individual is viewed from the front and when the back is straight.[16] This is the critical measurement; it can be achieved via adjustment in either table or chair height.

OPERATOR INPUT TO MACHINES.   Operator response to machines, be they hand tools, pedals, levers, or buttons, needs to be evaluated. Operations managers

[15]Henry Dreyfuss, *The Measure of Man* (New York: Whitney Library of Design, 1960).
[16]Edwin R. Tichauer, "Biomechanics Sustains Occupational Safety and Health," *Industrial Engineering* (February 1976): 46–55.

FIGURE 11.3 ■ Job Design and the Keyboard

Apple Computers' new adjustable keyboard is divided into two hinged sections that can be customized. (Apple Computers, Cupertino, California)

Most of the usual QWERTY letter layout is retained, but tests indicate that the keyboard is less physically demanding and more comfortable to use than a traditional computer keyboard. The keyboard is a closer fit to the natural shape of the hand. (Kinesis Corp., Bellevue, Washington)

The "DataHand" keyboard allows each hand to rest on its own ergonomically shaped and padded palm support. Five keys surround each fingertip and thumb. (Industrial Innovations, Inc., Scottsdale, Arizona)

need to be sure that operators have the strength, reflexes, perception, and mental capacity to provide the necessary control. The discussion of carpal tunnel syndrome in the photo shows what can happen when a tool as simple as a keyboard is poorly designed. Figure 11.3 indicates recent innovations designed to improve this common tool.

FEEDBACK TO OPERATORS. Feedback to operators is provided by sight, sound, and feel; it should not be left to chance. The mishap at the Three Mile Island nuclear facility, America's worst nuclear experience, was in large part the result of poor feedback to the operators about reactor performance. Nonfunctional groups of large, unclear instruments and inaccessible controls, combined with hundreds of confusing warning lights, contributed to that nuclear failure. Such relatively simple issues make a difference in operator response and therefore performance.

THE WORK ENVIRONMENT. The physical environment in which employees work affects their performance, safety, and quality of work life. Illumination, noise and vibration, temperature, humidity, and air quality are work environment factors under the control of the organization and the operations manager. The manager must approach them as controllable.

Illumination is necessary, but the proper level depends upon the work being performed. Figure 11.4 provides some guidelines. However, other factors of lighting are important. These other factors include reflective ability, contrast of the work surface with surroundings, glare, and shadows.

Noise of some form is usually present in the work area, and many employees seem to adjust well. However, high levels of sound will damage hearing. Figure 11.5 provides indications of the sound generated by various activities. Extended periods of exposure to decibel levels above 85 dB are permanently damaging to hearing. The Occupational Safety and Health Administration (OSHA) requires ear protection

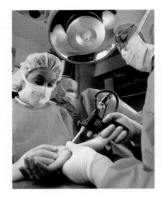

Carpal tunnel syndrome is a wrist disorder that afflicts 23,000 workers annually and costs employers and insurers an average of $30,000 per affected worker. Many of the tools, handles, and typewriter keyboards now in use put the wrists in an unnatural position. An unnatural position, combined with extended repetition can cause carpal tunnel syndrome. One of the medical procedures for carpal tunnel syndrome is the operation shown here that reduces the symptoms; but the cure is in the ergonomics of work place and tool design.

FIGURE 11.4   ■   Levels of Illumination Recommended for Various Task Conditions.

Task Condition	Type of Task or Area	Illumination Level (FT-C)*	Type of Illumination
Small detail, extreme accuracy	Sewing, inspecting dark materials	100	Overhead ceiling lights and desk lamp
Normal detail, prolonged periods	Reading, parts assembly, general office work	20–50	Overhead ceiling lights
Good contrast, fairly large objects	Recreational facilities	5–10	Overhead ceiling lights
Large objects	Restaurants, stairways, warehouses	2–5	Overhead ceiling lights

*FT-C (the footcandle) is a measure of illumination.

(*Source:* C. T. Morgan, J. S. Cook III, A. Chapanis, and M. W. Lund, eds., *Human Engineering Guide to Equipment Design* (New York: McGraw-Hill, 1963)).

FIGURE 11.5   ■   Decibel (dB) Levels for Various Sounds. Decibel levels are A-weighted sound levels measured with a sound-level meter.

Environment Noises	Common Noise Sources	Decibels	
	Jet takeoff (200 ft)	120	
Casting shakeout area	Riveting machine*	110	
Electric furnace area	Pneumatic peen hammer*	100	Very annoying
Printing press plant	Textile weaving plant* Subway train (20 ft)	90	
	Pneumatic drill (50 ft)	80	Ear protection required if exposed for 8 or more hours
Inside sports car (50 mph)	Freight train (100 ft)		
	Vacuum cleaner (10 ft)	70	
Near freeway (auto traffic)	Speech (1 ft)		Intrusive
Large store		60	
Private business office			
Light traffic (100 ft)	Large transformer (200 ft)	50	Quiet
Minimum levels, residential areas in Chicago at night		40	
	Soft whisper (5 ft)		
Studio (speech)		30	Very quiet
		20	
		10	Threshold of hearing

*At operator's position

(*Source:* Adapted from A. P. G. Peterson and E. E. Gross, Jr., *Handbook of Noise Measurement,* 7th ed. (New Concord, MA: General Radio Co.)).

above this level if exposure equals or exceeds 8 hours. Even at low levels, noise and vibration can be distracting. Therefore, most managers make substantial effort to reduce noise and vibration through good machine design, enclosures, or segregation of sources of noise and vibration.

Temperature and humidity parameters have been well established. Managers with activities operating outside of the established comfort zone should expect some adverse effect on performance.

METHODS ANALYSIS. Methods analysis focuses on *how* a task is accomplished. Whether controlling a machine or making or assembling components, how a task is done makes a difference in performance, safety, and quality. Using knowledge from ergonomics and methods analysis, methods engineers are charged with ensuring that quality and quantity standards are achieved efficiently and safely. Methods analysis and related techniques are useful in office environments as well as in the factory. The techniques include flow diagrams, process charts, activity charts, and operations charts.

Flow diagrams are schematics (drawings) used to investigate movement of people or material. They provide a systematic procedure for looking at long-cycle repetitive tasks (Figure 11.6). **Process charts** use symbols (Figure 11.7) to help us understand the movement of people or material. In this way, movement and delays can be reduced and operations made more efficient. Figure 11.7 shows a process chart used to supplement the flow diagram shown in Figure 11.6. An application of these techniques is discussed in the *POM in Action* box "Flow Diagrams and Process Charts Help an English Parts Factory."

Activity charts are used to study and improve utilization of an operator and a machine or some combination of operators (a "crew") and machines. Through observation, the analyst records the present method (see Figure 11.8) and then on a second chart the proposed improvement.

Flow diagrams

Process charts

Activity charts

FIGURE 11.6 ■ Flow Diagram of Axle-Stand Production Line at Paddy Hopkirk Factory. (a) Old method; (b) new method.

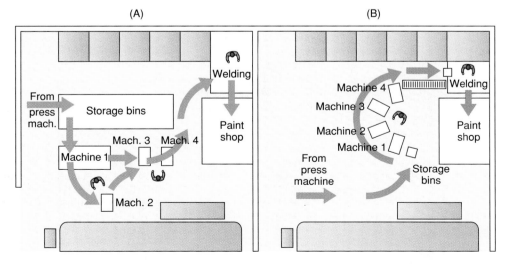

(*Source: Financial Times* (January 4, 1994):).

Flow Diagrams and Process Charts Help an English Parts Factory

It takes a brave manager to allow consultants—even ones well prepared with flow diagrams and process charts—to tear up a factory and rearrange it overnight. And it takes employees who are even more understanding to accept such changes. One morning, the Paddy Hopkirk car accessory factory in England was an untidy sprawl of production lines surrounded by piles of crates holding semifinished components. Two days later, when the 180-strong work force came to work, the machines had been brought together in tightly grouped "cells." The piles of components had disappeared, and the newly cleared floor space was neatly marked with color-coded lines mapping out the flow of materials.

Overnight, there were dramatic differences. In the first full day, productivity on some lines increased by up to 30%, the space needed for some processes had been halved, and work in progress had been cut considerably. The improved layout had allowed some jobs to be combined, freeing up operators for deployment elsewhere in the factory. "I was expecting a change, but nothing as dramatic as this," says board chairman, Paddy Hopkirk. "It is fantastic."

Source: Financial Times (January 4, 1994).

Disasters at nuclear power plants in the United States (Three Mile Island) and in the Ukraine (Chernobyl) have frightened federal and local regulators into increasingly stricter maintenance and reliability standards. Some experts believe that there is still insufficient attention given to the human side of reactor control systems. Designers, they believe, do not appreciate the fact that plants are man–machine systems. Here a worker with a geiger counter is checking the radiation level at the damaged Chernobyl plant.

FIGURE 11.7 ■ Process Chart of Axle-Stand Production Using Paddy Hopkirk's New Method Shown in the Flow Diagram (Figure 11.6b)

Present Method ☐
Proposed Method ☒

PROCESS CHART

SUBJECT CHARTED Axle-stand Production

DATE 1/1/96
CHART BY JH
CHART NO. 1

DEPARTMENT Work cell for axle stand

SHEET NO. 1 OF 1

DIST. IN FEET	TIME IN MINS.	CHART SYMBOLS	PROCESS DESCRIPTION
50		○ ⇨ ☐ D ▽	From press machine to storage bins at work cell
	3	○ ⇨ ☐ D ▽	Storage bins
5		○ ⇨ ☐ D ▽	Move to machine 1
	4	○ ⇨ ☐ D ▽	Operation at machine 1
4		○ ⇨ ☐ D ▽	Move to machine 2
	2.5	○ ⇨ ☐ D ▽	Operation at machine 2
4		○ ⇨ ☐ D ▽	Move to machine 3
	3.5	○ ⇨ ☐ D ▽	Operation at machine 3
4		○ ⇨ ☐ D ▽	Move to machine 4
	4	○ ⇨ ☐ D ▽	Operation at machine 4
20		○ ⇨ ☐ D ▽	Move to welding
	Poka-yoke	○ ⇨ ☐ D ▽	Poka-yoke inspection at welding
	4	○ ⇨ ☐ D ▽	Weld
10		○ ⇨ ☐ D ▽	Move to painting
	4	○ ⇨ ☐ D ▽	Paint
		○ ⇨ ☐ D ▽	
97	30		Total

○ = operation; ⇨ = transportation; ☐ = inspection; D = delay; ▽ = storage.

FIGURE 11.8 ■ Activity Chart

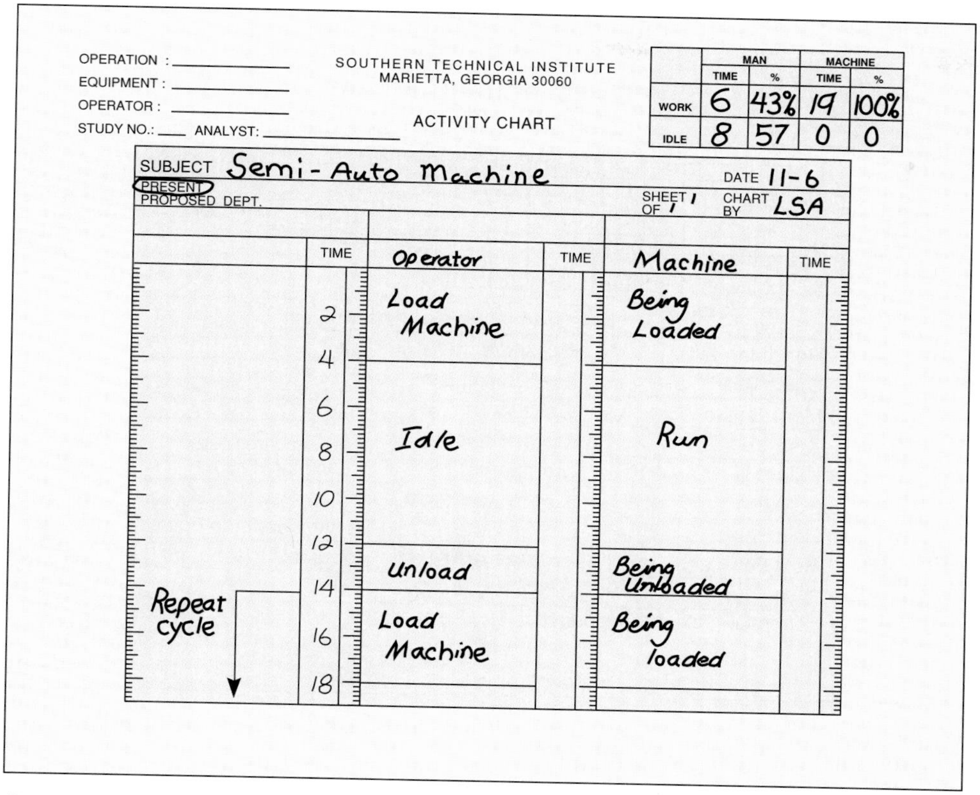

(Source: Adapted from L. S. Aft, *Productivity Measurement and Improvement*, © 1983, p. 67. Reprinted by permission of Prentice Hall, Inc., Englewood Cliffs, NJ.)

Body movement is analyzed by an **operations chart**. It is designed to show economy of motion by pointing out wasted motion and idle time (delay). The operations chart (also known as right-hand, left-hand chart) is shown in Figure 11.9.

Operations chart

LABOR STANDARDS

So far in this chapter, we have discussed labor planning and job design. The third requirement of an effective human resource strategy is the establishment of labor standards. Effective manpower planning is dependent upon a knowledge of the labor required.

Labor standards are the amount of time required to perform a job or part of a job. Every firm has labor standards, although they may vary from those established via informal methods to those established by professionals. Only when accurate labor standards exist can management know what its labor requirements are, what its costs should be, and what constitutes a fair day's work. Techniques for setting labor standards are presented in the supplement to this chapter.

Labor standards

FIGURE 11.9   ■   Operation Chart (Left-Hand/Right-Hand Chart) for Bolt–Washer Assembly.

LEFT-HAND / RIGHT-HAND CHART

SOUTHERN TECHNICAL INSTITUTE
MARIETTA, GEORGIA 30060

PROCESS Bolt Washer Assembly

STUDY NO.

OPERATOR SRA

ANALYST

DATE 11/ 6 / 95   SHEET NO. 1 of 1

METHOD (PRESENT PROPOSED)

REMARKS

SYMBOLS	PRESENT		PROPOSED		DIFFERENCE	
	LH	RH	LH	RH	LH	RH
○ OPERATIONS	5	10				
⇨ TRANSPORTATIONS						
☐ INSPECTIONS						
D DELAYS	10	5				
▽ STORAGES						
TOTALS	15	15				

LEFT-HAND ACTIVITY Present METHOD	DIST.	SYMBOLS	SYMBOLS	DIST.	RIGHT-HAND ACTIVITY Present METHOD
1 Reach for Bolt		●⇨☐D▽	○⇨☐D▽		Idle
2 Grasp Bolt		●⇨☐D▽	○⇨☐D▽		Idle
3 Move Bolt to Work		●⇨☐D▽	○⇨☐D▽		Idle
Area		○⇨☐D▽	○⇨☐D▽		
4 Hold Bolt		○⇨☐D▽	●⇨☐D▽		Reach for Washer
5 Hold Bolt		○⇨☐D▽	●⇨☐D▽		Grasp Washer
6 Hold Bolt		○⇨☐D▽	●⇨☐D▽		Move Washer to Bolt
7 Hold Bolt		○⇨☐D▽	●⇨☐D▽		Assemble Washer on
		○⇨☐D▽	○⇨☐D▽		Bolt

○ = operation; ⇨ = transportation; ☐ = inspection; D = delay; ▽ = storage.

(*Source*: Adapted from L. S. Aft, *Productivity Measurement and Improvement*, 1983, p. 75. Reprinted by permission of Prentice Hall, Inc., Englewood Cliffs, NJ.)

ACHIEVING WORLD-CLASS STANDARDS

World-class producers realize the importance of an effective human resource strategy. Good job design, manpower planning, and an environment of mutual commitment and trust are recognized by all members of the organization as critical to world-class performance. World-class firms have high training budgets, most well in excess of 40 hours per year per employee, and some as high as 200 hours. Employees are trained in problem solving and teamwork, and teams are encouraged and supported. Training also includes tools such as flow process diagrams and charts, activity charts, and micromotion charts. These organizations have designed jobs that use both the mental and physical capabilities of their employees. Most world-class organizations have a human resource strategy that has many of the attributes of lean production and provides a competitive advantage.

SUMMARY

How well a firm manages its human resource strategy ultimately determines its success. The P/OM activity usually has a large role to play in achieving human resource

Performance during a pit stop makes a difference between winning and losing a race. Activity charts are used to orchestrate the movement of members of a pit crew, an operating room staff, or machine operators in a factory. Solved Problem 11.1 shows an activity chart applied to a pit crew.

objectives. The first objective is to achieve efficient use of human resources within the operations function. This is often a major goal of a firm because operations is usually the function with the highest labor cost, and labor is often a large part of the total cost of the product. The second objective is the design of jobs that are effective, safe, and provide a reasonable quality of work life for the employee in an atmosphere of mutual respect.

KEY TERMS

Quality of work life (p. 480)
Mutual commitment (p. 480)
Mutual trust (p. 480)
Labor planning (p. 481)
Standard work schedule (p. 482)
Flextime (p. 482)
Flexible work week (p. 482)
Part-time status (p. 483)
Job design (p. 483)
Labor specialization (p. 483)
Job enlargement (p. 484)
Job rotation (p. 484)
Job enrichment (p. 484)
Employee empowerment (p. 484)

Self-directed team (p. 486)
Bonus (p. 489)
Profit sharing (p. 489)
Gain sharing (p. 489)
Incentive system (p. 489)
Measured daywork (p. 489)
Piece rate (p. 489)
Lean production (p. 489)
Ergonomics (p. 490)
Flow diagrams (p. 493)
Process charts (p. 493)
Activity charts (p. 493)
Operations charts (p. 495)
Labor standards (p. 495)

SOLVED PROBLEM

Solved Problem 11.1

As pit crew manager for Prototype Sports Car, you have just been given the pit stop rules for next season. You will be allowed only six people over the pit wall at any one time and one of these must be a designated *fire extinguisher/safety* crewman. This crewman must carry a fire extinguisher and may not service the car. However, the fire extinguisher/safety crewman may also signal the driver where to stop the car in the pit lane and when to leave the pit.

You expect to have air jacks on this year's car. These built-in jacks require the use of only an air hose to make them work. Fuel will also be supplied via a hose, with a second hose used for venting air from the fuel cells. The rate of flow for the fuel hose will be 1 gallon per second. The tank will hold 25 gallons. You expect to have to change all four tires on most pit stops. The length of the races will vary this year, but you expect that the longer races will also require the changing of drivers. Recent stopwatch studies have verified the following times for your experienced crew. These times are as follows:

ACTIVITY	TIME IN MINUTES
Install air hose	.075
Remove tire	.125
Mount new tire	.125
Move to air jack hose	.050
Move to rear of car	.050
Help driver	.175
Wipe windshield	.175
Load fuel (per gallon)	.016

Your job is to develop the initial plan for the best way to utilize your six-person pit crew. The six crewmen are identified with letters, as shown in Figure 11.10. You decide to use an activity chart similar to the one shown in Figure 11.8 to aid you.

FIGURE 11.10 ■ Position of Car and Six Crewmen (see chart on next page)

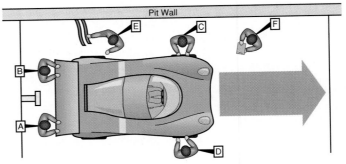

Solution
Your activity chart showing each member of the crew what they are to do during each second of the pit stop is shown in the chart.

FIGURE 11.10 ■ (Continued)

MULTIPLE ACTIVITY CHART

Chart No.:	Sheet No.:		Of:				S U M M A R Y		
PRODUCT:							PRESENT (min.)	PROPOSED	SAVING
						CYCLE TIME			
						Man			
PROCESS:	Pit stop for GTO cars					Machine			
						WORKING			
						Man			
						Machine			
MACHINE(S):						IDLE			
						Man			
						Machine			
OPERATIVE:		CLOCK NO.:				UTILIZATION			
CHARTED BY:		DATE:				Man			
						Machine			

TIME (min.)	CREW						TIME (min.)	NOTES
	A	B	C	D	E	F		

CREW columns (A–F) labels by time:

- E: Move to car /hoses, Gas flows
- F: SAFETY CREWMAN (vertical)
- A: Remove tire, Mount new tire, Move to air jack hose, Idle, Push
- B: Install air hose, Remove tire, Mount new tire, Move to rear, Idle, Push
- C: Remove tire, Mount new tire, Help driver, Idle
- D: Remove tire, Mount new tire, Wipe windshield, Idle
- E: 24.5 gal of gas, 24.5 seconds
- F: Idle

NOTES

Fire Extinguisher/ Safety crewman F, goes over the pit wall to signal the driver where to stop the car.

Crewmen A, C, D, move to the car with tires. B places the air jack hose in the connection at the rear of the car. B then returns to pit wall for the fourth tire. E moves to the car with two hoses (one for fuel & one to remove air).

F is ready with the fire extinguisher. If the driver is to change, the first driver is out in the first five seconds.

If there is a driver change, the new driver enters the car.

A, C, D, have their tires mounted. D wipes the windshield with towels from belt. C helps the driver as necessary with seat belt & ice to cool suit. A removes the air jack hose.

B has tire mounted.

B moves to the rear of the car. A removes the air jack hose when B, C, and D signal their tires are mounted.

A and B prepare to push car. E (fuel man) disconnects fuel lines. F signals completion of fuel loading.

F moves to front of car on the pit side and prepares to signal driver when to leave. A, B, C, and D, signal F when they are ready.

F signals driver when all is ready. A and B push car out of pits.

DISCUSSION QUESTIONS

1. What are some of the worst jobs you know about? Why are they bad jobs? Why do people want these jobs?

2. What factor would you add to, or delete from, the psychological factors given in the chapter?

3. If you were redesigning the job described in Question 1, what changes would you make? Are your changes realistic? Would they improve productivity (not just production, but productivity)?

4. How would you define a good quality of work life?

5. What is the difference between job enrichment, job enlargement, job rotation, job specialization, and employee empowerment?

6. Do you know of any jobs that push the man–machine interface to the limits of human capabilities?

7. Why prepare flow diagrams and process charts for tasks that are poorly done?

8. What are the six core characteristics of a good job design?

CRITICAL THINKING EXERCISE

The situation at the Lordstown, Ohio, airbag manufacturer was getting sticky. A skilled technician and member of the safety committee, Gregory White, suggested the line be shut down because of horrible fumes that were being created as employees inserted a chemical sensor into each airbag. The problem was that a new bonding agent for sealing the sensors was highly toxic as a liquid, but safe after drying. Additionally, the union steward was also questioning safety standards, saying perhaps the bonding agent remained toxic when drying. A recently installed ventilation system made little difference in the odor, but all tests had shown the chemical parts per million to be below the OSHA standard of 100. Steve Goodman, the plant manager, had discussed the issue with Nancy Kirschberg, the plant health and safety manager, who advised that although the OSHA standard is 100 ppm, the American Conference of Governmental Industrial Hygienists' (ACGIH) standard is only 50. Goodman was also well aware that the new employee empowerment program was important, but the automobile assembly plant 15 miles away needed the airbags now. The automaker had no airbags in stock and depended on JIT delivery from this plant. Therefore, shutting down airbag assembly would also shut down the assembly plant. Goodman's plant's reputation and the jobs of his people depended upon timely airbag delivery.

First, what decision would you make? Then justify your position and that of the union and Gregory White. Finally, propose a solution to deal with the very immediate problem.

PROBLEMS

• **11.1** Make a process chart for going from the living room to the kitchen for a glass, to the refrigerator for milk, and to a kitchen cabinet for cookies. Use a layout of your choosing. How can you make the task more efficient (that is, less time or fewer steps)?

• **11.2** Draw an activity chart for a machine operator with the following operation. The relevant times are as follows:

Prepare mill for loading (cleaning, oiling, and so on)	.50 min.
Load mill	1.75 min.
Mill operating (cutting material)	2.25 min.
Unload mill	.75 min.

⋮ **11.3** Draw an activity chart (a multiactivity chart) for a concert (for example, Phil Collins, Neil Diamond, Grateful Dead, Bruce Springsteen) and determine how to put the concert together so the star has reasonable breaks. For instance, at what point is there an instrumental number, a visual effect, a duet, a dance moment, that allows the star to pause and rest physically or at least rest his or her voice? Do other members of the show have moments of pause or rest?

· **11.4** Make an operations chart of one of the following:

   a) Putting a new eraser in (or on) a pencil.

   b) Putting a paper clip on two pieces of paper.

   c) Putting paper in a typewriter.

· **11.5** Having made the operations chart in Problem 11.4 and now being told that you were going to do the task 10,000 times, how would you improve the procedure? Prepare an operations chart of the improved task. What motion, time, and effort have you saved over the life of the task by redesigning it?

· **11.6** For a job you have had, rate each of Hackman and Oldham's core job characteristics on a scale from 1 to 10. What is your total score? What about the job could have been changed so you would be inclined to give it a higher score?

⋮ **11.7** Using the data provided in Solved Problem 11.1, prepare an activity chart (a crew chart) similar to the one in the solved problem, but based on having a total of only five crew members.

⋮ **11.8** Using the data provided in Solved Problem 11.1, prepare an activity chart similar to the one in the solved problem. However, fuel will now be delivered at the rate of 1½ gallons per second.

CASE STUDY

The Fleet That Wanders

Bill Southard runs Southard Truck Lines. He recently purchased 10 new tractors for his operation from ARC Trucks. His relations with his drivers have historically been excellent, but they do not like the new tractors. The complaint is that the new tractors are hard to control on the highway; they "wander." When the drivers have a choice, they choose the older tractors. Mr. Southard, after numerous discussions with the drivers, concludes that the new tractors do indeed have a problem. They get much better gas mileage, should have lower maintenance costs, and have the latest antilocking brakes. Because each tractor costs over $50,000, Mr. Southard's investment exceeds $500,000 in the new fleet. He is trying to improve his fleet performance by reducing maintenance and fuel costs. This has not happened. Additionally, he wants to keep his drivers happy. This has not happened either. Consequently, he has a rather serious talk with the manufacturer of the trucks.

The manufacturer, ARC Trucks of Canyon, Texas, redesigned the front suspension for this model of tractor. The firm tells him the new front end is great. Bill Southard finds out, however, that there have been minor changes in some front suspension parts on the model since he purchased his trucks.

ARC Trucks refuses to make any changes in the tractors Mr. Southard purchased. No one has suggested there is a safety problem, but the drivers are adamant that they have to work harder to keep the new tractors on the road. Mr. Southard has new tractors that spend much of their time sitting in the yard while drivers use the old tractors. His costs, therefore, are higher than they should be. He is considering court action, but legal counsel suggests that he document his case.

DISCUSSION QUESTIONS

1. What suggestions do you have for Mr. Southard?

2. Having been exposed to introductory material about ergonomics, can you imagine an analytical approach to documenting the problems reported by the drivers?

BIBLIOGRAPHY

Alexander, D. C. *Industrial Ergonomics: A Practitioner's Guide*. Norcross, GA: IE & MP Publishers, 1985.

Barnes, R. M. *Motion and Time Study, Design and Measurement of Work*. New York: John Wiley, 1968.

Berggren, C. *Alternatives to Lean Production: Work Organization in the Swedish Auto Industry*. Ithaca, NY: ILR Press, 1993.

————. "Point/Counterpoint: Nummi vs. Uddevalla." *Sloan Management Review*, 35, no. 2 (Winter 1994): 37–50.

Bowen, D. E., G. E. Ledford, Jr., and B. R. Nathan. "Hiring for the Organization, Not the Job." *The Executive*, 5, no. 4 (November 1991): 35.

Carson, R. "Ergonomically Designed Tools: Selecting the Right Tool for the Job." *Industrial Engineering*, 25, no. 7 (July 1993): 27–29.

Chapman, A. *Man-Machine Engineering*. Belmont, CA: Wadsworth, 1965.

Corlett, N., J. Wilson, F. Manencia, eds. *Ergonomics of Working Posture*. New York: Taylor and Francis, 1986.

Denton, D. K. "Redesigning A Job by Simplifying Every Task and Responsibility." *Industrial Engineering*, 24, no. 8 (August 1992): 46.

Dreyfuss, H. *The Measure of Man*. New York: Whitney Library of Design, 1970.

Franke, R. H. "The Ultimate Advantage: Creating the High-Involvement Organization." *The Executive*, 7, no. 1 (February 1993): 105–106.

Hall, G., J. Rosenthal, and J. Wade. "How to Make Reengineering Really Work." *Harvard Business Review*, 71, no. 6 (November/December 1993): 119–131.

Konz, S. *Work Design*. Columbia, OH: Grid, 1979.

McCormick, E. J. *Human Factors in Engineering and Design*, 4th ed. New York: McGraw-Hill, 1976.

Mesch, D. J., and D. R. Dalton. "Unexpected Consequences of Improving Workplace Justice: A Six-Year Time Series Assessment." *The Academy of Management Journal*, 35, no. 5 (December 1992): 1,099.

Meyer, C. "How the Right Measures Help Teams Excel." *Harvard Business Review* (May/June 1994): 95.

Snell, S., and J. Dean. "Integrated Manufacturing and Human Resource Management: A Human Capital Perspective." *The Academy of Management Journal*, 35, 3 (August 1992): 467–497.

Staughton, R. V. W., N. J. Kinnie, E. H. Davies, and R. L. C. Smith. "Modelling the Manufacturing Strategy Process: An Analysis of the Role Played by Human Resources Issues." *OM Review*, 9, no. 2 (April 1992): 48–68.

Stepkin, R. L., and R. E. Mosely, eds. *Noise Control: A Guide for Workers and Employers*. American Society of Safety Engineers, 1984.

Zammuto, R. F., and E. J. O'Connor. "Gaining Advanced Manufacturing Technologies' Benefits: The Roles of Organization Design and Culture." *The Academy of Management Review*, 17, no. 4 (October 1992): 701.

11 SUPPLEMENT

WORK MEASUREMENT

It was 2:36 P.M. and the 132 workers on the American Plastics Inc. factory floor were busy manning their noisy machines. When Bob Markland, a newly hired engineer, entered this production area through an office door, he was dressed in a white shirt and tie and carried a clipboard. He strode purposely to his destination, the lathe area where he was to time three workers whose labor standards had not been updated in a decade. One pair of eyes after another followed his movement, almost like a wave building as it approaches the shore. Before Markland was within 50 feet of his target, a loud whistle blew. The shop's union steward, Roscoe Davis, had just called a work stoppage. A "suit" was on the floor to time workers without union authorization. American Plastics was silent. ♦

LABOR STANDARDS AND WORK MEASUREMENT

Effective management of people requires knowledge of labor standards. Even though employees and unions may be opposed to jobs being observed and timed, as in the preceding quotation, labor standards are necessary. They help a firm determine the

1. labor content of items produced (the labor cost);
2. staffing needs of organizations (how many people it will take to make the required production);
3. cost and time estimates prior to production (to assist in a variety of decisions from developing cost estimates for customers, to the make-or-buy decision);
4. crew size and work balance (who does what on a group activity or assembly line);
5. production expected (both manager and worker should know what constitutes a fair day's work);
6. basis of wage-incentive plans (what provides a reasonable incentive);
7. efficiency of employees and supervision (a standard is necessary against which to determine efficiency).

Properly set labor standards represent the amount of time it should take an average employee to perform specific job activities under normal working conditions. The *POM in Action* box "Gain Sharing Drives Up Whirlpool's Productivity" indicates an incentive system application of effective labor standards.

How are labor, or production, standards set? Labor standards are set four ways:

1. historical experience;
2. time studies;
3. predetermined time standards;
4. work sampling.

This supplement covers each of these techniques.

HISTORICAL EXPERIENCE

Labor standards can be estimated based on *historical experience*, that is, how many labor-hours were required to do a task the last time it was performed. Historical standards do have the distinct advantage of being relatively easy and inexpensive to obtain. They are usually available from employee time cards or production records. But they are not objective, and we do not know their accuracy, whether they represent a reasonable or a poor work pace, and if unusual occurrences are included. Because these variables are unknown, their use is not recommended. Instead time studies, predetermined time standards, and work sampling are preferred to set production standards.

TIME STUDIES

Time study

The classical stopwatch study, or time study, originally proposed by Frederick W. Taylor in 1881, is still the most widely used time-study method. A **time-study** procedure

Gain Sharing Drives Up Whirlpool's Productivity

Lloyd Spoonholtz's first inclination when he heard about Whirlpool's proposed gain-sharing program "was to tell Whirlpool to go to hell." But the president of Machinists Local 1918 feared that his Benton Harbor, Michigan, plant was destined for the oblivion that befell many factories in his depressed town of 13,000. Other workers also doubted that the 40-year-old facility would be open much longer. Whirlpool had already closed two nearby plants. But the company assured them they had one hope: productivity.

The gain-share concept was simple. The bigger the gain in output, the larger the pool of money the workers share with the company. The precise percentage of the pool going to workers is determined by the quality of their output, as measured by the number of rejected parts.

Since gain share began, productivity at Benton Harbor has surged more than 19%, to 111 parts per man-hour, from 93. Moreover, the number of parts rejected sunk to a world-class 10 per million from 837 per million. To each of the plant's employees, this meant an extra $2,700 of pay last year. *And* it improved the workers' morale, reduced Whirlpool's costs, and bolstered its profits. A Whirlpool washer retails today for about $399, the same as it did several years ago, and its quality is better.

Sources: Wall Street Journal (May 4, 1992): A-1; and *Harvard Business Review* (May/June 1994): 100.

---

involves timing a sample of a worker's performance and using it to set a standard. A trained and experienced person can establish a standard by following these eight steps:

1. Define the task to be studied (after methods analysis has been conducted).
2. Divide the task into precise elements (parts of a task that often take no more than a few seconds).
3. Decide how many times to measure the task (the number of cycles or samples needed).
4. Time and record the elemental times and ratings of performance.
5. Compute the average actual cycle time. The **average actual cycle time** is the arithmetic mean of the times for *each* element measured, adjusted for unusual influence for each element:

   Average actual cycle time

$$\text{Average actual cycle time} = \frac{\left(\begin{array}{c}\text{sum of the times recorded} \\ \text{to perform each element}\end{array}\right)}{\text{number of cycles observed}} \quad \text{(S11.1)}$$

6. Compute the **normal time** for each element. This measure is a "performance rating" for the particular worker pace observed:

   Normal time

$$\text{Normal time} = (\text{average actual cycle time}) \times (\text{rating factor}) \quad \text{(S11.2)}$$

The performance rating adjusts the observed time to what a normal worker could expect to accomplish. For example, a normal worker should be able to walk 3 miles per hour. He or she should also be able to deal a deck of 52 cards into four equal piles in 30 seconds. There are numerous films specifying work pace on which professionals agree; and activity benchmarks have been

FIGURE S11.1 ■ Rest Allowances (in percentage) for Various Classes of Work.

1. Constant allowances:
    (A) Personal allowance 5
    (B) Basic fatigue allowance 4

2. Variable allowances:
    (A) Standing allowance 2
    (B) Abnormal position allowance:
        (i) Awkward (bending) 2
        (ii) Very awkward (lying, stretching) 7
    (C) Use of force or muscular energy in
        lifting, pulling, pushing
        Weight lifted (pounds):
        20 3
        40 9
        60 17
    (D) Bad light:
        (i) Well below recommended 2

        (ii) Quite inadequate 5
    (E) Atmospheric conditions (heat and humidity):
        Variable 0–10
    (F) Close attention:
        (i) Fine or exacting 2
        (ii) Very fine or very exacting 5
    (G) Noise level:
        (i) Intermittent—loud 2
        (ii) Intermittent—very loud or high-pitched . . . 5
    (H) Mental strain:
        (i) Complex or wide span of attention 4
        (ii) Very complex 8
    (I) Tediousness:
        (i) Tedious 2
        (ii) Very tedious 5

Source: Excerpted from B. W. Niebel, *Motion and Time Study*, 7th ed. (Homewood, IL: Richard D. Irwin, 1982) p. 393. Copyright © 1982 by Richard D. Irwin, Inc.

established by the Society for the Advancement of Management. However, performance rating is still something of an art.

7. Add the normal times for each element to develop a total normal time for the task.

Standard time

8. Compute the **standard time**. This adjustment to the total normal time provides for allowances such as *personal* needs, unavoidable work *delays*, and worker *fatigue*:

$$\text{Standard time} = \frac{\text{total normal time}}{1 - \text{allowance factor}} \qquad (\text{S}11.3)$$

Personal time allowances are often established in the range of 4% to 7% of total time, depending upon nearness to rest rooms, water fountains, and other facilities. Delay standards are often set as a result of the actual studies of the delay that occurs. Fatigue standards are based on our growing knowledge of human energy expenditure under various physical and environmental conditions. A sample set of personal and fatigue allowances is shown in Figure S11.1. Example S1 illustrates the computation of standard time.

EXAMPLE S1

The time study of a work operation yielded an average actual cycle time of 4.0 minutes. The analyst rated the observed worker at 85%. This means the worker performed at 85% of normal when the study was made. The firm uses a 13% allowance factor. We want to compute the standard time.

Average actual time = 4.0 min.

$$\text{Normal time} = (\text{average actual cycle time}) \times (\text{rating factor})$$
$$= (4.0)(.85)$$
$$= 3.4 \text{ min.}$$

$$\text{Standard time} = \frac{\text{normal time}}{1 - \text{allowance factor}} = \frac{3.4}{1 - .13} = \frac{3.4}{.87}$$
$$= 3.9 \text{ min.}$$

Example S2 works from a series of actual stopwatch times for each element.

EXAMPLE S2

Management Science Associates promotes its management development seminars by mailing thousands of individually typed letters to various firms. A time study has been done on the task of preparing letters for mailing. On the basis of the observations below, Management Science Associates wants to develop a time standard for the task. The firm's personal, delay, and fatigue allowance factor is 15%.

	CYCLE OBSERVED (IN MINUTES)					PERFORMANCE RATING
JOB ELEMENT	1	2	3	4	5	
(A) Type letter	8	10	9	21*	11	120%
(B) Type envelope address	2	3	2	1	3	105%
(C) Stuff, stamp, seal, and sort envelopes	2	1	5*	2	1	110%

The procedure after the data have been collected is as follows:

1. Delete all unusual or nonrecurring observations such as those marked with an asterisk (*). (They might be due to an unscheduled business interruption, a conference with the boss, or a mistake of an unusual nature; these are not part of the job.)

2. Compute the average cycle time for each job element:

$$\text{Average time for A} = \frac{8 + 10 + 9 + 11}{4}$$
$$= 9.5 \text{ min.}$$

$$\text{Average time for B} = \frac{2 + 3 + 2 + 1 + 3}{5}$$
$$= 2.2 \text{ min.}$$

$$\text{Average time for C} = \frac{2 + 1 + 2 + 1}{4}$$
$$= 1.5 \text{ min.}$$

3. Compute the normal time for each job element:

$$\text{Normal time for A} = (\text{Average actual time}) \times (\text{Rating})$$
$$= (9.5)(1.2)$$
$$= 11.4 \text{ min.}$$

$$\text{Normal time for B} = (2.2)(1.05)$$
$$= 2.31 \text{ min.}$$

$$\text{Normal time for C} = (1.5)(1.10)$$
$$= 1.65 \text{ min.}$$

Normal times are computed for each element because the rating factor may vary for each element, which it did in this case.

4. Add the normal times for each element to find the total normal time (the normal time for the whole job):

$$\text{Total normal time} = 11.40 + 2.31 + 1.65$$
$$= 15.36 \text{ min.}$$

5. Compute the standard time for the job:

$$\text{Standard time} = \frac{\text{total normal time}}{1 - \text{allowance factor}} = \frac{15.36}{1 - .15}$$
$$= 18.07 \text{ min.}$$

Thus, 18.07 minutes is the time standard for this job.

Sleep Inn is showing the world that big gains in productivity can be made not only by manufacturers, but in the service industry as well. Designed with labor efficiency in mind, Sleep Inn is staffed with 13% fewer employees than similar budget hotels. Its features include a laundry room that is almost completely automated, round shower stalls that eliminate dirty corners, and closets that have no doors for maids to open and shut.

Time study is a sampling process, and the question of sampling error in the average actual cycle time naturally arises. Error, according to statistics, varies inversely with sample size. In order to determine just how many cycles we should time, we must consider the variability of each element in the study.

To determine an adequate sample size, three items must be considered. They are as follows:

1. How accurate we want to be (for example, is ±5% of actual close enough?).
2. The desired level of confidence (for example, the z value; is 95% adequate or is 99% required?).
3. How much variation exists within the job elements (for example, if the variation is large, a larger sample will be required).

The formula for finding the appropriate sample size given these three variables is

$$n = \left(\frac{zs}{h\overline{x}}\right)^2 \tag{S11.4}$$

where h = accuracy level desired in percent of the job element, expressed as a decimal (5% = .05)
   z = number of standard deviations required for desired level of confidence (90% confidence = 1.65; see Table S11.1 for the more common z values)[1]

---

[1] The values of z for any desired confidence level can be found in Appendix A, "Normal Curve Areas."

TABLE S11.1

DESIRED CONFIDENCE (%)	Z VALUE (STANDARD DEVIATION REQUIRED FOR DESIRED LEVEL OF CONFIDENCE)
90.0	1.65
95.0	1.96
95.4	2.00
99.0	2.58
99.7	3.00

s = standard deviation of the initial sample
$\bar{x}$ = mean of the initial sample.

We demonstrate with Example S3.

EXAMPLE S3

Thomas W. Jones Mfg. has asked you to check a labor standard prepared by a recently terminated analyst. Your first task is to determine the correct sample size. Your accuracy is to be within 5% and your confidence level to be 95%. The standard deviation of the sample is 1.0 and the mean is 3.00.

Solution:

$$h = .05 \qquad \bar{x} = 3.00 \qquad s = 1.0$$

$$z = 1.96 \text{ (from Table S11.1 or Appendix A)}$$

$$n = \left(\frac{zs}{h\bar{x}}\right)^2$$

$$n = \left(\frac{(1.96 \times 1.0)}{(.05 \times 3)}\right)^2 = 170.74 \approx 171$$

Therefore, you recommend a sample size of 171.

Let us look at two variations of Example S3.

First, if h, the desired accuracy, is expressed as an absolute amount of error (say, 1 minute of error is acceptable), then substitute e for $h\bar{x}$, and the appropriate formula is

$$n = \left(\frac{zs}{e}\right)^2 \tag{S11.5}$$

where e is the absolute amount of acceptable error.

Second, for those cases when s, the standard deviation of the sample, is not provided (which is typically the case outside the classroom), it must be computed. The formula for doing so is

$$s = \sqrt{\frac{\Sigma(x_i - \bar{x})^2}{n-1}} = \sqrt{\frac{\Sigma(\text{each sample observation} - \bar{x})^2}{\text{number in sample} - 1}} \tag{S11.6}$$

where x_i = value of each observation
$\bar{x}$ = mean of the observations
n = number of observations

An example of this computation is provided in Solved Problem S11.3.

Time studies provide accuracy in setting labor standards (see the *POM in Action* box on UPS on page 512), but they have two disadvantages. First, they require a trained staff of analysts. Second, labor standards cannot be set before the task is actually performed. This leads us to two alternative work measurement techniques.

PREDETERMINED TIME STANDARDS

Predetermined time standards

A third way to set production standards is to use predetermined time standards. **Predetermined time standards** divide manual work into small basic elements that already have established times (based on very large samples of workers). To estimate the time for a particular task, the time factors for each basic element of that task are added together. For any given firm to develop a comprehensive system of predetermined time standards would be prohibitively expensive. Consequently, a number of systems are commercially available. Among these are MTM and CSD. The most common predetermined time standard is *methods time measurement* (MTM), which is a product of the MTM Association.[2] CSD (computerized standard data) is a product of Rath and Strong, a management consulting firm.

Predetermined time standards are an outgrowth of basic motions called therbligs. The term *therblig* was coined by Frank Gilbreth (*Gilbreth* spelled backwards with the *t* and *h* reversed). Therbligs include activities such as select, grasp, position, assemble, reach, hold, rest, and inspect. These activities are stated in terms of time measurement units (TMUs), which are each equal to only .00001 hour, or .0006 minute. MTM values for various therbligs are specified in very detailed tables. Figure S11.2 provides, as an example, the set of time standards for the motion REACH. Note that reaching 4 inches for a part will have a TMU very different from reaching 12 inches.

Example S4 shows the use of predetermined time standards.

EXAMPLE S4

Riveting a transistor board in an assembly process is assigned an MTM value of 70.0 TMU, based on industry data standards. Before riveting, a worker must reach 16 inches for a small part (17.0 TMU), grasp the part (9.1 TMU), move the part to the assembly (27.0 TMU), and position the transistor (32.3 TMU).

This very small task, which consists of five elements, takes a total of 155.4 TMU (17.0 + 9.1 + 27.0 + 32.3 + 70.0). Translating into minutes involves multiplying 155.4 TMU × .0006 minute = .0932 minute = 5.6 seconds.

[2]MTM is really a family of products available from the Methods Time Measure Association. For example, MTM-HC deals with the health care industry, MTM-C handles clerical activities, MTM-M involves microscope activities, MTM-V deals with machine shop tasks, and so on.

FIGURE S11.2 ■ Methods Time Measurement Data for REACH Motion.

Distance Moved (inches)	Time (TMU)				Hand in Motion	
	A	B	C or D	E	A	B
3/4 or less	2.0	2.0	2.0	2.0	1.6	1.6
1	2.5	2.5	3.6	2.4	2.3	2.3
2	4.0	4.0	5.9	3.8	3.5	2.7
4	6.1	6.4	8.4	6.8	4.9	4.3
6	7.0	8.6	10.1	8.0	5.7	5.7
8	7.9	10.1	11.5	9.3	6.5	7.2
10	8.7	11.5	12.9	10.5	7.3	8.6
12	9.6	12.9	14.2	11.8	8.1	10.1
14	10.5	14.4	15.6	13.0	8.9	11.5
16	11.4	15.8	17.0	14.2	9.7	12.9
18	12.3	17.2	18.4	15.5	10.5	14.4
20	13.1	18.6	19.8	16.7	11.3	15.8

Case and Description
A: Reach to object in fixed location, or to object in other hand or on which other hand rests.
B: Reach to single object in location that may vary slightly from cycle to cycle.
C: Reach to object jumbled with other objects in a group so that search and select occur.
D: Reach to a very small object or where accurate grasp is required.
E: Reach to indefinite location to get hand in position for body balance or next motion or out of way.

Source: Copyrighted by the MTM Association for Standards and Research. No reprint permission without written consent from the MTM Association, 16–01 Broadway, Fair Lawn, NJ 07410.

Predetermined time standards have several advantages over direct time studies. They may be established in a laboratory environment, which will not upset production activities (which time studies tend to do). The standard can be set before a task is done and can be used for planning. No performance ratings are necessary. Unions tend to accept this method as a fair means of setting standards. Predetermined time standards are particularly effective in firms that do substantial numbers of studies in which the tasks are similar. Some firms use both time studies and predetermined time standards to ensure accurate labor standards.

Examples from the Service Sector

MTM's health care and clerical (MTM-HC and MTM-C) standards have extended the use of predetermined time standards to help set *service* labor standards. Figure S11.3 provides the set of time standards for the motion GET and PLACE. To use GET and PLACE (the most complex motion in the MTM system), one needs to know what is "gotten," its approximate weight, and where and how far it is placed. Example S5 helps clarify this concept.

UPS: The Tightest Ship in the Shipping Business

United Parcel Service (UPS) employs 150,000 people and delivers an average of nine million packages a day to locations throughout the United States and 180 other countries. To achieve its claim of "running the tightest ship in the shipping business," UPS methodically trains its delivery drivers in how to do their jobs as efficiently as possible.

Industrial engineers at UPS have time-studied each driver's route and set standards for each delivery, stop, and pickup. These engineers have recorded every second taken up by stoplights, traffic volume, detours, doorbells, walkways, stairways, and coffee breaks. Even bathroom stops are put into the standards. All of this information is then fed into

company computers to provide detailed time standards for every driver, every day.

To meet their objective of 200 deliveries and pickups each day (versus only 80 stops a day at Federal Express), drivers must follow the engineers' procedures exactly. As they approach a delivery stop, drivers unbuckle their seat belts, honk their horns, and cut their engines. In one seamless motion, they are required to yank up their emergency brakes and push their gearshifts into first. The drivers slide to the ground with their clipboards under their right arms and their packages in their left hands. Their keys, teeth up, are in their right hands. They walk to the customer's door at the prescribed 3 feet per second and knock first to avoid lost seconds searching for the doorbell. After making the delivery, they do the paperwork on the way back to the truck.

Productivity experts describe UPS as one of the most efficient companies anywhere in applying the principles of scientific management.

Sources: Wall Street Journal (May 24, 1995): B1, B4; and S. P. Robbins, *Management*, 4th ed. (Englewood Cliffs, NJ: Prentice Hall, 1994), p. 28.

FIGURE S11.3   ■   Sample MTM Table for GET Motion. Time values are in TMUs.

GET AND PLACE			DISTANCE RANGE IN IN.	<8	>8 <20	>20 <32
WEIGHT	CONDITIONS OF GET	PLACE ACCURACY	CODE	1	2	3
<2 LBS	EASY	APPROXIMATE	AA	20	35	50
		LOOSE	AB	30	45	60
		TIGHT	AC	40	55	70
	DIFFICULT	APPROXIMATE	AD	20	45	60
		LOOSE	AE	30	55	70
		TIGHT	AF	40	65	80
	HANDFUL	APPROXIMATE	AG	40	65	80
>2 LBS <18 LBS		APPROXIMATE	AH	25	45	55
		LOOSE	AJ	40	65	75
		TIGHT	AK	50	75	85
>18 LBS <45 LBS		APPROXIMATE	AL	90	106	115
		LOOSE	AM	95	120	130
		TIGHT	AN	120	145	160

(*Source:* Copyrighted by the MTM Association for Standards and Research. No reprint permission without consent from the MTM Association, 16–01 Broadway, Fair Lawn, NJ 07410.)

EXAMPLE S5

Pouring a tube specimen in a hospital lab is a repetitive task for which the MTM data in Figure S11.3 may be used to develop standard times. The sample tube is in a rack and the centrifuge tubes are in a nearby box. A technician removes the sample tube from the rack, uncaps it, gets the centrifuge tube, pours, and places both tubes in the rack.

The first work element involves getting the tube from the rack. Suppose the conditions for GETTING the tube and PLACING it in front of the technician are

- weight (less than 2 pounds)   • place accuracy (approximate)
- conditions of GET (easy)   • distance range (8 to 20 inches)

Then the MTM element for this activity is AA2 (as seen from Figure S11.3). The rest of Table 11.2 is developed from similar MTM tables.

TABLE S11.2 ■ MTM-HC ANALYSIS: POURING TUBE SPECIMEN.

ELEMENT DESCRIPTION	ELEMENT	TIME	FREQUENCY	TOTAL
Get tube from rack	AA2	35	1	35
Get stopper, place on counter	AA2	35	1	35
Get centrifuge tube, place at sample tube	AD2	45	1	45
Pour (3 sec.)	PT	83	1	83
Place tubes in rack (simo)	PC2	40	1	40
			Total TMU	238

.0006 × 238 = Total Standard minutes = .14

Source: A. S. Helms, B. W. Shaw, and C. A. Lindner, "The Development of Laboratory Workload Standards through Computer-Based Work Measurement Technique, Part I," *Journal of Methods-Time Measurement,* 12, p. 43. Used with permission of MTM Association for Standards and Research.

Lincoln Electric pays its employees according to actual production results. Through a sophisticated point system, each employee is evaluated on performance. Managers at Lincoln Electric are held responsible for building a work environment that allows employees to perform at their maximum. Employees work diligently at improving work methods and production systems at a level of productivity that makes Lincoln Electric a world-class producer of arc-welding equipment. In this way, employees, stockholders, and customers benefit.

Most MTM calculations, by the way, are computerized, so the user need only key in the appropriate MTM codes, such as AA2 in Example S5.

WORK SAMPLING

Work sampling

The fourth method of developing labor or production standards, work sampling, was developed in England by L. Tippet in the 1930s. **Work sampling** estimates the percent of the time that a worker spends on various tasks. The method involves random observations to record the activity that the worker is performing.

Work sampling is used in the following:

1. *Ratio Delay Studies.* These estimate the percentage of time employees spend in unavoidable delays. The results are used to investigate work methods, to estimate activity costs, and to set allowances in labor standards.
2. *Setting Labor Standards.* For setting standard task times, the observer must be experienced enough to rate the worker's performance.
3. *Measuring Worker Performance.* Sampling can develop a performance index for workers for periodic evaluations.

The work-sampling procedure can be summarized in seven steps:

1. Take a preliminary sample to obtain an estimate of the parameter value (such as percent of time a worker is busy).
2. Compute the sample size required.
3. Prepare a schedule for observing the worker at appropriate times. The concept of random numbers (discussed in the supplement to Chapter 13) is used to provide for random observation.
4. Observe and record worker activities; rate the worker's performance.
5. Record the number of units produced during the applicable portion of the study.
6. Compute the normal time per part.
7. Compute the standard time per part.

To determine the number of observations required, management must decide the desired confidence level and accuracy. But, first, the work analyst must select a preliminary value of the parameter under study (step 1 above). The choice is usually based on a small sample of perhaps 50 observations. The following formula then gives the sample size for a desired confidence and accuracy:

$$n = \frac{z^2\, p(1-p)}{h^2} \tag{S11.7}$$

where n = required sample size

z = standard normal deviate for the desired confidence level ($z = 1$ for 68% confidence, $z = 2$ for 95.45% confidence, and $z = 3$ for 99.7% confidence—these values are obtained from Table S11.1 or the normal table in Appendix A)

p = estimated value of sample proportion (of time worker is observed busy or idle)

h = accuracy level desired, in percent

Example S6 shows how to apply the formula.

EXAMPLE S6

The head of one Western state's welfare office estimates that the assistants are idle 25% of the time. The supervisor would like to take a work sample that would be accurate within 3% and wants to have 95.45% confidence in the results.

In order to determine how many observations should be taken, the supervisor applies the equation:

$$n = \frac{z^2 \, p(1 - p)}{h^2}$$

where n = sample size required
  z = 2 for 95.45% confidence level
  p = estimate of idle proportion = 25% = .25
  h = accuracy desired of 3% = .03

It is found that

$$n = \frac{(2)^2(.25)(.75)}{(.03)^2} = 833 \text{ observations}$$

Thus, 833 observations should be taken. If the percent idle time noted is not close to 25% as the study progresses, then the number of observations may have to be recalculated and increased or decreased as appropriate.

Optical scanners at Giant Food Stores are used to read the codes on each item at the check-out counters. This procedure provides information for inventory control, quicker check-out, and monitoring of the cashier's speed. The food items and dollars rung by each cashier and the number of customers served are recorded on the printout, which Giant posts in the workplace.

Work sampling is used to set labor standards in a fashion similar to that used in time studies. The analyst, however, simply records whether a worker is busy or idle during the observation. After all the observations have been recorded, the worker rated, and the units produced counted (steps 4 and 5), we can determine the normal time by the formula

$$\text{Normal time} = \frac{\left(\begin{array}{c}\text{total study} \\ \text{time}\end{array}\right) \times \left(\begin{array}{c}\text{percent of time employee} \\ \text{observed working}\end{array}\right) \times \left(\begin{array}{c}\text{performance} \\ \text{rating factor}\end{array}\right)}{\text{number of pieces produced}}$$

The standard time is the normal time adjusted by the allowance factor, computed as

$$\text{Standard time} = \frac{\text{normal time}}{1 - \text{allowance factor}}$$

Example S7 demonstrates the calculation of normal and standard times.

EXAMPLE S7

A work-sample study conducted over the 80 hours (or 4,800 minutes) of a 2-week period yielded the following data. The number of parts produced was 225 by an operator who was performance rated at 100%. The operator's idle time was 20%, and the total allowance given by the company for this task is 25%.

$$\text{Normal time} = \frac{\left(\begin{matrix}\text{total} \\ \text{time}\end{matrix}\right) \times \left(\begin{matrix}\text{percent of time} \\ \text{working}\end{matrix}\right) \times \left(\begin{matrix}\text{rating} \\ \text{factor}\end{matrix}\right)}{\text{number of units completed}}$$

$$= \frac{(4{,}800 \text{ min.})(.80)(1.00)}{225} = 17.07 \text{ min./part}$$

$$\text{Standard time} = \frac{\text{normal time}}{1 - \text{allowance factor}}$$

$$= \frac{17.07}{1 - .25} = 22.76 \text{ min./part}$$

Work sampling offers several advantages over time-study methods. First, it is less expensive, because a single observer can observe several workers simultaneously. Second, observers usually do not require much training, and no timing devices are needed. Third, the study can be delayed temporarily at any time with little impact on the results. And fourth, because work sampling uses instantaneous observations over a long period, the worker has little chance of affecting the study's outcome.

The disadvantages of work sampling are that it does not divide work elements as completely as time studies, it can yield biased or incorrect results if the observer does not follow random routes of travel and observation, and it is less effective than time studies when cycle times are short.

SUMMARY

Labor standards are required for an efficient operations system. They are needed for production planning, labor planning, costing, and evaluating performance. They can also be used as a basis for incentive systems. They are used in both the factory and the office. Standards may be established via historical data, time studies, predetermined time standards, and work sampling.

KEY TERMS

Time study (p. 504)
Average actual cycle time (p. 505)
Normal time (p. 505)

Standard time (p. 506)
Predetermined time standards (p. 510)
Work sampling (p. 514)

USING SPREADSHEETS TO SOLVE WORK MEASUREMENT PROBLEMS

To illustrate spreadsheet software in solving for normal and standard times in a time study, we present Program S11.1. This "symbolic" spreadsheet shows all the formulas needed to solve Example S2.

PROGRAM S11.1 ■ Using Spreadsheets To Solve a Time-Study Problem. Example S2 is illustrated with the formulas shown.

	A	B	C	D	E	F	G	H	I
1	EXAMPLE S2 SOLVED BY SPREADSHEET—MANAGEMENT SCIENCE ASSOCIATES								
2									
3			PERFORM-	CYCLE OBSERVED					
4			ANCE	(IN MINUTES)				AVERAGE	NORMAL
5	JOB ELEMENT		RATING	1	2	3	4	5	TIME	TIME
6	(A) Type Letter	1.20	8	10	9		11	(C6+D6+E6+G6)/4	B6*H6
7	(B) Type envelope	1.05	2	3	2	1	3	(C7+D7+E7+F7+G7)/5	B6*H7
8	(C) Stuff, stamp, seal	1.10	2	1		2	1	(C8+D8+F8+G8)/4	B8*H8
9									
10									
11	Allowance factor	.15							
12								Total normal time	@sum(I6..I8)
13								Standard time	I10/(1-B11)
14									
15									

Solved Problem S11.1

A work operation consisting of three elements has been subjected to a stopwatch time study. The observations recorded are shown. By union contract, the allowance time for the operation is personal time 5%, delay 5%, and fatigue 10%. Determine the standard time for the work operation.

JOB ELEMENT	CYCLE OBSERVATIONS (IN MINUTES)						PERFORMANCE RATING (%)
	1	2	3	4	5	6	
A	.1	.3	.2	.9	.2	.1	90
B	.8	.6	.8	.5	3.2	.7	110
C	.5	.5	.4	.5	.6	.5	80

Solution

First, delete the two observations that appear to be very unusual (.9 minute for job element A and 3.2 minutes for job element B). Then,

$$\text{A's average cycle time} = \frac{.1 + .3 + .2 + .2 + .1}{5} = .18 \text{ min.}$$

$$\text{B's average cycle time} = \frac{.8 + .6 + .8 + .5 + .7}{5} = .68 \text{ min.}$$

$$\text{C's average cycle time} = \frac{.5 + .5 + .4 + .5 + .6 + .5}{6} = .50 \text{ min.}$$

$$A\text{'s normal time} = (.18)(.90) \qquad = .16 \text{ min}$$
$$B\text{'s normal time} = (.68)(1.10) \qquad = .75 \text{ min}$$
$$C\text{'s normal time} = (.50)(.80) \qquad = .40 \text{ min}$$
$$\text{Normal time for job} = .16 + .75 + .40 = 1.31 \text{ min.}$$

$$\text{Standard time} = \frac{1.31}{1 - .20} \qquad = 1.64 \text{ min.}$$

Solved Problem S11.2

A preliminary work sample of an operation indicates the following:

Number of times operator working	60
Number of times operator idle	40
Total number of preliminary observations	100

What is the required sample size for a 99.7% confidence level with ±4% precision?

Solution

$$n = \frac{z^2 \, p(1-p)}{h^2} = \frac{(3)^2(.6)(.4)}{(.04)^2} = 1,350 \text{ sample size}$$

Solved Problem S11.3

Amor Manufacturing Co. of Geneva, Switzerland, has just studied a job in its laboratory in anticipation of releasing the job to the factory. It wants rather good accuracy for costing and labor forecasting. Specifically, it wants you to provide a 99% confidence level and a cycle time that is within 3% of the true value. How many observations should it make? The data collected so far are as follows:

OBSERVATION	CYCLE TIME
1	1.7
2	1.6
3	1.4
4	1.4
5	1.4

Solution

First, solve for the mean, $\bar{x}$, and the sample standard deviation, s.

$$s = \sqrt{\frac{\Sigma(\text{each sample observation} - \bar{x})^2}{\text{number in sample} - 1}}$$

OBSERVATION	$\bar{x}_i$	$\bar{x}$	$x_i - \bar{x}$	$(x_i - \bar{x})^2$
1	1.7	1.5	.2	0.04
2	1.6	1.5	.1	0.01
3	1.4	1.5	−.1	0.01
4	1.4	1.5	−.1	0.01
5	1.4	1.5	−.1	0.01
	$\bar{x} = 1.5$	7.5		$0.08 = \Sigma(x_i - \bar{x})^2$

$$s = \sqrt{\frac{.08}{n-1}} = \sqrt{\frac{.08}{4}} = .141$$

Then, solve for $n = \left(\frac{zs}{h\bar{x}}\right)^2 = \left[\frac{(2.58)(.141)}{(.03)(1.5)}\right]^2 = 65.3$

where $\bar{x} = 1.5$

$\quad\quad\, s = .141$

$\quad\quad\, z = 2.58$

$\quad\quad\, h = .03$

Therefore, you recommend 65 observations.

Solved Problem S11.4

Each printed-circuit board at Maggard Micro Manufacturing, Inc., has a semiconductor pressed into predrilled slots. The elemental motions for normal time used by the company are as follows:

Reach 6 inches for semiconductors	10.5 TMU
Grasp the semiconductor	8.0 TMU
Move semiconductor to printed-circuit board	9.5 TMU
Position semiconductor	20.1 TMU
Press semiconductor into slots	20.3 TMU
Move board aside	15.8 TMU

(Each time measurement unit is equal to .0006 min.) Determine the normal time for this operation in minutes and in seconds.

Solution
Add the time measurement units:

$\quad\quad 10.5 + 8.0 + 9.5 + 20.1 + 20.3 + 15.8 = 84.2$

$\quad\quad$ Time in minutes $= (84.2)(.0006 \text{ min.}) = .05052 \text{ min.}$

$\quad\quad$ Time in seconds $= (.05052)(60 \text{ sec.}) = 3.0312 \text{ sec}$

Solved Problem S11.5

To obtain the random sample needed for work sampling, a manager divides a typical workday into 480 minutes. Using a random-number table to decide what time to go to an area to sample work occurrences, the manager records observations on a tally sheet such as the following:

STATUS	TALLY	FREQUENCY
Productively working	JHT JHT JHT I	16
Idle	IIII	4

Solution

In this case, the supervisor made 20 observations and found that employees were working 80% of the time. So, out of 480 minutes in an office workday, 20%, or 96 minutes, was idle time, and 384 minutes was productive. Note that this procedure describes what a worker *is* doing, not necessarily what he or she *should* be doing.

DISCUSSION QUESTIONS

1. Why do operations managers require labor standards?

2. How do we establish a fair day's work?

3. Is a "normal" pace the same thing as a 100% pace?

4. What is the difference between "normal" and "standard" times?

5. What kind of work pace would you expect from an employee during a time study? Why?

6. As a new time-study engineer in your plant, you are engaged in studying an employee operating a drill press. Somewhat to your surprise, one of the first things you notice is that the drill press operator is doing a lot of operations besides just drilling holes. Your problem is what to include in your time study. From the following examples, indicate how, as the individual responsible for labor standards in your plant, you would handle them.

   a) Every so often, perhaps every 50th unit or so, the drill press operator takes an extra-long look at the piece, which apparently is misshaped, and then typically throws it in the scrap barrel.

   b) Approximately 1 out of 100 units has a rough edge and will not fit in the jig properly; therefore, the drill press operator picks up the piece, hits the

   lower right-hand edge with a file a few times, puts the file down, and returns to normal operation.

   c) About every hour or so, the drill press operator stops to change the drill in the machine, even if he is in the middle of a job. (We can assume that the drill has become dull.)

   d) Between every job and sometimes in the middle of jobs, the drill press operator turns off the machine and goes for stock.

   e) The drill press operator is idle for a few minutes at the beginning of every job waiting for the setup man to complete the setup. Some of the setup time is used in going for stock, but the drill press operator typically returns with stock before the setup man is finished with the setup.

   f) The operator stops to talk to you.

   g) The operator lights up a cigarette.

   h) The operator opens his lunch pail (it is not lunch time), removes an apple, and takes an occasional bite.

   i) The operator drops a part, and you pick it up and hand it to him. Does this make any difference in the time study? How?

7. Describe Gilbreth's approach to setting work standards.

Although opposed by unions, computer monitoring has spread quickly at many companies, including AT&T Communications. AT&T uses a computer to check each telephone operator's "average work time," or AWT. AWT is the time consumed on each call and has been set at 30 seconds. A few years ago, one operator consistently averaged about 32 seconds and she was dismissed. When filing her grievance, the operator claimed that co-workers were under such pressure that they routinely risked disciplinary actions by cutting off callers so as to not ruin their daily AWTs. She further stated that she felt it was her job to help people who needed help, especially the elderly who would often need the name and number of a nearby pharmacy or other such time-consuming information.

Make the case for the operator and justify why the system should change. Then make the case for AT&T and justify why standards are needed.

At Northwest Airlines, data-entry workers are expected to type between 9,000 and 16,000 keystrokes per hour as they feed payroll and ticketing information into company computers. The computer keeps track of speed, and whereas slower typists can be penalized by losing pay, fast workers are rewarded with flexibility in arranging their schedules. A speed at least 75% as fast as the three fastest workers must be maintained by all workers or they can be dismissed.

Evaluate and critique Northwest's approach.

· **S11.1** The cycle time for performing a certain task was clocked at 10 minutes. The performance rating of the worker timed was estimated at 110%. Common practice in this department is to allow 5 minutes of personal time and 3 minutes of fatigue time per hour. In addition, it is estimated that there should be an extra allowance of 2 minutes per hour.

    a) Find the normal time for the operation.

    b) Compute the allowance factor and the standard time for the operation.

: **S11.2** A time study revealed an average cycle time of 5 minutes, with a standard deviation of 1.25 minutes. These figures were based on a sample of 75 cycles. Is this sample large enough that one can be 99% confident that the standard time is within 5% of the true value?

: **S11.3** The data in the following table represent time-study observations for an assembly process. On the basis of these observations, find the standard time for the process. Assume a 10% allowance factor.

		OBSERVATION (MINUTES PER CYCLE)				
ELEMENT	PERFORMANCE RATING (%)	1	2	3	4	5
1	100	1.5	1.6	1.4	1.5	1.5
2	90	2.3	2.5	2.1	2.2	2.4
3	120	1.7	1.9	1.9	1.4	1.6
4	100	3.5	3.6	3.6	3.6	3.2

: S11.4 The following data represent observations for the cycle time of an assembly process. How many observations would be necessary for the observer to be 99% confident that the average cycle time is within 5% of the true value?

OBSERVATION (IN MINUTES)				
1	2	3	4	5
1.5	1.6	1.4	1.5	1.5

(*Hint*: Compute the sample standard deviation as shown in Solved Problem S11.3.)

: S11.5 A work sample taken over a 100-hour work month produced the following results:

Units produced	200
Idle time	25%
Performance rating	110%
Allowance time	15%

What is the standard time for the job?

· S11.6 Rebecca Page clocked the cycle time for welding a part onto truck doors at 5.3 minutes. The performance rating of the worker timed was estimated at 105%. Find the normal time for this operation.

According to a local union contract, each welder is allowed 3 minutes of personal time per hour and 2 minutes of fatigue time per hour. Further, it is estimated that there should be an average delay allowance of 1 minute per hour. Compute the allowance factor, and then find the standard time for this welding activity.

: S11.7 A time study of a factory worker revealed an average cycle time of 3.20 minutes, with a standard deviation of 1.28 minutes. These figures were based on a sample of 45 cycles observed.

Is this sample adequate in size for the firm to be 99% confident that the standard time is within 5% of the true value? If not, what should be the proper number of observations?

: S11.8 The data in the following table represent time-study observations for a metalworking process. On the basis of these observations, find the standard time for the process, assuming a 25% allowance factor.

ELEMENT	PERFORMANCE RATING (%)	OBSERVATIONS (MINUTES PER CYCLE)						
		1	2	3	4	5	6	7
1	90	1.80	1.70	1.66	1.91	1.85	1.77	1.60
2	100	6.9	7.3	6.8	7.1	15.3*	7.0	6.4
3	115	3.0	9.0*	9.5*	3.8	2.9	3.1	3.2
4	90	10.1	11.1	12.3	9.9	12.0	11.9	12.0

*Disregard—unusual observation.

∶ S11.9 Based on a careful work study in the Honornell Sandling Company, the results shown in the table are observed:

	CYCLE (IN MINUTES)					PERFORMANCE
ELEMENT	1	2	3	4	5	RATING (%)
Prepare daily reports	35	40	33	42	39	120
Photocopy results	12	10	36*	15	13	110
Label and package reports	3	3	5	5	4	90
Distribute reports	15	18	21	17	45†	85

*Photocopying machine broken.
†Power outage.

a) Compute the normal time for each work element.

b) If the allowance for this type of work is 15%, what is the standard time?

c) How many observations are needed for a 95% confidence level within 5% accuracy? (*Hint:* Calculate the sample size of each element.)

∶S11.10 The Division of Continuing Education at Virginia College promotes a wide variety of executive training courses for its audience of firms in the Arlington, Virginia, region. The division's director, Christine Adams, believes that individually typed letters add a personal touch to marketing. To prepare letters for mailing, she conducts a time study of her secretaries. On the basis of the observations shown in the table, she wishes to develop a time standard for the whole job.

The college has an allowance factor of 12%. Adams decides to delete all unusual observations from the time study.

	CYCLE OBSERVED (IN MINUTES)						PERFORMANCE
ELEMENT	1	2	3	4	5	6	RATING (%)
Typing letter	2.5	3.5	2.8	2.1	2.6	3.3	85
Typing envelope	.8	.8	.6	.8	3.1	.7	100
Stuffing envelope	.4	.5	1.9	.3	.6	.5	95
Sealing, sorting	1.0	2.9	.9	1.0	4.4	.9	125

∶S11.11 A time study at the phone company observed a job that contained three elements. The times and ratings for 10 cycles are shown in the table.

	PERFOR-MANCE	OBSERVATIONS (MINUTES PER CYCLE)									
ELEMENT	RATING (%)	1	2	3	4	5	6	7	8	9	10
1	85	.40	.45	.39	.48	.41	.50	.45	.39	.50	.40
2	88	1.5	1.7	1.9	1.7	1.8	1.6	1.8	1.8	2.0	2.1
3	90	3.8	3.4	3.0	4.8	4.0	4.2	3.5	3.6	3.7	4.3

    a) Find the average cycle time for each element.

    b) Find the normal time for each element.

    c) Assuming an allowance factor for 20% of job time, determine the standard time for this job.

:S11.12 The Dubuque Cement Company packs 80-pound bags of concrete mix. Time-study data for the filling activity are shown in the table.

         The company's policy is a 20% allowance for workers. Compute the standard time for this work task. How many cycles are necessary for 99% confidence, within 5% accuracy?

	CYCLE TIME (SECONDS PER CYCLE)					PERFORMANCE
ELEMENT	1	2	3	4	5	RATING (%)
Grasp and place bag	8	9	8	11	7	110
Fill bag	36	41	39	35	112*	85
Seal bag	15	17	13	20	18	105
Place bag on conveyor	8	6	9	30†	35†	90

*Bag breaks open.
†Conveyor jams.

:S11.13 An office worker is clocked performing three work elements, with the results shown in the following table. The allowance for tasks such as this is 15%.

	MINUTES PER CYCLE						PERFORMANCE
ELEMENT	1	2	3	4	5	6	RATING (%)
1	13	11	14	16	51	15	100
2	68	21	25	73	26	23	110
3	3.0	3.3	3.1	2.9	3.4	2.8	100

    a) Find the normal time.

    b) Find the standard time.

:S11.14 Installing mufflers at the McElroy Garage in Sacramento involves five work elements. Judy McElroy times workers performing these tasks seven times with the results shown in the table.

	CYCLE OBSERVATIONS (MINUTES)							PERFORMANCE
JOB ELEMENT	1	2	3	4	5	6	7	RATING (%)
1. Select correct mufflers	4	5	4	6	4	15	4	110
2. Remove old muffler	6	8	7	6	7	6	7	90
3. Weld/install new muffler	15	14	14	12	15	16	13	105
4. Check/inspect work	3	4	24	5	4	3	18	100
5. Complete paperwork	5	6	8	—	7	6	7	130

By agreement with her workers, McElroy allows a 10% fatigue factor and a 10% personal-time factor. To compute standard time for the work operation, McElroy excludes all observations that appear to be unusual or nonrecurring. She does not want an error of more than 5%.

a) What is the standard time for the task?

b) How many cycles are needed to assure a 95% confidence level?

:S11.15 Sample observations of an assembly-line worker made over a 40-hour work week revealed that the worker produced a total of 320 completed parts. The performance rating was 125%. The sample also showed that the worker was busy assembling the parts 80% of the time. Allowances for work on the assembly line total 10%. Find the normal time and standard time for this task.

·S11.16 Bank manager Carrie Mattanini wants to determine the percent of time her tellers are working and idle. She decides to use work sampling, and its initial estimate is that the tellers are idle 30% of the time. How many observations should be taken to be 95.45% confident that the results will not be more than 5% away from the true result?

:S11.17 A work sample taken over a 160-hour work month produced the following results. What is the standard time for the job?

Units manufactured	220
Idle time	20%
Performance rating	90%
Allowance time	10%

·S11.18 Sharpening your pencil is an operation that may be divided into eight small elemental motions. In MTM terms, each element may be assigned a certain number of TMUs.

Reach 4 inches for the pencil	6 TMU
Grasp the pencil	2 TMU
Move the pencil 6 inches	10 TMU
Position the pencil	20 TMU
Insert the pencil into the sharpener	4 TMU
Sharpen the pencil	120 TMU
Disengage the pencil	10 TMU
Move the pencil 6 inches	10 TMU

What is the total normal time for sharpening one pencil? Convert this time to minutes and seconds.

CASE STUDY

Lincoln Electric's Incentive Pay System

Cleveland's Lincoln Electric was founded by John C. Lincoln in 1895 to make an electric motor he had developed. When his brother James joined the organization in 1907, they began emphasizing employee motivation. Since that time, the company has endorsed the message that the business must prosper if employees are to benefit. Today, Lincoln is a $440 million firm with 2,400 employees. About 90% of its

(Continued)

sales come from manufacturing arc-welding equipment and supplies.

The company has encouraged workers to own a stake in its property by allowing them to buy stock at book value. (The employees are required to sell the stock at book value when they leave.) Approximately 70% of the employees own stock, and together they hold nearly 50% of the outstanding shares. Most of the remaining stock is held by members of the Lincoln family who are not involved in company operations.

Factory workers at Lincoln receive piece-rate wages with no guaranteed minimum hourly pay. After working for the firm for 2 years, employees begin to participate in the year-end bonus plan. Determined by a formula that considers the company's gross profits and the employees' base piece rate and merit rating, it might be the most lucrative bonus system for factory workers in the United States. The *average* size of the bonus over the past 56 years has been 95.5% of base wages. Some Lincoln factory workers make more than $100,000 a year. In recent good years, average employees have earned about $85,000 a year, well above the average for U.S. manufacturing workers as a whole. But in a bad year, Lincoln employees' average might fall as much as 40%.

The company has a guaranteed-employment policy that it put in place in 1958. Since that time, it has not laid off a single worker. In return for job security, however, employees agree to several things. During slow times, they will accept reduced work periods. They also agree to accept work transfers, even to lower-paid jobs, if that is necessary to maintain a minimum of 30 hours of work per week.

The company calls the low cost of high wages its incentive-pay system. Each employee inspects his or her own parts and must correct any imperfect work on personal time. Each is responsible for the quality of his or her own work. Records are maintained reflecting who worked on each piece of equipment. Should inferior work slip by and be discovered by Lincoln's quality control people or by customers, the worker's merit rating, bonus, and pay are lowered.

However, some employees feel the system can cause some unfriendly competition as well. Because a certain number of merit points is allotted to each department, an exceptionally high rating for one person may mean a lower rating for another.

But the pressure has been good for productivity. One company executive estimates that Lincoln's overall productivity is about double that of its domestic competitors. The company has earned a profit every year since the depths of the 1930s' depression and has never missed a quarterly dividend. Lincoln has one of the lowest employee turnover rates in U.S. industry. Recently, *Fortune* magazine cited Lincoln's two U.S. plants as among the 10 best-managed in the country.

DISCUSSION QUESTIONS

1. How are labor standards used to establish an incentive system such as this?
2. How and why does Lincoln's approach to motivating people work?
3. What problems might this system create for management?
4. What types of employee would be happy working at Lincoln?

Sources: HR Magazine (November 1990): 73–76; *Inc.* (August 1988): 95–96; and *Success* (October 1989): 12.

BIBLIOGRAPHY

Barnes, R. M. *Motion and Time Study.* New York: John Wiley, 1980.

Flynn, B. B., C. Blair, and M. Walters. "Flexible Compensation for World Class Manufacturers: Creating a Labor Skill Inventory Using Skill-Based Pay" OM *Review,* 9, no. 3: 22–36.

Jacobs, L. W., and S. E. Bechtold. "Labor Utilization Effects of Labor Scheduling Flexibility Alternatives in a Tour Scheduling Environment." *Decision Sciences,* 24, no. 1 (January/February 1993): 148–166.

Karger, D. W. *Advanced Work Measurement.* New York: Industrial Press, 1982.

Konz, S. *Work Design.* Columbia, OH: Grid, 1975.

Neibel, B. W. *Motion and Time Study,* 7th ed. Homewood, IL: Irvin, 1982.

12

PURCHASING MANAGEMENT AND JUST-IN-TIME

LEARNING OBJECTIVES

When you complete this chapter you should be able to:

Identify or Define:
   Purchasing
   Vertical Integration
   Materials Management
   Virtual Companies
Explain:
   Just-in-time purchasing
   Make-or-buy decisions

BOEING FINDS COMPETITIVE ADVANTAGE WITH INTERNATIONAL PURCHASING

The relationship with suppliers in the aircraft business is complex. Aircraft system design and tremendous financial risk require that suppliers be a part of the concept from the very beginning.

The new Boeing 777 took an investment of about $4 billion. Boeing's out-of-pocket costs were about $2.5 billion, with suppliers investing the remaining $1.5 billion. With investments of this magnitude, Boeing designers and purchasing personnel work with suppliers early and in earnest. Engines, landing gear, and thousands of other parts and components procured from others are an integral part of plane design. Therefore, suppliers get on board in the early phases of design. Unless sales of the 777 reach 6 or 7 planes per month with total sales of 300 aircraft, Boeing may lose money on the plane. When the risks are this high, supplying "partners" must make a commitment, too.

Effective purchasing not only finds exceptional suppliers wherever they may be, but must also find suppliers who are willing to step up to the risk associated with new products. Those suppliers are diverse. Boeing finds such "partners" throughout the world, in over a dozen countries from the Middle East to the Pacific rim.

International procurement of components spreads Boeing's risk and has the added advantage of including local content in the plane. Countries that have a manufacturing stake in Boeing's 777 are more likely to buy from Boeing than from competing McDonnell Douglas or Airbus.

Boeing 777 International Purchasing. This figure shows the worldwide purchasing effort for Boeing's new 777, with 20% of the plane's structure contracted to a Japanese consortium.

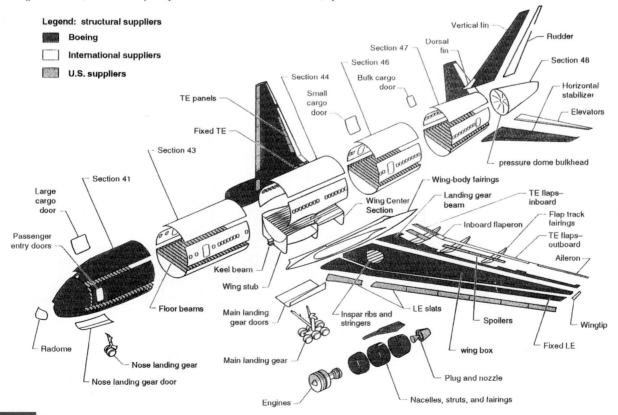

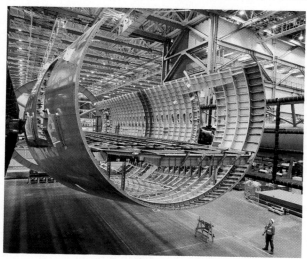

Boeing 777 Fuselage Rotated in Fixture. *The Boeing 777 aircraft fuselage section, or belly of the aircraft, is shown rotated upright after it was assembled in an inverted position. This 14,000-pound section housed the aft lower cargo hold and the economy section for the interior passenger cabin. Inverted sections give Boeing employees better access to all parts during assembly.*

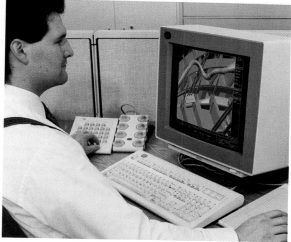

Computer-Aided Design Helps Boeing 777 Designers. *The Boeing 777 was designed entirely on computer screens and assembled without mockups. Designers created and manipulated full-color, 3-D solid images representing aircraft sections and systems. The Boeing 777 design was "paperless."*

Boeing 777 Being Assembled at Everett, Washington. *Purchasing personnel work with suppliers to develop contracts. These contracts ensure that quality components are delivered on time and within cost to Boeing's final assembly line in Everett, Washington.*

S uppliers for Chrysler Corporation's new Dodge Stratus were chosen before the parts were even designed. Chrysler evaluated suppliers on a number of criteria, but virtually eliminated traditional supplier bidding. As a part of this new and unique process, Chrysler has adopted contracts that extend for at least the life of the model. Additionally, the contracts call for periodic price reductions as the auto manufacturer helps suppliers eliminate the forces that push up costs. By working with Chrysler in these "partnerships," suppliers are to become more efficient, reducing prices as they move down the learning curve. ♦

As both Boeing and Chrysler have shown, no organization finds it economical to make all the material it uses. The advantages of specialization are too pervasive. Consequently, many items are purchased from others. The purchasing function often spends more money than any other function in the business, so purchasing provides a major opportunity to reduce costs and increase profit margins.

This leads to the creation of a purchasing (sometimes called procurement) department and the role of a purchasing agent. Purchasing is the acquisition of goods and services. The **purchasing** activity

Purchasing

1. helps identify the products and services that can best be obtained externally;
2. develops, evaluates, and determines the best supplier, price, and delivery for those products and services.

PURCHASING

Operations Environments

Purchasing agent

In operations environments, the purchasing function is usually managed by a **purchasing agent** who has legal authority to execute contracts on behalf of the firm. In a large firm, the purchasing agent may also have a staff that includes buyers and expediters. Buyers represent the company, performing all activities of the purchasing department except the signing of contracts. Expediters assist buyers in following up on purchases to ensure timely delivery. In *manufacturing* firms, the purchasing function is supported by product engineering drawings and specifications, quality control documents, and testing activities that evaluate the purchased items.

Service Environments

In many *service* environments, purchasing's role is less important because the primary product is an intellectual one. In legal and medical organizations, for example, the main items to be procured are office facilities, furniture and equipment, autos, and supplies. However, in other services such as transportation and restaurants, the purchasing function is critical. An airline that purchases planes that are not efficient for its route structure or a steak house that does not know how to buy steak is in trouble.

In the wholesale and retail segment of services, purchasing is performed by a **buyer** who has responsibility for the sale and profit margins on the purchased merchandise that will be resold. Buyers in this nonmanufacturing environment may have

Buyer

TABLE 12.1 ■ **CONSIDERATIONS FOR THE MAKE-OR-BUY DECISION**

REASONS FOR MAKING:	REASONS FOR BUYING:
1. Lower production cost	1. Lower acquisition cost
2. Unsuitable suppliers	2. Preserve supplier commitment
3. Assure adequate supply (quantity or delivery)	3. Obtain technical or management ability
4. Utilize surplus labor facilities and make a marginal contribution	4. Inadequate capacity
5. Obtain desired quality	5. Reduce inventory costs
6. Remove supplier collusion	6. Ensure alternative sources
7. Obtain unique item that would entail a prohibitive commitment for a supplier	7. Inadequate managerial or technical resources
8. Maintain organizational talents and protect personnel from a layoff	8. Reciprocity
9. Protect proprietary design or quality	9. Item is protected by a patent or trade secret
10. Increase or maintain size of the company (management preference)	10. Frees management to deal with its primary business

limited support in the form of documentation and specifications. They must often rely on the supplier's past performance or on standard grades. For instance, a USDA grade (such as AA eggs or U.S. choice meat), a textile standard or blend, or standard sizes may take the place of engineering drawings and quality control documents found in manufacturing environments.

Make or Buy

A wholesaler or retailer buys everything that he or she sells; a manufacturing operation hardly ever does. Manufacturers, restaurants, and assemblers of products buy components and subassemblies that go into final products. As we discussed in Chapter 6, choosing products and services that can be advantageously obtained externally as opposed to produced internally is known as the **make-or-buy decision**. Table 12.1 lists a wide variety of considerations in the make-or-buy decision. Usually, personnel from purchasing, engineering, and manufacturing participate in these decisions. However, the evaluation of alternative suppliers and preparation of data relevant to the buy alternative remain the responsibility of purchasing. Periodic review of the make-or-buy decision is necessary as vendor competence and costs change, and as costs and capabilities within the firm change.

Make-or-buy decision

THE PURCHASING OPPORTUNITY

With increasing specialization, our industrialized society spends an increasing proportion of revenue on purchases. This occurs because some part of a firm's product is very likely made more efficiently by someone else. The percent of revenue spent on purchases in a variety of industries is shown in Table 12.2. As the table suggests, many firms spend over half of their revenue on purchases. Consequently, improvements in

TABLE 12.2 ■ PERCENT OF SALES SPENT ON PURCHASES IN A VARIETY OF INDUSTRIES

INDUSTRY GROUP	PERCENT PURCHASES DIVIDED BY SALES	INDUSTRY GROUP	PERCENT PURCHASES DIVIDED BY SALES
All industries, total	54	Printing and publishing	35
Food and kindred products	63	Chemicals and allied products	48
Tobacco products	27	Petroleum and coal products	83
Apparel and other textile products	49	Stone, clay, and glass products	46
Lumber and wood products	60	Machinery, except electric	48
Furniture and fixtures	48	Electric and electronic equipment	45
Paper and allied products	54	Transportation equipment	60

Source: Derived from U.S. Bureau of the Census, Annual Survey of Manufacturers.

purchasing provide a tremendous opportunity for cost reduction. As the *POM in Action* box "The Dr. José Ignacio Lopez de Arriotua Escapade" suggests, both GM and Volkswagen understand the purchasing opportunity.

Table 12.3 illustrates the amount of leverage available to the operations manager through purchasing. Firms spending 50% of their sales dollar on purchases and having a net profit of 6% would require $3.57 worth of sales in order to equal the savings that accrues the company from a $1 savings in procurement. These numbers indicate the strong role that procurement can play in profitability. This is true in both manufacturing and service organizations.

EXAMPLE 1

The Goodwin Company spends 50% of its sales dollar on purchased goods. The firm has a net profit of 4%. Of the remaining 46%, 23% is fixed and the remaining 23% is variable. From Table 12.3, we see that the dollar value of sales needed to generate the same profit as results from $1 of purchase savings would be $3.70.

VERTICAL INTEGRATION

Vertical integration

Purchasing can be extended to take the form of vertical integration. By **vertical integration**, we mean developing the ability to produce goods or services previously purchased, or actually buying a supplier or a distributor. Vertical integration can take the form of forward or backward integration, as shown in Figure 12.1

Backward integration suggests a firm purchase its suppliers, as in the case of Ford Motor Company deciding to manufacture its own car radios. Forward integration, on the other hand, suggests that a firm make the finished product. An example is Texas Instruments, a manufacturer of integrated circuits; the firm also manufactures calculators and computers.

Vertical integration can offer a strategic opportunity for the operations manager. For firms whose internal analysis suggests that they have the necessary capital, managerial talent, and required demand, vertical integration may provide substantial opportunities for cost reduction. Other advantages in inventory reduction and scheduling can accrue to the company that effectively manages vertical integration or close, mutually beneficial relationships with suppliers.

TABLE 12.3 ■ DOLLARS OF ADDITIONAL SALES NEEDED TO EQUAL $1 SAVED THROUGH PURCHASING*

PERCENT NET PROFIT OF FIRM	PERCENT OF SALES SPENT FOR PURCHASES							
	20%	30%	40%	50%	60%	70%	80%	90%
2	$2.44	$2.78	$3.23	$3.85	$4.76	$6.25	$9.09	$16.67
4	$2.38	$2.70	$3.13	$3.70	$4.55	$5.88	$8.33	$14.29
6	$2.33	$2.63	$3.03	$3.57	$4.35	$5.56	$7.69	$12.50
8	$2.27	$2.56	$2.94	$3.45	$4.17	$5.26	$7.14	$11.11
10	$2.22	$2.50	$2.86	$3.33	$4.00	$5.00	$6.67	$10.00

*The required increase in sales assumes that 50% of the costs other than purchases are variable and that 1/2 of the remaining (less profit) are fixed. Therefore, at sales of $100 (50% purchases and 2% margin), $50 are purchases, $24 are other variable costs, $24 are fixed costs, and $2 profit. Increasing sales by $3.85 yields the following:

Purchases at 50%	$51.93
Other Variable Costs	24.92
Fixed Cost	24.00
Profit	3.00
	$103.85

Through $3.85 of additional sales, we have increased the profit by $1, from $2 to $3. The same increase in margin could have been obtained by reducing purchasing costs by $1.

Because purchased items represent such a large part of the costs of sales, it is obvious why so many organizations find interest in vertical integration. Vertical integration can yield cost reduction, quality adherence, and timely delivery. Additionally, vertical integration appears to work best when the organization has large market share or has the management talent to operate an acquired vendor successfully.[1] However, backward integration may be particularly dangerous for firms in industries

Each company in each industry makes its own judgment about the appropriate degree of vertical integration. Jaguar is changing its approach to vertical integration. In the past, Jaguar made virtually every part it could, even where it made little sense. It even manufactured some simple items such as washers. However, Jaguar is now focusing on those items that make a car unique: the body, engine, and suspension. Outside suppliers with their capabilities, expertise, and efficiencies provide most other components.

FIGURE 12.1 ■ Vertical Integration Can Be Forward or Backward

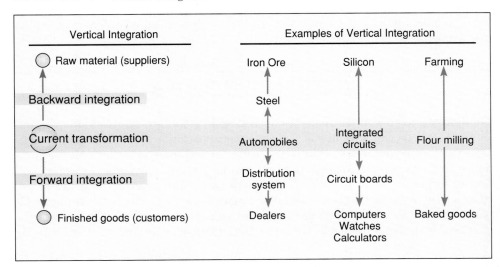

[1]Robert D. Buzzell, "Is Vertical Integration Profitable?" *Harvard Business Review*, 61, no. 1 (January/February 1983): 92–102.

The Dr. José Ignacio Lopez de Arriotua Escapade

When General Motors brought José Lopez from Europe to improve its purchasing and performance, he proceeded to challenge suppliers on cost, quality, and delivery. His methodology, called PICOS (Purchasing Input Concept Optimizing Systems), was to drive waste out of the procurement process while improving quality and responsiveness.

As the company's worldwide purchasing director, Lopez threatened both internal and outside suppliers. To GM divisions that make parts for the final product, he vowed to go to the "outside option" if costs were not slashed. To outside suppliers, who account for 30% of GM's parts needs, Lopez ordered price cuts of 20% immediately and 50% over the

next few years. The result was turmoil and rebellion among General Motors' suppliers. Nonetheless, most responded with improvements. By some estimates, supplier productivity improved 55% with similar reductions in lead time.

Watching GM's improvements, Volkswagen wanted Lopez to do the same for them. They made him an offer to return to Europe; GM counteroffered. Volkswagen made another offer. As GM held a news conference to announce that Lopez was staying with GM, he was instead boarding a plane to Germany. A number of key General Motors' purchasing personnel and several boxes of documents also ended up in Germany. The result is Dr. Lopez, Volkswagen, General Motors, and a number of associates have ended up in the German court system. This escapade points out just how important purchasing has become in today's organizations.

Sources: Wall Street Journal (May 18, 1994): A11, (April 4, 1994): B-3, and (December 1, 1993): A10.

---

undergoing technological change if management cannot keep abreast of those changes or invest the financial resources necessary for the next technological evolution.[2]

Keiretsu

Many large Japanese manufacturers have found a middle ground between purchasing from a subcontractor and vertical integration. These manufacturers are often financial supporters through ownership or loans to subcontractors. The subcontractors then become part of a company coalition known as a **keiretsu**. Members of the keiretsu are assured long-term relationships and are therefore expected to function as partners, lending technical expertise and stable quality production to the manufacturer. Members of the keiretsu may also operate as subcontractors to a chain of smaller subcontractors.

VIRTUAL COMPANIES

Virtual companies

The limitations to vertical integration, as noted before, are severe. Moreover, our technological society continually demands more specialization that further complicates vertical integration. Rather than letting vertical integration lock an organization into businesses that it may not understand, another approach is to find good flexible suppliers. A firm that has a department or division for everything may be too bureaucratic to be world-class. **Virtual companies** rely on a variety of supplier relationships to provide services on demand.[3] Virtual companies have fluid, moving organizational boundaries that allow them to create a unique enterprise to meet changing

[2]See, for instance, Robert H. Hayes and William J. Abernathy, "Managing Our Way to Economic Decline," *Harvard Business Review,* 58, no. 4 (July/August 1980): 72–73.

[3]Virtual companies are also known as *hollow corporations* or *network companies.* See *Business Week* (October 17, 1994): 86.

market demands. These relationships may provide a variety of services that include doing the payroll, hiring personnel, designing products, providing consulting services, manufacturing components, conducting tests, or distributing products. The relationships may be short-term or long-term, true partners or only collaborators, or simply able suppliers and subcontractors. But whatever the formal relationship, the result can be lean world-class performance. The advantages of virtual companies include specialized management expertise, low capital investment, flexibility, and speed. The result is efficiency.

As discussed in the *POM in Action* box "Purchasing Moves to Virtual Companies," Silicon Valley provides a contemporary example of virtual companies. The apparel business provides a *traditional* example of virtual organizations. The designers of clothes seldom manufacture their designs; they license the manufacture. The manufacturer may then rent a loft, lease sewing machines, and contract for the labor. The result is an organization that has low overhead, is flexible, and can respond rapidly to the market. In the virtual company, the purchasing function is demanding and dynamic.

Sanford Corporation is one of America's largest producers of highlighters and markers. Sanford is vertically integrated, making its own inks, which gives it a research, development, quality, and product flexibility advantage.

PURCHASING MANAGEMENT

A firm that decides to buy material rather than make it must manage a purchasing function. **Purchasing management** considers numerous factors, such as inventory and transportation costs, availability of supply, delivery performance, and quality of suppliers. A firm may have some competence in all areas of purchasing management, but exceptional competence may require a more narrow focus.

Purchasing management

The Purchasing Focus

One focus of purchasing is *source management*. **Source management** is concerned with developing new reliable suppliers. The product may be a high-technology, custom-made, or specialty item for which there are few, if any, suppliers. Management must be able to seek out likely suppliers, develop their ability to produce, and negotiate acceptable relationships.

Source management

Alternatively, purchasing may focus on *supply management*.[4] A **supply management** focus suggests a concern with long-term availability of high-dollar or critical purchases; future reliable supplies are critical to success of the enterprise. An example is General Motors' development of palladium and platinum suppliers so it would have reliable and reasonably priced raw materials for catalytic converters. The evaluation was global and development of the supplier was expensive. A supply management focus is also necessary if the dollar value of the purchases or fluctuations in cost are substantial. The extreme of this focus is for the firm to pursue backward integration to assure future supplies.

Supply management

Purchasing may be combined with various warehousing and inventory activities to form a materials management system. The purpose of **materials management** is to obtain efficiency of operations through the integration of all material acquisition, movement, and storage activities in the firm. When transportation and inventory

Materials management

[4]Peter Kraljic, "Purchasing Must Become Supply Management," *Harvard Business Review*, 61, no. 5 (September/October 1983): 109–117.

Purchasing Moves to "Virtual" Companies

Stripped-down, lean, world-class companies are farming out many activities, from payroll to design to manufacture. "People say we don't have companies, we have virtual companies," said Diosdado Banatao, who runs S3 Inc., a chip design company in Santa Clara. "Where once it was a one-stop shop, we have partners who do wafers and who do packaging and who do tests."

In the virtual factory, suppliers are freed up to concentrate on what they do best. The result is products that cost less and often perform better. At Visioneer, in Palo Alto, software is written by several partners, hardware is manufactured by a subcontractor in Silicon Valley, printed-circuit boards are made in Singapore, and plastic cases are made in Boston,

where the units are tested and packed for shipment. In this "hollow corporation" approach, the boundaries between firms, between customers and suppliers, and between competitors are blurred. These companies have fluid, moving, supplier–customer relationships that use exactly the organizational talents needed to create a competitive advantage.

However, there is a down side to virtual companies. Chips & Technology, a firm that designs innovative semiconductors, relies on Texas Instruments to build its product in TI's huge fabrication plants. This works well when the fabrication plants have excess capacity and prompt delivery. But when Chips & Technology had to wait 14 weeks for an important delivery from TI, it missed the market and saw red ink—a $57 million loss on revenues of $141 million in 1991. What looks like a smart, low-capital way to do business, has a down side.

Sources: Association for Manufacturing Excellence, Wheeling, Illinois; *New York Times* (July 17, 1994): ; *Forbes* (January 18, 1993): 88–89.

costs are substantial on both the input and output side of the production process, an emphasis of materials management may be appropriate. The potential for competitive advantage is found via both reduced costs and improved customer service. Many manufacturing companies have moved to some form of material management structure.[5]

Vendor Relations

The competitive advantage that can be obtained through purchasing can only be achieved with outstanding vendor relations. Viewing the supplier as an adversary is counterproductive. Long-term, close relationships with a few suppliers is a better way (see the *POM in Action* box "Firms Slash Vendor Rolls" on page 539). A healthy vendor relationship is one in which the supplier is committed to helping the purchaser improve its product and win orders. Suppliers can also be a source of ideas about new technology, materials, and processes, (as Chrysler discovered with its "SCORE" program (see Table 12.4). Purchasing is a way to convey such information to the proper people in the organization.

Likewise, healthy relationships also include those in which the purchaser is committed to keeping the supplier informed of possible changes in product and production schedule. The purchasing function and suppliers must develop mutually advantageous relationships. Because an outstanding operations function requires excellent vendor relations, purchasing conducts a three-stage process.

VENDOR EVALUATION.   The first stage, *vendor evaluation,* involves finding potential vendors and determining the likelihood of their becoming good suppliers.

[5]Jeffrey G. Miller and Peter Gilman, "Materials Managers: Who Needs Them?" *Harvard Business Review,* 57, no. 4 (July/August 1979): 143.

TABLE 12.4 ■ CHRYSLER'S SUPPLIER COST REDUCTION EFFORT (SCORE) HAS PRODUCED $161,000,000 IN SAVINGS IN 2 YEARS			
SUPPLIER	**SUGGESTION**	**MODEL**	**ANNUAL SAVINGS**
Rockwell	Use passenger car door locks on 1991 Dodge trucks	Dodge trucks	$280,000
Rockwell	Simplify design and substitute materials on manual window-regulator systems	Various	$300,000
3M	Change tooling for wood-grain panels to allow three parts to be made in one die instead of two	Caravan, Voyager	$1,500,000
Trico	Change wiper-blade formulations to eliminate the disposable plastic shield used during assembly and shipping	Various	$140,000
Leslie Metal Arts	Exterior lighting suggestions	Various	$1,500,000

Source: James Welch, Laddie Cook, and Joseph Blackburn, "The Bridge to Competitiveness, Building Supplier–Customer Linkages," *Target* (November/December 1992): 17–29. Reprinted from *Target* with permission of the Association for Manufacturing Excellence.

As a world-class telecommunications company, AT&T has an aggressive supplier evaluation and quality improvement program. Part of this program requires that vendors provide company profile and capability information. Providing this information is often done in formal presentations, as Hitachi Cable Ltd. is doing above. Once vendors are approved and orders placed, AT&T tracks key supplier variables, such as order cycle time and quality yield to determine effectiveness of the program.

This phase requires the development of evaluation criteria such as those in Figure 12.2. Both the criteria and the weights are dependent upon the needs of the organization. The selection of competent suppliers is critical. If good suppliers are not selected, then all other purchasing efforts are wasted. As firms move toward fewer longer-term suppliers, the issues of financial strength, quality, management, research, and technical ability play an increasingly important role. These attributes should be noted in the evaluation process. Note Motorola's approach discussed in the *POM in Action* box "Motorola Wants Shippers Who Deliver on Their Promises" on page 540.

VENDOR DEVELOPMENT. The second stage is *vendor development.* Assuming a firm wants to proceed with a particular vendor, how does it integrate this supplier into its system? Purchasing makes sure the vendor has an appreciation of quality requirements, engineering changes, schedules and delivery, the payment system, and procurement policies. Vendor development may include everything from training, to engineering and production help, to formats for electronic information transfer. Purchasing policies might include issues such as percent of business done with any one supplier or with minority businesses.

NEGOTIATIONS. The third stage is *negotiations.*[6] **Negotiation strategies** are of three classic types. First is the *cost-based price model.* This model requires that the supplier open its books to the purchaser. The contract price is then based on time and materials or on a fixed cost with an escalation clause to accommodate changes in the vendor's labor and materials cost.

 Second is the *market-based price model.* In this model, price is based on a published price or index. Paperboard prices, for instance, are published weekly in the "yellow sheet,"[7] and nonferrous metal prices in *Metals Week.*[8]

Negotiation strategies

[6]Gary J. Zenz, *Purchasing and the Management of Materials,* 7th ed. (New York: John Wiley, 1994).

[7]The "yellow sheet" is the commonly used name of the *Official Board Markets,* published by Magazines for Industry, Chicago. It contains announced paperboard prices for containerboard and boxboard.

[8]*Metals Week,* A. Patrick Ryan, editor and publisher, New York.

FIGURE 12.2 ■ Vendor Rating Form Used by J. M. Huber Corporation. Evaluation categories are weighted according to importance (for example, "Product" category is weighted 1.25; "Service" is next at 0.69). Individual factors (for example, quality, delivery, and so on) have descending values, from 4 points for excellent to 1 point for poor. Total of points in each category is multiplied by the weight for that category.

VENDOR   RATING   REPORT   J.M. HUBER CORPORATION

COMPANY   TOTAL RATING

Company:	Excellent (4)	Good (3)	Fair (2)	Poor (1)	Products:	Excellent (4)	Good (3)	Fair (2)	Poor (1)
Size and/or Capacity	4				Quality	4			
Financial Strength		3			Price		3		
Operational Profit		3			Packaging	4			
Manufacturing Range	4				Uniformity		3		
Research Facilities			2		Warranty	4			
Technical Service		3			Total 18	12	6		
Geographical Locations	4				1.25 x Total = 22.50				
Management		3			*Sales Personnel*				
Labor Relations		3			1. Knowledge				
Trade Relations		3			His company		3		
Total 32	12	18	2		His product	4			
.63 x Total = 20.16					Our industry		3		
Service					Our Company		3		
Deliveries on Time	4				2. Sales Calls				
Condition on Arrival		3			Properly Spaced	4			
Follow Instructions		3			By Appointment		3		
Number of Rejections	4				Planned and Prepared		3		
Handling of Complaints		3			Mutually Productive	4			
Technical Assistance			2		3. Sales-Service				
Emergency Aid		3			Obtain Information		3		
Supply Up to Date Catalogues, Etc.				1	Furnish Quotations Promptly	4			
Supply Price Changes Promptly	4				Follow Orders		3		
Total 27	12	12	2	1	Expedite Delivery		3		
.69 x Total = 18.63					Handle Complaints		3		
					Total 43	16	27		
					.48 x Total = 20.64				

Source: Stuart F. Heinritz, Paul V. Farrell, Larry Giunipero, and Michael Kolchin, *Purchasing: Principles and Applications,* 8th ed. (Englewood Cliffs, NJ: Prentice Hall, 1992), p. 180.

Both Levi Strauss as the purchaser and Milliken as the supplier have found advantages in a closer relationship. Milliken developed a *partners for profit* program so its customers could concentrate on their business rather than on the management of raw materials inventory. Shown here is a Levi Strauss factory that is benefiting from this program.

The third method is *competitive bidding*. In cases where suppliers are not willing to discuss costs or where near-perfect markets do not exist, competitive bidding is often appropriate. Competitive bidding is the typical policy in many firms for the majority of their purchases. The policy usually requires that the purchasing agent have several potential suppliers of the product (or its equivalent) and quotations from each. The major disadvantage of this method is that the development of long-term relations between the buyer and seller are hindered. Competitive bidding may effectively determine cost. But it may also make difficult the communication and performance that are vital for engineering changes, quality, and delivery.

Yet a fourth approach is to *combine one or more* of the preceding negotiation techniques. The supplier and purchaser may agree on review of certain cost data,

Firms Slash Vendor Rolls

Corporate America's drive for quality is squeezing thousands of suppliers. The pressure on suppliers results from American industry's struggle to slim down and tone up to meet global competition. Companies around the country are cutting back the number of suppliers they use by as much as 90%. They are demanding higher levels of service and product quality from the survivors. And they are willing to pay a premium on the theory that getting things right initially is cheaper in the long run.

"A revolution is going on in the relationships between suppliers and customers," says quality expert J. M. Juran.

In the change, many suppliers will eventually "fade away," says Richard Buetow, senior vice president of Motorola. In the current climate of worldwide competition, he adds, no one can "accept just sweat; you have to show results." Over the past several years, Motorola has cut its 10,000-company supplier base by 70% and is still slashing.

	NUMBER OF SUPPLIERS		
	CURRENT	PREVIOUS*	% CHANGE
Xerox	500	5,000	−90
Motorola	3,000	10,000	−70
General Motors	5,500	10,000	−45
Ford Motor	1,000	1,800	−44
Texas Instruments	14,000	22,000	−36

*The number of suppliers firm had prior to starting reduction programs.

Sources: Wall Street Journal (August 16, 1991): B1; and *Production & Inventory Management Journal* (Third Quarter 1991): 22–25.

accept some form of market data for raw material costs, or agree that the supplier will "remain competitive."

A good supplier relationship is one where both partners have established a degree of mutual trust and a belief in the competence of each other.

Purchasing Techniques

BLANKET ORDERS. Blanket orders are unfilled orders with a vendor.[9] A blanket order is a contract to purchase certain items from the vendor. It is not an authorization to ship anything. Shipment is made only upon receipt of an agreed-upon document, perhaps a shipping requisition or shipment release.

INVOICELESS PURCHASING. Invoiceless purchasing is an extension of good purchaser–supplier relations. In an invoiceless purchasing environment, there is typically one supplier for all units of a particular product. If the supplier provides all four wheels for each lawn mower produced, then management knows how many wheels it purchased. It just multiplies the quantity of lawn mowers produced times four and issues a check to the supplier for that amount.

ELECTRONIC ORDERING AND FUNDS TRANSFER. Electronic ordering and funds transfer reduce paper transactions. Paper transactions consist of a purchase

[9] Unfilled orders are also referred to as "open" orders or "incomplete" orders.

Motorola Wants Shippers Who Deliver on Their Promises

Motorola's drive for 100% customer satisfaction means it demands its suppliers and shipping agents "promise no more than they can deliver, then deliver on those promises." The firm has strict standards, for example, for its contract carriers who deliver company products to customers by sea, rail, or truck. The standard, almost impossible to meet, is that carriers will deliver on time 100% of the time, with no damage to goods.

Motorola spends up to a year investigating contract carriers, evaluating their quality records, on-time performance reports, employee standards of conduct, training systems, and safety records. Once the contract is signed, Motorola sets up a monitoring system that formally evaluates shipping criteria every 3 months. Performance is analyzed for on-time delivery, losses or damages to shipments, claims made by customers, billing accuracy, and customer service.

The giant firm also reaches out with visits to its shippers at least monthly to discuss ways to improve quality performance. Motorola's staff gets involved with training and support services, creative problem-solving teams, and sets up meetings among carriers and customers to examine ways to improve services. This win/win approach not only leads to innovations, but builds stronger relations and enhances communications with customers and shippers alike.

Sources: Business Week (April 13, 1992): 60–65; and Motorola, Inc., *Profiles in Quality* (Boston: Allyn and Bacon, 1991), pp. 15–16.

order, a purchase release, a receiving document, authorization to pay an invoice (which is matched with the approved receiving report), and finally the issuance of a check. Purchasing departments can reduce this barrage of paperwork by electronic ordering, acceptance of all parts as 100% good, and electronic funds transfer to pay for units received. Not only can electronic ordering reduce paperwork, but it also speeds up the traditionally long procurement cycle. General Motors has saved billions of dollars over the past few years through exactly this kind of electronic transfer.[10]

Electronic data interchange (EDI)

Transactions between firms are increasingly done via electronic data interchange. **Electronic data interchange (EDI)** is a standardized data transmittal format for computerized communications between organizations. EDI provides data transfer for virtually any business application, including purchasing. Data are transmitted directly from electronic media of the sender via a third party (usually, the phone company) to electronic media of the receiver. For instance, under EDI, data for a purchase order, such as order date, due date, quantity, part number, purchase order number, address, and so forth, are fitted into the standard EDI format. The data are then sent, usually from one computer to another, by phone line. The receiving organization knows where the data are on the standardized format; a computer program is used to read those data into the receiving company's files.

STOCKLESS PURCHASING.   The term *stockless purchasing* has come to mean that the supplier maintains the inventory for the purchaser. If the supplier can maintain the stock of inventory for a variety of customers who use the same product or whose differences are very minor, say, perhaps at the packaging stage, then there may be a net savings. Consignment inventories, discussed shortly, are a related option.

[10]See J. Carbonne, "G.M. After Lopez," *Electronic Business Buyer* (October 1993): 56–60.

STANDARDIZATION. The purchasing department should make special efforts toward increased levels of standardization. That is, rather than obtaining a variety of very similar components with labeling, coloring, packaging, or perhaps even slightly different engineering specifications, the purchasing agent should endeavor to have those components standardized.

JUST-IN-TIME (JIT) PURCHASING

In the traditional flow of material through the transformation process, there are many potential delays. Incoming material is delayed at receiving and incoming inspection; work-in-process is delayed at numerous workstations; and finished goods held at finished goods storage. **Just-in-time (JIT) purchasing** reduces the waste that is present at receiving and incoming inspection. It also reduces excess inventory, poor quality, and delay. This waste is present in virtually all production processes—and purchasing is a critical function in removing the waste and making JIT work. Every moment material is held should add value. And every movement of material should add value.

Just-in-time purchasing

Table 12.5 shows the characteristics of JIT purchasing, and the *POM in Action* box discusses Harley Davidson's drive toward JIT.

Goals of Just-in-Time Purchasing

The goals of JIT purchasing are:

1. *Elimination of Unnecessary Activities.* For instance, receiving activity and incoming inspection activity are unnecessary under just-in-time. If purchasing personnel have been effective in selecting and developing vendors, the purchased items can be received without formal counting, inspection, and testing procedures. To do its job well, the purchasing staff requires support from other sections of the operations function. Production can contribute by providing accurate, stable schedules, adequate lead time for engineering changes to be implemented, and time to develop ethical suppliers.

2. *Elimination of In-Plant Inventory.* Virtually no raw material inventory is necessary if materials that meet quality standards are delivered where and when they are needed. Raw material inventory is necessary only if there is reason to believe that supplies are undependable. Likewise, parts or components for processing at some intermediate stage should be delivered in small lots directly to the using department as needed. Reduction or elimination of inventory allows problems with other aspects of the production process to be observed and corrected. Inventory tends to hide problems.

3. *Elimination of In-Transit Inventory.* At any given time, over one-half of General Motors' inventory is moving between plants; it is in transit. For global manufacturers such as General Motors and Toyota, the problem is severe, but it also provides substantial opportunity for improvement.[11] Modern purchasing departments address in-transit inventory reduction by encouraging suppliers to locate

[11]See Joseph Bonney, "Toyota's Global Conveyorbelts," *American Shipper*, 36, no. 9 (September 1994): 50.

Automobile seats made 2 hours earlier are being delivered to Chrysler's Sterling Heights, Michigan, factory. The seats are then quickly transferred in proper sequence to the assembly line for JIT installation.

TABLE 12.5 ■ CHARACTERISTICS OF JIT PURCHASING

SUPPLIERS

Few suppliers

Nearby suppliers or clusters of remote suppliers

Repeat business with same suppliers

Active use of analysis to enable desirable suppliers to become/stay price competitive

Competitive bidding mostly limited to new purchases

Buyer resists vertical integration and subsequent wipeout of supplier business

Suppliers encouraged to extend JIT buying to *their* suppliers

QUANTITIES

Steady output rate (a desirable prerequisite)

Frequent deliveries in small lot quantities

Long-term contract agreements

Minimal paperwork to release orders

Delivery quantities variable from release to release but fixed for whole contract term

Little or no permissible overage or underage of receipts

Suppliers encouraged to package in exact quantities

Suppliers encouraged to reduce their production lot sizes (or store unreleased material)

QUALITY

Minimal product specifications imposed on supplier

Help suppliers to meet quality requirements

Close relationships between buyers' and suppliers' quality assurance people

Suppliers encouraged to use process control charts instead of lot sampling inspection

SHIPPING

Scheduling of inbound freight

Gain control by use of company-owned or contract shipping and warehousing

Source: Richard J. Schonberger and James P. Gilbert, "Just-in-Time Purchasing: A Challenge for U.S. Industry." Copyright 1983 by The Regents of the University of California. Reprinted from the *California Management Review,* Vol. 26, No. 1. By permission of The Regents.

near the plant and support rapid transportation of purchases. The shorter the flow of material and money in the resource "pipeline," the less inventory (see Figure 12.3). Another way to reduce in-transit inventory is to have inventory

Consignment

on **consignment**. Under a consignment arrangement, the supplier maintains title to the inventory. For instance, an assembly plant may find a hardware supplier that is willing to locate its warehouse where the user currently has its stockroom. In this manner, when hardware is needed, it is no farther than the stockroom. And the supplier can ship to other, perhaps smaller, purchasers from the "stockroom." The supplier bills the user on the basis of the signed pickup receipt or number of units shipped.

4. *Quality and Reliability Improvement.* Reducing the number of suppliers and increasing long-term commitments to suppliers tends to improve supplier quality

FIGURE 12.3 ■ Shorter Processing Time Also Lowers Costs.

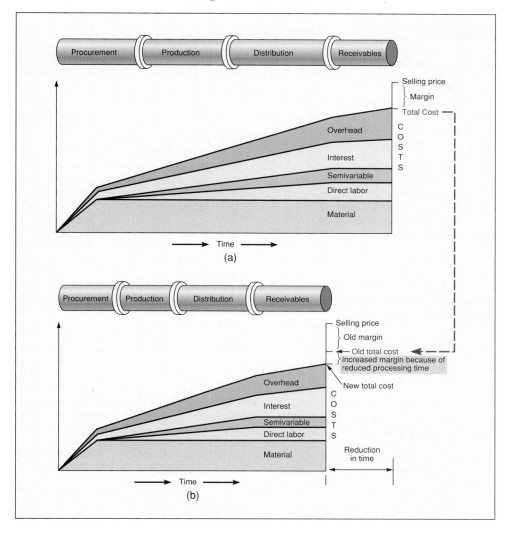

and reliability. Vendors and purchasers must have mutual understanding and trust. To achieve deliveries only when needed, in the exact quantities needed, also requires perfect quality—or as it is also known, zero defects. And, of course, both the supplier and the delivery system must be excellent. Notice in the *POM in Action* box, "Strangling General Motors with the Power of JIT", how a strike at one supplier can be devastating.

Supplier Concerns

To implement JIT purchasing successfully, purchasing personnel must work closely with suppliers to overcome supplier concerns. These supplier concerns include[12]

[12]This summary is based on a study by Tom Schmitt and Mary Connors, "A Survey of Suppliers' Attitudes Toward the Establishment of JIT," *Operations Management Review*, 3, no. 4 (Summer 1985): 36.

Harley's Drive Toward Just-in-Time

Harley Davidson's motorcycle business was on the ropes when it seriously began to look at just-in-time manufacturing.

In its initial efforts, Harley erred by taking a legalistic approach in trying to sign up suppliers for a just-in-time system. Contracts of 35 pages devoted to spelling out suppliers' obligations to Harley were used. Harley turned to more informal arrangements (with two-page contracts) when months passed and only a few companies signed up. As Harley realized it needed to take steps to enhance supplier relationships, groups of its buyers and engineers fanned out to visit suppliers. They began refining and simplifying designs, and assisted suppliers in reducing setup time between jobs by modifying equipment to allow for speedy die changes. Courses in statistics to teach workers how to chart small changes in the perfor-

mance of their equipment were given to suppliers by Harley. This system provided early warnings when machines were drifting out of tolerance.

For Harley and its suppliers, results have been excellent—Harley is profitable once again. Because of the refinement in the quality of its motorcycles, as well as greatly updated manufacturing techniques, Harley's bill for warranty repairs, scrap, and reworking of parts has been reduced 60%.

Harley's program improved what might be called the infrastructure of the system. Although it shifted business to suppliers closer to its plants, it also diminished the number of suppliers. For example, about three-quarters of the suppliers to its Milwaukee engine plant are now located within a 175-mile radius of the city's suburbs. The company has reduced the need for safety stocks—inventories kept as insurance against breakdowns in transportation—merely by reducing the distances from its suppliers.

Sources: Management Accounting (September 1990): 61–62; and *Industrial Management & Data Systems*, 90, no. 3 (1990): 12–17.

1. *Desire for Diversification.* Many suppliers do not want to tie themselves to long-term contracts with one customer. The suppliers' perception is that their risk is reduced if they have a variety of customers.

2. *Poor Customer Scheduling.* Many suppliers have little faith in the purchaser's ability to reduce orders to a smooth, coordinated schedule.

3. *Engineering Changes.* Frequent engineering changes with inadequate lead time for suppliers to implement tooling and process changes play havoc with JIT. Purchasing personnel must find ways to insulate their prospective JIT suppliers from these changes.

4. *Quality Assurance.* Production with "zero defects" is not considered realistic by many suppliers.

5. *Small Lot Sizes.* Suppliers often have processes that are designed for large lot sizes, and they see frequent delivery to the customer in small lots as a way to transfer holding costs to the supplier.

6. *Proximity.* Depending upon the customer's location, frequent supplier delivery of small lots may be seen as too expensive.

Purchasing may have to enlist the help of its own production personnel to assist suppliers in overcoming many of the preceding objections, but there is no doubt that those firms that have not developed JIT suppliers are at a distinct disadvantage. For those who remain skeptical of the use of JIT, we would point out that virtually every restaurant in the world practices JIT, and with minimal staff support.

Strangling General Motors with the Power of JIT

The 9-day strike by the United Auto Workers (UAW) union at General Motors die shop in Lordstown, Ohio, ended on September 5, 1992. Once again, thick rolls of steel were trucked in from the mills of Wheeling and Pittsburgh, so the Lordstown workers could stamp out Cadillac trunk lids, Saturn fenders, and Buick headlight brackets. But the walkout by 2,300 employees, to protest GM's plan to close the tool and die shop, will be long and sorely remembered as a confrontation over GM's drive for leanness.

The battle itself was costly enough, idling 43,000 GM workers in seven states and affecting production of 14 GM models. GM's financial loss exceeded $50 million. But ironically, the UAW used one of the cornerstones of GM's leanness strategy against it: the just-in-time delivery of parts. JIT, in theory, eliminates the need for costly stockpiling of parts. The GM Lordstown plant adopted JIT 18 months earlier.

"It's become a great weapon . . . the fact is, just-in-time puts the entire power of the UAW in just one local chapter," says Detroit auto analyst Arvid Jouppi. Supplies are kept so tight that sometimes helicopters have to fly in and out of the GM plant loaded with JIT deliveries. Strikers at the Lordstown plant say the policy's sloppy execution is a reason the plant remains so inefficient and vulnerable to a closing.

Sources: Boston Globe (September 6, 1992): 72; and *Wall Street Journal* (June 26, 1993): A-1.

BREAK-EVEN ANALYSIS APPLIED TO PURCHASING

When a purchaser understands the cost structure of suppliers, more intelligent negotiations and purchases can take place. Cost data may be obtained from the supplier, from financial statements, or from analysis of the supplier's sales or purchases, labor, and overhead costs. The objective is to determine both the fixed and variable portions of the supplier's cost. Once this is done, the purchaser is in a much better position to work with the supplier. If we know the approximate cost structure and related break-even of the supplier, then we know the impact of our purchases on the supplier. Under some conditions, an astute buyer can purchase more during the next buying cycle (say, a year) at lower cost and leave the supplier better off financially. Example 2 shows how this is done.

EXAMPLE 2

Using the data in Figure 12.4, Wilmington Auto Repair Stations (WARS) knows that Tarleton Tires makes a combination of units for various customers that moves them out on the (horizontal) percent capacity axis to point A. WARS also knows that it purchases about half of the tires made by Tarleton. Analysis in the WARS purchasing department suggests that Tarleton is not operating at capacity, but at about 70% of capacity. Tarleton's realistic capacity and top efficiency is point B on the capacity axis (about 85%). WARS can move some purchases from another supplier (with whom it has had quality problems) to Tarleton. It is therefore very interested in the impact of such a move on Tarleton. If Tarleton maintains its existing sales and adds 15% from WARS to its volume, Tarleton's profit corridor increases (the vertical distance X is larger than the vertical distance Y) even if the slope of the revenue line is slightly less. (With WARS paying less per tire, the revenue line drops to the proposed level.) But because volume has increased with an attendant increase in the profit corridor, Tarleton has more profit and WARS pays less for its tires.

FIGURE 12.4 ■ Purchasing Break-Even Analysis. WARS reduces costs whereas Tarleton Tire increases profit.

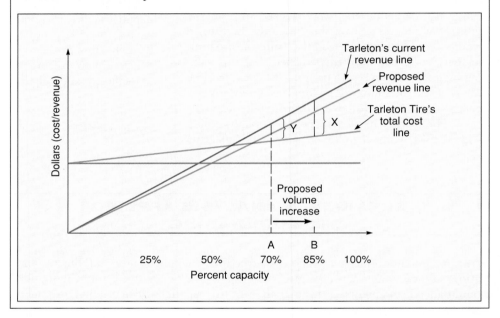

Example 2 shows one avenue a resourceful purchasing department can pursue to reduce costs *and* improve the strength of a supplier. There are, of course, some issues that the supplier, Tarleton Tires, must address. Among these issues is the concern that Tarleton may have if it devotes 50% of its capacity to one customer. Such a move may limit its flexibility in the marketplace. Second, if Tarleton thinks it can sell that capacity at a higher price, then the WARS offer may not be of interest.

ACHIEVING WORLD-CLASS STANDARDS

World-class firms understand that a huge part of revenue is spent on purchases and that a dollar saved in purchasing flows directly to profit. These firms find the right mix of vertical integration, traditional purchasing, and "virtual" organization techniques. Evaluation, selection, and development of suppliers ensure that suppliers warrant being partners in long-term relationships seeking to satisfy the same customers. JIT is the norm in world-class firms and JIT techniques are expected of suppliers as well.

World-class firms practice supply chain management. These firms see themselves in customer–supplier relationships where 100% good quality is always expected. As Table 12.6 shows, world-class firms do indeed set world-class benchmarks in purchasing.

TABLE 12.6 ■ PURCHASING PERFORMANCE IN WORLD-CLASS FIRMS

	TYPICAL FIRMS	WORLD-CLASS FIRMS
Number of suppliers per purchasing agent	34	5
Purchasing costs as percent of purchases	3.3%	.8%
Lead time for purchases (weeks)	15	8
Time spent placing an order	42 minutes	15 minutes
Percentage of late deliveries	33%	2%
Percentage of rejected material	1.5%	.0001%
Number of shortages per year	400	4

Source: Adapted from McKinsey & Company, as reported in *Business Week*, November 30, 1992, p. 72.

SUMMARY

Purchasing is responsible for a substantial portion of the cost of many firms, including most manufacturing, restaurant, wholesale, and retail firms. Consequently, procurement provides a great opportunity for such firms to develop a competitive advantage. The purchasing function may focus on traditional purchasing activities, source development, supply management, or materials management; but at some time, purchasing may have to engage in all of these activities regardless of the focus. Developing close, long-term relationships with suppliers of integrity is, for many organizations, a prerequisite to efficient operations. For many firms, just-in-time purchasing is another opportunity to obtain competitive advantage.

KEY TERMS

Purchasing agent (p. 530)
Buyer (p. 530)
Make-or-buy decision (p. 531)
Vertical integration (p. 532)
Keiretsu (p. 534)
Virtual companies (p. 534)
Purchasing management (p. 535)
Source management (p. 535)
Supply management (p. 535)
Materials management (p. 535)
Negotiation strategies (p. 537)
Electronic data interchange (EDI) (p. 540)
Just-in-time purchasing (p. 541)
Consignment (p. 546)

SOLVED PROBLEM

Solved Problem 12.1

Super Discount knows that Plastics, Inc., of San Diego makes a great plastic cabinet for small items for home and shop. Through its research, Super Discount suspects that Plastics is operating at only 75% of capacity. Super Discount wants to do a major promotion of the plastic cabinet and would like all of Plastics' remaining capacity. Super Discount judges that the maximum effective capacity of Plastics is 88%. (See the horizontal axis of Figure 12.5.)

Super Discount is interested in the impact of such a move on Plastics and thinks Plastics' profit corridor will increase. Super Discount's purchasing agent explains to the management of Plastics that the profit corridor (Z) is larger even if the slope of the Plastics, Inc., revenue line is slightly less. (The Plastics' revenue line moves from Plastics(a) to Plastics(b).) This means Super Discount is paying less per cabinet, but because volume has increased, with an attendant increase in the profit corridor (that is, Z is greater than X), Plastics has more profit and Super Discount pays less for its cabinets.

FIGURE 12.5 ■ Purchasing Break-Even Analysis

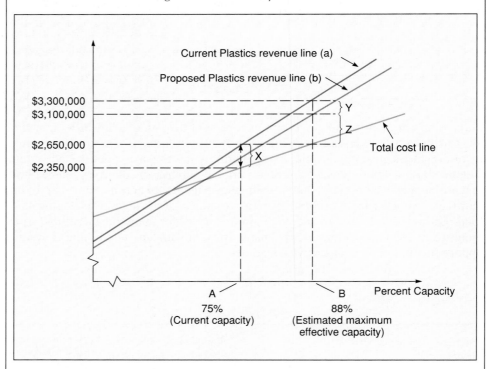

How much less can Super Discount expect to pay for cabinets? What is Plastics' increase in profit?

Solution
The dollar value of X is $300,000 ($2,650,000 – $2,350,000). This is Plastics' current profit. The dollar value of Y is $200,000 ($3,300,000 – $3,100,000), and this represents the savings to Super Discount. The dollar value of Z minus X is the increase in profit to Plastics if it accepts the contract, approximately $150,000 (Z – X = $450,000 – $300,000 = $150,000).

DISCUSSION QUESTIONS

1. Under what conditions might a firm decide to organize its purchasing function as a materials management function? As a supply management function? As a source management function?

2. What can the purchasing function do to implement just-in-time techniques with suppliers?

3. What information does purchasing receive from other functional areas of the firm?

4. How does an adversarial relationship with suppliers change when a firm makes a decision to move to just-in-time deliveries?

5. What are the three basic approaches to negotiations?

6. What are the characteristics of JIT purchasing?

7. What reservations do suppliers have about JIT purchasing?

8. How do restaurants implement JIT purchasing?

9. How does the apparel business have the characteristics of a "virtual" company?

CRITICAL THINKING EXERCISE

The *POM in Action* box about GM purchasing guru Dr. José Lopez noted that Lopez forced suppliers to cut costs quickly and sharply. Although Lopez saved GM billions of dollars, suppliers blamed him for demanding major sacrifices with little offered in return. Industry analysts wonder if GM sacrificed quality for the sake of low costs. Analyze Lopez's approach, discussing the advantages and disadvantages of that strategy. What are the long-term implications to GM and suppliers of these price cuts? Find out from newspapers and magazines what has become of Dr. Lopez since he left GM. Has GM's approach with suppliers changed?

PROBLEMS

· **12.1** Using Tables 12.2 and 12.3, determine how much a food firm with a net profit of 8% has to increase its sales to equal $1 of procurement savings.

⁞ **12.2** Using the data in Example 2, what is the impact on WARS' costs if WARS wants Tarleton Tires to have additional funds for research?

⁞ **12.3** Using the data in Solved Problem 12.1, what is the impact on Plastics if Super Discount wants Plastics to increase its engineering budget by $200,000 for a new plastic cabinet design?

⁞ **12.4** As purchasing agent for Woolsey Enterprises in Golden, Colorado, you ask your buyer to provide you with a ranking of "excellent," "good," "fair," or "poor" for a variety of characteristics for two potential vendors. You suggest that the rankings be consistent with the vendor rating form show in Figure 12.2. The buyer has returned the ranking shown on the next page.

How do you rank these potential vendors? (*Hint:* Figure 12.2 provides an excellent approach.)

DONNA INC. = D VENDOR RATING:										
KAY CORP. = K										
Company	Excellent	Good	Fair	Poor	Products	Excellent	Good	Fair	Poor	
	(4)	(3)	(2)	(1)		(4)	(3)	(2)	(1)	
Size and/or capacity		K	D		Quality	KD				
Financial strength			K	D	Price			KD		
Operational profit			K	D	Packaging			KD		
Manufacturing range			KD		Uniformity			KD		
Research facilities	K		D		Warranty			KD		
Technical service			K	D						
Geographical locations			K	D	*Sales Personnel*					
Management			K	D	1. Knowledge					
Labor relations			K	D	His company			D	K	
Trade relations			KD		His products			K	D	
					Our industry			KD		
Service					Our company			K	D	
Deliveries on time		KD			2. Sales calls					
Condition on arrival		KD			Properly spaced			D	K	
Follow instructions			D	K	By appointment				KD	
Number of rejections				KD	Planned and prepared			K	D	
Handling of complaints		KD			Mutually productive			K	D	
Technical assistance			K	D	3. Sales service					
Emergency aid				KD	Obtain information			D	K	
Supply up-to-date catalogues, etc.				KD	Furnish quotations promptly		K		D	
Supply price changes promptly				KD	Follow orders			D	K	
					Expedite delivery			K	D	
					Handle complaints		KD			

: 12.5 As a library assignment, identify organizations that are

   a) engaged in vertical integration

   b) engaged in reducing their vertical integration

   c) moving toward "virtual" companies

CASE STUDY

Hahn and Pinto Manufacturing

As purchasing manager of the consolidated purchasing department of Hahn and Pinto, you have decided to use decision-tree techniques to evaluate the cost of (1) a blanket contract from the home office, (2) individual large contracts from the home office, and (3) orders placed directly by the three company plants. Regardless of how the orders are placed, you expect the total quantity purchased to be 100,000 lineal feet of multistrand wire. You estimate the cost

and related probability for each of the three alternatives as follows:

ALTERNATIVES	PROBABILITY	COST
Individual orders placed by the home office	.50	$.71
	.25	.68
	.25	.74
Individual orders placed by each plant	.40	.82
	.50	.65
	.10	.70
Blanket order	1.0	.70

(Continued)

DISCUSSION QUESTIONS

1. Use a decision tree to analyze the alternatives, using highest expected monetary value as a decision criteria. (*Hint*: Review the supplement to Chapter 2 for examples and explanations of decision trees.)

2. As purchasing agent, what is your recommendation for the purchase?

3. What will be the expected total cost to the firm next year if your recommendation is followed?

CASE STUDY

Thomas Manufacturing Company

Mr. Thomas, president of Thomas Manufacturing Company, and Mr. McDonnell, the vice president, were discussing how future economic conditions would affect their product, home air purifiers. They were particularly concerned about cost increases. They increased selling prices last year, and thought another price increase would have an adverse affect on sales. They wondered if there was some way to reduce costs in order to maintain the existing price structure.

Mr. McDonnell had attended a purchasing association meeting the previous night and heard a presentation by the president of a tool company on how they were approaching cost reduction. The tool company had just hired a purchasing agent with a business degree who was reducing costs by 15%. Mr. McDonnell thought some of the ideas might be applicable to Thomas Manufacturing. The present purchasing agent, Mr. Older, had been with the company for 25 years and they had no complaints. Production never stopped for lack of material. Yet a 15% cost reduction was something that could not be ignored. Mr. Thomas suggested that Mr. McDonnell look into this area and come up with a recommendation.

Mr. McDonnell contacted several business schools in the area. He said he would be interested in hiring a new graduate. One of the requirements for applicants was a paper on how to improve the company's purchasing function. Several applicants visited the plant and analyzed the purchasing department before they wrote their papers. The most

dynamic paper was submitted by Tim Younger. He recommended:

1. Lower stock reorder levels (from 60 days to 45 days) for many items, thus reducing inventory.

2. Analyze specifications on many parts.

3. Standardize many of the parts to reduce the variety of items.

4. Analyze items to see whether more products can be purchased by blanket purchase orders, with the ultimate goal of reducing the purchasing staff.

5. Look for new and lower cost sources of supply.

6. Increase the number of requests for bids, to get still lower prices.

7. Be more aggressive in negotiations. Make fewer concessions.

8. Make sure all trade, quantity, and cash discounts are taken.

9. Buy from the lowest price source, disregarding local public relations.

10. Stop showing favoritism to customers who also buy from the company. Reciprocity comes second to price.

11. Purchase to current requirements rather than to market conditions. Too much money is tied up in inventory.

After reading all the papers Mr. McDonnell was debating with himself what he should recommend to Mr. Thomas. Just the previous week at the department meeting, Mr. Older was recommending

(Continued)

many of the opposite actions. In particular, he recommended an increase in inventory levels anticipating future rising prices. Mr. Older also stressed the good relations the company had with all their suppliers and how they can be relied upon for good service and a possible extension of credit, if the situation warrants it. Most of their suppliers bought their home air purifiers from Thomas Manufacturing. Yet Mr. Younger said the practice of favoring them was wrong and should be eliminated. Mr. McDonnell was hesitant about what action he should recommend; Mr. Thomas wanted a decision in the morning.

DISCUSSION QUESTIONS

1. What recommendation would you make if you were Mr. McDonnell? Why?
2. Analyze each of Mr. Younger's recommendations. Do you agree or disagree with them? Why?

Source: Professor Richard J. Tersine, University of Oklahoma

CASE STUDY

AT&T Buys a Printer

AT&T decided in 1991 to replace with state-of-the art technology the Troy brand of check printers that were being used in two of its operations sites. These sites printed checks for Payroll, Accounts Payable, Employee Reimbursements, and Billing Customer Refunds. Total annual print volume was estimated to be 13 million checks for 1992 and growing.

Treasury Operation's management thought that serving AT&T check printing needs in the future would require a major re-engineering of the check issuance process and that replacement of the printers was a first step. The current systems and equipment, for example, could not meet requirements for printing checks as part of AT&T marketing promotions. The marketing team, therefore, was forced to use outside services to print these checks. While the outside services met most of the requirements, the accounting transactions that were associated with these checks were often incorrect, and check reconciliation for these checks was almost impossible. Treasury Operations believed that they could eliminate the use of outside services and improve the quality and costs of their current service if they purchased print equipment that was computer

controlled. In addition, it was important that the magnetic ink character recognition (MICR) line that was printed at the bottom of the check be of high quality, because banks charge extra for processing checks with unreadable MICR lines.

The team looking into new printers had identified Siemens, Delphax, Xerox, IBM, and NCR as the vendors that had printers that should be considered. Team members then decided on the following six criteria:

1. Features: Documented the technical features of each printer, maintenance availability, and requirements.
2. User rating: Documented results of a survey of users of each of the printers.
3. Pros/cons: Documented overall team observations.
4. Cost: Cost analysis included purchase of printers, maintenance, supplies, and software.
5. MICR quality: Conformance to MICR standards.
6. Print quality: Conformance to print quality standards.

The team then assigned a point value (10 being the highest score), for each printer for each situation. Their final tabulation is shown on the next page.

(Continued)

CRITERIA	SIEMENS	DELPHAX	XEROX	IBM	NCR
Features	9.9	6.6	5.2	7.7	8.2
User ratings	8.0	8.3	6.7	8.6	8.6
Pros/cons	10.0	1.0	5.0	8.0	8.0
Cost	10.0	6.0	4.0	2.0	8.0
MICR quality	9.7	5.4	6.0	9.4	9.4
Print quality	9.7	5.7	8.0	8.4	8.6
Total	57.3	33.0	34.9	44.1	50.8
Ranking	1	5	4	3	2

DISCUSSION QUESTIONS

1. Is it appropriate that in the final analysis MICR Quality was given the same weight as Cost?

2. Recompute the comparisons, using the following weight factors: Features 15%, User Ratings 15%, Pros/Cons 15%, Cost 30%, MICR Quality 12.5%, Print Quality 12.5%. Does this change the end result?

Source: Written by Paula Beavers, under the supervision of Prof. B. Render, Rollins College

BIBLIOGRAPHY

Akinc, U. "Selecting a Set of Vendors in a Manufacturing Environment." *Journal of Operations Management*, 11, no. 2 (June 1993): 107–122.

Billington, C. "Supply Chain Management." *OR/MS Today*, 21, no. 2 (April 1994): 20–29.

Blumenfeld, D. E., L. D. Burns, C. F. Daganzo, M. D. Frick, and R. W. Hall. "Reducing Logistics Costs at General Motors." *Interfaces*, 17 (January/February 1987): 26–47.

Chapman, S. N., and P. L. Carter. "Supplier/Customer Inventory Relationships under JIT." *Decision Sciences* (Winter 1990): 35–51.

Davis, T. "Effective Supply Chain Management." *Sloan Management Review*, 34, no. 4 (Summer 1993): 35–46.

Datar, S., K. Sunder, T. Mukhopadyay, and E. Svaan. "Overloaded Overheads: Activity-Based Cost Analysis of Material Handling in Cell Manufacturing." *Journal of Operations Management*, 10, no. 1 (January 1993): 119–137.

Drtina, R. "The Outsourcing Decision." *Management Accounting*, 75, no. 9 (March 1994): 56–62.

Dyer, J. H., and W. G. Ouchi. "Japanese-Style Partnerships: Giving Companies A Competitive Edge." *Sloan Management Review*, 35, no. 1 (Fall 1993): 51–64.

Freeland, J. R. "A Survey of Just-in-Time Purchasing Practices in the United States." *Production and Inventory Management Journal*, vol. 32 (Second Quarter 1991): 43.

Frey, S. C., Jr., and M. M. Schlosser. "ABB and Ford: Creating Value Through Cooperation." *Sloan Management Review*, 35, no. 1 (Fall 1993): 65–72.

Fuller, J. B., J. O'Conor, and R. Rawlinson. "Tailored Logistics: The Next Advantage." *Harvard Business Review*, 71, no. 3 (May/June 1993): 87–98.

Golhar, D. Y. "JIT Purchasing Practices In Manufacturing Firms." *Production and Inventory Management Journal*, 34, no. 3 (Third Quarter 1993): 75–79.

Helper, S. "How Much Has Really Changed between U.S. Automakers and Their Suppliers?" *Sloan Management Review*, 32 (Summer 1991): 15.

Inman, A. R., and S. Mehra. "Determining the Critical Elements of Just-in-Time Implementation." *Decision Sciences*, 23 (January/February 1992): 160–174.

Tersine, R. J., and J. H. Campbell. *Modern Materials Management*. New York: North-Holland, 1977.

Venkatesan, R. "Strategic Sourcing: To Make or not to Make." *Harvard Business Review*, 70, no. 6 (November/December 1992): 98.

Zenz, G. J. *Purchasing and the Management of Materials*. New York: John Wiley, 1994.

12 SUPPLEMENT

LEARNING CURVES

Korean electronics giant Samsung entered the microwave oven market in 1978. On a makeshift assembly line, its production team began making one oven a day, then two, and then five, as employees began to learn the assembly process. With long hours spent redesigning the line at night, Samsung engineers worked out the bugs discovered by day. Production improved to 10 ovens a day, then 15, and soon to 50. By the end of 1981, the learning process allowed workers to produce 300 ovens a day, and by 1982, that number doubled again. By 1983, Samsung was making 2500 microwaves a day, and continuing to improve.[1] ♦

[1]Ira C. Magaziner and Mark Patinkin, "Fast Heat: How Korea Won the Microwave War," *Harvard Business Review*, 89, 10. (January/February 1989): 83–92.

In 1936, T. P. Wright of Curtis-Wright Corporation published the first report of **learning curves** applied to industry.[2] Learning curves, or as they are sometimes called, experience curves, are based on the premise that organizations, like people, become better at their tasks as the tasks are repeated. A learning curve graph, of labor-hours per unit versus the number of units produced, normally has the negative exponential distribution shape illustrated in Figure S12.1.

Learning curves

The learning curve is based on a doubling of productivity. That is, when production doubles, the decrease in time per unit effects the rate of the learning curve. So, if the learning curve is an 80% rate, the second unit takes 80% of the time of the first unit, the fourth unit takes 80% of the time of the second unit, the eighth unit takes 80% of the time of the fourth unit, and so forth. This is shown as

$$T \times L^n = \text{time required for the Nth unit} \qquad \text{(S12.1)}$$

where T = unit cost or unit time
L = learning curve rate
n = number of times Y is doubled

If the first unit of a particular product took 10 labor-hours, and if a 70% learning curve is present, the hours the fourth unit will take require doubling twice—from 1 to 2 to 4. Therefore, the formula is

$$\text{Hours required for unit } 4 = 10 \times (.7)^2 = 4.9 \text{ hours}$$

FIGURE S12.1 ■ The Learning Curve Effect States that Time Per Repetition Decreases as the Number of Repetitions Increases. This means *it takes less time to complete each additional unit a firm produces*. But the time savings in completing each unit decreases with each additional unit. These are the major implications of the learning curve effect.

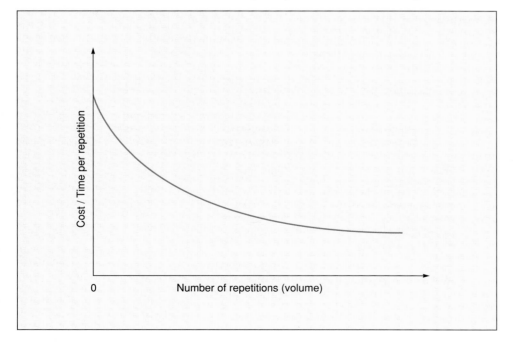

[2]T. P. Wright, "Factors Affecting the Cost of Airplanes," *Journal of the Aeronautical Sciences* (February 1936).

Different organizations, and different products, have different learning curves. The rate of learning varies depending upon the quality of management and the potential of the process and product. *Any change in process, product, or personnel disrupts the learning curve.* Caution should be exercised in assuming that a learning curve is continuing and permanent.

Industry learning curves vary widely, as shown in Table S12.1. The lower the number, such as 70% compared to 90%, the steeper the slope and the faster the drop in costs. By tradition, learning curves are defined in terms of the *complements* of their improvement rates. For example, a 70% learning curve implies a 30% decrease in time each time the number of repetitions is doubled. A 90% curve means there is a corresponding 10% rate of improvement.

Stable, standardized, labor-intensive products and processes tend to have costs that decline more steeply than others. Between 1929 and 1955, for instance, the steel industry was able to reduce labor-hours per unit to 79% each time cumulative production doubled. The *POM in Action* box, coincidentally, finds that doctors follow the same 79% learning curve in performing heart transplants.

Learning curves are useful for a variety of applications. These include

1. internal labor forecasting, production scheduling, establishing costs and budgets;
2. external purchasing and subcontracting of items (see the SMT case study at the end of this supplement);
3. strategic evaluation of company and industry performance.

APPLYING THE LEARNING CURVE

A mathematical relationship enables us to express the time it takes to produce a certain unit. This relationship is a function of how many units have been produced

TABLE S12.1 ■ EXAMPLES OF LEARNING CURVE EFFECTS IN U.S. INDUSTRY

EXAMPLE	IMPROVING PARAMETER	CUMULATIVE PARAMETER	LEARNING CURVE SLOPE (%)	TIME FRAME
1. Model T Ford production	Price	Units produced	86	1910–1926
2. Aircraft assembly	Direct labor-hours per unit	Units produced	80	1925–1957
3. Equipment maintenance at GE	Average time to replace a group of parts	Number of replacements	76	Around 1957
4. Steel production	Production worker labor-hours per unit produced	Units produced	79	1920–1955
5. Integrated circuits	Average price per unit	Units produced	72*	1964–1972
6. Hand-held calculator	Average factory selling price	Units produced	74	1975–1978
7. Disk memory drives	Average price per bit	Number of bits	76	1975–1978

*Constant dollars.

Source: James A. Cunningham, "Using the Learning Curve as a Management Tool," *IEEE Spectrum* (June 1980): 45. © 1980 IEEE.

The Impact of Learning Curves on Heart Transplants

The concept of the learning curve has long been documented in the production of goods and services. Studies now indicate that even the medical profession can look to learning curves to predict the success of surgeries. And today, as more hospitals face pressure from insurance companies and the government to enter fixed-priced negotiations for their services, their ability to learn from experience will become critical.

Temple University Hospital researchers evaluated learning effects for heart transplants. An expensive operation, averaging $60,000 in actual cost to a hospital, a transplant requires complex, precise coordination of a large team. In addition,

hospitals doing heart transplants rarely recover the full costs of these procedures and therefore have a strong incentive to reduce these costs whenever possible.

The results of a 3-year study of 62 patients receiving transplants revealed a 79% learning curve, as measured by 1-year death rates (that is, the number of patients dying within the first year of surgery). In this case, every three operations resulted in a halving of the death rate. This ultimate measure of improvement estimates not just the lives lost, but the loss of a scarce and valued medical resource—the donor heart.

This Temple University Hospital experience places learning curves for heart transplants on a par with what has been found almost universally in industrial production.

Source: David B. Smith and Jan L. Larsson "The Impact of Learning on Cost: The Case of Heart Transplantation," *Hospital and Health Services Administration* (Spring 1989): 85–97.

before it and how long it took to produce them. Although this procedure determines how long it takes to produce a given unit, the consequences of this analysis are more far-reaching. Costs drop and efficiency goes up for individual firms and the industry. Therefore, severe problems in scheduling occur if operations are not adjusted for implications of the learning curve. Learning curve improvement may result in labor and productive facilities being idle a portion of the time. Furthermore, firms may refuse additional work because they do not consider the improvement that results from learning. The foregoing are only a few of the ramifications of not considering the effect of learning. Learning curve effects occur in marketing and financial planning. From a purchasing perspective, our interest is in judging what a supplier's cost should be for further production.

Let us look at three approaches to learning curves: arithmetic analysis, logarithmic analysis, and learning curve coefficients.

Arithmetic Approach

The arithmetic approach is the simplest approach to learning curve problems. As we noted at the beginning of this supplement, each time production doubles, the labor per unit declines by a constant factor, known as the learning rate. So, if we know that the learning rate is 80% and that the first unit produced took 100 hours, the hours required to produce the second, fourth, eighth, and sixteenth units are:

NTH UNIT PRODUCED	HOURS FOR NTH UNIT
1	100.0
2	$80.0 = (.8 \times 100)$
4	$64.0 = (.8 \times 80)$
8	$51.2 = (.8 \times 64)$
16	$41.0 = (.8 \times 51.2)$

As long as we wish to find the hours required to produce n units and n is one of the doubled values, then this approach works. Arithmetic analysis does not answer the question for other units. However, the logarithmic approach does give us this flexibility.

Logarithmic Approach

The logarithmic approach allows us to determine labor for *any* unit, T_N, by the formula

$$T_N = T_1(N^b) \tag{S12.2}$$

where $T_1 =$ hours to produce the first unit,
  b is the slope of the learning curve, and is equal to

$$b = (\text{log of the learning rate})/(\text{log } 2)$$

Some of the values for b are presented in Table S12.2. Example S1 shows how this formula works.

TABLE S12.2
LEARNING CURVE VALUES OF B

LEARNING RATE (%)	B
70	−.515
75	−.415
80	−.322
85	−.234
90	−.152

EXAMPLE S1

The learning rate for a particular operation is 80% and the first unit of production took 100 hours. The hours required to produce the third unit may be computed as follows:

$$T_N = T_1(N^b)$$
$$T_3 = (100 \text{ hours})(3^b)$$
$$= (100)(3^{\log .8/\log 2})$$
$$= (100)(3^{-.322}) = 70.2 \text{ labor-hours}$$

The logarithmic approach allows us to determine the hours required for *any* unit produced, but there *is* a simpler method.

Learning Curve Coefficient Approach

The learning curve coefficient technique is embodied in Table S12.3 and the following equation:

$$T_N = T_1 C \tag{S12.3}$$

where T_N = number of labor-hours required to produce the Nth unit
T_1 = number of labor-hours required to produce the first unit
C = learning curve coefficient found in Table S12.3

TABLE S12.3 ■ LEARNING CURVE COEFFICIENTS

UNIT NUMBER (N)	70%		75%		80%		85%		90%	
	UNIT TIME	TOTAL TIME	UNIT TIME	TOTAL TIME	UNIT TIME	TOTAL TIME	UNIT TIME	TOTAL TIME	UNIT TIME	TOTAL TIME
1	1.000	1.000	1.000	1.000	1.000	1.000	1.000	1.000	1.000	1.000
2	.700	1.700	.750	1.750	.800	1.800	.850	1.850	.900	1.900
3	.568	2.268	.634	2.384	.702	2.502	.773	2.623	.846	2.746
4	.490	2.758	.562	2.946	.640	3.142	.723	3.345	.810	3.556
5	.437	3.195	.513	3.459	.596	3.738	.686	4.031	.783	4.339
6	.398	3.593	.475	3.934	.562	4.299	.657	4.688	.762	5.101
7	.367	3.960	.446	4.380	.534	4.834	.634	5.322	.744	5.845
8	.343	4.303	.422	4.802	.512	5.346	.614	5.936	.729	6.574
9	.323	4.626	.402	5.204	.493	5.839	.597	6.533	.716	7.290
10	.306	4.932	.385	5.589	.477	6.315	.583	7.116	.705	7.994
11	.291	5.223	.370	5.958	.462	6.777	.570	7.686	.695	8.689
12	.278	5.501	.357	6.315	.449	7.227	.558	8.244	.685	9.374
13	.267	5.769	.345	6.660	.438	7.665	.548	8.792	.685	10.052
14	.257	6.026	.334	6.994	.428	8.092	.539	9.331	.670	10.721
15	.248	6.274	.325	7.319	.418	8.511	.530	9.861	.663	11.384
16	.240	6.514	.316	7.635	.410	8.920	.522	10.383	.656	12.040
17	.233	6.747	.309	7.944	.402	9.322	.515	10.898	.650	12.690
18	.226	6.973	.301	8.245	.394	9.716	.508	11.405	.644	13.334
19	.220	7.192	.295	8.540	.388	10.104	.501	11.907	.639	13.974
20	.214	7.407	.288	8.828	.381	10.485	.495	12.402	.634	14.608
21	.209	7.615	.283	9.111	.375	10.860	.490	12.892	.630	15.237
22	.204	7.819	.277	9.388	.370	11.230	.484	13.376	.625	15.862
23	.199	8.018	.272	9.660	.364	11.594	.479	13.856	.625	16.483
24	.195	8.213	.267	9.928	.359	11.954	.475	14.331	.617	17.100
25	.191	8.404	.263	10.191	.355	12.309	.470	14.801	.613	17.713
26	.187	8.591	.259	10.449	.350	12.659	.466	15.267	.609	18.323
27	.183	8.774	.255	10.704	.346	13.005	.462	15.728	.606	18.929
28	.180	8.954	.251	10.955	.342	13.347	.458	16.186	.603	19.531
29	.177	9.131	.247	11.202	.338	13.685	.454	16.640	.599	20.131
30	.174	9.305	.244	11.446	.335	14.020	.450	17.091	.596	20.727
35	.160	10.133	.229	12.618	.318	15.643	.434	19.294	.583	23.666
40	.150	10.902	.216	13.723	.305	17.193	.421	21.425	.571	26.543
45	.141	11.625	.206	14.773	.294	18.684	.410	23.500	.561	29.366
50	.134	12.307	.197	15.776	.284	20.122	.400	25.513	.552	32.142

The learning curve coefficient, C, depends on the learning rate (70%, 75%, 80%, and so on) and the unit of interest.

Example S2 uses the preceding equation and Table S12.3 to calculate learning curve effects.

EXAMPLE S2

It took 125,000 labor-hours to produce the first of several tugboats you expect to purchase for your shipping company, Great Lakes Services, Inc. Boats 2 and 3 have been produced with a learning factor of 85%. At $40 per hour, what should you, as purchasing agent, expect to pay for the fourth unit?

First, search Table S12.3 for the fourth unit and a learning factor of 85%. The learning curve coefficient, C, is .723. To produce the fourth unit, then, takes

$$T_N = T_1 C$$
$$T_4 = (125{,}000 \text{ hours})(.723)$$
$$= 90{,}375 \text{ hours}$$

To find the cost, multiply by $40:

$$90{,}375 \text{ hours} \times \$40/\text{hour} = \$3{,}615{,}000$$

Table S12.3 also shows cumulative values. These allow us to compute the total number of hours needed to complete a specified number of units. Again, the computation is straightforward. Just multiply the table value times the time required for the first unit. Example S3 illustrates this concept.

EXAMPLE S3

Example S2 computed the time to complete the fourth tugboat Great Lakes Services plans to buy. How long will *all four* boats require?

Looking this time at the total column in Table S12.3, we find the cumulative coefficient is 3.345. Thus, the time required is

$$T_N = T_1 C$$
$$T_4 = (125{,}000)(3.345) = 418{,}125 \text{ hours in total for all four boats}$$

For an illustration of how AB:POM can be used to solve Examples S2 and S3, see Program S12.1 at the end of this supplement.

Using Table S12.3 requires that we know how long it takes to complete the first unit. But what happens if our most recent or most reliable information available pertains to some other unit? The answer is that we must use this data to find a revised estimate for the first unit, and then apply the table to that number. Example S4 illustrates this concept.

EXAMPLE S4

Great Lakes Services believes that unusual circumstances in producing the first boat (see Example S2) imply that the time estimate of 125,000 hours is not as valid a base as the time of the third boat. Boat number 3 was completed in 100,000 hours.

To solve for the revised estimate for boat number 1, we turn to Table S12.3 with a unit value of $N = 3$ and a learning curve coefficient of $C = .773$ in the 85% column. We divide the actual time for boat three, 100,000 hours, by $C = .773$ to find the revised estimate:

$$\frac{100,000}{.773} = 129,366 \text{ hours}$$

STRATEGIC IMPLICATIONS OF LEARNING CURVES

So far, we have shown how operations managers can forecast labor-hour requirements for a product. We have also shown how purchasing agents can determine a supplier's cost, which can help in price negotiations. An important additional application of learning curves concerns strategic planning.

The *POM in Action* box "Building Strategy on the Learning Curve at Texas Instruments" suggests segments of the semiconductor industry actively pursue a steep

FIGURE S12.2 ■ Industry Learning Curve for Price Compared with Company Learning Curve for Cost. *Note:* Both the vertical and horizontal axes of this figure are log scales. This is known as a log-log chart.

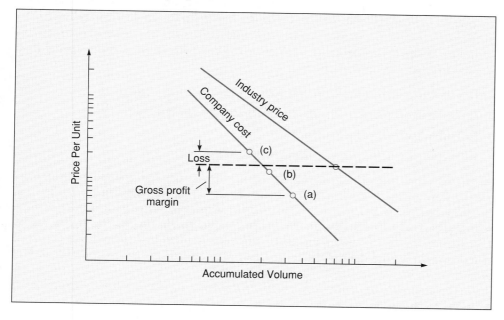

Building Strategy on the Learning Curve at Texas Instruments

Learning curve strategies are especially appropriate when products, such as hand calculators or PCs, are very sensitive to price changes. Texas Instruments (TI) found that cutting prices could lead to huge demand jumps. Extra demand in turn sped TI's progress down the learning curve by increasing output. Lower costs then provided the flexibility for more price cuts and for another cycle of this process.

In the case of the hand calculator, advances in semiconductor technology and a large price-sensitive demand provided chances for huge growth. When TI entered the fray with a learning curve strategy, costs per calculator plunged from thousands of dollars to under $10 in less than 10 years. Sales skyrocketed, and TI reaped the benefits of being a leader instead of a follower.

The PC market provides an ironic illustration of the same lesson. PCs, also price-sensitive, have a steep learning curve. But TI allowed others to lead in the cost-reduction and price-cutting game. It paid the price for its mistake with the fizzling of its PC line.

It is critical to understand competitors before embarking on a learning curve strategy. A competitor is weak if it is undercapitalized, stuck with high costs, or does not understand the logic of learning curves.

Strong and dangerous competitors control their costs, have solid financial positions for the large investments needed, and have a track record of using an aggressive learning curve strategy. Taking on such a competitor in a price war may help only the consumer.

Source: Harvard Business Review (March/April 1985): 148.

learning curve. An example of a steep semiconductor industry price line is so labeled in Figure S12.2. These learning curves are straight because the scales are both log scales. When the *rate* of change is constant, a log-log graph yields a straight line. If a particular company believes its cost line to be the "company cost" line and the industry price is indicated by the dashed horizontal line, then the company must have costs at the points below the dotted line (for example, points *a* or *b*) or else operate at a loss (point *c*). When a firm's strategy is to pursue the company curve, a curve steeper than the industry average, it does this by

1. following an aggressive pricing policy;

2. focusing on continuing cost reduction and productivity improvement;

3. building on shared experience;

4. keeping capacity growing ahead of demand.

Costs may drop as a firm pursues the learning curve, but volume must increase for the learning curve to exist. For instance, Figure S12.3 shows the units that have to be produced per year for a reduction of 25% when operating with a 60% or 80% learning curve. In recent years, much of the computer industry has operated at a 25% cost reduction. The volumes and cost reductions implied by learning curves and as demonstrated by the data of Table S12.1 and Figure S12.3 suggest the difficulty of achieving such an objective.

Developing a competitive strategy via the learning curve is not, as Example S5 suggests, a solution for everyone.

EXAMPLE S5

Seymore Computers, Inc., just completed production of the first Seymore Mark II Computer, a supercomputer that has established a world standard. The firm expects the industry to continue to reduce costs by 25% annually with an 80% learning curve. By the sixth year, how many computers will Seymore have to produce each year to keep up with the industry curve?

From Figure S12.3, we find the intersection of year 6 and the 80% curve. They intersect at 100. Therefore, Seymore has to establish marketing and production plans for production of 100 units per year by the sixth year.

Because the total worldwide demand for supercomputers is less than 20 per year, it seems unlikely that this is a reasonable strategy. Perhaps maintaining low levels of production with state-of-the-art technology is preferable to a standardized product for Seymore.

FIGURE S12.3 ■ The 80% and 60% Curves Show the Number of Units That Must Be Produced to Reduce Costs 25% Annually If the Firm Is Operating on One of Those Curves.

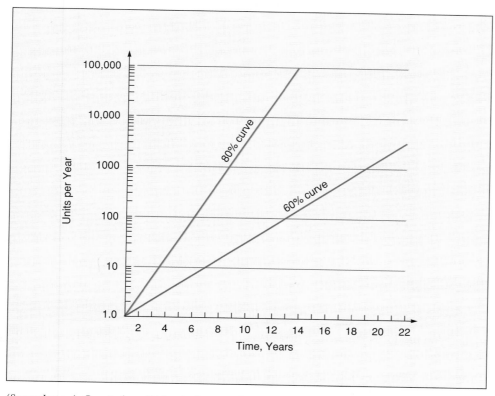

(*Source*: James A. Cunningham, "Using the Learning Curve as a Management Tool," *IEEE Spectrum* (June 1980): 47. © 1980 IEEE.)

SUMMARY

The learning curve is a powerful tool for the operations manager. This tool can assist operations managers in determining future cost standards for items produced as well as purchased. Additionally, the learning curve can provide understanding about company and industry performance. We saw three approaches to learning curves: arithmetic analysis, logarithmic analysis, and learning curve coefficients found in tables. AB:POM software can also help analyze learning curves.

KEY TERM

Learning curve (p. 555)

USING AB:POM FOR LEARNING CURVES

AB:POM's Learning Curve Module computes the length of time that future units will take, given the time required for the base unit and the learning rate (expressed as a number between 0 and 1). As an option, if the time required for the first and Nth units are already known, the learning *rate* can be computed.

PROGRAM S12.1 ■ AB:POM's Learning Curve Module Applied to Examples S2 and S3. The program also has graphic capability.

————————————————— Experience (learning) Curves ———————————— Solution ——

———————————————— Great Lakes Services, Inc. ——————————————

Unit Number	Production Time	Cumulative Time
1	125000.00	125000
2	106250.00	231250
3	96614.48	327864
4	90312.50	418177

Unit number of base unit   1
Labor time for base unit, T1   125000.0
Unit number of last unit, N   4
Learning coefficient   0.850

F1 = Help   F3 = Graph   F4 = Character Graph   F8 = All Print   F9 = Print ESC

SOLVED PROBLEMS

Solved Problem S12.1

Digicomp produces a new telephone system with built-in TV screens. Its learning rate is 80%.

a) How long does it take Digicomp to make the eleventh system when the first one took 56 hours?

b) How long will the first 11 systems take in total?

c) As a purchasing agent, you expect to buy units 12 through 15 of the new phone system. What would be your expected cost for the units if Digicomp charges $30 for each labor-hour?

Solution

a) $T_N = T_1 C$ (from Table S12.3 – 80% unit time)

$T_{11} = (56 \text{ hours})(.462) = 25,872 \text{ hours}$

b) Total time for the first 11 units $= (56 \text{ hours})(6.771) = 379.5 \text{ hours}$

(from Table S12.3 – 80% unit time)

c) To find the time for units 12 through 15, we take the total cumulative time for units 1 to 15 and subtract the total time for units 1 to 11, which was computed in part (b). Total time for the first 15 units $= (56 \text{ hours})(8.511) = 476.6$ hours. So the time for units 12 through 15 is $476.6 - 379.5 = 97.1$ hours. (This could also be confirmed by computing the times for units 12, 13, 14, and 15 separately using the unit time column and then adding them.) Expected cost for units 12 through 15 $= (97.1 \text{ hours})(\$30/\text{hour}) = \$2,913$.

Solved Problem S12.2

If the first time you perform a job takes 60 minutes, how long will the eighth job take if you are on an 80% learning curve?

Solution

Three doublings from 1 to 2 to 4 to 8 implies 8^3. Therefore, we have

$$60 \times (.8)^3 = 60 \times .512 = 30.72 \text{ minutes}$$

or, using Table S12.3, we have $C = .512$. Therefore:

$$60 \times .512 = 30.72 \text{ minutes}$$

DISCUSSION QUESTIONS

1. What are some of the limitations to the use of learning curves?

2. What techniques can a firm use to move to a steeper learning curve?

3. What are the approaches to solving learning curve problems?

4. What are the implications for Great Lakes Services, Inc., of Example S1 if the engineering department wants to change the engine in the third and subsequent tugboats Great Lakes Services purchases?

5. Under what conditions should a firm avoid "pricing on the learning curve"?

6. Why isn't the learning curve concept as applicable in a high-volume assembly line as it is in most other human activities?

7. What can cause a learning curve to vary from a smooth downward slope?

8. Explain the concept of the "doubling" effect in learning curves.

CRITICAL THINKING EXERCISE

The first *POM in Action* box in this chapter discusses how the learning effect was found to take place in predicting the decline in death rates for heart transplant operations. Yet the same researchers at Temple University Hospital found that the learning curve did not seem to be valid in predicting length of hospital stay for transplant survivors or in the average unit cost of a transplant. Explain why these two factors do not seem to follow the traditional learning curve concept whereas the death rates do. If necessary, visit a hospital administrator to discuss whether this issue has been addressed locally. Have learning curves been applied in any other areas of the hospital? Why?

PROBLEMS

: S12.1 Beth Zion Hospital has received initial certification from the State of California to become a center for kidney transplants. The hospital, however, must complete the first 18 transplants under great scrutiny and at no cost to the patients. The very first transplant, just completed, required 30 hours. On the basis of research at the hospital noted in the *POM in Action* box in this chapter, Beth Zion estimates it will have an 80% learning curve. Estimate the time it will take to complete the following:

  a) The fifth kidney transplant.

  b) All of the first five transplants.

  c) The eighteenth transplant.

  d) All eighteen transplants.

: S12.2 Beth Zion Hospital (see Problem S12.1) has just been informed that only the first 10 transplants must be performed at the hospital's expense. The cost per hour of surgery is estimated to be $5,000. Again, the learning rate is 80% and the first surgery took 30 hours.

  a) How long will the tenth surgery take?

  b) How much will the tenth surgery cost?

  c) How much will all ten cost the hospital?

: S12.3 If the fourth oil change/lube job at Trendo-Lube took 18 minutes and the second took 20 minutes, estimate how long:

  a) The first job took.

  b) The third job took.

  c) The eighth job will take.

  d) The actual learning rate.

· S12.4 A student at San Diego State University bought six bookcases for her dorm room. Each required unpacking of parts and assembly, which included some nailing and bolting. She completed the first bookcase in 5 hours and the second in 4 hours.

  a) What is her learning rate?

  b) Assuming the same rate continues, how long will the third bookcase take?

  c) The fourth, fifth, and sixth cases?

  d) All six cases?

· S12.5 Cleaning a toxic landfill took one EPA contractor 300 man-days. If the contractor follows an 85% learning rate, how long will it take in total to clean the next five, that is, landfills 2 through 6?

· **S12.6** The first vending machine that Smith Inc. assembled took 80 labor-hours. Estimate how long the fourth machine will require for each of the following learning rates:

a) 95%.

b) 87%.

c) 72%.

· **S12.7** In the previous problem, the time for the fourth unit was estimated. How long will the sixteenth vending machine take to assemble under the same three learning rates, namely:

a) 95%.

b) 87%.

c) 72%.

: **S12.8** As the purchasing agent for Northeast Airlines, you are interested in determining what you can expect to pay for airplane number 4 if the third plane took 20,000 hours to produce. What would you expect to pay for plane number 5? Number 6? Use an 85% learning curve and a $40/hr labor charge.

: **S12.9** Using the data from Problem S12.8, how long will it take to complete the twelfth plane? How long will it take to complete the fifteenth plane? How long will it take to complete planes 12 through 15 inclusive? At $40 per hour, what can you, as purchasing agent, expect to pay for the four planes?

: **S12.10** Dynamic RAM Corporation produces semiconductors and has a learning curve of .7. The price per bit is 100 millcents when the volume is $.7 \times 10^{12}$ bits. What is the expected price at 1.4×10^{12} bits? What is the expected price at 89.6×10^{12} bits?

· **S12.11** If it takes 80,000 hours to produce the first jet engine at T.R.'s aerospace division and the learning factor is 90%, how long does it take to produce the eighth engine?

: **S12.12** It takes 28,718 hours to produce the eighth locomotive at a large French manufacturing firm. If the learning factor is 80%, how long does it take to produce the tenth locomotive?

: **S12.13** If the first unit of a production run takes 1 hour and the firm is on an 80% learning curve, what will unit 100 take? (*Hint:* Apply the coefficient in Table S12.3 twice.)

: **S12.14** As the estimator for Umble Enterprises, your job is to prepare an estimate for a potential service contract from a customer. The potential contract is for the service of diesel locomotive cylinder heads. The shop has done some of these in the past on a sporadic basis. The time for each cylinder head has been exactly 4 hours and similar work has been accomplished at an 85% learning curve. The customer wants you to quote in batches of 12 and 20.

a) Prepare the quote.

b) After preparing the quote, you find a labor ticket for this customer for five locomotive cylinder heads. From the sundry notations on the labor ticket, you conclude that the fifth unit took 2.5 hours. What do you conclude about the learning curve and your quote?

: **S12.15** Goodwin & Goodwin Manufacturing is producing new sophisticated hip-joint replacements. Goodwin & Goodwin knows that the industry is on a 80% learning curve that reduces costs by 25% per year for similar products. To maintain the industry average, how many units must be produced in the first 3 years?

CASE STUDY

SMT's Negotiation with IBM

SMT and one other, much larger company were asked by IBM to bid on 85 more units of a particular computer product. The RFQ asked that the overall bid be broken down to show the hourly rate, the parts and materials component in the price, and any charges for subcontracted services. SMT quoted $1.62 million and supplied the cost breakdown as requested. The second company submitted only one total figure, $5.0 million, with no cost breakdown. The decision was made to negotiate with SMT.

The IBM negotiating team included two purchasing managers and two cost engineers. One cost engineer had developed manufacturing cost estimates for every component, working from engineering drawings and cost-data books that he had built up from previous experience and that contained time factors, both setup and run times, for a large variety of operations. He estimated materials costs by working both from data supplied by the IBM Corporate Purchasing Staff and from purchasing journals. He visited SMT facilities to see the tooling available so that he would know what processes were being used. He assumed that there would be perfect conditions and trained operators, and he developed cost estimates for the 158th unit (previous orders were for 25, 15, and 38 units). He added 5% for scrap-and-flow loss; 2% for the use of temporary tools, jigs, and fixtures; 5% for quality control; and 9% for purchasing burden. Then, using an 85% learning curve, he backed up his costs to get an estimate for the first unit. He next checked the data on hours and materials for the 25, 15, and 38 units already made and found that his estimate for the first unit was within 4% of actual cost. His check, however, had indicated a 90% learning curve effect on hours per unit.

In the negotiations, SMT was represented by one of the two owners of the business, two engineers, and one cost estimator. The sessions opened with a discussion of learning curves. The IBM cost estimator demonstrated that SMT had in fact been operating on a 90% learning curve. But, he argued, it should be possible to move to an 85% curve, given the longer runs, reduced setup time, and increased continuity of workers on the job that would be possible with an

order for 80 units. The owner agreed with this analysis and was willing to reduce his price by 4%.

However, as each operation in the manufacturing process was discussed, it became clear that some IBM cost estimates were too low because certain crating and shipping expenses had been overlooked. These oversights were minor, however, and in the following discussions, the two parties arrived at a common understanding of specifications and reached agreements on the costs of each manufacturing operation.

At this point, SMT representatives expressed great concern about the possibility of inflation in materials costs. The IBM negotiators volunteered to include a form of price escalation in the contract, as previously agreed among themselves. IBM representatives suggested that if overall materials costs changed by more than 10%, the price could be adjusted accordingly. However, if one party took the initiative to have the price revised, the other could require an analysis of *all* parts and materials invoices in arriving at the new price.

Another concern of the SMT representatives was that a large amount of overtime and subcontracting would be required to meet IBM's specified delivery schedule. IBM negotiators thought that a relaxation in the delivery schedule might be possible if a price concession could be obtained. In response, the SMT team offered a 5% discount, and this was accepted. As a result of these negotiations, the SMT price was reduced almost 20% below its original bid price.

In a subsequent meeting called to negotiate the prices of certain pipes to be used in the system, it became apparent to an IBM cost estimator that SMT representatives had seriously underestimated their costs. He pointed out this apparent error because he could not understand why SMT had quoted such a low figure. He wanted to be sure that SMT was using the correct manufacturing process. In any case, if SMT estimators had made a mistake, it should be noted. It was IBM's policy to seek a fair price both for itself and for its suppliers. IBM procurement managers believed that if a vendor was losing money on a job, there would be a tendency to cut corners. In addition, the IBM negotiator felt that by pointing out the error, he generated some goodwill that would help in future sessions.

(Continued)

DISCUSSION QUESTIONS

1. What are the advantages and disadvantages to IBM and SMT from this approach?

2. How does SMT's proposed learning rate compare with that of other companies?

Source: Adapted from E. Raymond Corey, *Procurement Management: Strategy, Organization, and Decision Making* (New York: Van Nostrand Reinhold).

BIBLIOGRAPHY

Abernathy, W. J., and K. Wayne. "Limits of the Learning Curve." *Harvard Business Review*, 52 (September/October 1974): 109–119.

Camm, J. "A Note on Learning Curve Parameters." *Decision Sciences* (Summer 1985): 325–327.

Hall, G., and S. Howell. "The Experience Curve from the Economist's Perspective." *Strategic Management Journal* (July/September 1985): 197–210.

Hart, C. W., G. Spizizen, and D. D. Wyckoff. "Scale Economies and the Experience Curve." *The Cornell H.R.A. Quarterly*, 25 (May 1984): 91–103.

Smith, D. B., and J. L. Larsson. "The Impact of Learning on Cost: The Case of Heart Transplantation." *Hospital & Health Services Administration*, 34 (Spring 1989): 85–97.

Smith, J. *Learning Curve for Cost Control*. Industrial Engineering & Management Press, 1989.

Taylor, M. L. "The Learning Curve—A Basic Cost Projection Tool." *N.A.A. Bulletin* (February 1961): 21–26.

13

INVENTORY MANAGEMENT AND JUST-IN-TIME TACTICS

JIT BRINGS A COMPETITIVE ADVANTAGE TO HARLEY-DAVIDSON

Harley-Davidson is a repetitive manufacturer. This means that they assemble modules. Like most repetitive manufacturers, Harley produces on an assembly line and the end product takes a variety of forms depending on the mix of modules. In Harley's case, the modules are motorcycle components in the form of two engine types in three displacement sizes for 20 street bike models, which are available in 13 colors and two wheel options. This adds up to 95 combinations. In addition, Harley produces 4 police, 2 Shrine, and 19 custom paint options. This requires that no fewer than 20,000 different pieces be assembled on

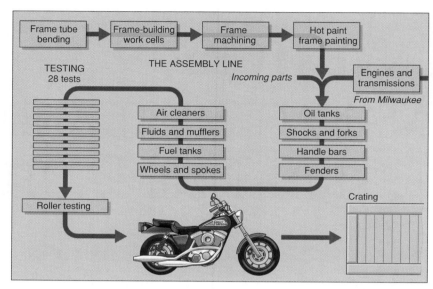

This is a flowchart of Harley-Davidson's York, Pennsylvania, assembly plant.

Most containers are specially made for individual parts, and many feature padding to protect the finish. Containers serve an important role in inventory reduction: the containers are the only place inventory is stored on the assembly line, so they serve as a signal to supply new parts to the line. After all the pieces have been removed, the container is returned to its originating cell, to signal the worker there to build more.

one product line. The use of modules reduces some of the management tasks associated with an inventory of 20,000 parts.

The Harley-Davidson engines are produced in Milwaukee and shipped to York, Pennsylvania. At the production facilities in York, both suppliers and the production departments deliver to the assembly line on a Just-in-Time (JIT) basis.

Harley-Davidson was founded in Milwaukee in 1903. Since that time, it has competed with hundreds of manufacturers, foreign and domestic. The competition has been tough, especially with the Japanese. Indeed, after almost nine decades, Harley is the only motorcycle company still producing in the United States.

a total quality control program driven by JIT.

By using JIT, large parts inventories with their inherent problems and high costs were eliminated. Now, management insists on delivery of small quantities of parts with no defects to the assembly line. The concept applies to suppliers as well as workers within Harley-Davidson. Indeed, Harley is so good at supplier development that they now do consulting in this area.

Laser trimming fenders at a fixture setup. Harley workers have standardized die and fixture setups and located them near the machine where they will be used. An operator simply rolls up the next fixture or die and sets up for the next job in an average of 12 minutes, saving an average of 30 minutes over Harley's earlier processes. With more than 500 operations requiring such setups, the saving is substantial enough to give Harley a competitive edge.

The Japanese motorcycle invasion of the 1970s caught Harley in the cross fire between Honda and Yamaha. The competition was so intense that Honda introduced 81 new models and Yamaha 34 in only 18 months. To meet the challenge, Harley-Davidson management emphasized quality improvement.

An emphasis on quality is a marvelous tonic for any management. And Just-in-Time tactics force operations managers to address improvements in virtually every area. At Harley-Davidson, this meant product and process improvement, JIT inventory, and a host of other modern manufacturing methods. But mostly it meant

Completed Harleys coming from the assembly line in preparation for a series of 28 tests and inspections.

573

Fansteel California supplies a critical steel part to Beckman Instruments, a medical instrument producer in Palo Alto, California. Beckman is a practitioner of Kanban, the famous Japanese system of inventory control. For Kanban to work, Beckman production personnel order parts directly by fax from Fansteel. There are no purchase orders and no bureaucratic go-between. The parts are shipped straight to the production line, so a high degree of trust in Fansteel's quality and reliability must exist. There is no excess inventory of parts to soften the blow of rejected pieces. A long-term commitment of both partners is required to achieve the economics of production inherent in Kanban. Results? Lead times are cut from 2 months to 5 days. Inventory and warehousing costs are slashed. Production schedules are coordinated. It works . . . if you have a partner you can trust. ♦

As Beckman and Fansteel both know, inventory is one of the most expensive assets of many companies, representing as much as 40% of total invested capital. Operations managers at these firms, at Harley-Davidson, and around the globe have long recognized that good inventory control is crucial. On one hand, a firm can try to reduce costs by reducing on-hand inventory levels. On the other hand, customers become dissatisfied when an item is frequently out of stock. Thus, companies must strike a balance between inventory investment and customer service levels. As you would expect, cost minimization is a major factor in obtaining this delicate balance.

All organizations have some type of inventory planning and control system. A bank has methods to control its inventory of cash. A hospital has methods used to control blood supplies and pharmaceuticals. Government agencies, schools, and, of course, virtually every manufacturing and production organization are concerned with inventory planning and control.

In cases of physical products, the organization must determine whether to produce goods or to purchase them. Once this has been determined, the next step is to forecast demand, as discussed in Chapter 5. Then operations managers determine the inventory necessary to service that demand. In this chapter, we discuss the functions, types, and management of inventory. We then address two basic inventory issues: how much to order and when to order.

FUNCTIONS AND TYPES OF INVENTORY

Inventory

Inventory is a stored resource that is used to satisfy a current or future need. In this section, we discuss the main functions of inventory and the four types of inventory.

Functions of Inventory

Inventory can serve several important functions that add flexibility to the operation of a firm. Six uses of inventory are

1. To provide a stock of goods to *meet anticipated demand* by customers.
2. To *separate production and distribution* processes. For example, if product demand is high only during summer, a firm may build up stock during the winter and thus avoid the costs of shortages and stockouts in summer. Similarly, if a firm's

supplies fluctuate, extra raw materials of inventory may be needed to separate (or "decouple") production processes.

3. To take advantage of *quantity discounts* because purchases in larger quantities can substantially reduce the cost of goods.

4. To *hedge against inflation* and price changes.

5. To *protect against stockouts* that can occur due to bad weather, supplier shortages, quality problems, or improper deliveries. "Safety stocks," namely, extra goods on hand, can reduce the risk of stockouts.

6. To *permit operations to continue smoothly* with the use of "work-in-process" inventory. This inventory exists because it takes time to make goods and because a pipeline of inventories is stocked throughout the process.

Types of Inventory

Firms maintain four types of inventories: raw material inventory, work-in-process inventory, maintenance/repair/operating supply (MRO) inventory, and finished goods inventory.

Raw material inventory has been purchased, but not processed. The items can be used to separate suppliers from the production process. However, the preferred approach is to eliminate supplier variability in quality, quantity, or delivery time so that separating is not needed. **Work-in-process (WIP) inventory** has undergone some change, but is not completed. WIP exists because of the time it takes for a product to be made (called cycle time). Reducing the cycle time reduces inventory. Often this is not difficult. As Figure 13.1 shows, most of the time a product is "being made," it is in fact sitting idle. Actual work time or "run" time is a small portion of the material flow time, perhaps as low as 5%.

MROs are inventories devoted to **maintenance/repair/operating** supplies. They exist because the need and timing for maintenance and repair of some equipment are unknown. Although the demand for MRO inventories is often a function of maintenance schedules, other MRO demands must be anticipated. Similarly, **finished goods inventory** is completed and awaiting shipment. Finished goods may be inventoried because customer demands for a given time period may be unknown.

Litton Industries uses bar-code readers to automate inventory control at its production and distribution facilities. The scanning device shown is linked to the central computer by wireless data transmission.

Raw material inventory

Work-in-process inventory

MRO

Finished goods inventory

INVENTORY MANAGEMENT

Operations managers establish systems for managing inventory. In this section, we briefly examine two ingredients of such systems: (1) how inventory items can be classified (called ABC analysis) and (2) how accurate inventory records can be maintained.

ABC Analysis

ABC analysis divides on-hand inventory into three classifications on the basis of annual dollar volume.[1] ABC analysis is an inventory application of what is known as

ABC analysis

---

[1]H. Ford Dickie, *Modern Manufacturing* (formerly *Factory Management and Maintenance*) (July 1951).

FIGURE 13.1 ■ The Material Flow Cycle

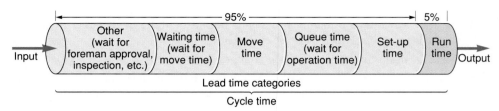

the Pareto principle. The Pareto principle states that there are a critical few and trivial many.[2] The idea is to focus resources on the critical few and not the trivial many.

To determine annual dollar volume for ABC analysis, we measure the *annual demand* of each inventory item times the *cost per unit*. Class A items are those on which the annual dollar volume is high. Such items may represent only about 15% of the total inventory items, but they represent 70 to 80% of the total inventory cost. Class B items are those inventory items of medium annual dollar volume. These items may represent about 30% of the items and 15 to 25% of the value. Those with low annual dollar volume are class C, which may represent only 5% of the annual dollar volume, but about 55% of the total items.

Graphically, the inventory of many organizations would appear as presented in Figure 13.2. An example of the use of ABC analysis is shown in Example 1.

Inventory items can be classified by criteria other than annual dollar-volume. For instance, anticipated engineering changes or high unit cost may dictate upgrading items to a higher classification. By dividing inventory items into classes, operations managers can set different policies and controls for each class.

FIGURE 13.2 ■ Graphic Representation of ABC Analysis

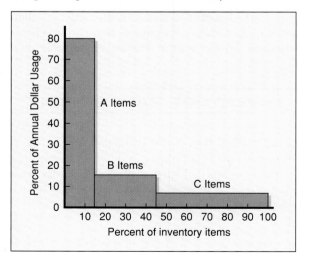

[2]Vilfredo Pareto, nineteenth-century Italian economist.

EXAMPLE 1

Silicon Chips, Inc., maker of super-fast 4-meg chips, has organized its 10 inventory items on an annual dollar volume basis. Shown below are the items, their annual demand, unit cost, annual dollar volume, and the percent each item represents of the total. In the last column on the right of the table below, we show these items grouped into ABC classifications.

ABC CALCULATION

ITEM STOCK NUMBER	PERCENT OF NUMBER OF ITEMS STOCKED	ANNUAL VOLUME (UNITS)	UNIT COST	ANNUAL DOLLAR VOLUME	PERCENT OF ANNUAL DOLLAR VOLUME		CLASS
#10286	20%	1,000	$ 90.00	$ 90,000	38.8%	72%	A
#11526		500	154.00	77,000	33.2%		A
#12760		1,550	17.00	26,350	11.4%		B
#10867	30%	350	42.86	15,001	6.5%	23%	B
#10500		1,000	12.50	12,500	5.4%		B
#12572		600	$ 14.17	8,502	3.7%		C
#14075		2,000	.60	1,200	.5%		C
#01036	50%	100	8.50	850	.4%	5%	C
#01307		1,200	.42	504	.2%		C
#10572		250	.60	150	.1%		C
		8,550		$232,057	100.0%		

Policies that may be based on ABC classification include the following:

1. Purchasing resources expended should be much higher for A items than for C items.

2. Physical inventory control should be tighter for A items; perhaps they belong in a more secure area, with the accuracy of their records being verified more frequently.

3. Forecasting A items may warrant more care than forecasting other items.

Better forecasting, physical control, supplier reliability, and an ultimate reduction in safety stock and inventory investment can all result from ABC analysis.

Record Accuracy

Inventory systems require accurate records. Without them, managers cannot make precise decisions about ordering, scheduling, and shipping. Record accuracy allows organizations to move away from being sure that "some of everything" is in inventory to focusing on only those items that are required.

These Levis are being scanned as part of the retailer's inventory control information system. Use of bar codes allows faster, more accurate data entry, better tracking of sales items, and reduced inventory costs. Bar-coding systems frequently pay for themselves within the first year of use.

Kmart's Remote Control Inventory Control

Bar codes are old hat in retailing. But top American stores, like Kmart, are learning to apply their bar-code data in ways that radically change inventory control.

Employees at Kmart scurry around the aisles with hand-held lasers to zap bar-coded labels on products still sitting on the shelf. A display window on the laser, which is called a "remote maintenance unit," provides an instant scorecard. It shows how many units of the product ought to be on the shelf, how many are still in the stockroom, the minimum number the store should have on hand, if an order has already been placed, what the price is, and whether that price is a sale or nonsale price.

Let's look at Kmart's new store at Auburn Hills, near Detroit, for example. Bar codes scanned at checkout counters are recorded in the store's point-of-sales computer. They are *also* sent by satel-

lite to Kmart's head office in Troy, Michigan. Troy logs the information for research purposes and then retransmits it to an inventory distribution center, where more computers decide reorder points and what restocking is needed at Auburn Hills. The fresh stock arrives within 48 hours.

About 90% of everything Kmart sells is now subject to this centralized merchandising system. Staff at the stores is left managing the other 10%, usually fast-changing items like greeting cards.

Systems like this one are transforming retailing by keeping track of shoppers' preferences daily, enabling headquarters staff to predict selling trends more accurately than an individual store manager could do. For example, the data showed that Kmart would do much better promoting a special line of soft toys by selling them next to infant's clothes, instead of in the toy section. The high-tech war in American retailing "is not going to be won by pilots flying around by the seat of their pants," concluded Kmart's MIS director.

Sources: Adapted from *The Economist* (May 29, 1993): 90–91; *Stores* (December 1992): 36–38.

To ensure accuracy, incoming and outgoing record keeping must be good, as must be stockroom security. A well-organized stockroom will have limited access, good housekeeping, and storage areas that hold fixed amounts of inventory. Bins, shelf space, and parts will be labeled accurately. Kmart's approach to improved inventory record accuracy is discussed in the *POM in Action* box "Kmart's Remote Control Inventory Control."

Cycle Counting

Cycle counting

Even though an organization may have gone to substantial efforts to maintain accurate inventory records, these records must be verified through continuing audits. Such audits are known as **cycle counting**. Historically, many firms take annual physical inventories. This procedure often involves shutting down the facility and having inexperienced people counting parts and material. Inventory records instead should be verified via cycle counting. Cycle counting uses inventory classifications developed through ABC analysis. With cycle counting procedure, items are counted, records are verified, and inaccuracies are periodically documented. The cause of inaccuracies is then traced, and appropriate action is taken. Most cycle counting procedures are established so that some of each classification are counted each day. "A" items will be counted frequently, perhaps once a month. "B" items will be counted less frequently, perhaps once a quarter. "C" items will be counted even less frequently, perhaps once every 6 months. Example 2 illustrates how many items of each classification to count.

EXAMPLE 2

Cole's Trucks, Inc., a builder of high-quality refuse trucks, has about 5,000 items in its inventory. After hiring Matt Clark, a bright young P/OM student, for the summer, the firm determined that it has 500 A items, 1,750 B items, and 2,750 C items. The policy is to count all A items every month (every 20 working days), all B items every quarter (every 60 working days), and all C items every 6 months (every 120 working days). How many items should be counted each day?

ITEM CLASS	QUANTITY	CYCLE COUNTING POLICY	NUMBER OF ITEMS COUNTED PER DAY
A	500	Each month (20 working days)	$500/20 = 25$/day
B	1,750	Each quarter (60 working days)	$1{,}750/60 = 29$/day
C	2,750	Every 6 months (120 working days)	$2{,}750/120 = \underline{23}$/day
			77/day

77 items are counted each day.

In Example 2, the particular items to be cycle counted are randomly selected each day. Another option is only to cycle count items when they are reordered.

Cycle counting also has the following advantages:

1. eliminating the shutdown and interruption of production necessary for annual physical inventories
2. eliminating annual inventory adjustments
3. providing professional personnel to audit the accuracy of inventory
4. allowing the cause of the errors to be identified and remedial action to be taken
5. maintaining accurate inventory records.

JUST-IN-TIME INVENTORY

Inventories in production and distribution systems often exist "just in case" something goes wrong, that is, just in case some variation from the production plan occurs. The "extra" inventory is then used to cover the variations or problems. We suggest that good inventory tactics require not "just-in-case," but "just-in-time" (JIT). **Just-in-time inventory** is the minimum inventory necessary to keep a perfect system running. With just-in-time inventory, the exact amount of good items arrive at the moment they are needed, not a minute before or a minute after the units are required.

Just-in-time inventory

Variability

To achieve just-in-time inventory, managers *reduce variability caused by both internal and external factors.* Inventory hides variability—a polite word for problems. The less variability in the system, the less inventory is required.

JIT's Revolution against Waste

The sweeping new JIT factory attacks four types of waste: inventories, changeovers, defects, and human resources. The days of long production lines and huge economic lots, with goods passing through monumental, single-operation machines, are gone. Now, each work cell, arranged in a U-shape, contains several small machines performing different operations. The cells produce goods one unit at a time, and they produce the units *only* after a customer buys them.

Inventory is waste. It wastes space; it wastes money; it wastes time. "Time is money!" said Benjamin Franklin. "Bolts are our enemies!" Japan's Shigeo Shingo tells us. Motion that does not add value to a product is waste. Single clamps replace most bolts. Workers can easily rearrange production cells to accommodate product improvements or even new designs. Almost nothing in this new factory is bolted down. Everything is on casters.

Defects are waste. When workers produce units one at a time, they can test each product or component at each production stage. Machines in work cells with "human-touch" functions sense defects and stop automatically when they occur. Before JIT, defective products were replaced from inventory. In a JIT factory there are no such buffers. Getting it right the first time is all-important.

Henry Ford was well versed in JIT practices when he wrote in 1926, "Our production cycle is about 81 hours from the mine to the finished machine in the freight car, or 3 days and 9 hours." (Note that 48 of those 81 hours were to move the iron ore from the mines to the docks.)

Sources: Manufacturing Engineering (January 1990): 104; *Today and Tomorrow* (Doubleday, 1926), p. 118.

Most variability is caused by tolerating waste or by poor management. (See the *POM in Action* box "JIT's Revolution against Waste.") Some of the reasons variability occurs are

1. employees, machines, and suppliers produce units that do not conform to standards, are late, or are not the proper quantity; or

2. engineering drawings or specifications are inaccurate; or

3. production personnel try to produce before drawings or specifications are complete; or

4. customer demands are unknown.

The idea is to eliminate variability and problems, as illustrated in Figure 13.3, which shows a stream full of rocks. The water in the stream represents inventory flow, and the rocks represent problems such as late deliveries, machine breakdown, and poor personnel performance. The water level in the stream hides variability and problems. Because problems are hidden by inventory, they are sometimes hard to find.

Therefore, to achieve just-in-time inventory, management must begin by reducing inventory. Reducing inventory uncovers the rocks that represent the variability and problems currently being tolerated. With reduced inventory, management chips away at the exposed problems until the stream is clear, and then makes additional cuts in inventory, chipping away at the next level of exposed problems. Ultimately, there will be virtually no inventory and no problems (variability).

Perhaps the manager who said, "Inventory is the root of operations management evil" was not far from the truth. If inventory is not evil, it tends to hide the evil at great cost.

Just-in-time has come to mean elimination of waste, synchronized manufacture, and little inventory. The key to JIT is producing small lot sizes to standards. Reducing

FIGURE 13.3 ■ Inventory Hides Problems, Just as Water in a Stream Hides the Rocks (a). Reduce inventory so the problems can be found (b); solve those problems, then reduce inventory again. Eventually the material should flow smoothly.

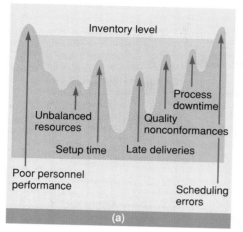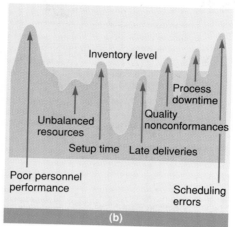

the size of batches can be a major help in reducing inventory and inventory costs. When inventory usage is constant, the average inventory level is the sum of the maximum inventory plus the minimum inventory divided by 2.

The average inventory drops as the inventory reorder quantity drops because the maximum inventory level drops. Moreover, the smaller the lot size (batch), the fewer problems are hidden. One way to achieve small lot sizes is to move inventory through the shop only as needed rather than *pushing* it on to the next workstation, whether the personnel there are ready for it or not. When inventory is moved only as needed, it is referred to as a *pull* system and the ideal lot size is one. The Japanese call this system *Kanban*.

Kanban

Kanban is a Japanese word for "card." In their effort to reduce inventory, the Japanese use systems that "pull" inventory through the shop. They often use a "card" to signal the need for more material, hence the name Kanban. The card is the authorization for the next batch of material to be produced. The Kanban *"pulls"* the material through the plant. The system has been modified in many facilities so that, even though it is called a Kanban, the card does not exist. In some cases, an empty position on the floor is indication that the next lot is needed (Figure 13.4). In other cases, some sort of signal, such as a flag or rag (Figure 13.5) is used to signify that it is time for the next batch.

Kanban

The batches are typically very small, usually a matter of a few hours' worth of production. Such a system requires tight schedules and frequent setups of machines. Small quantities of everything must be produced several times a day. Such a system must run smoothly because any shortage has an almost immediate impact on the entire system. Kanban places added emphasis on meeting schedules and reducing the time and cost required by setups.

Whether it is called Kanban or not, the advantages of small inventory and *pulling* material through the plant only when needed are significant. For instance,

FIGURE 13.4 ■ Diagram of Stockpoint Lanes at Tachikawa Spring Co. Press Shop. From the status shown in the diagram, the lane has just been filled with part G82; they may be working on part H31 and getting ready for part G30, but that depends on the pull signals.

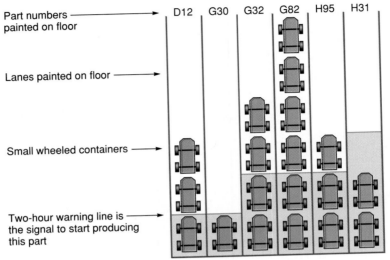

Part numbers painted on floor

Lanes painted on floor

Small wheeled containers

Two-hour warning line is the signal to start producing this part

(*Source:* Robert W. Hall, *Zero Inventories*, Homewood, IL: Dow Jones-Irwin, 1983, p. 51.)

small batches allow a very limited amount of faulty material. Numerous aspects of inventory are bad, and only one aspect, availability, is good. Among the bad aspects are poor quality, obsolescence, damage, occupied space, committed assets, increased insurance, increased material handling, and increased accidents. All of these negative aspects add to the costs associated with holding (carrying) inventory. The *POM in Action* box "Auto Parts Supplier Reduces Delays" describes how Libralter Plastics slashed inventory costs.

FIGURE 13.5 ■ Diagram of Outbound Stockpoint with Warning Signal Marker

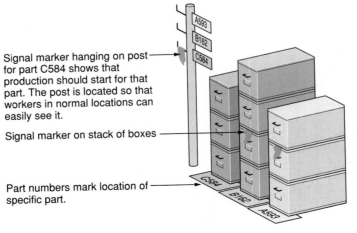

Signal marker hanging on post for part C584 shows that production should start for that part. The post is located so that workers in normal locations can easily see it.

Signal marker on stack of boxes

Part numbers mark location of specific part.

(*Source:* Robert W. Hall, *Zero Inventories*, Homewood, IL: Dow Jones-Irwin, 1983, p. 51.)

Auto Parts Supplier Reduces Delays

Libralter Plastics, in Walled Lake, Michigan, makes wheel covers, grilles, and other plastic parts for the Big Three auto makers. In only 3 years, the company went from chaos and waste to "the epitome of what every company is looking for in a supplier." Earning the 1994 *USA Today* Quality Cup Award for small organizations, Libralter employees developed new ways to respond to Big Three JIT demands. This meant being nimble enough to deliver parts on very short notice.

First, workers developed a computer system that sharply reduced inventory. Before, supplies would sit on Libralter's factory floor an average of 23 days. Down to 14 days now, the changes helped slash inventory holding costs almost $250,000 a year.

Libralter also responds to customers more quickly. Processing an order used to take 36 hours. Now, it takes less than 1 hour. Delivery trucks that used to sit idle until noon are loaded first thing in the morning.

The team of 10 employees formed to fix the problem came from accounting, production, and information systems. But most of the quality improvements at Libralter came after employees from the factory floor suggested them. As one Libralter manager says, "If you want to know the best way to do a job, ask the guy who's doing it."

Source: Adapted from *USA Today* (April 8, 1994): 2B.

INVENTORY MODELS

We now examine a variety of inventory models and the costs associated with them.

Independent versus Dependent Demand

Inventory control models assume that demand for an item is either independent of or dependent on the demand for other items. For example, the demand for refrigerators is *independent* of the demand for toaster ovens. However, the demand for toaster oven components is *dependent* on the production requirements of toaster ovens.

This chapter focuses on managing *independent* demand items. Chapter 14 presents the topic of *dependent* demand.

Holding, Ordering, and Setup Costs

Holding costs are the costs associated with holding or "carrying" inventory over time. Therefore, holding costs also include costs related to storage, such as insurance, extra staffing, and interest payments. Table 13.1 shows the kinds of costs that need to be evaluated to determine holding costs. Many firms fail to include all of the inventory holding costs. Consequently, inventory holding costs are often understated.[3]

Ordering cost includes costs of supplies, forms, order processing, clerical support, and so forth. When orders are being manufactured, ordering costs also exist, but they are known as setup costs. **Setup cost** is the cost to prepare a machine or process for manufacturing an order. Operations managers can lower ordering costs by reducing setup costs and by using such efficient procedures as electronic ordering and payment.

Holding costs

Ordering cost

Setup cost

[3]Jack G. Wacker, "Can Holding Costs Be Overstated for 'Just-in-Time' Manufacturing System?" *Production and Inventory Management,* **27** (Third Quarter, 1986): 11–14.

TABLE 13.1 ■ DETERMINING INVENTORY HOLDING COSTS

CATEGORY	COST AS A PERCENT OF INVENTORY VALUE*
Housing costs, such as building rent, depreciation, operating cost, taxes, insurance	6% (3 to 10%)
Material handling costs, including equipment, lease, or depreciation, power, operating cost	3% (1 to 3.5%)
Labor cost from extra handling	3% (3 to 5%)
Investment costs, such as borrowing costs, taxes, and insurance on inventory	11% (6 to 24%)
Pilferage, scrap, and obsolescence	3% (2 to 5%)
Overall carrying cost	26%

*All figures are approximate, as they vary substantially depending on the nature of the business, location, and current interest rates. Any inventory cost of less than 15% is suspect, but annual inventory costs often approach 40% of the value of inventory.

Setup time

In many environments setup cost is highly correlated with **setup time**. Setups usually require a substantial amount of work prior to an operation actually being accomplished at the work center. Much of the preparation required by a setup can be done prior to shutting down the machine or process. Setup times can be reduced substantially, as shown in Figure 13.6. Machines and processes that traditionally have taken hours to set up are now being set up in less than a minute by the more imaginative world-class manufacturers. As we shall see later in this chapter, reducing setup times is an excellent way to reduce inventory investment and to improve productivity.

Inventory Models for Independent Demand

In this section, we introduce three inventory models that address two important questions: *when to order* and *how much to order*. These *independent* demand models are

1. the basic economic order quantity (EOQ) model
2. production order quantity model
3. quantity discount model

The Basic Economic Order Quantity (EOQ) Model

The economic order quantity (EOQ) is one of the oldest and most commonly known inventory control techniques.[4] This technique is relatively easy to use but is based on several assumptions:

1. Demand is known and constant.

[4]The research on EOQ dates back to 1915; see Ford W. Harris, *Operations and Cost* (Chicago: A. W. Shaw, 1915).

FIGURE 13.6 ■ Steps to Reduce Setup Times. Reduced setup times are a major JIT component.

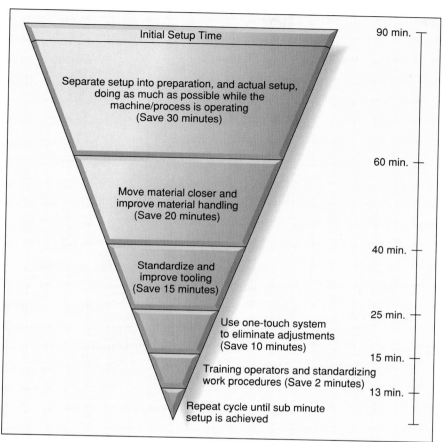

Initial Setup Time — 90 min.

Separate setup into preparation, and actual setup, doing as much as possible while the machine/process is operating (Save 30 minutes)

60 min.

Move material closer and improve material handling (Save 20 minutes)

40 min.

Standardize and improve tooling (Save 15 minutes)

25 min.

Use one-touch system to eliminate adjustments (Save 10 minutes)

15 min.

Training operators and standardizing work procedures (Save 2 minutes)

13 min.

Repeat cycle until sub minute setup is achieved

2. Lead time, that is, the time between the placement of the order and the receipt of the order, is known and constant.

3. Receipt of inventory is instantaneous. In other words, the inventory from an order arrives in one batch, at one time.

4. Quantity discounts are not possible.

5. The only variable costs are the cost of setting up or placing an order (setup cost) and the cost of holding or storing inventory over time (holding or carrying cost). These costs are discussed in the previous section.

6. Stockouts (shortages) can be completely avoided if orders are placed at the right time.

Under these assumptions, the graph of inventory usage over time has a sawtooth shape as in Figure 13.7. In Figure 13.7, Q represents the amount that is ordered. Let us say this amount is 500 Donna Karan dresses at a Chicago retail store. Then all 500 dresses arrive at one time when an order is received. Thus, the inventory level jumps from 0 to 500 dresses. In general, an inventory level increases from 0 to Q units when an order arrives.

FIGURE 13.7 ■ Inventory Usage Over Time

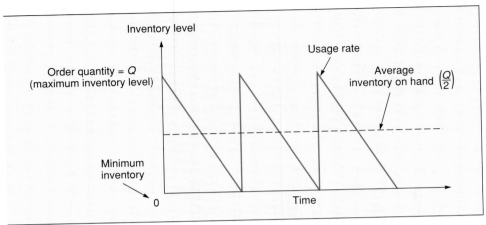

Because demand is constant over time, inventory drops at a uniform rate over time. (Refer to the sloped line in Figure 13.7.) When the inventory level reaches 0, the new order is placed and received, and the inventory level again jumps to Q units (represented by the vertical lines). This process continues indefinitely over time.

MINIMIZE COSTS. The objective of most inventory models is to minimize total costs. For the EOQ model, the significant costs are the setup (or ordering) cost and the holding (or carrying) cost. All other costs, such as the cost of the inventory itself, are constant. Therefore, if we minimize the sum of the setup and holding costs, we will also be minimizing the total costs. To help you visualize this situation, in Figure 13.8 we graph total costs as a function of the order quantity, Q. The optimal order size, $Q^\star$, will be the quantity that minimizes the total costs. As the quantity ordered

FIGURE 13.8 ■ Total Cost as a Function of Order Quantity

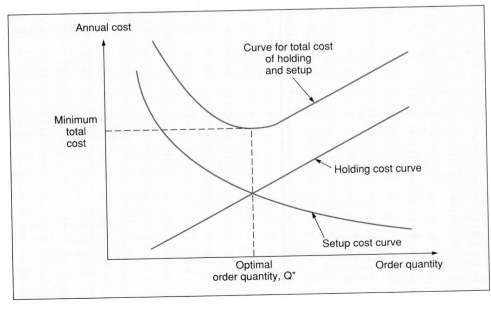

Small Lot Sizes Contribute to Toshiba's (and Japan's) Flexibility

It's a good news, bad news story. Here is the good news: The campaign in the United States to improve quality has paid off so well that the Japanese no longer enjoy a clear lead. Now the bad news: While the quality gaps disappear, a more challenging contest, called flexibility, faces world-class competitors. Flexibility's watchwords are change fast, keep costs low, and respond quickly to customers—all of which mean production of small lot sizes.

Flexibility is an explicit goal at Toshiba, Japan's $40 billion giant with products as diverse as computers, light bulbs, and power plants. The idea, explains company president Fumio Sato, is to push Toshiba's two dozen factories to adapt faster to markets. "Customers wanted choices. They wanted a washing machine or a TV set that was precisely right

for their needs. We needed variety, not mass production," says Sato.

The key to variety is finding ways to make money from ever-shorter production runs. Sato urges managers to reduce setup times, shrink lead times, and learn to make more products with the same equipment and people. "Smaller lot!" he yells at each plant he visits.

Toshiba's computer factory 30 miles outside of Tokyo got the message. Workers assemble 9 different word processors on the same line and, on an adjacent one, 20 varieties of laptop computers. Usually, they make a batch of 20 before changing models, but Toshiba can afford lot sizes as small as 10.

Product life cycles for low-end computers are now measured in months, not years, so flexible lines allow the company to guard against running short of a hot model or overproducing one whose sales have slowed. The results are less inventory, less space devoted to inventory, less obsolete inventory, lower holding costs, and a focus on the products currently in demand.

Sources: Adapted from *Fortune* (September 21, 1992): 62–72; *Network World* (August 12, 1991): 28.

---

increases, the total number of orders placed per year will decrease. Thus, as the quantity ordered increases, the annual setup or ordering cost will decrease. But as the order quantity increases, the holding cost will increase due to larger average inventories that are maintained.

As we can see in Figure 13.8, a reduction in either the holding cost or the setup cost will reduce the total cost curve. A reduction in the total cost curve also reduces the optimal order quantity (lot size). And smaller lot sizes have a positive impact on quality[5] and production flexibility. The *POM in Action* box "Small Lot Sizes Contribute to Toshiba's (and Japan's) Flexibility" discusses the competitive advantage found through smaller lot sizes.

You should note that in Figure 13.8, the optimal order quantity occurred at the point where the ordering cost curve and the carrying cost curve intersected. This was not by chance. With the EOQ model, the optimal order quantity will occur at a point where the total setup cost is equal to the total holding cost.[6] We can use this fact to develop equations that solve directly for $Q^\star$. We must

1. develop an expression for setup or ordering cost

---

[5]R. Anthony Inman, "The Impact of Lot-Size Reduction on Quality," *Production and Inventory Management Journal*, **35**, 1 (First Quarter 1994): 5–8.

[6]This is the case where holding costs are linear and begin at the origin—that is, when inventory costs do not decline (or increase) as inventory volume increases and all holding costs are in small increments. Additionally, there is probably some learning each time a setup (or order) is executed, which lowers subsequent setup costs. Consequently, the EOQ model is probably a special case. However, we abide by the conventional wisdom that this model is a reasonable approximation.

Blue Bell Company, the maker of Wrangler jeans, had severe inventory imbalances. Merchandisers reported months of supply of some styles, whereas others were out of stock. The EOQ model was implemented. By designing, testing, and providing a new production planning procedure, inventories were reduced more than 31% without a decrease in sales or customer service. The new procedure also reduced manufacturing costs by roughly $1 million.

2. develop an expression for holding cost

3. set setup cost equal to holding cost

4. solve the equation for the best order quantity.

Using the following variables, we can determine setup and holding costs and solve for $Q^\star$:

$$Q = \text{number of pieces per order}$$
$$Q^\star = \text{optimum number of pieces per order (EOQ)}$$
$$D = \text{annual demand in units for the inventory item}$$
$$S = \text{setup or ordering cost for each order}$$
$$H = \text{holding or carrying cost per unit per year}$$

1. Annual setup cost = (no. of orders placed/yr)(setup or order cost/order)

$$= \left(\frac{\text{annual demand}}{\text{no. units in each order}} \right) (\text{setup or order cost/order})$$

$$= \frac{D}{Q} S$$

2. Annual holding cost = (average inventory level)(holding cost/unit/yr)

$$= \left(\frac{\text{order quantity}}{2} \right) (\text{holding cost/unit/yr})$$

$$= \frac{Q}{2} H$$

3. Optimal order quantity is found when annual setup cost = annual holding cost, namely,

$$\frac{D}{Q} S = \frac{Q}{2} H$$

4. To solve for $Q^\star$, simply cross-multiply terms and isolate Q on the left of the equals sign.

$$2DS = Q^2H$$

$$Q^2 = \frac{2DS}{H}$$

$$Q^\star = \sqrt{\frac{2DS}{H}} \qquad (13.1)$$

Now that we have derived equations for the optimal order quantity, $Q^\star$, it is possible to solve inventory problems directly, as is done in Example 3.

EXAMPLE 3

Squirt, Inc., a company that markets hypodermic needles to hospitals, would like to reduce its inventory cost by determining the optimal number of hypodermic needles to obtain per order. The annual demand is 1,000 units, the setup or ordering cost is $10 per order, and the holding cost per unit per year is $0.50. Using these figures, we can calculate the optimal number of units per order:

1. $Q^\star = \sqrt{\dfrac{2DS}{H}}$ **3.** $Q^\star = \sqrt{4,000}$

2. $Q^\star = \sqrt{\dfrac{2(1,000)(10)}{0.50}}$ **4.** $Q^\star = 200$ units

We can also determine the expected number of orders placed during the year (N) and the expected time between orders (T) as follows:

$$\text{Expected number of orders} = N = \frac{\text{demand}}{\text{order quantity}} = \frac{D}{Q^\star} \qquad (13.2)$$

$$\text{Expected time between orders} = T = \frac{\text{number of working days in a year}}{\text{order quantity}} \qquad (13.3)$$

Example 4 illustrates this concept.

EXAMPLE 4

Using the data from Squirt, Inc., in Example 3, and a 250-day working year, we find the number of orders (N) and the expected time between orders (T) as:

$$N = \frac{\text{demand}}{\text{order quantity}} = \frac{1,000}{200} = 5 \text{ orders per year}$$

$$T = \frac{\text{number of working days /year}}{\text{expected number of orders}}$$

$$= \frac{250 \text{ working days/year}}{5 \text{ orders}} = 50 \text{ days between orders}$$

As mentioned earlier in this section, the total annual inventory cost is the sum of the setup and holding costs:

$$\text{Total annual cost} = \text{setup cost} + \text{holding cost} \qquad (13.4)$$

In terms of the variables in the model, we can express the total cost as

$$\text{Total cost} = \frac{D}{Q}S + \frac{Q}{2}H \qquad (13.5)$$

Example 5 shows how to use this formula.

EXAMPLE 5

Again using the Squirt, Inc., data (Examples 3 and 4), we determine that the total annual inventory costs are

$$\text{Total Cost} = \frac{D}{Q}S + \frac{Q}{2}H$$

$$= \frac{1{,}000}{200}(\$10) + \frac{200}{2}(\$0.50)$$

$$= (5)(\$10) + (100)(\$0.50)$$

$$= \$50 + \$50 = \$100$$

Often, the total inventory cost expression is written to include the actual cost of the material purchased. If we assume that the annual demand and the price per hypodermic are known values (for example, 1,000 hypodermics per year at $P = \$10$), total annual cost should include purchase cost. Material cost does not depend on the particular order policy found to be optimal, because regardless of how many units are ordered each time, we still incur an annual material cost of $D \times P = (1{,}000)(\$10) = \$10{,}000$. (Shortly, we discuss the case in which this may not be true, namely, when a quantity discount is available to the customer who orders a certain amount each time.)

Robust

ROBUST MODELS. A benefit of the EOQ model is that it is robust. By **robust** we mean that it gives satisfactory answers even with substantial variation in the parameters. As we have observed, determining accurate ordering costs and holding costs for inventory is often difficult. Consequently, a robust model is advantageous. Total cost of the EOQ changes little in the neighborhood of the minimum. The curve is very shallow. This means that variations in setup costs, holding costs, demand, or even EOQ make relatively modest differences in total cost. Example 6 shows how EOQ can be robust.

REORDER POINTS. Now that we have decided how much to order, we must determine when to order. Simple inventory models assume that receipt of an order is instantaneous. In other words, they assume that a firm will wait until its inventory level for a particular item reaches zero before placing an order, and that all of the order is

EXAMPLE 6

If management in the Squirt, Inc., example underestimated total annual demand by 50% (say it is actually 1,500 needles rather than 1,000 needles) while using the same Q, the annual inventory cost increases only $25.00 ($100 versus $125), or 25%. Similarly, if management cuts its order size by 50% from 200 to 100, cost increases by $25 ($100 versus $125), or 25%.

(a) If demand in Example 5 is actually 1,500 needles rather than 1,000, but management uses an EOQ of $Q = 200$ (when it should be $Q = 244.9$ based on $D = 1,500$), total costs increase 25%:

$$\text{Annual cost} = \frac{D}{Q}S + \frac{Q}{2}H$$

$$= \frac{1,500}{200}(\$10) + \frac{200}{2}(\$0.50)$$

$$= \$75.00 + \$50.00 = \$125.00$$

(b) If the order size is reduced from 200 to 100 needles, but other parameters remain the same, cost also increases 25%:

$$\text{Annual cost} = \frac{1,000}{100}(10) + \frac{100}{2}(\$0.50)$$

$$= \$100.00 + \$25.00 = \$125.00$$

received at once. However, the time between the placement and receipt of an order, called the **lead time** or delivery time, can be as short as a few hours to as long as months. Thus, the when-to-order decision is usually expressed in terms of a reorder point, the inventory level at which an order should be placed. See Figure 13.9.

Lead time

FIGURE 13.9 ■ The Reorder Point (ROP) Curve

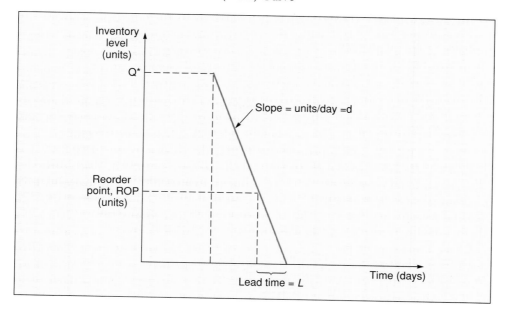

Reorder point (ROP)

The **reorder point (ROP)** is given as:

$$\text{ROP} = (\text{demand per day})(\text{lead time for a new order in days}) \qquad (13.6)$$
$$= d \times L$$

This equation for ROP *assumes that demand is uniform and constant.* When this is not the case, extra stock, often called **safety stock**, should be added.

Safety stock

The demand per day, d, is found by dividing the annual demand, D, by the number of working days in a year:

$$d = \frac{D}{\text{number of working days in a year}}$$

Computing the reorder point is demonstrated in Example 7.

EXAMPLE 7

Electronic Assembler, Inc., has a demand for TX512 VCRs of 8,000 per year. The firm operates a 200-day working year. On the average, delivery of an order takes 3 working days. We calculate the reorder point as follows:

$$d = \text{daily demand} = \frac{D}{\text{number of working days}} = \frac{8,000}{200}$$

$$= 40$$

$$\text{ROP} = \text{reorder point} = d \times L = 40 \text{ units/day} \times 3 \text{ days}$$

$$= 120 \text{ units}$$

Hence, when the inventory stock drops to 120, an order should be placed. The order will arrive 3 days later, just as the firm's stock is depleted.

Production Order Quantity Model

In the previous inventory model, we assumed that the entire inventory order was received at one time. There are times, however, when the firm may receive its inventory over a period of time. Such cases require a different model. This model applies when inventory continuously flows or builds up over a period of time after an order has been placed or when units are produced and sold simultaneously. Under these circumstances, we take into account the daily production (or inventory flow) rate and the daily demand rate. Figure 13.10 shows inventory levels as a function of time.

Production order quantity model

Because this model is especially suitable for the production environment, it is commonly called the **production order quantity model**. It is useful when inventory continuously builds up over time, but the other economic order quantity assumptions are valid. We derive this model by setting ordering or setup costs equal to holding costs and solving for $Q^{\star}$. Using the following symbols, we can determine the expression for annual inventory holding cost for the production run model:

$$Q = \text{number of pieces per order}$$
$$H = \text{holding cost per unit per year}$$
$$p = \text{daily production rate}$$

FIGURE 13.10 ■ Change in Inventory Levels over Time for the Production Model

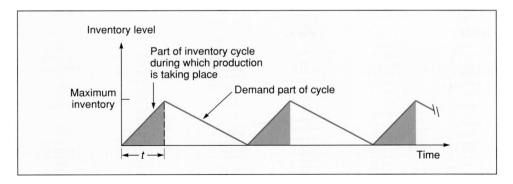

d = daily demand rate, or usage rate

t = length of the production run in days

1. $\left(\begin{array}{c}\text{Annual inventory}\\\text{holding cost}\end{array}\right)$ = (average inventory level) $\times \left(\begin{array}{c}\text{holding cost}\\\text{per unit per year}\end{array}\right)$

$\qquad$ = (average inventory level) $\times H$

2. $\left(\begin{array}{c}\text{Average inventory}\\\text{level}\end{array}\right)$ = (maximum inventory level)/2

3. $\left(\begin{array}{c}\text{Maximum}\\\text{inventory level}\end{array}\right) = \left(\begin{array}{c}\text{total produced during}\\\text{the production run}\end{array}\right) - \left(\begin{array}{c}\text{total used during}\\\text{the production run}\end{array}\right)$

$\qquad$ = $pt - dt$

But Q = total produced = pt, and thus $t = Q/p$. Therefore,

$$\text{Maximum inventory level} = p\left(\frac{Q}{p}\right) - d\left(\frac{Q}{p}\right)$$

$$= Q - \frac{d}{p}Q$$

$$= Q\left(1 - \frac{d}{p}\right)$$

4. Annual inventory holding cost (or simply holding cost)

$$= \frac{\text{maximum inventory level}}{2}(H) = \frac{Q}{2}\left[1 - \left(\frac{d}{p}\right)\right]H$$

Using the expression for holding cost above and the expression for setup cost developed in the basic EOQ model, we solve for the optimal number of pieces per order by equating setup cost and holding cost:

$$\text{Setup cost} = (D/Q)S$$

$$\text{Holding cost} = \frac{1}{2}\,HQ\,[1 - (d/p)]$$

Set ordering cost equal to holding cost to obtain $Q^\star$:

$$\frac{D}{Q}S = \tfrac{1}{2}HQ\,[1 - (d/p)]$$

$$Q^2 = \frac{2DS}{H\,[1 - (d/p)]}$$

$$Q_p^\star = \sqrt{\frac{2DS}{H[1 - (d/p)]}} \qquad (13.7)$$

Example 8 shows how to use the above equation, $Q_p^\star$, to solve for the optimum order or production quantity when inventory is consumed as it is produced.

EXAMPLE 8

Nathan Manufacturing, Inc., makes and sells specialty hubcaps for the retail automobile aftermarket. Nathan's forecast for its wire-wheel hubcap is 1,000 units next year, with an average daily demand of 6 units. However, the production process is most efficient at 8 units per day. So the company produces 8 per day but uses only 6 per day. Given the following values, solve for the optimum number of units per order.

$$\text{Annual demand} = D = 1{,}000 \text{ units}$$
$$\text{Setup cost} = S = \$10$$
$$\text{Holding cost} = H = \$0.50 \text{ per unit per year}$$
$$\text{Daily production rate} = p = 8 \text{ units daily}$$
$$\text{Daily demand rate} = d = 6 \text{ units daily}$$

1. $$Q_p^\star = \sqrt{\frac{2DS}{H[1 - (d/p)]}}$$

2. $$Q_p^\star = \sqrt{\frac{2(1{,}000)(10)}{0.50[1 - (6/8)]}}$$

$$= \sqrt{\frac{20{,}000}{0.50(1/4)}} = \sqrt{160{,}000}$$

$$= 400 \text{ hubcaps}$$

Also note that we can compute daily demand:

$$d = \frac{D}{\text{number of days the plant is open}}$$

and

$$\text{Number of days the plant is open} = \frac{D}{d}$$

Therefore, Nathan Manufacturing, Inc., in Example 8, is open only 167 days each year because

$$\text{Number of days the plant is open} = \frac{1{,}000}{6} = 167$$

You may want to compare the solution in Example 8 with the answer in Example 3. Eliminating the instantaneous receipt assumption, where $p = 8$ and $d = 6$, has resulted in an increase in $Q^\star$ from 200 in Example 3 to 400 in Example 8.

We can also calculate $Q_p^\star$ when annual data are available. When annual data are used, we can express $Q_p^\star$ as

$$Q_p^\star = \sqrt{\frac{2DS}{H[1 - (D/P)]}} \tag{13.8}$$

where D = annual demand rate
$\quad P$ = annual production rate

Quantity Discount Models

Quantity discount

To increase sales, many companies offer quantity discounts to their customers. A **quantity discount** is simply a reduced price (P) for the item when it is purchased in larger quantities. It is not uncommon to have a discount schedule with several discounts for large orders. A typical quantity discount schedule appears in Table 13.2.

As can be seen in the table, the normal price of the item is $5. When 1,000 to 1,999 units are ordered at one time, then the price per unit drops to $4.80; and when the quantity ordered at one time is 2,000 units or more, the price is $4.75 per unit. As always, management must decide when and how much to order. But with quantity discounts, how does the operations manager make these decisions?

As with other inventory models discussed so far, the overall objective will be to minimize the total cost. Because the unit cost for the third discount in Table 13.2 is the lowest, you might be tempted to order 2,000 units or more to take advantage of the lower product cost. Placing an order for that quantity with the greatest discount price, however, might not minimize the total inventory cost. As the discount quantity goes up, the product cost goes down, but the holding cost increases because the orders are large. Thus, the major trade-off when considering quantity discounts is between the reduced product cost and the increased holding cost. When we include the cost of the product, the equation for the total annual inventory cost becomes

$$\text{Total cost} = \text{setup cost} + \text{holding cost} + \text{product cost}$$

or

$$Total\ Cost = \frac{D}{Q}S + \frac{QH}{2} + PD \tag{13.9}$$

where D = annual demand in units
$\quad S$ = ordering or setup cost per order or per setup
$\quad P$ = price per unit
$\quad H$ = holding cost per unit per year

TABLE 13.2 ■ A QUANTITY DISCOUNT SCHEDULE

DISCOUNT NUMBER	DISCOUNT QUANTITY	DISCOUNT (%)	DISCOUNT PRICE (P)
1	0 to 999	0	$5.00
2	1,000 to 1,999	4	$4.80
3	2,000 and over	5	$4.75

Now, we have to determine the quantity that will minimize the total annual inventory cost. Because there are several discounts, this process involves four steps:

1. For each discount, calculate a value for $Q^\star$, using the following equation:

$$Q^\star = \sqrt{\frac{2DS}{IP}} \qquad (13.10)$$

You should note that the holding cost is IP instead of H. Because the price of the item is a factor in annual holding cost, we cannot assume that the holding cost is a constant when the price per unit changes for each quantity discount. Thus, it is common to express the holding cost (I) as a percentage of unit price (P) instead of as a constant cost per unit per year (H).

2. For any discount, if the order quantity is too low to qualify for the discount, adjust the order quantity upward to the lowest quantity that will qualify for the discount. For example, if $Q^\star$ for discount 2 in Table 13.2 were 500 units, you would adjust this value up to 1,000 units. Order quantities between 1,000 and 1,999 will qualify for the 4% discount.

The reasoning for step 2 may not be obvious. If the order quantity is below the quantity range that will qualify for a discount, a quantity within this range may still result in the lowest total cost.

As shown in Figure 13.11, the total cost curve is broken into three different total cost curves. There is a total cost curve for the first ($0 \le Q \le 999$), second ($1,000 \le Q \le 1,999$), and third ($2,000 \le Q$) discount. Look at the total cost curve for discount 2. $Q^\star$ for discount 2 is less than the allowable discount range, which is from 1,000 to 1,999 units. As the figure shows, the lowest allowable quantity in this range, which is 1,000 units, is the quantity that minimizes the total cost. Thus, the second step is needed to ensure that we do not discard an order quantity that may indeed produce the minimum cost. Note that an

FIGURE 13.11   ■   Total Cost Curve for the Quantity Discount Model

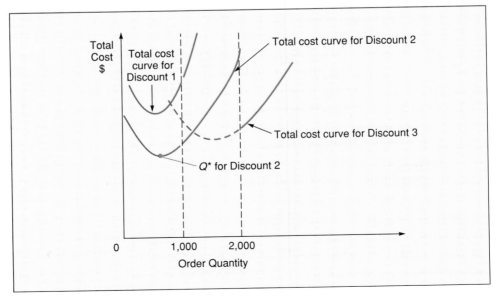

order quantity computed in step 1 that is greater than the range that would qualify it for a discount may be discarded.

3. Using the previous total cost equation, compute a total cost for every $Q^\star$ determined in steps 1 and 2. If you had to adjust $Q^\star$ upward because it was below the allowable quantity range, make sure to use the adjusted value for $Q^\star$.

4. Select that $Q^\star$ that has the lowest total cost as computed in step 3. It will be the quantity that will minimize the total inventory cost.

Example 9 shows how to apply this model.

EXAMPLE 9

Wohl's Discount Store stocks Cool Wheels cars. Recently, they have been given a quantity discount schedule for the cars. This quantity schedule was shown in Table 13.2. Thus, the normal cost for the Cool Wheels cars is $5. For orders between 1,000 and 1,999 units, the unit cost is $4.80; and for orders of 2,000 or more units, the unit cost is $4.75. Furthermore, the ordering cost is $49 per order, the annual demand is 5,000 Cool Wheels cars, and the inventory carrying charge as a percentage of cost, I, is 20% or .2. What order quantity will minimize the total inventory cost?

The first step is to compute $Q^\star$ for every discount in Table 13.2. This is done as follows:

$$Q_1^\star = \sqrt{\frac{2(5,000)(49)}{(.2)(5.00)}} = 700 \text{ cars/order}$$

$$Q_2^\star = \sqrt{\frac{2(5,000)(49)}{(.2)(4.80)}} = 714 \text{ cars/order}$$

$$Q_3^\star = \sqrt{\frac{2(5,000)(49)}{(.2)(4.75)}} = 718 \text{ cars/order}$$

The second step is to adjust upward those values of $Q^\star$ that are below the allowable discount range. Because $Q_1^\star$ is between 0 and 999, it does not have to be adjusted. $Q_2^\star$ is below the allowable range of 1,000 to 1,999, and therefore, it must be adjusted to 1,000 units. The same is true for $Q_3^\star$. It must be adjusted to 2,000 units. After this step, the following order quantities must be tested in the total cost equation:

$$Q_1^\star = 700$$

$$Q_2^\star = 1,000 - \text{adjusted}$$

$$Q_3^\star = 2,000 - \text{adjusted}$$

The third step is to use the total cost equation and compute a total cost for each of the order quantities. This is accomplished with the aid of Table 13.3.

The fourth step is to select that order quantity with the lowest total cost. Looking at Table 13.3, you can see that an order quantity of 1,000 Cool Wheels cars will minimize the total cost. It should be recognized, however, that the total cost for ordering 2,000 cars is only slightly greater than the total cost for ordering 1,000 cars. Thus, if the third discount cost is lowered to $4.65, for example, then this order quantity might be the one that minimizes the total inventory cost.

TABLE 13.3 ■ TOTAL COST COMPUTATIONS FOR WOHL'S DISCOUNT STORE

DISCOUNT NUMBER	UNIT PRICE	ORDER QUANTITY	ANNUAL PRODUCT COST	ANNUAL ORDERING COST	ANNUAL HOLDING COST	TOTAL
1	$5.00	700	$25,000	$350	$350	$25,700
2	$4.80	1,000	$24,000	$245	$480	$24,725
3	$4.75	2,000	$23,750	$122.5	$950	$24,822.5

PROBABILISTIC MODELS WITH CONSTANT LEAD TIME

Probabilistic models

All of the inventory models we have discussed so far make the assumption that the demand for a product is constant and uniform. We now relax this assumption. The following inventory models, known as **probabilistic models**, apply *when product demand is not constant* but can be specified by a probability distribution.

Service level

An important concern of management is maintaining an adequate service level in the face of uncertain demand. The **service level** is the complement of the probability of a stockout. For instance, if the probability of a stockout is .05, then the service level is .95. Uncertain demand raises the possibility of a stockout. One method of reducing stockouts is to hold extra units in inventory to avoid this possibility. Such inventory is usually referred to as *safety stock* and is added as a buffer to the reorder point. As you recall from our previous discussion:

$$\text{Reorder point} = \text{ROP} = d \times L$$
$$d = \text{daily demand}$$
$$L = \text{order lead time, or number of working days}$$
$$\text{it takes to deliver an order}$$

The inclusion of safety stock changes the expression to

$$\text{ROP} = d \times L + \text{safety stock} \tag{13.11}$$

The amount of safety stock depends on the cost of incurring a stockout and the cost of holding the extra inventory. Example 10 shows how this is done for David Rivera Optical.

EXAMPLE 10

David Rivera Optical has determined that its reorder point for eyeglass frames is 50 ($d \times L$) units. Its carrying cost per frame per year is $5, and stockout cost is $40 per frame. The optical store has experienced the following probability distribution for inventory demand during the reorder period. The optimum number of orders per year is six.

	NUMBER OF UNITS	PROBABILITY
	30	.2
	40	.2
ROP→	50	.3
	60	.2
	70	.1
		1.0

How much safety stock should David Rivera Optical keep on hand?

The objective is to find the safety stock that minimizes the total additional inventory holding costs and stockout costs on an annual basis. The annual holding cost is simply the holding cost multiplied by the units added to the ROP. For example, a safety stock of 20 frames, which implies that the new ROP, with safety stock, is 70 (= 50 + 20) raises the annual carrying cost by $5(20) = $100.

The stockout cost is more difficult to compute. For any level of safety stock, the stockout cost is the expected cost of stocking out. We can compute it by multiplying the number of frames short by the probability by the stockout cost by the number of times per year the stockout can occur (or the number of orders per year). Then we add stockout costs for each possible stockout level for a given ROP. For zero safety stock, a shortage of 10 frames will occur if demand is 60, and a shortage of 20 frames will occur if the demand is 70. Thus the stockout costs for zero safety stock are

$$(10 \text{ frames short})(.2)(\$40/\text{stockout})(6 \text{ possible stockouts per year})$$
$$+ (20 \text{ frames short})(.1)(\$40)(6) = \$960$$

The following table summarizes the total costs for each alternative.

SAFETY STOCK	ADDITIONAL HOLDING COST	STOCKOUT COST		TOTAL COST
20	(20)($5) = $100	$0		$100
10	(10)($5) = $50	(10)(.1)($40)(6)	= $240	$290
0	$0	(10)(.2)($40)(6) + (20)(.1)($40)(6) = $960		$960

The safety stock with the lowest total cost is 20 frames. This safety stock changes

When it is difficult or impossible to determine the cost of being out of stock, a manager may decide to follow a policy of keeping enough safety stock on hand to meet a prescribed customer service level. For instance, Figure 13.12 shows the use of safety stock when demand is probabilistic. We see that the safety stock in Figure 13.12 is 16.5, and the reorder point is also increased by 16.5.

The manager may want to define the service level as meeting 95% of the demand (or conversely having stockouts only 5% of the time). Assuming that demand during lead time (the reorder period) follows a normal curve, only the mean and

FIGURE 13.12   ■   Probabilistic Demand

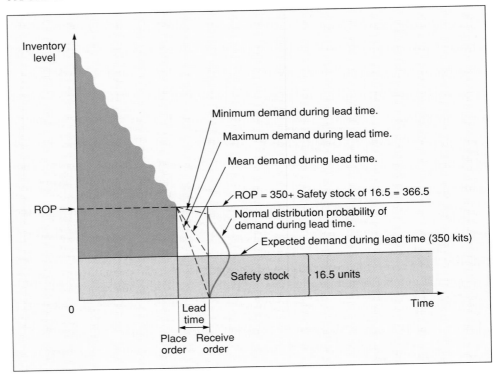

standard deviation are needed to define the inventory requirements for any given service level. Sales data are usually adequate for computing the mean and standard deviation. In the following example we use a normal curve with a known mean (μ) and standard deviation (σ) to determine the safety stock necessary for a 95% service level.

EXAMPLE 11

Memphis's Regional Hospital stocks a "code blue" resuscitation kit that has a normally distributed demand during the reorder period. The mean (average) demand during the reorder period is 350 kits, and the standard deviation is 10 kits. Regional Hospital wants to follow a policy that results in stockouts occurring only 5% of the time. How much safety stock should the hospital maintain? The following figure may help you visualize the example:

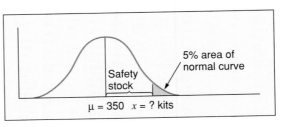

μ = mean demand = 350 kits
σ = standard deviation = 10 kits

or

$$\text{Safety stock} = x - \mu$$

Since

$$Z = \frac{x - \mu}{\sigma}$$

Then

$$\text{Safety stock} = Z\sigma \qquad (13.12)$$

We use the properties of a standardized normal curve to get a Z value for an area under the normal curve of .95 (or $1 - .05$). Using a normal table (see Appendix A), we find a Z value of 1.65 standard deviations from the mean. Also:

$$Z = \frac{x - \mu}{\sigma} = \frac{\text{safety stock}}{\sigma}$$

$$= 1.65 = \frac{\text{safety stock}}{\sigma}$$

Solving for safety stock, as in Equation 13.12, gives

$$\text{Safety stock} = 1.65(10) = 16.5 \text{ kits}$$

This is the situation illustrated in Figure 13.12. The reorder point becomes (350 kits + 16.5 kits of safety stock =) 366.5, or 367 kits.

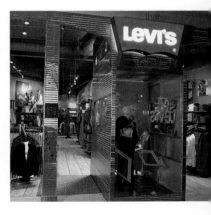

It typically takes this store 4 weeks to get an order for Levis 501 jeans filled by the manufacturer. If the store sells 10 pairs of size 30–32 Levis a week, the store manager could set up two containers, keep 40 pairs of jeans in the second container, and place an order whenever the first container is empty. This would be a fixed-point reordering system. It is also called a "two-bin" system and is an example of a very elementary, but effective, inventory approach.

Fixed-period system

FIXED-PERIOD SYSTEMS

The inventory models we have considered so far in this chapter all fall into a class called *fixed-quantity systems*. That is to say, the same fixed amount is added to inventory every time an order for an item is placed. We saw that orders are event-triggered with the event triggering a reorder point occurring any time.

In a **fixed-period system**, however, inventory is ordered at the end of a given period. Then, and only then, on-hand inventory is counted. Only the amount necessary to bring total inventory up to a prespecified target level is ordered. Figure 13.13 illustrates this concept.

The advantage of the fixed-period system is that there is no physical count of inventory items after an item is withdrawn—this occurs only when the time for the next review comes up. This procedure is also convenient administratively, especially if inventory control is only one of several duties of an employee.

FIGURE 13.13 ■ Inventory Level in a Fixed-Period System. Various amounts are ordered based on the quantity necessary to bring inventory up to the target maximum.

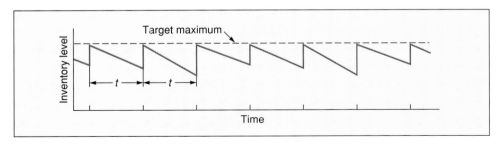

A fixed-period system is appropriate when vendors make routine (that is, at a fixed time interval) visits to customers to take fresh orders or when purchasers want to combine orders to save ordering and transportation costs (therefore, they will have the same review period for similar inventory items).

The disadvantage of this system is that since there is no tally of inventory during the time between reviews, there is the possibility of a stockout during this time. This scenario is possible if a large purchase draws the inventory level down to zero right after an order is placed. Therefore, a higher level of safety stock (as compared to a fixed-quantity system) needs to be maintained to provide protection against stockout both during the time between reviews and the lead time.

MARGINAL ANALYSIS

Marginal analysis

For many inventory models, the optimal stocking policy can be determined through **marginal analysis**, which takes into account marginal profit (MP) and marginal loss (ML). Given any inventory level, we would add an additional unit to the inventory level only if its expected marginal profit equals or exceeds its expected marginal loss. This relationship is expressed symbolically in what follows: First, we let

$$\hat{p} = \text{probability that demand will be greater than or equal}$$
$$\text{to a given supply (or the probability of selling at } \textit{least}$$
$$\text{one additional unit)}$$

$$1 - \hat{p} = \text{probability that demand will be less than supply}$$

The expected marginal profit is then found by multiplying the probability that a given unit will be sold by the marginal profit, $\hat{p}(\text{MP})$. Likewise, the expected marginal loss is the probability of not selling the unit multiplied by the marginal loss, or $(1 - \hat{p})(\text{ML})$. The decision rule is

$$\hat{p}(\text{MP}) \geq (1 - \hat{p})(\text{ML})$$

With some basic mathematical manipulations, we can determine the level of p that will help solve inventory problems:

$$\hat{p}(\text{MP}) \geq \text{ML} - \hat{p}(\text{ML})$$

or

$$\hat{p}(\text{MP}) + \hat{p}(\text{ML}) \geq \text{ML}$$

or

$$\hat{p}(\text{MP} + \text{ML}) \geq \text{ML}$$

or

$$\hat{p} \geq \frac{\text{ML}}{\text{MP} + \text{ML}} \tag{13.13}$$

We can use this relationship to solve inventory problems directly. This type of analysis is especially good for one-time inventory decisions when reordering and back-ordering are not possible. We present the use of marginal analysis in Example 12. Note that we have added three possible demands (5, 6, and 7 units, with probabilities of .2, .3, and .5, respectively). As long as the cumulative probability exceeds p, we keep stocking additional units.

EXAMPLE 12

Cases of paper towel rolls sell at Price-Mart for $6 each. The cost per case is $3, and unsold cases may be returned to the supplier, who will refund the cost for each case returned minus $1 per case for handling and storage. The probability distribution of demand is as follows:

DEMAND	PROBABILITY THAT DEMAND WILL BE AT THIS LEVEL
5	.2
6	.3
7	.5

1. From the previously developed relationship (Equation 13.13), we know that:

$$\hat{p} \geq \frac{ML}{MP + ML} \tag{13.13}$$

2. The next step is to determine $\hat{p}$. As you recall, $\hat{p}$ is the probability that demand will be at this level or greater. We can compute this *cumulative* probability as follows:

DEMAND	PROBABILITY THAT DEMAND WILL BE AT THIS LEVEL	(CUMULATIVE) PROBABILITY THAT DEMAND WILL BE AT THIS LEVEL OR GREATER
5	.2	$1.0 \geq 0.25$
6	.3	$.8 \geq 0.25$
7	.5	$.5 \geq 0.25$

$$ML = \text{marginal loss} = \$1$$
$$MP = \text{marginal profit} = \$6 - \$3 = \$3$$

Thus,

$$\hat{p} \geq \frac{1}{3+1} \geq .25$$

3. We keep adding additional cases as long as the $\hat{p} \geq ML/(MP + ML)$ relationship holds. If we stock 7 cases, our marginal profit will be greater than our marginal loss:

$$\hat{p} \text{ at 7 cases} \geq \frac{ML}{MP + ML}$$

Thus, the optimal policy is to stock 7 cases of paper towels.

ACHIEVING WORLD-CLASS STANDARDS

World-class firms *manage* their inventory. These firms know how much to order and when to place the order. They reduce inventory by driving down lot sizes. Inventories are not sitting and gathering dust. *Just-in-case* inventory does not exist. Material is moving or being worked on. JIT systems are commonplace, as are Kanban systems that pull material through the plant.

World-class organizations are also reducing inventory by developing computer information systems with increasingly accurate forecasts, or they have moved to short order cycles that allow them to produce to order. Incoming inventory is driven down, quality goes up, and cycle counting yields record accuracy. Orders can be filled faster so work-in-progress inventories are also reduced. The result of reduced inventory is less money tied up, increased quality, and, at the same time, increased responsiveness to customers. In world-class firms, "lean inventory" becomes a competitive advantage.

SUMMARY

Inventory represents a major investment for most firms. This investment is often larger than it should be because firms find it easier to have "just-in-case" inventory rather than "just-in-time" inventory. Inventories are of four types:

1. raw material and purchased components;
2. work-in-process;
3. maintenance, repair, and operating (MRO); and
4. finished goods.

In this chapter, we discussed independent inventory, ABC analysis, record accuracy, JIT, inventory costs, and inventory models used to control independent inventories. We presented the EOQ model, the production run model, the quantity discount model, the probabilistic model, the fixed-period system, and marginal analysis. The formulas for the inventory models presented in this chapter are summarized in Table 13.4.

KEY TERMS

Inventory (p. 574)
Raw materials inventories (p. 575)
Work-in-process (WIP) inventories (p. 575)
MRO (p. 575)
Finished goods inventory (p. 575)
ABC analysis (p. 575)
Cycle counting (p. 578)
Just-in-time inventory (p. 579)
Kanban (p. 581)
Holding costs (p. 583)
Ordering cost (p. 583)
Setup cost (p. 583)

Setup time (p. 585)
Robust (p. 590)
Lead time (p. 591)
Reorder point (ROP) (p. 592)
Safety stock (p. 592)
Production order quantity model (p. 592)
Quantity discount (p. 595)
Probabilistic models (p. 598)
Service level (p. 598)
Fixed-period system (p. 601)
Marginal analysis (p. 602)

TABLE 13.4 ■ STATISTICAL MODELS FOR INDEPENDENT DEMAND SUMMARIZED

Q = number of pieces per order

$Q^{\star}$ = EOQ = optimal order quantity

ROP = reorder point

D = annual demand in units

S = setup or ordering cost for each order

H = holding or carrying cost per unit per year in dollars

p = daily production rate

d = daily demand rate

t = length of production run in days

P = price

I = annual inventory carrying cost as a percentage of price

$\hat{p}$ = probability

MP = marginal profit

ML = marginal loss

μ = mean demand

σ = standard deviation

x = mean demand + safety stock

Z = standardized value under the normal curve

EOQ basic model

$$Q^{\star} = \sqrt{\frac{2DS}{H}} \tag{13.1}$$

Production run EOQ model

$$Q^{\star} = \sqrt{\frac{2DS}{H[1 - (d/p)]}} \tag{13.7}$$

Total cost

$$\text{total cost} = \text{setup cost} + \text{holding cost} + \text{product cost} = \frac{D}{Q}S + \frac{QH}{2} + PD \tag{13.9}$$

Quantity discount EOQ model

$$Q^{\star} = \sqrt{\frac{2DS}{IP}} \tag{13.10}$$

Probability model

$$\text{Safety stock} = Z\sigma \tag{13.12}$$

Marginal analysis

$$\hat{p} \geqslant \frac{ML}{MP + ML} \tag{13.13}$$

Solving Examples 8 and 9 with AB:POM

All three of the EOQ family of models presented in this chapter can be solved by AB:POM. We illustrate the production run model using the data from Example 8 in Program 13.1. The data we entered are on the left-hand side, and the computed output on the right.

Program 13.2 provides a second illustration of AB:POM, this time on the quantity discount data for Example 9.

PROGRAM 13.1 ■ AB:POM's Production Run Module. Note that Holding Cost (H) may be entered in dollars or as a percentage of the price of the item (by typing the percentage with the % sign). *Holding cost (H)* and *demand rate (D)* must both be in the same time unit, that is, either daily, annual, etc.

Days per year will vary depending on the *daily demand rate (d)*. If the *production rate (p)* and *daily demand rate (d)* are entered, then the *days per year* entry will be automatically computed and default to the appropriate value. If the *production rate (p)* is in days, but the *demand rate (D)* entry is annual, *days per year* must be entered.

Example 8

Production order quantity model

Model			
Demand Rate (D)	1000.00	Optimal order quantity (Q*)	400.00
Setup costs (S)	10.00	Maximum inventory level (Imax)	100.00
Holding costs (H)	0.50		
Production Rate (p)	8.00	Inventory $$ (Hold, Setup, Short)	$50.00
Days per year	166.6667	Unit costs (pD)	$1,000.00
or			
Daily demand rate (d)	6.00	Total cost	$1,050.00
Unit cost	1.00		

PROGRAM 13.2 ■ AB:POM's Quantity Discount Module. Starting and ending values for each price range must be input. The input is shown on the left of Program 13.2 and the answers on the right.

Wohl's Discount Store
EOQ with quantity discount

Model			
Demand Rate (D)	5000.00	Optimal order quantity (Q*)	1000.00
Setup cost (S)	49.00	Maximum inventory level (Imax)	1000.00
Holding cost (H)			
Price Ranges	20.00%	Inventory $$ (Hold, Setup, Short)	$725.00

From	To	Price	Unit costs (PD)	$24,000.00
1	999	5.00	Total Cost	$24,725.00
1000	1999	4.80		
2000	999999	4.75		

Using a Spreadsheet to Solve Examples 3 and 4

EOQ calculations can be easily determined using a spreadsheet, as seen in Program 13.3. The input data, from Examples 3 and 4, appear in cells B5 through B7 of this "symbolic" spreadsheet. The formulas representing output are in cells B11 through B13. The formula in B11, @SQRT (2 * B7 * B5/B6), for example, represents the economic order quantity.

PROGRAM 13.3 ■ Using a Spreadsheet to Solve the EOQ Model in Examples 3 and 4.

	A	B
1	Squirt Inc. Example-EOQ	
2		
3	Inventory Input Data	
4		
5	Ordering Cost	10
6	Carrying Cost	0.5
7	Annual Demand	1000
8		
9	Inventory Output Results	
10		
11	EOQ in Units (Q★)	@SQRT (2*B7*B5/B6)
12	Optimal Number of Orders/Year (N)	+B7/B11
13	Expected Time between Orders (T)	250/B12

SOLVED PROBLEMS

Solved Problem 13.1

Eric Severson's FAX manufacturing firm purchases 8,000 modems each year for use in the faxes it produces. The unit cost of each modem is $10, and the cost of carrying 1 modem in inventory for a year is $3. Ordering cost is $30 per order.

What are the optimal order quantity, the expected number of orders placed each year, and the expected time between orders? Assume that Severson operates a 200-day working year.

Solution

$$Q^\star = \sqrt{\frac{2DS}{H}} = \sqrt{\frac{2(8,000)(30)}{3}} = 400 \text{ modems}$$

$$N = \frac{D}{Q^\star} = \frac{8,000}{400} = 20 \text{ orders}$$

$$\text{Time between orders} = T = \frac{\text{no. working days}}{N} = \frac{200}{20} = 10 \text{ working days}$$

Hence, an order for 400 modems is placed every 10 days. Presumably, then, 20 orders are placed each year.

Solved Problem 13.2

Annual demand for the notebook binders at McClellan's Stationery Shop is 10,000 units. Jill McClellan operates her business 300 days per year and finds that deliveries from her supplier generally take 5 working days. Calculate the reorder point for the notebook binders that she stocks.

Solution

$$d = \frac{10,000}{300} = 33.3 \text{ units/day}$$

$$\text{ROP} = d \times L = (33.3 \text{ units/day})(5 \text{ days}) = 166.7 \text{ units}$$

Thus, Jill should reorder when her stock of notebook binders reaches 167.

Solved Problem 13.3

Joe Murray, Inc., a supplier to schools, has an annual demand rate of 1,000 blackboards but can produce at an average annual production rate of 2,000 blackboards. Setup cost is $10 and carrying cost is $1.00. What is the optimal number of blackboards to be produced each time?

Solution

$$Q^{\star} = \sqrt{\frac{2DS}{H[1 - (D/P)]}}$$

$$= \sqrt{\frac{2(1,000)(10)}{1[1 - (1,000/2,000)]}} = \sqrt{\frac{20,000}{1/2}} = \sqrt{40,000}$$

$$= 200 \text{ blackboards}$$

Solved Problem 13.4

What safety stock should Leslie Oliver Corporation maintain if mean sales are 80 during the reorder period, the standard deviation is 7, and Oliver can tolerate stockouts 10% of the time?

Solution

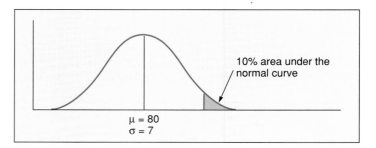

From Appendix A, Z at an area of .9 (or $1 - .10$) = 1.28

$$Z = 1.28 = \frac{x - \mu}{\sigma} = \frac{\text{safety stock}}{\sigma}$$

$$\text{Safety stock} = 1.28\sigma$$

$$= 1.28(7) = 8.96 \text{ units, or 9 units}$$

1. What are the main reasons that an organization has inventory?

2. Describe each of the four types of inventory.

3. Describe the costs that are associated with ordering and maintaining inventory.

4. With the advent of low-cost computing, do you see alternatives to the popular ABC classifications?

5. What is cycle counting and what are its benefits?

6. What is a Kanban?

7. How is a Kanban used?

8. What is the difference between the standard EOQ model and the production inventory model?

9. What are the assumptions of the EOQ model?

10. How sensitive is EOQ to variations in demand or costs?

11. Does the production model or the standard EOQ model yield a higher EOQ if setup costs and holding costs are the same? Why?

12. When is a good time for cycle counting personnel to proceed with auditing a particular item?

13. What impact does a decrease in setup time have on EOQ?

14. What is meant by service level?

15. How would a firm go about determining a service level?

16. What happens to total inventory costs (and EOQ) if inventory holding costs per unit increase (that is, increase at an increasing rate) as inventory increases?

17. What happens to total inventory costs (and EOQ) if there is a fixed cost associated with inventory holding costs (for example, leasing the warehouse)?

18. Describe the difference between a fixed-quantity and a fixed-period inventory system.

Wayne Hills Hospital, in tiny Wayne, Nebraska, faces a problem common to large, urban hospitals as well as small, remote ones like itself. That problem is deciding how much of each type of whole blood to keep in stock. Because blood is expensive and has a limited shelf life (up to 5 weeks under 1–6°C refrigeration), Wayne Hills naturally wants to keep its stock as low as possible. Unfortunately, disasters such as a major tornado in 1986 and a train wreck in 1991 illustrated that lives would be lost because not enough blood was available to handle massive needs. The hospital administrator wants to set an 85% service level based on demand over the past decade. Discuss the implications of this decision. What is the hospital's responsibility with regard to stocking lifesaving medicines that have short shelf lives? How would you set the inventory level for a commodity such as blood?

• **13.1** Ramona Sherman's company has compiled the following data on a small set of products:

STOCK KEEPING UNIT (SKU)	ANNUAL DEMAND	UNIT COST	STOCK KEEPING UNIT (SKU)	ANNUAL DEMAND	UNIT COST
A	100	$250	D	200	$150
B	75	$100	E	150	$75
C	50	$50			

Use her data to illustrate an ABC analysis.

· **13.2** Fernandes Enterprise has 10 items in inventory. Dennis Fernandes asks you, the recent P/OM graduate, to divide these items into three ABC classifications. What do you report back to Mr. Fernandes?

Item	Annual Demand	Cost/Unit	Item	Annual Demand	Cost/Unit
A2	3000	$50	F3	500	$ 500
B8	4000	12	G2	300	1,500
C7	1500	45	H2	600	20
D1	6000	10	I5	1750	10
E9	1000	20	J8	2500	5

· **13.3** Angelo Corio opened a new beauty products retail store. There are numerous items in inventory, and Angelo knows that there are costs associated with inventory. However, her time is limited, so she cannot carefully evaluate the inventory policy for all products. Angelo wants to classify the items according to the dollars invested in them. The following table provides information about the 10 items that she carries:

Item Number	Unit Cost	Demand (Units)
E102	$4.00	800
D23	8.00	1200
D27	3.00	700
R02	2.00	1000
R19	8.00	200
S107	6.00	500
S123	1.00	1200
U11	7.00	800
U23	1.00	1500
V75	4.00	1500

Use ABC analysis to classify these items into categories A, B, and C.

· **13.4** It takes approximately 2 weeks (14 days) for an order of steel bolts to arrive once the order has been placed. The demand for the bolts is fairly constant; on the average, the manager has observed that the hardware store sells 500 of these bolts each day. Because the demand is fairly constant, she believes she can avoid stockouts completely if she orders the bolts at the correct time. What is the reorder point?

· **13.5** Lead time for one of your fastest-moving products is 21 days. Demand during this period averages 100 units per day. What would be an appropriate reorder point?

: **13.6** Sande Johnson is attempting to perform an inventory analysis on one of her most popular products. Annual demand for this product is 5,000 units; unit cost is $200; carrying cost is considered to be approximately 25% of the unit price. Order costs for her company typically run nearly $30.00 per order and lead time averages 10 days. (Assume a 50-week year.)

a) What is the economic order quantity?

b) What is the reorder point?

c) What is the total inventory + ordering cost?

d) What is the optimal number of orders per year?

e) What is the optimal number of days between orders (assume 200 working days per year)?

· 13.7 Clarissa Seager is the purchasing agent for Central Valve Company, which sells industrial valves and fluid-control devices. One of its most popular valves is the Western, which has an annual demand of 4,000 units. The cost of each valve is $90.00, and the inventory carrying cost is estimated to be 10% of the cost of each valve. Clarissa has made a study of the costs involved in placing an order for any of the valves that Central Valve stocks, and she has concluded that the average ordering cost is $25.00 per order. Furthermore, it takes about 8 days for an order to arrive from the supplier. During this time, the demand per week for Central's valves is approximately 80.

a) What is the economic order quantity?

b) What is the reorder point?

c) What is the total annual inventory cost (carrying cost + ordering cost)?

d) What is the optimal number of orders per year?

e) What is the optimal number of days between any two orders assuming there are 200 working days per year?

: 13.8 Happy Pet, Inc., is a large pet store located in Long Beach Mall. Although the store specializes in dogs, it also sells fish, turtle, and bird supplies. Everlast Leader, a leather lead for dogs, costs Happy Pet $7.00 each. There is an annual demand for 6,000 Everlast Leaders. The manager of Happy Pet has determined that the ordering cost is $20 per order, and the carrying cost as a percentage of the unit cost is 15%. Happy Pet is now considering a new supplier of Everlast Leaders. Each lead would cost only $6.65; but in order to get this discount, Happy Pet would have to buy shipments of 3,000 Everlast Leaders at a time. Should Happy Pet use the new supplier and take this discount for quantity buying?

· 13.9 Paul Misselwitz uses 1,500 per year of a certain subassembly that has an annual holding cost of $45 per unit. Each order placed costs Paul $150. Paul operates 300 days per year and has found that an order must be placed with his supplier 6 working days before he can expect to receive that order. For this subassembly, find:

a) the economic order quantity   c) the annual ordering cost

b) the annual holding cost   d) the reorder point

: 13.10 Christine Adams, of Adams Plumbing, uses 1,200 of a certain spare part that costs $25 for each order and $24 annual holding cost. Calculate the total cost for order sizes of 25, 40, 50, 60, and 100. Identify the economic order quantity and consider the implications for making an error in calculating the economic order quantity.

· 13.11 Teresa Ryu's Dream Store sells water beds and assorted supplies. The best-selling bed in the store has an annual demand of 400 units. The ordering cost is $40; the holding cost is $5 per unit per year. There are 250 working days per year, and the lead time is 6 days.

a) To minimize the total cost, how many units should be ordered each time an order is placed?

b) If the holding cost per unit were $6 instead of $5, what would the optimal order quantity be?

: 13.12 Jim Spivey's Computer Store in Houston sells a printer for $200. Demand for this is constant during the year, and annual demand is forecasted to be 600 units. The holding cost is $20 per unit per year, and the cost of ordering is $60 per order. Currently, the company is ordering 12 times per year (50 units each time). There are 250 working days per year, and the lead time is 10 days.

     a) Given the current policy of ordering 50 units at a time, what is the total of the annual ordering cost and the annual holding cost?

     b) If the company used the absolute best inventory policy, what would the total of the ordering and holding costs be?

     c) What is the reorder point?

: 13.13 Jim Walsh is the owner of a small company that produces electric knives used to cut fabric. The annual demand is for 8,000 knives, and Jim produces them in batches. On average, Jim can produce 150 per day; during the production process, demand has been about 40 per day. The cost to set up production is $100.00, and it costs Jim $0.80 to carry a knife for 1 year. How many knives should Jim produce in each batch?

: 13.14 John Mayleben, inventory control manager for Cal-Tex, receives wheel bearings from Wheel-Rite, a small producer of metal parts. Wheel-Rite can produce only 500 wheel bearings per day. Cal-Tex receives 10,000 wheel bearings from Wheel-Rite each year. Because Cal-Tex operates 200 working days each year, the average daily demand of wheel bearings by Cal-Tex is 50. The ordering cost for Cal-Tex is $40 per order, and the carrying cost is $0.60 per wheel bearing per year. How many wheel bearings should Cal-Tex order at one time? Wheel-Rite has agreed to ship the maximum number of wheel bearings that it produces each day to Cal-Tex once an order has been received.

: 13.15 McLeavey Manufacturing has a demand for 1,000 pumps each year. The cost of a pump is $50. It costs McLeavey Manufacturing $40 to place an order, and the carrying cost is 25% of the unit cost. If pumps are ordered in quantities of 200, McLeavey Manufacturing can get a 3% discount on the cost of the pumps. Should McLeavey Manufacturing order 200 pumps at a time and take the 3% discount?

: 13.16 Froelich Products offers the following discount schedule for $4' \times 8'$ sheets of plywood:

ORDER	UNIT COST
9 sheets or less	$18.00
10 to 50 sheets	$17.50
More than 50 sheets	$17.25

Home Sweet Home Company orders plywood from Froelich Products. Home Sweet Home has an ordering cost of $45. The carrying cost is 20%, and the annual demand is 100 sheets. What ordering policy do you recommend?

: 13.17 Should the quantity discount be taken, given the following data on a hardware item stocked by the Steven Hazelwood and Sons Paint Store?

$$D = 2{,}000 \text{ units}$$
$$S = \$10$$
$$H = \$1$$
$$P = \$1$$
$$\text{Discount price} = \$.75$$
$$\left(\begin{matrix}\text{Quantity needed to} \\ \text{qualify for discount}\end{matrix}\right) = 2{,}000 \text{ units}$$

: **13.18** The regular price of a tape deck component is $20. On orders of 75 units or more, the price is discounted to $18.50. On orders of 100 units or more, the discount price is $15.75. At present, Sound Business, Inc., a manufacturer of stereo components, has an inventory carrying cost of 5% per unit per year, and its ordering cost is $10. Annual demand is 45 components. What should Sound Business, Inc., do?

: **13.19** A product is ordered once each year, and the reorder point without safety stock $(d \times L)$ is 100 units. Inventory carrying cost is $10 per unit per year, and the cost of a stockout is $50 per unit per year. Given the following demand probabilities during the reorder period, how much safety stock should be carried?

DEMAND DURING REORDER PERIOD		PROBABILITY
	0	.1
	50	.2
ROP→	100	.4
	150	.2
	200	.1
		1.0

: **13.20** For a given product, ML = $4 and MP = $1. What stocking policy would you recommend in regard to the following demand distribution?

DEMAND (IN UNITS)	PROBABILITY THAT DEMAND WILL BE AT THIS LEVEL	DEMAND (IN UNITS)	PROBABILITY THAT DEMAND WILL BE AT THIS LEVEL
0	.05	7	.10
1	.05	8	.05
2	.05	9	.05
3	.1	10	.03
4	.15	11	.02
5	.15		1.00
6	.20		

: **13.21** Carole Horton, Inc., an organization that sells children's art sets, has an ordering cost of $40 for the BB-1 set. The carrying cost for BB-1 is $5 per set per year. In order to meet demand, Carole orders large quantities of BB-1 seven times a year. The stockout cost for BB-1 is estimated to be $50 per set. Over the last several years, Carole has observed the following demand during the lead time for BB-1:

DEMAND DURING LEAD TIME	PROBABILITY	DEMAND DURING LEAD TIME	PROBABILITY
40	.1	70	.2
50	.2	80	.2
60	.2	90	.1
			1.0

The reorder point for BB-1 is 60 units. What level of safety stock should be maintained for BB-1?

▣ **: 13.22** Jon Ahlbrand's company produces a product for which the annual demand is 10,000. Production averages 200 per day, and demand is about 50 per day. Holding costs are $1.00 per unit per year; setup costs $200.00. If you wish to produce this product in batches, what size batch should be used?

: 13.23 For a given product, ML = $5 and MP = $2. What stocking policy would you recommend in regard to the following demand distribution?

DEMAND (IN UNITS)	PROBABILITY THAT DEMAND WILL BE AT THIS LEVEL (P)	PROBABILITY THAT DEMAND WILL BE AT THIS LEVEL OR GREATER (P)
0	.1	1.0
1	.1	.9
2	.2	.8
3	.2	.6
4	.3	.4
5	.1	.1

: 13.24 A product is delivered to Neil Marquardt's company once a year. The reorder point, without safety stock, is 200 units. Carrying cost is $15 per unit per year, and the cost of a stockout is $70 per unit per year. Given the following demand probabilities during the reorder period, how much safety stock should be carried?

DEMAND DURING REORDER PERIOD	PROBABILITY
0	.1
100	.1
200	.2
300	.2
400	.2

: 13.25 Demand during lead time for one brand of TV is normally distributed with a mean of 36 TVs and a standard deviation of 15 TVs. What safety stock should be carried for a 90% service level? What is the appropriate reorder point?

CASE STUDY

Sturdivant Sound Systems

Sturdivant Sound Systems manufactures and sells sound systems for both home and auto. All parts of the sound systems, with the exception of CD players, are produced in the Rochester, New York, plant. CD players used in the assembly of Sturdivant's systems are purchased from Morris Electronics of Concord, New Hampshire.

Mary Kim, purchasing agent for Sturdivant Sound Systems, submits a purchase requisition for the CD players once every 4 weeks. The company's annual requirements total 5,000 units (20 per working day), and the cost per unit is $60. (Sturdivant does not purchase in greater quantities because Morris Electronics, the supplier, does not offer quantity discounts.) Rarely does a shortage of CD players occur because Morris promises delivery within 1 week following receipt of a purchase requisition. (Total time between date of order and date of receipt is 10 days.)

Associated with the purchase of each shipment are procurement costs. These costs, which amount to $20 per order, include the costs of preparing the requisition, inspecting and storing the delivered goods, updating inventory records, and issuing a voucher and a check for payment. In addition to procurement costs, Sturdivant Sound Systems incurs inventory carrying costs that include insurance, storage, handling, taxes, and so forth. These costs equal $6 per unit per year.

Beginning in August of this year, management of Sturdivant Sound Systems will embark on a companywide cost control program in an attempt to improve its profits. One area to be closely scrutinized for possible cost savings is inventory procurement.

DISCUSSION QUESTIONS

1. Compute the optimal order quantity of CD players.
2. Determine the appropriate reorder point (in units).
3. Compute the cost savings that the company will realize if it implements the optimal inventory procurement decision.
4. Should procurement costs be considered a linear function of the number of orders?

Source: Professor Jerry Kinard, Western Carolina University.

CASE STUDY

Martin-Pullin Bicycle Corporation

Martin-Pullin Bicycle Corp. (MPBC), located in Dallas, is a wholesale distributor of bicycles and bicycle parts. Formed in 1981 by cousins Ray Martin and Jim Pullin, the firm's primary retail outlets are located within a 400-mile radius of the distribution center. These retail outlets receive the order from Martin-Pullin within 2 days after notifying the distribution center, provided the stock is available. However, if an order is not fulfilled by the company, then no backorder is placed; the retailers arrange to get their shipment from other distributors, and MPBC loses that amount of business.

The company distributes a wide variety of bicycles. The most popular model, and the major source of revenue to the company, is the AirWing. MPBC receives all the models from a single manufacturer overseas, and shipment takes as long as 4 weeks from the time an order is placed. With the cost of communication, paperwork, and customs clearance included, MPBC estimates that each time an order is placed, it incurs a cost of $65. The purchase price paid by MPBC, per bicycle, is roughly 60% of the suggested retail price for all the styles available, and the inventory carrying cost is 1% per

(Continued)

month (12% per year) of the purchase price paid by MPBC. The retail price (paid by the customers) for the AirWing is $170 per bicycle.

MPBC is interested in making the inventory plan for 1996. The firm wants to maintain a 95% service level with its customers to minimize the losses on the lost orders. The data collected for the last 2 years are summarized in Table 13.5. A forecast for Air Wing model sales in the upcoming year of 1996 has been developed and will be used to make an inventory plan for MPBC.

DISCUSSION QUESTIONS

1. Develop an inventory plan to help MPBC.
2. Discuss reorder points and total costs.
3. How can you address the demand that is not level of the planning horizon?

Source: Professor Kala Chand Seal, Loyola Marymount University.

TABLE 13.5 ■ DEMANDS FOR AirWing Model

	YEAR		
MONTHS	1994	1995	FORECAST FOR 1996
January	6	7	8
February	12	14	15
March	24	27	31
April	46	53	59
May	75	86	97
June	47	54	60
July	30	34	39
August	18	21	24
September	13	15	16
October	12	13	15
November	22	25	28
December	38	42	47
Totals	343	391	439

BIBLIOGRAPHY

Berkley, B. J. "Simulation Tests of FCFS and SPT Sequencing in Kanban Systems." *Decision Sciences*, **24**, 1 (January–February 1993): 218.

Brown, R. G. *Decision Rules for Inventory Management.* New York: Holt, Rinehart and Winston, 1967.

Freeland, J. R., J. P. Leschke, and E. N. Weiss. "Guidelines for Setup-Cost Reduction Programs to Achieve Zero Inventory." *Journal of Operations Management*, 9 (January 1990): 85.

Groenevelt, H., L. Pintelon, and A. Seidmann. "Production Lot Sizing with Machine Breakdowns." *Management Science*, **38**, 1 (January 1992): 104.

Hall, R. *Zero Inventories.* Homewood, IL: Dow Jones-Irwin, 1983.

Inman, R. A., and S. Mehra. "JIT Applications for Service Environments." *Production and Inventory Management Journal*, **32**, 3 (Third Quarter 1991): 16.

Jinchiro, N., and R. Hall. "Management Specs for Stockless Production." *Harvard Business Review*, **63** (May–June 1983): 89–91.

Landvater, D. V. *World Class Production and Inventory Management.* Newburg, NH: Oliver Wight Publications, 1993.

Louis, R. S. *How to Implement Kanban for American Industry.* Cambridge, MA: Productivity Press, 1992.

Schniederjans, M. *Topics in Just-in-Time Management.* Boston: Allyn & Bacon, 1993.

Shingo, S. *A Revolution in Manufacturing: The SMED System.* Cambridge, MA: Productivity Press, 1986.

Vollmann, T. E., W. L. Berry, and D. C. Whybark. *Manufacturing Planning and Control Systems.* Homewood, IL: Irwin, 1988.

Wight, O. W. *Production and Inventory Management in the Computer Age.* Boston: Cahners, 1974.

13 SUPPLEMENT

SIMULATION

A tlanta, July 30, 1996. The mother of all traffic jams. That day, 600,000 spectators, plus 120,000 athletes, judges, coaches, and reporters, will converge on Atlanta for the busiest 24 hours of competition in the 1996 Summer Olympics. Around 1:30 P.M. alone, 90,000 human beings will pour out of baseball and track and field contests. Stir in 2.8 million Atlantans, bake at 95° with 95% humidity, and the recipe is complete for traffic gridlock.

But if autos and buses spend that day moving briskly about, computer simulation models of traffic at the 1996 Olympics, developed by Georgia Tech, will likely earn the city's gratitude.[1] ♦

[1]*Wall Street Journal* (June 2, 1993): B-8.

Simulation models abound in our world. The city of Atlanta looks to them to control traffic. Boeing Aircraft uses them to test the aerodynamics of proposed jets. The U.S. Army simulates war games on computers. Business students use management gaming to simulate realistic business competition. And thousands of organizations develop simulation models to help make operations decisions.

Over half of the large manufacturing companies in the United States are estimated to use simulation models. Table S13.1 lists just a few areas in which simulation is now being applied.

TABLE S13.1 ■ SOME APPLICATIONS OF SIMULATION	
Ambulance location and dispatching	Bus scheduling
Assembly line balancing	Design of library operations
Parking lot and harbor design	Taxi, truck, and railroad dispatching
Distribution system design	Production facility scheduling
Scheduling aircraft	Plant layout
Labor-hiring decisions	Capital investments
Personnel scheduling	Production scheduling
Traffic-light timing	Sales forecasting
Voting pattern prediction	Inventory planning and control

SIMULATION DEFINED

Simulation

Simulation is the attempt to duplicate the features, appearance, and characteristics of a real system. In this supplement, we will show how to simulate part of an operations management system by building a mathematical model that comes as close as possible to representing the reality of the system. The model will then be used to estimate the effects of various actions. The idea behind simulation is (1) to imitate a real-world simulation mathematically, (2) then to study its properties and operating characteristics, and (3) finally to draw conclusions and make action decisions based on the results of the simulation. In this way, a real-life system need not be touched until the advantages and disadvantages of a major policy decision are first measured on the model.

To use simulation, a P/OM manager should:

1. define the problem;
2. introduce the important variables associated with the problem;
3. construct a numerical model;
4. set up possible courses of action for testing;
5. run the experiment;
6. consider the results (possibly modify the model or change data inputs);
7. decide what course of action to take.

These steps are illustrated in Figure S13.1.

The problems tackled by simulation may range from very simple to extremely complex, from bank teller lines to an analysis of the U.S. economy. Although small simulations could be conducted by hand, effective use of this technique requires a computer. Even large-scale models, simulating perhaps years of business decisions, can be handled by computer.

In this supplement, we examine the basic principles of simulation and then tackle some problems in the areas of waiting-line analysis and inventory control. Why do we use simulation in these areas when mathematical models described in other chapters can solve the problems? The answer is that simulation provides an alternative approach for problems that are very complex mathematically. It can handle, for example, inventory problems in which demand or lead time is not constant.

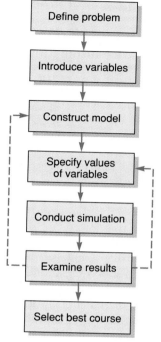

FIGURE S13.1 ■ The Process of Simulation

ADVANTAGES AND DISADVANTAGES OF SIMULATION

Simulation is a tool that has become widely accepted by managers for several reasons. The main *advantages* of simulation are as follows:

1. Simulation is relatively straightforward and flexible.

2. It can be used to analyze large and complex real-world situations that cannot be solved by conventional operations management models.

3. Real-world complications can be included that most P/OM models cannot permit. Simulation can use *any* probability distribution the user defines. It does not require standard distributions.

4. "Time compression" is possible with simulation. The effects of P/OM policies over many months or years can be obtained by computer simulation in a short time.

5. Simulation allows "what-if" types of questions. Managers like to know in advance what options will be most attractive. With a computerized model, a manager can try out several policy decisions within a matter of minutes.

6. Simulations do not interfere with the real-world system. It may be too disruptive, for example, actually to experiment with new policies or ideas in a hospital, manufacturing plant, or the U.S. Postal Service (as seen in the *POM in Action* box).

7. With simulation, we can study the interactive effect of individual components or variables in order to determine which ones are important.

The main *disadvantages* of simulation are as follows:

1. Good simulation models can be very expensive. They may take years to develop.

2. Simulation does not generate optimal solutions to problems as does linear programming. It is a trial-and-error approach that may produce different solutions in repeated runs.

3. Managers must generate all of the conditions and constraints for solutions that they want to examine. The simulation model does not produce answers without adequate, realistic input.

4. Each simulation model is unique. Its solutions and inferences are not usually transferable to other problems.

U.S. Postal Service Plans Its Automation through Simulation

No public agency, perhaps with the exception of the IRS, touches the lives of the American public as closely as the U.S. Postal Service (USPS). For two centuries, the post office has played a key role in the lives of all citizens.

Today, the USPS delivers over 500 million pieces of mail each day, or 166 billion pieces a year, to over 100 million delivery locations. It handles 40% of the world's volume at a unit cost that is the lowest in the world. With approximately 750,000 career employees, it is the nation's largest civilian employer. Faced with both rising mail volumes and escalating costs, USPS is always looking for ways to improve its mail-processing methods.

A major decision facing the Postal Service is automation—how much, what approach, and when. To keep up with increasing demands without adding more highly paid employees, capital investments of $12 billion have been proposed. Before spending that kind of money, USPS developed a huge simulation model called META.

META's job is to examine the impacts of changes in mail processing and delivery operations. Managers input the type and quantity of mail to be processed, the methods (equipment and people) used to sort mail, the flow of mail through the postal network of sorting operations, and unit costs. META models how the entire nationwide mail processing system would function given these inputs, and it produces figures for capacity utilization, total pieces handled, and the work hours and costs required.

Results achieved to date show total annual savings of one million work years of mail carrier labor, which will allow the USPS to maintain its lowest cost status and to continue to keep postage rate increases in the United States lower than inflation.

Sources: Interfaces (January/February 1992): 110–130; and B. Render and R. Stair, *Quantitative Analysis for Management,* 5th ed. (Boston: Allyn and Bacon, 1994): 700.

MONTE CARLO SIMULATION

Monte Carlo method

When a system contains elements that exhibit chance in their behavior, the **Monte Carlo method** of simulation may be applied. The basis of Monte Carlo simulation is experimentation on chance (or *probabilistic*) elements through random sampling.

The technique breaks down into five simple steps:

1. Setting up a probability distribution for important variables.
2. Building a cumulative probability distribution for each variable.
3. Establishing an interval of random numbers for each variable.
4. Generating random numbers.
5. Actually simulating a series of trials.

Let us examine these steps in turn.

Step 1. Establishing Probability Distributions. The basic idea in the Monte Carlo simulation is to generate values for the variables making up the model being studied. There are a lot of variables in real-world systems that are probabilistic in nature and that we might want to simulate. To name just a few:

1. inventory demand on a daily or weekly basis;
2. lead time for inventory orders to arrive;
3. times between machine breakdowns;

Computer simulation models have been developed to address a variety of productivity issues at Burger King. In one, the ideal distance between the drive-through order station and the pickup window was simulated. A longer distance reduced waiting time, and consequently 12 to 13 additional customers could be served per hour, a benefit of over $10,000 in extra sales per restaurant per year. In a second simulation, a second drive-through window was considered. This second window was to be placed in series to the first, rather than in a two-lane configuration. The simulation model predicted a sales increase of 15% during the busiest lunch hours or a sales increase of $13,000 per year per restaurant.

4. times between arrivals at a service facility;
5. service times;
6. times to complete project activities;
7. number of employees absent from work each day.

One common way to establish a *probability distribution* for a given variable is to examine historical outcomes. The probability, or relative frequency, for each possible outcome of a variable is found by dividing the frequency of observation by the total number of observations. Let us consider an example.

The daily demand for radial tires at Barry's Auto Tire over the past 200 days is shown in columns 1 and 2 of Table S13.2. We can convert this demand to a probability distribution (if we assume that past arrival rates will hold in the future) by dividing each demand frequency by the total demand, 200. The result is shown in column 3.

Step 2. Building a Cumulative Probability Distribution for Each Variable. The conversion from a regular probability distribution, such as in column 3 of Table S13.2, to a **cumulative probability distribution** is an easy job. In column 4, we see that the cumulative probability for each level of demand is the sum of the number in the probability column (column 3) added to the previous cumulative probability.

Cumulative probability distribution

Step 3. Setting Random-Number Intervals. Once we have established a cumulative probability distribution for each variable included in the simulation, we must assign a set of numbers to represent each possible value or outcome. These are referred to as **random-number intervals**. Basically, a **random number** is a series of digits

Random-number intervals
Random number

TABLE S13.2 ■ DEMAND FOR BARRY'S AUTO TIRE

(1) DEMAND FOR TIRES	(2) FREQUENCY	(3) PROBABILITY OF OCCURRENCE	(4) CUMULATIVE PROBABILITY
0	10	10/200 = .05	.05
1	20	20/200 = .10	.15
2	40	40/200 = .20	.35
3	60	60/200 = .30	.65
4	40	40/200 = .20	.85
5	30	30/200 = .15	1.00
	200 days	200/200 = 1.00	

(say, two digits from 01, 02, . . . , 98, 99, 00) that have been selected by a totally random process.

If there is a 5% chance that demand for a product (such as Barry's radial tires) will be 0 units per day, then we will want 5% of the random numbers available to correspond to a demand of 0 units. If a total of 100 two-digit numbers is used in the simulation, we could assign a demand of 0 units to the first five random numbers: 01, 02, 03, 04, and 05.[2] Then a simulated demand for 0 units would be created every time one of the numbers 01 to 05 was drawn. If there is also a 10% chance that demand for the same product will be one unit per day, we could let the next 10 random numbers (06, 07, 08, 09, 10, 11, 12, 13, 14, and 15) represent that demand—and so on for other demand levels.

Similarly, we can see in Table S13.3 that the length of each interval on the right corresponds to the probability of one of each of the possible daily demands. Hence, in assigning random numbers to the daily demand for three radial tires, the range of the random-number interval (36 to 65) corresponds *exactly* to the probability (or proportion) of that outcome. A daily demand for three radial tires occurs 30% of the time. Any of the 30 random numbers greater than 35 up to and including 65 are assigned to that event.

Step 4. Generating Random Numbers. Random numbers may be generated for simulation problems in two ways. If the problem is large and the process being studied

TABLE S13.3 ■ THE ASSIGNMENT OF RANDOM-NUMBER INTERVALS FOR BARRY'S AUTO TIRE

DAILY DEMAND	PROBABILITY	CUMULATIVE PROBABILITY	INTERVAL OF RANDOM NUMBERS
0	.05	.05	01 through 05
1	.10	.15	06 through 15
2	.20	.35	16 through 35
3	.30	.65	36 through 65
4	.20	.85	66 through 85
5	.15	1.00	86 through 00

[2]Alternatively, we could have assigned the random numbers 00, 01, 02, 03, and 04 to represent a demand of 0 units. The two digits 00 can be thought of as either 0 or 100. As long as five numbers out of one hundred are assigned to the 0 demand, it does not make any difference which five they are.

involves many simulation trials, computer programs are available to generate the random numbers needed. If the simulation is being done by hand, the numbers may be selected from a table of random digits.

Step 5. Simulating the Experiment. We may simulate outcomes of an experiment by simply selecting random numbers from Table S13.4. Beginning anywhere in the table, we note the interval in Table S13.3 into which each number falls. For example, if the random number chosen is 81 and the interval 66 to 85 represents a daily demand for four tires, then we select a demand of four tires. Example S1 carries the simulation further.

EXAMPLE S1

Let us illustrate the concept further by simulating 10 days of demand for radial tires at Barry's Auto Tire (see Table S13.3). We select the random numbers needed from Table S13.4, starting in the upper left-hand corner and continuing down the first column.

DAY NUMBER	RANDOM NUMBER	SIMULATED DAILY DEMAND
1	52	3
2	37	3
3	82	4
4	69	4
5	98	5
6	96	5
7	33	2
8	50	3
9	88	5
10	90	5

39   Total 10-day demand

39/10 = 3.9 = Tires average daily demand

It is interesting to note that the average demand of 3.9 tires in this 10-day simulation differs significantly from the *expected* daily demand, which we may calculate from the data in Table S13.3:

$$\text{Expected demand} = \sum_{i=1}^{5} (\text{probability of } i \text{ units}) \times (\text{demand of } i \text{ units})$$

$$= (.05)(0) + (.10)(1) + (.20)(2) + (.30)(3) + (.20)(4) + (.15)(5)$$

$$= 0 + .1 + .4 + .9 + .8 + .75$$

$$= 2.95 \text{ tires}$$

However, if this simulation were repeated hundreds or thousands of times, the average *simulated* demand would be nearly the same as the *expected* demand.

In the past, most simulations were done by mathematical experts, who developed long, complex computer printouts. But with graphic displays, simulation can be played out on the screen, step by step, for users to watch. "Animation gives managers confidence in the results," says simulation pioneer and creator of SLAM, Alan B. Pritsker. Such software can make a major contribution to productivity, with the United States being a world leader in developing user-friendly programs in all phases of manufacturing operation.

TABLE S13.4 ■ TABLE OF RANDOM NUMBERS

52	06	50	88	53	30	10	47	99	37	66	91	35	32	00	84	57	07
37	63	28	02	74	35	24	03	29	60	74	85	90	73	59	55	17	60
82	57	68	28	05	94	03	11	27	79	90	87	92	41	09	25	36	77
69	02	36	49	71	99	32	10	75	21	95	90	94	38	97	71	72	49
98	94	90	36	06	78	23	67	89	85	29	21	25	73	69	34	85	76
96	52	62	87	49	56	59	23	78	71	72	90	57	01	98	57	31	95
33	69	27	21	11	60	95	89	68	48	17	89	34	09	93	50	44	51
50	33	50	95	13	44	34	62	64	39	55	29	30	64	49	44	30	16
88	32	18	50	62	57	34	56	62	31	15	40	90	34	51	95	26	14
90	30	36	24	69	82	51	74	30	35	36	85	01	55	92	64	09	85
50	48	61	18	85	23	08	54	17	12	80	69	24	84	92	16	49	59
27	88	21	62	69	64	48	31	12	73	02	68	00	16	16	46	13	85
45	14	46	32	13	49	66	62	74	41	86	98	92	98	84	54	33	40
81	02	01	78	82	74	97	37	45	31	94	99	42	49	27	64	89	42
66	83	14	74	27	76	03	33	11	97	59	81	72	00	64	61	13	52
74	05	81	82	93	09	96	33	52	78	13	06	28	30	94	23	37	39
30	34	87	01	74	11	46	82	59	94	25	34	32	23	17	01	58	73
59	55	72	33	62	13	74	68	22	44	42	09	32	46	71	79	45	89
67	09	80	98	99	25	77	50	03	32	36	63	65	75	94	19	95	88
60	77	46	63	71	69	44	22	03	85	14	48	69	13	30	50	33	24
60	08	19	29	36	72	30	27	50	64	85	72	75	29	87	05	75	01
80	45	86	99	02	34	87	08	86	84	49	76	24	08	01	86	29	11
53	84	49	63	26	65	72	84	85	63	26	02	75	26	92	62	40	67
69	84	12	94	51	36	17	02	15	29	16	52	56	43	26	22	08	62
37	77	13	10	02	18	31	19	32	85	31	94	81	43	31	58	33	51

Source: Reprinted from *A Million Random Digits with 100,000 Normal Deviates,* Rand (New York: Free Press, 1995). Used by permission.

Naturally, it would be risky to draw any hard and fast conclusions regarding the operation of a firm from only a short simulation. It is also unlikely that anyone would actually want to go to the effort of simulating such a simple model containing only one variable. Simulating by hand does, however, demonstrate the important principles involved and may be useful in small-scale studies.

SIMULATION OF A QUEUING PROBLEM

An important use of simulation is in the analysis of waiting-line problems. As mentioned in Chapter 10's supplement, the assumptions required for solving queuing problems are quite restrictive. For most realistic queuing systems, simulation may be the only approach available.

Example S2 illustrates the use of simulation for a large unloading dock and its associated queue. Arrivals of barges at the dock are not Poisson-distributed, and unloading rates (service times) are not exponential or constant. As such, the mathematical waiting-line models of the Chapter 10 Supplement cannot be used.

Fully loaded barges arrive at night in New Orleans following their long trips down the Mississippi River from industrial midwestern cities. The number of barges docking on any given night ranges from 0 to 5. The probability of 0, 1, 2, 3, 4, and 5 arrivals is displayed in Table S13.5. In the same table, we establish cumulative probabilities and corresponding random-number intervals for each possible value.

TABLE S13.5 ■ OVERNIGHT BARGE ARRIVAL RATES AND RANDOM-NUMBER INTERVALS

NUMBER OF ARRIVALS	PROBABILITY	CUMULATIVE PROBABILITY	RANDOM-NUMBER INTERVAL
0	.13	.13	01 through 13
1	.17	.30	14 through 30
2	.15	.45	31 through 45
3	.25	.70	46 through 70
4	.20	.90	71 through 90
5	.10	1.00	91 through 00
	1.00		

A study by the dock superintendent reveals that the number of barges unloaded also tends to vary from day to day. The superintendent provides information from which we can create a probability distribution for the variable *daily unloading rate* (see Table S13.6). As we just did for the arrival variable, we can set up an interval of random numbers for the unloading rates.

TABLE S13.6 ■ UNLOADING RATES AND RANDOM NUMBER INTERVALS

DAILY UNLOADING RATES	PROBABILITY	CUMULATIVE PROBABILITY	RANDOM-NUMBER INTERVAL
1	.05	.05	01 through 05
2	.15	.20	06 through 20
3	.50	.70	21 through 70
4	.20	.90	71 through 90
5	.10	1.00	91 through 00
	1.00		

Barges are unloaded on a first-in, first-out basis. Any barges that are not unloaded the day of arrival must wait until the following day. Tying up a barge in dock is an expensive proposition, and the superintendent cannot ignore the angry phone calls from barge line owners reminding him that "time is money!" He decides that, before going to the Port of New Orlean's controller to request additional unloading crews, a simulation study of arrivals, unloadings, and delays should be conducted. A 100-day simulation would be ideal, but for purposes of illustration, the superintendent begins with a shorter 15-day analysis. Random numbers are drawn from the top row of Table S13.4 to generate daily arrival rates. They are drawn from the second row of Table S13.4 to create daily unloading rates. Table S13.7 shows the day-to-day port simulation.

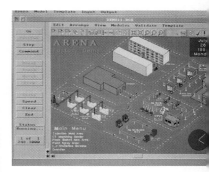

ARENA, a graphical simulation program developed by Systems Modeling Corporation of Sewickley, PA, takes advantage of new object-oriented technology. Virtually any process, from customer service banking to manufacturing assembly lines to material handling systems, can be simulated.

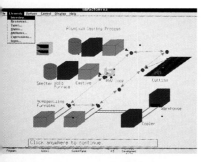

SIMSCRIPT, one of the most widely used special-purpose simulation languages, has graphic capabilities that include animation of the system being simulated. The software permits specialized simulations of such diverse applications as telecommunications systems, factories, and weather movement.

TABLE S13.7 ■ QUEUING SIMULATION OF PORT OF NEW ORLEANS BARGE UNLOADINGS

(1) DAY	(2) NUMBER DELAYED FROM PREVIOUS DAY	(3) RANDOM NUMBER	(4) NUMBER OF NIGHTLY ARRIVALS	(5) TOTAL TO BE UNLOADED	(6) RANDOM NUMBER	(7) NUMBER UNLOADED
1	—[1]	52	3	3	37	3
2	0	06	0	0	63	0[2]
3	0	50	3	3	28	3
4	0	88	4	4	02	1
5	3	53	3	6	74	4
6	2	30	1	3	35	3
7	0	10	0	0	24	0[3]
8	0	47	3	3	03	1
9	2	99	5	7	29	3
10	4	37	2	6	60	3
11	3	66	3	6	74	4
12	2	91	5	7	85	4
13	3	35	2	5	90	4
14	1	32	2	3	73	3[4]
15	0	00	5	5	59	3
	20		41			39
	Total delays		Total arrivals			Total unloadings

1. We can begin with no delays from the previous day. In a long simulation, even if we started with five overnight delays, that initial condition would be averaged out.
2. Three barges *could* have been unloaded on day 2. But because there were no arrivals and no backlog existed, zero unloadings took place.
3. The same situation as noted in footnote 2 takes place.
4. This time four barges could have been unloaded, but since only three were in queue, the number unloaded is recorded as 3.

The superintendent will likely be interested in at least three useful and important pieces of information:

$$\left(\begin{array}{c}\text{Average number of barges}\\ \text{delayed to the next day}\end{array}\right) = \frac{20 \text{ delays}}{15 \text{ days}}$$

$$= 1.33 \text{ barges delayed per day}$$

$$\text{Average number of nightly arrivals} = \frac{41 \text{ arrivals}}{15 \text{ days}}$$

$$= 2.73 \text{ arrivals per night}$$

$$\text{Average number of barges unloaded each day} = \frac{39 \text{ unloadings}}{15 \text{ days}}$$

$$= 2.60 \text{ unloadings per day}$$

When the data from Example S2 are analyzed in the context of delay costs, idle labor costs, and the cost of hiring extra unloading crew, it will be possible for the dock superintendent and port controller to make a better staffing decision. They may even elect to resimulate the process assuming different unloading rates that would correspond to increased crew sizes. Although simulation cannot guarantee an optimal solution to problems such as this, it can be helpful in recreating a process and identifying good decision alternatives.

SIMULATION AND INVENTORY ANALYSIS

In Chapter 13, we introduced inventory models. The commonly used EOQ models are based on the assumption that both product demand and reorder lead time are known, constant values. In most real-world inventory situations, though, demand and lead time are variables, and accurate analysis becomes extremely difficult to handle by any means other than simulation.

In this section, we present an inventory problem with two decision variables and two probabilistic components. The owner of the hardware store in Example S3 would like to establish *order quantity* and *reorder point* decisions for a particular product that has probabilistic (uncertain) daily demand and reorder lead time. He wants to make a series of simulation runs, trying out various order quantities and reorder points, in order to minimize his total inventory cost for the item. Inventory costs in this case will include ordering, holding, and stockout costs.

EXAMPLE S3

Simkin's Hardware sells the Ace model electric drill. Daily demand for the drill is relatively low but subject to some variability. Over the past 300 days, Simkin has observed the sales shown in column 2 of Table S13.8. He converts this historical frequency into a probability distribution for the variable daily demand (column 3). A cumulative probability distribution is formed in column 4 of Table S13.8. Finally, Simkin establishes an interval of random numbers to represent each possible daily demand (column 5).

TABLE S13.8 ■ PROBABILITIES AND RANDOM-NUMBER INTERVALS FOR DAILY ACE DRILL DEMAND

(1) DEMAND FOR ACE DRILL	(2) FREQUENCY	(3) PROBABILITY	(4) CUMULATIVE PROBABILITY	(5) INTERVAL OF RANDOM NUMBERS
0	15	.05	.05	01 through 05
1	30	.10	.15	06 through 15
2	60	.20	.35	16 through 35
3	120	.40	.75	36 through 75
4	45	.15	.90	76 through 90
5	30	.10	1.00	91 through 00
	300 days	1.00		

When Simkin places an order to replenish his inventory of Ace electric drills, there is a delivery lag of from 1 to 3 days. This means that lead time may also be considered a probabilistic variable. The number of days it took to receive the past 50 orders is presented in Table S13.9. In a fashion similar to that for the demand variable, Simkin establishes a probability distribution for the lead time variable (column 3 of Table S13.9), computes the cumulative distribution (column 4), and assigns random-number intervals for each possible time (column 5).

TABLE S13.9 ■ PROBABILITIES AND RANDOM-NUMBER INTERVALS FOR REORDER LEAD TIME

(1) LEAD TIME (DAYS)	(2) FREQUENCY	(3) PROBABILITY	(4) CUMULATIVE PROBABILITY	(5) RANDOM-NUMBER INTERVAL
1	10	.20	.20	01 through 20
2	25	.50	.70	21 through 70
3	15	.30	1.00	71 through 00
	50 orders	1.00		

The first inventory policy that Simkin's Hardware wants to simulate is an order quantity of 10 with a reorder point of 5. That is, every time the on-hand inventory level at the end of the day is 5 or less, Simkin will call his supplier and place an order for 10 more drills. If the lead time is 1 day, by the way, the order will not arrive the next morning, but rather at the beginning of the following work day.

The entire process is simulated in Table S13.10 for a 10-day period. We assume that beginning inventory is 10 units on day 1. We took the random numbers from column 2 of Table S13.4.

Table S13.10 was filled in by proceeding 1 day (or line) at a time, working from left to right. It was a four-step process:

1. Begin each simulated day by checking whether any ordered inventory has just arrived. If it has, increase the current inventory by the quantity ordered (10 units, in this case).

2. Generate a daily demand from the demand probability distribution by selecting a random number.

3. Compute ending inventory = beginning inventory minus demand. If on-hand inventory is insufficient to meet the day's demand, satisfy as much as possible and note the number of lost sales.

4. Determine whether the day's ending inventory has reached the reorder point (five units). If it has, and if there are no outstanding orders, place an order. Lead time for a new order is simulated by choosing a random number and using the distribution in Table S13.9.

Simkin's first inventory simulation yields some interesting results. The average daily ending inventory is

$$\text{Average ending inventory} = \frac{41 \text{ total units}}{10 \text{ days}} = 4.1 \text{ units/day}$$

We also note the average lost sales and number of orders placed per day:

$$\text{Average lost sales} = \frac{2 \text{ sales lost}}{10 \text{ days}} = .2 \text{ unit/day}$$

$$\text{Average number of orders placed} = \frac{3 \text{ orders}}{10 \text{ days}} = .3 \text{ order/day}$$

TABLE S13.10 ■ SIMKIN HARDWARE'S FIRST INVENTORY SIMULATION. ORDER QUANTITY = 10 UNITS; REORDER POINT = 5 UNITS

(1) DAY	(2) UNITS RECEIVED	(3) BEGINNING INVENTORY	(4) RANDOM NUMBER	(5) DEMAND	(6) ENDING INVENTORY	(7) LOST SALES	(8) ORDER?	(9) RANDOM NUMBER	(10) LEAD TIME
1		10	06	1	9	0	No		
2	0	9	63	3	6	0	No		
3	0	6	57	3	(3)[1]	0	Yes	(02)[2]	1
4	0	3	(94)[3]	5	0	2	No[4]		
5	(10)[5]	10	52	3	7	0	No		
6	0	7	69	3	4	0	Yes	33	2
7	0	4	32	2	2	0	No		
8	0	2	30	2	0	0	No		
9	(10)[6]	10	48	3	7	0	No		
10	0	7	88	4	3	0	Yes	14	
					Totals: 41	2			

1. This is the first time inventory dropped to the reorder point of five drills. Because no prior order was outstanding, an order is placed.
2. The random number 02 is generated to represent the first lead time. It was drawn from column 2 of Table S13.4 as the next number in the list being used. A separate column could have been used from which to draw lead time random numbers if we had wanted to do so, but in this example, we did not do so.
3. Again, notice that the random digits 02 were used for lead time (see footnote 2). So the next number in the column is 94.
4. No order is placed on day 4 because there is one outstanding from the previous day that has not yet arrived.
5. The lead time for the first order placed is one day, but as noted in the text, an order does not arrive the next morning, but rather the beginning of the following day. Thus, the first order arrives at the start of day 5.
6. This is the arrival of the order placed at the close of business on day 6. Fortunately for Simkin, no lost sales occurred during the two-day lead time until the order arrived.

Example S4 shows how these data can be useful in studying the inventory costs of the policy being simulated.

EXAMPLE S4

Simkin estimates that the cost of placing each order for Ace drills is \$10, the holding cost per drill held at the end of each day is \$.50, and the cost of each lost sale is \$8. This information enables us to compute the total daily inventory cost for the simulated policy in Example S3. Let us examine the three cost components:

AutoMod simulation software, designed by AutoSimulations Inc. in Utah, is a graphical system that allows users to model and analyze a variety of manufacturing problems with minimal programming knowledge. AutoMod features include three-dimensional computer-aided design (CAD)-like drawings and interactive, animated graphics. Here we see a 3D model of a transmission assembly line.

$$\text{Daily order cost} = (\text{cost of placing one order})$$
$$\times (\text{number of orders placed per day})$$
$$= \$10 \text{ per order} \times .3 \text{ order per day} = \$3$$

$$\text{Daily holding cost} = (\text{cost of holding one unit for 1 day})$$
$$\times (\text{average ending inventory})$$
$$= 50¢ \text{ per unit per day} \times 4.1 \text{ units per day} = \$2.05$$

$$\text{Daily stockout cost} = (\text{cost per lost sale})$$
$$\times (\text{average number of lost sales per day})$$
$$= \$8 \text{ per lost sale} \times .2 \text{ lost sales per day} = \$1.60$$

$$\text{Total daily inventory cost} = \text{daily order cost} + \text{daily holding cost}$$
$$+ \text{daily stockout cost} = \$6.65$$

After working through Example S3, we want to emphasize something very important. This simulation should be extended many more days before we draw any conclusions as to the cost of the order policy being tested. If a hand simulation is being conducted, 100 days would provide a better representation. If a computer is doing the calculations, 1,000 days would be helpful in reaching accurate cost estimates.[3]

Let us say that Simkin *does* complete a 1,000-day simulation of the policy from Example S3 (order quantity = 10 drills, reorder point = 5 drills). Does this complete his analysis? The answer is no—this is just the beginning! Simkin must now compare *this* potential strategy to other possibilities. For example, what about order quantity = 10, reorder point = 4; or order quantity = 12, reorder point = 6; or order quantity = 14, reorder point = 5? Perhaps every combination of values of order quantity from 6 to 20 drills, and reorder points from 3 to 10 should be simulated. After simulating all reasonable combinations of order quantities and reorder points, Simkin would likely select the pair yielding the lowest total inventory cost. Problem S13.12 gives you a chance to help Simkin begin this series of comparisons.

THE ROLE OF COMPUTERS IN SIMULATION

Computers are critical in simulating complex tasks. They can generate random numbers, simulate thousands of time periods in a matter of seconds or minutes, and provide management with reports that make decision making easier. A computer approach is almost a necessity in order to draw valid conclusions from a simulation.

Computer programming languages can help the simulation process. *General-purpose languages* such as FORTRAN, BASIC, COBOL, PL/1, or PASCAL are one approach. *Special-purpose simulation languages*, such as GPSS, SIMSCRIPT, and DYNAMO have a few advantages: (1) they require less programming time for large

---

[3]Moreover, even with a 1,000-day simulation, the generated distribution should be compared with the desired distribution to ensure valid results.

Taylor II is an example of a commercial, prewritten simulation program that contains simulations, animations (such as the airport luggage-sorting system one shown here), management reports, and graphs. The business version of this software costs about $50,000.

simulations, (2) they are usually more efficient and easier to check for errors, and (3) they have random-number generators already built in as subroutines.

Commercial, easy-to-use prewritten simulation programs are also available. Some are generalized to handle a wide variety of situations ranging from queuing to inventory. The names of a few such programs are: Witness, Xcell, MAP/1, Slam II, SIMFACTORY, ARENA, Micro Saint, and Taylor II.

Spreadsheet software can also be used to develop simulations quickly and easily. Such packages have built-in random-number generators (through the @ RAND command) and develop outputs through "data-fill" table commands.

SUMMARY

Simulation involves building mathematical models that attempt to act like real operating systems. In this way, a real-world situation can be studied without imposing on the actual system. Simulation models can be developed manually, but simulation by computer is generally more desirable. The Monte Carlo approach uses random numbers to represent variables, such as inventory demand or people waiting in line, which are then simulated in a series of trials. The advantages of simulation usually outweigh the disadvantages, leading to its wide use as an operations tool.

KEY TERMS	Simulation (p. 618)	Random-number intervals (p. 621)
	Monte Carlo method (p. 620)	Random number (p. 621)
	Cumulative probability distribution (p. 621)	

USING AB:POM AND SPREADSHEETS TO SOLVE SIMULATION PROBLEMS

Using AB:POM's Simulation Module

AB:POM's simulation module allows us to simulate one variable that has up to 10 possible outcomes. Program S13.1 takes the data for Barry's Auto Tire seen in Table S13.2 and conducts a simulation similar to Example S1.

PROGRAM S13.1 ■ AB:POM's Simulation Module. Users may select any number of trials and may choose their own seed number as the first random number. Users may also select random numbers from any row or column of Table S13.4.

———————————————— Simulation ———————————— Solution ————————

Number of categories (2–10)   6

Barry's Auto Tire

Options –>	NOStep	Cmputr			
# Trials –>	100	0	<– Seed or row or column		
	Freqncy	Probability	Cumulative	Occurrences	Percentage
Demand = 0	10.00	0.05	0.05	7	0.0769
1	20.00	0.10	0.15	10	0.1219
2	40.00	0.20	0.35	27	0.2700
3	60.00	0.30	0.65	23	0.2421
4	40.00	0.20	0.85	19	0.1938
5	30.00	0.15	1.00	14	0.1505
TOTAL	200.00			100	

Conducting a Simulation with Spreadsheets

Spreadsheet software has two features that make it a useful tool for conducting simulation analysis: (1) built-in random-number functions and generators (through the @ RAND command), and (2) lookup tables that easily permit us to match a simulated random number to a specific event (through the @ VLOOKUP command).

Program S13.2 illustrates these concepts on the Barry's Auto Tire example shown at the beginning of this supplement. The @ RAND function (in C15 through C24) returns a random number between 0 and 1, all values being equally likely. This

PROGRAM S13.2 ■ A Spreadsheet Simulation for Barry's Auto Tire Seen in Table S13.3. and Example S1. A symbolic spreadsheet, using formulas, is shown here.

	A	B	C	D
1	Note: This is a slightly restructured table (differing from Table S13.3)			
2		needed to accommodate the @VLOOKUP command		
3		Cumulative	Demand	
4	Probability	Probability	for Tires	
5	0.05	0	0	
6	0.1	0.05	1	
7	0.2	0.15	2	
8	0.3	0.35	3	
9	0.2	0.65	4	
10	0.15	0.85	5	
11				
12	Ten-day simulation of demand for radial tires (as in Example S1)			
13		Day	Random	Simulated Daily
14		Number	Number	Demand
15		1	@RAND	@VLOOKUP (C15, $B$5 . . $C$10, 1)
16		2	@RAND	@VLOOKUP (C16, $B$5 . . $C$10, 1)
17		3	@RAND	@VLOOKUP (C17, $B$5 . . $C$10, 1)
18		4	@RAND	@VLOOKUP (C18, $B$5 . . $C$10, 1)
19		5	@RAND	@VLOOKUP (C19, $B$5 . . $C$10, 1)
20		6	@RAND	@VLOOKUP (C20, $B$5 . . $C$10, 1)
21		7	@RAND	@VLOOKUP (C21, $B$5 . . $C$10, 1)
22		8	@RAND	@VLOOKUP (C22, $B$5 . . $C$10, 1)
23		9	@RAND	@VLOOKUP (C23, $B$5 . . $C$10, 1)
24		10	@RAND	@VLOOKUP (C24, $B$5 . . $C$10, 1)
25			Total	@SUM (D15 . . D24)
26			Aver.	+D25/10
27				
28	Press F9 to recalculate the numbers.			

is an example of a "continuous uniform distribution" in which each random number may take on any fractional value. The actual simulated demand is in cells D15 through D24 and employs the @ VLOOKUP function.

To simulate the first day's demand for tires, the @ VLOOKUP in cell D15 looks first to the random number just generated in C15. It then takes that number and moves to the small table of probabilities for demand just above it. Cells B5 through C10 comprise the "value lookup" table. These random variables for demand have one of several discrete values (0–5 in our case). Cumulative probabilities always start at zero. If the random number generated is between 0 and .05, a demand of 0 tires results. If the random number falls between .05 and .15, the lookup table indicates a demand for one tire, and so on. The "1" in the @ VLOOKUP command, by the way, means that demand is "looked up" in the first column to the right of the cumulative probability.

The F9 function key permits the entire simulation to be redone, with all new random numbers, each time it is pressed.

SOLVED PROBLEMS

Solved Problem S13.1

Higgins Plumbing and Heating maintains a stock of 30-gallon hot-water heaters that it sells to homeowners and installs for them. Owner Jerry Higgins likes the idea of having a large supply on hand to meet any customer demand. But he also recognizes that it is expensive to do so. He examines hot-water heater sales over the past 50 weeks and notes the following:

HOT-WATER HEATER SALES PER WEEK	NUMBER OF WEEKS THIS NUMBER WAS SOLD
4	6
5	5
6	9
7	12
8	8
9	7
10	3
	50 weeks total data

(a) If Higgins maintains a constant supply of eight hot-water heaters in any given week, how many times will he stock out during a 20-week simulation? We use random numbers from the seventh column of Table S13.4, beginning with the random digit 10.

(b) What is the average number of sales per week over the 20-week period?

(c) Using an analytic nonsimulation technique, what is the expected number of sales per week? How does this compare to the answer in part (b)?

Solution

HEATER SALES	PROBABILITY	RANDOM-NUMBER INTERVALS
4	.12	01 through 12
5	.10	13 through 22
6	.18	23 through 40
7	.24	41 through 64
8	.16	65 through 80
9	.14	81 through 94
10	.06	95 through 100
	1.00	

(a)

Week	Random Number	Simulated Sales	Week	Random Number	Simulated Sales
1	10	4	11	08	4
2	24	6	12	48	7
3	03	4	13	66	8
4	32	6	14	97	10
5	23	6	15	03	4
6	59	7	16	96	10
7	95	10	17	46	7
8	34	6	18	74	8
9	34	6	19	77	8
10	51	7	20	44	7

With a supply of eight heaters, Higgins will stock out three times during the 20-week period (in weeks 7, 14, and 16).

(b) Average sales by simulation = total sales/20 weeks = 135/20 = 6.75 per week

(c) Using expected values,

$$E \text{ (sales)} = .12(4 \text{ heaters}) + .10(5)$$
$$+ .18(6) + .24(7) + .16(8)$$
$$+ .14(9) + .06(10) = 6.88 \text{ heaters}$$

With a longer simulation, these two approaches will lead to even closer values.

Solved Problem S13.2

Random numbers may be used to simulate continuous distributions. As a simple example, assume that fixed cost equals $300, profit contribution equals $10 per item sold, and you expect an equally likely chance of 0 to 99 units to be sold. That is, profit equals $-\$300 + \$10X$, where X is the number sold. The mean amount you would expect to sell is 49.5 units.

(a) Calculate the expected value.

(b) Simulate the sale of 5 items, using the following double-digit random numbers: 37   77   13   10   85

(c) Calculate the expected value of part (b) and compare with the results of part (a).

Solution

(a) Expected value $= -300 + 10(49.5) = \$195$

(b) $-300 + \$10(37) = \$70$

$-300 + \$10(77) = \$470$

$-300 + \$10(13) = -\$170$

$-300 + \$10(10) = -\$200$

$-300 + \$10(85) = \$550$

(c) The mean of these simulated sales is $144. If the sample size were larger, we would expect the two values to be closer.

DISCUSSION QUESTIONS

1. What are the advantages and limitations of simulation models?

2. Why might a manager be forced to use simulation instead of an analytical model in dealing with a problem of:

   (a) inventory order policy?

   (b) ships docking in a port to unload?

   (c) bank teller service windows?

   (d) the U.S. economy?

3. What types of management problems can be solved more easily by techniques other than simulation?

4. What are the major steps in the simulation process?

5. What is Monte Carlo simulation? What principles underlie its use, and what steps are followed in applying it?

6. In the simulation of an order policy for drills at Simkin's Hardware, would the results (of Table S13.10) change significantly if a longer period were simulated? Why is the 10-day simulation valid or invalid?

7. Why is a computer necessary in conducting a real-world simulation?

8. Do you think the application of simulation will increase strongly in the next 10 years? Why?

9. Why would an analyst ever prefer a general-purpose language such as FORTRAN or BASIC in a simulation when there are advantages to using special-purpose languages such as GPSS or SIMSCRIPT?

10. What is the role of random numbers in a Monte Carlo simulation?

11. Why do the results of a simulation differ each time you make a run?

12. List six ways that simulation can be used in business.

13. Why is simulation such a widely used technique?

CRITICAL THINKING EXERCISE

The caption to the photo of cars waiting in line at a Burger King drive-through that you saw earlier in this supplement described two uses of simulation at Burger King. One application dealt with the distance between the drive-through order station and the pickup window. Saving $10,000 per restaurant translated to $15 million annual systemwide sale capacity. The second application hoped to expand sales capacity during peak drive-through hours by adding a second window. This small change added close to $20 million per year in sales to the corporation.

Examine any fast-food chain operation very carefully, and propose two more changes that could be tested by simulation before their actual implementations.

PROBLEMS

The problems that follow involve simulations that are to be done by hand. However, to obtain accurate and meaningful results, long periods must be simulated. This is usually handled by a computer. If you are able to program some of the problems by computer, we suggest you try to do so. If not, the hand simulations will still help you in understanding the simulation process.

• **S13.1** The daily demand for newspapers at a particular machine is either 20, 21, 22, or 23 with probabilities 0.4, 0.3, 0.2, or 0.1, respectively. Assume the following random numbers have been generated: 08, 54, 74, 66, 52, 58, 03, 22, 89, and 85. Using these numbers, generate the daily sales of newspaper for 10 days.

• **S13.2** The number of machine breakdowns in a day at Katie Park's factory is either 0, 1 or 2, with probabilities 0.5, 0.3, or 0.2, respectively. The following random numbers have been generated: 13, 14, 02, 18, 31, 19, 32, 85, 31, and 94. Use these numbers to generate the number of breakdowns for 10 consecutive days. What proportion of these days had at least 1 breakdown?

• **S13.3** The number of cars arriving at Dave Cole's self-service gasoline station during the last 50 hours of operation are as follows:

NUMBER OF CARS ARRIVING	FREQUENCY
6	10
7	12
8	20
9	8

The following random numbers have been generated: 44, 30, 26, 09, 49, 13, 33, 89, 13, and 37. Simulate 10 hours of arrivals at this station. What is the average number of arrivals during this period?

• **S13.4** Kate Moore has a newspaper stand where she sells papers for $.35. The papers cost her $.25, giving her a 10-cent profit on each one she sells. From past experience Kate knows that

20% of the time she sells 100 papers
20% of the time she sells 150 papers
30% of the time she sells 200 papers
30% of the time she sells 250 papers

Assuming that Kate believes that the cost of a lost sale is $.05 and any unsold papers cost her $.25, simulate her profit outlook over 5 days if she orders 200 papers for each of the 5 days. Use the following random numbers: 52, 06, 50, 88, and 53.

• **S13.5** Refer to Problem S13.4. Kate's new strategy is to order 175 papers for each of the 5 days. Use the same random numbers and simulate Kate's profits. What is the average daily profit?

⦂ **S13.6** Stacey Strahs' grocery store has noted the following figures with regard to the number of people who arrive at the store's three check-out stands ready to check out and the time it takes to check out the individuals.

ARRIVALS/MIN	FREQUENCY
0	.3
1	.5
2	.2

SERVICE TIME IN MIN	FREQUENCY
1	.1
2	.3
3	.4
4	.2

Simulate the utilization of the three check-out stands over 5 minutes, using the following random numbers: 07, 60, 77, 49, 76, 95, 51, and 16. Note the results at the end of the 5-minute period.

: **S13.7** Average daily sales of a product in Pam Lancaster's store are 8 units. The actual number of sales each day is either 7, 8, or 9 with probabilities 0.3, 0.4, or 0.3, respectively. The lead time for delivery averages 4 days, although the time may be 3, 4, or 5 days with probabilities .2, .6, and .2. The company plans to place an order when the inventory level drops to 32 units (based on the average demand and average lead time). The following random numbers have been generated:

60, 87, 46, 63 (set 1)

52, 78, 13, 06, 99, 98, 80, 09, 67, 89, 45 (set 2)

Use set 1 to generate lead times and use set 2 to simulate daily demand. Simulate two ordering periods and determine how often the company runs out of stock before the shipment arrives.

: **S13.8** The time between arrivals at a drive-through window of Jackie Senich's fast-food restaurant follows the distribution given below. The service time distribution is also given in the table. Use the random numbers provided to simulate the activity of the first five arrivals. Assume that the window opens at 11:00 A.M. and the first arrival is after this, based on the first interarrival time generated.

TIME BETWEEN ARRIVALS	PROBABILITY	SERVICE TIME	PROBABILITY
1	.2	1	.3
2	.3	2	.5
3	.3	3	.2
4	.2		

Random numbers for arrivals: 14, 74, 27, 03
Random numbers for service times: 88, 32, 36, 24

What time does the fourth customer leave the system?

• **S13.9** Ventra Property Management is responsible for the maintenance, rental, and day-to-day operation of a large apartment complex on the east side of New Brunswick. Mark Ventra is especially concerned about the cost projections for replacing air conditioner compressors. He would like to simulate the number of compressor failures each year over the next 20 years. Using data from a similar apartment building, he manages in a New Brunswick suburb, Ventra establishes a table of relative frequency of failures during a year as follows:

NUMBER OF A.C. COMPRESSOR FAILURES	PROBABILITY (RELATIVE FREQUENCY)
0	.06
1	.13
2	.25
3	.28
4	.20
5	.07
6	.01

He decides to simulate the 20-year period by selecting two-digit random numbers from column 3 of Table S13.4 (starting with the random number 50).

Conduct the simulation for Ventra. Is it common to have three or more consecutive years of operation with two or less compressor failures per year?

·S13.10 The number of cars arriving at Marcus Chapman's Car Wash during the last 200 hours of operation is observed to be the following:

NUMBER OF CARS ARRIVING	FREQUENCY
3 or less	0
4	20
5	30
6	50
7	60
8	40
9 or more	0
	200

a) Set up a probability and cumulative probability distribution for the variable of car arrivals.

b) Establish random-number intervals for the variable.

c) Simulate 15 hours of car arrivals and compute the average number of arrivals per hour. Select the random numbers needed from column 1, Table S13.4, beginning with the digits 52.

:S13.11 An increase in the size of the barge-unloading crew at the Port of New Orleans (see Example S2) has resulted in a new probability distribution for daily unloading rates. In particular, Table S13.6 may be revised as shown here.

DAILY UNLOADING RATE	PROBABILITY
1	.03
2	.12
3	.40
4	.28
5	.12
6	.05

a) Resimulate 15 days of barge unloading and compute the average number of barges delayed, average number of nightly arrivals, and average number of barges unloaded each day. Draw random numbers from the bottom row of Table S13.4 to generate daily arrivals and from the second-from-the-bottom row to generate daily unloading rates.

b) How do these simulated results compare to those in the supplement?

:S13.12 Simkin's Hardware Store simulated an inventory ordering policy for Ace electric drills that involved an order quantity of 10 drills with a reorder point of 5. This first attempt to develop a cost-effective ordering strategy was illustrated in Table S13.10 of Example S3. The brief simulation resulted in a total daily inventory cost of $6.65.

Simkin would now like to compare this strategy to one in which he orders 12 drills, with a reorder point of 6. Conduct a 10-day simulation for him and discuss the cost implications.

:S13.13 Carol Pharo, a Ph.D. student at Northern Virginia University, has been having problems balancing her checkbook. Her monthly income is derived from a graduate research assistantship; however, she also makes extra money in most months by tutoring undergraduates in their quantitative analysis course. Her chances of various income levels are shown here (on the left).

Pharo's expenditures also vary from month to month, and she estimates that they will follow the distribution on the right.

MONTHLY INCOME*	PROBABILITY	MONTHLY EXPENSES	PROBABILITY
$350	.40	$300	.10
$400	.20	$400	.45
$450	.30	$500	.30
$500	.10	$600	.15

*Assume this income is received at the beginning of each month.

She begins her final year with $600 in her checking account. Simulate the entire year (12 months) and discuss Pharo's financial picture.

•S13.14 Refer to the data in Solved Problem S13.1, which deals with Higgins Plumbing and Heating. Higgins has now collected 100 weeks of data and finds the following distribution for sales.

HOT WATER HEATER SALES PER WEEK	NUMBER OF WEEKS THIS NUMBER WAS SOLD	HOT WATER HEATER SALES PER WEEK	NUMBER OF WEEKS THIS NUMBER WAS SOLD
3	2	8	21
4	9	9	12
5	10	10	10
6	15	11	5
7	25		100

a) Resimulate the number of stockouts incurred over a 20-week period (assuming Higgins maintains a constant supply of 8 heaters).

b) Conduct this 20-week simulation two more times and compare your answers with those in part (a). Did they change significantly? Why or why not?

c) What is the new expected number of sales per week?

:S13.15 Helms Aircraft Co. operates a large number of computerized plotting machines. The plotting machines are highly reliable, with the exception of the four sophisticated built-in ink pens. The pens constantly clog and jam in a raised or lowered position. When this occurs, the plotter is unusable.

Currently, Helms Aircraft replaces every pen as it fails. The service manager has, however, proposed replacing all four pens every time one fails. This should cut down the frequency of plotter failures. At present, it takes 1 hour to replace one pen. All four pens could be replaced in 2 hours. The total cost of a plotter being unusable is $50 per hour. Each pen costs $8.

If only one pen is replaced each time a clog or jam occurs, the following break-down data are thought to be valid:

HOURS BETWEEN PLOTTER FAILURES IF ONE PEN IS REPLACED DURING A REPAIR	PROBABILITY
10	.05
20	.15
30	.15
40	.20
50	.20
60	.15
70	.10

Based on the service manager's estimates, if all four pens are replaced each time one pen fails, the probability distribution between failures is

HOURS BETWEEN PLOTTER FAILURES IF ALL FOUR PENS ARE REPLACED DURING A REPAIR	PROBABILITY
100	.15
110	.25
120	.35
130	.20
140	.05

a) Simulate Helms Aircraft's problem and determine the best policy. Should the firm replace one pen or all four pens on a plotter each time a failure occurs?

b) Develop a second approach to solving this problem (this time without simulation). Compare the results. How does it affect Helms' policy decision using simulation?

: S13.16 Tia Thompson owns and operates one of the largest Mercedes-Benz auto dealerships in Washington, D.C. In the past 36 months, her sales of this luxury car have ranged from a low of 6 new cars to a high of 12 new cars, as reflected in the following table:

SALES OF NEW CARS/MONTH	FREQUENCY
6	3
7	4
8	6
9	12
10	9
11	1
12	1
	36 months

She believes that sales will continue during the next 24 months at about the same historical rates, and that delivery times will also continue to follow this pace (stated in probability form):

DELIVERY TIME (IN MONTHS)	PROBABILITY
1	.44
2	.33
3	.16
4	.07
	1.00

Thompson's current policy is to order 14 cars at a time (two full truckloads, with 7 autos on each truck), and to place a new order whenever the stock on hand reaches 12 autos. What are the results of this policy when simulated over the next 2 years?

: **S13.17** Refer to Problem S13.16. Tia Thompson establishes the following relevant costs: (1) the carrying cost per Mercedes per month is $600; (2) the cost of a lost sale averages $4,350; and (3) the cost of placing an order is $570. What is the total inventory cost of the policy simulated in Problem S13.16?

: **S13.18** Tia Thompson (see Problems S13.16 and S13.17) wishes to try a new simulated policy, ordering 21 cars per order, with a reorder point of 10 autos. Which policy is better, this one or the one formulated in Problems S13.16 and S13.17?

: **S13.19** The Eichler Corporation is the nation's largest manufacturer of industrial-size washing machines. A main ingredient in the production process is 8-by 10-foot sheets of stainless steel. The steel is used for both interior washer drums and outer casings.

Steel is purchased weekly on a contractual basis from the RTT Foundry, which, because of limited availability and lot-sizing, can ship either 8,000 or 11,000 square feet of stainless steel each week. When Eichler's weekly order is placed, there is a 45% chance that 8,000 square feet will arrive and a 55% chance of receiving the larger-size order.

Eichler uses the stainless steel on a stochastic (nonconstant) basis. The probabilities of demand each week are

STEEL NEEDED PER WEEK (SQ. FT)	PROBABILITY
6,000	.05
7,000	.15
8,000	.20
9,000	.30
10,000	.20
11,000	.10

Eichler has a capacity to store no more than 25,000 square feet of steel at any time. Because of the contract, orders *must* be placed each week regardless of the on-hand supply.

a) Simulate stainless steel order arrivals and use for 20 weeks. (Begin the first week with a starting inventory of 0 stainless steel.) If an end-of-week inventory is ever negative, assume that "back orders" are permitted and fill the demand from the next arriving order.

b) Should Eichler add more storage area? If so, how much? If not, comment on the system.

:S13.20 Blacksburg, Virginia's General Hospital has an emergency room that is divided into six departments: (1) the initial exam station to treat minor problems or make diagnoses; (2) an X-ray department; (3) an operating room; (4) a cast-fitting room; (5) an observation room (for recovery and general observation before final diagnoses or release); and (6) an out-processing department (where clerks check out patients and arrange for payment or insurance forms).

The probabilities that a patient will go from one department to another are presented in the accompanying table.

a) Simulate the trail followed by 10 emergency room patients. Proceed, one patient at a time, from each one's entry at the initial exam station until he or she leaves through out-processing. You should be aware that a patient can enter the same department more than once.

b) Using your simulation data, what are the chances that a patient enters the X-ray department twice?

FROM	TO	PROBABILITY
Initial exam at	X-ray department	.45
emergency	Operating room	.15
room entrance	Observation room	.10
	Out-processing clerk	.30
X-ray department	Operating room	.10
	Cast-fitting room	.25
	Observation room	.35
	Out-processing clerk	.30
Operating room	Cast-fitting room	.25
	Observation room	.70
	Out-processing clerk	.05
Cast-fitting room	Observation room	.55
	X-ray department	.05
	Out-processing clerk	.40
Observation room	Operating room	.15
	X-ray department	.15
	Out-processing clerk	.70

:S13.21 Management of the First Syracuse Bank is concerned over a loss of customers at its main office downtown. One solution that has been proposed is to add one or more drive-through teller stations to make it easier for customers in cars to obtain quick service without parking. Steve Shoff, the bank president, thinks the bank should risk only the cost of installing one drive-through. He is informed by his staff that the cost (amortized over a 20-year period) of building a drive-through is $12,000 per year. It also costs $16,000 per year in wages and benefits to staff each new teller window.

The director of Management Analysis, Jennifer Jaenicke, believes that the following two factors encourage the immediate construction of two drive-through stations, however. According to a recent article in *Banking Research* magazine, customers who wait in long lines for drive-through teller service will cost banks an average of $1.00 per minute, in loss of goodwill. Also, adding a second drive-through will cost an additional $16,000 in staffing, but amortized construction costs can be cut to a total of $20,000 per year if two drive-throughs are installed together, instead of one at a time. To complete her analysis, Mrs. Jaenicke collected 1 month's worth of arrival and service rates at a competing downtown bank's drive-through stations. These data follow:

INTERARRIVAL TIMES FOR 1,000 OBSERVATIONS		CUSTOMER SERVICE TIME FOR 1,000 CUSTOMERS	
TIME BETWEEN ARRIVALS (IN MINUTES)	NUMBER OF OCCURRENCES	SERVICE TIME (IN MINUTES)	NUMBER OF OCCURRENCES
1	200	1	100
2	250	2	150
3	300	3	350
4	150	4	150
5	100	5	150
		6	100

a) Simulate a 1-hour time period, from 1 to 2 P.M., for a single-teller drive-through.

b) Simulate a 1-hour time period, from 1 to 2 P.M., for a two teller system.

c) Conduct a cost analysis of the two options. Assume the bank is open 7 hours per day and 200 days per year.

CASE STUDY

Alabama Airlines

Alabama Airlines opened it doors in June 1995 as a commuter service with its headquarters and only hub located in Birmingham. A product of airline deregulation, Alabama Air joined the growing number of successful short-haul, point-to-point airlines including Lone Star, Comair, Atlantic Southeast, Skywest, and Business Express.

Alabama Air was started and managed by two former pilots, David Douglas (who had been with the defunct Eastern Airlines) and Michael Hanna (formerly with Pan Am). It acquired a fleet of 12 used prop-jet planes and the airport gates vacated by Delta Airlines' 1994 downsizing.

With business growing quickly, Douglas turned his attention to Alabama Air's "800" reservations system. Between midnight and 6:00 A.M., only one telephone reservations agent had been on duty. The time between incoming calls during this period is distributed as shown in Table 1. Douglas carefully observed and timed the agent and estimated that the time taken to process passenger inquiries is distributed as shown in Table 2.

TABLE 1 ■ INCOMING CALL DISTRIBUTION

TIME BETWEEN CALLS (IN MINUTES)	PROBABILITY
1	.11
2	.21
3	.22
4	.20
5	.16
6	.10

TABLE 2 ■ SERVICE TIME DISTRIBUTION

TIME TO PROCESS CUSTOMER ENQUIRIES (IN MINUTES)	PROBABILITY
1	.20
2	.19
3	.18
4	.17
5	.13
6	.10
7	.03

(Continued)

All customers calling Alabama Air go "on hold" and are served in the order of the calls unless the reservations agent is available for immediate service. Douglas is deciding whether a second agent should be on duty to cope with customer demand. To maintain customer satisfaction, Alabama Air does not want a customer "on hold" for more than 3 to 4 minutes and also wants to maintain a "high" operator utilization.

Further, the airline is planning a new TV advertising campaign. As a result, it expects an increase in "800" line phone inquiries. Based on similar campaigns in the past, the incoming call distribution from midnight to 6 A.M. is expected to be as shown in Table 3. (The same service time distribution will apply).

TABLE 3 ■ INCOMING CALL DISTRIBUTION

TIME BETWEEN CALLS (IN MINUTES)	PROBABILITY
1	.22
2	.25
3	.19
4	.15
5	.12
6	.07

model carefully and justify the duration of the simulation, assumptions, and measures of performance.

2. What are your recommendations regarding operator utilization and customer satisfaction if the airline proceeds with the advertising campaign?

Source: Professor Zbigniew H. Przasnyski, Loyola Marymount University.

DISCUSSION QUESTIONS

1. What would you advise Alabama Air to do for the current reservation system based on the original call distribution? Create a simulation model to investigate the scenario. Describe the

BIBLIOGRAPHY

Abdou, G. and S. P. Dutta. "A Systematic Simulation Approach for the Design of JIT Manufacturing Systems." *Journal of Operations Management*, 11, no. 3 (September 1993): 25–38.

Brennan, J. E., B. L. Golden, and H. K. Rappoport. "Go with the Flow: Improving Red Cross Bloodmobiles Using Simulation Analysis." *Interfaces*, 22, no. 5 (September/October 1992): 1.

Buchanan, E., and R. Keeler. "Simulating Health Expenditures Under Alternative Insurance Plans." *Management Science* (September 1991): 1069–1088.

Evans, J. R. "A Little Knowledge Can Be Dangerous: Handle Simulation with Care." *Production and Inventory Management Journal*, 33, no. 2 (Second Quarter 1992): 51.

Fishman, G. S., and V. G. Kulkarni. "Improving Monte Carlo Efficiency by Increasing Variance." *Management Science*, 38, no. 10 (October 1992): 1432.

Flowers, A. D., and J. R. Cole. "An Application of Computer Simulation to Quality Control in Manufacturing," *IIE Transactions*, 17, no. 3 (September 1985): 277–283.

Greenwood, A. G., L. P. Rees, and I. W. M. Crouch. "Separating the Art and Science of Simulation Optimization: A Knowledge-Based Architecture Providing for Machine Learning." *IIE Transactions*, 25, no. 6 (November 1993): 70.

Heizer, J. H., and A. P. de la Garza. "Using Simulation to Evaluate Airplane Dealership Operations." *Airport Services Management*, 16, no. 6 (June 1976): 30–32.

Hendricks, K. B., and J. O. McClain. "The Output Processes of Serial Production Lines of General Machines with Finite Buffers." *Management Sciences*, 39, no. 10 (October 1993): 1194.

Hutchinson, J., G. K. Leong, and P. T. Ward. "Improving Delivery Performance in Gear Manufacturing at Jeffrey Division of Dresser Industries." *Interfaces*, 23, no. 2 (March/April 1993): 69–79.

Lev, B. "Simulation of Manufacturing Systems." *Interfaces*, 20, no. 3 (May/June 1990): 99.

Render, B., and R. M. Stair. *Introduction to Management Science*. Boston: Allyn and Bacon, 1992.

———. *Quantitative Analysis for Management*, 5th ed. Boston: Allyn and Bacon, 1994.

Render, B., R. M. Stair, and I. Greenberg. *Cases and Readings in Management Science*, 2nd ed. Boston: Allyn and Bacon, Inc., 1990.

Rosenblatt, M. J., Y. Roll, and V. Zyser. "A Combined Optimization and Simulation Approach for Designing Automated Storage/Retrieval Systems." *Industrial Engineering Research & Development*, 25, no. 1 (January 1993): 40–50.

Russell, R. A., and R. Hickle. "Simulation of a CD Portfolio." *Interfaces*, 16, no. 3 (May/June 1986): 49–54.

Solomon, S. L. *Simulation of Waiting Lines*. Englewood Cliffs, NJ: Prentice Hall, 1983.

Trunk, C. "Simulation for Success in the Automated Factory." *Material Handling Engineering* (May 1989): 64–76.

14

Material Requirements Planning (MRP)

LEARNING OBJECTIVES

*When you complete this
chapter you should be able to:*

Identify or Define:

   Lot-Sizing

   Low-Level Coding

   Planning Bills, Pseudo Bills, and
   Kits

   Phantom Bills

Explain:

   Material requirements planning

   Distribution requirements
   planning

MRP PROVIDES A COMPETITIVE ADVANTAGE FOR COLLINS INDUSTRIES

On the six parallel assembly lines, ambulances move forward each day to the next work-station. The MRP system makes certain that just the materials needed at each station arrive overnight for assembly the next day.

dustries has daily updates. The firm uses the MAPICS DB software on an IBM AS400 mini-computer. Effective use of MAPICS forces Collins to maintain accurate bills of material and inventory records. The system has reduced inventory by over 30% in just 2 years.

Collins insists that four key tasks be performed properly. First, the material plan must meet both the requirements of the master schedule and the capabilities of the production facility. Second, the plan must be executed as designed. Third, effective "time-phased" material deliveries, consignment inventories, and a constant review of purchase methods reduce inventory invest

Collins Industries, headquartered in Hutchinson, Kansas, is the largest manufacturer of ambulances in the world. The $150 million firm is an international competitor that sells more than 20% of its vehicles to markets outside the United States. In its largest ambulance plant, located in Winter Park, Florida, vehicles are produced on assembly lines (i.e., a repetitive process). There are 12 major ambulance designs assembled at the Florida plant, and they use 18,000 different inventory items, including 6,000 manufactured parts and 12,000 purchased parts.

This variety of products and the nature of the process demand good material requirements planning. The system at Collins In-

This cutaway of one ambulance interior indicates the complexity of the product, which for some rural locations may be the equivalent of a hospital emergency room in miniature. To complicate production, virtually every ambulance is custom-ordered, with 7,000 different options available. This necessitates precise orders and good bills of materials.

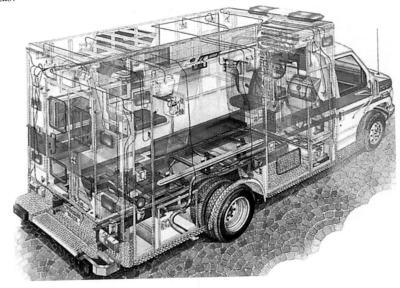

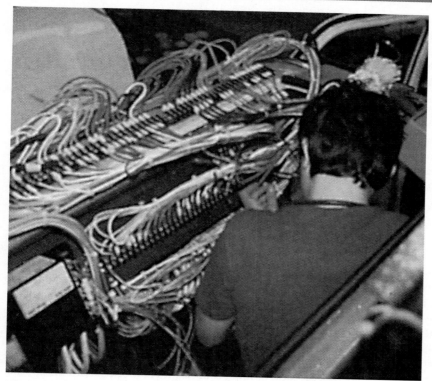

ment. Finally, Collins maintains record integrity. Record accuracy is recognized as a fundamental ingredient of its successful MRP program. Collins' cycle counters are charged with material audits that not only correct errors, but also investigate and correct problems.

Collins Industries has used MRP as the catalyst for low inventory, high quality, tight schedules, and accurate records. Collins has found competitive advantage via MRP.

This photo shows a worker wiring an electronic board. Ambulance wiring is so complex that there are an average of 15 miles of wire in a Collins vehicle. Compare this to the 16 miles in a sophisticated F-16 fighter jet.

The company uses a job shop environment to feed assembly-line needs. It maintains a complete carpentry shop (to provide interior cabinetry), a metal fabrication shop (to construct the shell of the ambulance), a paint shop (to prepare, paint, and detail each vehicle), an electrical shop (to provide for the complex electronics in a modern ambulance), and as shown here, an upholstery shop (to make interior seats and benches).

> N ancy Mueller turns quiche into cash. Her firm, Nancy's Specialty Foods, is designed for today's busy lifestyle, producing 750,000 prepackaged, frozen quiche hors d'ouevres each month. Material requirements planning (MRP) software has been key to her growing success. MRP is the primary management tool that keeps the ingredients and labor coming at the proper times and the schedule firm. Once Nancy's Specialty Foods knows the demand for her crab meat quiche, she knows the demand for all of the ingredients from dough, to cheese, to crab meat because *all of the ingredients are dependent.*[1] ◆

As we see at Collins Industries and Nancy's Specialty Foods, the demand for many items is dependent. By *dependent*, we mean the demand for one item is related to the demand for another item. Consider the Ford Explorer. Ford's demand for auto tires and radiators depends on the production of Explorers. Four tires and one radiator go into each finished Explorer. Demand for items is *dependent* when the relationship between the items can be determined. Therefore, once management can make a forecast of the demand for the final product, quantities required for all components can be computed, because all components are *dependent* items. The Boeing Aircraft operations manager scheduling production of one plane per week, for example, knows the requirements down to the last rivet. For any product, all components of that product are *dependent* demand items. *More generally, for any item where a schedule can be established, dependent techniques should be used.*

    Dependent models, when they can be used, are preferable to the models of Chapter 13.[2] Dependency exists for all component parts, subassemblies, and supplies when a schedule is known. Dependent models are better not only for manufacturers and distributors, but also for a wide variety of firms from restaurants[3] to hospitals.[4] When dependent techniques are used in a production environment, they are called **material requirements planning (MRP)**.

Material requirements planning (MRP)

DEPENDENT INVENTORY MODEL REQUIREMENTS

Effective use of dependent inventory models requires that the operations manager know the:

1. master production schedule (what is to be made and when);
2. specifications or bill of material (how to make the product);
3. inventory availability (what is in stock);
4. purchase orders outstanding (what is on order);
5. lead times (how long it takes to get various components.

---

[1]*Source:* Bob Sperber. "Computers Turn Quiche To Cash." *Food Processing,* vol. 53 (October 1992): 91–92.

[2]The inventory models discussed in Chapter 13 assumed that the demand for one item was independent of the demand for another item. For example, the demand for refrigerators may be *independent* of the demand for dishwashers. Moreover, the demand today may have little, if anything, to do with the demand tomorrow.

[3]John G. Wacker, "Effective Planning and Cost Control for Restaurants: Making Resource Requirements Planning Work," *Production and Inventory Management,* 26 (First Quarter 1985): 55–70.

[4]David W. Pentico, "Material Requirements Planning: A New Tool for Controlling Hospital Inventories," *Hospital Topics,* 57 (May/June 1979): 40–43.

In this chapter, we discuss each of these requirements in the context of material requirements planning (MRP). We then introduce a variation of MRP known as distribution resource planning (DRP).

Master Production Schedule

A **master production schedule** specifies what is to be made and when. The schedule must be in accordance with a production plan. The production plan sets the overall level of output in broad terms (for example, product families, standard hours, or dollar volume). Such plans include a variety of inputs, including financial plans, customer demand, engineering capabilities, labor availability, inventory fluctuations, supplier performance, and other considerations. Each contributes in its own way to the production plan, as shown in Figure 14.1, which shows the planning process from the production plan to execution. Each of the lower-level plans must be feasible. When it is not, feedback to the next higher level is used to make the necessary adjustment. One of the major strengths of MRP is its ability to determine precisely the feasibility of a schedule within capacity constraints. This planning process can yield excellent results. The production plan sets the upper and lower bounds on the master production schedule. From this production planning process, the master production schedule is developed.

Master production schedule

The master production schedule tells us what is required to satisfy demand and meet the production plan. This schedule establishes what items to make and when. Managers must adhere to the schedule for a reasonable length of time (usually a major portion of the production cycle). Many organizations establish a master production schedule and then "fix" the near-term portion of the plan. The fixed portion of the schedule is then referred to as the "fixed," "firm," or "frozen" schedule. Only changes beyond the fixed schedule are permitted. The schedule then becomes a rolling production schedule. For example, a fixed 7-week plan has an additional week added to it as each week is completed, so a 7-week fixed schedule is maintained. Note that the master production schedule is a statement of what is to be produced, not a forecast of demand. The master schedule can be expressed in terms of

1. an *end item in a continuous* (make-to-stock) company;
2. *modules in a repetitive* (assemble-to-stock) company;
3. a *customer order in a job shop* (make-to-order) company.

A master production schedule for two of Nancy's Specialty Foods' products, crab meat quiche and spinach quiche, might look like Table 14.1.

| **TABLE 14.1 ■ MASTER PRODUCTION SCHEDULE FOR PRODUCTS CRAB MEAT QUICHE AND SPINACH QUICHE** |

GROSS REQUIREMENTS FOR PRODUCT CRAB MEAT QUICHE

Day	6	7	8	9	10	11	12	13	14	and so on
Amount	50		100	47	60		110	75		

GROSS REQUIREMENTS FOR PRODUCT SPINACH QUICHE

Day	7	8	9	10	11	12	13	14	15	16	and so on
Amount	100	200	150			60	75		100		

FIGURE 14.1 ■ The Planning Process

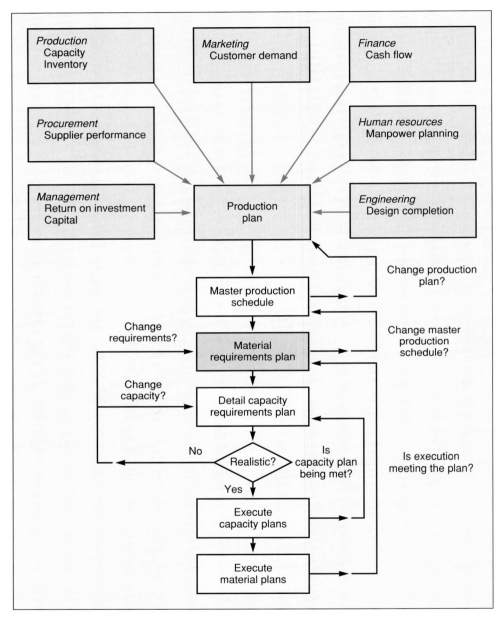

Specifications or Bills of Material

Determining what goes in a product may seem simple, but it can be difficult in practice. As we saw in Chapter 6, there is usually a rush to get a new product to market. Therefore, the drawings and specifications may be incomplete or even nonexistent. Moreover, complete drawings and specifications often contain errors in dimensions, quantities, or countless other areas. Then, engineering change notices (ECNs) are created, further complicating the process. An **engineering change notice (ECN)** is a change or correction to an engineering drawing or specification.

Engineering change notice (ECN)

Units to be produced are often specified via a bill of material, which we introduced in Chapter 6. A **bill of material (BOM)** is a list of quantities of components, ingredients, and materials required to make a product. The individual drawings describe not only physical dimensions, but also any special processing as well as the raw material from which each part is made. Nancy's Specialty Foods' recipe for quiche, specifying ingredients and quantities, and a full set of drawings for a Collins ambulance are both bills of material (although they do vary somewhat in scope).

A bill of material provides the product structure. Example 1 shows how to develop the product structure and "explode" it to reveal the requirements for each component. A bill of material for item A in Example 1 consists of items B and C. Items above any level are called *parents*; items below any level are called *components*, or *children*.

Bill of material (BOM)

EXAMPLE 1

Speaker Kits, Inc., packages high-fidelity components for mail order. The components for their top-of-the-line speaker kit, "Awesome" (A), includes two standard 12-inch speaker kits (B's) and three speaker kits with amp-boosters (C's).

Each B consists of two speakers (D's) and two shipping boxes with an installation kit (E's). Each of the three 300-watt stereo kits (C's) has two speaker boosters (F's) and two installation kits (E's). Each speaker booster (F) includes two speakers (D's), and one amp-booster (G). The total for each Awesome is four standard 12-inch speakers and twelve 12-inch speakers with the amp-booster. (Most purchasers require hearing aids within 2 years; and at least one court case is pending because of structural damage to a men's dormitory.) The demand for B, C, D, E, F, and G, as we can see, is completely dependent on the demand for A, actual orders for the "Awesome" speaker kits. Given this information, we can construct the product structure that follows.

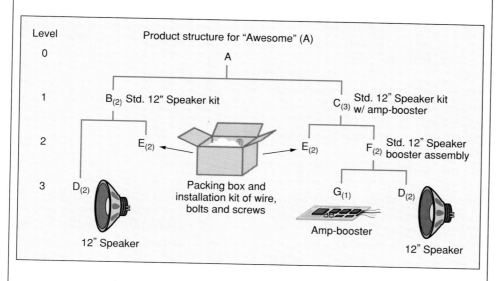

The structure has four levels: 0, 1, 2, and 3. There are four parents: A, B, C, and F. Each parent item has at least one level below it. Items B, C, D, E, F, and G

are components because each item has at least one level above it. In this structure, B, C, and F are parents and components. The number of parentheses indicates how many units of that particular item are needed to make the item immediately above it. Thus, $B_{(2)}$ means that it takes two units of B for every unit of A, and $F_{(2)}$ means that it takes two units of F for every unit of C.

Once we have developed the product structure, we can determine the number of units of each item required to satisfy demand for a new order of 50 Awesome speaker kits. This information is displayed in the following table:

Part B:	$2 \times$ number of A's =	(2)(50) =	100
Part C:	$3 \times$ number of A's =	(3)(50) =	150
Part D:	$2 \times$ number of B's + $2 \times$ number of F's =	(2)(100) + (2)(300) =	800
Part E:	$2 \times$ number of B's + $2 \times$ number of C's =	(2)(100) + (2)(150) =	500
Part F:	$2 \times$ number of C's =	(2)(150) =	300
Part G:	$1 \times$ number of F's =	(1)(300) =	300

Thus, for 50 units of A, we will need 100 units of B, 150 units of C, 800 units of D, 500 units of E, 300 units of F, and 300 units of G.

For manufacturers like Harley-Davidson who produce a large number of end products from a relatively small number of options, modular bills of material provide an effective solution.

Modular bills

Planning bills

Pseudo bills

Kit number

Phantom bills of material

Bills of material not only specify requirements, but are also useful for costing, and they can serve as a list of items to be issued to production or assembly personnel. When bills of material (BOM) are used in this way, they are usually called *pick lists*.

MODULAR BILLS. Bills of material may be organized around product modules (see Chapter 6). Modules are not final products to be sold, but are components that can be produced and assembled into units. They may be major components of the final product or product options. The bills of material for these modules are called **modular bills**. Bills of material are sometimes organized as modules (rather than as part of a final product) because production scheduling and production are often facilitated by organizing around relatively few modules rather than a multitude of final assemblies. For instance, a firm may make 138,000 different final products but have only 40 modules that are mixed and matched to produce the 138,000 final products. The firm forecasts, prepares its master production schedule, and builds to the 40 modules, not the 138,000 configurations of the final product. The 40 modules can be assembled for specific orders at final assembly.

PLANNING BILLS AND PHANTOM BILLS. Two other special kinds of bills of material are planning bills and phantom bills. **Planning bills** are created in order to assign an artificial parent to the bill of material. Such bills are used (1) when we want to group subassemblies together to reduce the number of items to be scheduled and (2) when we want to issue "kits" to the production department. For instance, it may not be efficient to issue inexpensive items such as washers and cotter pins with each of numerous subassemblies, so we call this a *kit* and generate a planning bill. The planning bill specifies the *kit* to be issued. A planning bill may also be known as **pseudo bill** or **kit number**. **Phantom bills of material** are bills of material for components, usually subassemblies that exist only temporarily. These components go directly into another assembly and are never inventoried. Therefore, components of phantom bills of material are coded to receive special treatment; lead times are zero, and they are handled as an integral part of their parent item.

LOW-LEVEL CODING.   Low-level coding of an item in a BOM is necessary when identical items exist at various levels in the BOM. **Low-level coding** means the item is coded at the lowest level at which it occurs. For example, item D in Example 1 is coded at the lowest level at which it is used. Item D could be coded as part of B and occur at level 2. But because D is also part of F, and F is level 2, item D becomes a level 3 item. Low-level coding is a convention to allow easy computing of the requirements of an item. When the BOM has thousands of items and when requirements are frequently recomputed, the ease and speed of computation become a major concern.

Low-level coding

Accurate Inventory Records

Knowledge of what is in stock is the result of good inventory management, as discussed in Chapter 13. Good inventory management is an absolute necessity for an MRP system to work. If the firm has not yet achieved at least 99% record accuracy, then material requirements planning will not work.

Purchase Orders Outstanding

Knowledge of outstanding orders should exist as a by-product of well-managed purchasing and inventory control departments. When purchase orders are executed, records of those orders and their scheduled delivery date must be available to production personnel. Only with good purchasing data can managers prepare good production plans and effectively execute an MRP system.

Lead Times for Each Component

Once managers determine when products are needed, they determine when to acquire them. The time required to acquire (that is, purchase, produce, or assemble) an item is known as **lead time**. Lead time for a manufactured item consists of move, setup, and assembly or run times for each component. For a purchased item, the lead time includes the time between when a part is ordered and when it is available for production.

Lead time

When the bill of material for Awesome speaker kits (A's), in Example 1, is turned on its side and lead times for each component are added (see Table 14.2), we then have a *time-phased product structure*. Time in this structure is shown on the horizontal axis (see Figure 14.2).

TABLE 14.2 ■ LEAD TIMES FOR AWESOME SPEAKER KITS (A'S)	
COMPONENT	**LEAD TIME**
A	1 week
B	2 weeks
C	1 week
D	1 week
E	2 weeks
F	3 weeks
G	2 weeks

MRP STRUCTURE

Although most MRP systems are computerized, the MRP procedure is straightforward and can be done by hand. A master production schedule, a bill of material, inventory and purchase records, and lead times for each item are ingredients of a material requirements planning system (see Figure 14.3 on page 658).

FIGURE 14.2   ■   Time-Phased Product Structure

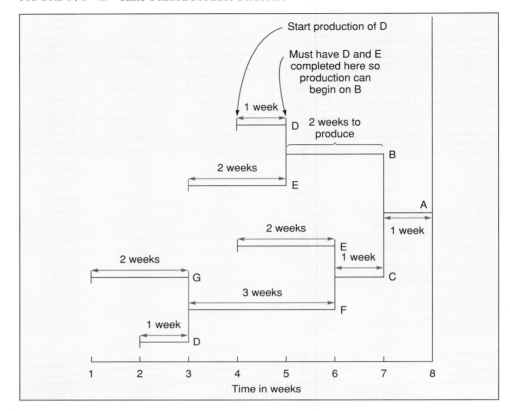

Once these ingredients are available and accurate, the next step is to construct a gross material requirements plan. The **gross material requirements plan** is a schedule. It combines a master production schedule (that requires a unit of A in week 8) and the time-phased schedule (Figure 14.2). It shows when an item must be ordered from suppliers if there is no inventory on hand or when the production of an item must be started in order to satisfy the demand for the finished product by a particular date.

Gross material requirements plan

EXAMPLE 2

Each Awesome speaker kit (item A of Example 1) requires all of the items in the product structure for A. The lead times were shown in Table 14.2. Using this information, we construct the gross material requirements plan and draw up a production schedule that will satisfy the demand of 50 units of A by week 8. This is shown in Table 14.3.

The interpretation of the gross material requirements is as follows: If you want 50 units of A at week 8, you must start assembling A in week 7. Thus, in week 7, you will need 100 units of B and 150 units of C. These two items take 2 weeks and 1 week, respectively, to produce. Production of B should start in week 5, and production of C should start in week 6 (lead time subtracted from the required date for these items). Working backward, we can perform the same computations for all of the other items. The material requirements plan shows when production of each item should begin and end in order to have 50 units of A at week 8.

TABLE 14.3 ■ GROSS MATERIAL REQUIREMENTS PLAN FOR 50 AWESOME SPEAKER KITS (A)

				WEEK					
	1	2	3	4	5	6	7	8	LEAD TIME
A. Required date								50	1 week
Order release date							50		
B. Required date							100		2 weeks
Order release date					100				
C. Required date							150		1 week
Order release date						150			
D. Required date					200				1 week
Order release date				200					
E. Required date					200	300			2 weeks
Order release date			200	300					
F. Required date						300			3 weeks
Order release date			300						
D. Required date			600						1 week
Order release date		600							
G. Required date			300						2 weeks
Order release date	300								

So far, we have considered *gross material requirements*, which assumes that there is no inventory on hand. When there is inventory on hand, we prepare a net requirements plan. When considering on-hand inventory, we must realize that many items in inventory contain subassemblies or parts. If the gross requirement for Awesome speaker kits (A's) is 100 and there are 20 of those speakers on hand, the net requirement for Awesome speaker kits (A's) is 80 (that is, 100 − 20). But each Awesome speaker kit on hand contains 2 B's. As a result, the requirement for B's drops by 40 B's (20 A kits on hand × 2 B's per A). Therefore, if inventory is on hand for a parent item, the requirements for the parent item and all its components decrease because each Awesome kit contains the components for lower-level items. Example 3 shows how to create a net requirements plan.

EXAMPLE 3

In Example 1, we developed a product structure from a bill of material (BOM), and in Example 2, we developed a gross requirements plan. Given the following on-hand inventory, we now construct a net requirements plan.

ITEM	ON HAND	ITEM	ON HAND
A	10	E	10
B	15	F	5
C	20	G	0
D	10		

FIGURE 14.3   ■   Structure of the MRP System

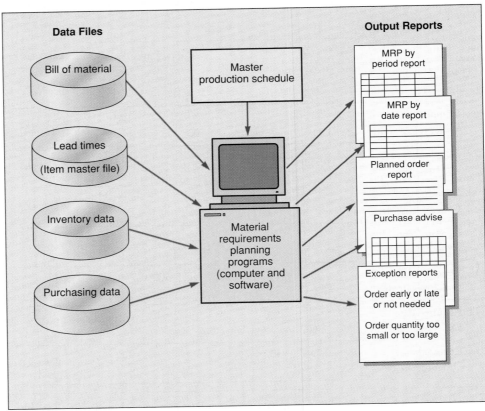

A net material requirements plan includes gross requirements, on-hand inventory, net requirements, planned order receipt, and planned order release for each item. We begin with A and work backward through the components. Shown in the chart is the net material requirements plan for product A.

Constructing a net requirements plan is similar to constructing the gross requirements plan. Starting with item A, we work backward to determine net requirements for all items. To do these computations, we refer to the product structure, on-hand inventory, and lead times. The gross requirement for A is 50 units in week 8. Ten items are on hand; therefore, the net requirements and planned order receipt both are 40 items in week 8. Because of the 1-week lead time, the planned order release is 40 items in week 7 (see the arrow connecting the order receipt and order release). Referring to week 7 and the product structure in Example 1, we can see 80 (2 × 40) items of B and 120 (3 × 40) items of C are required in week 7 in order to have a total for 50 items of A in week 8. The letter A to the right of the gross figure for items B and C was generated as a result of the demand for the parent, A. Performing the same type of analysis for B and C yields the net requirements for D, E, F, and G. Note the on-hand inventory in row E in week 6. It is zero because the on-hand inventory (10 units) was used to make B in week 5. By the same token, the inventory for D was used to make F.

Net Material Requirements Plan for Product A. Note that the superscript is the source of the demand.

Lot Size	Lead Time (weeks)	On Hand	Safety Stock	Allo-cated	Low-Level Code	Item Identi-fication			Week							
									1	2	3	4	5	6	7	8
Lot-for-Lot	1	10	—	—	0	A	Gross Requirements									50
							Scheduled Receipts									
							Projected on Hand	10	10	10	10	10	10	10	10	10
							Net Requirements									40
							Planned Order Receipts									40
							Planned Order Releases								40	
Lot-for-Lot	2	15	—	—	1	B	Gross Requirements								80^A	
							Scheduled Receipts									
							Projected on Hand	15	15	15	15	15	15	15	15	
							Net Requirements								65	
							Planned Order Receipts								65	
							Planned Order Releases							65		
Lot-for-Lot	1	20	—	—	1	C	Gross Requirements								120^A	
							Scheduled Receipts									
							Projected on Hand	20	20	20	20	20	20	20	20	
							Net Requirements								100	
							Planned Order Receipts								100	
							Planned Order Releases							100		
Lot-for-Lot	2	10	—	—	2	E	Gross Requirements							130^B	200^C	
							Scheduled Receipts									
							Projected on Hand	10	10	10	10	10	10			
							Net Requirements							120	200	
							Planned Order Receipts							120	200	
							Planned Order Releases					120	200			
Lot-for-Lot	3	5	—	—	2	F	Gross Requirements							200^C		
							Scheduled Receipts									
							Projected on Hand	5	5	5	5	5	5	5		
							Net Requirements							195		
							Planned Order Receipts							195		
							Planned Order Releases				195					
Lot-for-Lot	1	10	—	—	3	D	Gross Requirements				390^F		130^B			
							Scheduled Receipts									
							Projected on Hand	10	10	10	10					
							Net Requirements				380		130			
							Planned Order Receipts				380		130			
							Planned Order Releases			380		130				
Lot-for-Lot	2	0	—	—	3	G	Gross Requirements				195^F					
							Scheduled Receipts									
							Projected on Hand				0					
							Net Requirements				195					
							Planned Order Receipts				195					
							Planned Order Releases		195							

Examples 2 and 3 considered only product A, the Awesome speaker kit, and its completion only in week 8. Fifty units of A were required in week 8. Normally, there is a demand for many products over time. For each product, management must prepare a master production schedule (as we saw earlier in Table 14.1). Scheduled

3COM Corporation, headquartered in Santa Clara, CA, is a manufacturer of local and wide-area computer network systems. 3COM uses MRP to manage its production of printed-circuit boards. Timely and accurate information obtained from the system is forwarded to suppliers that deliver parts and material directly to the line on a Just-in-Time (JIT) basis. 3COM's MRP system allows them to keep inventory levels low and track vendor performance.

production of each product contributes to the master schedule and ultimately to the net material requirements plan. Figure 14.4 shows how several product schedules can contribute to one gross material requirements plan.

Most inventory systems also note the number of units in inventory that have been assigned to specific future production but not yet used. Such items are often referred to as *allocated* items. Allocated items may then be included in an MRP planning sheet, as shown in Figure 14.5.

The allocated quantity has the effect of increasing the requirements (or, alternatively, reducing the quantity on hand). The logic, then, of a net requirements MRP is

$$
\underbrace{\left[\left(\begin{array}{c}\text{gross}\\\text{requirements}\end{array}\right) + \left(\text{allocations}\right)\right]}_{\text{total requirements}} - \underbrace{\left[\left(\begin{array}{c}\text{on}\\\text{hand}\end{array}\right) + \left(\begin{array}{c}\text{scheduled}\\\text{receipts}\end{array}\right)\right]}_{\text{available inventory}} = \begin{array}{c}\text{net}\\\text{requirements}\end{array}
$$

MRP DYNAMICS

A material requirements plan is not static. Even though a bill of material and material requirements plan are established, changes in design, schedules, and production processes continue to occur. For example, if one of the production time estimates was 1 week less than it should have been, that week must be added to the material

FIGURE 14.4 ■ Several Schedules Contributing to a Gross Requirements Schedule for B. One "B" is in each A and one "B" in each S, and 10 B's are sold directly in week 1 and 10 more are sold directly in week 2.

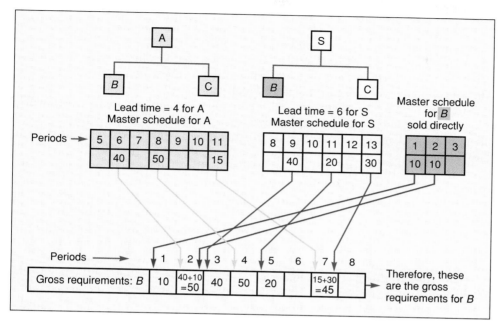

requirements plan. Likewise, if a design improvement allows construction of one of the intermediate inventory items with fewer parts, then the bill of material and the material requirements plan must be altered. Scrapped components, missed receiving dates, and machine breakdowns contribute to such alterations in the material requirements plan. Similarly, alterations occur in an MRP system when changes are made to the master production schedule. Regardless of the cause of any changes, the MRP model can be manipulated to reflect them. In this manner, an up-to-date schedule is possible. Such schedule changes reflect the most recent data so the production schedule can be satisfied.

Modifying the MRP schedule in response to changes is cumbersome if done by hand, and errors are likely when the plan is complex. Therefore, most MRP systems

FIGURE 14.5 ■ Sample MRP Planning Sheet for Item A

Lot Size	Lead Time	On Hand	Safety Stock	Allocated	Low-Level Code	Item ID		Period							
								1	2	3	4	5	6	7	8
Lot For Lot	1	0	0	10	0	B	Gross Requirements								80 90
							Scheduled Receipts								0
							Projected On Hand 0	0		0	0	0	0	0	0
							Net Requirements								90
							Planned Order Receipts								90
							Planned Order Releases								90	

are computerized. Indeed, only because they are computerized are they the popular and practical tool they have become.[5] Computerized programs perform the same types of calculations that we have demonstrated in this chapter and are widely used throughout the industrialized world.

A central strength of MRP is its timely and accurate replanning capability. Due to the variations that occur, it is not uncommon to recompute the MRP requirements about once a week. However, many firms find they do not want to respond to minor scheduling or changes even if they are aware of them. These frequent changes gener-

System nervousness

ate what is called **system nervousness**. Frequent changes can create havoc in purchasing and production departments if such changes are implemented. Consequently, P/OM personnel reduce the nervousness by evaluating the need and impact of changes prior to disseminating requests to other departments.[6] Two tools are particularly helpful.

Time fences

The first is the establishment of time fences. **Time fences** allow a segment of the master schedule to be designated as "not to be rescheduled." This segment of the master schedule is thus not changed during the periodic regeneration of schedules. The

Pegging

second tool available is pegging. **Pegging** means tracing upward in the BOM from the component to the parent item. By pegging upward, the production planner can determine the cause for the requirement and make a judgment about the necessity for a change in the schedule.

With MRP, the operations manager *can* react to the dynamics of the real world. How frequently the manager wishes to impose those changes on the firm requires professional judgment. Moreover, if the nervousness is caused by legitimate changes, then the proper response of operations management may be to investigate the production environment—not adjust via MRP.

LOT-SIZING TECHNIQUES

An MRP system is an excellent way to determine production schedules and net re-

Lot-sizing decisions

quirements. However, whenever we have a net requirement, a decision must be made about how much to order. These decisions are called **lot-sizing decisions**. There are a variety of ways to determine lot sizes in an MRP system; commercial MRP software usually includes the choice of several lot-sizing techniques. We will now review a few of them.

Lot-for-lot

LOT-FOR-LOT.   In Example 3, we used a lot-sizing technique known as **lot-for-lot**, which produced exactly what was required. This is consistent with the objective of an MRP system, which is to meet the requirements of *dependent* demand. Thus, an MRP system should produce units only as needed with no safety stock and no anticipation of further orders. When frequent orders are economical and just-in-time inventory techniques implemented, lot-for-lot can be very efficient. However, in cases where setup costs are significant or where management has been unable to implement JIT, lot-for-lot can be expensive. Example 4 uses the lot-for-lot criteria and determines its cost for 10 weeks of demand.

---

[5]As early as 1920, Al Sloan, president of GM, understood the basic ingredients of MRP. See Alfred P. Sloan, Jr., *My Years with General Motors* (Garden City, NY: Anchor Books, 1972), p. 145.

[6]Jay H. Heizer, "The Production Manager Can Be a Good Guy in the Factory with a Future," *APICS—The Performance Advantage* (July 1994): 30–34.

EXAMPLE 4

Speaker Kits, Inc., wishes to compute its ordering and carrying cost of inventory on lot-for-lot criteria. Speaker Kits has determined that, for the 12-inch speaker/booster assembly, setup cost is $100 and holding cost is $1 per period. The production schedule as reflected in net requirements for assemblies is as follows:

MRP LOT-SIZING PROBLEM: LOT-FOR-LOT TECHNIQUE

		1	2	3	4	5	6	7	8	9	10
Gross Requirements		35	30	40	0	10	40	30	0	30	55
Scheduled Receipts											
Projected On Hand	35	0	0	0	0	0	0	0	0	0	0
Net Requirements		0	30	40	0	10	40	30	0	30	55
Planned Order Receipts			30	40		10	40	30		30	55
Planned Order Releases		30	40		10	40	30		30	55	

Holding costs = $1/unit/week; setup cost = $100; gross requirements average per week = 27; lead time = 1 week.

    Shown is the lot-sizing solution using the lot-for-lot technique and its cost. The holding cost is zero, but seven separate setups yield a total cost of $700.

ECONOMIC ORDER QUANTITY.   As discussed in Chapter 13, EOQ can be used as a lot-sizing technique. But as we indicated there, EOQ is preferable where relatively constant independent demand exists, not where we know the demand. EOQ is a statistical technique using averages, typically average demand for a year, whereas our MRP procedure assumes known (dependent) demand. Operations managers should take advantage of this information, rather than assuming a constant demand. EOQ is examined in Example 5.

This Nissan pickup truck assembly line in Smyrna, Tennessee, has little inventory because Nissan schedules to a razor's edge. At Nissan Motor Company plants, MRP helps to reduce inventory to world-class standards. World-class automobile assembly requires that purchased parts have a turnover of slightly more than once a day and that overall turnover approaches 150 times per year.

EXAMPLE 5

Speaker Kits, Inc., with a setup cost of $100 and a holding cost per week of $1, examines its cost with lot sizes based on an EOQ criteria. The net requirements and lot sizes using the same requirements as in Example 4 follow:

MRP LOT-SIZING PROBLEM: EOQ TECHNIQUE

		1	2	3	4	5	6	7	8	9	10
Gross Requirements		35	30	40	0	10	40	30	0	30	55
Scheduled Receipts											
Projected On Hand	35	35	0	43	3	3	66	26	69	69	39
Net Requirements		0	30	0	0	7	26	4	0	0	16
Planned Order Receipts			73			73		73			73
Planned Order Releases		73			73		73		73		

Holding costs = $1/unit/week; setup cost = $100; gross requirements average per week = 27; lead time = 1 week.

Ten-week usage equals 270 units; therefore, weekly usage equals 27, and 52 weeks (annual usage) equals 1,404 units. From Chapter 13, the EOQ model is

$$Q^\star = \sqrt{\frac{2DS}{H}}$$

where D = annual usage = 1,404
S = setup cost = $100
H = holding (carrying) cost, on an annual basis per unit
= $1 × 52 weeks = $52

$$Q^\star = 73 \text{ units}$$

$$\text{Setups} = 1,404/73 = 19 \text{ per year}$$

$$\text{Setup cost} = 19 \times \$100 = \$1,900$$

$$\text{Holding cost} = \frac{73}{2} \times (\$1 \times 52 \text{ weeks}) = \$1,898$$

$$\text{Setup cost} + \text{holding cost} = \$1,900 + 1,898 = \$3,798$$

The EOQ solution yields a computed 10-week cost of $730 [$3,798 × (10 weeks/52 weeks) = $730].

Notice that actual holding cost will vary from the computed $730, depending upon the rate of actual usage. From the preceding table, we can see that in our 10-week example costs really are $400 for four setups, plus a holding cost of 375 units at $1 per week for a total of $775. Because usage was not constant, the actual computed cost was in fact more than the theoretical EOQ ($730) and more than the lot-for-lot rule ($700). If any stockouts had occurred, these costs too would need to be added to our actual EOQ of $775.

PART PERIOD BALANCING. Part period balancing (PPB) is a more dynamic approach to balance setup and holding cost.[7] PPB uses additional information by changing the lot size to reflect requirements of the next lot size in the future. PPB attempts to balance setup and holding cost for known demands. Part period balancing develops an **economic part period (EPP)**, which is the ratio of setup cost to holding cost. For our Speaker Kits example, EPP = $100/$1 = 100 units. Therefore, holding 100 units for one period would cost $100, exactly the cost of one setup. Similarly, holding 50 units for two periods also costs $100 (2 periods × $1 × 50 units). PPB merely adds requirements until the number of part periods approximates the EPP, in this case 100. Example 6 shows the application of part period balancing.

Part period balancing (PPB)

Economic part period (EPP)

EXAMPLE 6

Once again, Speaker Kits, Inc., computes the costs associated with a lot size by using a $100 setup cost and a $1 holding cost, only this time part period balancing is used. The data are shown in the following table:

PPB CALCULATIONS

PERIODS COMBINED	TRIAL LOT SIZE (CUMULATIVE NET REQUIREMENTS)	PART PERIODS	SETUP	HOLDING	TOTAL
2	30	0			
2, 3	70	$40 = 40 \times 1$			
2, 3, 4	70	40			
2, 3, 4, 5	80	$70 = \overline{40 \times 1} + \overline{10 \times 3}$	100 +	70 =	170
2, 3, 4, 5, 6	120	$230 = 40 \times 1 + 10 \times 3 + 40 \times 4$			

40 units held for 1 period = $40
10 units held for 3 periods = $30

(Therefore, combine periods 2 through 5; 70 is as close to our EPP of 100 as we are going to get.)

6	40	0			
6, 7	70	30			
6, 7, 8	70	30			
6, 7, 8, 9	100	$120 = 30 \times 1 + 30 \times 3$	100 +	120 =	220

(Therefore, combine periods 6 through 9; 120 is as close to our EPP of 100 as we are going to get.)

10	55	0	100 +	0 =	100
			300 +	190 =	490

MRP LOT-SIZING PROBLEM: PPB TECHNIQUE

		1	2	3	4	5	6	7	8	9	10
Gross Requirements		35	30	40	0	10	40	30	0	30	55
Scheduled Receipts											
Projected On Hand	35	35	0	50	10	10	0	60	30	30	0
Net Requirements		0	30	0	0	0	40	0	0	0	55
Planned Order Receipts			80				100				55
Planned Order Releases		80				100			55		

Holding costs = $1/unit/week; setup cost = $100; gross requirements average per week = 27; lead time = 1 week.

[7]J. J. DeMatteis, "An Economic Lot-Sizing Technique: The Part-Period Algorithms," *IBM Systems Journal*, 7 (1968): 30–38.

EPP is 100 (setup cost divided by holding cost = $100/$1). The first lot is to cover periods one, two, three, four, and five and is 80.

The total costs are $490, with setup costs totaling $300 and holding costs totaling $190.

Wagner–Whitin procedure

WAGNER–WHITIN ALGORITHM. The **Wagner–Whitin procedure** is a dynamic programming model that adds some complexity to the lot-size computation. It assumes a finite time horizon beyond which there are no additional net requirements. It does, however, provide good results.[8] The technique is seldom used in practice, but this may change with increasing understanding and software sophistication.

LOT-SIZING SUMMARY. In the three Speaker Kits lot-sizing examples, we found the following costs:

Lot-for-lot	$700
EOQ	$775
Part period balancing	$490

These examples should not, however, lead operations personnel to hasty conclusions about the preferred lot-sizing technique. In theory, new lot sizes should be computed whenever there is a schedule or lot-size change anywhere in the MRP hierarchy. But in practice such changes cause the instability and system nervousness referred to earlier in this chapter. Consequently, such frequent changes are not made. This means that all lot sizes are wrong because the production system can not respond to frequent changes.

In general, the lot-for-lot approach should be used wherever economical. Lot-for-lot is the goal. Lots can be modified as necessary for scrap allowances, process constraints (for example, a heat-treating process may require a lot of a given size), or raw material purchase lots (for example, a truckload of chemicals may be available in only one lot size). However, caution should be exercised prior to any modification of lot size because the modification can cause substantial distortion of actual requirements at lower levels in the MRP hierarchy. Where setup costs are significant and the demand is reasonably smooth, part period balancing (PPB), Wagner–Whitin, or even EOQ should provide satisfactory results. Too much concern with lot sizing yields false accuracy because of MRP dynamics. A correct lot size can be determined only after the fact, based on what actually happened in terms of requirements.[9]

---

[8]See James M. Fordyce and Francis M. Webster, "The Wagner–Whitin Algorithm Made Simple," *Production and Inventory Management* (Second Quarter 1984): 21–27. This article provides as straightforward an explanation of the Wagner–Whitin technique as the authors have found. The Wagner–Whitin Algorithm yields a cost of $455 for the data in Examples 4, 5, and 6.

[9]See discussions by Joseph Orlicky, *Material Requirements Planning* (New York: McGraw-Hill, 1975), pp. 136–137, and G. Nandakumar, "Lot-Sizing Techniques in a Multiproduct Multilevel Environment," *Production and Inventory Management*, 26 (First Quarter 1985): 46–54.

EXTENSIONS IN MRP

Recent years have seen the development of a number of extensions of MRP. In this section, we review three of them.

Closed-Loop MRP

Closed-loop material requirements planning implies an MRP system that provides feedback to scheduling from the inventory control system. Specifically, a **closed-loop MRP system** provides feedback to the capacity plan, master production schedule, and ultimately to the production plan (as shown in Figure 14.6). Virtually all commercial MRP systems are closed-loop.

Closed-loop MRP system

FIGURE 14.6 ■ Closed-Loop Material Requirements Planning

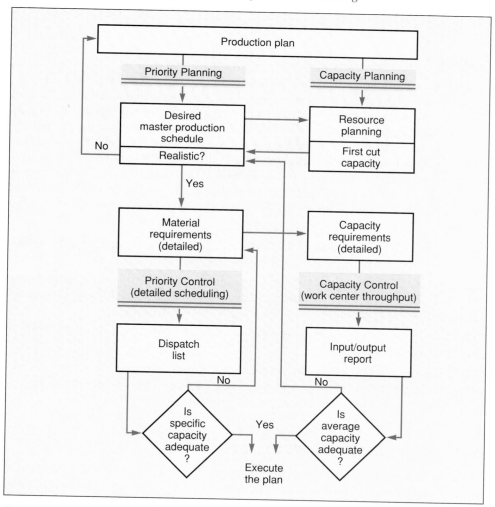

(*Source:* Adapted from *Capacity Planning and Control Study Guide.* Falls Church, VA: American Production and Inventory Control Society.)

FIGURE 14.7 ■ (a) Initial Resource Requirements Profile for a Milling Center
(b) Smoothed Resource Requirements Profile for a Milling Center

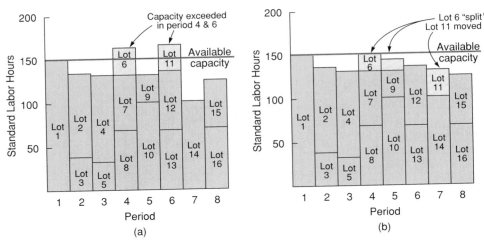

Capacity Planning

Load reports

In keeping with the definition of closed-loop MRP, feedback about work load is obtained from each work center. **Load reports** show the resource requirements in a work center for all work currently assigned to the work center, all work planned, and expected orders. Figure 14.7 shows that the initial load in the milling center exceeds capacity in weeks 4 and 6. Closed-loop MRP systems allow production planners to move the work between time periods to smooth the load or at least bring it within capacity. (This is the *capacity* side of Figure 14.6.) The closed-loop MRP system can then reschedule all items in the net requirements plan (see Figure 14.7). Tactics for smoothing the load and minimizing the impact of changed lead time include the following:

1. *Overlapping,* which reduces the lead time, entails sending pieces to the second operation before the entire lot is completed on the first operation.

2. *Operations splitting* sends the lot to two different machines for the same operation. This involves an additional setup, but results in shorter throughput times, because only part of the lot is processed on each machine.

3. *Lot splitting* involves breaking up the order and running part of it ahead of schedule.

When the work load consistently exceeds work center capacity, the tactics just discussed are not adequate. This may mean adding capacity. Options include adding capacity via personnel, machinery, overtime, or subcontracting.

Material Requirements Planning II (MRP II)

Material requirements planning II (MRP II)

Material requirements planning II is an extremely powerful technique. Once a firm has MRP in place, inventory data can be augmented by labor-hours, by material cost (rather than material quantity), by capital cost, or by virtually any resource. When MRP is used this way, it is usually referred to as **MRP II**, and *resource* is usually substituted for *requirements*. MRP then stands for material *resource* planning.

For instance, so far in our discussion of MRP, we have scheduled units (quantities), but each of these units requires resources in addition to its components. Those additional resources include labor-hours, machine-hours, and accounts payable (cash). Each of these resources can be used in an MRP format just as we used quantities. Table 14.4 shows how to determine the labor-hours, machine-hours, and cash that a sample master production schedule will require in each period. These requirements are then compared with the respective capacity (that is, labor-hours, machine-hours, cash, and so forth), so operations managers can make schedules that will work. The potential of MRP II, combined with other information, is discussed further in the *POM in Action* box "MRP II Builds Profits at Compaq."

Furthermore, most MRP II computer programs are tied into other computer programs that provide data to the MRP system or receive data from the MRP system. Order entry, invoicing, billing, purchasing, production scheduling, capacity planning, and warehouse management are a few examples. A schematic showing how these sources of data for a manufacturing organization tie together is shown in Figure 14.8.

MRP IN SERVICES

The demand for many services or service items is classified as dependent demand when it is directly related to or derived from the demand for other services. For example, in a restaurant where bread and vegetables are included in every meal ordered, the demand for bread and vegetables is dependent on the demand for meals. The meal is an end item and the bread and vegetables are component items.

Figure 14.9 on page 671 shows a bill of materials and accompanying product structure tree for veal picante, a top-selling entree in a New Orleans restaurant. Note that the various components of veal picante (that is, veal, sauce, and linguini) are

TABLE 14.4 ■ MATERIAL RESOURCE PLANNING (MRP II). BY UTILIZING THE LOGIC OF MRP, RESOURCES SUCH AS LABOR, MACHINE-HOURS, AND COST CAN BE ACCURATELY DETERMINED AND SCHEDULED. WEEKLY DEMAND FOR LABOR, MACHINE-HOURS, AND PAYABLES FOR 100 UNITS ARE SHOWN.

		WEEK		
	5	6	7	8
A. (lead time 1 week)				100
Labor: 10 hours each				1,000
Machine: 2 hours each				200
Payable: $0 each				0
B. (lead time 2 weeks, 2 each required)			200	
Labor: 10 hours each			2,000	
Machine: 2 hours each			400	
Payable: Raw material at $5 each			1,000	
C. (lead time 4 weeks, 3 each required)	300			
Labor: 2 hours each	600			
Machine: 1 hour each	300			
Payable: Raw material at $10 each	3,000			

MRP II Builds Profits at Compaq

Cal Monteith, Compaq's Manager of Master Planning and Production Control in Houston, was in the process of phasing out one of Compaq's personal computer models when he was told that Compaq had underestimated demand. The new schedule suggested he build 10,000 more PCs. Could he do it? Questions Monteith faced were: What parts were on hand and on order? What labor was available? Could the plant handle the capacity? Did vendors have the capacity? What product lines could be rescheduled?

Traditionally, amassing such information required not only MRP reports, but a variety of additional reports. Even then a response was based on partial information.

New software that includes a combination of spreadsheets, inquiry languages, and report writers allowed Monteith to search huge data bases, isolate the relevant data (customer orders, forecasts, inventory, and capacity), and do some quick calculations. One such piece of software is FastMRP, which is based in Ottawa, Canada. Another is Carp Systems International of Kanata, Ontario. The result: Compaq was able to make schedule adjustments that added millions of dollars to the bottom line.

Sources: New York Times (October 18, 1992): F9; Carp System International; and FastMRP.

---

prepared by different kitchen personnel (see part (a) of Figure 14.9). These preparations also require different amounts of time to complete. Figure 14.9(c) shows a bill of labor for the veal dish. It lists the operations to be performed, the order of operations, and the labor requirements for each operation (types of labor and labor-hours).

FIGURE 14.8   ■   MRP Information Flow Integrated with Other Information Systems.
Note: Arrowheads indicate the flow of data.

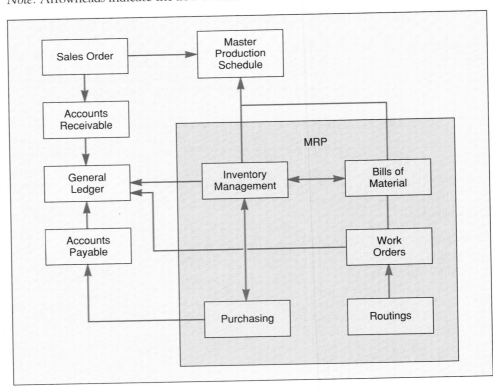

FIGURE 14.9 ■ Product Structure Tree, Bill of Material, and Bill of Labor for Veal Picante

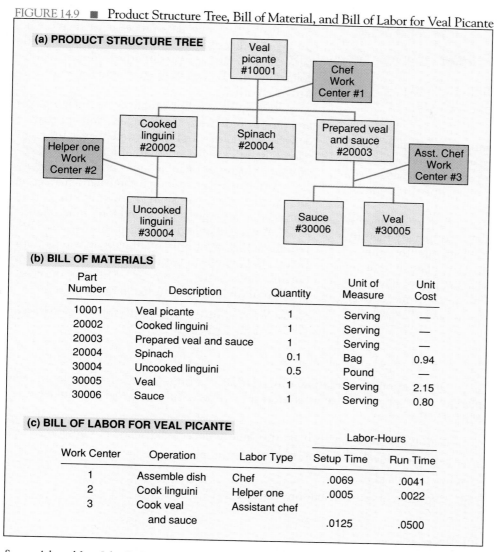

(a) PRODUCT STRUCTURE TREE

(b) BILL OF MATERIALS

Part Number	Description	Quantity	Unit of Measure	Unit Cost
10001	Veal picante	1	Serving	—
20002	Cooked linguini	1	Serving	—
20003	Prepared veal and sauce	1	Serving	—
20004	Spinach	0.1	Bag	0.94
30004	Uncooked linguini	0.5	Pound	—
30005	Veal	1	Serving	2.15
30006	Sauce	1	Serving	0.80

(c) BILL OF LABOR FOR VEAL PICANTE

Work Center	Operation	Labor Type	Labor-Hours Setup Time	Run Time
1	Assemble dish	Chef	.0069	.0041
2	Cook linguini	Helper one	.0005	.0022
3	Cook veal and sauce	Assistant chef	.0125	.0500

Source: Adopted from John G. Wacker "Effective Planning and Cost Control for Restaurants," *Production and Inventory Management,* First Quarter, 1985, p. 60.

MRP is also applied in hospitals, especially when dealing with surgeries that require equipment, materials, and supplies. Houston's Park Plaza Hospital, for example, uses the technique to improve the management of expensive surgical inventory.[10]

DISTRIBUTION RESOURCE PLANNING (DRP)

When dependent techniques are used in distribution environments, they are called distribution resource planning (DRP). See, for instance, the *POM in Action* box, "Moving the Pampers Faster Cuts Everyone's Costs."

[10]See E. Steinberg, B. Khumawala, and R. Scamell, "Requirements Planning in the Health Care Environment," *Journal of Operations Management,* 2, no. 4 (August 1982): 251–259.

Moving the Pampers Faster
Cuts Everyone's Costs

Experts cite Procter & Gamble as a foremost example of how packaged goods and food manufacturers can work closely and form partnerships with major retailers to prune costs in the pipeline that connects manufacturers to consumers.

Cutting inventories for both parties, smoothing out production schedules, and quickly identifying quality and service problems are the aims of these partnerships. The identical benefits that automakers and other industrial companies have been reaping in recent years from just-in-time delivery arrangements with suppliers are exactly what they are looking for.

Teams that mix data-processing experts, who automate order and record-keeping systems, with sales and purchasing representatives are assigned by companies like Procter & Gamble and Kmart to deal with each other.

To help Procter & Gamble avoid sudden spikes and dips in orders for, say, Pampers, and coordinate delivery schedules with Kmart's warehouses, the companies' logistics managers share information. To coordinate Procter & Gamble's new product introductions with Kmart's promotional campaigns, marketing and finance managers share both up-to-date sales data on the latest promotions and long-range plans.

"When we started looking at this, we saw a potential savings of $1 billion annually in the U.S. for Procter & Gamble and just as much, if not more, for our customers," said Lawrence D. Milligan, the company's senior vice president in charge of sales.

Sources: New York Times (July 14, 1991): 15; and *Supermarket Business* (May 1991): 29–37, 165–166.

Distribution resource planning (DRP)

Distribution resource planning (DRP) is a time-phased stock replenishment plan for all levels of a distribution network. Its procedures and logic are analogous to MRP. DRP requires

1. gross requirements, which are the same as expected demand or sales forecasts;
2. minimum levels of inventory to meet customer service levels;
3. accurate lead time;
4. definition of the distribution structure.

DRP Structure

When DRP is used, expected demand becomes gross requirements. Net requirements are determined by allocating available inventory to gross requirements. The DRP procedure starts with the forecast at the retail level (or the most distant point of the distribution network being supplied). All other levels are computed. As is the case with MRP, inventory is then reviewed with an aim to satisfying demand. So that stock will arrive when it is needed, net requirements are offset by the necessary lead time. A planned order release quantity becomes the gross requirement at the next level down the distribution chain.

Allocation

Pull system

The traditional DRP network, known as a **pull system**, is driven by the top or retail level ordering more stock. Allocations are made to the top level from available stock after being modified to obtain shipping economies. These modifications might include changing the shipping quantity to a truckload or a pallet load. The pull system has three notable problems. First, the pulls are often distorted (increased) at subsequent levels in the network.[11] Second, each ordering location ignores the replenishment requirements at other locations. Third, ordering locations also ignore the stock status at the supplying location.

The alternative system is the **push system**. In the push system, orders are received from upstream locations, but they are evaluated by the supplying location. The evaluation includes determining not only requirements at each requesting location but also total system requirements and stock availability at the supplying locations. Such a system is designed to combine information from both using and supplying locations. In theory, the combination yields an improved allocation of stock, because replenishment policies can be established based on both availability and system demand.

Push system

ACHIEVING WORLD-CLASS STANDARDS

Although MRP is complex, it improves scheduling and inventory management. World-class firms know this. They have found that MRP systems have a number of benefits. Among these benefits are (1) increased performance to schedules and improved customer service, (2) improved utilization of facilities and labor, (3) faster response to market changes, and (4) reduced inventory levels.

These benefits have allowed world-class organizations to build and achieve schedule performance. The result is improved customer service that wins orders and market share. World-class firms use MRP in a proactive way, not only to improve delivery to customers, but to gather materials from suppliers. Schedules are shared with suppliers to yield better coordination. The result is improved supplier relations that improve purchasing activities, from price and quality to delivery.

Utilization of facilities and labor yields higher productivity and return-on-investment, just as less inventory frees up capital and floor space for other uses. Inventory turnover in some world-class firms approaches 150 times per year. The improvement in utilization, supplier relations, and scheduling allows movement toward smaller lot sizes and shorter lead times. These improvements in turn allow better response to market.

Once the foregoing capabilities are demonstrated, world-class MRP users usually become innovative users of MRP II by scheduling resources such as product development and testing.

SUMMARY

Material requirements planning (MRP) is the preferred way to schedule production and inventory when demand is dependent. For MRP to work, management must have a master schedule, precise requirements for all components, accurate inventory and

---

[11]This is the same type of response recognized in Jay Forrester's *Industrial Dynamics*. Forrester noted that small changes in demand at the retail level stimulated wider variations at the wholesale level and even greater deviations at the factory level. J. Forrester, *Industrial Dynamics* (Cambridge, MA: MIT Press, 1964).

purchasing records, and accurate lead times. Distribution resource planning (DRP) is a time-phased stock replacement technique for distribution networks based on MRP procedures and logic.

Production should often be lot-for-lot in an MRP system, and replenishment orders in a DRP system should be small and frequent, given the constraints of ordering and transportation costs.

Both MRP and DRP, when properly implemented, can contribute in a major way to reduction in inventory while improving customer service levels. These techniques allow the operations manager to schedule and replenish stock on a "need-to-order" basis rather than simply a "time-to-order" basis.

KEY TERMS

Material requirements planning (MRP) (p. 650)
Master production schedule (p. 651)
Engineering change notice (ECN) (p. 652)
Bill of material (BOM) (p. 653)
Modular bills (p. 654)
Planning bills (p. 654)
Pseudo bills (p. 654)
Kit number (p. 654)
Phantom bills of material (p. 654)
Low-level coding (p. 655)
Lead time (p. 655)
Gross material requirements plan (p. 656)
System nervousness (p. 662)
Time fences (p. 662)

Pegging (p. 662)
Lot-sizing decisions (p. 662)
Lot-for-lot (p. 662)
Part period balancing (PPB) (p. 665)
Economic part period (EPP) (p. 665)
Wagner–Whitin procedure (p. 666)
Closed-loop MRP system (p. 667)
Load reports (p. 668)
Material requirements planning II (MRP II) (p. 668)
Distribution resource planning (DRP) (p. 672)
Pull system (p. 672)
Push system (p. 673)

USING AB:POM TO SOLVE MRP AND LOT-SIZING PROBLEMS

Solving Examples 1, 2, and 3 with AB:POM

Programs 14.1 and 14.2 show the detailed input and output respectively for solving Examples 1 to 3 using AB:POM. Here are the inputs used in Program 14.1

1. *Item names*. The item names are entered in the left column. The same item name will appear in more than one row if the item is used by two parent items. Each item must follow its parents, as shown in Program 14.1.
2. *Item level* (Lvl). The level in the indented BOM must be given here. The item *cannot* be placed at a level more than one below the item immediately above.
3. *Lead time* (ldtm). The lead time for an item is entered here. The default is 1 week.
4. *Number* (#per). The number of units of this subassembly needed for its parent is entered here. The default is one.
5. *On-hand* (nhnd). List current inventory on hand once, even if the subassembly is listed twice.
6. *Lot size* (Lot). The lot size can be specified here. A 0 or 1 will perform lot-for-lot ordering. If another number is placed here, then all orders for that item will be in integer multiples of that number.
7. *Demands* (entered in the first row). The demands are entered in the end item row in the period in which the items are demanded.
8. *Scheduled receipts*. If units are scheduled to be received in the future, they should be listed in the appropriate time period (column) and item (row). (An entry here in level one is a demand; all other levels are receipts.)

PROGRAM 14.1 ■ AB:POM's MRP Module Applied to Examples 1, 2, and 3. AB:POM's material requirements planning (MRP) module can be used to perform an MRP analysis for up to 18 periods. The data screen shown is generated by indicating the number of lines in the bill of materials. In our sample problem, we created a BOM with 7 items, but 9 lines.

Data File:HREX3 —————— Material Requirements Planning —————— Data Screen —

Number of BOM lines (1–90) 9   Number of demand periods (1–18) 8

Item	Level	Lead time	#per	On-hand inv	Lot size	pd1	pd2	pd3	pd4	pd5	pd6	pd7	pd8
A	0	1	0	10	0	0	0	0	0	0	0	0	50
B	1	2	2	15	0	0	0	0	0	0	0	0	0
D	2	1	2	10	0	0	0	0	0	0	0	0	0
E	2	2	2	0	0	0	0	0	0	0	0	0	0
C	1	1	3	20	0	0	0	0	0	0	0	0	0
E	2	2	2	10	0	0	0	0	0	0	0	0	0
F	2	3	2	5	0	0	0	0	0	0	0	0	0
G	3	2	1	0	0	0	0	0	0	0	0	0	0
D	3	1	2	0	0	0	0	0	0	0	0	0	0

PROGRAM 14.2 ■ Printed Solution to MRP Run on Examples 1, 2, and 3 Data. The printed solution for items A, B, and D in Examples 1, 2, and 3 is shown in this output of Program 14.1. The meaning of each item on the left-hand column of the printed output is explained in items 1 through 5 below.

1. *Total required.* The total number of units required in each week is listed in the first row. For the end item, the first row contains the demand schedule that was input on the data screen (Program 14.1). Other requirements are computed.
2. *On-hand.* The number on-hand is listed here. The on-hand amount starts as given on the data screen and is reduced according to needs.
3. *Order receipt.* The amount that was scheduled in the original data screen is shown here.
4. *Net required.* The net amount required is the amount needed after the on-hand inventory is used.
5. *Order release.* Order release is the net amount required, offset by the lead time.

Item A

	Week 1	Week 2	Week 3	Week 4	Week 5	Week 6	Week 7	Week 8
TOT. REQ.	0	0	0	0	0	0	0	50
ON HAND	10	10	10	10	10	10	10	10
ORD REC.	0	0	0	0	0	0	0	0
NET REQ.	0	0	0	0	0	0	0	40
ORD REL.	0	0	0	0	0	0	40	0

Item B

	Week 1	Week 2	Week 3	Week 4	Week 5	Week 6	Week 7	Week 8
TOT. REQ.	0	0	0	0	0	0	80	0
ON HAND	15	15	15	15	15	15	15	0
ORD REC.	0	0	0	0	0	0	0	0
NET REQ.	0	0	0	0	0	0	65	0
ORD REL.	0	0	0	0	65	0	0	0

Item D

	Week 1	Week 2	Week 3	Week 4	Week 5	Week 6	Week 7	Week 8
TOT. REQ.	0	0	390	0	130	0	0	0
ON HAND	10	10	10	0	0	0	0	0
ORD REC.	0	0	0	0	0	0	0	0
NET REQ.	0	0	380	0	130	0	0	0
ORD REL.	0	380	0	130	0	0	0	0

Solving Example 5 with AB:POM Lot-Sizing Module

Program 14.3 illustrates the use of AB:POM in solving lot-sizing problems.

PROGRAM 14.3 ■ Solving Example 5 with the AB:POM Lot-Sizing Module. The data screen for lot sizing is initialized by indicating the number of periods over which the lot sizing is to be performed. In this example we use 10 periods.

The lot-sizing module will perform lot sizing for minimizing total holding and setup costs when demands in each period are not equal. You may input your own ordering schedule, or use *economic order quantity (EOQ)*, *lot-for-lot, part period balancing*, or *Wagner–Whitin*. Use the toggle menu to select the desired option.

Data file:hrex5 ———————— Sizing, Lot ———————————— Solution ———

Number of time periods (1–98) 10

METHOD –> Economic Order Quantity

Total cost = $775.00

EOQ = 73

Holding cost   1.00
Setup cost   100.00
Initial inventory 35.00
Lead time   1

Period	Demand	Release	Receipt	Inventory	Holding $	Setup $
Period 1	35	73	0	0	0.00	
Period 2	30	0	73	43	43.00	100.00
Period 3	40	0	0	3	3.00	
Period 4	0	73	0	3	3.00	
Period 5	10	0	73	66	66.00	100.00
Period 6	40	73	0	26	26.00	
Period 7	30	0	73	69	69.00	100.00
Period 8	0	0	0	69	69.00	
Period 9	30	73	0	39	39.00	
Period 10	55	0	73	57	57.00	100.00
Totals	270	292	292	375	$375.00	$400.00

Solved Problem 14.1

Determine the low-level coding and the quantity of each component necessary to produce 10 units of an assembly we will call Alpha. The product structure and quantities of each component needed for each assembly are noted in parentheses.

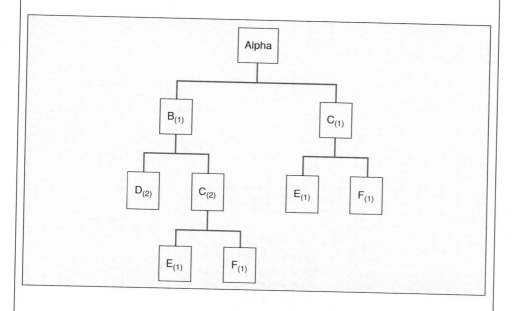

Solution

Redraw the product structure with low-level coding. Then multiply down the structure until the requirements of each branch are determined. Then add across the structure until the total for each is determined.

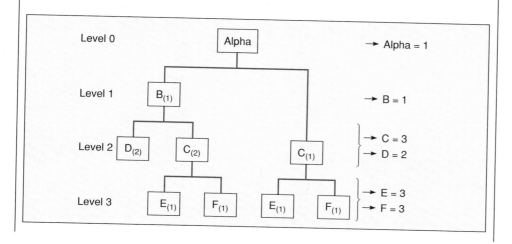

E's required for left branch:

$$(1_{alpha} \times 1_B \times 2_C \times 1_E) = 2$$

and E's required for right branch:

$$(1_{alpha} \times 1_C \times 1_E) = \underline{1}$$
$$3 \text{ E's required}$$

Then "explode" the requirements by multiplying each by 10, as shown in the following table.

LEVEL	ITEM	QUANTITY PER UNIT	TOTAL REQUIREMENTS FOR 10 ALPHA
0	Alpha	1	10
1	B	1	10
2	C	3	30
2	D	2	20
3	E	3	30
3	F	3	30

Solved Problem 14.2

Using the product structure for Alpha in Solved Problem 14.1, and the lead times, quantity on hand, and master production schedule shown below, prepare a net MRP table for Alphas.

ITEM	LEAD TIME	QTY ON HAND
Alpha	1	10
B	2	20
C	3	0
D	1	100
E	1	10
F	1	50

MASTER PRODUCTION SCHEDULE FOR ALPHA

PERIOD	6	7	8	9	10	11	12	13
Gross requirements			50			50		100

Solution
See the chart on the next page.

Net Material Requirements Planning Sheet for Alpha. *Note:* The letter in parentheses (A) is the source of the demand.

Lot Size	Lead Time (# of Periods)	On Hand	Safety Stock	Allocated	Low-Level Code	Item ID		Period (week,day) 1	2	3	4	5	6	7	8	9	10	11	12	13
Lot-for-Lot	1	10	—	—	0	Alpha (A)	Gross Requirements								50			50		100
							Scheduled Receipts													
							Projected on Hand 10								10			—		—
							Net Requirements								40			50		100
							Planned Order Receipts								40			50		100
							Planned Order Releases							40			50		100	
Lot-for-Lot	2	20	—	—	1	B	Gross Requirements							40(A)			50(A)		100(A)	
							Scheduled Receipts													
							Projected on Hand 20					—		20	—		—		—	
							Net Requirements							20			50		100	
							Planned Order Receipts							20			50		100	
							Planned Order Releases					20			50		100			
Lot-for-Lot	3	0	—	—	2	C	Gross Requirements					40(B)		40(A)	100(B)	200(B) + 50(A)			100(A)	
							Scheduled Receipts													
							Projected on Hand 0					—		—	—		—			
							Net Requirements					40		40	100		250		100	
							Planned Order Receipts					40		40	100		250		100	
							Planned Order Releases		40		40	100		250		100				
Lot-for-Lot	1	100	—	—	2	D	Gross Requirements					40(B)			100(B)		200(B)			
							Scheduled Receipts													
							Projected on Hand 100					100			60		—			
							Net Requirements				0	0			40		200			
							Planned Order Receipts					0			40		200			
							Planned Order Releases							40		200				
Lot-for-Lot	1	10	—	—	3	E	Gross Requirements		40(C)		40(C)	100(C)		250(C)		100(C)				
							Scheduled Receipts													
							Projected on Hand 10		10		—	—		—		—				
							Net Requirements		30		40	100		250		100				
							Planned Order Receipts		30		40	100		250		100				
							Planned Order Releases	30		40	100		250		100					
Lot-for-Lot	1	50	—	—	3	F	Gross Requirements		40(C)		40(C)	100(C)		250(C)		100(C)				
							Scheduled Receipts													
							Projected on Hand 50		50		10	—		—		—				
							Net Requirements		0		30	100		250		100				
							Planned Order Receipts				30	100		250		100				
							Planned Order Releases	—		30	100		250		100					

DISCUSSION QUESTIONS

1. What is the difference between a *gross* requirements plan and a *net* requirements plan?
2. Once a material requirements plan (MRP) has been established, what other managerial applications might be found for the technique?
3. What are the similarities between MRP and DRP?
4. How does MRP II differ from MRP?
5. Which is the best lot-sizing policy for manufacturing organizations?
6. What impact does ignoring carrying cost in the allocation of stock in a DRP system have on lot sizes?
7. What do we mean by *closed-loop* MRP?
8. What are the options for the production planner that has (a) scheduled more than capacity in a work center next week and (b) a consistent lack of capacity in that work center?
9. What types of resources might be scheduled via an MRP II?
10. What functions of the firm impact an MRP system? How?
11. What is the rationale for (a) a phantom bill of material, (b) a planning bill of material, and (c) a pseudo bill of material?
12. Identify five specific requirements of an effective MRP system.
13. What are some of the benefits of MRP?

CRITICAL THINKING EXERCISE

The very structure of MRP systems suggests fixed lead times. However, many firms are moving toward JIT and Kanban techniques. What are the issues and the impact of adding JIT inventory and purchasing techniques and Kanban to an organization that has MRP?

PROBLEMS

· **14.1** The product structure for a product we make, called Alpha, is shown below. We need 10 units of Alpha in week 6. Three units of D and two units of F are required for each Alpha. The lead time for Alpha is 1 week. We have no units of Alpha, D, or F on hand. Lead time for D is 1 week and lead time for F is 2 weeks. Using the format below, prepare a gross and net material requirements plan for Alpha. (*Hint:* For this and other problems in this chapter, a copy of the form on the page may be helpful.)

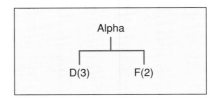

: **14.2** The demand for subassembly S is 100 units in week 7. Each unit of S requires one unit of T and .5 unit of U. Each unit of T requires one unit of V, two units of W, and one unit of X. Finally, each unit of U requires .5 units of Y and three units of Z. One firm manufactures all items. It takes 2 weeks to make S, 1 week to make T, 2 weeks to make U, 2 weeks to make V, 3 weeks to make W, 1 week to make X, 2 weeks to make Y, and 1 week to make Z.

Lot Size	Lead Time (# of periods)	On Hand	Safety Stock	Allo-cated	Low-Level Code	Item ID		Period (week,day)							
								1	2	3	4	5	6	7	8
							Gross Requirements								
							Scheduled Receipts								
							Projected on Hand								
							Net Requirements								
							Planned Order Receipts								
							Planned Order Releases								
							Gross Requirements								
							Scheduled Receipts								
							Projected on Hand								
							Net Requirements								
							Planned Order Receipts								
							Planned Order Releases								
							Gross Requirements								
							Scheduled Receipts								
							Projected on Hand								
							Net Requirements								
							Planned Order Receipts								
							Planned Order Releases								
							Gross Requirements								
							Scheduled Receipts								
							Projected on Hand								
							Net Requirements								
							Planned Order Receipts								
							Planned Order Releases								
							Gross Requirements								
							Scheduled Receipts								
							Projected on Hand								
							Net Requirements								
							Planned Order Receipts								
							Planned Order Releases								

a) Construct a product structure and a gross material requirements plan for the dependent inventory items. Identify all levels, parents, and components.

b) Construct a net material requirements plan from the product structure and the following on-hand inventory.

ITEM	ON-HAND INVENTORY	ITEM	ON-HAND INVENTORY
S	20	W	30
T	20	X	25
U	10	Y	15
V	30	Z	10

14.3 In addition to 100 units of S (per Problem 14.2), there is also a demand for 20 units of U, which is a component of S. The 20 units of U are needed for maintenance purposes. These units are needed 1 week before S, in week 6. Modify the gross and net material requirements plan to reflect this change.

: 14.4 Given the following bill of material, master production schedule, and inventory status, develop: (a) a gross requirements plan for all items and (b) net materials requirements (planned order release) for all items.

MASTER PRODUCTION SCHEDULE: X1						
PERIOD	7	8	9	10	11	12
Gross requirements		50		20		100

ITEM	LEAD TIME	ON HAND	ITEM	LEAD TIME	ON HAND
X1	1	50	C	3	10
B1	2	20	D	1	0
B2	2	20	E	1	0
A1	1	5			

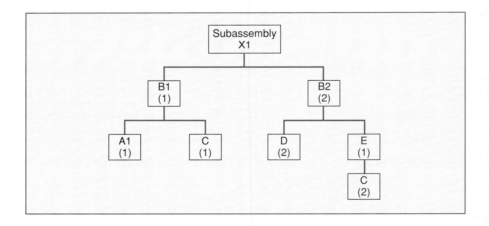

Problems 14.5 and 14.6 use the data shown below and at the top of the next page.

DATA FOR PROBLEMS 14.5 AND 14.6					
PERIOD	8	9	10	11	12
Gross requirements: A	100		50		150
Gross requirements: H		100		50	

DATA FOR PROBLEMS 14.5 AND 14.6 (CONT'D)					
ITEM	ON HAND	LEAD TIME	ITEM	ON HAND	LEAD TIME
A	0	1	F	75	2
B	100	2	G	75	1
C	50	2	H	0	1
D	50	1	J	100	2
E	75	2	K	100	2

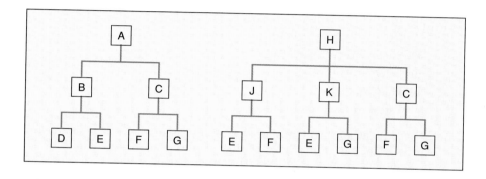

💻 : **14.5** Given the bill of material, master production schedule, and inventory status shown above, develop (a) a gross requirements plan for C and (b) a planned order release for C.

💻 : **14.6** Based on the preceding data, complete a net planned order release schedule for all items (10 schedules in all).

Problems 14.7 through 14.9 are based on an item that has the gross requirements shown in the following table and a beginning inventory of 40 units.

DATA FOR PROBLEMS 14.7–14.9												
PERIOD	1	2	3	4	5	6	7	8	9	10	11	12
Gross requirements	30		40		30	70	20		10	80		50

Holding cost = $2.50/unit/week; setup cost = $150; lead time = 1 week.

💻 : **14.7** Develop a lot-for-lot solution and calculate total relevant costs.

: **14.8 a)** Develop an EOQ solution and calculate total relevant costs. Stockout costs equal $10 per unit.

💻 **b)** Solve part (a) with lead time = 0.

: 14.9 **a)** Develop a PPB solution and calculate total relevant costs.

   b) Solve part (a) with lead time = 0.

:14.10 Keebock, a maker of outstanding running shoes, keeps the soles of its size 13 running shoes in inventory for one period at a cost of $.25 per unit. The setup costs are $50. Beginning inventory is zero and lead time is 1 week; stockout cost is $5 per unit. Shown in the following table are the net requirements per period.

DATA FOR PROBLEM 14.10

PERIOD	0	1	2	3	4	5	6	7	8	9	10
Net requirements		35	30	45	0	10	40	30	0	30	55

Determine Keebock's cost based on:

a) EOQ.

b) Lot-for-lot.

c) Part period balancing (PPB).

   Problems 14.11 through 14.14 are based on the data shown in the table below. The parent item has a 1-week lead time, and the lot-for-lot rule is employed. Beginning inventory is 20 units. The parent item has a component whose lead time is also 1 week and whose starting inventory position is 30 units. At the component level, production occurs in lot sizes to cover three periods of net requirements.

DATA FOR PROBLEMS 14.11–14.14

PERIOD	1	2	3	4	5	6	7	8	9	10
Gross requirements	0	40	30	40	10	70	40	10	30	60

:14.11 Develop the parent and component MRP tables to show the original planned positions.

:14.12 At the parent level, gross requirements for period 2 are canceled. Develop the parent and component net MRP tables to show the net effect of this cancellation.

:14.13 With the parent level gross requirements canceled for period 2, what is the effect on inventory quantity, setup costs, and holding costs?

:14.14 At the component level, there is enough capacity to produce 75 units in period 1. Gross requirements at the parent level increase from 40 to 50 units in period 2. What problem arises? What solution would you recommend?

:14.15 A part structure, lead time (weeks), and on-hand quantities for product A are shown on the next page.

   From the information shown, generate:

a) An indented bill of material for product A (see Figure 6.10).

b) A bill of material showing the quantity of each part required to produce one A.

c) An exploded bill of material showing the quantity of each part required to produce ten A's.

DATA FOR PROBLEMS 14.15, 14.16, 14.17, AND THE DATA BASE APPLICATION 14.19

PART	INVENTORY ON HAND
A	0
B	2
C	10
D	5
E	4
F	5
G	1
H	10

PART STRUCTURE TREE

LT = lead time in weeks

d) Net requirements for each part to produce ten A's in week 8 using lot-for-lot.

(*Hint:* The AB:POM can help with parts (b) and (c), but not produce an output other than in MRP format.)

14.16 You are product planner for product A (in Problem 14.15). The field service manager, Al Trostel, has just called and told you that the requirements for B and F should each be increased by 10 units for his repair requirements in the field.

a) Prepare an exploded bill of material showing the quantity of each part required to produce the requirements for the service manager *and* the production request of 10.

b) What are the net requirements (i.e., exploded bill of materials less on-hand inventory)?

c) Prepare a net requirement plan by date for the new requirements (for both production and field service), assuming that the field service manager wants his 10 units in week 6 and the 10 production units are still due in week 8.

14.17 You have just been notified via FAX that the lead time for component G of product A (Problem 14.16) has just been increased to 4 weeks.

a) Which items have changed and why?

b) What are the implications for the production plan?

c) As production planner, what can you do?

14.18 As director of operations, you have recently installed a distribution requirements planning (DRP) system. The company has an East Coast and a West Coast warehouse, as well as a main factory warehouse in Omaha, Nebraska. You have just received the orders for the next planning period from the managers at each of the three facilities. Their reports are shown below. The lead time to both the East Coast and the West Coast warehouses is 2 weeks and there is a 1-week lead time to bring material to the factory warehouse. Shipments are in truckload quantities of 100 each. There is no initial inventory in the system. The factory is having trouble installing the level of material work schedule and still has a lot size in multiples of 100.

DATA FOR EAST COAST WAREHOUSE

PERIOD	1	2	3	4	5	6	7	8	9	10	11	12
Forecast requirements			40	100	80	70	20	25	70	80	30	50

Lead time = 2 weeks

DATA FOR WEST COAST WAREHOUSE

PERIOD	1	2	3	4	5	6	7	8	9	10
Forecast requirements		30	45	60	70	40	80	70	80	55

Lead time = 2 weeks

DATA FOR FACTORY WAREHOUSE

PERIOD	1	2	3	4	5	6	7	8	9	10
Forecast requirements			30	40	10	70	40	10	30	60

Lead time = 1 week

a) Show the plan for *receipt* of orders from the factory.

b) If the factory requires 2 weeks to produce the merchandise, when must the orders be *released* to the factory?

DATA BASE APPLICATION

: 14.19 Your stockroom manager, Yamil Bermudez, arrived at your desk just after you had completed the net requirements plan for product A (use data in Problem 14.15), exclaiming that the cycle counter should be fired. It seems that the cycle counter was wrong; there are three A's available now, not zero as the original data showed; moreover, five E's are also available. About then, your boss, Sam Melnyk, who overheard the discussion, says, "You might as well extend the net requirements plan out to 16 weeks, because we just received an order for 10 more A's in week 12 and five more in week 15. Additionally, count on the field service department wanting three more B's in week 16, as well as those 10 units in week 8." You decide to use the lead times in Problem 14.15, but item G now has a lead time of 4 weeks.

Now you must prepare a new net requirements plan, based on the actual inventory (as reported) and the new schedule. Your assignment is to do so.

CASE STUDY

Service, Inc.

Service, Inc., is a distributor of automotive replacement parts. With no manufacturing capability, all products it sells are purchased, assembled, and repackaged. Service, Inc., does have extensive inventory and final assembly facilities. Among its products are private-label carburetor and ignition kits. The company has been experiencing difficulties for the last 2 years. First, profits have fallen considerably. Second, customer service levels have declined, with late deliveries now exceeding 25% of orders.

Third, customer returns have been rising at a rate of 3% per month.

Bob Hass, vice president of sales, claims that most of the problem lies with the assembly department. He says that they are not producing the proper mix of the product, they have poor quality control, their productivity has fallen, and their costs are too high.

Dick Houser, the treasurer, believes that problems have arisen due to investment in the wrong inventories. He thinks that marketing has too many options and products. Dick also thinks that the purchasing department buyers have been hedging their

(Continued)

inventories and requirements with excess purchasing commitments.

John Burnham, assembly manager, says, "The symptom is that we have a lot of parts in inventory, but no place to assemble them in the production schedule." An additional comment by John was, "When we have the right part, it is not very good, but we use it anyway to meet the schedule."

Freddy Fearon, manager of purchasing, has taken the stance that purchasing has not let Service, Inc., down. He has stuck by his old suppliers, used historical data to determine requirements, maintained what he views as excellent prices from suppli-

ers, and evaluated new sources of supply with an aim of lowering cost. Where possible, Freddy reacted to the increased pressure for profitability by emphasizing low cost and early delivery.

You are the president of Service, Inc., and must get the firm back on a course toward improved profitability.

DISCUSSION QUESTIONS

1. Identify both the symptoms and problems at Service, Inc.
2. What specific changes would you implement?

BIBLIOGRAPHY

Akinc, U. "A Practical Approach to Lot and Setup Scheduling at a Textile Firm." *Industrial Engineering Research & Development*, 25, no. 2 (March 1993): 54–64.

Bookbinder, J. H., and L. A. Koch. "Production Planning for Mixed Assembly/Arborescent Systems." *Journal of Operations Management*, 9, no. 1 (1990): 7–23.

Brown, R. G. *Advanced Service Parts Inventory Control.* Norwich, VT: Materials Management Systems, 1982.

Brucker, H. D., G. A. Flowers, and R. D. Peck. "MRP Shop-Floor Control in a Job Shop: Definitely Works." *Production and Inventory Management Journal*, 33, no. 2 (Second Quarter 1992): 43.

Campbell, G. M. "Master Production Scheduling Under Rolling Planning Horizons with Fixed Order Intervals." *Decision Sciences*, 23, no. 2 (March/April 1992): 312.

Davis, S. G. "Scheduling Economic Lot Size Production Runs." *Management Science*, 36, no. 8 (August 1990): 985–998.

Deleersnyder, J., T. J. Hodgson, R. E. King, P. J. O'Grady, and A. Savva. "Integrating Kanban Type Pull Systems and MRP Type Push Systems: Insights from a Markovian Model." *Industrial Engineering Research & Development*, 24, no. 3 (July 1992): 43.

Ding, F., and M. Yuen. "A Modified MRP for a Production System with the Coexistence of MRP and Kanbans." *Journal of Operations Management*, 10, no. 2 (April 1991): 267–277.

Dolinsky, L. R., T. E. Vollmann, and M. J. Maggard. "Adjusting Replenishment Orders to Reflect Learning in a Material Requirements Planning Environ-

ment." *Management Science*, 36 (December 1990): 1,532–1,547.

El-Najdawi, M. K., and P. R. Kleindorfer. "Common Cycle Lot-Size Scheduling for Multi-product, Multi-stage Production." *Management Science*, 39, no. 7 (July 1993): 872–885.

Freeland, J. R., J. P. Leschke, and E. N. Weiss. "Guidelines for Setup Cost Reduction Programs to Achieve Zero Inventory." *Journal of Operations Management*, 9 (January 1990): 85.

Gardiner, S. C., and J. H. Blackstone, Jr. "The Effects of Lot Sizing and Dispatching on Customer Service in an MRP Environment." *Journal of Operations Management*, 11, no. 2 (June 1993): 143–160.

Haddock, J., and D. E. Hubicki. "Which Lot-Sizing Techniques Are Used in Material Requirements Planning?" *Production and Inventory Management*, 30 (Third Quarter 1989): 57.

Hopp, W. J., M. L. Spearman, and I. Duenyas. "Economic Production Quotas for Pull Manufacturing Systems." *Industrial Engineering Research & Development*, 25, no. 2 (March 1993): 71–79.

Jacobs, F. R., and D. C. Whybark. "A Comparison of Reorder Point and Material Requirements Planning Inventory Control Logic." *Decision Sciences*, 23, no. 2 (March/April 1992): 332.

Ledbetter, M. E., C. A. Snyder, and S. C. Gardiner. "Work-in-Process Inventory Control for Repetitive Manufacturing in an MRP Environment: A Case Study." *Production and Inventory Management Journal*, 34, no. 2 (Second Quarter 1993): 48–52.

Martin, A. J. *DRP: Distribution Resource Planning.* Engle-wood Cliffs, NJ: Prentice Hall, 1983.

Meckler, V. A. "Setup Cost Reduction in the Dynamic Lot-Size Model." *Journal of Operations Management*, 11, no. 1 (March 1993): 35–44.

St. Johns, R. "The Evils of Lot Sizing in MRP." *Production and Inventory Management*, 25 (Fourth Quarter 1984): 75–85.

Sridharan, V., and R. Lawrence LaForge. "Freezing the Master Production Schedule: Implications for Customer Service." *Decision Sciences*, 25, no. 3 (May/June 1994): 461–469.

Sum, C., D. O. Png, and K. Yang. "Effects of Product Structure Complexity on Multi-level Lot Sizing." *Decision Sciences*, 24, no. 6 (November/December 1993): 1,135–1,156.

Wagner, H. M., and T. M. Whitin. "Dynamic Version of the Economic Lot Size Model." *Management Science*, 5, no. 1 (1958): 89–96.

Zhao, X., and T. S. Lee. "Freezing the Master Production Schedule for Material Requirements Planning Systems under Demand Uncertainty." *Journal of Operations Management*, 11, no. 2 (June 1993): 185–206.

15

AGGREGATE PLANNING

LEARNING OBJECTIVES

*When you complete this
chapter you should be able to:*

Identify or Define:

   Aggregate Planning

   Tactical Scheduling

   Graphic Technique for Aggregate
   Planning

   Mathematical Techniques for
   Planning

Explain:

   How to do aggregate planning

AGGREGATE PLANNING PROVIDES A COMPETITIVE ADVANTAGE AT ANHEUSER-BUSCH

In the starting cellar control room, process control uses computers to monitor the starting cellar process, where wort is in its final stage of preparation before being fermented into beer.

tion, a major factor in all high capital investment facilities.

Beer is produced in a product-focused facility, one that produces high volume and low variety. Product-focused production processes usually require high fixed cost, but typically have the benefit of low variable costs. Maintaining high use of such facilities is critical because high capital costs require high use to be competitive. Performance above the break-even point requires high use—and downtime is disastrous.

Beer production can be divided into four stages. The first stage is the selection and assurance of raw material delivery and quality. The second stage is the actual

Anheuser-Busch is a major beer producer, producing close to 40% of the beer consumed in the United States. The company achieves efficiency at such volume by doing an excellent job of matching capacity to demand.

Matching capacity and demand in the intermediate term (3–18 months) is the heart of aggregate planning. Anheuser-Busch matches fluctuating demand by brand to specific plant, labor, and inventory capacity. Meticulous cleaning between batches, effective maintenance, and efficient employee and facility scheduling contribute to high facility utiliza-

Shown are brew kettles where wort, later to become beer, is boiled and hops are added for the flavor and bitter character they impart.

Automated guided vehicles are used to transfer full kegs to storage prior to shipping.

brewing process from milling to aging. The third stage is packaging into the wide variety of containers desired by the market.

The fourth and final stage is distribution, which includes temperature-controlled delivery and storage. Each stage has its resource limitations. Developing the aggregate plan to make it all work is demanding.

Effective aggregate scheduling is a major ingredient in competitive advantage at Anheuser-Busch.

The canning line imprints on each can: a code that identifies the day, year, and 15-minute period of production; the plant at which the product was brewed and packaged; and the production line used. This allows any quality control problems to be tracked and corrected.

U nlike most other appliances, room air conditioners are heavily dependent on weather for sales. That makes decisions on aggregate
planning schedules a tough call for manufacturers like Whirlpool,
which produces air conditioners for Sears. If Whirlpool increases output and the
summer is warmer than usual, it stands to increase sales and market share. But if
the summer is cool, it may be stuck with expensive unsold machines. "You have
to plan for the average year," says Whirlpool's director of merchandising. "If not,
you are likely to go broke carrying over excessive inventory."[1] ◆

Aggregate planning

Planning for seasonal demands of air conditioners at Whirlpool is one aspect of aggregate planning. **Aggregate planning** is concerned with determining the quantity and
scheduling of production for the intermediate future, usually from 3 to 18 months
ahead. Operations managers try to determine the best way to meet forecasted demand
by adjusting production rates, labor levels, inventory levels, overtime work, subcontracting rates, and other controllable variables. *The objective of the process usually is to
minimize costs over the planning period.* Other objectives may be to minimize fluctuations in the work force or inventory levels, or to obtain a certain standard of service
performance.

Four things are needed for aggregate planning. First, the firm needs a logical
overall unit for measuring sales and output, such as air conditioning units in the case
of Whirlpool or cases of beer at Anheuser-Busch. Second, managers must be able to
forecast for a reasonable intermediate planning period in these aggregate terms.
Third, they must be able to determine the relevant costs we discuss in this chapter.
And fourth, operations managers need to develop a model that combines these forecasts and costs so that good scheduling decisions can be made for the planning period.

In this chapter, we describe the nature of the aggregate planning decisions in
both manufacturing and service sector firms. To this end, we will show how the aggregate plan fits into the overall planning process, as well as describe several techniques
that managers use in developing a plan.

THE PLANNING PROCESS

In Chapter 5, we saw that demand forecasting can address short-, medium-, and long-
range plans. Long-range forecasts help managers deal with capacity and strategic issues
and are the responsibility of top management (see Figure 15.1). Management formulates policy-related questions, such as facility location and expansion, new product development, research funding, and investment over a period of several years.

Tactical scheduling decisions

Once long-term capacity decisions are made, operations managers begin
medium-range planning that meets the objectives of the firm. **Tactical scheduling decisions** include making monthly or quarterly plans, which address the problem of
matching productivity to fluctuating demands. All of these plans need to be consistent with top management's long-range strategy and work within the resources allocated by earlier strategic decisions. The heart of the medium- (or "intermediate-")
range plan is the aggregate production plan.

[1]*New York Times* (February 23, 1989): D1, D4.

FIGURE 15.1 ■ Planning Tasks and Responsibilities

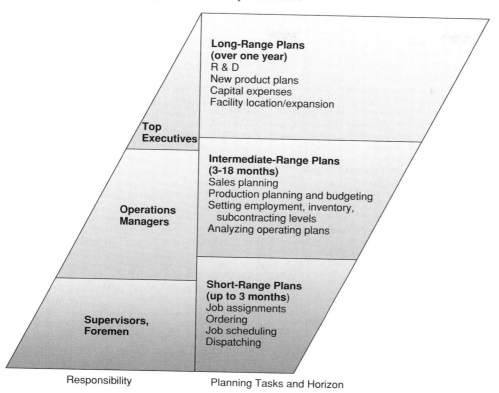

Responsibility   **Planning Tasks and Horizon**

Short-range planning extends up to a year but is usually less than 3 months. Operations managers make these plans in conjunction with supervisors and foremen, who "disaggregate" the intermediate plan into weekly, daily, and hourly schedules. Tactics for dealing with short-term planning involving loading, sequencing, expediting and dispatching, and other issues are discussed in Chapter 16.

Figure 15.1 illustrates the time horizons, features, and responsibilities for short-, intermediate-, and long-range planning.

THE NATURE OF AGGREGATE PLANNING

As the term *aggregate* implies, an aggregate plan means combining the appropriate resources into general, or overall, terms. Given the demand forecast, the facility capacity, overall inventory levels, the size of the work force, and related inputs, the operations manager has to select the rate of output for the facility over the next 3 to 18 months. The plan can be for manufacturing firms such as Whirlpool or Anheuser-Busch, for hospitals, for colleges, or for Prentice Hall, the company that published this textbook.

Take, for a manufacturing example, IBM or Compaq, each of which produces different models of microcomputers. They make: (1) laptops, (2) desktops, (3) notebook computers, and (4) advanced technology machines with high-speed chips. The aggregate plan for IBM or Compaq might have the following output (in units of production) for this "family" of microcomputers each month in the upcoming three quarters:

QUARTER 1			QUARTER 2			QUARTER 3		
Jan.	Feb.	Mar.	April	May	June	July	Aug.	Sept.
150,000	120,000	110,000	100,000	130,000	150,000	180,000	150,000	140,000

Note that the plan looks at production in the aggregate, not on a machine-by-machine breakdown.

An example from the service sector would be a company that provides microcomputer training for managers. The firm offers courses on Lotus, dBase, Harvard Graphics, WordPerfect, and a wide variety of other programs and subjects and employs several instructors to meet the demand from business and government for its services. Demand for training tends to be very low near holiday seasons and during summer, when many people take their vacations. To meet the fluctuating needs for courses, the company can perhaps hire and lay off instructors, advertise to increase demand in slow seasons, or subcontract its work to other training agencies during peak periods. Again, the operations planner will make decisions about intermediate-range capacity without getting into details of specific courses or instructors.

Aggregate planning is part of a larger production planning system; therefore, understanding the interfaces between the plan and several internal and external factors is useful. Figure 15.2 shows that not only does the operations manager receive input from the marketing department's demand forecast, but he or she has to deal with financial data, personnel, capacity, and availability of raw materials as well. In a manufacturing environment, the resulting master production schedule provides input to material requirements planning (MRP) systems, which address the procurement or production of parts or components needed to make the final product (see Chapter 14). Detailed work schedules for people and priority scheduling for products result as the final step of the production planning system (and are discussed in Chapter 16).

AGGREGATE PLANNING STRATEGIES

There are several questions the operations manager must answer when making an aggregate plan:

1. Should inventories be used to absorb changes in demand during the planning period?
2. Should changes in demand be accommodated by varying the size of the work force?
3. Should part-timers be used or should overtime and idle time absorb changing demand?
4. Should subcontractors be used during increased demand so that a stable work force can be maintained?
5. Should prices or other factors be changed to influence demand?

FIGURE 15.2 ■ Relationships of the Aggregate Plan

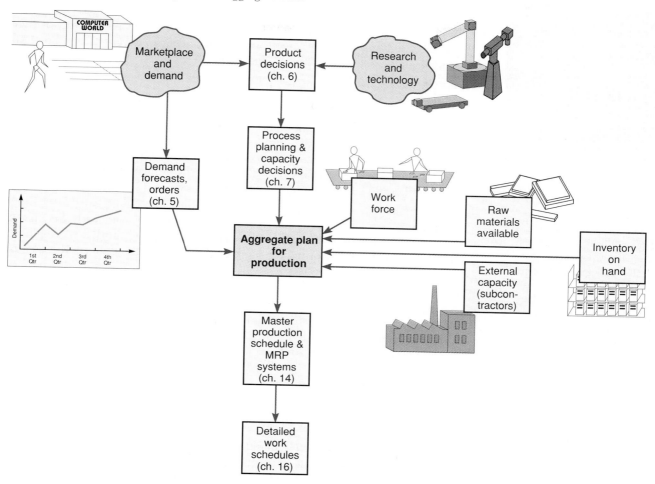

All of the foregoing are legitimate planning strategies available to management. They involve the manipulation of inventory, production rates, labor levels, capacity, and other controllable variables.

We will now examine eight options in more detail. The first five are called *capacity options* because they do not try to change demand but attempt to absorb the fluctuations in it. The last three are *demand options* through which firms try to influence the demand pattern to smooth out its changes over the planning period.

Capacity Options

The basic capacity (supply) options that a firm can choose are as follows:

1. *Changing Inventory Levels.* Managers can increase inventory during periods of low demand to meet high demand in future periods. Using this strategy increases costs associated with storage, insurance, handling, obsolescence, pilferage, and capital invested. (These costs typically range from 15 to 50% of the value of an item annually.) However, when the firm enters a period of increasing demand, shortages can result in lost sales due to potentially longer lead times and poorer customer service.

John Deere and Company, the "granddaddy" of farm equipment manufacturers, uses sales incentives to smooth demand. During the fall and winter off-seasons, sales are helped with price cuts and other incentives. About 70% of Deere's big machines are ordered in advance of seasonal use; this is about double the industry rate. The incentives hurt margins, but Deere keeps its market share and controls costs by producing more steadily all year long.

2. *Varying Work-Force Size by Hiring or Layoffs*. One way to meet demand is to hire or lay off production workers to match production rates. But often new employees need to be trained, and the average productivity drops temporarily as they are absorbed into the firm. Layoffs or firings, of course, lower the morale of all workers and can lead to lower productivity.

3. *Varying Production Rates Through Overtime or Idle Time*. Managers may be able to adjust for changes in demand by varying working hours. When demand is on a large upswing, though, there is a limit on how much overtime is realistic. Overtime pay requires more money, and too much overtime can wear workers down to the point that their overall productivity drops off. Overtime also implies increased overhead associated with keeping the facility open. On the other hand, when there is a period of decreased demand, the company must somehow absorb workers' idle time—usually a difficult process.

4. *Subcontracting*. A firm can handle peak demand periods by subcontracting some work. Subcontracting, however, has several pitfalls. First, it is costly. Second, it risks opening the door of your client to a competitor. And third, it is often hard to find the perfect subcontractor supplier, one who always delivers the quality product on time.

5. *Using Part-Time Workers*. Part-time workers can fill in for unskilled labor needs especially in the service sector. Hiring part-time workers is common practice at most supermarkets, retail stores, and restaurants like McDonald's and Wendy's. The *POM in Action* box describing Federal Express and United Parcel Service provides two views of this strategy.

Demand Options

The basic demand options are as follows:

1. *Influencing Demand*. When demand is low, a company can try to increase demand through advertising, promotion, increased personal selling, and price cuts. For example, airlines and hotels have long offered weekend discounts and off-season rates; telephone companies charge less at night; and air conditioners are least expensive in winter. Special advertising, promotions, selling, and pricing are not always able, however, to balance the demand with the production capacity.

2. *Back Ordering During High Demand Periods*. Back orders are orders for goods or services that a firm accepts but is unable (either on purpose or by chance) to fill at the moment. Back ordering works only if customers are willing to wait without loss of their goodwill or canceling their order. For instance, many auto dealers purposely back-order, but the approach is often unacceptable in the sale of many consumer goods.

3. *Counterseasonal Product Mixing*. Many manufacturing firms try to make several products that are sold in opposite seasons. Examples include companies that make both furnaces and air conditioners or lawn mowers and snowblowers. Service companies (and manufacturers also, for that matter) that follow this approach, however, may find themselves involved in services or products beyond their area of expertise or beyond their target market.[2]

---

[2] A good discussion of this subject in general is given by W. E. Sasser, "Match Supply and Demand in Service Industries," *Harvard Business Review*, 54, no. 6 (November/December 1976): 133–140.

These eight options, along with their advantages and disadvantages, are summarized in Table 15.1.

Mixing Options to Develop a Plan

Although each of the five capacity options and three demand options described above might produce a cost-effective aggregate plan, a combination of them—called a **mixed strategy**—often works best. Mixed strategies involve the combination of two or more controllable variables to set a feasible production plan. For example, a firm might use a combination of overtime, subcontracting, and inventory leveling as its strategy. Finding the one "optimal" aggregate plan is not always possible, though, because there are a huge number of combinations.

The mix of strategy options is different for service firms than for manufacturing firms. For instance, stocking inventory may not be an option and subcontracting may invite competition. Consequently, service firms often address aggregate scheduling via changes in personnel. They do this by changing labor requirements, cross-training, job rotation, and using part-time employees.

Mixed strategy

Level Scheduling

Level scheduling, or level capacity planning, is a strategy popularized by the Japanese and their desire for "lifetime employment." **Level scheduling** involves aggregate plans in which daily capacities from month to month are uniform. In effect, firms like Toyota and Nissan keep production systems at uniform levels and may let the finished

Level scheduling

TABLE 15.1 ■ AGGREGATE PLANNING OPTIONS: ADVANTAGES AND DISADVANTAGES

OPTION	ADVANTAGES	DISADVANTAGES	SOME COMMENTS
Changing inventory level.	Changes in human resources are gradual or none; no abrupt production changes.	Inventory holding costs. Shortages, resulting in lost sales, may occur if demand increases.	This applies mainly to production, not service, settings.
Varying work-force size by hiring or layoffs.	Avoids the costs of other alternatives.	Hiring, layoff, and training costs may be significant.	Used where many unskilled people seek extra income.
Varying production rates through overtime or idle time.	Matches seasonal fluctuations without hiring/training costs.	Overtime premiums; tired workers; may not meet demand.	Allows flexibility within the aggregate plan.
Subcontracting.	Permits flexibility and smoothing of the firm's output.	Loss of quality control; reduced profits; loss of future business.	Applies mainly in production settings.
Using part-time workers.	Is less costly and more flexible than full-time workers.	High turnover/training costs; quality suffers; scheduling difficult.	Good for unskilled jobs in areas with large temporary labor pools.
Influencing demand.	Tries to use excess capacity. Discounts draw new customers.	Uncertainty in demand. Hard to exactly match demand to supply.	Creates marketing ideas. Overbooking used in some businesses.
Back-ordering.	May avoid overtime. Keeps capacity constant.	Customer must be willing to wait, but goodwill is lost.	Many companies backlog.
Counterseasonal product and service mixing.	Fully utilizes resources; allows stable work force.	May require skills or equipment outside firm's areas of expertise.	Risky finding products or services with opposite demand patterns.

A Tale of Two Delivery Services

Federal Express and United Parcel Service are direct competitors in package delivery. Both firms are successful, but they approach aggregate planning quite differently.

Managers at Federal Express use a large number of part-time employees in their huge package-sorting facility. This Memphis facility is designed and staffed to sort over a million envelopes and packages in a short 4-hour shift during the middle of the night. Federal Express found that college students provide a good source of labor. These high-

energy part-timers help meet peak demands, whereas the firm believes that full-timers could not be effectively utilized for a full 8-hour shift.

At UPS's package-sorting hub, managers are also faced with the decision whether to staff with mostly full-time or part-time employees. UPS chose the full-time approach. The firm also researches job designs and work processes thoroughly, hoping to provide a high level of job satisfaction and a strong sense of teamwork. Hours at UPS are long, the work is hard, and UPS generates union complaints about its demanding levels of productivity. But when openings occur, UPS has never had a shortage of job applicants.

Sources: J. Heskett, W. E. Sasser, and C. Hart, *Service Breakthroughs* (New York: Free Press, 1990); and *Wall Street Journal* (May 24, 1995): B1, B4.

goods inventory of autos go up or down to buffer the difference between monthly demand and production level or find alternative work for production employees. Their philosophy is that stable employment leads to better-quality autos, less turnover, less absenteeism, and more employee commitment to corporate goals.

Level scheduling usually results in lower labor costs than other strategies. Workers tend to be more experienced, so supervision is easier, costs of hiring/firing and overtime are minimized, and the operation is smoother with less dramatic startups and shutdowns. The *POM in Action* box "Scheduling Swimsuits at Argentina's Porges-Ruiz Enterprises" discusses another approach to level scheduling.

METHODS FOR AGGREGATE PLANNING

Some companies have no formal aggregate planning process. They use the same plan from year to year, making adjustments up or down just enough to fit the new demand. This method certainly does not provide much flexibility, and if the original plan was suboptimal, the entire production process will be locked into suboptimal performance.

In this section, we introduce several techniques operations managers use in developing more useful and appropriate aggregate plans. They range from the widely used charting (or graphical) method, to a series of more formal mathematical approaches, including the transportation method of linear programming.

Graphical and Charting Methods

Graphical and charting methods

Graphical and charting methods are popular because they are easy to understand and use. Basically, these plans work with a few variables at a time to allow planners to compare projected demand with existing capacity. Although they are only trial-

and-error approaches that do not guarantee an optimal production plan, they are popular because they require only limited computations and can be performed by clerical staff.

In general, graphical methods follow five steps:

1. Determine the demand in each period.
2. Determine what the capacity is for regular time, overtime, and subcontracting each period.
3. Find the labor costs, hiring and layoff costs, and inventory holding costs.
4. Consider company policy that may apply to the workers or to stock levels.
5. Develop alternative plans and examine their total costs.

Examples 1 to 4 illustrate these steps.

Federal Express' huge aircraft fleet is used to near capacity for nighttime delivery of packages but is 100% idle during the daytime. In an attempt to better utilize its capacity (and leverage its assets), Federal Express considered two services with opposite or countercyclical demand patterns to its nighttime service— commuter passenger service and passenger charter service. However, after a thorough analysis of these new services, the 12% to 13% return on investment was judged insufficient for the risks involved.

EXAMPLE 1

Bill Wicker and Sons, a Charlotte manufacturer of roofing supplies, has developed monthly forecasts for roofing tiles and presented the period January–June in Table 15.2. The demand per day is computed by simply dividing the expected demand by the number of working days each month.

TABLE 15.2

MONTH	EXPECTED DEMAND	PRODUCTION DAYS	DEMAND PER DAY (COMPUTED)
January	900	22	41
February	700	18	39
March	800	21	38
April	1,200	21	57
May	1,500	22	68
June	1,100	20	55
	6,200	124	

To represent the projected demand, Wicker and Sons also draws a graph (Figure 15.3) that charts the daily demand each month. The dotted line across the chart represents the production rate required to meet average demand. It is computed by

$$\text{Average requirement} = \frac{\text{total expected demand}}{\text{number of production days}} = \frac{6{,}200}{124} = 50 \text{ units/day}$$

Scheduling Swimsuits at Argentina's Porges-Ruiz Enterprises

Porges-Ruiz Enterprises, a Buenos Aires manufacturer of swimwear, developed an innovative personnel policy that not only cut costs, but also made it more responsive to its customers. In a highly seasonal business, the company had to ship about three-quarters of its products in three summer months. Porges-Ruiz management had traditionally relied on overtime, temporary workers, and inventory buildup to deal with the huge increase in demand. But problems with this approach were numerous. For one thing, when the firm produced swimwear many months in advance, it was unable to meet changing style demands. For another, during the three busy months, customer complaints, urgent production needs, schedule changes, and outages all plagued management.

Porges-Ruiz's solution was to vary production schedules while maintaining the employees' regular 42-hour-per-week pay. Scheduling would change from August through mid-November to 52-hour production weeks.* Then when the peak period ended, a 30-hour-week schedule through April began. During slack time, swimsuit lines and stable model designs were produced.

This flexible use of workers helped Porges-Ruiz reduce its working capital needs by 40% and double its peak season capacity. Keeping a quality advantage, the firm is competitive in price and expanding its sales into Brazil, Chile, and Uruguay.

*Note that South America's summer season is during North America's winter.

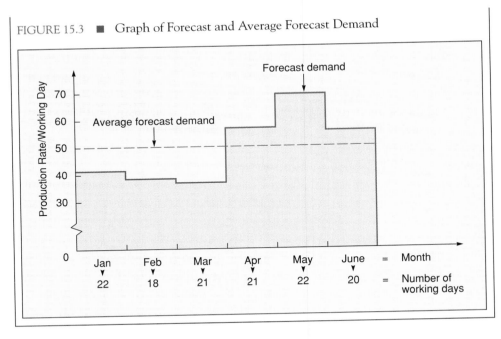

FIGURE 15.3 ■ Graph of Forecast and Average Forecast Demand

The graph in Figure 15.3 illustrates how the forecast differs from the average demand. Some strategies for meeting the forecast were listed earlier. The roofing firm, for example, might staff to yield a production rate that meets the average demand (as indicated by the dashed line). Or it might produce a steady rate of, say, 30 units and then subcontract excess demand to other roofing suppliers. A third plan might be to combine overtime work with some subcontracting to absorb demand. Examples 2 to 4 illustrate three possible strategies.

EXAMPLE 2

One possible strategy (call it Plan 1) for Wicker and Sons, the manufacturer described in Example 1, is to maintain a constant work force throughout the 6-month period. A second (Plan 2) is to maintain a constant work force at a level necessary for the lowest demand month (March), and to meet all demand above this level by subcontracting. Yet a third plan is to hire and lay off workers as needed to produce to exact monthly requirements. Table 15.3 provides cost information needed to analyze these plans.

TABLE 15.3 ■ **COST INFORMATION**

Inventory carrying cost	$5/unit/month
Subcontracting cost (marginal cost per unit above in-house manufacturing cost)	$10/unit
Average pay rate	$5/hour ($40/day)
Overtime pay rate	$7/hour (above 8 hours)
Labor-hours to produce a unit	1.6 hours/unit
Cost of increasing production rate (training and hiring)	$10/unit
Cost of decreasing production rate (layoffs)	$15/unit

ANALYSIS OF PLAN 1. When analyzing this approach, which assumes that 50 units are produced per day, we have a constant work force, no overtime or idle time, use no safety stock, and use no subcontractors. The firm accumulates inventory during the slack period of demand, which is January through March, and depletes it during the higher-demand warm season, April through June. We assume beginning inventory is 0, and planned ending inventory is 0.

MONTH	PRODUCTION AT 50 UNITS/DAY	DEMAND FORECAST	MONTHLY INVENTORY CHANGE	ENDING INVENTORY
January	1,100	900	+ 200	200
February	900	700	+ 200	400
March	1,050	800	+250	650
April	1,050	1,200	− 150	500
May	1,100	1,500	− 400	100
June	1,000	1,100	− 100	0
				1,850

$$\left(\begin{array}{l}\text{Total units of inventory carried over} \\ \text{from one month to the next month}\end{array}\right) = 1{,}850 \text{ units}$$

Work force required to produce 50 units/day = 10 workers

(Because each unit requires 1.6 labor-hours to produce, each worker can make 5 units in an 8-hour day. Hence to produce 50 units, 10 workers are needed.) Plan 1's costs are computed as follows:

COSTS		CALCULATIONS
Inventory carrying	$ 9,250	(= 1,850 units carried × $5/unit)
Regular time labor	49,600	(= 10 workers × $40/day × 124 days)
Other costs (overtime, hiring, layoffs, subcontracting)	0	
Total cost	$58,850	

The graph for Example 2 was shown in Figure 15.3. Some planners prefer a *cumulative* graph to display visually how the forecast deviates from the average requirements. Such a graph is provided in Figure 15.4.

FIGURE 15.4   ■   Cumulative Graph for Plan 1

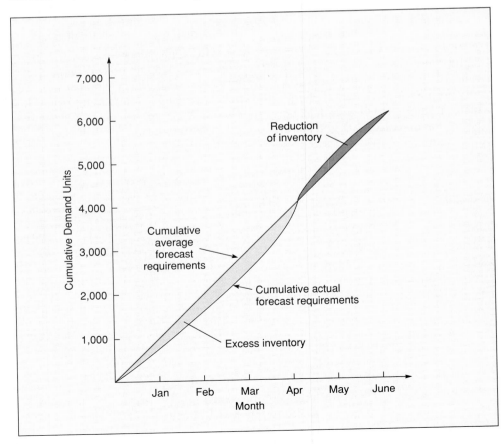

EXAMPLE 3

ANALYSIS OF PLAN 2. A constant work force is also maintained in Plan 2, but set low enough to meet demand in March, the lowest month. To produce 38 units/day in-house, 7.6 workers are needed. (You can think of this as 7 full-time workers and 1 part-timer.) All other demand is met by subcontracting, which is thus required in every month. No inventory holding costs are incurred in Plan 2.

Because 6,200 units are required during the aggregate plan period, we must compute how many can be made by the firm and how many subcontracted for:

$$\text{In-house production} = 38 \text{ units/day} \times 124 \text{ production days}$$
$$= 4,712 \text{ units}$$
$$\text{Subcontract units} = 6,200 - 4,712 = 1,488 \text{ units}$$

Plan 2's costs are:

Costs	Calculations	
Regular-time labor	$37,696	(= 7.6 workers × $40/day × 124 days)
Subcontracting	14,880	(= 1,488 units × $10/unit)
Total cost	$52,576	

EXAMPLE 4

ANALYSIS OF PLAN 3. The final strategy, Plan 3, involves varying the work-force size by hiring and firing as necessary. The production rate will equal the demand. Table 15.4 shows the calculations and the total cost of plan 3. Recall that it costs $15 per unit produced to reduce production from the previous month's level and $10 per unit change to increase production through hirings.

TABLE 15.4 ■ COST COMPUTATIONS FOR PLAN 3

Month	Forecast (Units)	Basic Production Cost (Demand × 1.6 Hr/Unit × $5/Hr)	Extra Cost of Increasing Production (Hiring Cost)	Extra Cost of Decreasing Production (Layoff Cost)	Total Cost
January	900	$ 7,200	—	—	$ 7,200
February	700	5,600	—	$3,000 (= 200 × $15)	8,600
March	800	6,400	$1,000 (= 100 × $10)	—	7,400
April	1,200	9,600	4,000 (= 400 × $10)	—	13,600
May	1,500	12,000	3,000 (= 300 × $10)	—	15,000
June	1,100	8,800	—	$6,000 (= 400 × $15)	14,800
		$49,600	$8,000	$9,000	$66,600

The final step in the graphical method is to compare the costs of each proposed plan and to select the approach with the least total cost. A summary analysis is provided in Table 15.5. We see there that Plan 2 has the lowest cost and is the best of the three options.

TABLE 15.5 ■ COMPARISON OF THE THREE PLANS

COST	PLAN 1 (CONSTANT WORK FORCE OF 10 WORKERS)	PLAN 2 (WORK FORCE OF 7.6 WORKERS PLUS SUBCONTRACT)	PLAN 3 (HIRING AND LAYOFFS TO MEET DEMAND)
Inventory carrying	$ 9,250	$ 0	$ 0
Regular labor	49,600	37,696	49,600
Overtime labor	0	0	0
Hiring	0	0	8,000
Layoffs	0	0	9,000
Subcontracting	0	14,880	0
Total cost	$58,850	$52,576	$66,600

Of course, many other feasible strategies can be considered in problems like this, including combinations that use some overtime. Although charting and graphing are popular management tools, their help is in evaluating strategies, not generating them. Managers need a systematic approach that considers all costs and produces an effective solution. Mathematical models provide one such approach.

Mathematical Methods for Planning

This section introduces some of the mathematical approaches to aggregate planning that have been developed over the past 40 years.

Transportation method of LP

THE TRANSPORTATION METHOD OF LINEAR PROGRAMMING.   Linear programming can be used in aggregate planning to allocate operating capacity to meet forecasted demand. The **transportation method of LP** (discussed in the supplement to Chapter 9) is not a trial-and-error approach like charting, but produces an optimal plan for minimizing costs. It is also flexible in that it can specify the regular and overtime production in each time period, the number of units to be subcontracted, extra shifts, and the inventory carryover from period to period.

In Example 5, the supply consists of on-hand inventory and units produced by regular time, overtime, and subcontracting. Costs, in the upper right-hand corner of each cell of the matrix, relate to units produced in a given period or units carried in inventory from an earlier period.

The optimal solution to the problem in Example 5 can be easily found using our AB:POM microcomputer software package described at the end of this chapter.

EXAMPLE 5

Harpell Radial Tire Company developed data that relate to production, demand, capacity, and costs at its West Virginia plant, as shown in Table 15.6. Table 15.7 illustrates the structure of the transportation table and an initial feasible solution.

TABLE 15.6 ■ HARPELL'S PRODUCTION, DEMAND, CAPACITY, AND COST DATA

	SALES PERIOD		
	MARCH	APRIL	MAY
Demand	800	1,000	750
Capacity			
Regular	700	700	700
Overtime	50	50	50
Subcontracting	150	150	130
Beginning inventory	100 tires		

COSTS	
Regular time	$40/tire
Overtime	$50/tire
Subcontract	$70/tire
Carrying cost	$2/tire/month

TABLE 15.7 ■ HARPELL'S TRANSPORTATION TABLE

SUPPLY FROM		Period 1 (March)	Period 2 (April)	Period 3 (May)	Unused Capacity (Dummy)	TOTAL CAPACITY AVAILABLE (SUPPLY)
Beginning inventory		0 / 100	2	4	0	100
Period 1	Regular time	40 / 700	42	44	0	700
	Overtime	50	52 / 50	54	0	50
	Subcontract	70	72 / 150	74	0	150
Period 2	Regular time		40 / 700	42	0	700
	Overtime		50 / 50	52	0	50
	Subcontract		70 / 50	72	0 / 100	150
Period 3	Regular time			40 / 700	0	700
	Overtime			50 / 50	0	50
	Subcontract			70	0 / 130	130
TOTAL DEMAND		800	1,000	750	230	2,780

You should note the following:

1. Carrying costs are \$2 per tire per month. Because holding cost is linear, 2 months' holdover costs \$4.

2. Transportation problems require that supply equal demand. Hence, a dummy column called "unused capacity" has been added. Costs of not using capacity are zero.

3. The quantities in each column of Table 15.7 are levels of inventory needed to meet demand requirements. We see that demand of 800 tires in March is met by using 100 tires from beginning inventory and 700 tires from regular time.

Using the transportation LP approach to solve aggregate planning problems works well in analyzing the effects of holding inventories, using overtime, and subcontracting. But it does not work when more factors are introduced.[3] So, when hiring and layoffs are introduced, the more general method of simplex linear programming, seen in the supplement to Chapter 6, must be used.

Linear decision rule

LINEAR DECISION RULE. The **linear decision rule** (LDR) is an aggregate planning method that attempts to specify an optimum production rate and workforce level over a specific period. It minimizes the total costs of payroll, hiring, layoffs, overtime, and inventory through a series of quadratic cost curves.[4]

MANAGEMENT COEFFICIENTS MODEL. A *heuristics decision rule* is a rule of thumb based on a manager's previous experiences in tackling a problem.

Management coefficient model

A classic heuristics application is E. H. Bowman's **management coefficient model**.[5] This unique approach builds a formal decision model around a manager's experience and performance. The theory is that the manager's past performance is fairly good, so it can be used as a basis for future decisions. This method uses a regression analysis of past production decisions made by managers. The regression line provides the relationship between variables (say, demand and labor) for future decisions. According to Bowman, managers' deficiencies were mostly inconsistencies in decision making.

Scheduling by simulation

SIMULATION. A computer model called **scheduling by simulation** was developed in 1966 by R. C. Vergin.[6] This simulation approach uses a search procedure to look for the minimum-cost combination of values for the size of the work force and the production rate.

---

[3]See R. DeMatta and T. Miller, "A Note on the Growth of a Production Planning System," *Interfaces*, 23 (April 1993): 27–31, for a description of how American Olean Tile Co. uses the transportation method. This large manufacturer of ceramic tiles generates plans that minimize total production and freight costs while meeting quarterly product demands.

[4]Because LDR was developed by Charles C. Holt, Franco Modigliani, John F. Muth, and Nobel Prize–winner Herbert Simon, it is popularly known as the HMMS rule. For details, see C. C. Holt et al., *Production Planning, Inventories, and Work Force* (Englewood Cliffs, NJ: Prentice Hall, 1960).

[5]E. H. Bowman, "Consistency and Optimality in Managerial Decision Making," *Management Science*, 9, no. 2 (January 1963): 310–321.

[6]R. C. Vergin, "Production Scheduling under Seasonal Demand," *Journal of Industrial Engineering*, 17, no. 5 (May 1966): 260–266.

SEARCH DECISION RULE. The **search decision rule**, developed by W. H. Taubert, is a pattern search algorithm that tries to find the minimum-cost combination of various work-force and production levels.[7] A computer makes the thousands of systematic searches for points that produce a cost reduction. Search rules such as this do not yield optimal solutions, but are flexible enough to be used on any type of cost function.

Search decision rule

Comparison of Aggregate Planning Methods

Although the search decision rule, linear programming, and other mathematical models have found some acceptance in industry, the fact is that most sophisticated planning models are not widely used.[8,9] Why? Perhaps it reflects the average manager's attitude about what he or she views as overly complex models. Planners, like all of us, like to understand how and why the models on which they are basing important decisions work. This may explain why the simpler charting and graphical approach is more generally accepted.

Table 15.8 highlights some of the main features of the planning methods we discussed in this chapter.

TABLE 15.8 ■ SUMMARY OF AGGREGATE PLANNING METHODS

TECHNIQUE	SOLUTION APPROACHES	IMPORTANT ASPECTS
Charting/graphical methods	Trial and error	Simple to understand and easy to use. Many solutions; one chosen may not be optimal.
Transportation method of linear programming	Optimization	LP software available; permits sensitivity analysis and new constraints; linear functions may not be realistic.
Linear decision rule	Optimization	Model takes 1 to 3 months to develop; complex cost functions not always valid; does not always produce a feasible solution.
Management coefficient model	Heuristic	Simple, easy to implement; tries to mimic manager's decision process; uses regression.
Simulation	Trial and error	Able to test many relationships among variables; can be costly; computerized; can handle any cost function.
Search decision rules	Heuristic	Widely used; permits any cost function; can test alternative decisions and do sensitivity analysis; 3 to 6 months to develop; expensive search cycle.

[7]W. H. Taubert, "A Search Decision Rule for the Aggregate Scheduling Problem," *Management Science,* 14, no. 6 (February 1968): 343–359.

[8]W. B. Lee and B. M. Khumawala, "Simulation Testing of Aggregate Production Planning Models in an Implementation Methodology," *Management Science,* 20, no. 6 (February 1974): 903–911.

[9]W. N. Ledbetter and J. F. Cox, "Operations Research in Production Management," *Production and Inventory Management* (Third Quarter 1977): 84–91.

DISAGGREGATION

Disaggregation
Master production schedule

The output of the aggregate planning process is usually a production schedule for family groupings of products. It tells an auto manufacturer how many cars to make, but not how many should be two-door versus four-door or red versus green. It tells a steel manufacturer how many tons of steel to produce, but does not differentiate rolled steel from sheet steel. However, firms still need a plan dealing with specific products: What quantities should each one be produced in, and by what date? The process of breaking the aggregate plan down into greater detail is called **disaggregation**. Disaggregation results in a **master production schedule**, which, as we saw in Chapter 14, specifies:

1. the sizing and timing of specific item production quantities;
2. the sizing and timing of manufactured or purchased components;
3. the sequencing of individual orders or jobs;
4. the short-term allocation of resources to individual operations.

AGGREGATE PLANNING IN SERVICES

Part-time workers are a proven planning resource tactic, especially in restaurants and supermarkets. McDonald's, for example, has found that hiring retired workers for part-time jobs pays off. Older workers are effective and loyal employees whose absentee rates are typically much lower than those of their teenage co-workers.

Some service organizations conduct aggregate planning in exactly the same way as we did in Examples 1 through 5 in this chapter. Most services pursue a number of the eight capacity and demand strategy options discussed earlier in Table 15.1 in combination, resulting in a *mixed* aggregate planning strategy for meeting demand. In actuality, in some firms, such as banking, trucking, and fast foods, aggregate planning may be even easier than in manufacturing.

Approaches to aggregate planning differ by the type of service provided. Here are five service scenarios.[10]

Restaurants

Aggregate planning in the case of a high-volume-product output business such as a restaurant is directed toward (1) smoothing the production rate, (2) finding the size of the work force to be employed, and (3) attempting to manage demand to keep equipment and employees working. The general approach usually requires building inventory during slack periods and depleting inventory during peak periods.

Because this is very similar to manufacturing, traditional aggregate planning methods may be applied to high-volume tangible services as well. One difference that should be noted is that in restaurants, inventory is perishable. In addition, the relevant units of time may be much smaller than in manufacturing. For example, in fast-food restaurants, peak and slack periods may be measured in hours and the "product" may be inventoried for only as long as 10 minutes.

[10]The first four of these scenarios and their discussion are excerpted from R. Murdick, B. Render, and R. Russell, *Service Operations Management* (Boston: Allyn and Bacon, 1990), pp. 219–221.

Miscellaneous Services

Most "miscellaneous" services—financial services, hospitality services, transportation services, and many communication and recreation services—provide a high-volume, but intangible output. Aggregate planning for these services deals mainly with planning for human resource requirements and managing demand. The goal is to level the demand peak and to design methods for fully utilizing labor resources during forecasted low-demand periods.

National Chains of Small Service Firms

With the advent of national chains of small service businesses such as funeral homes, fast-food outlets, photocopy/printing centers, and computer centers, the question of aggregate planning versus independent planning at each business establishment becomes an issue. One component of aggregate planning for a service chain is centralized purchasing, which has many advantages. Output also may be centrally planned when demand can be influenced through special promotions. This approach is advantageous because it reduces advertising costs and helps regulate cash flow at the independent sites.

Airline Industry

Another service example may be found in the airline industry. Consider an airline that has its headquarters in New York, two hub sites in cities such as Atlanta and Dallas, and 150 offices in airports throughout the country. Aggregate planning consists of tables or schedules of (1) number of flights in and out of each hub; (2) number of flights on all routes; (3) number of passengers to be serviced in all flights; and (4) number of air personnel and ground personnel required at each hub and airport.

This planning is considerably more complex than aggregate planning for a single site or a number of independent sites. Additional capacity decisions are focused on determining the percentage of seats to be allocated to various fare classes in order to maximize profit or yield. This type of capacity allocation problem is called **yield management**.

Yield management

Hospitals

Hospitals face the aggregate planning problem by allocating money, staff, and supplies to meet the demands of patients for their medical services. Michigan's Henry Ford Hospital, for example, plans for bed capacity and personnel needs in light of a patient load forecast developed by moving averages. Its aggregate plan has led to the creation of a new floating staff pool serving each nursing pod.[11]

---

[11]G. Buxey, "Production Planning for Seasonal Demand," *International Journal of Operations and Production Management*, 13, no. 7 (1993): 4–21.

ACHIEVING WORLD-CLASS STANDARDS

Aggregate planning provides companies with a competitive weapon to help capture market shares in the global economy. By looking at an intermediate planning horizon, the aggregate plan provides the ability to respond to changing customer demands while still producing at low-cost and high-quality levels.

Managers at world-class firms schedule well because they know what to schedule, how to schedule, and why. While their world-class orientation is toward level schedules, they effectively balance capacity, inventory, personnel, and supplier/subcontractors. They prefer to invest in optimizing methods such as linear programming rather than trial-and-error approaches. The result is an effective and efficient use of resources to meet market demands.

SUMMARY

The aggregate plan sets levels of inventory, production, subcontracting, and employment over an intermediate time range, usually 3 to 18 months. This chapter describes several aggregate planning techniques, ranging from the popular charting approach to a variety of mathematical and computer-oriented models such as linear programming.

The aggregate plan is an important tactical responsibility of an operations manager and a key to smooth production. Output from the aggregate plan leads to a more detailed master production schedule, which is the basis for disaggregation, job scheduling, and MRP systems.

Although the discussion in the early part of this chapter dealt mostly with the manufacturing environment, we just saw that aggregate plans for service systems are similar. Banks, restaurants, airlines, and auto repair facilities are all service systems that can employ the concepts developed here. Regardless of the industry or planning method, though, the most important issue is the implementation of the plan. Managers appear to be more comfortable with less complex and less mathematical approaches to planning, often because they are untrained in using quantitative methods.

KEY TERMS		
	Aggregate planning (p. 692)	Management coefficient model (p. 706)
	Tactical scheduling decisions (p. 692)	Scheduling by simulation (p. 706)
	Mixed strategy (p. 697)	Search decision rule (p. 707)
	Level scheduling (p. 697)	Disaggregation (p. 708)
	Graphical and charting methods (p. 698)	Master production schedule (p. 708)
	Transportation method of LP (p. 704)	Yield management (p. 709)
	Linear decision rule (p. 706)	

USING AB:POM TO SOLVE AGGREGATE PLANNING PROBLEMS

Solving Example 2 with AB:POM's Aggregate Planning Module

AB:POM's Aggregate Planning module performs aggregate or production planning for up to 12 time periods. Given a set of demands for future periods, you can try various plans to determine the lowest-cost plan based on holding, shortage, production, and changeover costs. The initial input is the number of periods in the planning horizon.

As shown in Program 15.1, four methods are available. More help is available on each of these methods *after* you choose the method.

In addition to the method, there is a *toggle* on the second row that lets you indicate whether excess demands should be handled first by overtime or by subcontracting. That is, if your *production amount* is larger than *regular-time* capacity—which option should be used next.

The table has two different sides. On the left side, capacities can be given, and on the right side, the costs can be given. Furthermore, the costs may be the same in each period or may vary from period to period. If they are the same, then the easiest way to enter the column is to go to the top of the column and place the cost.

Initial inventory is set at the top of the demand column.

Programs 15.1 and 15.2 illustrate the use of AB:POM for analyzing Plan 1 (the first strategy) for Example 2. That "user-defined" plan kept a constant work force throughout the 6-month planning period.

PROGRAM 15.1 ■ AB:POM's Aggregate Planning Program, with Options Menu and Data-Entry Screen for Plan 1 of Example 2. Note that on the left side of the table, capacities are input, and on the right-hand side, costs are input. "User-defined" method was chosen for this analysis.

———————— Toggle Menu ————————
Smooth production (let inventory vary)
Produce to demand (let work force vary)
Constant Reg time, then OT and sub
User defined

Data file: PLAN1 ———————— Aggregate Planning ———————— Data Screen ————————
Number of time periods (1–99) 6

ANALYSIS OF PLAN1 OF EXAMPLE 2

METHOD -> User defined

PRIORITY   Overtime precedes subcontracting

All Pds ->   0   0   0 $8.00 $11.20 $10. $5.0 $0.0 $0.0   0.00

| | | SCHEDULE | | | | | COSTS | | | |
Pd	Demnd	Regtm	Ovrtm	Subcn	Regtim	Ovrtim	Subcon	Holdng	Shortg	Incres	Decres
Init	0	0	0	0							
Pd1	900	1100	0	0	8.00	11.20	10.00	5.00	0.00	0.00	0.00
Pd2	700	900	0	0	8.00	11.20	10.00	5.00	0.00	0.00	0.00
Pd3	800	1050	0	0	8.00	11.20	10.00	5.00	0.00	0.00	0.00
Pd4	1200	1050	0	0	8.00	11.20	10.00	5.00	0.00	0.00	0.00
Pd5	1500	1100	0	0	8.00	11.20	10.00	5.00	0.00	0.00	0.00
Pd6	1100	1000	0	0	8.00	11.20	10.00	5.00	0.00	0.00	0.00

PROGRAM 15.2   ■   Output of AB:POM's Aggregate Planning Analysis of Plan 1

```
——————————————————— ANALYSIS OF PLAN1 OF EXAMPLE 2 ———————————————

METHOD ->  User defined
PRIORITY   Overtime precedes subcontracting
All Pds ->        0        0        0      8.00    11.20    10.00     5.00    $0.0    $0.0    0.00
              SCHEDULE                                 U N I T S
     Pd Demnd  Regtm  Ovrtm  Subcn   Regtim  Ovrtim  Subcon  Holdng  Shortg  Incres  Decres
```

Pd	Demnd	Regtm	Ovrtm	Subcn	Regtim	Ovrtim	Subcon	Holdng	Shortg	Incres	Decres
Init	0	0	0	0				200	0	1100	0
Pd1	900	1100	0	0	1100	0	0	400	0	0	200
Pd2	700	900	0	0	900	0	0	650	0	150	0
Pd3	800	1050	0	0	1050	0	0	500	0	0	0
Pd4	1200	1050	0	0	1050	0	0	100	0	50	0
Pd5	1500	1100	0	0	1100	0	0	0	0	0	100
Pd6	1100	1000	0	0	1000	0	0	1850	0	1300	300
TOTL	6200	6200	0	0	6200	0	0	1850	0	1300	300

```
               SUBTOTAL COSTS ->    49600      0       0     9250      0       0       0
               TOTAL COSTS = 58850
```

Solving Aggregate Planning Problems with AB:POM's Transportation LP Module

AB:POM's Transportation Model module was first introduced as a tool for facility location in the Supplement to Chapter 9. In using the transportation linear programming program, we can also view the "origins" as supply sources and the "destinations" as periods, usually months or quarters. The program may then be used to solve Example 6 (Harpell Radial Tire Company) and other problems. Origin and destination names should be edited to reflect the aggregate plan. Cells that are clearly not feasible for the plan (namely, those that require back ordering) should be given *very* high costs. This will force the computer to avoid producing in those sources. For details as to the use of this approach, refer back to Programs S9.1 and S9.2.

SOLVED PROBLEMS

Solved Problem 15.1

Bill Wicker and Sons, the roofing manufacturer described in Examples 1 to 4, wishes to consider yet a fourth planning strategy (Plan 4). This one maintains a constant work force of eight people and uses overtime whenever necessary to meet demand. Cost information in Table 15.3 is to be used. Again, assume beginning and ending inventories are equal to zero.

Solution
Employ eight workers and use overtime when necessary. Carrying costs will be encountered now.

Month	Production at 40 Units/Day	Beginning of Month Inventory	Forecast Demand This Month	Overtime Production Needed	Ending Inventory
Jan.	880	—	900	20	0
Feb.	720	0	700	0	20
Mar.	840	20	800	0	60
Apr.	840	60	1,200	300	0
May	880	0	1,500	620	0
June	800	0	1,100	300	0
				1,240 units	80 units

Carrying cost totals = 80 units × $5/unit/month = $400

To produce 1,240 units at overtime rate (of $7/hour) requires 1,984 hours.

Overtime pay = $7/hour × 1,984 hours = $13,888

Regular pay = 8 workers × $40/day × 124 days = $39,680

Cost	Plan 4 (Work Force of 8 plus Overtime)	
Carrying cost	$ 400	(80 units carried × $5/unit)
Regular labor	39,680	(8 workers × $40/day × 124 days)
Overtime	13,888	(1,984 hours × $7/hour)
Hiring or firing	0	
Subcontracting	0	
Total costs	$53,968	

Solved Problem 15.2

Trent-Herren, a bicycle manufacturer in Memphis, has developed the accompanying supply, demand, cost, and inventory data. The firm has a constant work force and meets all of its demand. Allocate the production capacity to satisfy demand at a minimum cost. What is the cost of this plan?

Supply Capacity Available (in Units)			
Period	Regular Time	Overtime	Subcontract
1	300	50	200
2	400	50	200
3	450	50	200

DEMAND FORECAST	
PERIOD	DEMAND (UNITS)
1	450
2	550
3	750

OTHER DATA

Initial inventory: 50 units
Regular-time cost per unit: $50
Overtime cost per unit: $65
Subcontract cost per unit: $80
Carrying cost per unit per period: $1

Solution

SUPPLY FROM		DEMAND FOR				TOTAL CAPACITY AVAILABLE (SUPPLY)
		Period 1	Period 2	Period 3	Unused Capacity (Dummy)	
Beginning inventory		0 50	1	2	0	50
Period 1	Regular time	50 300	51	52	0	300
	Overtime	65 50	66	67	0	50
	Subcontract	80 50	81	82	0 150	200
Period 2	Regular time		50 400	51	0	400
	Overtime		65 50	66	0	50
	Subcontract		80 100	81 50	0 50	200
Period 3	Regular time			50 450	0	450
	Overtime			65 50	0	50
	Subcontract			80 200	0	200
Total	DEMAND	450	550	750	200	1,950

Cost of plan:

Period 1: $50(\$0)\ + 300(\$50) +\ 50(\$65) +\ 50(\$80) = \$22{,}250$

Period 2: $400(\$50) +\ 50(\$65) + 100(\$80)\qquad\quad = \$31{,}250$

Period 3: $50(\$81) + 450(\$50) +\ 50(\$65) + 200(\$80) = \$45{,}800$

Total cost $\$99{,}300$

DISCUSSION QUESTIONS

1. What is the purpose of aggregate planning? Describe some demand and capacity options for implementing plans.

2. What is the difference between mixed production planning strategies and those eight demand and capacity options that are not mixed? Name four strategies that are not mixed.

3. Why are mathematical models not more widely used in aggregate planning?

4. What are the advantages and disadvantages of varying the size of the work force to meet demand requirements each period?

5. Why would some firms have longer planning horizons than others?

6. What is the relationship between the aggregate plan and the master production schedule?

7. Briefly describe four mathematical approaches to aggregate planning.

8. How does the aggregate planning differ for services versus manufacturing?

9. Why are graphical aggregate planning methods useful?

10. What are major limitations of using the transportation method for aggregate planning?

11. What impact on quality do you think each of eight production planning strategies might have?

12. What are the disadvantages that the following two strategies have in common: (1) varying inventory levels and (2) back ordering during periods of high demand?

CRITICAL THINKING EXERCISE

Many companies deal with aggregate planning by forcing overtime on their employees to adjust for the peaks of seasonal demand. For example, the *Wall Street Journal*'s report on long and irregular hours in the United States (July 14, 1994, p. B1) highlights Angie Clark, a J.C. Penney supervisor in Springfield, Virginia. Mrs. Clark works at least 44 hours a week, including evenings and frequent weekend shifts. Because of the recent recession, staffers are busier than 5 years earlier, when Mrs. Clark had 38 salespeople instead of the current 28. The result of this pressure is a 40% turnover. Because employee turnover is so large, training consists of the bare minimum—mostly how to operate the cash registers.

Discuss the implications of a strategy of heavy use of overtime in retailing, as well as in other fields such as manufacturing, hospitals, and airlines. How does this American approach compare to that in other countries?

PROBLEMS

⌨ ⦙ **15.1** Develop another plan for Bill Wicker and Sons, the roofing manufacturer described in Examples 1 to 4 and Solved Problem 15.1. For this plan, Plan 5, the firm wishes to maintain a constant work force of six and to pay overtime to meet demand. Is this plan preferable?

⌨ ⦙ **15.2** Bill Wicker and Sons, the roofing manufacturer in Examples 1 to 4 and Solved Problem 15.1, has yet a sixth plan. A constant work force of seven is selected and the remainder of demand is filled by subcontracting. Is this a better plan?

⌨ ⦙ **15.3** The president of King Enterprises, Kris King, projects the firm's aggregate demand requirements over the next 8 months as follows:

Jan.	1,400	May	2,200
Feb.	1,600	June	2,200
Mar.	1,800	July	1,800
Apr.	1,800	Aug.	1,400

Her operations manager is considering a new plan, which begins in January with 200 units on hand. Stockout cost of lost sales is $100 per unit. Inventory holding cost is $20 per unit per month. Ignore any idle time costs. The plan is called Plan A.

> Plan A—Vary the work-force level to meet exactly the demand requirements. The December rate of production is 1,600 units per month. The cost of hiring additional workers is $5,000 per 100 units. The cost of laying off workers is $7,500 per 100 units.

Evaluate this plan.

▪ : **15.4** Refer to Problem 15.3. King Enterprises is now looking at Plan B, below. Beginning inventory, stockout costs, and holding costs were provided in Problem 15.3.

> Plan B—Produce a constant rate of 1,400 units per month (which will meet minimum demands). Then subcontract additional units at a premium price of $75 per unit.

Evaluate this plan.

▪ : **15.5** Refer to Problem 15.3. Plan C is shown below. Beginning inventory, stockout costs, and holding costs were provided in Problem 15.3.

> Plan C—Keep a stable work force by maintaining a constant production rate equal to the average requirements and by varying inventory levels. Plot the demand with a histogram that also shows average requirements.

Evaluate this plan.

: **15.6** King's operations manager (see Problems 15.3 to 15.5) is also considering these two mixed strategies:

> Plan D—Keep the current work force stable at 1,600 units per month. Permit a maximum of 20% overtime at an additional cost of $50 per unit. A warehouse now constrains the maximum allowable inventory on hand to 400 units or less.

> Plan E—Keep the current work force, which is producing 1,600 units per month, and subcontract to meet the rest of the demand.

: **15.7** Mark and Ventra is a VCR manufacturer in need of an aggregate plan for July–December. The company has gathered the following data:

COSTS	
Holding cost	$8/VCR/month
Subcontracting	$80/VCR
Regular-time labor	$10/hour
Overtime labor	$16/hour above 8 hours/worker/day
Hiring cost	$40/worker
Layoff cost	$80/worker

DEMAND	
July	400
August	500
September	550
October	700
November	800
December	700

OTHER DATA	
Current work force	8
Labor-hours/VCR	4
Workdays/month	20
Beginning VCR inventory	150

What will the two following strategies cost?

a) Vary the work force to have exact production to meet the forecast demand. Begin with eight workers on board at the end of June.

b) Vary overtime only, and use a constant work force of eight.

⁞ 15.8 Develop your own aggregate plan for Mark and Ventra (see Problem 15.7). Justify your approach.

⁞ 15.9 Vanessa Juenger, the operations manager at Lauren Wallace Furniture, has received the following estimates of demand requirements.

APR.	MAY	JUNE	JULY	AUG.	SEPT.
1,000	1,200	1,400	1,800	1,800	1,600

Assuming stockout costs for lost sales are $100 and inventory carrying costs are $25/unit/month, evaluate these two plans on an *incremental* cost basis.

    Plan A—Produce at a steady rate (equal to minimum requirements) of 1,000 units per month and subcontract the additional units at a $60 per unit premium cost.

    Plan B—Vary the work force, which is at a current production level of 1,300 units per month. The cost of hiring additional workers is $3,000 per 100 units produced. The cost of layoffs is $6,000 per 100 units cut back.

⁞15.10 Vanessa Juenger (see Problem 15.9) is considering two more mixed strategies. Using the data of Problem 15.9, compare Plans C and D with the earlier ones and make a recommendation.

    Plan C—Keep the current work force steady at a level producing 1,300 units per month. Subcontract the remainder to meet demand. Assume 300 units remain from March that are available in April.

    Plan D—Keep the current work force at a level capable of producing 1,300 units per month. Permit a maximum of 20% overtime at a premium of $40 per unit. Assume warehouse limitations permit no more than 180 units carryover from month to month. This means that any time inventories reach 180, the plant is kept idle. Idle time per unit is $60. Any additional needs are subcontracted at a cost of $60 per incremental unit.

·15.11 Consider the following aggregate problem for one quarter.

	REGULAR TIME	OVERTIME	SUBCONTRACTING
Production capacity/month	1,000	200	150
Production cost/unit	$5	$7	$8

Assume there is no initial inventory and a forecasted demand of 1,250 units in each of the 3 months. Carrying cost is $1 per unit per month. Solve this aggregate planning problem.

💻 **: 15.12** Carrie Mattanini's firm had developed the accompanying supply, demand, cost, and inventory data. Allocate the production capacity to meet demand at a minimum cost. What is the cost?

SUPPLY AVAILABLE

PERIOD	REGULAR TIME	OVERTIME	DEMAND SUBCONTRACT	FORECAST
1	30	10	5	40
2	35	12	5	50
3	30	10	5	40

Initial inventory	20 units
Regular-time cost per unit	$100
Overtime cost per unit	$150
Subcontract cost per unit	$200
Carrying cost per unit per month	$4

💻 **: 15.13** The production planning period of 10-megabyte RAM boards for CDM personal computers is 4 months. Cost data are as follows:

Regular-time cost per board	$70
Overtime cost per board	$110
Subcontract cost per board	$120
Carrying cost per board per month	$4

Capacity and demand for RAM boards for each of the next 4 months are as follows:

	PERIOD			
	MONTH 1	**MONTH 2**	**MONTH 3***	**MONTH 4**
Demand	2,000	2,500	1,500	2,100
Capacity				
Regular time	1,500	1,600	750	1,600
Overtime	400	400	200	400
Subcontract	600	600	600	600

*Factory closes for 2 weeks of vacation.

CDM expects to enter the planning period with 500 RAM boards in stock. Back-ordering is not permitted (meaning, for example, that boards produced in the second month cannot be used in the first month). Set a production plan that minimizes costs.

:15.14 Haifa Instruments, an Israeli producer of portable kidney dialysis units and other medical products, develops a 4-month aggregate plan. Demand and capacity (in units) are forecast as follows:

CAPACITY SOURCE	MONTH 1	MONTH 2	MONTH 3	MONTH 4
Labor				
Regular time	235	255	290	300
Overtime	20	24	26	24
Subcontract	12	15	15	17
Demand	255	294	321	301

The cost of producing each dialysis unit is $985 on regular time, $1,310 on overtime, and $1,500 on a subcontract. Inventory carrying cost is $100 per unit per month. There is to be no beginning or ending inventory in stock. Set up a production plan that minimizes cost.

:15.15 A Birmingham, Alabama, factory produces cast iron ingots according to a 3-month capacity plan. The cost of labor averages $100 per regular shift-hour and $140 per overtime (O.T.) hour. Inventory carrying cost is thought to be $4 per labor-hour of inventory carried. There are 50 direct labor-hours of inventory left over from March. For the next 3 months, demand and capacity (in labor-hours) are as follows:

	CAPACITY		
MONTH	**REGULAR LABOR-HOURS**	**O.T. LABOR-HOURS**	**DEMAND**
April	2,880	355	3,000
May	2,780	315	2,750
June	2,760	305	2,950

Develop an aggregate plan for the 3-month period.

: 15.16 A large Omaha feed mill prepares its 6-month aggregate plan by forecasting demand for 50-pound bags of cattle feed as follows: January, 1,000 bags; February, 1,200; March, 1,250; April, 1,450; May 1,400; and June, 1,400. The feed mill plans to begin the new year with no inventory left over from the previous year. It projects that capacity (during regular hours) for producing bags of feed will remain constant at 800 until the end of April, and then increase to 1,100 bags per month when a planned expansion is completed on May 1. Overtime capacity is set at 300 bags per month until the expansion, at which time it will increase to 400 bags per month. A friendly competitor in Sioux City, Iowa, is also available as a backup source to meet demand—but it insists on a firm contract and can provide only 500 bags total during the 6-month period.

Cost data are as follows:

Regular-time cost per bag (until April 30)	$12
Regular-time cost per bag (after May 1)	$11
Overtime cost per bag (during entire period)	$16
Cost of outside purchase per bag	$18.50
Carrying cost per bag per month	$1

Develop a 6-month production plan for the feed mill.

: 15.17 The Todd Corbin Chemical Supply Company manufactures and packages expensive vials of mercury. Given the accompanying demand, supply, cost, and inventory data, allocate production capacity to meet demand at minimum cost. A constant work force is expected and no back orders are permitted.

	SUPPLY CAPACITY (IN UNITS)			DEMAND
PERIOD	REGULAR TIME	OVERTIME	SUBCONTRACT	(IN UNITS)
1	25	5	6	32
2	28	4	6	32
3	30	8	6	40
4	29	6	7	40

OTHER DATA	
Initial inventory	4 units
Ending inventory desired	3 units
Regular-time cost per unit	$2,000
Overtime cost per unit	$2,475
Subcontract cost per unit	$3,200
Carrying cost per unit per period	$200

:15.18 Given the following information, solve for the minimum-cost plan:

	PERIOD							
	1	**2**	**3**	**4**	**5**			
Demand	150	160	130	200	210	Subcontracting: 100 units available over the 5-month period		
Capacity								
Regular	150	150	150	150	150	Beginning inventory: 0 units		
Overtime	20	20	10	10	10	Ending inventory required: 20 units		

COST	
Regular-time cost per unit	$100
Overtime cost per unit	$125
Subcontract cost per unit	$135
Inventory cost per unit per period	$3

Assume that back orders are not permitted.

:15.19 Rich Rowe, owner of a dry-cleaning equipment manufacturer, develops an 8-month aggregate plan. Demand and capacity (in units) are forecast as follows:

CAPACITY SOURCE	JAN.	FEB.	MAR.	APR.	MAY	JUNE	JULY	AUG.
Labor								
Regular time	235	255	290	300	300	290	300	290
Overtime	20	24	26	24	30	28	30	30
Subcontract	12	16	15	17	17	19	19	20
Demand	255	294	321	301	330	320	345	340

The cost of producing each dry-cleaning unit is $1,000 on regular time, $1,300 on overtime, and $1,500 on a subcontract. Inventory carrying cost is $100 per unit per month. There is no beginning or ending inventory in stock and no back orders are permitted from period to period.

a) Set up a production plan that minimizes cost by producing exactly what the demand is each month and letting the work force vary. What is this plan's cost?

b) Through better planning, regular-time production can be set at exactly the same value, 275, per month. Does this alter the solution?

c) If overtime costs rise from $1,300 to $1,400, will your answer to part (a) change? What if they fall to $1,200?

CASE STUDY

Andrew-Carter, Inc.

Andrew-Carter, Inc. (A-C) is a major Canadian producer and distributor of outdoor lighting fixtures. Its fixture is distributed throughout North America and has been in high demand for several years. The company operates three plants that manufacture the fixture and distribute it to five distribution centers (warehouses).

During the present recession, A-C has seen a major drop in demand for its fixture as the housing market has declined. Based on the forecast of interest rates, the head of operations feels that demand for housing and thus for its product will remain depressed for the foreseeable future. A-C is considering closing one of its plants, as it is now operating with a forecasted excess capacity of 34,000 units per week. The forecasted weekly demands for the coming year are:

Warehouse 1	9,000 units
Warehouse 2	13,000 units
Warehouse 3	11,000 units
Warehouse 4	15,000 units
Warehouse 5	8,000 units

The plant capacities, in units per week, are

Plant 1, regular time	27,000 units
Plant 1, on overtime	7,000 units
Plant 2, regular time	20,000 units
Plant 2, on overtime	5,000 units
Plant 3, regular time	25,000 units
Plant 3, on overtime	6,000 units

If A-C shuts down any plants, its weekly costs will change, as fixed costs are lower for a nonoperating plant. Table 1 shows production costs at each plant, both variable at regular time and overtime, and fixed when operating and shut down. Table 2 shows distribution costs from each plant to each warehouse (distribution center).

DISCUSSION QUESTIONS

1. Evaluate the various configurations of operating and closed plants that will meet weekly demand. Determine which configuration minimizes total costs.

2. Discuss the implications of closing a plant.

Source: Professor Michael Ballot, University of the Pacific.

TABLE 1 ■ ANDREW-CARTER, INC. VARIABLE COSTS AND FIXED PRODUCTION COSTS PER WEEK

| PLANT | VARIABLE COST | FIXED COST PER WEEK | |
		OPERATING	NOT OPERATING
No. 1, regular time	$2.80/unit	$14,000	$6,000
No. 1, overtime	3.52		
No. 2, regular time	2.78	12,000	5,000
No. 2, overtime	3.48		
No. 3, regular time	2.72	15,000	7,500
No. 3, overtime	3.42		

TABLE 2 ■ ANDREW-CARTER, INC. DISTRIBUTION COSTS PER UNIT

| FROM PLANTS | TO DISTRIBUTION CENTERS | | | | |
	W1	W2	W3	W4	W5
No. 1	$0.50	$0.44	$0.49	$0.46	$0.56
No. 2	0.40	0.52	0.50	0.56	0.57
No. 3	0.56	0.53	0.51	0.54	0.35

BIBLIOGRAPHY

Armacost, R. L., R. J. Penlesky, and S. C. Ross. "Avoiding Problems Inherent in Spreadsheet-Based Simulation Models—An Aggregate Planning Application." *Production and Inventory Management*, 31 (Second Quarter 1990): 62–68.

Bowers, M. R., and J. P. Jarvis. "A Hierarchical Production Planning and Scheduling Model." *Decision Sciences*, 23 (January/February 1992): 144–157.

Buxey, G. "Production Planning and Scheduling for Seasonal Demand." *International Journal of Operations and Production Management*, 13, no. 7 (1993): 4–21.

Coker, J. L. "Analyzing Production Switching Heuristics for Aggregate Planning Models via an Application." *Production and Inventory Management* (Fourth Quarter 1985): 1–13.

DeMatta, R., and T. Miller. "A Note on the Growth of a Production Planning System." *Interfaces*, 23 (April 1993): 27–31.

Heskett, J., W. E. Sasser, and C. Hart. *Service Breakthroughs: Changing the Rules of the Game*. New York: Free Press, 1990.

Krajewski, L. J., and L. B. Ritzman. "Disaggregation in Manufacturing and Service Organizations." *Decision Sciences*, 8 (January 1977): 1–18.

Leone, R. A., and J. R. Meyer. "Capacity Strategies for the 1980's." *Harvard Business Review* 58 (November/December 1980): 133.

McLeavey, D. W., and S. L. Narasimham. *Production Planning and Inventory Control*. Boston: Allyn and Bacon, 1985.

Murdick, R., B. Render, and R. Russell. *Service Operations Management*. Boston: Allyn and Bacon, 1990.

Sasser, W. E. "Match Supply and Demand in Service Industries." *Harvard Business Review*, 54 (November/December 1976): 133–140.

Schramm, W. R., and L. E. Freund. "Application of Economic Control Charts by a Nursing Modeling Team." *Industrial Engineering*, 25 (April 1993): 27–31.

Vollmann, T. E., W. L. Berry, and D. C. Whybark. *Manufacturing Planning and Control Systems*, Third Edition. Homewood, IL: Irwin, 1992.

16

SHORT-TERM SCHEDULING TACTICS

LEARNING OBJECTIVES

When you complete this chapter you should be able to:

Identify or Define:
  Gantt Charts
  The Assignment Method
  Sequencing Rules
  Johnson's Rule
Explain:
  Shop loading
  Sequencing
  Scheduling

SCHEDULING AT LTV PROVIDES A COMPETITIVE ADVANTAGE

With the development of numerical control machines (machines controlled by computer software), companies now control (1) piece movement on the machine, (2) tool changing at the machine, and (3) the movement of materials between machines. When these capabilities are combined, we have a flexible machining system (FMS).

This FMS at LTV Aircraft Products Group in Dallas allows a number of good things to happen. Among these are rapid movement of pieces between machines, rapid tool setup, efficient waste handling, economical use of floor space, and high machine utilization. In a well-scheduled FMS, machine use can increase to 200% or 300% more than in a standard numerical control shop.

All machine and material movement instructions (computer code) are loaded into a mainframe computer. The mainframe computer downloads schedules to a computer at the FMS, where an on-site scheduler makes final determination about what job should be processed next. The on-site scheduler determines available tooling and risers (which hold the fixtures), as well as the final schedule.

The FMS makes possible the scheduling of parts in random order, handling similar or dissimilar parts and accommodating varying shapes and sizes without disrupting the production flow. This versatility results in parts being manufactured on a just-in-time (JIT) basis. Therefore, processing flexibility has improved.

Competitive advantage accrues to LTV in a variety of ways. First, machine utilization is about three times that of a normal machining center. Second, less than three hours are required to produce a piece, so work-in-process is less. Third, because the time to set up for one piece is low and throughput is rapid, customer service is improved.

Using computer-generated job instructions, planning and scheduling personnel determine the tooling necessary for each job. Then the appropriate tools for that job are loaded into the proper position at the machine to which the job has been assigned.

A carousel is shown receiving and delivering each fixture holder, called risers, which hold fixtures to the automated guided vehicle (AGV). The carousel has two workstations for mounting and dismounting pieces on the various risers. Here an operator on the far left is removing completed work and the operator in the red shirt determines the next order. Operators who do part loading and unloading also do a verification check prior to marking the part as complete and sending it on for inspection. The second floor control room in the background provides visual feedback to the scheduler.

The AGV releases its tooling holder (riser 35) to the loading conveyer of the washing station. The automatic washing station allows for complete rotation of the piece while it is being washed with high-pressure coolant. As each piece is washed, the metal chips flow into drainways in the floor to the central chip-sorting station.

T he problem of scheduling American League umpire crews from one series of games to the next is complicated by many restrictions on travel, ranging from coast-to-coast time changes, airline flight schedules, and night games running late.

The league strives to achieve two major objectives: (1) balance crew assignments relatively evenly among all teams over the course of a season and (2) minimize travel costs. These objectives are by nature conflicting, as attempting to balance crew assignments necessitates considerable airline travel and equipment moves, and hence increased travel costs. By using the assignment problem formulation described in this chapter, the time it takes the league to generate a schedule has been significantly decreased. And the quality of the schedule has improved.[1] ◆

Scheduling assigns resources, like equipment at LTV or umpires in baseball, over time to accomplish an organization's tasks. Table 16.1 illustrates scheduling decisions in four organizations, a hospital, a college, a factory, and an airline.

The process of scheduling (see Figure 16.1) begins with *capacity* planning, which involves facility and equipment acquisition. In the aggregate planning stage, decisions regarding the *use* of facilities, inventory, people, and outside contractors are made. Then the master schedule separates the aggregate plan and develops an *overall* schedule for outputs. Short-term schedules then translate capacity decisions, intermediate planning, and master schedules into job sequences, specific assignments of personnel, materials, and machinery. In this chapter, we describe the narrow issue of scheduling goods and services in the *short run* (that is, on a weekly, daily, or hourly basis).

SCHEDULING ISSUES

Scheduling involves assigning due dates to specific jobs, but many jobs compete simultaneously for the same resources. To help address the difficulties inherent in

TABLE 16.1 ■ **SCHEDULING DECISIONS**	
ORGANIZATION	**MANAGERS MUST SCHEDULE THE FOLLOWING:**
Hospital	Operating room use
	Patient admissions
	Nursing, security, maintenance staffs
	Outpatient treatments
University	Classrooms and audiovisual equipment
	Student and instructor schedules
	Graduate and undergraduate courses
Factory	Production of goods
	Purchases of materials
	Workers
Airline	Maintenance of aircraft
	Departure timetables
	Flight crews, catering, gate, and ticketing personnel

[1]James Evans, "Scheduling American League Umpires," *Interfaces* (November/December 1988): 42–51.

FIGURE 16.1 ■ The Relationship Between Capacity Planning, Aggregate Planning, Master Schedule, and Short-Term Scheduling

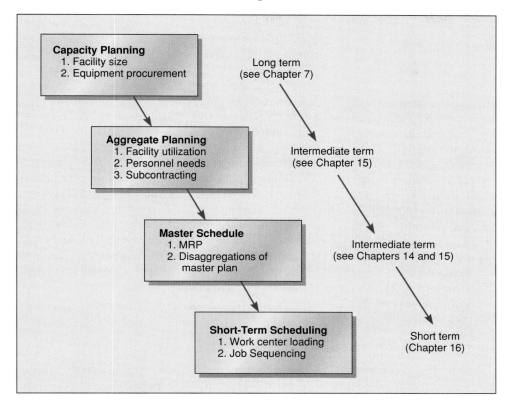

scheduling, we can categorize scheduling techniques as (1) forward scheduling and (2) backward scheduling.

Forward and Backward Scheduling

Forward scheduling starts the schedule as soon as the requirements are known. Forward scheduling is used in a variety of organizations such as hospitals, clinics, fine-dining restaurants, and machine tool manufacturers. In these facilities, jobs are performed to customer order and delivery is often requested as soon as possible. Forward scheduling is usually designed to produce a schedule that can be accomplished even if it means not meeting the due date. In many instances, forward scheduling causes a buildup of work-in-process inventory.

Forward scheduling

Backward scheduling begins with the due date, scheduling the final operation first. Steps in the job are then scheduled, one at a time, in reverse order. By subtracting the lead time for each item, the start time is obtained. However, the resources necessary to accomplish the schedule may not exist. Backward scheduling is used in many manufacturing environments, as well as service environments such as catering a banquet or scheduling surgery. In practice, a combination of forward and backward scheduling is often used to find a reasonable trade-off between what can be achieved and customer due dates.

Backward scheduling

Scheduling Workers Who Fall Asleep on the Job Is Not Easy

Unable to cope with a constantly changing work schedule, an operator at a big oil refinery dozes off in the middle of the night—and inadvertently dumps thousands of gallons of chemicals into a nearby river.

A similar story holds for pilots. Their inconsistent schedules often force them to snooze in the cockpit in order to get enough sleep. "There have been times I've been so sleepy, I'm nodding off as we're taxiing to get into take-off position," says a Federal Express pilot. "I've fallen asleep reading checklists. I've fallen asleep in the middle of a word."

An estimated 20 million people in the United States work in industries that maintain round-the-clock schedules. In interviews with researchers, employees from the graveyard shift report tales of seeing

sleeping assembly-line workers fall off their stools, batches of defective parts sliding past dozing inspectors, and exhausted forklift operators crashing into walls. "It's kind of too ugly. How can you admit that your nuclear power plant operators regularly fall asleep on the job?" says a Harvard researcher.

Scheduling is a major problem in firms with late shifts. Some companies, but far from all, are taking steps to deal with schedule-related sleep problems among workers. Dow Chemical, Detroit Edison, Pennzoil, and Exxon, for instance, are giving all workers several days off between shift changes. The Philadelphia Police Department is now using fewer and less random schedule changes and reports a 40% decline in officers' on-the-job auto accidents.

As more is learned about the economic toll of constant schedule changes, companies will find they cannot afford to continue ignoring the problem. As Dr. David Kupfer says, "Megabucks are involved, and, sometimes, lives."

Sources: Prevention (May 1994): 72–80; and *Wall Street Journal* (July 7, 1988): 1.

Machine breakdowns, absenteeism, quality problems, shortages, and other factors further complicate scheduling. (See the *POM in Action* box "Scheduling Workers Who Fall Asleep on the Job Is Not Easy.") Consequently, assignment of a date does not ensure that the work will be performed according to the schedule. Many specialized techniques, therefore, have been developed to aid us in preparing reliable schedules.

Scheduling Criteria

The correct scheduling technique depends on the volume of orders, the nature of operations, and the overall complexity of jobs, as well as importance placed on each of four criteria. Those four criteria are:

1. *Minimize Completion Time:* This is evaluated by determining the average completion time for each job.
2. *Maximize Utilization:* This is evaluated by determining the percent of the time the facility is utilized.
3. *Minimize Work-in-Process (WIP) Inventory:* This is evaluated by determining the average number of jobs in the system. The relationship between the number of jobs in the system and WIP inventory is high. Therefore, the fewer the number of jobs in the system, the lower the inventory.
4. *Minimize Customer Waiting Time:* This is evaluated by determining the average number of late days.

These four criteria are used in this chapter, as they are in industry, to evaluate scheduling performance. Additionally, good scheduling approaches should be simple, clear, easily understood, easy to carry out, flexible, and realistic. Given these considerations, *the objective of scheduling is to optimize the use of resources so the production objectives are met.* In this chapter, we examine scheduling in process-focused (intermittent) production, repetitive production, and the service sector.

SCHEDULING PROCESS-FOCUSED WORK CENTERS

Process-focused facilities (also known as intermittent or job shop facilities)[2] are high-variety, low-volume systems commonly found in manufacturing and service organizations. It is a production system in which products are made to order. Items made under this system usually differ considerably in terms of materials used, order of processing, processing requirements, time of processing, and setup requirements. Because of these differences, scheduling can be complex. To run a facility in a balanced and efficient manner, the manager needs a production planning and control system. This system should:

1. Schedule incoming orders without violating capacity constraints of individual work centers.
2. Check the availability of tools and materials before releasing an order to a department.
3. Establish due dates for each job and check progress against need dates and order lead times.
4. Check work in progress as jobs move through the shop.
5. Provide feedback on plant and production activities.
6. Provide work efficiency statistics and monitor operator times for payroll and labor distribution analyses.

Whether the scheduling system is manual or automated, it must be accurate and relevant. This means it requires a production data base with both planning and control files.[3] Three types of **planning files** are (1) an *item master file*, which contains information about each component the firm produces or purchases; (2) a *routing file*, which indicates each component's flow through the shop; and (3) a *work center master file*, which contains information about the work center, such as capacity and efficiency. **Control files** track the actual progress made against the plan for each work order.

Planning files

Control files

LOADING JOBS IN WORK CENTERS

Loading means the assignment of jobs to work or processing centers. Operations managers assign jobs to work centers so that costs, idle time, or completion times are kept to a minimum. Loading work centers takes two forms.[4] One is oriented to capacity; the second is related to assigning specific jobs to work centers. First, we examine

Loading

[2]Much of the literature on scheduling is about manufacturing; therefore, the traditional term *job shop scheduling* is often used.

[3]For an expanded discussion, see *APICS Training Aid—Shop Floor Control* (Falls Church, VA: American Production and Inventory Control Society).

[4]Note that this discussion can apply to work centers that might be called a "shop" in a manufacturing firm, or a "ward" in a hospital, or a "department" in an office or large kitchen.

loading from the perspective of capacity via a technique known as input–output control. Then, we present two approaches used for loading: *Gantt charts* and the *assignment method* of linear programming.

Input–Output Control

Many firms have difficulty scheduling (that is, achieving effective throughput) because they overload the production processes. This often occurs because they do not know actual performance in the work centers. Effective scheduling depends on matching the schedule to performance. Lack of knowledge about capacity and performance causes reduced throughput.

Input–output control

Input–output control is a technique that allows operations personnel to manage facility work flows. If the work is arriving faster than it is being processed, we are overloading the facility and a backlog develops. Overloading causes crowding in the facility, leading to inefficiencies and quality problems. If the work is arriving at a slower rate than it is being performed, we are underloading the facility and the work center may run out of work. Underloading the facility results in idle capacity and wasted resources. Example 1 shows the use of input–output controls.

EXAMPLE 1

Figure 16.2 shows the planned capacity for the DNC Milling work center for 8 weeks (weeks 6/6 through 7/25). The planned input is 280 standard hours per week. The actual input is close to this figure, varying between 250 and 285. Output is

FIGURE 16.2 ■ Input–Output Control

Work Center DNC Milling (In standard hours)								
Week ending	6/6	6/13	6/20	6/27	7/4	7/11	7/18	7/25
Planned Input	280	280	280	280	280	280	280	280
Actual Input	270	250	280	285	280	285		
Cumulative Deviation	–10	–40	–40	–35	–35	–30		
Planned Output	320	320	320	320				
Actual Output	270	270	270	270				
Cumulative Deviation	–50	–100	–150	–200				
Cumulative Change in Backlog*	0	–20	–10	+5				

*Sum of actual inputs minus sum of actual outputs = cumulative change in backlog

scheduled at 320 standard hours, which is the assumed capacity. A backlog of 300 hours exists in the work center. However, actual output (270 hours) is substantially less than planned. Therefore, neither the input plan nor the output plan is being achieved. Indeed, the backlog of work in this work center has actually increased by 5 hours by week 4. This increases work-in-process inventory, complicating the scheduling task and indicating the need for manager action.

The options available to operations personnel to manage facility work flow include

1. correction of performances;
2. increasing facility size;
3. increasing or reducing input to the work center by
   (a) routing work to or from other work centers,
   (b) increasing or decreasing subcontracting,
   (c) producing less (or producing more).

Producing less is not a popular solution for many managers, but the advantages can be substantial. First, the customer service level may improve because units may be produced on time. Second, efficiency may actually improve because of less work-in-process cluttering the work center and adding to overhead costs. Third, quality may improve because less work-in-process hides fewer problems.

Gantt Charts

Gantt charts are visual aids that are useful in loading and scheduling. Their name is derived from Henry Gantt, who developed them in the late 1800s. The charts help describe the use of resources, such as work centers and overtime.

Gantt charts

When used in *loading*, Gantt charts show the loading and idle time of several departments, machines, or facilities. They display the relative workloads in the system so that the manager knows what adjustments are appropriate. For example, when one work center becomes overloaded, employees from a low-load center can be transferred temporarily to increase the work force. Or if waiting jobs can be processed at different work centers, some jobs at high-load centers can be transferred to low-load centers. Versatile equipment may also be transferred among centers. Example 2 illustrates a simple Gantt load chart.

EXAMPLE 2

A New Orleans washing machine manufacturer accepts special orders for machines to be used in unique facilities such as submarines, hospitals, and large industrial laundries. The production of each machine requires varying tasks and durations. Figure 16.3 shows the load chart for the week of March 8.

The four work centers process several jobs during the week. This particular chart indicates that the Metal Works and Painting centers are completely loaded for the entire week. The Mechanical and Electronic centers have some idle time scattered during the week. We also note that the Metal Works center is unavailable on Tuesday, perhaps for preventive maintenance.

FIGURE 16.3   ■   Gantt Load Chart for the Week of March 8

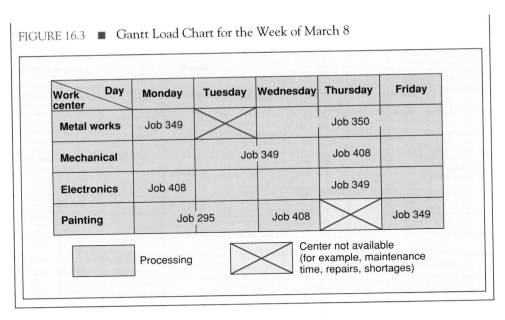

Work center \ Day	Monday	Tuesday	Wednesday	Thursday	Friday
Metal works	Job 349	✕		Job 350	
Mechanical			Job 349	Job 408	
Electronics	Job 408			Job 349	
Painting	Job 295		Job 408	✕	Job 349

☐ Processing   ☒ Center not available (for example, maintenance time, repairs, shortages)

The Gantt *load chart* does have some major limitations. For one, it does not account for production variability such as unexpected breakdowns or human errors that require reworking a job. The chart must also be updated regularly to account for new jobs and revised time estimates.

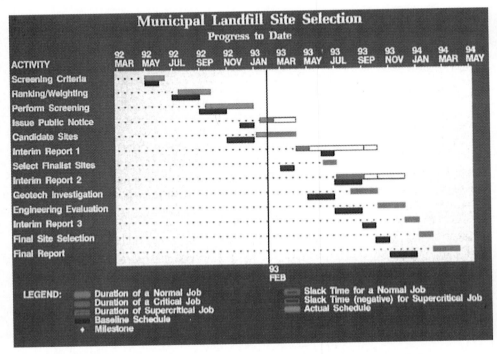

Gantt chart software, such as this one from the SAS Institute Inc. in Cary, N.C., helps managers schedule projects easily. Time, resource, and procedure constraints can be included to track project progress. Here the SAS Gantt chart monitors the selection process for a municipal landfill site.

A Gantt *schedule chart* is used to monitor jobs in progress.[5] It indicates which jobs are on schedule and which are ahead of or behind schedule. In practice, many versions of the chart are found. The schedule chart in Example 3 places jobs in progress on the vertical axis and time on the horizontal axis.

EXAMPLE 3

JH Products Corporation uses the Gantt chart in Figure 16.4 to show the scheduling of three orders, jobs A, B, and C. Each pair of brackets on the time axis denotes the estimated starting and finishing of a job enclosed within it. The solid bars reflect the actual status or progress of the job. Job A, for example, is about one-half day behind schedule at the end of day 5. Job B was completed after equipment maintenance. Job C is ahead of schedule.

FIGURE 16.4 ■ Gantt Scheduling Chart for Jobs A, B, and C

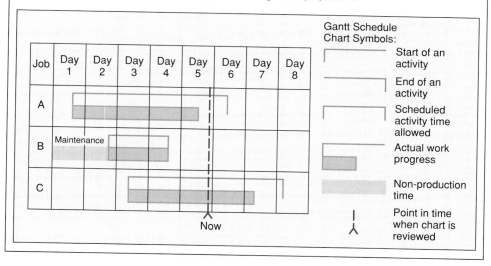

The Assignment Method

The **assignment method** is a special class of the linear programming model that involves assigning tasks or jobs to resources. Examples include assigning jobs to machines, contracts to bidders, people to projects, and salespeople to territories. The objective is most often to minimize total costs or time required to perform the tasks at hand. One important characteristic of assignment problems is that only one job (or worker) is assigned to one machine (or project).

Assignment method

Each assignment problem uses a table. The numbers in the table will be the costs or times associated with each particular assignment. For example, if a facility has three available machines (A, B, and C) and three new jobs to be completed, its table might appear as follows. The dollar entries represent the firm's estimate of what it will cost for each job to be completed on each machine.

[5]Gantt charts are also used for project scheduling and are again noted in Chapter 17, "Project Management."

MACHINE JOB	A	B	C
R-34	$11	$14	$6
S-66	$8	$10	$11
T-50	$9	$12	$7

The assignment method involves adding and subtracting appropriate numbers in the table in order to find the lowest *opportunity cost*[6] for each assignment. There are four steps to follow:

1. Subtract the smallest number in each row from every number in that row and then subtract the smallest number in each column from every number in that column. This step has the effect of reducing the numbers in the table until a series of zeros, meaning *zero opportunity costs*, appear. Even though the numbers change, this reduced problem is equivalent to the original one, and the same solution will be optimal.

2. Draw the minimum number of vertical and horizontal straight lines necessary to cover all zeros in the table. If the number of lines equals either the number of rows or the number of columns in the table, then we can make an optimal assignment (see step 4). If the number of lines is less than the number of rows or columns, we proceed to step 3.

3. Subtract the smallest number not covered by a line from every other uncovered number. Add the same number to any number(s) lying at the intersection of any two lines. Return to step 2 and continue until an optimal assignment is possible.

4. Optimal assignments will always be at zero locations in the table. One systematic way of making a valid assignment is first to select a row or column that contains only one zero square. We can make an assignment to that square and then draw lines through its row and column. From the uncovered rows and columns, we choose another row or column in which there is only one zero square. We make that assignment and continue the above procedure until we have assigned each person or machine to one task.

Example 4 shows how to use the assignment method.

EXAMPLE 4

The cost table shown earlier in this section is repeated below. We find the minimum total cost assignment of jobs to machines by applying steps 1 through 4.

MACHINE JOB	A	B	C
R-34	$11	$14	$6
S-66	$8	$10	$11
T-50	$9	$12	$7

[6]Opportunity costs are those profits forgone or not obtained.

Step 1a. Using the previous table, subtract the smallest number in each row from every number in the row. The result is shown below.

JOB \ MACHINE	A	B	C
R-34	5	8	0
S-66	0	2	3
T-50	2	5	0

Step 1b. Using the previous table, subtract the smallest number in each column from every number in the column. The result is shown below.

JOB \ MACHINE	A	B	C
R-34	5	6	0
S-66	0	0	3
T-50	2	3	0

Step 2. Draw the minimum number of straight lines needed to cover all zeroes. Because two lines suffice, the solution is not optimal.

JOB \ MACHINE	A	B	C
R-34	5	6	0
S-66	0	0	3
T-50	(2)	3	0

Smallest uncovered number

Step 3. Subtract the smallest uncovered number (2 in this table) from every other uncovered number and add it to numbers at the intersection of two lines.

JOB \ MACHINE	A	B	C
R-34	3	4	0
S-66	0	0	5
T-50	0	1	0

Return to step 2. Cover the zeroes with straight lines again.

MACHINE / JOB	A	B	C
R-34	3	4	0
S-66	0	0	5
T-50	0	1	0

Because three lines are necessary, an optimal assignment can be made (see step 4 on page 736). Assign R-34 to machine C, S-66 to machine B, and T-50 to machine A.

$$\text{Minimum cost} = \$6 + \$10 + \$9 = \$25$$

(*Note:* If we had S-66 assigned to machine A, we could not assign T-50 to a zero location.)

Some assignment problems entail *maximizing* the profit, effectiveness, or payoff of an assignment of people to tasks or of jobs to machines. It is easy to obtain an equivalent minimization problem by converting every number in the table to an *opportunity loss*. To convert a maximizing problem to an equivalent minimization problem, we subtract every number in the original payoff table from the largest single number in that table. We then proceed to step 1 of the four-step assignment method. It turns out that minimizing the opportunity loss produces the same assignment solution as the original maximization problem.

SEQUENCING JOBS IN WORK CENTERS

Sequencing

Scheduling provides a basis for assigning jobs to work centers. *Loading* is a capacity control technique that highlights overloads and underloads. **Sequencing** specifies the order in which jobs should be done at each center. For example, suppose that 10 patients are assigned to a medical clinic for treatment. In what order should they be treated? Should the first patient to be served be the one who arrived first or the one who needs emergency treatment? Sequencing methods provide such detailed information. These methods are referred to as priority rules for dispatching jobs to work centers.

Priority Rules for Dispatching Jobs

Priority rules

Priority rules provide guidelines for the sequence in which jobs should be worked. The rules are especially applicable for process-focused facilities such as clinics, print shops, and manufacturing job shops. We will examine a few of the most popular priority rules. Priority rules try to minimize completion time, number of jobs in the system, and job lateness, while maximizing facility utilization.

The most popular priority rules are:

FCFS: First-come, first-served. The first job to arrive at a work center is processed first. FCFS

SPT: Shortest processing time. The shortest jobs are handled first and completed. SPT

EDD: Earliest due date. The job with the earliest due date is selected first. EDD

LPT: Longest processing time. The longer, bigger jobs are often very important and are selected first. LPT

Example 5 compares these rules.

EXAMPLE 5

Five sheet metal jobs are waiting to be assigned at Ajax Company's Long Beach work center. Their work (processing) times and due dates are given below. We want to determine the sequence of processing according to (1) FCFS, (2) SPT, (3) EDD, and (4) LPT rules. Jobs were assigned a letter in the order they arrived.

JOB	JOB WORK (PROCESSING) TIME (DAYS)	JOB DUE DATE (DAYS)	JOB	JOB WORK (PROCESSING) TIME (DAYS)	JOB DUE DATE (DAYS)
A	6	8	D	3	15
B	2	6	E	9	23
C	8	18			

1. The *FCFS* sequence is simply A–B–C–D–E. The "flow time" in the system for this sequence measures the time each job spends waiting plus being processed. Job B, for example, waits 6 days while job A is being processed, then takes 2 more days of operation time itself; so it will be completed in 8 days—which is 2 days later than its due date.

JOB SEQUENCE	JOB WORK (PROCESSING) TIME	FLOW TIME	JOB DUE DATE	JOB LATENESS
A	6	6	8	0
B	2	8	6	2
C	8	16	18	0
D	3	19	15	4
E	9	28	23	5
	28	77		11

The first-come, first-served rule results in the following measures of effectiveness:

(a) Average completion time = $\dfrac{\text{sum of total flow time}}{\text{no. of jobs}}$

$$= \frac{77 \text{ days}}{5} = 15.4 \text{ days}$$

Your doctor may use a first-come-first-served priority rule satisfactorily. However, such a rule may be less than optimal for this emergency room. What priority rule might be best, and why? What priority rule was often used on the TV program M*A*S*H?

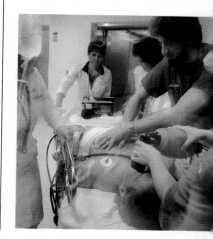

"We've been at it all night, J.B., and we've narrowed it down to 36,000 possibilities. We should have today's schedule firmed up by noon."
Source: CMCS News.

(b) Utilization = $\dfrac{\text{total job work (processing) time}}{\text{sum of total flow time}}$

$$= \frac{28}{77} = 36.4\%$$

(c) Average number of jobs in the system = $\dfrac{\text{sum of total flow time}}{\text{total job work (processing) time}}$

$$= \frac{77 \text{ days}}{28 \text{ days}} = 2.75 \text{ jobs}$$

(d) Average job lateness = $\dfrac{\text{total late days}}{\text{no. of jobs}} = \dfrac{11}{5} = 2.2 \text{ days}$

2. The *SPT* rule results in the sequence B–D–A–C–E (see below). Orders are sequenced according to processing time, with the highest priority given to the shortest job.

JOB SEQUENCE	JOB WORK (PROCESSING) TIME	FLOW TIME	JOB DUE DATE	JOB LATENESS
B	2	2	6	0
D	3	5	15	0
A	6	11	8	3
C	8	19	18	1
E	9	28	23	5
	28	65		9

Measurements of effectiveness for SPT are:

(a) Average completion time $= \dfrac{65}{5} = 13 \text{ days}$

(b) Utilization $= \dfrac{28}{65} = 43.1\%$

(c) Average number of jobs in the system $= \dfrac{65}{28} = 2.32$

(d) Average job lateness $= \dfrac{9}{5} = 1.8 \text{ days}$

3. The *EDD* rule gives the sequence B–A–D–C–E. Note that jobs are ordered by earliest due date first.

JOB SEQUENCE	JOB WORK (PROCESSING) TIME	FLOW TIME	JOB DUE DATE	JOB LATENESS
B	2	2	6	0
A	6	8	8	0
D	3	11	15	0
C	8	19	18	1
E	9	28	23	5
	28	68		6

Measurements of effectiveness for EDD are:

(a) Average completion time = $\dfrac{68}{5}$ = 13.6 days

(b) Utilization = $\dfrac{28}{68}$ = 41.2%

(c) Average number of jobs in the system = $\dfrac{68}{28}$ = 2.42

(d) Average job lateness = $\dfrac{6}{5}$ = 1.2 days

4. The *LPT* results in the order E–C–A–D–B.

JOB SEQUENCE	JOB WORK (PROCESSING) TIME	FLOW TIME	JOB DUE DATE	JOB LATENESS
E	9	9	23	0
C	8	17	18	0
A	6	23	8	15
D	3	26	15	11
B	2	28	6	22
	28	103		48

Measures of effectiveness for LPT are:

(a) Average completion time = $\dfrac{103}{5}$ = 20.6 days

(b) Utilization = $\dfrac{28}{103}$ = 28.2%

(c) Average number of jobs in the system = $\dfrac{103}{28}$ = 3.68

(d) Average job lateness = $\dfrac{48}{5}$ = 9.6 days

The results of these four rules are summarized below.

RULE	AVERAGE COMPLETION TIME (DAYS)	UTILIZATION (%)	AVERAGE NO. OF JOBS IN SYSTEM	AVERAGE LATENESS (DAYS)
FCFS	15.4	36.4	2.75	2.2
SPT	13.0	43.1	2.32	1.8
EDD	13.6	41.2	2.42	1.2
LPT	20.6	28.2	3.68	9.6

As we can see in Example 5, LPT is the least effective measurement of sequencing for the Ajax Company. SPT is superior in three measures and EDD in the fourth (average lateness). This is typically true in the real world also and has been supported by a number of simulation experiments.[7] We find that no one sequencing rule always excels on all criteria. Experience indicates the following:

1. Shortest processing time is generally the best technique for minimizing job flow and minimizing the average number of jobs in the system. Its chief disadvantage is that long-duration jobs may be continuously pushed back in priority in favor of short-duration jobs. Customers may view this dimly, and a periodic adjustment for longer jobs has to be made.

2. First-come, first-served does not score well on most criteria (but neither does it score particularly poorly). It has the advantage, however, of appearing fair to customers, which is important in service systems.

Critical Ratio

Critical ratio

Another type of sequencing rule is the **critical ratio**. The critical ratio (CR) is an index number computed by dividing the time remaining until due date by the work time remaining. As opposed to the priority rules, critical ratio is dynamic and easily updated. It tends to perform better than FCFS, SPT, EDD, or LPT on the average job lateness criterion.

The critical ratio gives priority to jobs that must be done to keep shipping on schedule. A job with a low critical ratio (less than 1.0) is one that is falling behind schedule. If CR is exactly 1.0, the job is on schedule. A CR greater than 1.0 means the job is ahead of schedule and has some slack.

The formula for critical ratio is

$$CR = \frac{\text{time remaining}}{\text{work days remaining}} = \frac{\text{due date} - \text{today's date}}{\text{work (lead) time remaining}}$$

Example 6 shows how to use the critical ratio.

EXAMPLE 6

Today is day 25 on S. Geraud Food's production schedule. Three jobs are on order, as indicated below:

JOB	DUE DATE	WORK DAYS REMAINING
A	30	4
B	28	5
C	27	2

We compute the critical ratios, using the formula for CR.

JOB	CRITICAL RATIO	PRIORITY ORDER
A	$(30 - 25)/4 = 1.25$	3
B	$(28 - 25)/5 = .60$	1
C	$(27 - 25)/2 = 1.00$	2

Job B has a critical ratio less than 1, meaning it will be late unless expedited. Thus, it has the highest priority. Job C is on time and job A has some slack.

[7]See R. W. Conway, W. L. Maxwell, and L. W. Miller, *Theory of Scheduling* (Reading, MA: Addison-Wesley, 1976).

The critical-ratio rule can help in most production scheduling systems to do the following:

1. Determine the status of a specific job.
2. Establish relative priority among jobs on a common basis.
3. Relate both stock and make-to-order jobs on a common basis.
4. Adjust priorities (and revise schedules) automatically for changes in both demand and job progress.
5. Dynamically track job progress and location.

Sequencing N Jobs on Two Machines: Johnson's Rule

The next step in complexity is the case where N jobs (where N is 2 or more) must go through two machines or work centers in the same order. This is called the $N/2$ problem.

Johnson's rule can be used to minimize the processing time for sequencing a group of jobs through two facilities.[8] It also minimizes total idle time on the machines. *Johnson's rule* involves four steps:

> **Johnson's rule**

1. All jobs are to be listed, and the time each requires on a machine is to be shown.
2. We select the job with the shortest activity time. If the shortest time lies with the first machine, the job is scheduled first. If the shortest time lies with the second machine, schedule the job last. Ties in activity times can be broken arbitrarily.
3. Once a job is scheduled, eliminate it.
4. Apply steps 2 and 3 to the remaining jobs, working toward the center of the sequence.

Example 7 shows how to apply Johnson's Rule.

EXAMPLE 7

Five specialty jobs at a Fredonia, New York, tool and die shop must be processed through two work centers (drill machine and lathe machine). The time for processing each job follows:

WORK (PROCESSING) TIME FOR JOBS (IN HOURS)

JOB	WORK CENTER 1 (DRILL)	WORK CENTER 2 (LATHE)
A	5	2
B	3	6
C	8	4
D	10	7
E	7	12

[8]S. M. Johnson, "Optimal Two and Three Stage Production Schedules with Set-Up Times Included," *Naval Research Logistics Quarterly*, 1, no. 1 (March 1954): 61–68.

Scheduling machines and people to provide the services on which we rely is an important part of P/OM. TV stations such as the one shown use algorithms to deal with the scheduling of tape editing machines. The news department's biggest job is taking several hours of video tape daily and editing it down to 7 or 8 one- to two-minute clips plus a four-minute feature and yet have everything in place by the evening news show deadline. Scheduling limited resources is a critical job. It is often tackled by operations personnel using the techniques of this chapter.

1. We wish to set the sequence that will minimize the total processing time for the five jobs. The job with the shortest processing time is A, in work center 2 (with a time of 2 hours). Because it is at the second center, schedule A last. Eliminate it from consideration.

				A

2. Job B has the next shortest time (3). Because that time is at the first work center, we schedule it first and eliminate it from consideration.

B				A

3. The next shortest time is job C (4) on the second machine. Therefore, it is placed as late as possible.

B			C	A

4. There is a tie (at 7 hours) for the shortest remaining job. We can place E, which was on the first work center, first. Then D is placed in the last sequencing position.

B	E	D	C	A

The sequential times are:

Work Center 1	3	7	10	8	5
Work Center 2	6	12	7	4	2

The time-phased flow of this job sequence is best illustrated graphically:

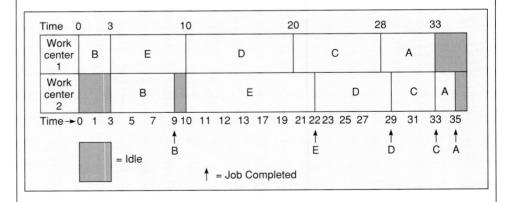

Thus, the five jobs are completed in 35 hours. The second work center will wait 3 hours for its first job, and it will also wait 1 hour after completing job B.

Sequencing N Jobs on Three Machines

The optimal solution to sequencing *N* jobs on three machines is quite complicated. However, if either or both of the following conditions are met, the solution is possible by Johnson's rule:

1. The smallest duration on machine 1 is at least as great as the largest duration on machine 2.

2. The smallest duration on machine 3 is at least as great as the largest duration on machine 2.

Example 8 illustrates this concept.

EXAMPLE 8

Consider the following jobs and their processing times at corresponding machines:

	DURATION (HOURS)		
JOB	MACHINE 1, T_1	MACHINE 2, T_2	MACHINE 3, T_3
A	13	5	9
B	5	3	7
C	6	4	5
D	7	2	6

We want to use Johnson's rule to find the optimal sequence. Because both conditions of Johnson's rule are met, we can apply it. First, form a new table as follows:

JOB	$T_1 + T_2$	$T_2 + T_3$
A	18	14
B	8	10
C	10	9
D	9	8

Now, using Johnson's rule for the $N/2$ problem, we get the optimal sequence: B, A, C, D.

Essentially, Johnson's rule converts an $N/3$ problem into an $N/2$ problem, provided that certain conditions are met. Even if these conditions are not met, the rule still provides a near-optimal solution.

Sequencing N Jobs on M Machines

When *several* jobs have to be processed through many facilities, finding an optimal sequence requires a complex search procedure. An efficient heuristic procedure is known as the CDS algorithm.[9] The CDS algorithm extends the $N/3$ Johnson's rule to a general N/M problem and provides a near-optimal solution.

[9]H. G. Campbell, R. A. Dudek, and M. L. Smith, "A Heuristic Algorithm for the (n) Job, (m) Machine Sequencing Problem," *Management Science*, 16, no. 10 (June 1970): 630–637.

Bottleneck Work Centers

Bottleneck work centers limit the output of production. Bottlenecks have less capacity than the prior or following work centers. Bottlenecks are a common occurrence because even well-designed systems are seldom balanced for very long. Changing products, product mixes, and volumes often create multiple and shifting bottlenecks. Consequently, bottleneck work centers occur in virtually all production processes, from hospitals and restaurants to factories. Approaches used to address bottlenecks include increasing capacity of the bottleneck, rerouting work, changing lot size, changing work sequence, or accepting idleness at other workstations. Substantial research has been done on the bottleneck issue;[10] an easy-to-read analysis of the bottleneck issue is found in *The Goal: A Process of Ongoing Improvement*.[11]

Limitations of Rule-Based Systems

Traditional rule-based systems have a number of limitations. Among those are

1. Scheduling is dynamic, therefore, rules need to be revised to adjust to changes in process, equipment, product mix, and so forth.
2. Rules do not look upstream or downstream; idle resources and bottleneck resources in other departments may not be recognized.
3. Rules do not look beyond due dates. For instance, two orders may have the same due date. One order involves restocking a distributor and the other is a custom order that will shut down the customer's factory if not completed. Both may have the same due date, but clearly the custom order is more important.

As may be obvious from this list of limitations and from the preceding discussion of bottleneck resources, scheduling can be complex to perform and still yield poor results—not a very fruitful combination. For instance, an operations manager may pick a decision rule such as *critical ratio* and "start the order with the least slack time remaining," or "start the order that uses the same machine setup." Both examples might seem like reasonable decisions. The first focuses on meeting customer due dates and the second focuses on improving efficiency. But the "order with least slack time remaining" may be a very inefficient setup, and the order with the "same setup" may not be needed for a week. Or it may be that the schedule really should include a new order that is to be shipped with an order going out tonight. Our point is that even with sophisticated rules, good scheduling is very difficult.

So how do schedulers tackle the sequencing decisions that have to be made everyday? The answer is that in spite of their limitations, they often use sequencing rules such as SPT, EDD, or critical ratio. They apply these methods periodically at each work center and then the scheduler modifies the sequence to deal with a multitude of real-world variables.

Bottleneck

To manage her hundreds of retail cookie outlets, Debbi Fields decided to capture her experience in an "expert system" that every store could access at any time. Her Retail Operations Intelligence System (ROIS) takes advantage of headquarters expertise in scheduling minimum-wage employees, the predominant counter help. The software draws up a work schedule, including breaks, to best use hourly employees' time. ROIS also creates a full-day projection of the amount of dough to be processed and charts progress and sales on an hourly basis. It even tells staff when to cut back production and start offering free samples to passing customers.

---

[10]See, for instance, Thomas E. Morton and David W. Pentico, *Heuristic Scheduling Systems* (New York: John Wiley, 1993).

[11]Eliyahu, M. Goldratt, and Jeff Cox, *The Goal: A Process of Ongoing Improvement* (Croton-on-Hudson, NY: North River Press, 1986).

ADVANCES IN SCHEDULING AND SEQUENCING

Two recent advances are proving very beneficial to operations scheduling. They are *expert systems* and *finite scheduling*.

Expert Systems

As described in Chapter 8, an **expert system** is a computer program that makes decisions and solves problems much as a human expert would handle them. The idea in scheduling is to use the knowledge and skills of a person who is an expert at sequencing and scheduling. The firm can then derive the benefits of expert judgment without having the expert present.

Expert system

There is a growing number of scheduling expert systems, dating back to *Intelligent Scheduling and Information System (ISIS)* in 1984.[12] ISIS works by searching for solutions that satisfy the scheduling constraints. When it cannot find a feasible solution, it relaxes the constraints based on their relative importance. Texas Instruments is a company that uses an expert system at its manufacturing plant in Carrolton, Texas. The TI system coordinates the scheduling, dispatching, and tool loading on the plant floor.[13]

Finite Scheduling

The second recent advance is interactive finite scheduling. **Finite scheduling** overcomes the disadvantages of rule-based systems by providing the scheduler with graphical interactive computing. This system is characterized by the ability of the scheduler to make changes based on up-to-the-minute information. These schedules are often displayed in Gantt chart form (see Figure 16.5). The scheduler has the flexibility to handle any situation, including order, labor, or machine changes.

Finite scheduling

Finite scheduling allows delivery needs to be balanced against efficiency based on today's conditions and today's orders, not according to some predefined rule. Many of the current finite scheduling computer programs offer resource constraint features, a multitude of rules, and the ability of the scheduler to work interactively with the scheduling system to create a realistic schedule.[14] These systems may also combine an expert system[15] and simulation techniques[16] and allow the scheduler to assign costs to various options. Finite scheduling helps the scheduler, but leaves it up to the scheduler to determine what constitutes a "good" schedule.

---

[12]M. S. Fox and S. F. Smith, "ISIS: A Knowledge-Based System for Factory Scheduling." *Expert Systems*, 1, no. 1 (July 1984): 25–49.

[13]J. Lyman, "Manufacturing," *Electronics* (October 16, 1986): 105–106.

[14]Andrew Gilman, "Interest in Finite Scheduling Is Growing . . . Why?" APICS: *The Performance Advantage*, 4, no. 8 (August 1994): 45–48.

[15]Factrol, Inc., West Lafayette, Indiana 47906.

[16]AutoSimulations, Bountiful, Utah 84010.

FIGURE 16.5 ■ Most Finite Scheduling Systems Generate a Gantt Chart That Can Be Manipulated by the User on a Computer Screen

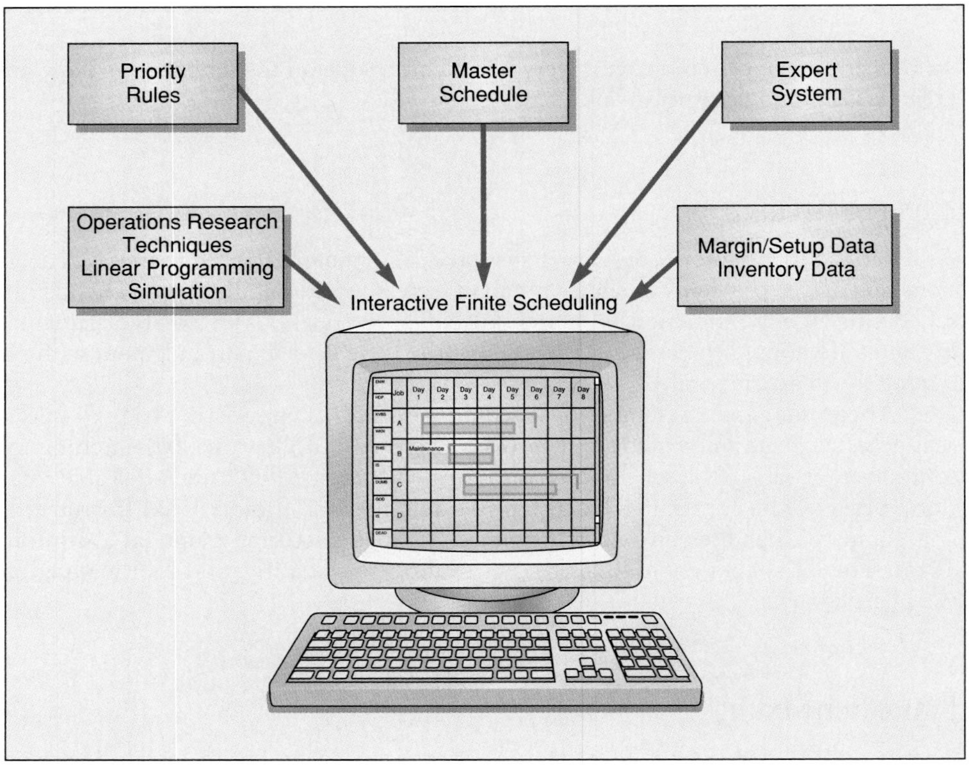

REPETITIVE MANUFACTURING

The scheduling goals as defined at the beginning of this chapter are also appropriate for repetitive production. You may recall from Chapter 7 that repetitive producers make standard products from modules. Repetitive producers want to satisfy customer demands, lower inventory investment, reduce the batch (or lot) size, and utilize equipment and processes. The way to move toward these goals is to move to a level material use schedule. **Level material use** means frequent, high-quality, small lot sizes that contribute to just-in-time production. This is exactly what world-class producers such as Harley-Davidson and John Deere do. The advantages of level material use are:

Level material use

1. Lower inventory levels, which release capital for other uses.

2. Faster product throughput (that is, shorter lead times).

3. Improved component quality and hence improved product quality.

4. Reduced floor-space requirements.

5. Improved communication among employees because they are closer together (which can result in improved teamwork and *esprit de corps*).

6. Smoother production process because large lots have not "hidden" the problems.

	TRADITIONAL BATCH SIZE (MONTHLY REQUIREMENT;	LEVEL MATERIAL USE SCHEDULE (DAILY REQUIREMENT
MODEL	**20-DAY MONTH)**	**TO MEET DEMAND)**
LA30	120	6
LB38	220	11
LB46	180	9
LC38	240	12
LC46	240	12
LD38	500	25
LE38	1,160	58
	2,660	133

TABLE 16.2 ■ L SERIES TRACTOR AT A U.S. TRACTOR MANUFACTURER

Suppose a repetitive producer runs large monthly batches. With a level material use schedule, management would move toward shortening this monthly cycle. Management might run this cycle every week, day, or hour.

Table 16.2 shows a *traditional batch* and a new *level material use* schedule for an actual Midwestern repetitive manufacturer of small tractors. Their daily level material use schedule meets daily demand with substantial savings over the costs of the batch system, which met a monthly demand. All direct costs except material handling have been reduced substantially.

One way to develop a level material use schedule is to determine first the minimum lot size that will keep the production process moving. Ideally, this is the one unit that is being moved from one adjacent process to the next. More realistically, analysis of the process, transportation time, and containers used for transport are considered when determining lot size. Such analysis typically results in a small lot size but a lot size larger than one. Once a lot size has been determined, the EOQ production-run model can be modified to determine the desired setup time. We saw in Chapter 13 that the production-run model takes the form

$$Q^\star = \sqrt{\frac{2DS}{H[1 - (d/p)]}}$$

where D = annual demand
  S = setup cost
  H = holding cost
  d = daily demand
  p = daily production

Example 9 shows how Crate Furniture, Inc., a firm that produces rustic furniture, moves toward a level material use schedule.

EXAMPLE 9

Crate Furniture's production analyst, Aleda Roth, determined that a 2-hour production cycle would be acceptable between two departments. Further, she concluded that a setup time that would accommodate the 2-hour cycle time could be achieved. Aleda developed the following data and procedure to determine analytically that optimum setup time:

$$D = \text{annual demand} = 400,000 \text{ units}$$
$$d = \text{daily demand} = 400,000/250 \text{ days} = 1,600 \text{ units per day}$$
$$p = \text{daily production rate} = 4,000 \text{ units per day}$$
$$Q = \text{EOQ desired} = 400 \text{ (which is the 2-hour demand,}$$
$$\text{that is, 1,600 per day/4 2-hour periods)}$$
$$H = \text{holding cost} = \$20 \text{ per unit per year}$$
$$S = \text{setup cost (to be determined)}$$

Aleda determines that the cost, on an hourly basis, of setting up equipment is $30. Further, she computes that the setup cost per setup should be

$$Q = \sqrt{\frac{2DS}{H(1 - d/p)}}$$

$$Q^2 = \frac{2DS}{H(1 - d/p)}$$

$$S = \frac{(Q^2)(H)(1 - d/p)}{2D}$$

$$S = \frac{(400)^2(20)(1 - 1,600/4,000)}{2(400,000)}$$

$$= \frac{(3,200,000)(0.6)}{800,000} = \$2.40$$

$$\text{Setup time} = \$2.40/(\text{hourly labor rate})$$
$$= \$2.40/(\$30 \text{ per hour})$$
$$= 0.08 \text{ hour, or } 4.8 \text{ minutes}$$

Now, rather than producing components in large lots, Crate Furniture can produce in a 2-hour cycle with the advantage of an inventory turnover of four *per day*.

Only two changes need to be made for this type of level material flow to work. First is the radical reduction in setup times, which is usually not difficult from a technical point of view. Second, changes may need to be made to improve material handling. With short production cycles, there can be very little wait time.

SCHEDULING FOR SERVICES

Scheduling service systems differs from scheduling manufacturing systems in several ways. First, in manufacturing, the scheduling emphasis of the operations manager is on materials, but in services, it is on staffing levels. Second, service systems do not store inventories of services. Third, services are labor-intensive, and the demand for this labor can be highly variable.

A hospital is an example of a service facility that may use a scheduling system every bit as complex as one found in a job shop. Hospitals seldom use a machine shop priority system such as first-come, first-served (FCFS) for treating emergency case patients. But they do schedule products (such as surgeries) just like a factory, even though finished goods inventories cannot be kept and capacities must meet wide variations in demand.

This section discusses scheduling in four typical service organizations: banks, hospitals, airlines, and restaurants.

Scheduling Bank Personnel with Linear Programming

Linear programming, as we saw in the Supplement to Chapter 6, can be a useful tool for scheduling service employees. Chase Manhattan Bank used this technique to deal with the work-load curve illustrated in Figure 16.6.[17] Employing part-time personnel effectively provided a variable capacity. Part-timers at Chase work at least 4 hours/day, take no lunch, and are not entitled to all of the bank's fringe benefits, making them less expensive than full-timers. But corporate considerations limited the extent to which part-timers could be hired in other departments. So Chase's problem was to find an optimal work-force schedule that would meet labor requirements (in the upper half of Table 16.3), and also be economical. A linear programming model with 18 variables and 21 constraints yielded the schedule seen in the lower half of Table 16.3.

A much larger LP application is discussed in the POM in Action box "Scheduling Crews with LP at American Airlines."

Scheduling Nurses with Cyclical Scheduling

Head nurses in large hospitals often spend more than 20 hours a month establishing schedules for their departments. They consider a fairly long planning period (say, 6 weeks) and then need to set timely and efficient schedules so that adequate health care can be delivered to patients while keeping personnel happy with their hours. Although there are several ways of tackling this problem, including linear programming, one approach that is both workable yet simple is *cyclical scheduling*.[18]

Cyclical scheduling has seven steps:

1. Plan a schedule equal in length to the number of people being scheduled.
2. Determine how many of each of the least desirable off-shifts must be covered each week.

---

[17]S. L. Moondra, "An L.P. Model for Workforce Scheduling for Banks," *Journal of Bank Research* (Winter 1976).

[18]For more details, see R. Murdick, B. Render, and R. Russell, *Service Operations Management* (Boston: Allyn and Bacon, 1990), pp. 336–340, or J. D. Megeath, "Successful Hospital Personnel Scheduling," *Interfaces*, 8, no. 6 (February 1978): 55–59.

TABLE 16.3 ■ RESULTS OF CHASE MANHATTAN LINEAR PROGRAMMING ANALYSIS FOR PERSONNEL SCHEDULING

WORK-FORCE SCHEDULE

TIME PERIOD	NUMBER OF PERSONS REQUIRED	NUMBER OF PERSONS AVAILABLE		
		FULL-TIME	PART-TIME	TOTAL
9–10 A.M.	14	29	—	29
10–11	25	29	—	29
11–12	26	15	11	26
12–1 P.M.	38	14	26	40
1–2	55	29	26	55
2–3	60	29	31	60
3–4	51	29	22	51
4–5	29	29	5	34
5–6	14	9	5	14
6–7	9	9	0	9

RESULTS USING LP: TIME SCHEDULES

NUMBER OF EMPLOYEES	STARTING TIME	FULL-TIME EMPLOYEES			
		NUMBER OF EMPLOYEES	LUNCH PERIOD	NUMBER OF EMPLOYEES	LEAVING TIME
29	9 A.M.	14	11–12	20	5 P.M.
		15	12–1	9	7 P.M.

NUMBER OF EMPLOYEES	PART-TIME EMPLOYEES		
	STARTING TIME	NUMBER OF EMPLOYEES	LEAVING TIME
11	11 A.M.	9	3 P.M.
		2	4 P.M.
15	12 noon	15	4 P.M.
5	2 P.M.	5	6 P.M.

FIGURE 16.6 ■ Work-Load Curve at Chase Manhattan Bank

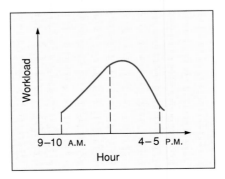

Scheduling Crews with LP at American Airlines

American Airlines employs more than 8,300 pilots and 16,200 flight attendants to fly more than 500 aircraft. Total crew cost exceeds $1.4 billion every year and is second only to fuel cost. But unlike fuel costs, a large part of crew costs is controllable. To develop crew assignment plans that achieve a high level of crew utilization, American relies heavily on linear programming.

Clearly, every airline flight needs a full crew of pilots and flight attendants, but because crew members are people and not machines, scheduling their deployment is considerably more complicated than scheduling the use of aircraft, gates, or other equipment. The FAA has established a complex set of work-time limitations designed to ensure that crew members can safely fulfill their duties.

In addition, financial issues affect scheduling practices. Union contracts specify that flight crews will be guaranteed pay for some number of hours each day or each trip. Therefore, airline planners must try to build crew schedules that meet or exceed the crews' pay guarantees to the maximum extent possible. A trip containing one or more days with small amounts of flying time might be very expensive, because the crews would receive extra pay over and above the assigned flying time.

The LP model, 15 labor-years in the making, assigns crews in 12 cities. It takes about 500 hours of mainframe computer time per month, but generates annual savings of over $20 million. Considered the best scheduling approach for problems of its type, the LP model has been sold by American to 10 other airlines and one railroad.

Sources: Interfaces (January/February 1991): 62–74; and *Management Science* (June 1993): 657–682.

3. Begin the schedule for one nurse by scheduling the days off during the planning cycle (at a rate of 2 days per week on the average).

4. Assign off-shifts for that first nurse using step 2. Here is an example of one nurse's 42-day schedule, where X is the day off, D is the day shift, and E is the evening shift:

S	M	T	W	T	F	S		S	M	T	W	T	F	S		S	M	T	W	T	F	S		S	M	T	W	T	F	S		S	M	T	W	T	F	S		S	M	T	W	T	F	S
E	E	E	E	E	X	X		X	X	E	E	E	E	E		E	D	X	D	D	D	D		D	D	X	X	D	E	X		X	E	E	E	E	E	X		D	E	D	D	X	X	E

5. Repeat this pattern for each of the other nurses, but offsetting each one by 1 week from the previous one.

6. Allow each nurse to pick his or her "slot" or "line" in order of seniority.

7. Mandate that any changes from a chosen schedule are strictly between the personnel wanting to switch.

When this approach was applied at Colorado General Hospital, the head nurse saved an average of 10 to 15 hours a month and found these advantages: (1) no computer was needed, (2) the nurses were happy with the schedule, (3) the cycles could be changed during different seasons (to accommodate avid skiers), and (4) recruiting was easier because of predictability and flexibility.

Large savings of time can also be found in scheduling at small businesses, such as restaurants. As the *POM in Action* box "Scheduling Employees at McDonald's Becomes a Lot Easier" notes, PC-based scheduling systems can be a great boon to managers.

Scheduling Employees at McDonald's Becomes a Lot Easier

Al Boxley, the progressive owner of four McDonald's restaurants in the Cumberland, Maryland, area, faced an operations problem that still haunts most small businesses. Every week, the manager in each of Boxley's restaurants was spending more than 8 hours to prepare manually the work schedules for 150 employees. This weekly routine involved forecasting sales by hour; translating these sales to hourly staff needs in the grill, counter, and drive-through work areas; and then matching the mostly part-time employee availabilities and work skills with McDonald's hourly needs. This time-consuming activity was further complicated by high turnover, movement of employees among restaurants, and constant change in the availability of student workers.

Boxley decided he needed a cheap, simple-to-use, PC-based scheduling system that could seriously cut the manager's time loss. Turning to linear programming, he found that for a restaurant with 3 work areas, 150 employees, and 30 possible work shifts, formulating a scheduling problem results in 100,000 decision variables and 3,000 constraints. Clearly, such a large problem could not be solved very quickly on a PC. But by dividing the LP problem into a number of simpler subproblems (in a process called "decomposition into network flows"), the schedule could actually be developed in only 15 minutes.

The results were impressive: Managers reported an 80–90% reduction in the time it took to generate employee schedules. Costs were kept down by eliminating overstaffing, and employee morale and efficiency were improved. Also, managers now had a valuable "what-if" tool to measure the sensitivity of employee schedules to a variety of operating conditions.

Source: Robert Love and James Hoey, *Interfaces* (March/April 1990): 21–29.

ACHIEVING WORLD-CLASS STANDARDS

Because customers expect deliveries on schedule, world-class firms perform scheduling correctly. Scheduling plays a very large role in employee morale, plant utilization, and winning orders. Consequently, world-class firms are moving toward scheduling systems that use a combination of both computers and people. Increasingly, this means using systems that include dispatching rules, expert systems, simulation, and finite scheduling systems. Computer-generated schedules, adjusted by humans, are proving to yield exceptionally good scheduling. World-class firms such as Pratt & Whitney, LTV, Texas Instruments, and NUCOR have verified this trend. All of these firms are now using one or more of these techniques.

SUMMARY

Scheduling involves the timing of operations to achieve the efficient movement of units through a system. This chapter addressed the issues of short-term scheduling in process-focused, repetitive, and service environments. We saw that process-focused facilities are production systems in which products are made to order, and that scheduling tasks in them can become complex. Several aspects and approaches to scheduling, loading, and sequencing of jobs were introduced. These ranged from Gantt charts and the assignment methods of scheduling to a series of priority rules, the critical-ratio rule, and Johnson's rule for sequencing. We also examined the use of level material flow in repetitive manufacturing environments.

Service systems generally differ from manufacturing systems. This leads to the use of appointment systems, first-come, first-served systems, and reservation systems, as well as to heuristics and mathematical programming approaches to servicing customers.

USING AB:POM TO SOLVE SCHEDULING PROBLEMS

AB:POM's assignment module is used to solve the traditional one-to-one assignment problem of people to tasks, machines to jobs, and such. Program 16.1 shows the input screen for a three-job, three-machine problem using Example 4's data. The very straightforward output and solution are seen in Program 16.2.

PROGRAM 16.1 ■ AB:POM's Assignment Model Program Using Example 4 Data as Input

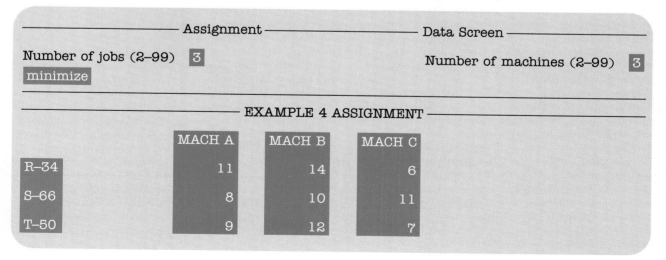

— Assignment —			Data Screen —		
Number of jobs (2–99) 3			Number of machines (2–99) 3		
minimize					

EXAMPLE 4 ASSIGNMENT	MACH A	MACH B	MACH C
R–34	11	14	6
S–66	8	10	11
T–50	9	12	7

PROGRAM 16.2 ■ Output from Assignment Program on Example 4 Data

EXAMPLE 4 ASSIGNMENT

SHIPMENTS	MACH A	MACH B	MACH C
R–34			1
S–66		1	
T–50	1		

The minimum total cost = $25

NOTE: alternate optimal solutions exist

Program 16.3 illustrates AB:POM's job shop scheduling module, which can solve a one- or two-machine job shop problem. Example 5's data are used as input. Outputs appear on the same screen.

PROGRAM 16.3 ■ AB:POM's Job Shop Scheduling Program Using Example 5 Data. Available priority rules include SPT, FCFS, EDD, and LPT. Each can be examined in turn once the data are all entered.

———————————— Job Shop Sequencing ———————————— Solution ———

Number of jobs (1–14) 5   Number of machines (1–2) 1

———————————————— AJAX COMPANY, EXAMPLE 5 ————————————————

SPT	mach. 1	Due Dat	EXTRA	Order	Flow tm	Tardy
JOB A	6	8	0	third	11	3
JOB B	2	6	0	first	2	0
JOB C	8	18	0	fourth	19	1
JOB D	3	15	0	second	5	0
JOB E	9	23	0	fifth	28	5
				TOTAL	65	9
				AVERAGE	13.00	1.80

Average # of jobs in system = 2.32

SEQUENCE

JOB B, JOB D, JOB A, JOB C, JOB E

SOLVED PROBLEMS

Solved Problem 16.1

King Finance Corporation, headquartered in New York, wants to assign three recently hired college graduates, Julie Jones, Al Smith, and Pat Wilson, to regional offices. But the firm also has an opening in New York and would send one of the three there if it were more economical than a move to Omaha, Dallas, or Miami. It will cost $1,000 to relocate Jones in New York, $800 to relocate Smith there, and $1,500 to move Wilson. What is the optimal assignment of personnel to offices?

OFFICE / HIREE	OMAHA	MIAMI	DALLAS
Jones	$800	$1,100	$1,200
Smith	$500	$1,600	$1,300
Wilson	$500	$1,000	$2,300

Solution

(a) The cost table has a fourth column to represent New York. To "balance" the problem, we add a "dummy" row (person) with a zero relocation cost to each city.

OFFICE / HIREE	OMAHA	MIAMI	DALLAS	NEW YORK
Jones	$800	$1,100	$1,200	$1,000
Smith	$500	$1,600	$1,300	$ 800
Wilson	$500	$1,000	$2,300	$1,500
Dummy	0	0	0	0

(b) Subtract the smallest number in each row and cover all zeroes (column subtraction will give the same numbers and therefore is not necessary).

OFFICE / HIREE	OMAHA	MIAMI	DALLAS	NEW YORK
Jones	0	300	400	200
Smith	0	1,100	800	300
Wilson	0	500	1,800	1,000
Dummy	0	0	0	0

(c) Subtract the smallest uncovered number (200), add it to each square where two lines intersect, and cover all zeroes.

OFFICE / HIREE	OMAHA	MIAMI	DALLAS	NEW YORK
Jones	0	100	200	0
Smith	0	900	600	100
Wilson	0	300	1,600	800
Dummy	200	0	0	0

(d) Subtract the smallest uncovered number (100), add it to each square where two lines intersect, and cover all zeroes.

OFFICE / HIREE	OMAHA	MIAMI	DALLAS	NEW YORK
Jones	0	0	100	0
Smith	0	800	500	100
Wilson	0	200	1,500	800
Dummy	300	0	0	100

(e) Subtract the smallest uncovered number (100), add it to squares where two lines intersect, and cover all zeroes.

OFFICE / HIREE	OMAHA	MIAMI	DALLAS	NEW YORK
Jones	100	0	100	0
Smith	0	700	400	0
Wilson	0	100	1,400	700
Dummy	400	0	0	100

(f) Because it takes four lines to cover all zeroes, an optimal assignment can be made at zero squares. We assign

> Dummy (no one) to Dallas
> Wilson to Omaha
> Smith to New York
> Jones to Miami

$$\text{Cost} = \$0 + \$500 + \$800 + \$1,100$$
$$= \$2,400$$

Solved Problem 16.2

A defense contractor in Dallas has six jobs awaiting processing. Processing time and due dates are given below. Assume jobs arrive in the order shown. Set the processing sequence according to FCFS and evaluate.

JOB	JOB PROCESSING TIME (DAYS)	JOB DUE DATE (DAYS)
A	6	22
B	12	14
C	14	30
D	2	18
E	10	25
F	4	34

Solution

FCFS has the sequence A–B–C–D–E–F.

JOB SEQUENCE	JOB PROCESSING TIME	FLOW TIME	DUE DATE	JOB LATENESS
A	6	6	22	0
B	12	18	14	4
C	14	32	30	2
D	2	34	18	16
E	10	44	25	19
F	4	48	34	14
	48	182		55

1. Average completion time = 182/6 = 30.33.
2. Average no. jobs in system = 182/48 = 3.79.
3. Average job lateness = 55/6 = 9.16 days.
4. Utilization = 48/182 = 26.4%.

Solved Problem 16.3

The Dallas firm noted in Solved Problem 16.2 wants also to consider job sequencing by the SPT priority rule. Apply SPT to the same data and provide a recommendation.

Solution

SPT has the sequence D–F–A–E–B–C.

JOB SEQUENCE	JOB PROCESSING TIME	FLOW TIME	DUE DATE	JOB LATENESS
D	2	2	18	0
F	4	6	34	0
A	6	12	22	0
E	10	22	25	0
B	12	34	14	20
C	14	48	30	18
	48	124		38

1. Average completion time = 124/6 = 20.67 days.

2. Average no. jobs in system = 124/48 = 2.58.

3. Average job lateness = 38/6 = 6.33 days.

4. Utilization = 48/124 = 38.7%.

SPT is superior to FCFS in this case on all four measures. If we were to also analyze EDD, we would, however, find its average job lateness to be lowest at 5.5 days. SPT is a good recommendation. SPT's major disadvantage is that it makes long jobs wait, sometimes for a long time.

Solved Problem 16.4

Use Johnson's rule to find the optimum sequence for processing the jobs below through two work centers. Times at each center are in hours.

JOB	WORK CENTER 1	WORK CENTER 2
A	6	12
B	3	7
C	18	9
D	15	14
E	16	8
F	10	15

Solution

B	A	F	D	C	E

The sequential times are

Work Center 1	3	6	10	15	18	16
Work Center 2	7	12	15	14	9	8

Solved Problem 16.5

Illustrate the throughput time and idle time at the two work centers in Solved Problem 16.4 by constructing a time-phased chart.

Solution

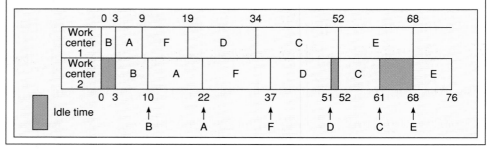

Solved Problem 16.6

Swearingen Products makes microwave ovens and desires to move to a level material use schedule for the various components used in those ovens. The firm has traditionally made both components and units in large batches and stored them in inventory until needed because the foreman liked it that way. Because the foreman retired last week, the president, John Swearingen, wants to move to a level material use schedule. When reviewing the flow of the first component, a control panel, the P/OM analyst found that the standard tote tray holds 2 hours of assembly-line work (100 units) and that move time is less than 1 hour even when allowing for the occasional delay that sometimes occurs. With these data, the analyst concludes that a 3-hour cycle would be a good place to begin. Swearingen's production data for control panels are:

$$\text{Annual demand} = 104{,}000$$
$$\text{Daily demand rate} = 400$$
$$\text{Daily production rate} = 1{,}000$$
$$\text{Desired lot size (a 3-hour supply)} = 300$$
$$\text{Holding cost} = \$10 \text{ per unit per year}$$
$$\text{Setup labor cost per hour} = \$12$$

What should be the setup time?

Solution

$$Q = \sqrt{\frac{2DS}{H(1 - d/p)}}$$

$$Q^2 = \frac{2DS}{H(1 - d/p)}$$

$$S = \frac{Q^2 H(1 - d/p)}{2D} = \text{setup cost per setup}$$

$$S = \frac{(300)^2(10)(1 - 400/1{,}000)}{2(104{,}000)} = (4.327)(.6) = \$2.59$$

$$\text{Setup time} = \$2.59/(\text{labor rate per hour})$$
$$= \$2.59/(\$12) = 0.1295 \text{ hour} = 7.77 \text{ minutes}$$

DISCUSSION QUESTIONS

1. Name five priority sequencing rules. Explain how each works to assign jobs.

2. When is Johnson's rule best applied in scheduling?

3. Describe the differences between forward and backward scheduling.

4. What is the difference between a Gantt load chart and a Gantt schedule chart?

5. Briefly describe how the assignment method works.

6. What is the most popular priority rule and why?

7. Why is the scheduling of services a difficult problem?

8. What is input–output control? How does it help the operations manager?

9. What are the criteria by which we evaluate sequencing rules?

10. What are the advantages of level material flow?

11. How does a bottleneck work center impact scheduling?

CRITICAL
THINKING
EXERCISE

Scheduling people to work the late, or "graveyard," shift is a problem in almost every 24-hour company. The *POM in Action* box "Scheduling Workers Who Fall Asleep on the Job Is Not Easy" describes night-shift dilemmas at an oil refinery and a police department. Scheduling is also difficult for airlines that fly long routes, such as El Al Airline's popular 11-hour nonstop Tel Aviv to New York flight.

Select five companies that require night shifts and discuss how each can deal with its staffing requirements. What are the major issues in each that impact on morale, productivity, alertness, and safety?

PROBLEMS

16.1 David Gillespie's company has scheduled five jobs. Today, which is day 7, David is reviewing the Gantt chart depicting these schedules.

■ Job A was scheduled to begin on day 3 and to take 6 days. As of now, it is 1 day ahead of schedule.

■ Job B was scheduled to begin on day 1 and take 4 days. It is currently on time.

■ Job C was scheduled to start on day 7 and take 3 days. It actually got started on day 6 and is progressing according to plan.

■ Job D was scheduled to begin on day 5, but missing equipment delayed it until day 6. It is progressing as expected and should take 3 days.

■ Job E was scheduled to begin on day 4 and take 5 days. It got started on time, but has since fallen behind 2 days.

Draw the Gantt chart as it looks to David.

16.2 Alice Harra's company wishes to assign a set of jobs to a set of machines. The following table provides data as to the productivity of each machine when performing the specific job.

a) Determine the most appropriate assignments of jobs to machines so as to maximize total productivity.

b) What is the total cost of your assignments?

JOB \ MACHINE	A	B	C	D
1	7	9	8	10
2	10	9	7	6
3	11	5	9	6
4	9	11	5	8

16.3 Bill Hendee's company wishes to assign a set of jobs to a set of machines. The following table provides data as to the cost of each job when performed on a specific machine.

a) Determine the most appropriate assignments of jobs to machines so as to minimize Bill's total cost.

b) What is the total cost of your assignments?

JOB \ MACHINE	A	B	C	D
1	7	9	8	10
2	10	9	7	6
3	11	5	9	6
4	9	11	5	8

: 16.4 JH Products Corporation has four more jobs to be scheduled, in addition to those shown in Example 3. JH production scheduling personnel are reviewing the Gantt chart at the end of day 4.

■ Job D was scheduled to begin early on day 2 and to end on the middle of day 9. As of now (the review point after day 4), it is 2 days ahead of schedule.

■ Job E should begin on day 1 and end on day 3. It was on time.

■ Job F was to begin on day 3, but maintenance forced a delay of 1½ days. The job should now take 5 full days. It is now on schedule.

■ Job G is a day behind schedule. It started at the beginning of day 2 and should require 6 days to complete.

Develop a Gantt schedule chart for JH Corporation.

· 16.5 The operations manager of King Manufacturing must assign three tasks to three machines. Cost data are presented below.

JOB \ MACHINE	#1	#2	#3
C-3	$800	$1,100	$1,200
C-5	$500	$1,600	$1,300
C-8	$500	$1,000	$2,300

Use the assignment algorithm to solve this problem.

: 16.6 The scheduler at a small southwestern U.S. plant has six jobs that can be processed on any of six machines, with respective times as shown (in hours) below. Determine the allocation of jobs to machines that will result in minimum time.

JOB	MACHINE #1	#2	#3	#4	#5	#6
A-52	60	22	34	42	30	60
A-53	22	52	16	32	18	48
A-56	29	16	58	28	22	55
A-59	42	32	28	46	15	30
A-60	30	18	25	15	45	42
A-61	50	48	57	30	44	60

▦ · **16.7** The hospital administrator at St. Charles General must appoint head nurses to four newly established departments: urology, cardiology, orthopedics, and obstetrics. In anticipation of this staffing problem, she had hired four nurses: Hawkins, Condriac, Bardot, and Hoolihan. Believing in the P/OM analysis approach to problem solving, the administrator has interviewed all the nurses; considered their backgrounds, personalities, and talents; and developed a cost scale ranging from 0 to 100 to be used in the assignment. A 0 for Nurse Hawkins being assigned to the cardiology unit implies that she would be perfectly suited to that task. A value close to 100, on the other hand, would imply that she is not at all suited to head that unit. The accompanying table gives the complete set of cost figures that the hospital administrator felt represented all possible assignments. Which nurse should be assigned to which unit?

	DEPARTMENT			
NURSE	**UROLOGY**	**CARDIOLOGY**	**ORTHOPEDICS**	**OBSTETRICS**
Hawkins	28	18	15	75
Condriac	32	48	23	38
Bardot	51	36	24	36
Hoolihan	25	38	55	12

▦ · **16.8** The Gleaming Company has just developed a new dishwashing liquid and is preparing for a national television promotional campaign. The firm has decided to schedule a series of 1-minute commercials during the peak housewife audience viewing hours of 1:00 to 5:00 P.M. To reach the widest possible audience, Gleaming wants to schedule one commercial on each of four networks and have one commercial appear during each of the four 1-hour time blocks. The exposure ratings for each hour, representing the number of viewers per $1,000 spent, are presented in the accompanying table. Which network should be scheduled each hour in order to provide the maximum audience exposure?

	NETWORKS			
TIME	**A**	**B**	**C**	**INDEPENDENT**
1:00–2:00 P.M.	27.1	18.1	11.3	9.5
2:00–3:00 P.M.	18.9	15.5	17.1	10.6
3:00–4:00 P.M.	19.2	18.5	9.9	7.7
4:00–5:00 P.M.	11.5	21.4	16.8	12.8

▦ ⦂ **16.9** The Kevin Johnson Manufacturing Company is putting out seven new electronic components. Each of Johnson's eight plants has the capacity to add one more product to its current line of electronic parts. The unit manufacturing costs for producing the different parts at the eight plants are shown in the accompanying table. How should Johnson assign the new products to the plants in order to minimize manufacturing costs?

ELECTRONIC COMPONENTS	PLANTS							
	1	2	3	4	5	6	7	8
C53	10¢	12¢	13¢	11¢	10¢	6¢	16¢	12¢
C81	5	6	4	8	4	9	6	6
D5	32	40	31	30	42	35	36	49
D44	17	14	19	15	10	16	19	12
E2	6	7	10	5	8	10	11	5
E35	8	10	12	8	9	10	9	6
G99	55	62	61	70	62	63	65	59

💻 : **16.10** The following jobs are waiting to be processed at the same machine center. Jobs are logged as they arrive:

JOB	DUE DATE	DURATION (DAYS)
A	313	8
B	312	16
C	325	40
D	314	5
E	314	3

In what sequence would the jobs be ranked according to the following decision rules: (a) FCFS, (b) EDD, (c) SPT, and (d) LPT? All dates are specified as manufacturing planning calendar days. Assume that all jobs arrive on day 275. Which decision is best and why?

• **16.11** Suppose that today is day 300 on the planning calendar and that we have not started any of the jobs given in Problem 16.10. Using the critical-ratio technique, in what sequence would you schedule these jobs?

💻 : **16.12** An Alabama lumber yard has four jobs on order, as shown below. Today is day 205 on the yard's schedule. Establish processing priorities.

JOB	DUE DATE	REMAINING TIME IN DAYS
A	212	6
B	209	3
C	208	3
D	210	8

:16.13 The following jobs are waiting to be processed at a small machine center:

JOB	DUE DATE	DURATION (DAYS)
010	260	30
020	258	16
030	260	8
040	270	20
050	275	10

In what sequence would the jobs be ranked according to the following decision rules: (a) FCFS, (b) EDD, (c) SPT, and (d) LPT? All dates are specified as manufacturing planning calendar days. Assume that all jobs arrive on day 210. Which is the best decision rule?

:16.14 The following jobs are waiting to be processed at Bill Leonard's machine center:

JOB	DATE ORDER RECEIVED	PRODUCTION DAYS NEEDED	DATE ORDER DUE
A	110	20	180
B	120	30	200
C	122	10	175
D	125	16	230
E	130	18	210

In what sequence would the jobs be ranked according to the following rules: (a) FCFS, (b) EDD, (c) SPT, and (d) LPT? All dates are according to shop calendar days. Today on the planning calendar is day 130. Which rule is best?

· 16.15 Suppose that today is day 150 on the planning calendar and that we have not yet started any of the jobs in Problem 16.14. Using the critical-ratio technique, in what sequence would you schedule these jobs?

:16.16 Barry Automation Company estimates the data entry and verifying times for four jobs as follows:

JOB	DATA ENTRY (HOURS)	VERIFY (HOURS)
A	2.5	1.7
B	3.8	2.6
C	1.9	1.0
D	1.8	3.0

In what order should the jobs be done if the company has one operator for each job? Illustrate the time-phased flow of this job sequence graphically.

:16.17 Six jobs are to be processed through a two-step operation. The first operation involves sanding and the second involves painting. Processing times are as follows:

JOB	OPERATION 1 (HOURS)	OPERATION 2 (HOURS)
A	10	5
B	7	4
C	5	7
D	3	8
E	2	6
F	4	3

Determine a sequence that will minimize the total completion time for these jobs. Illustrate graphically.

:16.18 Consider the following jobs and their processing times at the three machines. No passing of jobs is allowed.

JOB	MACHINE 1 (HOURS)	MACHINE 2 (HOURS)	MACHINE 3 (HOURS)
A	6	4	7
B	5	2	4
C	9	3	10
D	7	4	5
E	11	5	2

Using Johnson's rule, find the sequence in which the jobs are to be processed.

:16.19 Bill Penny has a repetitive manufacturing plant producing trailer hitches in Arlington. The plant has an average inventory of only 12 turns per year. He has, therefore, determined that he will reduce his component lot sizes. He has developed the following data for one component, the safety chain clip.

$$\text{Annual demand} = 31,200$$
$$\text{Daily demand} = 120$$
$$\text{Daily production} = 960$$
$$\text{Desired lot size (1 hour of production)} = 120 \text{ units}$$
$$\text{Holding cost per unit per year} = \$12$$
$$\text{Setup labor cost per hour} = \$20$$

What setup time should he have his plant manager aim for regarding this component?

:16.20 Mark Davis is the manager of the body shop at Cumberland Ford. On Monday morning, he arrived at work at 7:30 A.M. and discovered that the firm's wrecker service had towed in five automobiles involved in weekend accidents. In all cases, the owners had authorized Cumberland Ford to make all necessary repairs. Mark carefully analyzed the extent of damage to each car and noted the amount of time (in hours) that each car would require at each station in the body shop. The following table shows these time estimates.

AUTOMOBILE	METAL WORK AND REPLACEMENT OF PARTS	SANDING AND MASKING	PAINTING AND BAKING
Crown Victoria	9 hours	8 hours	2 hours
Mustang	12	6	3
Escort	10	3	5
Tempo	8	7	4
T Bird	14	2	1

Mark wanted to minimize waiting time and total time consumed in repairing the five automobiles. However, he was uncertain about the priority to give each car to accomplish this objective. After rechecking his time estimates for accuracy, he pondered his decision.

a) Suggest a scheduling method that Mark could substitute for his "trial-and-error, hit-or-miss" sequencing decisions. Illustrate.

b) In what sequence should the cars be routed through the various operations to minimize waiting time and total time consumed?

DATA BASE APPLICATION

:16.21 NASA's astronaut crew currently includes 10 mission specialists who hold a Ph.D. in either astrophysics or astromedicine. One of these specialists will be assigned to each of the 10 flights scheduled for the upcoming 9 months. Mission specialists are responsible for carrying out scientific and medical experiments in space or for launching, retrieving, or repairing satellites. The chief of astronaut personnel, himself a former crew member with three missions under his belt, must decide who should be assigned and trained for each of the very different missions. Clearly, astronauts with medical educations are more suited to missions involving biological or medical experiments, whereas those with engineering- or physics-oriented degrees are best suited to other types of missions. The chief assigns each astronaut a rating on a scale of 1 to 10 for each possible mission, with a 10 being a perfect match for the task at hand and a 1 being a mismatch. Only one specialist is assigned to each flight, and none is reassigned until all others have flown at least once.

ASTRONAUT	MISSION JAN. 12	JAN. 27	FEB. 5	FEB. 26	MAR. 26	APR. 12	MAY 1	JUN. 9	AUG. 20	SEP. 19
Vincze	9	7	2	1	10	9	8	9	2	6
Veit	8	8	3	4	7	9	7	7	4	4
Anderson	2	1	10	10	1	4	7	6	6	7
Herbert	4	4	10	9	9	9	1	2	3	4
Schatz	10	10	9	9	8	9	1	1	1	1
Plane	1	3	5	7	9	7	10	10	9	2
Certo	9	9	8	8	9	1	1	2	2	9
Moses	3	2	7	6	4	3	9	7	7	9
Brandon	5	4	5	9	10	10	5	4	9	8
Drtina	10	10	9	7	6	7	5	4	8	8

a) Who should be assigned to which flight?

b) We have just been notified that Anderson is getting married in February and he has been granted a highly sought publicity tour in Europe that month. (He intends to take his wife and let the trip double as a honeymoon.) How does this change the final schedule?

c) Certo has complained that he was misrated on his January mission. Both ratings should be 10's, he claims to the chief, who agrees and recomputes the schedule. Do any changes occur over the schedule set in part (b)?

d) What are the strengths and weaknesses of this approach to scheduling?

CASE STUDY

Old Oregon Wood Store

In 1995, George Brown started the Old Oregon Wood Store to manufacture Old Oregon tables. Each table is carefully constructed by hand, using the highest-quality oak.

The manufacturing process consists of four steps: preparation, assembly, finishing, and packaging. Each step is performed by one person. In addition to overseeing the entire operation, George does all of the finishing. Tom Surowski performs the preparation step, which involves cutting and forming the basic components of the tables. Leon Davis is in charge of the assembly, and Cathy Stark performs the packaging.

Although each person is responsible for only one step in the manufacturing process, everyone can perform any one of the steps. It is George's policy that occasionally everyone should complete several tables on his or her own without any help or assistance. A small competition is used to see who can complete an entire table in the least amount of time. George maintains average total and intermediate completion times. The data are shown in Figure 16.7.

FIGURE 16.7 ■ Manufacturing Time in Minutes

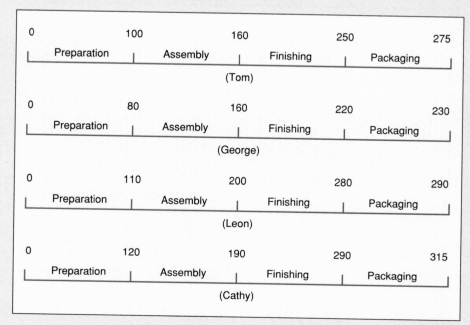

(Continued)

It takes Cathy longer than the other employees to construct an Old Oregon table. In addition to being slower than the other employees, Cathy is also unhappy about her current responsibility of packaging, which leaves her idle most of the day. Her first preference is finishing, and her second preference is preparation.

In addition to quality, George is concerned with costs and efficiency. When one of the employees misses a day, it causes major scheduling problems. Overtime is expensive, and waiting for the employee to return to work causes delay and sometimes stops the entire manufacturing process.

To overcome some of these problems, Randy Lane was hired. Randy's major duties are to perform miscellaneous jobs and to help out if one of the employees is absent. George has given Randy training in all phases of the manufacturing process, and he is pleased with the speed at which Randy has been able to learn how to completely assemble Old Oregon tables. Total and intermediate completion times for Randy are given in Figure 16.8.

DISCUSSION QUESTIONS

1. What is the fastest way to manufacture Old Oregon tables using the original crew? How many could be made per day?

2. Would production rates and quantities change significantly if George would allow Randy to perform one of the four functions and make one of the original crew the backup person?

3. What is the fastest time to manufacture a table with the original crew if Cathy is moved to either preparation or finishing?

4. Whoever performs the packaging function is severely underutilized. Can you find a better way of utilizing the 4- or 5-person crew than either giving each a single job or allowing each to manufacture an entire table? How many tables could be manufactured per day with this scheme?

Source: B. Render and R. M. Stair, *Quantitative Analysis for Management,* 5th ed. (Boston: Allyn and Bacon, 1994), p. 583.

FIGURE 16.8 ■ Manufacturing Time in Minutes for Randy Lane

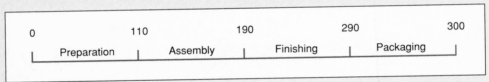

BIBLIOGRAPHY

Akinc, U. "A Practical Approach to Lot and Setup Scheduling at a Textile Firm." *IIE Transactions,* 25, no. 2 (March 1993): 54–64.

Anbil, R., E. Gelman, B. Patty, and R. Tanga. "Recent Advances in Crew-Pairing Optimization at American Airlines." *Interfaces,* 21, no. 1 (January/February 1991): 62–74.

Bauer, A., J. Browne, R. Bowden, J. Duggan, and G. Lyons. *Shop Floor Control Systems.* New York: Van Nostrand Reinhold, 1991.

Ghosh, S., and C. Gaimon. "Production Scheduling in a Flexible Manufacturing System with Setups." *IIE Transactions,* 25, no. 5 (September 1993): 21.

Gopalakrishnan, M., S. Gopalakrishnan, and D. M. Miller. "A Decision Support System for Scheduling Personnel in a Newspaper Publishing Environment." *Interfaces,* 23, no. 4 (July/August 1993): 104–115.

Kim, Y., and C. A. Yano. "Heuristic Approaches for Loading Problems in Flexible Manufacturing Systems." *Industrial Engineering Research & Development,* 25, no. 1 (January 1993): 26.

Morton, Thomas E., and David W. Pentico. *Heuristic Scheduling Systems.* New York: John Wiley, 1993.

Render, B., and R. M. Stair. *Quantitative Analysis for Management,* 5th ed. Boston: Allyn and Bacon, 1994.

Schartner, A., and J. M. Pruett. "Interactive Job Shop Scheduling: An Experiment." *Decision Sciences,* 22, no. 5 (November/December 1991).

Sivakumar, R. A., R. Batta, and K. Tehrani. "Scheduling Repairs at Texas Instruments." *Interfaces,* 23, no. 4 (July/August 1993): 68–74.

Vollmann, T. E., W. L. Berry, and D. C. Whybark. *Manufacturing Planning and Control Systems,* 3rd ed. Homewood, IL: Irwin, 1992.

17

PROJECT MANAGEMENT

LEARNING OBJECTIVES

When you complete this chapter you should be able to:

Identify or Define:

  Activity

  Event

  Critical Path

  PERT/Cost

  Dummy Activity

Explain:

  Critical path method (CPM)

  Program evaluation and review technique (PERT)

  Crashing a project

PROJECT MANAGEMENT PROVIDES A COMPETITIVE ADVANTAGE FOR BECHTEL

More than 200 lagoons filled with one million gallons of seawater were built. Pumps and hose lines to throw six thousand gallons of water a minute were installed.

Fire-fighting crews relied on explosives and heavy machinery to remove the hardened petroleum residue that had formed around many wells. Even a day after a fire is out, the surface is still hot enough to boil water.

In the late fall of 1990, Iraq invaded Kuwait. In one final devastating act before Iraq's defeat in "Operation Desert Storm," Saddam Hussein torched the oil wells of Kuwait. To begin the rebuilding of its lands, the government of Kuwait called in one of the world's largest construction firms, Bechtel, which is headquartered in San Francisco. When the

first three-member Bechtel advance team landed, within days of Desert Storm's end, the panorama of destruction was breathtaking.

Nearly 650 wells were ablaze, and others were gushing thousands of barrels of oil into dark lakes in the desert. Fire roared out of the ground from virtually every compass point.

Restoring the oil fields of Kuwait was a monumental project. There was no water, electricity, food, or facilities. Also, the country was littered with unexploded mines, bombs, grenades, and artillery shells. Finally, a good portion of the fires were inaccessible as lakes of oil-covered roads and fire spread to the ground surrounding many of the wells.

Even for Bechtel, whose competitive advantage is project management, this was a first-of-a-kind logistics problem. The number of specific project events that needed to be identified and accomplished was huge. Bechtel launched an on-site assessment effort, with a worldwide planning team to support the effort. A major global procurement program was needed. Bechtel equipment specialists in San Francisco, Houston, and London were called on to tap the company's computer network of buyers and suppliers worldwide.

Then the issue was how to feed, house, and equip a work force

The dense black clouds produced by burning oil wells turned day into night and added new meaning to "reading by firelight."

that would grow into thousands by the time the effort was fully mobilized.

About 550 miles to the southeast of Kuwait, at the port of Dubai, Bechtel established storage, docking, and warehousing facilities. As a central transshipment point into Kuwait, the port received and processed hundreds of shipments from chartered seacraft and aircraft.

The Bechtel project management team procured, shipped, and deployed 125,000 tons of equipment and supplies, including some 4,000 pieces of operating equipment, ranging from bulldozers to ambulances. The team also managed a work force that laid some 150 kilometers of pipeline, capable of delivering 20 million gallons of water a day to the fire site.

The Bechtel project management team also mobilized:

- an international force of nearly 8,000 manual workers
- 1,000 project and construction professionals
- 6 full-service dining halls
- 27,000 meals a day
- 2 helicopter evacuation teams
- a 40-bed field hospital
- a team of 100 medical personnel for seven medical stations

The fires are out. Kuwait is once again shipping oil and Bechtel has demonstrated its competitive advantage—project management.

Source: Adapted from *Bechtel Briefs*, San Francisco: Bechtel.

The damage was extensive to facilities as well as oil fields and each item had to be included in the schedule that the project managers developed to tackle this huge problem.

Davavid Cutler blasts through the door leading to Microsoft Corporation's lab. It is 10:20 A.M., Monday, May 3, 1993, and Mr. Cutler is checking on the progress of Window's NT, the biggest, most complex, and possibly most important program ever designed for a desktop computer. Cutler is not happy, and this project manager does not believe in bottling up emotion, as evidenced by the wall he cracked with a violent kick over programming failures. Time is about the only thing that matters to him and the 200 programmers who are bringing this network version of Windows to life. The product is already 6 months late, and Microsoft plans to begin shipping hundreds of thousands of copies to customers within 60 days. Failure to meet that deadline—or shipping bug-ridden NT—would mar the reputation of a computer program considered the most ambitious ever tried. Consisting of a staggering 4.3 million lines of code and costing more than $150 million to develop, Windows NT is designed to conquer new worlds for Microsoft. Immense stakes ride on this project being delivered on time.[1] ◆

At one point or another, almost every organization will take on a large and complex project like the one David Cutler managed for Microsoft Corp. A construction company like Bechtel, helping to restore Kuwait's oil wells, must complete thousands of costly activities. A government agency installing and debugging an expensive computer spends months preparing the details for smooth conversion to new equipment. An oil refinery about to shut down for a major maintenance project faces astronomical expenses if this difficult task is unduly delayed for any reason. The problem every time is how to manage such a complicated project effectively.

Large, often one-time, projects are difficult challenges to operations managers. The stakes are high. Millions of dollars in cost overruns can be wasted due to poor planning on projects. Unnecessary delays can occur due to poor scheduling. And companies can go bankrupt due to poor controls.

Special projects that take months or years to complete are usually developed outside the normal production system. Project organizations within the firm are set up to handle such jobs and are often disbanded when the project is complete. The management of large projects involves three phases (see Figure 17.1):

1. *Planning.* This includes goal setting, defining the project, and team organization. Note in Figure 17.1 that it is completed before the project even begins.

2. *Scheduling.* This relates people, money, and supplies to specific activities and relates activities to each other.

3. *Controlling.* Here the firm monitors resources, costs, quality, and budgets. It also revises/changes plans and shifts resources to meet time and cost demands.

PROJECT PLANNING

Project organization

Projects can usually be defined as a series of related tasks directed toward a major output. A **project organization** is developed to make sure existing programs continue to run smoothly on a day-to-day basis while new projects are successfully completed.

[1]*Wall Street Journal* (May 26, 1993): A1, A12.

FIGURE 17.1 ■ Project Planning, Scheduling, and Controlling

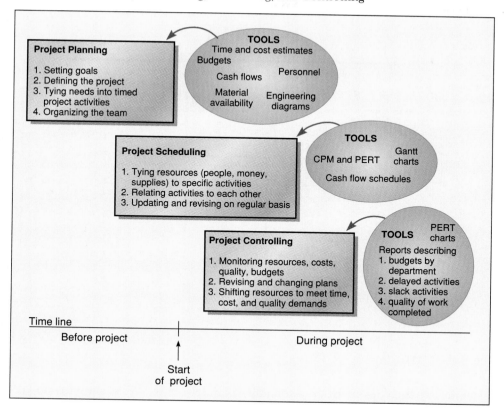

Project Planning

1. Setting goals
2. Defining the project
3. Tying needs into timed project activities
4. Organizing the team

TOOLS
Time and cost estimates
Budgets
Cash flows   Personnel
Material   Engineering
availability   diagrams

Project Scheduling

1. Tying resources (people, money, supplies) to specific activities
2. Relating activities to each other
3. Updating and revising on regular basis

TOOLS
CPM and PERT   Gantt charts
Cash flow schedules

Project Controlling

1. Monitoring resources, costs, quality, budgets
2. Revising and changing plans
3. Shifting resources to meet time, cost, and quality demands

TOOLS   PERT charts
Reports describing
1. budgets by department
2. delayed activities
3. slack activities
4. quality of work completed

Time line
Before project | During project
Start of project

A project organization is an effective way of pooling the people and physical resources needed for a limited time to complete a specific project. It is basically a temporary organization structure designed to achieve results by using specialists from throughout the firm. For many years, NASA successfully used the project approach to reach its goals. You may recall Project Gemini and Project Apollo. These terms were used to describe teams NASA organized to reach space exploration objectives.

The project organization works best when

1. work can be defined with a specific goal and deadline;
2. the job is unique or somewhat unfamiliar to the existing organization;
3. the work contains complex interrelated tasks requiring specialized skills;
4. the project is temporary but critical to the organization.

An example of a simplified project organization that is part of an ongoing firm is shown in Figure 17.2. The project team members are temporarily assigned to the project and report to the project manager. The manager heading the project coordinates its activities with other departments and reports directly to top management, often the president, of the company. Project managers receive high visibility in a firm and are a key element in the planning and control of project activities.

The project management team begins its task well in advance of the project so that a plan can be developed. One of its first steps is to set the project's objectives

FIGURE 17.2   ■   A Sample Project Organization

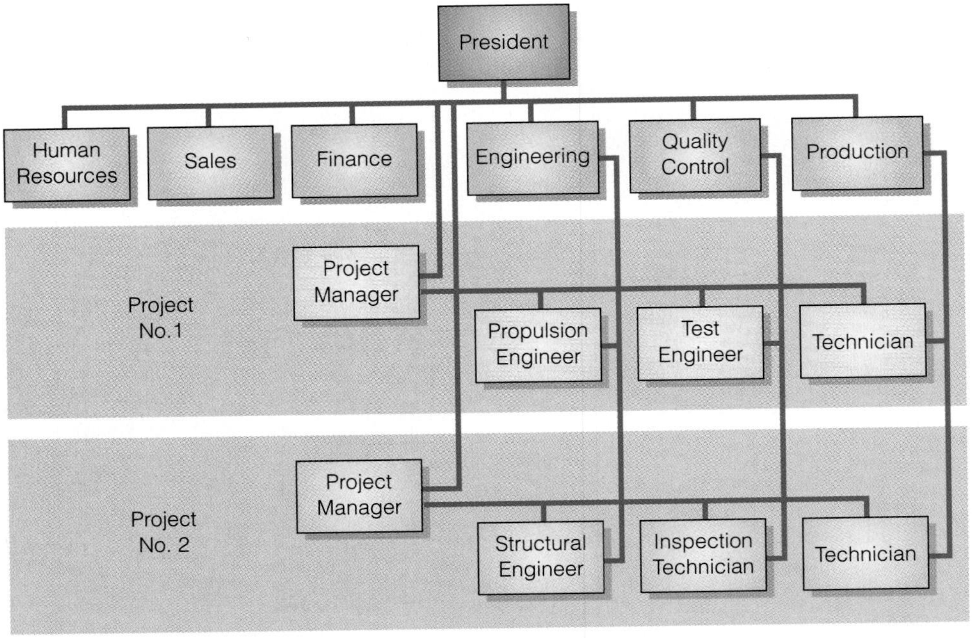

(*Source:* R. W. Mondy and S. R. Premeaux, *Management: Concepts, Practices and Skills*, 6th ed. (Boston: Allyn and Bacon, 1993), p. 247.)

carefully and then define the project and break it down into a set of activities and related costs. Gross requirements for people, supplies, and equipment are also estimated in the planning phase.

PROJECT SCHEDULING

Project scheduling involves sequencing and allotting time to all project activities. At this stage, managers decide how long each activity will take and compute how many people and materials will be needed at each stage of production. Managers also chart separate schedules for personnel needs by type of skill (management, engineering, or pouring concrete, for example). Charts also can be developed for scheduling materials.

Gantt charts

One popular project scheduling approach is the Gantt chart. **Gantt charts** are low-cost means of helping managers make sure that (1) all activities are planned for, (2) their order of performance is accounted for, (3) the activity time estimates are recorded, and (4) the overall project time is developed. As Figure 17.3 shows, Gantt charts are easy to understand. Horizontal bars are drawn for each project activity along a time line. The letters to the left of each bar tell the planner which other activities have to be completed before that one can begin.

Activity progress is noted, once the actual project is under way, by shading the horizontal bars as an activity is partially or fully completed. For example, we see in Figure 17.3 that activities a, b, c, and d are on schedule because their bars have been shaded up to the vertical status date line. The date line, July 1 in this case, is a status

FIGURE 17.3 ■ Sample Gantt Chart. Circled items represent precedence relationships (for example, activity c, construct collection stack, may not begin until activity a, which is circled, is completed).

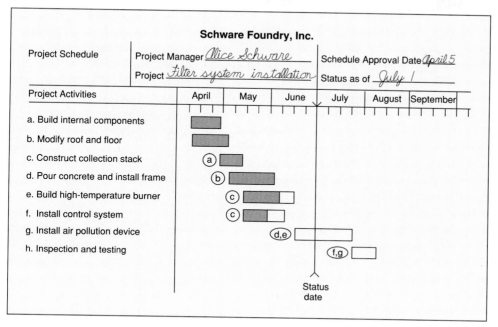

reporting period that lets participants see which tasks are on time, which are ahead of time, and which have fallen behind schedule. Activities e, f, and g are all behind schedule, because their bars are not shaded in their entirety or up to the status date line.

A second example of a Gantt chart is shown in Figure 17.4. This illustration of a routine servicing of a Delta jetliner during a 60-minute layover shows that Gantt charts also can be used for scheduling repetitive operations. In this case, the chart helps point out potential delays. The *POM in Action* box on Delta provides additional insights.

Scheduling charts such as these can be used alone on simple projects. They permit managers to observe the progress of each activity and to spot and tackle problem areas. Gantt charts are not easily updated, though. And more importantly, they do not adequately illustrate the interrelationships between the activities and the resources.

PERT and CPM, the two widely used network techniques that we shall discuss shortly, *do* have the ability to consider precedence relationships and interdependency of activities. On complex projects, the scheduling of which is almost always computerized, PERT and CPM thus hold an edge on the simpler Gantt charts. Even on huge projects, though, Gantt charts can be used as a summary of project status and may complement the other network approaches.

To summarize, whatever the approach taken by a project manager, project scheduling serves several purposes:

1. It shows the relationship of each activity to others and to the whole project.
2. It identifies the precedence relationships among activities.
3. It encourages the setting of realistic time and cost estimates for each activity.
4. It helps make better use of people, money, and material resources by identifying critical bottlenecks in the project.

FIGURE 17.4 ■ Service Activities for a Commercial Jetliner
During a 60-Minute Layover

Passengers	Deplaning					
	Baggage claim					
Baggage	Container offload					
Fueling	Pumping					
	Engine injection water					
Cargo and mail	Container offload					
Galley servicing	Main cabin door					
	Aft cabin door					
Lavatory servicing	Aft, Center, Forward					
Drinking water	Loading					
Cabin cleaning	First class section					
	Economy section					
Cargo and mail	Container/bulk loading					
Flight service	Galley/cabin check					
	Receive passengers					
Operating crew	Aircraft check					
Baggage	Loading					
Passengers	Boarding					

Time, minutes (0, 15, 30, 45, 60)

PROJECT CONTROLLING

The control of large projects, like the control of any management system, involves close monitoring of resources, costs, quality, and budgets. Control also means using a feedback loop to revise the project plan and having the ability to shift resources to where they are needed most. Computerized PERT/CPM reports and charts are widely

Being able to use powerful project manager software packages such as Primavera (shown here) first requires an understanding of the principles of PERT and CPM. In a competitive job environment, a graduate who has experience with one of the popular programs will find himself or herself a valued member of any organization involved in project planning.

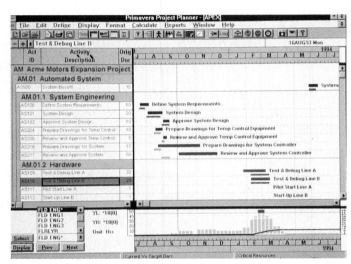

POM IN ACTION

Delta's Ground Crew Orchestrates a Smooth Takeoff

Flight 199's three engines screech its arrival as the wide-bodied L–1011 jet lumbers down Orlando's taxiway with 200 passengers arriving from San Juan. In an hour the plane is to be airborne again.

But before this jet can depart, there is business to attend to: hundreds of passengers and tons of luggage and cargo to unload and load; hundreds of meals, thousands of gallons of jet fuel, countless soft drinks and bottles of liquor to restock; cabin and restrooms to clean; toilet holding tanks to drain; and engines, wings, and landing gear to inspect.

The 12-person ground crew knows that a miscue anywhere—a broken cargo loader, lost baggage, misdirected passengers—can mean a late departure and trigger a chain reaction of headaches from Orlando to Dallas to every destination of a connecting flight.

Dennis Dettro, the operations manager for Delta's Orlando International Airport, likes to call the turnaround operation "a well-orchestrated symphony." Like a pit crew awaiting a race car, trained crews are in place for Flight 199 with baggage carts and tractors, hydraulic cargo loaders, a truck to load food and drinks, another to lift the cleanup crew, another to put fuel on, and a fourth to take water off. The "orchestra" usually performs so smoothly that most passengers never suspect the proportions of the effort. Gantt charts, such as the one in Figure 17.4, aid Delta and other airlines with the staffing and scheduling that are necessary for this symphony to perform.

Sources: Orlando Sentinel (December 21, 1993): A-1; *Distribution* (October 1991): 38–40; and *Aviation Week* (November 23, 1992): 42–43.

---

available today on personal computers. Some of the more popular of these programs are Harvard Total Project Manager (by Harvard Software, Inc.), Primavera (by Primavera Systems, Inc.), Project (by Microsoft Corp.), MacProject (by Apple Computer Corp.), Pertmaster (by Westminster Software, Inc.), VisiSchedule (by Paladin Software Corp.), and Time Line (by Symantec Corp.).

These programs produce a broad variety of reports including (1) detailed cost breakdowns for each task, (2) total program labor curves, (3) cost distribution tables, (4) functional cost and hour summaries, (5) raw material and expenditure forecasts, (6) variance reports, (7) time analysis reports, and (8) work status reports. When commercially available software does not provide all of the features a company wants, the company may even develop its own project management programs, as we see in the M. W. Kellogg Company *POM in Action* box.

PROJECT MANAGEMENT TECHNIQUES: PERT AND CPM

Program evaluation and review technique (PERT) and the **critical path method (CPM)** were both developed in the 1950s to help managers schedule, monitor, and control large and complex projects. CPM arrived first, in 1957, as a tool developed by J. E. Kelly of Remington Rand and M. R. Walker of duPont to assist in the building and maintenance of chemical plants at duPont. Independently, PERT was developed in 1958 by the Navy with Booz, Allen and Hamilton.

Program evaluation and review technique (PERT)

Critical path method (CPM)

Controlling Projects
at M. W. Kellogg Company

Houston's M. W. Kellogg Company is one of the world's largest construction contractors, specializing in engineering and building petroleum and petrochemical complexes. Until 10 years ago, it used commercial project management software to control its numerous and wide-ranging projects. When Kellogg outgrew the software, it decided to write its own program to integrate time analysis, scheduling, networking, and charting of project schedules, materials, and costs. The huge new program, called Integrated Project Control System (IPCS), had to manage about 20 projects at a time. A typical Kellogg project would involve 1,500 engineering activities, 1,100 requisitions, and forecasts for 4,000 cost account lines.

IPCS now tracks each project's performance every 2 weeks by measuring the actual hours expended against planned base lines. IPCS has cut the time for updating from 24 hours under the old software to a matter of minutes today. It also makes project management at Kellogg more efficient than at competing companies. In the dynamic, visible, and safety-conscious environment of large-scale engineering projects, IPCS is able to reduce risks, control projects, and give Kellogg's management more exact and flexible information.

Sources: A. M. Hickman, "Refining the Process of Project Control," *Production and Inventory Management* (February 1992): 26–27; and P. W. Stonebraker and G. K. Leong, *Operations Strategy* (Boston: Allyn and Bacon, 1994), p. 505.

The Framework of PERT and CPM

PERT and CPM both follow six basic steps:

1. Define the project and all of its significant activities or tasks.
2. Develop the relationships among the activities. Decide which activities must precede and which must follow others.
3. Draw the network connecting all of the activities.
4. Assign time and/or cost estimates to each activity.
5. Compute the longest time path through the network. This is called the **critical path**.
6. Use the network to help plan, schedule, monitor, and control the project.

Critical path

Step 5, finding the critical path, is a major part of controlling a project. The activities on the critical path represent tasks that will delay the entire project unless they are completed on time. Managers can gain the flexibility needed to complete critical tasks by identifying noncritical activities and replanning, rescheduling, and reallocating resources such as labor and finances.

Although PERT and CPM differ to some extent in terminology and in the construction of the network, their objectives are the same. Furthermore, the analysis used in both techniques is very similar. The major difference is that PERT employs three time estimates for each activity. Each estimate has an associated probability of occurrence, which, in turn, is used in computing expected values and standard deviations for the activity times. CPM makes the assumption that activity times are known with certainty, and hence requires only one time factor for each activity.

For purposes of illustration, the rest of this chapter concentrates on a discussion of PERT and PERT/Cost. PERT/Cost is a technique that combines the benefits of both PERT and CPM. Most of the comments and procedures described, however, apply just as well to CPM.

PERT, PERT/Cost, and CPM are important because they can help answer questions such as the following about projects with thousands of activities:

1. When will the entire project be completed?
2. What are the critical activities or tasks in the project, that is, the ones that will delay the entire project if they are late?
3. Which are the noncritical activities, that is, the ones that can run late without delaying the whole project's completion?
4. What is the probability that the project will be completed by a specific date?
5. At any particular date, is the project on schedule, behind schedule, or ahead of schedule?
6. On any given date, is the money spent equal to, less than, or greater than the budgeted amount?
7. Are there enough resources available to finish the project on time?
8. If the project is to be finished in a shorter amount of time, what is the best way to accomplish this at the least cost?

Activities, Events, and Networks

The first step in PERT is to divide the entire project into significant events and activities. An **event** marks the start or completion of a particular task or activity. An **activity** is a task or a subproject that occurs between two events. Table 17.1 shows the symbols used to represent events and activities.

Event
Activity

This approach is the most common one to drawing networks and is also referred to as the Activity-on-Arrow (AOA) convention. A less popular convention, called Activity-on-Node (AON), places activities on nodes. For simplicity, we will discuss only AOA.

Any project that can be described by activities and events may be analyzed by a PERT **network**. A network, illustrated in Example 1, is a sequence of activities defined by starting and ending events.

Network

The U.S. Navy, working with Booz, Allen, and Hamilton, devised PERT to help plan and control the Polaris missile program for submarines. That project involved the coordination of thousands of contractors, and PERT was credited with cutting 18 months off the project length.

TABLE 17.1 ■ EVENTS, ACTIVITIES, AND HOW THEY RELATE

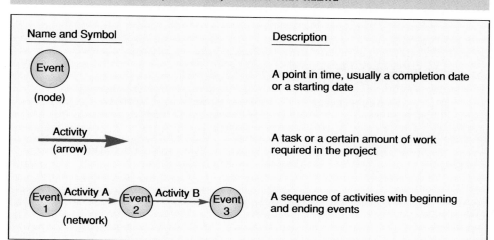

Name and Symbol	Description
Event (node)	A point in time, usually a completion date or a starting date
Activity (arrow)	A task or a certain amount of work required in the project
Event 1 — Activity A → Event 2 — Activity B → Event 3 (network)	A sequence of activities with beginning and ending events

EXAMPLE 1

Given the following information, develop a network.

ACTIVITY	IMMEDIATE PREDECESSOR(S)
A	—
B	—
C	A
D	B

In the network below, we assign each event a number. It is also possible to identify each activity with a beginning and an ending event or node. For example, activity A is the activity that starts with event 1 and ends at node, or event, 2. In general, we number nodes from left to right. The beginning node, or event, of the entire project is number 1, and the last node, or event, in the entire project bears the largest number. The last node below shows the number 4.

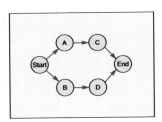

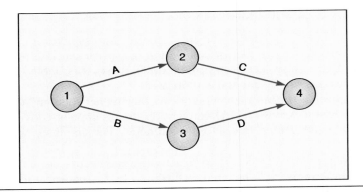

We can also specify networks by events and the activities that occur between events. Example 2 shows how to develop a network based on this type of specification scheme.

EXAMPLE 2

Given the following table, develop a network.

BEGINNING EVENT	ENDING EVENT	ACTIVITY
1	2	1–2
1	3	1–3
2	4	2–4
3	4	3–4
3	5	3–5
4	6	4–6
5	6	5–6

Instead of using a letter to signify activities and their predecessor activities, we can specify activities by their starting event and their ending event. Beginning with the activity that starts at event 1 and ends at event 2, we can construct the following network.

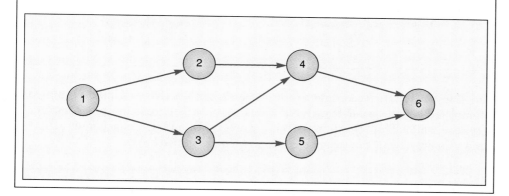

All that is required to construct a network is the starting and ending event for each activity.

Dummy Activities and Events

You may encounter a network that has two activities with identical starting and ending events. **Dummy activities** and events can be inserted into the network to deal with this problem. A dummy activity is defined as an activity using no time, but is inserted into a network to maintain the logic of the network. The use of dummy activities and events is especially important when computer programs are to be employed in determining the critical path and project completion time. Dummy activities and events can also ensure that the network properly reflects the project under consideration. A dummy activity has a completion time, t, of zero. Example 3 illustrates the use of dummy activities.

Dummy activities

EXAMPLE 3

Develop a network based on the following information:

ACTIVITY	IMMEDIATE PREDECESSOR(S)	ACTIVITY	IMMEDIATE PREDECESSOR(S)
A	—	E	C, D
B	—	F	D
C	A	G	E
D	B	H	F

Given these data, you might develop the following network.

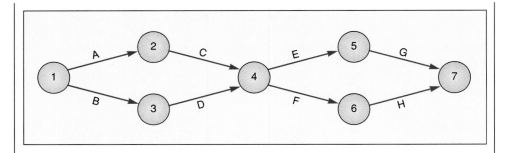

Look at activity F. According to the network, both activities C and D must be completed before we can start F, but in reality, only activity D must be completed (see the table). Thus, the network is not correct. The addition of a dummy activity and a dummy event can overcome this problem, as shown below.

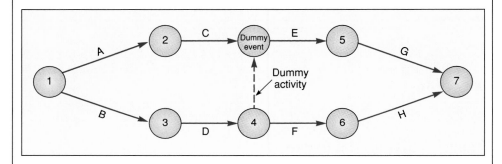

Now the network embodies all of the proper relationships and can be analyzed as usual.

PERT and Activity Time Estimates

Activity time estimates

As mentioned earlier, one distinguishing difference between PERT and CPM is the use of three **activity time estimates** for each activity in the PERT technique. Only one time factor is given for each activity in CPM.

Optimistic time
Probable time
Pessimistic time
Beta probability distribution

For each activity in PERT, we must specify an **optimistic time**, a most **probable** (or most likely) **time**, and a **pessimistic time** estimate. We then use these three time estimates to calculate an expected completion time and variance for each activity. If we assume, as many researchers do, that activity times follow a **beta probability distribution**,[2] we can use the formula:

$$t = \frac{a + 4m + b}{6} \quad \text{and} \quad v = \left(\frac{b-a}{6}\right)^2 \tag{17.1}$$

where a = optimistic time for activity completion
        b = pessimistic time for activity completion

[2]Although the beta distribution has been widely used in PERT analysis for 40 years, its applicability has been called into question. See M. W. Sasieni, "A Note on PERT Times," *Management Science*, 32, no. 12 (December 1986): 1,662–1,663.

m = most likely time for activity completion

t = expected time of activity completion

v = variance of activity completion time

In PERT, after we have developed the network, we compute expected times and variances for each activity. Example 4 shows these computations.

EXAMPLE 4

Compute expected times and variances of completion for each activity based on the following time estimates:

ACTIVITY	a	m	b
1–2	3	4	5
1–3	1	3	5
2–4	5	6	7
3–4	6	7	8

ACTIVITY	a + 4m + b	t	$\frac{b-a}{6}$	v
1–2	24	4	2/6	4/36
1–3	18	3	4/6	16/36
2–4	36	6	2/6	4/36
3–4	42	7	2/6	4/36

Critical Path Analysis

The objective of **critical path analysis** is to determine the following quantities for each activity:

Critical path analysis

ES: Earliest activity start time. *All predecessor activities* must be completed before an activity can be started. The ending time of the predecessor activities is the earliest time an activity can be started.

LS: Latest activity start time. *All following activities* must be completed without delaying the entire project. This is the latest time an activity can be started without delaying the entire project.

EF: Earliest activity finish time.

LF: Latest activity finish time.

S: Activity **slack time**, which is equal to (LS − ES) or (LF − EF).

Slack time

For any activity, if we can calculate ES and LS, we can find the other three quantities as follows:

$$EF = ES + t$$

$$LF = LS + t$$

$$S = LS - ES$$

PERT software is
also available from
SAS Institute, Inc.
Here early starts,
early finishes,
normal tasks, and
slack times are
indicated for a
factory expansion
project in
Lancaster, PA.

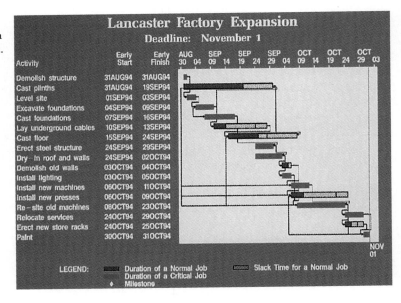

or

$$S = LF - EF$$

Once we know these quantities for every activity, we can analyze the overall project. Typically, this analysis includes an examination of the following:

1. The critical path—the group of activities in the project that have a slack time of zero. This path is *critical* because a delay in any activity along this path would delay the entire project.

2. T—the total project completion time, which is calculated by adding the expected time (t) values of those activities on the critical path.

3. V—variance of the critical path, which is computed by adding the variance (v) of those individual activities on the critical path.

Critical path analysis normally starts with the determination of ES and EF. Example 5 illustrates the procedure.

EXAMPLE 5

Given the following information, determine ES and EF for each activity.

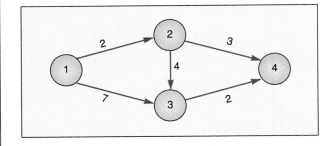

ACTIVITY	t
1–2	2
1–3	7
2–3	4
2–4	3
3–4	2

We find ES by moving from the starting activities of the project to the ending activities of the project. For the starting activities, ES is either zero or the actual starting date, say, August 1. For activities 1–2 and 1–3, ES is zero. (By convention, all projects start at time zero.)

There is one basic rule. Before an activity can be started, *all* of its predecessor activities must be completed. In other words, we search for the *longest* path leading to an activity in determining ES. For activity 2–3, ES is 2. Its only predecessor activity is 1–2, for which $t = 2$. By the same reasoning, ES for activity 2–4 also is 2. For activity 3–4, however, ES is 7. It has two predecessor paths: activity 1–3 with $t = 7$ and activities 1–2 and 2–3 with a total expected time of 6 (or 2 + 4). Thus, ES for activity 3–4 is 7 because activity 1–3 must be completed before activity 3–4 can be started. We compute EF next by adding t to ES for each activity.

See the following table.

ACTIVITY	ES	t	EF
1–2	0	2	2
1–3	0	7	7
2–3	2	4	6
2–4	2	3	5
3–4	7	2	9

The next step is to calculate LS, the latest starting time for each activity. We start with the last activities and work backward to the first activities to determine the latest possible starting time (LS) without increasing the earliest finishing time (EF). This task seems more difficult than it really is. Example 6 shows how to calculate LS.

EXAMPLE 6

Determine LS, LF, and S (the slack) for each activity based on the following data:

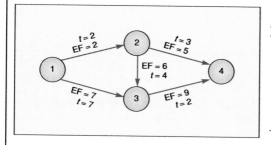

ACTIVITY	t	ES	EF
1–2	2	0	2
1–3	7	0	7
2–3	4	2	6
2–4	3	2	5
3–4	2	7	9

The earliest time by which the entire project can be finished is 9 because activities 2–4 (EF = 5) and 3–4 (EF = 9) *both* must be completed. Using 9 as a basis, we now will work backward by subtracting the appropriate values of t from 9.

The latest time we can start activity 3–4 is at time 7 (or 9 – 2) in order to still complete the project by time period 9. Thus, LS for activity 3–4 is 7. By using the same reasoning, LS for activity 2–4 is 6 (or 9 –3). If we start activity 2–4 at 6 and it takes 3 time units to complete the activity, we can still finish in 9 time units. The latest we can start activity 2–3 is 3 (or $9 - 2 - 4$). If we start activity 2–3 at 3 and it takes 2 and 4 time units for activities 2–3 and 3–4, respectively, we can still finish on time. Thus, LS for activity 2–3 is 3. By using the same reasoning, LS for activity 1–3 is 0 (or $9 - 2 - 7$). Analyzing activity 1–2 is more difficult because there are two paths. Both must be completed in 9 time units.

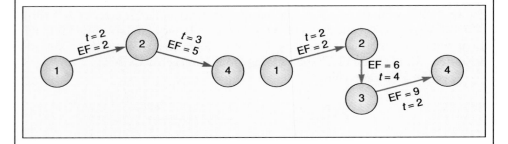

Because both of the above paths must be completed, LS for activity 1–2 is computed from the most binding, or slowest, path. Thus, LS for activity 1–2 *is* 1 (or $9 - 2 - 4 - 2$) and *not* 4 (or $9 - 3 - 2$). Noting the following relationships, we can construct a table summarizing the results.

$$LF = LS + t$$

$$S = LF - EF$$

or

$$S = LS - ES$$

Activity	ES	EF	LS	LF	S
1–2	0	2	1	3	1
1–3	0	7	0	7	0
2–3	2	6	3	7	1
2–4	2	5	6	9	4
3–4	7	9	7	9	0

Once we have computed ES, EF, LS, LF, and S, we can finish analyzing the entire project. Analysis includes determining the critical path, project completion time, and project variance. Example 7 shows this procedure.

EXAMPLE 7

We have computed times, activity variances, and other information for the following network. What is the critical path, total completion time T, and project variance V of this network?

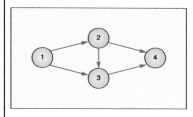

Activity	t	v	ES	EF	LS	LF	S
1–2	2	2/6	0	2	1	3	1
1–3	7	3/6	0	7	0	7	0
2–3	4	1/6	2	6	3	7	1
2–4	3	2/6	2	5	6	9	4
3–4	2	4/6	7	9	7	9	0

The critical path consists of those activities with zero slack. These are activities 1–3 and 3–4.

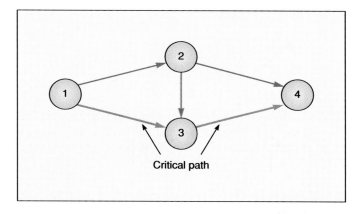

Critical path

The total project completion time is 9 (or 7 + 2). The project variance is the sum of the *activity variances* along the *critical path*, which is 7/6 (or 3/6 + 4/6).

The Probability of Project Completion

Having computed the expected completion time T and completion variance V, we can determine the probability that the project will be completed at a specified date. If we make the assumption that the distribution of completion dates follows a normal curve, we can calculate the probability of completion as in Example 8.

EXAMPLE 8

If the expected project completion time T is 20 weeks and the project variance V is 100, what is the probability that the project will be finished on or before week 25?

$$T = 20$$
$$V = 100$$
$$\sigma = \text{standard deviation} = \sqrt{\text{project variance}} = \sqrt{V}$$
$$= \sqrt{100} = 10$$
$$C = \text{desired completion date}$$
$$= 25 \text{ weeks}$$

The normal curve would appear as follows:

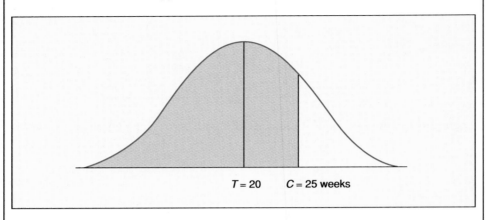

$$Z = \frac{C - T}{\sigma} = \frac{25 - 20}{10} = .5$$

where Z equals the number of standard deviations from the mean. The area under the curve for $Z = .5$ is .6915. (See the normal curve table in Appendix A.) Thus, the probability of completing the project in 25 weeks is approximately .69, or 69%.

We must point out that probability analysis should be used with caution. For example, a noncritical path activity with a large variance could become a critical path activity. This occurrence would cause the analysis to be in error. Consider the network pictured in Figure 17.5. The critical path is 1–3 and 3–4 with $T = 12$ and $V = 4$. If the desired completion date is 14, the value of Z is 1 [or $(14 -12)/\sqrt{4}$]. The chance of completion is 84% from the normal distribution in the appendix. What would happen if activities 1–2 and 2–4 became the critical path? Because of the high variance, this event is not unlikely. With the same values for C and T, Z becomes 0.4 [or $(14 - 12)/\sqrt{25}$]. Looking at the normal distribution, we see that the chance of project completion is 66%. If activities 1–2 and 2–4 became the critical path, the chance of project completion would drop significantly due to the large total variance $(25 = 16 + 9)$ of these activities. A simulation of the project could provide better data.

To transform the corporate image of an international airline is a huge task. Aircraft, check-in desks, lounges, shops, ground vehicles, printed materials—including company stationery, timetables, tickets, baggage tags, and, of course, uniforms—all need to be changed. To help British Airways (BA) plan the changes, a computerized project management package, PertMaster, was used. PertMaster uses the same concepts presented in this chapter. By understanding and using PERT, British Airways was able to make the project requirements fit together on schedule.

FIGURE 17.5   ■   Critical Path Analysis

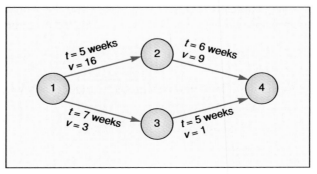

TABLE 17.2 ■	ACTIVITIES AND IMMEDIATE PREDECESSORS FOR SCHWARE FOUNDRY, INC.	
ACTIVITY	DESCRIPTION	IMMEDIATE PREDECESSOR(S)
A	Build internal components	—
B	Modify roof and floor	—
C	Construct collection stack	A
D	Pour concrete and install frame	B
E	Build high-temperature burner	C
F	Install control system	C
G	Install air pollution device	D, E
H	Inspection and testing	F, G

Case Study of PERT: Schware Foundry

Schware Foundry, Inc., a metalworks plant in Takoma Park, Maryland, has just decided to make a major investment in new air pollution control equipment. The plant, however, must be shut down during this installation process. Schware's board of directors estimates that the company can survive no more than 16 weeks without production in full swing. Alice Schware, the managing partner, wants to make sure the installation of the filtering system progresses smoothly and on time.

All activities involved in the foundry project are shown in Table 17.2. (You may recall seeing the same data earlier in the Gantt chart example of Figure 17.3.) We see in the table that before the collection stack can be constructed (activity C), the internal components must be built (activity A). Thus, activity A is the immediate predecessor to activity C. Likewise, both activities D and E must be performed just prior to installation of the air pollution device (activity G). The network for Schware Foundry is illustrated in Figure 17.6.

FIGURE 17.6 ■ Network for Schware Foundry, Inc.

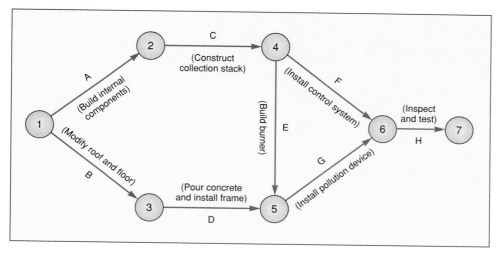

| | **TABLE 17.3** ■   TIME ESTIMATES (IN WEEKS) FOR SCHWARE FOUNDRY, INC. | | | | |

ACTIVITY	OPTIMISTIC a	MOST PROBABLE m	PESSIMISTIC b	EXPECTED TIME $t = (a + 4m + b)/6$	VARIANCE $[(b - a)/6]^2$
A	1	2	3	2	$\left(\dfrac{3-1}{6}\right)^2 = \dfrac{4}{36}$
B	2	3	4	3	$\left(\dfrac{4-2}{6}\right)^2 = \dfrac{4}{36}$
C	1	2	3	2	$\left(\dfrac{3-1}{6}\right)^2 = \dfrac{4}{36}$
D	2	4	6	4	$\left(\dfrac{6-2}{6}\right)^2 = \dfrac{16}{36}$
E	1	4	7	4	$\left(\dfrac{7-1}{6}\right)^2 = \dfrac{36}{36}$
F	1	2	9	3	$\left(\dfrac{9-1}{6}\right)^2 = \dfrac{64}{36}$
G	3	4	11	5	$\left(\dfrac{11-3}{6}\right)^2 = \dfrac{64}{36}$
H	1	2	3	2	$\left(\dfrac{3-1}{6}\right)^2 = \dfrac{4}{36}$
				Total: 25 weeks	

Table 17.3 shows Schware's optimistic, most probable, and pessimistic time estimates for each activity. It also reveals the expected time (t) and variance for each of the activities. Table 17.4 summarizes the critical path analysis for the activities and network. The total project completion time, 15 weeks, is seen as the largest number in the EF or LF columns of Table 17.4. Operations managers may refer to this as a boundary time table.

TABLE 17.4 ■   SCHWARE FOUNDRY'S SCHEDULE AND SLACK TIMES

ACTIVITY	EARLIEST START (ES)	EARLIEST FINISH (EF)	LATEST START (LS)	LATEST FINISH (LF)	SLACK (LS − ES)	ON CRITICAL PATH?
A	0	2	0	2	0	Yes
B	0	3	1	4	1	No
C	2	4	2	4	0	Yes
D	3	7	4	8	1	No
E	4	8	4	8	0	Yes
F	4	7	10	13	6	No
G	8	13	8	13	0	Yes
H	13	15	13	15	0	Yes

FIGURE 17.7 ■ Probability of Schware Foundry's Meeting the 16-Week Deadline

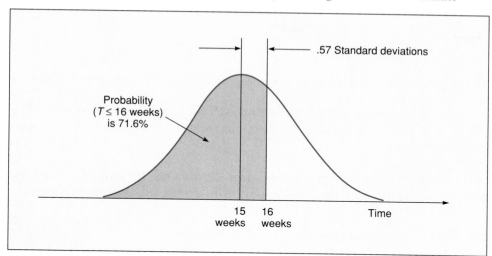

PROBABILITY OF PROJECT COMPLETION. The critical path analysis helped us determine that the foundry's expected project completion time is 15 weeks. Alice is aware, however, that there is significant variation in the time estimates for several activities. Variation in activities that are on the critical path can impact on overall project completion, possibly delaying it. This is one occurrence that worries Alice considerably.

PERT uses the variance of critical path activities to help determine the variance of the overall project. Project variance is computed by summing variances of critical activities.

From Table 17.3 and Equation (17.1), we know that

CRITICAL ACTIVITY	VARIANCE
A	4/36
C	4/36
E	36/36
G	64/36
H	4/36

Hence, the project variance = 4/36 + 4/36 + 36/36 + 64/36 + 4/36 = 3.111.

$$\text{Project standard deviation} = \sqrt{\text{project variance}}$$
$$= \sqrt{3.111} = 1.76 \text{ weeks}$$

In order for Alice to find the probability that her project will be finished on or before the 16-week deadline, she needs to determine the appropriate area under the normal curve in Figure 17.7. The standard normal equation can be applied as follows:

$$Z = \frac{\text{due date} - \text{expected date of completion}}{\text{standard deviation}} \qquad (17.2)$$

$$= \frac{16 \text{ weeks} - 15 \text{ weeks}}{1.76 \text{ weeks}} = \frac{1}{1.76} = .57$$

where Z is the number of standard deviations the due date or target date lies from the mean or expected date.

Referring to the normal table in Appendix A, we find a probability of .71567. Thus, there is a 71.6% chance that the pollution control equipment can be put in place in 16 weeks or less.

WHAT PERT WAS ABLE TO PROVIDE SCHWARE FOUNDRY.   PERT has thus far been able to provide Alice Schware with several valuable pieces of management information.

1. The project's expected completion date is 15 weeks.

2. There is a 71.6% chance the equipment will be in place within the 16-week deadline. And PERT can easily find the probability of finishing by any other date in which Alice is interested.

3. Five activities (A, C, E, G, H) are on the critical path. If any one of them is delayed for any reason, the whole project will be delayed.

4. Three activities (B, D, F) are not critical but have some slack time built in. This means Alice can borrow from their resources, and, if necessary, she may be able to speed up the whole project.

5. A detailed schedule of activity starting and ending dates has been made available (Table 17.4).

PERT/COST

Until now, we have assumed that it is not possible to reduce activity times. This is usually not the case, however. Perhaps additional resources can reduce activity times for certain activities within the project. These resources might be additional labor, more equipment, and so on. Although it can be expensive to shorten activity times, doing so might be worthwhile. If a company faces costly penalties for being late with a project, using additional resources to complete the project on time might be economical. There may be fixed costs every day the project is in process. Thus, it might be profitable to use additional resources to shorten the project time and save some of the daily fixed costs. But what activities should be shortened? How much will this action cost? Will a reduction in the activity time in turn reduce the time needed to complete the entire project? Ideally, we would like to find the least expensive method of shortening the entire project. This is the purpose of **PERT/Cost**.

Figure 17.8 shows cost–time curves for two activities. For activity 5–6, it costs $300 to complete the activity in 8 weeks, $400 for 7 weeks, and $600 for 6 weeks. Activity 2–4 requires $3,000 of additional resources for completion in 12 weeks and $1,000 for 14 weeks. Similar cost–time curves or relationships can usually be developed for all activities in the network.

PERT/Cost

FIGURE 17.8 ■ Cost–Time Curves Used in PERT/Cost Analysis

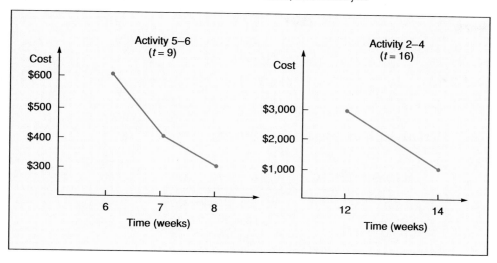

The objective of PERT/Cost is to reduce the entire project completion time by a certain amount at the least cost. To accomplish this objective, we must introduce a few more variables. For each activity, there will exist a reduction in activity time and the cost incurred for that time reduction. Let:

M_i = maximum reduction of time for activity i

C_i = additional cost associated with reducing activity time for activity i

K_i = cost of reducing activity time by one time unit for activity i

$$K_i = \frac{C_i}{M_i}$$ (17.3)

With this information, it is possible to determine the least cost of reducing the project completion date. Example 9 illustrates the procedure.

EXAMPLE 9

Given the following information, determine the least cost of reducing the project completion time by 1 week.

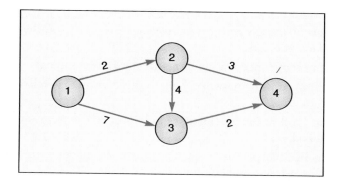

ACTIVITY	t (WEEKS)	M (WEEKS)	C	ACTIVITY	ES	EF	LS	LF	S
1–2	2	1	$ 300	1–2	0	2	1	3	1
1–3	7	4	2,000	1–3	0	7	0	7	0
2–3	4	2	2,000	2–3	2	6	3	7	1
2–4	3	2	4,000	2–4	2	5	6	9	4
3–4	2	1	2,000	3–4	7	9	7	9	0

The first step is to compute K for each activity:

ACTIVITY	M	C	K	CRITICAL PATH
1–2	1	$ 300	$ 300	No
1–3	4	2,000	500	Yes
2–3	2	2,000	1,000	No
2–4	2	4,000	2,000	No
3–4	1	2,000	2,000	Yes

The second step is to locate that activity on the critical path with the smallest value of K_i. The critical path consists of activities 1–3 and 3–4. Because activity 1–3 has a lower value of K_i, we can reduce the project completion time by 1 week, to 8 weeks, by incurring an additional cost of $500.

We must be very careful in using this procedure. Any further reduction in activity time along the critical path would cause the critical path also to include activities 1–2, 2–3, and 3–4. In other words, there would be two critical paths and activities on both would need to be "crashed" to reduce project completion time.

A CRITIQUE OF PERT AND CPM

As a critique of our discussions of PERT, here are some of its features about which operations managers need to be aware.

ADVANTAGES

1. Useful at several stages of project management, especially in the scheduling and control of large projects.
2. Straightforward in concept and not mathematically complex.
3. Graphical displays using networks help to perceive quickly relationships among project activities.
4. Critical path and slack time analyses help pinpoint activities that need to be closely watched.
5. Networks generated provide valuable project documentation and graphically point out who is responsible for various activities.

6. Applicable to a wide variety of projects and industries.

7. Useful in monitoring not only schedules, but costs as well.

LIMITATIONS

1. Project activities have to be clearly defined, independent, and stable in their relationships.

2. Precedence relationships must be specified and networked together.

3. Time estimates tend to be subjective and are subject to fudging by managers who fear the dangers of being overly optimistic or not pessimistic enough.

4. There is the inherent danger of too much emphasis being placed on the longest, or critical, path. Near-critical paths need to be monitored closely as well.

ACHIEVING WORLD-CLASS STANDARDS

World-class firms effectively manage projects and the resources required to accomplish those projects. Using project management tools, they manage numerous complex projects such as implementing computer systems, building factories, and automating warehouses. The tools used include computerized Gantt charts, PERT, CPM, and PERT/Cost. With these tools, managers understand the status of each activity and know which activities are critical and which have slack; in addition, they know where crashing makes the most sense. Projects are segmented into discrete activities and the specific resources are identified. This allows project managers in world-class organizations to respond aggressively to global competition. Moreover, effective project management also allows these firms to create products and services for global markets.

Such firms know the amount of human resources as well as capital resources necessary for each phase of a project. This knowledge allows managers to hire and train exactly the employees needed for each new challenge. The results are projects accomplished efficiently. This effective utilization of both labor and capital provides world-class firms, such as Bechtel (as we saw in the World-Class Profile that opened this chapter), a competitive advantage.

SUMMARY

PERT, CPM, and other scheduling techniques have proven to be valuable tools in controlling large and complex projects. A wide variety of software packages to help managers handle network modeling problems are also available.

PERT, CPM, and PERT/Cost will not, however, solve all the project scheduling and management problems of business and government. Good management practices, clear responsibilities for tasks, and straightforward and timely reporting systems are also needed. It is important to remember that the models we described in this chapter are only tools to aid managers make better decisions.

KEY TERMS

Project organization (p. 776)	Dummy activities (p. 785)
Gantt charts (p. 778)	Activity time estimates (p. 786)
Program evaluation and review technique (PERT) (p. 781)	Optimistic time (p. 786)
	Probable time (p. 786)
Critical path method (CPM) (p. 781)	Pessimistic time (p. 786)
Critical path (p. 782)	Beta probability distribution (p. 786)
Event (p. 783)	Critical path analysis (p. 787)
Activity (p. 783)	Slack time (p. 787)
Network (p. 783)	PERT/Cost (p. 796)

USING AB:POM AND SPREADSHEETS TO SOLVE PROJECT MANAGEMENT PROBLEMS

Solving the Schware Foundry Example with AB:POM's CPM/PERT Module

The project scheduling module will find the expected project completion time for a PERT and CPM network with either one or three time estimates. Program 17.1 contains the input data for Schware Foundry. Program 17.2 provides Schware Foundry's completed input repeated, as well as the final output. The CPM/PERT *one time estimate* program contains less output.

Using Spreadsheets for PERT/CPM

Spreadsheet formulas can easily be developed to compute expected values and variances for activities, as we did by hand for Schware Foundry in Table 17.3. Table 17.4 then summarized the PERT analysis for that firm. Program 17.3 performs that same analysis. ES for activity C is equal to EF for activity A (or + C13). EF for activity C is ES for activity C plus the activity time (or + B15 + B5). Note the use of the @MAX function to make sure that both activities leading into G and then both leading into H are completed before these activities are started. Computing ES and EF completes the "forward pass" through the network.

PROGRAM 17.1 ■ AB:POM's CPM/PERT Module, Data Entry Screen for Schware Foundry. The screen allows for naming of tasks and entry of times and predecessors for those activities that have predecessors.

———————————— CPM/PERT Project Scheduling ———————————— Data Screen ———

Number of activities (1–99) 8

———————————————————— SCHWARE FOUNDRY ————————————————————

Task	opt time	lik time	pes time	Predecessors			
a	1	2	3	—	—	—	—
b	2	3	4	—	—	—	—
c	1	2	3	a	—	—	—
d	2	4	6	b	—	—	—
e	1	4	7	c	—	—	—
f	1	2	9	c	—	—	—
g	3	4	11	d	—	—	—
h	1	2	3	f	g	—	—

PROGRAM 17.2 ■ Solution to Schware Foundry Example Using AB:POM. The critical path consists of those activities that have zero slack, namely, a, c, e, g, and h.

SCHWARE FOUNDRY

Project completion time = 15   Project standard deviation = 1.7638

Task	opt time	lik time	pes time	Time	ES	EF	LS	LF	slack	σ
a	1	2	3	2	0	2	0	2	0	.33
b	2	3	4	3	0	3	1	4	1	.33
c	1	2	3	2	2	4	2	4	0	.33
d	2	4	6	4	3	7	4	8	1	.67
e	1	4	7	4	4	8	4	8	0	1
f	1	2	9	3	4	7	10	13	6	1.33
g	3	4	11	5	8	13	8	13	0	1.33
h	1	2	3	2	13	15	13	15	0	.33

PROGRAM 17.3 ■ Using a Spreadsheet to Perform PERT Analysis. Input data (activity times, which are already calculated) appear in rows 3 through 10. Output appears in rows 13 through 20.

	A	B	C	D	E	F
1	Input Data					
2	Activity	Times				
3	A	2				
4	B	3				
5	C	2				
6	D	4				
7	E	4				
8	F	3				
9	G	5				
10	H	2				
11	Output Results					
12	Activity		ES	EF	LS	LF	Slack
13	A		0	+B3	+E13–B3	+D15	+E13–C13
14	B		0	+B4	+E14–B4	+D16	+E14–C14
15	C		+C13	+B15+B5	+E15–B5	@MIN(D17..D18)	+E15–C15
16	D		+C14	+B16+B6	+E16–B6	+D19	+E16–C16
17	E		+C15	+B17+B7	+E17–B7	+D19	+E17–C17
18	F		+C15	+B18+B8	+E18–B8	+D20	+E18–C18
19	G	@MAX(C16..C17)	+B19+B9	+E19–B9	+D20	+E19–C19
20	H	@MAX(C18..C19)	+B20+B10	+E20–B10	+C20	+E20–C20

The "backward pass" starts with the last activity—activity H. The LF value for activity H is the same as EF for this activity (15, or + C20). The LS value is computed by subtracting the activity time from the LF value. For activity H, this is + E20 – B10. The same calculations are then made for the other activities starting with activity G and proceeding to activity A. Note the use of @MIN for activity C. This is needed because there are two paths between activity C and the end of the network. After the backward pass has been completed, slack values are determined. This is done in column F. Slack is equal to LF minus EF.

SOLVED PROBLEMS

Solved Problem 17.1

Construct a network based on the following table.

ACTIVITY			
1–2	1–4	3–5	5–7
1–3	2–5	4–6	6–7

Solution

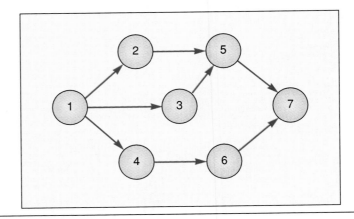

Solved Problem 17.2

Insert dummy activities and events to correct the following network:

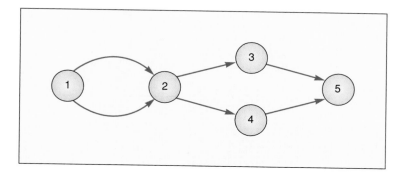

Solution

We can add the following dummy activity and dummy event to obtain the correct network:

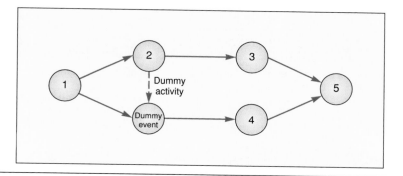

Solved Problem 17.3

Calculate the critical path, completion time T, and variance V based on the following information.

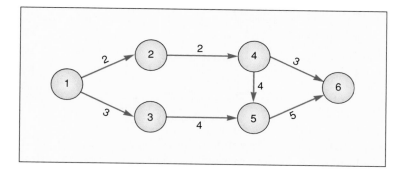

ACTIVITY	t	v	ES	EF	LS	LF	S
1–2	2	2/6	0	2	0	2	0
1–3	3	2/6	0	3	1	4	1
2–4	2	4/6	2	4	2	4	0
3–5	4	4/6	3	7	4	8	1
4–5	4	2/6	4	8	4	8	0
4–6	3	1/6	4	7	10	13	6
5–6	5	1/6	8	13	8	13	0

Solution

We conclude that the critical path is $1 \to 2 \to 4 \to 5 \to 6$.

$$T = 2 + 2 + 4 + 5 = 13$$

and

$$V = \frac{2}{6} + \frac{4}{6} + \frac{2}{6} + \frac{1}{6} = \frac{9}{6} = 1.5$$

Solved Problem 17.4

Given the following information, perform a critical path analysis.

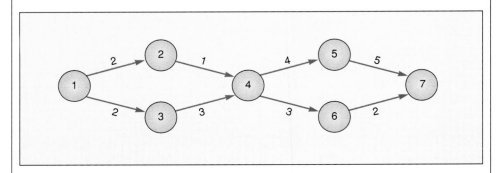

ACTIVITY	t	v	ACTIVITY	t	v
1–2	2	1/6	4–5	4	4/6
1–3	2	1/6	4–6	3	2/6
2–4	1	2/6	5–7	5	1/6
3–4	3	2/6	6–7	2	2/6

Solution

The solution begins with the determination of ES, EF, LS, LF, and S. We can find these values from the above information and then enter them into the following table:

ACTIVITY	t	V	ES	EF	LS	LF	S
1–2	2	1/6	0	2	2	4	2
1–3	2	1/6	0	2	0	2	0
2–4	1	2/6	2	3	4	5	2
3–4	3	2/6	2	5	2	5	0
4–5	4	4/6	5	9	5	9	0
4–6	3	2/6	5	8	9	12	4
5–7	5	1/6	9	14	9	14	0
6–7	2	2/6	8	10	12	14	4

Then we can find the critical path, T, and V. The critical path is 1–3, 3–4, 4–5, 5–7.

$$T = 2 + 3 + 4 + 5 = 14 \quad \text{and} \quad V = \frac{1}{6} + \frac{2}{6} + \frac{4}{6} + \frac{1}{6} = \frac{8}{6}$$

Solved Problem 17.5

The following information has been computed from a project:

$$T = 62 \text{ weeks}$$
$$V = 81$$

What is the probability that the project will be completed 18 weeks *before* its expected completion date?

Solution

The desired completion date is 18 weeks before the expected completion date, 62 weeks. The desired completion date is 44 (or 62 − 18) weeks.

$$Z = \frac{C - T}{\sigma} = \frac{44 - 62}{9} = \frac{-18}{9}$$

The normal curve appears as follows:

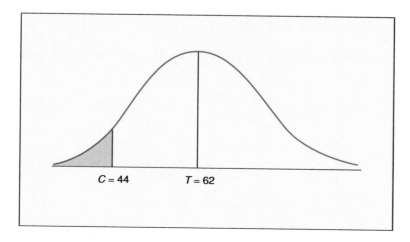

C = 44   T = 62

Because the normal curve is symmetrical and table values are calculated for positive values of Z, the area desired is equal to 1 − (table value). For Z = +2.0, the area from the table is .97725. Thus, the area corresponding to a Z value of −2.0 is .02275 (or 1 − 0.97725). Hence, the probability of completing the project 18 weeks before the expected completion date is approximately .02, or 2%.

Solved Problem 17.6

Determine the least cost of reducing the project completion date by 3 months based on the following information:

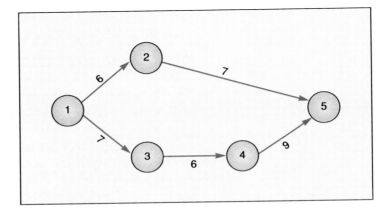

ACTIVITY	t (MONTHS)	M (MONTHS)	C
1–2	6	2	$400
1–3	7	2	500
2–5	7	1	300
3–4	6	2	600
4–5	9	1	200

Solution

The first step in this problem is to compute ES, EF, LS, LF, and S for each activity.

ACTIVITY	ES	EF	LS	LF	S
1–2	0	6	9	15	9
1–3	0	7	0	7	0
2–5	6	13	15	22	9
3–4	7	13	7	13	0
4–5	13	22	13	22	0

The critical path consists of activities 1–3, 3–4, and 4–5.

Next, K must be computed for each activity by dividing C by M for each activity.

ACTIVITY	M	C	K	CRITICAL PATH?
1–2	2	$400	$200/month	No
1–3	2	500	250/month	Yes
2–5	1	300	300/month	No
3–4	2	600	300/month	Yes
4–5	1	200	200/month	Yes

Finally, we will select that activity on the critical path with the smallest K_i value. This is activity 4–5. Thus, we can reduce the total project completion date by 1 month (because M = 1 month) for an additional cost of $200. We still need to reduce the project completion date by 2 more months. This reduction can be achieved at least cost along the critical path by reducing activity 1–3 by 2 months for an additional cost of $500. This solution is summarized in the following table:

ACTIVITY	MONTHS REDUCED	COST
4–5	1	$200
1–3	2	500
	Total:	$700

DISCUSSION QUESTIONS

1. What are some of the questions that can be answered with PERT and CPM?

2. What is an activity? What is an event? What is an immediate predecessor?

3. Describe how expected activity times and variances can be computed in a PERT network.

4. Briefly discuss what is meant by critical path analysis. What are critical path activities and why are they important?

5. What are the earliest activity start time and latest activity start time and how are they computed?

6. Describe the meaning of slack and discuss how it can be determined.

7. How can we determine the probability that a project will be completed by a certain date? What assumptions are made in this computation?

8. Briefly describe PERT/Cost and how it is used.

9. What is crashing and how is it done by hand?

10. What are the three phases involved in the management of a large project?

11. What is a dummy activity and when is it required?

12. What is the basic difference between PERT and CPM?

13. How is the variance of the total project computed in PERT?

14. How is the expected completion time of a PERT project computed?

15. What is a project organization?

16. Describe the differences between a Gantt chart and a PERT/CPM network.

17. Name some of the widely used project management software programs.

18. What is the difference between an Activity-on-Arrow (AOA) network and an Activity-on-Node (AON) network? Which is used in this chapter?

CRITICAL THINKING EXERCISE

The *POM in Action* box in this chapter that describes Delta Airlines' "well-orchestrated" ground turnaround procedures deals with a serious issue for all airlines. As a matter of fact, the *Wall Street Journal's* article "New Airline Fad: Faster Airport Turnarounds" (August 4, 1994, pp. B1–B2) describes similar scheduling improvements at USAir, Continental, and Southwest. For years, Southwest has turned its planes around in 15 minutes.

Provide detailed suggestions as to how airlines can speed up their turnaround times. What are Southwest's processes? What problems keep other airlines from emulating Southwest? Which is the preferable tool—Gantt charts or PERT/CPM, and why?

PROBLEMS

· **17.1** Draw the PERT network associated with the following activities for Bill Beville's next homework project.

ACTIVITY	IMMEDIATE PREDECESSOR(S)	ACTIVITY	IMMEDIATE PREDECESSOR(S)
A	—	E	B
B	A	F	C
C	A	G	D
D	B	H	E, F

· **17.2** Given the activities whose sequence is described by the following table:

ACTIVITY	IMMEDIATE PREDECESSOR(S)	ACTIVITY	IMMEDIATE PREDECESSOR(S)
A	—	F	C
B	A	G	E, F
C	A	H	D
D	B	I	G, H
E	B		

Draw the appropriate PERT diagram.

· **17.3** The following represent activities in Daniella Popoff's Construction Company project. Draw the network to represent this situation.

ACTIVITY	IMMEDIATE PREDECESSOR(S)	ACTIVITY	IMMEDIATE PREDECESSOR(S)
A	—	E	B
B	—	F	C, E
C	A	G	D
D	B	H	F, G

• **17.4** Sally McPherson is the personnel director of Babson and Willcount, a company that specializes in consulting and research. One of the training programs that Sally is considering for the middle-level managers of Babson and Willcount is leadership training. Sally has listed a number of activities that must be completed before a training program of this nature could be conducted. The activities and immediate predecessors appear in the accompanying table.

ACTIVITY	IMMEDIATE PREDECESSOR	ACTIVITY	IMMEDIATE PREDECESSOR
A	—	E	A, D
B	—	F	C
C	—	G	E, F
D	B		

Develop a network for this problem.

• **17.5** Sally McPherson was able to determine the activity times for the leadership training program. She would like to determine the total project completion time and the critical path. The activity times appear in the accompanying table. (See Problem 17.4).

ACTIVITY	TIME (DAYS)
A	2
B	5
C	1
D	10
E	3
F	6
G	8
Total:	35 days

• **17.6** The activities needed to build an experimental weed-harvesting machine at Timothy Urban Machinery Corp. are listed in the accompanying table. Construct a network for these activities.

ACTIVITY	IMMEDIATE PREDECESSORS	ACTIVITY	IMMEDIATE PREDECESSORS
A	—	E	B
B	—	F	B
C	A	G	C, E
D	A	H	D, F

🖳 · **17.7** Timothy Urban (see Problem 17.6) was able to determine the activity times for constructing his weed-harvesting machine. Urban would like to determine ES, EF, LS, LF, and slack for each activity. The total project completion time and the critical path should also be determined. Here are the activity times:

ACTIVITY	TIME (WEEKS)	ACTIVITY	TIME (WEEKS)
A	6	E	4
B	5	F	6
C	3	G	10
D	2	H	7

🖳 · **17.8** Riddick Wiring and Electric is a company that installs wiring and electrical fixtures in residential construction. Anne Riddick has been very concerned with the amount of time that it takes to complete wiring jobs. Some of her workers are very unreliable. A list of activities and their optimistic completion time, the pessimistic completion time, and the most likely completion time (all in days) is given in the table below.
      Determine the expected completion time and variance for each activity.

ACTIVITY	a	m	b	IMMEDIATE PREDECESSORS
A	3	6	8	—
B	2	4	4	—
C	1	2	3	—
D	6	7	8	C
E	2	4	6	B, D
F	6	10	14	A, E
G	1	2	4	A, E
H	3	6	9	F
I	10	11	12	G
J	14	16	20	C
K	2	8	10	H, I

🖳 : **17.9** Anne Riddick would like to determine the total project completion time and the critical path for installing electrical wiring and equipment in residential houses. See Problem 17.8 for details. In addition, determine ES, EF, LS, LF, and slack for each activity.

:**17.10** What is the probability that Riddick will finish the project described in Problems 17.8 and 17.9 in 40 days or less?

🖳 ·**17.11** The activities described by the following table are given for the Rivera Corporation:

ACTIVITY	IMMEDIATE PREDECESSOR(S)	TIME
A	—	9
B	A	7
C	A	3
D	B	6
E	B	9
F	C	4
G	E, F	6
H	D	5
I	G, H	3

a) Draw the appropriate PERT diagram for David Rivera's management team.

b) Find the critical path.

:17.12 A small software development project at Jack McGarrie's firm has four major activities. The times are estimated and provided in the table below. Find the expected time for completing McGarrie's project.

ACTIVITY	IMMEDIATE PREDECESSOR	a	m	b
A	—	2	5	8
B	—	3	6	9
C	A	4	7	10
D	B	2	5	14
E	C	3	3	3

a) What is the expected completion time for this project?

b) What variance would be used in finding probabilities of finishing by a certain time?

:17.13 Given the activities described by the following table:

ACTIVITY	EXPECTED TIME	STANDARD DEVIATION OF TIME ESTIMATE	IMMEDIATE PREDECESSOR(S)
A	7	2	—
B	3	1	A
C	9	3	A
D	4	1	B, C
E	5	1	B, C
F	8	2	E
G	8	1	D, F
H	6	2	G

a) Draw the appropriate PERT diagram.

b) Find the critical path and project completion time.

c) Find the probability that the project will take more than 49 time periods to complete.

:17.14 Development of a new deluxe version of a particular software product is being considered by Joan Blasco-Paul's software house. The activities necessary for the completion
of this are listed in the table below.

ACTIVITY	NORMAL TIME	CRASH TIME	NORMAL COST	CRASH COST	IMMEDIATE PREDECESSOR(S)
A	4	3	2,000	2,600	—
B	2	1	2,200	2,800	—
C	3	3	500	500	—
D	8	4	2,300	2,600	A
E	6	3	900	1,200	B
F	3	2	3,000	4,200	C
G	4	2	1,400	2,000	D, E

a) What is the project completion date?
b) What is the total cost required for completing this project on normal time?
c) If you wish to reduce the time required to complete this project by 1 week, which
   activity should be crashed, and how much will this increase the total cost?

:17.15 A project in Janice Laughlin's company has an expected completion time of 40 weeks
and a standard deviation of 5 weeks. It is assumed that the project completion time is
normally distributed.
a) What is the probability of finishing the project in 50 weeks or less?
b) What is the probability of finishing the project in 38 weeks or less?
c) The due date for the project is set so that there is a 90% chance that the project
   will be finished by this date. What is the due date?

:17.16 B&R Manufacturing produces custom-built pollution-control devices for medium-
sized steel mills. The most recent project undertaken by B&R requires 14 different activities. B&R's managers would like to determine the total project completion time
and those activities that lie along the critical path. The appropriate data are shown in
the table below.

ACTIVITY	IMMEDIATE PREDECESSORS	OPTIMISTIC TIME	MOST LIKELY TIME	PESSIMISTIC TIME
A	—	4	6	7
B	—	1	2	3
C	A	6	6	6
D	A	5	8	11
E	B, C	1	9	18
F	D	2	3	6
G	D	1	7	8
H	E, F	4	4	6
I	G, H	1	6	8
J	I	2	5	7
K	I	8	9	11
L	J	2	4	6
M	K	1	2	3
N	L, M	6	8	10

:17.17 Bill Trigiero, director of personnel of Trigiero Resources, Inc., is in the process of designing a program that his customers can use in the job-finding process. Some of the activities include preparing resumes, writing letters, making appointments to see prospective employers, researching companies and industries, and so on. Some of the information on the activities appears in the following table:

	TIME (DAYS)			IMMEDIATE
ACTIVITY	a	m	b	PREDECESSORS
A	8	10	12	—
B	6	7	9	—
C	3	3	4	—
D	10	20	30	A
E	6	7	8	C
F	9	10	11	B, D, E
G	6	7	10	B, D, E
H	14	15	16	F
I	10	11	13	F
J	6	7	8	G, H
K	4	7	8	I, J
L	1	2	4	G, H

a) Construct a network for this problem.
b) Determine the expected times and variances for each activity.
c) Determine ES, EF, LS, LF, and slack for each activity.
d) Determine the critical path and project completion time.
e) Determine the probability that the project will be finished in 70 days.
f) Determine the probability that the project will be finished in 80 days.
g) Determine the probability that the project will be finished in 90 days.

:17.18 Using PERT, Marcie Pleau-Watson was able to determine that the expected project completion time for the construction of a pleasure yacht is 21 months, and the project variance is 4.

a) What is the probability that the project will be completed in 17 months?
b) What is the probability that the project will be completed in 20 months?
c) What is the probability that the project will be completed in 23 months?
d) What is the probability that the project will be completed in 25 months?

:17.19 Norris Builders manufactures steel storage sheds for commercial use. Clay Norris, president of Norris Builders, is contemplating producing sheds for home use. The activities necessary to build an experimental model and related data are given in the accompanying table.

ACTIVITY	NORMAL TIME	CRASH TIME	NORMAL COST ($)	CRASH COST ($)	IMMEDIATE PREDECESSORS
A	3	2	1,600	1,600	—
B	2	1	2,700	2,700	—
C	1	0	300	600	—
D	7	3	1,300	1,600	A
E	6	3	850	1,000	B
F	2	1	4,000	5,000	C
G	4	2	1,500	2,000	D, E

a) What is the project completion date?

b) Crash this project to 10 weeks at the least cost.

: 17.20 The Maser is a new custom-designed sports car. An analysis of the task of building the Maser reveals the following list of relevant activities, their immediate predecessors, and their duration.[3]

JOB LETTER	DESCRIPTION	IMMEDIATE PREDECESSORS	NORMAL TIME (DAYS)
A	Start	—	0
B	Design	A	8
C	Order special accessories	B	0.1
D	Build frame	B	1
E	Build doors	B	1
F	Attach axles, wheels, gas tank	D	1
G	Build body shell	B	2
H	Build transmission and drivetrain	B	3
I	Fit doors to body shell	G, E	1
J	Build engine	B	4
K	Bench-test engine	J	2
L	Assemble chassis	F, H, K	1
M	Road-test chassis	L	0.5
N	Paint body	I	2
O	Install wiring	N	1
P	Install interior	N	1.5
Q	Accept delivery of special accessories	C	5
R	Mount body and accessories on chassis	M, O, P, Q	1
S	Road-test car	R	0.5
T	Attach exterior trim	S	1
U	Finish	T	0

a) Draw a network diagram for the project.

b) Mark the critical path and state its length.

c) If the Maser had to be completed 2 days earlier, would it help to:

  i) Buy preassembled transmissions and drivetrains?

  ii) Install robots to halve engine-building time?

  iii) Speed delivery of special accessories by 3 days?

d) How might resources be borrowed from activities on the noncritical path to speed activities on the critical path?

---

[3]*Source:* James A. F. Stoner and Charles Wankel, *Management*, 3rd ed. (Englewood Cliffs, NJ: Prentice Hall, 1986), p. 195.

:17.21 Getting a degree from a college or university is a long and difficult task. Certain courses must be completed before other courses may be taken. Develop a network diagram in which every activity is a particular course that must be taken for a given degree program. The immediate predecessors will be course prerequisites. Do not forget to include all university, college, and departmental course requirements. Then try to group these courses into semesters or quarters for your particular school. Which courses, if not taken in the proper sequence, could delay your graduation?

:17.22 The Van Voorhis Construction Company is involved with constructing municipal buildings and other structures that are used primarily by city and state municipalities. This requires developing legal documents, drafting feasibility studies, obtaining bond ratings, and so forth. Recently, Jamie Van Voorhis was given a request to submit a proposal for the construction of a municipal building. The first step is to develop legal documents and to perform all necessary steps before the construction contract is signed. This requires approximately 20 separate activities that must be completed. These activities, their immediate predecessors, and time requirements are given in the table shown below. As you can see, optimistic (a), most likely (m), and pessimistic (b) time estimates have been given for all of the activities described in the table. Using these data, determine the total project completion time for this preliminary step, the critical path, and slack time for all activities involved.

DATA BASE APPLICATION

ACTIVITY	TIME REQUIRED (WEEKS)			DESCRIPTION	IMMEDIATE PREDECESSOR(S)
	a	m	b		
1	1	4	5	Drafting legal documents	—
2	2	3	4	Preparation of financial statements	—
3	3	4	5	Draft of history	—
4	7	8	9	Draft demand portion of feasibility study	—
5	4	4	5	Review and approval of legal documents	1
6	1	2	4	Review and approval of history	3
7	4	5	6	Review feasibility study	4
8	1	2	4	Draft final financial portion of feasibility study	7
9	3	4	4	Draft facts relevant to the bond transaction	5
10	1	1	2	Review and approval of financial statements	2
11	18	20	26	Firm price received of project	—
12	1	2	3	Review and completion of financial portion of feasibility study	8
13	1	1	2	Draft statement completed	6, 9, 10, 11, 12
14	.10	.14	.16	All materials sent to bond rating services	13
15	.2	.3	.4	Statement printed and distributed to all interested parties	14
16	1	1	2	Presentation to bond rating services	14
17	1	2	3	Bond rating received	16
18	3	5	7	Marketing of bonds	15, 17
19	.1	.1	.2	Purchase contract executed	18
20	.1	.14	.16	Final statement authorized and completed	19
21	2	3	6	Purchase contract	19
22	.1	.1	.2	Bond proceeds available	20
23	.0	.2	.2	Sign construction contract	21, 22

CASE STUDY

The Family Planning Research Center of Nigeria

Dr. Adinombe Watage, deputy director of the Family Planning Research Center in Nigeria's Over-The-River Province was assigned the task of organizing and training five teams of field workers to do education and outreach as part of a large project to demonstrate acceptance of a new method of birth control. These workers had already had training in

"there aren't that many of us to go around. There are only 10 of us in this office."

"I can check whether we have enough heads and hands, once I have tentatively scheduled the activities," Dr. Watage responded. "If the schedule is too tight, I have permission from the Pathminder Fund to spend some funds to speed it up, just so long as I can prove that it can be done at the least cost necessary. Can you help me prove that? Here are the costs for the activities with the elapsed time that we planned and the costs and times, if we shorten them to an absolute minimum." Those data are in Table 2.

TABLE 1 ■ **THE FAMILY PLANNING RESEARCH CENTER**			
ACTIVITY	**MUST FOLLOW**	**TIME (IN DAYS)**	**STAFFING NEEDED**
A. Identify faculty and their schedules	—	5	2
B. Arrange transport to base	—	7	3
C. Identify and collect training materials	—	5	2
D. Arrange accommodations	A	3	1
E. Identify team	A	7	4
F. Bring in team	B, E	2	1
G. Transport faculty to base	A, B	3	2
H. Print program material	C	10	6
I. Have program materials delivered	H	7	3
J. Conduct training program	D, F, G, I	15	0
K. Perform fieldwork training	J	30	0

family planning education, but must receive specific training regarding the new method of contraception. Two types of materials must also be prepared: (1) those for use in training the workers, and (2) those for distribution in the field. Training faculty must be brought in and arrangements made for transportation and accommodations for the participants.

Dr. Watage first called a meeting of his office staff. Together they identified the activities that must be carried out, their necessary sequences, and the time that they would require. Their results are displayed in Table 1.

Louis Odaga, the chief clerk, noted that the project had to be completed in 60 days. Whipping out his solar-powered calculator, he added up the time needed. It came to 94 days. "An impossible task then," he noted. "No," Dr. Watage replied, "some of these tasks can go forward in parallel." "Be careful though," warned Mr. Oglagadu, the chief nurse,

DISCUSSION QUESTIONS

1. Some of the tasks in this project can be done in parallel. Prepare a diagram showing the required network of tasks and define the critical path. What is the length of the project without crashing?

2. At this point, can the project be done given the personnel constraint of 10 persons?

3. If the critical path is longer than 60 days, what is the least amount that Dr. Watage can spend and still achieve this schedule objective? How can he prove to Pathminder Foundation that this is the minimum cost alternative?

Source: Professor Curtis P. McLaughlin, Kenan-Flagler Business School, University of North Carolina at Chapel Hill.

(Continued)

TABLE 2 ■ THE FAMILY PLANNING RESEARCH CENTER

ACTIVITY	NORMAL		MINIMUM		AVERAGE COST PER DAY SAVED ($)
	TIME	COST ($)	TIME	COST ($)	
A. Identify faculty	5	400	2	700	100
B. Arrange transport	7	1,000	4	1,450	150
C. Identify materials	5	400	3	500	50
D. Make accommodations	3	2,500	1	3,000	250
E. Identify team	7	400	4	850	150
F. Bring team in	2	1,000	1	2,000	1,000
G. Transport faculty	3	1,500	2	2,000	500
H. Print materials	10	3,000	5	4,000	200
I. Deliver materials	7	200	2	600	80
J. Train team	15	5,000	10	7,000	400
K. Do fieldwork	30	10,000	20	14,000	400

CASE STUDY

Shale Oil Company

The Shale Oil Company contains several operating units that comprise its Aston, Ohio, manufacturing complex. These units process the crude oil that is pumped through and transform it into a multitude of hydrocarbon products. The units run 24 hours a day, 7 days a week, and must be shut down for maintenance on a predetermined schedule. One such unit is Distillation Unit No. 5, or DU5. Studies have shown that DU5 can operate only 3½ years without major equipment breakdowns and excessive loss of efficiency. Therefore, DU5 is shut down every 3½ years for cleaning, inspection, and repairs.

DU5 is the only distillation unit for crude oil in the Aston complex, and its shutdown severely af-

fects all other operating units. Some of the production can be compensated by Shale refineries in other locations, but the rest must be processed before the shutdown and stored. Without proper planning, a nationwide shortage of Shale gasoline could occur. The time of DU5's shutdown is critical, and the length of time the unit is down must be kept to a minimum to limit production loss. Shale uses PERT as a planning and controlling tool to minimize shutdown time.

The first phase of a shutdown is to open and clean the equipment. Inspectors can then enter the unit and examine the damage. Once damages are determined, the needed repairs can be carried out. Repair times can vary considerably depending on what damage the inspection reveals. Based on previous inspection records, some repair work is known ahead of time. Thorough cleaning of the equipment is also necessary to improve the unit's

(Continued)

operating efficiency. Table 3 lists the many maintenance activities and their estimated completion
times.

DISCUSSION QUESTIONS

1. Determine the expected shutdown time and
the probability the shutdown can be completed 1 week earlier.

2. What are the probabilities that Shale finishes
the maintenance project 1, 2, 3, 4, 5, or 6 days
earlier?

3. Shale Oil is considering increasing the budget
to shorten the shutdown. How do you suggest
the company proceed?

TABLE 3 ■ PREVENTIVE MAINTENANCE OF DU5

		TIME ESTIMATES (IN DAYS)		
ACTIVITIES		**OPTIMISTIC**	**MOST LIKELY**	**PESSIMISTIC**
1–2	Circulate wash water throughout unit	1	2	2.5
2–3	Install blinds	1.5	2	2.5
3–4	Open and clean vessels and columns	2	3	4
3–5	Open and clean heat exchangers; remove tube bundles	1	2	3
3–6	Open and clean furnaces	1	2	4
3–7	Open and clean mechanical equipment	2	2.5	3
3–8	Inspect instrumentation	2	4	5
4–9	Inspect vessels and columns	1	2	3
5–10	Inspect heat-exchanger shells	1	1.5	2
5–11	Inspect tube bundles	1	1.5	2
6–12	Inspect furnaces	2	2.5	3
6–17	Retube furnaces	15	20	30
7–13	Inspect mechanical equipment	1	1.5	2
7–18	Install new pump mechanical seals	3	5	8
8–19	Repair instrumentation	3	8	15
9–14	Repair vessels and columns	14	21	28
10–16	Repair heat-exchanger shells	1	5	10
11–15	Repair tube bundles; retube	2	5	10
12–17	Repair furnaces	5	10	20
13–18	Repair mechanical equipment	10	15	25
14–20	Test and close vessels and columns	4	5	8
15–16	Install tube bundles into heat-exchanger shells	1	2	3
16–20	Test and close heat exchangers	1	2	2.5
17–20	Test and close furnaces	1	2	3
18–20	Test and close mechanical equipment	1	2	3
19–20	Test instrumentation	2	4	6
20–21	Pull blinds	1.5	2	2.5
21–22	Purge all equipment with steam	1	3	5
22–23	Start up unit	3	5	10

BIBLIOGRAPHY

Cleland, D. I., and W. R. King. *Project Management Handbook*. New York: Van Nostrand Reinhold, 1984.

Dean, B. V. "Getting the Job Done! Managing Project Teams and Task Forces for Success." *The Executive*, 6, no. 4 (November 1992): 94.

Dusenberry, W. "CPM for New Product Introductions." *Harvard Business Review* (July/August 1967): 124–139.

Hickman, Anita. "Refining the Process of Project Control." *Production and Inventory Management* (February 1992): 26–27.

Keefer, D. L., and W. A. Verdini. "Better Estimation of PERT Activity Time Parameters." *Management Science*, 39, no. 9 (September 1993): 1,086.

Kerzner, H., and H. Thamhain. *Project Management for Small and Medium Size Business*. New York: Van Nostrand Reinhold, 1984.

Kim, S., and R. C. Leachman. "Multi-Project Scheduling with Explicit Lateness Costs." *IIE Transactions*, 25, no. 2 (March 1993): 34–44.

Pinto, M. B., J. K. Pinto, and J. E. Prescott. "Antecedents and Consequences of Project Team Cross-functional Cooperation." *Management Science*, 39, no. 10 (October 1993): 1,281.

Render, B., and R. M. Stair. *Introduction to Management Science*. Boston: Allyn and Bacon, 1992.

———. *Quantitative Analysis for Management*, 5th ed. Boston: Allyn and Bacon, 1994.

18

MAINTENANCE AND RELIABILITY

LEARNING OBJECTIVES

When you complete this chapter you should be able to:

Identify or Define:

   Maintenance

   Redundancy

   Preventive Maintenance

   Breakdown Maintenance

   Mean Time Between Failures

   Infant Mortality

Explain:

   How to measure system reliability

   How to improve maintenance

   How to evaluate maintenance
   performance

MAINTENANCE PROVIDES A COMPETITIVE ADVANTAGE FOR ORLANDO UTILITIES COMMISSION

The Orlando Utilities Commission (OUC) owns and operates power plants that supply power to 13 central Florida counties. Every year, OUC takes each one of its power-generating units off-line for 1 to 3 weeks to perform maintenance work.

Additionally, each unit is also taken off-line every 3 years for a complete overhaul and turbine generator inspection. Overhauls are scheduled for spring and fall, when the weather is mildest and demand for power is low. These overhauls last from 6 to 8 weeks.

Units at OUC's Stanton Energy Center require that maintenance personnel perform approximately 12,000 repair and preventive

maintenance tasks a year. To accomplish these tasks efficiently, many of these jobs are scheduled daily via a computerized maintenance management program. The computer generates preventive maintenance work orders and lists of required materials.

Every day that a plant is down for maintenance costs OUC about $55,000 extra for the replacement cost of power that must be generated elsewhere. However, these costs pale beside the costs associated with a forced outage. An unexpected outage could cost OUC an additional $250,000 to $500,000 each day!

Scheduled overhauls are not easy; each one has 1,800 distinct tasks

and requires 72,000 labor-hours. But the value of preventive maintenance was illustrated by the first overhaul of a new turbine generator. Workers discovered a cracked rotor blade, which could have destroyed a $27 million piece of equipment. To find such cracks, which are invisible to the naked eye, metals are examined by dye tests, X-rays, and ultrasound.

At OUC, preventive maintenance is worth its weight in gold. As a result, OUC's electric distribution system is ranked number 1 in Florida for reliability. Effective maintenance provides a competitive advantage for the Orlando Utilities Commission.

Maintenance of capital-intensive facilities requires good planning to minimize downtime. Here, turbine overhaul is under way. Organizing the thousands of parts and pieces necessary for a shutdown is a major effort.

The high pressure/low pressure section of turbine has been removed for overhaul. When steam first enters this 23-ton high-pressure rotor, it bears hurricane-strength force.

Inspection is proceeding on low pressure section of turbine. The tips of these turbine blades will travel at supersonic speeds of 1,300 miles per hour when the plant is in operation. And a crack in any one of these blades can cause a catastrophic failure.

Whendesign the United Airlines DC-10 left Denver, three engines and all three hydraulic systems were working. But at 3:17 P.M., an explosion shook the plane. Number 2 engine had torn itself apart. The three separate hydraulic lines ceased to work. Despite the work of dedicated designers and well-trained maintenance personnel, the engine failed. Despite having three separate hydraulic lines, the aircraft had no working hydraulic system. Despite eight million hours of no fatal United Airlines accidents, over one hundred people were about to die. ♦

Failure

This chapter is concerned with avoiding undesirable results of system failure. A **failure** is the change in a product or system from a satisfactory working condition to a condition that is below an acceptable standard. Even when the results are not catastrophic, the results of failure can be disruptive, inconvenient, wasteful, and expensive.

A study addressing the weaknesses in British productivity compared British and German firms.[1] The study found that although the machinery in the British plants was no older than that in the German plants, it was badly maintained. Breakdowns were found to be more frequent and lasted longer. Operators were found less able to do repairs themselves. Machine and product failures can have far-reaching effects on a firm's operation and profitability. In complex, highly mechanized plants, an out-of-tolerance process or a machine breakdown may result in idle employees and facilities, loss of customers and goodwill, and profits turning into losses. Likewise, in an office, the failure of a generator, an air-conditioning system, or a computer may halt operations.

Reliability is important to P/OM managers. Maintenance is important to P/OM managers. System failures cause undesirable results.

Good managers maintain a system while keeping maintenance and breakdown costs under control. Reliability and maintenance protect both a firm's performance and its investment. Systems must be designed and maintained to reach expected performance and quality standards. **Reliability** is the probability that a machine part or product will function properly for a given length of time. **Maintenance** includes all activities involved in keeping a system's equipment in working order. *The objective of reliability and maintenance is to maintain the capability of the system while controlling costs.*

In this chapter, we examine four tactics for improving reliability and maintenance of products and equipment as well as the systems that produce them. The four tactics are organized around reliability and maintenance.

The reliability tactics are

Reliability
Maintenance

1. improving individual components;
2. providing redundancy.

The maintenance tactics are

1. implementing or improving preventive maintenance;
2. increasing repair capabilities or speed.

---

[1]National Institute of Economic and Social Research as reported in "Britain's Economy," *The Economist* (March 9, 1985): 62–63.

FIGURE 18.1 ■ Overall System Reliability as a Function of Number of Components and Component Reliability with Components in a Series

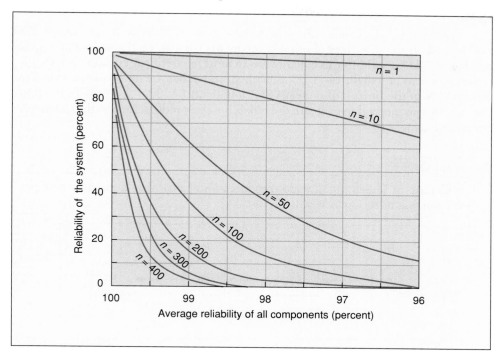

RELIABILITY

Systems are composed of a series of individual interrelated components, each performing a specific job. If any *one* component fails to perform, for whatever reason, the overall system (for example, an airplane or machine) can fail.

Improving Individual Components

As the story about United Airlines at the beginning of this chapter shows, failures do occur. That failures occur is an important reliability concept.

Figure 18.1 shows that as the number of components in a *series* increases, the reliability of the whole system declines very quickly. A system of $n = 50$ interacting parts, each of which has a 99.5% reliability, has an overall reliability of 78%. If the system or machine has 100 interacting parts, each with an individual reliability of 99.5%, the overall reliability will be only about 60%!

To measure system reliability in which each individual part or component may have its own unique rate of reliability, we cannot use the reliability curve in Figure 18.1. However, the method of computing system reliability (R_s) is simple. It consists of finding the product of individual reliabilities as follows:

$$R_s = R_1 \times R_2 \times R_3 \times \cdots \times R_n \qquad (18.1)$$

where R_1 = reliability of component 1
            R_2 = reliability of component 2

and so on.

Equation (18.1) assumes that the reliability of an individual component does not depend on the reliability of other components (that is, each component is independent). Additionally, in this equation, as in most reliability discussions, reliabilities are presented as probabilities. A .90 reliability means that the unit will perform as intended 90% of the time. It also means that it will fail $1 - .90 = .1 = 10\%$ of the time. We can use this method to evaluate the reliability of a product, such as the one we examine in Example 1.

EXAMPLE 1

Nels Electric of Greeley, Colorado, produces an electrical relay switch that has three components set up in series:

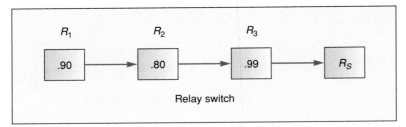

Relay switch

If the individual reliabilities are .90, .80, .99, then the reliability of the entire relay switch is

$$R_s = R_1 R_2 R_3 = (.90)(.80)(.99) = .713, \text{ or } 71.3\%$$

Component reliability is often a design or specification issue for which engineering design personnel may be responsible. However, purchasing personnel may be able to improve components of systems by staying abreast of suppliers' products and research efforts. Purchasing personnel can also directly contribute to evaluation of supplier performance.

The basic unit of measure for reliability is the product failure rate (FR). Firms producing high-technology equipment often provide failure rate data on their products. The failure rate measures the percentage of failures among the total number of products tested, FR(%), or a number of failures during a period of time, FR(N):

$$FR(\%) = \frac{\text{number of failures}}{\text{number of units tested}} \times 100\% \qquad (18.2)$$

$$FR(N) = \frac{\text{number of failures}}{\text{number of unit-hours of operating time}} \qquad (18.3)$$

Mean time between failures (MTBF)

Perhaps the most common term in reliability analysis is the **mean time between failures (MTBF)**, which is the reciprocal of FR(N):

$$MTBF = \frac{1}{FR(N)} \qquad (18.4)$$

In Example 2, we compute the percentage of failure FR(%), number of failures FR(N), and mean time between failures (MTBF).

EXAMPLE 2

Twenty air-conditioning systems to be used by astronauts in NASA space shuttles were operated for 1,000 hours at NASA's Huntsville, Alabama, test facility. Two of the systems failed during the test—one after 200 hours and the other after 600 hours. To compute the percentage of failures,

$$FR(\%) = \frac{\text{number of failures}}{\text{number tested}} = \frac{2}{20}(100\%) = 10\%$$

Next we compute the number of failures per operating hour:

$$FR(N) = \frac{\text{number of failures}}{\text{operating time}}$$

where

$$\text{Total time} = (1,000 \text{ hr})(20 \text{ units})$$

$$= 20,000 \text{ units-hr}$$

$$\text{Nonoperating time} = 800 \text{ hr for 1st failure} + 400 \text{ hr for 2nd failure}$$

$$= 1,200 \text{ unit-hr}$$

$$\text{Operating time} = \text{total time} - \text{nonoperating time}$$

$$FR(N) = \frac{2}{20,000 - 1,200} = \frac{2}{18,800}$$

$$= .000106 \text{ failure/unit-hr}$$

and because MTBF $= \dfrac{1}{FR(N)}$

$$MTBF = \frac{1}{.000106} = 9,434 \text{ hr}$$

If the typical space shuttle trip lasts 60 days, NASA may be interested in the failure rate per trip:

$$\text{Failure rate} = (\text{failures/unit-hr})(24 \text{ hr/day})(60 \text{ days/trip})$$

$$= (.000106)(24)(60)$$

$$= .152 \text{ failure/trip}$$

Today's jetliners are expected to be designed so that one system's failure doesn't automatically cripple others. But the 1989 crash of this United Airlines DC-10 in Sioux City, Iowa, seems to indicate that the McDonnell Douglas plane's hydraulic systems aren't providing good enough protection. The DC-10 has three separate mazes of half-inch pipes running throughout the plane. Each pipe is designed to continuously pump fluid that operates control devices. But federal investigators think the pipes in the plane's tail were severed by flying tail parts. Hydraulic fluid then sprayed out, causing loss of control and, ultimately, the crash.

Because the failure rate of Example 2 is likely too high, NASA will have to either increase the reliability of individual components, and hence of the system, or else install several backup air-conditioning units on each space shuttle. Backup units provide redundancy.

Providing Redundancy

To increase the reliability of systems, redundancy ("backing up" the components) is added. Redundancy is provided if one component fails, and the system has recourse to another. For instance, say reliability of a component is .80 and we back it up with another component with reliability of .80. Then the resulting reliability is the probability of the first component working plus the probability of the backup component working multiplied by the probability of needing the backup component $(1 - .8 = .2)$. Therefore:

$$\begin{pmatrix} \text{Probability} \\ \text{of first} \\ \text{component} \\ \text{working} \end{pmatrix} + \left[\begin{pmatrix} \text{Probability} \\ \text{of second} \\ \text{component} \\ \text{working} \end{pmatrix} \times \begin{pmatrix} \text{Probability} \\ \text{of needing} \\ \text{second} \\ \text{component} \end{pmatrix} \right] =$$

$$(.8) \quad + \quad [(.8) \quad \times \quad (1 - .8)] \qquad = .8 + .16 = .96$$

Example 3 shows how redundancy can improve the reliability of the system presented in Example 1.

EXAMPLE 3

Nels Electric is disturbed that its electrical relay has a reliability of only .713 (see Example 1). Therefore, Nels decides to provide redundancy for the two least reliable components. This results in the system shown below:

$$R_1 \qquad R_2 \qquad R_3$$

$$\boxed{0.90} \quad \boxed{0.8}$$
$$\downarrow \qquad \downarrow$$
$$\boxed{0.90} \rightarrow \boxed{0.8} \rightarrow \boxed{0.99} = [.9 + .9(1 - .9)] \times [.8 + .8(1 - .8)] \times .99$$

$$= [.9 + (.9)(.1)] \times [.8 + (.8)(.2)] \times .99$$

$$= .99 \times .96 \times .99 = .94$$

So by providing redundancy for two components, Nels has increased reliability of the switch from .713 to .94.

MAINTENANCE

Preventive maintenance

There are two types of maintenance: preventive maintenance and breakdown maintenance. **Preventive maintenance** involves performing routine inspections and servicing and keeping facilities in good repair. These activities are intended to build a system that will find potential failures and make changes or repairs that will prevent failure. Preventive maintenance is much more than just keeping machinery and equipment running. It also involves designing technical and human systems that will keep the productive process working within tolerance; it allows the system to perform. The emphasis of preventive maintenance is on understanding the process and allowing it to work without interruption. **Breakdown maintenance** occurs when equipment fails and then must be repaired on an emergency or priority basis.

Breakdown maintenance

FIGURE 18.2 ■ Lifetime Failure Rates

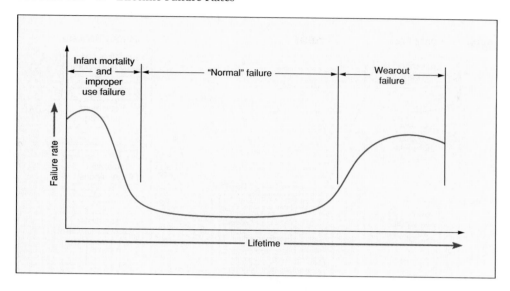

Implementing Preventive Maintenance

Preventive maintenance implies that we can determine when a system needs service or will need repair. Figure 18.2 indicates that failure occurs at different rates during the life of a product. This failure rate may follow different statistical distributions. A high initial failure rate, known as **infant mortality**, exists initially for many products. This is the reason many electronic firms "burn in" their products prior to shipment. That is to say, many firms execute a variety of tests to detect "startup" problems prior to shipment. Other firms provide 90-day warranties. We should note that many infant mortality failures are not product failures per se, but failure due to improper use. This fact points up the importance of operations management's building a maintenance system that includes training and personnel selection.

    Once the product, machine, or process "settles in," a study can be made of the MTBF (mean time between failure) distribution. When the distributions have a small standard deviation, then we know we have a candidate for preventive maintenance even if the maintenance is expensive.[2]

    Once we have a candidate for preventive maintenance, we want to determine when preventive maintenance is economical. Typically, the more expensive the maintenance, the narrower must be the MTBF distribution. Additionally, if the process is no more expensive to repair when it breaks down than the cost of preventive maintenance, perhaps we should let the process break down and then do the repair. However, the consequence of the breakdown must be fully considered. Some relatively minor breakdowns have catastrophic consequences. At the other extreme, preventive maintenance costs may be so incidental that preventive maintenance is appropriate even if the distribution is rather flat (that is, it has a large standard

Infant mortality

[2]See, for example, the work of P. M. Morse, *Queues, Inventories, and Maintenance* (New York: John Wiley, 1958), pp. 161–168; and "Using Statistical Thinking to Solve Maintenance Problems," *Quality Progress* (May 1989): 55–60.

FIGURE 18.3 ■ A Computerized Maintenance System

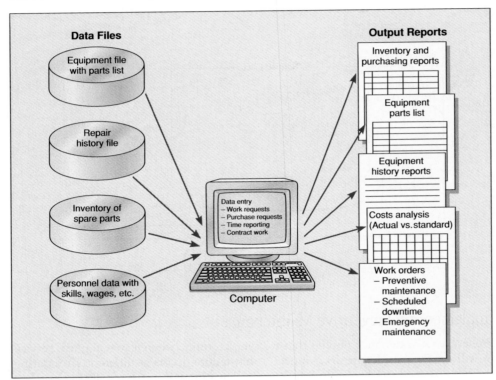

deviation). In any event, all machine operators must be held responsible for preventive maintenance of their own equipment and tools.

A variety of sensing devices exist to help determine when a process should receive maintenance. For instance, many aircraft engines have a sensor that indicates the presence of metals in the lubricating oils. This sensor indicates unusual wear and the need for preventive maintenance prior to a breakdown (which is a nice idea, particularly on airplanes). A variety of other devices, from vibration sensors to infrared thermography, are available to help determine preventive maintenance requirements.[3] Additionally, with good reporting techniques, firms can maintain records of individual processes, machines, or equipment. Such records can provide a profile of both the kinds of maintenance required and timing of maintenance needed. Maintaining equipment history is an important part of a preventive maintenance system, as is a record of the time and cost to make the repair. Such records can also contribute to similar information about the family of equipment as well as suppliers.

Record keeping is of such importance that most good maintenance systems are now computerized. Figure 18.3 shows the major components of such a system with files to be maintained on the left and reports generated on the right.

[3]Ronald L. Stiemsma, "Vibration Monitoring Proves Itself at Clinton Power Station," *Electric Light and Power*, 70, no. 6 (June 1992): 2; and Bruce D. Nordwall, "Engine Monitoring System May Provide 100-Hr. Warning Before Jet Failure," *Aviation Week and Space Technology*, 136, no. 10 (March 9, 1992): 54–56.

FIGURE 18.4 ■ Maintenance Costs

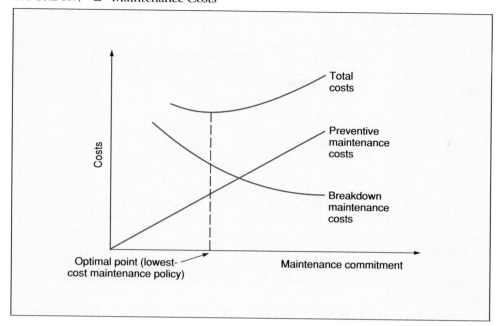

Figure 18.4 shows the relationship between preventive maintenance and break-down maintenance. Operations managers need to consider a balance between the two costs. Allocating more money and crew to preventive maintenance will reduce the number of breakdowns. But, at some point, the decrease in breakdown maintenance costs will be less than the increase in preventive maintenance costs, and the total cost curve will begin to rise. Beyond this optimal point, the firm will be better off waiting for breakdowns to occur and repairing them when they do.

Unfortunately, these cost curves seldom consider the full costs of a breakdown. Many costs are ignored because they are not directly related to the immediate breakdown. For instance, the cost of inventory maintained to compensate for this downtime is not typically considered; and downtime can have a devastating effect on morale. Employees may begin to believe that performance to standard and maintaining equipment are not important. In addition, downtime can adversely affect delivery schedules, destroying customer relations and future sales.

Assuming that all costs associated with downtime have been identified, the operations staff can compute the optimal level of maintenance activity on a theoretical basis. The analysis, of course, also requires accurate historical data on maintenance costs, breakdown probabilities, and repair times. Example 4 illustrates how to compare preventive and breakdown maintenance costs in order to select the least expensive maintenance policy.

EXAMPLE 4

Huntsman and Associates is a CPA firm specializing in payroll preparation. The accountants have been successful in automating much of their work, using computers for processing and report preparation. The computerized approach has problems, however. Over the past 20 months, the computer system has broken down, as indicated below.

NUMBER OF BREAKDOWNS	NUMBER OF MONTHS THAT BREAKDOWNS OCCURRED
0	4
1	8
2	6
3	2
	Total: 20

Each time the computer breaks down, the partners estimate that the firm loses an average of $300 in time and service expenses. One alternative is for the firm to accept a service contract for preventive maintenance. If they accept preventive maintenance, they expect an *average* of only one computer breakdown per month. The price for this service is $220 per month. We will follow a four-step approach to answer the question of whether the CPAs should contract for preventive maintenance:

Step 1. Compute the *expected number* of breakdowns (based on past history) if the firm continues as is, without the service contract.

Step 2. Compute the expected breakdown cost per month with no preventive maintenance contract.

Step 3. Compute the cost of preventive maintenance.

Step 4. Compare the two options and select the one that will cost less.

1.

NUMBER OF BREAKDOWNS	FREQUENCY	NUMBER OF BREAKDOWNS	FREQUENCY
0	4/20 = .2	2	6/20 = 0.3
1	8/20 = .4	3	2/20 = 0.1

$$\begin{pmatrix} \text{Expected number} \\ \text{of breakdowns} \end{pmatrix} = \Sigma \left[\begin{pmatrix} \text{number of} \\ \text{breakdowns} \end{pmatrix} \times \begin{pmatrix} \text{corresponding} \\ \text{frequency} \end{pmatrix} \right]$$

$$= (0)(.2) + (1)(.4) + (2)(.3) + (3)(.1)$$

$$= 0 + .4 + .6 + .3$$

$$= 1.3 \text{ breakdowns/month}$$

2. $\text{Expected breakdown cost} = \begin{pmatrix} \text{expected number} \\ \text{of breakdowns} \end{pmatrix} \times \begin{pmatrix} \text{cost per} \\ \text{breakdown} \end{pmatrix}$

$$= (1.3)(\$300)$$

$$= \$390/\text{month}$$

3. $\begin{pmatrix} \text{Preventive} \\ \text{maintenance cost} \end{pmatrix} = \begin{pmatrix} \text{cost of expected} \\ \text{breakdowns if service} \\ \text{contract signed} \end{pmatrix} + \begin{pmatrix} \text{cost of} \\ \text{service contract} \end{pmatrix}$

> $$= (1 \text{ breakdown/month})(\$300) + \$220/\text{month}$$
>
> $$= \$520/\text{month}$$
>
> **4.** Because it is less expensive to suffer the breakdowns *without* a maintenance service contract ($390) than with one ($520), the firm should continue its present policy.

Through variations of the technique shown in Example 4, operations managers can determine minimum-cost maintenance policies.

INCREASING REPAIR CAPABILITIES

When neither reliability nor preventive maintenance has been achieved, operations managers need good repair facilities. Enlarging or improving repair facilities can get the system back in operation faster. A good maintenance facility should have these six features:

1. well-trained personnel;
2. adequate resources;
3. ability to establish a repair plan and priorities;[4]
4. ability and authority to do material planning;
5. ability to identify the cause of breakdowns;
6. ability to design ways to extend MTBF.

However, not all repairs can be done in the firm's facility. Managers must therefore decide where repairs are to be performed. Figure 18.5 shows some of the options and how they rate in terms of speed, cost, and competence. Consistent with employee empowerment, a strong case can be made for employees' maintaining their own equipment, but this type of repair may also be the weakest link in the repair chain. Not every employee can be trained in all aspects of equipment repair.

Whichever preventive maintenance policies and techniques management chooses must include an emphasis on employees' accepting responsibility for the maintenance they are capable of doing. Employee maintenance may be only of the "clean, check, and observe" variety, but if each operator does those activities within his or her capability, the manager has made a step toward employee empowerment and toward maintaining system performance.

OTHER MAINTENANCE POLICY TECHNIQUES

Two other P/OM techniques have proven beneficial to maintenance systems: simulation and expert systems.

---

[4] You may recall from our discussion of network planning in Chapter 17 that duPont developed the critical path method (CPM) to improve the scheduling of maintenance projects.

FIGURE 18.5   ■   The Operations Manager Must Determine How Maintenance Will Be Performed

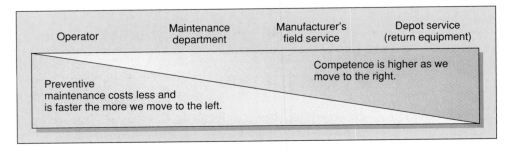

SIMULATION.   Because of the complexity of some maintenance decisions, simulation is a good tool for evaluating the impact of various maintenance policies. For instance, operations personnel can decide whether to add more maintenance staff on the basis of the trade-offs between machine downtime costs and the costs of additional labor. Management can also simulate replacing parts that have not yet failed as a way of preventing future breakdowns. Simulation via physical models can also be useful. For example, a physical model can vibrate an airplane to simulate thousands of hours of flight time in order to evaluate maintenance needs. The Supplement to Chapter 13 covers the topic of simulation in more detail.

EXPERT SYSTEMS.   P/OM managers use expert systems to assist staff in isolating and repairing various faults in machinery and equipment. For instance, General Electric's DELTA system asks a series of detailed questions leading and aiding the user in identifying the problem. Expert systems are discussed in Chapter 8.

ACHIEVING WORLD-CLASS STANDARDS

World-class firms have reliable systems. Such firms achieve reliability through systems design and effective maintenance. Companies like Orlando Utilities, featured earlier in this chapter, use sophisticated computer software to schedule maintenance projects, control inventory of spare parts, and track the failure of parts.

Other firms use automated sensors and controls to warn when production machinery is about to fail or is becoming damaged by heat, vibration, or fluid leaks. General Motors, for example, has developed a computer system to sense unusual vibrations of machines while they are running. DuPont uses expert systems to monitor equipment and to train repair personnel. The key is to avoid failures and to perform preventive maintenance before machines are damaged.

Finally, world-class companies give their employees a sense of "ownership" in their equipment. When a worker repairs or does preventive maintenance on his or her own machine, breakdowns are often avoided. Well-trained and empowered employees ensure reliable systems through preventive maintenance. Reliable, well-maintained equipment not only provides higher utilization, but also improves quality and performance to schedule. World-class firms build and maintain systems so their customers can count on products produced to specifications on time.

SUMMARY

Reliable systems are a necessity. In spite of our best efforts to design reliable components, systems sometimes fail. Consequently, backup components are used. Reliability improvements also can be obtained through the use of preventive maintenance and excellent repair facilities. Expert systems and comprehensive data collection and analysis assist reliability and maintenance management. Simulation techniques can also aid in determining maintenance policies. Reliable processes require well-designed systems, trained personnel, and good record keeping.

Failure (p. 822)
Reliability (p. 822)
Maintenance (p. 822)
Mean time between failures (MTBF)
  (p. 824)

Preventive maintenance (p. 826)
Breakdown maintenance (p. 826)
Infant mortality (p. 827)

KEY TERMS

Solving Example 3 Using AB:POM's Reliability Module

Program 18.1 illustrates the use of AB:POM in solving a reliability problem.

USING AB:POM TO SOLVE RELIABILITY PROBLEMS

PROGRAM 18.1 ■ AB:POM's Reliability Module Example. The entries for reliability are: **1.** *number of systems* (components) in the series (1 through 10); **2.** *number of backup or parallel components* (1 through 10); **3.** *component reliability*. Enter the reliability of each component in the body of the table. Series data are entered across the table and backup or parallel data down the table. The program will disregard any zeroes in the table.

	Reliability		Data Screen
Number of systems in series (1–10) ⬛3	Max # of parallel components (1–10)		
Parll Sys 1	Parll Sys 2	Parll Sys 3	⬛2
.9000	.8000	.0000	
.9000	.8000	.9900	
Output:	Reliability		Esc
Parll Sys 1	Parll Sys 2	Parll Sys 3	
.9000	.8000		
.9000	.8000	.9900	
.9900	.9600	.9900	
System reliability = .94090			

Notice that the entries that were 0 have been eliminated. The products for each column show the combined parallel (backup) component reliability.

SOLVED PROBLEMS

Solved Problem 18.1

The semiconductor used in the Sullivan Wrist Calculator has five parts, each of which has its own reliability rate. Component 1 has a reliability of .90; component 2, .95; component 3, .98; component 4, .90; and component 5, .99. What is the reliability of one semiconductor?

Solution

$$\text{Semiconductor reliability, } R_s = R_1 R_2 R_3 R_4 R_5$$

$$= (.90)(.95)(.98)(.90)(.99)$$

$$= .7466$$

Solved Problem 18.2

A recent engineering change at Sullivan Wrist Calculator places a backup component in each of the two least reliable transistor circuits. The new circuit will look like the following:

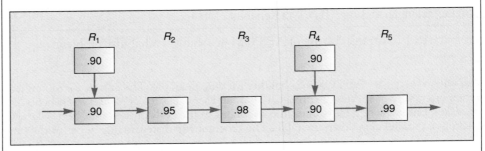

What is the reliability of the new system?

Solution

$$\text{Reliability} = [.9 + (1 - .9) \times .9] \times .95 \times .98 \times [.90 + (1 - .9) \times .9] \times .99$$

$$= [.9 + .09] \times .95 \times .98 \times [.90 + .09] \times .99$$

$$= .99 \times .95 \times .98 \times .99 \times .99$$

$$= .903$$

DISCUSSION QUESTIONS

1. What are the variables that contribute to infant mortality for new machinery?

2. What techniques can management use to improve system reliability?

3. Under what conditions is preventive maintenance likely to be appropriate?

4. Why is simulation often an appropriate technique for maintenance problems?

5. What is the trade-off between operator-performed maintenance versus supplier-performed maintenance?

6. How can the manager evaluate the effectiveness of the maintenance function?

7. What kind of records are helpful when developing a good maintenance system?

8. How do expert systems improve maintenance systems?

9. How can a firm improve or speed up its repair facilities?

The 1989 crash of a McDonnell Douglas DC-10 suggests that the plane's hydraulic systems may not provide enough protection. The DC-10 has three separate hydraulic systems, all of which failed when an engine exploded. The engine threw off shreds of metal that severed two of the lines, and the third line required power from the demolished engine that was no longer available. The DC-10, unlike other commercial jets, has no shutoff valves that might have stemmed the flow of hydraulic fluid. Lockheed's similar L-1011 trijet has four hydraulic systems. A McDonnell Douglas VP says, "You can always be extreme and not have a practical airplane. You can be perfectly safe and never get off the ground." Discuss the pros and cons of McDonnell's position. How might you design a reliability experiment?

PROBLEMS

· **18.1** The Beta II computer's electronic processing unit contains 50 components in series. The average reliability of each component is 99.0%. Using Figure 18.1, determine the overall reliability of the processing unit.

: **18.2** Holzwart Manufacturing, a medical equipment manufacturer, has subjected 100 heart pacemakers to 5,000 hours of testing. Halfway through the testing, 5 of the pacemakers failed. What was the failure rate in terms of:

a) Percent of failures?

b) Number of failures per unit-hour?

c) Number of failures per unit-year?

d) If 1,100 people receive pacemaker implants, how many units can we expect to fail during the following 1 year?

· **18.3** Given the probabilities that follow for a machine shop, find the expected breakdown cost.

NUMBER OF BREAKDOWNS	DAILY FREQUENCY
0	.3
1	.2
2	.2
3	.3
	1.0

The cost per breakdown is $10.

· **18.4** You have a system composed of four components in series. The reliability of each component is .95. What is the reliability of the system?

· **18.5** You have a system composed of a serial connection of four components with the following reliabilities:

COMPONENT	RELIABILITY
1	.90
2	.95
3	.80
4	.85

What is the reliability of the system?

: 18.6 You have a system composed of three components in parallel. The components have the following reliabilities:

$$R_1 = 0.90, \qquad R_2 = 0.95, \qquad R_3 = 0.85$$

What is the reliability of the system?

· 18.7 A hydraulic control system has three components in series with individual reliabilities (R_1, R_2, and R_3) as shown.

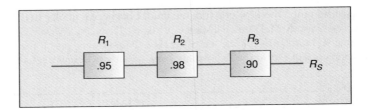

What is the reliability of the system?

: 18.8 What is the reliability of the system shown below?

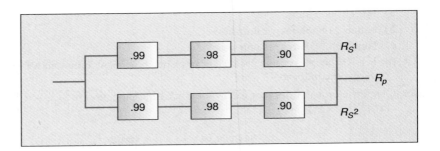

: 18.9 What is the impact on reliability if the hydraulic control system shown in Problem 18.7 is changed to the parallel system shown in Problem 18.8?

:18.10 Your design team has proposed the following system with component reliabilities as indicated.

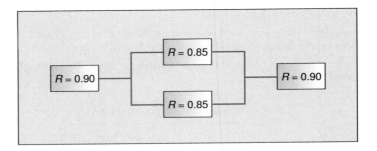

What is the reliability of the system?

:18.11 Randolph Manufacturing has tested 200 units of a product. After 2,000 hours, four units have failed; the remainder functioned for the full 4,000 hours of the testing.

a) What is the percent of failures?

b) What is the number of failures per unit hour?

c) What is the number of failures per unit year?

d) If you sell 500 units, how many are likely to fail within a 1-year time period?

: 18.12 Wharton Manufacturing Company operates its 23 large and expensive grinding and lathe machines from 7 A.M. to 11 P.M., 7 days a week. For the past year, the firm has been under contract with Simkin and Sons for daily preventive maintenance (lubrication, cleaning, inspection, and so on). Simkin's crew works between 11 P.M. and 2 A.M. so as not to interfere with the daily manufacturing crew. Simkin charges $645 per week for this service. Since signing the maintenance contract, Wharton Manufacturing has noted an average of only three breakdowns per week. When a grinding or lathe machine *does* break down during a working shift, it costs Wharton about $250 in lost production and repair costs.

   After reviewing past breakdown records (for the period before signing a preventive maintenance contract with Simkin and Sons), Wharton Manufacturing's production manager summarizes the patterns shown below.

   The production manager is not certain that the contract for preventive maintenance with Simkin is in the best financial interest of Wharton Manufacturing. He recognizes that much of his breakdown data are old but is fairly certain that they are representative of the present picture.

   What is your analysis of this situation and what recommendations do you think the production manager should make?

NUMBER OF BREAKDOWNS PER WEEK	NUMBER OF WEEKS IN WHICH BREAKDOWNS OCCURRED
0	1
1	1
2	3
3	5
4	9
5	11
6	7
7	8
8	5
Total weeks of historical data:	50

: 18.13 Alain Prost, salesman for Wave Soldering Systems, Inc. (WSSI), has provided you with a proposal for improving the temperature control on your present machine. The present machine uses a hot-air knife to remove cleanly excess solder from printed-circuit boards; this is a great concept, but the hot-air temperature control lacks reliability. The engineers at WSSI have, says Alain, improved the reliability of the critical temperature controls. The new system still has the four sensitive integrated circuits controlling the temperature, but the new machine has a backup for each. The four integrated circuits have reliabilities of .90, .92, .94, and .96. The four backup circuits all have a reliability of .90.

a) What is the reliability of the new temperature controller?

b) If you pay a premium, Alain says he can improve all four of the backup units to .93. What is the reliability of this option?

CASE STUDY

Worldwide Chemical Company

Jack Smith wiped the perspiration from his face. It was another scorching-hot summer day and one of the four process refrigeration units was down. The units were critical to the operation of Worldwide Chemical Company's Fibers Plant, which produced synthetic fibers and polymer flake for a global market.

Before long Al Henson, the day-shift production superintendent, was on the intercom, shouting his familiar proclamation that "heads would roll" if the unit was not back online within the hour. But Jack Smith, the maintenance superintendent, had heard it all before—nothing ever happened as a result of those temper tantrums. "Serves him right," he thought, "Henson is uncooperative when we want to perform scheduled maintenance, so it doesn't get done and the equipment goes down."

At that moment, Henson, furious over the impact the equipment breakdown would have on his process yield figures, was meeting with Beth Conner, the plant manager, charging that all the maintenance department did was to "sit around" and play cards like firemen waiting for an alarm to send them on their way to a three-alarm blaze across town. It was true that the "fix-it" approach to maintenance was costing the plant throughput that was vital to meeting standard costs and avoiding serious variances. Foreign competitors were delivering high-quality fibers in less time, at lower prices. Beth Conner had already been "on the carpet" at corporate headquarters over output levels that were significantly below the budgeted numbers. The business cycle contained seasonal variations that were predictable. That meant building inventories that would be carried for months, tying up scarce capital, a characteristic of most continuous processes. Monthly shipments would look bad. Year-to-date shipments would look even worse because of

machine breakdowns and lost output to date. Conner knew that something had to be done to develop machine reliability. Capacity on demand was needed to respond to the growing foreign competition. Unreliable production equipment was jeopardizing the company's TQM effort by causing process variations that affected first-quality product yields and on-time deliveries, but no one seemed to have the answer to the problem of machine breakdowns.

The maintenance department operated much as a fire department, rushing to a breakdown with a swarm of mechanics, some who disassembled the machine, others who poured over wiring schematics, and others who hunted spare parts in the maintenance warehouse. Eventually, they would have the machine back up, sometimes only after working through the night to get the production line going again. Maintenance had always been done this way. But, with new competitors, machine reliability had suddenly become a major barrier to competing successfully.

Rumors of a plant closing were beginning to circulate and morale was suffering, making good performance that much more difficult. Beth Conner knew she needed solutions if the plant had any chance of survival.

DISCUSSION QUESTIONS

1. Could Smith and Hensen do anything to improve performance?
2. Is there an alternative to the current operations approach of the maintenance department?
3. How would production make up for lost output resulting from scheduled maintenance?
4. How could maintenance mechanics be better utilized?
5. Is there any way to know when a machine breakdown is probable?

Source: Patrick Owings under the supervision of Professor Marilyn M. Helms, University of Tennessee at Chattanooga.

BIBLIOGRAPHY

Hayes, R. H., and K. B. Clark. "Why Some Factories Are More Productive than Others." *Harvard Business Review*, 64, no. 5 (September/October 1986): 66–73.

Joshi, S., and R. Gupta. "Scheduling of Routine Maintenance Using Production Schedules and Equipment Failure History." *Computers and Industrial Engineering*, 10, no. 1 (1986): 11–20.

Linder-Dutton, L., M. Jordan, and M. Karwan. "Beyond Mean Time to Failure." *OR/MS Today*, 21, no. 2 (April 1994): 30–33.

Maggard, B. N., and D. M. Rhyne. "Total Productive Maintenance: A Timely Integration of Production and Maintenance." *Production and Inventory Management Journal*, 33, no. 4 (Fourth Quarter 1992): 6–10.

Mann, L., Jr. *Maintenance Management*. Lexington, MA: Lexington Books, 1983.

Schneeweiss, C. A., and H. Schroder. "Planning and Scheduling the Repair Shops of the Deutsche Lufthansa AG: A Hierarchical Approach." *Production and Operations Management*, 1, no. 1 (Winter 1992): 22.

Sherwin, D. J. "Inspect or Monitor." *Engineering Costs and Production Economics*, 18 (January 1990): 223–231.

Vaziri, H. K. "Using Competitive Benchmarking to Set Goals." *Quality Progress*, 25, no. 10 (October 1992): 81.

APPENDICES

APPENDIX A   AREAS UNDER THE STANDARD NORMAL CURVE

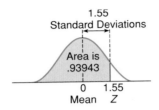

To find the area under the normal curve, you must know how many standard deviations that point is to the right of the mean. Then, the area under the normal curve can be read directly from the normal table. For example, the total area under the normal curve for a point that is 1.55 standard deviations to the right of the mean is .93943.

	.00	.01	.02	.03	.04	.05	.06	.07	.08	.09
.0	.50000	.50399	.50798	.51197	.51595	.51994	.52392	.52790	.53188	.53586
.1	.53983	.54380	.54776	.55172	.55567	.55962	.56356	.56749	.57142	.57535
.2	.57926	.58317	.58706	.59095	.59483	.59871	.60257	.60642	.61026	.61409
.3	.61791	.62172	.62552	.62930	.63307	.63683	.64058	.64431	.64803	.65173
.4	.65542	.65910	.66276	.66640	.67003	.67364	.67724	.68082	.68439	.68793
.5	.69146	.69497	.69847	.70194	.70540	.70884	.71226	.71566	.71904	.72240
.6	.72575	.72907	.73237	.73536	.73891	.74215	.74537	.74857	.75175	.75490
.7	.75804	.76115	.76424	.76730	.77035	.77337	.77637	.77935	.78230	.78524
.8	.78814	.79103	.79389	.79673	.79955	.80234	.80511	.80785	.81057	.81327
.9	.81594	.81859	.82121	.82381	.82639	.82894	.83147	.83398	.83646	.83891
1.0	.84134	.84375	.84614	.84849	.85083	.85314	.85543	.85769	.85993	.86214
1.1	.86433	.86650	.86864	.87076	.87286	.87493	.87698	.87900	.88100	.88298
1.2	.88493	.88686	.88877	.89065	.89251	.89435	.89617	.89796	.89973	.90147
1.3	.90320	.90490	.90658	.90824	.90988	.91149	.91309	.91466	.91621	.91774
1.4	.91924	.92073	.92220	.92364	.92507	.92647	.92785	.92922	.93056	.93189
1.5	.93319	.93448	.93574	.93699	.93822	.93943	.94062	.94179	.94295	.94408
1.6	.94520	.94630	.94738	.94845	.94950	.95053	.95154	.95254	.95352	.95449
1.7	.95543	.95637	.95728	.95818	.95907	.95994	.96080	.96164	.96246	.96327
1.8	.96407	.96485	.96562	.96638	.96712	.96784	.96856	.96926	.96995	.97062
1.9	.97128	.97193	.97257	.97320	.97381	.97441	.97500	.97558	.97615	.97670
2.0	.97725	.97784	.97831	.97882	.97932	.97982	.98030	.98077	.98124	.98169
2.1	.98214	.98257	.98300	.98341	.98382	.98422	.98461	.98500	.98537	.98574
2.2	.98610	.98645	.98679	.98713	.98745	.98778	.98809	.98840	.98870	.98899
2.3	.98928	.98956	.98983	.99010	.99036	.99061	.99086	.99111	.99134	.99158
2.4	.99180	.99202	.99224	.99245	.99266	.99286	.99305	.99324	.99343	.99361
2.5	.99379	.99396	.99413	.99430	.99446	.99461	.99477	.99492	.99506	.99520
2.6	.99534	.99547	.99560	.99573	.99585	.99598	.99609	.99621	.99632	.99643
2.7	.99653	.99664	.99674	.99683	.99693	.99702	.99711	.99720	.99728	.99736
2.8	.99744	.99752	.99760	.99767	.99774	.99781	.99788	.99795	.99801	.99807
2.9	.99813	.99819	.99825	.99831	.99836	.99841	.99846	.99851	.99856	.99861
3.0	.99865	.99869	.99874	.99878	.99882	.99886	.99899	.99893	.99896	.99900
3.1	.99903	.99906	.99910	.99913	.99916	.99918	.99921	.99924	.99926	.99929
3.2	.99931	.99934	.99936	.99938	.99940	.99942	.99944	.99946	.99948	.99950
3.3	.99952	.99953	.99955	.99957	.99958	.99960	.99961	.99962	.99964	.99965
3.4	.99966	.99968	.99969	.99970	.99971	.99972	.99973	.99974	.99975	.99976
3.5	.99977	.99978	.99978	.99979	.99980	.99981	.99981	.99982	.99983	.99983
3.6	.99984	.99985	.99985	.99986	.99986	.99987	.99987	.99988	.99988	.99989
3.7	.99989	.99990	.99990	.99990	.99991	.99991	.99992	.99992	.99992	.99992
3.8	.99993	.99993	.99993	.99994	.99994	.99994	.99994	.99995	.99995	.99995
3.9	.99995	.99995	.99996	.99996	.99996	.99996	.99996	.99996	.99997	.99997

Source: From *Quantitative Approaches to Management,* 4th ed., by Richard I. Levin and Charles A. Kirkpatrick. Copyright © 1978, 1975, 1971, 1965 by McGraw-Hill, Inc. Used with permission of McGraw-Hill Book Company.

APPENDIX B   POISSON DISTRIBUTION VALUES

$$P(X \leq c; \lambda) = \sum_0^c \frac{\lambda^x e^{-\lambda}}{x!}$$

Table shows 1000 times the probability of c or less occurrences of an event that has an average number of occurrences of λ.

λ	VALUES OF C										
	0	1	2	3	4	5	6	7	8	9	10
.02	980	1000									
.04	961	999	1000								
.06	942	998	1000								
.08	923	997	1000								
.10	905	995	1000								
.15	861	990	999	1000							
.20	819	982	999	1000							
.25	779	974	998	1000							
.30	741	963	996	1000							
.35	705	951	994	1000							
.40	670	938	992	999	1000						
.45	638	925	989	999	1000						
.50	607	910	986	998	1000						
.55	577	894	982	998	1000						
.60	549	878	977	997	1000						
.65	522	861	972	996	999	1000					
.70	497	844	966	994	999	1000					
.75	472	827	959	993	999	1000					
.80	449	809	953	991	999	1000					
.85	427	791	945	989	998	1000					
.90	407	772	937	987	998	1000					
.95	387	754	929	984	997	1000					
1.00	368	736	920	981	996	999	1000				
1.1	333	699	900	974	995	999	1000				
1.2	301	663	879	966	992	998	1000				
1.3	273	627	857	957	989	998	1000				
1.4	247	592	833	946	986	997	999	1000			
1.5	223	558	809	934	981	996	999	1000			
1.6	202	525	783	921	976	994	999	1000			
1.7	183	493	757	907	970	992	998	1000			
1.8	165	463	731	891	964	990	997	999	1000		
1.9	150	434	704	875	956	987	997	999	1000		
2.0	135	406	677	857	947	983	995	999	1000		

Source: Adapted from E. L. Grant, *Statistical Quality Control*, McGraw-Hill Book Company, New York, 1964. Reproduced by permission of the publisher.

APPENDIX B POISSON DISTRIBUTION VALUES (CONTINUED)

λ	0	1	2	3	4	5	6	7	8	9	10	11	12	13	14	15	16	17	18	19	20	21	22
2.2	111	359	623	819	928	975	993	998	1000														
2.4	091	308	570	779	904	964	988	997	999	1000													
2.6	074	267	518	736	877	951	983	995	999	1000													
2.8	061	231	469	692	848	935	976	992	998	999	1000												
3.0	050	199	423	647	815	916	966	988	996	999	1000												
3.2	041	171	380	603	781	895	955	983	994	998	1000												
3.4	033	147	340	558	744	871	942	977	992	997	999	1000											
3.6	027	126	303	515	706	844	927	969	988	996	999	1000											
3.8	022	107	269	473	668	816	909	960	984	994	998	999	1000										
4.0	018	092	238	433	629	785	889	949	979	992	997	999	1000										
4.2	015	078	210	395	590	753	867	936	972	989	996	999	1000										
4.4	012	066	185	359	551	720	844	921	964	985	994	998	999	1000									
4.6	010	056	163	326	513	686	818	905	955	980	992	997	999	1000									
4.8	008	048	143	294	476	651	791	887	944	975	990	996	999	1000									
5.0	007	040	125	265	440	616	762	867	932	968	986	995	998	999	1000								
5.2	006	034	109	238	406	581	732	845	918	960	982	993	997	999	1000								
5.4	005	029	095	213	373	546	702	822	903	951	977	990	996	999	1000								
5.6	004	024	082	191	342	512	670	797	886	941	972	988	995	998	999	1000							
5.8	003	021	072	170	313	478	638	771	867	929	965	984	993	997	999	1000							
6.0	002	017	062	151	285	446	606	744	847	916	957	980	991	996	999	999	1000						
6.2	002	015	054	134	259	414	574	716	826	902	949	975	989	995	998	999	1000						
6.4	002	012	046	119	235	384	542	687	803	886	939	969	986	994	997	999	1000						
6.6	001	010	040	105	213	355	511	658	780	869	927	963	982	992	997	999	999	1000					
6.8	001	009	034	093	192	327	480	628	755	850	915	955	978	990	996	998	999	1000					
7.0	001	007	030	082	173	301	450	599	729	830	901	947	973	987	994	998	999	1000					
7.2	001	006	025	072	156	276	420	569	703	810	887	937	967	984	993	997	999	999	1000				
7.4	001	005	022	063	140	253	392	539	676	788	871	926	961	980	991	996	998	999	1000				
7.6	001	004	019	055	125	231	365	510	648	765	854	915	954	976	989	995	998	999	1000				
7.8	000	004	016	048	112	210	338	481	620	741	835	902	945	971	986	993	997	999	1000				
8.0	000	003	014	042	100	191	313	453	593	717	816	888	936	966	983	992	996	998	999	1000			
8.5	000	002	009	030	074	150	256	386	523	653	763	849	909	949	973	986	993	997	999	999	1000		
9.0	000	001	006	021	055	116	207	324	456	587	706	803	876	926	959	978	989	995	998	999	1000		
9.5	000	001	004	015	040	089	165	269	392	522	645	752	836	898	940	967	982	991	996	998	999	1000	
10.0	000	000	003	010	029	067	130	220	333	458	583	697	792	864	917	951	973	986	993	997	998	999	1000

APPENDIX C   VALUES OF $e^{-\lambda}$ FOR USE IN THE POISSON DISTRIBUTION

VALUES OF $e^{-\lambda}$

λ	$e^{-\lambda}$	λ	$e^{-\lambda}$	λ	$e^{-\lambda}$	λ	$e^{-\lambda}$
.0	1.0000	1.6	.2019	3.1	.0450	4.6	.0101
.1	.9048	1.7	.1827	3.2	.0408	4.7	.0091
.2	.8187	1.8	.1653	3.3	.0369	4.8	.0082
.3	.7408	1.9	.1496	3.4	.0334	4.9	.0074
.4	.6703	2.0	.1353	3.5	.0302	5.0	.0067
.5	.6065	2.1	.1225	3.6	.0273	5.1	.0061
.6	.5488	2.2	.1108	3.7	.0247	5.2	.0055
.7	.4966	2.3	.1003	3.8	.0224	5.3	.0050
.8	.4493	2.4	.0907	3.9	.0202	5.4	.0045
.9	.4066	2.5	.0821	4.0	.0183	5.5	.0041
1.0	.3679	2.6	.0743	4.1	.0166	5.6	.0037
1.1	.3329	2.7	.0672	4.2	.0150	5.7	.0033
1.2	.3012	2.8	.0608	4.3	.0136	5.8	.0030
1.3	.2725	2.9	.0550	4.4	.0123	5.9	.0027
1.4	.2466	3.0	.0498	4.5	.0111	6.0	.0025
1.5	.2231						

APPENDIX D   TABLE OF RANDOM NUMBERS

52	06	50	88	53	30	10	47	99	37	66	91	35	32	00	84	57	07
37	63	28	02	74	35	24	03	29	60	74	85	90	73	59	55	17	60
82	57	68	28	05	94	03	11	27	79	90	87	92	41	09	25	36	77
69	02	36	49	71	99	32	10	75	21	95	90	94	38	97	71	72	49
98	94	90	36	06	78	23	67	89	85	29	21	25	73	69	34	85	76
96	52	62	87	49	56	59	23	78	71	72	90	57	01	98	57	31	95
33	69	27	21	11	60	95	89	68	48	17	89	34	09	93	50	44	51
50	33	50	95	13	44	34	62	64	39	55	29	30	64	49	44	30	16
88	32	18	50	62	57	34	56	62	31	15	40	90	34	51	95	26	14
90	30	36	24	69	82	51	74	30	35	36	85	01	55	92	64	09	85
50	48	61	18	85	23	08	54	17	12	80	69	24	84	92	16	49	59
27	88	21	62	69	64	48	31	12	73	02	68	00	16	16	46	13	85
45	14	46	32	13	49	66	62	74	41	86	98	92	98	84	54	33	40
81	02	01	78	82	74	97	37	45	31	94	99	42	49	27	64	89	42
66	83	14	74	27	76	03	33	11	97	59	81	72	00	64	61	13	52
74	05	81	82	93	09	96	33	52	78	13	06	28	30	94	23	37	39
30	34	87	01	74	11	46	82	59	94	25	34	32	23	17	01	58	73
59	55	72	33	62	13	74	68	22	44	42	09	32	46	71	79	45	89
67	09	80	98	99	25	77	50	03	32	36	63	65	75	94	19	95	88
60	77	46	63	71	69	44	22	03	85	14	48	69	13	30	50	33	24
60	08	19	29	36	72	30	27	50	64	85	72	75	29	87	05	75	01
80	45	86	99	02	34	87	08	86	84	49	76	24	08	01	86	29	11
53	84	49	63	26	65	72	84	85	63	26	02	75	26	92	62	40	67
69	84	12	94	51	36	17	02	15	29	16	52	56	43	'26	22	08	62
37	77	13	10	02	18	31	19	32	85	31	94	81	43	31	58	33	51

Source: Excerpted from *A Million Random Digits with 100,000 Normal Deviates,* The Free Press, 1955, p. 7, with permission of the Rand Corporation.

APPENDIX E   USING AB:POM

This technical appendix provides additional details as to the use of AB:POM. Specific program modules, such as Forecasting or Inventory, are illustrated in their respective chapters. The intent of this appendix is to discuss the overall program operations and to describe how the system may be run on your specific computer.

In this appendix, we first discuss (1) Hardware Requirements, then (2) the Main AB:POM Menu, (3) the Module Submenu Screen, (4) Entering/Editing data, and (5) Getting Started. This program is so user-friendly that, depending on your computer experience and skills, you may wish to go straight to the Getting Started section and proceed to the paragraphs called "Normal Startup."

HARDWARE REQUIREMENTS

AB:POM will work on any IBM or compatible personal computer. The programs themselves require less than 384K of available memory. The system has one 3.5-inch, 1.44-megabyte diskette. The programs also can be loaded onto a hard disk and run from there.

A printer is not required to run AB:POM. Of course, if you want a hard copy (printout), it is necessary to have a printer attached. No special features, characters, installation, or printer is required. It is possible to print the learning curve, Gantt charts, control charts, and linear programming graphs by running the DOS program GRAPHICS.EXE prior to starting up AB:POM and then pressing the **Prt Scn** key.

MAIN MENU

Program E.1 shows AB:POM's Main Menu, consisting of 19 individual application programs plus a **Help** command and an **Exit to DOS** command. Selections from this menu may be made by pressing the first letter (or highlighted letter) of each command on the screen or by moving the cursor to the program you want and then pressing the enter key.

If you request Help from this Main Menu, you may view four detailed Help screens. Program E.2 illustrates the program commands and how function keys may be used.

PROGRAM E.1 ■ The AB:POM Main Menu

─────────────────── Main Menu ───────────────────

Help   **I**nventory
Decision Tables   Sim**u**lation
Quality Control   **M**aterial Requirements Planning
Forecasting   **S**izing, Lot
Linear Programming   **A**ggregate Planning
Plant Location   **J**ob Shop Sequencing
Transportation   Assi**g**nment
Operations Layout   **C**PM/PERT Project Scheduling
Balancing, Assembly Line   **R**eliability
Waiting Line Models   Co**n**figure
Experience (learning) Curves E**x**it to DOS

──────────── INSTRUCTIONS ────────────

Use highlighted letter or point with
arrow keys and then press ENTER (↵) key
to select option or press ESC key to exit

PROGRAM E.2 ■ Optional Help Screen for Function Keys

─────────────── Submenu Options ───────────────

Submenu options appear on the last line of the data screen after a
module is chosen. The options are chosen by pressing the highlighted letter. When you press the ESC key while editing the data
the options will become available. It is also possible to access the
submenu options by using the function keys which are listed below.

F1–**H**elp–Displays the module or submodule help screen
F2–**N**ew–Use this to start a new problem
F3–**L**oad–Use this to load a file from disk
F4–**M**ain–This returns to the module menu
F5–**U**til–Customize colors, toggle sound, print to file, etc.
F6–**Q**uit–Exit AB:POM and go to DOS
F7–**S**ave–Save a problem/file on a disk
*F8–**T**itl–Change the problem title
F9–**P**rnt–Print the data or solution to a printer (or file)
F10–**R**un–Solve the problem

For most modules, **ESC** followed by the **INS**ert key can be used to insert

THE MODULE SUBMENU SCREEN

The module submenu will appear after the module has been chosen.

Submenu Options

Each submenu will have the following six options, which can be selected by typing the highlighted (first) letter or the corresponding function key as shown in Program E.2.

Help (F1)

This option will present a brief description of the module, the data required for input, the output results, and the available options. It is worthwhile to look at this screen at least one time in order to be certain that there are no unsuspected differences between your assumptions and the assumptions of the program. The same help screen also can be accessed from the data screen, where it is perhaps most useful, because you will then be looking at the data to which the help screen is referring. You can examine the help screen at any time; the screen appears instantaneously and takes little time to read.

Create a New Data Set (F2)

Creating a new data set will be a frequently chosen option. After the create option is chosen, one of three types of screens will appear, depending on the module. For some modules (decision tables, forecasting, inventory plant location, project scheduling, and quality control), a model submenu will appear, indicating that different programs are available within the broad context of the module. The desired choice is made in the usual way—by using the first letter or point and shoot. After selecting a model, it will be possible to give the problem a title.

Load a Data Set from the Disk (F3)

If you have previously stored data on a disk (which may be the AB:POM program disk or any blank, formatted disk), it is possible to load the data into memory. If you choose the load data option, a screen will appear that contains the name of the drive, the name of the subdirectory (if there is one), and a list of the available files.

To load a file, simply type its name and then press **Return**. Standard DOS file names *without* extensions are legal. In other words, you may type in up to eight characters, but a period is illegal. You may preface the file name with a drive letter (with its colon). Examples of legal file names are **sample**, **test**, **b:sample**, **problem 1**. It does not matter whether you use uppercase or lowercase characters. DOS treats all characters as uppercase. You may type them as uppercase, lowercase, or mixed. The following are examples of illegal file names.

sample.1p   The program will not allow you to type the period.

abcdefghij   The name is too long; the program will issue an error message.

lpt1   This is a reserved DOS word.

After the file is loaded, you will be placed in the data screen and can edit or run the data.

Return to the Main Menu (F4)

The next option on the submenu list in Program E.2 is to return to the main menu. This option is not necessary if all of your problems come from the same module. However, if you have homework problems from more than one chapter, this is one way to go from module to module.

Utilities (F5)

If the utilities option is chosen, a new submenu will appear. The submenu options are again chosen in the normal fashion.

CUSTOMIZE COLORS. The first option allows you to create a custom color file. The colors of 13 different items can be changed (in the usual way). For example, to change the color of the boxes in AB:POM, keep pressing **b** until you are satisfied with the color. The colors of the two boxes on the screen change each time you press **b**.

If you have a monochrome monitor, it may take eight presses of a button in order for the shades to change. Be patient.

After you have made all of the desired color changes, you have a few additional choices to make. For example, you must decide whether or not you want to keep a permanent file of these colors; if you do want to save the colors, select the save colors option. (Once saved, these colors can be used by starting the program with **pom u.**) If you plan to use these colors one time only, select the quit option. If you want to cancel the changes and revert to the colors that you started the program with, pick the restore initial colors option.

DELETE A FILE. This option can be used to delete (erase) files from your diskette. If you choose this option, a list of your files for the module currently in use will appear, along with a prompt asking you for the name of the file you wish to delete. To erase a file, simply type the file name. This option should be used if you have trouble saving files because your diskette is full. Obviously, an option that erases files should be used with great care.

PRINT TO DISK FILE OR PRINTER TOGGLE SWITCH. It is possible to send the output to a file rather than to the printer. If this option is chosen, the program will request a name for the output file. All output will be sent to the file named until this option is toggled back to the printer. It is possible to use an extension (file.ext) for this file name.

TOGGLE FIX FORMAT ON. For most of the modules, you can fix the number of decimal places displayed on output by setting on the toggle for fixed number of places. This option must be used with care. (We demonstrate this option later in this section.)

ERROR BEEPS/SOUND OFF. Use this toggle to turn off or on the beep that alerts you when an error has occurred.

FUNCTION KEY DISPLAY OFF/ON. Use this toggle to turn off or on the function key display or the last row of the data screen. The function keys will work even when they are not displayed.

Exit (F6)

The last option on the submenu screen is the exit option. This is the option to choose when you have completed all of your work. The exit option will return control to DOS. If you wish to return to AB:POM from DOS after selecting this option, you must restart the system in the usual manner—by typing **pom** with any desired options.

(*Note:* If DOS is not on your diskette, the computer will issue a message stating that COMMAND.COM is missing. If you wish to continue working, you must insert a DOS diskette; otherwise, you can simply turn off the machine.)

ENTERING AND EDITING DATA

Character Data and Numerical Data

When entering names and numbers, simply type the name or number and then press one of the direction keys, the enter key, or a function key. If you make a mistake while editing, there are two other direction keys to consider: **Back Space** and **Del**, both of which will delete the last character typed.

A beep indicates that you have typed an illegal key while entering data. One of the following messages will appear.

- Typing a character when a number is required.
- Trying to enter a number larger than permitted.
- Trying to enter a name longer than permitted.
- Trying to enter more digits after the decimal than permitted.
- Trying to enter a character that is not permitted for this entry.

(*Note:* The format of numerical displays is handled by the program. Furthermore, any number less than .00001 is displayed as 0.)

Toggle Entries

As mentioned previously, you will not always be entering data. Some entries are toggled—that is, the allowable entries have been preset. For example, in assembly-line balancing, the time unit can be toggled. You can change seconds to minutes to hours and back to seconds again by moving the cursor to the top of the cell of the column with zeroes and pressing the space bar three times. The time unit will change each time the space bar is pressed. So, when the desired unit appears, simply go on to the next cell. Alternatively, you can call up a menu of all available options by pressing the **Enter** key.

While you are editing the data, the function keys shown on the bottom row of the data screen are available. Program E.2 tells what each function key does. Notice that function keys **F1** through **F6** correspond exactly to the menu options from the submenu. We now explain the four options we have not discussed.

Save **(F7)**: This option is similar to the load a data file option. When you choose this option, a screen will appear with the names of your data files, and you will be asked for the name under which to save the data.

If you give the file the name of an existing file, you will be warned about replacing the existing file. The existing file will be replaced by the more recent one if you press **y** (or **Y**) or **Return**. After entering the name, press **Return** to save the data. As before, it is possible to change the drive by using the **F1** key option. It also is possible to use the shell option in the set utilities option from the data screen to change the drive or the directory.

Titl **(F8)**: When you press **F8**, the top line of the data requests that you enter a new title. You will be permitted to enter a title up to 37 characters in length. The title is entered in the usual manner, and will appear at the top of the data after **Return**, a direction key, or a function key is pressed.

Prnt **(F9)**: This option will print the contents of the data or solution screen. The bottom lines and the outside box will not be printed. (It is possible to have everything printed character for character; use **Shift-PrtScn**.) The program prints to the LPT1 file, the standard printer file. If your printer is not attached to LPT1 (if, for example, you have a serial printer), you need to use the DOS MODE statement to redirect the output to the appropriate place; see your DOS manual for instructions. In one or two cases (most notably, linear programming and MRP), the output will not be exactly as it appears on the screen. Changes have been made to fit more than one screen's worth of data onto the printer.

If you have used the utility option, you can print to a file. Later, you can use a word processor to edit this file. In most cases, one of two things will happen if you press **F9** and your computer is not attached to a printer or your printer is not turned on: Either you will get an error message or the program will think that it is printing when it is not—which is harmless. It is also possible that the printer will keep trying to print every 30 seconds or so. You can stop this by pressing the **Esc** key.

Run **(F10)**: After you have entered all of the data, you can press **F10** to solve the problem. Answers will appear either in addition to the data or in place of the data. In either case, the function key bar at the bottom of the screen will change. In all modules, **F9** will be available to print the solution. In some modules, additional function keys for displaying more information will be defined. These definitions will appear in the chapters for those modules. After viewing or printing the solution, press any key to return to the data screen.

Formats for Data

All of the formats for the data are determined by the program. In general, the maximum value that can be input for a number is determined by the width of the field in which the number appears. For example, the largest possible number in a field with six spaces is 999,999. The field width also determines the number of places after the decimal. In most cases, this will not pose a problem. However, there will be occasions when the number of places after the decimal varies within a column, even though the screen would appear orderly if there were no variations.

There is a trade-off involved in the use of this option: In order to have neat columns, we must express the data in round numbers. In many cases, rounding poses no problem, but we advise you to use the **format** option with great care.

GETTING STARTED

Regardless of the configuration of your system, you should begin by making a backup copy of AB:POM. Because AB:POM is not copy-protected, it is very easy to copy with the DOS **copy *.*** or **diskcopy** command.

Normal Startup from a Disk Drive

In order to run AB:POM, simply follow the procedure below. The description that follows assumes that you have a standard disk drive system and are not using a hard drive.

1. Insert a DOS diskette into drive a: (usually the top drive or the left drive).
2. Turn on the computer.
3. When the A> prompt appears on the screen, insert the AB:POM diskette into drive a:.
4. Type **pom** with any options (described in the following section).

If you have trouble starting, try typing **go** (with any options) rather than **pom**.

(*Note:* If you use a version of DOS less than DOS 3.00, a prompt will appear after you have typed **pom**. The machine will ask you to input the run-time module path. In order to run the system, you must type a backslash (\ ) or the drive name in which AB:POM is running (usually drive a:). When AB:POM is in drive a:, the proper response to the prompt is to type **a:** followed by **Return** or **Enter**. Notice that the third character is a backslash, not a slash. On some machines, the backslash is not required. Alternately, it is possible to begin the program by typing **path = ** prior to typing **pom**. The file GO.BAT will do this for you.)

Normal Startup from a Hard Drive

If you have a hard drive then the best way to run the system is to create a directory for AB:POM and run it from there. If a path is set it is possible to run AB:POM from any directory. To set the system up, perform the following steps:

1. From the C> prompt type **MD ABPOM**
2. Type **CD ABPOM**
3. Insert the 3.5″ AB:POM diskette into drive A: and type **COPY A:*.* C:**

Henceforth to use the AB:POM system

1. Boot the computer
2. Type **CD \ABPOM**
3. Type **POM** with any options

There is a file on the 3.5″ diskette named INSTALL that will perform the above steps. If you type INSTALL at the A:> prompt or type A:INSTALL at the C:> prompt with AB:POM in the A: drive then install will perform the steps above and create a directory named ABPOM on your C: drive and then copy all of the files from the AB:POM diskette to your drive.

Startup Options

The program starts with the command POM (or GO). The following options can be added.

DISK DRIVE FOR DATA.   The letters a, b, c, d, and e can be used to specify which drive contains the data. (This can be changed from within the program also.) There is enough room on the program disk to store all your data files, if you so desire.

EXAMPLE

> POM B will indicate to the program that the data files can be found on drive b:. The default drive is the drive from which AB:POM was started.

COLOR/MONITOR OPTIONS.   The letter **m** can be used to indicate that the monitor is a monochrome (single-color monitor). The number 1 can be used to indicate that the monitor is a color monitor, colors should be used, and the background color should be black. The number 2 indicates a color monitor and a background color that allows shadowing. The letter **u** indicates that a user file of colors called COLOR.POM should be used. (This file can be created and/or changed from the utility menu within AB:POM.) If you do not choose a color option at the command line, the program will ask you for one.

EXAMPLES

> POM M or POM m will use a monochrome monitor.
> POM 1 will use default colors that include a black background.
> POM 2 will use default colors that include a blue background and a shadowing effect.
> POM U will look for the file COLOR.POM and use those colors.

NUMBER OF LINES ON THE SCREEN.   The usual number of lines is 25 and this is the nicest display. However, if you use option H (high resolution), then 43 lines will be used (if your monitor allows this), and if you use option V (for VGA), then 50 lines will be used if your monitor allows this.

SOUND TOGGLE.   If you start the program with the letter S, then the beeps made when errors occur will be silenced. This can be changed from within the program, using the utility option.

COMBINING OPTIONS.   Options can be combined.

EXAMPLE

> POM smb
> will turn off beeps, display everything in black/white and look for data on drive b:.

FORMATTING PROCEDURES.   POM F will change the formatting procedure of AB:POM. Typically, AB:POM allows nine spaces for numbers and decimal points. If this option is chosen, the number of places after the decimal is fixed. This makes for a neater display, but it can lead to roundoff problems. As explained in the earlier section on formatting, this option should be used with great care.

SOLUTIONS TO
EVEN-NUMBERED PROBLEMS

Chapter 1

1.2 (a) 20 ornaments/hour.
(b) 26.7 ornaments/hour.
(c) 33.5%.

1.4

	LAST YEAR	THIS YEAR	% CHANGE
Labor	4.29	4.62	$\dfrac{.33}{4.29} = 7.7$
Capital	.10	.08	$\dfrac{-.02}{.1} = -20$
Energy	.50	.55	$\dfrac{.05}{.50} = 10$

Productivity of capital did drop, labor productivity increased as did energy (but only 10%, not 15%).

1.6 The business cycle impacts this number substantially, but for the economy as a whole probably less than 2%.

Chapter 2

2.2 (a) For a producer with high energy costs, major oil prices change the cost structure, result in higher selling prices, and, if the company is energy-inefficient compared to other producers, result in a change in competitive position.

Chapter 2 Supplement

S2.2 Major expansion; EMV = $250,000.
S2.4 8 cases.
S2.6 (a)

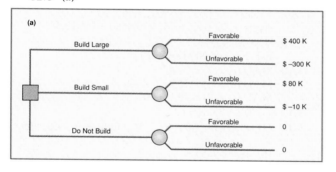

(b) Small plant with EMV = $26,000.
(c) EVPI = $134,000.
S2.8 (a) Max EMV = $11,700.
(b) EVPI = $13,200 − $11,700 = $1,500.

S2.10

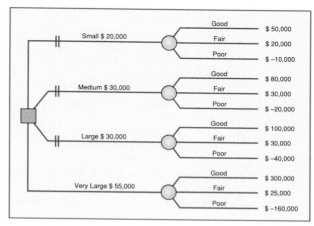

S2.12

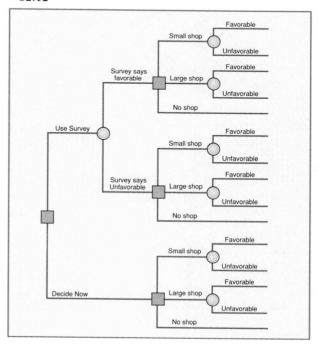

S2.14 No information and build large; $4,500.
S2.16 $12,000,000.

Chapter 3

3.2 Individual answer.

3.4 **(a)** 8′   ↓   move to trunk
                     ○   open trunk
                     ○   loosen tire and jack
                     ○   remove tire and jack
            8′   ↓   move the tire and jack to wheel
                     ○   position jack
                     □   inspect
                     ○   loosen wheel lugs
                     ○   jack-up car
                     ○   remove wheel lugs
                     ○   remove wheel
                     ○   position good wheel
                     ○   tighten lugs
                     ○   lower car
                     ○   finish tightening lugs
                     □   inspect
            8′   ↓   move tire and jack to trunk
                     ○   position tire and jack
                     ○   close trunk
            8′   ↓   move to driver's seat

3.6

Factors   Concern

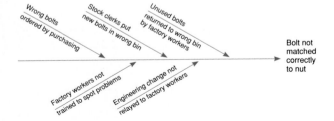

Bolt not matched correctly to nut

Chapter 4

4.2 $UCL_{\bar{x}} = 52.308$
$LCL_{\bar{x}} = 47.692$
$UCL_R = 8.456$
$LCL_R = 0.0$

4.4 $UCL_{\bar{x}} = 46.966$
$LCL_{\bar{x}} = 45.034$
$UCL_R = 4.008$
$LCL_R = 0$

4.6 $UCL_{\bar{x}} = 17.187$
$LCL_{\bar{x}} = 16.814$
$UCL_R = .932$
$LCL_R = .068$

4.8 $UCL_{\bar{x}} = 3.728$
$LCL_{\bar{x}} = 2.336$
$UCL_R = 2.29$
$LCL_R = 0.0$
The process is in control.

4.10 $UCL_p = .0596$
$LCL_p = .0104$

4.12 $UCL_p = .0311$ to $.1636$
$LCL_p = 0.0$ to $.0364$

4.14 $UCL_{\bar{x}} = 64.54$
$LCL_{\bar{x}} = 62.36$
$UCL_R = 3.423$
$LCL_R = 0$

4.16 $UCL_p = .0581$
$LCL_p = 0$

4.18 $UCL_c = 33.4$
$LCL_c = 7$

4.20

Fraction Defective	$P(x \leq 1)$
.01	.999
.10	.910
.20	.736
.40	.406
.60	.199
.80	.092
1.0	.040

4.22 The plan meets neither the products nor the consumers' requirement.

4.24 $UCL_{\bar{x}} = 61.13$
$LCL_{\bar{x}} = 38.42$
$UCL_R = 41.62$
$LCL_R = 0.0$
The process appears to be in control.

Chapter 4 Supplement

S4.2 5.45, 4.05.

S4.4 **(a)** .2743.
      (b) .5.

S4.6 **(a)** .1587.
      (b) .2347.
      (c) .1587.

S4.8 **(a)** .0548.
      (b) .6554.
      (c) .6554.
      (d) .2119.

Chapter 5

5.2 18.67, 16.67, 14, 14.33, 15.33, 17, 18.33, 19.33, 20.33, 21.33.

5.4 **(a)** 337;   **(b)** 380;   **(c)** 423.

5.6 2 year: 5, 5, 4.5, 7.5, 9.0, 7.5, 8.0, 10.5, 13.0.
4 year: 4.75, 6.25, 6.75, 7.50, 8.50, 9.00, 10.50.

5.8 Wtd. M.A. MAD = 2,312.
Exp. Smooth MAD = 2,581.

5.10 MAD $(\alpha = .3) = 74.6$.
MAD $(\alpha = .6) = 51.8$.
MAD $(\alpha = .9) = 38.1$ (best).

5.12 $y = 522 + 33.6x = 623$.

5.14 **(a)** 43.4, 47.4, 50.2, 53.7, 56.3 for $\alpha = .6$; 44.6, 49.5, 51.8, 55.6, 57.8 for $\alpha = .9$.
      (b) 49, 52.7, 55.3.
      (c) 45.8, 49.0, 52.2, 55.4, 58.6, 61.8.
      (d) Trend with MAD = .6.

5.16 5, 5.4, 6.12, 5.90, 6.52, 7.82.

5.18 MAD = 3.98; β = .8 is better than β = .2.

5.20 $y = 5.26 + 1.11x$.
Period 7 demand = 13.03.

5.22 (a) Moving average forecast for February is 13.6667.
(b) Weighted moving average forecast for February is 13.16.
(c) MAD for Avg is 2.2.
MAD for Weighted Avg is 2.7.
(d) seasonality, causal variables such as advertising budget.

5.24 (a) $\hat{y} = 1 + 1x$; $r = .45$.
(b) $S_{yx} = 3.65$.

5.26 $y = .972 + .0035 x$; $r^2 = 0.479$; $x = 350$; $y = 2.197$; $x = 800$; $y = 3.77$.

5.28 131.2 → 72.7 patients; 90.6 → 50.6 patients.

5.30 Fall = 270; Winter = 390; Spring = 189; Summer = 351.

5.32 (a) 1785.
(b) 1560.

5.34 (a) 17.00; 17.80; 18.04; 19.03; 18.83; 18.26; 18.61; 18.49; 19.19; 19.35; 18.48.
(b) 2.60.
(c) No, tracking signal exceeds 5 sigma at week 10.

5.36 (a, b)

WEEK	$\alpha = .1$ FORECAST	$\alpha = .6$ FORECAST
25	46.9	57.6

(c) On the basis of forecast and standard error of estimate, $\alpha = .6$ is better. But other α's should be tried.

5.38 Each answer will differ, but note the presence of both seasonal and trend factors.

5.40 150,000; 126,000; 120,000; and 207,000 for the four respective quarters.

Chapter 6

6.2 Assembly chart for a ballpoint pen.

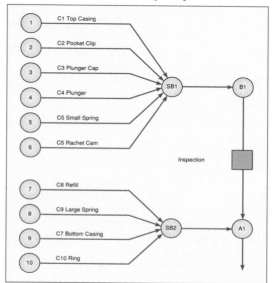

6.4

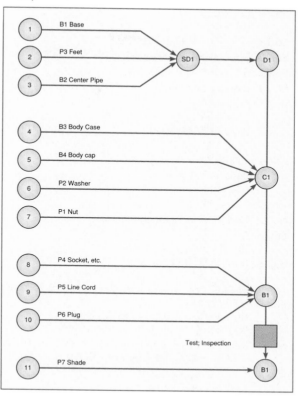

6.6 The lap top computer has contributed 30%, but sales are substantial, yielding 50% of the total contribution; conversely, the hand calculator has a high individual contribution, but only contributes 10% to the company's total contribution.

6.8 EMV of Proceed = $49,500,000.
EMV of Do Value Analysis = $55,025,000.
Therefore, Do Value Analysis.

6.10 EMV of Design A = $875,000.
EMV of Design B = $700,000.

Chapter 6 Supplement

S6.2 100 = profit at $x = 0$, $y = 10$.

S6.4 (a) $P = \$3,000$ at $x_1 = 75$, $x_2 = 75$ or $x_1 = 50$, $x_2 = 150$.
(b) Two solutions generate the same profit.

S6.6 (a) Minimize $x_1 + 2x_2$
$$x_1 + x_2 \geqslant 40$$
$$2x_1 + 4x_2 \geqslant 60$$
$$x_1 \leqslant 15$$
(b) Cost = 65¢ at $x_1 = 15$, $x_2 = 25$.
(c) 65¢.

S6.8 $x_1 = 200$, $x_2 = 0$, $P = \$18,000$.

S6.10 10 Alphas, 24 Betas, $P = \$55,200$.

S6.12 (a) $x_1 = 25.71$, $x_2 = 21.43$.
(b) Cost = $68.57.

S6.14 Objective function, first and fifth constraints.

S6.16 (a) 26¢.
    (b) $7.86.

S6.18 $x_1 = 60$, $x_2 = 90$, $P = \$3,930$.

S6.20 7,500 round, 5,000 square, cost = $115,000.

S6.22 (e) $x_1 = 8$, $x_2 = 4$, $P = \$60$.

S6.24 Basis for 1st tableau:
$$A_1 = 80$$
$$A_2 = 75$$
Basis for 2nd tableau:
$$A_1 = 55$$
$$x_1 = 25$$
Basis for 3rd tableau:
$$x_1 = 14$$
$$x_2 = 33$$
Cost = 221 at optimal solution.

S6.26 (a) x_1.
    (b) A_1.

S6.28 (a) $22.50–$30.00.
    (b) $5.00.
    Shadow price holds within the range 210–280 hours.

S6.30 (a) $5.00–∞.
    (b) –$5.00 is valid from 5,000–∞ hours.
    (c) –$3.00 is valid from 0–20,000 tables.

S6.32 Minimize $6X1A + 5X1B + 3X1C + 8X2A + 10X2B + 8X2C + 11X3A + 14X3B + 18X3C$

Subject to:
$$X1A + X2A + X3A = 7$$
$$X1B + X2B + X3B = 12$$
$$X1C + X2C + X3C = 5$$
$$X1A + X1B + X1C \leq 6$$
$$X2A + X2B + X2C \leq 8$$
$$X3A + X3B + X3C \leq 10$$

S6.34 61 medical beds, 29 surgical beds, annual profit = $9,551,668.

Chapter 7

7.2 (a) 4,590 in excess capacity.
    (b) 2,090 in excess capacity.

7.4 Design   = 81,806.
    Fabrication = 152,646.
    Finishing   = 62,899.

7.6 (a) $BEP_\$ = \$125,000$.
    (b) $BEP_\$ = \$140,000$.

7.8 (a) Proposal A is best; $a = \$18,000$; $b = \$15,000$.
    (b) Proposal B is best; $a = \$70,000$; $b = \$80,000$.

7.10 NPV = $19,800.

7.12 NPV = $1,764.

7.14 Present equipment = $1,000.
    New equipment = 0.

7.16 (a) $100,000.
    (b) 12,500 units.
    (c) $350,000.

7.18 (a) Purchase two large ovens.
    (b) Equal quality, equal capacity.

    (c) Payments are made at end of each time period. And future interest rates are known.

7.20 BEP(x) = 25,000.

7.22 BEP($) = $7,584.83.
    Daily meals = 9.

7.24 Payoff from small line equal $200,000; payoff from large line equals $133,000.

7.26 NPV for investment 1 = $17,127.
    NPV for investment 2 = $25,532.
    NPV for investment 3 = $18,962.

Chapter 8

8.2 GPE is best below 100,000; FMS is best between 100,000 and 300,000; DA is best above 300,000.

8.4 The optimum process will change with each additional 100,000 units.

Chapter 9

9.2 (b) Denver, 0–3570 units; Burlington, 3,571–24,999 units; Cleveland, more than 25,000 units.
    (c) Burlington.

9.4 Suburb B, rating = 6.35 but all are close.

9.6 Shopping is mall best.

9.8 Hyde Park with 54.5 points.

9.10 (a) Lyon, 3970; Bonn, 3915; The Hague, 3920.
    (b) Lyon, 3730; Berlin, 3585; The Hague, 3840.
    (c) Berlin, 3840; The Hague, 3840; Bonn, 3810.

Chapter 9 Supplement

S9.2 (a) A-1, 10; B-1, 30; C-2, 60; A-3, 40; C-3, 15.
    (b) $1,775.

S9.4 Houston, $19,500.

S9.6 Solution is optimal.

S9.8 (a) Initial solution is degenerate.
    (b) Cost = $2,750.

S9.10 W-A, 200; X-B, 100; X-C, 75; Y-C, 75; Dummy-A, 50.

S9.12 Fountainbleau is $1,530,000 vs. Dublin at a higher cost of $1,535,000.

S9.14 East St. Louis with a cost of $17,400 is higher than St. Louis with a cost of $17,250.

S9.16 A-1, 9; B-3, 8; C-1, 3; C-3, 7; D-1, 7; and D-2, 24.

Chapter 10

10.2 Yes, with AB:POM patient movement = 4,500 feet.

10.4 Layout #1, 600 = distance.
    Layout #2, 602 = distance.

10.6 Layout #4, 609 = distance.
    Layout #5, 372 = distance.

10.8 (a) Throughput of 3.75 people/hour possible.
    (b) Medical exam—16 minutes.
    (c) At least 5 per hour now.

10.10 Cycle time = 9.6 minutes; eight workstations with 63.8% efficiency is possible.

10.12 Station #1, tasks 1, 3; #2, task 5; #3, tasks 2, 4; #4, tasks 6, 8; #5, tasks 7, 9. Efficiency = 78%.

10.14 Cycle time = .5 minute/bottle. Possible assignments with four workstations yields efficiency = 90%.

10.16 Minimum (theoretical) = four stations. Efficiency = 80% with five stations. Several assignments with five are possible.

10.18 There are three alternatives each with an efficiency = 86.67%.

Chapter 10 Supplement

S10.2 (a) .5.
(b) .5.
(c) 1.
(d) .5.
(e) .05 hr.
(f) .1 hr.

S10.4 (a) .667.
(b) .667 min.
(c) 1.33.

S10.6 (a) .375.
(b) 1.6 hr.
(c) .225.

S10.8 (a) 2.25.
(b) .75.
(c) .857 min.
(d) .64 min.
(e) 42%, 32%, 24%.

S10.10 (a) 6 trucks.
(b) 12 min.
(c) .857.
(d) 54%.
(e) $1,728/day.
(f) Yes, save $3,096.

S10.12 (a) .666.
(b) 1.33.
(c) 10 sec.

S10.14 3, 2, 4 MDs, respectively.

S10.16 (a) .05.
(b) .743.
(c) .795.

Chapter 11

11.2

Time	Operator	Time	Machine	Time
	Prepare Mill			
1	Load Mill	1	Idle	1
2		2		2
3	Idle	3	Mill Operating (Cutting Material)	3
4		4		4
5	Unload Mill	5	Idle	5
6		6		6

11.4 The first 10 steps are shown below. The remaining 10 steps are similar.

OPERATIONS CHART		SUMMARY							
PROCESS: CHANGE ERASER		SYMBOL			PRESENT		DIFF.		
ANALYST:				LH	RH	LH	RH	LH	RH
DATE:		○ OPERATIONS		1	8				
SHEET: 1 of 2		⇨ TRANSPORTS		3	8				
METHOD: PRESENT PROPOSED		☐ INSPECTIONS		1					
REMARKS:		D DELAYS		15	4				
		▽ STORAGE							
		TOTALS		20	20				

LEFT HAND	DIST.	SYMBOL	SYMBOL	DIST.	RIGHT HAND
1 Reach for pencil		⇨	D		Idle
2 Grasp pencil		○	D		Idle
3 Move to work area		⇨	⇨		Move to pencil top
4 Hold pencil		D	○		Grasp pencil top
5 Hold pencil		D	○		Remove pencil top
6 Hold pencil		D	⇨		Set top aside
7 Hold pencil		D	⇨		Reach for old eraser
8 Hold pencil		D	○		Grasp old eraser
9 Hold pencil		D	○		Remove old eraser
10 Hold pencil		D	⇨		Set aside old eraser

11.6 Individual solution.

11.8 The answer is similar to Solved Problem 11.1, but crew activities C and D become the limiting activities.

Chapter 11 Supplement

S11.2 Sample size of 166 is required.

S11.4 Six observations are required.

S11.6 Normal time = 5.565 min.
Allowance = 10%.
Std. time = 6.183.

S11.8 29.8 min.

S11.10 5.4 or 6.67 depending upon the observation deleted.

S11.12 82.35 seconds, 106 samples.

S11.14 (a) 47.55 min.
(b) 60 observations are required for element 4.

S11.16 336.

S11.18 .1092 min, or 6.55 sec.

Chapter 12

12.2 WARS costs increase by the amount of Tarleton's research.

12.4 Donna Inc.: 47.04.
Kay Corp.: 54.15.

Chapter 12 Supplement

S12.2 (a) 14.31 hr.
(b) $71,550.
(c) $947,250.

S12.4 (a) 80%.
(b) 3.51.
(c) 3.2, 2.98, 2.81.
(d) 21.5.

S12.6 (a) 72.2 hr.
(b) 60.55 hr.
(c) 41.47 hr.

S12.8 $748,240 for fourth, $709,960 for fifth, and $679,942 for sixth.

S12.10 **(a)** 70 millicents/bit.
(b) 8.2 millicents/bit.

S12.12 26,755 hr.

S12.14 **(a)** 32.98 hr, 49.61 hr.
(b) Initial quote is high.

Chapter 13

13.2 A item is G2. B item is F3. All others = C.

13.4 7000.

13.6 **(a)** 78.
(b) 250.
(c) $3,873.08.
(d) 64.
(e) 3.125 days.

13.8 Qty discount cost = $41,436.25.

13.10 Total cost = total ordering cost + total holding cost.
Q = 25   TC = 1500
Q = 40   TC = 1230
Q = 50   TC = 1200
Q = 60   TC = 1220
Q = 100   TC = 1500
Small variations in order quantity will not have a significant impact on total cost.

13.12 **(a)** TSC + THC = $1220.
(b) If we order EOQ = 60 units TSC + THC = $1200.
(c) ROP = 24 units.

13.14 1217 units.

13.16 51 units, $1,901.22.

13.18 TC = 753 @ 34 units.

13.20 Stock for demand = 3.

13.22 2809 units.

13.24 100 units of safety stock.

Chapter 13 Supplement

S13.2 0, 0, 0, 0, 0, 0, 0, 2, 0, 2.

S13.4 Profits = 20, −15, 20, 17.50, 20; average equals 12.50.

S13.6 Simulations will differ, depending on random numbers selected.

S13.8

Arrivals	Arrival Time	Service Time	Departure Time
1	11:01	3	11:04
2	11:04	2	11:06
3	11:06	2	11:08
4	11:07	1	11:09

S13.10 **(a, b)**

No. Cars	Prob.	Cum. Prob.	R.N. Interval
3 or less	0	0	—
4	.10	.10	01–10
5	.15	.25	11–25
6	.25	.50	26–50
7	.30	.80	51–80
8	.20	1.00	81–00
9 or more	0	—	—

(c) Average no. arrivals/hour = 105/15 = 7 cars.

S13.12 Each simulation will differ. Using random numbers from right-hand column of the random number table, reading top to bottom, in the order used, results in a $9.20 cost. This is greater than the $6.65 in Example S3.

S13.14 **(a)** 5 times.
(b) 6.95 times, yes.
(c) 7.16 heaters.

S13.16 Average demand is about 8.75, average lead time is 1.86, average end inventory = 6.50, average lost sales = 4.04.

S13.18 Average end inventory = 8.90; average lost sales = 3.41; total cost = $488,568 or $20,357/month. This new policy seems preferable.

S13.20 Here are the random-number intervals for the first two departments.

From	To	R.N. Interval
Initial exam	X-ray	01–45
	OR	46–60
	Observ.	61–70
	Out	71–00

From	To	R.N. Interval
X-ray	OR	01–10
	Cast	11–35
	Observ.	36–70
	Out	71–00

Each simulation will produce different results. Some will indeed show a person entering X-ray twice.

Chapter 14

14.2 **(a)**

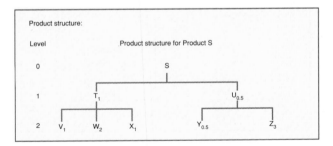

Product structure:

Level — Product structure for Product S

0 — S

1 — T_1 $U_{0.5}$

2 — V_1 W_2 X_1 $Y_{0.5}$ Z_3

Gross material requirements plan:

ITEM		WEEK								LEAD TIME (WKS)
		1	2	3	4	5	6	7	8	
S	Required date							100		
	Order release					100				2
T	Required date						100			
	Order release				100					1
U	Required date						50			
	Order release				50					2
V	Required date						100			
	Order release			100						2
W	Required date					200				
	Order release	200								3
X	Required date					100				
	Order release			100						1
Y	Required date				25					
	Order release	25								2
Z	Required date					150				
	Order release			150						1

(b) Net material requirements plan (only items S and T are shown):

ITEM		WEEK								LEAD TIME (WKS)
		1	2	3	4	5	6	7	8	
S	Gross required							100		
	On hand							20		
	Net required							80		2
	Order receipt							80		
	Order release					80				
T	Gross required						80			
	On hand						20			
	Net required						60			1
	Order receipt						60			
	Order release					60				

14.4 (a) Gross material requirements plan:

		WEEK											
		1	2	3	4	5	6	7	8	9	10	11	12
X_1	Required date								50		20		100
	Order release							50		20		100	
B_1	Required date								50		20		100
	Order release						50		20		100		
B_2	Required date							100		40		200	
	Order release						100		40		200		
A_1	Required date							50		20		100	
	Order release					50		20		100			
D	Required date						200		80		400		
	Order release					200		160		400			
E	Required date						100		40		200		
	Order release					100		40		200			
C	Required date					200	50	80	20	500			
	Order release	200	50	80	20	500							

(b) Net material requirements (planned order release) plan:

		WEEK											
		1	2	3	4	5	6	7	8	9	10	11	12
X_1	Required date										20		100
	Order release									20		100	
B_1	Required date												100
	Order release								100				
B_2	Required date										20		200
	Order release							20		200			
A_1	Required date									95			
	Order release							95					
D	Required date								40		400		
	Order release						40		400				
E	Required date								20		200		
	Order release						20		200				
C	Required date							30		400	100		
	Order release			30		400	100						

14.6 Net material requirements plan (only items A and H are shown):

		WEEK											
		1	2	3	4	5	6	7	8	9	10	11	12
A	Gross required								100		50		150
	On hand								0		0		0
	Net required								100		50		150
	Order receipt								100		50		150
	Order release							100		50		150	
H	Gross required								100		50		
	On hand								0		0		
	Net required								100		50		
	Order receipt								100		50		
	Order release							100		50			

14.8 **(a)** EOQ = 57.4 units.
Theoretical total cost: $1,723.42.
Actual total cost: $2,362.50.
(b) EOQ = 57.4 units.
Theoretical total cost: $1,723.42.
Actual total cost: $1,810.00.

14.10 **(a)** EOQ   = $1,992.50.
(b) Lot-for-lot = $400.
(c) PPB cost   = $220.

14.12 New master production schedule:

		WEEK									
		0	1	2	3	4	5	6	7	8	9	10
P	Gross required	0	0	30	40	10	70	40	10	30	60

Gross material requirements plan:

		WEEK									
		0	1	2	3	4	5	6	7	8	9	10
P	Required date				30	40	10	70	40	10	30	60
	Order release			30	40	10	70	40	10	30	60	
C	Required date				30	40	10	70	40	10	30	60
	Order release		80			120			90			

Net material requirements plan:

		WEEK									
		0	1	2	3	4	5	6	7	8	9	10
P	Gross required	0	0	0	30	40	10	70	40	10	30	60
	On hand	20	20	20	20	0	0	0	0	0	0	0
	Net required				10	40	10	70	40	10	30	60
	Order receipt				10	40	10	70	40	10	30	60
	Order release			10	40	10	70	40	10	30	60	
C	Gross required			10	40	10	70	40	10	30	60	
	On hand	30	30	30	20			0			0	
	Net required	0	0	0	100			80			60	
	Order receipt				100			80			60	
	Order release			100			80			60		

14.14 The limit of 75 components per week constrains component production in weeks 4 and 7. Some production will need to be moved to weeks 2 and 5.

14.16 **(a)** Ten units are required for production, and ten for field service repair.

(b)

COMPONENTS	QUANTITY
A	20
B	20
C	40
D	20
E	40
F	20
G	20
H	20

COMPONENTS	QUANTITY
A	20
B	18
C	18
D	13
E	30
F	15
G	14
H	10

(c) Not shown here.

14.18 **(a)**

REQUIREMENTS

	1	2	3	4	5	6	7	8	9	10	11	12
E.C.W.			40	100	80	70	20	25	70	80	30	50
W.C.W.		20	45	60	70	40	80	70	80	55		
F.W.			30	40	10	70	40	10	30	60		

REQUIREMENTS OFFSET FOR LEAD TIMES

	0	1	2	3	4	5	6	7	8	9	10	11	12
E.C.W.		40	100	80	70	20	25	70	80	30	50		
W.C.W.	20	45	60	70	40	80	70	80	55				
F.W.			30	40	10	70	40	10	30	60			

RECEIPTS FROM FACTORY AT FACTORY WAREHOUSE

	0	1	2	3	4	5	6	7	8	9	10	11	12
Gross required	20	85	190	190	120	170	135	160	165	90	50		
On hand		80	95	5	15	95	25	90	30	65	75	25	
Planned receipt from Factory	100	100	100	200	200	100	200	100	200	100			

(b) Release all orders 2 weeks prior to the schedule above (the planned "Receipts from Factory" date).

If the schedule is late, as suggested above, then the initial order for receipt in week 3 should be for all requirements needed prior to that (i.e., weeks 0, 1, 2, and 3, for a total of 500 units). The release schedule would then be

	WEEK						
	1	2	3	4	5	6	7
Planned order release	500	200	100	200	100	200	100

Chapter 15

15.2 Cost = $68,200.
No, plan 2 is better.

15.4 Cost = $214,000 for plan B.

15.6 Plan D; $122,000.

15.8 Each answer you develop will differ.

15.10 Plan C, $92,000; Plan D, $82,300 assuming initial inventory = 0.

15.12 $11,790.

15.14 $1,186,810.

15.16 $100,750.

15.18 $88,150.

Chapter 16

16.2 **(a)** 1-D, 2-A, 3-C, 4-B.
   (b) 40.

16.4

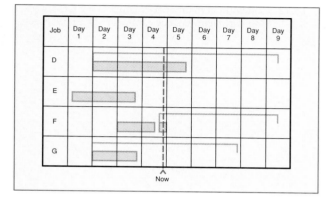

16.6 A-61 to 4; A-60 to 1; A-53 to 3; A-56 to 5; A-52 to 2; A-59 to 6; 150 hr.

16.8 1–2 P.M. on A; 2–3 P.M. on C; 3–4 P.M. on B; 4–5 P.M. on Independent; 75.5 rating.

16.10 **(a)** ABCDE.
   (b) BADEC.
   (c) EDABC.
   (d) CBADE.
   SPT is best.

16.12 DCAB sequence for critical ratio.

16.14 **(a)** A, B, C, D, E.
   (b) C, A, B, E, D.
   (c) C, D, E, A, B.
   (d) B, A, E, D, C.
   EDD is best on tardiness, SPT on other 2 measures.

16.16 D, B, A, C.

16.18 A, C, D, E, B.

16.20 4, 1, 2, 3, 5; makespan = 56 hr.

Chapter 17

17.2

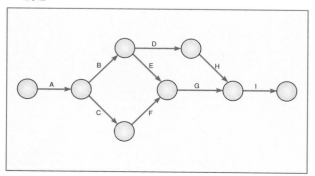

17.4

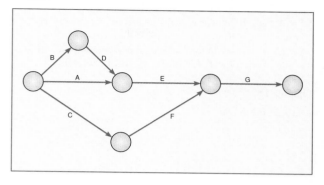

17.6

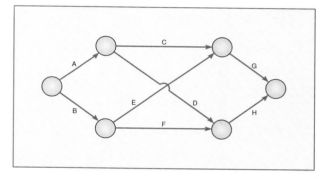

17.8 A, 5.83, 0.69.
   B, 3.67, 0.11.
   C, 2.00, 0.11.
   D, 7.00, 0.11.
   E, 4.00, 0.44.
   F, 10.00, 1.78.
   G, 2.17, 0.25.
   H, 6.00, 1.00.
   I, 11.00, 0.11.
   J, 16.33, 1.00.
   K, 7.33, 1.78.

17.10 .9463

17.12 **(a)** 15 (A, C, E).
   (b) 2.

17.14 **(a)** 16 (A, D, G).
   (b) $12,300.
   (c) D, 1 week for $75.

17.16 A, C, E, H, I, K, M, N; 50 weeks.

17.18 **(a)** .0228.
   (b) .3085.
   (c) .8413.
   (d) .9772.

17.20 **(a, b)** Critical path = A, B, J, K, L, M, R, S, T, U; time = 18.
   (c) Transmissions and drive trains are not on the critical path; halving engine time reduces the

critical path by 2 days; speeding accessory
delivery is not critical.

(d) Reallocating workers can reduce the critical
path length.

17.22 Length = 34 weeks; critical path is composed of
activities 11, 13, 14, 16, 17, 18, 19, 21, and 23.

Chapter 18

18.2 **(a)** 5.0%.

(b) .00001025 failures/unit-hr.

(c) .08979.

(d) 98.77.

18.4 $R_s = .8145$.

18.6 $R_p = .99925$.

18.8 $R_p = .984$.

18.10 $R = .7918$.

18.12 Cost without maintenance contract = \$1,255/week.
Cost with maintenance contract   = \$1,395/week.

GLOSSARY

ABC analysis (p. 575) A method for dividing on-hand inventory into three classifications based on annual dollar volume.

Acceptable quality level (AQL) (p. 124) The quality level of a lot considered good.

Acceptance sampling (p. 121) A method of measuring random samples of lots or batches of products against predetermined standards.

Activity (p. 781) A task or a subproject in a CPM or PERT network that occurs between two events; a flow over time.

Activity charts (p. 493) A way of depicting studies and the resultant suggestions for improvement of utilization of an operator and a machine or some combination of operators (a crew) and machines.

Activity time estimate (p. 784) The time it takes to complete an activity in a PERT or CPM network.

Adaptive smoothing (p. 186) An approach to exponential smoothing forecasting in which the smoothing constant is automatically changed to keep errors to a minimum.

Aggregate planning (p. 692) An approach to determine the quantity and timing of production for the intermediate future (usually 3 to 18 months ahead).

American Production and Inventory Control Society (APICS) (p. 13) A professional organization for production and inventory control personnel.

American Society for Quality Control (p. 14) An association of quality control professionals.

APT or automatically programmed tool (p. 327) A computer program language used to control numerically controlled machines.

Assembly chart (p. 227) A means of identifying the points of production where components flow into subassemblies and ultimately into a final product.

Assembly drawing (p. 227) An exploded view of the product, usually through a three-dimensional or isometric drawing.

Assembly line (p. 419) An approach that puts fabricated parts together at a series of workstations; used in repetitive processes.

Assembly-line balancing (p. 420) Obtaining output at each workstation on the production line so that it is nearly the same.

Assignable variations (p. 111) Variation in a production process that can be traced to specific causes.

Assignment method (p. 735) A special class of linear programming models that involves assigning tasks or jobs to resources.

Association for Systems Management (p. 14) An association for professionals in the systems and procedures occupations.

Attribute inspection (p. 96) An inspection that classifies items as being either good or defective regardless of degree.

Automated guided vehicle (AGV) (p. 329) Electronically guided and controlled carts used to move materials.

Automated storage and retrieval system (ASAR) (p. 328) Computer-controlled warehouses that provide for the automatic placement of parts into and from designated places within the warehouse.

Automatic identification system (AIS) (p. 335) A system for transforming data into electronic form, for example, bar codes.

Average actual cycle time (p. 505) The arithmetic mean of the times for each element measured, adjusted for unusual influences for each element.

Average outgoing quality (AOQ) (p. 127) The percent defective in an average lot of goods inspected through acceptance sampling.

Backward scheduling (p. 729) A job shop scheduling technique in which the last operation on the routing is scheduled first.

Benchmarking (p. 84) Selecting a demonstrated standard of performance that represents the very best performance for a process or activity.

Beta probability distribution (p. 784) A mathematical distribution that may describe the activity time estimate distributions in a PERT network.

Bill of material (BOM) (pp. 221, 652) A listing of the components, their description, and the quantity of each required to make one unit of a product.

Bonus (p. 489) A monetary reward, usually in cash or stock options, given to management or executives in an organization.

Bottleneck (p. 746) An operation that limits output in the production sequence.

Breakdown maintenance (p. 826) Remedial maintenance that occurs when equipment fails and must be repaired on an emergency or priority basis.

Break-even analysis (p. 301) A means of finding the point, in dollars and units, at which costs equal revenues.

Buyer (p. 530) A person in the retail profession responsible for the purchase, sale, and profit margins on merchandise that will be resold, or a person in manufacturing responsible for purchases, usually reporting to a purchasing agent.

Capacity (p. 296) The maximum output of a system in a given period.

c-charts (p. 120) A quality control chart used to control the number of defects per unit of output.

Center-of-gravity method (p. 354) A mathematical technique used for finding the best location for a single distribution point that services several stores or areas.

Central limit theorem (p. 112) The theoretical foundation for $\bar{x}$-charts that states that regardless of the distribution of the population of all parts or services, the distribution of x's will tend to follow a normal curve as the sample size grows large.

Closed-loop MRP system (p. 662) A system that provides feedback to the capacity plan, master production schedule, and production plan.

Coefficient of correlation (p. 182) A number measure, between −1 and +1, of the statistical relationship between variables.

Compact II (p. 327) A computer program language used to control numerically controlled machines.

Competitive advantage (p. 39) The creation of a unique advantage over competitors.

Computer-aided design (CAD) (p. 225) Use of a computer to develop the geometry of a design.

Computer-aided manufacturing (CAM) (p. 326) The use of information technology to control machinery.

Computer-integrated manufacturing (CIM) (p. 330) A manufacturing system in which electronically controlled machines are integrated with robots, transfer machines, or automated guided vehicles to create a complete manufacturing system.

Computer numerical control (CNC) (p. 327) The control of machines via their own computer.

Configuration management (p. 228) A system by which a product's planned and changing components are accurately identified and for which control and accountability of change are maintained.

Consignment (p. 546) An arrangement whereby the supplier maintains title to the inventory.

Constraints (p. 240) Restrictions that limit the degree to which a manager can pursue an objective.

Consumer market survey (p. 161) A forecasting method that solicits input from customers or potential customers regarding their future purchasing plans.

Consumer's risk (p. 125) The mistake of a customer's acceptance of a bad lot overlooked through sampling (a Type II error).

Continuous process (p. 287) A product-oriented, high-volume, low-variety process.

Control chart (p. 110) A graphic presentation of process data over time.

Control files (p. 731) All of the information in an MRP system pertaining to a particular order—the shop order master file and the shop order detail file.

Corner point method (p. 246) A method for solving graphical linear programming problems.

CRAFT (Computer Relative Allocation of Facilities Technique) (p. 411) A computer program that systematically examines alternative departmental rearrangements to reduce total material-handling cost.

Critical path (p. 780) The computed longest time path(s) through a network.

Critical path analysis (p. 785) A network model for finding the shortest possible schedule for a series of activities. It usually employs PERT or CPM.

Critical path method (p. 779) A network technique using only one time factor per activity that enables managers to schedule, monitor, and control large and complex projects.

Critical ratio (CR) (p. 742) A sequencing rule that is an index number computed by dividing the time remaining until the due date by the work time remaining.

Crossover chart (p. 305) A chart depicting more than one process with costs for the possible volumes.

Cumulative probability distribution (p. 621) The accumulation of individual probabilities of a distribution.

Cycle counting (p. 578) A continuing audit of inventory records.

Cycle time (p. 422) The time the product is available at each workstation in assembly-line balancing.

Data Processing Management Association (DPMA) (p. 14) An association for computer programmers, operators, and managers in the electronic data-processing field.

Decision Sciences Institute (p. 14) An association for individuals interested in advances in the use of applied quantitative techniques.

Decision support system (DSS) (p. 335) A logical extension of MIS that helps managers model decision alternatives by allowing "what-if" analysis given certain financial or operating parameters.

Decision table (p. 56) A tabular means of analyzing decision alternatives and states of nature.

Decision tree (p. 60) A graphical means of analyzing decision alternatives and states of nature.

Degeneracy (p. 382) An occurrence in transportation models when there are too few squares or shipping routes being used so that tracing a closed path for each unused square becomes impossible. Degeneracy exists when the number of rows plus the number of columns minus one does not equal the number of occupied cells.

Delphi method (p. 160) A forecasting technique using a group process that allows experts to make forecasts.

Demand forecast (p. 160) A projection of a company's sales for each time period in the planning horizon.

Design for manufacturability and value engineering teams (p. 218) Teams charged with improvement of designs and specifications at the research, development, design, and production stages of product development.

Direct numerical control (DNC) (p. 327) A machine that is directly (hard) wired to a control computer that supplies the electronic instructions and controls.

Disaggregation (p. 708) The process of breaking the aggregate plan into greater detail.

Discrete probability distribution (p. 144) A frequency distribution in which outcomes are not continuous. Outcomes from the roll of a die are discrete, whereas temperatures (which can take on any fractional value) are considered continuous variables.

Distribution resource planning (DRP) (p. 671) A time-phased stock replenishment plan for all levels of a distribution network.

Double sampling (p. 122) A form of inspection that takes a small sample and if the resulting defects fall within a marginal acceptance level, a second sampling may be drawn; cumulative results determine rejection or acceptance of the lot.

Dummy activity (p. 783) An activity having no time, inserted into the network to maintain the logic of the network.

Dummy destinations (p. 381) Artificial destination points created in the transportation method of linear programming when the total supply is greater than the total demand; they serve to equalize the total demand and supply.

Dummy sources (p. 387) Artificial shipping source points created in the transportation method when total demand is greater than total supply in order to effect a supply equal to the excess of demand over supply.

Earliest due date (EDD) (p. 739) A priority scheduling rule that means the earliest due date job is performed next.

Economic forecasts (p. 160) Planning indicators, often provided by forecasting services, valuable in helping organizations prepare medium- to long-range forecasts.

Economic part period (p. 655) That period of time when the ratio of setup cost to holding cost is equal.

Effective capacity or utilization (p. 296) The maximum capacity a firm can expect to achieve given its product mix, methods of scheduling, maintenance, and standards of quality.

Efficiency (p. 296) A measure of actual output over effective capacity.

Electronic data interchange (EDI) (p. 540)   A standardized data transmittal format for computerized communications between organizations.

Employee involvement (p. 82)   Inclusion of employee(s) in every step of the process from product design to final packaging.

Engineering change notice (ECN) (pp. 228, 651)   A correction or modification of an engineering drawing.

Engineering drawing (p. 220)   A drawing that shows the dimensions, tolerances, materials, and finishes of a component.

Equally likely (p. 57)   A criterion for decision making under certainty that assigns equal probability to each state of nature.

Ergonomics (p. 490)   The study of work; in the United States often called *human factor engineering*.

Event (p. 781)   A point in time that marks the start or completion of a task or activity in a network.

Expected monetary value (EMV) (p. 58)   The expected payout or value of a variable that has different possible states of nature, each with an associated probability.

Expected value (p. 145)   A measure of central tendency and the weighted average of the values of the variable.

Expected value of perfect information (EVPI) (p. 59)   The difference between the payoff under certainty and under risk.

Expected value under certainty (p. 60)   The expected or average return.

Expert system (ES) (p. 336, 747)   A computer program that mimics human logic and "solves" problems much as a human expert would.

Exponential smoothing (p. 167)   A weighted moving-average forecasting technique in which data points are weighted by an exponential function.

Fabrication line (p. 419)   A machine-paced, product-oriented facility for building components.

Failure (p. 822)   The change in a product or system from a satisfactory working condition to a condition that is below an acceptable standard.

Finite scheduling (p. 747)   An interactive computer technique that allows schedulers flexibility to handle any situation, including order, labor, or machine changes.

First-come, first-served (FCFS) (p. 739)   A priority job scheduling rule by which the jobs are completed in the order they arrived.

First-in, first-out (FIFO) (p. 448)   A queuing rule by which the first customers in line receive the first service; or in an inventory system, the first inventory received is the first inventory used.

Fish-bone chart (p. 92)   A schematic technique used to discover possible locations of quality problems in manufacturing; also known as an Ishikawa diagram or a cause-and-effect diagram.

Fixed costs (p. 302)   Costs that continue even if no units are produced.

Fixed-period system (p. 601)   A system that triggers inventory ordering on a uniform time frequency.

Fixed-position layout (p. 404)   Addresses the layout requirements of stationary projects or large bulky projects (such as ships or buildings).

Flexible manufacturing system (FMS) (p. 329)   A system using an automated work cell controlled by electronic signals from a common centralized computer facility.

Flexible work week (p. 482)   A work schedule that deviates from the normal or standard five 8-hour days (usually, four 10-hour days).

Flextime (p. 482)   A system that allows employees, within limits, to determine their own work schedules.

Flow diagram (p. 493)   A drawing used to analyze movement of people or material.

Focus forecasting (p. 187)   Forecasting that tries a variety of computer models and selects the best one for the particular application.

Focused factory (p. 414)   A permanent facility to produce a product or component in a product-oriented facility.

Focused work center (p. 414)   A permanent product-oriented arrangement of machines and personnel in what is ordinarily a process-oriented facility.

Forecasting (p. 158)   The art and science of forecasting future events.

Forward scheduling (p. 729)   Assumes that procurement of material and operations start as soon as the requirements are known.

Fuzzy logic (p. 337) A concept that deals with ambiguous and approximate information to make decisions.

Gain sharing (p. 489) A system of financial rewards to employees for improvements made in an organization's performance.

Gantt charts (p. 733, 776) Planning charts used to schedule resources and allocate time; developed by Henry L. Gantt in the late 1800s.

Graphical/charting methods (p. 698) An aggregate planning technique that works with a few variables at a time to allow planners to compare projected capacity with existing capacity.

Gross material requirements plan (p. 656) A schedule that shows the total demand for an item (prior to subtraction of on-hand inventory and scheduled receipts) and when it must be ordered from suppliers or production must be started in order to meet its demand by a particular date.

Group technology (p. 224) A system that requires that components be identified by a coding system that specifies the type of processing and the parameters of the processing; it allows similar products to be processed together.

Historical experience (p. 504) Estimating the time required to do a task based on the last time it was required.

Holding cost (p. 583) The cost to keep or carry inventory in stock.

Incentive system (p. 489) An employee reward system based on individual or group productivity.

Industrial engineering (p. 6) Analytical approaches applied to the improvement of productivity in both manufacturing and service sectors.

Infant mortality (p. 827) The failure rate early in the life of a product or process.

Information sciences (p. 6) The systematic processing of data to yield information.

Input–output control (p. 732) A system that allows operations personnel to manage facility work flows, by tracking work added to a work center and its work completed (in that work center).

Inspection (p. 94) A means of ensuring that an operation is producing at the quality level expected.

Institute of Industrial Engineers (IIE) (p. 14) A professional organization for industrial engineers.

Intangible costs (p. 350) A category of location costs that can be evaluated through weighting techniques.

Intermittent process (p. 286) A low-volume, high-variety process; also known as a process-oriented process.

Inventory (p. 594) A stored resource that is used to satisfy a current or future need.

ISO 9000 (p. 80) A set of quality standards developed by the European Community.

Iso-cost line approach (p. 249) An approach to solve a linear programming minimization problem graphically.

Iso-profit line method (p. 245) An approach to solving a linear programming maximization problem graphically.

Job design (p. 483) An approach that specifies the tasks that constitute a job for an individual or a group.

Job enlargement (p. 484) The grouping of a variety of tasks about the same skill level; horizontal enlargement.

Job enrichment (p. 484) A method of giving an employee more responsibility that includes some of the planning and control necessary for job accomplishment; vertical enlargement.

Job instructions (p. 228) A way of providing detailed instructions about how to perform a task.

Job lot (p. 407) A group or batch of parts processed together.

Job rotation (p. 484) A system in which an employee is moved from one specialized job to another.

Job shop (p. 731) A high-variety, low-volume system; intermittent processing.

Johnson's rule (p. 743) An approach that minimizes processing time for sequencing a group of jobs through two facilities and minimizes total idle time in the facilities.

Jury of executive opinion (p. 160) A forecasting technique that takes the opinion of a small group of high-level managers, often in combination with statistical models, and results in a group estimate of demand. The most widely used of all forecasting approaches.

Just-in-time (JIT) inventory (p. 579) The minimum inventory necessary to keep a perfect system running.

Just-in-time (JIT) purchasing (p. 541) Purchasing that reduces waste present at receiving and incoming inspection; it also reduces inventory, poor quality, and delay.

Kaizen (p. 82) The Japanese word for the ongoing process of incremental improvement.

Kanban or Kanban system (p. 581) The Japanese word for *card* that has come to mean "signal"; a Kanban system moves parts through production via a "pull" from a signal.

Keiretsu (p. 534) A Japanese word to describe subcontractors who become part of a company coalition.

Kit number (p. 654) See **Planning bill**.

Knowledge society (p. 19) A society in which much of the labor force has migrated from manual work to work based on knowledge.

Labor planning (p. 481) A means of determining staffing policies dealing with employment stability and work schedules.

Labor specialization (p. 483) The division of labor into unique ("special") tasks.

Labor standards (p. 495) The amount of time required to perform a job or part of a job.

Lead time (pp. 591, 655) In purchasing systems, the time between placing an order and receiving it; in production systems, it is the wait, move, queue, setup, and run times for each component produced.

Lean producers (p. 289) Repetitive producers who are world-class.

Lean production/lean manufacturing (p. 489) Using committed employees with ever expanding responsibility in an effort to achieve zero waste, 100% good product, delivered on time every time. The concept implies expanding each employee's job to the maximum and enhancing each employee's responsibility. It is the opposite of some repetitive manufacturing, which removes responsibility and thinking from a job to simplify it to the maximum.

Learning curve (p. 555) The premise that people and organizations get better at their tasks as the tasks are repeated; sometimes called an experience curve.

Level material use (p. 748) The use of frequent, high-quality, small lot sizes that contributes to just-in-time production.

Level scheduling (level material scheduling) (p. 697) Mixing products so that each day's production meets the demand for that day. (Large/long production runs of the same product for inventory are not allowed.)

Limited, or finite, population (p. 446) A queuing system in which there are only a limited number of potential users of the service.

Linear decision rule (p. 706) An aggregate planning model that attempts to specify an optimum production rate and work-force level over a specific period.

Linear programming (LP) (p. 240) A mathematical technique designed to help production and operations managers in planning and decision making relative to the trade-off necessary to allocate resources.

Linear-regression analysis (p. 178) A straight-line mathematical model to describe the functional relationships between independent and dependent variables; common quantitative causal forecasting model.

Load reports (p. 731) A report for showing the resource requirements in a work center for all work currently assigned there as well as all planned and expected orders.

Loading (p. 731) The assigning of jobs to work or processing centers.

Locational break-even analysis (p. 353) A cost–volume analysis to make an economic comparison of location alternatives.

Log-log graphs (p. 561) Graphs that use a logarithmic scale on both the x- and y-axis.

Longest processing time (LPT) (p. 739) A priority rule that assigns the highest priority to those jobs with the longest processing time.

Lot-for-lot (p. 662) A lot-sizing technique producing exactly what was required to meet the plan.

Lot-sizing decisions (p. 662) The process of, or techniques used in, determining lot size.

Lot tolerance percent defective (LTPD) (p. 124) The quality level of a lot considered bad.

Low-level coding (p. 655) A system in a bill of material when an item is coded at the lowest level at which it occurs.

Maintenance (p. 822) All activities involved in keeping a system's equipment in working order.

Make-or-buy decision (p. 223, 531) The choosing between producing a component or a service and purchasing it from an outside source.

Management coefficient model (p. 706) A formal planning model built around a manager's experience and performance; also known as Bowman's coefficient.

Management information system (MIS) (p. 335) A system dedicated to obtaining, formatting, manipulating, and presenting data as information to managers when needed.

Management process (p. 10) The application of planning, organizing, staffing, leading, and controlling to the achievement of objectives.

Management science (p. 6) A systematic approach to problem formulation and solution, typically utilizing interdisciplinary talents and making use of mathematical, behavioral, and computer skills.

Marginal analysis (p. 602) When applied to inventory, a technique that determines the optimal stocking policy by taking into account marginal profit (MP) and marginal loss (ML).

Master production schedule (pp. 651, 708) A timetable that specifies what is to be made and when.

Material requirements planning (MRP) (p. 650) A dependent demand technique that uses bill of material, inventory, expected receipts, and a master production schedule to determine material requirements.

Material Requirements Planning II (MRP II) (p. 668) A system that allows, with MRP in place, inventory data to be augmented by other resource variables; in this case, MRP becomes *material resource planning*.

Materials management (p. 535) An approach that seeks efficiency of operations through the integration of all material acquisition, movement, and storage activities in the firm.

Maximax (p. 57) A criterion for decision making under uncertainty that finds an alternative that maximizes the maximum outcome or consequence; hence, an optimistic criterion.

Maximin (p. 57) A criterion for decision making under uncertainty that finds an alternative that maximizes the minimum outcome or consequence; hence, a pessimistic criterion.

Mean absolute deviation (MAD) (p. 169) One measure of the overall forecast error for a model; it is computed by taking the sum of the absolute values of the individual forecast errors and dividing by the number of periods of data (n).

Mean squared error (MSE) (p. 170) The average of the squared differences between the forecasted and observed values.

Mean time between failures (MTBF) (p. 824) The expected time between a repair and the next failure of a component, machine, process, or product.

Measured daywork (p. 489) A standard time system whereby employees are paid based on the amount of standard time accomplished.

Mission (p. 33) The purpose or rationale for an organization's activity.

Mixed strategy (p. 697) A planning strategy that uses two or more controllable variables to set a feasible production plan.

Model (p. 53) A representation of reality; it may be graphic, physical, or mathematical.

Modified distribution (MODI) method (p. 383) A method that computes improvement indices for each unused square without drawing all of the closed paths in a transportation system.

Modular bills (p. 654) Bills of material organized by major subassemblies or by product options.

Modules (p. 287) Parts or components of a product previously prepared, often in a continuous process.

Monte Carlo method (p. 620) A simulation technique that uses random elements when chance exists in their behavior. The basis of this method is experimentation of the chance elements through random sampling.

Moving averages (p. 165) A forecasting method that uses an average of the n most recent periods of data to forecast the next period.

MRO (p. 575) Maintenance, repair, and operating systems.

Multiphase queuing system (p. 449) A system in which the customer receives services from several stations before exiting the system.

Multiple-channel queuing system (p. 449) A service system with one waiting line but with several servers.

Multiple regression (p. 184) A causal forecasting method with more than one independent variable.

Mutual commitment (p. 480)   The concept that both management and employees strive to meet common objectives.

Mutual trust (p. 480)   An atmosphere in which both management and employees operate with reasonable, documented employment policies that are honestly and equitably implemented.

Naive approach (p. 165)   A forecasting technique that assumes demand in the next period is equal to demand in the most recent period.

National Association for Purchasing Management (NAPM) (p. 14)   A professional purchasing organization.

Natural variations (p. 110)   Variabilities that affect almost every production process to some degree and are to be expected; also known as common causes.

Negative exponential probability distribution (p. 450)   A continuous probability distribution often used to describe the service time in a queuing system.

Negotiation strategies (p. 537)   Approaches taken by purchasing personnel to develop contractual relationships with suppliers.

Net present value (p. 308)   A means of determining the discounted value of a series of future cash receipts.

Network (p. 781)   A sequence of activities defined by starting and ending events and the activities that occur between them.

Neural networks (p. 337)   Computer programs modeled on the brain's meshlike network of interconnected cells and programmed to recognize patterns and to solve related problems.

Normal distribution (p. 147)   A continuous probability distribution characterized by a bell-shaped curve, the parameters of which are the mean and the standard deviation.

Normal time (p. 505)   The time, adjusted for performance, to complete a task observed during a time study.

Northwest-corner rule (p. 375)   A systematic procedure in the transportation model where one starts at the upper left-hand cell of a table (i.e., the northwest corner) and systematically allocates units to shipping routes.

Numerical control (NC) (p. 327)   The controlling of machines by computer programs on paper or magnetic tape.

Objective function (p. 240)   A mathematical expression in linear programming that maximizes or minimizes some quantity (usually profit or cost).

Office layout (p. 404)   The grouping of workers, their equipment, and spaces/offices to provide for comfort, safety, and movement of information.

Operating characteristic (OC) curve (p. 123)   A graph that describes how well an acceptance plan discriminates between good and bad lots.

Operations chart (p. 495)   A chart depicting right- and left-hand motions.

Optimistic time (p. 784)   The "best" activity completion time that could be obtained in a network plan.

Ordering cost (p. 583)   The cost of the ordering process and its supplies and personnel.

Part period balancing (PPB) (p. 655)   An inventory ordering technique that balances setup and holding costs by changing the lot size to reflect requirements of the next lot size in the future.

Part-time status (p. 483)   When an employee works less than a normal week; less than 32 hours per week often classifies an employee as "part-time."

p-chart (p. 118)   A quality control chart that is used to control attributes.

Pegging (p. 662)   In material requirements planning systems, tracing upward in the bill of material (BOM) from the component to parent item.

PERT/Cost (p. 794)   A network technique that finds the least expensive method of shortening the entire project.

Pessimistic time (p. 784)   The "worst" activity time that could be expected in a network activity.

Phantom bills (p. 654)   Bills of material for components, usually assemblies, that exist only temporarily; they are never inventoried.

Physical sciences (p. 6)   The fields of physics, chemistry, biology, and other related sciences.

Piece rate (p. 489)   A work system that assigns a standard time for each piece produced; the employee is paid based on the number of pieces made.

Pivot column (p. 253)   The column in a linear programming simplex table that indicates which variable will enter the solution next.

Pivot number (p. 253)   The number at the intersection of the pivot row and the pivot column in a linear programming simplex table.

Pivot row (p. 253) The row in a linear programming simplex table that indicates which variable will leave the solution next.

Planning bill (p. 654) Paperwork created in order to assign an artificial parent to the bill of material. An artificial group of components issued together to facilitate production; not a complete subassembly; also known as a "kit" or "pseudo bill."

Planning files (p. 731) An item master file, a routing file, and a work center master file in a material requirements planning system.

Poisson distribution (p. 447) An important discrete probability distribution that often describes the arrival rated in queuing theory; derived by Simeon Poisson in 1837.

Poka-yoke (p. 95) Literally translated, "foolproof"; it has come to mean a device or technique that ensures the production of a good unit every time.

Predetermined time standards (p. 510) An approach that divides manual work into small basic elements that have established and widely accepted times.

Preventive maintenance (p. 826) A plan that involves routine inspections, servicing, and keeping facilities in good repair to prevent failure.

Priority rules (p. 738) Rules that are used to determine the sequence of jobs in process-oriented facilities.

Probabilistic model (p. 598) A statistical model applicable when product demand or any other variable is not known, but can be specified by means of a probability distribution.

Probable time (p. 784) The most likely time to complete an activity in a PERT network.

Process chart (p. 91, 493) A chart using symbols to analyze the movement of people or material.

Process control (p. 327) The use of information technology to control a physical process.

Process focus (p. 286) A low-volume, high-variety process.

Process-oriented layout (p. 404) A layout that deals with low-volume, high-variety production; intermittent process; like machines and equipment are grouped together.

Process (or transformation) strategy (p. 286) The approach that an organization takes to transform resources into goods and services.

Producer's risk (p. 124) The mistake of having a producer's good lot rejected through sampling (a Type I error).

Product-by-value analysis (p. 220) A listing of products in descending order of their individual dollar contribution to the firm, as well as the *total annual* dollar contribution of the product.

Product development teams (p. 218) Teams charged with moving from market requirements for a product to achieving product success.

Product focus (p. 287) A product-oriented, high-volume, low-variety process.

Product-oriented layout (p. 404) A production process built around a product and seeking the best personnel and machine utilization via repetitive or continuous production.

Product strategy (p. 210) The selection, definition, and design of products.

Production (p. 4) The creation of goods and services.

Production and operations management (P/OM) (p. 4) Activities that relate to the creation of goods and services through the transformation of inputs to outputs.

Production order quantity model (p. 592) An economic order quantity technique applied to production orders.

Productivity (p. 15) The enhancement to the production process that results in a favorable comparison of the quantity of resources employed (inputs) to the quantity of goods and services produced (outputs).

Productivity variables (p. 18) The three factors critical to productivity improvement—labor, capital, and the arts and science of management.

Program Evaluation and Review Technique (PERT) (p. 779) A technique to enable managers to schedule, monitor, and control large and complex projects by employing three time estimates for each activity.

Project organization (p. 774) An organization formed to ensure that programs (projects) receive the proper management and attention.

Pseudo bill (p. 654) See **Planning bill**.

Pull system (p. 672) A distribution or production network driven by the top or end user level ordering more stock.

Purchasing (or procurement) (p. 530) The acquisition of goods and services.

Purchasing agent (p. 530) A person with legal authority to execute purchasing contracts on behalf of the firm.

Purchasing management (p. 535) The management of inventory, plus the transportation, availability of supply, and quality of suppliers.

Push system (p. 673) A distribution network in which orders are received from upstream locations (users) but are evaluated by the supplying location.

Qualitative forecasts (p. 160) Forecasts that incorporate important factors such as the decision maker's intuition, emotions, personal experiences, and value system.

Quality circle (p. 83) A group of employees meeting regularly with a facilitator to solve work-related problems in their work area; initiated by the Japanese in the 1970s.

Quality loss function (p. 89) A mathematical function that identifies all costs connected with poor quality and shows how these costs increase as product quality moves from what the customer wants.

Quality-of-work life (p. 480) Aims toward a job that is reasonably safe, is equitable in pay, and achieves an appropriate level of both physical and psychological requirements.

Quality robust (p. 89) Products that are consistently built to specifications in spite of adverse conditions.

Quality robust design (p. 218) A design that yields a good product in spite of small variations in the production process.

Quantitative forecast (p. 160) An approach that employs one or more mathematical models that use historical data and/or causal variables to forecast demand.

Quantity discount (p. 595) A reduced price for items purchased in large quantities.

Queuing theory (p. 445) The body of knowledge about waiting lines.

Random number (p. 621) A series of digits that have been selected by a totally random process; all digits have an equal chance of occurring.

Random-number intervals (p. 621) A set of numbers to represent each possible value or outcome in a computer simulation.

Rated capacity (p. 297) A measure of the maximum usable capacity of a particular facility.

R-chart (p. 112) A process control chart that tracks the "range" within a sample; indicates that a gain or loss in uniformity has occurred in a production process.

Reliability (p. 822) The probability that a machine part or product will function properly for a reasonable length of time.

Reorder point (p. 592) The inventory level (point) at which action is taken to replenish the stocked item.

Repetitive process (p. 287) A product-oriented production process that uses modules.

Retail/service layout (p. 404) An approach (often computerized) that allocates shelf space and responds to customer behavior.

Revenue function (p. 302) An element in break-even analysis that increases by the selling price of each unit.

Robot (p. 328) A flexible machine with the ability to hold, move, or grab items that functions through electronic impulses that activate motors or switches.

Robust model (p. 590) A model that gives satisfactory answers even with substantial variation in the parameters.

Robust quality (p. 89, 219) A product that can be produced to requirements even if minor variations occur in the production process.

Route sheet (p. 227) A listing of the operations necessary to produce the component with the material specified in the bill of material.

Safety stock (p. 592) Extra stock to allow for uneven demand; a buffer.

Sales force composite (p. 160) A forecasting technique based upon salespersons' estimates of expected sales.

Scheduling by simulation (p. 706) A computer model to find a minimum-cost combination for workforce size and production rate.

Search decision rule (p. 707) A pattern search algorithm that tries to find the minimum-cost combination of various force and production levels.

Sensitivity analysis (p. 257) An analysis that projects how much a solution might change if there were changes in the variables or input data.

Sequencing (p. 738) Determining the order in which jobs should be done at each work center.

Sequential sampling (p. 122)   An inspection system where units are randomly selected from a lot and tested one by one with a cumulative number of inspected pieces and defects recorded.

Service level (p. 598)   The complement of the probability of a stockout.

Service sector (p. 18)   That segment of the work force that includes trade, financial, education, legal, medical, and other professional occupations.

Setup cost (p. 583)   The cost to prepare a machine or process for manufacturing an order.

Setup time (p. 584)   The time required to prepare a machine or process for manufacturing an order.

Shadow price (p. 256)   The value of one additional unit of a resource in the form of one more hour of machine time or labor time or other scarce resource in linear programming.

Shortest processing time (SPT) (p. 739)   A priority job scheduling rule that assigns the shortest time job first.

Simplex method (p. 250)   An algorithm developed by Dantzig for solving linear programming problems of all sizes.

Simulation (p. 618)   The attempt to duplicate the features, appearance, and characteristics of a real system, usually a computerized model.

Single-channel queuing system (p. 449)   A service system with one line and one server, e.g., a drive-in bank with one open teller.

Single-phase queuing system (p. 449)   A system in which the customer receives service from only one station and then exits the system.

Single sampling (p. 121)   A form of inspection that specifies a number of items to be sampled and an acceptable number of defects.

Slack time (p. 785)   The amount of time an individual activity in a project management network can be delayed without delaying the entire project.

Smoothing constant (p. 167)   The weighting factor used in an exponential smoothing forecast; a number between 0 and 1.

Society of Manufacturing Engineers (SME) (p. 14)   A professional association.

Source inspection (p. 95)   Inspection at the supplier.

Source management (p. 535)   An approach that seeks likely suppliers, develops their ability to produce, and negotiates acceptable relationships.

SPACECRAFT (p. 411)   A three-dimensional layout system to minimize the cost of moving workers and materials.

Standard deviation (p. 146)   A measure of dispersion or spread; the square root of the variance.

Standard error of the estimate (p. 181)   A distribution within which samples of the process under study are expected to fall.

Standard for the Exchange of Product Data (STEP) (p. 326)   A standard for the electronic exchange of product design information, used internationally.

Standard time (p. 506)   A time-study adjustment to the total normal time; the adjustment provides allowances for personal needs, unavoidable work delays, and worker fatigue.

Standard work schedule (p. 482)   Five 8-hour days in the United States.

Standards manuals (p. 228)   Manuals that provide standard times for setup and information about speed, capacity, tolerance, and other pertinent data for each operation.

Statistical process control (SPC) (p. 93, 108, 110)   A process used to monitor standards, making measurements and taking corrective action as a product or service is being produced.

Stepping-stone method (p. 376)   An iterative technique for moving from an initial feasible solution to an optimal solution in the transportation method; it is used to evaluate the cost-effectiveness of shipping goods via transportation routes not currently in the system.

Strategy (p. 34)   How an organization expects to achieve its missions and goals.

Suboptimize (p. 33)   To operate at a level less than the best.

Supply management (p. 535)   The control of long-term availability of high-dollar or critical purchases.

Surplus variable (p. 258)   The amount over and above a required minimum level set on the right-hand side of a greater-than-or-equal-to constraint in a linear programming problem.

System (p. 32)   An aggregation of interacting variables.

System nervousness (p. 662)   A situation generated by frequent changes in the MRP system.

Tactical scheduling decisions (p. 692) Making monthly or quarterly plans that address fluctuating demands.

Taguchi technique (p. 88) A quality control technique that focuses on improving the product at the design stage.

Tangible costs (p. 350) Readily identifiable costs that can be measured with some precision.

Target value (p. 90) A philosophy of continuous improvement to produce products that are exactly on target.

Technological forecasts (p. 160) Long-term forecasts concerned with the rates of technological progress; such forecasts are critical in high-technology industries; usually performed by experts in each particular field.

Time-based competition (p. 220) Competition based on time; may take form of rapidly developing products and moving them to market or rapid product or service delivery.

Time fences (p. 662) A way of allowing a segment of the master schedule to be designated as "not to be rescheduled."

Time series (p. 161) A forecasting technique that uses a series of past data points to make a forecast.

Time study (p. 504) The timing of a sample of a worker's performance and using it to set a standard.

Total quality management (TQM) (p. 81) Management of an entire organization so that it excels in all aspects of products and services that are important to the customer.

Tracking signal (p. 185) A measurement of how well the forecast is predicting actual values.

Transaction processing system (p. 334) A system that processes the multitude of transactions that occur within and between firms.

Transportation method of LP (p. 704) A heuristic technique for solving a class of linear programming problems.

Transportation technique (pp. 357, 374) A linear programming technique that determines the best pattern of shipments from several points of demand to several destinations so as to minimize total production and transportation costs.

Trend projection (p. 174) A time-series forecasting method that fits a trend line to a series of historical data points and then projects the line into the future for forecasts.

Type I error (p. 125) Statistically, the probability of rejecting a good lot.

Type II error (p. 125) Statistically, the probability of a bad lot being accepted.

Unlimited, or infinite, population (p. 446) A queuing situation in which a virtually unlimited number of people or items that could request the services, or the number of customers or arrivals on hand at any given moment is a very small portion of potential arrivals.

Value analysis (p. 219) A review of products with long life cycles that takes place during the production process.

Variable (p. 620) A measurable quantity that may vary or is subject to change.

Variable costs (p. 302) Costs that vary with the volume of units produced; also known as direct costs.

Variable inspection (p. 96) As opposed to attribute inspection, the classifications of inspected items as falling on a continuum scale such as dimension size or strength.

Variance (p. 146) A number that reveals the overall spread or dispersion of the distribution.

Vertical integration (p. 532) Developing the ability to produce goods or services previously purchased by buying a supplier or distributor.

Virtual companies (p. 534) Companies that meet changing demands through flexible, fluid organizational boundaries by relying on a variety of supplier relationships.

Vision systems (p. 327) Using video cameras and computer technology in inspection roles.

Wagner–Whitin procedure (p. 666) A programming model for lot-size computation that assumes a finite time horizon beyond which there are no additional net requirements.

Waiting lines (p. 445) Queues; items or people in a line awaiting a service.

Warehouse layout (p. 404) A design that attempts to minimize total cost by addressing trade-offs between space and material handling.

Weighted approach technique (p. 351) A location method that instills objectivity into the process of identifying hard-to-evaluate costs.

Work cell (p. 413) A temporary product-oriented arrangement of machines and personnel in what is ordinarily a process-oriented facility.

Work order (p. 228) An instruction to make a given quantity of a particular item, usually to a given schedule.

Work sampling (p. 514) An estimate, via sampling, of the percent of the time that a worker spends working on various tasks.

World-class firms (p. 44) Firms that compete successfully in the international arena.

World-class manufacturing (p. 44) A strategic and tactical approach to the P/OM function that yields continuous improvement in meeting customer requirements through excellence in the transformation process.

World-class P/OM function (p. 44) See **World-class manufacturing**.

$\bar{x}$-chart (x-bar) (p. 111) A quality control chart for variables that indicates when changes occur in the central tendency of a production process.

Yield management (p. 709) The study of capacity allocation (such as airplane seats) in order to maximize profit or utilization.

NAME INDEX

COMPANY INDEX

GENERAL INDEX

Aaker, David A., 36, 36n
ABC analysis, 575–577
AB:POM,
    aggregate planning, 710–712
    assignment, 755–756
    center of gravity method, 361–362
    CPM/PERT, 798–799
    decision theory problems, 65–66
    entering and editing data, 850–852
    facility location, 361–362
    forecasting, 187, 189–190
    getting started, 852–854
    hardware requirements, 846
    help screens, 847
    inventory, 605–606
    job shop sequencing, 755–761
    layout, 424, 426–428
    learning curves, 564
    line balancing, 427–428
    linear programming, 257, 260,
      261–263
    lot sizing, 676
    main menu of, 846–847
    module submenu screen, 847–850
    MRP, 674–676
    PERT/CPM, 798–799
    plant location, 361–362
    quality control, 131
    queuing module, 463–464
    reliability, 833
    scheduling problems, 755–756
    simulation, 632
    transportation problems, 387–388
    using, 846
    waiting line models, *See* Queuing
      module
Acceptable quality level (AQL), 124
Acceptance sampling, 110, 121–130
    average outgoing quality and
      (AOQ), 127–130
    average outgoing quality limit
      (AOQL), 130
    operating characteristic curves and,
      123–124
    producer's and consumer's risk and,
      124–127
    sampling plans and, 121–122
Accurate records, inventory and,
    577–578
Activities,
    dummy, 783
    in PERT, 781–783
Activity charts, job design and, 493
Activity-on-Arrow (AOA), 781

Activity on Node, 781
Activity time estimates, in PERT,
    784–789
Ada, Countess of Lovelace, 6
Adaptive smoothing, 186
Aesthetics, layout strategy and, 406
AGV's, *See* Automatic guided vehicles
Aggregate planning, 689–723
    comparison of methods for, 707
    concern of, 692
    disaggregation and, 708
    graphical and charting methods in,
      698–704
    level material use schedule, 748–750
    mathematical methods for, 704–707
    methods for, 698–708
    strategies for, 694–698
    mixed strategies for, 697
    nature of, 693–694
    planning process and, 692–693
    planning strategies for, 694–698
    in services, 708–709
Aided, 411n
Airbus Industries, 158, 225
Airline industry
    aggregate planning in, 709
    scheduling in, 753
Alaska,
    Amoco, 55, 56
    Delphi method, 162
Alaska Airlines, 478–479
ALDEP, 412
Allocation, distribution resource
    planning and, 672–673
A M Manufacturing, 294
American Airlines, 239, 451, 753
American Express Company, 338
    Authorizer's Assistant expert system,
      338
American Hardware Supply, 187
American League umpires, scheduling,
    728
American Plastics, Inc., 503
American Production and Inventory
    Control Society (APICS), 13–14
American Society of Mechanical
    Engineers (ASME), 91
    symbols of, 91
American Society for Quality Control
    (ASQC), 14, 80
Ames Rubber, 81
Amoco, 55, 56
Anheuser-Busch, 690–691, 693
A-O-A, 781

A-O-N, 781
APICS, 13–14
Apple Computer, 491, 779
Applied Decision Analysis, 63
Area of feasible solutions, 244
Areas Under the Standard Normal
    Curve, 842
ARENA, 625, 631
Arithmetic approach, learning curves
    and, 557–558
Arrival characteristics, of waiting line
    systems, 446–448
Arrival population, 446–451
    behavior of, 447–448
    limited, 448
    pattern of arrivals and, 446–447
    unlimited, 448
Art and science of management, as
    productivity variable, 21
Artificial intelligence, 336–338
Artificial variables, simplex method
    and, 258
Assembly chart, 227
Assembly drawing, 227
Assembly line, product-oriented layout
    and, 419
Assembly line balancing, product-
    oriented layout and, 420–424
    objectives of, 420
Assignable variations, statistical
    process control and, 110–111
Assignment method, linear
    programming and, 735–738
Assignment method, loading and,
    735–738
Association for Systems Management,
    14
ASYBL (Assembly Line
    Configuration), 424
Atanasoff, John Vincent, 6
AT&T, 81, 218, 260, 322–324, 483
Attitudes, location and, 350
Attribute(s), control charts for,
    118–121
    p-charts and, 118–119
Attribute inspection, 96
Australia
    Brisbane International Airport, 377
Auto Desk, 416
Auto Simulations Inc., 630, 747n
Automated Storage and Retrieval
    Systems (ASRS), 328
Automatic guided vehicles (AGVs),
    329, 425